BEHAVIORAL SCIENCE
for Medical Students

BEHAVIORAL SCIENCE
for Medical Students

Edited by

Frederick S. Sierles, M.D.

Professor, Vice Chairman and Director of Medical Student Education
Department of Psychiatry and Behavioral Sciences
University of Health Sciences/the Chicago Medical School
North Chicago, Illinois

*A project of the Association of Directors of
Medical Student Education in Psychiatry*

WILLIAMS & WILKINS
BALTIMORE • HONG KONG • LONDON • MUNICH
PHILADELPHIA • SYDNEY • TOKYO

Editor: Timothy S. Satterfield
Managing Editor: Carol Eckhart
Copy Editor: Jennifer J. Conway
Designer: Wilma Rosenberger
Illustration Planner: Lorraine Wrzosek
Production Coordinator: Anne Stewart-Seitz
Indexer: Deborah Tourtlotte

Copyright © 1993
Williams & Wilkins
428 East Preston Street
Baltimore, Maryland 21202, USA

Accurate indications, adverse reactions, and dosage schedules for drugs are provided in this book, but it is possible that they may change. The reader is urged to review the package information data of the manufacturers of the medications mentioned.

Printed in the United States of America

Library of Congress Cataloging-in-Publication Data

Behavioral science for medical students / edited by Frederick S.
Sierles.
    p. cm.
    "A project of the Association of Directors of Medical Student Education in Psychiatry."
    Includes bibliographical references and index.
    ISBN 0-683-07730-9.
    1. Medicine and psychology. 2. Human behavior. I. Sierles, Frederick, 1942- . II. Association of Directors of Medical Student Education in Psychiatry.
    [DNLM: 1. Behavior. 2. Neuropsychology. BF 121 B419]
R726.5.B4268 1992
155--dc20
DNLM/DLC
for Library of Congress   91-44690
                                    CIP

92 93 94 95 96
1 2 3 4 5 6 7 8 9 10

to our students and mentors

FOREWORD

Many psychopathology and general psychiatry texts have been written specifically for medical students, but only a handful of "behavioral science" texts have been written for them. There is good reason for this. Few educational writers have been willing to tackle the essential dilemma of how to deal appropriately with the need to be comprehensive and content rich without being too detailed and just plain too long.

What informational areas are clinically important, useful, and interesting in the training of future physicians? Behavioral science is taught in many different formats by many different types of faculty whose interests and expertise are wide ranging. The essential solution for both students and educators must be that they have material available to them that is comprehensive, practical, and enjoyable enough to cover all important areas in sufficient depth to be meaningful and challenging. The text must be all these things without being ponderous in length or in style, and therefore unpalatable or useless for the medical student consumer.

Several good texts have solved the problem by limiting breadth by taking a very particular point of view, typically either developmental/dynamic or biological. Another solution has been to leave out many important topics, for example pregnancy, psychopathology, somatic treatments, violence, and accidents, viewing these topics as ones defined by general medicine or "psychiatry."

The authors of *Behavioral Science for Medical Students,* almost all being members of the Association of Directors of Medical Student Education in Psychiatry, found these solutions to be inadequate and chose to address the problem more pragmatically yet more ambitiously. Their solution involved finding a careful balance, sacrificing neither breadth nor depth, defining and thoroughly covering the topic areas without being too detailed, leaving no relevant or important topic out. An ambitious task indeed, but one that will enable course coordinators to breathe a sigh of relief in designing more workable courses and students to have a sense of satisfaction when using the book. Consideration has been given to covering important topic areas in sufficient depth to be of educational value to future physicians and to present the material in an engaging, interesting, and readable fashion. Certainly different course coordinators will emphasize different areas and thus define their institutions' and departments' educational perspective. However, as part of the general format of the book, chapter objectives, detailed references, and many case examples have been provided to make the text useful and user friendly.

Perhaps the most important factor to understand about *Behavioral Science for Medical Students* is that it has been written and edited by the educators themselves, those faculty who actually teach in the classrooms and at the bedside. This book is written by folks who want to use the book themselves at their own institutions, academicians who are seeking to fill specific educational needs defined by years of teaching and working with medical students. As a group, these educators have succeeded at fitting their individual areas of knowledge and expertise into a textual framework, which has been carefully designed to present the material in the most organized, useful way without losing any of the richness and complexity of the content. The editor's and authors' goal has been to present concepts and points of view that will help students learn by experience, become competent physicians, and, as much as possible, be content and gratified in their roles as physicians.

To understand how and why this textbook was written, it is necessary to be acquainted with the Association of Directors of Medical Student Education in Psychiatry (ADMSEP). Founded in 1974, ADMSEP is a group of medical school faculty who specialize in teaching and behavioral science and psychiatry to medical students. The organization exists solely to support and meet the needs of these educators and their constituents—the students. The idea for the book arose from discussion among the officers, primarily Irv Hassenfeld, ADMSEP's president at the time, and Fred Sierles, president elect. Truly it was Fred Sierles who made this text "happen." He organized all the ADMSEP members'

thoughts and ideas, solicited the authors, actually edited each chapter, and was an original contributor as well. Dr. Sierles is no stranger to this type of writing, this being his third behavioral science text. He brings almost 20 years of clinical and educational experience to the task and is thus uniquely qualified to be the editor of this unique text—one designed by educators specifically for fellow educators and students. The highest praise I can offer is that I am eagerly awaiting the release of the text so that I can use it myself!

—Deborah C. Roth, D.O.
Director of Medical Student Education
Department of Psychiatry
University of South Florida College of Medicine
Tampa, Florida
Immediate Past President
Association of Directors of Medical Student Education in Psychiatry

PREFACE

Behavioral Science for Medical Students endorses the universally held public health concept that behavior (including that of patients, physicians, and the community) plays a central role in the prevention, incidence, prevalence, manifestations, diagnosis, treatment, and prognosis of illness. Most readers already know that behaviors contribute to the causation of illness (e.g., that smoking, overeating, sedentary lifestyle, substance abuse, and noncompliance with antihypertensive drug prescription play major roles in causing cardiovascular and cerebrovascular diseases, the first and third leading causes of death in the United States [1]).

Many, but perhaps fewer, readers appreciate how an understanding of behavior and its application to patient care (a goal of this book) facilitate the prevention, early diagnosis, and effective treatment of illness. For example, learning theory (Chapter 6) underlies most smoking cessation and weight reduction programs, and skillfully conducted interviews (Chapter 16) employing techniques derived in part from psychoanalysis (Chapter 7) effectively elicit symptoms and signs of illness and foster patient cooperation with treatment. From another perspective, abnormal behaviors (e.g., panic attacks and delusions) may be the first or the only sign of medical or surgical as well as psychiatric illness.

What is behavior and what is "behavioral science"? Behavior is action in response to external and internal stimuli, the latter including thought and emotion. Behavior is a manifestation of brain function, and the modern concept of the mind requires the existence of brain structure and function, just as the concept hospital requires the existence of a spe-

cialized building, patients and staff, and medical procedures and treatments.

Before the early 1970s, the phrase "behavioral science" was not used routinely in medical schools. In 1972, the term was popularized by the introduction of a behavioral science test section into Part 1 of the certifying examination of the National Board of Medical Examiners (NBME). As conceptualized by the NBME and presented in this text, behavioral science spans many topics—from behavioral neurology to child development to psychopathology to health care financing and delivery—which have behavior as a central theme. The knowledge of these is fundamental to medical practice. Each of these topics fits a broad definition of science: a department of systematized knowledge as an object of study. Many of the topics also fit a more specific definition of science, as discussed in Chapter 2.

Behavioral Science for Medical Students presents these subjects in an organized, clinically meaningful fashion, using chapter objectives, patient vignettes, and many references. Following the first section, Approaches to Behavior, most of the chapters use the biopsychosocial model (2), meaning that for each person, states of disease as well as good health are simultaneously influenced by biological, psychological, and social factors. This model is explained in detail in Chapter 1.

Behavioral Science for Medical Students is a project of the Association of Directors of Medical Student Education in Psychiatry (ADMSEP), written by 46 authors at nearly as many medical schools and reflecting the state of the art in behavioral science teaching in the United States. It presents a common data base in the field of behavioral science that should be helpful in the production of, and medical student preparation for, Step 1 of NBME's United States Medical Licensure Examination (USMLE).

Although the text is only 455 pages long, it is reasonably comprehensive, for the following reasons: (1) most if not all the topics are clinically important; (2) across the United States, different subjects are emphasized at different schools, and we wanted the text to be useful in most medical schools; (3) for medical students doing "one-stop shopping" to prepare for Step 1 of the USMLE, this text, in conjunction with medical school coursework, offers a solid, substantial survey of the field. This comprehensive coverage includes both psychopathology and a variety of politically sensitive subjects (e.g., contraception, therapeutic abortion, gender psychology, and violence) that have literally life-and-death importance, and which are pertinent to the daily practice of medicine, but which are avoided in most behavioral science texts. Moreover, although this is not a textbook of preventive medicine, considerable attention is given to illness prevention, which is fundamental to modern medical practice and medical education.

ACKNOWLEDGEMENTS

Behavioral Science for Medical Students was an ambitious undertaking requiring the assistance, wisdom, and patience of many people at many medical schools. Identifying and thanking everyone who helped each of the authors would be impossible. There are, however, many people that I, as Editor, can thank.

Michael Alan Taylor and Irwin Hassenfeld suggested the idea for the book. At Williams and Wilkins, Timothy Satterfield, Michael Fisher, Nancy Evans, and Jennifer Conway provided timely, frank guidance. Jennifer Conway copy-edited superbly, and Anne Stewart Seitz and Carole Eckhart produced the final product efficiently while tolerating my delays with grace and good humor.

At the University of Health Sciences/the Chicago Medical School (UHS/CMS), my chairman (Dr. Taylor) and colleagues recognized how important this book was to me, and allowed me hundreds of hours of "protected" time for editing. Dolores Turowski, the undergraduate secretary, retyped edited manuscripts for hundreds of hours. At the UHS/CMS Computer Center, Anna Kepic, Frank Naeymi-Rad, and David Hammergren taught me how to operate my computer and responded to my "emergency" calls at odd hours when the computer misbehaved. At our Learning Resource Center, Sharyn Fradin filled in numerous gaps in the references, and Deborah Rubenstein added many fine illustrations. My students, on whom I field-tested early drafts of many of the manuscript's chapters, and Hannah Sierles, offered constructive criticisms from a consumer's perspective.

Many colleagues in ADMSEP, UHS/CMS, and elsewhere wrote perceptive chapter reviews. These included Sheri Berenbaum, George Balis, Carl Bell, Nancy Evans, Cory Franklin, David Garfield, Irwin Hassenfeld, V. Chowdary Jampala, Theresa Kepic, Elizabeth Kessler, Richard Lane, Phil Lebovitz, Noel List, Thomas Mackenzie, Allan Markle, Richard McNally, Gary Oltmans, Eugene Rogers, Deborah Roth, Bala Sarma, Michael Seidenberg, Michael Schrift, Ashok Srinivasaraghavan, Conrad Swartz, Michael Alan Taylor, Chandragupta Vedak, and Mark Young.

Finally, I thank my parents for providing moral support even while my father was very ill, and my son Josh and his friends for allowing me "protected time" at home after working hours and on weekends.

—Frederick S. Sierles, M.D.
North Chicago, Illinois
August 26, 1992

References

1. U.S. Department of Health and Human Services, Public Health Service, Centers for Disease Control, National Center for Health Statistics. Health United States 1990. DHHS pub. no. (PHS91-1232). Washington, DC: US Government Printing Office, 1990:80.
2. Engel GS. The clinical application of the biopsychosocial model. Am J Psychiatry 1980;137:535–544.

CONTRIBUTORS

Richard Balon, M.D.
Associate Professor of Psychiatry
Director, Junior Medical Student
Education Program
Wayne State University School of
Medicine
Detroit, Michigan

Robert W. Bloom, M.D.
Assistant Professor of Psychiatry
Rush Medical College
Chicago, Illinois

Patricia M. Butler, M.D.
Associate Professor of Psychiatry and
Associate Dean for Educational
Programs
University of Texas Health Sciences
Center at Houston
Houston, Texas

Steven Cody, Ph.D.
Associate Professor of Psychiatry
Marshall University School of Medicine
Huntington, West Virginia

Jennifer J. Conway
Editor
Leonard Davis Institute of Health
Economics
University of Pennsylvania
Philadelphia, Pennsylvania

Wayne C. Drevets, M.D.
Assistant Professor of Psychiatry
Washington University School of
Medicine
St. Louis, Missouri

Theodore B. Feldmann, M.D.
Associate Professor of Psychiatry &
Behavioral Sciences
Director of Medical Student Education in
Psychiatry and Behavioral Sciences
University of Louisville School of
Medicine
Louisville, Kentucky

Gregory Franchini, M.D.
Assistant Professor of Psychiatry
Director of Medical Student Education in
Psychiatry
University of New Mexico
Albuquerque, New Mexico

Phillip S. Freeman, M.D., D.M.H.
Assistant Professor of Psychiatry
Associate Director, Medical Student
Program in Psychiatry
Boston University Medical School
Boston, Massachusetts

Donald M. Gallant, M.D.
Professor Emeritus of Psychiatry and
Neurology
Tulane Medical School
New Orleans, Louisiana

Richard L. Grant, M.D.
Clinical Associate Professor of Psychiatry
Department of Psychiatry & Behavioral
Medicine
University of Illinois College of Medicine
at Peoria
Peoria, Illinois

Carl B. Greiner, M.D.
Associate Professor of Psychiatry &
Internal Medicine
Director of Medical Student Education in
Psychiatry
Nebraska-Creighton Department of
Psychiatry
University of Nebraska Medical Center
Omaha, Nebraska

N. Gregory Hamilton, M.D.
Associate Professor of Psychiatry
Oregon Health Sciences University
Portland, Oregon

Irwin N. Hassenfeld, M.D.
Professor of Clinical Psychiatry
Director of Psychiatric Education
Albany Medical College
Albany, New York

Abraham Heller, M.D.
Professor Emeritus of Psychiatry &
Community Health
Wright State University School of
Medicine
Dayton, Ohio

Charles R. Hillenbrand, M.D.
Clinical Associate Professor of Psychiatry
Loyola University
Stritch School of Medicine
Maywood, Illinois

Sanford Jacobson, M.D.
Professor of Psychiatry
Director of Medical Student Education in
Psychiatry
University of Miami School of Medicine
Coral Gables, Florida

Edward D. Joseph, M.D. (Deceased)
Formerly Professor of Psychiatry
Director of Medical Student Education in
Psychiatry
The Mount Sinai School of Medicine
New York, New York

Jerome Kroll, M.D.
Professor of Psychiatry
University of Minnesota Medical School
Minneapolis, Minnesota

Edward H. Leatherman, M.D.
Associate Professor of Psychiatry
Louisiana State University Medical Center
Shreveport, Louisiana

Freda C. Lewis-Hall, M.D.
Vice Chairperson
Department of Psychiatry
Howard University Hospital
Howard University College of Medicine
Washington, DC

Thomas B. Mackenzie, M.D.
Associate Profesor of Psychiatry
Director of Medical Student Education in
Psychiatry
University of Minnesota Medical School
Minneapolis, Minnesota

Myrl R.S. Manley, M.D.
Assistant Professor of Psychiatry
Director, of Undergraduate Education in
Psychiatry
State University of New York
Health Sciences Center, Brooklyn
Brooklyn, New York

Robert Margolies, Ph.D.
Clinical Assistant Professor of Psychiatry
College of Medicine
State University of New York (Downstate)
Brooklyn, New York

Philip K. McCullough, M.D.
Assistant Professor and Associate
Director, Medical Student Education
Department of Psychiatry & Behavioral
Sciences
Northwestern University Medical School
Chicago, Illinois

Mary Lou Meyers, M.D.
Associate Professor of Psychiatry
Director of Medical Student Education in
Psychiatry
University of Rochester School of
Medicine & Dentistry
Rochester, New York

Linda Nidelkoff, Ph.D.
University of Chicago
Chicago, Illinois

Linda F. Pessar, M.D.
Clinical Associate Professor of Psychiatry
Director of Medical Student Education in
    Psychiatry
State University of New York at Buffalo
Buffalo, New York

Janice L. Petersen, M.D.
Assistant Professor of Psychiatry
University of Colorado Health Sciences
    Center
Denver, Colorado

Martin D. Plutzer, M.D.
Associate Professor of Psychiatry
Medical College of Pennsylvania
Philadelphia, Pennsylvania

H. Jonathan Polan, M.D.
Associate Professor of Clinical Psychiatry
Director of Medical Student Education
Department of Psychiatry
Cornell University Medical College
New York, New York

John C. Racy, M.D.
Professor of Psychiatry
Director of Medical Student Education in
    Psychiatry
University of Arizona College of Medicine
Tucson, Arizona

Marc Rothman, M.D.
Associate Professor of Clinical Psychiatry
Robert Wood Johnson Medical School–
    Camden
University of Medicine and Dentistry of
    New Jersey
Camden, New Jersey

Jeffrey Colman Salloway, Ph.D.
Associate Professor of Health
    Management and Policy
Director, Center for Health Promotion
    and Research
University of New Hampshire
Durham, New Hampshire

Michael J. Schrift, D.O.
Assistant Professor & Director, Medical
    Student Education
Department of Psychiatry
Rush Medical College
Chicago, Illinois

Darlene L. Shaw, Ph.D.
Associate Professor of Psychiatry &
    Behavioral Sciences
Medical University of South Carolina
Charleston, South Carolina

Roger C. Sider, M.D.
Professor of Psychiatry
College of Human Medicine
Michigan State University
Grand Rapids, Michigan

Frederick S. Sierles, M.D.
Professor, Vice Chairman, and Director of
    Medical Student Education
Department of Psychiatry and Behavioral
    Sciences
University of Health Sciences/the Chicago
    Medical School
North Chicago, Illinois

Joel M. Silberberg, M.D.
Associate Professor of Clinical Psychiatry
Director of Medical Student Education
Loyola University Medical Center
Maywood, Illinois

Nada L. Stotland, M.D.
Associate Professor of Psychiatry
University of Chicago
Chicago, Illinois

Howard S. Sudak, M.D.
Professor of Psychiatry
Vice Dean, School of Medicine
Associate Vice President for Medical
    Affairs
Case Western Reserve University
School of Medicine
Cleveland, Ohio

Virginia L. Susman, M.D.
Associate Professor of Clinical Psychiatry
Coordinator, Medical Student Affairs
Department of Psychiatry
Cornell University Medical College
White Plains, New York

Marie D. Thomas, Ph.D.
Personnel Research Psychologist
Navy Personnel Research and
Development Center
San Diego, California

Terry A. Travis, M.D., M.S.Ed.
Professor of Psychiatry & Medical
Education
Southern Illinois University School of
Medicine
Springfield, Illinois

Danny Wedding, Ph.D.
Professor of Psychiatry
Director, Missouri Institute of Mental
Health
University of Missouri
Columbia, Missouri

Daniel R. Wilson, M.D.
Department of Psychiatry
Harvard Medical School
Boston, Massachusetts

CONTENTS

SECTION I.
APPROACHES TO BEHAVIOR

1/Acquired Immunodeficiency Syndrome: A Biopsychosocial Paradigm of Illness

H. Jonathan Polan, M.D.

OBJECTIVES

GENERAL OBJECTIVE: Given a patient's case history, address the biological, psychological, and social components of the patient's care.

SPECIFIC OBJECTIVES:
1. Define the biopsychosocial model, and state how it differs from the biomedical model.
2. Discuss two common misconceptions about the biopsychosocial model.
3. Discuss the epidemiology of the human immunodeficiency virus (HIV) and of the acquired immunodeficiency syndrome (AIDS).
4. Summarize the biology of HIV infection and AIDS, including the following: effect on the immune system and its consequences, and dementia and delirium secondary to HIV infection and AIDS.
5. Summarize the psychosocial factors involved in AIDS, including the following: depression, suicide, psychology of AIDS prevention, patient education and the health belief model, peer influence, physician sensitivity to cultural values, maintenance of hope, and social support.
6. Discuss the biological treatments of HIV infection and AIDS.
7. Discuss the psychosocial treatments of HIV infection and AIDS.
8. Summarize the data on pediatric AIDS.

THE BIOPSYCHOSOCIAL MODEL

In 1977, Dr. George Engel, an internist and psychoanalyst at the University of Rochester, proposed the biopsychosocial model as a response to medicine's increasingly narrow focus on the spectacular advances of molecular biology and other basic biological sciences of medicine, which Engel labeled the "biomedical model" (1). Following Engel, the biopsychosocial model is defined in this book as a broader new approach to medical practice that encompasses not only the biological factors that influence the prevention, causes, and outcome of disease, but the psychological and social factors as well. Each of these factors continuously interacts with the others, and together they constitute the unique state we call illness (Fig. 1.1). Although it is doubtful whether any basic scientist or medical educator would seriously claim that only the basic biological sciences should be applied to the panoply of clinical problems of patients with, for example, acquired immunodeficiency syndrome (AIDS), that message is, nevertheless, still implicit in much medical education and practice.

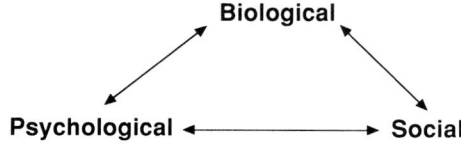

Figure 1.1. Biopsychosocial Model.

Weighing the Biomedical Model

The New England Journal of Medicine, possibly the world's most influential medical journal, carries a regular feature, "Case Records of the Massachusetts General Hospital." A clinicopathological correlation exercise, this report is read by many medical students, house officers, and practitioners. The exercise takes the biomedical approach, in which psychosocial information is presented only if it assists in discovering the biological diagnoses that are the exercise's objective. Such a focus may be heuristically useful in training students to think through biological pathogenic mechanisms of disease, but it may subtly imply that psychosocial problems are not, in their own right, the province of the well-educated physician.

AIDS was the subject of a recent Case Record (2). A 29-year-old man was admitted to the hospital for "an increasing cough and fever." At least one intriguing psychosocial glimpse of him is offered: his sexual partners included one man with Kaposi's sarcoma (a malignancy that is unusual except in patients with AIDS) and a Haitian man (presumably mentioned since Haitians have a higher prevalence of AIDS than the general population of the U.S.). A serologic test for antibodies to human immunodeficiency virus (HIV), the virus that causes AIDS, was positive. The presentation details the patient's physical findings, laboratory test procedures and results, and antibiotic treatments during four hospitalizations that occurred over 19 months. Never mentioned is who may have accompanied the patient to the hospital, with whom he was living (if anyone), who visited him in the hospital, whether he knew he was infected with HIV, or whether he practiced "safe sex" (i.e., took recommended precautions to prevent the spread of HIV to his sexual partners).

On the eighth hospital day of the fourth admission, he died from Kaposi's sarcoma that had spread within his lungs (determined on autopsy). The gross and microscopic anatomic postmortem findings are thoroughly described, but there is no mention of the patient's mood or thoughts before his death, what issues he struggled with, how he coped with his final illness, whether he requested that he be resuscitated in case of cardiopulmonary arrest, whom he designated to be informed of his death, or who may have grieved for him. Although the omission of important psychosocial information from the case record may have its heuristic rationale, it might seem artificial, even strange, to a first-year medical student reading such a record for the first time. What is the student to think? That acknowledging the patient as a person with a mind, experiences, emotions, and relationships is not relevant to understanding the course of his illness and the causes of his suffering?

Integrating the Biopsychosocial Model

In a 1980 paper (3) elaborating on the clinical implications of the biopsychosocial model, Engel presented a vignette that vividly illustrates how the three components of the model interact and how that interaction may literally make the difference between life and death.

Mr. Glover was a 55-year-old salesman brought to the emergency room from work for chest pain. He dismissed these symptoms as "fatigue" and "emotional tension" despite their similarity to the symptoms of his myocardial infarction (death of heart muscle tissue because of inadequate blood supply) 6 months earlier. His employer, knowing Mr. Glover's need to feel in control, overcame Mr. Glover's denial and escorted him to the hospital. There Mr. Glover felt calmer, and the pain subsided.

During the initial evaluation, the house staff had trouble with the arterial puncture, and as they left to get help without an explanation, Mr. Glover's fears of losing control returned. He felt hot and flushed, his chest pain recurred, and he went into ventricular fibrillation (worm-like uncoordinated contractions within the ventricular muscle, negating its pumping ability and producing cardiac arrest). Fortunately he was successfully resuscitated.

Mr. Glover's biological disease entity is ischemic heart disease, damage to a portion of cardiac muscle caused by an inadequate supply of oxygen to that muscle on the basis of an obstruction of one of the heart's arteries. The biological process was exquisitely sensitive to changes in Mr. Glover's psychological state. His emotional tension increased the demand on the injured muscle, exceeding the oxygen supply reaching that muscle through the blocked artery, resulting in chest pain. As he felt calmer, the pain subsided because the reduced oxygen supply through the blocked artery was adequate for the reduced demand. Mr. Glover's psychological state was, in turn, sensitive to the social environment. Arriving in the emergency room provided a sense of security and control, but this was shattered when the house staff failed to explain to him that their difficulty with the arterial puncture was a minor technical problem. As fear returned, demand on the heart muscle increased, again outstripping the oxygen supply, leading to recurrent pain and a sudden, near-fatal arrhythmia.

Functioning within the biomedical model, the house staff ignored critical psychosocial aspects of their patient's illness. Engel argued convincingly (3) that had the doctors recognized, and dealt with, Mr. Glover's emotional responses and the effects of their interaction with him, they might have prevented his arrhythmia. A reassuring explanation, taking no more than perhaps 20 seconds, would have been the appropriate biopsychosocial intervention. A humanistic physician might have done this anyway, out of compassion, but only a physician working within the biopsychosocial model would have done it with the knowledge that it was crucial to maintaining the delicate

balance among the biological, psychological, and social factors of this life-threatening illness.

Misconceptions About the Biopsychosocial Model

In the 15 years since Engel's proposal, the biopsychosocial model has been incorporated into the education and practice of such specialties as family medicine, developmental and behavioral pediatrics, internal medicine, and psychiatry. Despite this widening arena of application, the biopsychosocial model continues sometimes to be misunderstood, even at times by its proponents.

Two misunderstandings of the biopsychosocial model are (1) the humanistic view that it is synonymous with the compassionate practice of medicine, and (2) the reductionistic view that it can be expressed as a set of scientific principles from which diagnoses and treatments are derived with the same degree of certainty that one finds in applying the biomedical model to problems of pharmacology or molecular genetics.

The humanistic view equates biopsychosocial medicine with the physician's ethical, caring attitude but may neglect the body of scientific knowledge from psychology, sociology, anthropology, economics, and the other social sciences. A physician who ignores the biopsychosocial model may be as compassionate and ethical as the next. Yet compassion and ethics alone will not help the physician to formulate an effective intervention for a patient with asthma who continues to smoke, a patient with inflammatory bowel disease who cannot maintain a diet that has been proved effective in reducing symptoms, or a 50-year-old woman with a family history of breast cancer who "forgets" to perform breast self-examinations and has cancelled her last three annual checkups because she was "too busy" at her job.

Subscribers of the reductionistic view, on the other hand, seem to expect clinical problems to be neatly divisible into lists of distinct biological, psychological, and social problems, each of which should then be solved by selection of the relevant formulae of the respective sciences. But science is far from the point of explaining all clinical phenomena as instances of known principles; therefore, this view overestimates the role of science and underestimates the value of clinical experience and judgment.

The reductionistic misunderstanding can also be used, ironically, to distance medicine from patients' psychosocial problems and justify further fragmentation of modern subspecialized care. If clinical problems are separable into distinct biological, psychological, and social categories, then perhaps, some might argue, each problem is best served by separate attention from an expert in that field: a physician for the biomedical disease entity, a psychologist for the troubling emotional reaction to the disease, and a social worker for the disruptive impact of the illness on the patient's family. This scenario neglects that a knowledgeable physician, taking primary responsibility for a patient's care, can develop a therapeutic alliance that enhances the effectiveness of specialized interventions. In contrast to the humanistic and reductionistic views, this book proposes that the physician's success as a diagnostician, healer, teacher, and researcher depends on his or her ability to weave the relevant principles of the biological, psychological, and social sciences into an integrated approach to illness.

PARADIGM OF AIDS

At Cornell University Medical College, AIDS is taught to first-year students as a biopsychosocial paradigm of illness (4). AIDS is the late stage of HIV infection, a fatal condition characterized by opportunistic infections (i.e., taking advantage of failure of the immune system's defenses) and opportunistic malignant tumors, central nervous system disorders, and wasting. One of the world's leading causes of death, AIDS is a medically, socially, and psychologically complex disease. It requires continuing care over time, coordina-

tion of many services, and intensive psychosocial interventions. Education, counseling, and early diagnosis and treatment are critical elements in combating the epidemic. AIDS patients cannot simply be treated as bearers of a viral infection.

The impact of AIDS on medicine and society is profound. In 1977, just before the HIV epidemic began, it was widely believed that the eradication of smallpox marked medicine's final victory over the great infectious lethal epidemics. The major remaining epidemics were thought to be degenerative processes (e.g., cardiovascular disease, Alzheimer's disease, and cancer) that most often affected the elderly. AIDS has radically altered that view.

AIDS has additional biological, psychological, and social characteristics that account for its dramatic impact. It is predominantly an illness of the young, with a peak prevalence occurring among persons in their 30s. Over 50% of these young adults develop dementia (5). HIV has a mean incubation period (time from infection until onset of symptoms) of a decade (6), so that, once diagnosed, the HIV-infected person lives under a biological sword of Damocles. Persons with AIDS, many of whom have been discriminated against as members of stigmatized groups—intravenous (IV) drug users and homosexual men—face even greater discrimination as a result of their illness. The devastation of AIDS is concentrated within families and specific communities. On average, women with HIV infection transmit it to one third of their children perinatally (7). (Perinatal refers to the time immediately preceding, during, and following childbirth.) On average, each gay man in New York City knows six men who died of AIDS (8). AIDS raises special issues for health care workers: the occupational risk of accidental needle punctures and the attendant emotional reactions. A small percentage (0.3%) of injuries from needles used on patients with HIV infection have transmitted HIV to health care workers (9). Although this is a low percentage, the lethality of the disease requires that special precautions be taken in handling contaminated materials. A random survey of over

1,000 American primary care physicians revealed that, given the option, 50% would not treat patients with HIV infection (10).

Fear of contagion is a double-edged sword. One well-publicized report (11) of a dentist with AIDS who transmitted the virus to several patients during dental care (although the mechanism of transmission is unclear) led to controversial calls for HIV testing of health care workers. In July 1991, the United States Public Health Service's Centers for Disease Control (CDC) recommended HIV antibody testing for health care workers who perform certain "exposure-prone" procedures, and prohibited seropositive workers from performing those procedures (12). Organized medicine and civil rights organizations strenuously opposed these recommendations, citing the lack of scientific evidence that certain procedures were riskier than others. In the face of this criticism, the CDC replaced its proposal with guidelines that call for case-by-case decisions on whether HIV-infected health care workers may perform particular procedures based on their individual capabilities (13). The debate continues as more data are gathered. To establish appropriate procedures that will protect patients and health care workers without overreaction, members of the health care profession are reexamining their professional conduct and obligations.

Epidemiology of AIDS

AIDS is an international epidemic and a national health crisis. By the end of 1991, a total of 446,681 cases of AIDS had been reported to the World Health Organization (WHO) (14) from 162 countries on all six inhabited continents. The WHO estimates that the cumulative total of AIDS cases may reach 10 million, with 40 million persons infected with HIV by the year 2000 (15). In central and east Africa alone, an especially hard-hit region, one estimate predicts that, by the year 2000, AIDS will kill over a quarter of a million children under 5 years of age each year and produce between three and five million orphans during the 1990s (16).

In the United States, AIDS has as of this writing claimed more than twice as many lives as the 55,000 American servicemen and women lost during the Vietnam War. The nation's reported cases of AIDS (206,392 as of December 31, 1991 [17]) continue to rise steadily. The 15th leading cause of death in 1988 (18), it rose to 9th as of August 31, 1991 after heart disease, malignant tumor, stroke, accident, chronic obstructive pulmonary disease, pneumonia and influenza, diabetes mellitus, and suicide (19). Between 1988 and 1989, the age-adjusted rate of death from HIV infection increased by 32% (18). In the United States, the epidemic's destruction cuts across generations, ethnic groups, sexes, and geographic regions. Approximately 2% of all U.S. cases have occurred in children under 13 years of age (17); 54% have occurred in Euro-Americans, 20% in African-Americans, 16% in Hispanic-Americans, and 0.6% in Asian-Americans and Native Americans (17). Ten percent of adolescents or adults with AIDS have been women (17). Cases have been reported in all 50 states, the District of Columbia, Puerto Rico, and the Virgin Islands (17). Of the cases reported in 1991, 83% were in metropolitan areas with a population of 500,000 or more, 11% were in smaller cities of 50,000 to 500,000, and 6% were in towns or rural areas of less than 50,000 (17).

Among American men, having unprotected sex with an infected man has been the most common mode of transmission (65% of AIDS cases); sharing contaminated needles during drug injection is the second method (19%), but faster growing (17). Men who inject drugs *and* have sex with men account for 7% of total cases; heterosexual contact, receipt of contaminated transfusions or blood products, and undetermined factors each account for no more than 3%. Women account for an increasing proportion of AIDS cases in the United States: from 1988 to 1989, cases in women rose 29% compared with 18% in men (20). By 1987, in New Jersey and New York, AIDS had become the third leading cause of death among women aged 15–44 years and the leading cause of death among African-American women in the same age group, ahead of malignant tumor and heart disease (21). The disproportionate impact on nonwhite women is related to the higher rates of HIV infection among IV drug users and their sexual partners (20). Among American women, IV drug use accounts for half of their cases of AIDS, unprotected sex with an infected man one third, and contaminated transfusions and blood products and undetermined factors, the rest (17). Many American women are unaware they are at risk for HIV infection (22), making women's access to HIV education, testing, counseling, and treatment an urgent public health priority.

The incidence of AIDS is accelerating among children and adolescents in the United States. In 1987 AIDS became the ninth leading cause of death among children aged 1–4 years and the sixth cause of death among adolescents aged 15–24 years (23). Among adolescents aged 13–19 years, one fourth of cases have been transmitted through unprotected sex between males, whereas heterosexual contact and intravenous drug use each account for about one sixth (17). Over one third are transfusion or blood product related, and the remainder are associated with no known risk. Finally, in children under age 13 years, 85% are cases of perinatal transmission from an infected mother, which may include transmission through breast milk, 13% are associated with transfusions or blood products, and 2% are of unknown cause (17).

An estimated 1 million Americans have HIV infection (24), and about 40,000 Americans acquire new HIV infections annually and are expected to develop AIDS. About half of those who are HIV infected may also have CD4$^+$ cell counts of less than 500 per cu mm, an immunologic marker of an active HIV infection (24), and thus need medical treatment (25).

Biology of AIDS

The human immunodeficiency virus attaches to a type of lymphocyte, the CD4$^+$ helper T cell (pp. 403–404), a critical component of the body's immune system, and is incorporated into its genome. After an incubation period, during which the infected person remains well, HIV replicates and destroys the host cell. This incapacitates the body's immune system, resulting in nonspecific systemic symptoms of fever, night sweats, weight loss, and malaise, and opportunistic infections and malignancies, the defining disorders of AIDS (26). The opportunistic infections include the most common one, *Pneumocystis P. carinii*, caused by a protozoan parasite resembling a fungus; tuberculosis (p. 195), caused by a bacterium; toxoplasmosis, caused by a protozoan parasite which, during pregnancy, causes severe fetal abnormalities; candidiasis, caused by a fungus that most often affects the mouth; and other viral infections (e.g., cytomegalovirus, which causes a serious retinal infection that can cause blindness). The opportunistic malignancies include Kaposi's sarcoma, a purplish-brown tumor usually confined to the skin that spreads to other body sites in AIDS patients, and lymphoma, a malignancy of lymphocytes that can involve many tissues. Complications of AIDS arise in every organ system: cardiovascular, pulmonary, endocrinologic, hematologic, renal, gastrointestinal, dermatologic, and neurologic.

DEMENTIAS OF AIDS

The human immunodeficiency virus has an affinity for the nervous system (i.e., it is neurotropic). Soon after exposure to the virus occurs, at about the same time that seroconversion (production of antibodies to HIV) occurs, the virus enters the nervous system (27). After entry, it sometimes causes a transient encephalitis (brain infection), meningitis (infection of the meningeal membranes surrounding the brain and spinal cord), or myelopathy (spinal cord disease). These infections typically subside spontaneously, and the virus remains dormant. All of the above usually occur before HIV has damaged the immune system (27).

Eventually most HIV-infected patients develop a dementing illness called HIV encephalopathy (formerly called the AIDS dementia complex). Persons with dementia experience diffuse cognitive dysfunction in the presence of normal alertness, and have a prolonged, progressive, life-shortening course (pp. 278–285). In addition, patients with HIV encephalopathy usually show a subtype of dementia termed subcortical dementia. Subcortical dementias are characterized by psychomotor slowing, apathy, social withdrawal, movement abnormalities such as tremor, ataxia (unsteady gait), and myoclonus (brief muscle spasms), and mood disorder, most typically depression (28, 29). This corresponds to the predominant occurrence of the virus in the brain's basal ganglia (the putamen, caudate nucleus, globus pallidus, amygdala, claustrum, and thalamus, all masses of gray matter buried deep in the cerebral hemispheres, close to the ventricles), as well as in the deep hemispheric white matter. The electroencephalogram (p. 198) is abnormal in two thirds of AIDS patients (28, 30), and magnetic resonance imaging of the brain typically reveals brain atrophy (reduction in size and number of cells) with enlargement of the ventricles and lesions (discrete areas of disease) in the white matter around the ventricles (28). Interestingly, the HIV encephalopathy sometimes appears before the immune system is affected (27, 28).

HIV encephalopathy, by far the most common AIDS dementia, is not the only cause of dementia in AIDS. The opportunistic infections and cancers listed above may also affect the brain and produce dementia, which may or may not be of the subcortical type (28).

DELIRIUM IN AIDS

Delirium, like dementia, is a syndrome of diffuse intellectual dysfunction (31). Unlike dementia, delirium is characterized by deficits of arousal and attention (p. 287). Delirium has numerous causes, including metabolic derangement and infection. In AIDS, delirium can occur during pneumocystis pneumonia due to decreased oxygenation of the brain, high fever, or opportunistic infections of the brain. A drug user with AIDS may have delir-

ium as a result of substance intoxication or withdrawal (32).

Psychosocial Factors in AIDS

Depressed mood and depressive illnesses are common in AIDS for many reasons. Depressive illness may be secondary to viral infections of the brain, including all those noted above. Depression may be a side effect of drugs used to treat AIDS (32). Some patients who develop HIV infection have preexisting mood disorders, leaving them vulnerable to recurrence under the multiple stresses of the illness (33). In fact, persons at high risk for developing HIV infection may be at greater risk for developing mood disorders even if they never become infected (33).

Depression may also result from psychosocial stress. The psychosocial stressors for AIDS patients are numerous. A depressed mood (not necessarily a depressive illness) is a common experience for most persons who have received a fatal diagnosis (pp. 161–171) (34). For persons who are HIV-infected or have AIDS, there is the added stress of having to reveal previously confidential information (e.g., sexual behavior, drug use) to family or others and to bear the stigma of having AIDS. Many experience rejection by friends, family, coworkers, and neighbors once the diagnosis becomes public knowledge. In addition, the patient may fear or experience loss of independence, bowel or bladder control, or occupational competence as the illness progresses (35).

Not everyone is affected by these events in the same way, and not all develop depressive illness. The patient's adaptation to the illness is affected by what the illness means to him or her. Common meanings of illness include illness as a challenge, an enemy, a punishment, a weakness, a strategy for life, an irreparable loss or injury, or an incentive to change behaviors (36). If stressors overwhelm coping capacities, depressive illness may result.

The clinical findings in depressive illness are discussed at length in Chapter 20. Some of these include a sad, apathetic, or anxious mood, loss of self-esteem, guilt, hopeless or helpless feelings, and vegetative signs including insomnia, loss of appetite (anorexia), and suicidal thoughts.

SUICIDE IN AIDS

Suicide occurs in up to 15% of patients with depression. The risk of suicide among men with AIDS is 15 to 36 times that in the general male population (37). This is related to a clustering of risk factors for suicide in AIDS: depression, chronic illness, and drug dependence.

PSYCHOLOGY OF AIDS PREVENTION

Prevention is the best hope for controlling the HIV epidemic. The social behaviors— needle-sharing and unprotected sex—that transmit HIV are crucial aspects of the psychology of the disease. In this regard, AIDS is like other serious illnesses such as cancer and heart disease. Cigarette smoking, an addiction of millions of Americans, contributes to 350,000 deaths annually (p. 79). Despite knowing its dangers, people continue to smoke, denying their own vulnerability or believing that stopping is not worth the effort. For smoking, as well as AIDS-related risk behaviors, knowledge alone is not sufficient to change habits that are powerfully reinforced by pleasurable experiences. Guiding patients to adopt health-promoting behaviors is increasingly recognized as an important role of physicians. Effectiveness in that role requires an understanding of the principles of how people perceive a health risk and alter their behavior to reduce it.

Health Belief Model and Patient Education

Whereas knowledge of health risks may influence behavioral change in some persons, other factors may be important for others. The health belief model (p. 101) holds that certain perceptions are necessary to consolidate health-related behavioral changes (38). These perceptions are perceived vulnerability and susceptibility to the illness, perceived serious-ness of the illness, motivation to health, and perceived benefits and personal costs of behavioral change in the interest of health. Ultimately, is the benefit to health of changing behavior worth the money, time, inconvenience, or embarrassment necessary to make the change? Physicians in practice and the medical and public health community in general should make persons aware of their susceptibility, of the seriousness of the risk of AIDS, of the ease and benefits of care, and that the benefits outweigh the costs. When tested, this model has repeatedly proved effective.

Influence of Peers

People are strongly influenced by what they think their peers are doing (39). This was demonstrated by an experimental intervention in which persons identified as popular leaders of the gay community in a small city were trained to serve as "behavior change endorsers" to their peers (40). Two months after the intervention, the proportion of men who engaged in anal intercourse without a condom decreased from 37% to 28%, and the proportion of men who had more than one sexual partner decreased 18%. Likewise, IV drug users are more likely to use bleach to clean their syringes if they believe their friends and acquaintances have done so (39).

Physician Sensitivity to Cultural Values

Assessing behavioral risks for AIDS requires sensitivity, because IV drug use and certain sexual behaviors carry strong negative social sanctions. Patients therefore hide such behavior or regard it as privileged information. For example, African-American and Hispanic-American men may deny having sex with other men because of homophobic attitudes within their cultures (41) and fear of being labeled by professionals. Female sexual partners of men who have or are at risk for HIV infection may not follow advice to use condoms because they fear provoking the anger of their partners for making such a demand. Follow-up counseling sessions that include the male partner may help. All types of substance abuse are highly correlated with high-risk sexual behavior (i.e., increased number of partners, and not protected by a condom) (42). Thus, physicians must tactfully conduct a complete history of drug and alcohol use with all patients.

Maintaining the trust of patients also requires sensitivity to cultural values in general, regardless of their direct relevance to AIDS. For example, Hispanic-Americans are especially likely to prefer a physician with a friendly manner, one who makes physical contact through shaking hands or placing a hand on the patient's shoulder, and who treats the family, not just the patient (43).

Maintaining Hope

Coping with stress is easier for persons who maintain hope and face challenges. Despite the gravity of HIV infection and AIDS, most patients meet these challenges successfully. Clinicians experienced in the treatment of HIV infection are often struck by the courage and optimism of their patients. Compared with a control group of nondepressed, HIV-seronegative gay men, a community sample of nondepressed, HIV-positive gay men demonstrated (on a questionnaire) high levels of hope about the future in general (44).

Social Support

Social support, through emotional contact with valued individuals and groups, has emerged as an important determinant in coping with illness. Social support has protective effects on health. For example, social support reduces the likelihood that depression will complicate a stroke (45). A high level of social contact also was found to protect patients who had arthritis or heart trouble (and who also reported depression) against deterioration (46). Similarly, in a study of HIV-infected homosexual men, an active coping style was significantly related to greater perceived social support, whereas avoidance coping was related to lower social suport (47).

What is different about AIDS is that family ties have often been strained or severed by family rejection of a patient's homosexuality or drug use even before the diagnosis of HIV infection. Thus, same-sex lovers and drug use partners in spousal relationships have often provided the only support. AIDS has led many practitioners in medicine to reevaluate their concepts of social support and their images of family.

People benefit not only from the support of their families and friends, but also from societal support. The responses of countries to AIDS are as varied as their political systems and cultures. In Cuba, where HIV infection is rare (0.00009% of the adult population), most of the population over 15 years of age has been tested for HIV and those who test positive (several hundred persons) have been quarantined for life in "residential parks (48)." They may have weekend passes, but are chaperoned by health officials or medical students. The Cuban Ministry of Public Health justifies this policy as the only guarantee of safe sexual behavior by HIV-infected persons. This policy is reminiscent of leper colonies in Europe in the Middle Ages.

By contrast, in Amsterdam (49), the Dutch government has instituted policies that encourage voluntary behavior change among the city's IV drug users, whose prevalence of HIV infection is about 30%, providing information, condoms, and needle exchange. Studies have shown a marked reduction in sharing used needles after introduction of the needle exchange program. This was, in turn, followed by a decrease in the incidence (number of new cases) of HIV infection among Amsterdam's IV drug users.

Biological Treatments of AIDS

For HIV and AIDS, the antiviral agent zidovudine (AZT), which interferes with viral replication, is the mainstay of biological therapy. Drugs for specific opportunistic infections and malignancies are used when indicated. These include the antibiotics trimethoprim/sulfamethoxazole, pentamidine isethionate, and dapsone for prevention and treatment of *Pneumocystis carinii* pneumonia; interferon for

Kaposi's sarcoma; ganciclovir sodium, an antiviral used for cytomegalovirus retinitis; and acyclovir, an antiviral treatment useful against herpes simplex virus infection.

Drugs are also used to treat behavioral complications. For depression, the antidepressants imipramine and fluoxetine hydrochloride are effective and well tolerated (50, 51). The drug AZT ameliorates the cognitive symptoms of HIV dementia (52). Psychostimulants (dextroamphetamine, methylphenidate hydrochloride) counteract the apathy and psychomotor retardation of AIDS dementia (53). Delirium is treated by attending to the underlying condition and providing a supportive environment (e.g., night lights, visitors, conversation with staff) (pp. 288–290).

Medications often have behavioral side effects. AZT can cause insomnia and agitation (an increased frequency of purposeless movement in response to an intense mood); interferon can cause depression and weakness; the combination of trimethoprim and sulfamethoxazole can cause psychosis (inability to perform ordinary tasks of life because of delusions, hallucinations, formal thought disorder, or severe cognitive deficits), depression, anorexia (appetite loss), insomnia, headache, and apathy.

Finally, long-term maintenance treatment with dolophine hydrochloride (methadone), a synthetic narcotic agent that blocks the craving for heroin, is one of the most effective methods of treatment of narcotic addiction. Because it reduces intravenous drug use, it is also effective in preventing spread of HIV by needle sharing.

Psychosocial Treatments: HIV Test Counseling and Psychotherapy

Counseling and psychotherapy, which use clinician-patient communication in a variety of strategies (e.g., insight, education, and catharsis), can help manage stress and reduce suffering.

Counseling for the antibody test that diagnoses HIV infection is a paradigm of medical counseling. The objectives of HIV test coun-

seling have recently been formulated (54) and illustrate principles of counseling for other life-threatening conditions (e.g., genetic counseling or informing a patient of a diagnosis of cancer). All physicians should be able to perform HIV test counseling. The U.S. Public Health Service recommends pre- and posttest counseling sessions. The content of sessions depends on each patient's needs and concerns, but most sessions should contain certain basic elements (54). Before the test the physician explains the meaning of the test, takes steps to protect the patient's confidentiality, facilitates the decision to be tested, and assesses the patient's strengths and vulnerabilities likely to come into play when dealing with the result, whether positive or negative. Posttest counseling involves notification, reduction of immediate distress, education on the behavioral changes necessary to prevent the spread of infection (using condoms during sex, reducing the number of sex partners, avoiding drug use in association with sex, and cleaning needles with bleach), and planning for follow-up care. These principles are summarized in Table 1.1.

Although some physicians are understandably concerned that HIV testing could increase already high levels of distress in patients with histories of high-risk behaviors, test counseling combined with six sessions of stress reduction training has been shown to effectively reduce distress for seropositive persons after HIV testing (55). Most physicians are not experienced at stress reduction training, but

Table 1.1. Human Immunodeficiency Virus Test Counseling[a]

Pretest session
  Explain meaning of test
  Construct positive test-result scenario with patient.
  Anticipate responses and actions
Posttest sessions
  Review meaning of test
  Elicit responses
  Reinforce behavioral change (equally important for seronegative persons)
  Review medical follow-up, whom to tell, and support network

[a]Modified from Perry SW, Markowitz JC. Counseling for HIV testing. Hosp Comm Psychiatry 1988;39:731–739.

they may make referrals to experienced clinicians. Also, their ongoing relationship with the patient may supply many of the same supportive elements.

These principles of medical counseling presume a context of an effective doctor-patient relationship, the basis of which consists of four elements: acceptance, empathy, conceptualization, and competence (56). That is, the physician must treat the patient's illness in the context of understanding that person's unique background and responses to the illness. This relationship is affected by both persons' past experiences unconsciously projected into the present (called transference in the patient, and countertransference in the doctor) and by age, sex, ethnicity, culture, and social class. Each of these factors strikes powerful emotional chords in both patients and doctors.

Psychotherapy for seriously ill patients explores issues such as loss of function and social role, coping with discomfort and pain, facing dying and death, and forming a new self-concept that provides satisfaction and meaning within the constraints of the illness (57). Depression and demoralization are not the inevitable byproduct of serious illness. When they occur, the doctor recognizes that each stressor has unique meaning and potential for resolution for each patient. Two examples of psychotherapeutic interventions for patients with HIV or AIDS illustrate this point:

> A gay man diagnosed with HIV became depressed. He revealed to his doctor that his greatest concern was that he would lose the love and respect of his parents to whom he had never revealed his homosexuality. The conversation with the doctor enabled the patient to find the courage to confront his parents and his depression lifted.
>
> A widow with AIDS became despondent. Her husband, an intravenous drug user, had died of AIDS. She told the psychiatrist that she felt guilty at the prospect of dying because it meant leaving her children alone with no one to care for them. She had thought of asking her sister to adopt them, but resentment stemming from her sister's hostility towards her husband prevented

her from broaching the subject. With the psychiatrist's support, she approached her sister, who agreed to adopt the children. Following this, the patient's depression resolved.

Pediatric AIDS

The high rate of increase of new pediatric HIV infections is of great concern. In the United States, 1,700 infants were born infected with HIV in 1989 (55). Infants with HIV infection progress to AIDS faster than adults, on average 1 year as opposed to 10 years from time of infection (58). This is probably because the immune systems of infants are not as well developed as those of adults. Because AZT delays progression (59), however, early treatment can favorably alter the disease course.

A common syndrome of neurodevelopmental deterioration (loss of neurological developmental milestones) in infants, because of the direct effects of HIV infection of the brain, is the equivalent of HIV encephalopathy in adults (60). Some medical complications of AIDS are more common in young children than in adolescents and adults. These are lymphoid interstitial pneumonitis (infiltration of lung tissue by activated lymphocytes) and recurrent bacterial infections (61). On the other hand, Kaposi's sarcoma, common in adult AIDS, is unusual in childhood AIDS (62).

Treating children who have perinatal AIDS requires understanding of the biopsychosocial model of illness. Families of children with AIDS have multiple problems, including parental HIV infection, poverty, substance abuse, and depression (60). Treatment of these children requires instilling hope and offering support; it requires medical care, counseling and substance abuse treatment for their parents, and addressing the individual needs of the child. The latter may include, at times of maternal illness, arrangements for surrogate caregivers if there is no father at home (61). These interventions usually require the collaboration of a team of health professionals.

CASE HISTORY

You are an internist in practice in a large American city. You have begun interviewing a new patient.

Mr. R. is a 35-year-old Hispanic, Roman Catholic, New York City policeman who is the father of four children ages 16 months through 12 years. He was referred to you by the counselor at a confidential HIV test site where he went 2 weeks ago. He had received a letter telling him to come in to receive the results of his test, and there he was told that he had tested positive for the antibody that shows HIV infection. He is worried that he may already be suffering from AIDS.

He is not surprised. Although he does not consider himself bisexual or gay, he has sex with a man who was just diagnosed with AIDS. He has noticed weakness, weight loss, forgetfulness, and mistakes in judgment at work. His sergeant suspects he may be on drugs. Although he has never used drugs while on duty, he has used crack during sex with his lover.

At the testing center he was counseled about the treatments and prognosis of HIV infection, safer sex methods, and discussion of his condition with his wife. Many local physicians do not treat AIDS patients, so he was referred to you because you are known to have an interest in treating patients with this disease. He accepted the referral but did not reveal the infection to his wife; he was afraid she would leave him if she knew he had had sex with men. So as not to arouse her suspicions, he has not begun using condoms during sex with her. Now he has become distraught at the idea that he may have infected her.

She is 32 years old, a full-time homemaker, and currently healthy. She has been concerned that their 16-month-old daughter has not been developing as fast as her other children. Because this could be a sign of HIV infection, the pediatrician asks about, and she denies, risk factors for HIV in the family. However, the question has made her uneasy. She knows women in the neighborhood who acquired HIV from their husbands or boyfriends and then transmitted it to their children. She has thought of mentioning the subject to her husband, but its implications are too disturbing for her to deal with right now. Although recently he has had little interest in sex with her, their sex life was always good, and she cannot imagine that he might have sex with men. She has never seen any signs that he has used drugs; even wondering about his behavior makes her feel guilty.

From the data presented in this book, you could apply the biopsychosocial model to the care of Mr. R, a man with a fatal illness that he may have transmitted to his wife and infant daughter. Much is at stake at this time of crisis for his family. What can be salvaged?

The diagnoses of HIV infection and cocaine abuse are definite. Mr. R's report of weakness, weight loss, forgetfulness, and errors in judgment at work require that you consider diagnoses of AIDS with an opportunistic infection or cancer, HIV encephalopathy with subcortical dementia, and depressive illness with a risk of suicide.

To proceed with diagnosis and treatment, you must take into account your feelings about his risk-taking and self-centered behavior, so that you can appreciate his personality traits and accomplishments, and empathize with his dilemma. Your manner will be friendly and respectful. Among other courtesies, you will shake his hand at the beginning and at the end of your examination.

As you continue your interview, you will inquire further about Mr. R's memory and other mental abilities. Soon, you will formally assess his cognition with a screening instrument such as the "Minimental State" examination. You will ask about symptoms of depression, past episodes of mood disorder, past suicide attempts, and family history of psychiatric illness. You will assess his suicide risk, not hesitating to ask him about suicidal thoughts and intentions. This will include asking whether he keeps a loaded gun at home. Although you will be mindful of the epidemiology of suicide (more common in men than in women, more common in police work than in most other occupations, more frequent in chronically ill people; less frequent in Catholics), you will emphasize Mr. R's history and mental status in assessing his suicide risk (pp. 353–355).

You will question him systematically about symptoms in each organ system, because this is standard history-taking procedure (p. 180), and because AIDS can affect all organ systems. You will physically examine Mr. R. Following your examination, you will summarize your findings and conclusions, answer his questions, and ask for his opinion about your treatment plans. If he asks about the confidentiality of what he tells you, you will respond that you will make every effort to keep his communications confidential, but that under several circumstances (e.g., a life-threatening emergency, a court subpoena) you may have to breach it.

If he is seriously depressed, suicidal, demented, or otherwise seriously ill, he will need hospitalization. If there is serious depression or suicide risk, psychiatric consultation and psychiatric hospitalization are indicated, preferably in a general hospital where you can continue to participate in Mr. R's care. If Mr. R is suicidal and refuses admission, you or the consultant should arrange involuntary hospitalization.

Whatever the site of Mr. R's care, you will review his prior medical records. If laboratory testing has not been done recently, you will order the following studies: complete blood count and differential count; a T4 lymphocyte count and a T4:T8 lymphocyte ratio; an erythrocyte sedimentation rate; blood studies for electrolytes, urea nitrogen, uric acid, and enzyme levels; a urinanalysis and urine drug screen; a chest x-ray film; and an electrocardiogram. You will also order an electroencephalogram and (unless Mr. R. has to pay out of pocket) magnetic resonance brain imaging. The phlebotomist (the person who draws Mr.

R's blood) should wear latex gloves and goggles and dispose of the syringe and needle (without recapping the needle) in a special container. Neuropsychologic testing may be in order, especially if there is a question about Mr. R's intellectual capacities if and when he plans to return to work.

If there is evidence for HIV encephalopathy, or if the T4 lymphocyte count is below 500 per cu mm, you will likely prescribe AZT. You will treat infections with a well-chosen antibiotic and supportive measures (e.g., fluids, expectorants, and respiratory therapy for pneumonia). If Mr. R is depressed, the psychiatrist will recommend or provide an appropriate psychotherapy (pp. 310–320) and somatic treatment.

The above should be easy compared to your development with Mr. R of a strategy that will ensure that his wife's and child's health will be addressed. This will include HIV testing. Much of your care of Mr. R will be devoted to your persuading him that it is in his best interest to be considerate of his family, whatever its cost to him. Disclosure to Mrs. R of her health risk status is in her best interest, and probably in Mr. R's best interest as well. He will want his family's support, and to support them in return, in the months and years ahead. Perhaps Mrs. R will be irreparably furious, and justified in leaving Mr. R, when she is better informed about the situation. On the other hand, based on the data available, there are some strengths in the marital relationship that might withstand this crisis. At the appropriate time, you will arrange the first of several family counseling sessions. The biomedical model offers you no guidance in this regard.

2/Basic Research and Statistical Methods[a]

Robert Margolies, Ph.D., and Marie D. Thomas, Ph.D.

OBJECTIVES

GENERAL OBJECTIVE: Given a journal article, comment on the type and quality of the methodology.

SPECIFIC OBJECTIVES:
1. Discuss empiricism, inductive reasoning, and deductive reasoning.
2. Define nominal, ordinal, and interval-ratio data, and discuss how each type of data is presented in tables and graphs.
3. Define descriptive and inferential statistics.
4. Discuss central tendency, variability, and correlation.
5. Discuss null hypothesis, statistical significance, and type I and type II errors.
6. State when you should apply each of the tests of statistical significance.
7. Discuss reliability and validity.
8. State the essentials of experimental design that allow for reasonable conclusions.
9. State the pitfalls of published research to be considered in evaluating research conclusions.

Even if you never conduct medical research, you will use it in your daily practice of medicine each time you read a new journal article or review the literature in your field. Understanding basic research and statistical concepts will help you to evaluate critically the literature, and sort through what sometimes seems to be contradictory findings on a given issue (such as the recent controversy over the cholesterol-lowering effects of oat bran [1]). It will also help you to appreciate how the logical methods of science guide hypothesis testing and theory development.

HOW THE GOALS OF SCIENCE INFORM MEDICINE

Before Joseph Lister introduced the principle of antisepsis to surgery in 1865, surgeons operated in old, blood-stained coats under the most unsanitary conditions (2). Complete recovery from surgery was rare; if patients did not die on the operating table or from postoperative infection, their chances of having a limb amputated following hospital-acquired gangrene were strong. Such outcomes distressed surgeons, but infection was considered an inevitable consequence of surgery because of some type of corrosive action of oxygen on tissue, a theory that at the time could not be scientifically proved or disproved.

---

[a]The opinions expressed herein are those of the authors. They are not official and do not necessarily reflect the views of the Navy Department.

Lister felt this explanation was inadequate; after all, healthy tissue was surrounded by oxygen and did not become infected. His studies on blood coagulation and inflammation, and his replications of Louis Pasteur's work, convinced him that infection was the result of microorganisms introduced into the wound. He hypothesized that through antisepsis, the destruction of the microbes falling into the wound, he could prevent infection. His techniques, although cumbersome, resulted in fewer fatalities and many complete recoveries without infection.

Many physicians in Germany and France readily accepted and practiced "Listerism," but Lister's own British colleagues initially ignored his findings. In Victorian England, scientific observation often clashed with the tradition of authority, and authority said infection was inevitable.

Lister's research illustrates the goals of science: to *observe* and *describe*, to *understand* or *explain*, to *hypothesize* or *predict*, and, in the applied sciences, finally to *control* the phenomenon of interest. To describe the phenomenon (in the case of medicine, disease) observations must be made. Scientific observations are empiric, i.e., real, objective, measurable, and repeatable. Lister's observations of surgical outcomes and his empiric study of inflammation convinced him that putrefaction was caused by an unknown foreign substance. To explain his observations, he applied Pasteur's findings that microorganisms in the air fermented previously sterile solutions.

The data that Lister, Pasteur, and others collected were best explained by the germ theory of disease. This process of moving from the particular (data) to the general (eventually a theory) is inductive reasoning. Lister then hypothesized or predicted that if the germ theory was correct, then destroying the germs dropped into a wound during surgery should prevent infection. His surgical outcomes supported this theory.

Once a workable theory is developed, the process is reversed; scientists use the theory to predict new events consistent with the theory (3). This is deductive reasoning, moving from the general to the particular. Pasteur's communications with Lister led Pasteur to seek the cause of disease in microbes, to study the anthrax bacillus and, eventually, to develop a vaccine. The German physician and bacteriologist Robert Koch (1843–1910) also used deductive reasoning to link six types of surgical infection to six distinct bacteria (4, 5).

Eventually deductive reasoning led to the realization that a surgical wound need not be disinfected, but that anything that contacted the wound should be sterile. With this discovery, Lister's antiseptic surgery became outmoded and aseptic surgery was born. Such is the progress and attitude of science; the same sequence of observation, explanation, and prediction continues to be used to conquer modern medical problems.

BIOSTATISTICS

When Lister first presented his findings about antiseptic surgery in *Lancet*, he reported his results as a proportion: number of deaths per total number of cases, before and after "the antiseptic period" (2, 6). He used statistics to help him draw conclusions. Statistics is a branch of logic and mathematics that enables a researcher to organize and analyze numeric observations. Statistical analysis provide a way to evaluate the validity of study results and, ultimately, to propose hypotheses or theories.

Categories of Data

To apply statistics to scientific observations, the observations, or *data*, must be in numeric form. Data can be viewed at three levels of measurement: nominal, ordinal, and interval-ratio. The more information the numbers provide about each measured subject, the higher the level of measurement.

NOMINAL DATA

Nominal (categoric) data refers to the classification of objects or subjects into discrete categories, with no suggestion of an underlying continuum. For example, patients can be classified into diagnostic categories (e.g., hypertension–Group 1, gastritis–Group 2), but the numerals themselves have meaning only as labels. Further examples of nominal data are tumor types or psychiatric diagnoses. Information from categoric data can only be used to compare the number of frequencies of subjects classified into categories.

ORDINAL DATA

Ordinal scales imply a continuum; they specify the relative order or rank of subjects or objects. Burn depth, for example, is labeled as first, second, or third degree, an ordinal scale. The severity of two burns can be compared according to which one is deeper. Ordinal scales are not an exact ranking, however, and lack numeric properties; a second-degree burn is not twice as deep as a first-degree burn.

INTERVAL-RATIO DATA

Most physical scales (e.g., height, weight), and many psychologic measurements (e.g., IQ), lend themselves to true numeric status and can be treated as interval-ratio data. Such data are measured on scales with equal intervals between measurement units; thus, they can be subject to addition and subtraction (interval and ratio), and multiplication and division (ratio) without destroying the scale's integrity. Because interval-ratio scales have true numeric properties, they provide the most information and can be analyzed in more sophisticated ways.

Branches of Statistics

There are two major branches of statistics: descriptive and inferential. Descriptive statistics are used to list or summarize sets of data in a practical way. For example, taking the number of hours per day a first-year resident works in a week and averaging them to get one summary statistic (a mean) is a descriptive statistic task. Descriptive statistics do not support inferences; rather, data are organized like

an inventory so that they may be examined from a clear perspective.

Inferential statistics make probability-based assertions about a population (all existing or potentially existing subjects for which generalizations will be made), based on data from a sample (a subgroup of the population). For example, the activity level of a group of 30 children who have attention deficit disorder who are taking 10 mg of methylphenidate per day, and the activity level of another 30 children receiving a placebo (no drug) could be measured. Were there a difference in treatment outcome between the samples, it could be inferred, with a probability estimated from inferential statistics, whether such a difference is likely to be found in the population of similar subjects. The leap from descriptive to inferential statistics is made when generalizations or predictions are made from data obtained from a sample. Many advances in inferential statistics were made as computers became more powerful and widespread in the 1960s and 1970s.

DESCRIPTIVE STATISTICS

Using Tables and Graphs to Organize and Summarize Data

For nominal data, tables generally consist of frequencies and percentages. For example, an oncology nurse collects data about cancer patients who have been on her floor in the last month (this and all other raw data examples are hypothetical). The data could be displayed as shown in Table 2.1, or it could be presented in the form of a bar chart as shown in Figure 2.1.

Like nominal data, ordinal data are tabled by listing the frequency or percentage of each observation. The difference, of course, is that

Table 2.1. Frequency Distribution, Nominal Data

Type of Cancer	Number of Patients	Percent
Lung	20	40
Breast	15	30
Pancreas	10	20
Other	5	10
Total	50	100

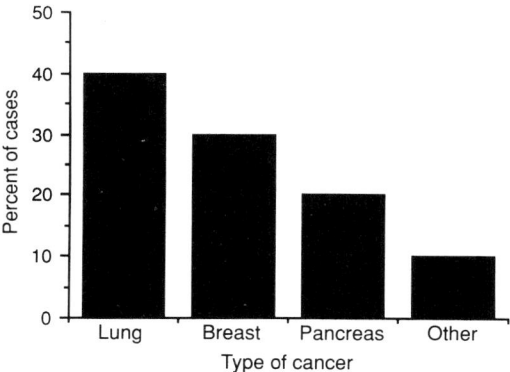

Figure 2.1. Bar chart.

ordinal categories suggest a continuum. Using the burn depth example, a severely burned person might be categorized according to the severity of the burn (Table 2.2). Naturally ordered data (e.g., stages of development) are of an ordinally ranked nature and can be correlated (see p. 23) with other ranked data. Ordinal data are rarely graphed.

When interval-ratio data are tabulated as a frequency distribution, the categories represent points (or sections) on a continuous, mathematically precise scale, such as inches, hours, or degrees. For example, the following are lengths in hours of the first stage of labor (the period during which the cervix is not yet fully dilated) for 20 women who gave birth in the same hospital during a 24-hour period: 11, 10, 13, 7, 6, 15, 10, 10, 12, 8, 9, 10, 9, 9, 11, 8, 12, 11, 10, 9. These data as they appear are meaningless, but they can be grouped into a frequency distribution from which information can be immediately extracted. For example, the most frequent length of labor was in the interval of 10 to 11 hours (Table 2.3).

Frequency distributions are generally graphed into frequency polygons as can be

seen in Figure 2.2. The curve is jagged because of the small sample size. Frequency polygons "smooth out" as the sample size increases.

Characteristics of frequency polygons (e.g., their shape, where they are located on the graph, how spread out they are) reflect important characteristics of the data. This will become clearer in the following discussions of measures of central tendency and variability.

Describing Data Using Averages

Measures of central tendency inform us about the general location of a frequency distribution. For example, in Figure 2.3, two sets of first-stage labor data are graphed. For day 1, the average number of hours is around 10; for day 2, the average is higher.

There are three measures of central tendency: the mode, the median, and the mean. The mode is the value of the most frequently occurring measurement. In a graphed frequency distribution, the mode is located at the peak of the distribution. For the first-stage labor data, the mode is 10 for day 1 and 16 for day 2. Some distributions have two modes; they are bimodal. Such a case would result, for example, if the heights of a large sample of men and women were graphed on the same axes.

When observations are ordered from least to most, the median is the middle value. For an odd number of observations, the median value is the exact middle value. With an even number, the median is the midpoint between the two most central observations. For example, the median of 1, 3, 5, 7, and 9 is 5. For the day 1 labor data the median is 10 and for day 2 the median is 15 (Fig. 2.3). Because the

Table 2.2. Frequency Distribution, Ordinal Data

Degree of Burn	Percent of Body Tissue Burned
No burn	30
First degree	10
Second degree	40
Third degree	20

Table 2.3. Frequency Distribution, Interval-Ratio Data

Hours, First Stage Labor	Frequency
14-15	1
12-13	3
10-11	8
8-9	6
6-7	2
TOTAL	20

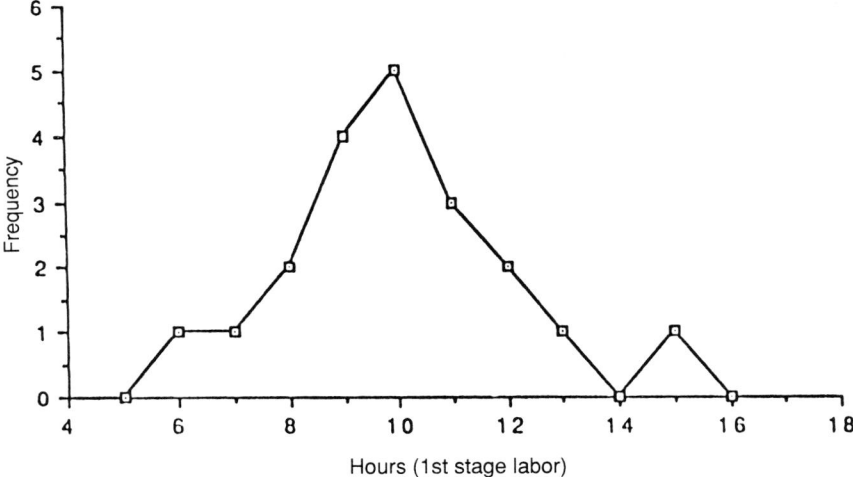

Figure 2.2.   Frequency polygon, Day 1 data.

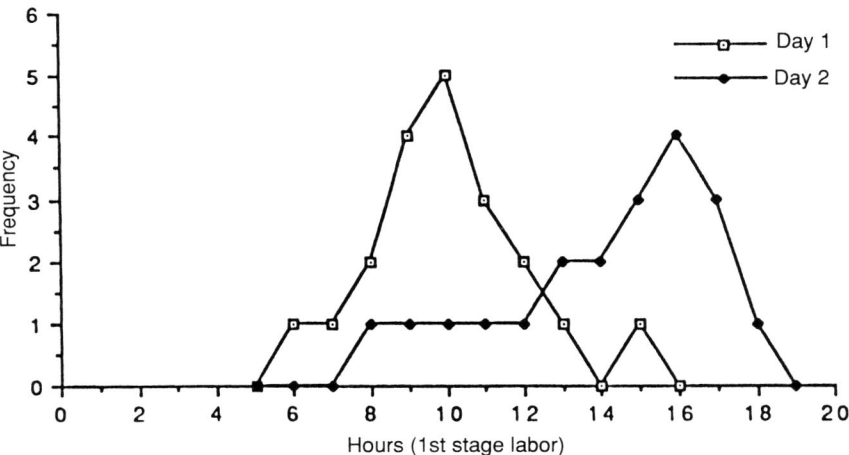

Figure 2.3.   Frequency polygons, Day 1 and Day 2 data.

median is the midpoint of a set of values, it divides the frequency distribution into two halves: 50% of the observations fall below the median and 50% fall above it.

The mean is what is popularly thought of as an average. It is found by summing all observations and dividing the sum by the number of observations. Some symbols will help:

X = an individual observation (score)
N = the total number of observations
Σ = "the sum of"
$\overline{X}$ = the mean

The mean is calculated from this formula: $\overline{X} = \frac{\Sigma X}{N}$ which reads: the mean equals the sum of the scores on variable X (a variable is anything that can be measured and for which the values can vary) divided by the total number of observations. For example, the number of hours per day a first-year resident works in 1 week are 12, 10, 14, 19, 11, 3, 15. The sum of the observations is 84; the number of observations is 7. The mean equals 84 divided by 7, or 12 hours per day.

The mean of the day 1 labor data is 10, and the day 2 data is 14.1. The mean is a fulcrum point, sensitive to all scores in a set of data; it reveals more about the set than does any individual observation. If, for example, the highest score in a data set were higher, the mean would shift upwards. This is in contrast to the median, which is not sensitive to the value of each score. If the highest score in a data set were higher, the median would stay the same because, regardless of its numeric value, the highest score is simply a score above the median.

Your selection of a central tendency measure depends on the level of measurement and the information you wish to convey. The mode is used primarily for nominal data (e.g., Which category is most frequent?), because it does not take into account characteristics of the entire distribution of scores. The mode can be cited, however, for any data if the goal is simply to identify the most frequent score or observation.

For ordinal data, the median is the appropriate measure of central tendency. For interval-ratio data, the mean or median may be most appropriate, depending on the shape of the frequency distribution. Distributions can have one of two general shapes, symmetrical or skewed. The day 1 labor data are approximately symmetrical; in a completely symmetrical distribution, one side of the frequency polygon is a mirror image of the other.

Now consider the day 2 data presented in Figure 2.3. On this day, a large number of primagravidas (woman pregnant for the first time; their lengths of labor tend to be longer) gave birth, and the overall length of labor was longer than on the previous day. The day 2 data are skewed; most of the data are bunched at one end of the distribution. This is a negatively skewed distribution because most of the scores fall at the high end of the distribution, with the tail pointing left. Distributions in which most scores fall at the lower end and only a few are at the positive extreme are positively skewed.

When a distribution is fairly symmetrical, the mean is the best indicator of the average. Where the distribution is approximately sym-

metrical, the mean, median, and mode will all be close to one another. However, when a distribution is highly skewed, positively or negatively, the median should be reported because it is not sensitive to extreme scores. For example, were the President of the United States to report the mean U.S. income as the national average, a rosy but inaccurate picture would be presented; extreme incomes raise the average. By reporting the median U.S. income, however, the salary that divides the upper and lower 50% of persons in the country would be given—a more accurate picture of the average income.

Measures of Variability

Frequency distributions (or sets of data) not only differ in shape or location; they also differ in how spread out or variable scores are. In Figure 2.4, distributions are juxtaposed. Each is symmetric and both have the same mean, but they differ in variability.

Variability is most important for interval-ratio data. The three measures of variability are the range, the standard deviation, and the variance. The range is the measured distance from the smallest observation to the largest. For example, in Figure 2.3, the range for day 1 is 9 and day 2 is 10. The range is not a preferred measure of variability, because it depends only on the two most extreme observations and does not reflect the variability of the scores in between.

The standard deviation (SD), a better measure of variability than the range, is the most

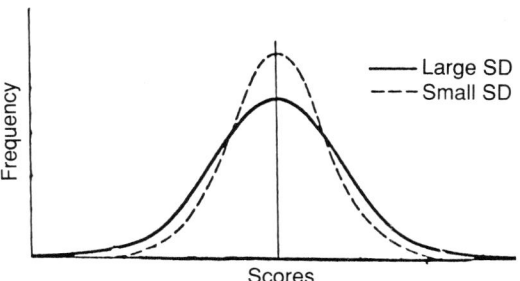

Figure 2.4. Frequency distributions with same mean but different SD.

Table 2.4.   Calculation Of The Standard Deviation

X (Score)	$\overline{X}$	$(X - \overline{X})$	$(X - \overline{X})^2$
1	5	-4	16
3	5	-2	4
5	5	0	0
7	5	$+2$	4
9	5	$+4$	16
		$\Sigma(X - \overline{X}) = 0$	$\Sigma(X - \overline{X})^2 = 40$

$$SD = \sqrt{\tfrac{40}{5}} = \sqrt{8} = 2.83$$

widely used measure. The SD is like (but not exactly like) an average of the distance from every score to the mean of the scores. That distance is called a deviation and is written: $X - \overline{X}$. Scores above the mean have a positive deviation; scores below the mean a negative deviation. The size of the "average" deviation depends on how variable or spread out the distribution is. If the distribution is very spread out, deviations tend to be large, and if the distribution is bunched up, deviations tend to be small.

Deviations cannot simply be added up and then divided by the number of observations; the negative and positive deviations cancel each other out, and the sum of deviation scores is always 0. The way around this problem is to square each deviation (to make them all positive). These squared deviations are then averaged, and the square root is taken to get back to the original units of measurement. The formula for the standard deviation therefore reads:

$$SD = \sqrt{\frac{\Sigma(X - \overline{X})^2}{N}}$$

The SD for the data 1, 3, 5, 7, 9 is calculated in Table 2.4. The SD is an average distance of every score to the mean. A standard deviation of 6.0 is larger than one of 2.83 and indicates a more variable set of scores.

The variance is the square of the SD. Conversely, the SD is the square root of the variance. The variance plays a role in more advanced statistics. The formula for the variance is the same as that for the SD but without the square root. The variance of the preceding data is, therefore, 8.

Normal Distributions, Z-Scores, and Percentile Ranks

A perfectly symmetric, bell-shaped frequency distribution of scores is a normal distribution. Almost all measurements of real-life phenomena (e.g., height, temperature, IQ) tend to yield distributions that have a normal bell shape. Such a distribution is symmetric, and the mean, median, and mode lie at the same point.

When measurements are normally distributed, it is useful to interpret scores by looking at their distance from the mean in SD units. Such scores are known as z-scores and are found by the formula $z = \frac{X - \overline{X}}{SD}$. A normal distribution of IQ scores with mean 100 and SD of 15 in terms of raw scores, z-scores, and percentile ranks is illustrated in Figure 2.5.

An IQ of 115, for example, falls at a z-score of $+1$: $z = \frac{115 - 100}{15} = +1$, meaning that the score is 1 SD above the mean. A score of 70 would be 2 SDs below the mean: $z = \frac{70 - 100}{15} = -2$.

Because all normal distributions are shaped alike, and the proportion of cases falling under each part of the curve is known, a table has been constructed that can convert any z-score into a percentile rank (the percentage scores exceeded by a particular score). This is the standard normal table. For example, an IQ of 115 converts to a z-score of $+1$, which surpasses 84% of the scores in the normal distribution (or has a percentile rank of 84). Percentile rank conversions are useful in many ways. In curving test scores, for example, z-scores can be positive or negative, indicating whether they are above or below the mean, respectively. A z-score of 0 represents the mean of the distribution.

The use of many common statistical techniques assumes that the population being measured is normally distributed. If this is not the case, special techniques are in order.

Measures of Relationships

Much of medical practice involves the use of relationships. For example, there is a positive relation between smoking and lung cancer

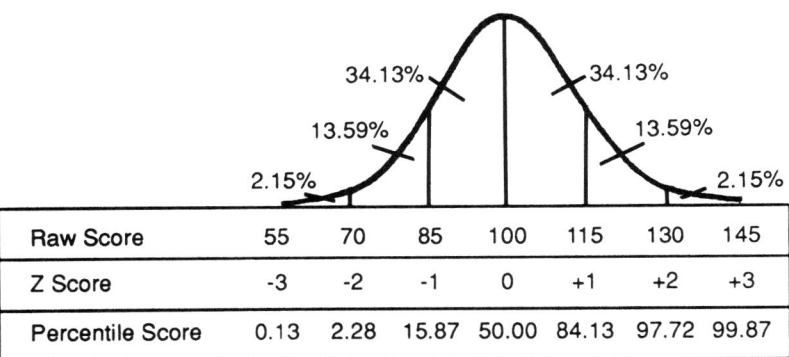

Raw Score	55	70	85	100	115	130	145
Z Score	-3	-2	-1	0	+1	+2	+3
Percentile Score	0.13	2.28	15.87	50.00	84.13	97.72	99.87

Figure 2.5. Relationships among raw scores, Z-scores, and percentile ranks of a normally distributed variable in which the mean equals 100 and the standard deviation equals 15.

(the more cigarettes smoked, the higher the chance of developing lung cancer). This is not a perfect relationship; many people who smoke heavily never develop cancer, whereas some lung cancer patients have never smoked.

Correlation Coefficients

A correlation coefficient is a numeric index that describes the direction and strength of the linear relationship between two variables. Many formulas can determine correlation coefficients depending on the nature of the data to be correlated. The two most widely used are the Spearman rank order coefficient (for ordinal data) and the Pearson product-moment correlation coefficient (for interval-ratio data). There are also correlation coefficients for nominal data and curvilinear relationships. Only the Pearson correlation (r) will be discussed here; however, most correlation coefficients have similar characteristics and can be interpreted similarly.

A Pearson correlation coefficient (r) can take any value between $+1$ and -1. A coefficient with a plus ($+$) sign indicates a positive correlation; as one variable increases, the second variable increases (e.g., number of cigarettes smoked and risk of lung cancer). One with a minus ($-$) sign indicates a negative correlation; as one variable increases, the second variable decreases (e.g., maternal smoking and birth weight of child). Correlations can take any value between $+1$ and -1, including 0. An r approaching $+1$ or -1 indi-

cates a strong relationship (either positive or negative), whereas an r approaching 0 indicates a weak relationship. Speaking loosely, an r from .60 to 1.0 is a strong correlation, from .30 to .60 a moderate correlation, and from 0 to .30 a weak correlation. A correlation of 1.0 indicates a perfect relation between two variables and is rare in real life except in trivial situations (e.g., the r between height in inches and height in centimeters).

Scatterplots

A scatterplot graphs subjects' scores on two variables, clarifying the direction of the relationship between these variables. Different kinds of correlations are illustrated in Figures 2.6–2.9. Each point represents one person's score on two variables.

A positive correlation results in a scatterplot in which the points cluster on a diagonal from lower left to upper right (Fig. 2.6 and 2.7). For a negative correlation, the points cluster diagonally from upper left to lower right (Fig. 2.8). Where there is little or no relation between two variables, the points are randomly distributed (Fig. 2.9).

Having established that a relationship is either positive or negative, note in Figure 2.6 how closely the cluster in the scatterplot approximates a straight line. The stronger the linear relation (positive or negative) between two variables, the more closely the points in the scatterplot cluster along a straight line. The Pearson r only measures linear relation-

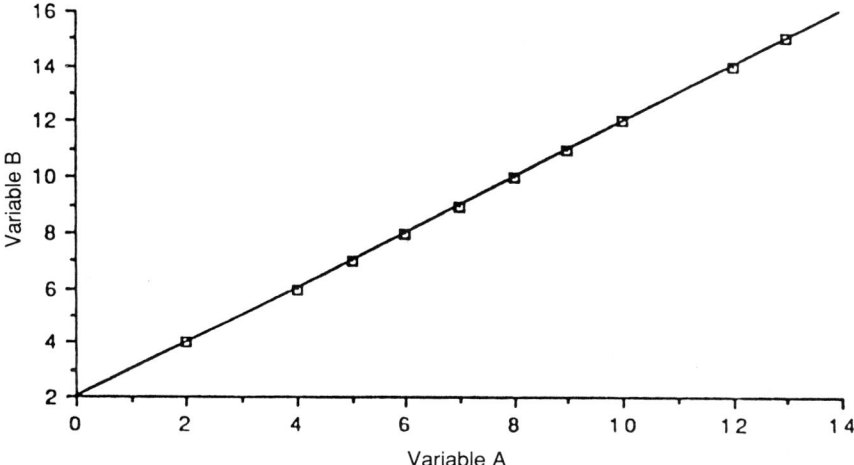

Figure 2.6. Scatterplot, perfect positive correlation ($r = +1.0$).

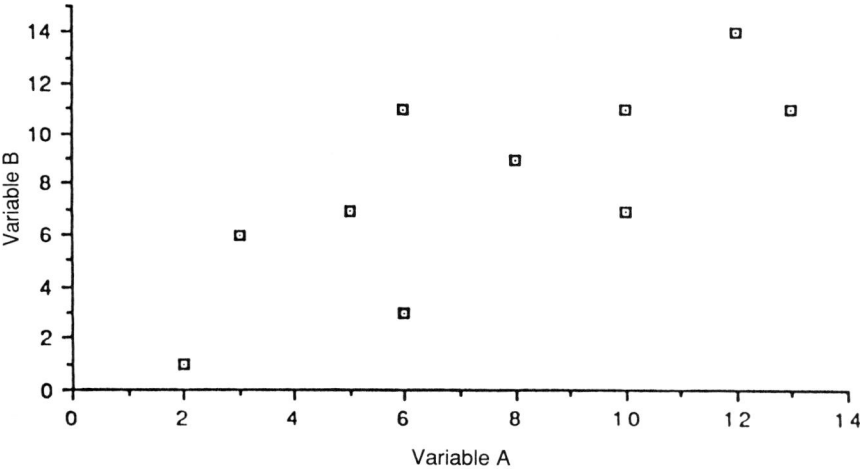

Figure 2.7. Scatterplot, positive correlation ($r = +.76$).

ships accurately. But not all relations are linear. For example, if the correlation between strength and age were graphed in a scatterplot, the relationship would be curvilinear because strength would rise and fall with age. Although the relation between these two variables is strong, a linear correlation analysis would yield a zero correlation. Other correlational measures must be used to assess the strength of nonlinear relationships. For data in which a simple curved relationship is observed, the correlation ratio is useful (4). For othr complex relationships, trend analysis or

goodness of fit can be used. It is *crucial*, in evaluating correlation, to first construct a scatterplot to determine linearity.

Interpretation of a Correlation Coefficient

A correlation coefficient describes the relation or association between two variables; it does not describe the causal relation between those variables. When a link between lung cancer and smoking was first reported, it was based on the fact that people who developed lung cancer were also likely to have been heavy smokers. Because the data were purely

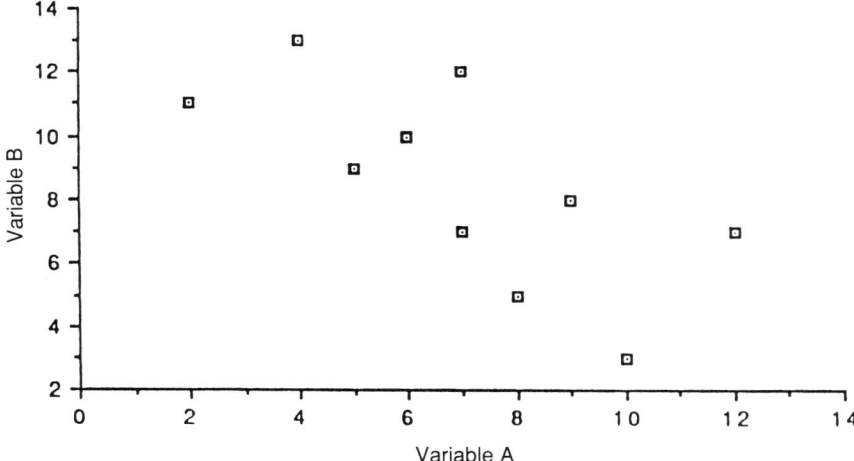

Figure 2.8. Scatterplot, negative correlation ($r = .69$).

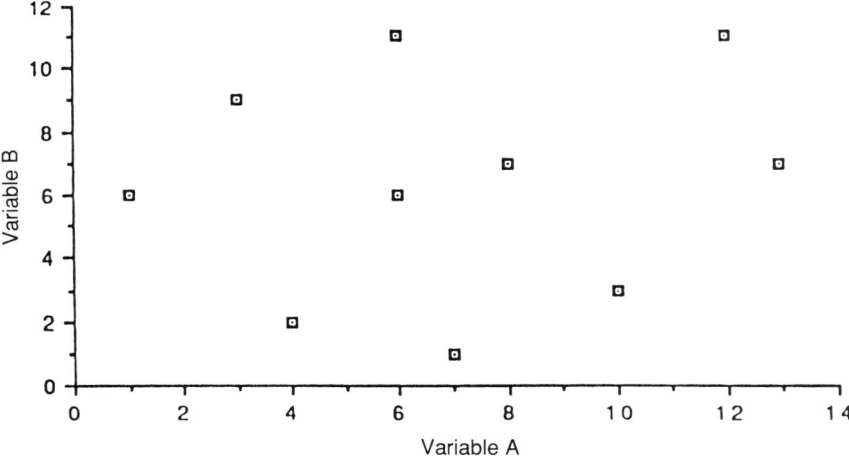

Figure 2.9. Scatterplot, weak correlation ($r = +.14$).

correlational, it could not be said that smoking caused lung cancer; the relationship could be the result of their common association with a third variable. *No matter what its size, a correlation coefficient provides no cause-and-effect information.* Once a correlation was demonstrated between smoking and lung cancer, experiments were then needed to determine cause and effect. Laboratory studies on animals established that cigarette tar is carcinogenic, and the causal link was made (despite continuing denials from tobacco companies).

Even if a cause-effect relationship cannot be established, strong correlations between two variables can be valuable because one variable can be predicted from another. For example, although the Medical College Aptitude Tests (MCATs) do not cause first-year medical school grades, if the correlation between MCATs and first-year medical school grades is substantial, the latter can be predicted with knowledge of the former. A correlational technique known as regression is used to predict one variable with a knowledge of another. Most predicted variables, however, are more

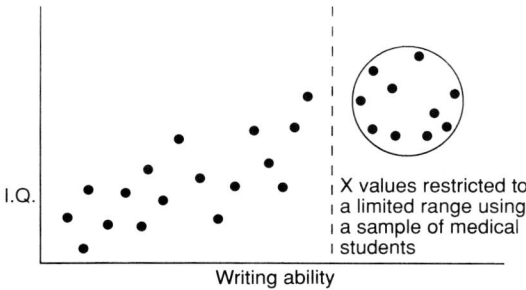

Figure 2.10. Full range of x and y values shows high, positive relationship, but a restricted range of scores produces a correlation near zero.

complex, having relationships with more than one other variable. Multiple regression techniques are used when there are multiple predictors (independent variables). These techniques account for the strength of the correlation between variables and the linearity in the relationship (7). Still other techniques, canonical correlation and factor analysis, are available when there are multiple predictors and multiple variables being predicted (8).

The size of a correlation depends in part on the homogeneity of the sample being studied. The more homogeneous a sample (i.e., how restricted the range of scores is), the lower the correlation between variables. Figure 2.10 shows a scatterplot of a high positive correlation between IQ and writing ability; when only a small section of the plot is considered (i.e., the range is restricted), the correlation is reduced to near zero. Low but significant correlations often occur in educational studies using college or medical student samples.

INFERENTIAL STATISTICS

Although inferential statistics are complex, knowledge of basic concepts is necessary for understanding the medical literature.

Null Hypothesis

As stated earlier, inferential statistics help researchers to generalize about a population from data collected on a random sample or samples. Without measuring the entire population, a researcher could never be sure that the conclusions are correct. Through hypothesis testing, however, inferences can be made

with a known degree of certainty. The first step in hypothesis testing is to state a null hypothesis, a hypothesis about some potential state of affairs in the real population. Commonly, this is a statement that "no difference exists" or that "no effect has occurred." For example, a researcher studying the relation between smoking and lung cancer might assert that tar does not cause cancer in the real population and that observed relations or comparisons between inhaling tar and developing lung cancer in samples studied are the result of chance. A study could, however, be conducted leading to acceptance of an alternative hypothesis, that tar is carcinogenic, with a known degree of certainty. By rejecting the null hypothesis, you assert that the research results are real and not caused by chance.

Probability and Significance

Generally, a researcher is not really interested in the data of a particular sample of subjects, but wants instead to know if what is observed in the sample is genuine, reproducible, and generalizable. With inferential statistics, you assess the probability that what you observe in a sample would be true for similar samples taken from the same or a similar population.

The concept of statistical significance refers to such a probability estimation. A finding is statistically significant if it is believed to be genuine and not the result of chance variations that affect all observations in samples. How significant does something have to be to be labelled statistically significant? By scientific convention, a certain known and calculated chance of being wrong is acceptable. Most commonly, the accepted probability of being wrong is less than 5 out of 100 (the .05 level of significance) or, more conservatively, less than 1 out of 100 (the .01 level). An example may help: a researcher wishes to learn whether a 60-day trial of a new drug lowers blood cholesterol. Two hundred subjects with cholesterol levels between 300 and 350 are randomly assigned to one of two groups; 100 subjects in group A are given the drug, and 100 subjects in group B receive a placebo. Examining the results, the researchers find that the mean cholesterol level of group A is 290, and the mean for group B is 310. A statistical test is conducted, and it is determined that the difference in levels is significant at the .05 level; that is, the difference between group A's mean of 290 and group B's mean of 310 can be attributed to the drug and not to chance variation in the groups' scores. By claiming that the result is statistically significant, the researcher expresses the belief that the finding is "real." According to probability, however, there are still 5 out of 100 chances that this belief is wrong.

Statistical significance says nothing about the magnitude or importance of the observed effect. In the above example, you might ask whether it is worth administering a drug with certain side effects to lower cholesterol level by 20 points. In other words, in examining results of studies, you need first to see if a result is statistically significant and then to examine if the result is important. The latter assessment is known as evaluating the magnitude (or utility) of the effect. Evaluating the magnitude of an observed effect is critical, but it is often ignored because of enthusiasm that there *is* some effect.

Type I and Type II Errors

Any decision based on statistical probabilities risks making one of two errors. A Type I error occurs when the null hypothesis is actually true but is rejected. For example, a drug is claimed to have an effect when, in fact,

there is no effect. Remember, at the .05 level of significance, there are five chances out of 100 that an incorrect rejection of the null hypothesis will be made (i.e., that the significant result is caused by chance factors). Type I errors are often discovered when an attempt to replicate (reproduce) a study yields different results.

Experimenters must account for multiple hypothesis tests conducted in the same experiment, because Type I errors increase in proportion to the number of tests. If 20 statistical tests are performed on one sample, by chance alone (at the .05 level of significance) one test will be statistically significant. Adjustments such as the Bonferroni correction can be applied: for example, if 25 tests are performed, the level of significance required is .05/25 = .002.

In a Type II error, the null hypothesis is accepted when, in fact, it is false. For example, a drug is effective but a clinical trial yields no statistical effect. Such errors can occur when the sample size or the experimental controls are inadequate.

Comparisons

The null hypothesis can be tested in a number of situations. A commonly tested null hypothesis is that the mean of one population does not differ from the mean of another. For example, in a study on the effectiveness of a new drug, the null hypotheses would be "no difference" in the populations from which the samples were drawn—those given the drug and those not. A variety of hypothesis tests exist; which statistic to use depends on the type and nature of the data and the comparisons desired. The calculations are easily conducted with hand calculators or computer programs.

The chi-square test is often used to examine hypotheses about nominal data. The question being tested is whether the observed frequencies, or proportions, differ from frequencies expected if the null hypothesis were true. For example, if a researcher observed that 8 of 30 AIDS patients treated with a certain drug survived beyond 1 year, compared with 1 of 30 without the drug, a chi-square test could test the null hypothesis that there is no difference between these outcomes (9).

For interval-ratio data, *t*-tests are commonly used to compare the mean of one group to the mean of another, or to a hypothesized population mean. The test evaluates the magnitude of the difference between means relative to the variability in the distributions being compared (9). When two groups are compared, and observations from one sample are not linked to observations from another, an independent groups *t*-test is appropriate. This would apply, for example, if we tested the effects of administering a drug thought to decrease blood pressure, with patients randomly assigned to placebo (no drug) or drug groups. Sometimes variability from extraneous factors (e.g., the subject's weight) is great enough to obscure the effects of the variable you wish to test. A dependent groups *t*-test is useful when subjects can be paired or matched on a relevant variable, or where subjects serve as their own controls. In the drug study example, because weight may strongly influence blood pressure, subjects could be paired by weight, then assigned to either the placebo or drug groups. The dependent groups *t*-test would provide greater precision in determining drug effect by accounting for blood pressure variability related to weight.

Analysis of variance (ANOVA) is a similar technique that allows simultaneous comparisons of two or more means (10). ANOVA designs would be necessary, for example, to compare effects of multiple dosages of drug in the above study. Variations of ANOVA (e.g., multivariate ANOVA) allow for the testing of numerous hypotheses of group (or combination of group) mean differences in a single experimental design (8).

MEASUREMENT CONCEPTS

The quality of the measurement device is an important aspect of any science. A basal body temperature thermometer is useful only if the readings it provides accurately reflect the temperature of the body (validity) and if conditions other than body temperature do not cause the readings to fluctuate (reliability).

Reliability

Reliability refers to consistency of measurements in the same subjects when reexamined with the same test or instrument on different occasions, or with different sets of equivalent test items, with different examiners, or under variable examining conditions (11). The ways to assess the reliability of a measure are numerous. The simplest is test-retest reliability, which involves the readministration of a test after a stated interval. A reliable test, that is, one not highly susceptible to random changes in the environment or the test-taker, should produce approximately equal scores on the two occasions. For example, height measurements taken 2 hours apart, with the same ruler on the same person, should be virtually the same. If a paper-and-pencil test can only be administered once, split-half reliability is sometimes used: the test is divided into two equivalent halves to measure consistency of content sampling.

There are certain types of instruments (e.g., diagnostic scales based upon clinical observation) in which scoring involves considerable judgment of the examiner. Scorer reliability, also known as inter-rater reliability, can be assessed simply by having two judges independently score the same protocol (12).

Validity

Validity concerns *what* is being measured by a test procedure, and *how well* it is measured (11). There are different ways of assessing validity; the method chosen depends on the type of test under study. When evaluating achievement tests (e.g., anatomy examinations), content-related validation is performed. Content validation involves assessing test content to determine whether the coverage of material is representative of the domain being measured (e.g., what has been taught).

Students often complain, for example, that classroom tests lack content validity when material lightly covered in class is weighted heavily on a test, and material emphasized in class is barely tested. Content validity should not be confused with face validity. Face validity is what a test superficially appears to measure— does the test appear plausible to those who will take it and to those who will use it? For example, popular magazines often contain questionnaires claiming to assess the quality of a social relationship. These measures appear to be valid (face validity), when in fact they are of limited value.

The construct validity of a test is the degree to which the test measures a theoretic trait or construct (11). For example, senior resident or attending physicians should be more skilled at clinical problem-solving in their specialty than medical students. Consequently, on a valid measure of clinical problem-solving skill in that specialty, specialist physicians will score higher than medical students (13).

In criterion-related validation, a characteristic (e.g., having a depressive illness, being a skilled diagnostician) is defined or measured by the instrument to be validated. The characteristic is then assessed by an independent (presumably valid) means. The two types of criterion-related validity are concurrent and predictive (10). If a test is designed to assess current status, as in a diagnostic procedure, concurrent validation (the collection of criterion data at approximately the same time as the obtaining of test scores) would be used. For example, to validate a depression scale, you would determine whether it could accurately differentiate between groups of normal patients and depressive patients diagnosed by other, well-validated strategies (e.g., diagnoses by experienced clinicians, or another depression rating scale). Tests such as the National Board of Medical Examiners (NBME) examination, used to anticipate some future status, would undergo predictive validation. For example, a recent study of part 2 of the NBME demonstrated, for the first time, the part's predictive validity of clinical performance in the first year of residency (14). It is hoped that

this can be replicated. For further discussion of types of validity, see Cook and Campbell (15).

DIAGNOSTIC CONFIDENCE

A research and clinical concept related to concurrent and construct validity of medical testing is diagnostic confidence (16). The diagnostic confidence of a test is assessed in two ways. Sensitivity is the proportion of patients with an illness (identified by other validated means) who manifest abnormal results on the test. This is the true positive rate, or

$$\text{sensitivity} = \frac{\text{number of true positives} \times 100}{\text{number of all cases of the illness}}$$

For example, of 82 persons who have the fictional disease exosis, 41 have abnormal (positive) results on the exosis identification test (EIT). The sensitivity of the EIT is therefore

$$\text{sensitivity} = \frac{41 \times 100}{82} = 50\%$$

Specificity equals the proportion of persons without the illness who have normal results on the test in question. This true negative rate is measured by

$$\text{specificity} = \frac{\text{number of true negatives} \times 100}{\text{number of all cases without the illness}}$$

For example, of 33 persons who do not have exosis, 22 have normal (negative) results on the EIT. The specificity of the EIT is therefore

$$\text{specificity} = \frac{22 \times 100}{33} = 66.7\%$$

EXPERIMENTAL DESIGN

As stated previously, a theory describes and explains observed and observable events and predicts the observations that will occur under specified conditions. Scientific progress requires continual observation and explanation. This is well served by the experimental method and other research designs.

In an experiment, researchers create an environment in which certain variables are manipulated, but all other variables that might affect the outcome are held constant. For example, a study was conducted to determine whether clonidine, which ameliorates opiate withdrawal, reduces tobacco withdrawal symptoms (17). Approximately half the subjects received clonidine and the other half a placebo for 1 month, during which they were to try to quit smoking. Subjects were seen individually by a research assistant each week for medication and daily diary exchange and to encourage them to continue abstinence or attempts to quit. Measures of effect included severity of withdrawal symptoms, quitting, and smoking-reduction behavior, all of which were found not to differ as a result of clonidine use.

The variable manipulated by the researchers, the independent variable, was clonidine use (and non-use). The variables being measured, the dependent variables, were severity of withdrawal symptoms, quitting, and smoke reduction behavior; these were expected to change because of manipulation of the independent variable.

Control variables are those that the researcher does not want to vary as the independent variable varies. The researchers exerted control over the experimental situation in many ways. Only those who smoked at least 20 cigarettes per day were included in the subject pool. People were excluded if they were pregnant, spoke no English, or were receiving an adrenergic pathway drug. These variables could confound their results.

After a pool of subjects is developed, how should a researcher divide subjects into drug (experimental), and no-drug (control) groups? One common method is to randomly assign subjects to groups. There may be individual differences among subjects, however, that might affect the dependent variable, and care must be taken so that the division of subjects does not allow this to happen. The researcher can exert additional control over these extraneous variables through matching. The researcher actually matches subjects on important characteristics (e.g., sex, degree of tobacco dependence) and then randomly assigns

one of each pair to each group. Additional levels of control can be exercised through stratifying subjects; this is done when there are important subgroups in the subject pool that should be represented in each experimental group. Subjects are first divided into the subgroups, and then are matched and randomly selected from the subgroups and placed in each treatment.

It is crucial to include some baseline comparison measure (a control group) in an experiment. In a drug study, this is often done with a "no drug" condition. However, the research literature has demonstrated a placebo effect; just believing one is taking medication can produce physiologic changes. It is also important, therefore, that subjects in the no-drug group ingest something they think is a drug.

This usually prevents subjects from knowing whether they are receiving the experimental treatment. Should they know which treatment group they are in? In the above experiment, if people knew they were taking a drug that might help them quit smoking, they might try harder to abstain than subjects who knew they were ingesting placebo. Thus, it helps that subjects do not know what group they are in, a design known as a single-blind experiment.

In the above experiment, subjects met weekly with a research assistant (RA). Should the RA know which group each subject is in? Because the RA's role included encouraging the subjects to stop smoking, unintended contamination (e.g., extra encouragement) could occur if the RA knew which subjects were taking the drug. When both the subject and the evaluator do not know what group the subject is in, the design is a double-blind experiment. Blinding further controls the experimental situation.

A more powerful statistical treatment employs a crossover design, illustrated in a study measuring the effect of increasing the frequency of meals on serum lipid concentrations in normal subjects (18). Two metabolically identical diets were used, one consisting of 17 meals per day and the other three meals per day. Subjects were randomly assigned to one of the two diets, followed that diet for 2 weeks, and then, after following their normal diet for a few weeks, were switched to the other experimental diet for 2 weeks. This design results in all subjects experiencing all conditions, but in different orders.

Two terms used inconsistently in the medical literature are prospective and retrospective. Rather than referring to a particular method, they indicate *when* the study is conducted (19). The two experiments described above were prospective, i.e., the subjects were chosen before the treatments occurred. Prospective designs are necessary for determining whether one variable causes another. But not all prospective designs are experimental; often, prospective studies follow people over time without the introduction of experimental manipulations. For example, a prospective study of relative weight, height, and risk of breast cancer was performed by following over 100,000 women who were cancer-free in 1976 until 1984 (20). The relative weight and height of the women who developed cancer pre- and postmenopausally were compared to the weight and height in women who did not develop cancer. This is a longitudinal design.

A retrospective study investigates a population after an event, illness, or treatment. For example, first trimester aspirin use was compared in mothers of infants who had cardiac defects and in mothers of infants who had other congenital malformations to determine whether ingestion of aspirin by pregnant women increased their infants' risk of certain heart defects (21). The researchers did not observe the course of pregnancy; they had access to data from postdelivery examinations. Although this type of study is popular because it is less expensive and less time-consuming, it is less useful in determining causality.

WEAKNESSES OF PUBLISHED RESEARCH

Journal articles in which original research is reported generally contain six basic sections: the abstract which summarizes the work, focusing on results; the introduction which usually consists of a literature review, background information and study purpose; the method section, which describes the study design, subject selection, measurement tools, and procedure; the results section, which presents the findings, often as tables and figures, and reports the results of statistical tests; the discussion or conclusion, which considers the meaning and significance of the study, often in light of previous research, while stating limitations of the study and alternative hypothesis which could explain the results; and the references. A number of issues can derail a study's validity and chances of being published.

LACK OF REFEREE BLINDNESS

Before gaining entrance into the scientific literature, a study must be evaluated impartially by research peers. Many journals use blind reviews; the paper is given to the reviewer with no identifying marks on it. In this way, research will, theoretically, be evaluated on its own merits; a well-known researcher will have no more chance of having a paper accepted for publication than a person starting out, if the papers are of equal quality.

Unfortunately, science is not free of controversy, pettiness, and favoritism. Even when a review is meant to be blind, experienced reviewers may be able to identify the authors, so that personal biases may color the review. Moreover, many journals send their reviewers the page listing the authors.

OVERSTATEMENTS IN ABSTRACTS

The abstract, a précis of the research, should identify for the reader whether the article is of sufficient interest to read further. Owing to the brevity of abstracts, findings must be discussed in a way that may not bring out subtleties or limitations in the study. Some readers read abstracts rather than full articles (an inappropriate practice). Overstatements in the abstracts can then be perpetuated as the real findings of the study.

INCOMPLETE LITERATURE REVIEWS

The literature review, an important part of all good research, reveals the theories, challenges, frustrations, and nuances of previous studies on the topic. An incomplete literature review may result in a deficient perspective on a subject or the assumption of credit for an idea already advanced or tested.

INADEQUATE METHODOLOGY

Research strategies and pitfalls have already been discussed. The good researcher or knowledgeable physician will be constantly alert to studies that use unreliable or invalid instruments, do not use proper controls or blinding, claim causality based on correlational analysis or retrospective designs, use inadequate sample size, do not account for Type 1 errors, and select the wrong tests for statistical significance (19).

NEGLECT OF ALTERNATIVE HYPOTHESES

To support a theory, it is not enough to demonstrate support from the study itself; alternative hypotheses must also be shown *not* to be supported. The placebo effect is an example of how the neglect of alternative hypotheses may mislead. An example: in the 1950s, the surgical technique of tying off the internal mammary arteries was developed to reduce anginal pain (chest pain due to insufficient coronary arterial blood flow) (19). The theory was that blood would be forced into collateral (auxiliary) cardiac blood vessels, which would eventually increase blood supply to the myocardium. Many patients who received the surgery reported improvement. Although electrocardiogram studies did not document a corresponding physiologic improvement, the researchers considered their theory supported and continued this surgery. Another research team tested an alternative hypothesis; half of their patients were given the angina operation, the other half (controls) received a sham operation. The most dramatic improvements occurred in the sham operation group.

SHUNNING OF REPLICATION STUDIES

For an observation to be scientific, it must be replicable (repeatable). Most research findings are published and publicized before replication has been performed. Sometimes, further research confirms the original findings. In other cases (cold fusion, for example), replication does not support the findings. Be alert to the fact that many dramatic findings reported in the literature have not been replicated, and may later turn out to be false. Unfortunately, many journals reject papers that replicate initial findings, because replication is often not perceived as "newsworthy."

SUMMARY

Given the powerful influence of published research on clinical practice, and the many possible pitfalls, it is crucial that everyone connected with the process of research (authors, reviewers, journal editors, readers) be vigilant about research methodology. Fortunately, this vigilance occurs with sufficient frequency to foster the health of our population dramatically.

3/Neurology of Behavior

Michael J. Schrift, D.O.

OBJECTIVES

GENERAL OBJECTIVE: Given the examination of a patient, associate each behavioral finding (normal and abnormal) with brain sites and pathways.

SPECIFIC OBJECTIVES:
1. State the functions of the five zones of the cerebral cortex and of each cerebral hemisphere.
2. Summarize the neuroanatomic pathways involved in language functions and discuss the pathophysiology of the aphasias, aprosodias, alexias, and agraphias.
3. Summarize the neuroanatomic pathways involved in motor skills and discuss the pathophysiology of the apraxias.
4. State the neuroanatomy involved in pattern recognition and discuss the pathophysiology of the agnosias.
5. List the functions and neural connections of the frontal lobe and describe the syndromes of frontal lobe dysfunction.
6. Discuss the syndromes of limbic system dysfunction, including epilepsy.

The brain is the body's organ of behavior. It governs all bodily functions, including sensation, perception, movement, language, thought, memory, emotion, systemic physiology and circadian rhythms. The neuroanatomic pathways of many human behaviors are presented in this chapter using the Wernicke-Geschwind model (1). Much of the data for this model were originally obtained from correlating abnormal patient behaviors with brain lesions (areas of discrete pathology). Our focus in this chapter is the highly developed human cerebral cortex, the general architecture of which is displayed in Figure 3.1.

FUNCTIONAL ORGANIZATION OF THE BRAIN

Five Zones of the Cerebral Cortex

The cerebral cortex is a five-part unit that bridges the internal physiologic milieu (e.g., electrolyte balance, temperature regulation, hormonal activity, and immune system regulation) and the external environment (Fig. 3.2). It has five behaviorally and histologically specialized zones: the limbic areas or system, paralimbic areas, heteromodal association areas, primary sensory/motor areas, and unimodal association areas.

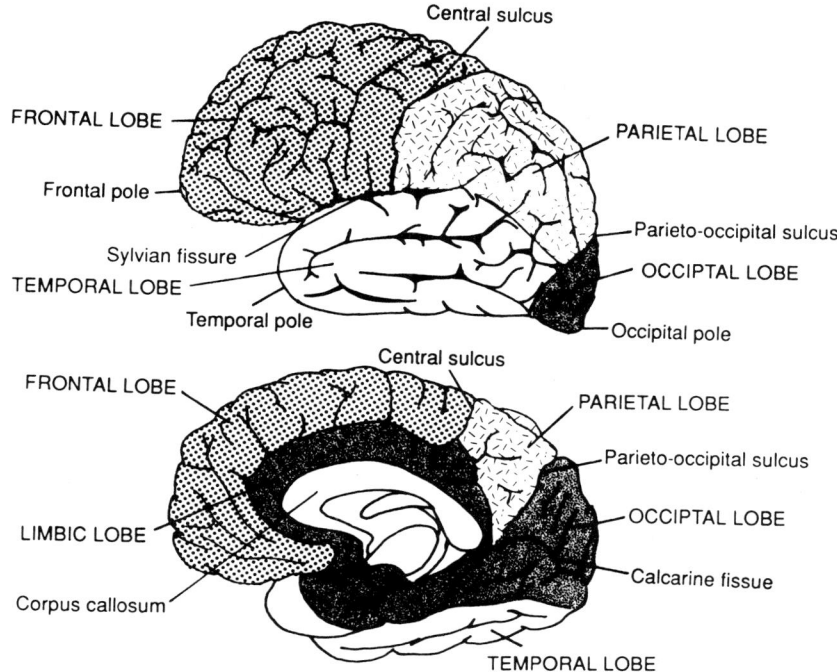

Figure 3.1. General architecture of the cerebral cortex. (Modified from Pansky B, Allen DJ. Review of neuroscience. New York: Macmillan, 1980: 89.)

EXTERNAL ENVIRONMENT

PRIMARY SENSORY/MOTOR AREAS (IDIOTYPIC)
UNIMODAL ASSOCIATION AREAS (HOMOTYPICAL)
HETEROMODAL ASSOCIATION AREAS (HOMOTYPICAL)
PARALIMBIC AREAS
LIMBIC AREAS

HYPOTHALAMUS

INTERNAL ENVIRONMENT

Figure 3.2. Cortical zones and their neural connectivity. (Modified from Mesulam M-M. Principles of behavioral neurology. Philadelphia: FA Davis, 1985.)

The limbic system (Fig. 3.3) is involved in control over the internal milieu, the emotional coloring of experience, the modulation of drives and instincts, and memory and learning (2). It includes the septum pellucidum and septal nuclei; the amygdaloid complex and its nuclei; the hippocampus; and the olfactory tubercle, bulb, and striae (Fig. 3.3).

The paralimbic areas (Fig. 3.4), better organized histologically, include the orbitofrontal cortex, insula, temporal pole (the anterior tip of the temporal lobe), parahippocampal gyrus, and cingulate gyrus. These areas form a girdle between the limbic system and the brain's heteromodal association areas.

The primary (ideotypic) cortex is responsive to the external environment. It includes areas such as the primary visual cortex (Brodmann's area 17, designated V in Fig. 3.4), primary auditory cortex (Heschl's gyrus, A in Fig. 3.4), primary sensory cortex (the sensory strip, S in Fig. 3.4) and primary motor cortex (the motor strip, M, Fig. 3.4). The primary sensory cortex receives primitive sensations (e.g., light, sound, pain, touch) from the external environment. The primary motor cortex gives rise to the corticospinal and cor-

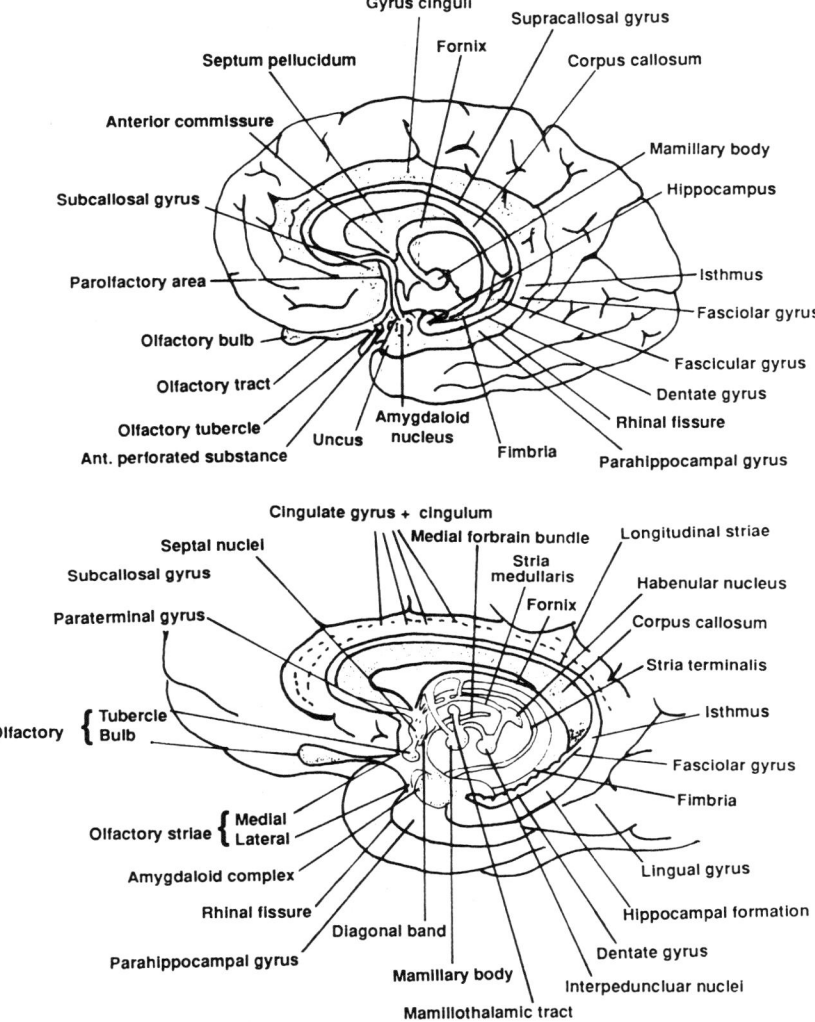

Figure 3.3. Limbic system. (Modified from Pansky B, Allen DJ. Review of neuroscience. New York: Macmillan, 1980: 339.)

ticobulbar tracts, which convey impulses down the spinal cord for muscle movement.

Each primary sensory and motor area is connected to a unimodal association area (unimodal, modality-specific isocortex). Unimodal sensory association areas organize sensations, such as light, into recognizable patterns, such as the image of a door. The unimodal isocortex and heteromodal isocortex (see below) are comprised in the homotypical isocortex, which is more behaviorally special-

ized and structurally complex than the rest of the brain.

The unimodal auditory association area (Wernicke's area, *AA* in Fig. 3.4) is in the superior temporal gyrus. The unimodal visual association cortex (Brodmann's areas 18 and 19, *VA* in Fig. 3.4) is in the peristriate, midtemporal, and inferotemporal regions; the unimodal somatosensory area is located in the superior parietal lobule (*SA*, Fig. 3.4). The unimodal motor association area (*MA*, Fig.

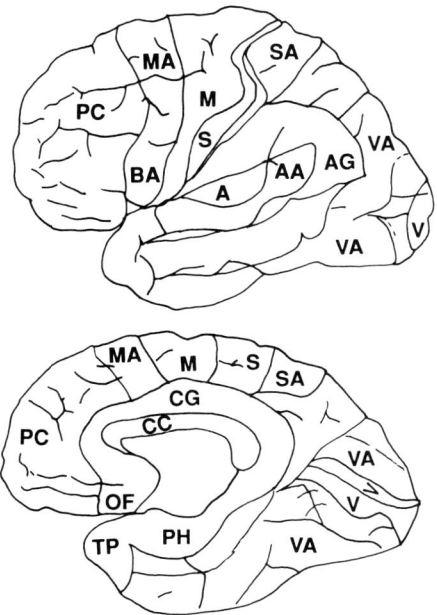

Figure 3.4. Schematic diagrams of the brain: left lateral surface view (top) and midline (sagittal) view (bottom), both depicting the distribution of functional areas of the brain. **V**-primary visual area; **VA**-unimodal visual association area; **A**-primary auditory area; **AA**-unimodal auditory association area (Wernicke's area); **S**-primary somatosensory area (sensory strip); **SA**-unimodal somatosensory association area; **M**-primary motor area (motor strip); **MA**-unimodal motor area; **BA**-Broca's area (type of unimodal motor area containing the "motor programs" for speech); **AG**-angular gyrus (heteromodal association area); PC-prefrontal cortex (heteromodal association area); **CC**-corpus callosum; **CG**-cingulate gyrus (paralimbic area); **OF**-orbitofrontal area (paralimbic area); **PH**-parahippocampal gyrus (paralimbic area); **TP**-temporal pole (paralimbic area). (Modified from Mesulam M-M. Principles of behavioral neurology. Philadelphia: FA Davis, 1985.)

3.4) is rostral to (in front of) the precentral gyrus (3–5). Unimodal association areas contain templates (central representations in the form of patterns) of items such as objects, speech sounds and words, and movements. When incoming sensory information from the primary sensory areas is matched to a particular template (2), which in turn is linked to memories of the pattern stored in the limbic system, recognition of that stimulus occurs. Damage to unimodal sensory association areas, or disconnection (disruption of neural connections) of the unimodal sensory association areas from

the limbic system, causes agnosia, or failure to recognize that stimulus (2), which is explained in the following case history.

> After a stroke (cerebrovascular accident), a 59-year-old man suddenly became unable to recognize his family and other familiar people. Shown photographs of celebrities, he could not recognize them. A computed tomographic (CT) scan revealed bilateral infarctions (death of tissue due to inadequate blood supply) involving occipitotemporal areas. The infarctions had disconnected the perception of faces (in occipital visual unimodal association areas) from previous memories of that face (located in temporal limbic areas), impeding recognition of the familiar.

The unimodal motor association areas contain motor programs for particular complex movements (e.g., speaking, figure skating, sewing). A motor program is a central representation of the strength, sequence, and position for muscle contractions, under sensory guidance, in carrying out a complex motor act without having to think through each step. These areas are also involved in the initiation, inhibition, planning, and learning of complex movements (6). Damage to unimodal motor association areas disturbs the performance of specific movements, such as those involved in speech, as the following case example illustrates:

> A 61-year-old woman developed speech problems after a stroke in the left frontal premotor area. Her verbal output was slow, hesitant, and dysarthric. Instead of stating "I want to go the bathroom," she would say "I ba ba bathroom," and struggled to do so.

The heteromodal association areas are in the inferior parietal lobule and the prefrontal cortex (Fig. 3.4, *PC*) (2). These areas handle cross-modal associations; they connect the unimodal motor and sensory association areas with each other and with the limbic system, and they permit these areas to communicate with one another. This enables us to do such things as put words to objects, name what we touch, express our feelings, and read and write. Damage to these areas leads to impairments such as dyslexia (impaired reading), dysgraphia (impaired writing), dysnomia (impaired naming), and dyscalculia (impaired calculation) (2).

Cerebral Lateralization

The left and right hemispheres differ in function and structure. Language was the first behavior in which cerebral asymmetries (in structure and function) were demonstrated. The left hemisphere is the major processor for language in 97% of persons. Damage to the left hemisphere leads, in most right-handed persons, to aphasias, or language disorders. The left hemisphere is also responsible for learning of fine motor movements (7, 8).

Constructional abilities (tested as the ability to copy the outline of a figure without lifting the pencil off the paper), visual-spatial orientation, appreciation and production of musical tones, facial recognition, and prosody (comprehension and production of the feelings associated with language) are mediated by the right hemisphere (6–9). In this chapter, the left hemisphere is considered dominant.

The two hemispheres are connected by the corpus callosum, a large white fiber bundle (Fig. 3.4, *CC*), which allows information to pass from one hemisphere to the other. It allows each hemisphere to know what the other is doing. One common way to test the function of your corpus callosum is to tie your shoelaces with your eyes closed.

APHASIAS AND APROSODIAS

Broca's Aphasia

In 1861, the French anatomist and surgeon Pierre Paul Broca (10) suggested that language problems in patients who had suffered strokes was the result of damage in the left posterior frontal region (Broca's area) (Fig. 3.4, *BA*, Fig. 3.5, diagram *I*). His work marked the beginning of the era of clinicoanatomic correlations in neurology. Broca's patients had impaired

speech fluency. They spoke slowly and struggled to produce words. Although filled with nouns and verbs, their speech lacked grammar, articles, prepositions, adverbs, and adjectives (11). Today, patients who have Broca's aphasia might say "I movies" instead of "I went to the movies." Their speech is slow, labored, and telegraphic, and they have trouble repeating statements, although they usually comprehend what others say.

Broca's aphasics are also weak on their right side, and the lower two thirds of the right side of their face droops. This is because the lesion is usually large enough to disrupt the ipsilateral (same side) corticospinal (brain to spinal cord) and corticobulbar (brain to face and head) tracts. The forehead is spared because it receives ipsilateral *and* contralateral (opposite side) corticobulbar connections. The eyes usually look left because the lesion typically involves the left frontal gaze center which, when normally stimulated, makes the eyes move right conjugately (simultaneously).

Broca's aphasics often develop depressive syndromes (12–14) that respond to cyclic antidepressants or electroconvulsive therapy. Once considered a psychologic reaction to the disability, this depression is now considered pathologic. Recent studies have shown that depressions are more frequent and severe in Broca's aphasics than in orthopaedic control subjects who have similar disabilities (12–14). The damage occurs in the inferior frontal gyrus, the lowest exterior segment of the prefrontal cortex (Fig. 3.4, *PC*), and insula, a small, deeply placed, anatomically distinct cortical lobe (not depicted).

A 63-year-old man developed Broca's aphasia after a stroke in the left frontal region. As his stroke evolved, he became severely depressed with crying spells, appetite loss, trouble staying asleep, and psychomotor retardation (he thought and moved slowly). He also developed a delusion that he was financially insolvent and the IRS would arrest him and his family. He was treated with a CA. Within a few weeks his depression totally remitted, although his language problems remained.

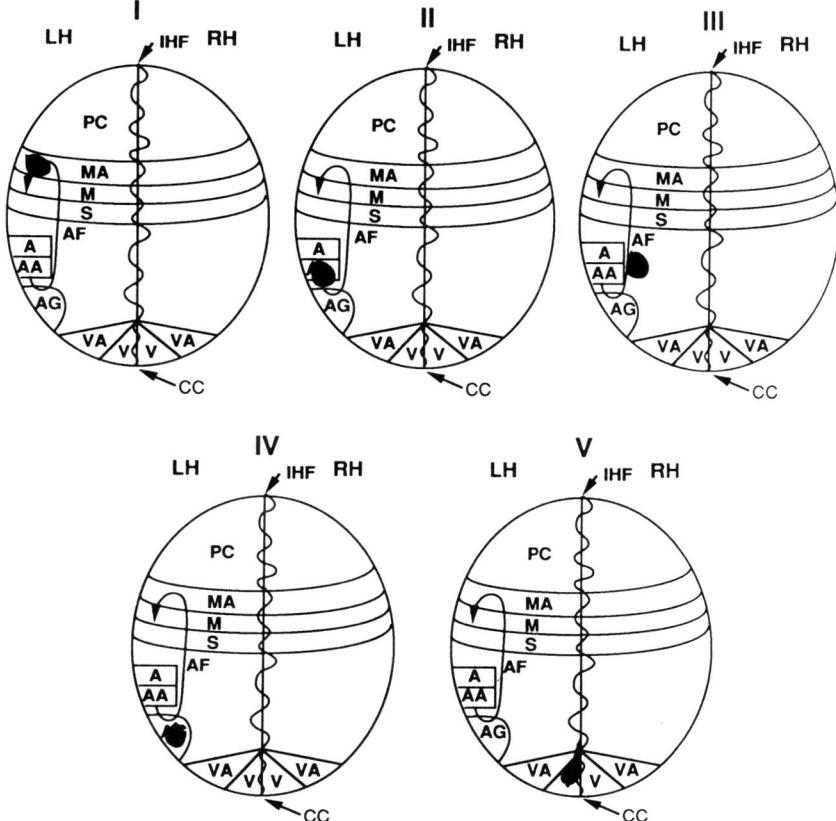

Figure 3.5. Schematic diagrams of the skull and brain (viewed from above) depicting the pathways and lesions involved in the aphasic disorders. **LH**-left hemisphere; **RH**-right hemisphere; **V**-primary visual area; **VA**-unimodal visual association area; **AG**-angular gyrus (heteromodal association area); **AA**-unimodal auditory association area (Wernicke's area); **A**-primary auditory area; **S**-primary sensory area; **M**-primary motor area; **MA**-unimodal motor association area; **PC**-prefrontal cortex; **AF**-arcuate fasciculus; **IHF**-interhemispheric fissure; **CC**-corpus callosum. **I**-shows the lesion location involved in Broca's aphasia; **II**- shows the lesion location involved in Wernicke's aphasia; **III**-shows the lesion location involved in conduction aphasia; **IV**-shows the lesion location involved in anomic aphasia and alexia with agraphia (also the angular gyrus syndrome); **V**-shows the lesion location involved in pure word blindness (alexia without agraphia).

Wernicke's Aphasia

Soon after Broca reported his cases, the German neurologist Karl Wernicke described aphasics whose signs differed from those of Broca's aphasia. Wernicke's patients had copious, abnormal verbal output. They spoke at a rapid or normal rate, manifested paraphasias, and had impaired language comprehension. Paraphasias are incorrect substitutions of one speech sound (a phoneme) or word for another. There are verbal paraphasias (substituting one word for another, such as *writer* for

pen), phonemic paraphasias (substituting one phoneme for another, such as *fen* for *pen*), and neologistic paraphasias (making up new words, such as *freuter*). Like Broca's aphasics, Wernicke's aphasia patients had trouble repeating statements. Wernicke's patients had damage to the left posterior-superior temporal gyrus (Fig. 3.4, *AA*; Fig. 3.5, diagram II) (15, 16). The unimodal auditory association area, known as Wernicke's area, is where templates for phonemes (speech sounds, such as *f* or *ph*) and words are linked to primitive auditory sensations received from the primary auditory

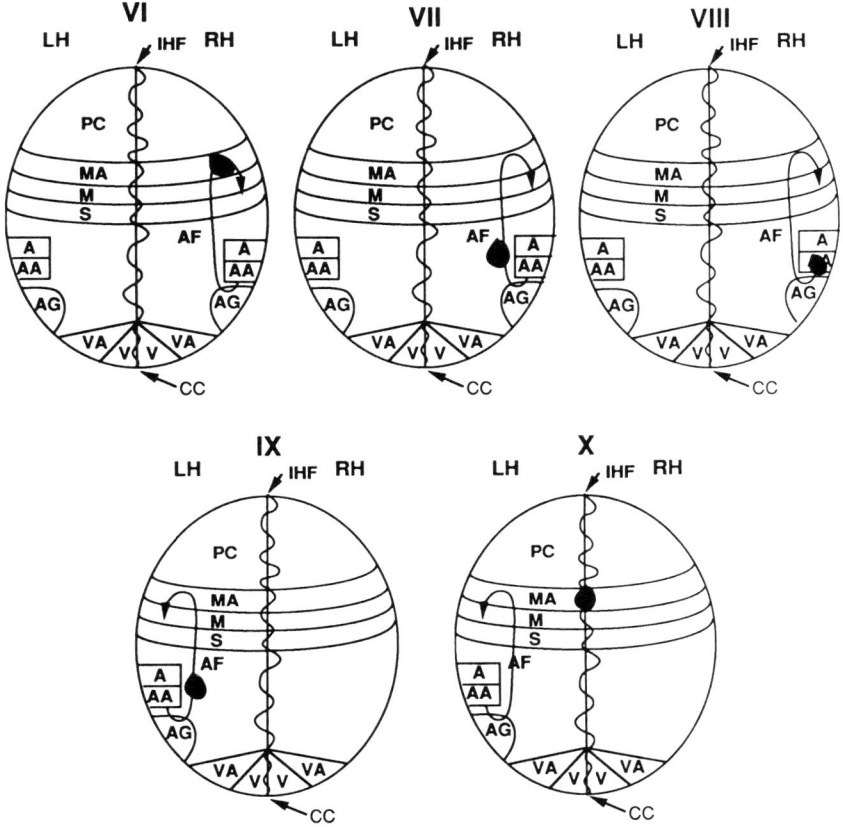

Figure 3.6. Schematic diagrams of the skull and brain (viewed from above) depicting the pathways and lesions involved in the aprosodic and apraxic disorders. **LH**-left hemisphere; **RH**-right hemisphere; **V**-primary visual area; **VA**-unimodal visual association area; **AG**-angular gyrus (heteromodal association area); **AA**-unimodal auditory association area (Wernicke's area); **A**-primary auditory area; **S**-primary sensory area; **M**-primary motor area; **MA**-unimodal motor association area; **PC**-prefrontal cortex; **AF**-arcuate fasciculus; **IHF**-interhemispheric fissure; **CC**-corpus callosum. **VI**-shows the lesion location involved in motor aprosodia (agestural-aprosodic syndrome); **VII**-shows the lesion location involved in conduction aprosodia; **VIII**-shows the lesion location involved in sensory (receptive) aprosodia; **IX**-shows the lesion location involved in parietal apraxia (bilateral ideomotor apraxia); **X**-shows the lesion location involved in callosal apraxia (left unilateral apraxia).

cortex (Fig. 3.4, A); these templates are also linked to auditory memories from the limbic system, and to visual, olfactory, and other cross-modal sensory patterns from the angular gyrus (Fig. 3.4, AG).

Wernicke's aphasics have no muscle weakness; the lesion spares the primary motor areas. Sensory loss on the body's right side occurs if the lesion extends to parietal sensory areas. Wernicke's aphasics are often mislabelled as psychotic because of their odd verbal output, which resembles (but is not identical to) a formal thought disorder (p. 190) (17).

These patients do, however, tend to develop a mania-like psychosis (16) characterized by hyperactivity, rapid speech and euphoric or irritable mood.

Conduction Aphasia

Wernicke (18) hypothesized how the brain was organized for language. He believed that Broca's and Wernicke's areas were connected by fibers of the arcuate fasciculus (Fig. 3.5, AF). He hypothesized that an arcuate fasciculus lesion would disconnect Broca's from Wernicke's area, impairing repetition of statements: although the patient understands what is being said (intact Wernicke's area), the message cannot be transmitted to the intact Broca's area that contains the motor programs for speech. By the same logic, the patient can read silently with comprehension, but cannot read aloud. Wernicke, who found a patient with this lesion and language problem, labelled this dysfunction conduction aphasia (Fig. 3.5, diagram *III*) (19).

Alexia With and Without Agraphia

In the late 1800s, the French neurologist Joseph Jules Déjèrine (20) described two other classic patients whose language disorders fit Wernicke's model. The first patient had a lesion in the angular gyrus (Fig. 3.5, diagram *IV*), the heteromodal association area that makes the cross-modal associations needed for reading, writing, and naming. To read, write, and name objects, the central representation of that visually perceived item (in the unimodal visual association area) must be linked to the phonemes (the smallest unit of spoken language needed to produce a sound [e.g., *f* and *ph*]) and words for that item (located in Wernicke's area, the unimodal auditory association area). Angular gyrus lesions produce the syndromes alexia with agraphia (difficulty reading and writing) and anomic aphasia (difficulty naming) (19–21).

Déjèrine's other patient had a lesion in the left primary visual cortex which extended to the splenium of the corpus callosum (Fig. 3.5, diagram *V*). This lesion produced right homonymous hemianopsia (inability to see out of the right half or the right visual field of both eyes) because the left primary visual cortex was destroyed. The same lesion cut off the left hemisphere from direct visual input. Because of the corpus callosal lesion and because visual information that enters the brain comes to the right hemisphere, the right hemisphere could not send visual information to the left hemisphere. Déjèrine's patient developed the syndrome alexia without agraphia, or pure word blindness, a condition in which the patient, al-

though able to perform most language functions, including writing, could not read. Reading is possible only if you can process visual information into words in the left hemisphere; writing, on the other hand, is possible if you know what you want to say and your motor systems for writing are intact. Alexia without agraphia patients cannot even read their own writing (19–21).

Global Aphasia

The most severe aphasia is global aphasia (19) in which most of the left perisylvian area (the area surrounding the arcuate fasciculus) becomes disrupted, producing nonfluent verbal output as well as severe language comprehension and repetition problems. Essentially, both Broca's and Wernicke's areas are impaired. These patients often have right-sided weakness and sensory loss because the corticospinal and corticobulbar tracts and parietal sensory areas (Fig. 3.4, *S*) are involved.

Transcortical Aphasias

Transcortical aphasias (19) occur following severe hypotensive or hypoxemic episodes in which the blood or oxygen supply to the brain is compromised. When this occurs, the brain's watershed areas (areas not supplied directly by an artery) are most vulnerable. Among the watershed areas are regions surrounding the speech areas. Hypoxemic or hypotensive episodes therefore often include disruption of connections between the speech areas and the rest of the cortex. If damage is between Broca's area and the rest of the frontal lobe, transcortical motor aphasia develops: the patient has severe problems initiating speech (a frontal lobe function) and tends to be apathetic and hypoactive. Although patients are able to repeat complex sentences, they are usually unable to spontaneously utter a word. Language comprehension remains good.

Transcortical sensory aphasia (19) occurs when Wernicke's area is disconnected from the rest of the cortex. Like Wernicke's aphasics, transcortical sensory aphasics have severe language comprehension problems and copious paraphasic speech. They differ from Wernicke's aphasics because they can repeat complex sentences (incoming sounds can be linked to templates for phonemes or words), but (like Wernicke's aphasics) they do not understand what they say. This is because Wernicke's area is disconnected from heteromodal association areas and the limbic system, so that auditory sensations cannot be linked to other sensations or prior memories.

The most severe transcortical aphasia occurs when the left perisylvian area is disconnected from the rest of the cortex because of hypoxemia or hypotension. The left perisylvian area, which surrounds the Sylvian fissure (Fig. 3.1), is responsible for syntax (organization of words into sentences), grammar (the rules of language), and semantics (the meaning of words). In this isolation of the speech area (19), transcortical motor and sensory aphasia occurs, with severe problems in the initiation of speech, nonfluent verbal output, and impaired language comprehension. All patients can do verbally is automatically repeat words, known as echolalia.

The Aprosodias

The left hemisphere is responsible for propositional speech: grammar, syntax, and semantics. The right hemisphere handles prosody, the emotional components of speech: rhythm, timing, melody, and gesturing (22). Normal speech combines prosodic and propositional language. When the right hemisphere is damaged, aprosodia occurs, in which the normal variations in the stress, pitch, and rhythm of speech are absent, or the prosody in others' speech is not comprehended (23). Aprosodias neuroanatomically are the mirror image of aphasias: when damage occurs to the right posterior frontal area (the mirror-image equivalent of Broca's area), patients often develop motor aprosodia, which is characterized by monotonous, agestural (scarcity or absence of gestures) speech that lacks normal emotional coloring. Like Broca's aphasics, these patients tend to be weak or paralyzed, with

lower facial droop and hemiplegia, now left-sided.

With damage to the mirror image of Wernicke's area, the patient develops a problem in comprehending and recognizing prosody. A normal quantity of gestures and emotional expression is produced, but it may be inappropriate for the situation. Aprosodic patients may have difficulty recognizing their own feelings (like Wernicke's aphasics, who cannot comprehend what they think and say). Conduction and transcortical aprosodias have also been described (23).

ALEXITHYMIA

Recently, alexithymia, or the inability to verbalize emotions, has been studied neurologically (24). The frequency of alexithymia is greater in patients who have psychosomatic disorders (e.g., inflammatory bowel diseases) (25), and posttraumatic stress disorder (PTSD) (26). One hypothesis (27) is that alexithymia is caused by a functional commissurotomy in which one's emotional right hemisphere cannot connect with one's verbal left hemisphere to describe how one feels. Patients who have had commissurotomies (longitudinal bisection of the corpus callosum for treatment of intractable epilepsy) often develop alexithymia (24). Deficits in tasks that measure the interhemispheric transfer of information have been found in alexithymic PTSD patients (28). Gazzaniga (29) has speculated that the unconscious, as described in psychoanalytic theory, could have nondominant hemispheric components.

THE APRAXIAS

Apraxia (19) is the inability of a person with normal strength, sensation and comprehension to carry out simple motions. To carry out a task with the right arm in response to a verbal command, the following steps must occur: (1) the auditory sensations (e.g., examiner's voice) must be processed through the ascending auditory system and reach the primary auditory cortex (Fig. 3.4, *A*); (*2*) from there, it is processed in the unimodal auditory association cortex (Fig. 3.4, *AA*) where the templates for phonemes and words are stored and sounds are recognized as words; (*3*) this information is further processed in the left inferior parietal lobule, a heteromodal association area linked to the limbic system (where memories about carrying out the task are located); (*4*) the information about carrying out this task is then sent by way of the arcuate fasciculus to the premotor areas (unimodal motor association cortex, Fig. 3.6, *MA*) in the left frontal lobe; (*5*) from there, the information is sent to the primary motor cortex (motor strip, Fig. 3.6, *M*) on the left, which gives rise to the corticospinal tracts that cross in the medulla to the right side of the body, eventually synapsing with the anterior horn cells of the spinal cord. The anterior horn cells innervate the muscles of the right arm to make it move. A similar process occurs if a person is asked to do the task with the left arm; that is, until the left premotor area is reached (see step 4, above). From there, the information must be sent first to the right premotor area through the corpus callosum, and then to the right primary motor strip where it eventually reaches the left arm.

Two types of apraxia are ideomotor and ideational. Ideomotor apraxia tends to result from focal brain damage, whereas ideational apraxia is often seen with diffuse damage.

Ideomotor Apraxia

Tasks that reveal whether a patient has ideomotor apraxia include asking the person to pantomime (first with the left arm, then with the right) saluting and using a hammer, key, and comb (19). Of the three types of ideomotor apraxia—parietal, sympathetic, and callosal—parietal apraxia is caused by a lesion that typically involves the arcuate fasciculus (Fig. 3.6, diagram *IX*); the information cannot reach either the left or the right motor area, resulting in bilateral apraxia. Moreover, when the arcuate fasciculus is affected, some of the patients develop conduction aphasia. Sympa-

thetic apraxia is caused by a lesion in the left frontal area, and typically occurs in Broca's aphasics. In this apraxia, the left premotor area is disrupted; information cannot be passed to the corpus callosum or the right hemisphere, which renders the left arm apractic in sympathy with the weak or paralyzed right arm. In callosal apraxia the information from the left premotor area cannot reach the right premotor area because of a corpus callosal lesion (Fig. 3.6, diagram *X*). The left arm therefore manifests the apraxia. This is why, to distinguish between parietal and callosal ideokinetic dyspraxias, one tests each arm (left first).

Ideational Apraxia

In ideational apraxia, typically seen in patients diagnosed with diffuse brain syndromes (delirium and dementia), the patient is asked to pantomime (produce from memory on command) a series of tasks. Patients who have ideational apraxia often cannot complete the tasks, or mix up the sequence, even though they can perform each task individually (19).

Dressing Apraxia

Patients with posterior right hemisphere damage may experience dressing apraxia (30), which is a combination of unilateral spatial neglect (inattention to the left half of space), visual agnosia (see p. 44), and apraxia. Patients cannot properly dress themselves: shirts may be put on upside down, inside out, on the legs, or on one half of the body.

> A 70-year-old man was brought to the hospital by his family after a sudden onset of confusion. Part of the confusion was that he could not dress himelf. He put his shirt on upside down, and inserted his left arm into his right sleeve. A CT scan revealed a cerebral hemorrhage in the right parieto-occipital region.

Constructional Apraxia

Constructional apraxia, the inability to copy simple drawings (31), is a condition that can develop in patients who have either left or right parietal damage (32). To copy simple drawings with the right hand, the "visuospatial" right hemisphere needs to connect with the motor-regulating component of the left hemisphere through the corpus callosum. Damage to the right hemisphere disturbs the gestalt (outlines and alignments) aspects of the drawing, whereas left hemisphere injury yields problems in motor sequencing, disordering the drawing's details (32).

Whole Body Apraxia?

Patients who have ideomotor apraxia may be able to carry out axial commands, such as opening or closing their eyes, bowing, or demonstrating use of a golf club. It is hypothesized (33) that damage to certain parietal areas could give rise to a whole-body apraxia, including axial abilities.

Buccofacial Apraxia

Finally, patients who have damage to left frontal premotor areas can develop a buccofacial apraxia; they can neither pantomime using a straw or blowing out a candle nor actually perform these acts (19). This often occurs in Broca's aphasics (19).

THE ALEXIAS

To read, one must have intact visual pathways, recognize graphemes (the smallest part of written language necessary to make a sound, such as f and ph), and comprehend the meaning of the words. Disruption in any of these steps can lead to alexia or dyslexia, a disorder of reading.

Developmentally, a person learns to read (assuming an intact visual system [eyes, retina, optic nerves, optic chiasm, lateral geniculate bodies, optic radiations, primary visual cortex]) by first recognizing graphemes and then speaking (out loud or subvocally) the phoneme associated with that grapheme, a grapheme-to-phoneme conversion. The templates for graphemes are stored in the visual associa-

tion cortices (Fig. 3.4, *VA*); the templates for phonemes and words are stored in Wernicke's area (2). Grapheme-to-phoneme conversions occur in the left angular gyrus (Figs. 3.4–6, *AG*) (2).

Patients who have aphasic syndromes typically also have alexia. Wernicke's aphasics have difficulty reading because their templates for phonemes and words are destroyed, so they cannot comprehend what they read. Patients who have anomic aphasia or alexia with agraphia have difficulty reading because they cannot convert graphemes to phonemes (16). Broca's aphasics are dyslexic because they have trouble comprehending grammar, and Broca's area handles grammar comprehension (16). Patients who have right parietal pathology may have dyslexia owing to neglect of the left side of the page, word, or sentence (16).

THE AGRAPHIAS

To write, one must have a word in mind, that is, to recall phonemes and words and convert them (in the arcuate fasciculus) into graphemes and written words. Once the words are thought of and converted in the angular gyrus, this must be transmitted to the brain's motor systems. This information is sent through the arcuate fasciculus to ipsilateral premotor areas involved with arm, hand, and finger movements (Fig. 3.4, *MA*), then to the motor strip (Fig. 3.4, *M*) ipsilaterally, and then to the corticospinal tracts which cross at the medulla and progress to the peripheral nerves involved in writing movements. Disruption of any of these processes can cause agraphia (16).

Aphasic patients typically have an associated agraphia (34). Wernicke's aphasic patients are agraphic because their templates for phonemes and words are disrupted. Their writing resembles the verbal, phonemic and neologistic paraphasias of their speech, termed paragraphias when errors are written. Although these patients tend to have intact syntax, their writing is empty, devoid of nouns.

Broca's aphasics also have difficulty writing because of the weakness of their right side, and they often have a sympathetic apraxia of the left arm. If they can use the left arm their writing resembles their speech, with impaired grammar and syntax and excessive use of nouns.

Patients who have right parietal pathology tend to neglect the left side of the page (a visuospatial agraphia). Those who have movement disorders often have dysgraphia. Patients who have Parkinsonism (pill-rolling tremor, shuffling gait, expressionless face, drooling) typically write small (micrographia). Chorea (jerky movements), tics, tremors, and ballistic (flailing) movements, resulting from numerous causes (p. 190), show up in patients' writing. Patients suffering from frontal lobe disorders and Tourette's syndrome (see p. 276) tend to perseverate or repeat words and letters (33).

THE AGNOSIAS

When unimodal sensory association areas, or the connections between unimodal sensory association areas and memories of a stimulus are disrupted, agnosia results (35). Visual object agnosia occurs when the visual association areas are disconnected from associated visual memories located in the temporal portion of the limbic system, which results in an inability to link visual perceptions to memories about that perception. For example, a patient wants to leave a conference room but cannot recognize the doorway, and walks aimlessly until directed out. Fortunately, patients can sometimes compensate by way of touch or sound. In prosopagnosia, familiar faces are not recognized (35). Prosopagnosic patients can develop Capgras' syndrome, or delusions that family members are impostors (36). Often, patients who have right hemispheric damage can develop Fregoli syndrome, delusions that strangers are familiar (sometimes famous) persons (37), or reverse Fregoli syndrome, in which familiar persons are strangers (but not impostors, as in Capgras' syndrome) (38).

Patients who have nondominant posterior cerebral lesions can develop facial agnosia, or difficulty matching faces. When presented with a target face, they have difficulty picking it out from a group of faces (39).

The inability to perceive more than one stimulus at a time, or more than one aspect of a complex picture, is simultanagnosia. In looking at a picture of scenery that contains multiple items, the patient focuses on one item and ignores the rest. These patients usually have posterior cerebral lesions (40–42).

The denial of one's illness can have a neurologic correlation known as anosognosia. Patient's who have right parietal lobe damage and who are paralyzed often believe they are not paralyzed, and may even deny their left arm belongs to them. This is called Babinski's agnosia (43). They can also develop duplication phenomena in which they believe they have a third arm (44), that there are doppelgänger or doubles of themselves (45), or that environments are doubled (reduplicative paramnesia) (46). They may exhibit pain asymbolia in which they are unable to locate a source of pain or have a very high pain tolerance (47).

Inability to recognize objects by touch is astereognosis (48). Patients who suffer from this cannot recognize and differentiate objects (e.g., denominations of coins) placed in their hands (with eyes closed) (48). The pathology is usually in the parietal lobe contralateral to the hand tested.

THE ACALCULIAS

There are many causes of calculation difficulties. Patients who have language disorders may appear unable to calculate, as is the case with patients who have number paraphasia (speech error) in which one number may be substituted for another (49). The patient knows the sum of $3 + 2$ is 5 but says 6. Number paralexia is a reading error in which one number may be misread for another. Number paragraphia is similar, except the error is in writing one number when another is meant

(50). Patients with visuospatial processing problems may misalign columns of numbers or neglect the left side of an equation (51). Some patients may develop difficulty calculating because they have trouble recognizing symbols (50). For example, a patient may not recognize that a plus sign (+) means to add, or that the number 8 represents eight objects placed before the person.

Patients who have dominant parietal lesions can lose the concept of arithmetic, known as anarithmetria (51–53). This is often part of the Gerstmann syndrome, as are left-right disorientation, finger anomia (trouble naming fingers), and agraphia (53).

THE FRONTAL–SUBCORTICAL AXIS AND BEHAVIOR

Frontal lobe functions include concentration and attention (such as spelling a five-letter word backwards or subtracting seven serially from 100); global orientation—to time, place, and person; language (discussed previously); problem-solving and abstracting ability (such as identifying the way in which two items are similar: a bird and a butterfly, an airplane and a bicycle, a fire and an oven); judgment (how does the patient handle daily problems?); and motor regulation (can the patient, for example, when directed reach for a piece of paper with the right or the left hand, then fold it in half with both hands, and then put it on the floor; or, when you touch your nose, can the patient touch his or her chin). Except for language and movement functions the two frontal lobes can be viewed as a single unit.

Four general areas are comprised in the frontal lobe. The precentral or primary motor area is discussed above (see section on The Apraxias). Damage leads to motor weakness.

The premotor area (Fig. 3.4, *MA*) is also discussed above. Lesions can disrupt motor programs for complex motor acts. For example, the patient may show ideokinetic apraxia, agestural or dysarthric speech, or buccofacial apraxia.

The prefrontal area (Figs. 3.4–6, *PC*), which occupies the rest of the frontal lobe anterior to the premotor cortex, is a heteromodal association area. It can be subdivided into the dorsolateral prefrontal cortex and the orbitomedial cortex. The dorsolateral prefrontal cortex receives highly integrated sensory input from the inferior temporal and parietal lobes which transmit external perceptual information. It also receives input from the thalamus, hypothalamus, hippocampus, and basal ganglia, all subcortical regions that send information about the state of the internal milieu. Sensory, motor, and cognitive processes are integrated in this region. The orbitomedial prefrontal paralimbic cortex is more intimately linked with limbic system structures than the dorsolateral area. It is the neocortical representation of the limbic system, and is a buffer between emotional arousal and behavioral response.

The frontal limbic cortex (the cingulate gyrus) (Fig. 3.3 and Fig. 3.4, *CG*) is linked with the amygdaloid complex, thalamus, and septal nuclei (54-58). The frontal limbic cortex sends information to the midbrain premotor cortex and basal ganglia.

Lesions in the dorsolateral prefrontal cortex often cause an apathetic lack of response, indifference to surroundings, and the slowing of thought and movement. Lesions involving the subcortical regions can also result in a similar behavioral pattern (59).

A 57-year-old man, an attorney, is hospitalized for depression. Two years prior to admission he had sustained a concussion in a car accident. According to his wife he lost all prior drive and motivation and has since been unable to make decisions. He has not been to work and watches TV all day. On examination he is unkempt. He displays hypoactivity (decreased frequency of movement) and bradykinesia (slow movement). He is apathetic and emotionally blunted. His speech is slow and low in volume. A magnetic resonance imaging (MRI) reveals his atrophied (reduced in size and cell number) frontal lobes, particularly the lateral convexities.

Lesions of the orbitofrontal prefrontal cortex (disrupting the buffer) result in disinhibited behavior; impulses are acted upon without considering social consequences. Patients often become emotionally labile in which moods shift rapidly with minimal provocation, and they develop witzelsucht, a silly shallow mood (59).

A 24-year-old man, an accountant with no prior history of neuropsychiatric problems or substance abuse, was in a motor vehicle accident and sustained a closed head injury with a concussion. At the accident scene he became violent and verbally abusive to police and accident witnesses, behaviors totally out of character. He continued this behavior in the hospital and began to parrot what others said to him (echolalia). He was examined by a neurologist (with no training in behavioral neurology) who stated that the patient was malingering. Two days after the accident, an MRI scan revealed a contusion (bruising) of the orbital aspects of the frontal lobe.

States of decreased movements, such as Parkinsonism and catatonia, often occur with lesions involving the orbitomedial prefrontal paralimbic cortex (60, 61).

THE LIMBIC SYSTEM AND BEHAVIOR

The limbic system was initially described by Papez (62), and then by MacLean (63). The Papez circuit consists of the hippocampal formation, the mammillary bodies, the anterior thalamic nuclei, and the cingulate gyrus (Fig. 3.3). The limbic system is central to formation of affective experience (feelings, emotions, moods). Diseases of the limbic system cause mood disorders and other psychopathology.

In the early 1900s, for example, a worldwide influenza epidemic caused encephalitis lethargica (64). This viral infection of the limbic system led to varieties of psychopathology (obsessive-compulsive, manic-depressive, and schizophrenia-like states) in the survivors (64). In 1951, Gibbs reported that psychiatric complications of epilepsy (e.g., manic-like and schizophrenic-like states) were more common in epileptics who had temporal-limbic disturbances (65). Other conditions involve the limbic system and cause various psychopathologies, such as herpes simplex encephalitis, limbic encephalitis in patients who have various cancers, rabies, and measles encephalitis.

Disorders of memory are also seen when certain limbic system structures are damaged. Korsakoff's psychosis involves the mammillary bodies (p. 35) and dorsomedial nucleus of the thalamus. (The thalamus is a relay station for sensory stimuli en route to the cerebral cortex.) Vitamin B1 (thiamine) deficiency, a cause of memory disorders in alcoholics, leads to a disruption in the ability to learn new information and to recall information prior to illness onset (66, 67).

EPILEPSY

Epilepsy is an intermittent derangement of the central nervous system due presumably to a sudden, excessive, disorderly discharge of cerebral neurons (67). There are two main categories: partial and generalized seizures. Partial seizures have a local (focal) onset, unlike generalized seizures which involve the whole brain from the onset. Partial seizures can be further divided into simple and complex partial seizures, as well as partial seizures that secondarily generalize to the whole brain (67).

Simple partial seizures could involve focal motor seizures, somatosensory or special sensory symptoms such as hallucinations, autonomic symptoms such as flushing and tachycardia (rapid pulse), or mental symptoms such as sudden mood changes, intrusive thoughts, or false remembrances (déjà vu). In simple partial seizures, consciousness is retained.

A 21-year-old woman came to the neuropsychiatric clinic with the chief complaint of depression. She stated the depression would come on suddenly. Specifically, she would experience sudden, overwhelming sadness with uncontrolled crying which would last for about 3 minutes. This was then followed by an intense frontal headache and a feeling that she had to sleep. She had attacks like this 3–4 times a week. An ambulatory 24-hour electroencephalogram (EEG) revealed epileptiform (spike-shaped) discharges emanating from the right temporal region. She was treated with carbamazepine (an anticonvulsant) which completely controlled the depressions.

In complex partial seizures, there is an impairment of consciousness that may be preceded by a simple partial seizure (termed an aura). Of the types of epilepsy, this one is most often associated with psychiatric disorders such as schizophrenia-like illnesses (65). It usually emanates from temporolimbic structures. Both simple and complex seizures can spread through the whole brain, causing a generalized seizure. Patients who have complex partial seizures sometimes develop a personality change in which they become overly religious and philosophical (out of proportion to their preillness background), hypergraphic (keeping overly detailed notes), circumstantial (giving many unimportant details in conversations and writings) viscous (interpersonal "stickiness"—the patient [and doctor] cannot easily break off conversation), and hyposexual (uninterested in sex) (68, 69).

A 72-year-old man has lived on a chronic ward of a public psychiatric hospital for 30 years. He has had chronic temporal lobe epilepsy (documented by EEG) for 40 years. Though he did not come from a religious family, he suddenly had a religious conversion 35 years ago. His room overflows with religious articles and pictures; almost every inch of his wall has pictures of saints. He writes detailed letters—5–10 daily—to religious leaders around the world. He never married and has never been interested in sex.

The two most common types of generalized seizures are tonic-clonic (grand mal) and absence (petit mal) seizures. In grand mal, consciousness is suddenly lost, followed by a tonic phase in which the major muscle groups suddenly have a sustained contraction. In this phase, the patient is apneic (stops breathing), becomes cyanotic (skin and mucus membranes develop a grayish or bluish hue owing to inadequate oxygenation or circulation of blood), typically bites his or her tongue or inner cheek and is incontinent. After a few moments, this evolves into the clonic phase, in which there are alternating flexion and extension movements of the extremities. The frequency and amplitude of these clonic movements slowly diminish into the postictal (after the seizure) phase in which the patient is in a coma (unresponsive). The patient then slowly regains consciousness over the next few hours.

In petit mal, the patient (often a child) suddenly has a brief impairment of consciousness, with an arrest of attention, which may be associated with eye blinking. The seizure typically lasts a moment or two, and the patient promptly regains full consciousness, usually unaware of the episode (67).

An 11-year-old boy was evaluated for multiple learning disabilities. He had been in special education classes since second grade. He was diagnosed with attention-deficit hyperactivity disorder (ADHD [p. 144] and was treated for ADHD with various medications. The teachers reported that he was inattentive in class—a daydreamer. An EEG revealed a three-per-second spike and wave abnormality consistent with absence seizures. He was treated with valproic acid (an anticonvulsant). He is now in a regular classroom, receiving A's and B's.

4/Neurochemistry of Behavior

Myrl R. S. Manley, M.D.

OBJECTIVES

GENERAL OBJECTIVE: Given the changes in neurotransmitter function caused by a particular drug, predict therapeutic and side effects.

SPECIFIC OBJECTIVES:
1. Describe the sequence of events in signal transmission between two brain neurons.
2. Explain how the same neurotransmitter can be both neuroexcitatory and neuroinhibitory.
3. Discuss the evidence for and against the dopamine hypothesis of schizophrenia, the monoamine hypothesis of mood disorders, the serotonin hypothesis of obsessive-compulsive disorder, and the cholinergic hypothesis of memory dysfunction.
4. Describe the effects on brain neurochemistry of antipsychotics, antidepressants, and benzodiazepine and barbiturate anxiolytics.
5. List several functions mediated by endogenous opiates.
6. With reference to Kandel's work, discuss neurochemical changes associated with learning and memory.
7. Explain the neurochemical changes associated with Parkinson's disease, with Parkinsonian movement disorders caused by antipsychotic drugs, with Huntington's disease, and with tardive dyskinesia.

The structure and function of neurons (nerve cells), as well as the fundamental units of the central nervous system (CNS) are discussed in relation to normal and abnormal behavior.

NEURONS

Neurons vary enormously in size and shape. A typical one (Fig. 4.1) has four regions: the soma, dendrites, axon, and synapse. The soma (cell body) contains the cell's nucleus and metabolic machinery. Dendrites are tentacle-like projections from the soma that contact other cells and receive intercellular communication. The axon is the elongated portion of the neuron along which an electrical impulse is sent. The synapse is the contact point between the axon of the transmitting neuron and some portion (dendrites, soma, or [rarely] axon) of the receiving neuron. The cell transmitting a signal is the presynaptic neuron, that receiving a signal is the postsynaptic neuron. Some neurons have few synaptic contacts, others have millions.

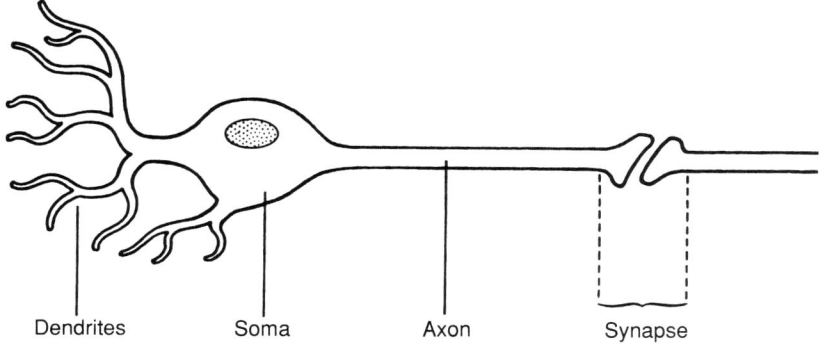

Figure 4.1.   Structure of the neuron.

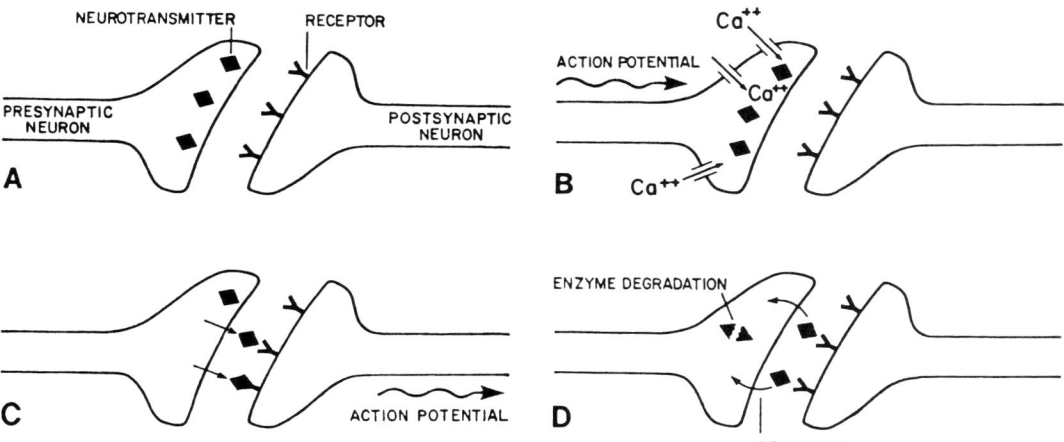

Figure 4.2.   Neurotransmitter action at the synapse. **A.** Neurotransmitter is stored in the presynaptic terminus. **B.** The action potential opens voltage-dependent calcium channels. **C.** The change in calcium concentration causes neurotransmitter to be released into the synaptic cleft where it binds to receptor proteins on the postsynaptic neuron. **D.** Transmitter is disposed of through reuptake into the presynaptic neuron and through enzyme degradation. Some neurotransmitter diffuses away.

TRANSMISSION OF SIGNALS BETWEEN NEURONS

In a few synapses, the presynaptic and postsynaptic neurons are in direct contact, and the electrical signal is transmitted uninterrupted. For most neurons, the cells are separated by the synaptic cleft (1), which disrupts the electrical signal and interposes another step in transmission (Fig. 4.2). When the depolarization wave reaches the presynaptic terminal, it triggers release of stored chemical (neurotransmitter) packets into the cleft. The neurotransmitter interacts with specific receptor sites on the postsynaptic neuron. The neurotransmitter-receptor interaction initiates changes in the postsynaptic neuron, resulting in a wave of depolarization moving along the cell membrane from the original point of contact towards and along the axon. Alternatively, the transmitter-receptor binding may inhibit the postsynaptic neuron from firing, even if it is signalled to fire by other neurons.

DEPOLARIZATION

The electrical pulse that travels along the cell membrane, unlike the current in a wire, is not the movement of electrons, but rather the progressive, sequential movement of ions across the cell membrane. The key to ion movement, and thus to mental activity, is an energy-dependent ion pump in the cell membrane. Fueled by the splitting of adenosine triphosphate (ATP), the pump extrudes sodium ions (Na^+) from the cell and brings in potassium ions (K^+), resulting in a high extracellular Na^+ concentration and a high intracellular K^+ concentration (2).

Ions enter or leave the cell through channels in the membrane. Each channel type is specific for one ion species. An ion channel has only two states: open or closed. Channels may be voltage-dependent or independent. Voltage-dependent channels are opened or closed by changes in the charge differential across the membrane. Voltage-independent channels are opened or closed by chemical changes in the membrane (e.g., changes in a receptor protein after binding neurotransmitter).

If a cell had only K^+ channels open, no other ions could cross the membrane. A few K^+ ions would leak across the open channels because the K^+ concentration is greater inside than outside the cell. The negative charges left inside make the area inside negative with respect to the outside. If only Na^+ channels were open, no other ions could cross, and Na^+ ions would enter because there is a higher concentration of Na^+ outside. These positive charges would make the inside positive with respect to the outside.

The ratio of open K^+ to open Na^+ channels determines the transmembrane potential. In a resting neuron with at least 10 times as many open K^+ channels as open Na^+ channels, transmembrane voltage is about $-70mV$ (always given as inside voltage with respect to the outside) (Fig. 4.3).

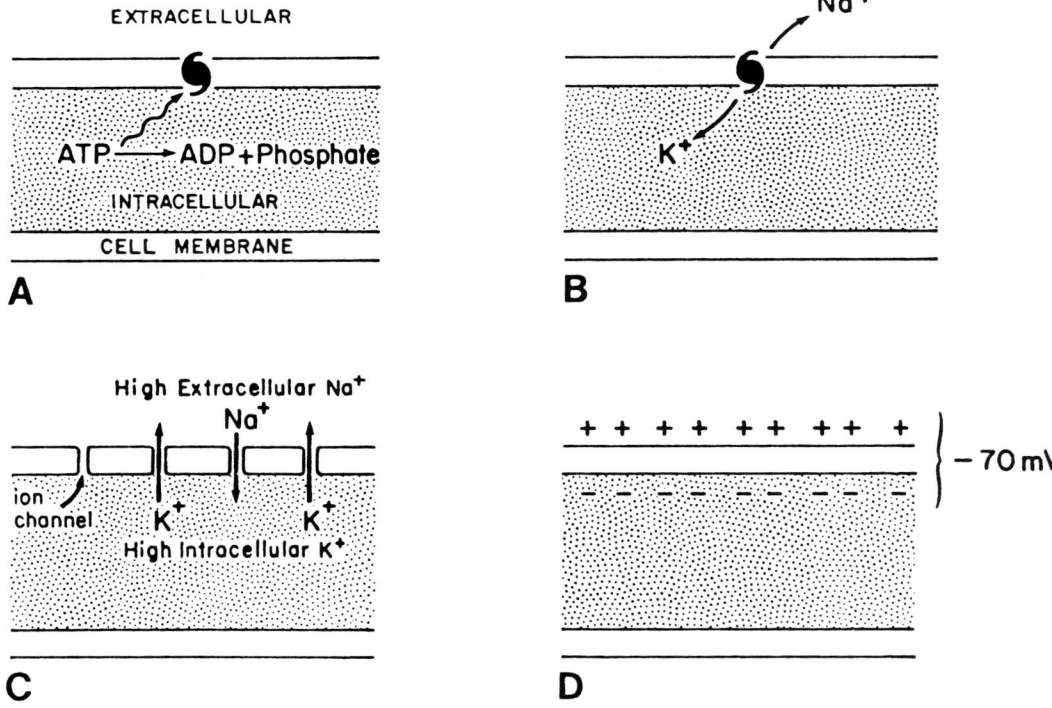

Figure 4.3. The membrane resting potential. **A.** An energy-dependent membrane pump is fueled by the splitting of ATP. **B.** The pump concentrates potassium ions inside the cell and sodium ions outside. **C.** Open ion channels permit leakage of sodium into and potassium out of the neuron. **D.** Because most resting neurons have more potassium than sodium channels open, there is a net buildup of negative charge inside with respect to outside.

Table 4.1.   Selected Neurotransmitters and Their Chemical Groups

Monoamines	Amino Acids	Peptides
Dopamine	γ-aminobutyric acid	β-endorphin
Norepinephrine	Glutamic acid	Dynorphin
Epinephrine		Luteinizing hormone releasing hormone
Acetylcholine		
Serotonin		

Any event that increases positive charge inside is said to depolarize the membrane. Any event that increases negative charge inside hyperpolarizes it. For example, if something triggers an influx of Na^+, the membrane is depolarized. But if something causes an influx (entry into the cell) from outside the cell of negatively charged chloride ions (Cl^-), the membrane is hyperpolarized. The wave of depolarization that sweeps down the cell towards and along the axon, the action potential, is caused by successive opening of adjacent voltage-dependent Na^+ channels (3). An increase in the resting potential from $-70mV$ to $-35mV$ opens voltage-dependent Na^+ channels, causing Na^+ influx. This further depolarizes the membrane, causing still more Na^+ channels to open. The resulting depolarization opens adjacent membrane channels in a wave moving down the length of the axon to the synapse, like a row of dominoes toppling. At the next synapse, another series of events is initiated, resulting in release of neurotransmitter from the presynaptic neuron into the synaptic cleft.

NEUROTRANSMITTERS

There are three classes of neurotransmitters: biogenic amines, amino acids, and peptides (4) (Table 4.1). Peptide transmitters are synthesized in the soma, moved by axonal transport to the presynaptic terminal, and stored. (Axonal transport is movement through the interior of the axon, probably through microtubules.) Biogenic amine transmitters are made in the presynaptic terminal; enzymes for their synthesis are made in the soma and transported down the axon to the cell terminal. Some amino acid transmitters are cleaved from peptides, but more are a by-product of the cell's carbohydrate metabolism. Once made, neurotransmitter is stored in the presynaptic terminal until the neuron fires. When the action potential arrives at the presynaptic terminal, it opens voltage-dependent calcium (Ca^{2+}) channels. The influx of Ca^{2+} causes extrusion of neurotransmitter into the synaptic cleft (5). Once released into the cleft it binds with receptor proteins on the postsynaptic membrane. This initiates events in the postsynaptic neuron that either depolarize or hyperpolarize its membrane. For any given transmitter there may be several subtypes of receptor. Different receptor subtypes bound to transmitter cause different changes within the postsynaptic cell. A transmitter may be excitatory or inhibitory depending on its receptor binding (6).

Neurotransmitter release transmits a signal from one neuron to another; transmitter removal ends the signal. After release, neurotransmitter is promptly removed in 3 ways: it may be taken back into the presynaptic neuron (reuptake), be degraded by enzymes (within the cell or extracellularly), or diffuse away.

Each neuron receives input from numerous other neurons. Whether a cell fires or not—whether an action potential is generated—is determined by the sum of inputs. If the net effect of all synaptic influences is depolarization to $-35mV$, it fires; otherwise, it will not (7). An action potential is not graded; a cell cannot partially fire; the process is all or none.

SIGNAL TRANSDUCTION

Neurotransmitter binding to postsynaptic receptors affects firing in one of two ways. It may directly alter membrane ion channels. If binding opens Na^+ channels, the postsynaptic neuron depolarizes and is more excitable. Opening Cl^- channels hyperpolarizes the cell, inhibiting firing. Reciprocal effects occur if ion channels close: when Na^+ channels close, the cell hyperpolarizes; when Cl^- channels close, it depolarizes. Most brain synapses use an amino acid transmitter whose receptor binding directly opens or closes channels. By contrast, the biogenic amines and peptides (affecting a tiny [but important] proportion of brain synapses) only indirectly affect ion channels, through a cascading sequence of events (8). Two such sequences, second messenger systems, have been identified: the adenylate cyclase and phosphoinositide systems. The two systems are widely distributed in the brain. Most neurons contain both. Which of the two is activated, and whether the transmitter is excitatory or inhibitory, is determined by the receptor subtype.

Adenylate Cyclase System (Fig. 4.4)

When a receptor binds transmitter, the resulting complex activates one of a family of G proteins, named for their affinity for guanosine triphosphate (GTP). Coupled with activated G protein, GTP either stimulates or inhibits adenylate cyclase: G_i protein causes inhibition, G_s causes stimulation (10). When adenylate cyclase is stimulated by GTP-G_s it activates formation of cyclic adenosine monophosphate (cAMP) from ATP. One effect of cAMP is to close K^+ channels, increasing neuron excitability.

The Phosphoinositide System (Fig. 4.5)

The phosphoinositide system also begins with transmitter-receptor binding. Receptor stimulation activates a G protein which in turn activates phospholipase C. Phospholipase C hydrolyzes a membrane phospholipid (PIP$_2$), producing two second messengers. One is inositol triphosphate (IP$_3$), which triggers Ca^{2+} release from within the cell when it binds to an intracellular receptor.

The other product of hydrolysis of PIP$_2$ is diacylglycerol, which activates protein-kinase C. Protein-kinase C blocks Ca^{2+} activated K^+

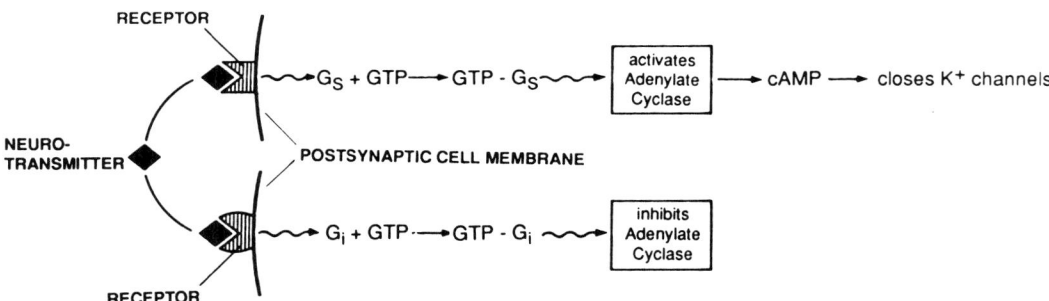

Figure 4.4. The adenylate cyclase second messenger system.

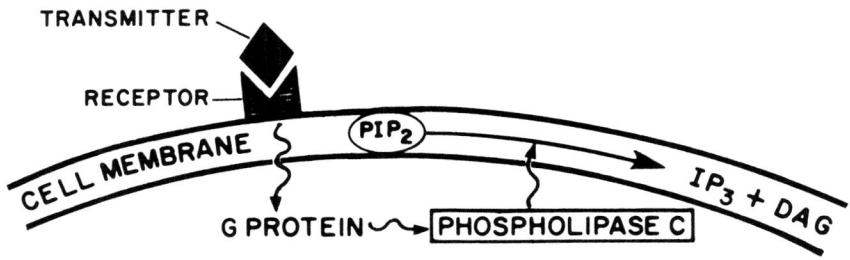

Figure 4.5. The phosphoinositide second messenger system.

channels, depolarizing the cell, increasing excitability. It also blocks inhibitory actions initiated by several neurotransmitters. Animal studies suggest that lithium carbonate, a drug highly effective for bipolar disorder (characterized by manic episodes [pressured speech, euphoric or irritable mood, hyperactivity, grandiosity, etc.] and *sometimes* by depressive episodes [sustained sad mood, appetite and sleep trouble, suicidal thoughts, etc.]), acts by suppressing the phosphoinositide system (8, 11).

The two second messenger systems themselves interact. For example, activation of the adenylate cyclase system sometimes inhibits the phosphoinositide system.

Neurotransmitters are not randomly scattered in the brain. Their location and action are specific. Mature neurons use either a single neurotransmitter or an unchanging combination of neurotransmitters (4). Neurons that use the same transmitter are often linked in tracts connecting parts of the brain.

STUDY TECHNIQUES

Several innovations permitted localization of neurotransmitter systems in the brain. Conventional histologic techniques such as electron and light microscopy can distinguish neuronal structures (e.g., mitochondria, synapses), but cannot distinguish neurotransmitter or receptor differences among neurons (2). Immunocytochemical studies use antibody against a specific transmitter (the antigen). The antibody is developed from lymphocytes from the spleens of mice immunized against the transmitter. When mouse lymphocyte immunoglobulin is applied to brain tissue sections, the antibody it contains binds to the antigenic transmitter. The section is next incubated with a second antibody carrying a visualizable marker (e.g., the enzyme peroxidase), which reveals the transmitter locations. Other techniques include autoradiography (12), positron emission tomography (13) using radioactive analogues of transmitter, and dye studies (14).

SELECTED NEUROTRANSMITTERS AND THE MENTAL EVENTS THEY INFLUENCE

Several neurotransmitters are thought to affect mental illnesses, learning, and memory. They include dopamine, norepinephrine, serotonin, γ-aminobutyric acid, acetylcholine, glutamate, and peptides.

Dopamine

The biogenic amine transmitter dopamine (DA) has long been presumed to have a role in schizophrenia. Schizophrenia is manifested by hallucinations and delusions (like many other conditions), as well as by first rank symptoms (FRS—specific types of delusions and hallucinations), formal thought disorders (FTD—aphasia-like language disorders), and emotional blunting (reduced emotional expressivity and concern). Antipsychotic drugs can reduce hallucinations, delusions, FRS, and FTD. They block postsynaptic DA receptors and probably produce their therapeutic effect by disrupting transmission in DA pathways (15).

Drugs that enhance DA activity (e.g., amphetamines, L-dopa) can also cause schizophrenia-like psychotic symptoms. These observations led to the dopamine hypothesis of schizophrenia, or the theory that schizophrenia is a hyperdopaminergic state.

There are problems with this hypothesis. Psychotic symptoms such as hallucinations, delusions, FRS, and FTD are seen in many other conditions (e.g., mania, drug-induced psychoses), and antipsychotic drugs are also effective for these. Moreover, antipsychotic drugs are minimally effective in controlling the functional impairment between acute psychotic episodes in schizophrenia. The DA hypothesis of schizophrenia is really a dopamine hypothesis of psychotic symptoms.

Another problem is that no one has conclusively demonstrated tissue or chemical pathology to correlate with the presumed increase in DA transmission. We could speculate that the core defect is synthesis of too much DA, a failure in presynaptic reuptake or enzymatic degradation of it, an excessive number of postsynaptic receptors, or receptors abnormally sensitive to DA. In 1986, D.F. Wong (13) reported increased numbers of DA receptors in young schizophrenic persons who had never been medicated. Previous work had shown increased numbers of postsynaptic DA receptors in schizophrenics who had received antipsychotic drugs, but it was not known whether the increase was the result of schizophrenia or its drug treatment. Wong's report was problematic, however. The increased DA receptors were in a pathway not conventionally associated with psychosis. Wong's research also has not yet been replicated.

A final problem with the old DA hypothesis is presented by the new antipsychotic drug clozapine. The potency of earlier antipsychotics was related to how well they blocked DA receptors: the greater the blockade, the more potent the drug (12, 16). Clozapine blocks DA receptors, but not as strongly as most other antipsychotics. Nevertheless, it does control psychotic symptoms, better than some drugs which are better DA antagonists (17–19). Thus, something else must also be involved in the chemistry of psychotic symptoms.

BIOSYNTHESIS AND PATHWAYS

DA is a catecholamine neurotransmitter, named for its catechol core (Fig. 4.6). Its synthesis is illustrated in Fig. 4.7. Like all major catecholamines, tyrosine hydroxylase is the enzyme that controls the rate of synthesis (20). There are five major DA pathways (Fig. 4.8) in the human brain (4). We understand the importance of three: the cell bodies of the nigrostriatal tract are in a midbrain area, the substantia nigra. Axons from these cells extend to the putamen and the caudate nucleus

(here, nucleus refers to a cluster of cell bodies), which form a larger structure, the corpus striatum (hence nigrostriatal). The substantia nigra and the corpus striatum are part of the basal ganglia, a neural system linked to the premotor and motor cortex, which helps to coordinate movement and possibly plays a role in intellectual functioning (21).

The mesocortical-mesolimbic tract is in the midbrain, where its cell bodies are near the substantia nigra. This tract extends to the limbic system and frontal cortex. The frontal cortex serves many functions, including reasoning. The limbic system helps modulate emotions. It was once assumed that pathologically increased transmission in the mesocortical-mesolimbic pathway was solely responsible for psychotic symptoms (as in schizophrenia), but this is questionable.

The short tuberoinfundibular tract links the hypothalamus and the anterior pituitary. In it,

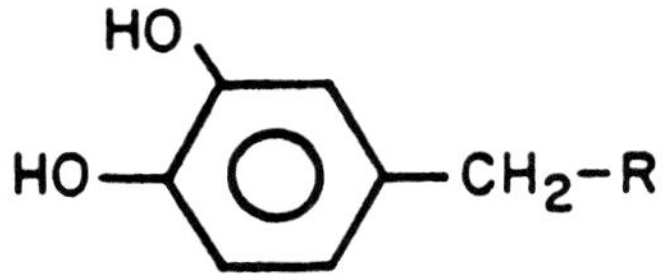

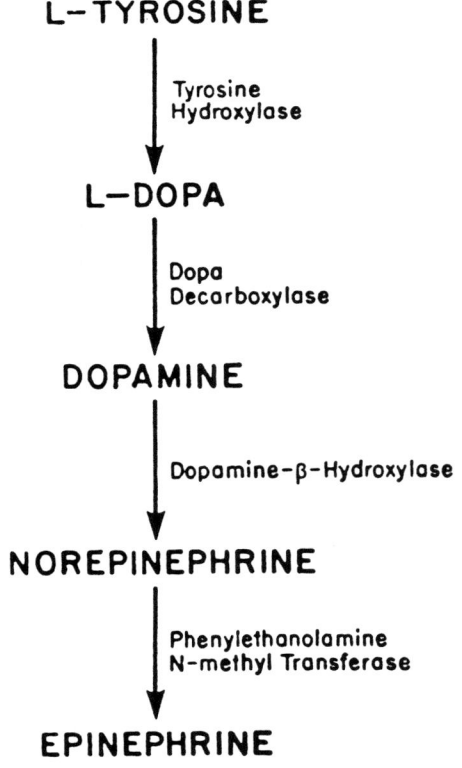

Figure 4.7. Catecholamine biosynthetic pathway.

HO, HO—⟨O⟩—CH₂–R

Figure 4.6. Catechol core.

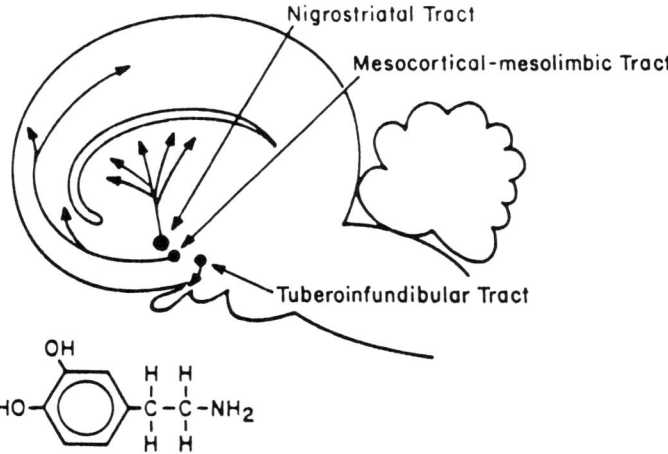

Figure 4.8. Dopamine structure and pathways. (Adapted with permission from Coyle JT. Neuroscience and psychiatry. In: Talbott JA, Hales RE, Yudofsky SC, eds. Textbook of psychiatry. Washington DC: American Psychiatric Press, 1988.)

DA continuously inhibits the release of prolactin, a hormone that stimulates milk production (22). The other two DA tracts are less well understood.

RECEPTORS

There is nothing intrinsic to the DA molecule to make it excitatory or inhibitory; this is determined by neurotransmitter-receptor binding. Two major subtypes of postsynaptic DA receptors, D_1 and D_2, are known (23). DA bound to D_1 receptors activates adenylate cyclase and is thus excitatory. DA bound to D_2 receptors inhibits adenylate cyclase and is inhibitory. A third subtype is found on presynaptic neurons and provides autoregulation.

The antipsychotic drugs bind and block D_2 receptors but do not affect the adenylate cyclase system. The blockade indiscriminately occurs wherever D_2 receptors are found. Because the three major DA tracts contain D_2 receptors, it is easy to predict some antipsychotic drug side effects. DA blockade in the nigrostriatal tract causes movement disorders; blockade in the tuberoinfundibular tract disinhibits prolactin release and stimulates (sometimes) milk production, which is disconcerting to women who have not recently given birth.

Norepinephrine

Norepinephrine (NE) is thought to play a role in causing depression (24). Like DA in schizophrenia, the evidence implicating NE in depression is indirect. Drugs that are effective for depression enhance transmission in pathways using NE (or serotonin, discussed in the section that follows). The antidepressant drugs comprise two groups: one (cyclic antidepressants) blocks the presynaptic reuptake of NE, the other (monoamine oxidase inhibitors) blocks enzymatic degradation. Either effect enhances NE transmission. Drugs that disrupt NE transmission (e.g., the antihypertensive reserpine) can cause depression. Because NE is a catecholamine, these observations led to formulation of the catecholamine hypothesis of mood disorders, which proposes that depression results from a functional deficiency of NE. Like the DA hypothesis, it has shortcomings.

No one has demonstrated characteristic tissue or neurochemical pathology in the brains of depressives, or characteristic catecholamine metabolite abnormalities in blood or urine. Moreover, drugs that block reuptake of serotonin (not a catecholamine) can be effective in depression.

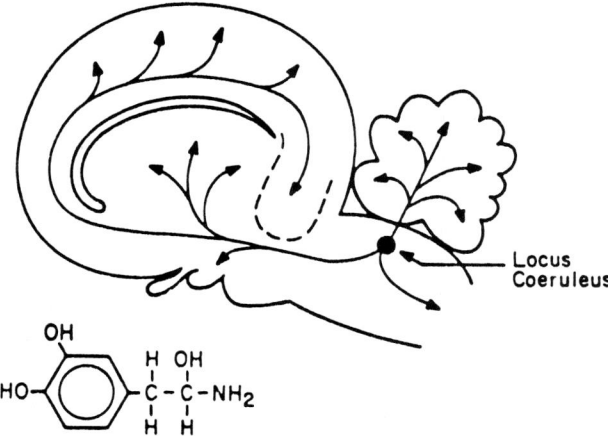

Figure 4.9. Norepinephrine structure and pathways. (Reproduced with permission from Coyle JT. Neuroscience and psychiatry. In: Talbott JA, Hales RE, Yudofsky SC, eds. Textbook of psychiatry. Washington DC: American Psychiatric Press, 1988.)

BIOSYNTHESIS, PATHWAYS, AND RECEPTORS

The synthesis of NE from DA is illustrated in Fig. 4.7. The main cluster of NE-containing cell bodies is the locus ceruleus ("blue place"; this locus is blue), a bilateral nucleus on the floor of the fourth ventricle. It contains cell bodies of over half the NE neurons in the CNS. Its neurons project throughout the CNS to synapse in the cortex, limbic system, cerebellum, and spinal cord (Fig. 4.9).

The importance of NE in anxiety states in general, and panic disorder in particular, is under investigation. Panic disorder is a vulnerability, probably inherited (25), to recurrent attacks of such dread that the afflicted person believes he or she is dying. The attack is accompanied by a massive autonomic discharge, with a rise in blood pressure and heart rate. In one primate model (26, 27), the attack is caused by paroxysmal locus ceruleus discharge. Evidence suggesting that this also occurs in humans is presented on page 258.

Four receptor subtypes have been identified (24): α-1, and α-2, β-1, and β-2. Norepinephrine binding to β-1 or 2 receptors activates adenylate cyclase and is therefore neuroexcitatory. Most postsynaptic receptors of NE tracts originating in the locus ceruleus are β-1 and β-2.

α-2 receptors are located on presynaptic neurons and are a means of autoregulation. Norepinephrine binding to α-2 receptors decreases NE release from the presynaptic neuron. An NE neuron with presynaptic α-2 receptors will eventually shut itself off after prolonged firing by depleting the neurotransmitter. The antihypertensive drugs clonidine and α-methyldopa are α-2 agonists. When they bind to α-2 receptors, they decrease NE release, decreasing central and peripheral NE transmission. Alpha 1 receptors, when activated by NE, appear to cause neuroexcitation, but the mechanism and importance are unclear.

Serotonin

Serotonin (5-hydroxytryptamine, 5-HT) is another monoamine neurotransmitter. Functional deficiencies of 5-HT transmission (as well as of NE functioning) have long been associated with depression (24). Drugs (e.g., reserpine) that deplete NE or 5-HT can cause depression and drugs that enhance their actions (e.g., imipramine) can alleviate depression. Some depressed patients respond better to drugs that are more serotonergic, whereas others respond to noradrenergic drugs.

Dysfunction of 5-HT *may* also underlie obsessive-compulsive disorder (OCD), formerly treatment-resistant. Obsessions are unwanted, intrusive, disturbing thoughts (e.g., "If I shake people's hands, I could transmit a serious infection.") that preoccupy patients even when they know the ideas are exaggerated or absurd. Compulsions are rituals performed in response to obsessions (e.g., repetitive hand washing to minimize spread of infection). Some drugs (e.g., clomipramine, fluoxetine) that block the presynaptic reuptake of serotonin and enhance its transmission, have antiobsessive effects (28, 29). Inconveniently, some 5-HT agonists increase OCD symptoms (30), and the potent serotonin-reuptake blocker sertraline is ineffective in OCD (31). Thus, a straightforward 5-HT theory of OCD is unsatisfactory.

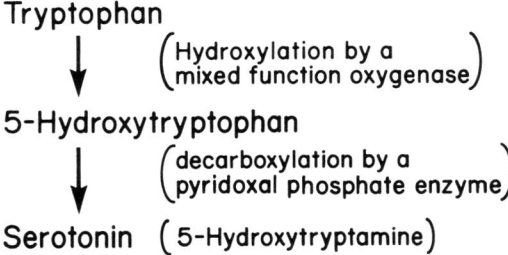

Figure 4.10. Tryptophan, an essential amino acid and a precursor of 5-HT.

Serotonin is thought to be a sleep-inducing neurotransmitter (32). Sleep consists of two physiologically distinct states: rapid eye movement (REM) sleep and non-REM (NREM) sleep (see pp. 375–377). A burst of 5-HT activity at the start of a normal night's sleep may initiate NREM sleep, after which 5-HT activity subsides.

A reasonable mistrust of sleeping pills led many insomniacs to try dietary supplements of typtophan, an essential amino acid and a precursor of 5-HT (Fig. 4.10). Increasing levels of tryptophan increase 5-HT synthesis and transmission in 5-HT pathways. This plausibly could enhance sleepiness, but it is less clear whether tryptophan supplements restore normal sleep (33, 34). Tryptophan tablets have been temporarily withdrawn from the market because of an allergy-inducing effect (35).

PATHWAYS AND RECEPTORS

Cell bodies of serotonin-containing neurons (the raphe nuclei) are concentrated in an area extending from the midbrain to the medulla along the aqueduct leading to the fourth cerebral ventricle. These neurons branch out to virtually all parts of the brain and spinal cord (Fig. 4.11) (4, 7).

Originally three classes of 5-HT receptors were identified: 5-HT$_1$, 5-HT$_2$, and 5-HT$_3$.

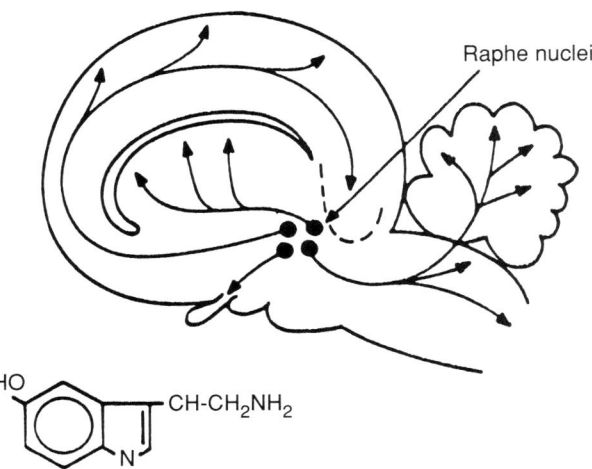

Figure 4.11. Serotonin structure and pathways. (Reproduced with permission from Coyle JT. Neuroscience and psychiatry. In: Talbott JA, Hales RE, Yudofsky SC. Textbook of psychiatry. Washington DC: American Psychiatric Press, 1988.)

There are four variations in the type 1 receptor, 5-HT$_{1A}$ through 5-HT$_{1D}$ (36). How transmitter-receptor binding of 5-HT causes depolarization or hyperpolarization of the postsynaptic neuron is not well understood. It is known that adenylate cyclase and phosphoinositide systems are involved, and that 5-HT may be excitatory or inhibitory (36).

Using compounds that selectively bind to one 5-HT receptor subtype but not others is how receptor subtypes and their functions are identified. Serotonin agonists that bind to 5-HT$_{1A}$ receptors and those that bind 5-HT$_2$ receptors have antidepressant properties. Antiobsessive drugs block presynaptic reuptake of the transmitter without regard to receptor subtype.

γ-Aminobutyric Acid (GABA)

An amino acid neurotransmitter, GABA is associated with modulating anxiety (37). Wherever bound to brain receptors it is inhibitory. When GABA neurons fire, they dampen excitement generated elsewhere in the CNS; when they are blocked, brain excitability increases and seizures may result. Postsynaptic receptor binding with GABA opens Cl$^-$ channels (38). The resulting influx of Cl$^-$ ions hyperpolarizes the cell membrane, decreasing the likelihood of firing.

Intimately associated with the GABA receptor is another receptor site, the benzodiazepine-binding site, that binds benzodiazepines (BDZ). BDZs are sedative hypnotics (e.g., diazepam) that have marked antianxiety properties. When BDZs enter the bloodstream and bind to their receptors, they increase the affinity of the nearby GABA receptor for GABA. The postsynaptic neuron is then hyperpolarized (and inhibited) by smaller concentrations of GABA than would otherwise be needed (39).

Barbiturates also enhance GABA activity. Another class of sedative hypnotics, barbiturates attach to the postsynaptic neuron close to GABA-controlled Cl$^-$ channels. When GABA-receptor binding opens Cl$^-$ channels, barbiturate binding keeps them open longer.

Changes in the amount of GABA transmission affect the likelihood of seizures: BDZs and barbiturates are antiepileptics, whereas high doses of isoniazid (INH) (a drug used for TB) inhibit GABA synthesis and cause seizures (38).

Identification of a BDZ receptor associated with the GABA receptor led to speculation (38, 39) about an endogenous anxiolytic that could quell anxiety. No such substance has yet been identified.

PATHWAYS AND RECEPTORS

Widely distributed (Fig. 4.12), GABA neurons are in the spinal cord, brain stem, cerebellum, limbic system, and cerebral cortex. Particularly high concentrations are found in extrapyramidal structures also innervated by the nigrostriatal DA tract. We know of two GABA receptors (23). GABA^A opens Cl$^-$ channels when activated by transmitter binding. GABA^B receptors are found on the terminals of nerve cells using another neurotransmitter, such as NE, DA, or 5-HT. When GABA^B receptors are activated by binding GABA, they decrease release of the other neurotransmitters.

Acetylcholine

Acetylcholine (ACh) is essential for memory (40). Part of the evidence is indirect, based on the effects of drugs. If healthy volunteers are given an anticholinergic drug (one that blocks ACh), they acquire memory deficits. If they then receive a second drug that counteracts the first, memory is restored (40).

Better evidence comes from studies of Alzheimer's disease, a neurodegenerative dementing illness (with prominent memory loss) that destroys neurons and is accompanied by amyloid (an amorphous protein) deposits throughout the brain. Acetycholine is synthesized from choline and acetyl coenzyme A under control of the enzyme choline acetyltransferase (Fig. 4.13). This enzyme is reduced by up to 90% below normal in the hippocampi of persons who have died from Alzheimer's (40, 41). These findings in volunteers and in Alzheimer's

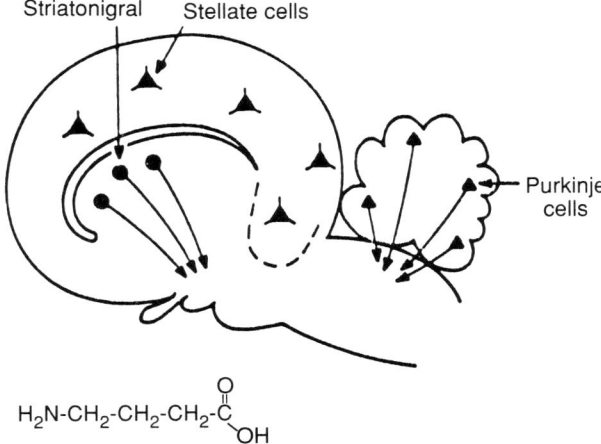

Striatonigral   Stellate cells

Purkinje cells

$$H_2N-CH_2-CH_2-CH_2-\overset{\overset{\displaystyle O}{\|}}{C}\diagdown_{OH}$$

Figure 4.12. Gamma aminobutyric acid structure and pathways. (Reproduced with permission from Coyle JT. Neuroscience and psychiatry. In: Talbott JA, Hales RE, Yudofsky SC, eds. Textbook of psychiatry. Washington DC: American Psychiatric Press, 1988.)

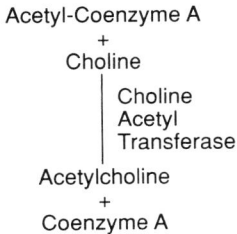

Acetyl-Coenzyme A
+
Choline

| Choline
| Acetyl
| Transferase

Acetylcholine
+
Coenzyme A

Figure 4.13. Acetycholine biosynthesis.

disease patients led to the cholinergic hypothesis (40, 41) of Alzheimer's disease and of memory function: intact cholinergic functioning is necessary for normal memory.

Unlike the DA hypothesis of psychosis and the monoamine hypothesis of depression, this hypothesis is supported by tissue pathology. A large concentration of cholinergic neurons is found in the basal forebrain in the nucleus basalis of Meynert. These neurons project throughout the cortex and innervate the neocortex (homotypical isocortex, pp. 35–37) and hippocampus. Researchers demonstrated in Alzheimer's disease a specific loss of neurons in and near the nucleus basalis that corresponds with a decrease in choline acetyltransferase. Because cells in the nucleus basalis project throughout the brain, their loss corresponds with decreased cholinergic transmission throughout the brain (41).

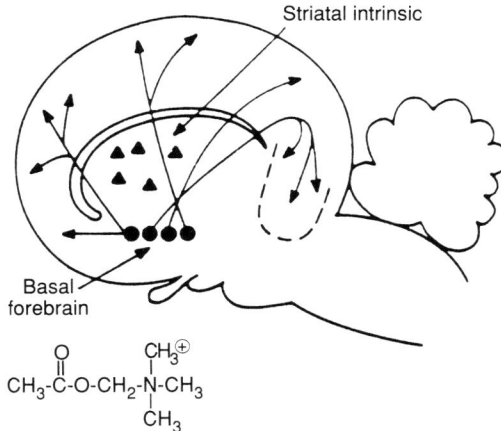

Striatal intrinsic

Basal forebrain

$$CH_3-\overset{\overset{\displaystyle O}{\|}}{C}-O-CH_2-\overset{\overset{\displaystyle CH_3^{\oplus}}{|}}{\underset{\underset{\displaystyle CH_3}{|}}{N}}-CH_3$$

Figure 4.14. Acetycholine structure and pathways. (Reproduced with permission from Coyle JT. Neuroscience and psychiatry. In: Talbott JA, Hales RE, Yudofsky SC. Textbook of psychiatry. Washington DC: American Psychiatric Press, 1988.)

PATHWAYS (Fig. 4.14)

The nucleus basalis is one of four major areas of cholinergic activity. The other three are the basal ganglia, nerves to voluntary muscles, and in the parasympathetic nervous system innervating smooth muscle such as heart, gut, and iris (40). Acetylcholine circuits in the basal ganglia are short and localized. Here ACh is in dynamic equilibrium with DA: increased DA activity inhibits release of ACh. Acting through GABA, ACh can inhibit DA firing. The ACh-DA interactions have clinical significance for movement disorders. Parkinson's disease (pill-rolling tremor, muscle rigidity, slow movements, shuffling gait, expressionless face, drooling) results from degeneration of DA neurons in the nigrostriatal tract. Anticholinergic drugs (e.g., diphenhydramine) can reduce Parkinsonian symptoms. Blocking ACh decreases GABA-mediated inhibition of DA, increasing DA firing in the remaining neurons. As noted above, the antipsychotic drugs block D_2 DA receptors throughout the brain, including the basal ganglia. Consequently, antipsychotics can cause movement disorders mimicking Parkinson's disease. Antipsychotic-caused Parkinson's symptoms are also relieved with anticholinergic drugs.

Huntington's disease is a genetically determined degeneration of ACh and GABA neurons in the basal ganglia (42) that produces dementia, psychosis, and mood and movement disorder. When the inhibitory effects of ACh and GABA are decreased, DA firing increases, causing choreoathetoid (jerky and writhing) movements.

The antipsychotic drugs, in addition to causing *hypo*dopaminergic Parkinsonian movements, can with prolonged administration cause an irreversible hyperdopaminergic choreoathetoid disorder (tardive dyskinesia [TD]). It is paradoxical that DA antagonists could cause a *hyper*dopaminergic problem. The answer could be that with prolonged D_2 receptor blockade, homeostatic mechanisms lead to increased numbers of receptors which eventually overcome DA antagonist properties of antipsychotics. This is based on animal studies; supersensitization (upregulation, increasing number) of D_2 receptors as a result of blockade has not yet been shown in humans. Other neurochemical mechanisms have been proposed for subgroups of TD patients (43).

Anticholinergic drugs make TD worse because they disinhibit DA in the basal ganglia. Increasing antipsychotic doses temporarily dampens the abnormal movements while worsening the underlying supersensitization.

RECEPTORS

There are two types of ACh receptors: nicotinic and muscarinic. Nicotinic receptors can be activated by nicotine as well as by ACh. Most are located outside the CNS, principally at the neuromuscular junction, where a motor neuron synapses on a voluntary muscle fiber.

Central ACh receptors, and those of the organs innervated by the parasympathetic system, are predominantly muscarinic. The known muscarinic receptors inhibit the adenylate cyclase system. Anticholinergic drugs block muscarinic receptors in the parasympathetic nervous system and in the brain. In addition to their intended effects, neuroleptic and cyclic antidepressant drugs block muscarinic receptors. This can cause tachycardia (rapid pulse), constipation, urinary retention, and blurred vision.

Glutamate

Of the five neurotransmitters discussed so far, DA, NE, 5-HT, and ACh collectively account for under 2% of brain synapses. 10% of synapses are GABAergic. Glutamate, another amino acid neurotransmitter, is used by roughly 60% of brain synapses. it is distributed throughout the brain, including pyramidal cells in the cortex and hippocampus, cerebellar granule cells, and sensory nerves returning to the brain (7).

Glutamate is excitatory. Glutamate receptor binding opens Na^+ ion channels, which results in depolarization and enhances neuronal excitability (44). Despite its ubiquity, glutamate is not yet associated with psychiatric symptoms and no current psychiatric drugs alter its transmission. (If this seems odd, consider the potentially staggering consequences of using a drug that affects 60% of synapses.)

Researchers are studying the possible role of glutamate in neurodegenerative diseases and epilepsies (44). Multiple conditions—Alzheimer's disease, Huntington's disease, strokes, and to a lesser extent normal aging—cause or result from neuron death. We cannot restore lost brain tissue, and the cause of cell

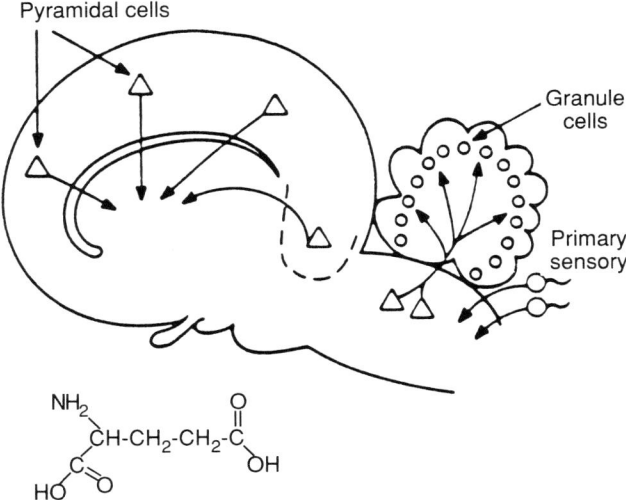

Figure 4.15. L-Glutamate structure and pathways. (Reproduced with permission from Coyle JT. Neuroscience and psychiatry. In: Talbott JA, Hales RE, Yudofsky SC. Textbook of psychiatry. Washington, DC: American Psychiatric Press, 1988.)

death remains unclear. Animal research implicates glutamate and other neuroexcitatory transmitters in neuron degeneration. Localized injections of glutamate agonists cause focal neuron death in animal brains, and cell death following ischemic (inadequate blood supply) damage can be prevented by localized injections of glutamate antagonist (44). But the relationship between cell excitation and cell death is unclear.

Either systemic or focal administration of glutamate agonists can cause seizures. And as you might suspect, glutamate antagonists (e.g., 2-amino-7-phosphono-hepatonoic acid) have anticonvulsant properties.

Peptides

Many peptide transmitters have been identified. Some peptides long known as hormones were found also to be neurotransmitters (45). Hormones are released into the blood and effect changes at some distance from their release. Transmitters act locally and immediately. Luteinizing hormone-releasing hormone (LHRH) is one of the peptides that is a neurotransmitter and a hormone. As a hormone, it is synthesized by hypothalamic neurons, released into the local portal venous system surrounding the hypothalamus and pituitary, and picked up by receptors in the anterior pituitary causing the release of luteinizing hormone into the systemic circulation. As a neurotransmitter, LHRH is released from synaptic terminals in a Ca^{2+}-dependent process after nerve stimulation in the sympathetic nervous system. It acts directly on the postsynaptic sympathetic neuron to cause depolarization. Finding the same peptide in nerve and endocrine cells has led to the speculation that in the phylogenetic development of a CNS, the newer, faster nervous system began coopting preexisting substances from the older, slower endocrine system (45).

Among the peptide transmitters are endogenous opiates, including enkephalins and endorphins. Eighteen peptides with opiate-like activity have been identified. Each arises from one of three polyprotein precursors: proopiomelanocortin (POMC), proenkephalin, and prodynorphin (46). When bound to receptors, opiate peptides induce responses that resemble those to heroin and morphine: analgesia, respiratory depression, decreased aggression, sedation, constipation, and decreased sex interest. Opiate receptors are distributed throughout the CNS, in areas that transmit pain signals (spinal cord, brain stem, thalamus), control attentiveness (locus ceruleus), and influence sexual and aggressive behavior (amygdala, stria terminalis). Seven receptor classes are known or proposed. Six have Greek letters: mu (μ), kappa (κ), gamma (γ), delta (δ), epsilon (ϵ), and sigma (Σ). A seventh, the cough-suppressant receptor, is on the floor of the fourth ventricle. It regulates cough reflexes and binds dextromethorphan.

Among the effects of opiate peptide binding to receptors are the following. μ-receptors mediate pain relief. μ is morphine-selective. μ_2 binds many opioid peptides. Neither μ-receptor is involved in respiratory depression. κ-receptors are selectively bound by dynorphin (from the prodynorphin line). They are in the deep layers of cortex and mediate mild pain relief. γ-receptors in the hippocampus explain opiate-caused cognitive disturbances. Σ-receptors are specific to β-endorphin, a proenkephalin product. Σ-receptors bind hallucinogenic opiates such as pentazocine and phencyclidine.

β-endorphin is one of the most powerful analgesics known. Injected into cerebral ventricles, it is 48 times more potent than morphine administered the same way (47). Unfortunately, repeated administrations of β-endorphin result in decreasing analgesic effectiveness.

Physical stress elevates plasma levels of β-endorphin (as well as adrenocorticotropin and cortisol, the stress hormones). Sometimes, the heightened endorphin levels produce analgesia. For example, mice given unavoidable foot shocks demonstrate increased β-endorphin levels and decreased sensitivity to other painful stimuli (47).

THE NEUROCHEMISTRY OF LEARNING

Kandel (48–50) describes a cell biology of learning and memory deriving from observations of the sea snail aplysia. Aplysia's nervous system is simple enough to allow correlation of changes in behavior with changes in single nerve cells One form of learning by aplysia is sensitization (see p. 75): the snail withdraws with increasing vigor to repeated mildly noxious stimuli. The neurons controlling withdrawal remember prior irritations and change biochemically, so that when again presented with the same stimulus, the response is greater. The irritant stimulates interneurons which facilitate transmission between the sensory neuron perceiving irritation and motor neurons causing withdrawal. Serotonin released from interneurons binds receptors on the membrane surface of the sensory neuron, activating adenylate cyclase. This closes K^+ channels, increasing neuron excitability and prolonging the action potential. With the action potential prolonged, more Ca^{2+} flows into the presynaptic terminal, increasing neurotransmitter release from the sensory nerve cell to the postsynaptic motor neuron. Serotonin from interneurons also activates the phosphoinositide system, which increases mobilization of neurotransmitter and prevents its depletion with repeated firing. The short-term memory demonstrated by aplysia's sensitization is thus accomplished by activation of second messenger systems.

By contrast, Kandel argues that long-term memory results not from alteration of existing intracellular proteins, but from the creation of new protein by transcription and translation, from the cell's genetic code. Protein synthesis fosters growth of new synaptic connections. Perhaps, psychotherapy (Chapter 23) fosters adaptive behavior by inducing protein synthesis, the branching of neurons, and the growth of new synaptic connections (50).

Acknowledgments

The author thanks Dr. James Ranck for his generous assistance with the manuscript and Drs. Douglas Evans and Martin Kesselman for their helpful review.

5/Genetics of Personality and Psychiatric Illness

Janice L. Petersen, M.D.

OBJECTIVES

GENERAL OBJECTIVE: Given a vignette of a patient with a family history of psychiatric illness, discuss the genetic counseling (if any) you would provide.

SPECIFIC OBJECTIVES:
1. Summarize methods by which genetic contributions to behavior are evaluated.
2. List personality traits and behavior disorders for which evidence of genetic transmission exists, and summarize this evidence.
3. Summarize Cloninger's biosocial hypothesis.
4. State potential uses of genetic recombination techniques for behavioral disorders.
5. Discuss the role of the family history in psychiatric practice.
6. Summarize the role of genetic counseling in psychiatry.

HOW CAN GENES AFFECT BEHAVIOR?

Considering how physically complex people are, it is a marvel that the physical substrate of the human body is only 46 strands of DNA. Yet one billion nucleotide base pairs, which code for 100,000 proteins interacting over time, create a person. Genes provide the code for species, sex, and physical characteristics, as well as the structures, functions, and capacities of all organs, including the brain (the main function of which is behavior).

In this chapter we examine evidence for genetic transmission of specific behaviors and behavioral disorders. How this occurs neurochemically is far from clear. We know how one gene can code for one enzyme, such as tyrosinase which transforms tyrosine (an amino acid) into precursors for melanin pigments that color hair, iris, and skin (1). How genes influence behavior is more elusive.

DNA chromosomal material is transcribed into RNA, which is then translated by ribosomes into proteins. Each protein is derived from a gene template. These proteins then perform the cell's functions, building its structures, regulating its physiology, and turning genes on and off during development (2).

Some genes directly affect neurotransmission. Examples include genes for the enzymes that synthesize dopamine (DA) and norepinephrine (NE). Any alteration of these enzymes can affect the activity of DA, NE, and their neurons. Another object of attention has been degradative enzymes such as monoamine oxidase (MAO), which metabolizes DA and NE intracellularly (3–7). Other sites at which mutations can alter neurotransmission include receptors, ion channels, second messenger systems, and regulator sites (see Chapter 4).

Another possible site of action is the migration and interconnection of the embryo's brain cells. Neural crest cells migrate, multiply, and organize into brain structures and tracts programmed by chemical organizers (2). A gene that specifies an altered gene product for an organizing factor, or a recognizing receptor, can alter the structure and function of a portion of the brain.

Major dysfunction of genes that regulate brain structure and function usually leads to major malformation or death of the organism, but more modest problems can create vulnerability revealed only under certain stresses. For example, in learned helplessness in experimental animals, a depression-like syndrome of inactivity and apathy is induced by inescapable electric shocks, retarding new learning in a nonstressful environment (8). This is a valuable model of depression because the manifestations can be reversed by the same antidepressant treatments given to depressed persons (9). Some inbred mouse strains are more vulnerable than others to learned helplessness under stress (10).

STRATEGIES FOR ASSESSING GENETIC CONTRIBUTIONS TO BEHAVIOR

Genetic and environmental factors act simultaneously throughout development. Because of this, discriminating the effect of each requires a methodic approach. The strategies are as discussed below.

Family Studies

Family studies involve observing the prevalence of an illness in the first-degree relatives (relatives who share 50% or more of one's genes) of probands (a proband is the person who first presents with the illness in a family under study). This prevalence is then compared to the rate in a control group of first-degree relatives of unaffected persons matched to the former group. The prevalence of the illness in relatives of probands divided by the prevalence in relatives of controls

yields the relative risk (Appendix 5.1) once age is taken into account. For example, a risk of 2.0 indicates that relatives of probands are twice as likely to show the disorder.

Acceptable methodology requires a sample of probands who show clear-cut evidence of the illness, evaluations of relatives made directly or through detailed descriptions from records and relatives, evaluators of relatives who are blind to proband diagnosis, and use of reliable diagnostic criteria (11).

Such study designs can tell us whether particular illnesses run in families (i.e., are familial), but they do not sort out what part of the aggregation (concentration of cases in the family of an affected person) is caused by common environmental factors and what part by genetic factors.

Studies of Twins Reared Together

The study of twins who have been reared together is another useful approach. Monozygotic (MZ, identical) twins come from the same fertilized egg and share 100% of their DNA. Dizygotic (fraternal, DZ) twins come from two eggs and share 50% of their DNA, like ordinary siblings. If MZ pairs have a significantly higher concordance (coexistence of a trait in both twins) for a trait or illness than do DZ pairs, this would seem to be (and often is) the result of 100% sharing of DNA by MZ twins. Diseases in which a genetic cause is conclusively proved show differential MZ to DZ concordance rates. Moreover, the variability of expression of a disorder in MZ twins informs us of the spectrum of illness associated with a given genetic diathesis (natural tendency).

But this is not the whole story. Many conditions, including TB and polio (which we tend not to view as genetic) could be considered heritable because MZ exceeds DZ concordance (12). Some MZ concordance also can result from sharing the placenta (DZ twins have separate placentas), spending time together, or being treated equally (13, 14). Discordance (when a twin pair does not share a trait) can result from unequal blood flow within the placenta (transfusion effect) (15–17), birth injury, postnatal disease, differential receipt of parenting or life stressors, or sampling errors (18). Multiple studies show no evidence, however, that MZ twin behavioral similarities result from their being treated equally (19, 20). For example, MZ twins dressed alike by their parents show no greater similarity in personality than MZ twins not dressed alike (21). In one study (14), the more time spent together, the greater the twin behavioral *discordance*.

In general, the MZ twin concordance for most major mental illnesses and many personality traits is significantly higher than DZ concordance. Although such data strongly suggest a role for genetic etiologic factors, the lack of 100% MZ concordance reveals that nongenetic factors are also important.

Adopted-Apart Twin Studies

As we noted, studies of twins reared together are not conclusive in determining genetic influence. An elegant approach to this problem is to study concordance for an illness or trait in MZ and DZ twins separated at birth and adopted into different homes. This negates the effect of shared postnatal environment (22).

Nontwin Adoption Studies

Nontwin adoption studies, of which there are several types, also show how genes influence behavior. In one type of study ill biologic parents who relinquished a child for adoption are identified. The adopted children are studied longitudinally, and their rate of illness is compared to that in adopted children whose biologic parents are unaffected (22). This eliminates the effect of being reared by a mentally ill parent. For example, an alcoholic parent's behavior can affect expression of alcoholism in the child. By observing the rate of alcoholism in alcoholics offspring adopted into nonalcoholic homes, we can estimate the genetic effect of having an alcoholic biologic parent. If genetic factors are influential, a higher rate of alcoholism will be apparent in the biologic children of alcoholics than in the adopted children of biologic nonalcoholic parents. This does occur (23–25).

Another type of adoption study starts with adopted children who have developed an illness. The prevalence of illness in their biologic parents is compared to the prevalence of illness in the biologic parents of nonaffected adopted children (20).

Cross-fostering studies involve children born to normal biologic parents and adopted by an affected parent. The rate of illness in these children is compared to the rate in children born to normal biologic parents and adopted by normal parents, and to the rate in children born to affected biologic parents and reared by normal parents. This approach allows estimation of the effect of being reared by a mentally ill parent (26).

Pedigree and Linkage Studies

Pedigree studies start with an ill person and assess the pattern of the illness in relatives. The study of such family trees can establish whether an illness is familial, and in large pedigrees (in which numerous family members in multiple generations have been studied) may suggest whether there is a genetic component, and whether inheritance is dominant or recessive (Appendix 5.1)

Linkage studies look at pedigrees to associate a behavioral trait with a marker trait (one for which the locus [position on a chromosome] is already known). Many such markers exist; examples include human blood group antigens (A, B, O), human leukocyte antigens (HLA) and color-blindness. If the trait being investigated is close to the marker gene on the same chromosome, the traits will usually be linked (inherited together) in the pedigree (22).

EVIDENCE FOR GENETIC FACTORS IN PSYCHIATRIC ILLNESS

The psychiatric disorders that have received the most attention regarding genetics are schizophrenia and bipolar and unipolar affective disorders (see pp. 246–255). Studies of schizophrenia show a prevalence of 8% in the first-degree relatives of probands and 1% in first-degree relatives of controls, an eight-fold relative risk. In one study (27), concordance for schizophrenia was 30.9% for MZ twins and 6.5% for DZ twins. Adoption studies show an increased risk for schizophrenia in biologic relatives of adopted schizophrenics but not in the biologic relatives of control adoptees. Kendler and Robinette's study (27) of schizophrenia in twins estimates heritability (the contribution of genes to the observable clinical manifestations; that is, the contribution of the genotype to the phenotype) to be 79% of the contribution to the phenotype (observable clinical manifestations) of schizophrenia.

Bipolar illness also shows strong familial aggregation. One pedigree study shows the risk of bipolar illness in first-degree relatives of bipolar probands (the morbidity risk) to be 8% compared to 0.5% in control families, a 16-fold relative risk for relatives of bipolar patients (28, 29). A survey of twin studies shows a MZ concordance of 65% and a DZ concordance of 14% (30). The case for genetic factors is strengthened by data that offspring of MZ twins discordant for bipolar disorder had a 10% chance of developing bipolar disorder, independent of whether the parent was the affected twin (31). Adoption studies reveal a 15-fold increased risk of mood disorder in biologic but not adopted relatives of bipolar probands (32). Some relation between bipolar and unipolar disorders is suggested by the fact that 9%–20% of the first-degree relatives of bipolar patients had unipolar illness compared to only 5% in control families (33–35). Some (not all) studies also show significant numbers of bipolar relatives of unipolar probands (33–35).

In contrast, genetic research on unipolar disorder is more mixed in its findings, probably because of unipolar disorder used. The relative risk for first-degree relatives of unipolar patients is twice that of the general population, more modest than for schizophrenia and bipolar disorder (35). Evidence suggests (Table 5.1) (23–25, 27–29, 31–58) that many other neuropsychiatric disorders have significant genetic etiologic factors.

EVIDENCE FOR GENETIC FACTORS IN INTELLIGENCE

Data on intelligence from over 100,000 twins reveal a striking genetic influence on intelligence. Recent studies show an 80%–90% correlation for IQ among MZ twins, even if the twins are reared apart. In contrast, the IQ correlation is 50% among DZ twins and only 5% among (virtually none) unrelated adoptees (13, 59). Heritability estimates of IQ range from 50% to 70%. Specific cognitive abilities such as verbal ability or spatial ability also have significant genetic factors (60, 61).

Mental retardation is sometimes associated with clear-cut Mendelian inheritance (straightforward inheritance patterns [dominant, recessive, incomplete penetrance] as originally described by Mendel) of an autosomal (each person has 44 autosomes and 2 sex chromosomes) recessive gene, or well-defined chromosomal abnormalities such as Down syndrome (trisomy 21), although the 2500 known causes of mental retardation comprise only 15% of cases of retardation (62) Major chromosomal (e.g., an extra chromosome) or single-gene defects usually result in moderate to severe impairment. Mild retardation is more often related to polygenetic and environmental effects.

EVIDENCE FOR GENETIC FACTORS IN PERSONALITY

Personality traits are enduring patterns of thinking, feeling, and behaving (63). In the past, clinicians viewed early childhood experience as the main determinant of personality. A growing body of literature demonstrates the contribution of genetic factors.

Table 5.1.   Illnesses, Syndromes With Known Genetic Factors

Illness	Family	Twin	Adoption	Remarks
Schizophrenia	+	+	+	(See text) (27)
Bipolar disorder	+	+	+	(See text) (28, 29, 31–35)
Unipolar depression	+	+	+	Significant hereditary component (36)
Anorexia nervosa	+	+		Increased rate of affective illness in relatives (37)
Alcoholism	+	+	+	Studies suggest different subtypes with different heritability (23–25, 38, 39)
Antisocial personality	+	+	+	Significant hereditary component (40, 41)
Anxiety disorders, overall	+	+		Significant hereditary component (42)
Agoraphobia	+			Increased rate of any anxiety disorder diagnoses in primary relatives (43)
Bulimia	+			Increased rate of affective disorder in primary relatives (44)
Attention deficit disorder	+			Increased rate in relatives (45)
Dyslexia	+			Increased rate in relatives (45)
Alzheimer's disease	+			Dominant inheritance suggested for presenile type, locus in chromosome 21 (46)
Lesch-Nyhan syndrome	+	+		X-linked recessive, known enzyme defect (hypoxanthine guanine phosphoribosyltransferse deficiency) (47)
Tourette's syndrome	+			May be autosomal dominant gene (48)
Huntington's disease	+	+		Dominant inheritance, mapped to 4th chromosome (49)
Somatization disorder	+		+	Increased rate of alcoholism and antisocial personality in male relatives (50, 51)
Obsessive compulsive disorder	+	+		Significant hereditary component (52, 53)
Cyclothymia	+			Increased rate of bipolar illness in relatives (54)
Autism	+	+		Possible recessive inheritance (55–57)
Panic disorder	+			Significant hereditary component (58)

Monozygotic twin studies of qualities of temperament (e.g., activity level, threshold of response to stimulation, distractibility) show little correlation before 2 years of age, but increasing correlation thereafter (64, 65). The timing of reaching developmental milestones such as separation anxiety (p. 132) and object constancy (p. 135), and manifesting traits such as fearfulness, are more similar in MZ than in DZ twins (64).

Multiple studies (66–68) that account for thousands of twins (MZ and DZ) reared together suggest considerable heritability of personality traits. Recent studies (69) of MZ and DZ twins reared apart and together reveal heritabilities of 39%–58% for many traits (Table 5.2). The MZ:DZ twin comparisons (70) even suggest heritability of attitudes on controversial subjects (e.g., the death penalty, censorship). When MZ twins who were adopted at birth into different homes meet as adults, researchers often find them eerily similar, as the following example (71) illustrates.

In the renowned case of Jim Springer and Jim Lewis, identical twins separated 4 weeks after their birth in Ohio and reunited 39 years later in a study on twins at the University of Minnesota, the twins discovered they had married and divorced women named Linda, married second wives named Betty and named their first sons James Allan and James Alan, respectively. The two men both drove the same model blue Chevrolet and enjoyed woodworking (having built identical benches around trees in their backyards). They often vacationed on the same small beach in St. Petersburg, Florida, and owned dogs named Toy.

Of course, adopted apart twins can also demonstrate strikingly different traits that demonstrate how profound the influence of environment can be.

One twin, separated from her identical sister at birth, grew up to be a professional-caliber pianist although her adoptive family was not at all musical. Her sister was adopted by a piano teacher and doesn't play it at all (71).

Table 5.2.   Behavioral Traits With High Heritability Inferred From Studies of Twins

	From Studies of Twins Reared Together	
1.	Aggressiveness	Readiness to argue or fight, vindictiveness
2.	Altruism	Tendency to give to others without expectation of personal gain
3.	Assertiveness	Willingness to stand up for one's rights, to obtain what is due, to take a position
4.	Empathy	Capacity to participate in another's feelings or ideas
5.	Extroversion	The combination of being sociable, lively, outgoing, carefree, changeable, impulsive, assertive, physically active, and optimistic (being sociable and being impulsive are independently heritable, but are frequently inherited together in the cluster of extroverted behaviors)
6.	Introversion	The combination of being quiet, passive, careful, thoughtful, reliable, mentally active, and pessimistic
7.	Neuroticism	Tendency to be nervous, anxious, touchy, moody, and restless, and to react anxiously to environmental stress
8.	Nurturance	The capacity to provide affectionate care and attention to another
	From Studies of Twins Reared Together and Apart	
1.	Absorption	Possession of vivid imagination readily captured by rich experience, but given to being unrealistic
2.	Achievement	Tendency to work hard, strive for mastery, and value accomplishment ahead of other things
3.	Aggressiveness	See above
4.	Alienation	Proneness to feeling used and mistreated
5.	Constraint	The combination of being self-restrictive, cautious, and traditional
6.	Control	Tendency to be cautious, plodding, rational and carefully planned
7.	Harm avoidance	Tendency to shun excitement, risk, and danger with preference for safe choices
8.	Negative emotionality	The combination of being anxious and angry, having diminished drive, and being a loner
9.	Positive emotionality	The combination of being joyful, cheerful, forceful, and hardworking
10.	Social closeness	Preference for emotional intimacy and close ties; tendency to seek help and comfort from others
11.	Social potency	Leadership, mastery, enjoyment of being center of attention
12.	Stress reaction	Feeling vulnerable, given to worry
13.	Traditionalism	Following of rules and authority, endorsing of strict discipline and high moral standards
14.	Well-being	Having a cheerful disposition; feeling confident and optimistic

CLONINGER'S BIOSOCIAL PERSONALITY THEORY

Recent discoveries about the biologic correlates of behavior have spurred several theories of personality that incorporate biologic, psychologic, and social components (72–76). The most extensive biopsychosocial theory of personality is C. Robert Cloninger's biosocial theory. Cloninger (72, 73) identifies three independent, heritable dimensions of personality: novelty seeking, harm avoidance, and reward dependence. Novelty seeking is an excitatory response to novel stimuli that leads to exploration and avoidance of monotony. For example, a child who prefers to be out of his or her seat examining items in the classroom exhibits novelty seeking. Harm avoidance is the tendency to respond intensely to aversive stimuli and to inhibit behavior to avoid punishment. A child who meekly submits after being told firmly by the teacher to stay seated, but who gets up when the teacher is out of the room, exhibits harm avoidance. Reward dependence is the tendency to respond intensely to signals of reward (especially social approval and positive emotion) or relief from punishment. A child who is especially attuned to the teacher's wishes, enjoys being the teacher's pet, and always follows the rules even when the teacher is out of the room shows reward dependence.

Cloninger maintains that novelty seeking is associated with the dopaminergic system (72, 73, 77), which he calls the brain's behavioral activation system. Harm avoidance reflects

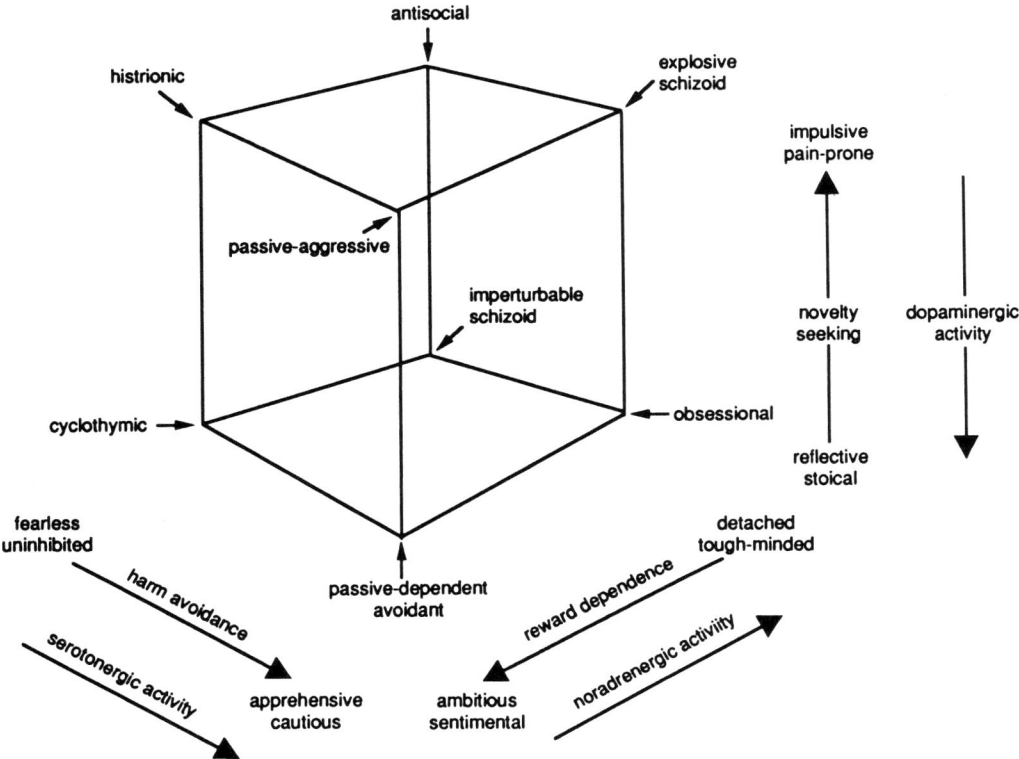

Figure 5.1. Cloninger's biosocial hypothesis linking heritable traits, neurotransmitters, and personality disorders. (Reprinted with permission from Cloninger CR. A proposal. A unified biosocial theory of personality and its role in the development of anxiety states. Psychiatr Dev 1986; 3:167–226.)

variation in the brain's behavioral inhibition system, linked to serotonin (78, 79). Reward dependence reflects variation in the behavioral maintenance system, linked to norepinephrine (72, 73, 80, 81).

Cloninger views personality disorders (lifelong maladaptive behavior patterns such as dependent personality disorder and antisocial personality disorder) as manifesting specific combinations of extreme variations of these three dimensions (Fig. 5.1). For example, antisocial personality (callous, selfish, lacking in guilt—a common disorder among criminals) is manifested by very high novelty seeking and very low harm avoidance, whereas obsessive-compulsive personality (perfectionistic, meticulous, workaholic) shows very low novelty seeking and very high harm avoidance.

The family environment also influences trait development. For example, the risk of

antisocial personality in adulthood is increased by low social status, lax or inconsistent discipline, instability of the early home environment, or rearing by a criminal parent (72, 73, 82–84).

Cloninger also addresses anxiety and anxiety disorders. He delineates two types of anxiety: somatic and cognitive (72). Somatic anxiety is manifested by diverse bodily pains and autonomic disturbance together with distractibility and a vague, general feeling of alarm not linked to specific stresses. An example of this would be:

A somatizing patient presents her physician a disjointed history of multiple vague physical complaints such as shortness of breath, trouble swallowing, and diffuse body pain. She is obviously in distress but is unable to articulate what it might be about. Extensive evaluation reveals this is due to somatization disorder (see p. 266).

One month later, the physican learns that prior to this presentation, the patient's 16-year-old son was arrested for selling cocaine. Although she had been aware that he was gone from home a great deal, sometimes stayed up all night, and seemed to be buying an unusual amount of expensive clothes, she had no previous idea of what he was doing.

Cloninger relates somatic anxiety to high novelty seeking and low harm avoidance, characteristic of histrionic and antisocial personality types. These persons have a hypovigilant information processing pattern that impedes their ability to learn from experience and to identify circumstances that should be avoided. When their environment produces stressful events, they are unable to avoid them and are sensitized (they respond more intensely over time [p. 75]) with chronic symptoms of anxiety.

In contrast, cognitive anxiety consists of anticipatory apprehension (fear of future events), ruminative anxiety (repetitive, unproductive thinking about feared events), and social anxiety (discomfort with and avoidance of contact with others), together with slow recovery after stress and minor illnesses and difficulty in muscular relaxation. An example of this would be:

> A first-year medical student presents to the student health service with headaches and difficulty sleeping. He readily explains that he received a low (but passing) grade on his biochemistry midterm. He has never received such a low grade. He fears failing his biochemistry final and then having to drop out of medical school. He cannot stop thinking about it; he has studied hard, but cannot be sure he has studied enough. He has withdrawn from all social activities because he is so afraid he will fail. The physician explains that this is a common response to the rigor of medical school. She reflects that it sounds like the student has studied extensively and needs to get some sleep before finals. She prescribes a few temazepam capsules. On the follow-up visit, after finals, she finds that the student did pass his exams and is exhausted, but that his sleep has improved and the headaches have disappeared.

Cloninger relates cognitive anxiety to high harm avoidance and such personality disorders as obsessive-compulsive and dependent personalities (excessive reliance on others). Persons who manifest these traits learn to avoid aversive stimuli more readily than others. If the environment provides numerous negatively toned experiences (such as angry, abusive parents), they become hypervigilant, manifesting cognitive anxiety, to avoid further abusive outcomes. Another example would be the development of a phobia:

> On several occasions a 2-year-old child is frightened by two large, friendly dogs at her mother's friend's house. She is inadvertently bowled over by them, resulting in a panicked, overwhelmed state that is difficult for her mother to soothe. Subsequently she fears all dogs; later she becomes afraid of dogs pictured on television; eventually she becomes afraid of large furry animals in general, such as bears and lions at the zoo.

Cloninger theorizes that these information-processing vulnerabilities interact with childhood circumstances to produce lifelong symptoms. For example, the child in the above example may develop a lifelong phobia of dogs. In histrionic personalities (theatrical, self-centered, seductive), a chaotic family life with inconsistent discipline increases the probability that these persons will develop chronic somatic anxiety states. Some evidence for this comes from a related disorder, somatization disorder (lifelong history of medically undocumented symptoms presented in a vague, dramatic fashion). In an adoption study of children of somatizing mothers, somatization in offspring occurred more frequently when they were reared in chaotic homes (85).

Cloninger's work needs replication at descriptive (Do the 3 personality dimensions indeed correlate with personality disorder?) and etiologic levels (Do the extremes of the personality dimensions indeed correlate with extremes of activity in the putative neurotransmitter system?). If so, how are these differences related to genetic and environmental factors? These are testable hypotheses.

FUTURE POSSIBILITIES OF GENETIC RECOMBINATION TECHNIQUES

Molecular biologists are now lobbying for the funds to complete the monumental task of mapping the entire human genome (composition and function of all genes on the 46 chromosomes) in the Human Genome Project (86).

Techniques used to determine the biologic basis of hereditary illness include restriction fragment length polymorphisms (RFLPs) and gene cloning. The RFLPs are patterns of DNA fragments that result when restriction enzymes (bacterial enzymes that recognize and cleave specific sequences of DNA base pairs) have acted on cellular DNA. After the DNA is cleaved, the fragments are separated and stained. Researchers take blood samples from an affected family with a large pedigree and examine the DNA for RFLP patterns associated with affected persons. If a particular RFLP pattern has a significant association with the illness, it suggests that the gene for the illness is near the locus of that RFLP.

For Huntington's chorea (a slowly fatal illness characterized by movement disorder and dementia), which is expressed as a completely penetrant dominant gene (50% of the offspring are fully affected; penetrance is the proportion of persons possessing a gene that express it in the phenotype), a large Venezuelan pedigree was used, and the affected gene was mapped to one end of chromosome 4 (49). Once the locus was identified, children of Huntington's patients could be tested by sampling their white blood cells to determine if they carried the gene. This requires supportive counseling because Huntington's patients are at higher risk for suicide (87). Fetuses can also be examined for the defective gene from tissue obtained by amniocentesis, allowing affected parents to choose whether to abort affected fetuses to avoid passing this disease to their offspring.

Much about genetic techniques has been learned from Duchenne's muscular dystrophy (which is not a psychiatric disorder). It is an X-linked (carried on the X chromosome) recessive gene that affects males and causes progressive muscle weakness leading to death in the late teens or twenties. Researchers learned the gene location and discovered the gene product by cloning (Appendix 5.1) the DNA from affected individuals and comparing it to the DNA of unaffected individuals. When unique DNA (i.e., DNA that might yield the normal gene product) was found in normals but not in Duchenne's patients, it was reproduced by cloning; once RNA was transcribed from the process, the mystery product could then be translated. This recently discovered protein, dystrophin, occurs in minute amounts in normal muscle. Research can now focus on learning its function, so corrective therapies can be proposed (88).

Possible therapies could include replacement of the defective gene with a functional gene, or replacement of the defective gene product with a normal one. One model uses a reverse transcriptase retrovirus (Appendix 5.1) to introduce the desired genetic material into the patient's cultured cells, which can be reinjected into the patient to produce the necessary protein product. Although safety of such genetic engineering must be addressed, prospects for this approach are striking (89).

ROLE OF THE FAMILY HISTORY IN MEDICAL PRACTICE

As knowledge of genetic factors increases, so does the utility of the family history (FH). Although an FH of a genetically transmitted illness does not assure a diagnosis for a particular patient, it provides some supportive diagnostic evidence. An FH of a disorder also has predictive value for treatment responsiveness. A patient may have a genetic vulnerability that expresses itself as a mild form of the illness, and knowledge of the FH may link the symptoms to the familial diagnosis.

Ms. A, a 32 year-old high school teacher, presented to her family practitioner with irritability, mood swings, tearfulness, and difficulty concentrating. These symptoms were present throughout each month, and especially troublesome premenstrually. She volunteered that she had been in psychotherapy for many years, but it was not relieving these symptoms, so she thought "I must have premenstrual syndrome."

During the history, the physician learned that the patient's mother had suffered from severe manic-depressive illness that had improved when lithium became available. Because the clinician knew that manic-depressive illness is hereditary, she wondered if the patient might have a similar vulnerability mildly expressed. Intrigued, she referred the patient for psychiatric consultation and was diagnosed as having cyclothymia, a mild form of bipolar disorder (90). The consultant suggested that the patient take lithium. The patient did so, and within a week noted improvement in her symptoms.

ROLE OF GENETIC COUNSELING

The issue of genetic counseling arises in the context of patients' or physicians' concerns in two areas: (1) the risk of hereditary illness in a child, given a patient's family or personal history of illness, or (2) the risk of developing an illness oneself. Principles of genetic counseling include the concept that most of the major psychiatric disorders (Table 5.1) have a significant genetic component; their mode of transmission is unknown; no genetic markers are currently available to determine which offspring will be affected; empirical risk estimates based on family studies are available (91). Counseling involves clarifying patient concerns, conveying the facts about the risk of the illness in question and available treatments, and discussing patient thoughts to foster informed decisions (92).

In general, the news is good. Because the risk of schizophrenia or bipolar illness in first-degree relatives is 8%, only a minority are affected. Although a person with a positive family history is at increased risk for developing a disorder, effective treatments are now available for many psychiatric disorders. Furthermore, early manifestations of the illness can be identified and treated promptly.

After several years, Ms. A. married and contemplated having children. There was no history of psychiatric illness in her husband's family. She was concerned that because she and her mother had affective illness, she might transmit it to her child. She consulted her psychiatrist, who advised her about the approximately 8% rate of bipolar illness in first-degree relatives and the availability of several good treatments. She was advised that if she decided to become pregnant, she should temporarily discontinue lithium, because it can be teratogenic. If she did so, her symptoms would be monitored and nonteratogenic treatments made available. She was also educated about the increased risk of a postpartum manic episode (see p. 126).

The patient and her husband mutually decided that the benefit of conceiving a child was worth the risk; if the child developed symptoms of mood disorder, treatment would probably be as effective as it had been for the mother and grandmother. The patient discontinued the lithium, and found her mood lability returning, but coped with it as she had before. She was delighted when she became pregnant and surprised that her mood stabilized without medication. The pregnancy proceeded uneventfully, and she delivered a healthy baby girl. After delivery her lability returned, and she restarted lithium.

Appendix 5.1. Additional Terms

Cloning—One method used in recombinant DNA technology. A selected DNA fragment is introduced into plasmids (DNA that bacteria possess in addition to chromosomes) which is then used to infect bacterial cells. The bacteria are then grown in media that discriminate between bacteria with the desired gene and those without. A suitably transformed cell will appear as a colony or clone on the plates. This clone is then grown to produce appreciable amounts of the desired product.

Dominant inheritance—A gene that is expressed when the individual inherits one copy of it.

Morbidity risk—An estimate of the risk of a population being affected by a given trait.

Recessive inheritance—A gene that requires 2 copies to be expressed.

Relative risk—The morbidity risk of a high-risk population compared to the risk in a control population.

Reverse transcriptase retrovirus—RNA virus with capacity to integrate DNA copies of itself into a host genome. RNA copies of desired DNA (e.g., dystrophin in muscular dystrophy) are introduced into the retrovirus which can then enter affected host cells and provide templates of the desired DNA.

6/Learning and Behavior Modification

Robert W. Bloom, M.D., Linda Nidelkoff, Ph.D., and Frederick S. Sierles, M.D.

OBJECTIVES

GENERAL OBJECTIVE: Given a history of a patient with a behavior problem, suggest behavioral techniques to help alleviate that problem.

SPECIFIC OBJECTIVES:
1. Define habituation, sensitization, and modeling, and state examples of each in daily life.
2. State uses of habituation and modeling in patient care.
3. Summarize classical conditioning.
4. Discuss operant conditioning in daily life and in medical care.
5. Define the various reinforcement schedules and give an example of each.
6. Summarize cognitive psychotherapy, biofeedback, behavioral rehearsal, counterconditioning, paradoxical intention, and response prevention.
7. Discuss strategies for smoking cessation and weight reduction.

Much of human behavior is learned—as infants, as children, and as adults. We continually learn throughout life. Learning is change in behavior based on experience. Use of learning principles in treatment is termed behavior modification.

NONASSOCIATIVE LEARNING

One type of learning is nonassociative learning, in which pairing of events (e.g., Pavlov's ringing a bell while presenting meat powder to a laboratory dog) is *not* required for behavior change. Three types of nonassociative learning are habituation, sensitization, and modeling.

Habituation

Habituation is a decline in responsiveness to the repeated presentation of a stimulus. Most medical students exposed weekly to a cadaver in an anatomy laboratory or to a hospital ward during a clerkship automatically become more comfortable in these settings. In psychiatry, patients who have phobias (intense, unreasonable fears of objects or situations such as going outside, animals, blood, social gatherings) and obsessive-compulsive disorder (incessant, troubling thoughts such as "there could be deadly germs on my hands") can benefit from the habituation offered by in vivo exposure (the planned "real life" experience of progressively more intense presentations of the feared situation) (1–5).

A 32-year-old married mother of a 6-month old infant became obsessed that she would stab the child with a kitchen knife. She is a self-controlled, responsible person who loves the infant and sees her infanticidal thoughts as absurd. Yet they persist and dramatically impede her comfort with her child. Sometimes she becomes angry with the child, but she has no obsession at these times.

Her treatment begins in the doctor's office by reading a gory scene (scripted by her psychologist) in which she stabs her child. Initially panicked by this, she begins to do it with comfort and humor. Weeks later, she is instructed to place knives throughout the room in which the infant's crib is located. Again, initially fearful, she learns to do it comfortably. Soon after, her obsession disappears.

Sensitization

Repeated presentations of certain stimuli can also intensify the response to the stimulus. For example, a medical student, uncomfortable with the first lecture of a series, becomes irritated (and then stops attending) at subsequent lectures because of a failure to understand what is presented. Augmentation of a response because of repeated stimuli is sensitization.

Observational (Imitative) Learning and Modeling

Much of what we learn occurs through imitation (imitative or observational learning). Planned imitative learning in an educational or therapeutic setting is called modeling. In imitative learning, we watch the behavior of another person, note the consequences, and then perform the behavior we saw. In learning to practice medicine, this includes watching experienced physicians interview, physically examine patients, and perform therapeutic procedures.

Modeling has been used in overcoming children's normal fears of surgery. In the film "Ethan Has an Operation," a 7-year-old boy narrates the steps of his hospitalization for a herniorrhaphy (hernia repair), describing his feelings and concerns. "Ethan" was shown to children scheduled for herniorrhaphy, tonsillectomy, and genitourinary surgery (6). These children also received conventional preoperative explanations and support, as did a control group of children who did not see the film. The children who watched the film had less preoperative and postoperative anxiety than did the controls.

Modeling is also used in treating animal phobias (e.g., fear of dogs) and dental phobias (fear of dental procedures) (7–9). Unfortunately, unwanted behaviors such as fighting or smoking can also be learned by imitation (10–13).

ASSOCIATIVE LEARNING

In associative learning, the pairing (contiguity) of events is essential. The two main categories of associative learning are classical and operant conditioning.

Classical Conditioning

In classical (respondent) or Pavlovian conditioning, named after the Nobel Prize-winning Russian physiologist who developed it, reflexive behavior is elicited in response to a stimulus that precedes it. For example, a dog salivates—an unconditioned response (UCR)—when presented with meat powder—an unconditioned stimulus (UCS). Then, when a bell—a conditioned stimulus (CS)—is paired with the meat powder, the dog also salivates. Eventually, the dog salivates—a conditioned response (CR)—at the sound of the bell alone. If the meat is never again paired with the bell, the conditioned response eventually ceases or becomes extinguished (14).

Conditioned reflexes in the medical setting include the following: many antineoplastic (anticancer) medications (UCS) often induce nausea and vomiting (UCR). For the occasional patient, some component of the medical setting (e.g., the hospital, the oncology [cancer-specializing] ward or clinic, the intravenous infusion bottles [CS]) becomes paired with the infusion process, eliciting retching

(CR) on sight. A similar phenomenon occurs when children become anxious or tearful (CR) at the sight of white medical coats (CS) after experiencing a stressful or painful medical procedure (UCS) (15). Classical conditioning techniques are occasionally used in the counter-conditioning treatment of pedophilia (p. 398) or alcoholism (p. 292), in which a noxious, aversive stimulus (UCS) such as an electric shock to a finger is paired with the ingestion of alcohol (a pleasurable UCS) in a clinically simulated bar (a discriminative stimulus [p. 77]) to produce an unpleasant CR (finger pain with withdrawal) to the originally pleasant UCS (15).

Operant (Instrumental) Conditioning

In operant (instrumental) or Skinnerian conditioning, named after B.F. Skinner, the psychologist who pioneered the concept, a behavior is emitted in anticipation of an event (a reinforcer) (16, 17). Types of operant conditioning include positive reinforcement, negative reinforcement, aversive conditioning, and stimulus control.

POSITIVE REINFORCEMENT

Positive reinforcement is when something valued or necessary (a reinforcer, a reward) is presented following a desired behavior. Primary reinforcers (e.g., food, water, affection, attention, sex) are biologically based. Conditioned reinforcers (e.g., gifts, praise, applause, smiling, deference, hearing one's name or seeing it in print, awards, good grades, job offers, promotions, job benefits such as days off and vacations, money) become reinforcing by pairing with other reinforcers. Money is a generalized reinforcer: it positively reinforces countless behaviors and can be exchanged for numerous other reinforcers (18).

Well-timed praise, respect, attentiveness, friendliness, and pleasant staff and office surroundings all foster patient compliance with treatment. Pediatricians giving lollipops to patients is another example. Scheduling occasional follow-up visits for patients when they are well can be a reinforcer (attention, concern) to pa-

tients for staying well, in contrast to scheduling visits exclusively in response to illness.

Some psychiatric wards use formal step systems, whereby progressively more privileges are granted for specific behaviors as the patient's condition progressively improves. The rules of the step system are prominently displayed for all patients to see (19). In some programs for chronically hospitalized schizophrenic patients, tokens (a generalized reinforcer redeemable for snacks, movies, clothing, etc.) are given to patients for desirable behaviors (e.g., participation in ward activities) or avoiding undesirable ones (e.g., not shouting in the hallway) in a token economy program (20).

Some events are reinforcing for unexpected reasons. For example, some persons appreciate and seek criticism if it is constructive. In some families, when a parent yells at or spanks a child, the child interprets this as attention. For this reason, not responding at all (combined with positive reinforcement for desired behaviors) often extinguishes temper tantrums.

NEGATIVE REINFORCEMENT

Negative reinforcement is removal of an unpleasant (aversive) stimulus, contingent on a desired response. Medical diagnosis and treatment remove or reduce suffering (e.g., pain, cough, diminished vision, weakness, sadness, short-windedness) associated with illness, fostering compliant patient behaviors as part of the sick role (21). *Negative reinforcement is therefore the basis for most contemporary medical care.* Unfortunately, for patients who have a disease but feel well (e.g., asymptomatic hypertension [high blood pressure]), negative reinforcement cannot come into play. Despite semantic similarities, negative reinforcement is very different from punishment and aversive conditioning.

PUNISHMENT AND AVERSIVE CONDITIONING

Sometimes rather than trying to increase behaviors, we strive to decrease them by delivering an unpleasant (aversive) stimulus or removing a pleasant one. In daily life, this is referred to as punishment. There are two categories of punishment: positive and negative. In positive punishment, an unpleasant stimulus (e.g., a spanking, a summons) is delivered. In negative punishment, a positively reinforcing stimulus is removed (e.g., a teenager is grounded from visiting friends for several days). Punishment is sometimes effective, but it (1) engenders resentment, (2) does not point to desirable alternative behaviors (so it must be accompanied by positive reinforcement), and (3) sometimes is positively reinforcing for some children, the attention given during a spanking outweighs its pain.

When an unpleasant stimulus is linked to an undesirable behavior in treatment, it is called aversive conditioning. Aversive conditioning strategies include rapid smoking, use of a "butt jar" in smoking cessation programs, and covert sensitization in alcoholism programs. Rapid smoking is a technique in which patients are instructed to take a puff every 6 seconds until they feel nauseated or finish their cigarette (22). Saving old cigarette butts in a conspicuous "butt jar" reinforces the unattractiveness of smoking (23). In covert sensitization, smokers or alcoholics read scripts depicting sickening scenes referring to their habit (e.g., "As the bartender is pouring your beer, vomit comes to your mouth.") (24).

DISCRIMINATIVE STIMULI AND STIMULUS CONTROL

A discriminative stimulus is an environmental cue meant to reinforce a given behavior in a certain way. For example, a red traffic light is a cue to come to a safe stop to avoid a collision (25). Your medical office is a cue for a patient to tell you information that would not be revealed had the person run into you at a museum. Your observations of a patient's appearance or mental status provide you with cues about how to proceed with an interview.

Because cues trigger behaviors, controlling them (stimulus control) can limit unwanted behaviors. Stimulus control is important in smoking cessation programs (e.g., suggesting that the patient sit in nonsmoking sections of

planes and restaurants) (23, 26), weight reduction programs (e.g., eating only in the kitchen, not eating while watching TV or doing other entertaining activities) (27–29), outpatient treatment of child molesters (e.g., a condition of treatment is that the person never be alone with a child), and the treatment of persistent sleep onset insomnia (trouble falling asleep not as a result of another disorder) (29–31). In the latter, the bed and bedroom are cues only for sleep and sex, as follows (30, 31):

1. Go to bed when you are tired, go to bed about the same time each evening, and arise at about the same time each morning.
2. If you do not fall asleep within 30–45 minutes after lying down, get up, go to another room, and do something until you get sleepy, then return to bed. Repeat continuously if you do not fall asleep within 30–45 minutes.
3. Do not do anything in bed except sleep and have sexual relations. Do not watch television, read, eat, and so forth in bed.
4. Do not eat or drink fluids after 7:00 PM, especially beverages containing caffeine.
5. Take no naps.

OTHER PERTINENT CONCEPTS IN OPERANT CONDITIONING

Reinforcement Schedules

The pattern of reinforcement and nonreinforcement of a given behavior is termed a reinforcement schedule. Unlike the psychology research laboratory, most medical settings do not allow for meticulous therapeutic use of reinforcement schedules. For example, it is not feasible or necessary for a ward nursing staff to give praise precisely every third time a patient produces a desired behavior. However, as we shall see below, reinforcement schedules help to explain some naturally occurring behaviors, such as cramming for tests or gambling. Of the four types of reinforcement schedules—fixed ratio, fixed interval, variable ratio, and variable interval—a fixed ratio reinforcement schedule rewards for performing a behavior a given number of times. For example, a physician performing cognitive testing on a cognitively impaired patient might praise the patient for every correct answer. This is a 1:1 ratio (continuous) reinforcement schedule. Salaried persons receive a monthly paycheck—a fixed interval schedule. When the quantity and quality of scheduled reinforcement (e.g., a high or low grade, bonus or no bonus, election or no election, research grant awarded or not awarded) vary for persons on fixed interval schedules, a scalloped response pattern occurs, in which more of the desired behavior occurs near the end of each interval (e.g., cramming for tests, intense legislative effort and the campaigning before election day, working late hours just before a grant deadline) (32).

In a variable ratio schedule, a seemingly random, uncertain number of behaviors precedes reinforcement. For example, a slot machine player receives a payoff after four lever pulls, the next payoff after 23 pulls. This schedule particularly resists extinction, which partly explains the popularity of gambling. In a variable interval schedule, unpredictable amounts of time elapse before reinforcement, e.g., trying to reach a busy doctor by phone.

Response Topography

Besides the presence or absence of a behavior, the quality of that behavior is often important. The varieties, refinements, and gradations of a behavior are its topography. For example, medical students learning to take a history often interview rigidly according to the sequence outlined in the textbook; later, using faculty models and acquiring experience from multiple interviews, their interview styles become more flexible.

BEHAVIOR MODIFICATION: TREATMENTS BASED ON LEARNING PRINCIPLES

We have discussed in vivo desensitization, positive reinforcement, aversive conditioning, and stimulus control. Other treatments based on learning principles include cognitive psychotherapy, biofeedback, behavioral rehearsal, counterconditioning, paradoxical intention and response prevention.

Cognitive Psychotherapy

A person's feelings and actions are not only influenced by environmental stimuli but by the person's thoughts and attitudes (cognitions) as well. A man who believes he will be humiliated in a social gathering is more likely to avoid that gathering or attend it anxiously than someone who is more confident. Distorted cognitions or perceptions of oneself often accompany depressions and phobias. Cognitive distortions include the following: (1) dichotomous thinking, in which the situation is perceived as either black or white (e.g., either the patient performs a task up to his or her perfectionist standards, or that patient believes he or she is a failure as a person); (2) personalization, or misinterpreting an event as reflecting on oneself when it has nothing to do with the person (e.g., a teacher incorrectly perceives two students smiling at each other as manifesting disdain for the teacher); (3) overgeneralization, in which one detail is taken to represent an entire experience (e.g., a teacher takes her incorrect answer to a student's question to mean the entire lesson was a failure); (4) magnification, in which an event or situation is exaggerated, and minimization, trivializing an accomplishment; and (5) arbitrary inference, misconstruing the meaning of an event (e.g., an employee misinterprets a boss's offer of assistance as an indication of poor performance) (33, 34). Techniques for correcting cognitive distortions constitute cognitive psychotherapy (see pp. 312–313), and are detailed by Beck (33, 34).

Biofeedback

Until late 1950s it was thought that persons could not voluntarily influence their autonomic (visceral) functions (35). Research on biofeedback taught us that continuous monitoring by some patients (e.g., by such devices as the electroencephalogram [EEG], electromyelogram [EMG], or blood pressure cuff) of their visceral or muscular functions, can be combined with techniques such as muscle relaxation to affect those functions. Eventually, patients are able to use the techniques in daily life without requiring feedback from the monitoring device.

Biofeedback is effective for muscle contraction headaches (bilateral headache from tension that causes overconstriction of forehead and temple muscles) using EMG feedback (36, 37), for anxiety associated with life stress (38) using devices that measure skin temperature or perspiration, and for postural hypotension (drop in blood pressure, with fainting on standing) using a blood pressure cuff on patients who have spinal cord injury (39). Biofeedback can affect blood pressure in patients who have hypertension (high blood pressure), but not sufficiently to replace antihypertensive medication (40). It *may* be useful for some cardiac arrhythmias such as atrial tachycardia (39), and for migraine headache (a unilateral headache with nausea and visual changes) (41, 42).

Other Behavioral Treatments

Behavioral rehearsal is a treatment in which the therapist coaches and models behaviors (e.g., dating skills, assertiveness) at which the patient is unskilled. Assertiveness training is a classic example in which the patient learns how to stand up for his or her rights (43–45).

The principle of reciprocal inhibition asserts that a person cannot be relaxed and anxious simultaneously (46). This principle was applied to a counter-conditioning technique in which patients were taught progressive muscle relaxation (47), and then relaxed while exposed sequentially during office visits to a hierarchy of anxiety-producing images (e.g., thinking about going to the dentist, calling for a dental appointment, getting in the car to go to the dentist's office, [eventually to] hearing the crunching sounds as your tooth is being pulled [an anxiety hierarchy]) (48, 49). This systematic desensitization is effective in a variety of anxiety disorders (49), but it has been replaced by in vivo exposure for treatment of phobias.

Paradoxical intention is a strategy to reduce pressure on a person who engages in an activity, such as sleeping, that requires relaxation. The patient is instructed to try *not* to perform the activity, thereby becoming free to act by choice, not by obligation; that is, having been instructed to stay awake all night if possible, the patient, no longer compelled to sleep, does so by choice when tired (50).

Response prevention is the essence of disulfiram (Antabuse) treatment of alcoholism. To deter further drinking, disulfiram is prescribed to alcoholics in doses of 250 mg/day after at least 12 hours of abstinence. Disulfiram blocks the metabolism of ingested alcohol, causing accumulation of acetaldehyde, with consequent unpleasant symptoms described below (51). The logic is that a sensible person will not drink if drinking is virtually certain to cause a dramatically unpleasant disulfiram-alcohol reaction (this does not deter all alcoholics). Analogously, sensible drivers do not speed when a police car is directly behind them (52). Supervised use of disulfiram (unsupervised, many alcoholics discontinue using the medication), as well as covert sensitization, can effectively control alcoholism (52–55).

> Several days after discontinuing alcohol intake, a 43-year-old divorced alcoholic man began taking 250 mg of Antabuse daily. His doctor had told him that "If you drink alcohol, eat alcohol-containing meat, fish, sauce, or vinegar, or use alcohol-containing shaving lotion or cough syrup, you will get flushing, headache, trouble breathing, vomiting, chest pain, and weakness. You will feel like you want to die, and you might even die if your general health is lousy. So don't drink." The patient responded "I get the picture."

Behavior Modification Applied to Smoking Cessation

Cigarette smoking is the largest preventable public health problem in the U.S., causing 350,000 deaths annually (56). Fortunately, since the 1964 U.S. Surgeon General's Report on Smoking and Health, smoking by adults in the U.S. has declined, in part because of concerted public health measures (25), many of which continue today.

The Houston Project, reported in 1981, was an antismoking public health campaign that used modeling to discourage teenagers from smoking (13). Groups of teenage students were exposed to posters and films in which high-status, similar-aged models demonstrated ways (e.g., putting counterpressure on the smoker by mentioning the risks of smoking) of resisting social pressures (e.g., from peers, smoking parents, cigarette ads) to smoke. This was the campaign in which the phrase "just say no" became popular. In other posters and films, physiologic consequences of smoking were depicted. Compared to groups of school children not exposed to them, students exposed to the messages smoked less and expressed less intention to smoke (57).

Most smokers say they would try to quit if told to by a physician. When told, one third try to quit, and 10% do quit (56, 58). Unfortunately, two thirds of smokers have never been told by their doctor to quit, or even to smoke less (57). Patients are more likely to try quitting when they become ill from smoking (59, 60), although it is better to prevent the onset (primary prevention) of smoking, or begin treatment early in the course of smoking (secondary prevention). Because nicotine is addicting, nicotine withdrawal symptoms (e.g., weight gain, irritability, insomnia) may induce relapse (61).

As a physician, you should energetically support antismoking public health programs, routinely recommend that your patients quit smoking, and educate patients on the health consequences of smoking. You should guide your patients through self-administered smoking cessation programs using printed materials from organizations such as the American Lung Association (23) and the U.S. Office of Health Promotion and Disease Prevention, refer patients to local smoking cessation programs, or develop a program yourself (62). Through the period of smoking reduction, cessation, and withdrawal, you also should arrange regular visits with your patients (62).

The American Lung Association's 20-day smoking cessation program is packaged as a clearly written, upbeat, 60 page booklet with photos of energetic nonsmokers enjoying themselves, *modeling* smoking-free activities. Readers choose rewards for completing each program component (self-reward, of uncertain efficacy [63, 64]), and report to others (first to someone with whom the smokers are close, then to others) that they have decided to quit smoking (soliciting positive reinforcement, using a promise as a stimulus for task completion). The booklet teaches patients how to respond to offers for cigarettes (assertion), or to persons who challenge the commitment to quit smoking (behavioral rehearsal). Relaxation techniques encourage slow, deep abdominal breathing and exercising (reciprocal inhibition, engaging in a behavior other than smoking, maintaining weight through the smoking withdrawal period).

Readers select from a list their reasons for quitting, adding some of their own (changing cognitions of self from that of a person ill from a habit to a person freer and healthier). For every cigarette smoked, the person records the time, intensity of need (on a 1–5 scale), location and persons present, and reason (identifying smoking cues or triggers). Later, for each cue, an alternative behavior (stimulus control) is selected. Cigarettes are bought by the pack, teeth are brushed after every meal, exercise is performed regularly, nonsmoking sections of planes and restaurants are chosen, more time is spent with nonsmokers and less with smokers, parties and bars are avoided at the beginning of the program, smoking accessories (matches, lighters, ashtrays, cigarette cases) are sequentially disposed of, and the lighting of cigarettes removed from the pack is delayed (stimulus control).

Cigarette butts are kept in a conspicuous butt jar (aversive conditioning). Cigarettes are inhaled less deeply, less of each is smoked, fewer are smoked daily, brands are changed every few days, moving to those that are lower in tar and nicotine (all strategies to minimize withdrawal symptoms, receive the negative reinforcement of feeling better, and remove the cue of a preferred brand).

If a relapse occurs, the program is simply resumed with the knowledge that multiple attempts at cessation increase the likelihood of eventual success (65). In some programs, nicotine gum is used to counter withdrawal symptoms as other strategies take hold (66, 67).

Behavior Modification Applied to Weight Reduction

About 34 million adult Americans (26% of those aged 20–75 years) are obese (overweight that is considered to be clinically significant), and 12.4 million are severely obese (68). Although observing the patient's girth is a passable method of estimating the extent of a patient's obesity, it is more objective to compare the patient's weight or body mass index to norms depicted in ideal weight or idea body mass index tables (68). Because aging is a fattening process (68), normal weight for height increases with age. To compute body mass index, multiply the patient's weight in pounds by 703.1 and divide this product by the square of the patient's height in inches (68).

Obesity is associated with increased risk for hypertension (p. 189); diabetes mellitus (p. 196); heart failure (inefficient pumping of the heart, associated with symptoms such as dyspnea [shortness of breath], and edema [fluid accumulation between cells in the soft tissues of the feet, shins and other gravity-dependent areas]); osteoarthritis (degenerative changes in bones and joints); cholesterol gallstones; and cancers in the endometrium (uterine lining), gallbladder, and biliary system disease in women. Severe obesity is associated with sleep apnea (p. 378) and respiratory problems.

Twin and adoption studies (69–74) suggest a strong genetic causal component in obesity. For example, there is a strong association between weight of adoptees and the body mass index of their biological parents, and no relationship between adoptee weight and body mass index of their adoptive parents (69).

There are different patterns of obesity. In the android or male pattern, excessive fat is distributed in the upper body above the waist. In the gynecoid or female pattern, fat excess is in the lower body in the lower abdomen, buttocks, hips, and thighs. Upper body fat is more closely correlated with increased morbidity and mortality.

Obese persons are more likely to be of lower socioeconomic status (75). Obese individuals have larger numbers of fat cells that cannot be reduced in quantity with weight loss; with weight loss, only the size of fat cells diminishes. Obese persons are less responsive than others to gastrointestinal cues of fullness (76, 77), and more responsive to external cues such as the sight of food (i.e., they are more stimulus-bound (78–81).

Although hypometabolism sometimes predisposes to obesity, obese persons actually expend more energy during activity—even though they are less active—than do thin people, because a heavier load must be transported. Although we often associate obesity with endocrine dysfunction, fewer than 1% of obese persons have endocrine disorders. Many medications, including virtually all psychotropic medications except molindone hydrochloride and fluoxetine hydrochloride (pp. 326), predispose to weight gain.

For the average obese person who has put on perhaps 40 pounds since early adulthood, a combination of behavior modification, educated dieting, and an exercise regimen is the management of choice. A nutritionally adequate diet is prescribed, tailored to the patient's tastes. Nutritional adequacy requires at least 1100 calories with adequate amount of vitamins and minerals. Crash diets are rarely effective and may be dangerous. A graded exercise program is tailored to the patient's daily activities and general health.

Weight reduction strategies resemble those for smoking cessation. Stimulus control includes limiting eating to one room and only at specific times, not eating during pleasurable activities such as watching television, not buying fattening foods, not shopping for food while hungry, shopping from a list with no "junk food," removing food from the table right after eating, storing food in opaque containers, and not using snack trays (75, 77).

Weight loss programs are usually successful (76), although relapses are frequent. Recently, an association was discovered between frequent body weight fluctuations (usually as a result of dieting followed by relapse) and coronary artery disease and death (78). Consequently, once weight has been lost through dieting, exercise, and behavior modification, the patient and physician should strive to maintain the patient's lower weight using the same principles (78). If obesity prevention takes heritability into account, then preventive efforts may best be focused on the dietary and exercise habits of children of obese parents (76).

For patients whose obesity exceeds 100% of desirable weight, and for whom dieting, exercise, and behavior modification have failed to reduce weight adequately, surgery may be considered (68). The latter is beyond the scope of this text.

7/Psychoanalytic and Psychodynamic Theories

Theodore B. Feldmann, M.D.

OBJECTIVES

GENERAL OBJECTIVE: Given a patient's history, state the ego defense mechanisms manifested.

SPECIFIC OBJECTIVES:
1. State the two basic assumptions of psychoanalytic theory.
2. Discuss the progression of Freud's practice from hypnosis to psychoanalysis.
3. Summarize Freud's topographic and structural models.
4. Define and give an example of each of the ego defense mechanisms.
5. Discuss the psychoanalytic treatment method.
6. List the contributions to theory and treatment of Freud's contemporaries and students, of the ego psychologists, and of the object relations theorists.
7. State the contributions of Kernberg and Kohut.

Behavior is affected by unconscious memories experienced in childhood which influence adult behavior outside of conscious awareness. The term psychodynamics refers to the internal psychological forces, conscious as well as unconscious, that influence the mind, shape the personality, and play a role in the development of psychopathology (1). Psychodynamic theories are derived from or influenced by the work of Sigmund Freud and are divisible into three categories: Freudian psychoanalytic theory, ego psychology, and object relations theory. Whereas Freud focused primarily on intrapsychic conflict and the neuroses, many contemporary psychodynamic theories examine self-esteem, identity, relationships, and personality disorders (2). Psychoanalytic theories are continually evolving. Their evolution is the focus of this chapter.

SIGMUND FREUD'S PSYCHOANALYTIC THEORY

Historical Perspective

Sigmund Freud (1856–1939), who founded psychoanalysis, is one of the most influential figures in the history of medicine. His theories shaped our views of mental illness and mental functioning and enriched our culture. From 1873 to 1881 he attended medical school. Following that he began a research career in neuroanatomy (3), only to be forced into the clinical practice of medicine (4) because of financial pressures and family responsibilities.

Freud was intrigued by patients suffering from hysteria (now called conversion disorder), whose symptoms resembled those of a neurologic disorder, but in whom no anatomical or physiological basis could be found. This led him to study in Paris with the neurologist Jean Martin Charcot (known for his descriptions of "Charcot's joints" and Charcot-Marie-Tooth syndrome), who used hypnosis to study hysterical seizures and paralysis. When he returned to Vienna, Freud used hypnosis to treat conversion disorder patients. He soon discovered that during the hypnotic state, patients often recalled traumatic experiences that seemed symbolically linked to their symptoms.

For example, a patient suffering from hysterical blindness would report having observed, as a child, some frightening, unacceptable scene. This discovery laid the foundation for psychoanalysis. Although patients temporarily improved following hypnosis, Freud eventually abandoned hypnosis in favor of an approach that was to become psychoanalysis, which is a theory and a treatment.

The late 19th and early 20th centuries were times of burgeoning basic science and clinical knowledge. Freud's contemporaries included Charles Darwin and Albert Einstein (4). Thus influenced, Freud attempted a scientific theory to explain the mind (5). Much of his terminology (e.g., "psychic energy") incorporated biologic concepts. Nevertheless, psychoanalytic theory was initially met with skepticism (6).

Freud's Models of the Mind

Based on his work with hysterical patients, Freud attempted to explain why traumatic experiences, not remembered by the patient, led to symptoms. This early work led to two basic assumptions on which psychoanalytic theory rests. The first is that much mental life is unconscious (based on Freud's study of "Anna O.") (7). The second is that previous experiences influence how a person feels and behaves at any point in time (psychic determinism).

In 1895, Freud's *Studies on Hysteria* (7) drew several conclusions. First, an early traumatic experience, usually sexual, leads to an intense, unpleasant affect (here defined as a feeling state). Freud initially believed that the affect resulted from a physical or sexual trauma. He later abandoned this seduction theory and concluded that the trauma is related to unacceptable sexual impulses. To minimize the unpleasant affect, the unacceptable idea is separated from consciousness, i.e., it is repressed. The idea is also associated with psychic energy (libido) which is converted into the hysterical symptom to further disguise its meaning. For example, aggressive impulses may be dealt with by pushing them into unconscious parts of the mind (repression), and by converting the psychic energy associated with the impulses into a physical symptom (e.g., paralysis of the arm). By bringing this repressed, unacceptable idea into consciousness through psychoanalysis, the psychic energy is discharged and symptom relief obtained. The libido is associated with drives or impulses that seek immediate, total gratification regardless of the consequences. Freud felt that these drives ultimately caused neurotic symptoms.

THE TOPOGRAPHICAL MODEL

Freud constructed and revised several models of the mind to explain his observations. In the first, the topographical model (8), the concepts of conscious, preconscious, and unconscious thought processes were introduced. Conscious thought consists of those things of which the person is aware. Preconscious thoughts are outside of awareness but can be brought into awareness with relative ease. Memories are an example of preconscious thought: at any moment you are probably not thinking about your telephone number, but if asked you easily recall it. Unconscious thoughts are outside of awareness and can be made conscious only with great difficulty and expenditure of much psychic energy. After a time, however, Freud perceived that although the topographical model was useful, it was insufficient to explain many of his patients' symptoms, such as anxiety. This led to a revision, the structural model (9, 10), in which the terms ego, id, and superego were introduced.

THE STRUCTURAL MODEL

The Id

The id is defined as an intrapsychic structure that is completely unconscious. It is the seat of human drives. Freud continually revised his notion of the drives and their importance. Drives, also referred to as instincts, can be defined as a pressure directing a person towards action (11). This pressure is a form of psychic energy (libido). Drives are thought to be primarily sexual (here, sexual includes oral, anal, and phallic libido) and aggressive, although Freud focused on the former. The intrapsychic energy or tension associated with the drives builds over time unless the drive is discharged or gratified. The tension is unpleasant, analogous to the discomfort generated by hunger. Discharge of the drive leads to tension relief and restoration of psychic equilibrium. The drives demand constant, immediate gratification, regardless of the consequences for the person, an expression of the pleasure principle. Total drive discharge relieves tension and yields pleasure. Drives may also be cognitively experienced as bizarre, convoluted, and symbolic thoughts, reflecting the id's unique type of thought or primary process. Dreams are a classic example of primary process thinking. The drives are constantly moving to escape from the id and be expressed in the external world. But uncensored expression of sexual or aggressive drives can harm the individual. What keeps the id in check? The two other intrapsychic components of the structural model play key roles in drive regulation, the ego and the superego.

The Ego

The ego is the interface and the mediator between the conscious and the unconscious, between fantasy and reality, and between the id and the external world. Whereas the id contains only unconscious mental processes, the ego has conscious and preconscious as well as unconscious elements. The ego limits the uncensored expression of the drives. This modulation of drive expression occurs through defense mechanisms (see p. 87), which transform the drives into a more acceptable form, relieving tension yet sparing the person from the consequences of uncensored expression, The id operates by the pleasure principle and the primary process; the ego functions by the reality principle and the secondary process. The reality principle takes into account the individual's role in society and the consequences of uncensored drive expression. Secondary process refers to thought that is logical and sequential, the opposite of primary process thought. Finally, there are certain conflict-free spheres of ego operation (12). These include thought, memory, and perception, the autonomous ego functions (see also p. 90).

The Superego

The final component of the structural model is the superego, which governs one's moral code and standards of behavior. It is a person's sense of right and wrong. It helps to determine which behaviors are appropriate and which drives must be modified. Thus, the superego augments the ego's modulation of the drives. Sometimes the superego acts in opposition to the ego, as in the case of an overly harsh, punitive superego. For example, some people have such rigid convictions about right and wrong that they have trouble functioning in our imperfect world. On the other hand, antisocial personalities (p. 272) lack a sense of right and wrong. Their superegos are too weak. The superego, influenced by parental values and self-expectations, consists of two parts: the conscience and the ego-ideal. The conscience governs the moral standard by which a person lives. It is the sense of right and wrong largely determined by internalization of parental values. When these standards are violated, the conscience exerts a punitive effect, experienced as guilt. The other component of the superego, the ego-ideal, refers to a person's expectations and aspirations—the kind of person we aspire to be. The ego-ideal can be thought of as our ideal self (13). When behavior, thought, or feelings violate the ideal perception of the self, the individual feels shame.

THE ROLE OF INTRAPSYCHIC CONFLICT IN SYMPTOM FORMATION

As described above, the ego and superego often oppose the id, producing intrapsychic conflict. The id pushes to have its drive completely gratified to relieve the tension resulting from the accumulation of libido. The ego opposes this because of cultural restrictions on behavior. The superego opposes uncensored drive expression that would violate a person's moral code (the conscience) or expectations of oneself (the ego-ideal).

A theory of neurosis (an illness [e.g., conversion disorder] caused by an unconscious conflict) can therefore be constructed: when a disturbance in psychic equilibrium results from drives threatening to erupt into consciousness, the ego and superego are alerted that action must be taken. This alert takes the form of transient anxiety called signal anxiety (14). The ego responds defensively. A basic defense mechanism is repression, used to push the drives back into the unconscious. If repression succeeds, the signal anxiety is relieved. Often, however, repression fails and the drives continue to impinge on consciousness. Auxiliary defense mechanisms are then used to disguise the drive and render it more acceptable to the ego and superego. This drive modification is a compromise formation. If the defenses used are adaptive, repression is augmented and the signal anxiety alleviated. Often the defenses used to assist repression are themselves pathologic. When this occurs, a neurotic symptom develops (13). The symptom is accompanied by anxiety, usually less intense than the signal anxiety initially experienced. Sometimes the anxiety is accompanied by a specific behavior (e.g., a phobia or compulsion). Sometimes it is a chronic low-grade symptom, as in generalized anxiety disorder. In generalized anxiety disorder, repression is the primary defense, whereas with phobias, displacement and avoidance occur along with repression. The common defense mechanisms are summarized in Table 7.1.

The defense mechanisms used are largely influenced by how the person dealt with the psychosexual stages of development, during each of which an anatomic area (erotogenic zone) is especially laden with libido (see p. 134). Freud described five psychosexual stages: oral, anal, phallic (Oedipal), latency, and genital. Each stage has defenses associated with it. Fixation caused by trauma during a given stage results in that defense being used to a greater extent. For example, isolation and undoing are associated with the late anal and early Oedipal stages. Fixation during this time restricts the options of the ego to these defenses. Hence, an obsessive-compulsive disorder (see p. 261) is likely to develop. Similarly, repression and displacement typify the Oedipal stage (p. 137). Oedipal fixation predisposes to the development of a phobia or generalized anxiety disorder. Not all fixation-based theories have held up to scrutiny, however. For example, alcoholics were thought to be orally fixated. Vaillant (15) prospectively studied a sample of Harvard college students using an orality rating scale, and then reinterviewed them at decade-long intervals. High orality during college did not predict adult alcoholism.

Although Freud focused on the neurotic disorders, psychoanalytic theory also explains personality disorders and psychoses. For example, in psychoses such as schizophrenia, the defense mechanism of projection is largely responsible for persecutory delusions (16).

Freud's Writings on Narcissism

Freud also contributed to the understanding of narcissism (the libidinal investment in the self) (17). He postulated that at birth a state of primary narcissism exists, during which all the child's libidinal energies are devoted to the satisfaction of personal needs. During this time, the child is unaware of others except to the extent that they meet his or her needs. As the child has more contact with others, classically the mother, his or her

Table 7.1.   Common Defense Mechanisms

Repression: the involuntary, automatic banishment of an unacceptable, threatening feeling or idea into the unconscious. Forgetting something unpleasant is an example. This defense operates in both normal and pathologic situations. Repression is the primary defense mechanism used by the ego.

Denial: the unconscious refusal to acknowledge or deal with a threatening idea or impulse. The person acts as if the threatening feeling or situation does not exist. A common example is the seriously ill patient's refusal to accept tihe severity of illness and its subsequent treatment. Denial is also commonly used by persons with substance abuse disorders.

Projection: a primitive defense in which persons unconsciously attribute to others their own unacceptable thoughts or feelings. For example, a person with much hostility comes to view others as being angry. Projection is the primary defense mechanism in delusions of persecution.

Identification: a mechanism in which one unconsciously patterns oneself after another, resulting in a change in the ego with development of self esteem and identity. This defense operates in everyone; for example, we all identify heroes or role models at different times in our lives. Identification with the same-sex parent is also important in resolving the Oedipal conflict and in superego formation.

Identification with the aggressor: in this variant of identification, common in children, a threatening object is identified with as a way of lessening anxiety about the object. An example is a child who plays doctor to allay anxiety about a doctor's appointment.

Introjection: a variant of identification. It is the unconscious, total symbolic internalization of another significant object, one that is loved or hated. Through this defense, anxiety related to separation or aggression is dealt with more effectively. Introjection is important in the development of some depressions.

Projective identification: this primitive defense contains elements of both projection and identification. It consists of a simultaneous projection of the unpleasant aspects of one's personality onto others, followed by identification with that person. This defense is commonly used by patients with personality disorders.

Splitting: another primitive defense characteristic of some personality disorders, classically the borderline personality. Objects are viewed in either an idealized or devalued light (all good or all bad) because the personality lacks the ability to handle ambivalent feelings.

Reaction formation: the adoption of attitudes or behaviors that are the opposite of one's unconscious feelings. This is commonly used in everyday life. An example is the person who is overly courteous or polite in response to underlying feelings of hostility.

Isolation: the separation of an unpleasant idea from its associated feeling. This defense, in combination with undoing (below), is characteristic of obsessive-compulsive disorder.

Undoing: a symbolic action that is the reverse of an unacceptable impulse or feeling, such as a compulsion to turn on and off gas jets to check on them.

Rationalization: irrational or unacceptable feelings are made more tolerable by providing logical and complex explanations, literally explaining something away. For example, a disappointment is dealt with by saying that it is not really important.

Intellectualization: similar to rationalization, it is the overuse of abstract concepts to avoid dealing with unpleasant feelings.

Regression: the partial or complete return to earlier patterns of adaptation to avoiding conflict. For example, an ill patient may temporarily become more demanding, dependent, and childlike, reflecting a wish to be taken care of or cured of their illness by someone more powerful. When regression results from a conscious decision to foster one's well-being, e.g., to take a vacation, it is called regression in the service of the ego (12).

Displacement: the redirection of an emotion from the original object to another one. Displacement, along with avoidance, characterizes phobias. Avoidance is simply the act of avoiding an unpleasant situation.

Dissociation: the segregation of any group of mental processes from the rest of a person's mental activities. Thoughts and feelings are literally walled off. Dissociation occurs in the dissociative disorders, such as psychogenic amnesia, psychogenic fugue states, and multiple personalities.

Conversion: the transfer of psychic energy into other bodily processes. As a result of this defense, unconscious impulses are transformed into medical symptoms, usually with symbolic relationship to the original impulse. This is the defense responsible for the hysterical symptoms that were first studied by Freud. Conversion is commonly seen in conversion disorder and somatization disorder.

Sublimation: a defense in which the energy associated with unacceptable impulses is diverted into a socially acceptable channel. Sublimation is the most mature and the healthiest of the defense mechanisms.

libido becomes progressively more invested in others (object libido). With stress, object libido can be reinvested in the ego; this is regression to a state of secondary narcissism.

Freud viewed narcissism primary within the context of object relations (relationships with others), and viewed secondary narcissism as pathologic. Freud viewed the narcissistic disorders (e.g., certain personality disorders) as particularly regressed and pathologic, more related to the psychoses than to the neuroses. Freud felt that these patients could be identified by their nonresponse to interpretations (properly timed explanations) of Oedipal conflict, were not neurotic, and consequently were not responsive to psychoanalysis. However, some contemporary analysts psychoanalyze patients who have borderline or narcissistic personality disorders (18).

THE NATURE OF THE DRIVES

As mentioned earlier, Freud initially emphasized the sexual drives and paid minimal attention to aggressive drives (19). Presented, however, with complex examples, such as when a patient experienced pleasure in pain, in 1915 he speculated that other instincts existed and delineated ego instincts (20), the source of the psychic energy necessary for ego functioning and self-preservation. Aggression remained minimally explained. From 1920 to 1923 Freud considered additional aggressive drives. The role of sexuality and aggression in driving behavior led to Freud's concept of opposing life and death instincts (eros and thanatos). The death instinct (thanatos) consists largely of aggressive drives. The life instinct (eros) is related to the sexual drives.

PSYCHOANALYSIS AS A TREATMENT

Because Freud's development of psychoanalytic theory arose from his care of patients, psychoanalysis simultaneously emerged as a theory and a treatment. The basic premise of psychoanalytic treatment is the uncovering of conflicts or traumas that cause symptoms. To do this, repressed memories have to be made conscious. One way this occurs is free association (21). The patient is instructed to talk about whatever comes to mind in an uncensored manner, thus determining the direction of the session. Examination of dreams, fantasies, and slips of the tongue also help uncover traumatic experiences, conflicts, and feelings. By understanding these, the patient (the analysand) can make more rational choices and function better. With the help of the analyst's interpretations, pathologic defenses and behaviors are transformed into more adaptive ones. Free association is fostered by an environment relatively free of distractions; Freud's patients lay on a couch and he sat behind them out of view. This minimized the analyst's influence on what the patient talked about. The analyst also assumed a neutral stance toward the patient, speaking minimally and acting nonjudgmentally. Previous conflicts with significant figures from the past were experienced with the analyst as transference reactions. For example, a patient who had a highly critical father might develop adulthood problems with people in authority. These will be reexperienced with the analyst, who is then perceived as acting like her father. Transference exemplifies psychic determinism; the past influences the present.

Uncovering of repressed material through free association fosters regression, a defense mechanism integral to the psychoanalytic process. When repressed memories emerge, there is a tendency to relive the event and its associated feelings, and temporarily behave in a more dependent or immature manner commensurate with the time of the original trauma or memory. By examining these regressive episodes, both patient and analyst better understand the impact of the traumatic event.

FREUD'S CONTEMPORARIES AND STUDENTS

Freud's work remains influential in contemporary theory and therapy. Many of his theories were expanded and modified by members of his "inner circle" in Vienna, by the ego psychologists, and by object relations theorists. Some of the ideas propounded (e.g., Jung's collective unconscious theory, Rank's birth trauma theory) by Freud's inner circle are rarely incorporated into practice, but are of historical interest.

Carl Jung (1875–1961) came to disagree with Freud's emphasis on sexual libido. Jung explored the possibility that a collective unconscious existed for all persons. This contained remnants of unconscious material passed from one generation to the next, in the form of archetypes from mankind's past. These archetypes help to shape the personality and the expression of psychopathology.

Jung noted that all personalities possess introversion and extroversion in different proportions. Introverts focus more on thoughts and emotions; extroverts are more oriented toward other people and the external world. At times the real personality is masked by the persona (Greek for mask), the facade that the individual presents to others. All personalities also have both masculine and feminine traits. (Anima described the feminine traits possessed by men, animus the masculine traits of women). The personality is composed of mixtures of the above traits. Psychopathology results from imbalances of these traits (22, 23).

Like Jung, *Alfred Adler* (1870–1937) ultimately disagreed with Freud over the roles of sexuality in psychopathology. He focused on feelings of inferiority and superiority in personality development. For Adler, inferiority is the original psychologic state for all persons, resulting from the infant's helpless dependency. As the personality develops, the person strives to overcome inferiority feelings by gaining power and mastery. A woman's striving for superiority in a male-dominated world is termed masculine protest (24).

Otto Rank (1884–1939) disagreed with Freud's emphasis on the Oedipal complex as causing neuroses; he thought anxiety originated in the birth trauma, the helplessness experienced by the newborn infant (25). A component of birth trauma is separation anxiety, addressed by later theorists.

Rank also questioned the psychoanalyst's relatively passive stance. He felt that treatment length could be shortened considerably by the therapist actively examining the birth trauma with the patient (26).

Like Rank, *Sandor Ferenczi* (1873–1935) advocated a more active therapist role (active therapy) and proposed that psychoanalytic treatment length could be shortened dramatically (2). He recommended routinely confronting the patient with reality, a process that Freud advised against.

Rather than focus exclusively on neurotic disorders, *Wilhelm Reich* (1897–1957) described personality types that defend (character armor) against instinctual drives and external pressures (27). Reich defined several personality types. For the hysterical (histrionic) character, anxiety and sexual preoccupation predominate. The compulsive character is rigid, controlled, indecisive, and perfectionistic. Narcissistic characters are self-centered, and require constant praise and attention. Reich's personality types correspond to many currently diagnosed personality disorders.

Karl Abraham (1877–1925) contributed a formulation of depression as arising from introjection of an ambivalently loved lost object. Following the loss (or anticipated loss) by rejection, departure, or death of a person who was ambivalently loved (simultaneously loved and hated) by the patient, the patient's ego incorporates the mental image (the introject) of the lost person. The patient's superego then directs anger at this introject (now within the patient's ego), contributing to the depression (28).

Adolph Meyer (1866–1950) focused more on observable behavior and less on unconscious factors. In his theory of psychobiology, personality and psychopathology result from a complex interaction of psychologic, physical, genetic, and environmental factors (2, 15). He constructed autobiographic histories of his patients, which were used in an active, goal-oriented therapy.

Franz Alexander (1891–1964) advocated face-to-face contact between patient and analyst, discarding the couch. He conceptualized the corrective emotional experience, in which the analyst relates to the patient more constructively about certain issues than did the patient's parents (29). Alexander hypothesized psychologic influences on certain medical illnesses (duodenal ulcer, essential hypertension, ulcerative colitis, syncope, thyrotoxicosis, rheumatoid arthritis, and bronchial asthma—now affectionately called the "Chicago seven") (30).

Karen Horney (1885–1952) was one of the first American-born psychoanalysts to make important contributions. In her holistic psychology, she placed greater emphasis on environmental interactions than on libidinal material (31). Horney discussed concepts of the self. These included the well-adjusted person, or real self; the image of what the person feels he or she should be, the idealized self; and the total of the person's experience, the actual self. When disharmony occurs in this system, the self experiences self-hatred, leading to basic anxiety and a lack of trust. Horney's therapy fostered self realization, the establishment of a more realistic view of the self.

Harry Stack Sullivan (1892-1949) described three levels of thinking: the prototaxic mode, parataxic mode, and syntaxic mode (32). The prototaxic mode is primitive thought characteristic of infants and seen in schizophrenic patients; parataxic thought is concrete (i.e., not abstract); syntaxic thought is logical and rational. Although all three are present in every person, the predominant type a person uses determines the overall level of functioning. Sullivan elaborated on the importance of self-esteem for mental health (33), and recommended an active therapist role in therapy, viewing the therapist as a participant-observer.

EGO PSYCHOLOGY

Ego psychology theories emphasize the role of the ego. Some ego psychologists such as Anna Freud stress the ego's role in mediating unconscious conflict. Others such as Heinz Hartmann stress the ego's role in dealing with the external world, moving away from instinc-

tual conflict, and examining the conflict-free spheres of ego (2). The ego's functions are nine: (1) defense mechanisms; (2) perception and reality testing; (3) motility; (4) intentionality (or impulse control); (5) anticipation; (6) adaptation; (7) cognition; (8) object relations (i.e., relationships with others); and (9) modulation of feelings or affects. The defensive functions of the ego, and their role in symptom formation, were elaborated on by *Anna Freud* (1895–1983) in *The Ego and the Mechanisms of Defense* (34).

Heinz Hartmann (1894–1970) believed that the child is born with a unique psychologic endowment that begins as an undifferentiated matrix and develops gradually into the ego independent of instinctual urges, i.e., in an autonomous (conflict-free) sphere (12). Only later, after the ego has developed, do the drives exert pressure on it. Hartmann believed that as the ego matured it developed object representations (internal representations of external objects [i.e., persons important to the individual]), even in the absence of the actual object (object constancy).

Hartmann (and *Ernest Kris* [1900–1957]) described how this ego defense mechanism of identification develops the ego and superego, so the ego depends less on objects (ego autonomy). For example, identification with the parents facilitates personality development in the child, resulting in the child becoming more independent. Hartmann also described neutralization, the transfer of libido from the id to the ego, diminishing drive intensity and strengthening the ego (35).

Erik Erikson (1902–) discussed ego development throughout the life cycle. His epigenetic model unfolds from the effective resolution of normative crises (36). These crises are: (1) basic trust versus mistrust (the child feels safe rather than viewing the world as dangerous); (2) autonomy versus shame and doubt (the child feels a sense of mastery); (3) initiative versus guilt (the child sets goals and strives to attain them); (4) industry versus inferiority (the child accomplishes goals and becomes more social); (5) identity versus role confusion (a sense of sameness over time); (6)

intimacy versus isolation (lasting relationships are formed); (7) generativity versus stagnation (family and occupational goals are reached, and younger persons are mentored); and (8) ego integrity versus despair (the aging adult reflects positively on his or her life).

Margaret Mahler (1897–1985) directly observed the interaction between children and their mothers and described stages of separation and individuation (37). These stages are the normal autistic stage, in which the child is unaware of the external world; the normal symbiotic stage, during which the child views self and mother (or other principal care giver) as one unit, with mother providing all of the child's needs; and the separation-individuation stage, during which the child gradually realizes self as a separate being from mother.

René Spitz (1887–1974) posited that ego organization occurs through the relationship between mother (or other nurturing person) and child (another bridge between ego psychology and object relations theory). The ego progresses through a sequence of tasks (ego organizers), each furthering the person's autonomy (38). These include social smiling at about 3 months of age (then thought to be the first recognition of an object outside oneself), stranger anxiety at 6 months (the first recognition that people are different), accompanied by bonding (attachment) with the parents, and negative head shaking at 18 months (a major assertion of autonomy).

OBJECT RELATIONS THEORY

We have seen how object relations theory extends from ego psychology. Object relations are observable relationships of a person with others (objects), and intrapsychic relationships between self representations and object representations (the intrapsychic images we have of ourselves and others) (39). Self-representations arise from internalizations, by identification and introjection, of objects (40). In object relations theory, ego development is related to object relations development, which is central.

According to *Melanie Klein* (1882–1960) (41), libido is experienced at birth as either pleasurable or unpleasurable based on the mother-child interaction. This is the basis for the ego defense of splitting, in which the child views the mother as all good or all bad (42). This mechanism may persist into adult life. Predominantly negative experiences with the mother in the first year of life yield the paranoid-schizoid position, characterized by lifelong feelings of isolation and persecution. Klein also originated play therapy with children: a child's comments about and attitudes toward toys, dolls, and other play objects reflect attitudes toward and relations with important people in the child's life.

Ronald Fairbairn (1889–1964) emphasized the importance of the environment in object relations: the ego always seeks objects, and can develop only in their presence. Libido is object-seeking rather than seeking discharge of tension, and aggression is an expression of frustration, not an instinct (43, 44).

David Winnicott (1896–1971) described the holding (facilitating) environment and transitional objects (45, 46). He discussed development of a real self versus a false self in response to the quality of early object relations. A false self (characterized by inadequacy, overcompliance, and lack of autonomy) develops in response to unempathic responses from the mother. A holding environment (i.e., an empathic environment) is necessary for the real self to develop. During the transition between object merger (primary narcissism) and object constancy, transitional objects (e.g., a teddy bear) are needed. These protect the child from overwhelming separation anxiety.

Otto Kernberg (1928–   ), a contemporary object relations theorist, writes extensively on borderline and narcissistic personalities (see p. 274). Borderline personalities manifest poor frustration tolerance, poor impulse control, impaired self-esteem, and impaired sense of identity (47), which result from faulty internalization of objects and frequent use of the primitive defenses splitting and projective identification. Kernberg developed expressive psychotherapy for patients who had this disorder (48).

His therapy emphasizes interpretation of pathologic transferences and defenses with emphasis on reality-oriented changes by patients to eliminate pathologic behaviors. For example, self-mutilation is a frequent behavior in borderline personalities. Kernberg would interpret the anger that leads to it, set limits prohibiting it, and point out alternative behaviors.

Self psychology is a psychoanalytic theory developed by *Heinz Kohut* (1913–1982). It addresses normal and pathologic narcissism by examining the development of the self, which Kohut defines as the center of a person's identity and initiative. His theories have enhanced our understanding of the narcissistic personality disorder (49).

Kohut disagreed with Freud's portrayal of secondary narcissism as regressive and pathologic. In fact, he believed that object relations required a healthy sense of narcissism. Furthermore, he felt that objects (self-objects) are viewed as extensions of the self (50).

According to Kohut, the primary narcissism that Freud described has two components, the grandiose self and the parent imago (idealized parent image). As development proceeds, these two components (the bipolar self) fuse to lay the foundation for healthy self-esteem (51). Defects in either the grandiose self or the parent imago result from unempathic responses from the parents (or other care givers). The result is that the narcissistic personality (see p. 274) overreacts to criticism, has a high anxiety level, and overrelies on the esteem from external objects (self-objects) to feel confident (52).

8/Medical Sociology

Jeffrey Colman Salloway, Ph.D.

OBJECTIVES

GENERAL OBJECTIVE: Given a patient who presents with a sickness, discuss the social factors that influence whether the patient will receive proper diagnosis and treatment that will achieve an optimal outcome.

SPECIFIC OBJECTIVES:
1. Discuss the effects of ethnicity, social class, occupation, age, and sex on health and health-related behavior.
2. Identify the historical shifts in primary causes of mortality and hypothesize about future epidemics.
3. Discuss the interaction of host, agent, and environment and state the value of primary prevention in light of these factors.
4. Contrast disease, sickness, and illness.
5. Characterize the sick role and show how Suchman's model uses this concept.
6. Discuss the health belief model and Andersen's health care utilization model.
7. State how health locus of control is useful in patient care.

Chances are you will practice in a western industrialized society whose prevailing Judaeo-Christian culture emphasizes the principles of rational thought and individual responsibility for behavior. Within medicine this leads naturally to a focus on forces that affect or are affected by individual patient behavior. It is on this basis that we explore individual psychopathology, accountability for prevention, and physician-patient relations. Western societies teach that each person has free will and is responsible for his or her own decisions. Such is our ideology of individualism that we use it post hoc to justify the good and evil that befall us. Yet the social forces that are a major determinant of individual behavior are all but invisible to the unpracticed eye. Those social forces, typically implicit but which affect patients'—as well as our own behavior—are the subject of this chapter.

Picture a freshman sociology class at any American university. The instructor labors to convince the students that social forces—demographics, class, race, sex—operate on their lives in ways of which they are not conscious. The students, in turn, argue vehemently against mysterious social forces and for their individualism and free will. Suddenly, at the click of the clock to noon, these free-willed students rise as a mass, don identical down-filled jackets with discreet labels from Freeport, Maine, lift identical backpacks, and exit on muffled soles of identical running shoes, each proudly proclaiming uniqueness.

The similarities in our behaviors are far more common than the differences. It is the difference that fascinates because, in truth, we behave so much alike. In this chapter, however, we consider not how people differ as individuals, but how they behave much like others in the groups to which they belong. We consider, therefore, the social forces that propel us and our patients to behave similarly in similar circumstances, and that affect the decisions we and our patients make.

SOCIAL STRUCTURE AND HUMAN BEHAVIOR

Life is lived in groups. For example, few groups live in closer proximity than medical students. Students in a medical school class identify subgroups with well-defined characteristics. These cliques can be named (e.g., gunners, drinkers, marrieds), are assigned behavioral characteristics (e.g., studious, weekend drinker, clannish, at home studier), interact more within than between cliques, and share expectations for their medical school performance and their career paths (e.g., high grades and academic medicine, careers in surgery, family practitioners). Once it is apparent to you that life is lived in group context, you can ask a series of questions about individuals and groups. One question is, what determines group life? These determinants powerfully predict individual behavior, especially health-related behavior. Major predictors include ethnicity, social class, age, occupation, and sex.

Ethnicity and Behavior

Unlike many countries, America is populated largely by multiple ethnic groups who originated elsewhere. Even when ethnic groups have belonged to our society for a long time, they maintain bonds within their own group that affect their behavior. Ethnic bonds are multidimensional and include religion, geography, language, family and intermarriage, and values. These bonds affect behavior in three fundamental ways.

First, people who belong to ethnic groups share an ethnic culture. Their values, perceptions of reality, and norms tend to have more in common with members of their ethnic group than with outsiders. Thus, you can make limited generalizations about behavior based on ethnicity. Investigators have linked perceptions of pain and reporting of symptom severity to ethnic origins (1, 2). This does not mean that every Irish-American represses pain perceptions, or that every Italian- or Jewish-American floridly describes symptoms. It merely alerts us to the fact that behavior can be colored by ethnic identity.

The sensitive practitioner considers culture and ethnicity when assessing symptoms, teaching compliance, or dealing with a family in distress. The non-Latino physician who assesses a Latino woman for depression should have some understanding of Latino culture. The white, Anglo-Saxon, Protestant physician reared in New England may need to shift cultural gears and perceptions when interacting with a patient from, say, Southeast Asia, the Middle East, Africa, Eastern Europe, or, for that matter, the Bayou or South Bronx.

Second, ethnic groups are variously placed in the status hierarchy (social class) of American life. Not only is income distributed differentially along ethnic and class lines, but so too is education, access to health care, and the nature of patient interaction with physicians. In addition to ethnicity, social class powerfully predicts—and controls—behavior.

Third, because ethnicity is often a common bond for marriage behavior, it becomes a vehicle for the transmission of genetic disorders (3). For example, Eastern European Jews have an increased likelihood of developing Tay-Sachs disease, white South Africans variegate porphyria (3).

Ethnicity and Social Class in Patient Behavior

To illustrate the interaction of ethnicity and social class on patient behavior, consider four concerned mothers of ill children. Each mother has an infant who is cranky, eating poorly, and appears to be ill. One, a poor Latino woman, is not eligible for Medicaid and cannot afford private insurance. She is a garment worker whose employer provides no health insurance. Because she is uninsured, her access to health care is extremely limited, although she can receive some care through her local hospital emergency room. She describes her child's symptoms in Spanish in terms that have specific meaning in her culture (4–6) but make little sense to the busy intern in the overcrowded emergency room who knows only high school-level Spanish. The problems of poor access (7–13) and limited communication (14, 15) are unsatisfying for all participants: they impede the physician's ability to fully diagnose and therefore treat the infant, and they retard the mother's sense that her baby will be well treated.

In the second scenario, the mother also is a Latino but is middle class, better educated, and has health insurance through her employer. She belongs to a health maintenance organization that staffs several bilingual pediatricians with whom she is able to communicate in more educated Spanish that avoids colloquialisms. Because she has health insurance, her child's care is not limited to the rushed, overcrowded conditions of the typical hospital emergency room (where most of the nation's uninsured receive care [16, 17] [p. 444]). Her better access to care enables her to interact more comfortably with her pediatrician concerning the nature of her child's problems and the treatment.

The third mother is not Latino but is of the lowest socioeconomic class and is therefore eligible for Medicaid. Although this is certainly better than no coverage, many care providers do not take Medicaid patients, or they limit the number of Medicaid patients served. This may say less about the ethics of health care providers than it does about Medicaid, which pays minimally (p. 444) and takes a long time to reimburse. In this case, the mother receives care through a local clinic and is not burdened by a language difference. She describes her baby as "colicky," a term with no more specificity of meaning than *mal ojo,* which the first mother used to describe her baby's sickness (literal meaning: evil eye, colloquial translation: failure to thrive). However, the physician has a notion of infant colic (p. 135), which passes for a diagnosis. The physician's affirmation of the diagnosis and supporting interaction style make this a more satisfying exchange than that between the physician and the poor Latino mother.

Our fourth mother is middle class and from the majority culture, which changes the situation yet again. She has access to care and easier communication with her physician. The health care workers who treat her and her child have middle class orientations and speak the same English. She feels more comfortable among these care providers than her middle class Latino counterpart.

The differences among these four situations are neither intrapsychic nor biologic in origin. Instead, differences in access to care, diagnosis, satisfaction, and ultimately patient compliance with prescribed regimen have far-reaching clinical implications for outcome. Table 8.1 lists additional medically relevant correlates of lower socioeconomic status (18–37).

Membership in Other Structural Groups

Every person belongs to multiple subgroups. These subgroups share ways of looking at the world, norms for behavior, values, and opportunities. They have unequal access to certain resources. Three important categories are age, occupation, and sex.

AGE GROUPS

Behavior varies throughout the life cycle, as discussed on pp. 119–175. In addition to age-related effects, there are also generational effects. Persons who grew up in the Great Depression may differ from those who grew up in the 1950s.

Use of medical services tends to vary substantially across a person's life cycle. The infectious diseases of childhood (measles, chicken pox, etc.) often confer lifetime immunity. At the other end of the age spectrum, many chronic diseases do not appear until late

Table 8.1. Health-Related Characteristics of Low Socioeconomic Status[a]

I.   Family and Social Factors
 Higher rates of parental death, separation, and divorce
 More hazardous occupations
 Higher rates of job-related death
 More maternal heads of household
 Increased competition for the attention of the single parent
 More marriage at earlier ages
 Greater sex role differentiation, with more distinctions in who performs which family tasks and who has higher
   status
 Less joint participation of both parents in leisure activities
 Less delay of gratification
 Membership in fewer organizations
 Greater reliance on nonverbal cues
 Greater feeling of alienation from society

II. Primary Prevention
 Less knowledge and sophistication about human physiology and pathology
 Less likelihood of eating a balanced diet
 Lower chance of obtaining health checkups costing money, or to get free immunization
 Less chance of preventive health visits
 Less dental and orthodontic care

III. Prevalence of Illness
 Higher infant mortality from numerous causes
 Higher incidence of premature births
 Higher incidence of
   mental retardation
   obesity
   chronic illness
   high blood pressure
   blindness
   speech problems
   coronary artery disease
   lung disease
   tuberculosis
   venereal (sexually transmitted) disease
   days lost from work or school because of illness
 Mental illness in general, specifically
   psychosis
   sociopathy
   schizophrenia
   Briquet's syndrome
 More homicide, rape, and robbery
 More psychological dependency
 Lower self-esteem
 Greater fears of change

IV. Sick Role Behavior
 Greater responsiveness to crises than to future objectives
 Diminished adherence to time-bound schedules
 Less interest in medical care when ill
 Less chance of self-referral to doctors when ill
 More self-medication
 Greater chance of using nonmedical personnel for treatment
 Less trust of the health care system
 Greater severity of illness once admitted to the hospital
 Greater likelihood of systemic or somatic presentation of mental illness
 Greater chance of being treated on a hospital ward by a "committee" of housestaff and students
 Longer hospital stays
 Greater chance of dying from cancer once it occurs
 Lower life expectancy

[a]Modified from Sierles FS. Behavioral science for the boreds. Miami: Medmaster, 1989:17-19.

life, typically adult onset diabetes, glaucoma (increased ocular fluid pressure), as well as cardiovascular and neoplastic diseases. The use of medical services also increases from the adult years into old age. Large numbers of people now live beyond 80 years, a previously unheard of figure (38). This portends a greater increase in the demand for geriatric and long-term care services (p. 450).

OCCUPATIONAL GROUPS

Another structural variable that implies differences in health care behavior is occupational groups. There are substantial health risks associated with different occupational groups (39–45). Examples include accidental death in loggers and timber cutters (43), burns in restaurant workers (45), mood disorders in professional writers (46), and cancers in chemical workers (40, 41). Moreover, occupational diseases arise as rapidly as does new technology. In the clinical interview, therefore, consideration of job and work environment can be as important as the patient's medical history.

SEX AND HEALTH

Women have different health risks than do men. Men are at higher risk for fatal accidents. Additionally, they seem to be at a higher risk for cardiovascular disease, although this may be cultural rather than sex-based. Clearly, reproductive health differs for men and women. Osteoporosis (decreased bone density with increased risk for fracture) is a common health risk for women, not men. It is a physiological risk related to premenopausal calcium metabolism and to estrogen production.

During the past decade, we have seen a change in women's health risk behavior. The number of women who smoke has been rising. As a result, lung cancer has surpassed neoplastic breast disease as the most frequent cancer among women (47). At the same time, women see physicians more often, respond faster to symptoms by seeing a physician, and are more often insured (48, 49). Associations between sex and health are discussed in detail on pages 154–162.

MULTIPLE GROUP MEMBERSHIP AND HEALTH

We have examined the impact of group membership on health risk and health care behavior of group membership as it relates to ethnicity, social class, age, occupation, and sex. In addition, the memberships cluster together. For example, migrant farm workers are most often minorities, largely Latino. This cluster includes Spanish-speaking people, most often of low educational status, poor, and in late adolescence or middle adulthood. They share other risks as well. They are exposed to chemical fertilizers and pesticides in the fields, and they risk back injury, accidental injury, heat exhaustion, dehydration, and perhaps malignant melanoma (a pigmented skin cancer). Migrant farm workers are rarely insured for medical care, seldom have a regular source of care, and therefore do not have accessible medical records, a source of payment, or prospects for continuing care. The net result is a high risk of disease, poor access to care, and problems in relating to non-Latino professionals. Their location in the social structure is a grave risk to their well-being. Migrant farm workers are but one example of how the confluence of group memberships affects health.

SOCIAL STRUCTURE AND THE EPIDEMIOLOGY OF DISEASE

We have alluded to differential risks of disease among groups. Analysis of the relation between disease risk and social groupings is the domain of social epidemiology. A two-part revolution has occurred in social epidemiology: one in the most prevalent causes of disease mortality in industrial society and another in our approach to disease.

The Revolution in Disease Epidemiology

Disease evolves as mankind evolves (50). As new technology and the ways in which we organize work, leisure, health care, and public health reduce the threat of any given disease, that same technology and organization lead to the primacy of new diseases. We have seen, especially within this century, the primary causes of mortality shift from environmental threat (famine, exposure, animal attacks) to acute and infectious diseases (e.g., smallpox, plague), to chronic diseases. Today the major causes of morbidity and mortality are chronic and degenerative diseases, principally cardiovascular disease, stroke, cancer, diabetes, and chronic obstructive lung disease (COPD) (51). What is compelling about these chronic diseases is that their incidence (new cases) and prevalence (active cases) are affected substantially by behavior: dietary fat, sedentary lifestyle, high sodium diets, work exposure to carcinogens, smoking, and so forth. Thus, the distribution of social behaviors in a population is also the path of distribution of disease. For example, as more women began smoking, their rate of lung cancer increased.

There is currently a shift in the prevalence of one disease over another. Since 1965 the rates of mortality from cardiovascular disease and stroke have dropped steadily (52). Reasons include reduction of dietary cholesterol, more exercise, and aggressive management of hypertension. However, the cancer death rate is rising, and within our lifetime will likely supplant cardiovascular disease as the major cause of death in the United States (52).

Cancer is a disease of industrial society. More prevalent in industrialized regions of the U.S. (41), it manifests itself as a set of diseases related to exposures to radiation, carcinogenic chemicals, air pollution, and asbestos (41). The U.S. is struggling to deal with such exposures to reduce cancer mortality. Like cardiovascular disease, cancer is a product of social behaviors unevenly distributed in the society along predictable lines.

If Dubos (50) is correct, and we successfully reduce cancer risk, will a new set of diseases in the postindustrial age succeed cancer as the leading cause of death? This is possible, even likely. Postindustrial society may be beset by iatrogenic diseases (diseases *caused* by medical care), fast-mutating retroviruses, or autoimmune diseases (diseases of allergy to one's own tissues). Much depends on our new technology and our behavior. If we depend heavily on radiation as a new technological tool, will we see an increase in cancers and blood dyscrasias (abnormalities of the blood's cells or its other components)? Will high-energy electrical transmissions produce disease?

Several predictions are possible. There will be a new round of diseases. Distribution of these diseases will be uneven, following the tracks of ethnicity, social class, occupation, age, and sex, as always. Life expectancy will continue to rise. And, still more medical practice will focus on the elderly.

The Revolution in Disease Intervention

Just as we have seen a shift from primary prevalence of acute, infectious diseases to chronic, degenerative ones, the medical model of disease has also shifted. Prior to Virchow's *Cellular Pathology* (53), notions of disease were confounded with theories of four humors (black bile, yellow bile, phlegm, and mucus), the imbalance of which caused disease. With the work of Pasteur, Lister, and Koch, a germ theory of disease ushered in laboratory medicine, yielding vaccines, antibiotics, and laboratory tests.

There is now another shift. We appreciate better that disease in the real world does not act as if in the laboratory, that the pathogen does not itself explain the disease (i.e., it is a necessary but not sufficient cause). Often the patient does not become ill unless compromised immunologically by poor nutrition, immunosuppressive agents, or stress. Looking at disease in the real world, therefore, requires not only looking for the agent of disease (the pathogen), but also asking, What is the nature of the reservoir (the host, the organism or substance sustaining the pathogen; often the person in human disease)? Further, one must ask, What environmental forces bring the host and agent symbolically together? Host, agent, and environment are variables in an epidemiological model (actually, a biopsychosocial model) wherein disease must be understood in its ecologic framework.

This alerts us to new modes of disease intervention. Instead of simply treating disease, we consider primary prevention: altering the relation between the host, agent, and environment so the disease never occurs. Instead of treating St. Louis encephalitis in a hospital, we can prevent the agent, a virus, from travelling from its blackbird host by a mosquito vector (an insect or other invertebrate that transmits the infection by inoculation) to its human victim. We can spray for mosquitoes or advise people to use insect repellent. We can encourage people toward physical activity, reduced fat intake, smoking cessation, and control of hypertension to lessen the incidence of cardiovascular disease. Likewise, rather than treating HIV infection, we can influence the behavior of needle users and sexually active people. By understanding the social epidemiology of disease, we can reduce its incidence and prevalence.

SOCIAL STRUCTURE AND BEHAVIORAL RESPONSE TO DISEASE

Group memberships also can affect people's response to illness. The medical model of disease assumes a direct relation between pathophysiology and illness. This is not always the case: 1000 college students were asked if they had any of 12 symptoms (e.g., runny nose, raw, scratchy throat), and 80% reported having at least one (54). All were in class, however, and not ill. They gave evidence of disease, a state of identifiable pathophysiology, but they were not ill by virtue of having claimed a reduced function.

Health, Illness, Sickness, and Disease

We distinguish between disease, sickness, and illness. Disease is the dimension with which most physicians are most comfortable. Disease is evidenced through clinical examination or laboratory diagnosis. The principal indicator of disease to the physician is a pathological finding.

Sickness is the patient's experience of not being well; the evidence of sickness is the experience of symptoms—pain, fatigue, and so forth. Often, however, the physician diagnoses disease when the patient feels no sickness. This often occurs with the diagnoses of hypertension, hypercholesterolemia, or premature ventricular contraction. How then can you convey to the patient the need for prompt medical intervention?

The distinctions between sickness and disease are illustrated by two examples:

Mr. Archer suffered a ruptured vertebral disk which placed pressure on the sciatic nerve. He suffered pain along the nerve tract and "foot drop" (loss of control of the left foot), so he was given a medical leave from his job as a mailman. He stayed at home and had subsequent surgery for removal of a ruptured disk. Following surgery, he complained of continued loss of function and was fitted for a leg brace. He can now walk with the leg brace and has been referred for physical therapy. It is expected that with physical therapy and an exercise program, he will regain full ability to walk. However, he continues to complain of pain and inability to walk easily. He has not attended physical therapy treatments regularly. His wife and family report that he has been permanently incapacitated by his back problems. His physician and the Post Office's consulting physician no longer see evidence of disease. *He may not be diseased, but he is sick.* (It is likely that he is suffering from somatic anxiety [p. 69]).

Mrs. Bartlett was seen for a routine gynecologic examination, at which time her gynecologist found her blood pressure (BP) elevated to 180/120. She was referred to her internist, who found a consistently elevated BP over a 3-week period. The internist prescribed a low sodium diet, weight loss of 30 pounds, a program of walking for exercise, attention to easing job stress, antihypertensive medication, and a return visit after 6 weeks. It has now been over a year. Mrs. Bartlett was intercepted in a routine public health screening by a public health nurse who found her BP to be 200/130. Mrs. Bartlett told the nurse that, indeed, her physician had identified the hypertension earlier, but that she felt fine except for some morning headaches and saw no reason to take drugs and get everyone upset. "After all," she said, "if you get everyone all riled up, you can't enjoy your health." *Mrs. Bartlett has a disease but is not sick.*

The practitioner's frustration at being unable to convince a patient who feels well that he or she has a disease is understandable. So, too, is the frustration of the patient who feels sick but cannot demonstrate disease. The patient who has dysmenorrhea, chronic fatigue syndrome, or insomnia may have difficulties translating these symptoms into understandable diagnostic criteria of disease, and so may drift from physician to physician looking for one who will properly diagnose the complaint.

This is doubly problematic when the patient is from a minority group, has limited English fluency, and faces a physician unfamiliar with "folk" diagnosis. Among Mexican-Americans, some middle-aged women suffer from *susto* (marked by lethargy, fatigue, and malaise) (13–15), for which there is no diagnosis in the American medical lexicon. Faced with a woman who has susto, the practitioner has trouble finding a disease label. For the patient and her family, this is a real sickness with consequences.

When the physician and the patient agree, the physician noting disease and the patient feeling sick, the patient can be considered ill. Illness is the legitimate, socially validated status of being sick and diseased. With illness comes the sick role.

THE STRUCTURE OF THE SICK ROLE

The sick role links the worlds of patient and physician. It is a specific role the patient enters when all players agree that the patient is unable to handle normal obligations because of illness. It contains for the patient two rights and two obligations (55).

The two rights are blamelessness and relaxed role obligations, powerful incentives for entering the role. Blamelessness implies that the patient will not be held responsible for his or her illness. This is usually unproblematic. The alcoholic wishing to be labelled ill rather than deviant, however, may have difficulty achieving blamelessness, as may the smoker who has COPD, the teenager who is pregnant, and the person who has AIDS. Yet the health practitioner's role is to treat, not judge. The ill are admitted to the sick role on evidence of disease and sickness. Nevertheless, when the diseased claim entry into the sick role and their blamelessness is questioned, they may be stigmatized.

Relaxed role obligations release the ill person from being responsible for fulfilling other role obligations because of the illness. This relaxation of role obligations, coupled with blamelessness, is a desirable status to the extent that it relieves the ill person of having to do and be responsible for the tasks of everyday life, while having the right to be cared for. The potential for wholesale claims of incapacity based on illness are so seductive that powerful disincentives are in place to prevent an epidemic of unwarranted claims of illness. Such disincentives as loss of salary, loss of important family roles, and the need to undergo treatment in order to validate illness work to limit the numbers of persons who claim illness when symptoms are minor or absent.

The patient's two obligations as part of the sick role are to seek professional help and to comply with the prescribed regimen. To gain access to the sick role, the ill person must present to a certified agent of treatment, usually a physician, for care. Implicit also is that this agent of care is competent to discriminate if the patient is diseased as well as sick. The physician serves two masters here: the patient and society. On one hand, the physician is the agent of the patient in assessing symptoms and in diagnosing and organizing treatment. On the other hand, the physician acts as an agent of society in diagnosing and denying access to the sick role to those not truly ill. In submitting to diagnostic and treatment procedures, the patient agrees to the second obligation to comply with physician orders, despite discomfort and difficulty. The classic question, "Don't you want to get well?" reflects that compliance is the price of entry into the sick role.

SOCIAL STRUCTURE AND MODELS OF HEALTH CARE UTILIZATION

Once patients have identified symptoms or health risks and wish to submit to being ill or to prevent illness, they must consider using the health care system. One of the key assumptions in this system is that patients seek service on their own. The system is a vendor of services to clients in a marketplace (56). Although this is not the only model of health care delivery, it is the most common in our society. Other models have been seen in an army at war, in rural health care delivery in China, or in a public health model. In these the system comes to the patient and not vice-versa (57).

This assumption has a corollary. Health care delivery is driven by patient demand for services (sickness), not medical need (disease) for services. Patients seek services they want. They may want attention to a cosmetic problem or a routine physical examination with certification of good health. They may not appreciate the physician's unsolicited lecture on stopping smoking (although physicians should recommend that smokers stop), reducing saturated fat intake, or exercising, although this is what the practitioner feels is most needed.

The Health Belief Model

The most accepted theoretical model of health care utilization, the health belief model (57–59), is based on the value-expectancy theory that people have sets of values, health among them, and decide logically how to implement those values. The model posits six variables that predict who will and will not seek care. These are (1) perceived susceptibility to illness, (2) perceived seriousness of the illness, (3) perceived benefits of seeking care, (4) perceived costs of care, (5) cues to action, and (6) motivation to health (57–59).

The model is simple. In research, it asks the potential users of health services if they perceive they are susceptible to an illness, if the illness has serious consequences, and if care will reduce susceptibility to the disease or reduce its seriousness. If so, is the cost in money, time, inconvenience, or embarrassment worth the reduced risk? What cues led to contemplating the risk? Perhaps a friend was ill with a similar diagnosis, or an ad campaign pointed out the risk. How motivated is the patient to maintain health?

The health belief model has been tested repeatedly, and it repeatedly predicts health care utilization. It consequently has spawned educational campaigns to raise people's awareness of susceptibility, seriousness of the disease, benefits of care, ease of care, and the importance of health. Patient education by professionals is based on this model.

The model works well for persons who have the socioeconomic resources to make rational decisions. But we have seen that the perceived susceptibility, consequences, and benefits of care are not the only determinants of whether care is sought. The poor face barriers that make it virtually impossible for them to exercise initiative in seeking care. The health belief model seems applicable primarily to America's urban middle class. The urban and rural poor, persons who are non-English-speaking, older adults who have limited physical mobility, all find barriers to access. For them, the model is irrelevant (60).

Alternative Models of Health Care Utilization

SUCHMAN'S MODEL

Although the health belief model is the most widely used theory of utilization, it is not the only one. Edward Suchman's model (61, 62) is rooted in the concept of the sick role. Suchman based his work on the notion of illness career in which the patient experiences stages of illness that call for different approaches. The career refers to the course of an illness. The first stage is symptom experience. The person feels something is wrong and attempts folk remedies, over-the-counter medication, and alteration of daily routine. When this fails to relieve symptoms, especially when symptoms interfere with daily roles, the person relinquishes some of these roles and claims the sick role as a reason. The sick role can be provisionally validated by the person's lay network, but formal responsibilities such as job and school require authoritative validation. Many persons never reach this stage; if access to care is unavailable, they may languish in a self-assigned sick role with no physician to legitimize their incapacity or to invalidate the claim. Nevertheless, there is now social pressure on the person to seek care. The pressures of symptoms, role loss, and need for legitimate entry into the sick role are balanced by social barriers to care. If these barriers are surmountable and the pressures are sufficient, the sick person makes medical care contact, becomes a patient, and must then accept the obligations of the sick role.

Suchman's model underscores some dilemmas the patient experiences in reaching the point of health care utilization. The alert physician can ask meaningfully what symptoms let the patient know something was wrong. How did those symptoms affect other roles? What nostrums or adaptations were tried? What circumstances caused the patient to seek care?

This model does not deal as adeptly with chronic diseases as it does with acute ones. This true in the last stages of the patient's illness career, the stages of treatment and rehabilitation.

ANDERSEN'S MODEL

Ronald Andersen (63) attempts to develop a comprehensive model of health care utilization, positing that three factors affect health care behavior: predisposing, enabling, and need variables. Predisposing variables describe lifestyle, the social behaviors that produce risk of disease in a population. Enabling variables are the family and community resources that making health care utilization possible. They include income, geographic location, and knowledge of the health care system. Need, as Andersen defines it, refers to the patient's perception of need. This is not need as we have termed it, but demand. The patient may perceive the need for liposuction for a weight problem, whereas the physician may feel this is a demand, not a need. For Andersen, the perception of need is what matters. His model is often used by researchers and theorists because it predicts the health care utilization behavior of *groups* of persons. Unlike the health belief model, which poses patient education as an appropriate *clinical* intervention, Andersen's model does not point toward techniques for changing the behavior of specific patients. Thus, it has less utility for clinical decision making.

ADHERENCE TO A PRESCRIBED REGIMEN

Primary prevention implies behavioral change: helping patients to stop smoking (p. 79), curtail drinking (p. 292), modify diet (p. 81), eliminate toxic exposures, change sedentary lifestyles, and reduce stress. This requires patient adherence to a regimen.

If primary prevention is not possible and the patient becomes ill, chronic disease management usually requires long-term medication and behavioral change to prevent complications and early death. For physicians, as agents of change, to assume their job is done when the diagnosis is complete and the treatment explained is to practice half of medicine. Medicine includes not only insightful diagnosis but also sensitivity to the patient's need for help in modifying those behaviors that affect the disease. This requires that the patient adhere to the treatment regimen.

To achieve successful compliance, physicians may first need to ease the transition for patients from seeing themselves as sick or healthy to seeing themselves as ill. Such transition may require explaining to the hypertensive (or hypercholesterolemic, etc.) patient that although he or she feels fine, there is an imminent threat to health. This means assessing the patient's health beliefs and addressing susceptibility, consequences, costs of and barriers to treatment, and the patient's motivation.

Patients who have hypertension and hyper-cholesterolemia therefore need careful explanation of their susceptibility to cardiovascular disease, the consequences of their two conditions for their arteries, and the costs of treatment in terms of altered diet, medication, routine medical monitoring, and time allotted for exercise and relaxation. Moreover, patients should face and assess their motives toward health and, if necessary, discuss with their physician the reasons why they should work at moderating their lifestyle. These are all elements of the health belief model.

In addition, however, another variable in the model must be addressed: barriers to treatment. Physicians must help their patients assess access to a continuum of care. Is there a nurse at the factory who can monitor the person's blood pressure? Is there a local laboratory where blood samples can be drawn? Does the person have access at the community hospital to a dietician? Is there a program on dealing with stress offered at the adult education center, an exercise group at the local department of recreation? Facilitating the patient's access to a continuum of care is part of the medical treatment. To offer a prescription for behavioral change that the patient cannot fill is to miss half of the obligation of treatment.

The patient's obligation, mandated by the sick role, is to try to get well. This means adherence to the prescribed regimen. The same variables of the health belief model that predict the use of treatment services predict adherence to prescribed regimen as well. Facilitating access to care and encouraging adherence are part of the physician's job.

Locus of Control

Two of the physician's tools in managing patient adherence are the health belief model and Suchman's model. Another is the health locus of control (64, 65), which asks the patient to identify what forces control the person's health. The concept of health locus of control identifies three types of controls: internal, powerful others, and chance (or fate).

Patients who have an internal locus see themselves as in charge of their own health, i.e., if they take care of themselves they will not become ill. If they become ill, their own caregiving makes them well. They take direct responsibility for their health.

Those who have a powerful others locus do not see themselves as responsible for their health. They see the physician as responsible for their care, their spouses as responsible for their nutrition, their bosses for their safety on the job, others for their stress. The final group has a chance or fate locus in which health is controlled by fate, chance, or God. Nothing the person can do changes health outcomes. If you are meant to be ill or to die, it will be so. The latter two types of locus of control are often merged into an external locus in which the patient delegates control of his or her health, taking no responsibility.

You might assume that the patient whose locus is internal would be easy to manage and the patient with an external locus frustrating. In fact, both are easy and both are frustrating. Patients with an internal locus typically take charge of their health in an outpatient setting. They follow a prescribed regimen well. But they will also make independent decisions on drug dosages, exercise, and nutritional regimens. They are in control, not the physician. This is fine, of course, until the patient suffers a drug interaction or the medication is ineffective because of the changed dose. Such patients can be troublesome in inpatient settings, when they insist on active participation in continued control over treatment (normally desirable) while you want them assured, unworried, and on bed rest.

Patients whose locus is external usually do well as inpatients. They have their orders, they are closely monitored, and they have few decisions to make. Bed rest is usually an easy order to follow. As outpatients, however, they cannot be relied on to attend to symptoms, to respond to subtle changes in their condition, or come for an office visit without pressure from someone.

As a physician, your best tool in dealing with these two types of patients is your interaction style. Patients who have an internal locus of control are poised to be team members. They are most comfortable as your partner in negotiating the nature of the treatment and what is expected. A physician interaction style that emphasizes openness, transmission of information, and willingness to negotiate aspects of the treatment works well here. Being authoritative, nondisclosive, or asking them to follow orders leaves them dissatisfied.

Offering autonomy to patients whose locus is external may also be counterproductive. They need to be told exactly what to do. They do well with written instructions. A valuable adjunct in promoting their adherence to a regimen is having a family member in the office to listen to the regimen along with the patient. This patient does well with an authoritative interaction style. In summary, you need to assess the patient's behavior and prescribe both a medical and a behavioral regimen.

Tailoring Behavioral Interventions to Patient Needs

Making a behavioral diagnosis means evaluating the patient according to the health belief model, the patient's course throgh an illness career, and locus of control. Once you have a sense of the social forces that impinge on the patient, and the person's health beliefs, you can better draw on resources for intervention. You can provide individual counselling, include a family member, or refer the patient to a health educator at the local hospital or service agency (Alzheimer's Association, Ileostomy and Colostomy Association, Planned Parenthood, etc.). These agencies provide group lectures, audio-visual aids, printed materials, and peer group discussions. They uniformly welcome physician referrals and are glad to consult with the patient and the physician. If you are unfamiliar with community resources, the social service department at your hospital will help. These departments have lists of community resources that accept physician referrals.

Finally, you must understand that the practice of medicine cannot solve all problems. Some patients are in situations in which behavioral change is impossible. When your effort has not achieved results with persistent attempts, you must be able to counsel the patient that you have done as good a job as can be done, and go on to the next patient.

9/Evolutionary Biology and Human Behavior

Thomas B. Mackenzie, M.D., and Jerome Kroll, M.D.

OBJECTIVES

GENERAL OBJECTIVE: Given a common human behavior, explain it in sociobiologic terms.

SPECIFIC OBJECTIVES:
1. Discuss the steps in human evolution from *Australopithecus* to *Homo sapiens*, noting regional continuity and Noah's Ark theories.
2. List characteristics that distinguish humans from other hominids.
3. Discuss the three competing explanations of bipedalism.
4. Explain sexual dimorphism, reproductive fitness, inclusive fitness, and K and R strategies.
5. Discuss ecologic pressure, niches, phylogenetic inertia, genetic variation, and kin recognition.
6. Provide sociobiologic explanations of altruism, ritualized fighting, sibling rivalry, hierarchies, and cooperation.
7. Discuss strengths and weaknesses of sociobiologic theory.

In trying to understand human behavior, the prospect of ignoring upbringing and experience seems foolish. Neither can human behavior be understood without knowledge of human evolution. Yet that is what modern psychiatry does. Open most psychiatry textbooks and you will find nary a word about the evolution of the human race. How can we be so mindful of ontogeny, the history of the individual, and so ignorant of phylogeny, the history of our species? The history of our species can tell us much about our behavior. The basic tasks of mammalian existence—self preservation, resource acquisition and defense, mate selection, courtship, reproduction, childrearing, and development and maintenance of hierarchies and alliances within social systems—are not unique to humans. As we evolved from ancestors, we did not eliminate their behavioral adaptations; we modified and extended them. Our everyday behavior is based on behavioral patterns tens of thousands to millions of years old, the influence of which is largely out of our awareness.

TAXONOMY

An understanding of the history of our species begins with the taxonomy that positions us in the animal kingdom. Binomial classification (1) was developed by Linnaeus (1707–1778). Every living thing has a species, genus, family, order, class, and phylum. Modern humans are identified in Table 9.1. Included in the order primates are monkeys, lemurs,

Table 9.1.   Classification of Modern Humans

Phylum	Chordata (having a notochord*)
Class	Mammalia (mammals)
Order	Primates
Superfamily	Hominoidea (also hominoids)
Family	Hominidae (also hominids)
Genus	Homo (meaning man)
Species	Sapiens (meaning wise)

*A notochord is a flexible rod that constitutes a primitive back-bone and is present in all chordates at some point in their development. In virtually all vertebrates, the notochord is replaced by the vertebral column.

Table 9.2.   Chronology of the Earth

Creation of Earth	4.5 billion years ago
First life (algae, bacteria)	3.5 billion years ago
Amphibians on land	345 million years ago
Reptiles on land	300 million years ago
First mammals	200 million years ago
First hominids (human ancestors)	5 million years ago
Last ice age	12,000 years ago
Agriculture begins	10,000 years ago

apes, and humans. The superfamily *Hominoidea* (hominoids) consists of the lesser and greater apes and humans, and the family *Hominidea* (hominids) is confined to humans and our extinct relatives distinct from the apes.

To put our emergence into perspective, it is useful to view our planet's history (Table 9.2). Mammals appeared roughly 200 million years ago; our first ancestors (hominids) emerged about 5 million years ago.

EVOLUTIONARY BIOLOGY

The known record of human evolution begins with *Australopithecus* ("southern ape"), named by Dart in 1924 when he discovered the skull of a child near Taung, South Africa. Remains of similar beings were subsequently found at several African sites, although some were not directly in the human evolutionary line. The most famous find is the skeleton of "Lucy," recovered in Ethiopia in 1974 (2). Several distinct species of *Australopithecus* roamed Africa, upright, as early as 5 million years ago. Anatomic differences from their hominoid ancestors reflected a shift to bipedal locomotion: a longer lower limb, alignment of

the great toe and a broadened heel, straightening of the lateral toes, and a low broadened pelvic girdle. Skull volumes indicate that enlargement of the brain had not begun (brain size ranged from 350–530 cubic centimeters [cc] compared to 1330 cc in modern humans), and the external cerebral cortical architecture resembled that of apes rather than human descendants. Growth and development of these creatures corresponded more closely to that of apes than to the prolonged childhood maturation of modern humans. Size estimates of *Australopithecus* suggest a marked difference between males and females, the average male being 5 feet and 150 pounds, compared to 3 feet and 75 pounds for females. No evidence exists that these hominids used spoken language, tools, or fire, or that they built habitations (3). Rather than hunting, they probably scavenged off kills of carnivores. They probably slept in trees or on cliffs to avoid predators.

The next evolutionary step was unearthed in 1964 by Louis Leakey and named *Homo habilis* (handy man)—they were the first to manufacture and use simple pebble tools (4). These habilines lived in East Africa from about 1.5 to 2 million years ago. Although no larger than australopithecines, they had larger brains (about 600 cc). It is tempting to relate their capacity to use tools to their increased brain size.

In 1984 a skeleton dated to 1.6 million years ago was recovered in Kenya. It was an early representative of *Homo erectus* (upright man), the next step in the path to *Homo sapiens*. Brain volume was 900 cc, 50% larger than in *Homo habilis*. However, the chest was conical, rather than barrel shaped like modern *Homo sapiens*. *Homo erectus* gathered seeds and fruits, hunted in an organized manner, fashioned tools, and used fire (5).

Paleontologists believe that *Homo erectus* migrated out of Africa about 1 million years ago. Remains of *H. erectus* have been found in Java, Peking, and Eurasia. *Homo erectus* in Africa continued to evolve, eventually becoming archaic or early modern man (*Homo sapiens*). Although not along lines identical to their African relatives, *H. erectus* in Europe, Asia, Indonesia, and Australia also evolved. The differences in evolution undoubtedly reflected different ecologic variables (e.g., diet, climate, predators). By 100,000 years ago, one branch of European *H. erectus* had become *Homo sapiens neanderthalensis*, or Neandertal man (the first specimen was found in Germany's Neander Valley). Neandertal man was heavily muscled with powerful jaws and a prominent brow. His brain volume equalled that of modern man (about 1330 cc). Neandertals buried their dead with ceremony, suggesting symbolic thinking. Although the neuroanatomic substrates for speech (reflected by brain markings etched on fossil skulls) were developed in some Neandertal brains, whether they used language is uncertain—most had tiny throats.

Theories of the Evolutionary Step to *Homo Sapiens Sapiens*

Two theories, not mutually exclusive, attempt to explain the final step in human evolution (6). The regional continuity (multiregional origins) theory posits that modern humans (*Homo sapiens sapiens*) evolved from *H. erectus* simultaneously, but independently, at multiple sites around the world. There was breeding between neighboring groups (gene flow) sufficient to maintain similarities and prevent emergence of novel species. In this theory, only one major migration out of Eastern Africa (about 1 million years ago) occurred. This migrant, *H. erectus*, was the blueprint for modern man.

The Noah's Ark (Mother of us all, single origin) theory proposes that African *H. erectus* evolved into a regional version of archaic *H. sapiens*, which about 200,000 years ago migrated from Africa (the second recent migration) and triumphed over locally evolved versions of archaic *H. sapiens* like Neandertal man. The nature of this triumph is not clear. In Europe, for example, Neandertals could have been outcompeted by the African *H. sapiens*, or destroyed by genocide. The latter explanation is credible because fossil evidence of the Neandertals dramatically disappears about 35,000 years ago. Possibly the muscular, thickskulled Neandertals were vanquished because they relied on their powerful jaws and lacked sophisticated hunting weapons (perhaps the first arms race).

Molecular Genetics and Emergence of *Homo Sapiens Sapiens*

Molecular genetics informs this controversy. Mitochondria contain DNA inherited exclusively from the mother and thus not altered by sexual reproduction. By studying the base composition of mitochondrial DNA in modern humans, proponents of the two-migration theory deduce that current (relatively slight) differences across regional groups correspond to the change expected if all beings had started with the same mitochondrial DNA (i.e., the same mother) about 250,000 years ago (7). More differences in mitochondrial DNA are seen within than between groups, evidence that the groups came from the same stem. At the regional sites there is little fossil evidence of evolution from *H. erectus* to modern *H. sapiens*; had the latter occurred, intermediate forms should exist. Opponents of the Noah's Ark theory debunk the precision of time estimates based on mutation rates, claiming the mitochondrial clock could be off by hundreds of thousands of years.

It seems that the truth lies between these two theories, and that there was no unitary emergence of modern man. Although we have written of *Homo erectus* as a uniform species, it is clear that once they migrated across the world 1 million years ago, different types emerged. One branch, the African type, was able to best other types in a variety of ecologic conditions.

The Role of Bipedalism

Five characteristics separate man from other hominoids: bipedality, reduced anterior dentition with molar predominance, unique sexual and reproductive behavior, a large neocortex, and material culture (8). Likely, the first step toward modern man was adoption of bipedal locomotion. Mary Leakey (9) commented that the outstanding evolutionary question is, What selection pressures produced bipedalism? There are three theories. One is that by liberating the hands, bipedalism enabled *Australopithecus* to produce tools and weapons, enhancing the hunting efficiency and protection from predation. However, evidence of tool-making postdates the origin of bipedality by about 1 million years. Presumably, the adaptive advantages conferred on those who walked upright had to be more immediate to favor their survival. A variant of this theory is that the hands were not liberated as much as the feet enslaved. Committed to a striding gait, the neurologic connections giving the feet the same adroitness as the arms in climbing were released to further refine arm action (9). Calvin (10) asked, "Did throwing stones lead to bigger brains?" To throw a stone accurately at 20 feet, the stone must be released at a critical moment lasting 1/1600 of a second. Released before or after this launch window, it misses its target. Such timing requires an extraordinarily precise neurologic sequencer.

The second explanation of the advantage conferred by bipedality is that its possessors filled the unoccupied niche of migrating scavenger. This pictures the upright *Australopithecus* following herds of ungulates (e.g., zebras), providing greater access to carcasses than scavenging in a fixed territory. This assumes the earliest hominid was a meat eater. Evidence suggests, however, that dentition was evolving from prominent canines and incisors to broad molars, opposing what would be expected if scavenging were a dominant feeding mode.

Lovejoy (8) advanced a third possibility, the provisioning thesis: ecologic conditions and reproductive pressures at the time of *Australopithecus* favored upright posture because it allowed males to carry provisions back to monogamous females and their offspring. To clarify, we introduce several concepts regarding sexual reproduction.

Sexual Reproduction, Dimorphism, and Mating Strategies

Sexual reproduction involves participation of two organisms to produce an offspring by uniting a gamete from each, each gamete contributing half the genetic material. This method of reproduction increases genetic diversity, fostering survival under varied environmental conditions. As each gamete is produced in meiosis, the paired chromosomes exchange genetic material, creating gene combinations on a single chromosome novel to the gamete. The gamete combines with a distinct set of chromosomes from the other partner. These sources of variation dwarf changes that could occur by mutation.

In theory, both gametes could consist of only genetic material, which would be precarious for the new organism because it would lack nutrients and a constant environment. Perhaps to efficiently ensure nutrients and a constant environment, sexual reproduction evolved so that the contribution of each parent is distinct and unequal. One of the two gametes, the egg, has nutrients as well as genetic material. One of the two parents often provides the fertilized egg with a supportive environment. These features lead to sexual dimorphism—different structure and function of the two parents contributing the gametes. These differences in the sexes lead to distinct reproductive organs, cycles, metabolic demands and mating strategies. Among mammals, the female has a finite number of eggs, can produce only a limited number of offspring across her reproductive cycle, and must nourish the fetus and then the child through a dependent, vulnerable period. This investment in time and energy is considerable. The male produces millions of gametes with little energy expenditure. The limitation to the number of offspring he can sire is his access to reproductively competent females. The optimal reproductive strategy for the female is to be impregnated by a male with high genetic fitness and then foster his contribution to rearing their offspring. To the extent that genetic fitness (size, strength, speed, etc.) and commitment to assist in childrearing (willingness to gather food, defend against aggressors, etc.) do not coexist in a given male, females may have to choose between them. For the male, the issue is which of two strategies to pursue: either copulate with as many females as possible and let them rear the young (perhaps fighting other males for access to females), or bond with a single female with the greatest genetic fitness and contribute to the rearing of the offspring in multiple ways, including protection, food acquisition, and child supervision. An intermediate strategy for a male would be to ally with a powerful male and copulate when opportunity presents itself. The female is always certain of her contribution to the offspring; the male can never be absolutely certain of his contribution. Perhaps for this reason, the commonest cause of marital homicide is jealousy (11).

Natural Selection

We elaborate on several evolutionary principles. The first is natural selection, introduced by Darwin. This favors the survival and reproductive success of individual animals possessing genetically determined attributes that allow them to function more effectively in a given environment. These attributes are passed to their offspring who then have an advantage in survival and reproduction over other members of the species. The attribute could be size, strength, stamina, quickness, visual acuity, capacity to nurture, to chew or digest certain food sources, perform precise manipulations, and so forth. The capacity of an attribute to confer advantage is determined by the environment in which it arises. Greater size could be advantageous or disadvantageous, depending on the setting (e.g., small size in a species might be favored because of concealment). Natural selection is the engine that drives evolution. As we have seen on p. 106, although the fossil record may permit identification of structural attributes that must have conferred advantage on their bearers (or those with the attribute would not have flourished), it is hard to reconstruct what aspect of the environment determined the adaptive advantage.

Reproductive Fitness and Altruism

Reproductive fitness (individual fitness) measures the number of offspring an individual produces relative to the number of offspring produced by others of the same species. One way to assess fitness is to determine how many of an animal's offspring survive into the next generation and bear offspring. Does an animal with no offspring have zero fitness? In 1964, Hamilton advanced the seminal concept of inclusive fitness (12). Unlike individual fitness, which measures only an individual's direct offspring, inclusive fitness accounts for the fact that one's relatives possess a certain percentage of genes identical to one's own. In first-degree relatives (see p. 64), the percentage is 50%, in second-degree relatives 25%, and so forth. Therefore, some of an individual's genes may pass into the next generation even if he has no offspring. An animal might have no offspring, but have high inclusive fitness because of successful efforts to rear or protect a sibling's offspring. This is kin selection, which posits that individuals will act altruistically toward others based upon degree of genetic relatedness. Altruism is defined as increasing the individual fitness of another (e.g., a second cousin) at the expense of *your* individual fitness. Sacrifice towards one's offspring is not genetic altruism; one's individual fitness is increased by enhancing the fitness of offspring.

Natural selection makes no distinction between females and males. The term sexual selection denotes adaptive changes that appear in only one gender. Logically, changes that occur in one sex but not the other involve functions unique to that sex. Two types of sexual selection are identified. Epigamic selection refers to evolutionary changes designed to better attract the opposite sex. If appearance among males (e.g., brightness of color attractive to females) gave an advantage in courtship or mating, such a trait, if heritable, would become more plentiful because males with it would have more mating opportunities. However, advantages conferred by bright coloration might be offset by easier predator detection. Emergence of traits adaptive in one area is often constrained by liabilities of the same trait. Epigamic selection among females would be evident when monogamous relationships are the rule: females might evolve features that make them more attractive to the fittest male, the one evidencing the most adaptive genetic constitution.

Intrasexual selection involves direct competition between members of the same sex. In males, this involves evolution of traits (e.g., size, strength, incisor size, cleverness) that give the bearer an advantage in competition for females.

K and r are reproductive strategies that represent opposite ends of a continuum. In the r strategy the number of offspring is maximized, with progeny receiving minimal parental care, e.g., frogs. The K strategy is reduction in number of offspring, with maximal parental investment in each progeny, e.g., humans.

Returning to Lovejoy's provisioning hypothesis (8), the primate order shows a trend toward an increased individual life span. Increases in a species' life span are accompanied by tendencies toward longer infant dependency, prolonged gestation, single births, later sexual maturity, and longer interval between pregnancies. An increase in these variables favors a K strategy with greater parental investment for longer periods in fewer offspring. For advanced primates to maintain population stability in face of increased longevity and the concomitant changes in reproductive physiology, there must be reduction in infant mortality and shortening of the interval between births (the latter is the only physiologic variable enumerated above that the organism can control). Mortality rates reflect both genetic and ecological variables, only the latter accessible to short-term modification. Causes of death such as predation, accident, infection, and famine could be mitigated by strong social bonds, high intelligence, intense parenting, and long periods of learning (8).

Lovejoy (8) posits that to survive and increase in numbers, terrestrial bipedal hominids of 5 million years ago must have modified both the space between births and survival of offspring. This could not have depended on either material culture (tools) or brain expansion, because neither appeared for at least 2 million years. The critical modification, he believes, came in social behavior.

To increase infant survival, more attention from the female would be necessary. Yet attention would be limited by the mother having to forage for the infant and herself. Lovejoy pictures the ecology of Africa at that time (grasslands, savannah, woodland, forests) as requiring movement between relatively sparse food sites. Infant mortality secondary to accidents would be least if females with infants foraged in a central area, while males were far-reaching in search of food. However, such a division of resource acquisition would be cost effective only if males supported the survival of their progeny and did not lose consort relationships. Such obstacles would be minimized by monogamous pair bonds. A male would then forage at a distance in order not to compete with his offspring and mate for food (also allowing more maternal attention to the offspring) and also return to the family with supplies, transportation of which was permitted by having the arms free. This is the provisioning dimension of the theory. Thus assisted, the female would have greater food supplies, allowing shortening of the interval between pregnancies. The first tools may have been devices for carrying provisions, not weapons (8).

Increasing K-type demographics forced greater involvement in the reproductive process upon the male. Monogamy led to a direct contribution of both parents to the care of the offspring. Polygynous (males mate with two or more females) patterns require the male to constantly rebuff male competitors, reducing the opportunity to contribute to the viability of his offspring by providing food and supervision. Further, conditions postulated to exist 5 million years ago indicate no superabundance of food, which disadvantaged single-parent (maternal) nutrition of offspring.

Lovejoy points to human sexual behavior as favoring monogamous bonding. Human females are continuously receptive sexually, and have no recognizable indicator of their menstrual phase. Male approach is continuous, and copulation is not synchronized with ovulation. Because no markers identify optimal breeding periods, regular copulation would be necessary to ensure fertilization. That random, promiscuous copulation might not lead to fertilization would give repeated intercourse with the same mate equal footing as a reproductive strategy. Also, in contrast to monogamously sired offspring, promiscuously sired offspring would not receive the support of the male parent, if the male consort suspected he was not the parent. Consequently, marital fidelity would have roots in biology.

A monogamous mating structure tends to select for epigamic dimorphism in both sexes, with males and females both adorned with characteristics that attract members of the opposite sex. In polygynous mammals, only the male is adorned. In monogamous mammals, females do not share the fittest male, but have to compete among themselves for him. This competition may take the form of adornment, such as makeup, jewelry, and attractive clothing.

Lovejoy emphasizes that a K-strategy model postulates that intensified parenting, monogamy, specialized sexual-reproductive behavior, and bipedality all predated tools and brain development. If so, the most basic feature of our ancestors was sociability and capacity for bonding, not language, abstract thought, ceremonies, or material culture. This might explain why emotional attachments, losses, dependency, and loyalty inspire eloquence, while defying precision of language. For example, a parent's love for a child cannot be expressed as a formula. These dimensions of human nature may be only dimly accessible to introspection and language, more recent characteristics of our mental evolution.

If changes in social systems and social behavior mark our ancestors' emergence, how can we account for these shifts? First, ecologic conditions must have favored a particular social structure such as pair bonding or male–male alliances. How could these shifts come about? Social behavior, as other behavior, is under genetic control. Did the emergence of pair bonding represent a change in the frequency of a gene for inclination towards monogamous relationships, conferring an adaptive advantage? More likely, genetic instructions that establish and constrain our social behavior as well as development of an elaborate forebrain allow considerable plasticity. Thus, the position of an organism on this bonding continuum is responsive to ecologic conditions such as food distribution, predators, male/female ratio, seasonality, and population density. In the latter case, appearance of pair bonding would not necessarily involve a change in gene frequency, but a change in ecology. Variation in the amount or type of behavior contingent on the stage of life cycle, population density, or other aspects of the environment is labelled behavioral scaling. A broader application of this concept emerges in life history analysis. A life history describes the genetically organized allocation of energy, time, or resources to reproduction, growth, or survival during different stages of an organism's life cycle (13). Different life histories of members of the same species can reflect either different genotypes or identical genotypes exposed to different environments— two ends of a continuum. Within the life history of a species, certain periodic events (zeitgebers) may influence the phase alignment of intrinsic biologic rhythms such as sleep, energy, concentration, and libido. Disturbances in the occurrence of social zeitgebers (e.g., daily routines, proximity to and physical contact with specific persons, hearing someone's voice, sharing of food) has been postulated as a factor in initiating depression (14).

However we imagine the emergence of such crucial human social behavior, we wonder how genes could serve as a blueprint for sociability. What components of social behavior are alterable, and which cannot be adjusted? What does the organism monitor to tell it whether it is succeeding or failing in its efforts? Because much human social behavior probably emerged before encephalization, we must seek the foundations for social behavior in processes not necessarily part of our verbal awareness. One would not expect introspection to be a powerful tool if the basic patterns it is trying to explain originate in biologic structures that antedate the capacity to introspect.

New language, concepts, and models are needed to understand the emergence of human characteristics from what came before. These models will emerge from disciplines such as ethology, sociobiology, evolutionary biology, and ecology.

Ethology

Ethology is the study of animal behavior, using precise description of behavior in natural settings. The behavioral units observed are not idiosyncratic to one individual, but evident in numerous individuals in the species. Observations of the behaviors have high inter-rater agreement, and require no interpretation. The settings in which the behavior occurs are recorded without regard to theory. Rather than focusing exclusively on a single aspect of the environment (e.g., presence of a parent), ethologic studies record the temperature, the type and amount of space, the number of individuals present, the time of day, etc. Such painstaking observations have been disregarded by psychiatry in favor of models focusing on a single variable.

Ethology emerged as a discipline in the last 50 years. Its evolution was affected by the revision of Darwinian theory. Darwin's original tenet was that natural selection operated at the level of the species. Modern genetics forced a shift from the species to the individual as the unit of evolution. Neo-Darwinism studies adaptive advantages that arise within an individual. If the issue of survival exists not at the species but at the individual level, then interactions between individuals must be explained in terms of the adaptive advantage

they confer. This line of thought leads to the biology of social interactions. How is the drive of the individual to survive and reproduce (natural selection) compatible with social organization? This question led to the development of sociobiology, a subdiscipline of ethology.

Sociobiology

Sociobiology was defined by E.O. Wilson in 1975 as the systematic study of the biological basis of social behavior (15). It rests on several ideas about social behavior: animals exhibit stable and quantifiable social behaviors; the social behavior of one species differs from that of another; differences in social behavior have come about through evolution, and evolution occurs through natural selection within a population.

Evolution favors the social behavior of individuals that increases their inclusive fitness. Change in social behavior is determined by ecologic pressure and the potential for genotypic changes within the population. Environments inevitably change over time. This change could be with respect to climate, availability and distribution of food, presence of more or new predators, population density, virulence of infections, and, for humans, changes in the inclusive fitness of competing groups (16). These changes create opportunities (niches) that could be exploited by individuals with particular capabilities, allowing them an advantage over others. Once the genotypic basis for such a capability appears, its frequency among members of the species will be increased, as animals possessing it produce more offspring. Of course, the changes an animal can undergo are constrained by the starting point (an elephant cannot readily become mouse-sized) and by the amount of genetic variation in the population over time. If the amount of variation is low, the phylogenetic inertia (resistance to change) is high.

What determines the amount of genetic variation in a population over time? Mutation is a source of genetic change, but because the mutation rate is 10^{-4}/cell/generation, this is not the likely source of genetic variation (15). Another source is gene flow. This occurs when individuals of the same species immigrate into the population from an outside group, usually geographically isolated, and introduce novel genetic material. A more dramatic example of gene flow is when two different species mate to produce hybridization. Less common than gene flow between populations of the same species, this introduces a change of greater magnitude when it occurs. Finally, sexual reproduction, with the creation of distinct gene combinations during meiosis, is a source of variation. New alleles are not introduced, as they are in mutation and gene flow, but new combinations are created (e.g., a gene coding for a given gene product may be combined with a gene controlling the rate of synthesis of the product).

KIN RECOGNITION

Wilson writes that social behavior, especially its complex forms, is based on kinship. The strength of social relations is determined by the degree of consanguinity. One expends resources on others only to the extent that such an expenditure enhances inclusive fitness. Preferential treatment of kin depends on accurate kin recognition. How do animals recognize kin? Four theories have been advanced (17). Phenotypic matching involves creation of a gestalt (a pattern, not the details comprised in the pattern) based on self and others (presumably the mother and siblings) with which the animal determines the relatedness of others. The nature of the gestalt (visual, auditory, olfactory or a combination) has not been defined, and probably varies among species. Spatial distribution theory posits that offspring are recognized by their proximity, such as within the nest, at the time of birth. The third theory, association, involves imprinting; kin recognition is determined by those with whom the animal is reared. The theory of recognition alleles posits that there are genetic sites that can be recognized by the individual. One breed of mice can detect apparent differences in histocompatibility loci in otherwise identical animals (17). How this occurs is unclear.

Kin recognition is important not only as a determinant of how much resource should be expended on another but also for mate selection. Most animals do not breed with siblings, presumably because this reduces genetic variation, thereby producing phylogenetic inertia. On the other hand, outbreeding with strangers may reduce the frequency of genes important for adaptive advantage over others. In fact, most animals breed with cousins to balance pluses and minuses of these two strategies.

RECIPROCAL ALTRUISM AND FIGHTING

Humans, unlike most other animals, behave altruistically not only toward close kin, but also toward strangers. This is termed reciprocal altruism (18). For reciprocal altruism to work, an animal must remember those animals who owe it debts and those to whom it owes debts. Because humans can plan, altruistic acts may be bestowed to create a future obligation. Reciprocal altruism may involve positive activities, such as sharing food and shelter and assisting in defense, but it may also involve withholding negative activities, such as maiming or killing. Most fighting between animals is ritualized, involving actions designed not to lethally injure the opponent. A defeated animal can escape harm by indicating its intention to withdraw. Maynard Smith (19) observed that most animals display two forms of fighting, ritualized and escalated, the latter intended to harm the opponent. Using game theory analysis, a theory of the rational behavior of individuals in competing situations, Smith demonstrated that it was disadvantageous for an animal to engage in escalated fighting too often *or* not at all. The former carries an unacceptably high risk of injury. The latter reduces the credibility of signs that one may resist, inviting persistent exploitation. Thus a ratio between the two modes, favoring ritualized fighting, is an evolutionary stable strategy. This means that the gene frequencies that determine this behavior are not likely to shift, because any general shift would be disadvantageous to its practitioners (i.e., there is no better alternative strategy).

SIBLING RIVALRY

In addition to situations in which it is advantageous to assist others, in other situations conflict is probable. An example is sibling rivalry. Some conflict between siblings is likely not because they are ill-bred or pathologically selfish, but because parental resources are limited, and distributed in relationship to members of the sibship asserting their need. Offspring that cannot claim their share within a litter may become casualties. Sociobiology does not propose a gene for sibling rivalry but rather a behavioral program that operates to maximize access to supplies critical to survival (protection, food, learning, warmth). Some conflict among sibs, depending on the abundance of resources, individual temperaments, and other variables, may be inevitable and not evidence of parental failure. The balance of competition and cooperation between sibs depends on inheritance rules, family traditions, economic opportunities, sex, resource availability, and life experiences.

A corollary concept is that of parental investment. Ordinarily one thinks of parental investment in offspring as limitless, and one often encounters examples among humans of protracted parental investment, such as sending a child through medical school. Among animals, however, parent-offspring conflict about the quantity of resources bestowed on each offspring is recognized. Stronger, older siblings may monopolize resources, depriving younger ones. Parents may curtail access of the older sib, eventuating in conflict between parent and child when emancipation is enforced.

ACQUISITION AND HOLDING
OF RESOURCES

Resources, mentioned before, are materials, possession of which is desirable and which correlate with enhanced survival of self and kin. An animal's capacity to gain and maintain control of these materials is measured as resource holding power, which depends on variables such as size, age, fighting skill, and motivation. In animals, these are related to the animal's genetic fitness. For humans, resource holding power reflects even more complex variables, many of which are not expressive of genotype as much as they are of cultural determinants (e.g., family of origin, inherited wealth, social class). Many inequalities in resource holding potential are culturally determined, and can be altered by political events, an extreme example being the toppling of an oppressive government and the subsequent trial of its leaders.

DOMINANCE

The access to resources in social animals is not determined in every instance by a struggle between individuals but is also influenced by a dominance system, a set of sustained aggressive-submissive relations among animals of the same species living in a territory (11). Most dominance systems are hierarchies with multiple ranks, the dominant member referred to as the alpha individual. Rank order determines access to resources, more dominant individuals having greater access to food, reproductive opportunities, and shelter, enhancing their inclusive fitness. An individual's rank is determined by multiple factors including size, strength, agility, ability to bluff, and lineage. But rank is not always decisive in determining the outcome of a conflict with another member. Factors such as proximity to home quarters ("fighting with one's back against the wall") may distort the outcome predicted by rank order. Hierarchies, once established, are often automatically maintained, group members accepting their rank until circumstances produce an encounter in which the rank order does not dictate an outcome satisfactory to the participants. A challenge or conflict, with a potential for change in the rank of the protagonists, may ensue. The outcome is often signified by the victor's exhilaration and the despondency and withdrawal of the vanquished. A benefit to the group of a stable hierarchy is enhancement of its ability to compete with other groups. *Thus, cooperation is not simply the opposite of competition; it is a strategy in competition between groups* (20).

A stranger threatens every member of a dominance hierarchy. Group cooperation is maximized in repelling the advances of an outsider (perhaps explaining the fixation on a common enemy used to solidify group cohesion in humans).

Development of culture and institutions that transmit information across generations is uniquely human. The appearance of advanced material culture corresponds to the emergence of agriculture, which allowed the accumulation of wisdom and resources in one place over generations. Did culture emerge as an expression of genetically determined social behavior, or is it independent of biology? Because culture is built on rudimentary social behaviors, and its evolution reflects the needs and limitations of its creators, it surely is influenced by our genetic potential. Culture and the institutions that maintain it are derived from our ability to recall the past and plan for the future. In imagining a future, humans can experience anxiety, joy, and sadness. The beliefs and institutions of a culture enable individuals and groups to master anxiety about the future through planning, shared optimism, and worship.

CRITIQUE

Applying sociobiologic analysis to human evolution is confounded by several factors. The breeding time is so long that using inclusive fitness as a variable is impossible. The pace of cultural evolution is so rapid that instances of sociobiologic process may be dwarfed by cultural or ecologic changes affected by human activity. Also, the effect of any change in genes that affect our social behavior may be relatively small, requiring large samples to detect and many generations to become evident.

Owing to these difficulties, sociobiology has been pictured as the "emperor's new clothes."

The basis of this critique is threefold. As noted, it is hard to demonstrate sociobiologic principles at work in human evolution, and easy to spin just-so yarns that explain why things turned out as they did. Thus, to postulate (a modest example) that humans are not covered with hair because precise recognition of kin is facilitated by having features undisguised by hair may seem plausible. But there is no evidence that this is true and no experimental design that could prove it. One might show that abundant hair makes it hard to recognize individuals, but this would not prove that the hair disappeared for that reason. Nevertheless, sociobiologic analyses such as these are heuristically useful in that they broaden the range of variables contemplated in studying human behavior.

A second knock on human sociobiology is that it becomes a pseudoscientific rationale for the political and social status quo, a form of determinism. This is particularly so in considering sex roles. Is it biologically inevitable that women will be subordinate in certain ways to men? The only inevitability is that men will not bear children, nor women sire them. Beyond that, although biology may create propensities for likely outcomes in a certain setting, these can be neutralized by chance, cultural evolution, or personal commitment. To study mammalian evolution (in which culture and political institutions play no role) of the differential functions of males and females, however, and conclude that observed differences in humans are unrelated to biology seems strikingly problematic. Nor is it true that a claim for genetically determined differences in social behavior means that this explains everything. Evidence that a social behavior changes from one generation to another indicates that a change in gene frequency is not involved. Such a change may be a result of behavioral scaling in which the shift reflects a genetic program, expression of which is sensitive to environmental factors, such as nutrition, crowding, competition from other species, or intraspecies competition.

Finally, human sociobiology has received fire because it is misrepresented as postulating a lawful progression toward perfection rather than accounting for accidents and coincidences. According to Gould (21), for example, if an asteroid had not hit the earth and led to the extinction of dinosaurs, mammals completely overshadowed by the larger species would never have flourished, and humans would never have emerged. Nothing about sociobiology contradicts Gould's trenchant view of human evolution.

The ultimate question may be, To what extent have we behaviorally outstripped our mammalian forebears? To the extent that our similarity to animals and their social behaviors is trivial, sociobiology may have little to contribute to understanding human behavior. Of course, encephalization has allowed us great innovative ability. But to the extent that it has also bestowed enormous powers to deceive ourselves about our self-control and motivation, we may not be far removed from the rudimentary behavioral algorithms that unfold to produce animal behavior. If this is the case, and we think it is, sociobiology is a reasonable approach to understanding our behavioral foundations.

SECTION II.
DEVELOPMENT

10/Pregnancy

Virginia L. Susman, M.D.

OBJECTIVES

GENERAL OBJECTIVE: Given the examination of a woman during any stage of pregnancy, identify the emotional, socioeconomic, and medical issues that will need attention during the remainder of her pregnancy.

SPECIFIC OBJECTIVES:
1. Outline the contraceptive methods and state their efficacy and risks.
2. Summarize the three trimesters of pregnancy.
3. Discuss guidelines of prenatal care.
4. Define high-risk pregnancy and state the management of high-risk pregnancies.
5. Discuss the unique characteristics of pregnancy in adolescents, older mothers, and physicians.
6. Describe the procedures used to induce abortion and the psychologic reactions to abortion.
7. Discuss the postpartum psychiatric disorders.
8. State the interventions for infertility.

Anticipation and onset of pregnancy mark the beginning of parenthood. Choices about whether to become pregnant or continue a pregnancy, how to care for the fetus and oneself during pregnancy, or what to do about infertility are influenced by one's history, identity, and other biologic, psychologic, and social factors.

For the 37 weeks of pregnancy, the fetus experiences dramatic growth and maturation, the quality of which is influenced by prenatal care. Is it a boy or a girl? is the first question asked in the delivery room. Although techniques such as ultrasound may afford a preview, confirmation of sex at birth will be central to the child's identity.

CONTRACEPTION

Freedom from unwanted pregnancy became a reality in the last 35 years. Oral contraceptives, which received FDA approval in 1960, made birth control easier and more effective. Induced abortion, legal since 1973, is much used (over 370 per 1,000 live births in 1982) but controversial. Methods of birth control include barrier devices (condom, diaphragm, or cervical cap), spermicidal agents (vaginal creams, foams, suppositories, jellies, films, or sponges), intrauterine devices (IUDs) that interfere with implantation of a fertilized ovum, levonorgestrel implants, and unreliable methods (withdrawal and monthly abstinence or rhythm). In 1987, 24% of U.S. women of reproductive age relied on surgical sterilization of themselves or partners to prevent pregnancy (1). Educate your patients about the physiology, mechanics, risks and benefits of each contraceptive method, facilitating informed choice. Besides the method itself, motivation for contraception influences its effectiveness.

Sterilization is meant to be permanent, so it must be carefully considered by the patient. Although surgical reconnection of vas deferens and Fallopian tubes can be accomplished, this is often unsuccessful. The risks associated with vasectomy and tubal ligation are minor surgical complications (e.g., infection), occasional spontaneous reanastomosis of the vas, and an ectopic (nonuterine) pregnancy rate of 16% in the 1–6/1000 "failures," (i.e., pregnancies after tubal ligation) (1).

Popularity of oral contraceptives has varied over the years owing to concerns about side-effects and long-term health risks. Recently, some concerns (e.g., higher incidence of breast cancer) were disproved by rigorous studies (1). Minimizing the estrogen and progestin doses in the pill reduced the rates of several (e.g., cardiovascular) complications. Only smokers over age 35 years have heightened risk for cardiovascular complications. In 1987, 23% of U.S. women of reproductive age used the pill. The failure rate of the most prescribed oral contraceptives, low-dose estrogen-progestin combinations, is 0.27/100 woman-years (0.27 pregnancies per 100 women per year) (1). The estrogen component may cause nausea, breast tenderness, fluid retention, and depression. Progestin-only oral contraceptives are somewhat less effective than estrogen-progestin forms, and can cause weight gain, acne, anxiety, and failure of withdrawal bleeding (i.e., bleeding on drug discontinuation). Choice of oral contraceptive is based on the most tolerable side-effect profile. Oral contraceptives seem to protect against endometrial (uterine lining) and ovarian cancer. Oral contraceptive users seem to have higher rates of cervical cancer, benign hepatic adenomas, and gallstones (1).

Levonorgestrel (Norplant) is a progestin that, contained in silicon capsules, is easily implanted surgically under the skin of the arm. It produces continuous contraception by suppression of ovulation for more than 5 years. Because it requires no effort once implanted, its failure rate is only 0.6/100 woman-years. For 70% of patients, menstruation becomes irregular, but it becomes more regular after a year's use. Acne, breast discharge, and headache each occur in 5%–20% of patients. When the implant is removed, pregnancy readily occurs (2).

Barrier contraceptives require self-discipline and manual dexterity. The failure rate of the diaphragm is 1.9/100 woman-years, the condom 3.6/100 woman-years; failure is related to improper use or placement. One-year pregnancy rate among cervical cap users is 8%–17%. For reasons (e.g., increased fertility, more frequent intercourse, less maturity) not yet certain, failure rates are higher for women under age 25 (1). Condoms may reduce penile sensation but have no other side effects. Diaphragm users more frequently have urinary tract infections, presumably because of mechanical obstruction of bladder emptying. One advantage of diaphragm and condom use is decreased transmission of AIDS and other sexually transmitted disease (STD). Condom and diaphragm users have lower rates of cervical neoplasia, presumably because these are barriers to the human papilloma virus, strains of which are etiologically linked to cervical neoplasia (tumor production). Vaginal spermicidal agents (which have antibacterial and antiviral properties) also have lower rates of STD and cervical neoplasia. However, there is a higher failure rate (11.9/100 woman-years) with spermicidal agents.

Use of IUDs among American women of reproductive age dropped from 4% in 1982 to 2% in 1987 (1). IUDs can cause perforation of the uterus during insertion, increased menstural blood loss, and infertility by way of chronic infections of the Fallopian tubes. When pregnancy occurs with an IUD in place (1.5/100 woman-years) miscarriage and premature delivery are more likely. Infections associated with IUD use are more common in women with multiple sex partners. The IUDs are most appropriate for older, monogamous women who have completed their families.

ANTICIPATING PREGNANCY

Care of a woman who anticipates childbearing must address infection. Rubella (German measles) is highly teratogenic. Rubella during the first trimester (first third) of pregnancy can cause congenital hearing loss, mental retardation, cardiac malformations, and ocular defects. Although children have been routinely vaccinated against rubella since 1969, up to 15% of adults are not immune because they were never exposed (3). Some states require premarital rubella antibody titers. Preventive care of the future mother includes measuring titers, and vaccination if not immune. Because syphilis can cause profound congenital abnormalities before conception, screen for syphilis with rapid plasma reagin (RPR); if positive, test with fluorescent treponema antibody (FTA). Other STDs (e.g., gonorrhea, chlamydia) can cause infertility. Although there are no vaccines for these, patient education and screening can be preventive.

Good nutrition and avoidance of substance abuse are necessary. Underweight women have a greater risk for delivering low-birth-weight infants. Smoking during pregnancy is associated with decreased birth weight. Excessive alcohol consumption can cause fetal alcohol syndrome (growth retardation, facial anomalies and CNS abnormalities like mental retardation or ADHD [p. 144]). Use of street drugs also results in a higher rate of pregnancy complications, neonatal addictions, and long-term neurologic impairments in the children.

You should obtain a family health history. For some women, genetic counseling (p. 72) before conception is advisable. Patients from families with known heritable diseases can use counseling to help plan their families while sorting out the facts from fantasies and myths. Anticipatory counselling can help women who have chronic diseases (e.g., diabetes, PKU [p.

123], cardiac disease, epilepsy) because treatment of these disorders before, during, and after pregnancy requires refinements (4).

PREGNANCY

Profound physiologic and psychologic changes precede the visible anatomic changes of pregnancy. During the first trimester, the most frequent symptoms are breast tenderness owing to hormonal stimulation, and nausea and fatigue (probably hormonally caused). Nausea and vomiting of early pregnancy may cause weight loss. Weight gain should be negligible. For several reasons, ranging from superstition to knowing the risk for miscarriage peaks in the first trimester, many couples do not reveal the pregnancy until late in this trimester.

During the second trimester, weight gain begins, nausea and fatigue recede, and the pregnancy becomes obvious. With lower risk for miscarriage and less nausea and fatigue, there is some relief, and passage of time and recognition by others make it seem more real. Often, the highlight of the second trimester is the first experience (usually by the 20th week) of fetal movement (quickening), soon followed by increasingly strong jumps, jabs, kicks, and pokes that are felt by the partner and may be seen by others. This follows completion of the production of the embryo's cerebral cortical neurons on the 125th day (E125), a process that began on about E40 (5).

The third (final) trimester involves continued weight gain and return of discomfort. Swollen ankles, shortness of breath, heartburn, hemorrhoids (swollen perianal veins), increasing fatigue, and difficulty sleeping prompt a wish for it to be over. As the due date approaches, anxiety about the labor, delivery, and health of the baby increases. Freud, whose reputation does not rest on his incisive understanding of the psychology of women, perceived pregnancy as a time of calm, bliss, and self-absorption. But according to several women analysts (Benedek, Deutsch, Bibring) (6, 7), pregnant women become concerned with dependency (e.g., worry about financial security), identity, and relationships with their mother and spouse. There is no uniformity of emotional responses to pregnancy—every pregnancy presents unique situations and concerns (8). The pregnant adolescent who used no contraception for lack of availability, or believed "it can't happen to me," differs from the 35-year-old who conceived after multiple infertility interventions. Women who had prior miscarriages or stillbirths react differently from those who accidentally conceive after having all the children they planned. Family finances, relationships with partners, and attitudes about staying home or working also color responses.

Pregnant women tend to focus more on an inner world of concepts than an outer world of actions and persons, and are less apt than controls to describe themselves as self-accepting and independent-thinking (9). Six-month-pregnant women were asked to report if symptoms were present before (or only during) pregnancy, and if symptoms worsened with pregnancy. They reported both a worsening of preexisting symptoms and onset of new ones (unrelated to pregnancy), but increases were not of pathologic proportion (10).

Fathers-to-be receive modest attention in studies of adjustment to pregnancy. The couvade syndrome, in which men develop some somatic or behavioral symptoms of pregnant partners, occurs in up to 50% of fathers-to-be (11).

PRENATAL CARE

Comprehensive prenatal care is definitively associated with lower maternal and infant mortality and fewer low-weight births (12). Ideal prenatal care includes regular monitoring of the mother and fetus, education, and psychologic support (13). Routine obstetric visits should be more frequent as the pregnancy progresses. Each visit involves checking the mother's weight and blood pressure, screening urine for glucose and protein (which might reveal gestational diabetes, or preeclampsia [fluid retention, elevated blood pressure, and spillage of protein in urine], respectively), measuring uterine growth and determining fetal position. Routine blood tests early in pregnancy are a complete blood count (CBC), blood type and Rh antibody screen, rubella titer, serologic test for syphilis and a screen for hepatitis B. Later, another CBC and a glucose tolerance test (a test for diabetes) are given. The mother-to-be should be counselled about diet, vitamins, and appropriate weight gain. Pregnancy increases the need for calories, protein, folic acid, calcium, zinc, and iron. Need for increased amounts of other vitamins is less well documented, but advisable (3). The expected pattern of weight gain is none or minimal in the first trimester, with steady gain thereafter at the rate of 0.4 kg/wk during the second and third trimesters. Total gain of 24–28 pounds is advised. Women underweight or overweight before pregnancy are encouraged to gain more or less, respectively. Moderate exercise is recommended; work not involving excessive standing, lifting, or stair climbing in the third trimester is allowable until the end of pregnancy. Over-the-counter medications (exception: acetaminophen and selected antihistamines) should be avoided and prescription medication limited to the drugs absolutely required for the underlying illness and relatively safe for the fetus. The known safety of any prescription drug during pregnancy is discussed in the *Physician's Desk Reference* (14). Likewise, exposure to x-rays is avoided if possible. Sexual intercourse is generally safe for the first 32 weeks of gestation; infrequently, it may introduce amniotic fluid infections leading to premature delivery and fetal morbidity. Orgasm after 32 weeks gestation predisposes to premature labor (3). Early in pregnancy, begin education about signs and symptoms (e.g., bleeding, cramping) of complications. Also important is a dialogue between you and the patient welcoming openness and questions.

Provision and acceptance of prenatal care in the U.S. lag behind many countries. In 1986, only 76% of pregnant women began prenatal care in the first trimester (12). Obstacles include inadequate insurance, inadequacies (e.g., unavailability of an ongoing relationship with one physician) in care provision, and negative attitudes toward the pregnancy or medical procedures. Other reasons for not seeking it are unawareness of the pregnancy, fear of parents discovering the pregnancy, fear of deportation for illegals, and fear that smoking or substance abuse will be identified. Women who do not obtain adequate prenatal care are more likely to be members of a minority group, single, poor, homeless, under age 18 or over age 30 and have less than a high school diploma (12). Women allowed to see their babies on ultrasound (a safe method of imaging the fetus) are more apt to follow prenatal advice than controls not shown the ultrasound, suggesting its value beyond its monitoring function (15).

High-Risk Pregnancies

High-risk pregnancies include those of women at either end of the reproductive age range (16), diabetics (p. 196), women who have certain other chronic illnesses (e.g., asthma, rheumatoid arthritis), exposed to certain drugs or infections, or carrying multiple pregnancies. Pregnancies become high risk if there is threatened abortion (symptoms include bleeding or cramping) or hypertension secondary to the pregnancy. A history of congenital abnormalities, growth retardation, or preterm labor in a prior pregnancy also means high risk (17).

High-risk pregnancies require more intensive and frequent assessments. When there is risk for premature labor, such as a woman with a previous history of preterm delivery or threatened abortion, an individually determined period of bed rest may be advised. Diabetic and phenylketonuric (inadequate breakdown of the amino acid phenylalanine because of an autosomal recessive disorder which, if diagnosed by screening of blood neonatally, can be controlled by dietary restriction of phenylalanine) women require dietary controls. Serial ultrasound examinations track intrauterine growth rate. Diagnostic ultrasound is used to determine if there is a multiple gestation (twins, triplets), to identify and locate placental abnormalities, to locate the site of vaginal bleeding of undetermined cause, and to locate the placenta so it is not unnecessarily punctured during amniocentesis (17). In some cases of premature labor, drugs such as ritodrine (a drug that inhibits uterine smooth muscle contractility) are administered to try to halt the labor.

The psychologic stress of high-risk pregnancies may be attenuated by some interventions (18, 19). Amniocentesis (inserting a needle into the uterus and withdrawing amniotic fluid, at about 16 weeks) has a low (0.5%) miscarriage rate and no other notable risks. It is routinely recommended to women at risk for having a baby with chromosomal abnormalities, such as women over age 35, history of a child with a chromosomal abnormality, or family history of such an abnormality (20). It identifies about 100 inherited diseases (e.g., Tay-Sachs, sickle cell anemia, thalassemia, Duchenne's muscular dystrophy, cystic fibrosis, and Huntington's disease). Women undergoing amniocentesis are more anxious just after their procedures than controls at the same point in their pregnancies (18). However, the amniocentesis patients do better than controls later in pregnancy, showing more attachment to their fetuses and less anxiety (18, 19). A newer procedure is chorionic villus sampling, which has a slightly higher risk for miscarriage and occasionally fails to obtain the tissue needed. It can identify almost as many disorders as amniocentesis and can be performed in the first trimester, giving the patient the opportunity to keep confidential an abortion secondary to detected abnormalities (21). First trimester therapeutic abortion is safer than a later one.

Delivery

The pregnant woman can choose among several sites to deliver. Once the rule, home childbirth is uncommon, and some doctors think it unwise. Nonetheless, some families elect it, usually under a midwife's supervision. Birthing centers offer a compromise between the comfort and familiarity of home and the relatively impersonal hospital environment. Many hospitals provide birthing rooms where labor and delivery occur in the same room and bed (21), replacing labor rooms where patients are confined to bed until birth is imminent and then transported to a delivery room resembling an operating room. For uncomplicated pregnancies, the ready medical expertise and equipment of a hospital may be unnecessary, but a complication is best managed there.

The idea that stress can complicate, precipitate, or lengthen a delivery is entrenched in lay views. Studies of this yield inconsistent results, but there is a trend toward anxiety, depression, and above average numbers of stressful life events correlating with obstetrical complications (22–24).

Special Circumstances

THE PREGNANT ADOLESCENT

Adolescent pregnancy is increasing in frequency and is a major public health problem (25). There are adverse consequences for the teenage mother and her baby: the woman often experiences disruption of her education and relationships. Immaturity and lack of support can lead to inadequate or abusive mothering. It is uncertain whether the high rate of prematurity, growth retardation, and perinatal complications associated with adolescent pregnancy are caused by the mother's age or her health practices. Pregnant adolescents tend to be less well nourished and underweight or of low-normal weight. They gain less weight during pregnancy, and are more likely to smoke, use drugs, and not obtain adequate prenatal care (26). Intensive sex education programs are associated with decreased numbers of adolescent pregnancies just after such interventions. Aggressive, supportive programs of prenatal care for pregnant adolescents produce better outcomes.

THE OLDER MOTHER

The woman who postpones childbearing until after age 35 is also unique. Complications of pregnancy, chromosomal abnormalities, and perinatal difficulties are more likely. Psychologic adjustment may be harder (27) because of the multiple risks and the intrapsychic conflict involved in becoming a mother relatively late, often in midcareer with a strong professional identity. The older, first-time mother might, like the adolescent, feel out of step with age peers and lack support or role models (28). Later childbearing is becoming more common, but the older mother who "does it all" by combining childrearing and a career might not take time to use support.

THE PREGNANT PHYSICIAN

The pregnant physician also faces a conflict. Ideal years for childbearing coincide with those usually devoted to professional training, often with grueling time demands. Consequently, many women physicians begin families during residency or medical school, despite it being easier to coordinate working and childrearing after residency. Studies of obstetric risk during residency reach different conclusions. One (29) showed more frequent low-weight birth and growth retardation from pregnancy during residency. Another (30) reported more postmaturity (p. 129), over-average birth weight, and threatened placental abruption (tearing of the placenta from the uterine wall) compared to controls. A third (31) showed higher rates of hypertension. But another study (32) of 8700 subjects with an 86% return rate revealed no increase in obstetric risk for resident physicians (compared to well-chosen controls) except when the resident worked over 100 hours weekly. But even if all goes well medically, the challenges of balancing professional goals and obligations with personal ones are formidable.

INDUCED ABORTION

Induced abortion is the deliberate termination of a pregnancy. Prior to its legalization in the 1973 *Roe vs. Wade* decision, there were about 0.25–1.25 million illegal abortions yearly in the U.S. Since then, the abortion rate has been estimated from 273/1000 live births in 1975 (for the entire U.S.) (33) to a high of over 370/1000 live births in 1982 (13 state reporting area) (34). Worldwide, about 25% of pregnancies are terminated by induced abortion (33). There are significant socioeconomic differences in abortion rate (34). In 1987, African-American women obtained abortions twice as often as Euro-American women; 58% of the women having abortions were under 25; 80% were unmarried. There were black-white differences in the relationship between educational level and abortion rate. The lowest rate among Euro-American women was in those best educated; the rate among African-American women was lowest among those least educated. Overall, poor, unmarried minority women are the first to lose access to abortion when its availability is limited by law.

Procedures and safety differ according to trimester. In 1987, 90% were in the first trimester. Suction curettage (dilation of the cervix followed by insertion of a suction cannula into the uterus) was used for 96% of these (34). Complications occur in under 2% of suction curettages, and mortality is under 2/100,000 patients.

Complications for second trimester abortions are 3–4 times higher (1) because procedures are more complex. Dilation of the cervix is followed by insertion of a prostaglandin (produced by the breakdown of arachidonic acid in cell membranes, prostaglandins induce inflammation and uterine and bronchial constriction) suppository into the vagina to induce labor. Alternatively, injection of hypertonic saline into the amniotic sac can induce labor. Any invasive abortion procedure could cause hemorrhage, cervical laceration, uterine preforation, or bowel injury. Prostaglandins can cause hyperthermia (very high body temperature) and other autonomic side effects. Saline can cause disseminated intravascular coagulation (abnormal gathering of clotting elements of blood, leading to their unavailability, with consequent bleeding tendency) and

hypernatremia (excessive serum sodium) (1, 34).

Although the most frequently documented short-term psychologic reaction to abortion is relief, some women also experience sadness, guilt, or anxiety (usually mild). The vast majority report no regrets. Long-term follow-up reveals predominantly positive psychologic effects in the majority (61%–90%, depending on the study) of women who underwent induced abortion (35).

Studies of women who wanted but were denied abortion reveal that 40% obtain abortion elsewhere (36). Of the remainder, 6%–19% give their child for adoption. Of those who rear the children, 59% are glad they did so, but another 34% perceive the child as a burden (37). The world literature on infanticide reveals that 83% of newborns killed by their mothers were from unwanted pregnancies (38). Children born following denial of abortion had more illnesses and poorer school performance than controls (39). As each pregnancy involves myriad personal concerns, each decision to abort reflects the sum of a host of emotions and circumstances. In treating a woman undergoing abortion, help her explore her motivations and provide nonjudgmental education, support, and contraceptive counselling.

THE POSTPARTUM PERIOD

Immediate postpartum care involves monitoring for complications (e.g., hemorrhage, infection) (40). In the absence of these, early discharge home with a follow-up 6 weeks later completes hands-on care. Education about postpartum bleeding, breast feeding, nutrition, weight loss, and resumption of sexual intercourse and contraception are essential. Bleeding decreases gradually over several weeks; breast feeding requires higher caloric intake than pregnancy, necessitating a balanced diet. Intercourse can be resumed as soon as the woman feels comfortable. Inform the patient that although breast feeding may delay resumption of ovulation, ovulation could occur as soon as 6 weeks postpartum, dictating attention to contraception when intercourse resumes.

Women experience higher rates of psychiatric disorders postpartum (41) as well as intense emotional reactions not reaching the magnitude of illness. Most common, occurring in up to 50% of women postpartum, is a benign self-limited condition termed postpartum blues, characterized by rapid mood swings, irritability, decreased concentration, and tearfulness. Women experiencing them can be told that this is common and usually transient. Nevertheless, postpartum major depression, next in severity, is more likely in patients who have had postpartum blues (42, 43). Postpartum major depression affects up to 10% of postpartum patients (44). Most severe is postpartum psychosis, which occurs in 1–2/1,000 postpartum women. Postpartum psychosis typically begins within 2–3 weeks after childbirth, and can be life-threatening to both mother and infant (45). There is a debate about whether postpartum psychosis is a discrete condition, or whether it is an episode of affective disorder or schizophrenia triggered by postpartum stress or endocrine changes (46–49). Regardless, it responds to conventional treatment of the presenting syndrome (e.g., lithium for mania, ECT for major depression with melancholia and psychosis) and has a good prognosis.

Women with preexisting psychiatric disorders need careful assessment during pregnancy and postpartum. Prospective studies of women with prior psychosis (especially postpartum) show high rates of psychiatric disturbance during pregnancy (50, 51). The rates of recurrence for postpartum psychosis and depression are at least 25% (44, 52, 53). Postpartum illness has a suicide rate of 5% and an infanticide rate of 4% (53).

Treating a psychiatrically ill, pregnant woman poses a clinical dilemma. Ensuring the well-being of the mother invites aggressive intervention, but available treatments pose a risk to the fetus. Current literature indicates that low-dose high potency neuroleptics, tricyclic antidepressants, and ECT can be used safely (54–56).

PSEUDOCYESIS

Pseudocyesis (false pregnancy) is uncommon. When in occurs, usually it is in women near menopause or younger women eager to be pregnant. Patients imagine they are pregnant, experience symptoms of pregnancy such as amenorrhea (absence of menses) and galactorrhea (production of breast milk), but examination demonstrates no pregnancy (3). The combination of amenorrhea and galactorrhea is associated with hyperprolactinemia (excessive prolactin production) 50%–70% of the time and with prolactinomas (prolactin-producing tumors) in 35%–60% (57). For patients with no endocrine abnormalities, supportive psychotherapy (p. 310), addressing the conflict between wish and reality, is recommended. Patients should also be shown ultrasound examinations. Prognosis varies; 50% recur (58).

INFERTILITY

Infertility is defined as the inability of a couple having normal sexual relations to conceive within a year. It affects about one in six U.S. couples (59–61) and is increasingly prevalent. There is a growing literature on the psychologic sequelae of infertility and its innovative treatments (61–69).

Hypotheses about this increase in infertility include postponement of childbearing beyond the biologically optimal time, increased numbers of sexual partners with concomitant increased exposure to venereal diseases, complications of which can impair fertility, and an artifact of increased reporting of infertility (61).

Absent, poorly formed, or inadequately motile sperm account for male factor infertility. Failure to ovulate or maintain necessary hormone levels for fertilization and implantation, occluded Fallopian tubes, a uterus with scars or fibroid tumors, or an incompetent cervix that dilates and releases the fetal tissues, are female factors.

Effects of infertility may include depression, anxiety, a damaged self-image, an aversion to sex regimented by the calendar rather than spontaneous, a sense of alienation, and conjugal conflict. Infertile couples often report not always being emotionally "in synch" with each other during protracted treatment for infertility. Menstrual cycles become an emotional roller coaster of hope and despair. Infertile couples tend to be more troubled than controls (62), but it is not known which of the following is true: stress causes infertility, infertility causes stress, or both mutually interact.

Medical advances offer opportunity to infertile couples (63). For male factor infertility, interventions include treatment of the man's sperm and artificial insemination with the treated sperm; artificial insemination with donor sperm, gamete intra-fallopian transfer (GIFT, the transfer of collected oocytes and sperm into the Fallopian tubes); and in vitro fertilization and embryo transfer (IVF-ET) (the transfer of developing embryos into the uterus after extracorporeal incubation of collected sperm with oocytes retrieved by laparoscopic surgery or by ultrasound-guided transvaginal aspiration). In vitro fertilization is also used when there is occlusion of the Fallopian tubes; GIFT and IVF-ET are useful for infertility from endometriosis (uterine lining tissue implanted outside the uterus). When anovulation or other endocrine problems cause female factor infertility, interventions include clomiphene (an ovulation-inducing drug) and human menopausal gonadotropin. Use of surrogate mothers and donated oocytes are biologically efficacious but highly controversial (e.g., the Baby M case) (60).

Couples who undergo donor insemination have a low divorce rate, and in one study, psychologic profiles of husbands of women who had undergone donor insemination did not differ from controls (64). But other studies identify decreased self-esteem and transient sexual dysfunction in husbands and anger and guilt among wives (65, 66). Studies of couples who undergo IVF revealed overoptimism about the outcome (67, 68), and that one motivation for undergoing the procedure was fear that if they did not use IVF, they would regret it later (68). Women who undergo IVF tended to believe they would be less fulfilled if they bore no children, but also thought that they could find satisfaction in other areas of their lives, and that their marriage could withstand the stress (67). In a study of semen quality before and during the in vitro procedure (69), deterioration in quality of semen sufficient to reduce fertility, attributed to stress, occurred in 8% of the men.

MISCARRIAGE AND STILLBIRTH

For any couple, loss of a baby through miscarriage (expulsion of the products of pregnancy before the middle of the second trimester) or stillbirth (when the infant is born dead) is overwhelming. Complicating grief associated with miscarriage is the lack of rituals that deal with the loss—no funeral or public mourning. Sometimes the couple have told no one, or others first learn of the pregnancy after its loss (70). Also, women tend to bond to the unborn baby earlier and stronger than men, so the loss may not be shared equally. Both partners may experience irrational guilt over how they might have "caused" the miscarriage (71). A stillbirth can involve the traumatic experience of labor and delivery shortly after learning that the baby has died, or the shock of all being well until the delivery. The hopes and arrangements that developed over months are suddenly wrested away.

Encourage bereaved parents to hold their baby, name it, and arrange a memorial compatible with the practices of their culture (72, 73). Well-meaning comments (e.g., "You'll have another," "It's all for the best") are usually unhelpful. Support groups and individual and marital counseling help many couples.

11/Child and Adolescent Development and Psychopathology

Patricia M. Butler, M.D., and Frederick S. Sierles, M.D.

OBJECTIVES

GENERAL OBJECTIVE: Given an examination of a child or adolescent, state whether a given behavior is normal.

SPECIFIC OBJECTIVES:
1. List generalizations about growth, maturation, and development.
2. Discuss factors that affect development.
3. Discuss temperament.
4. Discuss bonding and attachment.
5. For each stage of childhood, summarize motor, cognitive, emotional, and interpersonal development, and provide anticipatory guidance.
6. Discuss the psychology of adoption, hospitalization, divorce, and child abuse.
7. State recommendations for pediatric interviewing.
8. Summarize (etiology, manifestations, treatment, and prognosis) mental retardation, autistic disorder, attention deficit hyperactivity disorder, conduct disorder, depression, encopresis, enuresis, and anorexia nervosa.

GENERALIZATIONS ABOUT DEVELOPMENT

Development is the progress of a person's functioning that results from growth (increase in number and size of cells and size of the organism), maturation (genetically programmed unfolding of the organism's physiologic capacities), and interaction with the environment.

We do not begin life as undifferentiated clay to be molded (1). Individual differences in behavior (e.g., motor activity, response to experimental interventions) (2) are noted from birth. Maturation and development progress sequentially (e.g., endogenous smiling [p. 134] before social smiling before

laughter) (3). An adult learning to read has many of the same struggles as a child learning to read (4).

The rates at which growth and development occur vary among individuals. For each person, growth and development are not continuous; they occur in spurts and lulls (5). Organs grow at different rates. An adolescent's arms, legs, nose or chin may seem to enlarge individually with no apparent respect for overall body harmony, contributing to an appearance and feelings of gangliness, gawkiness, and self-consciousness (6). Under stress, transient loss of developmental milestones (regression) can occur (e.g., some toilet-trained children briefly bedwet when a sibling is born).

Development of a skill requires that other abilities be present (e.g., using past or future tenses in grammar requires understanding time) (7). When facilitating functions are impaired, skills may lag (e.g., blind children walk later than sighted ones) (8). Timing matters (e.g., following left hemisphere damage in children under age five years, the right hemisphere assumes language functions) (9).

Often (not always), childhood behaviors predict later behaviors: Intelligence tends to predict school performance (10). Two year olds with difficult temperaments are more apt to require later psychiatric care (11, 12). Children who have poor peer relations have an increased risk for adult psychopathology (13, 14). Boys who enjoy wearing girls' clothing are more apt to be gay as adults (15). "Blind" observers of home movies taken during the childhood of adult schizophrenics can identify them, in contrast to siblings, as preschizophrenic (16). High birth weight correlates with adult obesity (17).

Also, the child shapes the environment. For example, relatively inactive premature babies evoke more responses from their mothers than active ones (18), and active newborns receive more attention from nurses than less active ones (19).

Understanding normal development helps patient care. For example, children from age 6 months to 2–3 years, routinely frightened by strangers (stranger anxiety), are best examined in their parents' laps. Before age 6 months, an infant tends not to be frightened by strangers and can be examined while being held, rocked, or stroked (20). Stranger anxiety also explains why it is optimal for adoption to occur before 6 months (21).

FACTORS INFLUENCING DEVELOPMENT

Heredity

There is a genetic contribution to temperament, intelligence, personality traits, and susceptibility to many illnesses. Age of onset of social smiling (22), rhythms of lags and spurts in development (23), handedness (24), and age of first menstruation (25) are also heritable.

Pregnancy (Gestation) and Delivery

Obtaining good prenatal care and complying with it are associated with better child health. (p. 122) Before prescribing medication or radiographs for women of childbearing age, consider the possibility of pregnancy. Many drugs, maternal medical conditions, toxins, infections, and uterine abnormalities (Table 11.1) can be teratogenic (causing fetal pathology) (26).

Malnutrition in pregnant women increases risk of stillbirths (p. 127) and premature births. Prolonged undernutrition before and during pregnancy is usually more harmful than acute nutritional disturbance in a well-nourished mother (21). Age is pertinent: pregnant teenagers often do not obtain prenatal care, and children born to mothers (to a lesser extent, fathers) older than age 35 have greater risk of Down syndrome (p. 66)

Labor and delivery have risks, although most labors are uncomplicated. Fetal hypoxia during labor can result from respiratory depression because of drugs given the mother, maternal convulsions, or low blood pressure. Brain injury can result from mechanical problems (e.g., prolonged labor, cephalopelvic disproportion [pelvic narrowness in relation to fetal head size], breech delivery [buttocks before head], mid- and high-forceps delivery [the forceps is an instrument that facilitates extraction of the fetus], and prolonged labor).

Premature birth (younger than 37 weeks) and low birth weight (especially when the infant is small for gestational age) are associated with later cognitive deficits, behavior problems, and seizure disorders. Causes of prematurity (more common among the poor) include poor maternal health, inadequate prenatal care, preeclampsia (p. 122) and eclampsia (preeclampsia plus seizures) and multiple pregnancies (e.g., twins). Postmature birth (more than 42 weeks) can be as-

Table 11.1. Teratogenic Agents in Humans [a]

Drugs Taken By Pregnant Mother

Aminopterin or amethopterin (folic acid antagonist): hydrocephalus (excess cerebrospinal fluid in ventricles with head enlargement), craniosynostosis (premature bone formation in skull), shortened limbs, absent digits, mental deficiency

Cocaine: growth retardation, cerebrovascular accident (stroke) in utero, abruptio placentae (tearing of placenta from uterine wall)

Diethylstilbestrol (an estrogenic compound): carcinoma (cancer) in exposed females, genitourinary anomalies in exposed males

Iodides and propylthiouracil (a thyroid hormone-suppressing agent): goiter (enlarged thyroid), fetal hypothyroidism

Isotretinoin: brain malformations, smallness of the auricle or pinna of the ear, defective thymus gland formation, heart defects

Lithium: heart defects

Phenytoin (an anticonvulsant): heart defects, defective nail formation, growth retardation

Progestins (p. 120) contaminated with testosterone: masculinization of female fetus

Tetracyclines (a type of antibiotic): abnormal enamel development

Thalidomide (a banned hypnotic agent): phocomelia (hands or feet appear to come from trunk owing to absent arms or legs), anomalies of ears, teeth, eyes, and intestine

Valproic acid (p. 332): Spina bifida (p. 146), facial anomalies, developmental delay

Warfarin (vitamin K antagonist that slows clotting): defective nose formation, shortened digits, abnormalities at ends of bones, mental deficiency

Maternal Conditions

Alcoholism: Growth and mental retardation, microcephaly (small head), heart defects, flexion contractures (permanent muscle contractions)

Diabetes mellitus (p. 146): Numerous birth defects

Lupus erythematosus (an autoimmune disease [p. 196]): Blockage of cardiac conduction

Smoking: Low birth weight, abnormal attachment of placenta

Trace Metals

Lead: Decreased intelligence

Mercury: Microcephaly, spasticity, mental deficiency

Intrauterine Infections

Cytomegalovirus: Microcephaly, mental deficiency

Rubella (German measles): Heart defects, microcephaly, cataracts (lens opacities), deafness, mental deficiency

Toxoplasmosis: Macrocephaly (enlarged head) or microcephaly, small eyes, mental deficiency

Varicella: Skin scars, defective limb formation, small eyes, cataracts, mental deficiency

Uterine Factors

Amniotic band deformity (defect in the membrane surrounding the fetus): Amputation or constriction bands on one or more extremities

Severe oligohydramnios (insufficient amniotic fluid [fluid surrounding the fetus]): Deficient lung formation, pressure deformities

---

[a]Modified from Holmes LB. Genetic counseling. In: Behrman RE, Vaughan VC, Nelson WE, eds. Nelson textbook of pediatrics. Philadelphia: Saunders, 1987:272.

sociated with placental degeneration and anoxia (21).

General Health and Other Influences

Following birth, good nutrition, good supervision, and regular immunization are essential to development. Brain infection may have lifelong neuropsychiatric sequelae. Lead toxicity (anemia, mental retardation, seizures) from eating chipped paint can be devastating.

Low socioeconomic status (SES) is associated with greater risks to health and poorer medical care (p. 96). Low SES parents play less with their children (27, 28), supervise them less outside of the home (29, 30), and more often give directions rather than explain or ask questions (31, 32).

Although delinquency is more common among the poor, poverty alone does not explain it. Even in the toughest poverty-stricken areas, many children are considerate of others. These nondelinquents are more popular among their peers than delinquents (33–36). Also, poor children tend to be more generous and grateful than middle-class children (37, 38).

Gender (pp. 154–162) is important. The key determinant of sexual identity is the sex *assigned* by the parents (39–41). Children (97% in one study) reared by gay or transsexual parents show normal, typical psychosexual development (42). The prevalence of nearly all child psychiatric disorders is greater for boys than for girls (M>F) (43).

Ethnic differences occur. African-American, Mexican, Eastern Indian, and Middle Eastern children reach motor milestones before Euro-Americans (44). Euro-Americans become bladder-trained before African-Americans (45). Childrearing also differs: Japanese children sleep in their parents' room until age 10, inconceivable for U.S. families (46). Swedish and Australian parents begin toilet training children far earlier than American parents (outcomes are the same) (47, 48). Frequency of transitional object use (p. 135) varies among societies (49).

Birth order and family size are related to academic achievement. First-borns tend to score higher academically (50). Academic performance tends to decrease with family size (perhaps related to exposure to adult conversation) (51).

Major environmental changes can affect comfort and functioning. Children placed in supportive environments, after several years in deprived circumstances or residential nurseries, show major gains in health (52). Children from deprived families adopted into middle-class homes show higher IQs than nonadopted peers (53).

Personal characteristics and social backgrounds of pupils in a school better predict its students' academic achievements than any other variable (54). When schools in similar districts are compared, however, there are differences in achievement, attendance, and delinquency rates, attributable to administration, teaching, and morale (55, 56). Preschool programs (e.g. Head Start) improve children's achievements, but unless special interventions continue when the children begin school, effects of the enrichment wash out (10).

Attractiveness may play a role in development. Children rated by peers or teachers as attractive tend to be more popular and confident and less apt to be delinquent (57–59).

TEMPERAMENT

Temperament, or behavioral style, has nine components: activity level, rhythmicity (regularity of biologic functions such as sleep), tendency to approach or withdraw from new persons or situations, adaptability, responsiveness to stimulation, intensity, quality of mood (pleased and friendly or crying and unfriendly), distractibility, and attention span (60).

Many children show clusters of these characteristics. The easy child (about 40% of children) is adaptable, regular, and pleased. The difficult child (about 10%) reacts intensely, shows irregularity of functions, tends to withdraw, and adopts poorly. The slow-to-warm-up child (15%) first shows mild negative responses to new situations, but adapts eventually. The remaining 35% show varying combinations of traits (60).

Temperament has a heritable component (61). For many persons, temperament continues from infancy to adulthood. Outcome is influenced, however, by the relationship (goodness of fit) of the child's temperament with parental responsiveness and expectations (62, 63). Environmental changes can alter parent-child relations and outcome. For example, the death of a supportive, limit-setting father was followed by disruptive behavior in a teenage girl when her overtaxed mother could not provide enough support or limit-setting. A difficult child revealed musical talent highly valued by her parents, increasing their sensitivity to her artistic temperament (6).

PARENT-CHILD RELATIONSHIP

Besides parental contribution to a child's genes, nourishment, protection, and so forth, it is in the context of the parent-child relationship that development unfolds.

Bonding and Attachment

EARLY YEARS

Konrad Lorenz (64) discovered a sensitive period in a gosling's life when it became attached to (imprinted on) a moving figure. If a goose imprinted on a human, it ignored adult geese when the time came to mate. But there is no evidence for equivalent critical periods in human development.

Parent-child bonding is a mutual interaction that begins during pregnancy. As early as 12 hours postdelivery, newborns synchronize their actions with an adult voice (65). By 5 days, an infant can differentiate by smell his mother's breast pad from that of other mothers (66). Within weeks, infants can differentiate (e.g., by voice) their parents from other adults (67, 68).

Three-month-old infants will search a room until they find their parents, and then move their extremities excitedly and extend their arms to urge their parents to notice (69). Infants will start a dialogue by cooing, and the parents will respond with conversational speech. The baby listens, waits for the parent to stop, and coos again (reciprocity) (62, 70).

Infants, long aware of parent-stranger differences, prefer their parents' company. This development shows a quantum change between age 5–9 months, when infants become fearful and withdraw when a stranger is present. Stranger anxiety is normal, reflecting attachment to parents. This attachment provides security: in a parent's presence, infants are more willing to speak, explore, or play with a stranger, returning to the parent for reassurance (secure base effect) (71–74). Intensity and duration of stranger anxiety vary with the child's temperament. It often has a second

peak at 18–20 months and begins to subside by age 2½–3 years (75, 76).

Related (not identical) to stranger anxiety is separation anxiety. At 6–7 months (usually ending by 2–3 years), infants show distress when their parent departs, leaving them alone. The child cries, explores less, follows the departing parent, and calls for the mother or father to return (77). Over half of 2 year olds cry when left by the mother, and over 40% of 2½ year olds, but only 20% of 3 year olds (78). The more secure the attachment, the *less* crying on separation (79).

Attachment does not occur with just one caregiver but rather to a hierarchy of persons (80). Usually, the difference between the intensity of the attachment to the person atop the hierarchy compared to attachment to the person second in the hierarchy is not more than that between those who are second and third (67, 81). Although all studies show that most infants are most closely attached to their mother, these studies also show that infants bond to multiple others, the father especially. By age 18 months, 75% of infants are strongly bonded to their fathers (80, 82).

The amount of time spent in caretaking (dressing, etc.) is largely irrelevant; e.g., kibbutz-raised Israeli children are more strongly attached to their parents than to the nurse who supervises them daily. The key is active reciprocal interaction with persons responsive to the infant's cues (67, 72, 77, 83).

Although it is optimal for bonding to begin with the primary caretakers in the first days of life, close parent-child attachment can begin with adoptive parents in late childhood (84). Institution-reared children tend to be more clinging, less attached to individual caretakers, more attention-seeking and disobedient at school, less academically skilled, less articulate, and less popular than family-reared children. But adoption with family rearing can reverse some of this (67, 85–87). At the other pole, Spitz studied infants who were reared in a prison nursery, receiving minimal attention, with no access to parents (87). If they were not reunited with parents or adopted, they developed anaclitic depression: they lost their appetite and weight, initially cried and then became apathetic and developmentally retarded, and often died from infection or emaciation (marasmus).

LATER DEVELOPMENT

Autonomy increases over the years. Children move about freely, feed themselves easily, and convey needs through language. Optimal development occurs if the parents allow the child to enter uncharted territory without being too restrictive. They also promote socialization, sphincter control, awareness and handling of feelings, self-observation and self-esteem, and the development of a conscience (21).

STAGES OF CHILDHOOD

Pregnancy

The newborn can be viewed as 37 weeks old—massive maturation has occurred. During embryonic days 40–125, the cerebral cortical neurons were produced while migrating from the cerebral ventricular surface along glial columns to their final location (88). The cochlea (ear structure responsive to position change) works as early as 4 months prior to birth. The fetus responds to sounds and manifests all the reflexes (p. 134) of the newborn (3).

Some pediatricians encourage a third trimester prenatal visit (89) to assess risk factors, encourage the father's participation, and plan for the birth. Anticipatory guidance is provided in a question-answer format (e.g., Have you purchased a car seat?) rather than as directives. Parents' interest is praised.

The baby's return from the hospital should be in a proper car restraint. The child is *not* safest when held by the parent. Car accidents are the foremost preventable cause of death in children, and most injuries to children occur at slow speeds close to home (90). A child's behavior improves when in a safety seat (91).

Circumcision is performed on most newborn boys, usually 24 hours after birth. Ask the parents if they wish this procedure done.

Circumcision is associated with fewer urinary tract infections, and uncircumcised men are at greater risk for AIDS (70, 92). The infant has pain with circumcision that can be attenuated with dorsal penile nerve block (93).

Address sibling rivalry, a normal response to a new sibling. An older child normally attached to parents receives less attention and resents it. Regressions (e.g., clinging, demanding, sleep disturbances, stuttering, thumb sucking, bed wetting, baby talk) are common. The older child needs more attention (94). Paternal attention to older children predicts better adjustment (95). The older child will learn to laugh at the baby's antics, and develops confidence in making the infant laugh, play games, and imitate. Demands that the older child act like a big boy or girl are unfair (96).

The Newborn (Neonate)

IMMEDIATE ASSESSMENT

At 1 and 5 minutes after birth, rate the neonate by an Apgar Score (Table 11.2). Scores lower than 7 suggest a high-risk situation (97). Medication given the mother during labor and delivery affects the infant's behavior (e.g., diminished muscle tone, depressed respirations, diminished responsiveness to the mother [and vice versa]) (98).

The somatosensory cortex is the best developed part of the neonate's brain (90). During the first hours after delivery, the infant is particularly alert. If the mother plans breast feeding, this is the best time to begin (99). Newborns can distinguish degrees of sweet taste, reject aversive tastes, act pleased by fruity odors, and look displeased with noxious odors (100). They turn their head to the spoken word in the first hour and synchronize actions with an adult voice at 12 hours (101). They tend not to respond to loud noises (3) but may cry in response to another child's cry (early empathy?) (102). Visually they respond best to high-contrast, three-dimensional, and moving objects, bright colors, contours, curved lines, and faces (67). They may mimic interesting

Table 11.2. The APGAR Scale[a]

Sign	0	1	2
Heart rate	Absent	Below 100	Over 100
Respiratory effort	Absent	Slow, irregular	Good and crying
Muscle tone	Flaccid	Some flexion of extremities	Active motion
Reflex irritability	No response	Cry	Vigorous cry
Color	Blue, pale	Body pink, extremities blue	Completely pink

[a]Reprinted with permission from Klaus MH, Fanaroff AA. Care of the high-risk neonate. Philadelphia: WB Saunders, 1973.

Table 11.3. Ontogeny and Manifestations of Neonatal Reflexes[a]

Reflex	Normal Response	Age It Appears	Age It Disappears
Palmar grasp	Hand closes over finger placed in it	28 wks gestation	2 mos
Tonic neck	When head is turned, same-side leg extends, other-side arm and leg flex	35 wks, peaks at 44 wks	7–8 mos
Stepping, walking	With arms uplifted to make body erect, neonate takes steps	37 wks	2–4 mos
Moro	Responding to loud noise or other startling event, neonate extends and abducts arms, then flexes and adducts (brings toward trunk) them	28 wks complete at 37 wks	3–6 mos
Pupillary	Constriction of pupils when light shines on them	32 wks	Never
Babinski	Extension (upgoing) of great toe when lateral surface of sole is stroked		1 year
Deep tendon			
Biceps	Arm flexion when biceps tendon is tapped		Never
Knee	Knee jerk when patellar tendon is tapped		Never
Ankle	Ankle jerk when Achilles tendon is tapped		Never

[a]Modified from Volpe JJ. Neurology of the newborn. Philadelphia: WB Saunders, 1971.

visual displays (e.g., protruding the tongue if a parent does this) (103).

Infants sleep about 75% of the time, 50% of which is rapid eye movement (REM) sleep (p. 375). Many reflexes are present at birth (Table 11.3). Breast-fed babies are more resistant to infection and less susceptible to hyponatremia (low sodium) than formula-fed babies (99). But bottle feeding lets more caregivers participate.

Infancy (Birth to 18 Months)

EMOTIONAL DEVELOPMENT

Erikson wrote that consistency in meeting infants' needs engenders basic trust (104). Freud labelled infancy the oral period (much time is spent in pleasurable sucking), positing that tender care in meeting the child's oral and other needs leads to a capacity to be caring and self-reliant (105).

Low intensity, spontaneous smiling (endogenous smiling) occurs within several days after birth, disappearing at age 3 months (106). The 3-month-old has new facial expressions to convey emotions: pouting, coyness, disgruntlement, teasing, wariness, insulted, fearful, bored. The infant can imitate facial expressions and sounds, draws attention with forced coughs, bubble-blowing, and raspberries (blowing air through opposable lips), and explores faces by looking, swiping, poking, and pulling (69).

At age 2 months, infants smile at a face (social smile), and within several weeks smile at familiar faces or when pleased. They laugh at 4 months of age, best elicited by vigorously kissing their abdomen or looming towards them while talking, concluding with a tickle (106).

From birth, babies cry to express discomfort from pain, hunger, wetness, cold, excess stimulation, and fatigue. Often, parents can associate types of cry with cause (70, 107).

Quantity of crying peaks at 6 weeks of age (about 2¾ hours per 24 hours) and is most frequent from 4–6 PM (108). Some infants from 2–3 weeks to 3–4 months have colic, i.e., when an infant otherwise healthy and well fed has paroxysms of irritability or crying totaling over 3 hours daily for more than 3 days in any week (109). The cause is unknown, although air-trapping because of autonomic dysfunction is possible, based on (1) frequent termination of a colicky spell upon expulsion of flatus, and (2) routine spontaneous recovery by 4 months when the nervous system is more mature (110). Treatments may include routine holding of the infant for 3 hours daily, avoiding overstimulation, short vacations for the parents, or antispasmodic medication (111).

Stranger anxiety intensifies with unfamiliar surroundings, proximity to the stranger, and eye-to-eye contact. It decreases if the stranger is near the mother, holds toys, or responds to the infant's cues, or if the infant is familiar with the setting (112). Child strangers cause less anxiety than adult strangers (113).

Two thirds of U.S. children have a transitional object, a cuddly object that comforts them when tired, frightened, or hungry. Children select the object as early as age 7 months and as late as 2 years. Most children discard it by age 4, but many retain it into school years (112).

LANGUAGE AND OTHER INTELLECTUAL DEVELOPMENT

Virtually all parents and older siblings in all cultures speak to infants in baby talk (high pitch, short, slow, distinct utterances; a special intonation, here-and-now content stressing what the child attends to, and frequent repetition). This better holds the child's attention (114).

At age 3–4 months, the infant babbles (mixes vowels and consonants). Congenitally deaf children also babble. The congenitally deaf may be identified by responsiveness to gesturing compared to voice (114). When children first talk, they often echo the last few words of what is said to them. This echolalia persists to about age 2½ years (115). After echolalia, the first words children speak refer to familiar persons or objects (e.g., dada). This occurs at age 10–15 months. At first, children are highly specific in their use of words (e.g., dada for their father and nobody else), and later generalize (e.g., daddy for any man, which can embarrass the parents) (114).

Piaget termed birth-age 2 the sensorimotor period, when learning occurs through direct perception and action on the environment. Initially, the infant perceives that an object out of sight is gone, but at 12–18 months knows it is retrievable, (object permanence, reinforced by playing peek-a-boo) (116).

MOTOR DEVELOPMENT

Grasping progresses stepwise (117): Primitive reflexes appear before voluntary behavior. The grasp reflex, present at birth, disappears at age 2 months. There is proximal to distal (shoulder to fingers) progression: reach precedes grasp (4 months). There is ulnar to radial progression; the infant first picks up objects on the "little finger side" (4–5 months), and later (6–7 months) uses the "thumb side." Pronation precedes supination; palm-down maneuvers such as picking up objects occur before palm-up actions. Grasp precedes release. Release occurs at age 9–10 months. Between ages 1 and 3 years, hand preference begins.

Infants can roll over at age 2–4 months, sit without support at age 5–7 months, and pull themselves up to stand at age 6–10 months. At about 1 year of age they can walk forward if someone holds a hand, and can walk alone by around age 13 months. Initial walking is with the shoulders abducted, elbows flexed, and gait broad-based, with tremendous energy expenditure (118).

OTHER DEVELOPMENT

By age 3 months, babies usually sleep through the night. About one third of mothers of 1-year-olds report genital play by the infants (119).

ANTICIPATORY GUIDANCE

At age 4–6 months, before children crawl (not all children can crawl before they walk), physicians should discuss child-proofing the house with the parents. Medicines, toxic chemicals, and sharp objects should be out of reach, but all rooms should have something with which the children can play. Stranger anxiety should be anticipated, so that parents can forewarn visitors. Until they walk well, children should not eat and walk simultaneously. Education about the normal quantity of child crying can alleviate guilt (120).

The Toddler (18 Months to 3 Years)

The 18-month-old typically weighs 3½ times more than at birth, and pulse has slowed from 140 (2SD = 50) to 110 (2SD = 40). Climbing stairs, running (awkwardly), and throwing a ball are characteristic. Most children can run well at age 24 months (120, 121).

Speech by age 17–21 months is in telegraphic (e.g., "Mommy go"), two-word sentences (122). Children aged 18–25 months can express over 50 words, with receptive vocabulary 10 times that, which enables them to process brief, clear statements. By age 24–36 months, children can speak 200 words (123, 124). Stuttering is common and normal before age 3, reflecting thought faster than speech. Beyond age 3 or 4, it merits speech therapy referral (124).

The 2–3-year-old cannot distinguish TV ads from regular programs and is unusually vulnerable to advertising (125). There is more comprehension of spatial relations (e.g., rather than trying to fit a round object in a square hole by trial-and-error, many 2-year-olds select a round hole from a variety of shapes).

Toddlers readily play alone (solitary play) or alongside other children. But children do not mutually participate; play is independent (parallel play). At about age 18 months, children begin to say (or shake their head) no even if motivated to say yes; this normal negatism reflects developing autonomy. Erikson identified autonomy (vs. shame and doubt) as a key development in toddlers.

Bowel training is usually completed by age 3 years, bladder training by age 4. This follows the capacity for sphincter control at age 18–24 months, corresponding to the ability to run and then suddenly stop (122). Clues include the child's interest in the toilet, displeasure following soiling, and squatting for defecation after a meal. Despite recommendations to wait for this readiness, most mothers in many countries begin "potting" their infants before 1 year, with no proven good or bad outcome (126). Freud labelled this the anal period. He postulated that parental overcontrol in toilet training led to parsimony, over-cleanliness, or obsessiveness (105). Coerciveness in toilet training is insensitive and ineffectual.

Common fears at age 2 are noises, falling, and strange objects and persons. At age 3, fears of animals are common (106). Toddlers cannot easily delay gratification, suppress anger, or see others' perspectives, so tantrums occur, with frequency and intensity related to temperament and parental response.

Because most women who have children work outside the home (127), daytime supervision by grandparents, day care centers, or others is commonplace. Research on children in day care centers reveals no increase in behavioral problems. In fact, they show short-term decreases in stranger and separation anxiety, and have less traditional ideas of the family and sex roles. Supervised in day care, children from disadvantaged homes show short-term enhancement of development and health. For middle-class children, there is a short-term increase in frequency of colds, followed by a long-term decrease (112). Parents considering day care should visit the center and expect the center to be able to meet the child's physical needs; provide opportunities for play and conversation; and have consistent supervision by qualified staff (128).

Encourage use of toys whose use is child-determined (e.g., blocks, balls, puppets, crayons). For toilet training, emphasize the child's control, not the parents'. Tantrums can be handled by distracting the child, appearing not to notice, or giving the child a "time out" in his or her room with an explanation ("You will stay in your room until you stop crying. I'll be in the kitchen and you can come to me when you stop.") (129). Children should be encouraged to *use words* when angry. When children stutter, comments such as "relax" or "think before you speak" are unhelpful (120).

The Preschool/Kindergarten Child (Ages 3–6 Years)

Between 3 and 4 years of age, the child's vocabulary increases from several hundred to several thousand words. The 3-year-old can speak in fluent three-word sentences, the 4-year-old in four-word sentences, the 5-year-old in five-word sentences. The 5-year-old enters kindergarten (age $^+5 =$ grade in school).

The 3-year-old can use plurals and pronouns, state her age, sex, and full name, and is intelligible to strangers 75% of the time (130). The 4-year-old can use prepositions, knows common colors and animals, and the meaning of tired, cold, and hungry, and follows a two-stage command. The child at age 4 can use the past tense, making minor errors (e.g., "I wented to Granny's") that parents find cute and do not correct (correct usage comes naturally, not from parental teaching). Parents do, however, correct errors of fact (e.g., if he didn't go to Granny's) (131).

Five-year-olds can use the future tense, understand numbers, and follow three-stage commands. Thus, the office examination of a 3–5-year-old with a parent can include useful 3-way verbal interchanges. Form perception remains imperfect; 96% of kindergarteners confuse p with q in reading and writing (132).

During ages 2½–6, the child develops cause-and-effect theories that typify Piaget's preoperational cognitive stage. All objects have feelings and motives. All moving things are alive ("Where do boats go at night?" "They sleep like we do.") (animism). All things are made by humans for humans, all questions have answers, and adults have the answers ("What causes rain?" "Someone emptying a water can.") (artificialism). Events of-

ten occur for the child's benefit ("Why does the sun shine?" "To keep me warm.") (egocentrism) (133). Unrelated events perceived together are often causally related (e.g., the child had to take medicine *because* the doctor put an otoscope in his ear) (transductive reasoning) (134).

A 3-year-old can ride a tricycle, climb stairs alone, and put on shoes without tying laces. A 4-year-old can throw a ball overhand. Many 5-year-olds can skip, hop on one foot, and learn other complex activities, e.g., figure skating. Handedness is fully expressed by age 5 (134). Because it is heritable, left-handedness in a child in a strictly right-handed pedigree warrants investigation (112).

Between ages 3 and 4, cooperative play begins. From age 3 through the rest of childhood, similar-age play is preferred (135). About 20% of children ages 3–6 have an imaginary friend. These are more often created by girls, first-borns, and only children (136). The 3–4-year-old child also notices differences between individuals (e.g., differences in weight, ethnicity [ethnic identity]) (136). Two thirds of 3-year-olds know their sex, first by hairstyle and clothing (137), and begin to show sex-typical behavior (e.g., roughhousing for boys, doll play for girls) (138).

Freud described ages 3–6 as the time of the Oedipus complex and its resolution: the child wants to marry the opposite-sex parent, feels rivalry towards the same-sex parent, and fears retribution (for boys, by castration) from this parent. This resolves by the child's identification with the same-sex parent. This identification includes incorporating parental moral values, the content of a developing superego.

Are Oedipal phenomena universal and normal? Systematic observations of children suggest they are common but not inevitable. Children ages 5–13, who at some point had observed the genitals of the opposite sex, were interviewed: 33% thought girls had had a penis that had shrunk or was cut off, but most were not perturbed by this (137). Most children have a phase of antipathy to the same sex parent while continuing to love *both* parents, particularly the mother (139). Generally, children prefer the parent who is most responsive, not necessarily the opposite-sex parent (21). Between ages 2–5, 80% of children engage in genital play, and 55% of boys and 16% of girls masturbate (41).

The School-Age Child (Ages 6–12)

Pediatricians and parents readily appreciate the school-age child: For physicians, who consider these children a pleasure to examine, they rarely present any problems (140). The child is industrious (Erikson's normative crisis for this stage is industry vs. inferiority), proud of mastering tasks at school and in organized athletic and artistic activities (104).

Attention span is increased and the child will practice. Riddles and jokes are fun. At age 7, the child can copy a diamond, at age 9 a Red Cross sign, and at age 12 a cube. Piaget's stage of concrete operations (116) begins by age 7, and continues to ages 12–13: the child learns to categorize and to discern that an item has more than one property (e.g., when given wooden beads, some red and more white, and asked if there are more red or white beads, the child answers white. Then, if asked if there are more white or *wood* beads, the child replies wood.) (21). The understanding of the concept of conservation also develops: knowing that a given quantity of a substance is fixed regardless of its container or distribution. A ball of clay molded into another shape has the same *amount* of clay, and an amount of liquid poured into a different-shaped container stays the same.

Another achievement is reversibility: Before age 7, children can add 6 + 4 and know it equals 10; after age 7, they will also conclude that 10 minus 4 equals 6. Questioning about an event (e.g., a summer vacation), activity, or person is a good test of memory ("Where did you go on your vacation?"), problem-solving ("What did you like best and least about the trip?" "Why?"), and creativity ("Where would you like to go if you could go anywhere?" "Why?") (141). By age 6, the

brain reaches adult size (142). At age 10, sleep reaches the adult balance of 20% REM, 80% non-REM (143).

Contact with peers increases throughout childhood, increasing from 10% of contact time at age 2 to 50% for school age (144). By ages 8–10, the child lists two to three best friends instead of one. Same-sex peer relations become especially close. Empathy develops considerably in relations with chums (145).

Freud named this period latency, during which sexual drives are channeled into learning and peer relations (105). But this sublimation is incomplete. In sexually permissive cultures, sex play and even lovemaking are common during middle childhood (146, 147). Also, frequency of masturbation by boys increases progressively from ages 6–12 (148).

About 15% of children ages 5–12 sleepwalk (p. 380) at least once. Sleepwalking is most frequent during times of stress and usually ceases spontaneously by young adulthood (149). Night terrors, which occur in 1%–3% of children (p. 381), tend *not* to be associated with daytime anxiety and usually cease spontaneously by young adulthood (150).

Adolescence

Adolescence starts with puberty and ends in adulthood. Puberty refers to the physical changes initiating sexual maturation. It usually begins between ages 8–13 in girls, 10–14 in boys. A growth spurt accompanies puberty. Because organs grow at different rates, the adolescent often appears gangly and gawky and feels self-conscious.

> Some youngsters feel they are growing too fast or too slowly, too soon or too late. These apprehensions are most often revealed by nonverbal or obtuse patterns of communication. Hence, the girl whose breasts are developing more quickly than those of her peers may adopt a hunched posture. . . . The boy whose genitals are not as big as those of his friends may suddenly find excuses not to take gym or go to the locker room (6).

Adolescents may spend hours before a mirror or in the bathroom becoming acquainted with their own bodies. There is preoccupation with grooming, cleanliness, and dieting. Do not tease teenagers about their appearance (6).

Teenage boys who mature earlier physically tend to be more self-assured and poised (21). In contrast, *late*-maturing teenage girls tend to be more self-assured. Boys and girls who experience earlier puberty tend to have earlier and more sexual experience (151). This also occurs for precociously pubescent (before age 8 in girls, age 10 in boys) children.

In the past 80 years, puberty has begun at progressively earlier ages. The average age of menarche (first menstruation) was 14.5 years in 1900, compared to 12.5 in 1980 (152). With each succeeding generation, height also increases (153).

Adolescents experience major development of the following: cognitive ability, which approaches its highest level during adolescence; identity (Who am I? What are my interests, skills, strengths and weaknesses? How do I appear to others?); independence from parents, resulting in a more equal relationship with them, and a capacity for self-support and autonomous living; career development; and sexual object choice with a capacity to be intimate (concerned, affectionate) as well as erotic. Adolescence is often divided into early (ages 11–13), middle (ages 14–16), and late (age 17 and over).

COGNITIVE AND MOTOR DEVELOPMENT

Individuals vary widely in judgment, abstract thinking, problem-solving and planning. Although these are refined throughout life as wisdom, the extent to which a person has these *capacities* is established by late adolescence. This is why debating teams are formed or plane geometry is taught for the first time in high school. Piaget (116) labelled these tasks formal operations. After age 11 children know that death is irreversible. Acquisition of postconventional morality (applying universal ethical principles, regardless of the rules) re-

quires formal operations (154). Despite early adolescent gangliness, motor development approaches adult level, with capacities for professional-caliber athletic performance from exceptional persons.

SOCIAL DEVELOPMENT

The early adolescent maintains close same-sex friendships, a major source of information about sex, and a sounding board for new ideas (6). There is a teen culture, with its own music, dress, and language. This allows some separateness while the adolescent remains influenced by the parents' values (21). Adolescents view reasonable parental limit-setting as evidence of concern (155).

The midadolescent enters heterosexual peer groups and begins dating and sexual experimentation. Members of the opposite sex, however, are viewed primarily as sex objects; one component of dating is pride from telling same-sex peers about the date. Late adolescents begin more intimate, empathic relationships, and some marry.

SEXUALITY

All adolescent boys and most adolescent girls masturbate. About 30% of 16–year-old girls from all social classes have had coitus before marriage, as have 60% of 19 year old women (156). The lower the socioeconomic status and the less the occupational aspiration, the earlier the sex. About 33% of sexually active teenagers become pregnant, and 40% of these obtain abortions (157). Sexually transmitted disease (STD) is common and increasing in prevalence (158). Homosexual fantasies are common among heterosexual teenagers and adults (159). About 4% of the population is exclusively homosexual (160). Gay sexual behavior usually starts in adolescence.

RISK-TAKING

Risk-taking is common in teenagers. Transitory delinquencies (e.g., stealing, vandalism) and pranks are common, and unrelated to socioeconomic status. Repeated delinquency often presages antisocial personality disorder (161). Although adolescent drug abuse and smoking have declined, 54% of high school seniors have smoked marijuana at least once, and teenage drinking and smoking are common (162).

HEALTH CARE

Ages 5–18 are usually the healthiest years with the fewest doctor visits. The four most common causes of death in U.S. teenagers are accidents, suicide, homicide, and cancer. Because of the adolescent's developing autonomy, need for privacy, and cognitive capacity, the topical sensitivity of sex and drug abuse, and laws in many states supporting treatment of STD and management (prenatal care or abortion) of teenage pregnancy without parental consent, a portion of most visits should be conducted alone with the adolescent. Most parents support a physician's maintaining confidentiality despite the minor status of most under age 18 adolescents, and most adolescents welcome some sharing of information with parents. The teenager and parent should be promptly told the rules of confidentiality (p. 434).

Take a sexual history from every adolescent, and (unless the teenager broaches the subject spontaneously) obtain this matter-of-factly during the review of systems in a private interview (163). A contraceptive display of pills, condoms, and so forth should be available if the subject of contraception arises (164). Often, when a teenager asks about contraception, the person has been sexually active for months (165). Symptoms of pregnancy may be the reason for a teenager's first visit to you (156). Inform the pregnant teenager of the diagnosis and options, and encourage her to discuss the pregnancy with her parents (perhaps in your office) and the baby's father. The decision of what to do about the pregnancy is hers (164).

Screening for STD is indicated for all teenagers who are sexually active, rape or incest victims, pregnant, gay and male, imprisoned,

have pyuria (pus in the urine), or have a past STD history (157, 166). A drug abuse history should be obtained matter-of-factly and nonjudgmentally (e.g., Do you *do* drugs? *Drop* acid?, or by asking first if the teen's peers do drugs).

Pelvic examinations of teenage girls are indicated for amenorrhea (absent menses), painful menses, excessive quantity or numbers of days of menstrual flow, vaginal discharge, contraceptive prescription, cytologic studies (for precancerous conditions or cancer) if the teenager is sexually active, or if the patient asks to be evaluated. A patient's report of rape usually requires examination by a specialist (167). A patient experiencing her first pelvic examination is often anxious, embarrassed, or puzzled about what to expect. Before asking her to undress, explain the procedure and your reason for performing it. This is best done by a demonstration of the examination that includes insertion of a speculum into a three-dimensional pelvic anatomic model, and discussion of the pelvic anatomy (167). Tell the patient that the examination does not affect her virginity, and ask if she has questions. The remainder of the examination is discussed elsewhere (167). Following the examination, discuss your findings with the patient.

Teach teenage girls about breast self-examination after explaining its purpose and answering questions. To show her what her normal breast feels like, have her palpate her breast after you have done so. Then, have her place her tongue in her cheek and palpate her face over the cheek to demonstrate what a firm rubbery abnormal mass feels like. Models are available from supply houses (164). Instruct teenage boys to notify you if they notice a testicular or scrotal lump; though testicular cancer in teenagers is rare, it does occur (164, 168).

SPECIAL SITUATIONS

Adoption

Between 2%–3% of infants become adopted children. About 50% of adoptions are by relatives. Adoption should ideally occur within several days after birth. Next best is before the sixth month. However, adoptions of older children may work well if the child does not have major behavioral problems, has not had multiple foster home placements, and is not intensely attached to the biologic mother (21).

The adoption agency should inform the adoptive parents about major medical problems of the families of the biologic parents, to permit prompt addressing of heritable disorders, if they occur. Although comprehension of adoption does not occur until school age, children should be told they are adopted long before this age by their adoptive parents, lest this information come unexpectedly, leading to mistrust. Adopted children are twice as likely as nonadopted children to be referred for behavioral problems (21, 169).

Hospitalization

About 30% of children are hospitalized at least once. About 5% have multiple admissions (120). Hospitalization involves many stresses for the child: separation from parents (unless there is a rooming-in policy), strangers and medical procedures, the illness itself, and parental anxiety. Expect some regression after the hospital stay, regardless of the child's age (20, 170).

Distress with hospitalization is greatest between 6 months and 4 years of age. The 4 year old knows the separation from parents will not be permanent, but the child may feel he or she caused the illness. The school age child can make friends on the ward. The adolescent can comprehend the medical problem well, but self-image may suffer (170).

Stein (170) recommends the following: avoid hospitalization if possible; give the child an age-appropriate reason for the hospitalization; for elective procedures, describe in advance the hospital setting and procedures; allow flexible visiting hours and rooming-in by parents. Parent participation is so helpful that it outweighs the occasional problems that parents present; hospitalize in a setting designed for children; allow the child to participate in the care (e.g., "Which arm should I take the blood from?").

Divorce

Before children in the United States today reach age 18, about 40% will experience the breakup of their parents marriage. Research (171–174) documents that children of divorced parents experience more behavioral problems than children living with both biologic parents. But the divorce itself does not sufficiently explain the behavioral problems that typically *precede* the divorce by several years (175). If the postdivorce situation stabilizes, children in a stable single-parent family tend to function better than children in conflict-ridden nuclear families (171).

Once the divorce occurs, only 10% of children feel relieved (172). The rest experience the initial postdivorce period as painful. Family conflict tends to *escalate* after the divorce (173). The following are common initial responses to divorce: children ages 2.5–5 experience regression, sleep disturbances, irritability, separation anxiety, demands for physical contact, inhibition of play, fear of abandonment (by the remaining parent), and feeling responsible for the separation. Children 5–8 years of age manifest open grieving, sobbing, feelings of rejection, longing for the departed parent, fantasies of return of the departed parent, marked decline in school work, and fears of being thrown out (in boys whose fathers have left). Children 9–12 years of age show feigned nonchalance, reluctance to discuss the problem, intense anger at one or both parents, decline in school performance, and deterioration in peer relations. Adolescents show depression, truancy, sexual activity, drug abuse, and suicidal behaviors (174).

Socioeconomic problems influence the situation. Poor people are more apt to divorce, and divorce usually lowers the living standard for one or both partners, usually the mother (171). Few divorce settlements address college education; half the children of divorce becomes less well educated than their parents

(172). Divorce is one of the few crises in which social supports (e.g., friends who think they will have to take sides) decrease. Children of divorce form supportive friendships and may benefit from support groups sponsored by schools (172).

For many children, improvement in behavior occurs by the second year following divorce. About 33% (boys more than girls) continue, however, to have behavior problems after 5 years (171). Problems are greatest when there is continued fighting between parents or the custodial parent is depressed (120). Children of divorce are more likely to divorce as adults (172).

If divorce cannot be forestalled by marital counseling, the physician should foster continued involvement with the child by both parents. Psychotherapy is often indicated for children of divorce whose adaptation is impaired. Children should be told they were not responsible for the divorce, that they need not take sides, and that they cannot mend the divorce (120).

Child Abuse

Estimates are that between 1–4 million cases of child abuse occur yearly in the U.S. The imprecision of the estimates results in part from the fact that most cases are unreported. They account for 10% of injuries in children under age 5 seen in emergency rooms and about 2000 deaths a year (120).

Abused children are more apt to be under age 5, boys, handicapped, of difficult temperament, behaviorally different (e.g., hyperactive), or a foster child. Contributing factors include poverty, unemployment, social isolation, geographic mobility, poor housing, parental discord or a dominant-submissive relationship between parents, problems in parent-child attachment, punitive child-rearing style, scapegoating of a child, role reversals with a parent expecting a child to meet dependency needs, and child being unwanted (120). Abuse also occurs in middle- and upper-class families. Abusive parents often have low self-esteem, depressed mood, substance abuse,

personality disorder, ignorance of childrearing strategies, and unrealistic expectations of children. Parents tend themselves to have been abused as children. There is an increased risk of child abuse by mothers with postpartum psychosis (p. 126). But 90% of abusing parents are neither psychotic nor habitual criminals. Immediate triggers include family crises and child behaviors such as persistent crying, wetting or soiling, spilling or disobedience (120). Psychologic complications are numerous and include delayed development, depression, low self-esteem, self-destructive behavior, school problems, and an increased likelihood of becoming an abusive parent.

Some injuries are not obviously the result of abuse. Often the parent who accompanies the child hides the fact of the abuse, but experienced personnel can recognize distinctive injury patterns (176). Accidental bruises most often occur over the forehead, anterior tibia, and bony prominences. Bruises on the buttocks or lower back are usually from abuse. Subdural hematomas (bleeding under the brain's dural membrane) and abdominal injuries can occur from shaking or squeezing without external signs of injury.

When you suspect abuse, ask nonjudgmentally for details of how the injury occurred, and consider whether the family's explanation jibes with the physical findings. If possible, obtain some information separately from involved adults and from the child. In obtaining and charting information, attend to detail (e.g., circumstances of the injury, past abuse, size, shape, color and locations of injuries, height and weight percentiles, bone surveys for children under age 5, bleeding studies [if bruises are present]).

Protect the child from further injury. Physicians are legally required to report documented or suspected abuse to the local Department of Child and Family Services. Hospital admission may be needed to treat injuries and assure the child's safety. By law, this can be done against a parent's wishes if necessary to protect the child. Services should be provided to abusing families, including childrearing support and parenting education.

Over 250,000 cases of sexual abuse of children are reported each year. Extrafamilial sexual abusers of girls are more often acquaintances than strangers or friends. Uncles are the most frequent intrafamilial perpetrators, followed by stepfathers and fathers, first cousins, and brothers (177). Behavioral manifestations may include the child's simulation of sex acts with dolls, inclusion of genitalia in drawings, verbal references to molestation, sleep and appetite disorders, phobias, depression, and suicidal behaviors. Findings may include genital or anal trauma, signs of STD, recurrent urinary tract infections, vaginitis, genital warts, or pregnancy. Pregnancy can be prevented within 72 hours of intercourse by giving two norgestrel or ethinyl estradiol tablets after examination and another two 12 hours later.

PEDIATRIC INTERVIEWING

Participants

As in other specialities, the pediatric interview usually yields more information than the physical examination (140) or laboratory tests. Before the child is 13 years of age, the interview is triangular, with doctor-parent, doctor-child, and child-parent communication. The child *and* the parent are the patient (120, 178). Although the parent usually can present the history articulately, only the child knows how much he or she is suffering (179). Some children by age 3, and most by age 8, can provide some history. The adolescent should be viewed as the primary informant (178). Regardless of the child's age, to assess patient cognition and ensure that the patient feels valued, some comments or questions should be directed at the child (20).

Often after several visits one parent accompanies the child exclusively. This reveals how the family operates (e.g., sex roles, availability). If the physician invites it, the other parent usually is willing to attend the next visit. Involvement of the father in the child's activities correlates with better functioning by the child (180).

Time

Except for emergencies, initial assessments require at least 30–40 minutes. An initial 10-minute visit appears incomplete. Although emergencies may require briefer interviews, you must continue assembling data while treating a critically ill child (178, 179).

Communication

Position yourself at the same level as parent and child to avoid one-upsmanship. A 6-month to 3-year-old child is best seated in the parent's lap. Before age 2, early in the examination, direct eye contact with the child is frightening and should be avoided (20). Sometimes a first encounter with a child is easier when introduced in a whisper, to which the child often whispers in response (178).

Talk with a child as you would with any patient, and use age-appropriate words. Respect what the child says; do not convey that an idea is childish. Do not laugh at what a child says unless he or she is trying to be humorous. Do not try to be routinely amusing. A child should not be teased unless you know the patient very well and are prepared to be teased in return. Ask *why* questions cautiously (e.g., Why did you do something like that?); they are judgmental. Do not blatantly challenge the truth of what the child says.

Principles of adult interviewing (pp. 179–184) apply to the parents. Address parental concerns in every visit. This, combined with a friendly attitude, are associated with increased compliance (181). When parents seem dissatisfied with an explanation, ask if you have left any questions unanswered.

CHILD PSYCHIATRIC SYNDROMES

Mental Retardation

Mental retardation (M>F) is characterized by significant subaverage intellectual functioning (IQ<70) associated with deficits in adaptive behavior (documented on a social maturity scale). Population prevalence is about 1%–

3% (43); 80% of this group are mildly retarded (IQ 50–70; can learn to sixth grade level), 12% are moderately retarded (IQ 35–49; can talk; poor awareness of social conventions), 7% are severely retarded (IQ 20–34; may learn to talk, can be trained in elementary hygiene); and 1% are profoundly retarded (IQ<20; require lifetime care for survival).

The prevalence of coexisting psychiatric disorders in retarded children is 2–4 times higher than in normal children. Tolerance for anxiety and frustration is lower. Disturbed social relationships, aggressive behaviors, and school problems are the commonest presenting complaints (182, 183).

Mental retardation is a syndrome with hundreds of causes (psychosocial, hereditary, infectious, etc.) (43). The patient's adaptive capacities, relationships, financial supports, and parents' reactions to the child should be assessed. Treatment is individualized, involving educational placement and special services (e.g., speech therapy). Supportive psychotherapy (play therapy with younger children) could address self-esteem, identity, self-control, and expression of feelings, including sexuality. Medications are prescribed if a coexisting syndrome requires it (e.g., stimulants for attention deficit hyperactivity disorder [see below]).

Autistic Disorder

A rare disorder (2–4/10,000 children, M>F), autism is characterized by a *pervasive disruption of social relatedness and language*. The child usually lacks a social smile, is not cuddly, and does not look at people. Language impairment may include mutism, aprosodia (p. 41), or echolalia. Retardation occurs 70%-75% of the time, with an IQ lower than 50 40% of the time. Stereotypic (repetitive, complex, purposeless) behaviors include head-banging, toe-walking, arm-flapping, and posturing. Between 35%–50% of autistic children develop seizures. Minor physical anomalies are common. Hallucinations and delusions are *not* typical. Occasionally, the child demonstrates excellence of a single intellectual ability (savant syndrome).

Laboratory abnormalities often occur and are discussed elsewhere (43). The monozygotic to dizygotic concordance ratio (p. 64) of 36:0 suggests a genetic factor, but there is an elevated incidence of early diseases (e.g., brain infections, congenital rubella, phenylketonuria [p. 123]). About 2%–5% of autistic children have fragile X syndrome (increased number of fragile sites on the long arm of the X chromosome) (184, 185).

Treatment includes behavior modification in a structured classroom, and an individualized education program including speech training, with strong involvement of the parents. Prescribe anticonvulsants for seizures. Full recovery does not occur; adults remain aloof with cognitive deficits. But language function tends to improve and occasionally an adult can function at a rote job and live independently (43, 186).

Attention Deficit Hyperactivity Disorder

Attention deficit hyperactivity disorder (ADHD) is the most commonly diagnosed child psychiatric disorder, occurring in 5%–12% of school age boys (M:F = 6:1). The child shows inability to maintain attention, poor impulse control, low frustration tolerance, and excessive activity level. About 50% have learning impairment owing to attentional difficulties. About 15% have a specific learning disability. Attention dysfunction can occur without hyperactivity.

The frequency of neurologic soft signs (e.g., clumsiness, dysgraphia) and EEG abnormalities increases, as does the frequency of frontal lobe dysfunction on neuropsychologic testing. Computed tomographic scans measuring cerebral blood flow often reveal hypoperfusion in frontal lobes and caudate nuclei (reversible by the stimulant methylphenidate), and increased blood flow in temporal and occipital sensory regions (43, 187). ADHD children have higher blood lead levels than do siblings.

ADHD often coexists with retardation, autism, conduct disorder, Tourette's disorder (p. 276), mood disorder, and disease of the right hemisphere. Thus, ADHD may be a final outcome of a variety of disorders, not a separate disease. It runs in families, often along with alcoholism and antisocial personality disorder, as well as mood and anxiety disorders (43).

The patient should be assessed for other disorders. Patients require structure and accommodation in educational placements and at home. Special education classes may help, ideally with a small, self-contained classroom, careful seating selection, and high teacher to student ratio. At home, an ideal situation includes quiet spaces, subdued colors, simple furniture, keeping toys in the closet, visits from only one friend at a time, and avoiding parties and supermarkets.

Treatment also includes behavior modification, and individual and family therapy. In about 75% of ADHD children, stimulants (p. 332) help considerably. Cyclic antidepressants and clonidine can also help (43). The most common adult outcome is normality. However, 50% maintain some impulsivity as adults (often responsive to stimulants), and 25% develop antisocial personality disorder (188).

Conduct Disorder

Conduct disorder (M>F), formerly called delinquency, is a recurrent, persistent pattern of violation of the rights of others and major social norms. Common behaviors include lying, cruelty toward people or animals, running away from home, truancy, stealing, coercing others into sexual activity, and fire-setting. Prevalence is 3%–10%. It is more common in low socioeconomic status families. Severe family discord, parental neglect or abusiveness, and overcrowding often influence a child of difficult temperament in producing conduct disorder. The most effective treatment appears to be behavior modification in a structured therapeutic program.

Childhood Depression and Suicide

Childhood depression is underdiagnosed, in part because manifestations may differ from those of depression in adults. About 10%–25% of psychiatrically treated children have depressive disorders (189). Manifestations vary by age (190). Environmentally deprived infants show failure to thrive, with weight below the third percentile for age, frozen watchfulness, minimal smiling or vocalizing, and resistance to being held. Often, the child responds to several weeks of attentive inpatient pediatric care (120).

The depressed preschool child may manifest separation anxiety, school refusal, and somatic symptoms. Treatment includes play therapy and family counseling. Depression in the school-age child sometimes resembles adult depression. Also, school refusal, learning problems, psychosomatic symptoms, and other behavior problems may occur. Antidepressants can help. Depression in teenagers resembles adult depression (p. 246), but symptoms may include declining school performance, drug abuse, truancy, promiscuity, or psychosis. Suicide is the second (in some studies, the third) leading cause of death in adolescents (p. 350). Treatments should resemble those for adult depressive disorders (p. 253). Family involvement is crucial. Hospitalize the suicidal adolescent.

Although the incidence of suicide in children is low, suicide attempts are increasing. At one outpatient psychiatric clinic, 33% of children had contemplated or attempted suicide (191). Childhood suicide attempts tend to be impulsive, a response to perceived ill treatment, or motivated by a desire to get even. The school-age child attempts suicide by jumping from high places, hanging, or running in front of a car. A young child does not understand death's permanence, so suicidal behavior may reflect a wish to join temporarily a deceased relative, to decrease loneliness, or to eliminate stress and obtain peace.

Encopresis

Encopresis (M>F) is fecal soiling after bowel control is physiologically possible and bowel training should be completed (before age 4). Most encopresis is involuntary; only occasionally is it deliberate. In most children, it is primary (the child never had continuous [for a year] bowel control). In secondary encopresis, the child had good control of bowel movements for a year and then regressed. It accounts for up to 3% of child psychiatric outpatients. It is familial; 15% of fathers of encopretics had childhood encopresis (43).

There is no unitary etiology. Some reflect developmental delay associated with poor coordination, speech disorder, enuresis, or retardation. Some occur in chaotic families that have not systematically encouraged sociable behavior including bowel training. Sometimes, the child is afraid to defecate because of pain from large bowel movements or an anal fissure, or fear of the toilet itself (e.g., the noise of flushing). In the latter, the child withholds defecation until it is uncontrollable. Persistent withholding often leads to impaction (large quantity of hard stools difficult to expel) and leakage around the impaction. Some cases are attributed to unresolved anger at especially controlling parents expressed by soiling (192). Care includes correction of fecal impaction when present (effective 50%–75% of the time), positive reinforcement of nonwithholding continent behavior, and psychotherapy (193).

Enuresis

Enuresis is involuntary urination after age 4, before which voluntary control is usually established. Occasional enuresis occurs in 25% of boys. Repetitive enuresis occurs in 5%–7% of boys and 3% of girls (43). By age 12, the prevalence is 1%. For 80% of enuretics, the problem is primary (bladder control never occurred), and for 20% the child has regressed (sometimes because of excessive anger and frustration, or the stress of start-ing kindergarten, separation from parents, or arrival of a newborn sibling). For 80%, it occurs only in sleep, for 5% in daytime only. For 15%, it is nocturnal *and* diurnal. It is familial; 70% of enuretics have a first-degree relative who was enuretic (43). Etiologies include development immaturity and abnormalities of bladder functioning (126). It is sometimes associated with sickle cell disease, diabetes mellitus or insipidus (which cause *excessive* urination), intestinal parasites, urinary tract infection, spina bifida (spinal column defect with protrusion of the spinal cord), and polycystic kidneys. Daytime enuresis is especially associated with spina bifida or polycystic kidneys.

Treatment includes restriction of fluids before bedtime, midsleep awakenings for voiding, and either imipramine (25–100 mg at bedtime) or use of a bell-and-pad feedback device that sets off an alarm on urination in bed. Most bedwetters are well adjusted, but there is an increased frequency of behavior problems in enuretics (194).

Anorexia Nervosa

Anorexia nervosa is an often lethal (9% of cases) syndrome most common in teenage girls or young women. It begins with the patient perceiving herself as obese (this belief persists even when she becomes gaunt) and dieting to a point of starvation with a risk of death from electrolyte imbalance, dehydration, or infection. Despite the term anorexia, appetite is normal. Many patients gorge themselves with food and then induce vomiting, or use diuretics or laxatives to avoid weight gain (bulimia, which can occur alone as well as with anorexia nervosa). Amenorrhea (absent menses) is typical, often *preceding* weight loss. A past or family history of depression is common. Anorexia nervosa might be a variant of affective disorder. Treatment includes hospitalization, positive reinforcement of normal eating and weight gain, psychotherapies, and cyclic antidepressants or monoamine oxidase inhibitors (195).

12/Adult Development

Edward D. Joseph, M.D.

OBJECTIVES

GENERAL OBJECTIVE: Given an examination of an adult, state whether or not a given behavior is normal.

SPECIFIC OBJECTIVES:
1. List the physiologic changes associated with early and middle adulthood.
2. Summarize the adulthood stage theories of Erikson, Benedek, Jacques, Vaillant, Levinson, and Gould.
3. Define the phrase marker event, and contrast stage theory with marker event theory.
4. List common experiences of adults who divorce.
5. Summarize family development, including grandparenting.

Adulthood covers approximately the ages 25–60 years, with young adulthood ranging from about age 25–45 and middle age from about age 45–60. Neither age nor physiology alone makes precise boundaries. We have conflicting images rather than stereotypes of age; the 70 year old can be in a wheelchair or on a tennis court; the 18 year old can be married and supporting a family or a college student who brings laundry home to mother each week (1).

BIOLOGIC CHANGES

Most persons enter adulthood in their physiologic prime. For example, muscle mass (and total body mass) and contractility peak at the onset of adulthood and are maintained until about age 35, after which they gradually diminish for the remainder of life.

Adulthood physiologic changes (2–5) usually occur slowly. Almost everyone aged 40–50 has presbyopia (diminished accommodation or adjustment of the lens for near vision because of a loss of lens flexibility). Lens changes begin earlier, but it is not until age 40–50 that the near (focusing) point recedes beyond the point that the eye can read easily. Recession in the near point continues through old age.

Another change is the menopause in women, which typically occurs between the ages of 40 and 50 years, marking loss of the reproductive function. This function, the production of ova and estrogen by the ovary, is controlled by interaction between the hypothalamus and anterior pituitary and negative feedback from the ovary. From menarche until about age 35, this interaction yields a monthly production of ova and increased production of progesterone by the corpus luteum which builds the uterine mucosa. Without fertilization, progesterone secretion falls off and the menses ensue. Some time after age 35, oocyte production and hormonal activity gradually decreases, leading to cessation of production of ova and uterine mucosal proliferation. The menses stop and the production of estrogen and progesterone gradually diminishes, although ovarian production of testosterone continues. The loss of stimulation by estrogen and progesterone also affects the breast, vaginal wall (which thins out), labia, and clitoris (which diminish in size). There may be vasomotor instability, sweating, and paroxysmal tachycardia, the combination constituting a hot flash. After menopause, osteoclastic activity (bone breakdown) increases, contributing to osteoporosis in many women.

It is uncertain whether there is a male equivalent of menopause. Although circulating testosterone begins to decrease in early adulthood, studies conflict as to how much it declines. Spermatocyte production continues throughout adulthood, although the amount of sperm decreases. Sperm motility may also change, but men can reproduce to advanced ages. There is a loss of penile tumescence associated with REM sleep. At the beginning of adulthood, about 80% of REM periods are associated with erections; by the end of middle age, this percent is halved.

Age also affects the time it takes for a man to have an erection as well as the refractory period following orgasm. Men aged 45–60 years take 2–3 times longer than young adult men to have an erection. And, by middle age, the refractory period after orgasm may increase to as much as 24 hours before another erection can occur because of the loss of elasticity of the blood vessels supplying the corpora cavernosa of the penis. Sexual behavior changes during adulthood. On average, sexual intercourse among married couples occurs about three times weekly at age 25, decreasing to about twice a week at age 40, and about once a week from ages 45–60. Degree of satisfaction is more important than absolute frequency, however. Although some of this change may be the result of decreased hormone production, some also is the result of lifestyle change. For many, middle age provides more free time and self confidence; for others, middle age involves intense competition with more stress.

Changes in the central nervous system (CNS) also gradually occur. Brain weight peaks in the early twenties and slowly declines thereafter. The ratio of gray to white matter changes, with white matter increasing and gray decreasing. This change in the brain from ages 20–50 is caused primarily by the loss of about 50,000 neurons daily (from a total of 10 billion that exist early in gestation). Memory, learning, and other cognitive functions usually remain unaffected. Roose and Pardes (6) suggest that throughout life, the brain's dendrites and synapses continue to develop from stimulation by mental activity. Within the CNS, an older person's responses to stimuli tend to be slower than a younger person's. Consequently, a 45 year old sports coach may respond more calmly to stress but have slower reflexes as an athlete.

Cardiovascular changes include gradual loss of arterial elasticity and increased tortuosity of the veins, which leads to increased peripheral resistance. The loss of elasticity ordinarily starts at age 40 and continues at about 1% a year. Cerebral blood flow and kidney perfusion decrease after age 40. This change in the vascular bed is associated with an increase of collagen and calcium deposition in the endothelium (inner lining of blood vessels). Changes in the endothelium are associated with arteriosclerotic changes with an increased incidence of myocardial infarcts (death of heart muscle due to insufficient blood supply) from age 40 onward. About 5% of all heart attacks occur in persons younger than age 40, and 45% in persons younger than age 65 (7). Myocardial infarcts are the principal cause of death in middle age (under age 38, accidents are the principal cause). In women, the shift to cardiovascular disease as the principal cause of death occurs ten years later, although the gender gap has narrowed in recent years. This should warn young physicians and their young adult patients to exercise, stop smoking, control weight, blood pressure, and serum cholesterol. The consequences by middle age could be severe.

The skin gradually loses its subcutaneous fat and elasticity, leading to wrinkles and folds, which are most noticeable in the face. Gradual graying of bodily hairs occurs after age 30 and affects particularly the axilla and pubic regions. Gradual scalp hair loss also occurs, starting in the periphery and moving rostrally, but graying of scalp hair, more genetic than other graying of other hair, may begin early in adulthood if genetic factors are dominant.

PSYCHOSOCIAL DEVELOPMENT IN ADULTHOOD

Adulthood involves momentous psychosocial developments which occur in response to events and the unfolding of recognizable patterns. According to the Navajo philosophy of life, "All is order. Look for the pattern" (8). Ecclesiastes says, "There is a time for everything . . . A time to embrace and a time to sow and a time to reap." Understanding adulthood requires appreciating these patterns.

In the 1950s, Erik Erikson (9–11) proposed that the life span followed certain patterns (i.e., developmental sequences) that were comparable for most people, an innovative idea for behavioral science of that time. He proposed that there were developmental tasks (normative crises) appropriate to each age level, the successful accomplishment of which left its mark on the person's character. Erikson used the term crisis uniquely: "crisis at any age does not necessarily connote a threat of catastrophe but rather a turning point, a crucial period of increased vulnerability and heightened potential" (9). He proposed that for early and middle adulthood, there were two stages, the early adult stage whose normative crisis is intimacy vs. isolation, and the mature adult stage, whose normative crisis is generativity vs. stagnation. In the first stage, the essential life cycle task is to establish intimacy with another person, usually in the form of dating, courting, and romance ending in marriage. This has been the pattern in our western culture for much of this century, but in earlier periods marriages were arranged by elders and often included a dowry, a practice that continues in some other cultures today.

Accompanying this is the development of loving feelings and of closeness to another person, with a desire and ability to share feelings and events with someone who reciprocates in kind. Failure to establish intimacy, because of personality characteristics inherited or derived from childhood experience, leads to isolation from others.

A 24-year-old graduate student sought treatment because he felt unhappy with his career choice and with his seeming inability to form a steady relationship with a woman. He had no difficulty attracting the interest of women during his adolescence and early twenties, but he had never become attached to any, thinking of them primarily as potential sexual partners. Through counseling, he explored his childhood and adolescent relationships with his mother and grandmother, an understanding of which helped him establish a relationship with a woman that lasted two years before it ended. He then experienced loneliness and emptiness which became productive in therapy by demonstrating his fear of close attachment with the potential for loss and painful mourning.

As this experience was worked through, he developed an intense relationship with another woman and contemplated marriage; he had begun to attain an age-typical sense of intimacy. The intimacy involved some displeasure, but gave him more satisfaction than the previous isolation. Simultaneously he changed his career direction from one reflecting the family's interests toward one suiting his talents.

The next stage (9) is marked by a crisis concerning generativity, which is more than reproduction; it refers to creativity in multiple areas, including career development and childrearing. Career development actually starts earlier, usually in adolescence. For a medical student, career development means years of education before settling into a specialty. For a business graduate, this often means starting at the bottom of the corporate ladder with gradual advancement into the person's 50's. For a blue collar worker, it involves learning trade skills and finding employment using those skills.

Whatever the career development path, the essence is growth achieved over time. In former years, such career development was routinely regarded primarily as the province of men. In the past 20 years, many more women have pursued careers paralleling those of men, and have delayed marriage to the late twenties and early thirties. This in turn has deferred the time of childbearing and changed the nature of current childrearing, because often a woman continues her career during her reproductive period.

One generative path is in producing and aiding in the development of children. The desire to have children arises in the intimacy between a man and woman and carries the obligation, pleasure, and difficulties of rearing children.

Verification of Erikson's concept were provided by Benedek, Gould, Jacques, Levinson, and Vaillant. Therese Benedek (12) studied the impact of biologic change on adult development, citing menopause as an event influencing development. Whereas for some women, menopause signaled the end of a feminine role which diminished self-esteem, for many others it fostered greater sexual freedom and enhanced self-esteem as well as the sense of femininity and freedom to change to other generative activities, including resuming or inaugurating careers.

Jacques (13) reviewed the impact of recognition of the passage of time and the increasing nearness of death. He studied creative people, principally artists, and found that there was a time in their mid-thirties when the recognition of the inevitability of death produced a mid-life crisis (the first use of this phrase) with many effects in personality and career development. Some, like Gauguin, became productive and began to create. Others ceased creativity. There was an increased death rate between age 35–45 among these creative persons. All who survived showed a change in their work, becoming more mellow and deliberate.

Vaillant (14, 15) studied 258 men for 40 years. They were selected from a college class in the early 1940s after evaluations revealed good psychologic and general health and academic achievement. Vaillant's data support Erikson's concept of developmental patterns, with intimacy and generativity dominating adulthood. But Vaillant's primary interest was not the patterns, but rather in adaptations to life's vicissitudes. He found that despite mistakes, neurotic behaviors, even alcoholic bouts, these men had ego defense mechanisms that served them well. The more successful (in career, health, and family relationships) these people were, the more often they used mature defenses—humor, altruism, sublimation, suppression, and anticipation. Those who were less successful used defenses (e.g., isolation and dissociation) typical of earlier periods of life.

> A 48-year-old woman, a successful business executive and mother of two grown children, lost her position when her firm merged with another. Despite her education and experience, she could not find an equivalent position, so she retired. She maintained an active social life with fine humor, and resumed gardening, a prior hobby. As her garden expanded, she sought more knowledge about plants. Friends began to consult her about their gardens. Then, altruistically, she began lecture-demonstrations, first in senior citizens homes, then a local college. This led to a position on the faculty teaching courses on botany and gardening. She maintained her successful adjustment by a combination of humor, altruism, and sublimation.

Vaillant concluded that successful development depended on defense mechanisms used, many of which fully emerged only during adulthood. But he could not determine the biopsychosocial mechanisms that fostered the emergence and utilization of mature defenses.

A contemporary of Vaillant, Levinson (16) studied 84 persons longitudinally. He detailed the patterns of career and family growth and depicted development as more dynamic and turbulent than was previously described. Levinson (16–18) views adulthood as a sequence of phases within the framework of the life cycle rather than as a smooth progression. He delineated four periods of stability between ages 22 and 60, each separated from the other by a transition period. The stable periods are about 5–7 years long; the transitions last about 5 years. Each stable period is marked by the consolidation of achievements, manifested by self-satisfaction (internal world) and accomplishments (in the external world). The transitions are characterized by changes in either the external or the internal world. At the end of the transitional period these two worlds are again in balance for another period of stability. Although notable events (e.g., marriage, birth of children, career advancement, loss) all affect the person's psychological equilibrium, the result is adaptation to events.

A minister in his mid-forties sought consultation because of general dissatisfaction. He reported that after graduating from the seminary, he was called to be assistant pastor in his home town church. He provided fine leadership and highly regarded sermons. He married, had two children, and seemed well established.

Nine years after the minister assumed the job, his father died. Shortly thereafter, he left his position, even though he was assured that he would become chief pastor of the church if he remained. Instead, he sought a graduate degree in pastoral counseling. This was a hardship for his family, because their only assets were modest savings; his wife had to go to work to support the family. There were tensions, but the family stayed together.

Four years later, having completed his training, he took a university position as the coordinator for students in his denomination. Again, he seemed content, and harmony returned to his family life.

But as his children were leaving home for college, he began finding his work distasteful. He thought of starting a private counseling practice and moving to a new city. His relations with his wife again became strained; this led him to seek consultation. He eventually took a position as a university health service counselor in another city. The new location enabled his wife to develop her own career, and they soon resumed a harmonious relationship.

Gould (19), another contemporary of Vaillant, perceived an orderly sequence of people's concerns and priorities during adult life. He studied 524 people between ages 16–50. He described a continuous theme of balancing childhood fantasies (e.g., rewards will come automatically if we do what we're supposed to do.) and dependencies with adult reality and autonomy. But each phase of adulthood is characterized by certain emphases and concerns; the early twenties deal with leaving the parental world and becoming independent. The later twenties involve developing relationships and closeness with another individual (or deciding not to). The decision is based on a growing sense of inner freedom which often is associated with career development. The early thirties begin a time of greater concern with one's spouse and children than with oneself. Between ages 35–45 issues of health, loss, and death come to the fore.

Gould also described an ongoing inner developmental struggle involving increasing distance from childhood fantasies and parental influences (i.e., a change from What would my parents want me to do? to What do I want to do?) Growth toward adulthood therefore means replacing parental controls with newer, age-appropriate expectations associated with career and family (e.g., I will do the best I can as a parent for my children, but I am not perfect and will make mistakes.)

A 42-year-old businessman sought advice because he could not decide whether to leave the family business (in which he had worked for 20 years) to start his own business. It became clear in the course of treatment that he regarded himself as a small, inadequate person unable to shoulder the burdens of the business and dependent on his father who started and still headed the business. The reality was that he was an active participant in many decisions; his father, 35 years older, was unable to keep abreast of all the activities of the business. Still, he felt unable to make a significant move without his father's approval, just as had been the situation when he was a child. Treatment consisted of showing him the incongruity between this inner image of weakness in comparison to a powerful father, in contrast to the reality in which he was now a strong person capable of heading the business.

Primacy of the stage concepts of Vaillant, Levinson, and Gould has been challenged during the past decade by those emphasizing the impact of planned or chance marker events of adult life; milestones such as marrying, having children, graduating, and being promoted, and traumas such as illness, losing a job, death of loved ones, being in combat, or being raped or kidnapped (21). Each of these marker events calls for adaptations under stress, and these adaptations may change the course of a person's life. Wallerstein (22) described the impact of divorce on the lives of the people involved.

The impact of divorce often lasts for years and requires extensive adaptations to changed circumstances. Effects on adults (typically, after divorce, one partner functions better than the other) include financial reverses, derailment of careers, failed second marriages, inadequate social and sexual life, loneliness, and dependence on children. Divorce is rarely a mutual decision. Typically, one spouse wants out and the other complies reluctantly or opposes the divorce. Ten years after divorce, 50% of women and 33% of men remain intensely angry at their former spouses (22). Depressed persons often accept their ex-spouses' view of them as unattractive. Effects are also felt by the children (p. 141). Unfortunately, as vivid, rich, and accurate as Wallerstein's observations were, she did not include a control group of families who remained together despite troubled marriages.

This study typifies many during the past decade that trace the impact of events on development. Aging of parents and its effects on the adult, who must adapt to parents requiring care rather than providing it, is well recognized by geriatric social workers. Other events such as the death of parents, job loss, illness or death of loved ones (sibling, child, friend) are all events affecting development (21).

The stage theories have also been criticized (23, 24) as reflecting the cohort of persons studied and the social condition in which that cohort matured. Vaillant, Gould, and Levinson described a cohort of adults who experienced the Great Depression, a World War, and an economic boom. The current cohort of adults is less affected by social timetables regarding marriage, family development, and career choice. With the divorce rate now so high, intimacy is harder to accomplish. Some authors (25) maintain that with so many more women in the work force and as single parents, adulthood is even more stressful for women today. However, women now have more opportunities for personal development.

The concept of adult stages of personal development remains valuable, as long as the greater time variability in contemporary society and the vicissitudes of life for individuals are addressed. When individual lives are studied in detail, in clinical experience and in the literature, they conform to these broader principles, although the timetable is not as precise as Levinson maintained. Finally, the person's endowment of heritable personality traits (p. 68), talents, and illness vulnerability is yet another critical variable.

FAMILY DEVELOPMENT

Families have their own cycles. The family begins when two persons consent to be together for an extended period. This requires adjustments (of habits, of living styles, of consideration for each other) by both to maintain the relationship. This period of adaptation and increasing intimacy produces strains on each, which are usually successfully faced. From this union comes the begetting and rearing of children which is both a powerful source of pleasure and a source of additional stress. The previous bonds of intimacy and closeness that existed between husband and wife are stretched as they expand to include a third person, or more.

Generativity is not only the period when children are produced, but also the time when their development is fostered within the family. It involves allowing the children sufficient freedom as well as sufficient care and discipline that limits that freedom. Such generativity requires constant modification and change as children mature, so that what was appropriate behavior toward children in their early years must give way as they grow into adolescence and begin a quest toward independence and intimacy. Further change comes when the children leave home for college, for career development, or to start new families. Following the departure of children, parents have to readjust to the empty nest and readapt to each other. At this phase, many women who had devoted themselves to the family begin careers or other activities that take them away from home. Adults face both mortality and recognition that they may never achieve some of their ambitions, and must accept having less authority in their children's lives.

In the final stage of the family cycle, the original family members become grandparents. Grandparenting has been little studied. However, from clinical experiences it is evident that the grandparent role is important for the grandchildren, and vice versa. Grandparents and grandchildren often have a special relationship, marked by less ambivalence, allowing many grandparents to be indulgent toward the grandchildren. This indulgence reflects an extension of the generative phase into a new generation, and the pleasure at seeing still another extension of oneself into the future. If parents have divorced, grandparents can be of assistance and can serve as role models for their grandchildren. Grandparents can also be a source of accumulated experience and wisdom which provides a link with the past. Not all grandparents fit this mold, and may be standoffish with grandchildren. As today's population ages, more families are called on to care for elderly parents, requiring adaptation to the new role of parenting the parents. No doubt there will be more research on the grandparenting role as the population ages and grandparents live longer.

13/Gender-Related Psychology

Nada L. Stotland, M.D.

OBJECTIVES

GENERAL OBJECTIVE: Given an examination of a patient, discuss the influence of the patient's sex on the person's behavior and on the doctor-patient relationship.

SPECIFIC OBJECTIVES:
1. Discuss the impact of a person's sex on medical care.
2. Discuss the impact of recent social changes in sexual roles on stress and health care needs.
3. Summarize the embryology of sex.
4. Explain the socialization of boys and girls into their sexual roles.
5. State the impact of a person's sex on the tendency to seek medical care.
6. Discuss the effects of sexual expectations on the medical care provided to men and women.
7. List ongoing instances of sexual discrimination in western society.
8. Discuss psychologic considerations related to menstruation, menopause, the postpartum period, and induced abortion.
9. List the medical considerations following rape or spouse abuse.

Gender-related factors may affect your choice of specialty (1) and the quality and sensitivity of your practice of that specialty (2). They may affect health promotion practices, quality and style of life (1, 3, 4), illness prevalence (5, 6), sick role behaviors of patients (7, 8), response to and side effects of treatments (9), and survival itself (5, 10). Every doctor and patient brings to their relationship a unique combination of inherited and learned sex role attitudes and other behaviors that influence the relationship.

To effectively treat patients, you need to understand the patient's gender-related roles, attitudes, and experiences. How does the person feel about depending on a health care provider? How does the illness affect the person's employment and relations with others? How will gender-related feelings and behaviors affect compliance with treatment? It is a mistake to assume that a patient engages in specific gender-related behaviors, as in this vignette:

Ms. G. was the 36-year-old executive director of a professional organization. She had never married. At the office, she sat at her desk for long hours, building the organization while the members, trustees, and staff made conflicting demands. After work, she relaxed by playing bridge all evening with friends. Then she develped severe lower back pain.

She consulted an orthopaedic surgeon in her suburb. He examined her and diagnosed muscle strain. Never asking about the realities of her life, he exhorted her to "stop driving all those Cub Scouts around in the station wagon and carrying in all those heavy bags of groceries." He never determined that she spent many hours sitting, which aggravated the strain on her back. He took no opportunity to advise her to correct her sitting posture, or to determine whether her job stress was increasing her muscle tension.

Her work performance and her recreation were both hampered. Her condition worsened daily, and she was concerned about the multiple muscle relaxants and analgesics she took. After the orthopaedist repeated his uninformed advice a second time, she cancelled her next appointment and saw another doctor.

Unfortunately, medical training and journals may reinforce traditional images and myths about the sexes (2, 11, 12). Researchers have studied how a person's sex is depicted in medical textbooks and journal ads and found that women are portrayed as sex objects, in demeaning ways, and in stereotyped roles (13).

Physicians are also affected by recent changes in sexual roles and expectations. Although the number of women in the paid work force, including medical practice, have increased dramatically, changes in the domestic sphere have not changed proportionately (14); for example, homemaking and parenting largely remain women's tasks (5).

A person's sex influences primary, secondary, and tertiary prevention. Women have a major influence on family diet and other aspects of life that affect health. For example, women visit doctors more often than men and make decisions about the medical care of relatives in many families. Recently, health providers have begun to recognize these family responsibilities and now market services specifically to women (15).

Too little scientific attention has been paid to a person's sex as it affects physician behavior and patient health. Some professionals fear this attention would validate prejudices about sexual differences that limit participation of both men and women in society (16). Neglect of these questions could be even more damaging, however. An example is initial testing of medications only on men, and then generalizing the findings to women without exploring possible differences in effects (17). Aspirin for the prevention of coronary artery disease (a major cause of death in women) was tested only on men. Another example gaining widespread attention is lack of serious research conducted on health issues specific to women, notably research on breast cancer.

SOCIOCULTURAL INFLUENCES

We begin with, and return as a central theme to, sociocultural influences on observed sexual differences. For example, parental attitudes towards children are gender-related even before birth (18). Childrearing practices are gender-dependent; we not only name and dress children according to sex, but we also talk to and touch them differently (19). Boys and girls tend to be assigned different tasks (e.g., boys mow the lawn; girls babysit). Men and women still do not enjoy the same opportunities (3). Men seldom have the chance to take primary responsibility for the hands-on care of home and children, whereas women have not advanced in significant numbers into upper corporate and management ranks (1). Women care for dependent relatives at home; men control workplace hiring and promotion. When roles change, our adaptation to new opportunities is complicated by the failure of social supports and expectations to keep pace. Few doctors and clinics have evening hours for employed patients; few workplaces provide day care for children; homemakers are expected to behave like traditional women, employed persons like traditional men. Much of the literature labelled gender psychology focuses on the psychology of women because male development and behavior was portrayed as the norm for humanity until recently. We would benefit from more studies focused on males as males.

Historical and anthropological studies enlighten the attempt to determine what behaviors are inherently masculine or feminine. If similar behaviors are associated with each sex in many societies separated by time and distance, we could reasonably define them as masculine or feminine.

Historically, most human societies have defined complementary but different gender roles for men and women. For example, women cooked animals for which men hunted. Women kept small children safe at home, while men defended the group from enemies. Differences in behaviors of females and males are also found in other species.

We frequently use other species for examples of normal sexual behaviors, but selectively, to support our biases. We note the devotion of the mother snake or bird to her eggs and young, and even the fierceness of many mammalian mothers in defense of their young offspring. However, among nonhuman primates, males may also be very attached to infants, and in some other species, males care for the very young. Male birds bear brilliant plumage to attract females, in contrast to the somber male and colorful female garb in most human societies (20).

Women care for their children in almost all human civilizations, although in many the responsibility for care is divided among many female group members. American society differentiates names, nursery decor, toys, and dress for male and female infants, and encourages gender-related behaviors for young children. At or before puberty in most societies, boys spend almost all their time with men and girls with women. Socialization and education then focus on mastering gender-related behaviors. Often, a ceremony marks the adolescent's entry into adult society as a man or woman. Many societies have menstrual taboos, which further segregate men from women for certain days in the menstrual cycle.

Many of us view as progress the recent cultural trend toward overlap in sexual roles (e.g., more men involved in child care, more women holding advanced degrees), and the gradual evolution toward increased legal rights for women. But some people are nostalgic for the "good old days" when men voted, financially supported women and children, and limited domestic duties to stable, garage, and grounds, while women cared for children, cooked, handled clothing, and cleaned homes.

But the good old days do not have a long history. The woman who spent all her time preparing meals and enriching children's lives is more a creature of the 1950s than of the 1700s or 1800s. And, although men have long been viewed as stronger and more competent than women, sexual roles varied greatly as circumstances changed. Poor women, mothers or not, had to earn money or help with the family farm or business, while privileged families hired servants. Nevertheless, the fantasy that the normal woman is entirely occupied with childrearing pervades our society, contributing to the lack of social and domestic supports for women as they take more responsibility outside the home. These duties are typically added to the responsibilities for home and family, whereas the male partner, if there is one at home, is seen as an assistant, not equally responsible.

Some studies suggest that motherhood and employment combine to add stress and worsen health; other studies demonstrate no worsening, or positive effects (21). For each person, personality traits, quality of the marriage, job, and the degree of financial disadvantage contribute to outcome.

EMBRYOLOGY AND PHYSIOLOGY

The sex of an embryo is determined at conception. Either the fertilized egg contains two X chromosomes, and becomes female, or an X and a Y, and becomes male. A single gene on the Y chromosome (testis-determining factor gene [TDF], probably the SRY gene) (22, 23) is responsible for sex differentiation. Without a Y chromosome, or when a genetic aberration blocks its effect, the embryo becomes female. The Y chromosome causes the embryonic gonad to differentiate from an ovary to a testis during the seventh week of embryonic life.

Then, testes secrete androgens which direct the development of the primitive urogenital structures into the male internal and external genitalia and inhibit the development of female genitalia. This differentiation is bound to precise stages of embryonic development. The same hormones do not have the same effects at other stages. In the absence of male hormones, or when a tissue defect blocks their action (androgen insensitivity), the embryo develops into a fetus and newborn that appears female (24, 25).

What are the causal links between sexual differentiation and outcomes and behaviors after birth? Both before and after birth, more male infants die. At all ages in childhood and adulthood, the life expectancy for females exceeds that for males (5). Men and women differ in their susceptibility to various conditions, and some of the differences are linked to sex hormones (5, 25). For example, women in their forties have fewer heart attacks than men. The administration of estrogens after the menopause, when they naturally fall, may prolong women's resistance to heart attacks. The vast majority of childhood psychiatric disorders are more common in boys (26). Young men have a higher incidence of sports injuries. Women are more vulnerable to breast cancer.

Males are heavier and longer at birth and throughout life except at ages 11 and 12, when girls experience a pubertal growth spurt 2 years, on average, before boys (27). Infant boys are somewhat more active (28) and more difficult to soothe than girls (28). (Even small effects such as these could be important for a given person.) Nevertheless, observers can reliably identify the sex of newborns only if they can see their genitals. Throughout life, males tend to be more aggressive than females (29). This has medical implications. Male adolescents are injured in fights and are more apt to die in accidents. Women are injured by male domestic partners. Doctors treat these injuries, and should attend to detection and prevention.

It is well established that boys and girls are regarded and treated differently (29–34). Parents have different plans and expectations for male and female children: before they are born, they are future beauty queens or nurses and football stars or doctors to their parents. Adults who do not know a newborn's sex will vary their behavior towards it depending on whether they are told it is a boy or a girl (35). They will handle gently a baby they are told is a girl, and comment on her good looks. They will bounce what they think is a baby boy more vigorously and comment on his vigor and strength. Newly delivered mothers talk more to their daughters than to their sons (36).

Especially in the U.S., as mentioned earlier, names, nursery decor, clothing, and toys for the newborn are designated by sex: the little girl in her pink ruffles shakes a flower-shaped rattle; the little boy in his blue baseball uniform sucks on toy boxing gloves. Sex is a core component of identity. When children become toddlers, they know what sex they are, which parent is the same sex, and how persons of each sex are expected to look and behave (37). Sexual identity arises primarily from the sex of rearing (which is virtually always based on biologic sex) (38). It also develops from behaviors encouraged by adults and peers, and from admiration and identification with the parent of the same sex. Children's fathers playfully taunt and punch their sons and flirt with their daughters (39). With infant sons (compared with daughters), fathers are more physically rough, use toys less, and play more gross motor games (29, 34, 39, 40). Boys' clothes are designed for active play, girls' for sedentary decoration. The depiction of girls and boys in advertisements and toy packages relentlessly portrays the male as involved with building, action, and aggression, and the female involved with appearance, domestic duties, and childrearing.

Girls have been expected to be demure and passive, subordinating their opinions and preferences to those of others, while boys are rewarded for being active, assertive, competitive, and dominant. In accordance with the preference for males and male behavior, girls who display tomboyish qualities are better accepted than boys who are sissies (41, 42).

Many successful adult women report being tomboys in childhood (42).

What is the scientific evidence for the origins of these differences? Researchers have observed children born with abnormalities which cause their genetic and gonadal sex to be at variance with the appearance of their external genitals, and thus, with the sex assigned them at birth. The influence of sexual assignment and expectation predominates. Children reared as females identify themselves as female and are satisfied most or all of the time to be female (38, 43). This is true even in female children who have been exposed to abnormally large amounts of male hormones (as in congenital adrenal hyperplasia) and are more physically active, more interested in boys' activities, and less interested in frilly clothing and motherhood, than other girls their age (38, 44–46).

There are detectable differences between males and females (also on average), with males excelling in mathematical, spatial, and gross motor skills (e.g., those involved in bicycle riding), and females excelling in certain language skills (29, 47). It is difficult to separate nature from nurture, given the differential encouragement adults give boys and girls in developing these skills (48). The overlap is so great that there is no justification for expecting or advising certain behaviors and life choices based on a person's sex alone. The presence of women role models, and deterrents to women's advancement in traditionally male endeavors, are more influential on women's entry into those activities than any sexual differences in ability. The increasing percentages of women successfully entering the professions confirms this. Since women have been equitably encouraged and accepted into medical school, the proportion of female students has risen to nearly 50%.

SEXUAL DEVELOPMENT DURING ADOLESCENCE

Puberty is a crucial step in the development of both women and men. Physical matu-
ration is marked by secondary sexual characteristics: breasts and a female body shape for girls, larger genitals, lower voice, and body and facial hair for boys. Girls begin to menstruate; boys have nocturnal emissions (wet dreams). Girls reach puberty and become interested in heterosexual relations sooner than boys, contributing to the embarrassment and awkwardness between the sexes during junior high school years.

Behavioral differentiation accompanies physical differentiation. Girls tend to dissociate themselves from roughhousing. They swoon over movie stars, gossip about boys, and dream of romance and family. Boys, too, are preoccupied with the opposite sex, although (especially during midadolescence) their fantasies tend to focus on conquest rather than domesticity. Both boys and girls become attentive to grooming and dress (49).

Homosexual adolescents confront painful conflicts. They share other teenagers' intense desire to be part of the group and to dress and behave like their peers. But their sexual object choice varies from social norms. Although many boys (including many with a primarily heterosexual orientation) have had homosexual fantasies since earlier in childhood, heterosexual behavior is expected to begin at adolescence. They must find a way to deal with dating and rituals such as high school proms. A gay organization in Chicago arranges a city-wide prom.

Traditional and changing sexual roles and mores complicate the development of responsible sexual behavior in adolescents. Sexual intercourse is tolerated by society at ever earlier ages, and there is not enough prevention of sexual activity by chaperoning or other supervision. Boys are expected to be sexually aggressive and to prove virility by having intercourse. Girls are expected to be the limiting force, but their ability to do so is constrained because they are socialized to acquiesce to others' wishes. School sex education is limited. These factors contribute to a socially disastrous incidence of adolescent pregnancy, parenthood, abortion, and sexually transmitted diseases including AIDS.

ADULT SEXUAL DIFFERENCES

Personality traits and sexual roles established in childhood and reinforced during adolescence merge into the traits and role divisions of adult life. As for childhood, it is virtually impossible to sort out the respective contributions of nature and nurture to observed differences. For example, differences in central nervous system anatomy and physiology (50–52) may result from differences in environmental stimuli, just as development of the brain's visual cortex depends upon retinal stimulation. An infant born with lens opacities will never see normally unless treated within 6 months. So, too, the brain may develop differently depending on whether the child spends hours running rather than cuddling. Conversely, biologic differences could underlie traditional sexual roles.

Whatever the genesis of sexual differences, they can be observed and measured. But this information can be misused. The following are statistical (not absolute) differences of indeterminate (probably multidimensional) cause, to be viewed as data (not judgments): men tend to be more skilled at spatial and mathematical thinking (25); they more often couch problems in terms of abstract right and wrong and feel more impelled to intervene with action (53); women tend to think in terms of the interconnecting webs of human relationships and feelings; "most women's sense of self and of self-worth is grounded in their ability to make and maintain relationships" (28). Men derive more satisfaction from achievement in employment, and tend to be more comfortable with competition than women.

Sexual differences in style can complicate diagnosis and treatment. For example, women are emotional; that is, they display and dwell on feelings more. Doctors sometimes downplay women's medical complaints, assuming that women exaggerate discomfort. This can be disastrous for the outcome of an illness, the relation between a woman and her doctor, and women and the medical profession.

Recently the consumer movement in health care has questioned such assumptions.

Women established women's health centers that excluded physicians or subordinated their authority to nonphysician managers. Publications (44, 54) criticized medicine and educated consumers about their health. Many doctors, especially men, felt unjustly accused and ignored after devoting so much to medical training to offer expert care. Situations such as these sometimes make both men and women, doctors and patients, feel the other is incomprehensible.

Differences between men and women in expressed emotion are well established in early childhood and persist throughout adulthood. As people move from middle to old age, the contrast between the sexes becomes less marked. Older adults tend to feel more comfortable behaving as they please, and less apt to behave as others expect. Men (and many women) have made their careers and may shift their attention from competition to more contemplative or humanistic endeavors. Having reared their children, women who devoted their lives to home and family often develop other skills and interests, less concerned about appearing passive and feminine.

OTHER SOCIAL AND ENVIRONMENTAL FACTORS

As stated earlier, differences in parental attitudes toward a child depend on its sex from before it is born (55, 56). Boys are valued preferentially worldwide. In China, with its billion people, sons and their families care for parents during sickness or old age. The preference for boys is so compelling that the government campaigned against that preference in attempting to control the rise in the Chinese population. Posters extolling the virtues of limiting each married couple to one child picture a daughter.

In western culture, boys are socialized into team sports, playing by strict rules and hiding feelings of weakness (57). Sports metaphors pervade adult enterprises: "the ball is in your court," "he made an end run," and so forth. Much is written about the "old boys' network" and its exclusion of women from major decision-making in medicine and society (1, 58). Only recently have sizeable numbers of girls been encouraged to develop educational and career aspirations like those of boys. Women have been defined by their fathers' or husbands' careers. Married women took their husbands' last names and first names (e.g., Mrs. John Smith, meaning wife of John Smith). When a family was described in the media, the sons tended to be defined by their employment and the daughters by their marriages and children. Motherhood was considered a full-time occupation, fatherhood an after-hours activity. Men were expected to support their families financially, women to be supported. These mores were largely limited to the white middle class, but this class set the cultural tone for North America.

Boys, who are slower to develop fine motor skills and a lengthened attention span, do not perform as well in the early school years. Good little girls sit still and produce neat work. But by junior high, teachers begin to encourage boys preferentially and expect girls to have less interest or aptitude, especially for math and science. Soon girls fall behind in these areas.

Many cultures throughout history have imposed strict taboos on menstruating women and on others' contact with them (59). Although these conspicuous forms of avoidance are no longer part of our culture, people still have strong, often unacknowledged, feelings about menstruation and menopause. Cultural beliefs about women's moodiness focus on the menstrual cycle; comparable variability and intensity in men's mood states are ignored or seen as character traits and eccentricities.

SEX AND REPRODUCTION

Reproduction is crucial for sexual roles. Difficulties with reproductive capacity are deeply upsetting to a couple, making them question their adequacy. Women are more psychosocially defined by their reproductive roles, however, expecting to make motherhood their central activity, or considered deviant if they do not. Feelings about one's sex influence the use of contraception and the timing of childbearing. For example, in some nonwestern societies and for some Americans, girls and boys are not considered full members of the adult sexual group until they have sired or borne children.

SEX AND ILLNESS

Certain conditions and illnesses (e.g., pregnancy, erectile dysfunction, prostatic enlargement, ovarian cancer) occur in one sex. This includes psychiatric syndromes associated with reproductive functions (e.g., postpartum psychosis [p. 126]). Little attention has been given to this association in men. In women, menstruation, abortion, childbirth, and menopause have been studied (60, 61).

It is debated whether some women have symptoms in the days preceding menstruation severe enough to constitute a psychiatric syndrome (60). This question is complicated because many women are taught to expect symptoms, which may reflect negative feelings about menstruation and womanhood, and because people typically view irritability and aggression as character traits in men (e.g., a "typical aggressive surgeon") and as illness in women.

Research on menstrually related symptoms underscores another dilemma. Overlooking gender-related conditions deprives us of the chance to understand them and relieve suffering. But focusing on them can reinforce unjustified stereotypes. Consideration of women candidates for positions of high responsibility often gives rise to concern about "raging hormones." And although there have been huge increases in the numbers of women in the professions and management, there are still few at the highest levels, including tenured professorships, chairs, and deanships (which would provide role models for women students) (1). The reasons for this relative paucity, beyond the fact that far fewer women were admitted to these fields when the current senior cohort was in training, include the ongoing disproportionate domestic responsibilities (notably the care of children, the ill, and the elderly) assumed by women, and promotion policies that reward characteristics (competition, assertiveness) nurtured in men (14). Consequently, some women may feel they must suppress symptoms connected with menstruation, pregnancy, and menopause to avoid discrimination. There is some cross-cultural evidence that women who have rewarding lives tend not to experience disabling symptoms.

Studies of women during menopause (62, 63) and after hysterectomy for nonmalignant conditions reveal that they do not have an increased rate of clinical depression, as had been believed previously. But the rate of depression and other serious psychiatric illness does increase postpartum (p. 126).

Psychiatric outcome after induced abortion has also been studied. The woman undergoing an induced abortion is doing so because she has experienced a pregnancy she finds untenable in her current highly stressful circumstances. The incidence, however, of major psychiatric illness after abortion is lower than that following childbirth (61), the pregnant woman's only other alternative. Counseling that helps the woman identify her values, circumstances, preferences, and supports, and minimizes the pressure from others, improves outcome so that she may feel better psychologically and contracept better after an abortion than before (61).

GENDER-RELATED VIOLENCE

Medical professionals play a major role in the care of victims of gender-related violence. Rape victims, most often women, are brought to hospitals for examination, treatment of injuries, and gathering of evidence for criminal investigation. Insensitivity of professionals at this vulnerable time increases the trauma suffered and decreases the victim's ability to feel safe and trusting. Victims of domestic abuse, most often children, women, and elders, visit the clinic or emergency room. They may need care for acute injuries, or complain of pain, but rarely report the abuse itself. If the abusive situation is not recognized and help not offered, even if the patient refuses it at first, the abuse will almost always continue, and some patients will be murdered. Even when the outcome is not so dramatic, the situation traumatizes the victim as well as children in the home and tends be repeated in the next generation when the children have children of their own (42, 60, 61, 64, 65).

Rape is a common, underreported crime (66, 67). There are popular misconceptions that most rape victims somehow tempted their attackers, that rape is perpetrated only on attractive young women, and that no woman can be forced to have intercourse against her will. But victims range in age from toddlers to the elderly, and looks and provocation have little to do with rape, a crime of violence and humiliation (66). Sexuality is merely the vehicle by which the rapist expresses his rage. Rape victims feel sullied, worthless, and guilty, regardless of whether their own behavior was a factor in the circumstances of the attack. Most rapes are committed by someone known to the victim, and many take place in the victim's home (62). In date rape, a man feels entitled to have intercourse with a date, forcing it on her if she does not agree.

The physical and psychological abuse of spouses, children, and the elderly within a family is also common, crossing all socioeconomic boundaries. Spouses are abused in approximately 3–6 million families in the U.S. (68). Victims of domestic violence also feel helpless, guilty, and worthless, contributing to a tendency among health providers to feel that the victims willingly submit to their plight. Rape and domestic violence (which may include rape) are so upsetting to us that we tend to deny they exist, even when evidence is clear. This often leads to blaming the victim (66, 67). An examination insensitive to these matters feels to the patient like another assault. To counter our tendency to deny these tragic situations, laws now mandate the reporting of child and elder abuse.

Many communities and medical centers have programs for the victims of violent, sex-related crimes. They include the use of female staff; having a supportive advocate accompany the patient throughout the examination, treatment, and questioning by police; emergency housing if the victim is uncomfortable going home alone; and follow-up counseling. The consequences of rape and domestic violence are serious and long-lasting. Victims are often psychologically disabled; their lowered self-esteem decreases their chances for success, and their persistent anxiety interferes with their enjoyment of heterosexual relations. Because patients usually do not volunteer this information, the physician should include inquiries about abuse whenever taking a history.

14/Geriatric Development

Philip K. McCullough, M.D., and Steven Cody, Ph.D.

OBJECTIVES

GENERAL OBJECTIVE: Given an examination of an elderly person, discuss the contributions of psychosocial factors, normal aging, and disease to the person's health.

SPECIFIC OBJECTIVES:
1. Compare successful and unsuccessful adaptation in the older adult.
2. List demographic trends and health care costs for the elderly.
3. State general theories of the biology of aging.
4. Discuss psychosocial problems facing very old people.
5. Discuss the aging of each organ system.
6. Summarize the importance of lifestyle in the elderly.
7. List common psychiatric disorders of old age.
8. Discuss general strategies in the medical care of seniors.

Adaptation to the challenges of aging is a formidable task. In coping with physical decine, role changes, and loss, the older adult must use inner resources developed over a lifetime to preserve integrity and vitality (1, 2).

Erikson (3) defines the normative conflict for the elderly as ego integrity versus despair. A sense of integrity results from the development of maturity, satisfaction with one's accomplishments, and the wisdom of experience. Maintaining this integrity in the face of physical decline is difficult (4), and it is a developmental task that involves negotiating a new role with society. In contrast is despair. Despairing older adults may be bitterly preoccupied with the past and consumed with concerns about their own demise. They may become more self-centered.

Successful adaptation earlier in life helps but does not ensure good adjustment for the older adult.

Many senior citizens enjoy retirement, leisure activities, and productive labor either as volunteers on in part- or full-time work. Elders can make a special contribution to grandchildren and other young people. Adaptation requires coping with gradual changes in biology, chronic and acute illness, and changing roles (5).

DEMOGRAPHIC TRENDS

The elderly are the fastest growing age group in the United States (6). For the first time, the number of Americans aged 65 years or older exceeds the number aged 25 years or younger. The fastest growing segment is 80 years of age or older. With the growth in the elderly as a percentage of the population, a growing dichotomy is developing between those elderly who are younger and healthier (the young-old) and those who are older and chronically ill or need nursing home care (the old-old (6, 7). Although the elderly as a group share many characteristics, they demonstrate much heterogeneity. There is a growing disparity between the longevity of women and men in our society. Currently there are slightly more than 1.5 women for each man aged 65 years older. Overall, African-Americans have a lower survival rate than Euro-Americans because of high mortality rates earlier in life, but rates for blacks 65 years of age or older approximate those for whites. The leading causes of death in the elderly are cardiovascular disease, cancer, and cerebrovascular disease. Functional disability, on the other hand, is more often caused by arthritis, dementia, and loss of hearing and vision (6).

HEALTH CARE COSTS

Americans aged 65 years and older use more health care resources than younger adults. The elderly represent 12% of the total U.S. population but account for 30% of the nation's annual health care costs. Thirty percent of Medicare expenditures are provided during the last year of life. Nursing home costs (most of which is spent on the 5% of the elderly requiring nursing home care) exceed $20 billion annually. These trends should intensify, because of longer life expectancy, in part resulting from decreasing cardiovascular mortality. By 2030, it is projected that the elderly may consume 50% of all U.S. health care costs (6, 7).

The elderly as a group have recently begun to flex considerable political muscle as a powerful lobby. As health resources become scarcer, however, a debate grows over how much of the health care pie to divide among prenatal, pediatric, adolescent, and elderly medical needs.

THE CAUSES OF AGING

All organisms experience aging, the essence of which is not well understood and thus cannot be applied in assessing a person. Normal aging must be differentiated from changes caused by a specific disease, although disease in an organ system often accelerates changes because of the aging process.

There are two general theories of the biology of aging. One postulates that the process is genetically programmed. Another postulates a more random occurrence of events that are cumulative, such as random mutation, problems in protein synthesis, wear and tear of genetic material, and development of free radicals that impede cell metabolism (6).

Environmental factors (e.g., exposure to carcinogens and other toxins) also can accelerate aging. Habits (e.g., smoking, drinking) can accelerate organ dysfunction. The systemic effects of aging render the individual more vulnerable to disease.

The rate of change in different organs and organ systems is highly variable. Routine measurements of organ function may yield normal results, but this can be misleading; the reserve capacity of organ systems may not be adequate to deal with the added demands of infection or injury.

PSYCHOSOCIAL PROBLEMS

Psychosocial problems often confront the older adult, necessitating new adaptive strategies. Lifelong psychosocial supports may be lost. Retirement, loss, and isolation may exacerbate the aging adult's physical problems (8).

Social isolation is common among the elderly. More than 8 million seniors live alone (7). Older women are likely to be widowed. Geographic mobility makes it less likely that the adult children of the elderly will live close enough to assist. Isolation may be intensified by ailments that limit mobility, by a decline in the sensory organs that make reading and listening harder, and by lack of convenient, affordable transportation (7).

Role changes that accompany retirement provide another stressor. The circumstances of retirement influence the person's experience. Forced retirement because of poor health, performance, or economic factors tends to cause more disruption than voluntary retirement. A person with interests or hobbies that can be developed or expanded is more likely to cope well with retirement's transitions. Volunteerism and continuing educational opportunities can help.

Loss and mourning are common themes and can lead to despair. Loss may include aspects of the self (e.g., strength, endurance), be related to loss of role functioning, or encompass the death of friends or relatives. And, the elderly must face their own mortality as an ultimate loss. Older adults who have lost a spouse have higher mortality rates during the first 2 years of widowhood. Pathologic grieving may require hospitalization and intensive treatment. Successful mourning, however, may liberate a person's creative energy (9).

Mistreatment of the older adult (elder abuse) is now recognized as a common, serious problem. Annually, about 1 million elderly Americans are abused (10). Most cases are not reported. Abuse may involve deliberate or inadvertent neglect, financial exploitation, verbal insults, or physical harm. Most commonly it is perpetrated by a spouse, but adult children or institutional caregivers may be implicated. Because victims may be afraid and ashamed, the physician may need to inquire explicitly about such problems. Reporting of elder abuse is required by law in 36 states.

Age discrimination causes older adults to become victims of age stereotypes. Physicians are not immune from such biases (11), and this may be detrimental to the care of the elderly. Commonly, an older patient with a treatable medical problem is shrugged off by the physician as having a symptom of "old age." Providers may be unenthusiastic about working with older adults because of the perception that the chronic illnesses and "inevitable" debilitations of age will make geriatric practice unrewarding.

Often, an older patient's attitude toward illness will result in a passive, accepting stance rather than an effort to seek more aggressive treatment. Anxiety and uncertainty about health requires that the physician and patient have ample time to communicate effectively (12).

BIOLOGIC CORRELATES

As mentioned earlier, the process of aging and associated disability varies greatly among persons. Many older adults continue to walk and to function intellectually well into their eighth, ninth, or tenth decades. For them, the physiologic decline associated with aging does not produce significant functional incapacity. In any person, most organ systems may remain functional, but one system may demonstrate accelerated aging or overt pathology. In those persons who have problems in multiple systems, risk of a catastrophic reaction to illness is greater (6, 13).

Problems in some organ systems may cause more functional disability than problems in others. The sensory system is important in this regard. Half of persons who are blind are elderly. Cataracts (opacities of the lens) and glaucoma (increased intraocular pressure) are common in the elderly and may cause problems with reading and walking (especially in negotiating stairs and curbs). Night vision is seriously affected, with only one third of the illumination reaching the retina in patients over age 60 years. The lens loses its ability to focus on near objects (presbyopia [p. 147]), causing problems with reading and fine work (14–16).

Hearing problems affect 30% of the elderly and may produce social withdrawal because of embarrassment over an inability to converse (17). Changes in smell and taste (e.g., fewer taste buds) may decrease the appetite of older adults and their ability to enjoy meals, leading to malnutrition. Problems with taste are related to aging, specific illnesses, and some medications (18).

Normal sexual interest and functioning continue in many older adults. Medications are a frequent cause of erectile dysfunction in this group (19, 20).

The older adult is less able to regulate body temperature and may not respond to severe infection by developing fever. This may cause problems in diagnosing infections. In addition, heat stroke in summer and hypothermia in winter are problematic and potentially lethal conditions in this population. Older adults may have a diminished ability to appreciate changes in body temperature, conserve heat, and generate body heat (21, 22).

There are skin changes accelerated by chronic exposure to sunlight. Gray hair and wrinkling are common, and alopecia (hair loss) in men accelerates with aging. As life expectancies increase, there is an increased prevalence of skin cancers in the elderly. Prevention of such lesions involves minimizing sunlight exposure and using sunblocks. Wound healing may decrease as much as fourfold (23).

Cardiac output and cardiac reserve gradually decrease with a tendency toward increased systolic blood pressure (pressure during cardiac contraction). Resting heart rate does not change with age, but maximal heart rate is diminished. Fifty percent of older adults have significant narrowing of coronary vessels. However, seniors who exercise regularly will have greater cardiac reserves than those with a sedentary lifestyle (24). Because pain is a less effective warning sign of disease in the elderly, silent (without pain) myocardial infarctions (death of heart muscle tissue from decreased blood supply) are more common (25).

A decrease in total lung capacity and a diminished resiliency of the lungs may lead to shortness of breath. Older adults are more prone to pulmonary infections. Forced expiratory volume in one second decreases by 30 ml annually in nonsmokers. Respiratory musculature is less contractile. These problems are greater in persons who smoked or are exposed to toxins. Exercise helps maintain the work capacity of the lungs (26).

Musculoskeletal changes are the leading cause of disability in the elderly. The body gradually loses muscle mass and strength as muscle fibers are replaced by fibrous tissue. Routine exercise may preserve muscle function. An unfortunate sequel of these changes is the tendency toward falls and fractures. Falls, the leading cause of injury in the elderly, often lead to serious problems such as hip fractures. Degenerative osteoarthritis is the leading cause of disability in the elderly; over 80% have radiologic signs of it. Pain and lost mobility may be extensive (27–29).

Renal structure and function gradually diminish with age. There are fewer kidney glomeruli (filtering structures) and glomerular filtration rate is reduced. An embarrassing problem for about 30% of the elderly is loss of bladder control. Women are more commonly affected than men. Embarrassment often prevents patients from discussing such topics. Physicians should ask elderly patients about incontinence. It has many causes; some are reversible (30–33).

The immune system changes with aging. Impaired T-cell lymphocyte function is present, and a reduced antibody response to antigens is typical. At the same time, there is an increased tendency to autoimmune (antibodies to one's own tissues) response. The generalized inflammatory response is weakened. Response to infection is diminished, and rates of infection of the respiratory, urinary, and gastrointestinal tract increase. The increased rate of death from influenza and pneumonia in the elderly is notable (34–36).

Metabolism of drugs by the older adult may be significantly diminished. This may lead to high blood levels of drugs and their active metabolites on doses of medication that are normal for younger persons. The elderly may be much more sensitive to specific side effects (e.g., anticholinergic effects) (p. 328). Seniors are more likely to develop delirium (p. 277) owing to anticholinergic effects of prescription and over-the-counter medications (6, 37). Initial doses of medications should be lower (one third to two thirds of routine adult doses) for the elderly (38).

Diminished reserve capacity in various organ systems, multiple-system illness, and chronic illness complicate treatment of the older adult. Combining medications, each with side effects, produces yet more complex clinical reactions. Often treatment needed for one illness is risky because of illness in another organ system.

In 16% of autopsies in older adults, no specific disease can be found that itself would produce a fatal outcome in a younger person, so it is reasonable to conclude the death was caused by a cumulative effect of multiple dysfunctions (i.e., death from old age). According to Gompertz's actuarial calculations (39), at advanced ages the age-specific death rate increases geometrically.

LIFESTYLE

Lifestyle is important in assessment. The cumulative effects of smoking, lack of exercise, obesity, and alcoholism may only take their toll as patients age. Past exposure to toxins may become evident as carcinoma (cancer). Although little can be done to alter the effects of past lifestyle, the current lifestyle of the older adult can be influenced with good results.

Maintenance of adequate nutrition in a balanced diet is important. Poor dentition often causes inadequate intake. Vitamin deficiencies are common because of malnutrition or malabsorption. Intramuscular vitamin supplementation may be more effective than by the oral route (40). Adequate dietary fiber is necessary. At the same time, obesity is the leading nutritional problem in the U.S., affecting one in five senior citizens.

Older adults tend to awaken more frequently and to sleep fewer hours at night. Daytime naps often compensate for lessened nighttime sleep (41). Insomnia must be carefully evaluated and not treated indiscriminately with hypnotic agents. Often an underlying treatable illness is present. Regular exercise is needed to maintain muscle tone and cardiovascular reserves. Stretching, walking, or cycling several times weekly also helps to maintain healthy body weight. Exercise may also help postmenopausal women prone to osteoporosis (42).

Accidents are a leading cause of death and disability in the elderly. A safe home environment (p. 345) is mandatory (28, 43). Patients who have major impairments should not operate motor vehicles or may require night driving restrictions. Seat belts should always be used (6).

COUNTERBALANCES

The complexities and challenges involved in the care of older adults are especially enjoyable for physicians willing to care for the elderly. The older patient and family are usually grateful for the care, and many acute medical conditions respond promptly and thoroughly.

GEROPSYCHIATRY

Psychiatric disorders in seniors often involve general medical illness or subtle brain diseases. Conditions that occur earlier in life, such as recurrent affective disorder, may recur during later life. Other psychiatric problems may become less severe as the patient grows older. For example, sociopathic (p. 272) tendencies tend to decrease (44, 45).

Some psychiatric problems begin in old age. Brain diseases commonly occur in the elderly. A change in mental status requires medical evaluation, because half of such cases result from underlying systemic or central nervous system (CNS) disease (46). Drug-induced delirium (p. 277) should also be assessed. Depressive pseudodementia (diffuse cognitive dysfunction owing to major depression [p. 248]) presents primarily with cognitive impairment (42, 47).

As many as 20% of persons aged 80 years or older have some degree of dementia. Alzheimer's disease (p. 280) is the most common dementia in the elderly. It affects about 2 million Americans and accounts for over half of the population in long-term care facilities.

No effective treatment has yet been found. In evaluating a patient for possible Alzheimer's, physicians also should look for treatable causes of dementia (48).

Affective illness (p. 246) is common in the elderly (7, 49), who are more prone to manifest psychotic features (e.g., hallucinations, delusions) during episodes of depression. Depression is often secondary to other medical illness (50). Primary depressions usually respond to a variety of antidepressants. Psychotic depressive disorders are especially responsive to electroconvulsive therapy. Suicide rates increase with age in men and women. In women, the rates reach a plateau starting in middle age.

Older patients previously diagnosed as schizophrenic may experience a decreased intensity of psychotic symptoms, although a larger number of negative symptoms (defect symptoms, e.g., loss of caring or of emotional expressiveness) appear (51). Patients who have a long history of neuroleptic medication (p. 324) use are at high risk for tardive dyskinesia (jerky and writhing movements owing to long-term use of antipsychotic drugs) (52). Late onset psychotic disorder (late paraphrenia) occurs in this population. Paraphrenic patients have no previous history of psychosis; they gradually develop a syndrome of persecutory delusions and hallucinations (53).

Anxiety symptoms first presenting in an older person must be carefully evaluated; general medical illness, dementia, and depression are commonly present with anxiety in the elderly. Once other causes of anxiety have been excluded, treatment of anxiety disorders must be instituted and monitored cautiously because of sensitivity of seniors to medication side effects (37).

Alcoholism in the elderly is common, with a prevalence of 10%–15%. Approximately one third of alcoholics began drinking excessively later in life. Alcoholic dementia occurs in some cases, and behavioral abnormalities may be secondary to other alcohol-related diseases (e.g., cirrhosis). Recognition of alcoholism requires appreciation of its high prevalence so that pertinent questions can be directed to the patient and family. Treatment is discussed on pages 304–308.

In general, elderly patients respond well to both pharmacotherapy and psychotherapy. Age is no contraindication to intensive psychotherapy.

GENERAL MEDICAL STRATEGIES

Comprehensive examinations should be performed. For patients having difficulty presenting a clear, complete history, prior medical records and interviews with family are invaluable. Elderly people require routine physicals at reasonable intervals (54). Such examinations must include psychosocial issues (6).

A physical examination should focus not only on detection of serious illness but also on conditions that interfere with functional ability. A screening examination of cognitive functioning (e.g., the Mini-mental state (55, 56) is mandatory. Seemingly minor interventions such as removal of cerumen from the ear canal can dramatically improve the day-to-day experience of the older adult (41).

All medications, including over-the-counter drugs, that the patient takes should be reviewed. Ask the patient to bring in *all* medications currently being taken. Compliance may be a problem in the forgetful patient. Medications should be limited only to what is absolutely necessary. This is especially true of drugs with CNS side effects. When there is a question of the need for medication, or if drugs are producing major side effects, attempt a drug-free trial. When prescribing medication for an older adult, use the adage start low and go slow—use lower doses (p. 166). Immunizations for pneumonia, influenza, and diphtheria-tetanus should routinely be offered.

15/Dying, Death, and Bereavement

Carl B. Greiner, M.D.

OBJECTIVES

GENERAL OBJECTIVE: Given an examination of a dying patient, state a plan for the person's care.

SPECIFIC OBJECTIVES:
1. Discuss the stages of dying according to Kübler-Ross and Weisman.
2. Differentiate among impersonal death, intrapersonal death, and interpersonal death.
3. List the components of appropriate death.
4. Discuss common complications (including pain and depression) in dying patients.
5. Discuss the importance of autonomy in the care of dying patients.
6. List the benefits of autopsy and organ donation.
7. Discuss manifestations of grief in families and physicians.

A biopsychosocially informed understanding of dying will improve patient care. Pain management, nutrition, infection control, and major organ failure are critical subjects. Patients face diverse psychologic concerns as they approach death, particularly in our pluralistic society which gives no common meaning to the term or to the process. We must consider the reactions of and towards family members, who can aid or hinder the process of dying.

Since the 1960s, death and dying have been increasingly addressed. The psychologic aspects were initially elucidated by Kübler-Ross (1), a psychiatrist who identified five stages of dying: denial, disbelief about the diagnosis or prognosis; anger at oneself, one's doctors, God, whomever one holds responsible; bargaining, being on one's best behavior to improve the future (e.g., less suffering, more time, a reward in heaven); depression;

and acceptance. For example, almost all patients experience initial disbelief when told of having cancer, and some later assert they were never told their diagnosis.

Weisman (2) provided an alternate staging based on the patient's health: existential plight, the shock of discovering one's vulnerability, and the questions "What does it mean?" "What can be done?"; mitigation and accommodation, convalescence with resumption of activities; decline and deterioration (denial is harder to maintain); and preterminality and terminality, where only palliation helps, and then a death watch begins. The patient who is experiencing existential plight may seek counseling and advice. In contrast, the preterminal patient may wish to be left alone.

Our responses to death depend on whose death we contemplate (2). Learning of a stranger's death (impersonal death) may or may not affect us. The idea of our own death

169

(intrapersonal death) often is hard to believe and leads to anxiety. Loss of a loved one (interpersonal death) changes our life and is most closely associated with classic bereavement.

Weisman (2) also offered the concept of appropriate death, marked by care, control, composure, communication, continuity, and closure. The following vignette has many of these features:

> A 40-year-old married woman diagnosed with metastatic breast cancer underwent a mastectomy. She wished an extended life and was planning to undergo a bone marrow transplantation for palliative treatment. She felt a sense of estrangement from her husband because of his prior infidelity. She sought psychotherapy to come to terms with him and to face her fear that she would "burn others out" with her illness. Through personal reflection, she developed a greater acceptance of her disappointment with her husband, her physical appearance, and her domineering mother. She felt relief at not having to hide her anger. Her concern for her children and friends provided anchoring points for her. She died during the course of therapy for her cancer, but she felt freer in allowing her friends to comfort her. She felt cared for by the medical staff and her friends.

The patient developed a sense of closure about her life and the disappointments she had encountered. She felt composure after successfully addressing her adequacy as a person. Her control was expressed in choosing the type of treatment. She experienced continuity in sharing with her friends and children. In coming to terms with her disappointment, she became more open to communicating her needs and receiving the care of her friends and physicians. She concluded that she had had a fulfilling life.

The quality of dying is also an important concept. Many patients wish to address unfinished business. Just as we have hopes for the way we will express ourselves in daily life, we have similar hopes for the way we will die. This ranges from accepting death and expressing one's deepest convictions, to avoiding important issues and resorting to substance abuse. An example of sharing one's convictions was demonstrated in the following case:

> A physician in his fifties had metastatic carcinoma (cancer spreading to other organs). He felt strongly about reconciliation and finding peaceful solutions to difficult social issues. Despite fatigue and a 40-pound weight loss, he sponsored a medical conference that brought together a group that had been beset by ill will. His approaching death provided further conviction of the importance of bringing peace.

MANAGEMENT OF PAIN AND OTHER COMPLICATIONS

Minimizing the suffering that often accompanies end-stage illness is a physician's responsibility. Unfortunately, this is often clouded by our tendency to limit contact with the dying, fear of producing a narcotic addiction (physicians tend to *undertreat* patients with narcotics) (3), and hesitation to acknowledge death's imminence (4).

An additional challenge is the differential diagnosis of pain. The pain from a tumor can be intensified by anxiety and depression. Here, the hospice team, (often an oncologist, psychiatrist, nurse, social worker, and clinical pharmacologist) can help. The pharmacologist can suggest narcotic strategies to reduce the pain of cancer; the psychiatrist can identify psychologic distress contributing to the pain. The following patient benefitted from the hospice service.

> A 29-year-old married woman developed metastatic cervical cancer. Her gynecologist was unfamiliar with pain management and had prescribed a minimal regimen of analgesics at eight-hour intervals. She was incapacitated with discomfort in the hospital bed and could not see her young children, which accentuated her pain. Recommendations were made for a continuous morphine pump which produced considerable relief, allowing her to return home and continue an active relationship with her husband and children until she died several months later.

Levy (5) presents a hierarchy of pain medication, with an increasing level of analgesia relative to greater suffering. As a rule, accept the patient's report of pain unless there is reason to doubt the person's honesty; for example, if the patient is known to be a narcotic abuser or is a sociopath (p. 272) (6).

You should know some of the pathophysiology of dying. Cassileth (7) lists common general complications as follows: decreased appetite, fever, dysphagia (trouble swallowing), malabsorption of ingested food, constipation, infection, dyspnea (trouble breathing), hematologic complications (e.g., insufficient blood cells, bleeding), bladder dysfunction and incontinence, edema (extracellular fluid retention), hypercalcemia (excessive calcium in blood), liver failure, and kidney failure. One of the kindest interventions a physician can make is to identify a medical complication and treat it effectively. A general medical complication (e.g., weight loss, fatigue) can be misread as depression, particularly in the terminal patient. For example, it could be most helpful to identify that a patient's fatigue and distress are caused by dyspnea (trouble breathing) from a pleural effusion (gathering of fluid in the pleural cavity).

Major Depression

Depression is a common complication for the dying patient, but not all terminally ill patients become clinically depressed. Think about complications that can mimic depression; weight loss or decreased energy and appetite can be symptoms of the terminal illness itself. You need to address the psychologic dimension of depression. For example, a patient who develops sadness or anxiety unresponsive to a sensitive interview, prominent feelings of guilt or worthlessness, and suicidal ideation is probably suffering from major depression. Be particularly attentive to depressive symptoms in a patient who has a prior history of mania or depression.

Antidepressants (p. 327) can diminish symptoms of major depression. For example, nortriptyline can be started at 25 mg at bedtime and increased by increments of 10–25 mg to a dosage level of 75–125 mg/day, or until side effects become excessive. Blood levels can be monitored. The inception of therapeutic effect can range from 10–21 days, although full recovery may not occur for 4–6 weeks. If suicidal ideas are present, consider hospitalization. Older, male, isolated patients with a substance abuse history are at greater risk.

HOSPICE CARE AND ADVANCE DIRECTIVES

Informed consent, hospice care, and the advance directives are means of expression of patient autonomy (p. 427). Current medical management includes offering the patient legitimate choices so that he or she can give informed consent (p. 427). There is increasing interest in choosing the location and character of terminal care. The encouragement of advance directives (e.g., organ donation, durable power of attorney) is a major contribution of the ethics movement.

The modern hospice movement, founded by the English physician Cicely Saunders in 1967, utilizes palliative, interdisciplinary, family-oriented assistance, an alternative to traditional medical intervention aggressively directed towards cure. It may address spiritual issues and include a chaplain's services. Although hospice consultation can form a part of institutional care, many terminally ill patients can be well cared for at home through the physician-directed involvement of family members, visiting nurses, dietitians, and physical therapists. Be explicit with families in assessing for home care; with inadequate family interest, dying at home can be an emotional disaster. Hospital or hospice care by interested professionals is preferable to home care by an uninterested, guilt-ridden family.

In 1990, Congress passed the Patient Self-Determination Act which became effective on December 1, 1991. It respected the right of a patient (1) to refuse medical care; (2) to specify in advance (advance directives) what measures the patient would want or would refuse (e.g., to be put on a breathing machine) under a variety of possible future circumstances (e.g., irreversible coma) if the patient is unable to express his or her preferences; and (3) to grant to a specific individual the authority to make medical decisions (Durable Power of Attorney) if the patient is unable to make them (8, 9). Two vignettes illustrate the importance of advance directives:

> A patient in his late forties had extensive surgical complications and diminished mental capacity. The question was raised about cardiopulmonary resuscitation and mechanical ventilation. He was unable to make his preferences known. Before his surgical procedure, he had not expressed his opinion about terminal care to the surgical team or his wife. Unfortunately, his wife was left with the decision about continuing his care. She felt guilty about making a "do not resuscitate" decision. She wondered if she were responding to her own wishes rather than his.

A different outcome would occur with early participation by team and patient in discussing treatment choices in advance of the patient suddenly becoming incapacitated.

> A lively man in his sixties is undergoing dialysis for end-stage renal failure. He expects a premature death. He has discussed with his wife and physician that he does not wish cardiopulmonary resuscitation, mechanical ventilation, or intravenous feeding. His physician has agreed to his requests, and he has written advance directives. His family feels secure that his wishes were clearly known.

An advance directive document may exclude measures such as mechanical respiration, cardiopulmonary resuscitation, and intravenous feeding. If the dying patient's wishes conflict with those of the family, respect the patient's wishes, provided the person appears competent to decide. Many hospitals have ethics committees to help in circumstances such as patient-family-staff conflict.

THE DEFINITIONS OF DEATH

It is said that the only certainties in life are death and taxes, but what constitutes death is not as certain as it was. There is confusion even among experienced physicians regarding definitions (10). The definition of death has shifted from one based on heart-lung criteria to one based on brain criteria. The current definition involves entire brain death, including the brain stem, so long as cessation of function is not secondary to drug intoxication or hypothermia (11). Cortical death, an alternate proposed definition, allows that death occurs even when there is a persistence of brain stem activity. If accepted, this would have implications for both extended care and organ transplantation.

Beyond the technical definitions, other factors contribute to acceptance of a death. To many, there is honor in death in battle, memorialized on Veterans Day (Fig. 15.1). When someone dies young or unexpectedly, however, it can be particularly difficult to accept. Death of a child or fetus can be particularly challenging:

> A 37-year-old married woman had attempted to conceive for several years. Finally she became pregnant. During her first trimester, she was discovered to have a lymphoma requiring intensive chemotherapy. She had a therapeutic abortion and underwent chemotherapy. She had lost both her long-awaited child and her fertility.

A patient with terminal illness early in life has concerns about appropriateness:

> A single gay man in his twenties from New Orleans tested positive for HIV. When he developed symptoms of AIDS, he returned to Nebraska to be with friends and family. He reflected on his illness as "playing Russian roulette and losing." Although he felt comfortable sharing his experiences with medical students, he regretted having a shortened life.

In chaotic social circumstances, such as revolutions or natural disasters, the community

Figure 15.1. Winslow Homer
American, 1836–1910

TROOPER MEDITATING BESIDE A GRAVE, c.1865
oil on canvas, 16 × 8in.
signed lower right: HOMER

Gift of Dr. Harold Gifford and Ann Gifford Forbes
1960.298. Collection, Joslyn Art Museum, Omaha,
Nebraska.

may be overwhelmed and less responsive to individuals (bereavement overload).

AUTOPSY AND ORGAN DONATION

When your patient dies, ask the family to allow an autopsy or organ donation. Most hospitals have policies regarding obtaining consent. If it is unclear who is the next of kin, your hospital's attorney can help interpret your state's laws. Following your explanation of the benefits that accrue from autopsy or organ donation, respect the family's decision.

The autopsy can help the family come to terms with the death. For example, the provision of autopsy results at a family conference 3 weeks after a sudden infant death was helpful in alleviating guilt (12). Often autopsies reduce suspicion, provide reassurance, and substitute facts for conjecture (13).

Autopsies provide you with a continuing education on medical uncertainty (14). The rate of discrepancy between premortem and postmortem diagnosis is 33%. The autopsy underscores the scientific nature of medicine. It is troubling that autopsy rates have declined from 50% in 1950 to 12% in U.S. hospitals in 1985 (15).

Organ donation standards vary among countries. Several European nations presume consent; donation is made unless there has been a specific denial. In the U.S., volunteering is the standard. However, 1987 federal law requires that hospitals identify potential donors and make families aware of an organ donation option. Hospital nurses, physicians, or organ procurement officers will discuss this situation with the families of patients who are not expected to survive and would be suitable donors. Organ procurement officers note that most families feel something meaningful has come from the death if an organ is donated.

TASKS AND COMPLICATIONS OF THE GRIEVING PROCESS

Although there may be anticipatory grief before a patient dies, the greatest impact is often after the death, for both the family and the medical team. The resultant grieving process has been described by Parkes as a painful relearning (16). One family described the experience as saying goodbye to the dead family member and hello to a new life without him. This letting go of attachments to the deceased moves by fits and starts and often lasts for years. C.S. Lewis (17) eloquently described the waves of grief he felt after his wife's death.

Clayton studied symptoms of bereavement in relatives of patients who died in a general

Table 15.1. Symptoms Experienced by Bereaved Relatives at 2 Weeks and at 1–4 Months[a]

Symptom	At First Interview (%)	At Follow-up (%)
Depressed mood	87	12
Sleep disturbance	85	27
Crying	79	12
Difficulty concentrating	47	27
Loss of interest in TV, news, friends	42	19
Anxiety attacks	36	31
Irritability	36	9
Anorexia or weight loss	49	27
Self-condemnation	13	12
Suicidal thoughts	13	15
Feeling tired	29	27
Diurnal variation	21	8
Hallucinations	3	7
Depersonalization, derealization	6	7
Somatic symptoms (three or more)	19	30
Use of medicine	36	27
Loss of interest in job or church	11	12
Fear of losing mind	3	4

[a]Reprinted with permission from Clayton P, Desmarais L, Winokur G. A study of normal bereavement. Am J Psychiatry 1968; 125:168–178.

hospital (Table 15.1) (18). During the period of grief, suicidal thoughts occur in 13% of family members, who may feel that there is no purpose in living without the deceased or feel responsible for the death. This must be addressed seriously, for there is an increased prevalence of psychiatric and general medical illness during the grieving period.

The biology of grief includes impaired white cell functioning and alteration in endocrine function, particularly increased cortisol levels (19). The notion of a broken heart in grief *may* have a basis in fact. Engel, who studied sudden death, noted that psychologic uncertainty can bring cardiac instability (20). In retrospectively studying (without controls) 275 cases of sudden death, he noted that 21% had occurred at the news of the death of someone close, 9% at the threat of loss, 20% during the first 3 weeks of acute grief, and 3% during mourning or on the anniversary of the death.

Helping the Family

Worden (21) identifies four tasks the survivor must accomplish: to accept the reality of the loss; to experience the pain of grief; to adjust to the environment in which the deceased is missing; and to withdraw emotional energy and reinvest that energy in another relationship. Physicians can encourage this process by helping survivors identify and express their feelings. There are additional supports for dealing with loss. Many religious and community organizations have support groups such as Widow-to-Widow programs, Widowers Support, or Survivors of Suicide, and public schools may sponsor small groups for children who have lost loved ones.

A family-oriented perspective is important. The widow and widower have lost a companion, sexual partner, and friend. Children have lost a parent, a sense of security, and a way of life. Be alert to the implications of the death for family members, and ask how they are managing. In my work with transplantation patients, for example, I find that families with limited social resources, low socioeconomic status (p. 96), histories of substance abuse, and multiple marriages tend to be as chaotic in grief as in life in general.

> An elderly woman had a complicated surgical history and a progressively downhill course. Her husband is a passive, alcoholic man who copes with her failing health by increased drinking and isolation. He does not accept recommendations for alcohol treatment, and has increased irritability and denial about his wife's condition.

Although some families appreciate the availability of additional resources to deal with their grief, most do not use medical services. Religious rituals often help. The participation of others in one's grief is an opportunity, not a requirement.

How long does grief last? Some aspects of grief, such as wondering about the deceased on birthdays or holidays, may last a lifetime. Yet the greatest intensity of grief lasts 1–2 years. Our society emphasizes speed and efficiency, so the length of time to recover from grief appears incongruous with contemporary standards. Anniversary reactions occur on the date of the death:

> A surviving parent remembers the anniversary of his child's death, both with fondness for the good experiences, and sadness about the premature death. The anniversary period is marked by reflection and tearfulness. There are occasional intrusive memories about the terminal parts of the illness.

Grief involves addressing thousands of memories of the lost person; this helps to explain its duration. One of your kindest acts as a physician is to acknowledge the length of time it takes to come to terms.

Grieving can also foster personal growth. We can develop a deeper sense of our values, and a greater appreciation for our own life and those of others. Storr (22) posits a role of grief in artistic production. As you participate with families during their times of loss, you can reflect, share, and learn, as well as support.

Physicians and medical students grieve when patients die. Unexpressed, your grief can manifest itself in delaying, distancing, or hyperintellectualizing (23). It is often considered weak to feel the loss of a patient, yet the loss of patients affects us. Part of the art of medicine is to find a personally acceptable way to say goodbye to those who have died. This can range from moments of reflection to memorial services on the ward. There is usually enrichment for both patients' families and physicians when the grief work is done.

SECTION III.
ASSESSMENT

16/Interviewing

Terry A. Travis, M.D., M.S.Ed.

OBJECTIVES

GENERAL OBJECTIVE: After observing a patient interview, offer a critique of the interviewer's technique.

SPECIFIC OBJECTIVES:
1. List the topics of an initial interview and written history.
2. List the information used to characterize each current or historically important symptom.
3. Discuss the following components of an initial interview: information already available, participants, getting started, combining open-ended and closed-ended questions, the psychotic or cognitively impaired patient, facilitating techniques, and ending the interview.
4. Summarize the following subjects related to interviewing: advice, reassurance, self-revelation, and strong feelings of patients.

Assessment and treatment of the patient begins with the history: the spoken and written summary of the patient's present and past health, and the factors influencing it. The physician obtains most of this information during the patient's first visit and augments it during subsequent visits, from collateral interviews with such persons as family members and professionals who have treated the patient, and from prior medical records. Also necessary are the physical examination (PE) and laboratory testing. The initial interview draws on all a physician's skills and knowledge of the art and science of medicine. The art of medicine establishes the doctor-patient relationship, facilitates communication, maximizes the quantity and quality of information the doctor elicits, and fosters patient compliance or cooperation with treatment. The science of medicine assures the physician that by applying reliable diagnostic standards (1), the diagnoses made using the history, PE, and lab testing can reasonably estimate the outcome of medical care provided (predictive validity) (2).

Physicians should observe and listen carefully to their patients—most convey how they wish to be helped and provide key diagnostic clues. Some accurately know their problem (e.g., "My diabetes is out of control") which a medical diagnosis will confirm. Physicians may ask any question about intimate, personal topics, as long as the question is well timed and pertinent to the diagnosis and the patient's health. You will make informed, individualized recommendations and interact with the patient as a unique person. This individualized treatment fosters your relationship with each patient and keeps medicine from becoming dull or routine, as you will learn from all your patients. Your concern and compassion for each patient as an individual becomes part of your treating of and caring for the person.

Issues addressed in this chapter concern universal truths about the initial interview— those commonly accepted, commonly published (3–12) guidelines that apply to most patients most of the time and that have not been empirically refuted. One truth is that most rules have exceptions—the art of medicine requires making exceptions if necessary.

BASIC DATA OBTAINED IN THE INITIAL INTERVIEW

Components

The initial interview and written history have six components:

1. Identifying data: age, sex, marital status, ethnicity, occupation, living circumstances, whether there were prior episodes of care at your medical center, and chief complaint: the problem that caused the patient to seek care, and the duration of that problem
2. History of the present illness: the patient's current problems, as mutually understood by the physician and patient
3. Past health: general health, childhood health, adulthood health (to include medical illnesses, surgical procedures, psychiatric illnesses, obstetrical history), accidents and injuries, allergies, and immunizations
4. Family health: health of the entire family, living and dead, emphasizing genetic and environmental determinants of disease
5. Personal and social history: past development, life experiences, personal relationships, and current situation
6. Review of systems: questions about common symptoms not yet covered in the interview, the review of which (in contrast to the rest of your history-taking) will progress in a head-to-toe fashion (skin, head, eyes, ears, etc.) (3).

The written history is entered in the patient's chart in the above (items 1-6) order. Although the interview must always begin with the present illness and the patient's current problems must be assessed to plan treatment, cues from the patient (comfort at each point in the interview, historical data that is reported, and diagnostically important observations the physician makes) should guide the sequence of the physician's questions and comments. You will learn the data needed to assess each organ system during your courses and clerkships, augmented by PE and interviewing texts (13, 14). The neuropsychiatric part of the assessment is covered in detail on pp. 185–200 and addressed throughout this book.

History-Taking in Different Specialties

The principles of interviewing and history-writing apply to all specialties. Even though the symptoms emphasized vary among specialties, all areas should be addressed in an initial assessment—for any patient new problems may develop at any time, and may affect any aspect of the patient's health.

Characterizing the Patient's Symptoms

A symptom is what the patient reports (e.g., "my head hurts over my eyes"); a sign is what the physician observes (e.g., the patient's sclerae [the whites of the eyes] are icteric [jaundiced, yellow]). Basic information for each current or historically important symptom (deciding what is important requires experience) contains the following:

1. Location and changes in location of the symptom (e.g., the pain of an inflamed appendix is often in the right lower abdominal quadrant)
2. Quality of the symptom (e.g., the pain of a myocardial infarction [death of heart muscle owing to inadequate coronary blood supply] is often experienced as crushing)
3. Severity or quantity of the symptom (e.g., the pain of a stone in the ureter often comes in waves [colicky pain] and is often the worst pain the patient ever experienced)
4. Chronology (changes with time) of the symptom (e.g., the sadness or anxiety of a melancholic pa-

tient is typically greatest when the person awakens in the AM)
5. Circumstances in which the symptom occurs (e.g., socially phobic patients are most anxious just before and during social gatherings or public speaking)
6. What intensifies the symptom (e.g., patients diagnosed with heart failure [inadequate pumping efficiency of the heart] often become short of breath when climbing stairs or lying flat)
7. What relieves the symptom (e.g., patients who have hiatus hernia [protrusion of the upper stomach into the lower esophagus] sleep better with their head elevated by several pillows)
8. What else accompanies the symptom (e.g., people with migraine headaches often vomit while experiencing their unilateral headache)
9. How does the patient react to the symptom (e.g., some patients with chest pain dismiss it as indigestion, many are very anxious about it)

Because the physician must obtain so many details, it is easy to overlook some. In such instances, unapologetically consult the patient, who will appreciate your concern and thoroughness and not view your questions as incompetence.

CONDUCT OF THE INTERVIEW

Information Already Available

Physicians often have information about patients before interviewing them. Typical known facts are whether the person is self-referred, or referred by a physician, minister, or the courts, and why the patient is being seen at that particular time for what problem (10). Employment, health insurance, address, age, education, ethnic group, and religion are other details that emerge from the patient's initial telephone call, referring physician, chart, or other sources.

Participants

Relatives or friends may accompany the patient. They are a valuable source of information, and their involvement with the patient is often important and should be clarified. By tradition, for confidentiality, adult patients are interviewed alone. After establishing a relationship with the patient, physicians may reserve the right, if more information is needed, to talk to the other person. The patient should be told of such intentions, what information is sought, and that all patient confidences will be honored (p. 434). This tradition has exceptions. Couples who seek family therapy (p. 315) are interviewed together. Interviews with patients who have severe cognitive dysfunction or who are psychotic (unable to perform ordinary roles or tasks of life because of hallucinations, delusions, thought disorders, or cognitive impairment) are often best conducted with a relative or friend present. If the physician and the patient do not speak the same language, a translator (friend or relative of the patient, hospital volunteer, etc.) is needed.

Starting the Interview

Adult patients should be addressed by their last names (children and teenagers prefer to be called by first names) and titles (e.g., Ms., Mr., Sgt., Dr.). Do not use first names with adults. This implies a familiarity that does not, or a paternalism that should not, exist. First names should prevail only in special circumstances, usually after a relationship with a particular patient has existed for some time, and only if you are willing to be addressed by your first name.

Make eye contact and (unless there is likelihood of hand-to-hand transmission of infection) shake hands. Your grooming, friendliness, manners, concern, and pleasure in your work all set the tone. Within limits, maintain your individuality. When I grew a beard in the early 70s, I was concerned that my patients, from a conservative rural part of Iowa, would see me as an inexperienced, hippie doctor. Because they perceived me as competent (at least I think they did), my beard became a unique identifier of me as their physician: "the doctor with the red beard is my doctor."

If the patient is seated or in bed, do not stand and tower over the person. Note and address discomfort (e.g., a patient short of breath may need the head of the bed raised). A separation of 3–5 feet between the two of you is usually comfortable (there is some ethnic variation [p. 11]) enough to maintain the patient's private space without distancing you (8, 13). Tell the patient your role in his or her care—are you a medical student, a resident, consultant, or the physician ultimately responsible? Explain the purpose of the interview.

In most interviews (and almost all interviews with well-spoken, insightful patients), begin each topic with an open-ended question. For example, taking the history of the present illness usually begins with such an open-ended question as, "Tell me what brings you here. How can I be of help? What are you concerned about?" An open-ended question invites a spontaneous, detailed response. Patients will usually explain what they consider most important, their concerns, and their misunderstandings. As long as information is being provided that is useful for your history of the patient, do not interrupt. You can become more specific or courteously change topics if patients become repetitive or excessively detailed. Once the patient has spontaneously elaborated on a topic, fill in details (if needed) with questions that become progressively more closed-ended (e.g., "Tell me more about the pain. When did it begin? Did anything make it go away?"). These questions further detail the symptom's location, quality, and so forth. The interview with a well-spoken, insightful patient (most patients fit this category) thus consists of a series of open-ended questions, each followed by increasingly closed, direct questions, until the history is completed. Choice of questions is guided simultaneously by (1) cues from the patient, and (2) your perception of what is diagnostically and therapeutically crucial (1 and 2 usually correspond well). Studies have shown that this sequencing is effective (8, 15–17).

An exception involves some patients who are psychotic or who have profound cognitive impairment. Here, you may increase their comfort and cooperativeness, and the clarity of what they say, if you speak softly, ask clear, brief, closed-ended questions, and sit relatively still.

The Remainder of the Interview

The interview should be as spontaneous and conversational as possible. It should not be conducted formally according to the order of a written chart history or case conference presentation. Cues from the patient guide your choice of questions. A man who talks about his chest pain, and then says his father had similar chest pain, provides a cue to ask (immediately or later) about family history of heart disease. Thus, the interview is a dynamic process between you and the patient. This style takes no longer, and yields more data and better rapport than a rigidly structured question-and-answer style (16, 17). Ask one question at a time; double-barrelled questions (e.g., "Where is the pain and what makes you think it's due to an ulcer?") yield unclear answers (16).

Note-Taking

You may take notes, so long as it does not impede your observation and interaction with the patient. You cannot see facial expressions and body language while writing. Thus, notes should be terse phrases that remind you of key details. You do not need to ask permission to take notes unless you see that this upsets the patient. Then briefly explain why (e.g., "I want to be sure I get the details correct").

Fostering the Patient's Spontaneity and Cooperation

The patient's openness, spontaneity, and cooperation can be facilitated in many ways.

Silence: When the patient is spontaneously providing helpful data, just listen, punctuating your listening with eye contact, nodding, and saying, "uh, huh," "I see," etc. When the patient is thinking about what to say, or unable to talk because of emotions, a few moments of attentive waiting is supportive and does not interrupt the flow of the patient's thoughts. If the patient is struggling to find a correct word, do not provide it yourself (that would be infantilizing) unless the patient asks you to do so.

Reflection: Restating something just said by the patient (e.g., "You've had pain in your chest several times? Your wife is worried about your breaking out sweating?") is often facilitating (16).

Empathic Observations: The patient's statements, your observation of nonverbal behavior, and your feelings, intuition, and reflection, contribute to your empathy (feeling what the other person is feeling; putting yourself in the patient's position). Often, tactfully stating what the patient appears to be feeling (e.g., "That must make you furious," or "You look as if you're holding back tears.") encourages the person to elaborate and fosters rapport. But empathic comments are sometimes unsuitable. For example, if you say to a frightened, mistrustful patient "You look like you'd like to stop the interview and leave," the person will probably exit your office promptly.

Support: Support includes simply stating that you understand how the patient feels, that you recognize the importance of what is being said, or that you admire the person's efforts to function better.

Praise: Occasional praise for the patient is often helpful. With the exception of cognitively impaired patients who require praise to maintain their participation in your examination, however, repetitive praise appears insincere and loses all meaning for the patient.

Reassurance: Reassurance is helpful if it is realistic (e.g., "80%–90% of patients respond excellently to this treatment"; "You have handled these demands well in the past and will again"). But guarantees and generic reassurances (e.g., "Everything will be done"; "Don't worry") can worsen your relationship. Why should the patient not worry when the situation is worrisome? Patients expect and deserve an honest relationship. Likewise, simplistic advice (e.g., "You should lose weight") unaccompanied by recommendations for change (e.g., "Let's make a plan for losing weight") is worthless.

Confidentiality: At some point in most initial interviews the physician tells the patient that all confidences will be honored within certain limits. Confidentiality, a cornerstone of the doctor-patient relationship, is discussed on pp. 434–435.

Self-Revelation: Physicians may ask patients almost anything, as long as it is done in the interest and context of their health. The reverse—giving patients detailed information about yourself—is not expected or even encouraged, except to the extent that it informs the patient generally about your professional qualifications and experience. If you think it will facilitate an interview, you might briefly answer an occasional question (e.g., "How do you like working here?, Where are you from?"). Toward the end of an interview, you might use a personal anecdote for the sake of illustration or empathy.

If a patient correctly notes that you are preoccupied (which you strive not to be), you should agree and tell the patient that you are distracted for reasons unrelated to him or her (if this is so), and that you will be more attentive. Revealing this, rather than denying it or being defensive, will add to your relationship with the patient. If you practice in a small community, your patient may know your family well, and you could answer a question or two about them warmly and succinctly. Except for answering a sequence of patient questions about diagnosis and treatment at the end of the interview, do not become the interviewee by responding to a series of questions. For any question in which self-revelation would be uncomfortable or would impede your relationship with the patient (decide and understand this *before* you are asked), it is best not to answer, perhaps stating "I'm not clear why you need this information about me," or "I want to focus on your health," or "I'd rather not get into details about myself."

Strong Patient Feelings: Allow patients to cry or express anger or other intense emotions (e.g., by listening, making eye contact, nodding, commenting empathically, offering a tissue), unless the emotion continues to intensify and threatens to disrupt the interview. In the latter case, intervene by tactfully changing the subject, suggesting the patient slow down, or requesting assistance (e.g., through a silent alarm that signals hospital security [p. 363]) to modify the emotion.

Ending the Interview

Allow time to conclude the interview. Present the diagnoses you are considering (and the rationale for these), studies you plan that would clarify the diagnosis, and treatment recommendations with their rationale. Conclude on a hopeful note; you can always identify something hopeful.

17/The Psychiatric Evaluation

Marc Rothman, M.D.

OBJECTIVES

GENERAL OBJECTIVE: Given an interview of a patient with a behavioral problem, summarize the findings and discuss how you would establish whether the cause was a general medical condition, a psychiatric illness, a personality trait, or a normal reaction to stress.

SPECIFIC OBJECTIVES:
1. Discuss the association of general medical illness with behavioral problems.
2. Summarize the contribution of the physical examination in psychiatry.
3. Define the mental status examination (MSE) and list its general categories.
4. For each category of the MSE, list common abnormalities and their common causes.
5. Discuss the laboratory assessment of the patient with a behavioral problem.
6. Discuss the role of observation in the assessment of an undiagnosed patient.

When a patient manifests a behavioral disturbance, the cause could be a general medical illness (e.g., pernicious anemia, meningitis), a psychiatric illness (e.g., panic disorder, mania), a drug side effect (e.g., corticosteroid-induced depression), a personality trait, or a natural response to stress. How the history, physical examination (including the mental status examination), laboratory tests, and bedside examinations are used to assess the patient with a behavioral problem are the focus of this chapter.

Many classic psychiatric disorders manifest brain dysfunction (Table 17.1) (1–16), and many systemic and coarse brain diseases can cause behavioral abnormalities that mimic classic psychiatric illness (17–25). For this reason, instead of making the old-fashioned "mental-physical" and "organic-functional" distinctions (distinctions the *Diagnostic and Statistical Manual, 4th Edition* of the Ameri-

can Psychiatric Association [DSM-IV; p. 240] will avoid [26]), phrases such as secondary psychiatric disorder, general medical illness, and so forth prevail here.

SYSTEMIC AND COARSE BRAIN DISORDERS IN PSYCHIATRIC PATIENTS

In assessing a patient with mental symptoms, the possibility of a systemic or coarse brain disease causing or worsening the problem must be considered. Seventeen studies on psychiatric inpatients and outpatients revealed that systemic disease caused or worsened psychiatric symptoms in 5%–46% of cases (17). The prevalence of nonpsychiatric disease in the psychiatric patients ranged from 15%–80%, and a new illness was diagnosed as often as 80% of the time. The following is an example of a psychiatric patient whose behavior deteriorated because of lung disease:

Table 17.1. Laboratory Evidence of Brain Dysfunction in Selected Psychiatric Disorders[a]

Modality	Findings
Neurologic Exam	70% of adult schizophrenics and manic-depressives have neurologic soft signs (p. 244).
	50% of children at risk for schizophrenia have neurologic soft signs.
Neuropsychologic Tests	75% of adult schizophrenics and 50% of manic-depressives have moderate to severe impairment (schizophrenia bilateral; manic-depressive bifrontal, nondominant).
	Many obsessive-compulsive and Tourette's patients have nondominant frontal impairments.
Eye Pursuit	75% of schizophrenics (ill and recovered) have abnormalities.
	50% of non-ill relatives of schizophrenics have abnormalities.
Electroencephalogram	50% of schizophrenics and 25% of manic-depressives have nonspecific abnormalities.
EEG Evoked Potentials	Many schizophrenics and manic-depressives have abnormalities.
Computerized Tomographic Scan/Magnetic Resonance Imaging	50% of schizophrenics have some cortical atrophy and ventricular enlargement.
	20% of schizophrenics have some cerebellar atrophy or agenesis.
	25–30% of manics and depressives have some cortical atrophy and ventricular enlargement.
Positron Emission Tomography/Cerebral Blood Flow	Many schizophrenics and manic-depressives have hypofrontality and increased posterior activity.
	Anxiety disorders often associated with right-sided hippocampal and parahippocampal abnormalities.
	Many obsessive-compulsive and Tourette's patients have right frontal and basal ganglia abnormalities.
Autopsy	Cell loss in the cerebellum, hippocampi, and frontal regions of many schizophrenics.
	Cellular disorganization in the hippocampi of many schizophrenics.
Endocrine	50%–60% of depressives (melancholic) have hypothalamic-pituitary abnormalities.
Biochemical	Lactate infusion induces panic attacks in 80% of panic disorder patients.
	Dopaminergic abnormalities found in some schizophrenics; all neuroleptic drugs are dopamine blockers.
Genetic	Schizophrenia, major affective disorders, obsessive-compulsive and Tourette's disorder, anxiety disorders, alcoholism, antisocial personality disorder are familial.
	Familial findings confirmed in twin and adoption studies.

[a]Source: Adapted with permission from Taylor MA. The practice of neuropsychiatry. New York: Free Press, 1992 (in press).

A 64-year-old woman with a past history of schizophrenia and hypertension (high blood pressure) came to the emergency room complaining that for the past week she had become increasingly short of breath. She reported no edema (fluid retention, often visible in the legs and feet), orthopnea (shortness of breath while lying flat), asthma, respiratory infection, or smoking. She had been compliant with her medications: captopril (an antihypertensive that inhibits angiotensin production), furosemide (a diuretic and antihypertensive agent that inhibits sodium reabsorption in the kidney), and haloperidol (p. 325).

She stated that a spirit was causing her short-windedness and had done so for 20 years. She revealed multiple related delusions and hallucinations. She was obese, and pulse and respirations were rapid. Lab findings revealed hypoxemia (subnormal content of oxygen in the arterial blood). Chest x-ray and electrocardiogram

(ECG) were normal. She was admitted for observation.

In the hospital she had shortness of breath throughout the day. The medical staff hesitated to proceed with diagnosis and treatment until a psychiatrist had evaluated her, thinking that her abnormal ideas were caused by her schizophrenia. The patient eventually underwent pulmonary function testing (PFT) after receiving a psychiatric evaluation. PFTs demonstrated obstruction of bronchi and bronchioles relieved by a bronchodilator. Prescription of a bronchodilator alleviated her behavioral and respiratory symptoms.

When a psychiatric presentation is secondary to another illness, patients (and to a lesser extent their physicians) are often unaware of the underlying cause (18). The most common causes in men are cardiovascular and respiratory, and in women endocrinologic and metabolic illnesses (19). Systemic illness is a more common cause of psychiatric symptomatology in a new psychiatric patient rather than a recurrently ill one, although (noted above) in the latter group the rate of general medical illness is high (20).

Any psychiatric symptom or sign could be caused by a nonpsychiatric disease (17–25). Often, the primary illness presents as a psychosis (inability to perform routine life tasks or roles because of hallucinations [p. 192], delusions [p. 191], thought disorder [p. 192], or severe cognitive impairment) (21). Anxiety, depression, irritability, and cognitive dysfunction are even more common (22).

If a patient has a well-documented systemic illness, you must consider the possibility that a newly developed behavior problem is caused by the systemic illness or side effects from treatment of that illness (hundreds of medications can produce behavioral side effects) (27). For example, a metastasis (spread), a remote complication (e.g., CNS damage from metabolic products of the cancer), or a chemotherapy side effect could easily cause new behavioral symptoms in a patient with cancer. Although you must be familiar with normal responses (pp. 169, 170) to having a serious illness such as cancer, do not automatically assume the cause of a symptom is a normal response to having the illness. Moreover, the presence of extensive cognitive abnormality (e.g., delirium, dementia, multiple parietal lobe signs [pp. 41–43]) suggests that the abnormal behavior stems from nonpsychiatric illness.

Often there is poor integration of psychiatric and other medical care (28, 29). Nonpsychiatrists and psychiatrists may each assume the other will coordinate the assessment of general health and not communicate adequately. The statement "The patient is medically cleared," often used in emergency rooms (ERs), is dangerous. "It does not convey what conditions were considered and how they were ruled out . . . implies that everything was done and nothing was found, [and] offers false assurance to the next professional who sees the patient, impeding the evaluation" (28).

A 40-year-old man with no serious past illnesses was transferred from a general hospital ER to a public psychiatric hospital 20 miles away. The transfer diagnosis was "paranoid schizophrenia." The transfer form included little more than "complains of pain all over body," "flat affect," and "cleared by medicine for transfer." No lab testing was done. When the patient was examined at the public hospital, it was clear that his total body "pain" was from muscle cramping, and his soft, monotonous voice, initially misinterpreted as "flat affect" (he had no other signs of emotional blunting) was from weakness. No wonder he had these symptoms: His serum glucose level was 1040 mg/dL, and his urine ketone level was 4 +, both reflecting a life-threatening diabetic ketoacidosis (p. 196), which was promptly and successfully treated.

This case reflects the meaninglessness of the phrase "medical clearance," and the risks inherent in a cursory evaluation.

As Teitelbaum states, "It seems easiest for us to look at illness as a product of either physical or emotional disturbance alone [in] trying to simplify what in reality is extraordinarily complex" (29). There is a danger when faced with behavioral symptoms alone to assume a diagnosis of psychiatric disorder. One would do better to acknowledge the diagnostic uncertainty (30).

PHYSICAL EXAMINATION IN PSYCHIATRY

Physical examination (PE) is essential for all psychiatric patients. Who does the PE depends on circumstances. Despite admonitions in the psychiatric literature of the examination's importance (31–34), most psychiatrists do not routinely perform PEs themselves, although they are trained to do (and can even teach) (35) them. In one study (31) it was reported that psychiatrists had performed PEs on 5% of outpatients and 37% of inpatients. Nonpsychiatric physicians may give cursory attention to the PE in patients presumed psychiatric.

Anderson (32) recommends, for the outpatient psychiatric office, a PE stressing observation and minimally intrusive procedures. Observation of body habitus, skin, and motor activity can provide the first clue to systemic illnesses. Check vital signs (blood pressure [BP], pulse, respirations, temperature), pupillary size and dynamics, the neck for rigidity or thyroid enlargement, and do a neurologic examination. Important components of the PE, as well as common abnormalities that may point to the primary cause of an abnormal behavior, are listed in Table 17.2.

When doing a PE on a psychotic, highly apprehensive, restless, or uncooperative patient, be opportunistic, as in the pediatric PE. Save the most intrusive or uncomfortable procedures, such as fundoscopic (examination of the retina), otoscopic (examination of the external ear canal and eardrum), rectal or pelvic exam, for last (or for another day) if the patient is irritable or uncooperative.

For general medical patients, 7.5% of PEs uncover an unexpected finding leading to a diagnosis, and 30% refine the differential diagnosis (39). A study of PEs on 75 psychiatric inpatients found that almost 66% of the positive physical findings had been unsuspected by history and led to further evaluation (40). In 32 of the patients, the findings led to consideration of a new diagnosis.

Mental Status Examination

The mental status examination (MSE), the psychiatric component of the PE, is an assessment of the patient's behaviors during the interview and PE. The emphasis is on objective observation, augmented by the physician's empathy, intuition, and reactions to the patient. The MSE observations can be made reliably (41–45).

Just as for the neurologic examination, there is no official format for the MSE as long as all areas are covered systematically. What follows is from multiple sources (41–69) and my clinical experiences. The sequence given is suggested for recording or presenting data and is not an interview outline.

Specific terminology must be mastered to clearly communicate your findings. But when in doubt about terminology, use lay terms.

Correlate the MSE with the patient's history, the rest of the PE, and lab studies. For example, if the history, recent chart entries, and the initial inspection portion of the PE suggest that abnormal behavior is secondary to coarse brain disease, focus more on cognitive assessment in the MSE.

The first portion of the MSE a physician should record is the first thing observed: the patient's appearance (p. 189). Along with appearance, note the level of consciousness. This varies from comatose (no meaningful behavioral response), to stuporous (torpid, lethargic, slow, sleepy, difficult to arouse), to alert, to hyperalert. Hyperalertness occurs with severe anxiety, intense mistrust, stimulant intoxication, or sedative withdrawal. A person may be in an impaired state of consciousness yet oriented, or disoriented while conscious.

Observe motor activity. Hyperactive patients over-respond to stimuli (e.g., by intruding into conversations, visiting the nursing station incessantly). Hyperactivity is a classic sign of mania and is sometimes seen with frontal lobe disease. Agitated patients have an increased frequency of purposeless movements (e.g., pacing, handwringing) in response to an intense mood (most often severe anxiety).

Catatonia is a syndrome of stimulus-bound motor dysregulation most frequently seen with the affective disorders. It can also be observed in schizophrenia, fluoride toxicity, hyperparathyroidism (p. 195), systemic lupus erythematosus (p. 196), akinetic mutism (absent speech and diminished movement owing to upper brainstem disease), tuberous sclerosis (a genetic disorder with skin nodules, seizures, and behavioral problems), syphilis, epilepsy, alcoholism, poisonings, head trauma, viral encephalopathy, arteriovenous malformation (a mass of intertwined arteries and veins in the CNS), and as a side effect of neuroleptic (formerly called antipsychotic) drugs (49–52).

Common catatonic findings include the following: posturing, assuming odd positions; waxy flexibility, the ability to pose the patient into postures; and echopraxia, when the patient mimics your posture or gestures.

Table 17.2.   Selected Physical Findings Pertinent to the Psychiatric Examination [a]

Appearance: Manics often wear highly decorated, brightly colored clothing. Chronically ill, hospitalized schizophrenics and demented patients often wear ill-fitting, poorly matched unfashionable or stained clothes. Parkinson's disease or neuroleptic-induced Parkinsonism patients have an expressionless face. Anxious and depressed patients often have furrowing of the forehead over the bridge of the nose. Major affective disorder patients are more apt to have an endomorphic build (broad-framed, high fat to muscle ratio), schizophrenics an ectomorphic (low fat and muscle mass) or dysplastic (malproportioned) build, sociopaths (p. 272) a mesomorphic build (high muscle to fat ratio).

IV drug abusers often have needle-track scars over veins, prior suicide attempters wrist scars, Briquet's syndrome patients (p. 266) abdominal surgical scars, hypothyroid or hypoparathyroid patients surgical neck scars, sociopaths tattoos and motorcycle-gang style of dress.

Alcoholics often have bulbous, red noses (rhinophyma) and ruddy complexion. Manics are often rosy-cheeked during manic episodes. Sunburn, anticholinergic drugs, and polycythemia (excess production of red blood cells [RBCs]) cause skin reddening. Jaundice (yellow sclerae [whites of the eyes] and skin) is common in liver disease, biliary tract blockage, and hemolytic (excess RBC breakdown) anemias (e.g., sickle cell anemia, anemia due to infectious mononucleosis, or lupus erythematosus [SLE]).

Pallor typifies anemias (low RBC count) and occurs with acute anxiety and heart disease. Cyanosis (dusky or bluish coloration of skin or mucus membranes) accompanies obstructive lung disease, respiratory depression, upper airway obstruction, cardiac anomalies, circulatory collapse, and grand mal seizures (p. 47). Psychotropic and other medications, many infections (e.g., measles), and allergies cause rashes. Bruises on a child's buttocks or back suggest abuse.

Vital Signs: Fever occurs with infections, collagen diseases (multiple-system auto-immune connective tissue disease [e.g., SLE]), inflammatory diseases (e.g., Crohn's disease of the bowel), drugs, cancers, hematopoeitic abnormalities (e.g., pernicious anemia [p. 195]), vascular diseases (e.g., pulmonary embolus [blood clot from vein in abdomen or leg dislodges and travels to lung]), and malingering (faking illness).

Tachycardia (rapid pulse) accompanies exercise, anxiety, fever, anticholinergic and sympathomimetic (e.g., amphetamines) medication, anemia, hypoxia (low blood O_2), cardiac disease, and hyperthyroidism (p. 196). Hypertension (elevated BP [HBP]) can be essential (unknown cause, very common) or due to kidney disease, sympathomimetic drugs, toxemia of pregnancy (p. 122), Conn's disease (adrenal gland overproduction of aldosterone), Cushing's disease (p. 198), pheochromocytoma (epinephrine- or norepinephrine-secreting tumor that causes episodic or continuous HBP, tachycardia, pallor, sweating, and anxiety), increased intracranial pressure, aortic valvular insufficiency (systolic BP is high, diastolic BP low, e.g., 160/60), aortic coarctation (local narrowing, producing HBP in arms, low BP in legs).

Hypotension (low BP) occurs with shock (diminished tissue perfusion with blood owing to blood or fluid loss, heart disease, infection, allergy, etc.), Addison's disease (p. 195), antihypertensive medications. Postural hypotension (BP drop on arising from lying-down or sitting position) occurs with neuroleptic, cyclic antidepressant and other medications, and viral infections.

Eyes: Marijuana intoxication causes dilated conjunctival blood vessels, opiate intoxication narrow pupils, sympathomimetic or anticholinergic drugs wide pupils, syphilis and anticholinergic drug use unreactive pupils. Nystagmus (eye jiggling on horizontal or vertical gaze) occurs in alcohol and sedative-hypnotic intoxication and Wernicke's encephalopathy (p. 302). Paralysis of eye movement may accompany Wernicke's encephalopathy (sixth nerve, lateral gaze) or brainstem disease. Illumination of retina could reveal blurring of the optic disc margin (papilledema) owing to increased intracranial pressure or severe HBP. Optic atrophy (whitening and flattening of the disk) is common in multiple sclerosis (p. 199). Retinal arterial narrowing, "nicking" of arteries by veins, hemorrhages or cotton-wool exudates (small, fluffy white patches) occur with HBP. Diabetic retinal pathology includes hard, yellowish-white exudates and blood vessel proliferation.

Ears: Hearing difficulty is frequent in the elderly and leads to misdiagnosis of dementia. Impacted cerumen (ear wax) often causes hearing loss.

Mouth: Dryness occurs with dehydration, fever, anticholinergic medication, and anxiety. Nonrhythmic chewing, puckering or writhing of tongue, mouth, or cheek may be caused by chronic neuroleptic drug use (tardive dyskinesia). Dental care is often neglected by poor people and chronic psychiatric patients. Tongue or inner cheek scars may result from grand mal seizures.

Neck: Thyroid enlargement often occurs with thyroid disease (which often presents with behavioral abnormalities [p. 196]). Enlarged lymph nodes occur with infections, AIDS, cancers (nodes may be hard and irregular), and many other causes. Severe neck stiffness with immobility accompanies hemorrhage under the arachnoid membrane (from rupture of an aneurysm [ballooned blood vessel] of the circle of Willis) and meningitis. Mild neck stiffness occurs with neuroleptic drugs.

Table 17.2. Selected Physical Findings Pertinent to the Psychiatric Examination[a] *(continued)*

Pulmonary: Chronic obstructive pulmonary disease (COPD) often causes increased anterior-posterior chest diameter. Asthmatic (and many COPD and some cardiac) patients have wheezing respirations. Upper or extensive lower airway obstruction causes retraction (pulling inward) of soft tissues between ribs or above the clavicles.

Cardiac: Enlarged heart occurs with alcoholic cardiomyopathy and other cardiac diseases. Murmurs (whooshing sounds) occur with anemia, dehydration, heart valve disease, and endocarditis (valvular infection, common in IV drug users).

Abdomen: Distention (swelling) may be caused by pregnancy, obesity, ascites (gathering of fluid from infection, tumor, heart failure, liver failure, or kidney failure), protein deficiency, intestinal obstruction, bladder obstruction with retained urine, or massive enlargements of an ovary, kidney, or liver. Liver enlargement may be the result of cirrhosis (accumulation of fibrous tissue and impaired function, most often from alcoholism), viral hepatitis (often due to IV drug use), and liver cancer.

Genitalia: Alcoholism can cause testicular atrophy (shrinkage).

Rectal: Fecal impaction (large quantity of hardened stools, difficult to expel) is common in patients receiving neuroleptics or antidepressants.

Neurologic: Brain diseases are uniformly associated with behavioral abnormality. Parkinson's disease shows shuffling gait, pill-rolling tremor, stooped posture, expressionless face, drooling, depression (frequent), and dementia (20%–40% of patients). Huntington's chorea shows choreoathetoid (jerky and writhing) movements of extremities, mouth and trunk, and depression, psychosis, and dementia. Left frontal stroke causes right-sided paralysis and pathologic reflexes (e.g., Babinski [p. 134], clonus [to-and-fro movements on foot flexion or knee extension]), Broca's aphasia (p. 37), and major depression (p. 246). Normal-pressure hydrocephalus causes ataxic (unsteady) gait, urinary incontinence, and dementia.

Alcohol and sedative-hypnotic withdrawal cause coarse tremor and delirium (delirium tremens). Liver, pulmonary, and kidney failure cause asterixis (flapping hand tremor). Lithium, cyclic antidepressants, and neuroleptics cause tremor and other neurologic complications (p. 325).

[a]Modified from Summers WK, Munoz RA, Read MR. The psychiatric physical examination. I. Methodology. J Clin Psychiatry 1981;42:95-98; Yater WM, Oliver WF. Symptom diagnosis. New York: Appleton-Century-Crofts, 1961; Wyngaarden JB, Smith LH Jr., eds. Cecil textbook of medicine, 17th ed. Philadelphia: WB Saunders, 1985; and Schwartz SO, Hartz WH, Robbins JH. Hematology in practice. New York: McGraw-Hill, 1961.

Usually echopraxia does not occur spontaneously and must be elicited: tell patients that when you touch one part of your body (e.g., your nose), they should touch a different part of their body (e.g., their mouth); for instance, "When I touch my nose, you touch your mouth." Often echopraxic patients will mimic your action instead of doing what you requested (e.g., when you touch your nose, they touch their nose). In mitgehen, light pressure to a limb results in movement, despite your instructions to the patient not to move (e.g., "I'm going to try to raise your arm, but don't let me.") There then can be a slow return (mitmachen) to the previous position. Gegenhalten occurs when the patient exerts resistance equal and opposite to the force you apply to a muscle group (e.g., the extensors of the hand at the wrist). A stereotypy is a complex, purposeless, repetitive action (e.g., patients continually pat their own head).

Speech is a major source of information. When describing speech, consider the rate, volume, pitch, inflection, syntax (p. 41) and accent. Poverty of speech (very brief [monosyllabic, one-word] answers with minimal spontaneity) is common in schizophrenia and in major depression with melancholia (44). A continuous stream of speech (often hard to interrupt) is called pressure of speech (logomania, logorrhea) and is often seen in mania. Rapidity of speech (tachylogia) often occurs with mania or severe anxiety. Although physicians do not count words at the bedside, rapid speech corresponds to over 150 words per minute (53). Dysarthric speech is slurred or indistinct and is seen in sedative intoxication or left frontal stroke (p. 37).

Thought processes are reflected by the logic, coherency, and efficiency with which the patient expresses ideas. Formal thought disorder, a language abnormality resembling

Wernicke's aphasia (54, 55), is commonly seen in schizophrenia. Compared to Wernicke's aphasics, however, schizophrenics and manics with formal thought disorders are more apt to understand what is said to them, better able to use long, complex words, and less likely to have trouble with naming and word-finding (56, 57). Some thought disorders (e.g., clang associations, circumstantiality, flight of ideas) are not formal (i.e., they do not resemble Wernicke's aphasia). Clang associations and flight of ideas are most often seen in mania (p. 250); circumstantiality is common in mania, alcoholism, and epilepsy. The term loose associations has been used "so loosely as to be nearly meaningless" (53). Thought disorders are summarized in Table 17.3 (53, 58).

Thought content describes what concepts, experiences, and concerns are expressed through the patient's thought processes. The thought processes are the "bottle" that contain and give form to the "wine" of thought content (46). Of the components of thought content the most important is which themes predominate. For example, is the person preoccupied with a family problem? Unhappiness over an illness?

Look for delusions. A delusion is a false belief not correctable by rational argument and not reflecting the beliefs of the patient's culture. Delusion reflects form; what the patient is deluded about is content. Ideas of reference are delusions that a neutral environmental event has an intentional personalized meaning. For example, a psychotic patient may believe that songs or statements on TV are broadcast to communicate a message just to him or her. Ideas of reference are also examples of the first rank symptom called delusional perceptions (see below). Delusions are not pathognomonic (a pathognomonic finding is one that, when present, makes the diagnosis certain). A delusion can be mood-congruent or incongruent. Congruency refers to how much the delusion reflects the patient's mood. For example, a severely depressed patient with severe guilt feelings may believe that a minor transgression is a terrible crime deserving punishment. This is mood-congruent. The belief of being persecuted but not knowing why is mood-incongruent.

Hallucinations (Table 17.4) are the experience of perceiving a sensory phenomenon when no source of the sensory event occurred in the material world.

An illusion is a misinterpretation of a real sensory stimulus (e.g., a tree mistaken at night for a human figure, a magician sawing a person in half.) Distortion is when actual sensory input is exaggerated, as in macropsia (an object looking larger than it is), or micropsia (when it looks smaller). Distortion can occur in epilepsy, illusions in delirium (p. 277), and in histrionic or other suggestible people.

Kurt Schneider (59) described eight first-rank symptoms he thought to be pathognomonic of schizophrenia. They are common in schizophrenia, but not pathognomonic of it (60–62). These eight can be boiled down to five (60): (1) complete auditory hallucination in which a clear, sustained voice, speaking full sentences, is perceived as coming from outside the patient's body; (2) thought broadcasting, in which patients can feel thoughts audibly escaping from their head; (3) experiences of influence, when thoughts or actions are experienced as externally controlled; (4) experiences of alienation, when thoughts, feelings, or movements have a quality of not belonging to the person (e.g., a patient believes his own tears are not his); and (5) delusional perception, in which a correctly perceived neutral event is perceived as having a special, delusional, meaning unrelated to the event (e.g., seeing a taxi driving by is interpreted by a patient as a sign that the Messiah has come).

A 42-year-old woman believes that a metal transmitter was implanted in her heart during her appendectomy 20 years ago. That transmitter broadcasts her thoughts to her coworkers and neighbors through her heartbeats, and comments by people she knows are often a response to these broadcasts. The transmitter is in turn controlled by a man in another city who has a book

Table 17.3. Thought Disorders[a]

Thought Disorder	Definition	Associated Illness
Non-Formal		
Flight of ideas	Jumping from topic to topic. Topics may be obliquely related and progress farther from the track, or totally unrelated (often in response to external stimuli). Individual sentences are understandable.	Mania
Clang associations	Associations by the sound rather than the meaning of words.	Mania
Circumstantiality	Tightly linked associations with extra, nonessential associations interspersed. Speech takes a circuitous route before reaching the goal.	Mania, major depression, alcoholism, temporal lobe epilepsy, common in non-ill
Formal		
Drivelling	Fluent speech with normal rhythm and melody, and good balance of nouns, verbs, adverbs, articles, and prepositions, all of which would appear to have normal syntax to a person who did not speak the language. But content is meaningless doubletalk. Word salad is its most severe form.	Schizophrenia, chronic coarse brain disease, and mania may each cause any of the formal thought disorders.
Perseveration	Repetition of stock words, phrases, and ideas automatically placed in the flow of speech.	
Nonsequiturs	The patient's responses are totally unrelated to the physician's questions, and there is no evidence of flight of ideas.	
Paraphasias	Misuse of words: word approximations (imprecise word usage such as ink pencil for pen, handshoe for glove), neologisms (words not in the dictionary, e.g., diatral), phonemic paraphasias (mispronunciations owing to incorrect phonemes or sounds, such as trookie for cookie).	
Tangentiality	Sentences have adequate grammar and syntax, associations are tightly linked, the content is on the right topic, but the response does not answer your question, and the answer is vague. Applies to questions, not spontaneous speech.	
Verbigeration	A verbal stereotype in which the patient automatically repeats phrases, words, or syllables, typically at the end of a thought (e.g., "I went to the store, the store").	

[a]Modified from Taylor MA, Sierles FS, Abrams R. General hospital psychiatry. New York: Free Press, 1985; and Andreasen NC. Thought, language and communication disorders. I. Clinical assessment, definitions of terms and evaluation of their reliability. Arch Gen Psychiatry 1979;36:1315-1321.

Table 17.4. Types of Hallucinations[a]

Type of Hallucination	Definition	Most Frequent Association
Pseudo-hallucination	Any vague, poorly formed hallucination	Can occur in non-ill
Hypnagogic/hypnopompic	Hallucination occurring while falling asleep or awakening	If pseudo-hallucination, can occur in non-ill; vivid and hypnogogic may be narcolepsy (p. 377)
Incomplete auditory	Most common hallucination. A muffled or whispered voice saying a few words.	Nonspecific
Complete auditory	A clear, sustained voice, speaking full sentences, perceived as coming from outside the patient's body.	Schizophrenia
Elementary	Unformed hallucinations (e.g., smells, tastes, flashes of light, unidentified voices)	Epileptic (p. 46) and toxic states
Functional	Occurs immediately after ordinary stimulation in that modality (e.g., hearing voices only when the faucet is on)	Epileptic and toxic states
Extracampine	A hallucination outside the normal sensory field (e.g., seeing people behind you)	Epileptic and toxic states, schizophrenia

[a]Modified from Taylor MA, Sierles FS, Abrams R. General hospital psychiatry. New York: Free Press, 1985.

about the patient's past and future. There are no hallucinations.

The patient also has episodes of depression, and of euphoria with hyperactivity, during which time the above beliefs preoccupy her more, but the beliefs exist even when her mood is normal.

This patient exhibits thought broadcasting and experiences of influence, both mood-incongruent.

Assessment for suicidal (p. 349), homicidal (p. 360), or assaultive thinking is also part of the MSE.

Affect, the capacity to experience and express feelings, has two principal categories: emotional expression (e.g., facial expressivity, mood intensity, modulation of mood, and animation and melody of voice) and volition (how much the patient cares about his or her current life situation, relationships, and future). Mood is the patient's feeling tone (e.g., sadness, anger, anxiety, euphoria) at a point in time (e.g., the length of an interview). Note whether the mood is sustained. In major depression with melancholia, the sad or anxious mood is sustained, whereas in dysthymic or reactive depression, a sad mood often "lifts" during a sensitively conducted interview. Flatness (blunting) of affect (Table 17.5) is a multidimensional finding (e.g., a composite of expressionless face, monotonous voice, lack of spontaneity) (42, 43, 63) most

common in schizophrenia (in which emotional expression and volition are impaired), major depression with melancholia (in which emotional expression reflects sustained sadness or anxiety, with volition intact), and dorsolateral prefrontal convexity syndrome (p. 45) (63). Lability of affect describes rapid changes of mood. It is seen in mania, dementia, delirium, and histrionic or borderline personality.

Insight about one's illness proceeds along a continuum from nonrecognition of a problem, to a feeling of subjective distress, to recognition of a psychiatric problem, to understanding the biopsychosocial factors (pp. 3–15) contributing to the problem. Anyone can lack insight, but it is most often impaired in patients who have coarse brain disease, certain personality disorders, psychoses, and substance dependence.

Judgment is the extent to which a person can solve problems in life, including moral, legal, social, and health-related decisions. Problems in judgment are most pronounced in schizophrenia, mania, coarse brain disease, mental retardation, and various personality disorders. Milder judgment problems may occur in anxiety disorders such as social phobia, in which patients misperceive that they will be the center of attention and their flaws will be exposed.

Your feelings toward the patient can be a clue to the diagnosis. Irritable, combative, or mistrustful patients can elicit fear, borderline patients anger, histrionic patients sexual interest, and manic patients amusement. Proverb testing is often included as a routine component of the MSE, but use of proverb testing has been challenged as being of little value in diagnosis (56).

Initial screening for coarse brain disease is readily addressed by any of several scored cognitive screening examinations with proven reliability and concurrent validity. They can be repeated to track a patient's clinical improvement or deterioration, are easy to administer, and can be used by diverse clinical staff.

Table 17.5.   Emotional Blunting Scale[a]

Item	Score*		
Emotional Expression			
1. Absent, shallow, incongruous mood	0	1	2
2. Constricted affect (narrow range)	0	1	2
3. Unvarying affect (lacks modulation)	0	1	2
4. Expressionless face	0	1	2
5. Unvarying, monotonous voice	0	1	2
6. Difficult to excite emotions (unresponsive)	0	1	2
Volition			
7. Indifference or unconcern for own present situation	0	1	2
8. Indifference or unconcern for own future (lacks plans, ambition, desires, drive)	0	1	2
Total Score_____			

[a]Modified from Berenbaum SA, Abrams R, Rosenberg S, Taylor MA. The nature of emotional blunting: a factor-analytic study. Psychiatric Res 1986;20:57-67.
*Total score of more than 7 = severe blunting, common in schizophrenia; 4–7 = mild blunting.

Table 17.6. The Mini-Mental State Examination[a]

Specific Test	Function	Maximum Score*
1. What is the year/season/ date/day/month?	orientation	5
2. What is the state/county/ town/hospital/floor?	orientation	5
3. Repeat 3 items (after you have said all 3).	registration	3
4. Serially subtract 7's from 100 (or spell "world" backwards).	concentration	5
5. Name wristwatch and pencil.	naming	2
6. Say "No ifs, ands, or buts."	expressive speech	1
7. "Take this paper in your right hand, fold it in half, and put it on the floor."	motor regulation	3
8. Read "close your eyes" and do it.	reading	1
9. Remember the 3 items from part 3.	memory	3
10. Write a sentence.	writing	1
11. Copy intersecting penta- gons.	construction	1

[a]Modified from Folstein MF, Folstein SE, McHugh PR. "Mini-mental state": a practical method for grading the cognitive state of patients for the clinician. J Psychiatric Res 1975;12:189-198 [with permission from the holder].
*Range of scores of patients with psychiatric disorders is 8–30. Average score for demented patients is 9.7, range 0–23.

The Mini-mental State Examination (Table 17.6) is the structured screening exam I most often use. It is useful in raising the red flag for coarse brain disease. Other tests are the Cognitive Capacity Screening Examination (CCSE) (65), the Short Portable Mental Status Questionnaire (66), and the Reitan-Indiana Aphasia Screening Test (67). Use of the CCSE led to an accurate diagnosis of coarse brain disease in 38 of 39 ER patients who scored in the range for "organicity" (68).

Poor performance on cognitive screening examinations strongly suggests brain disease. Sometimes the cause (e.g., Alzheimer's disease, meningitis) is already known. If not, a vigorous search for the cause is in order. But good performance on a screening examination does not exclude the possibility of brain disease causing abnormal behavior. Hence, a complete behavioral neurologic examination (46, 69), neuropsychologic testing (pp. 205–208), and other lab tests are in order when patients have behavioral abnormalities of unknown cause.

LABORATORY TESTS

The diverse causes of behavioral dysfunction may require a variety of diagnostic laboratory studies (Table 17.7). Although use of costly resources is an important ethical and fiscal issue, the consistent findings of nonpsychiatric illnesses causing or exacerbating the problems of patients with behavioral disorders compels proper lab investigation. But ordering lab tests is not a shotgun exercise. The choice of tests depends on the patient's unique clinical presentation.

In the emergency room (ER), the first priority is to rule out life-threatening systemic illness. To this end, the ER physician may order a complete blood count (CBC), blood glucose, electrolytes, blood urea nitrogen, and ECG in the absence of indications for other studies based on the history and PE (71).

For patients admitted to a psychiatric inpatient service, 90% of medical illnesses missed by history and PE will be detected by a 34 item automated blood chemistry analysis (including fasting blood sugar), ECG, CBC, urinalysis, and electroencephalogram (72). Serum treponemal antibody test (for syphilis), triiodothyronine resin uptake, total serum thyroxine, free thyroxine index, serum folate, and vitamin B_{12} levels are also useful in detecting systemic illnesses (17, 20, 73).

Because of the high prevalence of substance abuse (74), a drug screen of urine (in which all common drugs of abuse [except LSD] can be identified) (75) and blood (for alcohol or PCP), or a breathylizer (for alcohol) should be liberally used. Such testing is especially useful in new, acute presentations in ER and inpatient settings.

Lab tests are used to establish positively the diagnosis in some coarse brain diseases and intoxication states, and to provide a fuller characterization (but not definitive diagnosis) of classic psychiatric disorders (Table 17.1).

Table 17.7. Selected Laboratory Findings Pertinent to the Psychiatric Evaluation[a]

Test or Procedure	Examples	Comments
BLOOD		
Complete blood count (CBC)		
Increased white cells (WBC) (leukocytosis)	Mercury toxicity	Occupational exposure causes Mad Hatter's syndrome: hypersalivation, tremulousness, anxiety, irritability
	Bacterial infection	Fever, pus formation
Increased lymphocytes (lymphocytosis)	Tuberculosis	Poverty, crowding. Caused by TB bacillus. Typical granulomas in lungs, other organs. Fever, weight loss typical. Depression, hypomania, other behavioral problems
	Mononucleosis	Weakness; tiredness; fever; enlarged lymph nodes, spleen and liver; depression
	Leukemia	Overproduction of "cancerous" WBCs
Increased monocytes (monocytosis)	Brucellosis	Bacterial infection with brucella. Reservoir is farm animals. Fever, chills, weakness, headache, anxiety, depression
Decreased white cells (leukopenia)	Rickettsial infection	Examples: typhus, Rocky Mountain spotted fever. Insect-borne bacteria cause fever, rash, mental changes
	AIDS	(pp. 3–15).
	Viral encephalitis	Viral brain infection. Can cause obsessive-compulsive or mood disorder, psychosis, delirium, Parkinson's disease, seizures, coma
Increased eosinophils (eosinophilia)	Parasitic infections	Examples are worm infestations, malaria, amebic dysentery
Anemia (decreased red cells) (RBC)	Collagen disease	Multiple-system connective tissue autoimmune diseases, e.g., systemic lupus erythematosus, polyarteritis nodosa
	Lead toxicity	Occupational exposure (adult) or eating paint chips (children). Blue stipples in RBC, GI disturbance, peripheral neuropathy (leg weakness, decreased Achilles reflex), dementia, seizures
	Iron deficiency	Most common cause is chronic blood loss; RBCs small
	Folic acid or B_{12} deficiency	Impaired ingestion, absorption or utilization of folic acid or B_{12} causes pernicious anemia with large RBCs and megaloblastic madness (cognitive deficit, mood disorder, or psychosis)
Erythrocyte sedimentation rate	Autoimmune disease, infection, tumor	
Electrolytes		
Hyponatremia (low Na^+)	Addison's disease	Adrenal insufficiency because of TB, autoimmunity, fungal infection, cancer. Low BP, weakness, skin pigmentation, anxiety, depression.
	Water intoxication	Excess water drinking due to mental illness, alcoholic gastritis, teenage dare, excess dilute IV fluid. Excess blood volume, hyponatremia, stupor, delirium, convulsions
Hypernatremia (high Na^+)	Diabetes insipidus	Inadequate production of antidiuretic hormone, or inability of kidney to use it (nephrogenic), yields enormous output of dilute urine with increased serum Na^+. The latter causes stupor and delirium. Causes: genetic; hypothalamic or pituitary disease; nephrogenic (Li_2CO_3 can cause).
Hyperkalemia (high K^+)	Renal or adrenal disease or excessive K^+ therapy	Hyperkalemia can cause severe cardiac arrhythmia.
Hypokalemia (low K^+)	Diuretic medications	These cause increased urine production and can cause hypokalemia with muscle weakness or cardiac arrhythmia.
Hypercalcemia (high Ca^{2+})	Hyperparathyroidism	Overproduction of parathormone (PTH) from a PTH-producing tumor in parathyroid or elsewhere. PTH increase causes hypercalcemia with tiredness, kidney stones, bone disease, mood change, cognitive deficits.

Table 17.7. Selected Laboratory Findings Pertinent to the Psychiatric Evaluation[a] *(continued)*

Test or Procedure	Examples	Comments
Hypocalcemia (low Ca^{2+})	Hypoparathyroidism	Causes: accident of thyroid surgery, idiopathic (= cause ?). Decreased resorption of Ca^{2+} from bone. Hypocalcemia causes tetany with spasm of wrists, feet, bronchi or larynx; anxiety, depression, irritability, delusions.
Hyperglycemia (elevated glucose)	Diabetes mellitus	Impaired pancreatic insulin production causes decreased metabolism of glucose, hyperglycemia, increased sugar in urine with increased urination, dehydration, increased thirst, decreased blood volume. Inadequate insulin also causes decreased ketoacid metabolism, causing acidotic blood. Nausea, vomiting; rapid, deep sighing respiration; delirium. Long-term increased risk of stroke, myocardial infarction, blindness, peripheral and other neuropathy.
	Cushing's disease	(p. 198).
Other Blood Work		
Elevated blood urea nitrogen (BUN) and creatinine	Kidney disease	Consequences of severe kidney disease include HBP (p. 189), anemia (p. 195), hyperkalemia (p. 195), delirium, stupor, seizures.
Elevated creatine phosphokinase (CPK)	Neuroleptic malignant syndrome	(p. 326)
Elevated cholesterol	Thyroid disease, atherosclerosis	Causes of hypercholesterolemia include genetic, diet, hypothyroidism. Hypercholesterolemia predisposes to atherosclerosis (occlusion of arteries due to cholesterol deposits), which often causes cerebral infarction (death of brain tissue due to inadequate blood supply) or myocardial infarction (death of heart muscle tissue due to inadequate coronary blood supply).
Positive VDRL (Venereal Disease Research Laboratory) test	Syphilis	Sexually transmitted disease caused by spirochete (spiral microorganism) treponema pallidum. Causes local sore (chancre), rash (often on palms and soles), lesions anywhere in CNS, cognitive dysfunction, mania-like illness, and dementia.
	Systemic lupus erythematosus (SLE)	A collagen disease with exacerbations (spontaneous recurrences) and remissions (spontaneous recoveries) often associated with recurring mania-like psychosis, recurring schizophrenia-like psychosis, catatonia (p. 188), and dementia.
Elevated alkaline phosphatase (an enzyme)	Pernicious anemia	(see folic acid or B_{12} deficiency, above.)
	Scurvy	Vitamin C deficiency. Causes: alcoholism, food faddism, other types of malnutrition. Bleeding gums, bruising, secondary folic acid deficiency with anemia, weakness, depression, irritability.
Thyroxine (T4), Triiodothyronine (T3), TSH (Thyroid-stimulating hormone)	Hyperthyroidism	Overproduction of iodine-containing amino acids T3 and T4 from Graves' disease (likely autoimmune), hormone-secreting thyroid nodules or tumors. Rapid pulse, wide difference between systolic and diastolic BP (e.g., 160/60), atrial fibrillation (an arrhythmia), bulging eyes, tremor, heat intolerance, anxiety (99% of cases), peripheral neuropathy, mood disorder, psychosis, or delirium.
	Hypothyroidism	T3, T4 deficiency from Hashimoto's disease, thyroidectomy, iodine deficiency, Li_2CO_3 treatment, hypothalamic or pituitary disease. Coarse voice, weight gain with anorexia, anemia, cold intolerance, cognitive dysfunction or psychosis (myxedema madness).
Heavy metal screening	Arsenic toxicity	Occupational exposure or (rare) homicidal poisoning causes gastrointestinal disturbance, hemolytic anemia (p. 189), liver disease, kidney disease, peripheral neuropathy, cognitive dysfunction, mood changes, psychosis.

Table 17.7. Selected Laboratory Findings Pertinent to the Psychiatric Evaluation[a] *(continued)*

Test or Procedure	Examples	Comments
	Mercury, lead	See mercury toxicity, lead toxicity, above.
Ceruloplasmin decrease	Wilson's disease	Recessive defect on chromosome 13 causes copper deposition in liver, cornea and brain with cirrhosis (p. 190), brown ring in cornea, tremor, choreoathetoid movements (p. 190), dementia. Free ceruloplasmin decreases; copper binds the remainder.
Arterial blood gases	Hypoxia	Causes: diminished drive to breathe, obstructive lung disease, upper airway obstruction, inadequate O_2 diffusion due to alveolar disease, pulmonary embolus (p. 189). Common manifestations: agitation, delirium.
	Hypercapnia	Excess blood CO_2. Acutely causes drowsiness, delirium, coma. Chronically causes muscle twitching, asterixis (p. 190), papilledema (p. 189), headache, drowsiness, cognitive dysfunction.
Folate or B_{12} deficiency	Pernicious anemia	See anemia above.
Antinuclear antibodies present	SLE, other autoimmune diseases	See SLE above.
Ammonia elevation	Hepatic encephalopathy	With liver failure, toxic nitrogenous substances absorbed from the gut bypass the liver. Apathy, delirium, stupor, coma may occur.
HIV antibody present	AIDS	(pp. 3–15).
URINE		
Urinalysis	Diabetes mellitus	Glucose present in urine.
	Urinary tract infection	WBC (pus) in urine.
	Severe kidney disease	Casts of renal tubules, RBC, protein in urine.
Urinary catecholamine elevation	Pheochromocytoma	(p. 189)
Urinary steroid levels	Elevated in Cushing's	(p. 198)
	Reduced in Addison's	See hyponatremia above.
PROCEDURES		
ECG	Myocardial infarction	(p. 196)
	Cardiac arrhythmia	Irregular heartbeat; if severe, can cause shock (p. 189)
EEG	(p. 198).	
Cerebrospinal fluid abnormality	Bleeding into spinal fluid, tumor, infection	Depending on brain location (pp. 33–47) and extent of intracranial pressure, these cause sensory, motor, and cognitive abnormalities, mood disorder, psychosis, delirium, dementia, seizures, etc.
Tine skin test	Tuberculosis	See lymphocytosis, tuberculosis above.
RADIOGRAPHY		
Chest x-ray	Chronic obstructive lung disease, tumor, infection	Cardinal symptom is labored breathing, feeling unable to obtain air. Anxiety, agitation, depression, delirium occur.
Skull x-ray	Skull fracture	Fracture often causes brain injury. Signs as for blood clot, tumor.
CT and MRI	Hydrocephalus	Excessive spinal fluid in cerebral ventricles, dilating these cavities (p. 216). Multiple causes.
	Cerebral atrophy	Diminished size of brain and number of neurons. Enlarged ventricles, flattening of gyri, widening of sulci. Many conditions cause it (including schizophrenia and major affective disorder, in which atrophy is mild).
	Tumor, blood clot, abscess	See above.
	Multiple sclerosis	See p. 199. MRI good for locating patches of demyelination.

[a]Modified from Harry SW, Markowitz J. Organic mental disorders. In: Talbott JA, Hales RE, Yudofsky SC, eds. Textbook of psychiatry. Washington DC: American Psychiatric Press, 1988; Wyngaarden JB, Smith LH Jr., eds. Cecil textbook of medicine, 17th ed. Philadelphia: WB Saunders, 1985; and Hall RCW, ed. Psychiatric manifestations of medical illness: somatopsychic disorders. Jamaica, NY: SP Medical and Scientific Books, 1980.

Neuroendocrine Testing

Several tests are based on the abnormalities of the hypothalamic/pituitary axis sometimes accompanying mood disorders. The best established abnormality is the hypersecretion of cortisol in depression, evaluated with the dexamethasone suppression test (DST) (76).

The synthetic glucocorticoid dexamethasone is given at 11:30 PM and plasma cortisol levels are drawn the next day at 8 AM, 4 PM, and 11 PM. If the cortisol levels are less than 5 μg/dL, the test is negative. A positive result (failure to suppress leading to values of 5 μg/dL or greater at any of the above times) occurs in about 50% of patients who have major depression with melancholia, a group that generally responds well to somatic therapies for depression. If the DST remains positive after symptomatic remission occurs, relapse risk is higher. Unfortunately, the DST is not pathognomonic for melancholia; pregnancy, numerous systemic illnesses, schizophrenia, nonmelancholic depression, and medications can also give false-positive results. Five percent of normal controls are also nonsuppressors (76–79).

A 28-year-old woman had a history of depression for 1 year, with two prior psychiatric hospitalizations. The current admission was precipitated by increasing depression over the prior 3 months since losing her job. She was tearful, sad, irritable, restless, and had poor sleep and appetite. BP was 140/100. The MSE showed her to be neat, restless, and making poor eye contact. Speech was slow, fluent, and monotonous. She had poverty of thought and suicidal ideation. She was irritable, terminating the interview prematurely. She was oriented but refused to cooperate for formal intellectual assessment. Initial laboratory testing was normal except for low serum potassium (hypokalemia).

A DST was ordered to evaluate for major depression with melancholia. The result was non-suppression of cortisol at 47 μg/dL at 8 AM, 35 μg/dL at 4 PM, and 28 μg/dL at 11 PM.

The abnormal body habitus, hypertension, hypokalemia, and abnormal DST led to consideration of Cushing's syndrome (excessive production of cortisol because of an overactive pituitary or adrenal gland), prompting consultation with an endocrinologist. After further evaluation, the patient went to surgery and an adrenal adenoma (a benign hormone-secreting tumor) was removed. She has since been symptom-free.

This illustrates how, despite history suggesting a psychiatric disorder, the initial PE and lab evaluation, coupled with a fortuitous false-positive DST, led to diagnosis of an endocrine disorder.

In the thyrotropin-releasing test, give 0.5 mg. of thyrotropin-releasing hormone (TRH) and draw a thyroid-stimulating hormone (TSH) level 30 minutes later. In depressed or manic patients, the rise in TSH from the pretest TSH level can be blunted compared to the TSH rise in controls. The incidence of this abnormality in depression is about 25% (79).

Electroencephalography

An electroencephalogram (EEG) (80) is a record of the fluctuations in the brain's electrical activity from the surface of the scalp. The signal recorded represents only an average of the electrical events generated by the neurons in the superficial cortical layers. It is the graded sum of the excitatory and inhibitory potentials from the many thousands of neurons just beneath the recording electrode.

To record the EEG, at least two electrodes are needed: an active electrode and a reference (indifferent) one. The active electrode is placed over the presumed site of neuronal activity, and the reference electrode at some distance from this site. The recording electrodes are typically placed on the scalp over the frontal, parietal, occipital, and temporal lobes according to a conventional scheme.

The frequencies recorded from the scalp of a person in good health range from 1–50 cycles per second (Hertz [Hz]). The amplitude of the signal ranges from 20–100 microvolts. Alpha waves (8–13 Hz) are generally associated with relaxed wakefulness, more abundant when the eyes are closed, and best recorded over the parietal and occipital lobes. Beta waves (13–30 Hz) are normally observed over the frontal regions, have the smallest voltages, and are more abundant and diffuse with intense mental activity. Theta (4–7 Hz) and delta (0.5–4 Hz) waves, are associated with stages of sleep in normal adults, can be seen diffusely in awake states in patients with delirium and dementia, and focally in patients with specific brain lesions. Spike waves occur in epilepsy (p. 46). In petit mal epilepsy (p. 47), the spike frequency is specifically 3 Hz.

The frequency of EEG abnormalities (slowing, or changed characteristics of beta waves) increases in schizophrenia and major affective disorders, but these abnormalities are not pathognomonic (81–83).

EEG EVOKED POTENTIALS

The waves seen in a standard EEG recording are relatively high in voltage compared to the small voltage generated by simple stimuli (light, sound, touch). But in an evoked potentials EEG the high-voltage waves are cancelled by a special technique, allowing visualization of the stimulus-generated low-voltage waves. Thus, when a visual, auditory, or tactile stimulus is presented, the brain's response can be followed from the brainstem to the cortex or even across the corpus callosum. Evoked potential EEG is particularly helpful in diagnosing multiple sclerosis (myelin degeneration in multiple CNS sites, cause unknown).

BEDSIDE TESTS

The response of patients to intravenous (IV) sodium amobarbital (Amytal) and sodium lactate can enhance diagnostic thinking. In the Amytal interview, the patient is slowly given several hundred mg of Amytal IV as the interview progresses. Patients mute from psychosis or overwhelming anxiety may relax sufficiently to speak and may speak lucidly (84). Patients who have conversion disorders (p. 276) may show temporary improvement. But a demented or delirious patient will manifest increased cognitive impairment (85).

Intravenous sodium lactate induces panic attacks in patients with panic disorder, or flashbacks in patients who have posttraumatic stress disorder plus panic disorder. There is a 28% false-negative response. The specificity and sensitivity (p. 29) must be clarified before the test becomes a routine diagnostic tool (86, 87).

BRIEF OBSERVATION PERIOD

In differentiating between psychiatric and general medical disorders, and among psychiatric disorders, time and observation are valuable tools. Avoid premature labeling of patients' problems as either psychiatric or systemic; this risks inappropriate treatment which can obscure the diagnosis or even lead to death. For newly admitted, undiagnosed patients on the psychiatric ward, give supportive care and maintain a safe environment for patients and staff alike while observation and systematic investigation proceed vigorously. Reassurance and explanations by staff, on a constant one-on-one basis if needed, along with a calm, orderly immediate environment, lessen the need for sedation, restraints, or seclusion room use. Physical restraints can be used judiciously, but you must ensure that patients do not exhaust, injure, or dehydrate themselves by struggling against the restraints. An excellent alternative to restraints is the seclusion (locked, but carefully supervised) room.

If medicine is needed for the newly admitted, undiagnosed patient who is combative, agitated, or hyperactive, lorazepam 1–2 mg intramuscularly [IM] or slowly IV, or amobarbital 300–500 mg (IM or slowly IV) can induce sleep, during which time a PE and lab testing can be done. Afterwards, the medication completely wears off, allowing further observation in the unmedicated state, and spontaneous recovery in 10% of patients (58).

Some physicians recommend antipsychotic or neuroleptic medications (p. 324) for the control of agitated or threatening behavior in undiagnosed patients with acute psychosis, delirium, or dementia with psychosis, while vigorous efforts of diagnosis continue. Examples include oral or IM thiothixene, haloperidol, or fluphenazine, or IV haloperidol (88–90). Older or debilitated patients should receive half the standard adult dosage.

DIAGNOSIS AND DYNAMIC FORMULATION

As evaluation progresses, you establish a differential diagnosis (the list of conditions that could explain the patient's problems) and a working diagnosis (the most likely diagnosis on which initial management is predicated). In so doing, you also incorporate psychosocial factors into your understanding of the patient. This is the biopsychosocial perspective. Psychodynamic assessment includes evaluating the patient's ego and superego (p. 85) functioning (structural formulation), unconscious conflicts (dynamic formulation), and childhood and adult interpersonal contributions to the problem (genetic formulation) (48, 91).

18/Psychological Testing

Darlene L. Shaw, Ph.D., and Danny Wedding, Ph.D.

OBJECTIVES

GENERAL OBJECTIVE: Given a case history or patient interview, write an appropriate request for psychological testing for that patient.

SPECIFIC OBJECTIVES:
1. Summarize the purposes of psychological tests in medical settings.
2. Discuss the psychometric principles (standardization, reliability, validity) that determine a test's usefulness.
3. State the characteristics of the Wechsler and Stanford-Binet intelligence tests, including the age groups for which they are used.
4. List the four levels of inference that neuropsychologists use in assessing the likelihood of brain disease.
5. Discuss the Halstead-Reitan and Luria-Nebraska test batteries and the tests of specific brain functions.
6. Compare the characteristics and tenets of objective and projective personality tests.
7. Describe the Minnesota Multiphasic Personality Inventory, the Rorschach Test, and the Thematic Apperception Test, and specify the type of information each provides.

Psychological tests are a logical extension of the mental status examination (pp. 188–194) in that they measure differences among people and variability over time and situation of individuals while minimizing the faults of bedside evaluations. The tests do this by using a standard set of techniques to elicit a representative sample of behavior objectively recorded and analyzed.

Clinically, psychological tests serve many purposes. They measure acquisition and retention of information and skills, and they describe the patient's behavior and identify specific symptomatic behaviors. The tests also are used to classify persons along a particular dimension (e.g., intellectual ability) and to aid in diagnosis.

They aid decisions on specific issues (e.g., competency to handle funds) and in treatment (e.g., suitability for group therapy) and discharge planning. They supplement bedside judgment by helping predict behavior such as response to psychotherapy or suicide risk. In addition, some tests provide information about a person's psychodynamics (i.e., the underlying conflicts and issues that motivate behavior) and personality characteristics (e.g., introversion or capacity for insight). Tests can also establish baseline levels of a behavior to monitor changes in that behavior. For example, a clinician might collect psychological measures before and after prescribing a drug to determine whether the drug affected depressive symptomatology.

Data obtained from psychological tests are interpreted and written as reports by psychologists. In hospital settings these psychologists most often have a Ph.D. in clinical psychology. Some others may have a Ph.D in counseling psychology. In either case, they have had at least 4 years of postbaccalaureate education, a 12-month clinical internship, and 1 or 2 years of supervised postdoctoral work. They then have taken a written exam and an oral exam which, if passed, qualify them as licensed psychologists. Only 10% of applicants are accepted into American Psychological Association-approved clinical psychology doctoral programs—programs that are highly competitive and rigorous (1). In addition to interpreting the results of psychological testing, clinical psychologists are skilled diagnosticians, therapists, and researchers.

PRINCIPLES OF PSYCHOMETRIC TESTING

A psychological test must have standardization, reliability, and validity. Although some tests possess these characteristics more than others, together they determine the confidence clinicians place in the results of a particular test.

Standardization is when a test is administered to a large group of persons who typify the group for whom the test was devised using identical materials, instructions, administration, and scoring. Standardization provides a frame of reference or normative group to which a person's or group's scores can be compared. Many tests are "normed" on several groups including those of different sex, ages, and educational levels. For example, if a test of basic science knowledge is used to select medical school applicants, the normative group could be the general population. A better standardization group, however, would be medical school freshmen or senior premedical students.

Reliability is the consistency of the scores received by the same person on each administration or equivalent form of the test. If chance or random error largely determines a person's test score, the test is unreliable and therefore useless. A test's reliability is expressed as a correlation coefficient (p. 23) with a maximum of 1.0 and a minimum of 0. For psychological tests used in clinical settings, reliability coefficients of .80 or above are usually considered good. A test, however, may be standardized and reliable and still not measure what it purports to measure. Reliability is necessary, therefore, but not sufficient for validity.

Validity is the extent to which a test measures what it is intended to measure. Typically the validity of a test is determined by correlating the results of the test with a criterion (e.g., the validity of a test of depression might be determined by comparing its results with diagnoses made by expert clinicians [concurrent validity, p. 29]).

Even when a test has fine reliability and validity, psychologists rarely interpret its results in isolation. Data from a test are considered in the context of information from the patient's history, physical exam, other lab tests, and collateral sources (p. 185). Age, ethnic group, education, occupation, and current situation are also considered when interpreting results.

TYPES OF PSYCHOLOGICAL MEASURES

Psychological tests differ in content and administration. Most tests used in clinical settings are administered individually (versus group-administered tests used in educational settings). Psychological measures can be grouped as tests of cognitive ability which measure intellectual functioning and academic achievement, neuropsychologic tests which measure brain-behavior relationships, and personality tests which describe character traits. Behavioral assessments use observational techniques to quantify problematic behaviors and the environmental events that maintain them; developmental tests (e.g., the Denver Developmental Screening Test) measure the extent to which children and adolescents have achieved maturational milestones; and vocational tests measure interests, abilities, and aptitudes to aid educational and vocational planning.

SPECIFIC TESTS

Tests of Cognitive Ability

INTELLIGENCE TESTS

Intelligence is a construct (p. 29) used to describe a group of complex mental abilities. We cannot measure it directly; we infer it by measuring observable behaviors. These behaviors include the ability to learn from experience, acquire, store, access, and manipulate information, think abstractly, solve problems through insight, adjust to new situations, and focus and sustain direction in activities. Consequently, persons who obtain the same score on an intelligence test may have completely different patterns of abilities and deficiencies. Whereas one person might excel on manual skill items, another might do best on verbal tasks.

Development of intellectual ability depends on genetic factors and environmental encounters that promote learning of information or skills. Scores that measure IQ both predict scholastic achievement and are enhanced by formal education; consequently, they correlate with educational achievement. For example, although individual exceptions abound, Ph.D.'s and M.D.'s have an average IQ of 125, college graduates average 115, and high school graduates 105 (2).

Intelligence is stable over time (especially in persons tested after age 15–18 years), and test-retest reliability is high (.80–.90) for most IQ tests, even when administered to children 2 to 3 years of age with several months between test administrations. If, however, the test-retest interval is several years for a child, lower reliability is obtained. IQ scores can also change over several years in response to dramatic environmental changes, illness, or variations in motivation; thus, measured intelligence cannot be considered as fixed.

The first intelligence test was devised by the French psychologist Alfred Binet in 1905.

Known as the Binet-Simon Scale, the test was used in the Paris school system to identify children who were not expected to benefit from attending school. After numerous revisions over the years since it was first developed, the Stanford-Binet Scale (3) is now widely used to measure intellectual functioning. Although it can be used with persons aged 2–18 years, it is especially useful with children under 6 years of age. Moreover, because it assesses rudimentary as well as advanced skills, it is particularly helpful in evaluating severely impaired and exceptionally bright children. The scale consists of 142 brief tests, arranged in age-appropriate levels. Although the items measure manual manipulation skills in younger children, for older children they predominately test verbal abilities. Intelligence quotients (IQs) derived from the Stanford-Binet are expressed as standard scores with a mean of 100 and a standard deviation (SD) (p. 21) of 16.

The most frequently used intelligence tests were devised by David Wechsler. The Wechsler Adult Intelligence Scale–Revised (WAIS-R) (4) is used to evaluate persons 16 years of age or older, with norms existing to age 74 years. The WAIS-R consists of a Verbal Scale composed of six subtests which measure fund of knowledge, vocabulary, abstract reasoning, and practical problem solving, and a Performance Scale composed of five subtests which assess perceptual organization, visual-spatial-motor skills, and ability to sustain effort. Within each subtest the items are arranged in order of increasing difficulty, and each subtest is scored separately and converted to a standard score. The WAIS-R yields a Verbal IQ (VIQ) score, a Performance IQ (PIQ), and a Full Scale IQ score, each expressed as a standard score with a mean of 100 and an SD of 15 for each normative age group. The WAIS-R provides clear scoring criteria for each item, and test-retest reliability is .90 or above for each of the three IQ scores derived from the test (4).

In interpreting test performance, the psychologist classifies the VIQ, PIQ, and Full Scale IQ scores using the numerical ranges,

Table 18.1.   WAIS-R Intelligence Classifications[a]

IQ Score	Classification	Approximate % of Population
130 + above	Very Superior	2
120 - 129	Superior	7
110 - 119	High Average	16
90 - 109	Average	50
80 - 89	Low Average	16
70 - 79	Borderline	7
69 + below	Mentally Retarded	2

[a] Adapted from Wechsler Adult Intelligence Scale–Revised. Copyright 1981, 1955 by The Psychological Corporation. Reproduced by permission. All rights reserved.

classification labels, and percentile ranks presented in Table 18.1. The disparity between the VIQ and PIQ scores is evaluated. Relatively higher VIQ scores are associated with good academic achievement, whereas relatively higher PIQ scores are associated with academic underachievement and lower socioeconomic status. Although a 10-point discrepancy between these scores occurs in 30% of normal adults, a discrepancy of 15 points or greater in which the VIQ is lower may reflect, especially in males, left hemisphere brain dysfunction. Conversely, a PIQ score 15 or more points lower than the VIQ may reflect a right hemisphere lesion (5).

When interpreting the WAIS-R, the clinician also examines the patient's relative performance on the different subtests (intersubtest scatter) and pattern of performance within each subtest (intrasubtest scatter). Different patterns of intersubtest variability reflect a person's cognitive strengths and weaknesses, and a notable intrasubtest scatter may reflect inattention or other problems such as the memory loss of dementia (p. 277). Psychologists also examine the content of the person's responses particularly on such verbal subtests as vocabulary and comprehension. These may reflect important personality traits. But inferences about a person's cognitive abilities are rarely made solely on the basis of an IQ score; IQ is examined in the context of indicators such as social and vocational functioning.

Clinically, IQ tests are used for a variety of reasons, including to aid in diagnosis (e.g., de-

mentia vs. depression), educational planning (e.g., Can this person benefit from a training program?), discharge planning, and treatment planning (e.g., Can this patient follow a complicated medication regimen?). IQ tests may also help determine eligibility for Social Security disability benefits, or aid in vocational planning, as illustrated here:

Mr. Wells, a 52-year-old man, was referred for IQ testing to determine whether he was intellectually capable of maintaining gainful employment. Mr. Wells, who had dropped out of school in the sixth grade, has been employed for 24 years as a brickmason's assistant on a construction crew until he sustained a back injury which left him unable to perform hard labor. He applied for Social Security disability benefits, claiming he was unable to maintain any employment.

Testing with the WAIS-R indicated Mr. Wells had a PIQ of 68, a VIQ of 64, and a Full Scale IQ of 64, placing him in the range of mild mental retardation. His performance was uniformly poor across the various subtests, with the exception that he performed relatively better on a task that required him to attend to details and identify missing parts of common objects. His general fund of knowledge and practical reasoning skills were very poor. He could crudely sign his name, but was unable to read or perform even very simple addition. He had a pleasant demeanor and related to the examiner cooperatively.

Based on this information, the psychologist concluded that Mr. Wells could be employed, but only in a position that provided close supervision and required only very simple, repetitive behaviors (e.g., busboy, dishwasher, sheltered workshop worker). It was noted that his good interpersonal skills would be an asset at work.

In addition to the WAIS-R, used for adults, the Wechsler series also contains the Wechsler Intelligence Scale for Children–Revised (WISC-R) (6) used to assess the intellectual abilities of children aged 6–16 years. The WISC-R consists of the 11 subtests from the WAIS-R plus an optional subtest, Mazes, which assesses planning ability and visual-motor coordination. The WISC-R is similar to the WAIS-R in administration, scoring, and interpretation. It is also well standardized, and its validity and reliability are comparable to those of the WAIS-R.

The Wechsler Preschool & Primary Scale of Intelligence (WPPSI) (7) is used to assess children aged 4–6 1/2 years. The WPPSI also contains 11 subtests, some of which share items with the WISC-R, and others of which differ from the WISC-R subtests.

ACHIEVEMENT TESTS

Achievement tests measure information acquired through instruction. They are often paired with IQ tests to determine whether a person's academic skills correspond with IQ scores. This combination helps in educational and vocational planning and in diagnosing learning disabilities. The achievement test most often used in medical settings is the Wide-Range Achievement Test (WRAT) which assesses reading, written spelling, and arithmetic. Other achievement tests commonly used by school systems are the Stanford Achievement Test and the California Achievement Test. Most achievement tests can be administered in a group format. Their standardization, reliability, and validity are good.

Neuropsychological Tests

Neuropsychology is the study of the relation between the brain and behavior. Clinical neuropsychology applies knowledge of brain-behavior relations to the assessment and treatment of patients. Many neuropsychological (NP) tests can describe and quantify the effects of brain dysfunctions and diseases, extending mental status examination (MSE) findings or revealing subtle cognitive changes missed by the MSE. They may also localize lesions, but neuroimaging (p. 213) is preferable in definitively identifying and localizing lesions, If, however, the task is to identify how a lesion is affecting a patient's life, there is no substitute for NP testing. NP tests entail virtually no risk to the patient, but are time-consuming (5–8 hours for a complete test battery, depending on the patient) and expensive ($300–$800, depending on the tests used).

The neuropsychologist assesses patients using four levels of inference: (1) level of performance, (2) patterns of performance, (3) right-left differences, and (4) presence of pathognomonic signs (see below). This reflects that brain damage often causes a generalized decrement of performance across multiple tasks, may produce specific patterns of impairment (e.g., defective language skills with spared spatial abilities), and may produce deficits that rarely occur unless there is localizable brain disease (i.e., pathognomonic findings such as Wernicke's aphasia, which is seen almost exclusively with disease of the posterior superior temporal gyrus [p. 38]).

TEST BATTERIES

Most NP evaluations assess motor skills, perceptual abilities, verbal abilities, memory functions, abstract reasoning, and problem-solving skills. To ensure that each domain is sampled adequately, an established test battery is used. The Halstead-Reitan and the Luria-Nebraska batteries are the two most widely used.

HALSTEAD-REITAN NEUROPSYCHOLOGICAL BATTERY

The Halstead-Reitan Battery (HRB) (8) includes a variety of individual tests, many of which were widely used in clinical psychology and behavioral neurology long before they were included in the HRB by Ward Halstead or, later, by his student Ralph Reitan. The HRB is the battery most widely used in the United States.

The HRB includes the WAIS-R, the MMPI (p. 208), and five other measures.

1. The Category Test requires the patient to identify the principle (e.g., shape) presented in each of six sets of visually presented stimuli. It measures abstract concept formation, and is the HRB's most sensitive measure of brain dysfunction.
2. The Tactile Performance Test requires the patient, blindfolded, to fit 10 geometric forms into correspondingly shaped spaces on a board, using first the preferred hand, then the nonpreferred hand, and then both hands. This requires tactual, spatial

analysis and cognitive visualization and is the most sensitive measure of lateralized brain dysfunction.

3. The Speech Sounds Perception Test requires the patient to listen to 60 tape-recorded sets of four nonsense syllables and indicate on a multiple-choice form what was heard in each set. This task is sensitive to brain damage generally and to left hemisphere damage in particular.

4. The Seashore Rhythm Test, which requires the patient to discriminate between like and unlike pairs of recorded musical rhythms, measures nonverbal auditory functions and is particularly sensitive to right temporal lobe lesions.

5. The Trail Making Test requires the patient to draw lines to connect consecutively numbered circles (Part A), and then (Part B) to connect consecutively numbered and lettered circles, alternating between the two sequences (e.g., connect 1 to A, A to 2, 2 to B, B to 3, etc.). It measures visuomotor tracking and conceptual flexibility and is highly sensitive to brain damage. In addition, there are specific tests of gross and fine motor skills (e.g., grip strength and finger oscillation), as well as tests of auditory, tactile, and visual perception. The patient's response to two stimuli simultaneously presented is also assessed for hearing, touch, and vision.

The HRB reports include an Impairment Index, in a single decimal (ranging from 0–1), reflecting the proportion of those tests most sensitive to brain impairment on which the patient's score fell in the range characteristic of brain-injured subjects.

The HRB has adequate reliability, and numerous validity studies have demonstrated its effectiveness (90% accuracy) for distinguishing patients who have brain disease from neurologically intact controls (9). Its practical usefulness is illustrated by this case:

> Mr. Thomas, a 42-year-old technical school graduate, was referred for NP testing, to aid vocational planning, 3 months after the resection of a slow-growing tumor in his right anterior parietal lobe. The HRB revealed that the patient had retained well-learned verbal skills (e.g., vocabulary, verbal comprehension) in the High Average range, but his verbal abstract reasoning skills were only Average. He scored in the Defective range on tasks of concentration, visuospatial or-

ganization, and visual reasoning (particularly tasks dealing with unfamiliar, poorly structured stimuli). Consequently, the neuropsychologist predicted that the patient could not work effectively at his job as the "layout" man at the local newspaper; rather, he was encouraged to seek a position that would capitalize on his good verbal skills and provide him with supervision and a well-structured task dealing with familiar objects (e.g., a sales clerk).

THE LURIA-NEBRASKA NEUROPSYCHOLOGICAL BATTERY

The Luria-Nebraska Neuropsychological Battery (LNNB) is another commonly used NP test battery. This collection of short, easily administered tests is based on the work of A. R. Luria, a Soviet neurologist and psychologist whose techniques were organized in the United States by Anne-Lisa Christensen and later published and popularized by Charles Golden (10).

The LNNB has 269 items that are combined to produce the following 11 ability scales: motor, rhythm, tactile, visual, receptive speech, expressive speech, writing, reading, arithmetic, memory, and intellectual processes. Three additional scales attempt to identify pathognomonic signs and the extent to which damage is lateralized.

Although many neuropsychologists believe the LNNB is a helpful tool, it has many flaws (e.g., scales containing heterogenous items that confound the functions being tested) and questionable reliability and validity. Consequently, practitioners should be cautious about drawing conclusions based solely on LNNB scores (9).

TESTS OF SPECIFIC FUNCTIONING

Instead of using an NP test battery, many neuropsychologists administer several tests of specific functions because they believe these tests achieve the same results with less time and effort. For example, many neuropsychologists assess language skills with the Boston Aphasia Examination (11). Another popular test is the Wechsler Memory Scale-Revised (WMS-R) (12), which is included with IQ testing in almost every comprehensive assessment of a patient with suspected Alzheimer's or Pick's disease (p. 282). The WMS-R contains many subtests for comprehensive assessment of major memory functions. Its use is illustrated by this case:

Mrs. Smith, a 74-year-old widow, was hospitalized for treatment of a fractured bone in her foot. She was a high school graduate who had worked for 50 years as a hotel receptionist. Because of a successful physical rehabilitation program, she could walk while her foot was in a cast, and could perform personal hygiene tasks and other activities of daily living (e.g., fix simple meals). As she neared discharge, Mrs. Smith insisted on returning home. Her children, however, wanted her placed in a nursing home because they felt she was senile and unable to care for herself.

IQ testing with the WAIS-R established that Mrs. Smith's cognitive abilities were intact (Full Scale IQ=104) and not significantly changed from her premorbid intellectual level, which was estimated to be in the Average range. The test also revealed that her abstract reasoning skills and problem-solving abilities in practical situations were intact. Although the Performance tests indicated her fine motor coordination was slightly impaired, she demonstrated adequate visual-motor ability to manipulate small objects (i.e., blocks and puzzle pieces) similar in size to those required in daily living.

Testing with the WMS-R substantiated the findings of the WAIS-R (Mrs. Smith obtained a General Memory Quotient of 99, placing her at the 50th percentile), and provided additional evidence that her memory for recent and remote events was intact. The WMS-R also indicated she was fully oriented, her concentration was intact, and she could recall important facts from a paragraph read to her. She demonstrated an average ability to learn new associations. Consequently, the diagnosis of dementia was ruled out, and Mrs. Smith has functioned well at home for the past 3 years.

Psychologists who do not use the WMS-R usually assess story recall, which involves reading a standardized story to a patient and having the person recall, after a brief delay, as many details as possible (9). It is often shock-

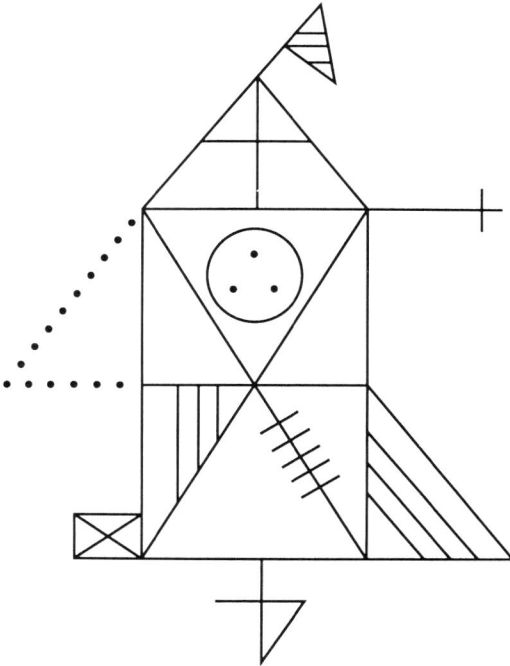

Figure 18.1. Complex figure similar to the Rey-Osterrieth figure.

ing to see how this simple measure can reveal dramatic impairment in an articulate, socially skilled patient who would otherwise appear normal.

Spatial skills can be assessed by having patients copy simple drawings. However, interpretation of these drawings is somewhat subjective. More systematic analysis of spatial problem-solving ability occurs with Raven's Progressive Matrices (13). Initially designed to measure culture-free intelligence, this test requires that the patient identify which of several patterns is the missing piece "cut" from a stimulus figure. The test requires good spatial abilities and general intelligence. A purer measure of spatial ability is the Rey-Osterrieth Complex Figure Test (14) which requires the patient to reproduce a detailed figure from memory. The figure is too complex to be effectively recalled from verbal memory alone. Figure 18.1 is a complex figure similar to the Rey-Osterrieth Figure.

Another widely used test of spatial skill is the Bender Visual-Motor Gestalt Test (15). It

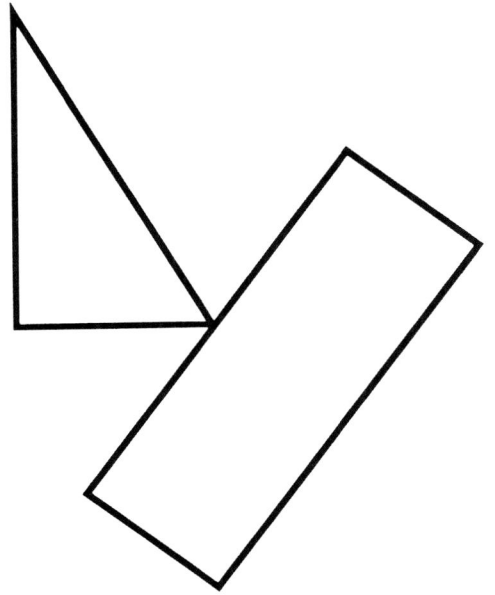

Figure 18.2. Design similar to the Bender-Gestalt designs.

requires that the patient copy nine complex figures. Figure 18.2 is a design similar to those on the Bender Gestalt. Although the Bender-Gestalt was once used as a global measure of cortical integrity, it is most sensitive to parietal lesions (especially right hemisphere lesions) and should not be used as an overall indicator of brain function.

The Wisconsin Card Sorting Test (WCST) (16) is sensitive to damage to the prefrontal cortex (p. 45). It assesses the patient's ability to shift conceptual sets (e.g., from color to shape to number) by recognizing the pattern (e.g., color, shape, or number) underlying the matching of a series of cards. Considerable cognitive flexibility is necessary because the category changes without warning (e.g., from purple objects to pentagons), and the patient must again decipher the rule for correct matching. Patients who have isolated prefrontal lesions often perform well on IQ tests, but not on the WCST.

Patients who have psychiatric disorders often perform poorly on NP tests. This used to be considered a weakness of the tests themselves; increasing evidence (p. 186) suggests,

however, that many psychiatric disorders result from underlying brain disease and are not simply the product of abnormal learning. Schizophrenic patients are especially likely to perform poorly on NP tests, and multiple studies (17–19) demonstrate a correlation between the severity of this impairment and the presence of enlarged cerebral ventricles.

Depressed patients often perform poorly on most NP tests, especially tests that require rapid responding. Differentiating between dementia and the pseudodementia of depression is complex, and these patients benefit from evaluation by a neuropsychologist as well as by a psychiatrist. Alcoholics perform poorly on general measures of cerebral integrity and have characteristic difficulties on tests of memory and new learning. These findings typically occur before liver damage or other systemic signs of alcoholism.

Tests of Personality Functioning

OBJECTIVE MEASURES OF PERSONALITY

Objective personality tests are usually paper-and-pencil tests consisting of specific, relatively unambiguous questions with a structured response format (e.g., true/false). Responses can be objectively scored and interpreted by comparing the person's scores with those of a normative group.

The Minnesota Multiphasic Personality Inventory (MMPI) is the most widely used and researched (over 6,000 articles) psychological test in the United States (20, 21). Its clinical utility is well established (22), and in our experience, it is the best of the psychological tests of psychopathology. When it was developed in 1943, its authors (Starke Hathaway and Charnley McKinley) empirically chose items on the basis of whether the item differentiated between specific patient groups (e.g., schizophrenics versus depressives) and between a specific diagnostic group and normal subjects. In 1990 new norms, based on a national sample tested with a slightly modified version of the MMPI (the MMPI-2), were published (23).

The MMPI-2 can aid in psychiatric diagnosis, prediction of treatment response, assessment of personality characteristics and overall adjustment, forensic evaluations, and evaluation of symptom clusters (e.g., depressive symptomatology).

The MMPI-2 consists of 567 statements which the patient answers "true or false" as applied to the person (e.g., I believe my sins are unforgivable). A "cannot say" option is for items the patient deems unanswerable. Responses are scored objectively to yield four validity scales and 10 basic clinical scales. The raw score for each scale is converted to a standard score (T scores having a mean of 50 and an SD of 10) and plotted on a profile sheet which is differentiated for males and females and which allows comparison of the person's scores on the scales with those obtained by the normative group.

The four validity scales (i.e., the Cannot Say, L (Lie), F (Faking), and K (Correction) scales) of the MMPI-2 reflect the patient's test-taking attitude and the presence of deviant response sets (e.g., defensiveness or exaggeration of problems). The 10 clinical scales provide information about personality characteristics and symptom patterns as follows: (1) hypochondriasis (Hs)–bodily concern; (2) depression (D)–symptoms of depression; (3) hysteria (Hy)–denial and somatization; (4) psychopathic deviance (Pd)–impulsiveness and problems with authority; (5) masculinity/ femininity (MF)–endorsement of interests more typical of the opposite sex; (6) paranoia (Pa)–suspiciousness and hypersensitivity to criticism; (7) psychasthenia (Pt)–anxiety and psychologic distress; (8) schizophrenia (Sc)– unusual thoughts and social alienation; (9) mania (Ma)–restlessness and excessive activity; and (0) social introversion (Si)–social discomfort.

Interpretation of the MMPI is based on an analysis of the pattern of scores generated by the patient. Scores that fall approximately 2 SD above the mean are viewed as clinically significant, but lower scores, the relationship among scores, and the configuration of the profile are also important. Hence, the score on a single scale cannot be taken at face value. For example, a high Sc score does not necessarily mean a patient is schizophrenic. The patient's profile type (coded by the highest two or three scales) is usually compared to established profile patterns whose associated personality characteristics have been well documented. For example, persons who have an elevated 2–7 profile often report feelings of tension, anxiety, depression, and pessimism. This profile type is common among psychiatric outpatients and patients who worry excessively and overreact to minor stress. Patients who have this profile tend to be perfectionistic and obsessive, often feel inadequate, and are passive-dependent in relationships, but their prognosis for psychotherapy is good (22).

Test-retest reliability of the MMPI is relatively high (.70–.80) over brief intervals but considerably lower for intervals of more than 1 year (22). However, individuals often produce the same code type on different test administrations, and when a person's code type changes there are often concomitant behavioral changes (22). Many validity studies have demonstrated consistent nontest correlates for MMPI code types. For example, moderate scores on scales 4 and 6 suggest immaturity and repressed anger (22).

Several other objective, self-report tests of personality functioning are also often used. They can be administered individually or in groups, and have acceptable reliability, validity, and normative data. The Millon Clinical Multiaxial Inventory (MCMI) (24) is a 175-item questionnaire with 20 clinical scales reflecting persistent traits, current symptom states, and levels of severity of pathology. The Symptom Checklist-90-Revised (25) provides information about degree of distress and nine symptom dimensions (e.g., somatic concern, obsessiveness, depression, and anxiety). Two other measures, the California Personality Inventory (26) and the Sixteen Personality Factor Inventory (27) identify nonpathologic personality traits.

Other tests address specific clinical syndromes. For example, the 21-item Beck Depression Inventory (28) assesses the physiolog-

Figure 18.3.   Inkblot resembling a plate on the Rorschach Inkblot Test (created by Deborah Rubenstein).

ical, cognitive, and affective symptoms of depression, and the Jenkins Activity Survey (29) assesses the degree to which a person endorses Type A personality characteristics (e.g., competitiveness, hostility, impatience, rushing) which have been associated with poor prognosis in the presence of arteriosclerotic heart disease.

PROJECTIVE TESTS

Projective techniques are based on the assumption (the projective hypothesis) that a person's personality traits, needs, conflicts, and unconscious motives determine how the person perceives an ambiguous stimulus like an inkblot, and that by revealing the principles by which the stimulus is organized, the person reveals the unconscious influences on his or her behavior. Some psychologists believe projective tests are an important part of a personality test battery, and that the information the tests provide about the patient's unconscious (e.g., defense mechanisms and degree of self-focus) is important in diagnosing and understanding the person.

The most frequently used projective test, the Rorschach Test, consists of 10 cards, each depicting a bilaterally symmetrical inkblot similar to that in Figure 18.3. Five of the blots are in black and white; the remaining 5 include other colors. The cards are individually presented and the examiner asks the patient, "What might this be?" The patient's responses are recorded verbatim during the free association portion of the test administration. The examiner then reviews that card and asks the patient which aspects of the card (e.g., overall form or color) were used to determine responses.

Several scoring systems for the Rorschach are available. The most psychometrically sound was developed by Exner (30). Psychologists note the number of responses, the reaction time, and the total time devoted to each card. Scoring converts the important aspects of each response into categories that are then quantified and compared to patient and nonpatient groups using norms collected by Exner and others. The response characteristics that are scored include: the portion of the blot used as the basis of the response (location), the characteristic (e.g., shape, color, texture) of the blot that made it appear a certain way to the patient (determinants), and the content areas (e.g., animal or human) identified. The number of popular (most frequently perceived) responses is also noted. Scores are used to generate indices on which inferences about the patient are based. For example, patients with a high proportion of popular responses are viewed as conventional and overly conforming. Schizophrenic inpatients, and others (creative or ill) who have difficulty seeing the world as others see it, produce low proportions of popular responses. The Rorschach's reliability and validity have long been questioned. But with Exner's system, adequate test-retest (.66–.90) and interrater (.85) reliability were established (31, 32), and validity studies suggested its value in predicting suicide (31, 33).

The Thematic Apperception Test (TAT) (34) is a projective personality test devised to assess inhibited and unconscious factors (e.g., needs, emotions, values, and conflicts) that motivate behavior. It is a series of 29 cards containing ambiguous pictures, and one blank card. The test requires the patient to make up a story describing what is happening in the picture, the thoughts and feelings of the characters, the preceding events, and the outcome. Usually, only 10–12 of the stimulus pictures are presented, with selection based in large part on the conflicts and issues (e.g., male/female relationships, suicide, achievement motivation) the examiner wishes to test in the patient.

Several systems exist for scoring the TAT, but most psychologists rely on subjective clinical judgment to interpret results. The patient's stories are evaluated for unusual and recurrent themes. The pictured figure (hero or heroine) with whom the patient seems to identify is also located, and the wishes and conflicts attributed to that person are noted. In addition, the environmental pressures on the hero or heroine, characteristics attributed to other figures in the picture (who may represent others in the patient's life), and the story's outcome are analyzed. For example, in interpreting a response to a picture of two women, one of whom looks menacing, psychologists would evaluate the relationships and personality characteristics attributed to the two women on the assumption that the picture often elicits descriptions of mother figures.

Attempts to establish the TAT's test-retest reliability and validity have failed. But some psychologists maintain that the TAT provides valuable information about relationships and motivations.

A third projective measure, sentence completion tests, requires the patient to complete a stem (e.g., "I feel . . . .," "My father . . . .") with the first thought that comes to mind. Often 50–100 stems are used, and the test is thought to elicit information regarding conscious issues (e.g., feelings, fears, attitudes) that are important to the patient. Although copyrighted forms are available, many psychologists create their own. Interpretation is usually based on an inspection of the items, noting particularly repetitive, unusual, or strongly worded responses.

Projective drawings such as the Draw-A-Person (35, 36) and House-Tree-Person (37) tests are sometimes included in a personality battery. These require the patient to draw the specified object, and interpretation is usually based on a simple inspection of the drawing, noting aspects such as placement and size. The assumption for this technique is that the drawings express the self-image and mood of the patient. Reliability and validity of these tests is generally lacking.

THE PHYSICIAN'S ROLE

Given the myriad tests available, selection of a specific psychological test or battery of tests is best left to a psychologist. Being familiar with the tests available and the information they provide is nevertheless important for the physician because situations in which testing would help can then be identified. Familiarity with these tests also helps in understanding test interpretations and reports, data which ultimately can be integrated with other information concerning care of the patient. Physicians can help psychologists choose the most appropriate tests by specifying the question to be answered by the testing (e.g., can this patient learn peritoneal dialysis procedures), data relevant to the question (e.g., the patient's physical limitations and educational history), and the purpose of the testing (e.g., to be used for planning patient's training for home-based dialysis).

19/Brain Imaging in Psychiatry

Wayne C. Drevets, M.D.

OBJECTIVES

GENERAL OBJECTIVE: Given an article that uses a brain imaging technique to identify abnormalities in a psychiatrically ill sample, critically assess the author's ability to test his or her hypotheses based on the strengths and limitations of the imaging tool used.

SPECIFIC OBJECTIVES:
1. Discuss current applications of brain imaging to psychiatric research.
2. Summarize the underlying technology and relative strengths and weaknesses of computed tomography and nuclear magnetic resonance imaging.
3. Review consistent structural abnormalities identified in patients with schizophrenia, affective disorders, and other psychiatric disorders.
4. Describe the methods by which functional imaging tools produce three-dimensional pictures of cerebral blood flow and metabolism.
5. Contrast positron emission tomography, single photon emission computed tomography, and regional nontomographic methods for measuring physiologic differences associated with psychiatric illnesses or their symptoms.
6. Review major findings of functional imaging studies in schizophrenia, affective disorders, and anxiety disorders.
7. Suggest potential applications of neuroreceptor imaging in studying the pathophysiology and pharmacotherapy of psychiatric disorders.
8. Discuss the importance, limitations, and preliminary applications of computerized EEG and evoked potential mapping in psychiatry.

Evidence demonstrating a neurobiologic basis for the major psychiatric disorders continues to accumulate. Much of this information has been obtained through family studies, pharmacologic effects, and measurements of neurotransmitter or neuroendocrine indices. More recently, a variety of brain imaging techniques have emerged to identify structural and functional abnormalities in psychiatric illness, and to illuminate the neuroanatomic correlates of human emotion and higher cognitive function. Because many symptoms of psychiatric disease represent distortions or loss of these functions, understanding normal neurophysiology is essential for elucidating the pathophysiology of psychiatric disorders.

The application of brain imaging for studying psychiatric illness is only in its infancy, slowed in part by the continuing evolution of imaging technology. Its clinical utility remains confined to differential diagnosis, for ruling out (generally with magnetic resonance imaging [MRI] or computed tomographic [CT] scanning) coarse brain diseases that present with psychiatric signs or symptoms. Yet it demonstrates increasing promise in psychiatric research, particularly as methodologic problems are progressively resolved and instrumentation and computer analysis capabilities improved. Besides illuminating pathophysiologic and morphologic abnormalities, imaging holds potential for directing neuropathologists to specific brain regions for receptor and cell measurements, for subgrouping patients in clinical or epidemiologic studies, and for identifying genotypic carriers not yet manifesting phenotypic changes in family linkage analyses. As larger groups of patients are studied, imaging may also become a useful clinical tool to establish diagnosis, provide treatment recommendations, or indicate prognosis.

Requirements for this to be realized include studying larger numbers of patients, replicating findings across multiple centers, and establishing diagnostic sensitivity and specificity (p. 29). Although no imaging finding in any psychiatric disorder yet fulfills all these criteria, the next decade should see methods that meet these standards, allowing us to better evaluate important findings already made (1).

In vivo brain imaging consists of structural and dynamic techniques. The structural techniques include x-ray CT and MRI, which are used to evaluate morphology and elements of tissue composition. The dynamic techniques assess functional activity and include regional cerebral blood flow (RCBF), single photon emission computed tomography (SPECT) and positron emission tomography (PET) (Fig. 19.1). MRI possesses important capabilities for both types of imaging.

STRUCTURAL IMAGING

Psychiatric disorders were previously termed "functional" illnesses, when early neuropathologic studies failed to identify histologic brain abnormalities. This was in part because structural differences identifiable in psychiatric illnesses are subtle, relative to the gross changes occurring in neurologic illnesses (e.g., cerebrovascular disease, degenerative basal ganglia diseases). However, recent systematic volumetric investigations using CT and MRI and quantifications of relatively small lesions with MRI are consistently revealing structural differences in major psychiatric illnesses. These have sparked new interest in neuropathologic studies of such disorders, many of which have already come to fruition (2–4).

Computed Tomography

X-ray computed tomography (CT) was the first imaging system to yield a direct in vivo image of the human brain. The major technical advance allowing its development (for which Cormack and Hounsfield received the Nobel Prize in 1979) was the analytic procedure known as projection reconstruction imaging. It involves computer reconstruction of a two-dimensional view of a tissue slice from a set of one-dimensional projections taken at multiple angles. The initial signals for generating a CT image consist of density profiles derived from the relative attenuation of an x-ray beam as it passes through tissue. The beam is projected from a series of points as the radiation source rotates around the subject. The corresponding two-dimensional density profile is then reconstructed by a computer. Other tomographic techniques such as MRI, PET, and SPECT utilize projection reconstruction, but differ in the origin of the initial signals.

CT scanning remains the most commonly available imaging modality. Its spatial resolution (the ability to display two closely associated small structures as distinct objects) is in the range of 1–2 mm in the xy (transverse) dimension. Although coronal or sagittal reconstructions may be computed, their spatial resolution is much lower, a major disadvantage of CT. *A greater limitation of CT is its contrast resolution.* Relative to MRI, CT provides much less contrast between gray and white matter and between normal and diseased tis-

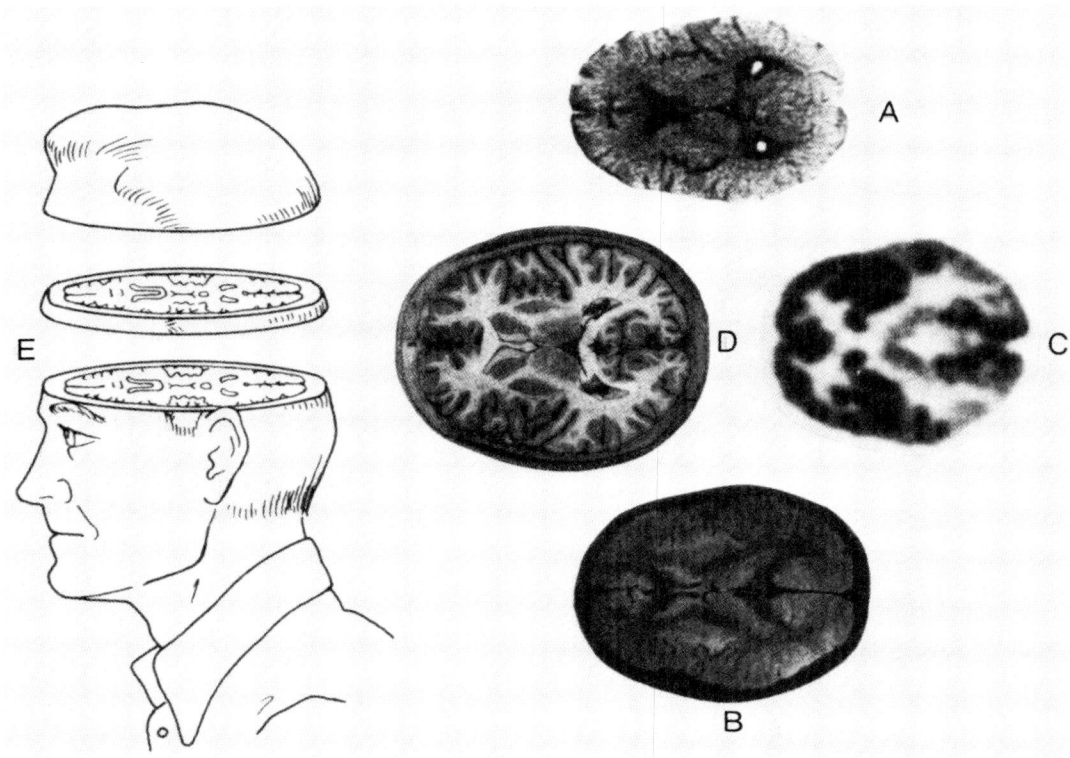

Figure 19.1. Images of the normal adult human brain obtained with **a.** x-ray computed tomography; **b.** nuclear magnetic resonance (NMR); and **c.** positron emission tomography (PET). These images, obtained in living human subjects, are to be compared with a representative anatomic section of the human brain obtained in the same horizontal plane **d.** The approximate orientation of these images is shown in the line drawing on the left **e.** The CT image reflects the density of the tissue to x-rays, thus bone and calcified tissue appear most dense (white), brain parenchyma less dense (grey), and fluid bathing the brain least dense (black). The NMR image reflects the proton density of the tissue. In contrast to the CT image, bone is not visualized. Note the striking demarcation between grey and white matter in the brain and the exquisite anatomic detail as revealed by the presence of small blood vessels (fine black lines within the brain). The PET image represents a quantitative map of local glucose utilization in the structures depicted in the other images and the anatomic section. Areas highest in glucose utilization are dark. Areas with lower glucose utilization appear lighter. (Reprinted with permission from Raichle ME. Images of the brain in action. In: Gregory RL, ed. The Oxford companion to the mind. New York: Oxford University Press, 1987:348.)

sue. CT is also subject to artifacts from beam hardening (the progressive absorption of lower energy photons as the polychromatic x-ray beam traverses tissue, causing the beam to consist of photons of increasing energy) which produces artifactual attenuation values, particularly near dense bony structures. Such artifacts, seen as dark streaks, obscure regions such as posterior fossa, inferior surfaces of frontal and temporal lobes, and other tissues adjacent to the skull edge. CT imaging also requires exposure to ionizing radiation.

Nuclear Magnetic Resonance Imaging

Nuclear magnetic resonance imaging (MRI) currently provides the highest spatial and contrast resolution pictures of in vivo brain structure. It holds great potential for functional imaging as well. MRI generates its images by manipulating the electromagnetic forces in tissues and reconstructing images based on changes in these forces. The most common nucleus targeted with MRI is hydrogen, because of its abundant distribution

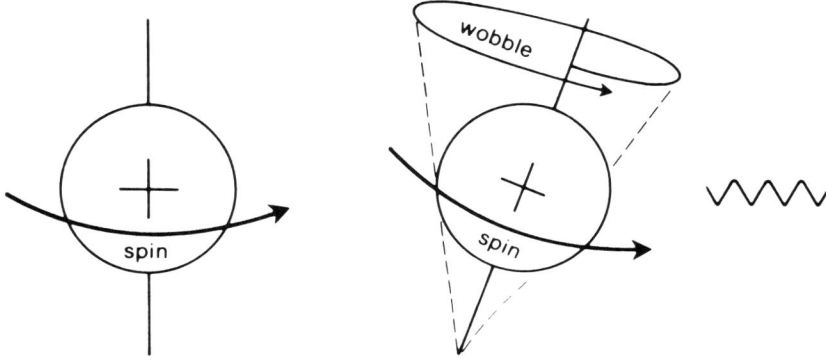

The spin is even.

The spin WOBBLES like a top, or precesses, with a resonant frequency specific to the nuclear species.

WITHOUT AN EXTERNAL FIELD   WITH AN EXTERNAL FIELD

Figure 19.2. How an external field produces resonance (precession): the *Resonance* in NMR. (Reprinted with permission from Andreasen NC. Nuclear magnetic resonance imaging. In: Andreasen NC, ed. Brain imaging: applications in psychiatry. Washington, DC: American Psychiatric Press, 1989:72.)

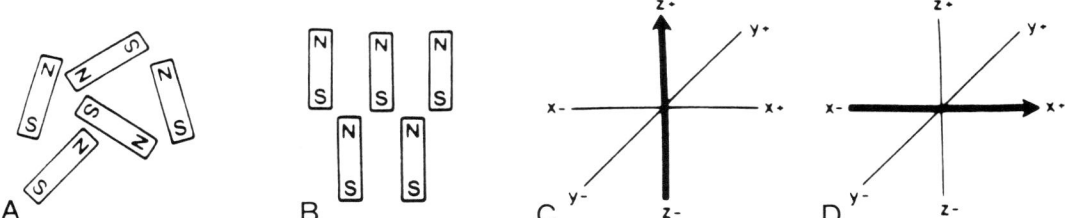

Figure 19.3. The sequence of effects to the magnetic moment of protons during MR imaging. **a.** Without application of the external magnetic field, the magnetic moments of spinning protons lie in random orientation. **b.** When placed in the external field of the MRI magnet, they become aligned in the direction of the external field, **c.** producing a net positive magnetization. **d.** When a radio frequency signal is administered at the protons' Larmor frequency, their magnetic moments tip 90° into the X axis, changing the direction of the net magnetic moment. (Modified from Andreasen NC. Nuclear magnetic resonance imaging. In: Andreasen NC, ed. Brain imaging: applications in psychiatry. Washington, DC: American Psychiatric Press, 1989:67–121.)

throughout the body. Other nuclei (e.g., phosphorus-31, carbon-13, sodium-23, potassium-39) will be important in the future.

These nuclei behave as spinning charged particles that induce a magnetic field, the strength and orientation of which is termed the magnetic moment. The magnetic moments of tissue nuclei lie in random directions. Inside the MRI scanner, an external magnetic field is applied so that all such magnetic moments are aligned in the same direction, producing a net

positive magnetization. When aligned with this magnetic field, the spinning nuclei wobble around the longitudinal axis of the field like a child's spinning top (Fig. 19.2). Each nuclear species has a characteristic wobble, called its Larmor frequency. While in the magnetic field, a radio signal is administered at the Larmor frequency of the specific nuclei (e.g., hydrogen) being imaged, giving them additional energy, and causing them to tip into the XY axis so that their net magnetic moment points in a different direction (Fig. 19.3). When the radio signal is discontinued, the increased energy imparted to the protons gradually diminishes, or relaxes, emitting a radio wave detected by a radio frequency receiver. The degree of relaxation over time is measured to generate the MRI image. As different tissues contain disparate amounts of hydrogen, relaxation varies, and the radio frequency signals produced during relaxation are of differing strengths. Magnetic resonance images are produced by assigning shades of gray to the signal strengths produced by the relaxing protons.

The MRI signal is produced by three components: (*1*) proton density, a measure of the number of hydrogen nuclei in tissue; (*2*) T1 relaxation time, the time required for net magnetization in the Z axis to return to 63% of its original value; and (*3*) T2 relaxation time, the time required for net magnetization to decay to 37% of the original value in the XY plane (5). At a given field strength and radio frequency strength, different tissues have characteristic T1s and T2s. The radio transmitter pulse sequence applied to the protons spinning in the magnetic field may be varied to emphasize one or more components of the MRI signal. Scanners in clinical use rely primarily on two types of pulse sequences: inversion recovery and spin echo. The former allow best gray and white matter resolution and provide T1 weighted images. Spin echo sequence allow better detection of small focal lesions such as tumors or multiple sclerosis plaques (p. 199) and are more commonly used clinically.

MRI holds several advantages over CT. It is free from bony artifacts, allowing clearer views of the posterior fossa. It provides superior spatial resolution (about 0.5 mm), obtainable in sagittal, coronal, or transverse planes. MRI allows better contrast resolution between gray and white matter, permitting visualization of small structures such as cranial nerves, basal ganglia nuclei, and limbic structures. Moreover, fine shades of tissue abnormality can be identified (e.g., multiple sclerosis plaques). And, it does not involve exposure to ionizing radiation.

MRI has thus proved superior to CT for psychiatric indications. Clinically these involve rul-

ing out gross neurologic brain disturbances that may produce psychiatric symptoms or signs. Its research uses include volumetric assessment and lesion quantitation. It possesses even greater potential for future functional studies. Examples include measures of oxygen metabolism (6), cerebral blood flow, oxidative metabolism [through the ratio of adenosine triphosphate (ATP) to other phosphates using the resonance frequencies of ^{31}P (7)], and neurotransmitter uptake using paramagnetic tracers.

Structural Imaging Studies in Psychiatry

Most structural imaging studies of patients with psychiatric illness have involved measures of cerebral ventricle size. The significance of ventricular enlargement is that it may reflect atrophy (shrinkage [in organ size, number of cells]) or hypoplasia (incomplete development) in the structures lining the ventricles. The lateral ventricles are in close proximity to basal ganglia, thalamus (a relay station for sensory stimuli to the cerebral cortex), limbic structures (p. 35) and hypothalamus, and the third ventricle to thalamus, hypothalamus, fornix, and habenula (the latter two are limbic structures).

Earlier linear indices used to measure lateral ventricular size included the Hutchinson index (ratio of the span of the anterior horns of the lateral ventricles to brain width at the same point) and the cella media index (ratio of maximum anterior horn width to brain width). These lacked the sensitivity to detect subtle changes and did not correlate well with ventricular volume (8). They have largely been replaced by computing a ventricular brain ratio (VBR) (9).

Structural Imaging in Schizophrenia

CT STUDIES IN SCHIZOPHRENIA

Of 40 studies (10) in which the lateral ventricle system in schizophrenia (p. 241) was measured, 31 demonstrated significant enlargement compared with various control groups. Among these, 90% in which normal controls were used found a difference, compared to 50% of those using neurologic patients as controls. The finding of lateral ventricular enlargement (LVE) has been corroborated in neuropathologic studies of schizophrenic patients at autopsy (11).

The LVE did not correlate with age or illness chronicity, which suggests that it occurs early in the illness and changes little over time (12–16). This is consistent with the conspicuous absence of gliosis (overgrowth of neuroglia [central nervous system "supporting cells"]) in most postmortem studies that report decreased tissue volume (17), and with the finding of abnormal cytoarchitecture (4), which implies an early developmental neuropathologic process. In addition, little relationship has been found between the degree of LVE and extent or duration of neuroleptic treatment, use of electroconvulsive therapy (ECT) or length of hospitalization (12, 18–21).

The LVE is positively correlated (p. 23), however, with illness severity and social impairment. It appears to be associated with a subtype of schizophrenia characterized by greater cognitive impairment (18, 22–25) and negative symptomatology (apathy, anhedonia [absence of enjoyment], avolition, [p. 193], paucity of speech [p. 242]). Other clinical findings associated with LVE include poor premorbid adjustment, persistent unemployment, lower incidence of psychotic symptoms, poor response to neuroleptic medications, and increased incidence of extrapyramidal side effects with neuroleptics (26–34). In a study of seven monozygotic twin pairs discordant for schizophrenia, the ill twins had significantly larger ventricles than their unaffected cotwins (35). This was replicated in a larger group of twins using MRI (see below).

Third ventricle size is usually assessed by measuring its maximum width, although some groups use a third-ventricular:brain ratio. (12, 36). Of 15 studies of third ventricle size in schizophrenia, 13 showed significant enlargement relative to controls (10). Nine of 11 in which medical or neurologic patients were used as controls were positive, as were each of two using normal controls. Associations of third ventricular enlargement and clinical variables such as chronicity, age, and so forth have been inconsistent, suggesting that it may be present in a broader segment of schizophrenic patients than LVE.

Cortical sulcal widening (sulci are grooves on the brain's surface) is generally associated with shrinkage of the cortical gyri. Sulcal measurements have been performed in 3 ways: (1) measuring widths of certain sulci and fissures, (2) subjective visual inspection for degree of atrophy, and (3) using computer algorithms to compare pixel quantities (a pixel is a 2-dimensional measure of square surface area, usually 1 mm × 1 mm) of criterion densities, corresponding to tissue versus CSF. Fourteen of 21 studies (10) reported significant sulcal widening in schizophrenia—six of 11 using medical or neurologic patients as controls, and five of six using normal controls. The sulcal widening usually involves frontal or temporal lobes (37–40). As with ventricular enlargement, age did not correlate with degree of cortical atrophy in most studies. There is some evidence for correlation between degree of cognitive impairment and sulcal widening (12, 41).

Cerebellar atrophy has also been reported in schizophrenia (The cerebellum is a large bilateral posterior brain structure with cortical connections. Two of its functions are motor coordination and balance.) Of 10 studies evaluating this, seven found more atrophy in schizophrenics (10). Rates of subjects with cerebellar atrophy varied between 5% and 17% in patients, and about 1% in controls. These rates notably *do not* differ from those observed in affective disorders. Other studies have assessed cerebral hemispheric asymmetry and brain density (tissue radiodensity). Abnormalities have been inconsistently reported (42).

MRI STUDIES OF SCHIZOPHRENIA

MRI studies of schizophrenia found similar structural abnormalities in the lateral and third ventricles, and also identified regional volumetric differences. Perhaps the most intriguing study was Suddath et al's (43) comparison of 15 monozygotic (MZ) twin pairs (p. 64) discordant for schizophrenia. They used unaffected MZ co-

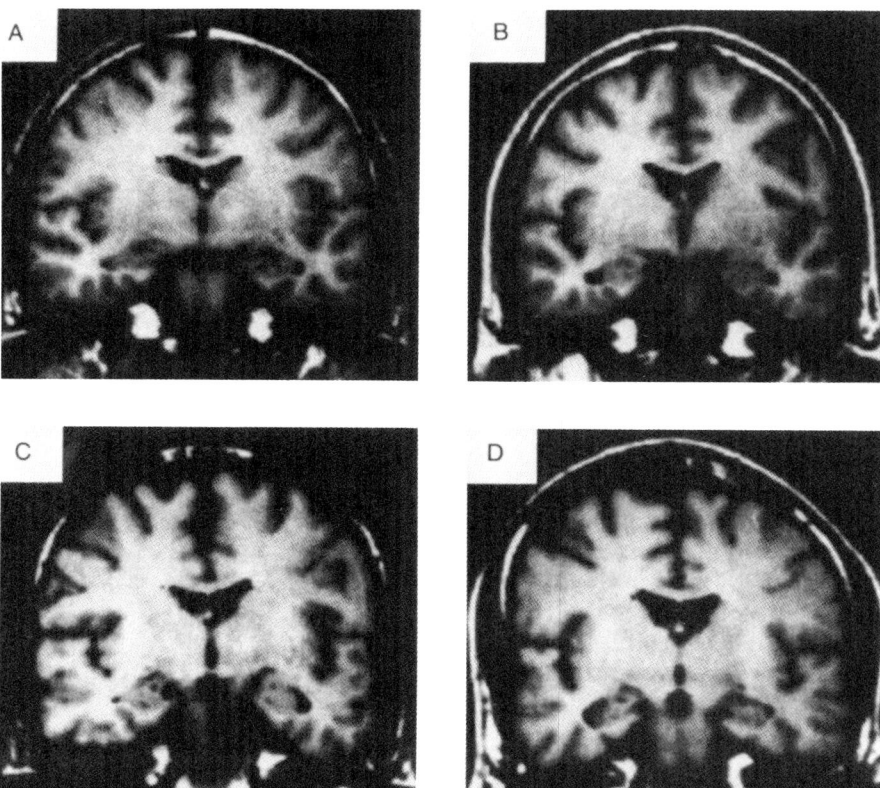

Figure 19.4. MRI coronal views from two sets of monozygotic twins discordant for schizophrenia showing subtle enlargement of the lateral ventricles in the affected twins (panels **B** and **D**) as compared with the unaffected twins (panels **A** and **C**), even when the affected twin had small ventricles. (Reprinted with permission from Suddath RL, Christison GW, Torrey EF, Casanova MF, Weinberger DR. Anatomical abnormalities in the brains of monozygotic twins discordant for schizophrenia. New Engl J Med 1990;322:791.)

twins as controls for anatomic variation from genetic and jointly experienced nongenetic factors (e.g., socioeconomic, psychological, traumatic, infectious). In the schizophrenic twins, lateral ventricles were larger on the left in 14 of the 15 pairs, and on the right in 13 of the pairs, relative to their unaffected co-twins (Fig. 19.4). The third venticle was larger in the affected twin in 13 of the pairs. Also, the hippocampus was smaller on the left in 14 of the 15 schizophrenic twins, and on the right in 13, consistent with a finding of reduced hippocampal volume in chronic schizophrenic patients at autopsy (3). Finally, the total volume of left temporal gray matter was decreased in 13 of the schizophrenics. Consistent with data from CT studies, none

of these anatomic measures correlated with age at onset, illness duration, or antipsychotic drug exposure. These findings suggest that subtle enlargements of the lateral and third ventricles are consistent features of schizophrenia, as opposed to being present in only a subgroup of such patients. They also imply that the cause of such abnormalities is in part not genetic. The latter has been suspected because MZ concordance rates, although substantially greater than those for dizygotic (DZ) twins, are less than 100% (44), implicating both heritable and nongenetic causal factors.

Other MRI investigations of schizophrenia reveal enlarged lateral (62%–67% volume increase) and third ventricle systems (73% increase) (45, 46). Reductions of temporal lobe volume have been inconsistently found; some investigators report such differences (43, 46) others do not (45). In contrast to Suddath's findings, other researchers have not identified differences in hippocampal size (5, 45).

Highlighting the importance of selecting an optimally matched control group, Andreasen et al. (47) compared schizophrenics with a control group of hospital staff and found significant decreases in both frontal and cerebral size in the patients. Their subsequent study using controls matched with the patients for socioeconomic variables found no differences, however, in any of these morphometric parameters between a new patient group and these more carefully matched controls (5). Other groups also could not identify differences in frontal lobe volume in schizophrenia (45, 46).

In contrast to the CT literature in which cerebellar atrophy was reported in some schizophrenics, MRI studies have not found cerebellar abnormalities (48, 49). Studies assessing size and shape of the corpus callosum have also been performed in schizophrenics (50, 51), but findings have been inconsistent. This is in part because there is no standard method for measuring callosal dimensions.

Finally, measurements of T1 and T2 relaxation times have been compared between schizophrenics and controls. Besson et al. (52) found that patients who display prominent negative symptoms demonstrate increased left frontal T1. Patients with tardive dyskinesia (p. 326) also demonstrate increased T1 in basal ganglia. Fujimoto et al. (53) reported decreased T1 in frontal white matter and increased T1 in putamen. The functional significance of such findings remains obscure.

Structural Imaging in Affective Illness

As in schizophrenia, numerous CT imaging studies of manic patients have demonstrated enlarged VBR (54–59). Two other studies comparing manics and controls did not find increased VBR, but did find third ventricle enlargement (60, 61). In contrast, MRI studies have not found abnormal VBR (62, 63).

Sulcal widening (54, 56, 57, 59–61, 64–68) and cerebellar atrophy (58, 69–71) have also been demonstrated in CT studies of manics. Clinical correlates of these findings have not been established. The only MRI study of cerebellar size found no differences between bipolar patients and controls (72).

Depressed patients who are elderly or psychotic also show ventricular enlargement (64–66, 68). Other groups found LVE in elderly depressives (64, 68). Thus far, studies of young, unipolar, nondelusional depressed patients (65, 68, 73) and unipolar depressives (p. 249) with early age of onset have not identified structural abnormalities (64, 73, 74). Biologic correlates of enlarged ventricles in affectively ill patients include higher urinary cortisol levels (75), nonsuppression of cortisol by dexamethasone (68), hypothyroidism (76), and increased CSF 5-HIAA levels (p. 353) (77). Pertinent to such correlations, therapeutically or pathologically induced hypercortisolism is associated with cerebral atrophy (78, 79).

Volumetric MRI studies have demonstrated regional differences between affectively ill patients and controls. Decreased frontal lobe size was reported in bipolar patients (80) and in elderly depressed patients (81). Bipolar patients also had abnormally small temporal lobe volumes (82). McDonald et al. (83) recently found reduced caudate volume in patients with major depression, which could be related to PET findings of decreased blood flow and metabolism in the caudate of depressed patients (see below). Pituitary enlargement has also been described (84) and may be a correlate of cortisol hypersecretion (frequent in depression).

Notably enlarged ventricles, sulcal widening, and reduced lobar volumes could result from fluid shifts. Lithium and tricylic antidepressants can produce fluid shifts (85). Therefore, medication-induced water movement from intracellular to extracellular spaces may be responsible for the aforementioned structural differences. Moreover, abnormalities in the central noradrenergic system have

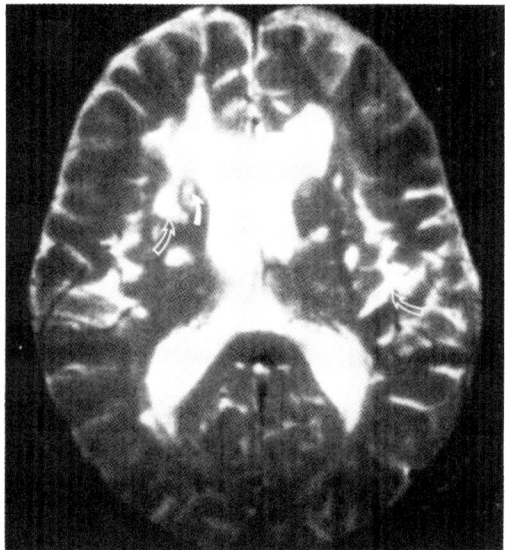

Figure 19.5. Brain MRI, axial scan through base of lateral ventricals showing large, confluent, deep white matter hyperintensities (*open arrows*), and hyperintensity in right caudate head in an elderly depressed patient. (Reproduced with permission from Figiel GS, Washington University School of Medicine, St. Louis, Missouri.)

been demonstrated in affective illness. As this system plays a prominent role in blood-brain barrier permeability (not all substances freely enter brain tissue from the blood), such abnormalities may also be associated with fluid shifts. It will be important to determine whether the morphometric changes described above reverse when patients are no longer symptomatic or on medications.

In addition to the morphometric studies, quantitative lesion studies have found abnormalities in affectively ill samples. Signal hyperintensities occur with greater frequency and size in elderly depressives than with matched controls (86, 87). These were specifically noted in the caudate heads and deep white matter of patients receiving initial treatment for depression after age 60. Figure 19.5 is an example. One autopsy series (88) and one phosphorus-31 MR-spectroscopy study (7) suggests such lesions are arteriosclerotic and ischemic. Elderly depressives with late illness onset may thus have a variant of post-stroke mood disorders (89).

Structural Imaging in Anxiety Disorders

Structural imagining has also identified abnormalities in patients with anxiety disorders. Luxenberg et al. (90), using CT for volumetric analyses in obsessive-compulsive (OCD) patients, reported significantly reduced caudate size bilaterally in patients versus controls. This finding is interesting in light of caudate abnormalities on PET (see below) and evidence that the cortical-striatal-pallidal-thalamic loop is involved in OCD pathophysiology (91, 92).

Neuroanatomic abnormalities involving the right temporal lobe were also found on MRI in a group of lactate-sensitive panic disorder (p. 255) patients (93). Forty-three percent of patients compared with 10% of controls had abnormalities in this region. Patients with temporal lobe abnormalities had younger age of onset and had experienced more panic attacks compared with patients with normal MRI scans. Notably PET imaging during panic attacks demonstrated activation of the temporal polar cortex (see below).

Structural Imaging in Other Psychiatric Disorders

Hypoplasia of cerebellar vermal lobules VI and VII was found in 14 of 18 autistic (p. 144) patients (94). This fits with postmortem studies that demonstrate fewer Purkinje and granule cells in the cerebellum of autistic patients (95, 96). One PET study of regional glucose metabolism in the cerebellum found no significant abnormalities (97).

Cerebral atrophy has been observed in alcoholics (98). Patients with Wernicke-Korsakoff syndrome (p. 302) have showed cerebellar, brainstem, and cortical atrophy. CT abnormalities have also been reported in anorexia nervosa (p. 146) (99–102) and attention deficit disorder (p. 144) (103, 104).

FUNCTIONAL IMAGING

Decades of investigation have demonstrated that blood flow and metabolism are related to the functioning of the brain. Functional imaging techniques yield accurate, detailed pictures of human brain function in terms of local metabolism or blood flow. Reviews of the development of regional cerebral blood flow and metabolism measurement techniques and the application of tracer kinetics underlying these methods are found elsewhere (105–108).

Studies of brain function measuring local blood flow and metabolism assume that neuronal activity, energy metabolism, and blood flow are tightly coupled. Such measurements should then provide indirect (blood flow) or direct (metabolism) assessments of local neuronal work. There is evidence that synaptic activity in the neuropil (a complicated network of axons, dendrites, and their cell bodies) rather than changes in the chemistry of cell bodies, accounts for nearly all of the metabolic changes observed during activation (105–113).

This has important implications for interpreting functional studies. Observed local changes in metabolism may be the product of metabolic activity that originates from distant cell bodies, as well as from local intercellular communication. For example, a blood flow increase in a prefrontal cortical region may occur from increased cortical-cortical neurotransmission within that region, or from increased synaptic transmission from a projecting structure such as the thalamus or amygdala. Moreover, either excitatory or inhibitory transmission (p. 49) results in increased chemical activity in the neuropil, and thus in increased local blood flow or metabolism.

Alternatively, observed functional differences may also be caused by differences in cell number. For example, decreased regional cerebral blood flow (rCBF) and cerebral metabolic rate for glucose (rCMRglu) found in the corpus striatum (the caudate and lenticular nuclei taken as one structure) of depressed patients (see below) could be the result of fewer neurons from hypoplasia or atrophy there.

The brain stores little glucose and no oxygen, depending on blood flow to provide these nutrients as needed. The blood flow response to a local alteration in neuronal activity is rapid, occurring within no more than 2 seconds (114–116) and probably within less than 500 milliseconds (117–119). A more complex, poorly characterized relation exists between local blood flow and metabolism. A local increase in the cerebral metabolic rate of glucose (rCMRglu) occurs with physiologic stimulation (109, 110, 112, 113, 120). Quantitative paired determinations of rCBF and rCMRglu using PET demonstrate that during neural activity, glucose uptake, and rCBF rise to the same extent (51% and 50% respectively) during visual stimulation (121). In contrast, there is considerable evidence that focal physiologic uncoupling of cerebral blood flow (CBF) and oxidative metabolism occurs during somatosensory (105, 122, 123) and visual stimulation (121) in humans. For example, quantitative paired determinations of regional blood flow and oxygen metabolic rates found that during neural activation from somatosensory stimulation, the local augmentation of CBF (29% mean) far exceeded the concomitant local increase in the cerebral metabolic rate for oxygen ($CMRO_2$) (5% mean) (122).

The ability to image regional brain activity has permitted mapping of cortical regions associated with various functions, using activation paradigms that compare dynamic images obtained during rest with those during a task. Studies have thus identified neurophysiologic correlates of motor, somatosensory, visual, auditory, linguistic, and purely cognitive tasks (124–126). Such paradigms will likely prove fruitful in studying the experience, evaluation, and expression of emotion. An example is a study of anticipatory anxiety (127) discussed below.

Similarly, functional imaging allows comparisons between patients and controls in resting versus activated states, each providing different information about illness pathophysiology. For example, differences in performing neuropsychological tests may have demonstrable circulatory correlates as measured by PET, providing insights into brain regions that are functioning abnormally but appearing normal at rest.

Finally, because functional measurements are sensitive to brain activity, intergroup differences (e.g., between patients and controls) of CBF or metabolism have many possible explanations. They may describe trait (a lifelong personality characteristic) pathophysiologic abnormalities associated with the genetic or environmental predisposition to a disorder; pathophysiologic state (occurring only during illness) changes corresponding to a symptom (e.g., hallucinations or anxiety) or effects of a symptom (e.g., sleep deprivation); cerebral activation associated with certain signs or cognitions (e.g., psychomotor activity, negative cognitions [pp. 78, 312]); or cytologic changes resulting from illness (e.g., degenerative changes resulting from sustained excitatory amino acid neurotransmission) or past treatment (e.g., receptor changes associated with medication). Moreover, disparate states within a single diagnostic group may give varying functional patterns. For example, ruminating about sad memories may show different rCBF patterns from suicidal ideation, yet both may occur in depression.

Techniques for measuring rCBF and metabolism can be grouped into two categories: nontomographic and tomographic. The former includes RCBF measurements performed with xenon-133 (^{133}Xe) inhalation. The latter includes SPECT and PET.

Regional Nontomographic Methods for Functional Imaging

The first successful technique for in vivo functional imaging was measurement of regional cerebral blood flow (RCBF). (note the use of upper case *R*, distinguishing nontomographic measurements from PET measurements of regional cerebral blood flow [rCBF]). Measurement of RCBF was based on principles of inert gas exchange following intracarotid (injected into the internal carotid artery) administration of ^{133}Xe or ^{85}Kr (krypton-85) (128). Most current studies modify this technique to permit inhalation of ^{133}Xe, to avoid carotid catheterization and to distribute radiotracer to all brain regions (not only the

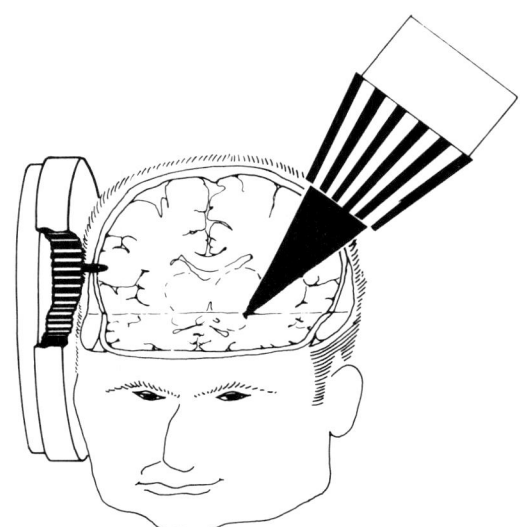

Figure 19.6. Geometry of regional nontomographic techniques for measurement of blood flow and metabolism in the human brain. Techniques are based on external detection of radioactive tracers administered by intracarotid or intravenous injection or by inhalation. Geometry of monitored region(s) of the brain depends on number and size of radiation detectors and on energy of tracer. *Left:* multidetector system with many small detectors; *right:* large single detector. Dark shadows extending as truncated cones from surface of detectors depict origin of data obtained with lower energy (81 keV) ^{133}Xe (*left*) and much higher energy (511 keV) of ^{15}O-labeled radiopharmaceuticals (*right*). Multidetector systems with ^{133}Xe are widely used in studies of regional brain blood flow in humans. (Reprinted with permission from Raichle ME. Circulatory and metabolic correlates of brain function in normal humans. In: Brookhart JM, Mountcastle VB, eds. Handbook of physiology—the nervous system V. Baltimore, MD: American Physiological Society 1977:645.)

region ipsilateral to injection site). The quantitation method depends on the rate at which the tracer clears from tissue, not the amount of tracer present. This is determined by detecting gamma rays emitted during the decay of ^{133}Xe with external detectors placed over the scalp (Fig. 19.6).

Recent nontomographic RCBF measurement systems involve up to 254 crystal detectors that monitor underlying brain tissue as an array of truncated cones. Detector sensitivity is greatest for brain tissue closest to the detector surface, and declines rapidly as tissue depth increases. This effect is most obvious with ^{133}Xe, and least with the more energetic [^{15}O]–H$_2$O. (Usually measured with PET, [^{15}O]–H$_2$O is sometimes nontomographically measured with single probe detectors [Fig. 19.6].) Because ^{133}Xe decays by emitting low energy radiation (88 KeV [kiloelectron volt], compared to 511 KeV for the annihilation photon emitted during positron decay), detectors record activity originating almost entirely from the cortical surface.

Most investigators employ a technique in which only data from the first 2 minutes of the tracer clearance curve are used to compute an index of blood flow, the initial slope index (ISI). This shortens measurement time, and permits repeat studies in rapid succession in the same subject (important for activation paradigms evaluating cortical function). However, it emphasizes data from gray matter, because clearance from gray matter is approximately four times faster than from white. Thus, for several reasons nontomographic methods using ^{133}Xe inhalation measure blood flow almost exclusively from superficial cortical gray matter.

Finally, when inhaled, ^{133}Xe enters the systemic circulation. Because it is nontomographic, this technique has trouble distinguishing radioactivity between infra- and extracranial tissues, confounding analysis. Hence caution is required when interpreting subtle changes in blood flow observed during activation.

Regional Tomographic Measurements in Functional Imaging

Regional tomographic (deriving three-dimensional information from two-dimensional data) measurements use modifications of the original autoradiographic techniques for measuring local blood flow and metabolism in tissue sections of animals following systemic radiotracer administration. Improved instrumentation with the development of PET allowed direct extension of these methods to study humans in vivo. PET and SPECT derive their basic principles from the application of noninvasive techniques to measure brain

blood flow and the development of tomographic technologies that use projection reconstruction for the measurement of brain structure. The marriage of these technologies permits physiologic measurement of brain function.

For measuring blood flow, modifications of the Kety autoradiographic method (129) are generally used. The most widely used tracer is [^{15}O]–H$_2$O. Its short physical half life (122 sec) leaves low residual activity in tissue after measurement (which requires only 40 seconds). Therefore, studies can be repeated in rapid succession, letting the subject serve as his or her own control, a highly desirable feature.

Measurements of glucose utilization usually employ radiolabeled deoxyglucose (with ^{18}F [fluorine] or ^{11}C [carbon]) and adaptations of the Sokoloff autoradiographic method (130, 131). Deoxyglucose enters the brain through the blood-brain-barrier transport system for glucose and is phosphorylated by hexokinase. Deoxyglucose 6-phosphate is then trapped within brain cells for about 45 minutes (132). Measurements of local brain glucose metabolism generally require 45 minutes (130, 132), making activation paradigms difficult. The data obtained in the tomographic image reflect a summary of events occurring as deoxyglucose is variably shifting from vascular to extravascular (precursor) pool, until it is metabolized.

Oxygen consumption may also be measured tomographically. This is complex and time consuming, requiring sequential administration of three ^{15}O-labeled tracers: O$_2$, CO, and either H$_2$O or CO$_2$. Moreover, it is a less sensitive indicator of neuronal activity than rCBF or rCMRglu.

Several areas require improvement in tomographic functional imaging methodology. Among these are anatomic localization techniques for correlating physiology and anatomy. Tomographic studies frequently rely on simple visual inspection of images to correlate anatomy and physiology. This is not sensitive enough to detect areas of subtle difference or to delineate specific subcortical structures. Alternatives involve localization schemes using MRI or CT (133). One of the most successful techniques currently employed for PET uses the coordinate system of a stereotactic neurosurgical atlas (134, 135). Measurements made from a lateral skull x-ray film and a tomographic transmission scan form the basis for this method. It allows regional comparison of multiple subjects in single study, and of different subject populations within a laboratory. Newer generation PET scanners should improve localization because their higher spatial resolution allows direct visualization of landmark structures (136).

Another area of need is statistical approaches for identifying differences between patient and control brain images. An average PET slice consists of about 7000 volume elements (voxels). Modern tomographic instruments obtain seven or more such slices during a single scan. Dealing with so many comparisons poses a serious statistical problem. Studies have thus used regions of interest (ROIs) specified a priori for making mean regional comparisons between patients and controls. Unfortunately, this substantially reduces sensitivity in psychiatric studies, because the obscurity of the pathophysiology of such disorders precludes sensitive a priori selection of ROIs. A solution to this problem was recently proposed (137).

The presence of atrophy in various clinical populations (e.g., dementia) also creates methodologic difficulties. Regional tomographic techniques provide measurements per unit volume of intracranial contents. Data are therefore affected by metabolically inactive cerebrospinal fluid spaces resulting from atrophy in a given ROI (the partial volume effect). It is difficult to determine whether observed differences in blood flow or metabolism result from meaningful changes in these, atrophy, or both. Future studies will require concomitant quantitations of anatomic differences using MRI or CT to accurately correlate physiology and anatomy. Notably, nontomographic measurements are not affected by atrophy or other anatomic variations because they record data only per unit of extant tissue.

TOMOGRAPHIC SYSTEMS

Positron Emission Tomography

PET is based on the in vivo detection of two 511-keV annihilation radiation photons emerging simultaneously, or coincidentally, from tissue after the interaction of a positron (a positively charged electron) and an ordinary electron (Fig. 19.7). Radioisotopes that decay by positron emission include ^{15}O ($t\frac{1}{2}$, 122 sec), ^{13}N (10 min), ^{11}C (20 min), and ^{18}F (110 min). Detecting annihilation events in tissue involves coincident circuits in which an activity count is recorded only when two opposing detectors are coincidentally struck by photons (Fig 19.8). The process by which PET measurements of tissue radioactivity are converted to quantitative three dimensional representations of circulatory or metabolic correlates is reviewed elsewhere (138).

The spatial resolution of PET is defined as the width of distribution of radioactivity at one half the maximum counting rate for a point source, called full width at half maximum (FWHM). Two point sources of radioactivity cannot be distinguished if they are closer than one FWHM (though point sources smaller than one FWHM may still be detected). Many operational PET devices have spatial resolutions in the range of 10–15 mm. Newer systems have resolutions of 5–6 mm using [^{18}F]deoxyglucose imaging. The ultimate resolution of PET has not been established, but will be limited by factors such as the 2–3 mm distance the positron may travel in tissue before colliding with an electron. However, for functional activation studies with PET, methods use spatial discrimination of sequential changes in local radioactivity. By detecting shifts in the point of maximum change in radioactivity from a control state, structures separated by less than 1 FWHM can be discriminated (139).

PET holds many advantages over other functional imaging techniques. It is superior to RCBF measurements using xenon 133 inhalation, for it provides three-dimensional data and far greater sensitivity for evaluating subcortical and deep cortical structures. Com-

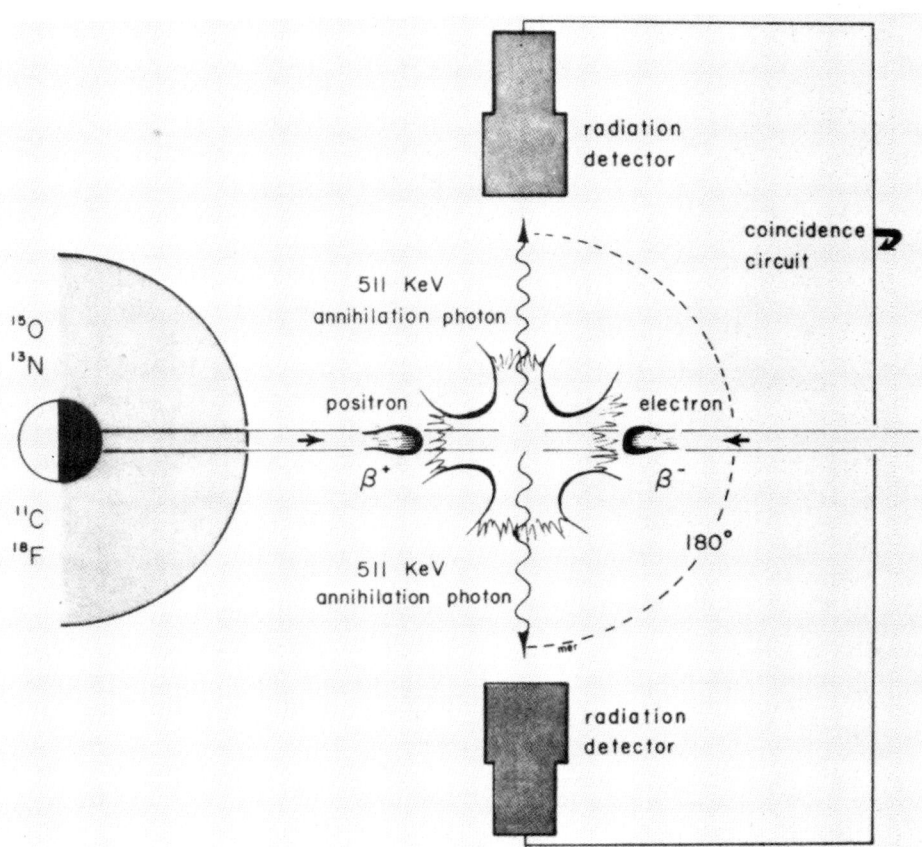

Figure 19.7.   Detection scheme for PET. Radionuclides employed in PET decay by emission of positrons ($\beta +$) from nuclei unstable because of deficiency of neutrons. Positrons lose their kinetic energy in matter after traveling a finite distance (~1–6 mm) and, when brought to rest, interact with electrons ($\beta -$). The two particles are annihilated, and their mass is converted to two annihilation photons traveling at ~180° from each other with an energy of 511 keV. Annihilation photons are detected by imaging device, using opposing radiation detectors connected by electronic coincidence circuits that record an event only when two photons arrive simultaneously. A major factor determining the ultimate resolution of PET is distance traveled by the positron before its annihilation. (Reprinted with permission from Raichle ME. Positron emission tomography. Ann Rev Neurosci 1983;6:249–267.)

pared with SPECT, PET affords better spatial resolution, fewer artifacts from scatter and attenuation of radiation, the ability to make both absolute and relative measurements, and the potential for a greater variety of measurements (1). Finally, unlike MRI, PET has potential for measuring characteristics of biologic compounds (e.g., neurotransmitters, neuroreceptors) that exist in minute concentrations. PET's greatest limitation is its high expense for installation, operation, and radiopharmaceutical preparation, which restricts its availability.

SINGLE PHOTON EMISSION COMPUTED TOMOGRAPHY

Early SPECT involved measurements of rCBF using diffusible indicators such as xenon-133 and rotating four detector systems or ring detector systems. Newer SPECT systems measure the distribution of statically distributed radiopharmaceuticals (radiotracers [including I-123-labeled amines] trapped in the brain whose distribution remains stable over time) that reflect perfusion patterns. Recent innovations in SPECT technology produced

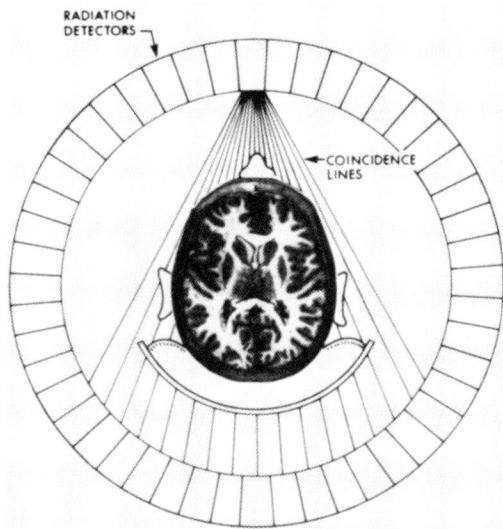

Figure 19.8. Geometry employed in PET. Multiple radiation detectors are arranged about subject's head and connected by coincidence circuits. Data from coincidence lines between detectors form quantitative image of distribution of radiopharmaceutical within the brain. Resulting image is equivalent to quantitative tissue autoradiogram obtained by exposing tissue containing radioactivity to x-ray film. Spatial geometry of resulting image is very different from that obtained by multidetector, nontomographic systems. (cf. Fig. 19.6). (Reprinted with permission from Raichle ME. Quantitative in vivo autoradiography with positron emission tomography. Brain Res Rev 1979;1:50.)

systems capable of 8 mm resolution and imaging times as short as 2 to 3 minutes.

The radiopharmaceuticals for SPECT emit single gamma rays, as opposed to PET radiopharmaceuticals that emit two simultaneous gamma rays traveling in opposite directions. This distinction leads to the instrumentation differences between SPECT and PET. Single photon tomographs are designed to detect single photons (gamma rays) and determine their point of origin based solely on their trajectory. This presents some technical problems that reduce SPECT's sensitivity for measuring changes in rCBF, particularly for deeper structures. These include difficulties in dealing with artifacts from the attenuation of radiation. The principles for SPECT imaging are reviewed elsewhere (140).

Radiopharmaceuticals currently available for SPECT fall into 4 categories: (1) diffusible

indicators such as ^{133}Xe (quantitative analyses with SPECT are presently limited to dynamic ^{133}Xe rCBF imaging; this technique has the same disadvantages as described for ^{133}Xe under nontomographic methods above); (2) I-123 labeled-lipophilic agents including I-123-labeled iodoamphetamine (IMP) which provide a relative distribution of rCBF but are not easily quantitated; (3) technetium-99m-labeled lipophilic agents, including Tc-99m HMPAO which distribute in a manner similar to the I-123 labeled amines; and (4) I-123 labeled neurotransmitter ligands such as I-123-labeled-QNB, a muscarinic cholinergic agonist (p. 60). In addition, I-123 labeled ligands for dopamine and benzodiazepine receptor studies (pp. 55, 58) have been developed. Because of its use of statically distributed radiopharmaceuticals, SPECT measurements of neuroreceptor systems could overcome modeling problems better than some PET receptor ligands. Notably, no pharmaceutical for SPECT is available for distribution related to glucose metabolism.

The major advantage of SPECT is that the instrumentation and radiopharmaceuticals used are routinely available in most nuclear medicine departments. The radiopharmaceuticals can be obtained from commercial manufacturers and do not require an on-site cyclotron for their production as do PET radiopharmaceuticals. Consequently SPECT costs much less than PET.

Functional Imaging Studies in Schizophrenia

Most studies of chronic, previously medicated patients with schizophrenia have demonstrated hypofrontality, or lower frontal/whole brain blood flow and metabolism relative to controls (141–151). Others have not found such hypofrontality (152–155). Notably, four studies using only never-medicated patients did not confirm this finding (156–159). Pertinent to this discrepancy, several studies found a reduced frontal relative to nonfrontal blood flow or metabolism following administration of antipsychotic medication (150, 151,

160), suggesting that hypofrontality may reflect a long-lasting effect of antipsychotic medication, rather than the pathophysiology of schizophrenia. This issue remains controversial, however, as other studies find increases in absolute (as opposed to relative) frontal CBF or metabolism with treatment (161).

In contrast, schizophrenic patients, medicated or not, demonstrate less activation (decreased augmentation of rCBF relative to controls) of frontal cortex when imaged while performing the Wisconsin Card Sorting Test (Fig. 19.9), which assesses prefrontal functioning (pp. 45, 208) (145, 146, 162). Most studies demonstrating this finding have used nontomographic RCBF measurements. A recent ^{133}Xe dynamic SPECT study demonstrated reversal of this abnormality when amphetamine (p. 332) was administered prior to testing (163). Another investigation of functional differences during neuropsychological testing with PET identified less augmentation of rCMRglu in the middle prefrontal cortex of schizophrenic subjects compared with controls during an auditory discrimination task, though performance accuracy did not differ (164).

Subcortical abnormalities have also been reported (subcortex consists of basal ganglia, hypothalamus, brainstem and cerebellum, the "reptilian, paleomammalian brains"). One PET study (159) demonstrated increased rCBF in the globus pallidus of never-medicated schizophrenics. A recent post mortem anatomic study indicating reduced pallidal volume in schizophrenic patients corroborates the importance of this structure in schizophrenia research (3). Most other studies have not evaluated individual basal ganglia structures.

Finally, rCMRglu for the left temporal lobe was found abnormal in some studies of schizophrenia (151, 165). In one of these, right temporal cortex exhibited increased rCMRglu following neuroleptic treatment (151). In a different study, rCMRglu in left temporal lobe and left caudate increased following treatment (150).

FUNCTIONAL IMAGING IN AFFECTIVE DISORDERS

Numerous PET, SPECT, and RCBF studies have been performed in subjects with affective illness. Findings are widely discrepant, partly because of methodologic differences in choosing ROIs, anatomic localization procedures, behavioral states during image acquisition, and subject selection. Because of the former two issues, many studies have not assessed the same brain regions, precluding comparisons across studies. Because functional imaging techniques are sensitive to cognitive and behavioral activation, studies involving different behavioral states may obtain disparate results.

Finally, homogeneity of the subject sample is critical. Some extant studies were performed with subjects on medications, others were not. Yet most studies comparing pre- and posttreatment scans find (apparently) drug-induced functional changes. Moreover, most studies do not separate unipolar (patients with only depressive episodes) and bipolar (patients with both manic and [sometimes] depressive episodes) subjects, although differences exist in their respective circulatory and metabolic correlates (166–171). This makes studies combining unipolar and bipolar patients into a single group difficult to interpret.

PET studies in unipolar depressed patients have demonstrated some consistent findings (137, 166, 168, 172). They have generally found no significant global differences in CBF or metabolism between patients and controls. They have all identified decreased rCBF or metabolism in the basal ganglia (three groups specifically identified this region as caudate). In fact, two groups reported metabolic increases in this region with antidepressant treatment (166, 172). Drevets et al. (137) found that decreased rCBF in caudate was also present in the unmedicated, remitted state (following resolution of depressive symptoms). Finally, each PET study of unipolar depression identified abnormalities in the prefrontal cortex (PFC), although the direction and location of such differences have varied. Buchsbaum et al. (168) reported increased

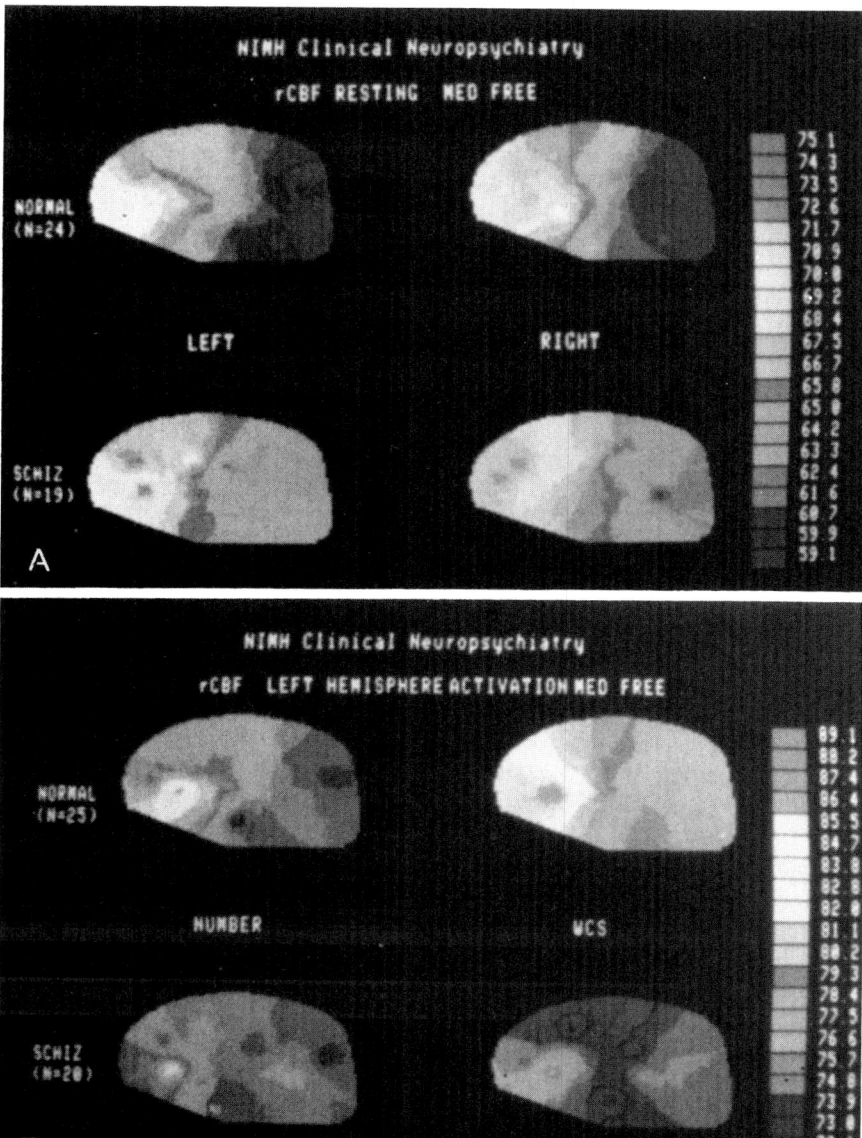

Figure 19.9. Topographic gray-matter group mean regional cerebral blood flow (rCBF) maps showing lateral view of cerebral cortex with anterior pole pointing to left. Monochromatic scale keyed to initial slope values. Note that scales are anchored to values for each figure and are comparable across figures. NIMH represents National Institute of Mental Health; med, medication; and schiz, schizophrenic. **A,** Resting state, corrected for carbon dioxide partial pressure (Pco₂). **B,** and **C,** Number matching (NM) and Wisconsin Card Sort (WSC) maps for left and right hemispheres, Pco₂, uncorrected. **D,** Percentage change maps: (WCS/NM) × 100. The NM condition was created as a control for those aspects of the WCS condition that were thought not to involve specific functions executed in the dorsal aspects of the WCS condition thought to not involve specific functions executed in the dorsal lateral prefrontal cortex. Hence, the percentage change map affords the analysis with greatest potential for displaying regional specialization related to performing the WCS in terms of rCBF changes. The lightest shades (white or off-white) correspond to greater rCBF. During activation by the WCS, normals manifest greater prefrontal rCBF. (Modified from Weinberger DR, Berman KF, Zec RF. Physiologic dysfunction of dorsolateral prefrontal cortex in schizophrenia. I. Regional cerebral blood flow evidence. Arch Gen Psychiatry 1986;43: 114–124.)

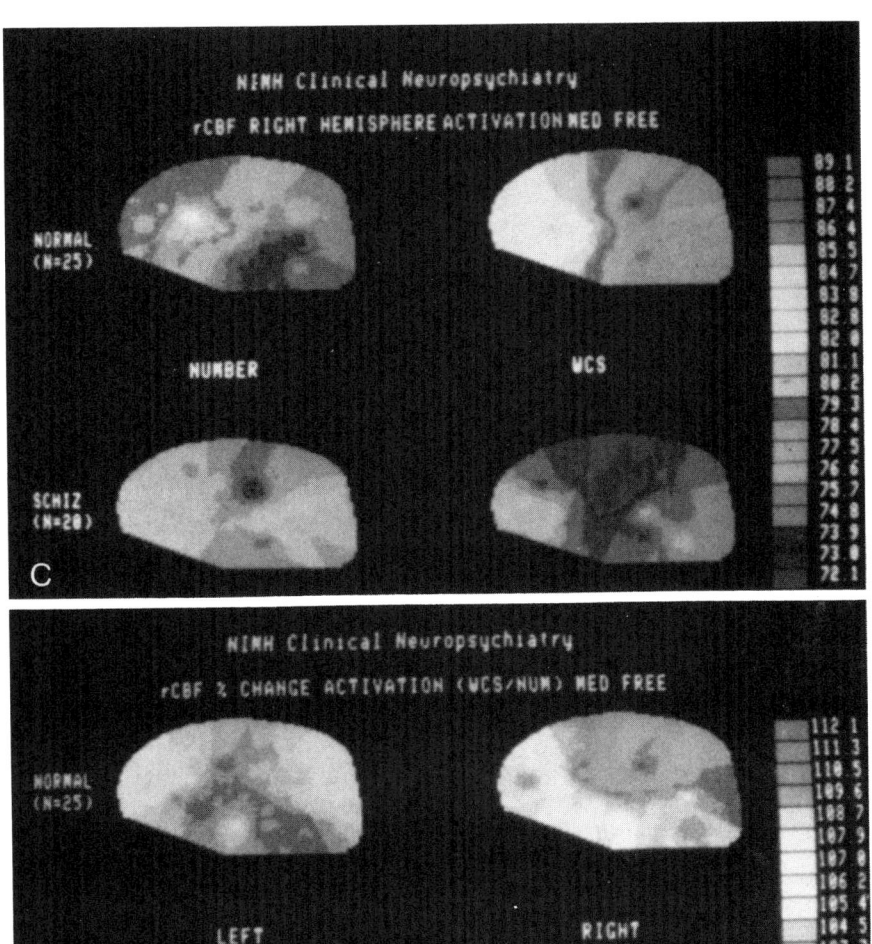

frontal/occipital ratio; Baxter et al. (173) identified a region in the left dorsal anterolateral prefrontal cortex (PFC) with decreased metabolism (common to both unipolar and bipolar depression, and correlated with depression rating scores); and Drevets et al. (137) found increased cerebral blood flow in frontal polar cortex and left ventrolateral PFC. The latter rCBF abnormality returned to normal in the remitted state.

SPECT studies in depression yield more varied results. This may be the result of technical problems in measuring CBF and SPECT. Notably, however, two studies in which subcortical rCBF was examined (170, 174) found regional decreases in basal ganglia consistent with PET literature, although in one of these the decrease was not significant after Bonferroni correction (p. 27) (174).

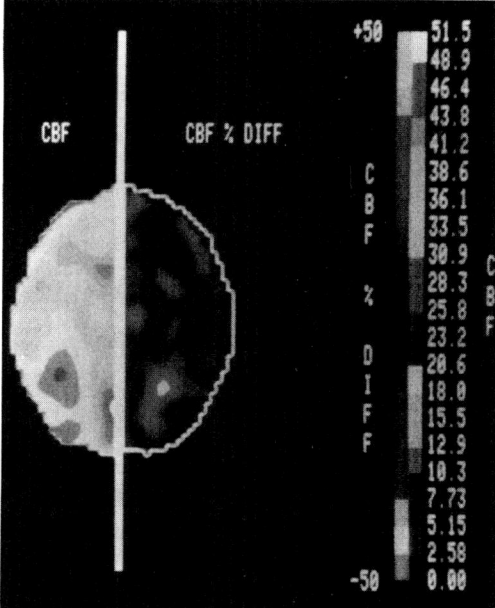

Figure 19.10. PET image of local cerebral blood flow in a resting awake subject with panic disorder, a severe form of anxiety. Left half of image is a quantitative representation of cerebral blood flow corresponding to left side of the calibrated monochromatic scale. Right half of image represents the difference between right and left hemispheres expressed as percent of the left hemisphere blood flow in right half of the calibrated monochromatic scale. Image is oriented with subject's left at 9:00 and anterior at 12:00. Note striking asymmetry in posterior aspect of image. With a complex localization technique, this regional asymmetry was determined to reside in region of the parahippocampal gyrus. Other asymmetries appearing in image vary randomly among subjects. (Reprinted with permission from Reiman EM, Raichle ME, Butler FK, Herscovitch P, Robins E. A focal brain abnormality in panic disorder, a severe form of anxiety. Nature 1984;310:684.)

Regional nontomographic studies of RCBF using xenon-133 inhalation have usually involved subject groups of mixed polarity. The majority of these have found no differences in either global or regional blood flow relative to controls (175–180), although one recent study found globally reduced flow and multiple regional abnormalities (181). In contrast, two studies involving only unipolar patients (182, 183) identified increased RCBF in the left frontal region, consistent with some PET series (137, 168). (It should be recalled that nontomographic techniques only measure

RCBF at the cortical surface, not in subcortical structures such as caudate.)

PET studies of bipolar disorder (p. 250) have variably reported abnormalities in global CMRglu. Whole brain metabolic rates were found significantly decreased by Baxter et al. (166) and increased by Buchsbaum et al. (168) in bipolar depressed patients. The former group was scanned at rest, and the latter while receiving electrical shocks to the arm. This difference may explain the discrepant result. In the former study, global CMRglu increased when converting to either a manic or euthymic (asymptomatic) state, but did not differ between manic and euthymic states (166). Regional abnormalities also varied. Buchsbaum et al. reported decreased metabolism in the caudate bilaterally for bipolar depressives, but no caudate difference was found by Baxter et al. Interestingly, Schwartz et al. (184) recently reported that the ratio of rCMRglu caudate/rCMRglu PFC distinguished unipolar and bipolar depressives with unipolar being lower in every case, and the ratio of rCMRglu caudate/rCMRglu parahippocampal gyrus distinguished both types of depressives from controls, with ratios for unipolar and bipolar patients being nearly equal. Regional reductions in frontal cortex were found by both groups, with Baxter et al. (173) locating this decrease in left dorsal anterolateral PFC.

Of SPECT studies measuring CBF in bipolar subjects, one reported no differences between medicated manic patients and controls (170). Another found increased mean global CBF in manic patients and no global differences in depressed patients (185). Regional CBF increases were found in the depressed group, however, in left parietal and temporal lobes (171).

FUNCTIONAL IMAGING STUDIES OF ANXIETY DISORDERS

Reivich et al. (186) reported that the level of anxiety in control subjects positively correlated with metabolic rates in posterior orbital frontal and middle frontal regions (which contain projections of the limbic system). Reiman et al. (127), using controls to study the neuro-anatomic correlates of anticipatory anxiety (during anticipation of a painful electric shock) observed bilateral rCBF increases in the temporal poles. Reiman et al. (187–189) also studied a pathologic anxiety state, panic disorder (p. 255), scanning patients before and during a panic attack elicited by IV lactate (p. 257). During the panic attack, rCBF increased in the same temporal polar region activated in the anticipatory anxiety paradigm. Regional CBF increases were also identified in insula and cerebellar vermis. Moreover, in the resting state, persons vulnerable to lactate-induced panic demonstrated abnormal hemispheric asymmetry of parahippocampal rCBF, blood volume, and oxygen metabolism, and abnormally high whole brain metabolism (Fig. 19.10).

Subjects with obsessive-compulsive disorder (OCD) were studied with PET measurements of [^{18}F]deoxyglucose. Baxter et al. (190, 191) found increased rCMRglu in the orbital gyri and in the caudate heads bilaterally. Global CMRglu was also elevated, and after normalizing regional values to ipsilateral hemispheric metabolism, only the orbital gyri differed from controls. Following successful pharmacotherapy, it was noted that the caudate/hemisphere metabolic ratio significantly increased bilaterally, whereas the orbital/hemisphere ratio remained unchanged. Similarly, Nordahl et al. (192) found a bilateral increase in normalized metabolic rates for the orbital gyri bilaterally and no significant differences in normalized regional values for caudate. However, they did not find differences in global CMRglu relative to controls. A third group also identified no global differences (193). They reported increased absolute rCMRglu in the left orbital gyrus only, and in contrast to the other two groups, this regional difference was no longer significant after normalizing for global metabolism. Also in contrast to other groups, Swedo et al. (193) found a significantly increased ratio of regional CMRglu/mean cortical gray matter metabo-lism for right prefrontal and left anterior cingulate cortices.

NEURORECEPTOR IMAGING

Imaging of neuroreceptors is also promising for PET and SPECT research. There are several methods for in vivo measurement of receptor density. For PET, ligands have been developed for dopamine (both D_1 and D_2), benzodiazepine, and opiate receptors, although methodologic problems (such as receptor modeling) remain to be solved (194–198). Such problems have been blamed for discrepancies between findings of D_2 receptor density in never-medicated (important because medications may produce long-lasting receptor changes) schizophrenic subjects. Wong et al. (p. 54) (197), using PET and [^{11}C]N-methylspiperone to examine D_2 dopamine receptor densities, found a two- to threefold elevation in receptor density in the caudate nucleus bilaterally (Fig. 19.11). Using the more selective D_2 receptor antagonist [^{11}C]raclopride as a ligand, however, Farde et al. (199) found no significant differences in B_{max} or K_d in caudate or putamen. They did find significantly higher densities in left versus right putamen in patients, but not controls. Another ligand [^{76}Br]bromospiperone has also been used for the same purpose by Martinot et al. (200), who reported no significant differences in D_2 dopamine receptor density between untreated schizophrenics and controls.

SPECT also holds great potential for neuroreceptor imaging. Muscarinic cholinergic (Fig. 19.12), dopamine D_2, and benzodiazepine receptor ligands have been developed (201). One such SPECT study in schizophrenic subjects reported a 10% increase in the striatal uptake of [^{77}Br]spiperone (202).

Another application of D_2 receptor ligands involves determining receptor occupancy for antipsychotic drugs (203). These have provided important information concerning the relationship of D_2 receptor occupancy and serum drug concentrations. This may eventually

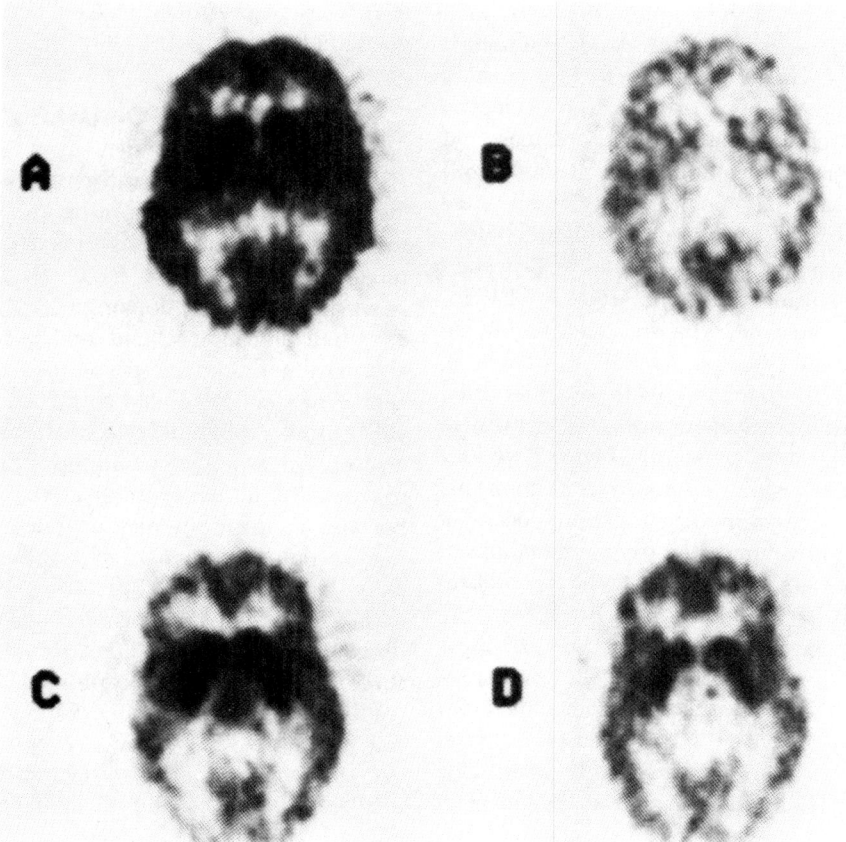

Figure 19.11. PET scan images of the radioactivity distribution obtained at the level of the caudate nucleus and putamen 65 to 95 minutes after injection of [¹¹C]NMSP in a normal subject (**A** and **B**) and in a schizophrenic patient (**C** and **D**) in the unblocked (**A** and **C**) and the blocked state (**B**) and (**D**). Both subjects, males aged 24 years, received a single dose of 7.5 mg haloperidol before the second PET scan. This illustrates the more pronounced block of [¹¹C]NMSP uptake in the caudate and putamen in the normal subject as compared to the patient, despite the fact that serum haloperidol was lower in the normal (2.5 ng/mL) than in the patient (4 ng/mL). B_{max} values in the normal and the schizophrenic subjects were 11.5 and 36.2 pmol/g, respectively. (Reprinted with permission from Wong DF, Wagner HN, Tune LE, et al. Positron emission tomography reveals elevated D_2 dopamine receptors in drug-naive schizophrenics. Science 1986;234:1558–1563.)

suggest when dosage increases are likely to be beneficial.

COMPUTERIZED EEG AND EVOKED POTENTIAL MAPPING

A final type of functional imaging involves generating topographic maps of brain electrical activity recorded with multichannel electroencephalography (EEG). Numeric values of chosen parameters of EEG or event-related potential (ERP) activity, such as the power in the alpha band or voltage at a peak of a sensory-evoked response, are obtained from specific locations on the side or top of the head. Points lying between electrode locations are assigned values by interpolation. The numeric values are then assigned to a color scale and plotted to produce a graphic representation of the scalp distribution of activity. This method has been popularized as brain electrical activity mapping (BEAM). Data are commonly dis-

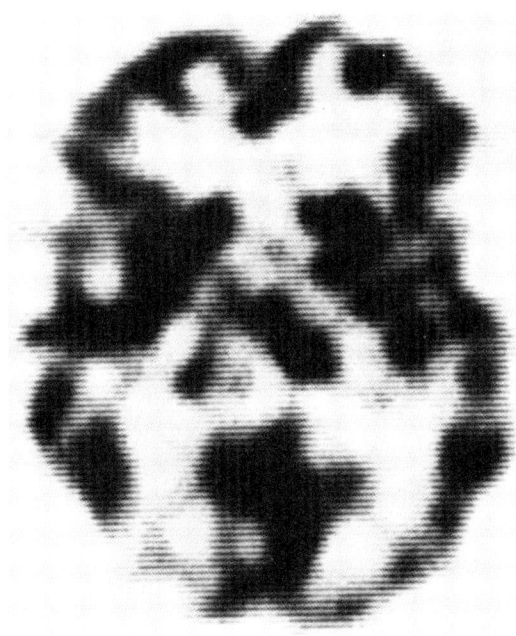

Figure 19.12.   A single tomographic slice obtained parallel to the orbital medial line through the region of the basal ganglia. The study was performed 20 minutes after injection of 4.9 mCi of 4-[¹²³I]IQNB. The images were obtained in 20 minutes on the Harvard Multidetector Brain Scanning System. The system resolution is 10 mm full width at half maximum with a slice thickness of 9.8 mm. The image shows increased uptake in the area of the caudate putamen having a high m-AChR concentration. Activity conforming to the convolutions of the gyral architecture of the cerebral cortex is visualized; more centrally in the area of white matter and ventricles, no activity is seen. (Reprinted with permission from Eckelman WC, Reba RC, Rzeszotarski WJ, et al. External imaging of cerebral muscarinic acetylcholine receptors. Science 1984;223:291–293.)

played in the form of a Z (p. 22) or t score, representing the degree of deviation of the subject's activity from a normative group. This type of statistical transformation typically involves computations for a few thousand pixels. Because of the problem of multiple comparisons, such information cannot be relied on for statistical probability, and is instead used for qualitative interpretation.

Computer mapping of electrical activity (CME) does not produce an image of the brain itself, but rather provides quasianatomical graphs of scalp-recorded EEG or ERP activity. Because of the lateral spread of EEG

current across the scalp, it has limited spatial resolution. More importantly, the nature of the neural generators responsible for the electrical phenomena measured is poorly understood. CME measurements are susceptible to artifactual contamination from eye movements, muscle activity, and 60 Hz interference. Recent clinical studies have demonstrated the importance of eliminating such artifacts from the EEG by showing that doing so changed findings from earlier studies of schizophrenia (204).

Advantages of brain electrical mapping include its unsurpassed temporal resolution. Electrical events can be measured with submillisecond resolution (compared to the fastest PET method of 40 seconds). For example, it is possible to visualize occipital cortex activation 100 milliseconds following a visual stimulus, the cognitive P300 wave associated with stimulus discrimination, or event-related desynchronization (ERD) associated with sensory or motor events (205). EEG mapping is also noninvasive, free of radiation exposure, and inexpensive. It can thus be repeatedly administered in within-subject designs for cognitive activation paradigms, studies of medication effects (pre- and posttreatment), and so forth.

Computerized Topographic EEG Mapping in Psychiatry

Relatively few studies of EEG topography have been performed in psychiatric populations. Early studies in schizophrenics found bilateral slowing (increased delta activity) in frontal regions relative to controls (206–209). However, more recent studies that included corrections for eye movement artifacts found no regional differences between patients and controls (204, 210). They did replicate previous findings of increased delta (slow) activity overall (207, 211). Delta activity of the EEG is associated with disturbed (usually depressed) function in awake adults.

Multiple CME studies in schizophrenia have found left-sided regional abnormalities. These include increased beta activity (212,

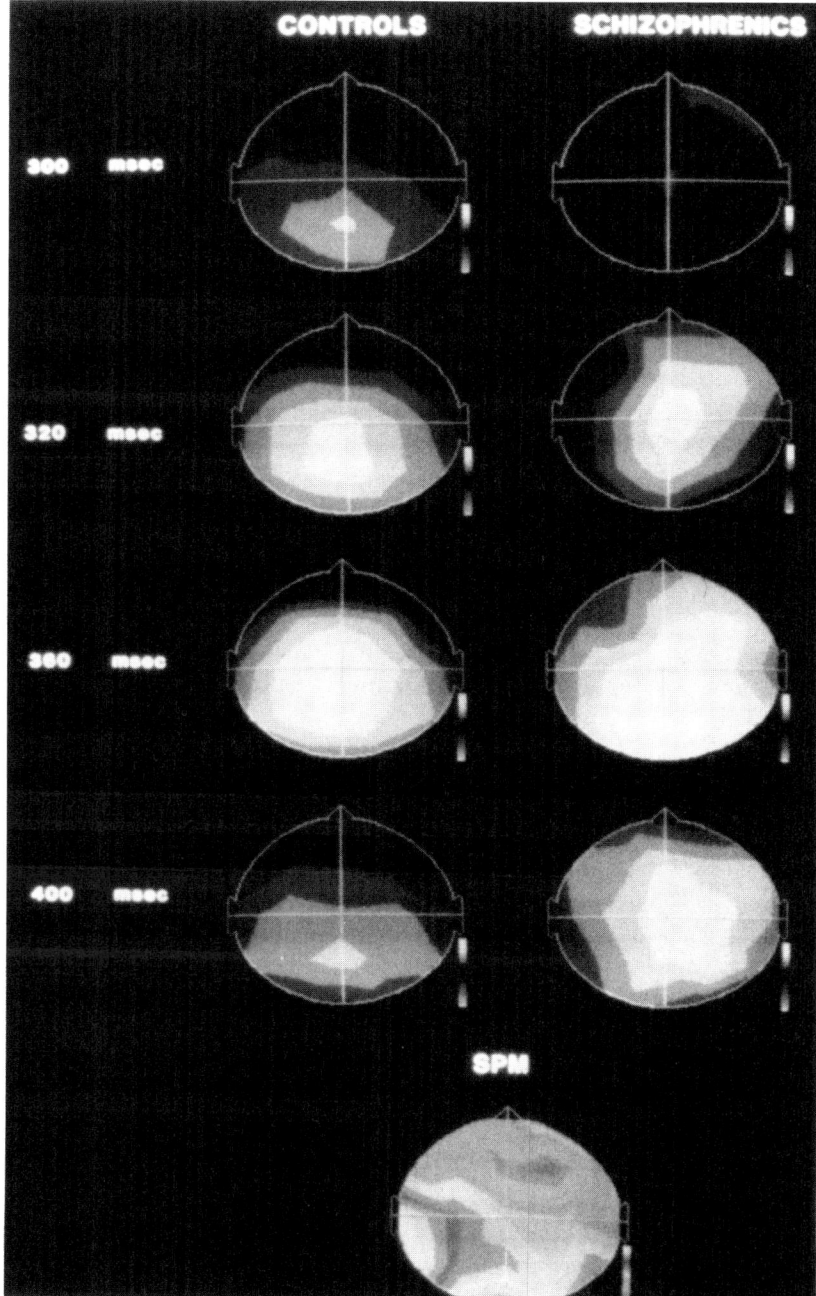

Figure 19.13. Topographic distribution of P300 activity at 300, 320, 360, and 400 msec after stimulus. Scaling of black and white was adjusted to allow topography in lower amplitude schizophrenic group to be clearly visible; scale ranges from −5 to +5 μV in controls and −2 to +2 μV in schizophrenics. Compared with controls, P300 development in schizophrenics shows maxima that are displaced anteriorly and to right and deficiency of activity in left temporal region. (Reprinted with permission from Torello MW, McCarley RW. The use of topographic mapping techniques in clinical studies in psychiatry. In: Duffy FH, ed. Topographic mapping of brain electrical activity. Boston: Butterworths 1986:383–387.)

213) and augmented visual evoked potential amplitudes (following a light flash [212]) in the left posterior quadrant relative to controls. Increased beta activity was reported using conventional EEG (214, 215), and has been considered indicative of increased cortical arousal. In the left temporal area a schizophrenic group was shown to have deficient activity in the P300 wave form (thought to indicate attentional deployment) compared to controls (Fig. 19.13) (216). The latter is consistent with several standard ERP studies (217) demonstrating reduced P300 amplitude in schizophrenics. In addition, Buchsbaum et al. (218) found that left-sided somatosensory ERP activity in schizophrenics was more diffuse and failed to exhibit the stimulus intensity-linked variation shown by normal controls. Finally, during complex motor tasks, a medicated schizophrenic sample showed markedly reduced changes in theta, beta, and delta frequency bands relative to controls in the left primary sensory and motor areas (209).

CME studies in other psychiatric disorders have not consistently discriminated between patient groups and normals. Schatzberg et al. (219) reported increased slowing (delta and theta) in the right posterior temporal region, and increased frontal beta bilaterally, predominantly on the left, in a group of chronically depressed patients relative to controls. Small et al. (211), however, found no differences between drug-free manic, depressed, or obsessive-compulsive patients and matched normal controls.

Computer mapping of electrical activity is sensitive to drug effects. Distinctive EEG changes were observed during treatment with lithium and carbamazepine in patients with affective disorders (211) and in patients with schizophrenia associated with the antipsychotic agents clozapine, chlorpromazine, and haloperidol (210, 211). This has implications for interpreting studies in which subjects were medicated. If replicated, a finding with potential clinical utility was that higher left frontal alpha amplitudes in schizophrenia were associated with favorable response to clozapine (p. 326) (210).

Author's note: Recent data suggest that the previously reported increase in regional blood flow in the temporal poles of the cerebral cortex during anticipatory anxiety or panic may be an artifact of increased blood flow in the temporalis and masseter muscles when these muscles are clenched during anxiety (Drevets WC, Videen TO, MacLeod AK, Haller JW, Raichle ME. PET images of blood flow changes during anxiety: correction. Science 1992;256: 1696).

SECTION IV. NEUROPSYCHIATRIC DISORDERS AND THEIR TREATMENT

20/Psychopathology

Philip S. Freeman, M.D., Daniel R. Wilson, M.D.,
and Frederick S. Sierles, M.D.

OBJECTIVES

GENERAL OBJECTIVE: Given the examination of a patient who has a behavioral problem, give a differential diagnosis of the cause of that problem.

SPECIFIC OBJECTIVES:

1. Discuss the reliability and validity of psychiatric diagnosis, including how reliability is maximized and how validity is confirmed.
2. Summarize the rationale and components of the five-axis system of the American Psychiatric Association's Diagnostic and Statistical Manuals.
3. Discuss the history of the concept of schizophrenia.
4. Discuss the symptoms, signs, prognosis, subtyping, epidemiology, etiology, and treatment of schizophrenia.
5. For affective disorders, discuss the following:
   a. Historical milestones
   b. Symptoms, signs, course, complications, and laboratory tests in major depression, the melancholic subtype of major depression, dysthymic disorder, bereavement, unipolar affective disorder, bipolar disorder and its variants, and depression in the presence of a preexisting psychiatric disorder
   c. Epidemiology
   d. Etiology
   e. Treatment
   f. Depression secondary to general medical illness
6. Discuss the historical milestones, symptoms, signs, course, complications, laboratory findings, epidemiology, etiology, and treatment for the following anxiety disorders: panic disorder, agoraphobia, social phobia, simple phobias, obsessive-compulsive disorder, generalized anxiety disorder, and posttraumatic stress disorder.
7. Discuss the symptoms, signs, course, complications, laboratory findings, epidemiology, etiology, and treatment of somatization disorder.
8. Define personality and personality disorders.
9. Discuss the problems of diagnostic overlap, reliability, and validity of personality disorders in general.
10. For each of the following personality disorders, discuss symptoms, signs, etiology and treatment: paranoid, schizotypal, schizoid, borderline, narcissistic, histrionic, obsessive-compulsive, dependent, and avoidant.

11. For antisocial personality disorder, discuss symptoms, signs, course and complications, epidemiology, etiology, and treatment.

DIAGNOSIS IN PSYCHIATRY

An accurate diagnosis predicts prognosis and directs treatment selection. Accurate diagnosis requires a good system of diagnostic classification. A diagnostic category is established when groups of patients who have a given diagnosis share common demographic characteristics (e.g., typical age of onset, sexual differences in prevalence), symptoms, signs, laboratory findings, and treatment response, course, prognosis, and tendency to run in families (1, 2).

Classification is easy when the pathogenic agent (e.g., the tubercle bacillus) is known and readily identified by pathognomonic (when present, the diagnosis is certain) lab tests (e.g., observing the bacillus on bacterial staining) suggested by clinical findings (e.g., fever, coughing blood, and weight loss).

In psychiatry, bedside diagnosis can be made reliably (3) and much data are available to *suggest* causes of illness (e.g., family, twin and adoption studies to *suggest* a genetic contribution to cause). However, in psychiatry, causation is not known with certainty, and there are no pathognomonic lab tests. In fact, historically, when a specific pathogenic process and pathognomonic lab test were established beyond question for a psychiatric disorder, as was the case for neurosyphilis, treatment of the disease became the province of other medical specialties.

With causes not conclusively established, psychiatric researchers and clinicians must be especially attentive to reliability and validity of diagnosis. Interrelater reliability is determined by the weighted kappa statistic, for which a kappa value of 1.0 reflects perfect interrater agreement, a value above 0.9 is ideal, and above 0.6 is usually acceptable (3–5).

To foster diagnostic reliability and acceptance of our system of diagnostic classification, diagnostic criteria are *operationalized* and *athe-oretical*. This means that diagnoses are based largely on observable signs and symptoms, and clinicians need not have a specific theory (e.g., learning theory, psychic determinism, inheritance) of behavior to diagnose the same patients the same way as would their colleagues.

The first operationalized criteria, those of Feighner et al. at Washington University, were published in 1972 (6). Over an 8-year span, these and the 1978 Research Diagnostic Criteria (7) were modified and expanded by an American Psychiatric Association Task Force directed by Dr. Robert Spitzer, and published in 1980 as the *Diagnostic and Statistical Manual of the American Psychiatric Association, Third Edition* (DSM-III) (8). Clinicians were expected to use DSM-III criteria, and the DSM system gained worldwide acceptance. The DSM-III was modified in 1987 (3) as the DSM-III-Revised (DSM-III-R); a fourth edition is expected in 1993.

Although not specifically stated in the DSM manual, the DSM system is attentive to the biopsychosocial model (pp. 3–15). Each patient should be assessed from five perspectives, termed its five Axes (3). Axis I is for the vast majority of psychiatric disorders (e.g., schizophrenia, mood disorders, anxiety disorders, substance abuse disorders). Axis II is for personality disorders (e.g., schizotypal personality disorder, antisocial personality disorder) and developmental disorders (e.g., mental retardation, pervasive developmental disorders such as autism, and specific developmental disorders such as developmental reading disorder [dyslexia]).

Axis III is for general medical disorders (e.g., arteriosclerotic heart disease, psoriasis), regardless of whether these cause behavioral disturbances. Axis IV addresses the severity of psychosocial stressors—at the time of assessment and during the year prior to assessment—that could have contributed to the de-

Table 20.1. Robins-Guze Standards for Establishing Validity of a Psychiatric Disorder[a]

For a putative syndrome to be considered a clinically discrete (valid) entity, groups of patients who have the syndrome will have common characteristics for each of the following:

1. **Clinical Description:** Common symptoms, signs, demographic characteristics (e.g., typical age of onset, gender difference in prevalence)
2. **Laboratory Studies:** Common laboratory findings (e.g., lactate sensitivity, dexamethasone nonsuppression), even though findings are not pathognomonic
3. **Delimitation from Other Disorders:** Symptoms and signs cannot routinely be explained by another disorder; for example, endocrine disease must be excluded to make a diagnosis of bipolar disorder.
4. **Follow-up Studies:** (a) When reexamined months or years later, patients do not have a different condition that would explain original signs and symptoms; (b) ideally, patients who have the putative diagnosis will have similar outcomes.
5. **Family Studies:** Regardless of etiology, many psychiatric illnesses run in families. Increased prevalence of the putative disorder in close family members strongly suggests validity.

[a]Modified from Robins E, Guze SB. Establishment of diagnostic validity in psychiatric illness: its application to schizophrenia. Am J Psychiatry 1970;126:107–111.

velopment, recurrence, maintenance, or intensification of the patient's mental illness. It is quantified on an ordinal scale (p. 18) of 1–6, in which 1 signifies no acute contributing events, and 6 reflects catastrophic events such as the death of one's child. Axis V details the patient's overall level of functioning at the time of the examination and during the prior year. It is recorded on a scale of 1–90, in which 1–10 identifies patients being in persistent danger of hurting themselves or others, and 81–90 represents minimal symptoms beyond everyday concerns.

Diagnostic classification must be valid as well as reliable. Diagnostic validity is usually assessed according to the 1970 Robins-Guze standards (1). For a diagnosis to represent a discrete, homogeneous clinical entity that suggests specific treatments and predicts a typical outcome, groups of patients who have the putative diagnosis should have the characteristics listed in Table 20.1. Some have suggested that response to specific treatments be included among the standards for validation (2).

In the rest of this chapter we present many of the psychiatric disorders organized along traditional lines of schizophrenia, affective disorders, anxiety disorders, somatization disorder, and personality disorders. Focal brain disorders, childhood psychiatric disorders, dementia and delirium, substance abuse, sleep disorders, and sexual dysfunctions are presented in Chapters 3, 11, 21, 22, 28, and 29, respectively. For pragmatic reasons, many of the several hundred DSM disorders cannot be covered in this text. For these, the reader should refer to the most current DSM and to standard textbooks of psychiatry.

SCHIZOPHRENIA

In 1860, the Austrian psychiatrist Benedict Morel described a patient diagnosed with an insidious illness onset in teenage and chronic deterioration of cognitive function and other behavior. He termed the disorder dementia praecox, meaning dementia starting in puberty (9). In 1896, Emil Kraepelin, the German psychiatrist who pioneered psychiatric classification, reported that 5% of the patients at his Munich Clinic had dementia praecox. He distinguished dementia praecox patients from those who had "manic depressive insanity" (now called bipolar and unipolar affective disorder), for which the course was usually one of intermittent acute episodes followed by full recovery. He wrote that the most important characteristics in dementia praecox were emotional indifference and impaired volition (p. 193) (10–12).

In 1911, the Swiss psychiatrist Eugen Bleuler further characterized dementia praecox and renamed it schizophrenia (13). By schizophrenia, he meant "splitting of the psychic functions" (*not* synonymous with multiple personality), which he divided into feelings, thoughts, and behaviors (the old tripartite mind concept). Examples of this splitting of functions included a patient's feelings being unrelated to events (e.g., laughing on hearing bad news) and words in a sentence being unrelated to each other (e.g., in one fluent com-

Table 20.2.   Negative and Positive Symptoms in Schizophrenic Patients[a]

Negative Symptoms	Positive Symptoms
Affective Flattening	**Hallucinations**
Unchanging facial expression	Auditory
Decreased spontaneous movements	Voices commenting
Paucity of expressive gestures	Voices conversing
Poor eye contact	Somatic
Affective nonresponsivity	Olfactory (only 6% of patients)
Inappropriate affect	Visual
Lack of vocal inflections	
	Delusions
Alogia	Persecutory
Poverty of speech	Jealous (only 4% of patients)
Poverty of content of speech	Guilt or sin
Blocking (interruption of thought)	Grandiose
Increased response latency	Religious
	Somatic
	Ideas of reference (belief that events are special
Avolition, Apathy	messages to oneself)
Impaired grooming and hygiene	Delusions of being controlled (ideas of influence [p.
Lack of persistence at work or school	191])
Anergia (doing virtually nothing; lack of spontaneous ac-	Delusions of mind reading
tivity)	Thought broadcasting
	Thought insertion (a type of experience of alienation [p.
	191])
Anhedonia and Asociality	Thought withdrawal
Few recreational interests or activities	
Little sexual interest or activity	**Bizarre Behavior**
Impaired intimacy and closeness	Clothing and appearance
Few relationships with friends and peers	Social or sexual behavior
	Aggressiveness or agitation
	Repetitive, stereotyped
Inattentiveness	
Social inattentiveness	**Positive Thought Disorder**
Inattentiveness during examination	Derailment
	Tangentiality (p. 192)
	Incoherence
	Illogicality
	Pressure of speech (p. 190)
	Distractible speech
	Clang associations (only 3% of patients)

[a]Modified from Andreasen NC, Black DW. Introductory textbook of psychiatry. Washington DC: American Psychiatric Press, 1991.

ment, the patient mentions, incomprehensibly, naval battles, Druids, and the Acropolis).

Bleuler wrote that certain signs were fundamental to schizophrenia. The most cited of these are called the four A's: affective blunting (p. 193), autism (living in one's own world), associational loosening (formal thought disorder [p. 190]), and ambivalence (coexistence of contradictory emotions toward a person or situation, such as by raising a spoonful of food to one's mouth without eating it, putting it down, and then repeating the process).

Bleuler also described accessory symptoms, which often occurred in schizophrenia and in other conditions, but were not fundamental to the diagnosis. These included hallucinations, delusions, intellectual abnormalities (e.g., abnormalities of language and judgment), involuntary muscle movements, impaired coordination, and menstrual abnormalities.

The late 20th century saw further characterization of symptoms that Kraepelin and Bleuler considered fundamental. Some contemporary psychiatrists (14–19) focused on

Table 20.3.   First-Rank Symptoms of Schneider[a]

I. **Complete Auditory Hallucinations:** A clear, sustained voice, speaking full sentences, perceived as coming from outside one's body
   A. Voices arguing
   B. Voices heard commenting on one's actions
II. **Experiences of Influence:** Experience that one's feelings and actions are one's own but are externally controlled
III. **Experiences of Alienation:** Experience that one's feelings and actions are not one's own, but are the work of someone or something else
IV. **Thought Broadcasting:** The perception that one's thoughts are audibly escaping from one's head
   A. Audible thoughts
   B. Thought withdrawal
   C. Thought insertion
V. **Delusional Perceptions:** The patient perceives a correctly perceived neutral event as having a special, delusional meaning unrelated to the event

[a]Modified from Schneider K. Clinical psychopathology. New York: Grune & Stratton, 1959:133; and Taylor MA. Schneiderian first rank symptoms and clinical prognostic features in schizophrenia. Arch Gen Psychiatry 1972;26:64–67.

symptoms that Crow (14) termed negative (deficit) symptoms (Table 20.2) that elaborated on Kraepelin's and Bleuler's descriptions of emotional indifference, lack of volition, and autism. The contemporary researchers found that the more negative symptoms a person has, the more likely that the patient will have a family history of psychiatric illness, laboratory test abnormalities, poor treatment response, and a deteriorating course.

Schizophrenics also have positive (productive) symptoms (Table 20.2). Compared to negative symptoms, positive symptoms usually appear more dramatic to observers and often precipitate hospitalization. However, positive symptoms are more responsive to treatment, less often associated with lab abnormalities, and less diagnostically specific for schizophrenia. They also occur in major affective disorders, drug-induced psychosis, and psychosis secondary to brain diseases (19–23).

The German psychiatrist Kurt Schneider (1887–1967) believed that eight symptoms (24) were pathognomonic of schizophrenia (i.e., symptoms of the first rank). Although 60% of schizophrenics manifest at least one of these eight first-rank symptoms (FRS), FRS

occur in other disorders (25–27). For simplicity, these eight can be reduced to five (Table 20.3) (28).

Additional research identified an increased frequency of neurologic soft signs (Table 20.4) among schizophrenics (29–31), as well as impaired smooth eye pursuit movements (20), and multiple lab abnormalities (pp. 186, 216, 226). Although common in schizophrenia, these abnormalities are not pathognomonic.

A patient who would meet Kraepelin's, Bleuler's, and modern diagnostic criteria for schizophrenia manifests (1) emotional blunting and other negative symptoms and (2) any positive symptom that impairs functioning. The patient would not have (1) coarse brain disease or psychotomimetic drug abuse that could explain symptoms or (2) a mood disorder. Most patients who meet these criteria (termed narrow or restrictive) have an insidious onset and deteriorating course. By age 30–40 years, the patient is likely to be unemployed or working in a sheltered workshop; living in his or her parents' home, on the streets, in a homeless shelter, or in a public hospital, and has no friends (32).

The diagnosis of schizophrenia in the U.S. was influenced by views that the fundamental symptoms did not occur in manic-depressive illness, and that classic manic-depressive symptoms (e.g., hyperactivity, severe guilt) did occur in schizophrenia. In part for this reason, until the late 1970s, American psychiatrists often diagnosed schizophrenia in patients who would now be diagnosed as having affective disorder (p. 246). This overdiagnosis of schizophrenia in the United States (33–37) was documented in the United States/United Kingdom (US/UK) Project (35), in which 250 patients hospitalized in London and 250 hospitalized in New York were examined by project psychiatrists. In New York, 65% of the 250 patients received a diagnosis of schizophrenia from their own psychiatrists. In London, 34% of the 250 patients received that diagnosis from their psychiatrists. However, when the US/UK Project psychiatrists examined these same 500 patients using standardized criteria, they diagnosed schizophrenia in

Table 20.4.   Soft Neurologic Signs[a]

Sign	Test	Abnormal Response
Palmomental reflex	Repeated scratching of base of thumb	Slight downward movement of the mouth and jaw which does not extinguish
Grasp reflex	Pressure (examiner's fingers) exerted on palm	Subject's fingers close about examiner's (grasps them)
Gegenhalten	Passive movement of subject's limbs	Subject resists with equal pressure to that of examiner's
Snout/Rooting reflex	Stroking corner of subject's mouth	Subject's lips purse and move towards stimulation
Motor impersistence	Subject makes a fist, closes eyes tightly, protrudes tongue	Unable to maintain each of these behaviors for 20 seconds
Adventitious motor overflow	Rhythmic and rapid tapping with fingers. Each hand separately	Movements also seen in inactive hand (chorea [p. 190] also an overflow movement)
Double simultaneous discrimination	Examiner simultaneously lightly touches cheeks and hands in sequence	Tendency to not perceive the touch on the hands

[a]Modified from Taylor MA. The behavioral neurologic examination. In: Sierles FS. Clinical behavioral science. New York: SP Medical & Scientific Books, 1982:14.

only 32% of the 250 American patients and in 26% of the British patients. Use of modern diagnostic criteria has reduced this tendency to overdiagnosis.

If a diagnostic system excludes a diagnosis of affective disorder when a patient has any of the signs depicted in Table 20.2, or if it permits a diagnosis of schizophrenia when the patient shows signs of affective disorder, using that system yields a higher population prevalence of schizophrenia and a lower prevalence of affective disorder (38–40). Further, use of criteria (termed broad criteria) that increase the frequency of a diagnosis of schizophrenia and reduce the frequency of a diagnosis of affective disorder leads to a conclusion that schizophrenics have a variety of outcomes, not just poor outcomes. Outcomes (45, 49, 50) range from never requiring hospital readmission (good outcome, 13%–20% of patients) to continuous hospitalization or extensive social or intellectual impairment (bad outcome, 45% of patients) (41–46). Factors that influence outcome are depicted in Table 20.5 (41–46).

In summary, for each patient, the prognosis can be estimated according to the following rule: The larger the number of affective disorder symptoms, and the fewer the negative symptoms, the better the prognosis (32).

Subtyping

Historically psychiatrists have identified schizophrenic subtypes (8, 12, 13, 50–52). The disorganized (hebephrenic) subtype corresponds to poor prognosis schizophrenia and is characterized by early age of onset, formal thought disorder, and many negative symptoms. In contrast, the paranoid subtype has a later age of onset, predominantly positive symptoms, and a better outcome (50, 51). Some schizophrenics have catatonia (p. 188), and thus a catatonic subtype. However, catatonia occurs in many other disorders, most often affective disorder (52). The validity of other subtyping is dubious (53); often, a patient receives different subtype diagnoses during different hospital admissions (54).

Epidemiology

Depending on which criteria are used, the population prevalence of schizophrenia varies between 0.4%–1.9% (55–57). The 1.9 figure was obtained in the Epidemiologic Catchment Area (ECA) study (57), where interviewers were laypersons using the Diagnostic Interview Schedule, which has modest reliability (58). Schizophrenia occurs in all cultures and

Table 20.5. Factors that Influence Outcome in Schizophrenia[a]

Factor	Good Outcome	Poor Outcome
Onset	Acute	Insidious
Duration	Short	Chronic
Psychiatric history	Absent	Present
Affective symptoms	Present	Absent
Sensorium	Clouded	Clear
Obsessions or compulsions	Absent	Present
Assaultiveness	Absent	Present
Premorbid functioning	Good	Poor
Marital history	Married	Never married
Psychosexual functioning	Good	Poor
Neurologic functioning	Normal	Soft signs present
Structural brain abnormalities	None	Present
Social class	High	Low
Family history of schizophrenia	Negative	Positive

[a]Reprinted with permission from Black DW, Yates WR, Andreasen NC. Schizophrenia, schizophreniform disorder, and delusional (paranoid) disorders. In: Talbott JA, Hales RE, Yudofsky SC, eds. Textbook of psychiatry. Washington DC: American Psychiatric Press, 1988:370.

social classes (32, 59, 60). Because it is so disabling, however, schizophrenics experience downward social class mobility (downward drift) and are usually of lower socioeconomic status (SES) than their parents (59–62). For first admissions, schizophrenia is equally common in men and in women. There is a slight tendency for schizophrenics to be born in late winter or early spring (63–65), which to some (65) suggests a viral contribution to etiology. The mean age of onset is 21 years in men, for whom the disorder is more likely to become chronic, and 26 for women. Life expectancy is shortened (66), primarily by suicide or accidental death (67).

Etiology

The etiology is unknown. All studies in which broad criteria have been used have concluded that it is familial (68–70). The MZ:DZ twin concordance ratio of 46:14 reflects significant heritability (18, 71, 72). (See p. 64 for a discussion of MZ:DZ concordance and heritability.) Adoption studies (69, 74–76) also suggest a genetic component, as does the fact that children of nonschizophrenic members of discordant MZ pairs are just as likely to become schizophrenic as the children of schizophrenic co-twins (77).

Many researchers hypothesize that insults to the central nervous system (CNS) contribute to the development of schizophrenia. These insults include viral infection (78), drug abuse (79), head trauma (80), or problems during gestation (81). During gestation, embryonic days 40–125 are probably the most vulnerable, because this is when primordial nerve cells migrate from the walls of the ventricles along glial columns to their final location (82).

Dopaminergic (DA) transmission (83) is abnormal in schizophrenia (p. 53). This does not translate, however, into clinically useful diagnostic lab testing. The abnormalities of DA transmission do not appear to be specific for schizophrenia (p. 53). Other neurotransmitter systems are also affected.

During the 1950s, it was posited (84–87) that impaired family communication caused schizophrenia. These hypotheses were based on observations of families *after* onset of a patient's psychosis. *Prospective* controlled data suggest, though, that impaired family communication can exacerbate schizophrenia: family therapy that reduces stress by educating family members about schizophrenia and teaching them to express positive and negative feelings more constructively, reduces the number of readmissions. The authors maintained that family treatment diminished a cluster of family behaviors termed "excessive expressed emotionality": critical comments and hostility directed at the patient, and emotional overinvolvement with the patient (88–90).

Treatment

Neuroleptic drugs (p. 324) are the mainstay of treatment for schizophrenia (32, 46, 53, 91, 92). During the initial hospitalization, a neuroleptic in a dosage equivalent of 200–600 mg chlorpromazine should suffice. If the patient has been ill for less than 3 years, neuroleptics combined with the interventions discussed below will effect improvement sufficient for the patient to return to the community (92).

Following discharge, the neuroleptic should be maintained at full dose for about 8 months and then gradually tapered and discontinued by the end of 1 year, the latter to reduce the risk of tardive dyskinesia (p. 326). This maintenance reduces the risk of relapse: with it, 30%–50% of patients relapse, without it, 50%–75% relapse (93–95). Following a second admission, another year of maintenance therapy is indicated (31, 93–95).

For some patients for whom neuroleptics are minimally effective, supplementing the neuroleptic with lithium may help (96). Some neuroleptic-resistant patients may respond to clozapine (p. 326) or to electroconvulsive therapy (ECT) (p. 335), especially if the patient is not emotionally blunted (97).

Somatic treatments of schizophrenia are best combined with other interventions. In the hospital, small units with a high staff to patient ratios, an organized system of granting privileges based upon improvements in behavior (32, 98), practical problem-solving approaches in supportive individual psychotherapy and ward group meetings (98), and education of the family to reduce excessive expressed emotionality (88–90, 99, 100), are all helpful. Following discharge, a combination of pharmacotherapy with supportive individual therapy, family therapy, and sheltered workshops or day hospital care are better than pharmacotherapy alone (88–90, 99–101).

AFFECTIVE (MOOD) DISORDERS

Everyone has experienced sad, anxious, irritable, and euphoric moods. After the loss of a job, for example, or the death of a loved one, a person's sad or anxious mood may be intense and may last for months. When sadness, anxiety, irritability, or euphoria occur daily and relentlessly, reduce a person's functioning, and cannot be explained by bereavement (p. 173), we speak of a mood (affective) disorder. Treatment of mood disorders can be especially gratifying. Most (70%–80% of) patients respond well, experiencing relief from intense suffering, restoration of effective functioning, and (considering the high suicide rate in depression) preservation of life.

History of the Diagnosis and Treatment of Affective Disorders

Unlike schizophrenia, descriptions of which first appeared during the Industrial Revolution, affective disorders were described through the millennia. Hippocrates described the depressive syndrome of melancholia, which he so named because he thought it was caused by excessive black bile (122). Other milestones in the history of the study of mood disorders are listed in Table 20.6 (11, 102–113).

Classification of Affective Disorders

The classification of mood disorders, especially depressions, is controversial (18, 32, 114–116). Accurate classification is important because it predicts the effectiveness of specific treatments. For example, the psychotic and melancholic subtypes of major depression are more responsive to somatic treatments (e.g., antidepressants, lithium, ECT) than to psychotherapies (18, 116–120). However, dysthymic disorder and nonmelancholic, nonpsychotic major depressions can be treated by psychotherapy alone, often respond to monoamine oxidase inhibitors (MAOIs), and often do not respond to ECT (118–122).

MAJOR DEPRESSION

The most severe forms of mood disorder are termed major depression and mania. Characteristics of major depression (8) are listed in Table 20.7.

Table 20.6. Historical Milestones in Study of Affective Disorders

Clinician	Milestone
Hippocrates (Greece; 460–377 BC)	Described melancholia
Aretaeus (Cappadocia [now Turkey]; 50–130 AD)	Reported manic and depressive states in same individual
Emil Kraepelin (Germany; 1856–1926)	Distinguished between manic depressive illness and schizophrenia by signs and prognosis
Sigmund Freud (Vienna, London; 1856–1939) and Karl Abraham (Germany; 1877–1925)	Distinguished between mourning and melancholia; psychodynamics of depression
Ugo Cerletti (Italy; 1877–1963)	Reported efficacy of ECT in depression (1938)
John Cade (Australia)	Reported efficacy of lithium in mania (1949)
Karl Leonhard (Germany)	Distinguished between unipolar and bipolar disorders (1957)
Julian Mendlewicz (U.S.A.) and John Rainer (U.S.A.)	Adoption study suggesting genetic transmission of manic depressive illness (1977)
Gerald Klerman (U.S.A.; 1929–1992) and Myrna Weissman (U.S.A.)	Controlled study of efficacy of interpersonal psychotherapy in depression (1974)
A. John Rush (U.S.A.) and Aaron Beck (U.S.A.)	Controlled study of efficacy of cognitive psychotherapy in depression (1977)
Bernard Carroll (U.S.A.)	Dexamethasone suppression test for melancholia (1982)

Table 20.7. Characteristics of Major Depression and Dysthymic Disorder

Major Depression	Dysthymic Disorder
Depressed mood	Depressed mood
Increased appetite and weight gain or decreased appetite and weight loss	Overeating or poor appetite
Insomnia or hypersomnia (excessive sleeping)	Insomnia or hypersomnia
Trouble concentrating or indecisiveness	Trouble concentrating or indecisiveness
Fatigue or reduced energy	Fatigue or reduced energy
Agitation or psychomotor slowing	
Anhedonia (inability to enjoy)	
Feelings of worthlessness	
Excessive guilt	
Thoughts of death or of suicide or suicide attempts	
	Feelings of hopelessness
	No past manic episode

Major Depression, Melancholic Subtype

The melancholic subtype of major depression has a cluster of characteristics (8, 123–127), not all of which occur in a given melancholic patient. The mood, which is sad, anxious, or dysphoric (restlessly irritable), is sustained and unresponsive to pleasurable events or to a sensitively conducted interview. Patients derive little or no pleasure from previously enjoyed thoughts or activities (anhedonia). Their inability to feel joy makes them feel yet more troubled.

Patients awaken well before the usual time of arising and usually cannot return to sleep. The sadness, anxiety, or dysphoria is most intense in the morning, with gradual, slight improvement as the day progresses (diurnal mood swing). Rarely, the reverse pattern occurs: the mood routinely worsens gradually as the day progresses (18).

Often, there is psychomotor slowing or agitation (p. 188); occasionally, a patient simultaneously manifests both (18). With slowing, tasks ordinarily handled with alacrity are performed at a snail's pace. For example, a teacher takes a month to prepare an examination that she would ordinarily produce in a few days. Patients perceive this pace as slow motion and time as passing slowly (117, 128). The patient may spend hours staring into space, or become stuporous (p. 188). The agitated melancholic may engage in pacing, rocking, hand-wringing, finger-tapping, or excoriating of the skin. An occasional patient shouts in anguish (32).

Appetite usually diminishes (anorexia), with consequent weight loss. Also common are a preoccupied, worried appearance, reduced emotional expressivity (volition is normal, however) and concentration (32), diminished cognitive ability which in the elderly may reach the point of dementia (129), constipation, dry mouth, diminished sex drive, menstrual irregularity, and an inability to cry. If dementia results from depression, it is reversed by treating the depression (129).

Feelings of worthlessness, hopelessness, and intense guilt are common. Worthless feelings in melancholia are qualitatively different from a trait of low self-esteem. For example, one melancholic described himself as "a mole on the face of society" whose family "would be better off if I died."

Hopeless feelings in depression differ from traits of pessimism or cynicism. Melancholics often anticipate continued suffering, deterioration, or premature death, sometimes by suicide. Melancholic guilt far exceeds the guilt that many people feel after acting insensitively. The guilt can reach delusional proportions, as in a man who believed that his sins caused the deaths of several world leaders.

This experience is one of nightmarish suffering. Professional writers who have suffered melancholia have depicted it thus:

> Depression is so mysteriously painful in the way it becomes known to the self—to the mediating intellect—as to verge close to being beyond description. . . . (It is) a form of torment so alien to everyday experience. For myself, the pain is most closely connected to drowning or suffocating—but even these images are off the mark (130).
>
> It is a positive and active anguish, a sort of psychical neuralgia wholly unknown to normal life (131).

Often the suffering is intensified by a memory of once having been well, combined with hopelessness about the possibility of recovery—one reason why suicidal thoughts and attempts (to end the suffering) are common. A review of 17 studies shows a lifetime risk of completed suicide of 15% in patients with major affective disorders (132).

About 20% of patients who have major depression, usually melancholics, are psychotic, with delusions, hallucinations, or first-rank symptoms (18). Circumstantiality, paucity of thought, and thought-blocking are the only thought disorders that occur in depression (19). Often, the psychotic signs fit the depressed mood (i.e., are mood-congruent), such as with delusions of guilt or hallucinations in which the patient is criticized or hears suggestions of suicide. Sometimes, psychotic features are mood-incongruent, such as when a patient believes he or she is being unfairly persecuted. If criteria for mood disorder are otherwise met, mood-incongruent psychotic features should not change the diagnosis (53, 116, 133, 134).

The more severe the depression, the more likely that lab abnormalities will occur. In about 50% of melancholics (113), there is a blunted response on the dexamethasone suppression test (DST, p. 198). Unfortunately, the specificity (p. 29) of the DST is only 70%, because a blunted response also occurs with pregnancy, malnutrition with weight loss, enzyme-inducing drugs (e.g., barbiturates), Cushing's disease, schizophrenia, and 5% of normal controls (32, 113, 135, 136). Also in melancholia, there is sometimes deficient production of thyroid-stimulating hormone in response to intravenous infusion of thyrotropin-releasing hormone (137, 138), and deficient production of corticotropin is response to corticotropin-releasing hormone (139). Because of lost sleep, rapid eye movement (REM) latency decreases, REM duration increases early in the evening, a greater proportion of REM sleep occurs early in the night, the frequency of eye movements increases during REM sleep, and quantity of slow-wave sleep decreases (140).

Severely depressed patients, especially those who are psychotic, have elevated cortisol levels, or respond poorly to treatment, often show mild brain atrophy with widening of sulci and ventricular enlargement, especially in the frontotemporal regions or basal ganglia (141–143). When patients respond to treatment, this atrophy sometimes disappears

Table 20.8. Differential Diagnosis Between Mild Melancholia and Dysthymia

	Mild Melancholia	Dysthymia
Preexisting psychiatric illness	No	Anxiety disorders Fearful, anxious personality disorders
Family history	Bipolar disorder Unipolar disorder Schizophrenia	Anxiety disorders

(141). Also, about 25% of seriously depressed people have EEG abnormalities (32, 144), and 50% have noteworthy abnormalities, particularly in the nondominant hemisphere and in the frontal lobes bilaterally on neuropsychologic testing (145).

Unipolar Affective Illness

When patients have one or more major depressive episodes, but no manic or hypomanic episodes, they have unipolar affective illness. Similarities and differences between unipolar and bipolar (p. 250) disorders are discussed later.

DYSTHYMIC DISORDER

At various times, dysthymic disorder (Table 20.7) has been called reactive, neurotic, minor, or characterologic depression, or hysteroid dysphoria (146). Many symptoms of dysthymia are the same as those of major depression, but dysthymic patients have few symptoms of melancholia, and have never had prior psychotic or manic episodes. Occasionally, however, mania occurs in patients previously diagnosed as dysthymic. Although dysthymia and melancholia share some symptoms in common, each syndrome has typical features. When symptoms overlap in mild cases, it is difficult to distinguish between mild melancholia and dysthymia. For such situations, several distinctions facilitate the diagnosis (Table 20.8).

DEPRESSION SECONDARY TO GENERAL MEDICAL ILLNESS

Hundreds of systemic medical conditions, coarse brain diseases, and drugs cause depression (147). Especially depressogenic are left frontal stroke (p. 37), cancer of the head of the pancreas, subcortical dementias (p. 283), viral infections, endocrine diseases, multiple sclerosis (p. 199), end-stage renal disease, steroids, and reserpine (147–154). In such cases, one should treat, if possible, the underlying general medical illness (148, 155).

DEPRESSION IN THE PRESENCE OF A PREEXISTING PSYCHIATRIC DISORDER

Sometimes, depression appears for the first time in a patient who has a prior correct diagnosis of another psychiatric disorder. Examples include depression following well-established onset of anxiety disorders, alcoholism, or antisocial personality disorder (6, 156, 157). Although the initial condition may have no causal relationship to the depression, the latter is termed secondary affective disorder. Its validity is based on how it differs from primary mood disorders. In secondary depressions, prognosis for recovery is poorer, but the risk of suicide is less than for primary affective illness. Management includes treatment of the preexisting psychiatric illness (156, 157).

BEREAVEMENT

Bereavement (p. 173) shares many symptoms in common with depressive illness. However, unlike patients with mood disorders, bereaved persons typically do not hallucinate, feel worthless, contemplate suicide, or believe they are ill. Bereavement itself never causes delusions. Most bereaved persons have gradual, spontaneous symptom reduction within 6 months (158).

BIPOLAR DISORDER

By convention, *the diagnosis of bipolar disorder is given to patients who manifest one or more episodes of mania or hypomania* (mild mania) not secondary to coarse brain disease, systemic illness, or drugs (8, 104). Such patients are at high risk for developing future episodes of major depression, but *occurrence of depression is not necessary for a diagnosis of bipolar disorder.*

Manic Episode

Mania is dramatic (11, 18, 32, 53). Typically, the speech is rapid and pressured (p. 190). Often, circumstantiality, flight of ideas, and clang associations occur (p. 192). Formal thought disorders (p. 190) are rare. Thought content is often grandiose. Manics may have delusions that they are supremely talented (e.g., better at basketball than Michael Jordan, holder of 5 Ph.D. degrees), hold high political office, are God, or are *all* of the above. Common themes include financial enterprises, religion, inventions, sex, and conspiracies by others.

The mood is euphoric, irritable, or labile (p. 193). A depressive mood may intrude in the midst of a manic episode. Manics often manifest stimulus-bound hyperactivity (p. 188). For example, they may intrude into others' conversations, attend to the slightest distraction, or approach the nurses' station whenever its door opens. Agitation (which is not the same as stimulus-bound hyperactivity) is common. Also, patients may relentlessly write letters, make notes, or call on the telephone.

Appetite may increase. The patient may feel less need to sleep and spend entire nights awake and active, without feeling tired. The patient may speak loudly, profanely, and incessantly, regardless of who is present. Irritable patients may be assaultive or menacing. Increased sex drive, sexual provocativeness, public nudity, or exhibitionistic behavior may occur. Spending sprees, gift-giving, writing bad checks, gambling large sums, sudden trips, and other extravagances could be finan-

cially ruinous. For obvious reasons, marital problems are common. Manics often dress in bright colors and excessively decorate themselves. Sporting odd haircuts, hats, and wigs is common, as is wearing many bracelets and flowers in lapels. Manics can manifest first-rank signs, delusions of grandeur or persecution, or hallucinations in any modality. Twenty percent develop catatonia (52). Manics may drive recklessly, provoke fights, and become exhausted and dehydrated (sometimes fatally). Thus, mania is an emergency requiring hospitalization. Fortunately, manics usually respond well to treatment.

Laboratory Testing in Bipolar Patients

About 50% of manics have notable neuropsychological test abnormalities (159), and 25% have abnormal electroencephalograms (EEGs) (31, 144). Compared to findings in controls, the CT and MRI in bipolars (during manic or depressed episodes) are more likely to show mild cortical atrophy with enlarged ventricles. Atrophy is most prominent in the frontal and temporal lobes, and may affect the cerebellum (160–162). MRI in bipolars are more likely to show abnormal T1 values (p. 216), which may resolve with lithium treatment (163). Unfortunately, these findings are not specific for bipolars; they also occur in schizophrenia.

Milder Variants of Bipolar Disorder

Mild episodes of mania are termed hypomania. In cyclothymia, patients have mild hypomanic and mild depressive episodes that, like mania, respond to lithium (164). A cluster of traits (extroverted, talkative, uninhibited, cheerful) termed "hyperthermic temperament" is also a variant of bipolar disorder (165).

DISTINCTION BETWEEN UNIPOLAR AND BIPOLAR DISORDER

Unipolar and bipolar disorder have so far been presented as distinct, based on demographic and clinical differences (53, 104, 123, 166): Average age of onset for unipolars is 30–

50 years, compared with 20–30 years for bipolars. A greater proportion of unipolar patients (70%–80%) compared to bipolars (50%–60%) are women. By a 10:1 ratio, unipolar disorder is much more common. Family members of bipolars are twice as likely to have mood disorders (although the mood disorder is often unipolar in the family members) than family members of unipolars. Bipolars are more likely to have recurrences. Bipolar disorder is uncommon (1%) in relatives of unipolars. PET findings are different in the two conditions (167). Bipolar depression is more responsive to lithium than is unipolar depression (166).

Despite these distinctions, some researchers (18, 168, 169) have suggested that bipolar disorder is a severe version and unipolar disorder a milder version of the same disorder: 7%–20% of relatives of bipolar patients have unipolar disorder (18). And, curiously, to demonstrate heritability of either disorder, twin pairs must be considered concordant if one co-twin is bipolar and other is unipolar (32).

COURSE AND COMPLICATIONS OF UNIPOLAR AND BIPOLAR DISORDERS

Major depressive episodes tend to begin gradually. Manic episodes tend to begin abruptly (18). Lengths of either depressed or manic episodes can range from days to a chronic lifetime course (53). The average duration of an untreated manic episode is 4–6 months, and is 6–13 months for an untreated major depression (116, 117). Properly treated, episodes of either can be limited to several weeks or several months, the latter if the initial treatment fails and other treatments must be used. For 61% of bipolars and 80% of unipolars, recovery from the first episode is complete (170). For the remainder, symptoms persist, even when the patient is able to return home.

Prompt treatment and follow-up maintenance treatment of mood disorders is important to stave off short-term complications, recurrence, and chronicity (32). Regardless of whether the patient is unipolar or bipolar, short-term complications of untreated or inadequately treated major depression include suicide (132); poor judgment leading to unwise decisions such as leaving a job, quitting school, or separating from a spouse (53, 171); or catatonia (which can lead to dehydration, malnutrition, and death) (32, 52). Complications of mania were discussed earlier.

Beyond what has been said, there is additional reason to treat promptly and provide maintenance treatment following recovery. Following recovery from an initial illness episode in unipolars or bipolars, there is a 75%–80% likelihood of one or more recurrences (172). Twelve percent of patients relapse within 4 weeks, and 25% within 12 weeks. The larger the number of prior episodes, the greater the chance of recurrence. The longer the patient remains well, the less the chance of relapse (173, 174). For bipolars, each subsequent episode tends to last longer, and interepisode duration decreases (32). For 20%–30% of patients, the mood disorder becomes chronic (123). Overall, patients who have major affective disorders have a decreased life expectancy, largely because of increased mortality from suicide and cancer (175, 176).

In bipolars, the first episode is manic 60%–80% of the time, and depressive 20%–40% of the time (133). Following an initial episode of major depression, 4%–18% of patients eventually have a manic episode, changing the diagnosis from unipolar to bipolar (177). Almost all bipolars eventually have at least one depression; unipolar mania is rare (117). Bipolars average 7–9 lifetime episodes (177).

EPIDEMIOLOGY OF AFFECTIVE DISORDERS

Mood disorders are common. The lifetime population prevalence of major depression (one type of mood disorder) is 5%–9% in women and 2%–4% in men (178, 179). At any time, 3.4%–4.3% of the population has some type of depressive illness (18). The lifetime prevalence of dysthymia is 3% (180). The lifetime prevalence of bipolar disorder is 0.5%–1% (178, 179), but manic episodes are so dramatic that in some psychiatric units, 25% of inpatients are manic (181). Because depression affects general health, causing symptoms such as anorexia, insomnia, and loss of libido, many depressives present themselves for the first time in the offices of nonpsychiatric physicians (182).

Mood disorders are more frequent in creative persons and those of high occupational achievement than in the general population (183, 184). For example, members of the Iowa Writers Workshop (and their family members) were more likely to have affective disorders than controls in the general population (183).

There are no racial differences in prevalence. Bipolar disorder occurs more frequently in persons of upper SES (179, 184). The greatest risk factor for a major affective disorder is a family history of it (117). The postpartum period is a time of increased risk for mood disorders (32). Women diagnosed with major affective disorder have an increased risk of postpartum mood disorders, especially if they have had prior postpartum illnesses. When affective disorder runs in a family, the age of illness onset also tends to be familial (32, 185).

Etiology

The etiology of primary mood disorders is unknown. There are multiple hypotheses which are not necessarily contradictory.

GENETIC HYPOTHESES

Major affective disorders run in families. Compared to the general population, unipolars are more likely to have unipolar relatives. Bipolars have increased familial occurrence of both bipolar and unipolar disorder (18). The MZ:DZ twin concordance for bipolar and unipolar patients taken together is 65:14 (18). This includes the 20% of concordant pairs in which one twin is bipolar, the other unipolar. In adoption studies, the biologic relatives of affectively ill adoptees are more likely to have affective disorder than are the biologic relatives of nonill persons or the adoptive relatives

of probands (109, 186). This strongly suggests a genetic component.

LIFE EVENTS

Bereavement is not classified as a depressive illness because it is a normal response that rarely requires treatment. There is debate about the extent to which depressive illness can be precipitated by life events in susceptible persons (18). Retrospective studies reveal an increased likelihood of negative events such as loss of a family member, friend or job in the months before depression is diagnosed (187). One confound is the effect of illness on events. Once a person has experienced depression or mania, especially if it is not treated promptly, there is an increased risk for divorce, job loss, and poor academic performance (18).

ANIMAL MODELS

Learned helplessness (p. 64) has been suggested as a model for human depression (188), although it does not explain mania. Based on primate studies, maternal deprivation has also been offered as a model.

PSYCHODYNAMIC THEORIES

Psychoanalytic theories posit that real, anticipated, or fantasized events can precipitate depression in susceptible people. One mechanism (107, 108) is that following real or fantasized loss, anger is directed at an introjected (p. 87) ambivalently loved lost love object. Another mechanism is that in persons whose self-esteem depends on attention and praise from others, real or anticipated rejections or failures trigger loss of self-esteem (189, 190).

Psychodynamic explanations of mania include that it is a defense against depression, a suspension of superego functioning following atonement for guilt, or an overcompensation for low self-esteem (191). The former theory is enhanced by the occurrence of depressive symptoms during manic episodes (18).

BIOCHEMICAL HYPOTHESES

The catecholamine hypothesis of affective disorder (p. 55) posits deficient catecholamine at brain receptor sites in depression, and catecholamine excess at receptor sites in mania. An indoleamine or serotonin hypothesis suggests deficits at receptor sites in both mania and depression. Other transmitters, as well as biogenic amines and enzymes, have also been implicated. None of these theories satisfactorily explains affective disorders. Although endocrine disease (e.g., Cushing's disease) frequently causes affective illness (p. 198), and although there is abnormality in the neuroendocrine axis in many affectively ill people, the contribution of neuroendocrine abnormality to primary affective illnesses is unknown (117).

SENSITIZATION

The sensitization or kindling model of mood disorder (192) makes an analogy to the ignition of paper and kindling wood in a fireplace to generate enough heat to cause logs to burn. In animal research, repeated applications of electrical current (or analeptic [convulsant] drug) below seizure threshold eventually sensitizes the brain's neurons to respond by seizure activity to further subthreshhold administrations of current (or drug).

This model was originally used to explain cocaine and amphetamine psychoses, and later to explain affective disorder. In the latter, repeated stresses, among the most serious of which is an illness episode itself, might sensitize the brain to the point where less stress is required to produce recurrence. Other stresses are the social consequences of the illness (e.g., divorce, job loss). This could explain why successive illness episodes tend to become longer with time, and why antikindling treatments (e.g., anticonvulsants or ECT) are effective in affective disorder.

Initial Treatment

BEREAVEMENT

Most bereaved persons seek no treatment and mourn alone or with family and friends. Mourning is discussed on p. 173. Occasionally,

reduced functioning (e.g., reduced concentration with falling grades) leads some bereaved persons to seek treatment. Supportive psychotherapy is helpful. The physician facilitates mourning through discussing the deceased person, reappraising guilt feelings, and reviewing plans.

DYSTHYMIC DISORDER OR NONMELANCHOLIC, NONPSYCHOTIC UNIPOLAR DISORDER

For dysthymia, or for nonpsychotic nonmelancholic major depression in unipolars, cognitive psychotherapy and interpersonal psychotherapy have proved effective in controlled trials (110–112). In cognitive psychotherapy (pp. 78, 312) of depression (193), the therapist assists the patient in correcting self-deprecatory cognitive distortions such as exaggeration of the negative implications of a minor event, or drawing an erroneous self-critical conclusion about an event. Interpersonal psychotherapy (IPT) is a brief (12–16 weeks) treatment derived from psychodynamic psychotherapy, which includes realistic reassurance, discussion of strategies for coping with the disorder, clarification of feeling states, testing of cognitions, and improvement of interpersonal skills (194). If insight-oriented psychotherapy is used, themes include modifying the patient's goal from obtaining approval to living for him- or herself, and analyzing past and current relationships.

Pharmacotherapy with cyclic antidepressants (CAs), monoamine oxidase inhibitors (MAOIs), or fluoxetine, alone or combined with psychotherapy, are all effective (18, 110–112). Use of CAs and MAOIs is discussed on pages 327–330. Of these alternatives, combined psychotherapy and pharmacotherapy is best (110–112). For nonmelancholic, nonpsychotic major depression in unipolars, or for dysthymia, hospitalization is not usually necessary unless the symptoms are severe or the patient is suicidal. Patients receiving antidepressants must be told about side effects and that improvement may not occur for 2–4 weeks.

SEVERE MAJOR DEPRESSION

Most patients diagnosed with severe major depression may need to be hospitalized. Hospitalization and its controls may reduce the anxiety associated with the patient's depression. In such cases, hospitalization itself is therapeutic. The patient should be told that he or she did not cause the illness, and that the odds strongly favor a full, relatively prompt recovery. Most melancholics cannot participate fully in ward activities or in long family visits on the ward, and should not be pushed to do so (32). Their inability to participate and to express affection for family may intensify their guilt and low self-esteem. For the same reason, expressive psychotherapy (p. 311) is contraindicated during severe major depression (32).

Nursing and other staff should explain unit policy, educate the patient about the illness and its treatment, provide reassurance and support, encourage compliance with treatment, and observe the patient for signs of suicidal ideation. Psychiatric units have suicide precaution policies (e.g., half hourly nursing observation for minimally suicidal patients, continuous observation for patients with a severe suicide risk [pp. 349–357]). Weight and sleep should be monitored and charted daily. For severe insomnia, sedative-hypnotic medication should be prescribed. The family should be educated about the patient's illness, and told that neither they nor the patient is responsible for causing it (32).

Treatment for Melancholia as Part of Unipolar Disorder

For melancholia as part of unipolar disorder, a variety of treatments are effective (18, 32, 116, 195–197). If the patient is not psychotic, CAs or ECT are effective. If the patient is psychotic, ECT is effective. If the patient refuses ECT, or if a course of the latter does not effect improvement, the following are alternatives: (1) a CA plus lithium, (2) a CA plus thyroid hormone, (3) carbamazepine, or (4) a CA plus a neuroleptic.

Treatment for Melancholia as Part of Bipolar Disorder

For melancholia as part of bipolar disorder, a variety of treatments are also effective. If the patient is not psychotic, lithium is a fine antidepressant. If the patient is psychotic, he or she can be treated with (1) ECT, (2) a CA plus lithium, (3) a CA plus thyroid hormone, (4) carbamazepine, or (5) a CA plus a neuroleptic. Dosing strategies are discussed on pages 324–332.

Hypomania and Mania

Some hypomanic patients can be treated as outpatients, but some should be hospitalized. If the patient is willing to take oral lithium carbonate or liquid lithium citrate, and the family or staff is willing to tolerate annoying hypomanic behaviors for the 5–7 days that it takes lithium to work, lithium is the treatment of choice. If allergy, other severe side effects, or prior lithium failure preclude use of lithium, then carbamazepine, valproic acid, neuroleptics, or clonazepam could be effective. Anticonvulsants are preferable to neuroleptics or clonazepam because the latter two have no preventive value once the initial episode is over. Unlike most melancholics, most hypomanics are energetic and sometimes benefit from well-organized, focused ward activities with minimal distractions.

Acute mania requires hospitalization. Euphoria and hyperactivity readily give way to irritability and argumentativeness (198). The unmedicated irritable manic should not be interviewed alone in a closed room (32). Once the diagnosis of mania is established (the diagnosis is usually obvious, but coarse brain diseases, systemic illnesses and drugs must be promptly excluded as causes), effective doses of high-potency intramuscular (IM) neuroleptic medications should be given promptly and regularly (e.g., haloperidol 20 mg IM immediately and twice daily), and not in as-needed (PRN) doses that are reactive responses to escalation of symptoms. As the patient becomes more self-controlled, it is time to begin the neuroleptic in an oral (PO) format at a dose

50% greater than the IM dose. For 2–3 days prior to discontinuing the IM medication, there is an overlap period in which the full PO and IM doses are given simultaneously. The IM dose is then discontinued. After a week of successful neuroleptic treatment, lithium can be instituted, and after several weeks the neuroleptic can be discontinued. Failure of response of manics to IM neuroleptics within several days may require use of ECT (199).

Maintenance Treatment

To prevent recurrence following successful somatic treatment of a first episode of dysthymia, major depression, or mania, pharmacotherapy for 1 year is indicated. Pharmacotherapy should be accompanied by psychotherapy designed to reduce stress. Choice of maintenance medication is based on the syndrome treated and the somatic therapy that helped the patient (117, 123). Following recovery from a first melancholic episode, a CA or lithium is the likely choice (200). Following recovery from a first episode of dysthymia, a CA or MAOI is the likely choice. After recovery from a first manic or hypomanic episode, lithium or an anticonvulsant would be best.

For recurrent depressions in unipolars, continuous indefinite follow-up treatment with lithium (201), an anticonvulsant, or both is in order. Maintenance ECT may be indicated if episodes occur less than 2 years apart.

In bipolars, for recurrences of mania or depression that occur more than 5 years apart (to a maximum of three episodes total), a year's maintenance treatment with lithium (201) or an anticonvulsant (202) is in order. The CAs predispose to recurrence of mania. If episodes recur less than 3 years apart, or if the patient has had more than three episodes lifetime, continuous indefinite pharmacotherapy with lithium, an anticonvulsant, or the combination is indicated.

ANXIETY DISORDERS

The physiologic concomitants of anxiety (e.g., rapid pulse, increased blood pressure,

shunting of blood to muscles, increased muscle tone) are part of the fight and flight reaction (p. 400) needed for survival. In moderation, anxiety can enhance performance. When excessive for the situation in which it occurs, it causes suffering and reduces efficiency. Mild to severe anxiety may accompany any psychiatric or general medical disorder (203).

The anxiety disorders include panic disorder (PD), agoraphobia, social phobia, simple phobia, obsessive-compulsive disorder (OCD), generalized anxiety disorder (GAD), and posttraumatic stress disorder (PTSD). Anxiety disorders are common (203–207). The lifetime prevalence of anxiety disorders in the general population is 15% (204).

Often, anxiety disorders coexist (e.g., PD with agoraphobia) (53). For all but the simple phobias, secondary nonmelancholic depression is a common complication (18, 32, 208–210). Although some patients who have agoraphobia, OCD or PTSD may need hospitalization, the vast majority can be treated as outpatients, and many never seek treatment. Anxiety disorder patients have an increased prevalence (27%–58%) of preexisting personality disorders, especially avoidant, dependent, or obsessive-compulsive personalities (211–215). They are also more likely to have preexisting anxious traits and social introversion (216).

Panic disorder (formerly called anxiety neurosis), OCD (formerly obsessive-compulsive neurosis), and the three types of phobia (phobic neurosis) are among the conditions sometimes termed neuroses. Freud wrote (p. 86) that neuroses arose from the ego's defensive attempt to reduce signal anxiety generated by unacceptable id impulses (217). The term neurosis was coined by the Scottish physician William Cullen (1712–1790), who believed that many conditions *not* characterized by fever were caused by nervous system disease (218).

Panic Disorder

The defining feature of panic disorder (PD) is attacks of intense anxiety (panic) in

Table 20.9.   Symptoms of Panic Disorder[a]

Symptom	Percentage Panic Disorder Patients with Symptom	Percentage Controls with Symptom
Palpitation	97	9
Tires easily	93	19
Breathlessness	90	13
Nervousness	88	27
Chest pain	85	10
Sighing	79	16
Dizziness	78	16
Faintness	70	12
Apprehensiveness	61	3
Headache	58	26
Paresthesias	58	7
Weakness	56	3
Trembling	54	17
Unsatisfactory breathing	53	4
Insomnia	53	4
Unhappiness	50	2
Shakiness	47	16
Fatigued all the time	45	6
Sweating	42	33
Fear of death	42	2
Smothering	40	3
Syncope (fainting)	37	11
Nervous chill	24	0
Frequent urination	18	2
Vomiting or diarrhea	14	0
Anorexia	12	3

[a]Modified from Goodwin DW, Guze SB. Psychiatric diagnosis. New York: Oxford, 1989; and Cohen M, White P. Life situations, emotions and neurocirculatory asthenia (anxiety neurosis, neurasthenia, effort syndrome). Assoc Res Nerv Dis Proc 1950;29:832–869.

the absence of apparent precipitating events or situations. The attacks usually last from 5–30 minutes (rarely, as long as an hour). They may occur as infrequently as once yearly and as often as several times daily (53, 207). Occurrence several times monthly, or less often if an attack is followed by a month's continual anxiety about recurrence of panic, is needed to satisfy DSM criteria (8). The frequency of symptom occurrence in panic disorder patients is listed in Table 20.9 (53, 219).

Anxiety attacks can occur in the course of psychiatric illnesses other than anxiety disorders, most commonly major depression, somatization disorder, and alcohol withdrawal (53). Anxiety attacks are common with thyrotoxicosis (p. 196), psychomotor epilepsy (p. 47), pheochromocytoma, hypoglycemia, cardiopulmonary emergencies, intense pain, stimulant drugs (e.g., caffeine, nasal decongestants, amphetamine), and drug withdrawal states (p. 301).

COURSE AND COMPLICATIONS

Panic disorder usually begins between the ages of 15 and 35 years, with a mean age of onset of 25 years (218–220). Onset after age 35 suggests that one of the above medical conditions is causing the attacks. The most typical patient response to the first episode is to seek emergency medical care. If PD is the emergency physician's working diagnosis, the patient should be told that the tentative diagnosis is panic disorder, a treatable anxiety disorder. If the anxiety attack continues once the patient has reached the emergency room, the patient should receive diazepam or chlordiazepoxide (p. 333) PO or IV. Then the patient should be referred to a psychiatric consultant to confirm the diagnosis and to provide treatment. Too often, the patient is told "It's due to stress," and then referred for completeness' sake to a nonpsychiatric consultant. Psychiatric referral is usually preceded by consultation with several nonpsychiatric specialists (18, 221).

On long-term follow-up, 50%–70% of PD patients are recovered or much improved, and 20% are disabled by PD or its complications (221). The longer the duration of untreated PD, the more likely that it will become chronic (222).

About 50% of PD patients develop secondary depressions, usually nonmelancholic and sometimes associated with demoralization from lack of improvement (203, 204, 208, 210). The frequency of suicide attempts (223) and the lifetime risk of suicide (224) is greater in PD patients than in the population. These suicide attempts may occur during secondary depressions (203, 207).

Some PD patients self-medicate with alcohol or other drugs to alleviate symptoms. For those who become alcoholic (typically it is Type I alcoholism [p. 297]), prognosis for abstinence is better if the PD is properly treated after detoxification (225).

Patients who have PD have increased risk for peptic ulcer, irritable bowel syndrome, chest wall tenderness from excessive thoracic breathing, hypertension, and other cardiovascular disease (18, 226). Among the latter is prolapse of the heart's mitral valve (MVP), which occurs in 30%–50% of PD patients (227) compared to 5% of the general population (228, 229). Usually, MVP is asymptomatic, but it can be associated with palpitations (awareness of one's heartbeat because of changes in its intensity, rate, or rhythm), fatigue, and chest pain, all of which are *also* common in PD. Physical findings in MVP include systolic clicks or murmurs, and an abnormal EKG, with T wave or ST segment abnormalities, or atrial or ventricular ectopic beats (53, 229, 230). The physiologic relationship of PD and MVP is unknown (53). However, PD might intensify MVP, which in turn could contribute to the increased cardiovascular mortality associated with PD. Equally likely, this increased mortality is associated with the typical sedentary lifestyles of PD patients (207).

Some authors (8, 53, 231) believe that most cases of agoraphobia (see below) are complications of PD by the following mechanism: one of the patient's initial panic attacks occurs in a location (e.g., in traffic, a tunnel, a marketplace) in which help is not immediately available. The panic attack then becomes paired in the patient's mind with the site at which it occurred, which the patient then avoids. Many cases of PD do not progress to agoraphobia, however (232).

LABORATORY FINDINGS

Patients who have PD have an increased frequency of certain lab abnormalities. Intravenous infusion over 20 minutes of 0.5 molar sodium lactate (10 mg/kg) induces a panic attack in 70%–100% of PD patients, but not controls (233–235). Placebo does not produce this response in PD patients. In patients for whom lactate induces panic, PET reveals asymmetry of parahippocampal blood flow prior to the lactate infusion (236). Inhaling 5% CO_2 in room air (237, 238), inhaling the beta

adrenergic drug isoproterenol (239), or receiving IV sodium bicarbonate (32) are each more likely to produce panic (in placebo-controlled studies) in PD patients than in controls. In part because PD is readily diagnosed in the office, these tests are not routinely used in everyday practice.

An increased frequency of MRI scan abnormalities (240), particularly in the right temporal horn, occurs in PD patients (40%) compared to controls (10%), a finding that has been associated with benzodiazepine (BDZ) use (241). Of PD patients, 10%–27% have EEG abnormalities that resemble those of epileptics, but these patients should be treated as if they had epilepsy manifested as panic attacks (242).

ETIOLOGY

Genetic and Conditioning Hypotheses

Panic disorder is familial: 25% of first-degree relatives of PD patients have PD compared to 2% of the general population (220). In various studies, MZ:DZ twin concordance ratios are reported as 40:4 and 50:15 (243, 244). This suggests a genetic causal component. To date, no adoption studies have been conducted.

Patients who have PD or phobias are more likely to have anxious and fearful personality disorders (211, 212, 245, 246) that are characterized by heritable traits of high harm avoidance, low novelty-seeking, and high reward dependence (247, 248). Harm avoidance is a tendency to respond strongly to aversive stimuli and to avoid novelty and punishment. Novelty seeking is the tendency towards exploratory behavior and enjoyment of novel stimuli. Reward dependence is the tendency to respond intensely to positive reinforcement and to maintain rewarded behavior. High harm avoidance in anxiety disorders generates high baseline levels of physiologic arousal with a predisposition to being conditioned to aversive external or internal stimuli. Life experience would then determine whether such conditioning would occur (247, 249).

Anatomic and Physiologic Hypotheses

Anatomic areas of interest are the locus ceruleus (LC) (p. 56) and the septohippocampal system. The former contains over half of the noradrenergic (NA) neurons in the nervous system, and over 70% of the brain's noradrenaline (32, 207). Activating the LC leads to the physiology of fight or flight. In animal studies, electrically stimulating the LC produces fear, and ablating it makes the animal less fearful when threatened (250). Drugs (e.g., yohimbine) and other substances (e.g., CO_2 added to room air) that cause LC discharge in animal studies also produce anxiety attacks in healthy persons and in PD patients (251). Drugs (e.g., propranolol, clonidine, morphine, CAs, endorphins, BDZs) that reduce firing of LC neurons also reduce anxiety (207).

The NA and serotoninergic neurons of the septohippocampal system respond to unfamiliar stimuli, drawing on memory to predict the stimulus's effect and then initiating a response. If this system malfunctions, overreaction to stimuli or needless spontaneous firing could occur (252). In animal studies, electrical stimulation of this system produces a fightflight response (252). In PET studies of PD patients, there is increased metabolism in parahippocampal regions (236). On MRI, PD patients are more likely than controls to show temporal lobe abnormalities (32).

Psychoanalytic Hypotheses

Freud identified anxiety as the core issue in neurotic disorders such as PD, phobias, OCD, and neurotic depression (p. 249). He wrote that in neuroses, id impulses threaten the ego, which responds with signal anxiety (p. 86) and then pairs repression, to keep the impulse from conscious awareness, with other defense mechanisms (217–253). In *Studies on Hysteria*, Breuer and Freud described how a woman's incomplete repression of sexual interest in an uncle caused her panic attacks (253).

TREATMENT

Treatment of PD often requires pharmacotherapy and psychotherapy. Cyclic antidepressants (imipramine, desipramine, and chlorimipramine have been systematically studied for PD) and phenelzine block panic attacks effectively (254–259). The benzodiazepine (BDZ) alprazolam (and possibly other BDZs) is also effective, but its risk of dependence indicates it only if CAs, phenelzine, and fluoxetine fail to work (260).

Because PD patients are more likely than affectively ill patients to become jittery when they first take a CA or MAOI, the initial dosage of either should be low (e.g., imipramine 10 mg daily). However, the eventual therapeutic dose will be as high as that for affective disorder (e.g., imipramine 150–300 mg/day, phenelzine 60–90 mg/day) (32). Initial jitteriness does not occur with alprazolam, the eventual dose of which will usually be 3–10 mg/day. The above drugs are safe in the presence of asymptomatic MVP. In fact, imipramine may alleviate MVP (261).

Patients are instructed to reduce caffeine intake and are taught about the physiology of panic, with emphasis on the physiology of hyperventilation and how to control it with slow abdominal breathing techniques. Their predictions about the catastrophic outcomes of panic are reviewed and modified. Most psychotherapies of PD address assertiveness, social relationships, and self-esteem.

In cognitive and behavioral therapies, patients are instructed to maintain diaries about physical sensations and external situations that accompany panic. They are taught to induce physical sensations (e.g., sweating, dizziness) through exercise that elicit a conditioned panic reaction, and then to overcome the situation through controlled breathing and modified cognitions. They receive homework assignments to face external triggering situations (e.g., shopping malls, tunnels) along a gradual progressive hierarchy (262, 263).

In insight-oriented psychotherapy, patients review the psychological triggers of the attacks and their predictions of catastrophe. The childhood genesis of the anxiety (e.g., separation or Oedipally caused anxiety) and the need to repress impulses are also addressed.

During pregnancy, psychotherapy alone is preferable (32). Pharmacotherapy and psychotherapy may work on the same brain receptor sites (264–266).

Phobic Disorders

A phobia is an intense, unreasonable fear of an activity, situation, or object that causes a compelling desire to avoid that activity, situation, or object (53). The term phobia was first used in medicine 2000 years ago in Rome, where hydrophobia, a *realistic* fear of drinking fluids, was identified as a symptom of rabies. (Hydrophobia occurs because the rabies virus often produces diaphragmatic and respiratory muscle spasm when the patient tries to drink, or even *sees* fluids [267]). In 1871, the German neurologist Kurt Westphal identified and named agoraphobia (originally, fear of the marketplace or of public assemblies) and prescribed companionship, alcohol, and use of a cane (268). Another component of phobias is fear of being fearful.

AGORAPHOBIA

Agoraphobia is a fear of a situation in which one could panic, lose self-control (e.g., by fainting, vomiting, urinating, or crying out), and not have prompt access to help. Situations feared by agoraphobics include crowds, theaters, elevators, restaurants, malls, waiting in line, department stores, crowded rooms, barbers' chairs, tunnels, bridges, airplanes, being home alone, leaving home, and leaving the neighborhood. Each agoraphobic fears a unique *combination* of these situations. A person who fears only *one* of these (e.g., elevators) may have a simple phobia, a different disorder.

The agoraphobic has anticipatory anxiety and avoids the feared situations. In its severest form, the patient becomes housebound and relies on friends and relatives or hires persons to perform tasks such as driving children to school. When a patient ventures into feared situations, anxiety is somewhat reduced in the company of a trusted companion.

Although pure PD and pure agoraphobia occur (232), several observations suggest that agoraphobia *may* be a severe form of PD: (1) most agoraphobics have panic attacks independent of anticipating or facing a feared situation; (2) illness onset in many agoraphobics follows an unanticipated panic attack in a previously safe situation, following which the patient fears that and related situations; (3) there is a high prevalence of PD in relatives of agoraphobics; (4) demographic features (e.g., sex ratios, ages of onset) are similar for both; (5) the two conditions respond to the same drugs; and (6) agoraphobics respond to IV lactate with panic and have an increased cooccurrence of MVP (269).

Course and Complications

Illness severity varies among agoraphobics; most do not become housebound. Like PD, the illness also waxes and wanes (18). Depression and substance abuse are common. Over half of agoraphobics experience at least one depressive episode. Agoraphobic symptoms often intensify during depressions (203). One third to one half of alcoholics suffer from social phobia or agoraphobia, suggesting that self-medication of anxiety is causally related to the alcoholism (225, 270).

Epidemiology

The population prevalence of agoraphobia is 1%–2% of men, and 3% of women (32). For PD, the typical age of onset is 18–35 years, with a mean age of 25 years.

Etiologic Hypotheses and Laboratory Studies

Agoraphobia is familial. Twelve percent of relatives (and 9% of first-degree relatives) of agoraphobics have agoraphobia (271, 272). Thirty-two percent of first-degree relatives of agoraphobics have some type of anxiety disorder (271). That mood disorders are more frequent in the relatives of nonanxious controls than in the relatives of agoraphobics (271) suggests that it is *not* a variant of mood disorder. There are no twin or adoption studies. The above data suggest but do not prove a genetic contribution.

In retrospective studies of agoraphobics, an increased occurrence of overprotective behavior by parents (273) and of childhood separation anxiety (274) have been reported. The former could be a parental reaction to an anxious child, however, and the latter a childhood manifestation of agoraphobia (203). Many agoraphobics maintain that they were self-sufficient prior to their illness onset (203).

Treatment

As for PD, treatment of agoraphobia often requires psychotherapy and pharmacotherapy. Initially, housebound patients may require home visits. Patients are taught about agoraphobia as well as about the physiology of panic. The panic component of agoraphobia is addressed as for PD. Essential to the treatment of any phobia is that the patient must face the feared situation (203, 275, 276). In cognitive behavioral therapy for agoraphobia, this is done in a gradual progressive fashion based on a hierarchy of fearfulness of situations constructed by the patient. The patient receives homework assignments according to the hierarchy. Patient groups visit places together. Cognitive distortions concerning loss of self-control, humiliation, and personal safety are addressed.

In psychodynamic therapies, the therapist and patient address concerns about loss of self-control, humiliation, and personal safety, and the patient is expected to face feared situations. The therapist and patient try to identify the childhood genesis of the fear (which often includes separation anxiety), and discuss the secondary gains (the "benefits") of being ill.

Pharmacotherapy is the same as for PD (207).

SOCIAL PHOBIA

Social phobia affects 3%–7% of the population, is equally frequent in men and in women, and is the most common phobia in

men (277, 278). The mean age of onset is 19 years (279). Unlike PD, agoraphobia and *most other psychiatric conditions*, it is *not* familial (280).

Its defining feature is anxiety in anticipation of and during social situations in which the patient perceives (almost always inaccurately) being scrutinized by others who will detect the patient's anxiety (e.g., by noticing the patient's blushing or trembling) and then act disparagingly (207). Feared situations include public speaking, interviews, dating, parties, weddings, dances, eating or writing in public, and urinating in public lavatories (207). Each social phobic fears a unique combination of these situations. For example, one social phobic may skillfully present well-practiced speeches, while avoiding unstructured situations such as parties. Another might enjoy well-chosen parties but refuse to give a talk. As some social interaction is necessary, social phobics develop coping strategies. These include avoidance (e.g., by working at jobs like electronics repair) or direct anxiety reduction (e.g., self-medication with alcohol or anxiolytic drugs).

According to most (not all) studies, social phobics are more vulnerable to alcoholism (280, 281). Nonmelancholic depression also commonly occurs. Compared to PD patients, social phobics are much less likely (less than 10%) to panic during lactate infusions (282).

One treatment is cognitive behavioral therapy in which cognitive distortions about scrutiny and humiliation are addressed and reduced, and in which the patient is guided to face social situations in a gradual, progressive fashion (p. 312). If psychotherapy alone does not cure the condition, MAOIs or fluoxetine can be effective (18). Psychotherapy and pharmacotherapy can be combined. Prescription of beta blocking agents such as propranolol or a BDZ as needed prior to a feared event is only palliative. These drugs may diminish performance by reducing alertness or memory. Also, BDZ may be habit-forming in social phobics, who are at risk for drug dependence.

Table 20.10. Common Simple Phobias[a]

Phobia	Feared Object or Situation
Acrophobia	Heights
AIDS phobia	AIDS
Ailurophobia	Cats
Arachnophobia	Spiders
Claustrophobia	Closed spaces
Cynophobia	Dogs
Hemophobia	Blood
Keraunophobia	Thunder
Ophidophobia	Snakes
Phonophobia	Loud noises
Pyrophobia	Fire
Topophobia	Stage fright

[a]Modified from Andreasen NC, Black DW. Introductory textbook of psychiatry. Washington DC. American Psychiatric Press, 1991.

SIMPLE PHOBIAS

Unlike agoraphobia or social phobia, simple phobias are fears of a very *specific* object or situation (e.g., snakes, thunderstorms, blood). The patient does not become anxious unless he or she is exposed to the phobic situation or anticipates exposure to it. The most common simple phobias are fear of animals; situations such as heights or flying, storms, and speaking on the phone; and blood and injury (18, 32, 53). Virtually anything can be feared. Common simple phobias are listed in Table 20.10.

How much the phobia is disabling depends on the extent to which the phobic person must face the feared situation. Most ophidophobic people who live in large cities experience little or no disability. In contrast, a medical student who has a blood or AIDS phobia requires treatment.

Most persons who have simple phobias view their fear as trivial and simply avoid the feared situation. This partially explains why, despite the lifetime population prevalence for simple phobia of 12.5% (204), it is the primary complaint in only 2%–3% of psychiatric outpatients (206, 283). When persons who have simple phobias seek treatment, often the phobia has existed for years or decades (203). Sometimes the decision to enter treatment follows a change in circumstances requiring exposure to the feared situation (e.g., an ophidophobe must move to a small town).

Simple phobias are more common in females than males by 3:2 (206, 283). Of the phobias, simple phobias are the most likely to have childhood onset. Of the childhood-onset phobias, school phobias and animal phobias are the most common. The mean age of onset of animal phobias is 4.4 years (284). The earlier the age of onset of a phobia, the better the prognosis.

Some simple phobias are acquired by conditioning following traumatic events (285). For example, a fear of driving might follow an auto accident. But most patients cannot recall such an event. Persons who have traits of high harm avoidance with high baseline arousal levels might be predisposed to pair aversive experiences with a fearful response (249).

In psychoanalytic theory, the feared object may represent symbolically a displacement from another feared object. For example, in Freud's case of Little Hans, Hans's fear of horses was a displacement of his fear of his father (286). There may be a phylogenetic basis for some phobias; for example, our distant ancestors may have naturally feared snakes to survive.

A variety of psychotherapies is effective. All require that the patient face the feared situation (18, 53). The most systematically studied of these are systematic desensitization and in vivo exposure (18, 53, 277).

OBSESSIVE-COMPULSIVE DISORDER

Early descriptions of obsessive-compulsive disorder (OCD) were provided by Westphal and the French psychiatrist Etienne Esquirol (1772–1840) (288). The essential symptom is recurrent, irresistible, intrusive thoughts perceived (early in the illness) as illogical or improbable. These are termed obsessions. Common obsessions are depicted in Table 20.11 (53, 289–291). Over half of OCD patients have more than one obsession (290).

Between 75% and 93% of OCD patients also have compulsions (290, 292), which are repetitive actions usually (not always) driven by obsessions. Unfortunately, performing the compulsive act does not relieve the suffering.

Table 20.11. Common Obsessions and Compulsions

Obsession	Example
Daily decisions	What shirt should I wear?
Destructive and injurious behaviors	Self-harm (e.g., jumping in front of a train)
Order and symmetry	Proper placements and arrangements of items
Dirt and contamination	Feces, urine, semen, infection, dirt, dust
Religious and philosophical	Existence of God, extent of the universe, usefulness of religious practices

Compulsion	Example
Washing. Driven by contamination obsession	Incessant handwashing to eliminate dirt or viruses; extreme example: washing garbage
Counting	Counting cards in a collection, tiles on a floor
Checking. Driven by urge to avoid catastrophe	Driving around a block to ensure car did not hit a pedestrian.
Ordering	Rearranging items on a dresser or in a closet

Habitual pleasurable actions (e.g., gambling, sex) are not typically considered compulsions, although possibly they are variants of OCD. Over 80% of OCD patients have more than one compulsion (290). Common compulsions are depicted in Table 20.11. The most common are cleaning (51%), avoiding (51%), repeating (40%), checking (38%), completeness (11%), and meticulousness (9%). About 7%–25% of OCD patients are pure obsessionals; they have no compulsions (291, 292).

There are modest similarities between obsessions and delusions, and between obsessions and phobias. Each may involve fear of an unwanted occurrence. Unlike patients who have delusions, however, early in their illness course OCD patients doubt the accuracy of their troubling ideas. Unlike phobics, who avoid what they fear, OCD patients struggle with their ideas in thought and by compulsions. Sometimes OCD patients have coexisting phobias (53, 293).

Course and Complications

Onset may be insidious or acute (293). Some cases begin as early as 6 years of age. The mean age of onset is about 20 years. Most cases begin before 25 years of age; 75% begin before age 30, and less than 15% begin after age 35 (290, 294, 295). First psychiatric contact is, on average, 7 years after onset (296).

The relation between premorbid obsessive-compulsive personality disorder (p. 275) and OCD is uncertain. Some studies (293, 296,

297) show such a relation. Other studies (214, 215) show more abnormal premorbid personality traits, but not necessarily obsessive-compulsive traits.

Long-term follow-up studies (294, 298, 300) were conducted before the availability of serotonin reuptake blockers (pp. 57, 329). These studies describe a variable course for OCD ranging from phasic with full remission (11%–14%) to fluctuating (24%–33%), to constant and progressive (54%–61% of cases). Total disability with long-term hospitalization is rare. Prognosis is best when (1) premorbid personality is good, (2) onset follows a precipitating event, (3) onset is in adulthood, (4) symptoms are mild, (5) obsessions are more prominent than compulsions, (6) treatment is sought promptly, and (7) the course fluctuates rather than progresses (293, 294, 296, 299, 301). The content of obsessions has no prognostic significance (53). OCD patients have an increased likelihood of having neurologic soft signs (302).

Secondary depression is common (301, 303). Unfortunately, successful treatment of the secondary depression does not usually reduce obsessive symptoms, which have a life of their own. In population surveys, there is a high prevalence of OCD in persons who have PTSD, but the relation between OCD and PTSD is not known (215). Also, certain complications tend *not* to occur. Despite the high frequency of secondary depression, suicide occurs in less than 1% of OCD patients, a low frequency for a major psychiatric illness (53, 295, 301). Also, despite the commonness of obsessions about violent events, in the absence of a coexisting disorder, the likelihood of an OCD patient acting violently is almost nil (293, 294).

Laboratory Studies

Neuropsychologic testing often reveals deficits in nonverbal cognitive functions (304). The EEG shows increased beta activity and decreased alpha activity (p. 198), suggesting that OCD is a hyperarousal state (32). Positron emission tomography often shows increased metabolism in anterior brain areas, the cingulate gyrus, and the caudate nucleus (305, 306). The CT scan often shows ventricular enlargement and reduced caudate volume (307). Magnetic resonance imaging often shows abnormal right frontal T1 values, and T1 asymmetry (right more than left) in orbitofrontal regions, both associated with symptom severity (32).

Epidemiology

Once thought to be uncommon, OCD's population prevalence was recently found to be 2% (216, 307). If so, then many OCD patients receive no psychiatric treatment. Occasionally, the severity of OCD requires that the patient be hospitalized. The prevalence of OCD in adult men equals that for adult women, but boys are more likely to have OCD than girls, the pattern for most child psychiatric disorders (300). OCD is associated with increased SES, educational level, and IQ (294, 298, 299). Compared to the general population, OCD patients (especially men) are much more likely to be celibate (celibacy rates are 40%–50%), to marry later, and to have fewer children. Patients who have OCD are more likely than controls to have histories of abnormal birth events (308).

Etiology

Genetic Hypotheses. Obsessive-compulsive disorder is familial; 7%–10% of first-degree relatives of OCD patients have the disorder, and another 10% have obsessional traits (309, 310). In addition to OCD and obsessive traits, there is also an increased prevalence of other disorders (including Giles de la Tourette's syndrome [p. 276]) in families of OCD patients (311–313). Twin studies reveal heritability. Concordance ratios for MZ:DZ twins have variously been reported at 80–90:50 and 30–60:10–30 (32, 313). Further suggesting a genetic contribution is the increased frequency of type A blood groups in OCD patients (310).

Neuropathologic Hypotheses. Cases of OCD are reported in patients who have temporal lobe epilepsy (p. 47), encephalitis lethargia (a viral infection which affects the basal ganglia), Parkinson's disease (p. 282), Huntington's disease (p. 282), and arteriosclerotic dementias (18, 32, 53, 314, 315).

Biochemical Hypotheses. There is also evidence of an abnormality in serotonin metabolism. The serotonin reuptake blocking agents clomipramine, fluoxitene, and fluvoxamine are all effective in OCD. Symptom reduction is associated with reduction in serotonin metabolites in cerebrospinal fluid and with reduced platelet serotonin (310, 316).

Psychoanalytic Hypotheses. Psychoanalytic hypotheses explain the content of obsessions and compulsions. Conflicts in the Oedipal stage of development lead to regression to the anal stage (p. 136), with increased use of the defense mechanisms (p. 87) of undoing, isolation, reaction formation, and intellectualization (317, 318).

TREATMENT

The most effective treatments of OCD are serotonin reuptake blocking agents and in vivo exposure combined with response prevention (303, 319–323). The pharmacotherapy and behavior modification may be employed singly or in combination. Clomipramine is far better than placebo and other CAs and is effective for most patients (319). Its dosage is gradually built to 150–300 mg per day. Following improvement, the patient should take it for one year and then should taper it over 3 months. If symptoms recur, treatment should be restarted and maintained for another year with another effort at tapering (320). Fluoxitene and fluvoxamine, or the combination of either with buspirone, are also effective, but efficacy is not as well established as it is for clomipramine (321–323).

In vivo exposure (324–326) based on the theory of habituation (p. 74) is conducted in the therapist's office and by homework assignments for the patient with assistance from relatives. In a gradual, progressive fashion, the patient is assigned to experience the provocative situation. Simultaneously the patient is directed not to engage in the compulsive act to counteract the situation (response prevention). For example, a man who has obsessions of dirt and contamination is instructed to carry dirty handkerchief in his briefcase, and directed not to wash his hands.

Expressive/psychodynamic psychotherapies and relaxation training have not proved effective (324). If ECT is given for secondary depressions, it usually does not relieve the obsessions (327). Furthermore, if (as is usually the case in OCD) the secondary depression is nonmelancholic and nonpsychotic, ECT will often be ineffective for the depression itself. If OCD continues to worsen after full trials of the above treatments, surgery by stereotactic cingulotomy is effective in about 30% of patients. This procedure has been used for several decades. Patients in good general health, with supportive families and no disruptive personality disorders, are the best candidates for this procedure. The procedure involves section of cingulate gyrus (p. 35) fibers connecting the limbic system to the prefrontal cortex (328).

GENERALIZED ANXIETY DISORDER

Generalized anxiety disorder (GAD) is diagnosed in the 2.5%–6% of the population who have the chronic anxiety symptoms of worry about daily events, muscle tension, increased vigilance, and autonomic hyperactivity without having anxiety attacks (8, 217, 329); 25% of GAD patients worry about having occasional anxiety attacks (226, 330, 331). The patient worries continually and excessively about day-to-day events but does not have anticipatory anxiety about panicking (329). Although autonomic symptoms (e.g., palpitations, sweating, paresthesias [p. 300]) occur, they are less frequent than in PD (332). The GAD syndrome was first separated from the other anxiety disorders in 1980 (3); thus, research on GAD is relatively sparse.

The most common age of onset is the late teens (332). GAD often occurs in patients who later develop PD (333, 334), in patients who have PD during long intervals when panic attacks are not occurring (333, 335), and in PD patients after they stop having panic attacks (333, 336). Secondary nonmelancholic depressions occur in 37% of GAD patients (332).

POSTTRAUMATIC STRESS DISORDER

Following exposure to a severely stressful event, people naturally experience behavioral symptoms. Symptoms following divorce and bereavement are discussed on pages 141, 152, and 173. Posttraumatic stress disorder (PTSD) is characterized by a specific cluster of symptoms following experience of a profound trauma (e.g., rape, combat, natural disaster, concentration camp) that is unlike the stressful events experienced by most people. The syndrome, most often studied in combat veterans, was labelled shell shock in World War I combatants, and combat neurosis in World War II veterans (337).

The symptoms fit into three categories: reexperiencing the event, social withdrawal, and increased arousal (8). Reexperiencing may occur as nightmares, daydreams, obsessions, hallucinations, illusions, or feeling as if the event were recurring. Combat veterans label these experiences flashbacks. In children, reexperiencing may take the form of repetitive play.

The withdrawal may include avoiding activities associated with the trauma (e.g., movies about war or rape), feeling detached from others (especially those who have not experienced a similar event), or reduced capacity to feel close to others and to enjoy activities. Hyperarousal may appear as insomnia, irritability, hypervigilance, an intense startle response, or severe anxiety in situations resembling the traumatic event.

Course, Comorbidity, and Complications

After experiencing a profound trauma, most people experience *some* PTSD symptoms (8). Of those who develop the full PTSD syndrome, most do so within 2 weeks of the event (18, 338). The majority recover. For example, in one study of rape victims, the percentage who met PTSD criteria at 2 weeks, 1 month, 3 months and 6 months after the assault were 95%, 63%, 46%, and 42%, respectively (339). However, some become chronically ill (338). Good outcome is associated with good premorbid functioning, rapid symptom onset, good social support, absence of concurrent psychiatric or other illness, and no family history of psychiatric illness (18, 340, 341). Age also affects outcome: 80% of severely burned children have PTSD 1–2 years afterward, compared to 30% of burned adults (342).

There is debate about whether PTSD can appear, for the first time, years after the event (delayed PTSD). Many delayed cases are intensifications of mild cases, recurrences of acute PTSD, and delayed help-seeking in chronically ill patients (338, 343).

Many (57%–99%) PTSD patients have coexisting (current and lifetime) psychiatric disorders (338, 344–346). It is not known whether these concurrent illnesses predispose to PTSD, express a common vulnerability, are complications of PTSD, or are independent of PTSD. In the ECA survey (205), OCD often coexisted with PTSD. In all *patient* samples, depression and PD frequently coexist with PTSD (338, 344–346).

In most combat veteran PTSD samples, alcoholism, drug dependence, and sociopathy are common, as are violent, rebellious, and impulsive behavior. However, these are common in young men in general (347, 348). When control groups of combat veterans without PTSD, and age-matched civilian men are studied, these conditions occur as frequently as with combat veterans with PTSD (347, 349). Postcombat violent behavior in veterans tends to occur in those who were violent prior to service (350, 351). When patient samples more representative of the general population in age and sex (e.g., dam disaster victims) are studied, coexisting sociopathy and substance abuse are uncommon. There is, however, a greater tendency for death by suicide and vehicular accidents in Viet Nam combat veterans compared to male civilian controls (352).

Cultural factors also affect comorbidity. For example, alcoholism does not occur in Israeli combat veterans who have PTSD, despite their high comorbidity of depression and PD (353).

Laboratory Studies

Patients who have PTSD show normal dexamethasone suppression, even when depression coexists (354, 355). Lactate infusion induces flashbacks in most PTSD patients with concurrent PD (356). There are no studies of lactate infusion in PTSD patients who do not have PD.

Epidemiology

The ECA study revealed a population prevalence of 1%–1.3%. In that study, 3.5% of persons exposed to civilian or military violence, 3.3% of sexual assault victims, and 20% of wounded Viet Nam combat veterans had PTSD (205, 338). When high-risk samples (e.g., combat veterans, rape victims) are studied exclusively, however, the prevalence of PTSD rises dramatically. For example, it has been asserted that as many as 480,000 American Viet Nam veterans have PTSD (338, 357). There are no known sex or ethnic differences in predisposition. Naturally, there are sex differences in exposure to given stressors (e.g., rape, combat).

Etiology

Many persons exposed to such trauma do not develop PTSD. Whether PTSD will occur and how severe it will be is affected by age at exposure to the trauma, intensity of the trauma, and predisposition to illness (338, 357–361). Among combat veterans, the greatest risk for PTSD is among those who killed noncombatants, participated in atrocities, or were wounded (338). Also associated with increased risk for PTSD are a history of childhood or teenage behavior problems, parental poverty, and preexisting psychiatric illness (338, 340, 341, 357). There could be a familial predisposition. Among American combat veterans who have PTSD, there is an increased prevalence of anxiety disorders in relatives (346). Harder to explain is that compared to Israeli combat veterans without PTSD, Israeli combat veterans with it are more likely to have parents who survived the Holocaust (362).

Treatment

Before publication of PTSD criteria in 1980 there were no systematic treatment studies in PTSD. Coexisting disorders should be treated (18, 32). Alcoholics should be treated in a chemical dependency program prior to treatment for PTSD. Patients who have coexisting depression are good candidates for antidepressant treatment. A broad variety of psychotherapies and pharmacotherapies are used, but efficacy data are only preliminary. Treatments include individual, group, and family psychotherapies, relaxation training, CAs, MAOIs, fluoxetine, carbamazepine, and valproic acid (18, 363).

SOMATIZATION DISORDER

Familiarity with somatization disorder (SD), coupled with willingness to question a patient systematically about symptoms in each organ system (p. 267), sometimes solves a diagnostic puzzle in a patient who has experienced symptoms in multiple systems that have not been explained to the patient's satis-

faction. Until SD is diagnosed, the patient has likely had needless, invasive, and expensive procedures (including surgery), and considerable discouragement and frustration at the lack of an explanation, or an explanation that "it's all in your head."

For a diagnosis of SD, the patient must have experienced at least 13 medically unexplained symptoms from the list in Table 20.12. The symptom has to concern the patient enough to cause him or her to take medication (other than over-the-counter drugs), to change behavior (e.g., to miss work), or to consult a physician (8).

This multisystem, chronic condition that fluctuates in severity was first described by the French psychiatrist Pierre Briquet in 1859 (364). The validity of "Briquet's syndrome" was established by studies conducted in St. Louis in the 1950s (365–367). The original criteria (6, 366) required that the patient have experienced 20–24 medically unexplained symptoms for a probable diagnosis, and 25 or more for a definite diagnosis, from a list of 59 symptoms (Table 20.12).

Course and Complications

Although SD patients usually report that they had some unexplained symptoms during childhood, SD is rarely diagnosable before age 14 years (368). Usually by the time the patient is 25 years of age, SD can be diagnosed (365, 367). If multiple unexplained symptoms have not appeared by age 30 years, SD cannot be diagnosed.

The course fluctuates. Episodes of intense symptoms typically lasting 6–9 months are often followed by periods of relative quiescence typically lasting 9–12 months (369). The condition is lifelong, although (compared to when they were younger) many middle-aged patients consult with doctors less frequently about their symptoms. Perhaps they have learned to tolerate their symptoms better and have become cynical about their care (369).

Patients who have SD perceive themselves as very ill. They report their health as being worse than do patients who have chronic med-

Table 20.12.   Symptoms of Briquet's† Syndrome and of Somatization Disorder*ᵃ

Group 1
Headaches
Sickly majority of life

Group 2
(SD) Blindness
(SD) Paralysis
Anesthesia
(SD) Aphonia (loss of voice)
(SD) Fits or convulsions
(SD) Unconsciousness
(SD) Amnesia
(SD) Deafness
Hallucinations
(SD) Urinary retention
(SD) Trouble walking
Other unexplained "neurologic" symptoms
(SD only) Double vision

Group 3
Fatigue
Lump in throat
Fainting spells
(SD) Visual blurring
Weakness
Dysuria
(SD only) Trouble swallowing

Group 4
(SD) Breathing difficulty
(SD) Palpitation
Anxiety attacks
(SD) Chest pain
(SD) Dizziness

Group 5
Anorexia
Weight loss
Marked fluctuations in weight
(SD) Nausea
(SD) Abdominal bloating
(SD) Food intolerances
(SD) Diarrhea
Constipation

Group 6
(SD) Abdominal pain
(SD) Vomiting

Group 7
(SD) Dysmenorrhea (painful menstruation)
(SD) Menstrual irregularity
Amenorrhea
(SD) Excessive bleeding

Group 8
(SD) Sexual indifference
Frigidity
(SD) Dyspareunia (painful intercourse)
Other sexual difficulties
(SD) Vomiting all 9 months of pregnancy at least once,
   or hospitalization for hyperemesis gravidarum
   (excessive vomiting during pregnancy)
(SD only) Impotence

Group 9
(SD) Back pain
(SD) Joint pain
(SD) Extremity pain
(SD) Burning pains of the sexual organs, mouth, or
   rectum
(SD only) Pain on urination
(SD only) Other pains

Group 10
Nervousness
Fears
Depressed feelings
Need to quit working, or inability to carry on regular
   duties because of feeling sick
Crying easily
Feeling life hopeless
Thinking a good deal about dying
Wanting to die
Thinking about suicide
Suicide attempts

†For Briquet's syndrome, 20–24 medically unexplained symptoms are needed from the list of 59 for a probable diagnosis, and 25 or more are needed for a definite diagnosis.
*For somatization disorder, 13 medically unexplained symptoms are required from the list of 35 symptoms marked (SD) for a definite diagnosis.
ᵃModified from Feighner JP, Robins E, Guze SB, Woodruff RA, Winokur G, Munoz RA. Diagnostic criteria for use in psychiatric research. Arch Gen Psychiatry 1972;26:56-63; and American Psychiatric Association. Diagnostic and statistical manual of mental disorders, 3rd ed, rev. Washington DC: American Psychiatric Press, 1987.

ical conditions such as chronic lung disease (370). Eighty-six percent report that their disability limits their ability to work (369). In the ECA study, 75% of SD patients were not employed full time, compared to 33% of persons who had other psychiatric diagnoses (370).

Logically, then, SD patients are more likely to visit doctors, be hospitalized, and receive needless surgery than the general population. In the ECA study, 95% of SD patients had seen health care providers in the prior 6 months, compared to 56% of the population (371); 45% of these patients had been hospitalized in the prior year compared to 12% of the population (371). On average, SD patients have had 4–5 surgical procedures, compared with two for hospitalized ill control subjects (369–372).

Patients who have SD comprise 27% of women who have hysterectomies for non-cancer-related causes (373), 17%–28% of patients who have irritable bowel syndrome (374), and 12% of chronic pain patients (375). These patients are also more likely to use psychiatric services, and 80%–90% report past depression (369). There is also increased risk for PD, phobias, GAD, OCD, PTSD, and alcoholism (369). Patients diagnosed with SD are more likely than others to marry persons who suffer from sociopathy, alcoholism, and drug dependence (32, 369).

Coexisting personality disorders occur in 47% of SD patients, the most common being avoidant, paranoid, and histrionic and antisocial personality (369, 376–378). Perhaps one third of patients who have conversion disorders (p. 276) have SD (379). SD patients are also prone to making suicide attempts, but completed suicide is rare (380). Although there is no known link of SD to malingering, malingering may occur (381, 382). Surprisingly, although complications are many, life expectancy is not shortened (383).

Signs and Laboratory Findings

The history is usually presented in a dramatic, vague fashion (384). The vagueness is due to mild circumstantiality or tangentiality (p. 192). Often, the patient is suggestible, eager to answer affirmatively when asked about symptoms. This suggestibility *supports* the diagnosis. A history of a symptom is considered positive regardless of whether the doctor believes that the symptom actually occurred (369).

Patients who have SD have lower pain thresholds than do controls (385). There is an increased likelihood of bilateral symmetrical frontal lobe impairment on neuropsychologic testing (386). Neuropsychologic assessment also reveals distractability, difficulty distinguishing target and nontarget stimuli, and failure to habituate (p. 74) to repeated stimuli (387–390).

Are Somatization Disorder and Briquet's Syndrome Identical?

The DSM criteria for SD were designed to simplify its diagnosis. Unfortunately, of a sample of patients diagnosed with either SD or Briquet's syndrome, only 63% received both diagnoses. Thus, the conditions are not identical (391). Because Briquet's syndrome is better validated than SD, Cloninger (391) recommends using Briquet's syndrome criteria.

Epidemiology

Reported prevalences for SD vary. When the diagnosis is made by experienced clinicians, prevalences are reported as higher than when the diagnosis is made by lay interviewers, as in the ECA study (384, 392). This is because a physician is less likely to consider a symptom as medically well explained than is a layperson (384, 392). For example, a physician would be less likely than a layperson to accept the explanation "They told me it might be an ulcer," unless there are additional data (e.g., a history of gastroscopic evidence or classic ulcer symptoms). Thus, in the ECA study, the prevalence of SD is 0.2%–0.3% of the population, compared to a 1%–3.8% prevalence in other studies (384, 393, 394). Somatization disorder is much more common in women than in men. Different studies variously report female to male ratios ranging between 2:1 and 20:1 (369, 371, 395). When it occurs in men, there is an increased likelihood that the patient is seeking compensation (53, 396). It is more common in people of low SES (384).

Etiology

GENETIC HYPOTHESES

Somatization disorder in women is familial. About 10%–20% of female first-degree relatives of SD patients also have SD (369, 384, 391, 397, 398). Male first-degree relatives of women who have SD have an increased prevalence of sociopathy, alcoholism, and drug dependence (397–400). In turn, female first-degree relatives of male convicted felons (most of whom have sociopathy) have an increased prevalence of SD (401). The adopted-away daughters of men with sociopathy have an increased frequency of SD (402, 403). Birth order of SD patients is random. The above family data strongly suggest a genetic component in SD, and, although the phenotypes for SD in women and sociopathy in men differ, they may share the same genotype. In men, SD is not familial (391).

Noted above, many SD patients have histrionic or antisocial personality disorders, which are characterized by heritable traits of low harm avoidance and high novelty seeking. They are more likely to experience what Cloninger labels somatic anxiety, characterized by diverse bodily pains, autonomic disturbance, distractibility and a vague general feeling of alarm not linked to specific stresses (247, 248, 404). Persons who somatize are more likely to have trouble articulating their emotions and more likely to experience emotions as bodily sensations (405).

Adoption studies also reveal that rearing in chaotic homes increases the likelihood of developing SD in biologic children of sociopaths or alcoholics (406). Fifty-five percent of SD patients report having been sexually abused as children, compared to 16% of affective disorder patients (407). Psychodynamically, the inability to identify and articulate emotions may result from denial and repression (p. 87) (408, 409). In learning theory terms, the failure of SD patients to habituate to stimuli (390) is paired with the positive reinforcement of medical attention to symptoms (384).

Treatment

No treatment cures SD. However, patient resentment and suffering can be reduced by the following strategy (370, 384, 410). Once the diagnosis is established, the patient should be taught about SD and its course. Some patients are relieved to hear what is the first cohesive explanation of their lifelong problem. Care should be orchestrated by one primary physician who knows the patient well, and the number of physicians who see the patient should be minimized. The patient should be taught a relaxation procedure and be told that most symptoms will subside spontaneously. If consultation must be obtained, the consultant should be told about the diagnosis. With patient consent, SD should be explained to family members.

Brief, regularly scheduled visits should replace visits responsive to patient symptoms. This reinforces good health and does not reward symptoms. An annual physical exam and routine lab work should be scheduled. The physician should direct the conversation toward the patient's personal life, deemphasizing symptoms.

Patients who have SD can develop other diseases like anyone else. Thus, if a new symptom arises, the pertinent system should be briefly examined, and lab tests kept to a minimum. Medications should be avoided if possible. The patient should try to tolerate symptoms and be praised for doing so.

PERSONALITY DISORDERS

Personality is the composite of individual traits; that is, characteristic behaviors, appearance, attitudes, and styles of relating that are stable over time. Some personality traits are maladaptive. When a person has a group of maladaptive traits that persist throughout life

Table 20.13.   DSM-III-R Personality Disorders

A: Odd or Eccentric Cluster
Paranoid personality disorder
Schizoid personality disorder
Schizotypal personality disorder
B: Dramatic, Emotional, or Erratic Cluster
Antisocial personality disorder (sociopathy)
Borderline personality disorder
Histrionic personality disorder
Narcissistic personality disorder
C: Anxious or Fearful Cluster
Avoidant personality disorder
Dependent personality disorder
Obsessive-compulsive personality disorder
Passive aggressive personality disorder

and markedly impede functioning or cause distress, a personality disorder is diagnosed.

The DSM system divides the personality disorders into three clusters based on common traits: (*a*) an odd or eccentric cluster; (*b*) a dramatic, emotional, or erratic cluster; and (*c*) an anxious or fearful cluster (Table 20.13) (8). A categorical approach to the diagnosis of these disorders would argue that they represent discrete disorders with distinctive presentations, courses, and etiologies. The dimensional approach to personality disorders posits that each is a combination of extremes of independently inherited or acquired traits. In general, severe personality disorders (e.g., paranoid, schizotypal, borderline, antisocial) may represent more discrete (categorical) illnesses, whereas the less severe disorders (avoidant, histrionic, obsessive-compulsive, dependent, passive-aggressive) may be more usefully approached from a dimensional perspective (411). One example of the dimensional approach is that of Cloninger (p. 69), in which personality disorders are viewed as extremes of the traits of harm avoidance, novelty-seeking, and reward dependence (247, 248).

Overlap, Reliability, and Validity of Personality Disorder Categories

Some traits occur in several different disorders. Thus, most patients who receive one

personality disorder diagnosis also receive at least one other such diagnosis (411–414). This blurring of demarcations between diagnoses raises questions about the reliability and validity of each disorder. Except for sociopathy, diagnostic reliability is poor. The kappa value for clinical ability to discern whether a patient simply has a personality disorder, let alone which one, is only 0.41–0.56 (415, 416).

Reports of validity studies for the other disorders began appearing only in the 1980s. As the evidence develops, it suggests only modest validity. Supporting syndromal validity is the following: cluster analyses show cooccurrence of traits within each of the following categories: antisocial, dependent and obsessive-compulsive (417). Follow-up studies reveal stability over time for schizotypal, borderline, and antisocial personalities (18, 413, 418). There are also common patterns of comorbidity between Axis II and Axis I disorders. For example, borderline personality is often associated with mood disorders (18, 419). Axis I disorders tend to be more resistant to treatment when accompanied by personality disorders. On the other hand, improvement in a patient with a personality disorder is more likely when an Axis I disorder coexists.

Epidemiology

Ten to twenty percent of the population have personality disorders (18, 420, 421). Onset is in adolescence or earlier. Late-onset personality disorder suggests an Axis I diagnosis or a coarse brain disease (18). Antisocial, schizoid and obsessive-compulsive personality are more often diagnosed in men, avoidant histrionic, and dependent personality in women. Borderline and schizotypal are equally prevalent in men and in women (18).

Specific Disorders

PARANOID PERSONALITY DISORDER

A 30-year-old political organizer for victims groups considered himself the only righteous man in a corrupt world. He felt justified in committing larceny to avenge perceived exploitation by his landlord, insurance company, automobile warranter, and eventually his therapist whom he left without paying his bill. He said his therapist had been amply rewarded by having access to the patient's unique personality. His inability to consider evidence of motives other than hostile ones ultimately isolated him and greatly impeded his functioning. His suspicion that his wife was unfaithful and that his boss had "ulterior motives" led him to make wild public accusations against each of them, leading to his wife divorcing him and his employer firing him.

People who have paranoid personality are mistrustful, suspicious, hypervigilant, and preoccupied with others' fidelity and trustworthiness. Prevalence of the disorder is unknown. Some evidence supports a heritable link to delusional disorder and schizophrenia (422, 423).

The symptoms can be understood from a psychodynamic perspective as a product of the patient's use of the ego defense of projection (p. 87). Projections rid the patient of unacceptable unconscious wishes (e.g., aggressive or passive wishes) by attributing these wishes to others, making the world threatening and confusing. The paranoid patient's suspicions serve to organize and "make sense" of these threats, now perceived as coming from the outside, thereby restoring to the patient a measure of control. The cost is isolation. The patient's suspicions, usually involving attributions of hostile intent, do not reach delusional intensity.

Suspiciousness makes it hard for these patients to request, and to remain in, treatment. Treatment recommendations call for supportive, nonconfrontational psychotherapy. Although low-dose antipsychotic medication may alleviate acute anxiety, medication is generally resisted by the patient as a challenge to the patient's autonomy (424). Compliance depends on establishing an alliance between patient and doctor.

SCHIZOTYPAL PERSONALITY DISORDER

Schizotypal personality disorder (STPD) is a relatively new diagnostic category that de-scribes a syndrome of odd but not quite psychotic symptoms. It was previously termed latent or ambulatory schizophrenia. Schizotypal traits include mild emotional blunting, mild thought disorder, magical thinking, or odd beliefs (not shared by others in the person's community) such as clairvoyance and telepathy, eccentric behaviors (e.g., unusual mannerisms) and lack of friends or confidants (except first-degree relatives) (8, 32). Patients also function poorly in the workplace, if they work at all. There is an increased risk of STPD among the family members of schizophrenics (32, 425–427). STPD patients also exhibit the impaired eye pursuit movements commonly found in schizophrenics (32, 428).

Patients who have STPD and patients with schizoid personality both exhibit aloofness. STPD is distinguished from schizoid personality disorder (see below) by the clinical prominence of the above behavioral oddities in STPD in contrast to the prominence of signs of aloofness in schizoid patients.

Treatment aims at bolstering the patient's fragile grasp on reality and facilitating social ties through supportive psychotherapies and rehabilitative settings (411, 429, 430). Expressive/psychodynamic psychotherapies that induce regressions (p. 87) are poorly tolerated. Low-dose neuroleptics may be useful in reducing symptoms and signs (431). Overall prognosis for social functioning is poor (418).

SCHIZOID PERSONALITY DISORDER

The schizoid personality disorder person is cold, aloof, and indifferent. Traditionally, such persons have been distinguished from those who have avoidant personality disorder by a deficient motivation for relationships in the former and fearful avoidance of relationships in the latter. Over the course of the illness, the schizoid patient retreats from social relationships into solitary activity and thought, often involving inanimate and mechanical themes or fantasies of fame and power. Psychotherapy involves efforts by the therapist to be warm but nonintrusive, to help the patient connect feelings to behavior, and to help the person understand the actions and motivations of others. An excellent outcome is one in which the patient finds a job and other roles in which his or her skills are appreciated, but at a comfortable distance for the patient (432).

ANTISOCIAL PERSONALITY DISORDER

The earliest descriptions of sociopathy are attributed to the British psychiatrist James Prichard (433) and the American psychiatrist Benjamin Rush (434). Sociopaths are callous, lack remorse, and are selfish. Many are superficially charming (making them good "con artists"), but this charm readily gives way to irritability when their needs are unmet. They learn minimally from experience (435). Sociopathy begins in childhood (436) and continues throughout life. In middle age or late life, those who are criminals tend to commit fewer crimes. Life expectancy is shortened by accidents, homicide, and consequences of substance abuse (437, 438).

Given these traits, the associated behaviors are easy to understand. In childhood, they include truancy, running away from home, starting fights, using a weapon in fights, committing rape, vandalism, firesetting, habitual lying, burglary, robbery with confrontation of a victim (e.g., mugging, extortion, armed robbery), and cruelty to animals (8, 53).

In adulthood, common behaviors include not working when jobs are available, abandoning jobs, committing felonies (whether arrested or not), frequent fighting, abusing or neglecting family members, marital infidelity, habitual lying, malingering, using aliases, and reckless behavior such as drunk driving (8, 53). About three quarters of convicted felons are sociopaths (438, 439). Associated behaviors include promiscuity, prostitution, unwanted pregnancy, veneral disease, conversion disorder (p. 276), and suicide attempts (53).

In a nonjudgmental, sensitively conducted interview, most sociopaths readily report their antisocial behaviors. Partly for this reason, these behaviors can be objectively identified, contributing to the realibility of the diagnosis (18). However, the personality traits (e.g., cal-

lousness) are what is central to the diagnosis (18, 440). There are callous, selfish people who habitually misuse others, but who do not meet the diagnostic criteria. They, too, are sociopaths.

Many sociopaths have a mesomorphic build, a motorcycle-gang style of dress, tattoos, needletracks, and a swaggering gait. The callousness, lack of remorse, superficial charm, and irritability are observable. Some sociopaths (especially those who are alcoholic) may cry and express guilt about a prior action, but then repeat similar actions (53). Many sociopaths maintain that past mistreatment justifies their behaviors and convey a sense of entitlement (441). On lab testing, sociopaths have an increased frequency of nonspecific EEG abnormalities (442) and reduced autonomic responsivity (measured by galvanic skin responsivity to sweating) to guilt-evoking stimuli such as contemplating a crime (443).

EPIDEMIOLOGY

Sociopathy occurs in 1%–3% of the population (421). In one psychiatric outpatient sample, 15% of men and 3% of women had this disorder, which is much more common in men than in women (444).

ETIOLOGIC HYPOTHESES

Psychopathy is familial. Also frequent in families of sociopaths are relatives with SD, alcoholism and drug dependence (399, 400, 447). Adoption studies strongly suggest a genetic causal component (53, 402, 446).

Sociopaths tend to marry people who have SD, and are sociopaths, alcoholics, and drug dependent. This nonrandom (assortative) mating contributes to illness in children (447). Most sociopaths are reared with one or both parents absent because of death, separation, or divorce (53, 448, 449). Children are often exposed to abusive or neglectful parenting, which generates resentment, leaves needs unfulfilled, and provides poor role modeling. Nevertheless, the upbringing of some sociopaths occurs in apparently intact, caring families. This has been explained psychodynamically as the result of vicarious parental enjoyment of the child's behaviors (450).

Treatment

Sociopaths are difficult to treat (18, 53, 411, 420, 429, 435, 451, 452). Most clinicians would agree with Vaillant (452) that "before treatment can begin with a sociopath, the therapist must find a way to deal with the patient's self-destructive behavior. Be it via parole, commitment to a prison hospital, or the ideological grip of (an altruistic movement), real control over behavior is a sine qua non of treatment." Low motivation, lack of trust, and blame of others tend to subvert treatment, whereas anxiety and a capacity for insight are more hopeful signs. Within the constraints of external controls, many sociopaths act responsibly.

> On a long-term chemical dependency unit in a large veteran's hospital, the patients, most of whom meet criteria for antisocial personality disorder, are among the most cooperative in the hospital. As a condition of remaining in the program, early in their hospital stay they must demonstrate self-control in activities that include helping to maintain (e.g., cooking, cleaning) the unit, which is the sole responsibility of the patient group. During the last few months of their 9-month stay, as a condition of discharge, they must obtain and retain jobs in the community, and return to the hospital in the evening. Medical students are routinely assigned to the unit, and patients enthusiastically consent to videotaped teaching interviews. However, this is not the full story. Half the patients on the unit have "chosen" to be admitted there and complete treatment as an alternative to imprisonment. Also, although many remain abstinent from drugs on return to the community, most do not.

In such specialized units, confrontation in group therapies by peers who have similar problems is helpful in addressing conflicts with authorities, establishing an alliance, and diminishing usual defensive patterns based on bravado (32).

On the other hand, during admissions to general hospital units, sociopaths are often disruptive, "preying upon the relative helplessness of other patients." (451) Furthermore, for many sociopaths convicted of felonies, particularly those who have been violent, imprisonment is the only option, if only to protect the community.

BORDERLINE PERSONALITY DISORDER

> A 20-year-old student was brought to the emergency room by her parents after they found her cutting her name into her forearm in the hallway outside their bedroom door. She told the psychiatric resident who evaluated her that she did not want to die. She had cut herself because she didn't feel "real," and found the sight of blood exciting and, at the same time, reassuring. She hated life, her parents, and her boyfriend, but she felt much better now that she accepted a referral to an outpatient clinic. Later that night, the resident was called from another emergency room by a doctor who said that the patient had swallowed a small quantity of sleeping pills and now would only speak to the resident whom she described as "my therapist."

The central characteristic of the borderline personality is an intolerance of feeling alone. Patients who have the borderline diagnosis often act dramatically and self-destructively, apparently to provoke rescues that are taken as evidence of the rescuer's love. Their feelings and their relations with other (453) are characterized by instability. Relationships fluctuate between intense, idealizing love and admiration, and violent disruptions with devaluing of others. Moods range widely between rage, boredom, and emptiness. The patient's sense of identity (p. 139) is poorly developed (8, 453–455).

There is an increased occurrence of EEG abnormalities, typically mild slowing, in borderline patients (456). In some (not all) studies, there is an increased likelihood of dexamethasone nonsuppression and a blunted TSH response to TRH (430, 457–459).

The disorder is probably not familial (413). Mood disorders are common in the families of borderline patients. For this reason and because of the tendency to mood swings, neuro-endocrine abnormalities, and responsiveness to mood-stabilizing medications, some authors (419) maintain that the disorder is a variant of affective disorder, but this remains debatable.

Psychodynamic theories focus on deficiencies in ego functions (pp. 90, 91) in borderline patients. These include deficits in tolerance for painful moods (e.g., anxiety and depression) precipitated by separations and crisis, the ability to accommodate loving and hating feelings towards the same person, and the ability to differentiate well between oneself and others. These functions are developed during the process of separation during early childhood. Deficits in these ego capacities in borderline patients suggest disruption of the process by which separation is gradually mastered through identification with caring and consistent parents (453). This disruption can occur in numerous ways: parental inconsistency, neglect, or overinvolvement, or mismatch between infant temperament and parental inclinations. Consistent with this hypothesis are data about the high frequency of violence and sexual abuse in the childhood histories of borderline patients (35, 460).

Psychotherapy alone, or combined psychotherapy and pharmacotherapy, are the standard treatments. To some extent, the borderline diagnosis arose out of efforts by psychotherapists to describe the complications that regularly occurred in psychotherapy. Specifically, the crises that arose, and the alternation between idealizing and devaluing of the therapist, often elicit strong countertransference responses of overinvolvement or withdrawal. Regular supervision or consultation with peers is often helpful to the therapist in treating borderline patients. Also important are regularity and structure in appointment times, fees, and roles (461). In addition to limit-setting, relatively high therapist activity is often helpful. Medications (lithium, carbamazepine, and low-dose neuroleptics) have a limited role in treatment of concurrent depressions or other illnesses (462). Hospitalization may be necessary (38).

NARCISSISTIC PERSONALITY DISORDER

Narcissistic personality disorder patients have an inflated sense of their importance, although their grandiosity does not reach delusional proportions. They view their relations with others as opportunities to be appreciated (463, 464). Any criticism or evidence that contradicts the patient's inflated self-esteem can precipitate rage or despair. This grandiosity has been explained psychodynamically as a means of protecting a highly vulnerable sense of self-esteem (463, 464). These patients are usually seen in outpatient practices where thay are treated with psychoanalysis and psychoanalytic psychotherapies.

AVOIDANT PERSONALITY DISORDER

A 30-year-old single woman, an office worker, soft-spoken, modest, serious, scrupulously polite, and attentive to her appearance, refuses all invitations to office functions where she might be "in the spotlight," declines team sports where she fears she will be judged overweight, and investigates but avoids further job training because she might "seem stupid."

Patients diagnosed with this disorder are introverted, avoiding situations and relations that present risks of rejection, embarrassment, criticism, or arousal. They strive to reduce severe anxiety precipitated by these situations. Avoidant traits are broadly distributed among psychiatric patients. Because avoidant personality disorder overlaps social phobia and may be related to other anxiety disorders (423), the validity of avoidant personality disorder as a discrete illness is uncertain.

DEPENDENT PERSONALITY DISORDER

Dependent personality disorder patients demonstrate extremes of submissiveness and self-doubt. They subjugate their own needs to those of others to obtain emotional support and to have others assume responsibility for decision making. They often present for treatment when circumstances demand independent functioning. Both behavioral and psychodynamic psychotherapies may be useful. The patient's inclination to dependent functioning transfers readily to the treatment setting, where the therapist can occasionally use the patient's wish for approval to facilitate the patient's progress towards more independent, adaptive functioning.

PASSIVE-AGGRESSIVE PERSONALITY DISORDER

A 35-year-old roofer intimates in therapy his frustration at work where he feels his efforts are unappreciated. He mentions in passing that he has been late several times recently, and the previous day he did not go to work because he felt tired. He feels that his girlfriend is pressing him for a commitment to marriage that he cannot give. She prepared a special dinner commemorating the anniversary of their relationship, but he forgot to attend "because I was working late."

He requests early appointments for therapy, and then arrives with a few minutes left in the hour. He accumulates a large unpaid bill. When the therapist confronts him with evidence of the hostility expressed by these actions, he sighs and acknowledges the truth of the therapist's observations. In fact, he describes himself as "passive-aggressive." The therapist often feels frustrated and defeated.

Patients who have passive-aggressive personality disorder demonstrate covert noncompliance with authority. They do so through actions such as dawdling, procrastinating, forgetting, arriving late, and giving less than their best effort. They may whine, complain, or express discontent without being forthrightly assertive or angry. Psychotherapy is the treatment of choice.

HISTRIONIC PERSONALITY DISORDER

Histrionic personality disorder patients are self-dramatizing, flirtatious, and attention-seeking. They are often described as superficial and fragile, and elicit protectiveness or sexual attraction in others. They are seductive but disclaim their own sexual intentions. Family studies find an increased prevalence of somatization, alcoholism, and antisocial personality disorder in relatives (465).

From a psychodynamic perspective, the patient's traits traverse a spectrum ranging from seductive behavior accompanied by guilty repression of incestuous fantasies to sexualization of interactions to satisfy covert dependency needs.

Psychotherapy is the treatment of choice. Like persons who have borderline and dependent personality disorders, these patients attempt to elicit behavior from the therapist that will confirm the patient's fantasies of the therapist's love for the patient. Ultimately, this will disappoint the patient. Two goals of the psychotherapy are to demonstrate the unrealistic nature of the patient's fantasies, and to promote the patient's seeking of alternatives to dramatic and often self-abasing behaviors designed to obtain satisfaction (54).

OBSESSIVE-COMPULSIVE PERSONALITY DISORDER

A 40-year-old bank clerk began each day dreading work because he anticipated that somebody would disrupt the order that he had achieved the day before. He took each new assignment with anxiety and rage until he brought it under control. He rarely delegated work to assistants because he feared they might overlook details, and that these oversights would prove to be his professional undoing.

Patients who suffer from obsessive-compulsive personality disorder are perfectionistic, formal, and intellectualized. They are preoccupied with details, lists, and rules, often losing the main point. Their meticulousness and perfectionism leaves tasks incomplete or delayed beyond deadlines. They are workaholic, taking no leisure. Their speech is excessively detailed (circumstantial).

There is an association between this and obsessive-compulsive disorder, but many persons who have the personality disorder do not develop OCD, and many OCD patients do not have the personality disorder (32, 466, 467). Historically Freud (5, 468) identified a characteristic disorder in which a triad of behaviors—orderliness, parsimony, and obstinacy—occurred together in patients whose

Table 20.14. Selected Other Disorders

Delusional Disorder: A rare condition characterized by well-organized delusions about mundane subjects such as sex (e.g., a delusion of infidelity), money (e.g., a delusion of being cheated out of money), or work (e.g., a delusion about a plot to have the patient fired). Hallucinations may occur, but if they do, they have the same content as the delusions. Crucial is the *absence* of other symptoms and signs (e.g., no emotional blunting, no appetite or weight loss, no formal thought disorder) that would suggest one of the more common psychotic disorders (8, 469, 470).

Schizoaffective Disorder: Some patients simultaneously exhibit symptoms and signs characteristic of both schizophrenia (e.g., formal thought disorder, emotional blunting) and unipolar or bipolar affective disorder (e.g., appetite and weight loss, rapid and pressured speech). It is widely debated whether schizoaffective disorder is (1) a discrete illness; (2) a variant of schizophrenia; (3) a variant of unipolar or bipolar disorder; or (4) an intermediate-severity manifestation of a "unitary psychosis," of which schizophrenia and major affective disorder are themselves variants; in other words, that schizophrenia and the major affective disorders are examples of the same illness (8, 471, 472).

Tourette's Disorder: A condition characterized by motor or verbal tics. Motor tics include involuntary twitching movements of the face, neck, trunk, or extremities. Verbal tics include involuntary grunts, coughs, barks, or words. For some patients, the words spoken are curses (coprolalia). Risk for OCD is increased in families of Tourette's patients (8).

Conversion Disorder: A pseudoneurologic condition whose signs and symptoms incompletely resemble those of neurologic disorders. These include paralysis, numbness, blindness, gait disturbance, and seizures. However, unless a classic neurologic disease (e.g., multiple sclerosis) is superimposed, the physical findings in conversion disorder differ from those found in the classic neurologic disease. For example, persons whose blindness is caused by multiple sclerosis often show optic atrophy (whitening and flattening of the optic disc in the retina), but patients who have conversion disorder do not have optic atrophy. Sometimes, follow up reveals that the original diagnosis of conversion disorder was wrong and that another disease (e.g., lupus erythematosus, psychomotor epilepsy) exists. Conversion disorder is more frequent in patients who have SD or sociopathy. The psychodynamic explanation of conversion disorder is the somatic (e.g., by paralysis of an arm) resolution of a conflict between an unconscious wish (e.g., a wish to strike someone) and a counterwish (this wish is unacceptable and merits punishment) (473–475).

histories were remarkable for prolonged struggles around toilet training. Psychotherapy is the treatment of choice for this personality disorder.

OTHER SELECTED DISORDERS

As explained at the chapter's beginning, this text cannot cover all of the several hundred psychiatric disorders listed in the DSM-III-R. Table 20.14 includes a brief description of four other conditions (469–475) mentioned elsewhere in the book but not discussed within this chapter.

21/Dementia and Delirium

Frederick S. Sierles, M.D.

<table>
<tr><td>

OBJECTIVES

GENERAL OBJECTIVE: Given a patient examination, ascertain whether the patient is demented or delirious and state a diagnostic and therapeutic plan.

SPECIFIC OBJECTIVES:

1. State the common features of dementia and delirium.
2. Discuss the differences between the two syndromes.
3. State the prevalence of each.
4. List the causes of dementia.
5. For each of the following, discuss the neuropathology, etiology, clinical diagnosis, treatment, and course: Alzheimer's disease, multi-infarct dementia, Pick's disease, Huntington's disease. Parkinson's disease, Wilson's disease, obstructive hydrocephalus, dementias of AIDS (p. 8), Creutzfeldt-Jakob disease, progressive multifocal leukoencephalopathy, neurosyphilis, and traumatic dementias.
6. List the causes of delirium.
7. Describe the clinical manifestations of delirium.
8. Discuss the management of delirium.
9. Summarize the psychosocial and environmental management of demented and delirious patients. Specifically, discuss the objectives of management, specific strategies during the hospital stay, and management once the *demented* patient returns home.

</td></tr>
</table>

Syndromes of focal, localized brain disease (e.g., Wernicke's aphasia) were presented in Chapter 3. When the brain is *diffusely* affected, dementia or delirium occurs.

COMMON FEATURES

In both of these common syndromes, the diffuse dysfunction is manifested by impaired memory, intellect, and other higher cortical functions that might include orientation, language (e.g., aphasia, dyslexia, dysgraphia), complex motor functions (e.g., dyspraxias, mo-

tor perseveration), and recognition of familiar objects (agnosias). These cognitive dysfunctions are documented by screening instruments such as the "Minimental State" examination (p. 194) (1), in which demented and delirious patients usually score between 0 and 23 (mean score for demented patients = 9.7). Hallucinations, delusions, illusions, and mood changes (e.g., lability [p. 193] and irritability) are common but not always present.

Each of the two syndromes has dozens of causes (2–5). Although some diseases (e.g., subdural hematoma, AIDS, thyrotoxicosis) can

Table 21.1.   Differential Diagnosis of Diffuse Cognitive Dysfunction (Dementia versus Delirium)

Characteristic	Dementia	Delirium
Level of alertness and consciousness	Typically normal unless delirium is superimposed	Invariably impaired
Electroencephalogram	Highly variable, ranging from normal, to focal abnormality, to diffuse slowing	Diffuse abnormality is typical (almost always diffuse slowing)
Most common causes	Degenerative, arteriosclerotic, genetic, AIDS	Toxic (including drugs), metabolic, infectious
Onset	Usually insidious	Usually sudden
Circadian rhythm patterns	Variable	Excessive daytime sleep (often >3 hours), diminished nighttime sleep (usually <5 hours)
Course	Slowly progressive downhill course over years in 85–90% of cases, recovery in 10–15%	Full recovery in majority of cases, but death within 3–4 months in 25%

produce either dementia or delirium, the two syndromes are distinguishable on the basis of level of consciousness, most common causes, onset, circadian rhythm changes, electroencephalogram (EEG) findings, course, and prognosis (Table 21.1) (5–8).

DIFFERENCES

In dementia ("falling away of the mind"), the patient's level of consciousness is typically normal (5–8). For most demented patients, onset is gradual. For 85%–90% of demented patients, the course is chronic, with deterioration occurring over multiple years, usually leading to premature death. On average, life expectancy of demented patients is 6–8 years less than for age-matched nondemented patients (9). The remaining 10%–15% have treatable, reversible dementias curable with proper management. Reversible dementias include normal-pressure hydrocephalus, central nervous system tumor or cyst, drug toxicity, subdural hematoma, major depression with melancholia (p. 247), hypothyroidism (p. 196), hyperthyroidism (p. 196), alcoholic dementias (p. 302), and general paresis (6, 10–12).

The cardinal, invariate feature of delirium is altered alertness and consciousness, which either fluctuates in intensity during each day, or occurs only at certain times of day (most often in the evening [sundowning], when the room is dark, visitors have left, the patient is fatigued, and fever from infection may have appeared). Onset is often sudden, and the cause is often toxic or metabolic. The EEG is diffusely abnormal most of the time (diffusely slowed in the vast majority, low-voltage fast waves diffusely in delirium tremens [p. 301] and some other agitated states) (13–15). Most patients recover fully within days to weeks. If recovery is not spontaneous, however, or correct diagnosis and treatment are not provided, dementia or death will follow; 25% of delirious patients die within 3–4 months from the underlying condition or complications (6, 8, 16–18).

Dementia and delirium may coexist in the same patient. For example, a patient who has dementia of the Alzheimer type may develop pneumonia with toxic delirium. Furthermore, being demented increases the likelihood of developing delirium (13, 19, 20). Deafness, certain aphasias, and catatonia may be mistaken for dementia—the patient *seems* to have diffuse cognitive dysfunction, but does not (pseudodementia).

PREVALENCE

Dementia and delirium are not only serious, but they also are very common. The Epidemiologic Catchment Area study (p. 244) (21) found a 1.0%–1.3% prevalence of severe cognitive dysfunction in the general population. Fifteen percent of persons aged 65 years

Table 21.2. Causes of Dementia[a]

Alzheimer's disease

Multi-infarct dementia

Pick's disease

Dementias with basal ganglia disease
  Huntington's disease
  Parkinson's disease
  Wilson's disease
  Progressive supranuclear palsy[b]
  Spinocerebellar degenerations[b]

Hydrocephalic dementias
  Nonobstructive hydrocephalus
  Obstructive hydrocephalus
    Noncommunicating
      Intraventricular blockade
      Obstruction of ventricular outlet foramina (apertures)
    Communicating (normal-pressure hydrocephalus)

Infectious dementias
  Viral dementias
    AIDS (pp. 8 and 9)
      HIV virus infection
      Opportunistic infection
    Creutzfeldt-Jakob disease
    Progressive multifocal leukoencephalopathy
    Paraneoplastic limbic encephalitis[b]
    Subacute sclerosing panencephalitis[b]
    Progressive rubella panencephalitis[b]
  Bacterial dementias
    Syphilis
    Whipple's disease[b]
    Tuberculosis[b]
    Fungal infections[b]
    Parasitic infestations[b]

Traumatic dementias
  Lacerations
  Contusions
  Subdural hematoma
  Epidural hematoma
  Dementia pugilistica

Dementias associated with psychiatric disorders
  Major depression with melancholia
  Schizophrenia

Metabolic and toxic dementias
  Metabolic
    Hypoxia
      Cardiopulmonary disease or failure[b]
      Anemia (see p. 195)[b]
    Uremia and dialysis dementia[b]

Hepatic encephalopathy[b]
Vitamin deficiencies
  B_{12} deficiency (see p. 195)[b]
  Folate deficiency (see p. 195)[b]
  Niacin deficiency[b]
Endocrine diseases
  Hypothyroidism (see p. 196)[b]
  Hyperthyroidism (see p. 196)[b]
  Hyperparathyroidism (see p. 195)[b]
  Hypoparathyroidism (see p. 195)[b]
  Cushing's disease (see p. 198)[b]
  Addison's disease (see p. 195)[b]
Toxic
  Drugs
    Psychotropic agents (see pp. 319–333)[b]
    Anticholinergic agents[b]
    Antihypertensive agents
    Antineoplastic drugs[b]
    Antibiotics[b]
    Alcohol and street drugs (see pp. 290–307)[b]
  Metals
    Lead (see p. 195)[b]
    Mercury (see p. 195)[b]
    Manganese
    Arsenic (see p. 196)[b]
    Thallium[b]
  Industrial agents
    Organic solvents[b]
    Organophosphate insecticides[b]
    Carbon monoxide[b]

Primary and secondary cancers[b]

Multiple sclerosis[b]

[a]Modified from Cummings JL. Neurology and clinical neuropsychiatry. Orlando, FL: Grune and Stratton, 1985: 75–93.
[b]Because there are so many causes of dementia, coverage of each is beyond the scope of this text. These syndromes are discussed in Cummings JL. Neurology and clinical neuropsychiatry, or in Cummings JL, Benson DF. Dementia: a clinical approach. 2nd ed. Boston: Butterworth, 1992.
[c]Page references are for syndromes whose capsule or detailed descriptions appear elsewhere in this text.

and older suffer from dementia (22, 23). Depending on the ward, between 5% and 80% of medical/surgical patients manifest delirium, with the highest risk among elderly patients, children, postcardiotomy, burn and intensive care unit patients, and drug-addicted patients (4, 6, 13, 24, 25). The diagnosis of dementia or delirium is easy if the physician's index of suspicion is high (as it will be on med/surg units) and if cognitive screening tests are used. Unfortunately, clinicians often miss the diagnosis (26–30).

MANAGEMENT OVERVIEW

Care of demented and delirious patients includes determining the cause and whether treating the cause is feasible (e.g., neurosurgical shunting for normal-presssure hydrocephalus, physostigmine for anticholineric delirium), managing the environment (e.g., using night lights, clearly explaining events) to optimize supportive and orienting stimuli and to reduce stimuli that exceed the patient's cognitive capacities (e.g., not asking long, complicated questions), and helping the patient's family cope and find necessary support and social services (2, 5, 6, 31).

SPECIFIC DEMENTIAS

Causes of dementia are listed in Table 21.2. Because there are so many causes, coverage of each is beyond the scope of this text. Some particularly common or illustrative conditions are discussed. For coverage of syndromes not discussed in this text, see Cummings (2), Cummings and Benson (32), and Mayeux (33).

Dementia of the Alzheimer Type

Alois Alzheimer was a neurologist in the hospital directed by Emil Kraepelin (p. 241), a pioneer of psychiatric diagnostic classification. In 1911, Alzheimer described the now-classic symptoms, signs, course, and autopsy findings of a 55-year-old demented woman (34). Definitive diagnosis of Alzheimer's disease requires specific brain tissue findings (e.g., dense concentration of neurofibrillary tangles and senile plaques) by brain biopsy or autopsy. Because brain biopsy is rarely performed, the bedside diagnosis is usually made by the pattern and progression of clinical signs and by excluding other causes (2). When the syndrome is diagnosed clinically, it is best termed dementia of the Alzheimer type (DAT) (2).

DAT is common, constituting 50%–60% of all dementias (35–38). It is one of the leading causes of death in the United States (39).

Rarely, it occurs as early as the third decade, but it is primarily a disease of the elderly. Prevalence increases with age (from 5% of the population aged 65 years, to 20%–50% of the population aged 90 years) (40). Probably it is equally common in women and men. It is familial, sometimes accompanied in the family by Down syndrome (trisomy 21) and blood or bone marrow cancers (e.g., leukemia, Hodgkin's disease, lymphoma) (41, 42). For some DAT patients, there is a specific defect on chromosome 21 (43).

On autopsy, the brain is atrophic (p. 197) with neuronal loss, dense concentrations of neurofibrillary tangles, senile plaques, granulovacuolar degeneration and amyloid angiopathy, especially in the parietal and frontal association areas and the hippocampus (2, 37). The density of neurofibrillary tangles, senile plaques and other degenerations is positively correlated with the severity of dementia (44–46). There is notable destruction in acetylcholine (ACh)-producing cells in the nucleus basalis of Meynert—a finding that led to a cholinergic hypothesis of DAT's pathophysiology (47, 48). Further supporting this hypothesis is that physostigmine (which inhibits ACh breakdown by cholinesterase) transiently improves memory in some DAT patients (49–51). Physostigmine is unsafe for routine daily use, however. A long-acting oral form is being tested for safety and efficacy. Inconsistent with the cholinergic hypothesis is that the ACh precursors choline and lecithin are ineffective for DAT (52–54). Several other transmitters besides ACh are affected (e.g., the noradrenergic locus ceruleus [p. 56] shows neuron loss) (43, 55).

Clinically DAT often progresses through three stages (2, 40). In stage 1, speech becomes empty with a paucity of substantial words and ideas. Words are generated with minimal or no spontaneity (e.g., when the patient is asked to list, within 1 minute, words beginning with the letter *a*), naming and memory (especially short-term memory) are impaired and a depressive mood is common. Lab findings are normal.

In stage 2, cognitive deterioration progresses. Transcortical sensory aphasia (p. 38) occurs. Memory worsens, patients lose their way, and constructional abilities and other praxic functions decline. Symmetrical EEG slowing is common (and highly correlated with extent of cognitive impairment [43, 56]), and some computed tomography (CT) and magnetic resonance imaging (MRI) scans reveal atrophy. Positron emission tomography (PET) and single photoemission computed tomography (SPECT) studies often reveal biparietal hypometabolism and hypoperfusion.

In stage 3, sphincter control is lost, the patient's limbs become rigid and flexed, the patient becomes mute or language is limited to verbigeration (p. 192) or echolalia (p. 41), and custodial care is required. Death follows, usually from aspiration pneumonia (owing to involuntary entry of food or fluid into the trachea) or urinary tract infection. The CT or MRI, PET scan, and EEG (diffuse, symmetrical slowing) are all abnormal. No drugs reverse DAT (2, 43). Preliminary reports suggest that selegiline (a monoamine oxidase inhibitor [p. 329] that selectively inhibits the MAO-B isoenzyme) effects some behavioral improvements (57). Psychosocial interventions (2, 5, 6, 26) are presented on pages 288–291. Delusions, hallucinations, agitation and depression are sometimes responsive to pharmacologic interventions, but the latter do not alter the progess of the illness.

Multi-infarct Dementia

Accumulation of multiple small cerebral infarctions (death of brain tissue owing to inadequate blood supply) produce a multi-infarct dementia (MID) whose deficits are determined by the location of these small strokes (2). MID is the second most common cause of dementia (10% of dementias) (32, 58, 59). Causes are arteriosclerosis related to hypertension, diabetes mellitus, or smoking; emboli from the heart (blood clots extruded from valve surfaces, often from atrial fibrillation [irregularly irregular heartbeat originating in the atria]); inflammatory conditions, or blood disorders (2, 59). Because arteriosclerosis is more common in men than in women, MID is more common in men.

In contrast to DAT, onset is sudden and progression is stepwise, consistent with the suddenness of the small brain injuries. Often the history includes prior hypertension, strokes or transient ischemic episodes (signs of a stroke, disappearing within 24 hours). Common nonbehavioral findings in stroke include hemiparalysis, cranial nerve palsies, and seizures. In contrast to DAT patients, many MID patients have insight into their problem. Signs of arteriosclerosis (e.g., small, hard, yellowish-white plaques in the retinal artery) are often noted elsewhere in the body. The EEG shows slowing at the infarction sites. The CT or MRI often reveals radiolucencies at the infarction sites and sometimes shows dilated ventricles (2, 5, 32, 58, 59).

Hypertension, clotting tendencies, and cardiac arrhythmias should be treated when present (e.g., with antihypertensives, aspirin, low-cholesterol diets or carotid arterial surgery, and antiarrhythmic drugs, respectively). Modify other risk factors such as smoking and obesity (pp. 78–92). Speech therapy benefits aphasic patients and physical therapy helps those who have motor deficits (2, 5).

Pick's Disease

Pick's disease is a degenerative disease of unknown causes that accounts for 5% of dementias. It resembles DAT in its insidious onset in middle or late life, gradual progression through stages with normal lab findings early in the disease, and incurability (2). In contrast to DAT, its pathology is more localized to the frontal and temporal lobes (60), it is more common in men, personality changes are more prominent, and cognitive functions are better preserved initially (61, 62). It does not selectively affect any neurotransmitter (63).

Frontal degeneration in Pick's leads to dorsolateral frontal convexity syndrome (p. 45) with loss of social graces, disinhibition, and avolition (p. 193) and sparing of emotional expression. Its onset after age 40 distinguishes it from schizophrenia. Bilateral temporal degeneration sometimes leads to Klüver-Bucy syndrome (placidity, oral ingestive behavior [including objects other than food], sexual disinhibition [e.g., masturbation in public], and visual agnosia [p. 44] [64, 65]). Midway through the illness, EEG shows frontal and temporal slowing, and the CT and MRI show frontal and temporal atrophy (64, 66).

> A retired teacher was brought to the hospital by his wife, prompted by his urinating in the sink and losing bowel control in public places. He was irritable, raising his fist at any suggestion of fault. His wife did not appreciate his being "more affectionate" than he had been for years. The CT scan showed marked frontal atrophy with a "walnut" appearance.

At autopsy, frontal and temporal lobes show severe atrophy and cells with large globules in the cytoplasm (Pick's bodies) which are pathognomonic (when present, the diagnosis is certain).

Dementias Associated with Disease of the Basal Ganglia

Several dementing diseases show severe, prominent pathology in the basal ganglia, thalamus, and associated frontal cortex. McHugh and Folstein (67), Albert (68), and Cummings and Benson (69, 70) noted that these dementias have a typical cluster of signs (psychomotor slowing with sparse verbal output, mood disturbances [depression especially common], speech and motor abnormalities [e.g., choreoathetosis, tremor], and memory and cognitive abnormality) and termed these subcortical dementias. These include Huntington's, Parkinson's, and Wilson's diseases. Some cases of MID, AIDS (p. 6), and melancholia present as subcortical dementias.

HUNTINGTON'S DISEASE

Huntington's disease is an autosomal dominant disease (chromosome 4) with complete penetrance (all persons who have the genotype have the phenotype if they live long enough) (71–74). Its pathology is marked atrophy of the caudate nucleus and putamen, less prominent atrophy of the globus pallidus, thalamus, and cerebral cortex, and occasional atrophy in the brainstem and spinal cord (60, 75). There is depletion of GABA (p. 58) and reduced number of GABA receptors (76–78). Although each normal caudate nucleus protrudes into its adjacent lateral ventricle, causing concavity of the ventricle's lateral edge, caudate atrophy leads to convexity of the ventricle's lateral edge, giving a pathognomonic butterfly appearance to the ventricles on CT or MRI (79, 80).

In the fourth or fifth decade (mean ages of onset are 35–42 years, range of ages of onset are much broader), the patient develops behavioral abnormalities (dementia, assaultiveness, depression, suicide are each common [81–83]) and choreoathetoid (p. 190) movements. The behavioral abnormalities may appear months or years *before or after* the choreoathetoid movements (71, 84, 85). Haloperidol, lithium, and carbamazepine slightly reduce behavioral symptomatology, but do not alter the gradually progressive, multiyear, ultimately fatal course (71, 84, 85). Treatments designed to restore GABA levels are ineffective (71).

Because the dominant Huntington's gene is completely penetrant, parents of an embryo at risk may request amniocentesis to determine if the embryo is affected, and to consider therapeutic abortion if it is. For teenagers or young adults at risk but who are currently well, a complex blood sampling procedure can identify the genotypic status of those who wish to know (71). Sometimes the phenotype is presaged by mild cognitive impairment in childhood revealed by neuropsychological testing (86).

PARKINSON'S DISEASE

In Parkinson's disease, which affects 1% of the population aged 50 years or older (87), there is degeneration in dopaminergic cells in the substantia nigra and ventral tegmentum (88–90). This produces the classic expressionless face, drooling, stooped posture with flexed extremities, shuffling gait, pill-rolling tremor (rhythmic, with apposition of thumb and forefinger [91]), and bradykinesia (slow movements). Depression is common (92). Dementia (usually with prominent frontal abnormalities and forgetfulness) occurs in 60% of Parkinson's patients (69, 92–94).

The dopamine (DA) precursor L-dopa is helpful, as are to a lesser extent dopa agonists (e.g., bromocryptine and pergolide) and the DA-releasing antiviral agent amantidine (contraindicated in patients who have major psychiatric illness) as well as to a still lesser extent anticholinergic antihistamines (e.g., benztropine) (95). Case reports suggest that for refractory cases, electroconvulsive therapy (ECT) helps (96). Transplantation of autologous (from the patient's own body) adrenal medullary tissues or fetal neural tissue into the caudate nuclei may also help in refractory cases, but the procedure is fraught with complications (97).

WILSON'S DISEASE

In Wilson's disease (98, 99), an autosomal recessive abnormality on the long arm of chromosome 13 leads to deficient excretion of copper in bile (the main problem) and underproduction of the copper-binding plasma protein ceruloplasmin. Consequently, there is accumulation of copper stores with copper deposits in (1) the cornea, usually causing a pathognomonic green or golden-brown Kayser-Fleischer ring (which may be visible only with a slit lamp); (2) the liver, with cirrhosis (p. 190); (3) the blood (with hemolytic anemia [p. 189]); (4) the basal ganglia (especially the putamen), with wing-beating tremor of wide excursion of the upper extremities, dystonia (p. 325) of the upper extremities and mouth, ataxia, psychosis and dementia; and (5) the cerebral cortex (with prominent frontal lobe signs [40]).

Unlike the dementias presented above, Wilson's disease is rare (prevalence = 30 per million population). Onset is usually between 8–20 years of age, but it can begin as early as age 4 and as late as age 60. Early diagnosis and prescription of d-penicillamine (which binds copper and increases its urinary excretion) and a low-copper diet make the difference between early death and a normal length and quality of life.

Hydrocephalic Dementias

In hydrocephalus, there is excess cerebrospinal fluid (CSF) in the cranial cavity manifested by enlarged cerebral ventricles visible on CT and MRI. Causes include brain tissue loss with replacement by CSF (hydrocephalus ex vacuo, nonobstructive hydrocephalus) and blockage of CSF circulation (obstructive hydrocephalus). Obstructive hydrocephalus can be caused by physical obstruction (e.g., by tumor) within the ventricles (noncommunicating hydrocephalus) or impaired absorption of CSF by the arachnoid membrane surrounding the brain, often owing to subarachnoid bleeding. CSF pressure in noncommunicating hydrocephalus is normal (normal-pressure hydrocephalus) (2, 32, 100).

Patients who have obstructive hydrocephalus (6% of dementias [101, 102]) have a classic triad of dementia (with prominent frontal lobe findings), gait disturbance (of many types, including ataxic or marionette-like [2, 40, 103]) and urinary incontinence. Between 40% and 60% improve following ventriculoperitoneal (between the ventricular system and the peritoneal [abdominal] cavity) surgical shunting (104, 105). Long-term prognosis depends on the underlying condition.

Dementias Associated with Infection

Some dementias and deliria are caused by viruses or bacteria.

VIRAL DEMENTIAS

Dementias of AIDS

Acquired immunodeficiency syndrome (AIDS) (pp. 6–15) often causes dementia. The human immunodeficiency virus (HIV) that causes AIDS is neurotropic (has an affinity for nervous tissue), causing many neurologic complications (106, 107). The opportunistic infections and cancers that frequently complicate it account for 30% of its neurologic complications (106).

Creutzfeldt-Jakob Disease

Creutzfeldt-Jakob disease is rare and incurable. It is caused by a slow virus (long delay between infection and symptom onset) that is not visible by electron microscopy and (uniquely) does not evoke an inflammatory response (108, 109). Human-to-human transmission through infected brain tissue can occur during corneal transplantation, from contaminated neurosurgical instruments or EEG depth electrodes, or prescription of growth hormone from cadaver pituitary (110, 111).

In the early stage, patients have fatigue, depression, insomnia, and anxiety. In addition to dementia, motor and sensory signs occur because many parts of the CNS are affected: (1) the cortex, often with aphasia, dysarthria, mutism, or blindness; (2) extrapyramidal system, with rigidity; (3) pyramidal tracts, with increased deep tendon (e.g., knee-jerk) reflexes; (4) cerebellum, with ataxia; and (5) anterior horn cells of the spinal cord, with fasciculations (worm-like contractions within muscles). Myoclonic jerking movements are common. Late in the disease, the EEG shows slowing and triphasic sharp waves (112, 113), but definitive diagnosis can be made only by brain biopsy or autopsy. Death occurs within 3–12 months after onset.

Progressive Multifocal Leukoencephalopathy

Progressive multifocal leukoencephalopathy is an infection of brain and blood by the JC virus, an opportunistic (p. 6) papovavirus (the tiniest virus) infection (114–117) that complicates AIDS (115), blood and bone marrow cancers and granulomatous and autoimmune diseases (118, 119). It causes patches of demyelination (loss of myelin, the lipid-containing substance that ensheathes axons and comprises the brain's white matter) throughout the brain, sparing neurons. Patches of de-

myelination are visible on MRI (preferable) or CT.

Fever appears in only a minority of cases. Neuropsychiatric findings depend on the sites of demyelination. Definitive diagnosis can be made only by brain biopsy or autopsy. There is no effective treatment. It is almost always fatal, but several cases of spontaneous remission (recovery) have been reported (8, 98).

BACTERIAL DEMENTIAS

Any acute bacterial infection of the brain or meninges can produce delirium. If the underlying condition is not properly treated, it causes dementia or death. Several bacterial infections of the brain and meninges (e.g., meningovascular syphilis) have a slow, progressive course that often includes dementia.

Syphilis (Lues)

Syphilis (107, 120–122), almost always sexually transmitted and more common in men than women, is caused by the spirochete (spiral bacterium) treponema pallidum. The initial (primary) lesion is a chancre (an ulcer that has hard, raised margins) at the point of bacterial entry (inoculation) on the genital or perianal skin or mucus membrane, in the pharynx, or in or near the mouth, lips, nipples or fingers. If diagnosed, proper administration of penicillin (107, 123) cures the condition. Untreated, the chancre heals spontaneously within several weeks, leaving a small scar in 30% of cases.

Four to 8 weeks after the chancre appears, untreated patients develop secondary syphilis. This typically includes fever, headache, sore throat, swollen lymph nodes, and rashes. Rashes are usually widespread and symmetrical. Location on the palms and soles (uncommon for rashes of other causes) suggest lues. Rarely are these rashes blisterlike (termed vesicular or bullous) or pruritic (itchy). Wartlike excrescences (condylomata lata) in warm, moist sites (e.g., the perineum) are common. Hepatitis (p. 303) occurs in up to 10% of cases. Occasionally, the eyes, bones or stomach are inflamed. Again, proper penicillin treatment is curative (107, 123). Untreated, the secondary lesions disappear and a long latent period begins.

One to 30 years after the primary infection, tertiary lues occurs, with many possible presentations:

1. A gumma is a granulomatous lesion (a distinctive focal inflammatory lesion, as seen in TB or leprosy) that can affect any organ, including the brain.
2. In syphilitic aortitis, the ascending aorta or the ring around the aortic value cusp is affected, producing an aortic aneurysm (a sac-like bulge of the aortic wall, which could rupture) or aortic valvular insufficiency (which may cause death in heart failure).
3. In tabes dorsalis, the posterior (dorsal) columns of the spinal cord are affected, impairing position and vibratory sensation with a broad-based, unsteady gait, proneness to chronic destruction (Charcot's joints) of large joints and to urinary incontinence or erectile dysfunction. Sudden, severe lightning pains (cause unknown) may occur in the abdomen or extremities.
4. In luetic myelitis, various other portions of the spinal cord are affected (e.g., the corticospinal tracts with Erb's paralysis).
5. In general paresis, there is a frontal lobe meningovascular infection with dementia (with frontal lobe signs) or psychosis (often resembling mania) (107, 120–122).
6. Argyll-Robertson pupils (small, irregularly shaped, and unresponsive to light, but responsive when the patient's gaze is transferred [accommodates] from a distant point to your finger placed 12 inches from the patient's nose) are common when the brain is affected (91).

Although primary syphilis is common (often predisposing to or coexisting with AIDS), general paresis is now rare owing to penicillin treatment of primary and secondary syphilis.

If a pregnant woman develops syphilis, the fetus is at risk for congenital syphilis, causing stillbirth or multiple-system disease.

Diagnosis of syphilis is supported by examining the plasma for antibodies to cardiolipin (not specific for treponemal infection) in the Venereal Disease Research Laboratory (VDRL) or rapid plasma reagin (RPR) tests, and confirmed by finding anti-treponemal antibodies in the fluorescent treponema antibody (FTA) test. Diagnosis of neurosyphilis is confirmed by finding characteristic abnormalities in the CSF (including a positive VDRL) obtained by lumbar puncture. All pregnant women should have plasma VDRL testing on diagnosis of the pregnancy and several months later.

Penicillin is highly effective for all forms of syphilis except latent syphilis, cardiovascular syphilis, and tabes dorsalis. For these three, penicillin should *still* be prescribed to prevent further progression of the disease (107, 123).

TRAUMATIC DEMENTIAS

Head injury, often sustained in vehicular accidents, is the most common cause of dementia in teenagers and young adults (2, 124). In the elderly, minimal head trauma may cause injury. The frontal and temporal poles are most vulnerable anatomically to trauma, but any part of the brain may be injured.

Injury may take the form of laceration (tearing) or contusion (bruising) of brain tissue, or space-occupying blood clot formation under (subdural hematoma) or over (epidural hematoma) the dural membrane. If acute and severe, these lead to delirium, seizures, coma, and (often) death. If subdural bleeding is slow and unrecognized, and the patient survives, chronic subdural hematoma results, often producing dementia. Predisposing factors for chronic subdurals include age (60 years or older) epilepsy, alcoholism, and being a dialysis patient (125).

Diagnostic suspicion is raised by a history of head trauma followed by loss of consciousness (LOC) (the longer the LOC, the likelier are neurobehavioral consequences such as amnesia), neurologic and mental status abnormalities, and visualization of blood collections (if they do not have the same density [isodensity] as brain tissue) on CT or MRI. In the elderly, minor head trauma without LOC may cause subdural hematomas. Sometimes there is no head trauma history, and diagnosis is made based on clinical suspicion (e.g., risk factors, exclusion of other causes) followed by CT or MRI.

The blood clot, if accessible, should be surgically evacuated. If seizures occur pre- or postoperatively, prescribe an anticonvulsant.

Dementia Pugilistica

Prizefighters sustain repeated blows to the head (some producing concussion, a transient disruption of brain structure and function with momentary LOC). The more prizefights a boxer has, the more likely his CT scan will show atrophy, and the greater the atrophy (126). After years of fighting, many fighters develop a dementia with ataxia and Parkinsonian signs (dementia pugilistica) (127–129).

DEMENTIAS FROM PSYCHIATRIC DISORDERS

Elderly patients who have major depression with melancholia sometimes develop a dementia with psychomotor slowing and bowed posture reversed by cyclic antidepressants or ECT (130). Occasionally schizophrenics (typically those who have emotional blunting, CT scan abnormalities and poor prognosis) have severe cognitive deficits (131–133). In the first half of the 19th century, schizophrenia was called dementia praecox because of its frequent teenage onset and downhill course (134). However, although 50% of melancholics and 75% of schizophrenics show notable cognitive abnormalities on neuropsychologic testing, the vast majority are not demented.

DELIRIUM

Engel and Romano (135) characterized delirium* as a syndrome of brain insufficiency fully analogous to heart, lung, liver or kidney insufficiency. Like these other insufficiencies, delirium has many causes (Table 21.3) leading to a characteristic clinical presentation (i.e., a final common pathway). Typically delirious

---

*The term delirium has over 24 synonyms (e.g., acute brain syndrome, acute confusional state, metabolic encephalopathy) (13).

Table 21.3. Common Causes of Delirium[a]

SYSTEMIC
  Metabolic
    Cardiac insufficiency, pulmonary insufficiency, hepatic failure, renal failure, electrolyte imbalance, malnutrition, vitamin deficiencies, metabolic effects secondary to carcinoma, trauma, infection, and allergic reactions
  Endocrine
    Adrenal insufficiency, Cushing's disease, pituitary insufficiency, diabetes and other causes of hyper- and hypo-glycemia, hyper- and hypo-thyroidism, hyper- and hypo-parathyroidism
  Drug-Related
    Withdrawal syndromes (especially alcohol, barbiturates, sedatives, narcotics), acute and chronic intoxication (especially from steroids, L-Dopa, bromides, alcohol, sedatives, barbiturates, minor tranquilizers, narcotics, and anticholinergics)
CENTRAL NERVOUS SYSTEM
  Vascular
    Embolism, ischemia, hemorrhage, collagen vascular disease
  Trauma
    Concussion, subdural hematoma, hemorrhage
  Tumor
    Primary and metastatic carcinoma
  Infections
    Meningitis, encephalitis (viral, bacterial, fungal spirochetal), abscess

[a]From DeVaul RA, Hall RCW. Hallucinations. In: Hall RCW, ed. Psychiatric presentations of medical illness: somatopsychic disorders. Costa Mesa, CA: PMA Publishing Corporation, 1980.

patients have impaired alertness and attentiveness, requiring you to refocus their attention by raising your voice, calling their name, tapping their shoulder, or reentering their field of vision to continue the interview (6, 8). This inability to attend can be quantified by a letter cancellation test. Read a list of letters (Fig. 21.1) to the patient, who should be asked to tap the table every time you read the letter A. Two or more errors document inattentiveness (136).

Patients may fall asleep in mid-interview. Their sleep-wake schedule is usually abnormal: daytime sleeping sometimes is more than 3 hours, and nighttime sleep often is less than 5 hours (40).

A perplexed facial appearance is characteristic, as are impaired memory, orientation, and many other cognitive functions. Anxiety or agitation with tremor, tachycardia, and sweating

LTPEAOAICTDALAA
ANIABFSAMRZEOAD
PAKLAUCJTOEABAA
ZYFMUSAHEVAARART

Figure 21.1. Letter Cancellation Test: The "A" Test of Attention, Alertness and Vigilance. (Reprinted with permission from Strub RL, Black FW. Organic brain syndromes: an introduction to neurobehavioral disorders. Philadelphia: FA Davis, 1982.)

are common (40). Like other organ insufficiencies, asterixis (rhythmic, flapping coarse tremor of the patient's hand when you extend it at the wrist) may occur (6).

Hallucinations may occur in any sensory modality. Picking at bedclothes or sheets in response to tactile hallucinations of bugs crawling on the skin (formication), visual hallucinations (which occur in 40%–75% of delirious patients), and misinterpretations of stimuli (illusions) are common (5). Correlates of the inability to attend to, perceive, and comprehend the environment include a suspicious mood and delusional ideas (40), as in this example:

> During an episode of delirium, an 89-year-old retired professor developed the notion that the TV in his intensive care unit room was malevolently directing the flow of his urine in his indwelling urinary catheter, and (oblivious to the numerous catheters and IV lines to which he was attached) arose from his bed to change the channel to prevent this.

Irritability, emotional lability and assaultiveness may occur. As in dementias, catastrophic reactions (137) are common. In a catastrophic reaction, patients become angry or panicky (and may terminate the interview abruptly) when they become acutely aware of their cognitive deficits during an interview or conversation.

ASSESSMENT AND TREATMENT

Because the management of dementia and delirium are similar, their management is discussed concurrently.

Diagnosis

For many demented or delirious patients previously unknown, most of their history must be obtained from sources (e.g., family, prior charts) other than themselves. Sometimes the diffuse dysfunction and its cause are already documented. If not, the history, mental status, and cognitive assessments reveal the cognitive dysfunction. Often, the physical exam will narrow the list of possible causes (the differential diagnosis). For example, onset of delirium an hour after starting an intravenous antiarrhythmic drug suggests a drug side effect or a cardiovascular cause.

After a differential diagnosis is established, lab tests are usually selected to finalize the diagnosis. Commonly used tests are listed in Table 17.7 (p. 195). A blanket "dementia work-up" or "delirium work-up" is needless. Sometimes, cognitive dysfunction has multiple simultaneous causes (e.g., abdominal infection from a perforated bowel plus anemia due to blood loss). Lab testing, especially when the patient must leave the ward for it, is stressful. Be efficient (the fewer venipunctures and off-ward trips the better) and provide clear explanation. Prior to CT or MRI scanning (which is time-consuming and requires sustained patient cooperation), a single dose of a benzodiazepine (p. 333) often helps. The legal issue of competence to consent for care is discussed on page 437.

Definitive Treatment

For reversible conditions (10%–15% of dementias, almost all deliria), treat the cause. Treatment of reversible dementias has been discussed. Specific treatment of the many conditions causing delirium is beyond the scope of this book and is covered in standard medical texts (138, 139). These treatments include dose reduction, discontinuation, or antidotes for offending drugs; antibiotics for bacterial infections; surgery for space-occupying lesions; antihypertensives for hypertensive encephalopathy; replacement therapy for vitamin or endocrine deficiencies (including thiamine for alcoholics); and fluids for dehydration. For *some* properly treated delirious patients (especially elderly ones), full recovery occurs only after 1–2 weeks of gradual improvement.

Principles of Psychosocial and Environmental Management

From the outset, psychosocial and environmental management are pivotal for patient cooperation, comfort, safety and successful outcome. Psychosocial care often obviates the need for sedative and neuroleptic drugs, which reduce alertness and can induce or intensify delirium (6). It is negligent practice to rely primarily on sedation or physical restraints to control a delirious patient's behavior solely because staffing and visiting arrangements are inadequate. Delirious or newly admitted demented patients on medical/surgical units should stay on these units, where lab testing and invasive treatments (e.g., IVs) are performed more efficiently, and (in contrast to psychiatric wards) bed rest is routine. Transfer to psychiatry delays care and requires acclimation to a new setting (5). If diagnostic evaluation is complete and invasive treatment or bed rest is not needed, some combative or psychotic demented patients are best treated in psychiatric wards.

Objectives of psychosocial and environmental management of demented and delirious patients include providing supportive, clear, and orienting stimuli and reducing stimuli that overtax cognitive capacities and cause catastrophic reactions (5, 6, 31). For example, dark rooms at night provide no orienting stimuli and intensify illusions. Busy, noisy, cluttered rooms visited by unfamiliar people who do not explain their actions are overstimulating, intensifying anxiety and irritability.

Problems addressed by psychosocial management include disorientation; impaired attention, memory, judgment, insight, and language comprehension; misinterpretation of stimuli with accompanying mistrust; incoordination; and (in many older adults) impaired hearing and vision. If a demented patient is to be discharged home, the patient's illness and the topics presented below should be discussed with the family. Part of educating the family should perhaps include encouraging them to read *The 36-Hour Day* (31) or join a support group such as Alzheimer's Disease and Related Disorders Association. Most demented patients return to the family after initial hospital discharge.

SPECIFIC STRATEGIES DURING THE HOSPITAL STAY

For each patient, trial and error (5) determines which of many suggested interventions are suitable. The unit should establish a simple, predictable routine for meals, medications, procedures and bedtimes. When possible, on each shift the same staff should attend to the patient each day.

Patient's Room

The patient's room should be neat and contain only essential machinery. A room with a window helps orient the patient to diurnal cues (140). If the patient has eyeglasses or a hearing aid, they should be used. A night light should be on at night. A readily visible clock and calendar, and familiar objects (e.g., photos of family, religious articles) kept in the same place can facilitate orientation. A TV or radio responsively tuned at the patient's direction often helps.

Interactions With Patient

Staff and visitors should explain, even narrate, their actions and converse with the patient in brief, understandable sentences (e.g., "I'm leaving for lunch; I'll be back in an hour." Or, "I'm changing your bandage now."). Talking about the patient in his or her presence should be minimized, and if necessary should be conducted in a respectful tone with a presumption that the patient is listening (e.g., "Mr. Smith's blood count is low, so we're giving him packed red cells.").

Praise cooperative behaviors (e.g., "You did that breathing exercise well."). Do not respond with anger or scolding to insults from patients whose brain disease does not permit tact; they are being honest but not intentionally unkind (31).

Staff or visitors can read to the patient from favorite periodicals, and help with other activities (e.g., choosing from a menu) while soliciting the patient's participation in decision making. Encourage patient participation. For example, a patient requiring spoon-feeding may like holding a roll. At times, the patient (and visitor) prefer rest and silence while the visitor remains in the room.

Respect must be accorded the patient. Use titles instead of first names, "you" instead of "we," and conventional (e.g., "Try to sleep") instead of childish (e.g., "Go night-night") terms (40).

Delirious patients "should have a constant attendant both to monitor behavior and to provide reorientation and assurance" (6). Visiting hours should be unlimited or minimally restricted, and staffing of units caring for delirious patients should be maximal. Private duty nursing is not usually covered by insurance. A less expensive way of attending to a patient when visitors and ward staff cannot is a sitter (e.g., a nursing assistant working off-hours) who exclusively performs supportive, reorienting tasks and answers the patient's phone. A less desirable option is placing the patient in a chair next to the nurses station.

Patients need chairs with armrests and high, firm seats, side rails on the bed, and handrails in the bathroom. For many, soup is easier to drink from a mug than spooned from a bowl, and eating finger foods is easier than using utensils. Eating courses presented one dish at a time is easier than eating from a tray with multiple dishes. Someone should offer to season the food. Step-by-step narration or hands-on assistance for some activities (e.g., eating, dressing, standing) may be necessary (31).

Exercise (even passive movement controlled by a staff member) reduces the occurrence of thrombophlebitis (inflamed leg veins prone to clots that may dislodge and travel to the lungs [pulmonary emboli]) or decubitus ulcers (bedsores).

Patients hospitalized for dementia on long-term psychiatric, geriatric, or rehabilitation medicine units enjoy activities that befit their interests and abilities. Accompanied walking, singing, and music listening, and playing simplified games (e.g., having a catch instead of playing baseball) provide pleasure and exercise. Dementia does not require a joyless life (31).

Symptomatic Pharmacotherapy

Occasionally, agitation or irritability (especially when caused by delusions or hallucinations) cannot be managed by psychosocial interventions alone. Then, modest doses of high-potency neuroleptics (e.g., haloperidol or fluphenazine, which have the lowest frequencies of postural hypotension and anticholinergic effects) or of benzodiazepine anxiolytics (p. 333) are indicated.

Discharge Planning

For patients whose dementias are not expected to clear, start discharge planning soon after admission. The extent of a dementia influences the plan. For example, early in DAT, it may suffice for the patient to retire from work. Later, adult day care (p. 451) allows activity, socialization and exercise. In advanced stages, continuous custodial care is usually needed. Families needn't feel guilty about such placement; the patient usually benefits (31).

Neuropsychologic evaluation (pp. 201–211) and occupational therapy consultation can clarify a patient's capacities for activities of daily living (ADLs). The patient is observed in a controlled setting to see if she or he can manage money, dress self, and prepare a simple meal. The nurse can instruct the family about giving baths, handling eating problems, maneuvering a wheelchair, preventing and coping with catastrophic reactions, and addressing other situations.

STRATEGIES ONCE PATIENT RETURNS HOME

General Health

High-fiber diets (vegetables, fruits, whole grain cereal) and fluids reduce constipation. If the patient has nighttime urinary incontinence, fluids should be limited after dinner. Keep medications to a minimum. Exercise is important; prolonged sitting or lying down induces sores.

For elderly patients, routine physical exams are indicated. Correcting minor problems can help dramatically (p. 168). Untreated cuts can be irritating. Minor infections can induce delirium. Patients who wear contact lenses may find glasses easier. If a hearing aid is needed, it should be purchased with the agreement that it can be returned if it does not work out (31).

Home Environment

Like the hospital room, rooms at home should be tidy and well lighted with minimal clutter and objects in the same place. Routines should be predictably regular. Closets should have lights. Rooms used by the patient should have night lights. Reflecting tape on hallway walls between rooms the patient traverses at night may help. When possible, adjacent furniture, floors, and walls should be in bright, contrasting colors without distracting patterns (31).

Sliding glass patio doors should be marked with decals. Family should supervise bathing or showering to some extent. Tub baths are safer than showers, but bubble baths or bath oils make the tub slippery and predispose to vaginal infections. If showering is the only option, grab bars should be installed. Towel racks and soap dishes should be well anchored to wall studs. Soft toilet seats are more comfortable than hard ones (31).

Water heater temperature should be lowered so the patient cannot be scalded. If water heater temperature cannot be controlled, hot water taps can be painted red. Family should check the temperature of bath water.

If the patient can read and the family leaves the person alone at home, notes with reminders and phone numbers may compensate for memory gaps. Commonly used phone numbers should be accessible, unless the patient telephones relentlessly. The family dog or cat usually adjusts to the patient's limitations, remaining a source of pleasure (31).

Activities of Daily Living

Complex tasks can be simplified by breaking them down into steps and narrating them. A person who can no longer tie shoelaces can use slip-on shoes. For someone who once enjoyed organizing and preparing meals, peeling the vegetables or helping to clear the table might be enjoyable. Matching articles of clothing can be placed together.

Driving

Very early in a dementing illness, some patients drive safely under certain circumstances. Many states issue licenses for driving only under specified conditions (e.g., in daylight) that the patient can master. If the patient cannot drive safely, others can drive and try to maintain the person's pride (e.g., "I'll drive today so you can enjoy the scenery").

If the patient cannot drive safely but insists on doing so, the physician's respected role can be enlisted to tell the person not to drive. If this does not work, the car keys can be taken away, or the distributor cap (readily replaced when others need to drive) removed. To ensure that the patient has identification in lieu of a driver's license, many states provide ID cards (31).

Taking Items from Stores

Many stimulus-bound patients take items from store shelves without viewing this as stealing. The patient could be asked to push the shopping cart, and pockets should be checked after the person leaves (31).

Urinary and Fecal Incontinence

Many demented persons have trouble finding the bathroom, especially in an unfamiliar setting, and then urinate or defecate in wastebaskets, flower pots, or closets. Responses include putting a sign on the bathroom door or painting it a bright color, putting a lid on the wastebasket, locking closets, and taking the patient to the bathroom regularly.

If the patient is incontinent at night, postdinner fluid intake can be limited, the person can be awakened once nightly, and a bedside commode can be installed. Following an incontinent episode, the patient's skin should be washed to avoid rashes and infections. Disposable adult diapers are available (31).

Wandering

Demented persons often wander from home and cannot find their way back. The patient should have an ID necklace or bracelet listing the person's name, the family's phone number, and other information (e.g., "memory impaired") that will help if he or she becomes lost (31).

22/Substance Abuse

Donald M. Gallant, M.D.

OBJECTIVES

GENERAL OBJECTIVE: Given a patient examination, state whether the patient has a substance abuse problem and, if so, propose a treatment plan.

SPECIFIC OBJECTIVES:
1. Define substance abuse.
2. Discuss the problem of underdiagnosis of substance abuse.
3. Summarize substance abuse morbidity, comorbidity, and mortality.
4. State the psychosocial correlates of drug abuse, including the denial defense, learning theory, and cultural values.
5. Review the genetics of alcoholism.
6. Summarize strategies for early diagnosis and intervention in substance abuse.
7. List signs, symptoms, and treatment of substance abuse and withdrawal.
8. State the general medical complications of drug abuse.
9. Summarize the treatment of chronic or relapsing substance abusers.
10. Discuss the problem of the substance-abusing physician.
11. Discuss substance abuse prevention.

A substance (alcohol or other drug) abuse problem exists if use of the substance continues despite its interference in any one of five areas of a person's life: (1) academic performance or employment (e.g., missing classes or work); (2) relations with family or friends, who complain about the problem; (3) a social life in which most contacts are substance abusers, which indicates that the drug controls the person's choice of friends (e.g., a marijuana smoker's association with other marijuana smokers indicates that marijuana controls the person's social life); (4) legal problems (e.g., driving under the influence [DUI], arrests for drug possession, child abuse, spouse battering); and (5) medical complications (e.g.,

cirrhosis). Defining substance abuse behavior gives the family more confidence about the need for treatment, and makes it easier to penetrate the substance abuser's denial mechanism, so the person can accept that a problem exists. This vignette portrays an early substance abuser.

Mrs. A. meets her family physician for an appointment to discuss Mr. A, her 34-year-old husband. Their photography business was starting to suffer because of Mr. A's cocaine use. One of his friends told her that he had seen Mr. A snorting cocaine several times at work. On reviewing recent checking accounts, Mrs. A discovered checks made out to cash totaling $4,500. When she confronted Mr. A with his friend's observations and the check stubs, he admitted he occasionally used cocaine, but claimed it was not affecting his work. She replied that he had missed work at the shop on several Mondays after disappearing the previous Sunday evenings.

She also described his increasingly irritable and uncharacteristic behavior: he became short-tempered with the children and had slapped her several times. This had never occurred before he began to use cocaine. He began to associate with a "swinging" crowd, and asked her to attend parties at which cocaine was available. She refused these invitations, and raised the possibility that she and the children would leave him if he did not enter treatment and continued to use cocaine despite her ultimatum. He treated this confrontation flippantly, saying he was only using the drug for recreational purposes. He said he could stop using it whenever he wanted.

In the early phase of substance abuse, Mr. A is already threatened by financial and marital problems and is letting the drug choose his associates. At this stage, he is using a strong denial mechanism, not recognizing an obvious problem, and will seek treatment only if a confronting intervention (p. 298) is used.

The next patient is in the advanced phase, needing immediate treatment.

Mrs. B, the wife of an alcoholic, called for an appointment because her husband was "killing himself with his drinking." Mr. B, a 60-year-old banker, had been given an early retirement from work because of his drinking problem. He had long-standing high blood pressure and diabetes but was not complying with treatment for either condition. Although Mrs. B had called the family physician about her husband's heavy drinking, the physician was not direct enough with her husband about the need for abstinence. This physician, a family friend, had been Mr. B's fraternity brother in college. During the past 2 years, Mr. and Mrs. B's attempts at sexual intercourse had been thwarted by his alcohol intake; they had had no sex during this time.

We arranged a meeting with Mr. and Mrs. B, their two adult children, and Mr. B's ex-boss. During the confrontation, the family told Mr. B they would stop all communication with him unless he sought treatment.

His blood pressure was 180/100. His diabetes was out of control (blood sugar was 385 mg%), and his liver profile showed damage. We advised immediate hospitalization to stabilize his medical condition, to be followed by enrollment in an inpatient rehabilitation program.

In this case, the family and employer had waited too long before insisting that the patient seek help. The patient had lost his job and was seriously ill. On average, an alcoholic's wife waits 7 years after the first gross evidence of alcoholic behavior before seeking help for herself or for her husband (1).

UNDERDIAGNOSING BY PHYSICIANS

Given the ubiquity of fatal substance abuse-caused medical problems (e.g., cirrhosis [degeneration of liver cells with replacement by connective tissue], cardiomyopathy [heart enlargement with inefficient pumping], depression, and violence), and that substance abuse includes smoking, substance abuse is a leading cause of death in the U.S. (2, 9, 11, 12, 39). A working knowledge of substance abuse should therefore be mandatory in all branches of medicine. Time and again, however, substance abuse specialists see a patient who was treated for years in their own hospitals for drug-related illnesses (e.g., hypertension of unknown etiology, pancreatitis [pancreatic inflammation with abdominal pain and elevated serum amylase], hepatitis [liver inflammation caused by toxic effects of alcohol or viral infection from needles], duodenal ulcer, and buccal cavity cancer) without referral to a substance abuse treatment program.

In one university hospital study, all new adult admissions were screened for alcoholism (2). Detection rates by faculty and residents were as low as 25% on surgery and obstetrics/gynecology wards, 25%–50% in neurology and medicine, and 65% in psychiatry. Alcoholic women and patients of high socioeconomic status were less apt to be diagnosed. Pivotally, the extent to which physicians intervened therapeutically with the hospitalized patient correlated with the patient's reduction in alcohol use after discharge (3).

Part of the fault lies in deficiencies in medical education—substance abuse is inadequately taught in many medical schools (4)—and much of the fault lies in denial by faculty and trainees that the problem often is so close to home. Only 5% of first-year medical students smoke cigarettes, but 80% use alcohol at least twice weekly, 16% of whom consume an average of more than 6 drinks each time they drink (5). On questionnaires, these students rated reduced alcohol intake by patients as a less important health-promoting factor than sleep, nutrition, or exercise (5).

Thirty-six percent of a sample of senior medical students had used cocaine at some time, including 17% in the prior year, 6% in the prior month (6). Although these rates were lower than for age-matched controls, acceptance of a drug by future physicians is significant. The implicit denial that their use of cocaine—or alcohol in considerable amounts—is abusive and potentially addictive may lead these future doctors to continue their substance abuse, minimize or not recognize the seriousness of their patients' substance abuse, and not refer patients for treatment.

The same denial is reflected in prescriptions by medical residents for nonpatients (3). Of 335 residents surveyed about psychoactive drug prescriptions (e.g., narcotic analgesics) for nonpatients in the prior 8 months, 23% had written such prescriptions for family members, friends, and fellow house officers. These prescriptions were written *without* proper evaluation or follow-up, an inappropriate and hazardous model for health care.

The frequency of alcoholism-related problems that require hospital admission is high: 32% of men and 8% of women on medical wards, and 26.3% of patients admitted for overnight observation or casualty wards (7). The rate of alcoholism was 28% in one general hospital walk-in clinic and 38% for emergency room (ER) visits (7).

MORBIDITY, COMORBIDITY, AND MORTALITY

The Epidemiologic Catchment Area (ECA) study (p. 244) (8) identified lifetime prevalence (the proportion of persons who ever experienced that disorder) of alcohol abuse and dependence between 11%–16%, and of nonalcohol drug abuse and dependence from 5%–6%, with overlap between these two groups.

The validity of the substance abuse and substance dependence distinction is doubted by some investigators (9). On follow-up, most persons diagnosed as alcohol abusers eventually are diagnosed as dependent. In studying alcohol-related deaths that include homicide and accidents, however, many persons are better classified as abusers.

About 33% of psychiatric disorders are substance abuse illnesses, making substance abuse the most common psychiatric illness in the U.S. (9). Men outnumber women by 2.5 times. Half of adolescent ER visits are substance-related.

Some substance abuse statistics are hopeful; many are troubling. Since 1981, per capita alcohol consumption has been slowly declining in the U.S., and the number of abstainers among men has been rising. Cross-sectional and longitudinal studies from 1980–1987 have shown an age-related decline of alcohol intake among the healthy elderly (10). Yet the proportion of heavy drinkers among men and women in their 20's has been increasing (10). In a reported prospective study of 7,725 middle-aged men, alcohol-related illnesses were the most frequent cause of death (11). The suicide rate among untreated alcoholics is about 300 times that for nonabusers (12).

Although the number of current occasional cocaine users fell by half from 1985–1989, the frequency of use among low-income African- and Hispanic-Americans rose, and medical emergencies from cocaine abuse have increased fivefold. This increase is related to availability of crack, the inexpensive smokeable form of cocaine.

The dual diagnosis (comorbidity) of substance abuse with other psychiatric disorders is increasing (13). The prevalence of substance use in psychiatric patients newly admitted to inpatient or outpatient units is 40%–60%. Two decades ago, it was less than 10% (13). Dual-diagnosis patients present serious treatment problems. They do not respond to treatment for their mental illness alone. Their suicide rate is 100–200 times that of the general population. Violence and suicide are more than twice as frequent among substance-abusing young chronic schizophrenics as among nondrug-abusing schizophrenics. To ensure that diagnoses are made and treatment is begun, all psychiatric patients should have urine drug screens on admission to the hospital and each time they return from pass. Random drug screens should be conducted on wards; in one study, as many as 30% of dual-diagnosis patients used contraband substances on the ward (13).

A primary major depression (p. 246) that coexists with substance dependence frequently requires both antidepressant medication and counseling. Undertreatment of major depression predicts subsequent relapse of the abuse and suicide attempts (12).

Although there are fewer violent deaths among benzodiazepine (BDZ) users, BDZs cause psychomotor and other cognitive impairment. Users of BDZ are more apt to have accidents than nonusers (14).

In the U.S. the mortality rate from cirrhosis decreased between 1981 and 1987, and the percentage of alcohol-related traffic deaths steadied since 1980 (13). Total traffic deaths decreased by 10%.

PSYCHOSOCIAL CORRELATES

There is no single personality type or psychodynamic formulation (p. 200) that explains substance abuse. In most cases, however, denial plays a major role and can complicate treatment even once the abuser admits to the addiction.

> During one family meeting on a rehabilitation unit, the physician was reviewing with a patient his alcohol history in his wife's presence; this included beating his wife, pawning her jewelry, two DUI's, and three arrests for assault. He had been unsuccessfully treated in two other programs. After this review, the physician explained the benefits and risks of disulfiram (Antabuse) (p. 79), which was being prescribed. The patient became angry and said, "I don't need Antabuse or A.A. or N.A. (Narcotic Anonymous). I can make it on my own. I may have a drinking problem, but I can control my drinking."

Yet another example involved a man who requested an interview concerning his 74-year-old father, Mr. C, a successful businessman.

> The son reported that Mr. C had been a controlled social drinker for many years until Mrs. C died 4 years earlier. Since her death, his alcohol intake increased to the point that he was intoxicated daily and was sometimes drunk on the floor when the children visited his home. They hired a housekeeper to care for Mr. C and his home. Mr. C said he fell frequently because of poor eyesight and because the housekeeper misplaced the furniture when she cleaned. He claimed the smell of alcohol on his breath was from his cough medicine.
>
> He started to display inappropriate behavior with the housekeeper (he believed she was flirting with him) during his drinking episodes, and she threatened to quit.

Sometimes physicians can explain the denial mechanism to the patient in this way: "Here you are, a mentally competent person who is certainly not stupid. So you have to deceive (or con) yourself to let yourself continue to drink. You may fool others or minimize the seriousness of your drinking problem, but above all, you have to deceive yourself. You are now an expert at deceiving yourself. You may go on denying your drinking problem until it is too late. You are losing the respect of your children and grandchildren and giving them a memory of you as a drunk, interfering with their good memories of you when they were growing up."

A tragic case of denial involved a young man, Mr. D, who had been sentenced for compulsory administration of Antabuse after two DUI's. He attended several sessions in the outpatient clinic and then dropped out. He subsequently drove and drank, even though his license was suspended. Several months later, his car crashed into another, killing two girls. He was driving on the wrong side of the road, and his blood alcohol level was more than 200 mg%. (The legal limit of intoxication is less than 100 mg% in most states.) For this, he was jailed. His lawyer arranged for Mr. D to enter an inpatient alcoholism treatment program prior to sentencing. During a staffing session, Mr. D made light of the tragedy, claiming the accident would have happened even if he had not been drinking. He talked about the bad roads and the rain.

Patient histories of substance abuse are notoriously unreliable because of denial or dishonesty. Although 63% of cardiac patients reported as long as 18 months after their last heart attack that they no longer smoked, urine assays showed that 20% of them still smoked. Of alcoholics whose urine was (covertly) found positive for alcohol at a clinic, 52% reported they had been abstinent for 24 hours (15).

The learning theory of chemical dependency posits that anxiety or depression leads to substance intake, with a short-term reduction in discomfort. In one study, 33%–50% of drug abusers had preexisting phobic disorders (16). Peer influence is also important. In a study of adolescents, exposure to cigarette or marijuana use by peers predicted use of other drugs 2 years later.

As substance abuse progresses, new psychologic problems emerge in relationships or employment, leading to guilt and diminished self-esteem.

Cultural values and sociologic patterns are important. Labelling alcohol use as deviant and intoxication as shameful contribute to a low prevalence of alcoholism among Mormons and Amish, and may explain the high rate of opiate abuse (cultural acceptance) but low rate of alcoholism (rejection) in the Meo of Southeast Asia (17). Migration affects cultural attitudes. Apaches, who had few problems with alcohol abuse, developed increasing rates of problem drinking, and Sioux and Navajo experienced more deaths from cirrhosis, as they moved from their ancestral villages to integrated (Native American-Euro-American) towns (17). On the other hand, in some Native American reservations, the prevalence of alcoholism is especially high (17a), the reasons for which are complex and beyond the scope of this book. Geographically, the prevalence of substance abuse in the inner cities of the United States as compared to rural areas is 4:3 (9).

Asian-Americans have the lowest rates of heavy drinking and drinking-related problems, possibly reflecting genetic traits, such as the cutaneous skin flush from alcohol ingestion (17).

GENETICS

Alcoholism is three times more prevalent in adopted-away daughters of alcoholic biologic mothers than in adopted-away daughters of nonalcoholic mothers (18). In adopted-away sons of male alcoholics the incidence is seven times greater than in male adoptees of nonalcoholic biologic parents. The genetic transmission of alcoholism appears to be sex linked according to one study which showed that the incidence of alcoholism in daughters of alcoholic men was no higher than in adopted daughters of nonalcoholic biologic fathers (19).

In a follow-up of the male alcoholics in the above study, Cloninger (20) postulated two genetic types: Type 1 with a penetrance (p. 281) of 30% and Type 2 with a striking penetrance of 90% (Table 22.1). Some investigators (8) think Type 2 alcoholism is secondary to (the heritable) antisocial personality disorder. Nevertheless, many substance abusers have no genetic family history of substance abuse. Substance abuse is so complex that it would be wrong to conclude that it is strictly genetic or environmental; it is a final common pathway with multiple simultaneous determinants.

Table 22.1.   Characteristic Features of Two Types of Alcoholism

Characteristic Features	Type of Alcoholism Type 1	Type 2
Alcohol-related Problems		
Usual age of onset (years)	After age 25	Before age 25
Spontaneous alcohol-seeking (inability to abstain)	Infrequent	Frequent
Fighting and arrests when drinking	Infrequent	Frequent
Psychologic dependence (loss of control)	Frequent	Infrequent
Guilt and fear about alcohol dependence	Frequent	Infrequent
Personality Traits		
Novelty seeking	Low	High
Harm avoidance	High	Low
Reward dependence	High	Low

Modified from Cloninger CR. Neurogenic adaptive mechanisms in alcoholism. Science 1987;236:410–416.

EARLY DIAGNOSIS

Interviewing the patient sensitively to obtain a reliable history is the physician's fundamental skill and best diagnostic tool. Like other illnesses, the earlier the patient is diagnosed and treated, the better the prognosis. Several problems may interfere with the interview and the ability to develop a reliable patient history, the most common among which are the patient's or the doctor's denial or embarrassment about discussing substance abuse (15). The physician should be honest, nonjudgmental (except for well-timed praise), and concerned. Such labels as alcoholic or addict should be avoided initially, unless the patient frankly and spontaneously uses these terms.

Some clinicians begin the chemical use history with the least threatening subjects: socially acceptable chemicals (e.g., cups of caffeinated beverages consumed daily, then the number of cigarettes, filtered or unfiltered, then the number of glasses of wine, beer, and ounces of liquor). After each drug is discussed, ask the patient about the effects of the drug behavior on others, starting with coffee (e.g., "Has anyone ever commented that you may be drinking too much coffee? Do you be-

come irritable after four or five cups?"). Then ask the same questions about cigarettes, wine, beer, and so forth. Other clinicians ask more directly (e.g., "Have you or anyone else ever thought you had a drinking problem? Did you ever do any drugs?")

Ask about mood disturbance, impulsiveness, suicide attempts or violence while intoxicated, impaired sexual functioning, or conditioned responses to seductive cues in the environment (e.g., becoming intoxicated after intending to have only one drink with buddies). A history of chemical use by family members may yield additional information.

Beyond the classic signs and symptoms of substance abuse discussed earlier, a physician should be alert to other findings, common early in the illness: frequent headaches, recurrent gastrointestinal complaints, absences from work or school for vague reasons, sudden mood changes, frequent injuries, becoming isolated from nondrug-abusing friends, losing sedative prescriptions, unexplained episodic high blood pressure, needle puncture wounds, nodding off, or lethargy. In adolescents, findings include their association with substance abusers, impulsivity, rebelliousness, deteriorating hygiene, dropping grades, tardiness, absenteeism, and decreasing athletic participation. Early symptoms in physicians include friction with peers, staff, and patients, decreased sense of humor, repeated mistakes in writing orders, forgetfulness concerning orders, workaholic behavior, and overprescription of hypnotics or stimulants.

Common symptoms are included in brief screening questionnaires. The physician should memorize many of these questions for interviews. The shortest is the four-question CAGE: "Have you ever tried to **C**ut down on alcohol intake and not succeeded? Have you ever been **A**nnoyed about criticism concerning your drinking? Have you ever felt **G**uilty about your drinking behavior? Have you ever had to take a drink or **E**ye opener in the morning to relieve the anxiety and shakiness?" The reliability of the CAGE increases if a friend or relative corroborates the patient's history.

Ninety-six percent of 1,350 alcoholics were correctly diagnosed if they answered yes to any of the following 3 questions (derived from the 26-item Michigan Alcoholism Screening Test [MAST]) (21): "Has your family ever objected to your drinking? Did you ever think you drank too much in general? Have others ever said you drink too much for your own good?" Diagnosing alcoholism based only on quantity and type of beverage without assessing psychosocial effects leads to misdiagnosis.

Urine drug screening can be used therapeutically, with immediate feedback to the patient, as well as for early diagnosis and referral or disciplinary purposes. Illegal drug use dropped in Methadone (p. 302) maintenance patients who learned they would receive their urine reports the same day they presented their samples (22). Immediate confrontation of illegal drug behavior and immediate positive reinforcement (p. 76) for a negative screen are more effective than delayed feedback. When a physician tests for disciplinary action (e.g., DUI charges, medical license suspension), precautions to protect the person should be taken. Accusing a patient of substance use without adequate assessment is destructive; false accusations infuriate and permanently alienate patients.

A nonalcoholic skin cleanser should be used prior to venipuncture because swabbing with absolute alcohol can raise the blood alcohol level as high as 18 mg% (23). Urine drug screens by thin layer chromatography lead to both false positives and false negatives; gas chromatography or mass spectrometry is more sensitive. All drug specimens should be split and a confirmation test performed if the first test is positive. To maximize reliability, all laboratories should periodically submit split comparison samples to other labs.

Compounds vary in their detection periods. Amphetamines, short-acting barbiturates, cocaine, opiates, and methaqualone may last from 2–4 days in the urine, whereas BDZs, cannabinoids, and phencyclidine (PCP) remain for up to 30 days.

Other early indicators of alcoholism are an increase in the γ-glutamyltransferase, glu-tamic-oxaloacetic transaminase, glutamic-pyruvic transaminase, or alkaline phosphatase, macrocytosis (enlarged red cells) without anemia, fracture of a rib or thoracic vertebra observed on routine chest x-ray (10–15 times more frequent in alcoholics), and anorexia nervosa or bulimia (which are more frequently associated with substance abuse).

EARLY INTERVENTION

Early intervention with the substance abuser compresses the past crises caused by the substance misuse into a dramatic confrontation designed to penetrate the denial mechanism and persuade the patient to seek treatment. The goal is to help the patient now, not to wait interminably for the person to hit bottom and destroy self, family, health, and job or education.

Mrs. E phoned me about Mr. E, an attorney, who was abusing alcohol and cocaine. Their 11-year-old daughter, Lynn, spent most of her time sulking around the house. Their 16-year-old son, Bill, had been doing well at school and on the football team, but during the last 6 months, his grades dropped and he quit the team. He started staying out late and hardly talked to either parent. According to Mrs. E during our first session, the early years of her marriage were good, but Mr. E's drinking and cocaine use was now ruining their marriage. When Mr. E would return home from his drinking or cocaine binges, he would undress, eat a little, retire to the bedroom, and sleep. Occasionally he would become abrupt and irritated if his children's friends were visiting and playing records or engaging in other normal activities. I suggested to Mrs. E that the children join the next session.

The children validated Mrs. E's history and related several embarrassing situations. Lynn's ballet class graduation was in a local auditorium where a bar was set up in the back of the room. By the end of the graduation, Mr. E was totally intoxicated. When Lynn introduced some friends to him, he made obscene remarks about their tutus, which she found unforgivable. Bill talked about Mr. E never attending the football games and never praising his achievements. He only saw his father shortly after he came home from work and in the morning just before school. The next meeting was with Mr. E's two best friends, the two children, and Mrs. E. Before each of these sessions, Mr. E was notified about the meetings by his wife and invited to attend if he agreed to treatment, which would consist of either inpatient therapy for 6 weeks or outpatient treatment consisting of disulfiram and married couples therapy.

Each time Mr. E was notified about the meetings, he said angrily, "What right does this shrink have butting into our family affairs?". Mrs. E replied that *she* was the patient, and my evaluation had shown that his substance abuse was affecting her emotional state—that was the reason for the invitation.

During the third meeting, Mrs. E, the children, and Mr. E's two friends attended. The friends were surprised to learn Mr. E was using cocaine although they were aware of his abuse of alcohol. They then recalled occasions when he appeared high, and two episodes of nosebleeds. During this meeting, Mrs. E stated that she would leave her husband unless he faced his problem. The children supported her decision, and all present agreed to a confrontation with Mr. E. I asked the group to prepare the list of painful events associated with Mr. E's substance abuse and to rehearse the intervention.

At the fourth meeting, I said that the confrontation should emphasize caring, nonjudgmental statements and honesty. Each person was asked to list the episodes that caused anger, embarrassment, or anxiety. Because there was no severe depression or suicidal intent in Mr. E, it was decided to allow Mrs. E to arrange the confrontation on a Saturday morning at home, shortly after her husband awakened. I was available by telephone if the intervention took an unexpected turn.

The meeting was successful. The participants read their lists to avoid any angry eye contact. (This technique is more comfortable for everyone. The goal is to convince the substance abuser to seek treatment, not to anger him.) He agreed to see me, as long as his friends would no longer be involved. We arranged the meeting with Mr. E, his wife, the children, and a couple, Mr. & Mrs. F, who had successfully completed therapy in our program. I used this couple as an auxiliary therapeutic team to draw some of Mr. E's anger away from me.

During the session, I presented educational material to Mr. E and his family. We reviewed the genetics of alcoholism (the paternal predisposition in his family was strong) and discussed the meaning of Mr. E's blackouts (while sober following a drinking binge, the patient forgets events that occurred during the binge), and his loss of control in cocaine use. Mr. and Mrs. F subsequently did most of the interviewing. Mr. F explained that he had experienced the same type of denial and had felt furious when people asked him to seek help. He presented the denial as a normal accompaniment of substance abuse.

Mr. E was then given the choice of entering our inpatient service for 4–6 weeks, joining our outpatient married couples group while taking disulfiram daily at breakfast with his wife and children present, or facing a separation from them. If he agreed to the help, he also would have to present at least two random urine samples for drug screens weekly. He chose the outpatient program and attended regularly for 12 months. Then, he asked to discontinue the disulfiram and group therapy, because he believed he had progressed sufficiently. During that year, Lynn did well in all phases of her life, and Bill returned to the football team and did well in school.

The members of the married couples group were asked for their opinions of whether Mr. E was ready for discharge. They agreed that he had shown much progress, but that he should continue for 6 more months and use A.A. and N.A. regularly after he terminated from the group. Mr. E was now communicating well with Lynn and Bill, was more involved in their activities, and was confiding well with Mrs. E. Their marriage had improved. Mr. E was discharged after an additional 6 months of married couples' group therapy. Mr. and Mrs. E were told to promptly call me if Mr. E showed any tendency toward relapse.

Physicians should make every effort to intervene early. It could save years of hardship. Delay frequently results in tragedy. Several interventions are possible (15), each of which should be modified according to the physician's and patient's available resources and attitudes about confrontation. At Tulane, the options are inpatient treatment *or* outpatient therapy with disulfiram (p. 79). If the patient does not accept one of these options, the family is asked to temporarily separate from the abuser until the person seeks help. Offering options allows the patient to select a therapy without fully backing the person into a corner. Again, as stated earlier, three attitudes are required: the physician should convey concern, maintain a nonjudgmental attitude, and be honest.

The team approach is used when family or friends have tried unsuccessfully to persuade the substance abuser to discontinue chemical use. Individual attempts at confrontation may only intensify the denial mechanism. In addition, well-intentioned family or friends who lack experience in handling such a problem may do more harm than good, causing angry, defensive reactions. Under these circumstances the team approach generally has a better chance of succeeding (15).

DRUG INTOXICATION SIGNS AND SYMPTOMS

The signs and symptoms of drug intoxication and withdrawal are shown in Table 22.2. As in reactions to other pharmacologic agents, the effects of abused substances on a person depend on many factors: social setting, drug dose, route of administration, absorption rate, hepatic and other organ metabolic rate, excretion rate, tolerance of brain cells to the chemical, and expectations of the person taking the drug.

When an intoxicated patient is semicomatose, hospitalization is required; immediate steps may be needed in the ER to sustain the airway and regular respiration and maintain circulation. In comatose undiagnosed patients, several emergency steps can be taken while waiting for the test results. To rule out and treat severe hypoglycemia (which occurs when a diabetic takes more insulin than necessary), give 50 cc of 50% glucose intravenously (IV) with 100 mg thiamine. If thiamine is not administered simultaneously, the patient may develop additional brain damage, manifested by ataxia (unsteady gait), ophthalmoplegia (paralysis of lateral gaze), and delirium (p. 279) (Wernicke-Korsakoff syndrome). If the comatose patient has needle marks, or intoxication with an unknown drug is suspected, naloxone (a narcotic antidote or antagonist) 0.4–2.0 mg IV repeated at 2–3-minute intervals, 2–3 times, may be lifesaving. If IV naloxone dramatically awakens the patient, observe the person frequently for reemergence of the intoxication once naloxone's effects have dissipated.

Patients may be admitted to ERs with lysergic acid diethylamide (LSD) or phencyclidine (PCP) psychosis. Some hallucinogenic compounds have proven toxic effects to the central nervous system. For example, PCP (and related agents such as ketamine) induces acute brain damage (with interruption of conditioned responses and ataxia) in rats (24). To treat acute intoxication with these hallucinogens (or amphetamines or cocaine), acidify the urine with vitamin C or cranberry juice, which enhances excretion of these compounds by 10–50 times. To calm the patient, IM lorazepam (p. 333) 2–4 mg may be necessary. Because these compounds in toxic dosages may cause seizures, carbamazepine (CBZ) or another anticonvulsant may be necessary.

In prisons, where it is sometimes hard to obtain street drugs, patients may steal from the pharmacy, barter with a convict or corrupt security officer, or trick a physician into prescribing anticholinergic agents (e.g., trihexyphenidyl) for a buzz. Some patients have described smoking compounds that have anticholinergic properties (e.g., doxepin) by emptying capsules on their cigarettes.

WITHDRAWAL SYNDROMES

As a rule, for most substance withdrawal symptoms, the signs are the opposite of intoxication (Table 22.2).

Alcohol

In mild to moderate alcohol withdrawal, it is not always necessary to hospitalize the patient, particularly if the prior history shows no

Table 22.2. Signs and Symptoms of Drug Intoxication and Withdrawal

Substance	Intoxication	Withdrawal
Stimulant	Anorexia, dilated pupils, dry mouth, delusions, euphoria, hallucinations, hyperactivity, hyperpyrexia (high temperature), hypertension, insomnia, irritability, labile mood, mistrust, paresthesia, restlessness, stereotypic behavior, sweating, tachycardia, tremor. Higher doses: delirium, seizures, coma	Constricted pupils, cravings, depression, hyperphagia (increased appetite and eating), hypersomnia (oversleeping), hypotension (lowered blood pressure), muscle cramping, muscle twitching, nasal congestion, nausea
Hypnosedative	Ataxia, clumsiness, cognitive impairment, depressed respiratory rate and reflexes, disinhibition, dizziness, drowsiness, dysarthria, dysmetria (inaccurate pointing), hypotension, hypotonia (decreased muscle tone), lethargy, nystagmus, stupor. High doses: shock, coma, respiratory arrest, coma.	Abdominal cramps, anorexia, anxiety, delirium, fever, flushed face, hallucinations, insomnia, irritability, nightmares, paresthesias (abnormal sensations such as "pins and needles"), postural hypotension, seizures, shock, tremors
Opiate, opioid	Anxiety, cyanosis (p. 189), depressed respirations, euphoria, floating feeling, hypothermia (low body temperature), hypotension, meiosis (narrow pupils), needle marks or tracks, nodding drowsiness, shock (p. 189), tachycardia. Overdose: pulmonary edema (frothy pink fluid in lungs), apnea (absent breathing), coma	Anorexia, anxiety, craving for opiates, diarrhea, dilated pupils, hypertension, insomnia, irritability, lacrimation (tearing), leg spasms, nausea, pains (abdomen, muscles, joints, bones), piloerection (gooseflesh), restlessness, rhinorrhea (runny nose), spontaneous ejaculation, tachycardia, vomiting, yawning

postalcohol convulsions or delirium tremens (DTs/delirium with coarse tremor), if tremor is nonexistent or minimal, and if the patient is not debilitated. A thorough outpatient assessment is necessary, however. Discomfort of the withdrawal symptoms should be alleviated. Early use of medication for withdrawal symptoms may decrease the risk of brain damage during subsequent withdrawal episodes (25). Scales for measuring the severity of the withdrawal symptoms can help in deciding about hospitalization (25). One of these should be used in evaluating any patient admitted to a detoxification unit.

Recent advances have occurred in alcohol withdrawal treatment. For mild to moderate symptoms, clonidine (p. 334) is as good as BDZ but is less sedating. Clonidine has no anticonvulsant or antihallucinogenic properties in man, however, making it unsuitable for severe withdrawal (e.g., delirium, severe agitation, hallucinations, impulsive suicide attempts). The BDZs, effective for alcohol withdrawal since the 1960s, are better for severe withdrawal syndromes. In double-blind comparisons with the anticonvulsant CBZ, however, CBZ was as effective for all components

of the withdrawal syndrome and had fewer side effects (including less sedation) (26).

Although magnesium sulfate and phenytoin have been used for alcohol withdrawal, no prospective studies show their efficacy for alcohol withdrawal (or withdrawal convulsions), and their use is not recommended. Paraldehyde is effective in alcohol withdrawal, but it has an offensive odor and more side effects than BDZ or CBZ.

Withdrawal symptoms occur after 2–3 months of BDZ treatment (e.g., tinnitus [ringing in the ears], muscle twitching, illusions [p. 191]) (27). Increasing numbers of alcoholics also abuse other drugs (polydrug abuse); the younger the alcoholic, the more likely the person is to abuse other drugs, often cocaine or BDZ. The alcohol-BDZ or alcohol-barbiturate patient is even more apt to have withdrawal seizures. Both CBZ and BDZ can treat alcohol-BDZ or alcohol-barbiturate withdrawal, but CBZ is better because BDZ may prolong the withdrawal phase and reinforce continuing dependence (28).

The best proof of opiate addiction is development of an abstinence syndrome (p. 300) after administering naloxone. Treating opiate withdrawal often involves substituting dolophine (Methadone, a long-acting opioid), with starting doses that should not exceed 30 mg/day, and that are slowly tapered by 5 mg/week, until the final 2 weeks, when the dosage should be reduced by 2.5 mg/wk.

Another method is clonidine (p. 334) 0.1 mg four times (QID) the first day, adjusting to a dose as high as 0.2 mg QID during days 2 and 3. An initial order to skip a dose of clonidine if necessary (PRN) should be written if blood pressure falls below 90/60. Clonidine should be slowly withdrawn during days 4–7. Because not all withdrawal symptoms are alleviated by clonidine (insomnia and muscle tension may remain), a hypnotic (e.g., flurazepam) is often used concurrently. Clonidine may be the preferred method, because, unlike dolophine, it does not give positive reinforcement to the patient, making withdrawal faster.

Nonpharmacologic approaches to cocaine withdrawal and maintaining abstinence include covert sensitization (p. 77) (29). Pharmacologic reduction of craving for cocaine includes desipramine (a cyclic antidepressant with alpha-1-DA agonist properties [p. 56], bromocriptine, mazindol, amantadine (which increase CNS DA), and CBZ. No double-blind studies have proved any of these to be superior to another for cocaine withdrawal. Mild cocaine withdrawal can be treated nonpharmacologically, but for severe withdrawal (severe depression and hypersomnia), one of these DA-facilitating agents should be used.

In intoxication with or withdrawal from PCP or amphetamines, the urine should be acidified with vitamin C to about pH 5.5 to increase excretion.

There are several pharmacologic treatments of cigarette cessation with its associated nicotine withdrawal: clonidine, diazepam, and a medicated gum or patch. Of 188 smokers who received clonidine, diazepam, or a placebo, craving in the clonidine group was less than in the other two groups. Long-term abstinence was no greater with clonidine, however (30). Nicotine polacrilex gum requires accompanying behavioral techniques (p. 77) to be effective.

About 30% of American adults drink more than 500 mg of caffeine daily, a dose that can cause anxiety, insomnia, irritability, and chronic fatigue (31). Sudden cessation of a daily dose of 500 mg may result in withdrawal symptoms within 12–24 hours that could last up to a week (31). Physicians should look for caffeine withdrawal when a patient enters the hospital and reduces caffeine intake, because such withdrawal can be mistaken for psychiatric illness or side effects of medications. Treat with caffeine sodium benzoate 500 mg (2 cc) IM.

GENERAL MEDICAL CONSEQUENCES OF CHRONIC SUBSTANCE ABUSE

Common diseases associated with alcoholism are cirrhosis (p. 293); alcoholic hepatitis (fever, enlarged, tender liver, jaundice [yellow skin and sclerae]); pancreatitis (p. 293); gastric or duodenal ulcer; esophageal varices (enlarged esophageal veins from increased pressure in the hepatic portal venous system, with risk for profuse hemorrhage); middle-age onset of diabetes; buccal and GI cancer; hypertension (p. 189); peripheral neuropathies (weakness and atrophy of leg muscles; diminished Achilles tendon reflexes; leg and foot numbness or paresthesias [abnormal sensations, e.g., pins and needles]); myopathies (weakness and atrophy of proximal muscles [shoulders, thighs]; cardiomyopathy (p. 293); cerebral vascular accidents; erectile dysfunction; deficiencies of any vitamin (e.g., scurvy [p. 195], pernicious anemia [p. 196]); and brain disease.

Types of alcoholic brain damage are Korsakoff's psychosis (p. 46) and Wernicke's encephalopathy, the latter a genetically caused inability to use thiamine which, with malnourishment (e.g., alcoholism, starvation, anorexia nervosa), causes diplopia (double vision) from weakness of the external rectus muscles, nystagmus (eye jiggling during lateral movement), unsteady gait, cognitive impairment, and peripheral neuropathy. Other types of damage are cerebellar degeneration (unsteady gait with falling, poor coordination, nystagmus), and central pontine myelinolysis (weakness of facial muscles and tongue, impaired speech and swallowing, emotional lability [p. 193], quadriplegia [four-limb paralysis] with Babinski signs [p. 134], which rapidly progresses over 2–3 weeks, ending in coma and death. Accumulation of acetaldehyde (the initial metabolic product of ethanol) causes much of the above organ damage and dysfunction by binding to proteins. In the liver, acetaldehyde stimulates collagen (connective tissue) production, contributing to cirrhosis.

The following vignette depicts clinical consequences of alcohol-induced tissue damage:

> A malnourished patient arrived in ER with evidence of alcoholism including gynecomastia (breast tissue development in men), rhinophyma (dilated capillaries with thickened skin in the nose), and the odor of digesting alcohol on his breath. He had external rectus palsy with diplopia (double vision), severe ataxia (he fell to the floor whenever he tried to get up from the examining table), disorientation, and abnormally high liver enzymes (a sign of liver disease).
>
> Wernicke's encephalopathy was diagnosed and 100 mg of thiamine IV was immediately administered. Within two hours, the eye palsy and the ataxia disappeared. Subsequent examinations revealed a peripheral neuropathy and confabulation (the patient stated it was 1942, not 1989) as a result of Korsakoff's psychosis, which gradually improved over several months with some residual cognitive deficits.

These patients should be diagnosed promptly. The mortality rate is 50% in untreated Wernicke's patients. In one study of 51 patients with this disease first diagnosed at autopsy, 45 were alcoholics, only 7 of whom had been diagnosed as alcoholic while alive. Many died of brainstem hemorrhage which damaged their cardiac and respiratory nuclei (32).

Brain damage is seen in heavy social drinkers who are not alcoholics; it is manifested on neuropsychologic testing by impaired problem-solving, planning, organizing, learning, and visual-spatial processing (the same cognitive functions affected in alcoholism) (33).

Other than the addictive properties of BDZ, barbiturates, and other sedative-hypnotics, their administration and withdrawal decrease cognitive performance and manual dexterity. This makes driving, handling heavy equipment, and other risky tasks more dangerous. Elderly persons are prone to hip fractures from falls that result from sedative-hypnotics.

Diseases related to IV opioid use are hepatitis (a serious viral liver infection with fever, weakness, appetite loss, tender enlargement of the liver, and elevated serum bilirubin and liver enzymes); skin and lung abscesses; pneumonia (including TB); pulmonary hypertension (foreign substances such as talc in drugs can cause pulmonary infarcts [death of lung tissue from inadequate blood supply] with resultant fibrosis and rigidity of lung structure); severe chronic constipation; bacterial endocarditis (infected heart valves with weight loss, fever, anemia, heart murmurs, heart failure, retinal red spots [Roth's spots]); and meningitis (infection of the membranous outer lining of the brain). The risk of HIV infection (pp. 6–15) among IV drug and crack users is also considerable because of needle sharing and unprotected sex. In one study of narcotic-related deaths in New York City, HIV infection was found in 44% of pneumonia cases, 32% of endocarditis cases, and 69% of TB cases (34).

Overdose deaths can occur with any drug of abuse, most often heroin or cocaine. All these drugs cross the placental barrier, and neonates born to addicted mothers often develop a generic neonatal withdrawal syndrome (hyperactivity, irritability, and gastrointestinal disturbances with consequent metabolic abnormalities).

Cocaine and amphetamines can produce grandiosity, irritability, and suspiciousness, leading to the patient being misdiagnosed as manic or schizophrenic. Even in moderate doses, stimulants such as cocaine can produce cardiac arhythmias, including ventricular fibrillation with sudden death. Some cocaine addicts have convulsions.

The drug MDMA (Ecstasy—3,4-methylenedioxymethamphetamine) and its metabolite MDA (3,4-methylenedioxyamphetamine) selectively destroy brain serotonin receptors in rats and monkeys (35). *If similar destruction occurs in people, it will produce serious mental illness.*

The effects of marijuana smoking on the respiratory system (increase of carboxyhemoglobin and tars) is well known. Long-term behavioral effects can occur. When they entered active duty at 20 years of age, 45,000 Swedish Army conscripts were evaluated for psychologic problems and general health. At a 15-year follow-up, a schizophrenia-like psychosis was 2.4 times more prevalent in conscripts who had reported any cannabis use, and 6 times more frequent among those who had used cannabis more than 50 times by age 20 (36). It was impossible to distinguish the men who had a diathesis (genetic or other predisposition) for schizophrenia potentiated by cannabis from those in whom cannabis caused the schizophrenia-like syndrome. Even if the psychosis occurred in conscripts who had a schizophrenia genotype, however, onset of the psychosis may have been delayed or nonexistent without the cannabis. Given this and the data on MDMA, it is extremely unsafe and unwise for anyone ever to experiment with marijuana, hallucinogens, cocaine, or amphetamines.

By definition, hallucinogens impair perception. This includes hallucinations (p. 192), illusions (p. 191), and synesthesias (distorted double perceptions, such as hearing a smell). In overdose, hallucinogens can cause convulsions and coma.

Chronic use of anabolic steroids by persons preoccupied with their musculature causes multiple complications: skin atrophy and spontaneous bruising; cardiomyopathy (p. 302), myopathy, bone mineral loss with osteoporosis in later years, hypertension, diabetes, and dangerously low serum K+ levels. Mood lability, depression, irritable mania, or atypical psychosis can be precipitated by steroids. When steroid use is suspected, urine should be tested for steroid metabolites.

Nicotine fosters dependence on cigarettes, and cigarette tars cause lung and other cancers. Nicotine also increases heart rate, blood pressure, and stomach acidity. The number of persons injured by involuntary (passive) smoking exceeds the number injured by toxins already government regulated (37). Separating smokers from nonsmokers within the same physical space (e.g., airline cabins) does not reduce passive smoking meaningfully. Children exposed to parental smoking have an increased risk of respiratory and middle ear disease. These data mandate that medical students and physicians protest working in buildings in which smoking is permitted (37).

Effects of Maternal Substance Abuse on the Fetus

The effects of maternal ingestion of alcohol on the fetus and neonate can be devastating, as in fetal alcohol syndrome (p. 130) and behavioral teratogenicity (behavioral deficits without morphologic abnormalities). Ethanol in breast milk has a detrimental effect on motor (but not cognitive) development (38). All these drugs cross the placental barrier. Marijuana or cocaine use during pregnancy also impairs fetal growth. Follow-up of children of drinking mothers reveals cognitive deficits at age 6 years.

TREATMENT OF CHRONIC OR RELAPSING ABUSERS

Self-reporting of substance abuse is unreliable, so that in treatment outcome studies, interviews with significant others, urine drug screens, and alcohol breathalyzer tests should be, but often are not, used (15). Treatment strategies also vary among rehabilitation centers, and treatment success varies according to the patient's support system, employment history, and antisocial personality traits.

Reports on controlled use of alcohol by alcoholics are contradictory (39). Possibly a subgroup of alcoholics with no family history of alcoholism could limit intake to social drinking (15). Until the data are definitive, however, abstinence is the goal. When we encounter patients who refuse abstinence but accept treatment, we offer controlled drinking, or gradual reduction of use, with a signed contract stating that if controlled drinking fails, the patient must abstain. The importance of abstinence from alcohol, even in addicts who are not alcoholics, is shown in a study of social-drinking cocaine addicts (40); resuming social drinking (1–2 drinks/day) predicted relapse of cocaine abuse.

Family meetings, when families or friends are available, are invaluable. If the employer is aware of the problem, that person could also participate, with the patient's written permission. Prognosis is good for patients who live with a caring spouse, have strong interpersonal support, or exhibit a stable work history. Also important are compulsory supervision and use of disulfiram, parole supervision for recently released prisoners, obtaining new social supports, and joining inspirational groups (e.g., Alcoholics Anonymous [AA]). Though there are no controlled studies proving AA's effectiveness, this layperson's group has helped hundreds of thousands of alcoholics, and most U.S. chemical dependency units include AA in their programs.

One objective in treating substance abusers is matching the specific patient with an appropriate treatment. Treatment efficacy studies are summarized in Table 22.3 (30, 41–55). Making policy decisions about treatment without adequate data can be disastrous. Methadone maintenance patients were terminated from a publicly subsidized California program because of its high expense. Patients unable or unwilling to transfer to private programs had poorer outcomes (higher crime rates, more drug abuse) (56).

Buprenorphine is an opioid that facilitates μ receptors while mildly antagonizing the opioid effects. This inhibits the patient from escalating the dosages and has less addiction potential than a pure opioid agonist (e.g., dolophine). The patient can feel comfortable without having the rush of IV heroin. It is less addicting than heroin, and treatment retention is higher than in those programs that expect their patients to be abstinent after withdrawal from heroin.

SUBSTANCE-ABUSING PHYSICIANS

The pharmacologic information gained by medical students leads some to believe they know what dosages of habituating medicines they can use without developing tolerance (requiring progressively increasing doses to obtain the same effect) and addiction. Such omnipotent feelings can lead to addiction.

Although the prevalence of substance abuse among physicians is uncertain, treatment results for doctors who accept care are encouraging. Follow-up of 50 treated doctors revealed that 50% of those under 40 years of age and 72% of those over 40 were practicing and abstinent. Earlier treatment yields better results. The physician's peers must facilitate treatment, however (57). Medical students and practitioners are obligated to do so, for the sake of the ill physician and the person's patients. Delayed treatment can result in tragedy, including suicide, which as reported in one study, happened epidemically in physicians whose licenses had been suspended with no requirement of therapy (58).

There are effective strategies for ill physicians and medical students to obtain help. Naturally, if professional performance is impaired, the ill physician's peers and supervisors must address this administratively (focusing on performance, not intimate details) to protect the physician, his or her patients, and the institution. However, if the doctor is performing competently or on leave of absence complying with treatment, the problem can be addressed by a state's Impaired Physician Committee or an Impaired Medical Student Group (at Tulane, the Phoenix Society) separately from the state licensing board or school dean's office. Some outstanding supervisory physicians and deans are finely tuned to this problem and can ensure that treatment occurs and performance is monitored without inti-

Table 22.3. Treatment Efficacy Studies of Patients with Substance Abuse Disorders

Study	Sample Composition	Design	Duration	Final Outcome	Limitations
Gallant et al. (1968) (41)	Criminal alcoholics on parole from a state penitentiary (N = 20)	Compulsory vs. voluntary treatment	24 mo.	Success rate significantly higher than in voluntary group (54% to 10%)	Small N and relied only on self-reporting and significant others
Gallant et al. (1973) (42)	Skid-row, revolving-door alcoholics (N = 210)	Compulsory vs. voluntary treatment	12 mo.	<10% success rate in both groups	Severely "deteriorated" population
Gallant et al. (1966) (43)	Outpatient alcoholics (N = 110)	Group intake "first contact" session vs. individual session	9 mo.	Group intake more effective than individual session	Only evaluated return rate after initial clinic session
Marlatt and Gordon (1985) (44)	Several studies with alcohol and drug patients (adequate N)	Relapse prevention maintenance strategies with controls	6-12 mo.	Relapse prevention strategies increase the abstinence rate	Reporting mainly relies upon patient and significant others
Miller and Taylor (1980) (45)	Evaluation of behavioral self-control training vs. 3 control groups of alcoholics (N = 41)	Clients provided with a self-help manual were compared to groups of patients provided with counselors	3- and 12-month follow-up	Cost effectiveness of bibliotherapy approach was significant	Small N; evaluations depended mainly on self-reports and lab tests
McCrady et al. (1986) (46)	Evaluation of spouse involvement in therapy with 2 control groups of alcoholics (N = 53)	Three types of spouse involvement were compared	6 mo.	Alcohol-focused spouse involvement plus behavioral marital therapy had highest success rate	Relatively small N in each group; evaluation did not use adequate lab follow-up
Chick et al. (1988) (47)	Newly admitted alcoholic patients (N = 154)	Simple advice vs. relatively intensive counseling	2 yrs.	Extended treatment patients showed greater improvement in behavior within their families and a trend towards less drinking. However, total abstinence rate was not significantly different	Only good prognosis patients were selected; lack of continued weekly follow-up outpatient therapy in the extended group
Helzer et al. (1985) (48)	Patients with alcoholism documented by treatment records (N = 1,289)	Follow-up evaluation of patients and informants	36 mo.	Abstinence rate of only 15%	Treatment was inadequate for 40% of the patients; many poor prognostic features in the initial population. No control group
Glaser and Osborne (1982) (49)	Review of studies of AA results	Survey	—	AA efficacy results are unknown	Authors recommend a series of studies that should evaluate the efficacy of AA and offer guidelines for such a study

Table 22.3.   Treatment Efficacy Studies of Patients with Substance Abuse Disorders *(continued)*

Study	Sample Composition	Design	Duration	Final Outcome	Limitations
Fuller and Roth (1979) (50)	Alcoholics in a Veteran's Affairs hospital setting (N = 128)	Antabuse vs. 2 control groups	12 mo.	Antabuse group had a significantly greater number of abstinent days than the other 2 groups	Select group of patients. In order to be eligible for the study, the patient had to be living with a relative
Azrin et al. (1982) (51)	Alcoholics in outpatient settings (N = 43)	Traditional Antabuse treatment vs. Antabuse adherence training group with job counseling and behavior therapy	6 mo.	The job counseling and behavior group had a significantly greater abstinence rate and better social adjustment	Laboratory measures of drinking were not used; population was rural and results may not apply to urban populations
Kristensen et al. (1983) (52)	Screening program of 11,643 Malmo, Sweden, residents	Top 10% GGT values (p. 298) assigned to either follow-up consultation with positive reinforcement to reduce GGT or an "advice" group	24–60 mo.	Positive reinforcement group had fewer hospitalization days, fewer sick days from work, and 50% lower mortality rate	Homogenous population relatively easy to locate for follow-up
Vaillant (1988) (53)	Alcoholic patients discharged after 10 days of inpatient treatment (N = 100)	Patients were followed for abstinence and rehospitalization rates	10-year follow-up	Predictors of relapse prevention were compulsory supervision, substitute dependency, inspirational groups, and new social support systems	Uncontrolled; data depended on self-reports
de la Fuente et al. (1989) (54)	Alcoholic patients discharged from a 4-week inpatient program (N = 53)	Lithium vs. placebo double-blind	6 mo.	Lithium no better than placebo in producing total abstinence	High drop-out and low compliance rates
Bullock, Culliton and Olander (1989) (55)	Severe, recidivist alcoholics (N = 80)	Placebo-controlled evaluation of acupuncture	6 mo.	Acupuncture more effective than placebo control with significantly fewer drinking episodes and admissions to detox units	Impossible to "blind" the therapist and data relied on self-reports
Wei and Young (1988) (30)	Chronic cigarette smokers who all received at least 3 sessions of behavioral treatment (N = 118)	Double-blind trial of clonidine vs. diazepam vs. placebo	4.5 mo.	Clonidine more effective than diazepam and placebo in alleviating withdrawal symptoms and in abstinence rates	Failure to validate self-reports by biologic measurements; abstinence rates in all groups were unusually high which further questions validity of self-reports

mate details entering a permanent record. A successful early intervention with a physician is illustrated in the case of Dr. F.

> Dr. G, a former patient in a substance program, now practicing successfully, called about Dr. F. Dr. F's wife told Dr. G that she was worried about her husband's drinking and its effect on his practice. Some of the nurses told Mrs. F that Dr. F. was forgetting to write orders, and sometimes wrote the wrong orders. They had smelled digesting alcohol on his breath, and complained to another ward doctor about the situation, but nothing had been done.
>
> Mrs. F reported that a few clinic patients had noticed Dr. F coming in hung over, and that he fell asleep while taking one patient's history. Dr. F was an excellent physician, and his patients were worried about him. Mrs. F was told that the situation would be reported to the Impaired Physician's Committee, but there would be no report to the state licensing board; the records would be confidential so long as there was no evidence of negligent medical practice and he accepted therapy.
>
> The Impaired Physician Committee made a confidential investigation which included interviews with the nurses, Mrs. F, and her children. An intervention meeting was then conducted with Dr. F.
>
> Initially defensive, Dr. F minimized his drinking. However, after the nurses read their lists of his mistakes on patient charts and recalled smelling alcohol on his breath, and after his wife and children summarized his abusive behavior at home, he abandoned his denial. He entered married couples' therapy and began taking disulfiram. He also wrote a contract with the Impaired Physician's Committee that if he stopped disulfiram or resumed drinking, he would admit himself to an inpatient rehabilitation program.
>
> Dr. F has been abstinent and practicing successfully for the past 5 years.

Any practitioner who is aware of a fellow physician's or student's substance abuse and does nothing about it is morally responsible for subsequent damage to the person and to any patients who may be affected by that behavior.

PREVENTION

Primary prevention (p. 99) is more effective and less expensive than secondary and tertiary prevention. Despite few controlled evaluations of primary prevention of substance abuse, some retrospective data cannot be ignored. Major tax increases on alcoholic beverages are associated with decreasing per capita consumption and cirrhosis prevalence (an indirect indicator of alcoholism prevalence) (44). In this distribution of consumption model, the availability of alcoholic beverages directly affects total alcohol consumption and indirectly affects the prevalence of alcohol-related damage (15).

Strong DUI laws are associated with fewer motor vehicles injuries and deaths. Every decade, about 250,000 Americans die because of drunk driving (15). The risks of accidents for those with blood alcohol concentration over 160 mg% is 21 times higher than if they were sober (15).

Increases in the minimum drinking age are consistently correlated with reduced traffic mortality for younger people (15). One state increased DUI penalties in 1982 and raised the drinking age to 21 in 1984. Subsequent alcohol-related motor vehicle deaths declined 38% among persons aged 19 and 20 years, and 33% among those aged 15–18 (15). This was because the drinking age was raised; persons older than 21 years of age showed no changes in accident mortality during this period.

Additional creative, inexpensive policies are recommended by Mothers Against Drunk Drivers (MADD): having newspapers print names and addresses of citizens whose licenses are revoked after a drunk driving accident; basing fines for drunk drivers on the costs of driving instruction, and teaching schoolchildren about substance abuse.

Compared to reduction of demand for drugs, efforts to reduce the supply of drugs have not worked well in recent decades. Because farmers in cocaine-producing countries earn 5–10 times more in coca fields than in other types of farming, problems in decreasing supply are obvious (59). When coca farmers are threatened in one region, they move their fields elsewhere. Intimidation and violence play a part; for example, in 1989, Barbara D'Achille, the distinguished Peruvian environmental journalist who lived for two decades in the Amazon and detailed its destruction by coca growers, was murdered (60).

More must be done to decrease consumption. Use of illegal drugs must become a public embarrassment, not a weekend social activity. The phrase recreational drugs is abhorrent. Drug legalization (61) is another possibility. However, legalization of heroin for narcotic addicts was ineffectual in the United Kingdom (UK); use of opioids, particularly illegal heroin, grew tenfold in the UK from 1970–1983 (62). There have been successful bans on smoking in medical centers and other buildings. Six months after a ban on smoking in one medical center, the percentage of persons who smoked at work declined from 82% before the ban to 43% following it (63). Nicotine vapor in the lounges declined 26-fold from 1 month prior to the ban to 6 months afterward.

Hospitals and medical schools should completely ban smoking. Students who find this not to be the case in their medical school should form a student committee to accomplish this goal. Other primary preventive measures include prohibition of the sale of tobacco to minors, a required warning at the point of sale, a ban on cigarette vending machines, a reward for reporting violators of vending laws, and strict penalties for violators.

Early diagnosis and treatment have been detailed. Secondary prevention efforts should include routine blood alcohol and urine drug screening in ERs (15). In one study of ER patients, 25% had positive alcohol levels and 16% had readings greater than 100 mg% (64). Patients with psychiatric illnesses had higher blood alcohol levels and displayed more intoxicated behaviors than other patients. These persons require prompt referral for psychiatric treatment; they are at greater risk of injuring themselves or others (64). Not documenting adequate referral of a substance abuser after treatment of the acute medical complication is negligent medical practice.

23/Psychotherapy

Linda F. Pessar, M.D., N. Gregory Hamilton, M.D., and Mary Lou Meyers, M.D.

OBJECTIVES

GENERAL OBJECTIVE: Given a patient with a behavioral or emotional problem, state how psychotherapy can contribute to his or her care.

SPECIFIC OBJECTIVES:
1. Compare expressive and supportive psychotherapies.
2. Summarize the individual psychotherapies and state their indications.
3. Discuss the indications for and strategies of family therapy.
4. Discuss the indications for and therapeutic mechanisms of group therapy.
5. Summarize the types of group psychotherapy.

The doctor–patient relationship powerfully affects the patient's ability to heal and cope with illness. In the last 100 years, knowledge about treating mental disturbances in a way that encourages coping and personality growth has evolved into the treatment known as psychotherapy. Psychotherapy occurs when a clinician and patient meet in a professional setting to help the patient with a problem, most often a mental or emotional problem, by communicating verbally and nonverbally (1). Treatment may be offered to the patient alone, the patient and family, or in a patient group.

INDIVIDUAL PSYCHOTHERAPY

All individual psychotherapies have common elements (2). The therapist, sanctioned by society in a healing role, understands the patient in a theoretical framework and expects the person to improve. The patient expects that help is possible and that the therapist is trustworthy. The collaboration influences patient and therapist. The therapist communicates attitudes and understandings so that the patient discovers new meanings, hopes, and alternative behaviors. Likewise, the patient conveys opinions and knowledge that are incorporated into the therapist's understanding of the patient and the problem.

Although modern psychotherapists agree on basic principles and work more similarly than differently, there are well-respected differences in technique. Psychotherapies may be viewed on a continuum from supportive to expressive, although all have some supportive and some expressive qualities.

Supportive therapies (3–5) build on the patient's strengths and shore up weaknesses without altering basic coping patterns. They involve face-to-face interactions with a therapist who is open and friendly but not controlling. Supportive elements include positive regard, encouragement, advice, education, and sometimes disapproval of actions; support never includes condemning the person.

Expressive (exploratory, uncovering, psychodynamic) therapies (3–5) give patients access to previously unrecognized aspects of themselves that affect their behaviors. Treatment emphasizes self-discovery (insight) (4). It deemphasizes the patient's practical daily choices. The clinician is more reserved and quiet (and in psychoanalysis, out of the patient's view, sitting behind a psychoanalytic couch). Therapists avoid supportive interventions and emphasize questioning and interpreting. Expressive psychotherapy requires greater preexisting personality strengths in the patient than does supportive psychotherapy because of the stresses of self-discovery.

Common to both types of therapy are empathy, containment, and interpretation (6). Empathy is understanding another person by looking at our own experience (7). Containment is bearing the weight of the patient's emotions while formulating what we have heard so that the patient can understand and accept it (6, 8). Interpretation is pointing out emotional connections (4).

Types of Individual Psychotherapy

PSYCHOANALYSIS

Psychoanalysis is the most expressive of psychotherapies. It is based on the idea that personality development results from the internalization of important past relations (6, 9), the continuous influence of the dynamic unconscious (pp. 83, 84) (4–10), and the use of defense mechanisms (11).

Awareness of the unconscious is partial because defense mechanisms keep unacceptable ideas from awareness. Many defenses (e.g., sublimation) are adaptive, but others produce symptoms or disturb relationships.

Internalized relationships of early life tend to repeat themselves in subsequent relations, including the therapeutic situation, through transference and projection (6). Transference (12) is the perception of a current person (e.g., the physician) as if that person had the

characteristics of a previous person (e.g., a parent). In medicine, we rely on the transference expectation that doctors provide parental functions such as caretaking and guidance. Projection is perceiving others as having our own characteristics (6). Countertransference once had a more specific meaning but now pertains to all the therapist's feelings in the therapy situation.

Psychoanalysis helps by uncovering the unconscious. Careful questioning and occasional interpretation elucidate defense mechanisms and clarify transferences, providing insight about unconscious self-deceptions that distort relationships. For example, if a patient acknowledges her rationalizations of her husband's rejection, she can then recognize and confront his behavior. Provision of a new, analytic relationship that is internalized (13) is fundamental, although this "supportive" element is not emphasized.

Sessions are 3–5 times weekly for 2–5 years. The analyst sits unobtrusively behind the patient, who lies on a couch. Psychoanalysis is thorough and allows adequate time for growth. Disadvantages are that it is expensive in time and money and limited to introspective persons able to delay gratification and maintain self-esteem in the face of deprivation.

PSYCHODYNAMIC PSYCHOTHERAPY

Psychodynamic psychotherapy can be tailored to the patient's circumstances and may lie anywhere on the supportive-expressive continuum. Like analysis, it is based on understanding the dynamic unconscious, defense mechanisms, and transference. But biopsychosocial factors such as a genetic diathesis for depression, or ability to tolerate stress, are also important and addressed.

For example, if a man taking blood pressure medication develops depression as a side effect, and secondarily perceives his wife as not loving him, the psychiatrist should (in concert with a colleague treating the patient's hypertension) discontinue that antihypertensive and recognize that the patient's description of his wife is influenced by the projection of his depressive lack of self-regard. As the depression clears, the therapist will help the patient understand the effects of his depression on his family and himself. Later, they may consider marital difficulties that remain.

The following example illustrates how expressive and supportive aspects of psychotherapy are interwoven to form the fabric of successful psychodynamic treatment:

> A successful 35-year-old school administrator was referred with gastritis (stomach inflammation) and anxiety. He had recently advanced to a middle management position. His supervisor had a directive, top-down management style, and the patient believed in administration by consulting with subordinates. Thus, he had to modulate the demands and frustration of the teachers he supervised as well as administrative directives. The psychiatrist understood the patient's dilemma, and this support relieved some tension. The psychiatrist introduced another supportive element by teaching relaxation techniques.
>
> The psychiatrist also asked about relations at home and past relations. The patient had a strict, domineering mother who ran the household with an iron hand. He resented this authority and now treated his students, supervisees, wife, and children with the consideration he wished he had received. He remained strict with himself, however, so that he could always be thoughtful of others.
>
> The patient was relieved to have the therapist understand and help him with a difficult boss. As a boy, he had always wished his father would help him with his difficult mother, rather than abandoning the home front through excessive work.
>
> The patient completed treatment after 8 months, functioning better at work and home.

Mixing supportive and expressive techniques and biologic, psychologic, and social viewpoints flexibly tailors treatment to the patient. It is, therefore, more focused and briefer than psychoanalysis. Sessions are less frequent, often once weekly; thus, treatment is less expensive. As the interaction takes place face-to-face with a therapist who is more open than in psychoanalysis, a more vivid model for identification is provided. For these reasons, it is the most commonly practiced psychotherapy.

COGNITIVE THERAPY

Cognitive therapy posits that cognitions (conscious ideas) influence our moods (14, 15), just as moods can affect our cognitions. Anxiety and depression can result from maladaptive cognitions (e.g., those in Table 23.1). Cognitions can be changed to foster comfort and adaptation.

Table 23.1. Cognitive Errors that Contribute to Social Anxiety[a]

1. Perfectionism; unrealistic expectations of self to perform perfectly or anxiety-free; fear of making even the slightest mistake; fear of taking risks; difficulty making decisions; procrastination.
2. Perceiving things in extreme "black or white" terms without consideration of the possibilities in between (example: viewing experience as either success or failure); typically expecting the worst possible outcome while insisting on the best, neither of which may be realistic; difficulty identifying options when faced with anxiety.
3. Focusing on and exaggerating minor negative aspects of an experience so that the perception of the entire situation is negative (example, evaluating your public presentation as "terrible" based solely on initial nervousness).
4. Discounting or minimizing positive experiences by attributing them to external factors, rather than giving yourself credit for accomplishments (e.g., "But I was on medication").
5. Drawing erroneous conclusions based on limited information that does not adequately support a negative interpretation; assuming that you know how others perceive you (example: "They'll notice my nervousness and think I'm strange or incompetent").
6. Self-criticism; tendency to compare self to others or to own past experiences that were more positive; perceiving self as inferior in comparison (example: "He's so confident" or "I used to do this without a problem"); minimization of personal accomplishments; avoidance of competitive situations.
7. Overconcern with others' perceptions of you; particular concern that others will readily detect the anxiety you experience; assumption that others view you with criticism; self-preoccupation with the assumption that you are the center of attention.

[a]Reprinted with permission from Louro C, Lorenz M. Unpublished protocol. Arlington Heights, IL: Agoraphobia Treatment Center, 1990.

Only current cognitive patterns are explored. This typically takes place in once-weekly sessions for 15–20 weeks. Treatment is face-to-face with a therapist who functions as an open, friendly, collaborative teacher. The therapist asks the patient to keep track of cognitions, helps assess their validity, and teaches new cognitions.

A 38-year-old radiologist sought treatment of a 20-year-long social phobia in which she feared humiliation if she blushed during a radiologic procedure or social event. Consequently, she limited the number of radiologic procedures she performed and social events she attended, despite superior clinical and interpersonal skill. She took diazepam 6 mg twice daily, plus 4–10 mg once daily as needed 30–60 minutes before procedures or events she anticipated would be stressful. She attributed her successful performance to the diazepam (not to her own skill), but resented the memory difficulties it produced.

Her psychotherapist assigned her to write a list, in hierarchical order of perceived stress, of those events for which she took extra diazepam. She placed intravenous pyelograms and wedding receptions atop it. She agreed to participate in events at the bottom of the list, taking lower preevent doses of diazepam. She and her therapist discussed in detail her perceptions (cognitions) of what others thought of her performance of medical and social tasks. To assist with the latter, the patient was given the list of "cognitive distortions related to anxiety" (Table 23.1) all of which she correctly believed applied to her.

Several weeks after therapy began, she had to record behaviors of people she thought were anxious, and found this strikingly difficult. Days passes in which she could not identify an anxious person. She also learned that she cared minimally whether others were anxious, as long as they did workmanlike jobs and treated her courteously. Her therapist persuaded her that most people were like her, and she frequently stated: "Who cares if my face gets red? They have other things to worry about."

After 2 months, she joined a therapy group of socially anxious patients who shared similar experiences and provided feedback, such as, "I had no idea you were anxious until you told us." By 6 months, she routinely performed tasks atop the list, stopped taking diazepam, and became more adventurous socially and professionally.

Cognitive therapy is brief, inexpensive, and easily learned and standardized, making it accessible to extensive research, which demonstrates its effectiveness for nonmelancholic depression and some anxiety disorders (14). Its major disadvantage is that cognitive therapists address transference and countertransference minimally.

SUPPORTIVE PSYCHOTHERAPY

Supportive psychotherapy (3–5, 16) avoids uncovering the unconscious. It presumes the underlying conflicts should not be addressed directly because the patient is on precarious ground psychologically. This is caused by personality deficits (e.g., inability to tolerate frustrations) or to an overwhelming circumstance (e.g., loss of a loved one) that requires all the strengths and defenses of a healthy person.

A 45-year-old divorced stockbroker with prior episodic depressions sought treatment the spring before her daughter's departure for college. The patient feared she was having another depression, and had been greatly helped by psychotherapy at the time of her divorce 4 years ago.

During the psychiatric consultation, the patient described a childhood in which both parents were remote and critical. When she was 6 years old, her parents separated, and for several years she felt responsible for this. As she talked about her past and present, she was briefly overcome by sadness and anger, during which time she lost concentration and forgot what she said.

Although the psychiatrist believed the patient's experience of rejection and guilt in childhood contributed to her anxiety about her daughter's leaving, he was concerned by her psychologic fragility and decided to use supportive psychotherapy. Consequently, he helped her recognize how the good aspects of her daughter leaving outweighed the bad, and how well she was coping with changes. He did not explore underlying feelings of rejection and guilt.

The therapist focuses on strengths, accepts limitations of introspection or unfavorable conditions, and provides guidance in the area of difficulty. For instance, an impulsive patient is asked to weigh pros and cons of a possible course of action and to consider alternatives. A patient with low self-esteem may be praised for strengths and encouraged to focus on these. The therapist does not interpret defenses or transference. The treatment can be as brief as one session to help a patient over a hurdle or be lifelong.

It can be tailored to patients of any intellectual level, and is less demanding, expensive and time-consuming than expressive therapies. Among its liabilities are that it tends to stabilize the status quo, and it is difficult to teach and standardize.

TIME-LIMITED THERAPIES

Many of the psychotherapies already described can be time-limited (i.e., have a set termination date), supportive and cognitive therapy in particular. There are also psychodynamically oriented expressive therapies designed for brief use (4, 17): focal psychotherapy (18), short-term anxiety-provoking psychotherapy (19), time-limited psychotherapy (20), and interpersonal psychotherapy (21). Economical and focused, they require an experienced therapist and a patient who is psychologically minded, highly motivated, able to form close relationships, tolerant of anxiety, and whose problems have one psychodynamic or interpersonal focus (4).

Choice of Therapies

In its broadest definition, psychotherapy includes any doctor–patient relationship and can help most patients. Simply consulting an understanding physician can be salutary. But each type of psychotherapy has indications.

In general, crises are best resolved with supportive treatment, because expressive techniques may sidetrack energies needed for coping, worsening the situation. Nonmelancholic depression, anxiety, phobias, and sexual inhibitions can often be relieved by psychodynamic psychotherapy, cognitive therapy, or behavior modification (pp. 74–82). Psycho-

analysis is not sufficiently focused, and supportive psychotherapy does not produce enough behavior change.

Addictions, paraphilias, and eating disorders are best treated with supportive therapy which includes admonition, support of self-esteem, and behavioral modification. More expressive approaches can be experienced as giving tacit permission for continuing that behavior. Psychotic persons usually need a combination of medication, social support, and supportive psychotherapy.

Personality disorders are best treated with psychoanalysis or expressive psychoanalytic psychotherapy. Cognitive therapies, pure supportive therapy, and behavior modification can help with specific personality traits and are more focused and limited in their goals.

A few patients function worse when anyone tries to help them—they do better without treatment. For example, a narcissistic patient felt so offended that anyone was in a position to help him that he defeated therapeutic efforts by developing worsening symptoms. He improved when therapy stopped.

Approximately 20% of the population has a diagnosable psychiatric disorder (22). In addition, many people need time-limited help with specific problems. Thus, perhaps one third of persons will benefit from psychotherapy. Psychotherapies may be combined with other treatments. Individual therapy is often combined with pharmacotherapy, social services, family and group therapy, substance abuse programs, or self-help approaches. Research has demonstrated that psychotherapies are effective for most disorders for which they are used (23–31).

Psychotherapists

Psychotherapeutic elements exist in all doctor–patient relationships. When a brief intervention by the general physician is insufficient, it is best to refer to a specialist. Psychiatrists are trained in psychotherapies. Clinical psychologists, social workers, pastoral counselors, and psychiatric nurse-practitioners are also trained in psychotherapy.

Psychotherapy is complex and requires extensive training and self-scrutiny. Complicated interactions of biologic, psychologic, and social factors also occur in psychiatric disorders. Patients referred for psychotherapy should be evaluated initially by a psychiatrist, because psychiatrists have the requisite training and experience in the biology of behavior.

FAMILY THERAPY

For individual psychotherapy, it is expected that as the person's mental health improves, the social environment will adapt, with everybody benefiting. Family and couples therapy, on the other hand, emphasizes the communication patterns and social reinforcements that contribute to prevention, onset, and outcome of behavioral problems. It is expected that the person will adapt to family changes, fostering individual and family health. Individual and family therapy are complimentary; each can stand alone or be used with the other.

Family or couples therapy is indicated for marital maladjustment, sexual dysfunction, and treatment of children with certain behavior problems (e.g., eating disorders, conduct disturbances). Involvement of the family, often in family therapy, is important in the treatment of persons who have major psychiatric illness (e.g., schizophrenia) (32). It also supplements individual therapy when a patient's family does not accommodate to the person's improved functioning during individual treatment.

> A 20-year-old woman with a history of anorexia nervosa in adolescence began to lose weight after marriage. Through individual psychotherapy she understood her refusal to eat as anger at her controlling husband. As she resumed normal eating, her husband insensitively cautioned her against getting plump. Marital therapy, which explored the couple's difficulty sharing decision-making, enabled her to maintain weight.

Marital therapy explores the behavioral, interpersonal, and intrapsychic components of the relationship. The behavioral focus explores how the couple negotiates satisfaction of needs and reinforces behaviors. Treatment helps the couple communicate individual needs and plan reinforcement strategies to maximize each partner's satisfaction and reduce conflict.

> Mrs. A responded to her husband's gifts as if they were points on a scale of devotion. If disappointed, she would pout and be resentful. Mr. A experienced each gift as a marital crisis. She was encouraged to give gift suggestions so that both could enjoy these occasions.

The interpersonal focus addresses how the couple satisfies or thwarts needs of intimacy. Feelings of disappointment and mistrust are explored to foster reestablishment of intimacy.

> As therapy continued with Mr. and Mrs. A, Mr. A stated he felt rejected by Mrs. A's emotional withdrawal when she was angry. Mrs. A, afraid to show her anger directly, was impressed by her husband's wish to please her, and realized that her withdrawal threatened their closeness.

The intrapsychic focus investigates psychologic distortions in the present based on assumptions derived from important past relations, as well as projections of individual needs and fears upon the partner. Intrapsychic factors are clarified to free the couple from reenacting unconscious conflicts of the past.

> Mrs. A described her father as an alcoholic who would leave home after a family fight and return drunk and abusive. She feared her husband would act irrationally and destructively if she voiced anger or disappointment directly.

Sex therapy includes psychological and interpersonal components of the couple's adjustment. Consequently, individual and marital psychotherapy may be indicated in addition to sex therapy (33). Sex therapy is highly effective in treating premature or retarded ejaculation, erectile dysfunction, orgasmic dysfunction, and vaginismus (p. 397) (34).

A child's life is so pervasively influenced by the family that family therapy should be used for most childhood behavior problems, often combined with individual treatment of the child, school tutoring, or pharmacotherapy. All strategies of family therapy view the child's symptom in terms of the family's functioning.

> A family was referred by the school guidance counselor after the second grade child developed school avoidance and other symptoms of separation anxiety. During early family sessions it was learned that the father had recently begun law school after a 10 year hiatus and felt overwhelmed by the academic demands. The mother had encouraged this change in plans but was now depressed and unable to ask her husband for support. The child had responded to the emotional withdrawal of both parents by developing fears of leaving home.
>
> The therapist encouraged family members to discuss their responses to this transition. The father learned to set priorities to free time to spend with his family. The mother was encouraged to use the extended family for support when her husband was unavailable. When her depressive symptoms persisted, an antidepressant was prescribed with good results. As the family became more comfortable expressing its needs to one another, and spent more time together, the child began to attend school without difficulty.

Family therapy is useful for children who have eating and conduct disorders. For conduct disorders, family therapy also reduces the risk of similiar behavior occurring among siblings of the identified patient (the person whose symptoms brought the family to treatment) (35).

As treatment for severe, chronic psychiatric illness moved from institutions (typically state hospitals) into the community in the late 1960s and the 1970s, family therapy became more important. The objectives are to educate the family about the illness, help them set realistic goals, and foster coping with the vicissitudes of living with an impaired family member.

Family treatment has been studied for families of schizophrenics persons. Families are taught about family behavior such as expressed emotionality (a triad of overcriticalness, hostility, and intrusiveness) associated with exacerbations of illness (36), and are helped to reinforce the patient's health. Groups are offered for families to obtain practical and emotional support for living with a chronically ill relative. Family treatment in schizophrenia is useful in preventing relapse (35). Although family treatment for mood and anxiety disorders is less often advocated, it is helpful (35).

In initial assessment, several strategies are used. Because the family is the patient, the couple or family is seen together from the outset or first meeting. A joint first session allows observations of family interactions missing in individual reports.

History-taking focuses on the here and now, but it also considers the evolution of present family difficulties. Whenever possible, the presenting problem is elucidated in family terms, avoiding a focus on one member as the cause of the problem. This defocusing usually provides relief for the often scapegoated identified patient.

The complexity of addressing multiple relationships requires considerable therapist activity. The therapist is relatively open about responses to family members and encourages the family to be candid. For example, interviewing a family whose adolescent daughter has cut her wrists daily for the prior week, the therapist said, "whenever I ask Betty a question, I'm fearful I will make her angry and she will cut herself. How do you feel?"

The therapist must intervene to stop scapegoating of a family member or to stop unmodulated displays of anger which demoralize the family and compromise the therapy.

> A family was referred for therapy when the 14-year-old son began to vandalize the schoolyard months after the father lost his job and the family had to move from a working class suburb to the inner city. After a family tirade against the son's "criminal tendencies," the therapist inter-

vened. "I wonder if it's easier for the family to focus on Robert's behavior than to face their sadness and anxiety about the move."

Many family therapists use behavioral treatments as the first intervention. The family is asked to make contracts to reward desired behavior. For example, if an adolescent keeps her room clean for week, she can resume phoning friends. The family may be asked to practice new behaviors between sessions. When phone privileges were resumed, the girl's brothers were to practice being polite to her friends. If this straightforward approach is ineffective, the therapist, having observed communication patterns that interfere with problem-solving, introduces new strategies.

Observations from family therapy pertain to general medical practice. First, the family is a crucial resource in treating the patient who has a serious or chronic disabling illness, so that educating the family about the illness, with patient consent, is usually indicated. Living with a person who has a serious illness is often burdensome, and families require the physician's support and reasonable availability. National support networks exist for specific illnesses, and families should be referred to them.

Second, many marital, family, and sexual problems respond readily to treatment. The stigma surrounding these difficulties makes it hard, however, for the patient to reveal those problems. The physician should routinely inquire about sexual and family adjustment during initial interviews, and be familiar with family therapists to whom patients can be referred for assessment and treatment.

GROUP THERAPY

This powerful treatment method has its roots in general medicine, where it emerged as a solution to the problem of too many patients and too little time. Initially it was used to deliver medical information and advice to large groups of tuberculosis patients at a single sitting (37). Today, it is a form of psycho-

therapy that has flourished because of our social nature.

Interpersonal relations mold us and can curse or save us. Treatment that draws on our social affinity can introduce us to ourselves. Maladaptive patterns of relating as well as distorted views and expectations of others can often be identified in ways that encourage insight and therapeutic change.

Indications for Group Psychotherapy

Research has shown that individual and group treatment are equally effective for most patients (38). Often practical considerations about availability of services and patient preferences influence the choice of treatment. There are, however, three general indications for group treatment: difficulty with interpersonal relations, impulsive behavior, and transference behavior that hinders individual therapy (39).

DIFFICULTY WITH INTERPERSONAL RELATIONS

Some patients have long-standing problems maintaining successful relationships. Group work helps the patient recognize, understand, and change problematic behavior patterns.

A 45-year-old accountant became lonely, withdrawn, and isolated over the course of 6 months. His children were grown and his wife had left 8 months previously after telling him, "you're cold, unfeeling, and don't want to change." After initial psychiatric evaluation, the patient was referred to a long-term interactional group.

He attended every meeting, dutifully at first, but gradually became more involved with the other members. His early group behavior was intellectualized and he appeared unfeeling. The group commented on this, and he began to see himself as others did, and gained insight about why feelings frightened him. After months of treatment, he reconciled with his wife.

IMPULSIVE BEHAVIOR

Many patients who have difficulty controlling their feelings—tending to act on them immediately—are helped by groups. The group, with its structure and limits, is a safe place to display some problematic behavior, receive group feedback, and gain insight. Some patients who have personality disorders are particularly prone to action in response to feelings. Group therapy helps modify this tendency by teaching the patient to think rather than react.

TRANSFERENCE BEHAVIOR THAT HINDERS INDIVIDUAL THERAPY

Some patients need more help and support than one therapist can offer. In group treatment, members provide additional support. Some patients have difficulty separating realistic perceptions about the therapist from transferences. Group members can help the patient make these distinctions.

> When the male cotherapist spoke in group, one young woman frequently complained of being "singled out for criticism." She would announce that the therapist was just like her father and favored the others. The other group members pointed out that the therapist did not single her out and did treat members equally.

Contraindications for Group Psychotherapy

Refusal to accept a group referral is a contraindication for group therapy; coercion results in early dropping out (40). Another contraindication is when the patient is profoundly ill. Following resolution of the acute problem, appropriateness for group referral can be reassessed.

Heterogeneous and Homogeneous Groups

Patients for whom heterogeneous groups (members have varied diagnoses or problems) are not indicated may benefit from homogeneous groups in which members share a common problem (e.g., social phobia, bipolar disorder). Homogeneous groups are often useful for patients who are poorly motivated, non-

compliant, or have highly stigmatized problems (e.g., child abusers) (41).

> A 32-year-old single man sought medical attention for fatigue, malaise, and weight loss, and learned he had AIDS. As his anxiety and depression grew, he was dismayed to realize that many of his family and friends were not supportive. Some were shocked, frightened, or angry. He began feeling isolated and afraid to discuss his situation further. His physician referred him to a group known to its members as the "HIV Positive Club." He found that what was previously alienating had become his password for acceptance, support, and advice. Because of the group's interventions, he began to approach others again, and made meaningful future plans.

Therapeutic Mechanisms for Group Treatment

According to Yalom (42), 11 therapeutic elements underlie all group treatments:

Instillation of Hope: Hearing others describe how treatment has helped and observing others improve increases belief in the efficacy of group treatment and fosters optimism.

Universality: Discovering that one's problems are not unique (consensual validation) is reassuring.

Imparting of Information: Ranging from teaching by the therapist to advice from members, education can be therapeutic.

Altruism: Group therapy offers members the opportunity to help others, often increasing self-esteem.

Development of Socializing Techniques: Through interactions with others, group members develop and modify social skills.

Imitative Behavior: Group participation offers members an opportunity to observe the behavior, struggles, and treatment of others. Valuable imitating occurs and should be encouraged.

Catharsis: Overrated by Hollywood as a therapeutic maneuver, sharing feelings is nonetheless useful. Acceptance of our emotions by others helps us accept our feelings.

Corrective Recapitulation of the Primary Family Group: The group is ripe for reenactment of unsettled family scores. Group work explores family conflict so that the person gains the insight necessary to move beyond old behavior patterns.

Existential Factors: Existential realities such as aloneness, mortality, and responsibility for self are faced when the group copes with bereavement or life-threatening illnesses.

Group Cohesiveness: This is shared loyalty to the group because the members feel accepted. It is crucial for group success, providing the "safety" needed for individual exploration and growth.

Interpersonal Learning: Just as leftover family conflict is likely to be revealed in group, so, too, are characteristic patterns of relating. As problematic patterns appear, the group work of observation and feedback helps members.

The Structure and Function of Groups

The leader's work begins with selecting and orienting new members. In most groups, this involves one or more individual sessions to screen each prospective member. The therapist looks for persons who are motivated to change and have problems compatible with the group's focus. The therapist educates the new patient about the treatment and the group itself, explaining ground rules such as regular attendance, anticipating problems such as early discouragement or frustration, and correcting misconceptions about treatment.

The therapist strives for a group size consistent with therapeutic goals. Most group psychotherapy is done in groups with 6–8 members. The therapist secures a comfortable, private room that allows all members to see each other clearly when seated, and arranges a convenient regular meeting time. The usual session is 90 minutes. Meetings may be shorter if patient limitations require it (e.g., inpatient groups).

Often the therapist works with a cotherapist, one who uses the same theoretical framework. Individual styles can vary but should be complementary. Usually cotherapy teams are male–female, in part to recapitulate feelings about important relationships. Cotherapists provide each other with moral support, feedback, advice, and coverage during absence.

Once planning and selection are done, therapeutic work begins. Although there is

overlap in how individual, family, and group psychotherapists work, some techniques are unique to groups. Much happens in a group at any time. The therapist chooses from this material to promote the group goals by examining here-and-now interactions. Although group members may resist this, members are asked to risk sharing feelings about themselves and others as they occur, rather than from the safety of time passed. The therapist can help this process by describing here-and-now work in pregroup education, by role-modeling self-revelation, and by redirecting attention to the here and now.

The therapist, who starts and ends the meeting, addresses lateness, absence, dropping out, and socializing outside the group (which pregroup preparation can reduce but not eliminate). Extragroup socialization is usually discouraged because it often leads to subgroups (persons more loyal to each other than to the group), which undermine the group's work.

Conflict between members is inevitable and sometimes desirable. The conflict is treated like any other communication, but the therapist must keep the conflict at a level tolerable to the group.

When should treatment end? Crisis resolution and relief of symptoms can often occur within weeks or months, but treatment may proceed for a year or two to achieve lasting personality change. This termination phase is an important part of treatment, not simply a final session. Termination from group can be timely and well planned, occurring after growth and change, or premature, perhaps impulsive, with much work undone. Sometimes when the group is designed for a time-limited course, the group terminates together.

Types of Groups

Of the many types of psychotherapy groups, the most common are briefly described here.

Higher functioning interactional groups usually consist of 6–8 outpatients. Regular attendance is required and extragroup socializing discouraged. It is usually open: new members can be added by the therapist to keep membership size optimal for the group's work. Treatment length is indefinite; it may be many years for the group itself and 1–2 years for each member. The major therapeutic factors are interpersonal learning and corrective recapitulation of the primary family group. Efficacy is good, especially if patients continue beyond 50 sessions (43).

Inpatient group size varies but is usually 6–8. Group members bring multiple disorders and symptoms, some of which may be psychotic. If a psychotic patients disrupts the group's work, that person may be temporarily excluded. Meetings are often 30 minutes or less. Attendance may be mandatory. The duration of the group is indefinite, but each member's stay in the group reflects hospitalization length. The major therapeutic factors are instillation of hope and self-esteem and improvement of social skills. Outcome data are variable (36).

Aftercare and medication clinic group size may be larger than 6–8 persons depending on the structure of the clinic or treatment program. Members participate as long as they are involved in the treatment, often indefinitely. Attendance is strongly encouraged. Therapeutic factors include instillation of hope, universality, socialization techniques, and imparting of information.

Support and education groups are homogeneous groups that usually consist of members who share a specific reason for membership (e.g., a specific medical disorder or bereavement). Usually these groups are time-limited, spanning 6–12 sessions. Attendance is voluntary and flexible, often on an as needed basis. The therapeutic factors include imparting of information, existential factors, cohesiveness, and universality.

The typical behavior modification group treats a specific disorder (e.g., an eating disorder) or a specific behavior (e.g., smoking). Patients are asked to attend for the life of the group, usually 6–12 sessions. Behavior modification techniques are used. The therapeutic factors include universality, imitative behavior, and behavioral rehearsal.

24/Psychopharmacology and Electroconvulsive Therapy

Richard Balon, M.D., and Edward H. Leatherman, M.D.

OBJECTIVES

GENERAL OBJECTIVE: Given a patient with a well-documented psychiatric disorder, discuss psychopharmacologic (or electroconvulsive) treatment, if indicated, for the patient.

SPECIFIC OBJECTIVES:
1. State general principles of psychopharmacologic treatment.
2. Summarize the historical background, proposed mechanism of action, indications, contraindications, strategies of use, and side effects of the following: neuroleptics, cyclic antidepressants, monoamine oxidase inhibitors, lithium, anticonvulsants (in psychiatry), stimulants, buspirone, β-adrenergic blockers, clonidine, sedative-hyponotics, and electroconvulsive therapy.

GENERAL PRINCIPLES OF PHARMACOTHERAPY

Good diagnosis is the cornerstone of treatment. The following are needed for diagnosis: patient history, physical examination (including mental status), and pertinent lab tests (1). Brief observation periods help in cases of diagnostic uncertainty, which are frequent. Sometimes initial emergency sedation with a nonspecific agent (e.g., lorazepam) is part of this observation period in hospitalized patients (2, 3).

Choice of drug is another difficult decision. A familiar one should be used. Physicians should familiarize themselves with 2–3 from each group, and use them most of the time. Knowing a patient's prior response to a drug may be a clue, as may response of a family member to it. The drug's side-effect profile is another important consideration. Certain side effects should be avoided for certain patients;

they may be more harmful (e.g., increased risk of postural hypotension [p. 189] in older patients). Other side effects can, however, be used to advantage in treatment management (e.g., higher sedation with certain intramuscular [IM] neuroleptic drugs during manic hyperactivity). As much as possible, polypharmacy should be avoided. The consequences of polypharmacy are illustrated in this vignette:

Mr. E was a 60-year-old married store manager who, after years of outstanding peformance, was losing interest in his job. He felt incompetent at work and was looking forward to retirement for the first time. Despite this attitude, he was not clinically depressed. He was taking clorazepate dipotassium (a benzodiazepine [p. 333] for well-documented panic disorder of 35 years' duration; nifedipine and diltiazem hydrochloride (calcium channel blockers) as well as nitroglycerin for his angina pectoris (chest pain from arteriosclerotic heart disease), gemfibrozil (a cholesterol-lowering agent) for his hypercholesterolemia; ranitidine hydrochloride (a histamine H₂-receptor antagonist) for duodenal peptic ulcer; insulin for his diabetes mellitus; sulindac and acetaminophen (anti-inflammatory agents) for his degenerative arthritis; simethicone for flatulence; trazodone (an antidepressant) for a doctor's (mistaken) impression of depression; and temazepam (a benzodiazepine) for his occasional initial insomnia due to anxiety.

He was obese, friendly, and cooperative. He had difficulty concentrating. His mood was euthymic. Minimental state score was 18/30, reflecting diffuse cognitive dysfunction owing to drug-induced delirium (p. 287).

Temazepam, trazodone, simethicone, nifedipine, and acetaminophen were discontinued, and doses of several other medications were reduced. His delirium subsided and he was again able to perform well, and proudly, at work.

Patients (and the patient's family in many circumstances) should be informed about the diagnosis, target symptoms, expected effects of the medication, and side effects. Terms used should be ones the patient understands. Patients tolerate side effects better when they know what to expect, what to do if a side effect occurs, and how long it will likely take before the drug starts to work. Informed consent (p. 427) is always required. Some centers require written patient consent for neuroleptic drugs because of the risk of tardive dyskinesia (p. 326).

Psychopharmacotherapy does not preclude psychotherapy. For example, cognitive psychotherapy is often part of the management of nonmelancholic depression.

Although combining agents is usually not recommended, combinations are sometimes necessary. For example, neuroleptics plus cyclic antidepressants (CAs) are preferable to CAs alone for psychotic depression (4), although ECT alone is the best treatment for psychotic depression (5). Agents from the same group (e.g., two neuroleptics) should not be combined.

Sensitive interviewing, patient education, positive reinforcement for compliance, and use of single (or two) daily doses (CAs, neuroleptics, lithium, and monoamine oxidase in-

hibitors all have long half-lives [p. 333], and it is easier to remember and take one or two doses than three or four) all foster compliance. Sometimes people forget to take medication. Often, side effects are bothersome, or the patient is delusional about the medication and refuses to take it (or hides it under the tongue or in the cheek and later throws it away). Compliance for severely ill patients in supervised settings may be fostered by oral administration of liquid medication or intramuscular (IM) administration. Two neuroleptics (fluphenazine and haloperidol decanoate) exist in depot form administered IM on an outpatient basis once every 1–4 weeks; this method is useful for patients willing to accept an injection every few weeks rather than to take medication daily. Some agents are used but not approved by the Food and Drug Administration (FDA) (p. 452) for certain diagnoses (e.g., imipramine in panic disorder, carbamazepine in mood disorders). Use for "non-approved" indications is based on peer-reviewed research and on prior FDA approval for the original indication (e.g., imipramine in depression).

Monitoring plasma levels may help assess dosage and compliance. Therapeutic range of several antidepressants (Table 24.1), lithium, carbamazepine, and valproic acid has been established. There are no established therapeutic levels of neuroleptics (except haloperidol whose recommended level is 5–15 ng/mL).

Long-term consequences of the psychotropic drugs on the brains of children are not known. The initial approach, therefore, should be nonpharmacologic if possible. Children and their parents should be questioned actively about side effects; as a child's ability to report side effects may be limited.

The principles of use for each psychotropic drug are similar for children and adults, but pediatric dosage (based on child's weight) is usually lower. Neuroleptics are used in childhood psychoses and sometimes in attention deficit disorder (ADHD). Antidepressants have been used in mood disorders, enuresis, and ADHD. Lithium is not often used in chil-

Table 24.1. Cyclic Antidepressants

Generic Name	Brand Name	Daily Dose for Depression (mg)	Usual Starting Dose (mg/day)	Therapeutic Level (ng/mL)[a]
Amitriptyline	Elavil	100–300	75	100–250 (combined with nortryptiline)
Amoxapine	Asendin	200–400	100–150	unknown
Buproprion	Wellbutrin	300–450	200	unknown
Desipramine	Norpramin Pertofrane	100–300	75	150–300
Doxepin	Sinequan, Adapin	100–300	50–100	100–250
Fluoxetine	Prozac	10–80	10–20	unknown
Imipramine	Tofranil	150–300	75	150–300 (combined with desipramine)
Maprotiline	Ludiomil	100–225	75	150–300
Nortriptyline	Pamelor	50–150	25	50–150
Protriptyline	Vivactil	15–60	15	75–250
Trazadone	Desyrel	150–600	75	unknown
Trimipramine	Surmontil	100–300	75	unknown

[a]Slight variations in different laboratories.

dren, but it has its place in bipolar disorder, or in ADHD with severe, violent mood swings. Stimulants are used in ADHD. Pediatric psychopharmacology is detailed by Weiner (6).

NEUROLEPTICS

Neuroleptics (antipsychotics) have eight main classes with different structures: phenothiazines (aliphatic, piperidine, and piperazine subclasses), thioxanthenes, butyrophenones, diphenylbutylpiperidines, dibenzoxazepines, dihydroindolones, dibenzodiazepines, and benzamides. The first neuroleptic, chlorpromazine, was developed in France, and introduced to psychiatry by Delay and Deniker in 1952 (7). Neuroleptics became used worldwide, starting a deinstitutionalization revolution in psychiatry in the 1960s (p. 452). Thousands of patients were discharged from public long-term hospitals (with varying results, including wellness or homelessness) because neuroleptics helped the patients to be more self-controlled.

Neuroleptics may be used in the treatment of schizophrenia, schizoaffective disorder (p. 276), mania and delusional disorder (p. 276), psychoses that are substance induced or secondary to brain disease (e.g., psychosis secondary to brain tumor), delusional depression (combined with a CA), combative behavior,

and Tourette's syndrome (pimozide or haloperidol). Because so many conditions respond to neuroleptics, *neuroleptic responsiveness is not specific for any diagnosis.*

Antipsychotic efficacy is connected to neuroleptic blockade of dopamine 2 receptors (p. 55) in mesolimbic and mesocortical brain areas. Unfortunately, they also block receptors elsewhere in the brain (e.g., nigrostriatal), causing a plethora of side effects.

Pretreatment liver function tests, a complete blood count (CBC), and an electrocardiogram (ECG) should be ordered. Agranulocytosis (dramatically reduced white blood cell [WBC] count with susceptibility to death from rampant infection) has been reported during treatment with clozapine (also possible, but less frequent, with other neuroleptics), for which pretreatment and weekly CBCs are required.

Neuroleptics are contraindicated in coma, severe cardiac disease, or a severe seizure disorder (neuroleptics lower seizure threshold). Drugs with anticholinergic side effects (e.g., thioridazine) may be contraindicated in narrow angle glaucoma (increased intraocular pressure). Patients allergic to a given neuroleptic subtype should not receive drugs of that subtype. Clozapine is contraindicated in patients who have a history of agranulocytosis or myeloproliferative disorder. Patients should be screened for abnormal movements prior

Table 24.2. Abnormal Involuntary Movement Scale (AIMS)[a]

Instructions to Examiner

General

Either before or after completing the examination, observe the patient unobtrusively at rest (e.g., in waiting room). The patient's chair should be hard and firm without arms. After observing the patient for each component of the examination, rate on a scale of 0 (none), 1 (minimal), 2 (mild), 3 (moderate), 4 (severe) according to symptom severity. Rate the highest severity observed. Rate movements that occur upon activation one less than those occurring spontaneously.

Ask the patient whether there is anything in his or her mouth (e.g., gum), and if there is, to remove it. Ask the patient about the current condition of his or her teeth and whether dentures are worn.

Specific Maneuvers

1. Have patient sit in chair with hands on knees, legs slightly apart, and feet flat on floor.
2. Ask patient to sit with hand hanging unsupported.
3. Ask patient to open mouth, and then protrude tongue.
4. Ask patient to tap thumb with each finger as rapidly as possible for 10–15 seconds, separately with right hand, then with left hand (observe facial and leg movements).
5. Flex and extend patient's left and right arm (one at a time).
6. Ask patient to stand.
7. Ask patient to extend both arms outstretched in front with palms down (observe trunk, legs, and reach).
8. Have patient walk a few paces, turn, and walk back to chair (observe hands and gait).

Specific Abnormalities

Facial and Oral Movements

1. Muscles of facial expression (e.g., movements of forehead, eyebrows, periorbital area. Include frowning, blinking, grimacing of upper face) 0 1 2 3 4
2. Lips and perioral area (e.g., puckering, pouting, smacking) 0 1 2 3 4
3. Jaw (e.g., biting, clenching, chewing, mouth opening, lateral movement) 0 1 2 3 4
4. Tongue (rate only increase in movement both in and out of mouth, NOT inability to sustain movement) 0 1 2 3 4

Extremity Movements

5. Upper (arms, wrists, hands, fingers). Include choreic movements (rapid, objectively purposeless, irregular, spontaneous) and athetoid movements (slow, irregular, complex, serpentine). DO NOT include tremor (repetitive, regular, rhythmic). 0 1 2 3 4
6. Lower (legs, knees, ankles, toes). Include lateral knee movement, foot tapping, heel dropping, foot squirming, inversion and eversion of foot. 0 1 2 3 4

Trunk Movements

7. Neck, shoulders, hips (e.g., rocking, twisting, squirming, pelvic gyrations). Include diaphragmatic movements. 0 1 2 3 4

Global Judgments

8. Severity of abnormal movements (Score based on highest single score on items 1–7 above) 0 1 2 3 4
9. Incapacitation owing to abnormal movements 0 1 2 3 4
10. Patient's awareness of abnormal movements

No awareness	0
Aware, no distress	1
Aware, mild distress	2
Aware, moderate distress	3
Aware, severe distress	4

Dental

11. Current problems with teeth or dentures

No	0
Yes	1

12. Does patient usually wear dentures?

No	0
Yes	1

[a]Modified from Guy W. ECDEU assessment manual for psychopharmacology, revised. Washington, DC: U.S. Department of Health, Education & Welfare, Public Health Service 1976: 534–537.

and during treatment, using the Abnormal Involuntary Movement Scale (AIMS) (Table 24.2) (8).

When the ideal dose has been reached for each patient, all neuroleptics have equal antipsychotic efficacy (9). As stated earlier, choice of an agent should be based on the physician's familiarity with the drug, the patient's previous response to it, and its side effect profile. For example, sedation that is desirable at some times (e.g., psychotic agitation) is dangerous at others (e.g., driving).

There is no standard dose of neuroleptic for any disorder: doses should be individualized. The usual recommended oral starting dose is an equivalent of 200–400 milligrams (mg) of chlorpromazine (Table 24.3) Higher or IM (which has greater potency/mg) doses may be necessary. The daily dose of thioridazine should not exceed 800 mg, or pigmentary retinopathy (which causes blindness) may occur.

The initial dose should be gradually increased until the psychosis resolves, as long as side effects are tolerated. Underdosing frequently causes treatment failure. The full treatment effect may be reached in several weeks. A twice-daily (BID) dose may be switched to a single dose at bedtime in a week or so.

Once the patient's condition is stabilized, the daily dose of neuroleptic should be gradually reduced to the lowest effective dose. Schizophrenic patients should be treated for at least 8 months after the improvement, and then an attempt should be made to discontinue the neuroleptic gradually. Some patients, however, may require longer maintenance therapy with neuroleptics (p. 246). Even then, periodic efforts at dosage reduction or removal are in order. The most common long-term maintenance dose is an equivalent of 100–200 mg chlorpromazine.

Mr. A, a 60-year-old African-American factory worker, was treated for schizophrenia on and off for 25 years. He was doing fine on fluphenazine decanoate 25 mg IM every 3 weeks for 3 years. A few months after the decrease of his medication to 7.5 mg IM every 3 weeks, he started to hear voices again. He felt that women were trying to control him and read his mind. His medication was increased back to fluphenazine decanoate 25 mg IM every 3 weeks. He improved and has been symptom free, except for blunted affect, for 2 years.

Neuroleptics (which affect multiple receptor sites) cause numerous side effects. Extrapyramidal symptoms or side effects (EPS) include the following: (1) dystonia (involuntary contraction) of muscle groups, Dystonia of laryngeal muscles may cause suffocation and death. IM or IV benztropine mesylate or diphenhydramine hydrochloride dramatically cures dystonia. (2) Akathisia, an inner restlessness not associated with obvious reasons for anxiety, is a common side effect often confused with worsening of psychosis. Reduction of the dosage is the best management, but beta adrenergic blockers (e.g., propranolol) may be useful, too (10, 11). (3) Pseudoparkinsonism includes muscle stiffness, expressionless face, greasy skin, cogwheel rigidity, drooling, shuffling gait and pill-rolling tremor (identical with the findings in Parkinson's disease). Anticholinergic antiparkinson drugs such as benztropine mesylate, trihexyphenidyl hydrochloride, and amantadine hydrochloride are helpful. (4) Neuroleptic malignant syndrome is a life-threatening side effect characterized by muscle rigidity, hyperpyrexia (very high fever), and increased blood pressure. Bromocriptine mesylate and dantrolene sodium are useful in this condition (12). (5) Tardive dyskinesia (TD), a common, permanent side effect of months of years of neuroleptic treatment, is characterized by choreoathetoid (jerky and writhing) movements of the head, neck, trunk, and limbs. Almost all neuroleptics cause TD, but there are no confirmed cases with clozapine. Prevention by using treatments other than neuroleptics, or by prescribing neuroleptics in the lowest effective dose, is the best approach.

Table 24.3. Frequently Used Neuroleptic Drugs

Generic Name	Brand Name	100 mg Chlorpromazine Equivalent	Daily Dose (mg)	EPS	Side Effects ACh	Sedat.
Phenothiazines						
Aliphatic						
Chlorpromazine	Thorazine	100	100–1000	2+	3+	4+
Piperidine						
Thioridazine	Mellaril	100	100–600	1+	4+	4+
Mesoridazine	Serentil	50	75–400	1+	3+	4+
Piperazine						
Fluphenazine	Prolixin Permitil	2	1–40	4+	2+	2+
Perphenazine	Trilafon	10	8–64	4+	2+	3+
Trifluoperazine	Stelazine	3–5	5–30	4+	2+	1+
Thioxanthenes						
Chlorprothixene	Taractan	50	50–600	3+	2+	4+
Thiothixene	Navane	3–5	5–60	3+	2+	2+
Butyrophenones						
Haloperidol	Haldol	2–5	2–100	4+	1+	2+
Diphenylbutylpiperidines						
Pimozide	Orap	*	2–10	2+	1+	1+
Dibenzoxazepines						
Loxapine	Loxitane	10–15	30–200	3+	3+	2+
Dihydroindolones						
Molindone	Moban	10	10–200	3+	2+	1+
Dibenzodiazepines						
Clozapine	Clozaril	75	300–600	1+	4+	3+

*Equivalent for pimozide not available.
Neuroleptics from the class of benzamides are not available in the U.S.

Anticholinergic side effects include dry mouth, blurred vision, constipation, urinary retention, and (occasionally) delirium. Neuroleptics can also cause sedation, weight gain (except for molindone hydrochloride), ECG changes or arrhythmias, intrahepatic cholestatic allergic jaundice, hematologic side effects (leukopenia [p. 195), or agranulocytosis [a WBC count should be taken if the patient reports fever or sore throat]). Ophthalmologic side effects include pigmentary retinopathy with daily doses of thioridazine >800 mg and photosensitivity (rash on exposure to sunlight preventable with a sun block in susceptible patients). Futher side effects include gray skin discoloration (neuroleptics are stored in the skin), lowering of seizure threshold, endocrinologic changes such as lactation (dopamine blockade increases prolactin production, causing milk production), menstrual irregularity or amenorrhea, and altered glucose tolerance (elevated fasting blood sugar).

Concurrent use of other psychotropic drugs is usually not recommended. Lithium is often used along with a neuroleptic during initial treatment of mania, but the neuroleptic should later be discontinued and lithium continued alone. Lithium does not work as promptly as an IM neuroleptic for the combativeness or hyperactivity of a manic episode (7).

CYCLIC ANTIDEPRESSANTS

The antidepressant effect of imipramine hydrochloride was identified in 1957 when Kuhn (13) noted improved mood in patients during the clinical trial of imipramine in schizophrenia. Originally, only cyclic antidepressants (CAs) with a three ring-nucleus (tricyclics, e.g., amitriptyline) were used. Newer (second and third generation) CAs include compounds with one-, two- or four-ring nuclei.

The CAs have primarily been used for major depression (p. 246). They are also effective in panic disorder (14), agoraphobia (14), generalized anxiety disorder (14), obsessive-compulsive disorder (clomipramine) (14), eating disorders (15, 16), chronic pain (amitriptyline) (17), enuresis (imipramine) (18), ADHD (19) and peptic ulcer (doxepin).

Inhibition of reuptake of brain neurotransmitters such as norepinephrine, serotonin, or dopamine by CAs was originally postulated as their mechanism of action. However, some drugs increase neurotransmitter levels without improving mood. Moreover, although antidepressants increase monoamine levels quickly, there is a time lag in the onset of antidepressant action. Other explanations (e.g., down-regulation of beta adrenergic receptors) (20) are more plausible.

Use of Cyclic Antidepressants

MAJOR DEPRESSION

In addition to a history, physical, and standard lab tests (1), the recommended pretreatment tests for CAs include liver function tests, CBC with differential, and ECG.

The CAs are contraindicated during acute myocardial infarction (p. 4), and narrow-angle glaucoma. Caution is required before prescribing CAs in the presence of cardiac conduction deficits, ECG abnormalities, seizure disorder, severe prostatism (enlarged prostate causing urinary retention *and* frequent urination), pregnancy, and lactation. Care should be taken in dispensing CAs (as well as lithium, neuroleptics, and barbiturates) to suicidal outpatients; the overdose can be fatal.

Efficacy of all CAs is similar. Some authors claim amoxapine helps in psychotic depression (21). The pretreatment dexamethasone test and 3-hydroxy-4-methoxyphenylglycol levels do not predict outcome (22) or help in choosing an antidepressant. Some CAs are more sedative (e.g., amitriptyline, doxepin, trazodone), and the bedtime dose may induce sleep (which is often welcome) well before the depression begins to lift. The CAs are administered orally. One or two daily doses are more efficient than, and as effective as, three- or four-time-daily (TID or QID) doses. Dosage should be adjusted to the patient's response and side effects. The usual ranges of daily doses are summarized in Table 24.1.

The dose of most CAs (exceptions include nortriptyline, and protriptyline hydrochloride) should be gradually increased by about 25 mg every other day up to a maximally therapeutic dose. The patient should be informed that it takes 2–6 weeks for the CAs to take full effect. Once maximum improvement is achieved, the therapeutic dose should be continued for the time of greatest risk of recurrence (usually 6–9 months), roughly the duration of an untreated depressive episode. If the patient is asymptomatic, a trial to discontinue the medication could then be started. The CAs should be discontinued gradually, because the cholinergic rebound syndrome (nausea, sweating, headache) or rebound hypomania or mania are possible. The recommended dosage decrease is 25 mg every 3 days, while watching for reemergence of the depression. If it recurs, the dose should be increased to the previous therapeutic dose.

Prolonged maintenance therapy with CAs is usually safe, without permanent side effects. The indication for such therapy is frequently relapsing major depression. The usual recommended maintenance dose of CAs is about half the therapeutic dose, and the time of prolonged treatment begins after one year (23, 24).

Plasma levels of CAs are useful in assessing treatment response and compliance. Therapeutic range of several CAs is known (Table 24.1). But *remember that you treat patients, not blood levels.* Sometimes patients respond well at low levels, or can tolerate high levels without therapeutic or side effects.

Anticholinergic effects and sedation are the most frequent side effects. Often these can be alleviated by a decrease in dose, or by bethanechol chloride 10–30 mg TID (25). Dry mouth may be helped by chewing sugarless gum (sugared gums foster yeast infection) or having a pitcher of water handy. Bulk fiber laxatives (e.g., psyllium) reduce constipation. One bedtime dose helps patients with insomnia. Orthostatic hypotension (dropping blood pressure upon arising, with faintness) is unpleasant and dangerous, especially in elderly patients. Nortriptyline has a low frequency of this problem. Instruct posturally hypotensive patients to arise slowly from the lying-down or sitting position. Another approach may be the addition of fludrocortisone. Other frequent side effects are cardiac (e.g., tachycardia, quinidine-like [tending to decrease cardiac muscle excitability, contractility, and speed of conduction] effect), weight gain, and erectile dysfunction. Maprotiline and buproprion hydrochloride pose a greater risk of seizures than other CAs. Amoxapine may cause akathisia and pseudoparkinsonism, likely owing to the dopamine blockade.

> Mr. B was a 30-year-old Euro-American who worked as a clerk. He complained of depressed mood, feeling down, no energy, and inability to enjoy anything. He was waking up during the night. Appetite was poor, and he lost 15 pounds within 2 months. The rest of his physical examination and lab tests were normal. He was started on imipramine hydrochloride 25 mg at bedtime, and the dosage was gradually increased to 250 mg/day over 2 weeks. At that time, he complained of a dry mouth, constipation, and blurred vision, but he slept better. Dosage was decreased to 200 mg/day, and several weeks later his depression began to subside, and then disappeared. He ate better and felt better about himself. He continued to receive 200 mg imipramine for 6 months without any problem.

Cyclic antidepressants can be combined with other medications. Lithium could augment the treatment response in depression, as can levothyroxine sodium (in women). During the first few weeks of CA treatment, if the CA alone does not induce sleep, benzodiazepines may be added for sleep induction. Combining CAs with monoamine oxidase inhibitors should be left for a psychiatrist experienced in using this combination.

PANIC DISORDER OR AGORAPHOBIA

The CAs (most often imipramine) are also used for panic disorder or agoraphobia. Patients who have panic disorder are more sensitive to side effects of antidepressants than depressed patients, and may become jittery. A low initial dose, usually 10 mg, with a daily increase of 10 mg, is recommended. Onset of action may be earlier than in depression. The maximum dose for the patient depends on the person's clinical response and may reach the maximum dose for depression. Other CAs such as desipramine, nortriptyline, and fluoxetine hydrochloride are also effective in panic disorder.

> Mr. C was a 47-year-old teacher who suffered from panic attacks since his childhood. He was given 10 mg imipramine, which was gradually increased to 100 mg/day. His panic attacks disappeared within 3 weeks. He complained of constipation and sexual dysfunction, so imipramine was decreased to 50 mg/day, keeping him symptom-free.

GENERALIZED ANXIETY DISORDER

The CAs (specifically doxepin, amitriptyline, desipramine, and imipramine) are useful for generalized anxiety disorder (GAD), sometimes in combination with benzodiazepines. The CAs are especially useful in substance-abusing patients who have GAD.

EATING DISORDERS

Imipramine and desipramine have been used successfully in bulimia (p. 146) (15, 16). Buproprion is contraindicated because of an increased incidence of seizures in bulimics receiving this drug.

OBSESSIVE-COMPULSIVE DISORDER

This formerly treatment-resistant disorder responds to drugs (e.g., clomipramine, fluoxetine) that block serotonin reuptake (14). Clomipramine hydrochloride is the drug of choice. Starting dose should be about 75 mg/day in divided doses, gradually increased by about 25 mg every other day. A trial on a maximum dose of up to 300 mg should last at least 6 weeks.

MONOAMINE OXIDASE INHIBITORS

Monoamine oxidase inhibitors (MAOIs) have been used for mental disorders since the late 1950s, when improved mood was noted in patients treated for tuberculosis with isoniazid (structurally similar to MAOIs) (26). Phenelzine sulfate is the most commonly used. Tranylcypromine sulfate and isocarboxazid are also used. The MAOIs are effective for atypical, dysthymic, or reactive depression (27), panic disorder, agoraphobia, social phobia (28), posttraumatic stress disorder (29), and eating disorders (30). They may also be useful in ADHD (31, 32), narcolepsy (33), and some pain syndromes (34). The MAOIs inhibit monoamine oxidase (MAO), the enzyme that deaminates (breaks down) monoamines intracellularly. The MAOIs increase the availability of monoamines at synapses, which may explain their action. There may be other explanations, however, because MAO inhibition occurs acutely, whereas the antidepressant action usually takes a few weeks.

Liver function tests are indicated prior to MAOI therapy. An ECG is indicated prior to treatment with tranylcypromine sulfate. The MAOIs are contraindicated in patients who have pheochromocytoma (tumor of chromaffin issue secreting biogenic amines), congestive heart failure, and liver disease. They should not be combined with certain medications (Table 24.4) or used during elective surgery. They also should not be combined with fluoxetine hydrochloride or buspirone. Tranylcypromine is contraindicated in patients who have cerebrovascular disease, hypertension, or cardiovascular disease.

Patients must avoid food with high tyramine content (Table 24.4); these may cause a hypertensive reaction during MAOI treatment. The diet should continue for 2 weeks after treatment is stopped. At least 10 days should elapse following discontinuation of MAOIs prior to initiating CAs, to avoid hypertensive crisis. About a week without medication is recommended when switching from CAs to MAOIs (for fluoxetine, 5 weeks are required.

Initial dosage should be 15 mg phenelzine daily, and gradually increased by 15 mg/day to a maximally effective dose, or a maximum of 90 mg/day. Doses should be once daily or BID. Tranylcypromine should be started at 10 mg/day and gradually increased to a maximally effective dose or a maximum of 60 mg/day. Isocarboxazid dose should usually not exceed 30 mg/day. MAOIs are administered orally.

Again, maintenance with the lowest effective dose may be useful after a few months of acute treatment with the original therapeutic dose. Plasma monitoring of MAOIs is not done.

Side effects of MAOIs include orthostatic hypotension, weight gain, hypertensive reaction with certain foods, sexual dysfunctions, dry mouth, constipation, and urinary hesitancy. The orthostatic hypotension may be handled by support stockings, adequate hydration or fludrocortisone (an adrenal corticosteroid) (25). The patient should be instructed to arise slowly from a lying-down or sitting position. In case of hypertensive reaction, phentolamine mesylate (an alpha blocker) 5 mg IV is the treatment of choice. Prescribe one or two 10 mg nifedipine (a calcium channel blocker) tablets for the patient to keep readily available at all times, and instruct the patient to take one in the event that hypertension develops (symptoms of which are occipital headache, neck soreness, nausea, sweating, and photosensitivity), in which case the person should

Table 24.4.   Foods and Drugs to be Avoided During MAOI Treatment

Foods	Drugs
Aged cheese (fresh cottage and cream cheese are allowed)	Amphetamines
Beer, red wine* (small amounts of liquor or white wine allowed)	Asthma medications (including inhalants)
Dry sausage	Antihypertensives (alphamethyldopa, guanethidine, reserpine)
Fava or broad beans	Cocaine
Liver (beef, chicken)	Cold medications
Meat extracts	
Smoked or pickled fish and other meats	Epinephrine, hay fever medication, L-dopa, tryptophan, nasal decongestants
Yeast flavoring or yeast vitamin supplements	Sinus medications, stimulants
Large amounts of avocado, eggplant, plums, ripe bananas, raisins, sour cream, yogurt	Weight loss pills, L-dopa, meperidine, fluoxetine, buspirone

*Alcohol content not important

be driven immediately to the hospital. If side effects of one MAOI are intolerable, decrease the dosage, switch to another MAOI (after 2 weeks without medication), or discontinue the MAOI.

Lithium and MAOIs can be combined. Benzodiazepines can be combined with MAOIs, especially in MAOI-associated insomnia.

LITHIUM

Cade's 1949 (35) report on improvement of mania with lithium sparked an interest in this element. Lithium use in the U.S. was delayed until the late 1960s because of problems with unmonitored side effects.

Lithium is indicated in the acute treatment of manic (its main indication), hypomanic (mildly manic), or depressive episodes in patients with bipolar disorder; in maintenance treatment of bipolar disorder; in major depressive episodes in patients who have unipolar depression (as an adjunct to antidepressants); in cyclothymia (according to some researchers a mild variant of bipolar disorder

[36]); in schizoaffective disorder (which may be a variant of major affective disorder) (37, 38); in anorexia nervosa and bulimia (39); in some cases of schizophrenia (40); and in patients who manifest impulsively aggressive behavior (41–43). It is useless for patients whose violence is planned. Lithium used to raise WBC counts (utilizing its side effect of leukocytosis [p. 195]) in patients who have leukopenia [p. 195] from antineoplastic agents), and in cluster or migraine headaches. Its mechanism of action is unknown. Some theories are its effect on cell membranes and second messenger systems, and its causing the release of brain monoamines.

Pretreatment laboratory tests include electrolytes, creatinine, blood urea nitrogen (BUN), fasting blood sugar, urinalysis, CBC, thyroid function tests (T3, T4, TSH) and ECG. A pregnancy test should be done if there is a possibility of pregnancy. Thyroid function tests should be repeated every 6 months during maintenance therapy, and the other tests should be repeated annually.

Lithium should not be administered in severe cardiovascular or renal disease, severe dehydration, in pregnancy, during lactation, in most patients taking salt-depleting diuretics (exception: furosemide) or in patients taking indomethacin (a nonsteroidal antiinflammatory agent used for arthritis).

It is available in tablets or capsules (lithium carbonate) and elixir (lithium citrate), the latter for supervised settings if compliance is questionable. Otherwise, there is no difference in preparations.

Dosage is guided by clinical response and serum lithium levels. The initial daily lithium dose is 1200–1800 mg in one or two doses. Starting lithium doses in elderly or frail patients should be lower. Obtain a serum level in 3-5 days, and adjust the dose to achieve a range of 1.0–1.5 mEq/L (0.8–1.2 mEq/L if 24 hour total lithium exposure is computed [44]) in the acute phase of the treatment, which clinically corresponds to fine tremor and loss of ruddiness in the cheeks. The acute phase of lithium treatment should last for a year. Then, reassess continued use (p. 255).

The maintenance dose of lithium is guided by clinical observation and the serum level. The desirable lithium maintenance level is debated (45–47), lying within the range of 0.6–1.2 mEq/L. If 24-hour total daily lithium exposure is used, the level should be 0.8–1.2 mEq/L (44). Lithium maintenance is safe (48), and should be indefinite for most patients who have had prior *frequent* episodes of depression or mania (p. 255). The dosage strategies for various indications are the same. Again, as for CAs, treat patients, not blood levels.

Monitor lithium levels regularly, twice weekly during the acute phase, once weekly when the blood level stabilizes and the patient is improved, monthly during initial follow-up, and then at follow-up visits. Typically, blood for lithium level is drawn about 12 hours after the last dose, but if you have 15 minutes to calculate a 24-hour total lithium exposure level, blood can be drawn any time (44).

Mr. D is a 47-year-old African-American with a 15-year history of bipolar disorder. He was maintained on lithium carbonate 1200 mg/day for the last 3 years, and his lithium level varied between 0.6–0.8 mEq/L. He missed several appointments and stopped taking lithium. He was admitted to the hospital within 3 months after he stopped lithium. He was grandiose, with elevated mood and delusions. He was started on lithium carbonate again, and chlorpromazine was added for 2 weeks. He rapidly improved and has done well on lithium for 2 years.

Properly prescribed and monitored, lithium is remarkably safe. But it can cause many side effects, and the range between therapeutic and toxic dose is narrow. The most common side effects are nausea, tremor, mild cognitive impairment, hypothyroid, goiter, weight gain, diarrhea, polyuria and polydipsia, skin eruptions (e.g., worsening of psoriasis), and cardiac effects (flattening of T wave, depression of sinus node activity). There is a debate about whether kidney damage occurs; if so, it is minimal, and patients most at risk are those who develop nephrogenic diabetes insipidus. Some side effects can be minimized by lowering dosage. Tremor, if troubling, is usually alleviated by propranolol. Thyroid preparations are indicated in hypothyroid goiter. Lithium is contraindicated during the first trimester of pregnancy. It can cause fetal cardiac anomalies. The treatment of choice for a manic or melancholic episode during pregnancy (49, 50) is ECT. Nausea is often reduced by prescribing lithium with meals. Polyuria and polydipsia often reflect lithium-induced nephrogenic diabetes insipidus (the kidney is unresponsive to antidiuretic hormone; urine-specific gravity is low [less than 1.005], serum sodium is high, and there is no glucose in the urine). This diabetes insipidus is treated with the sulfanylurea diuretics chlorothiazide or hydrochlorothiazide, which are otherwise contraindicated for patients on lithium.

Lithium can be administered with neuroleptics, antidepressants, carbamazepine, and benzodiazepines. It should be discontinued for 3 days prior to ECT.

ANTICONVULSANTS

Three anticonvulsants, carbamazepine, valproic acid, and clonazepam, are often used in psychiatry, primarily as alternatives to lithium in the treatment of mania and prophylaxis of bipolar disorder (51, 52). Carbamazepine was originally used for trigeminal neuralgia (severe facial pain in the distribution of trigeminal nerve) and psychomotor epilepsy (p. 47), but research (53) in Japan in the 1970s suggested its efficacy in bipolar disorder. It is also effective in alcohol withdrawal (p. 301). Valproic acid has also been used in benzodiazepine withdrawal and panic disorder.

The hypothesized mechanism of action of anticonvulsants is either inhibition of kindling (prolonged stimulation with subthreshold stimuli finally eliciting an excitatory response) (54), γ-aminobutyric acid (GABA) agonism (p. 58) or norepinephrine blockade.

Liver function tests and CBC with differential are required before carbamazepine treatment. Liver function tests should also precede treatment with valproic acid, which is contraindicated with liver disease.

Carbamazepine, valproic acid, and clonazepam are good second-line medications in bipolar disorder. The usual starting dose of carbamazepine is 100 mg BID the first week, and 200 mg BID the second week. It is gradually increased to 600–2000 mg/day based on serum levels and outcome. The therapeutic serum level of carbamazepine is between 4 and 12 mg/L.

Valproic acid should be started at 250 mg TID and increased by 250 mg every 4–7 days to a serum level of 50–100 μgs/mL. Daily doses will then range from 750–3000 mg. Clonazepam can be started at 0.5 mg BID and gradually increased to 4–20 mg/day for manic episodes. Carbamazepine and valproic acid (52) can be used for prophylaxis.

Common side effects of carbamazepine include sedation, drowsiness, nausea, vomiting, ataxia, and dizziness; it is best to increase the dose slowly. Carbamazepine can also cause liver damage and bone marrow suppression (aplastic anemia or agranulocytosis). Follow-up liver function tests are indicated every 3–6 months, and follow-up CBCs weekly for 8 weeks, monthly after that.

Valproic acid can also cause nausea and vomiting, and may cause tremor, ataxia (unsteady gait), alopecia (hair loss), and sedation. Anticonvulsants can be combined with antidepressants, lithium, and neuroleptics.

SYMPATHOMIMETICS (STIMULANTS)

Three sympathomimetics are usually used in psychiatry: dextroamphetamine, methylphenidate hydrochloride, and magnesium pemoline. Sympathomimetics or stimulants have been used since the 1930s for ADHD, narcolepsy, and depression.

Dextroamphetamine and methylphenidate are used in ADHD (in children, or adults with ADHD persisting from childhood), narcolepsy (p. 377), and chronic treatment-resistant depression in older persons (55). Magnesium pemoline is used in ADHD.

The probable mechanism of action of these drugs is the release of dopamine into the synapse, and possibly dopaminergic and noradrenergic reuptake blockade. Liver function should be tested prior to use of pemoline.

Sympathomimetics should not be used in glaucoma, substance abuse, psychosis, tics, or Tourette's disorder. Pemoline should not be used if there is liver damage. The usual daily dose of methylphenidate for ADHD in children is 10–40 mg, and should rarely exceed 60 mg. The daily dose of dextroamphetamine for ADHD in children is 5–40 mg, and for narcolepsy in adults 5–60 mg. Dextroamphetamine and methylphenidate are Class II controlled substances which must be prescribed on triplicate forms in some states. The usual daily dose of pemoline for ADHD in children is 37.5–75 mg and should not exceed 112.5 mg. Frequent side effects include nervousness, insomnia, anorexia, nausea, tachycardia, increased blood pressure, and dizziness. Adjusting dosage or switching to another drug may be necessary because of side effects. Sympathomimetics should be periodically discontinued in children.

> E. is a 10-year-old girl who was evaluated for poor attention, daydreaming, failing grades, hyperactivity, and inability to sit still. According to her mother, E. has been like that for as long as she could remember. The girl was started on methylphenidate 10 mg in the morning and at noon, and she improved dramatically within a few days.

Sympathomimetics could be combined with CAs in chronic, treatment-resistant depression.

BENZODIAZEPINES

Fourteen benzodiazepines (BZPs) are used in psychiatry in the United States (another, midazolam hydrochloride, is used in anesthesia). They can be categorized by structure, but practically they are classified according to half-life (the time it takes for the plasma concentration to fall by 50%) (Table 24.5). Benzodiazepines, introduced in the early 1960s, quickly became widely prescribed and abused.

They are used for anxiety disorders, insomnia, alcohol withdrawal, muscle relaxation,

Table 24.5. Benzodiazepines

Generic Name	Brand Name	Dosage Range (mg/day)
Long-Acting		
Chlordiazepoxide	Librium	15–100
Clonazepam	Klonopin	1–3
Clorazepate	Tranxene	15–60
Diazepam	Valium	4–40
Flurazepam	Dalmane	15–30
Halazepam	Paxipam	60–160
Prazepam	Centrax	20–60
Quazepam	Doral	7.5–15
Intermediate-Acting		
Alprazolam	Xanax	0.75–4
Lorazepam	Ativan	2–6
Oxazepam	Serax	30–120
Temazepam	Restoril	15–30
Estazolam	Pro Som	1–2
Short-Acting		
Triazolam	Halcion	0.125–0.5

preoperative anesthesia, status epilepticus (diazepam), myoclonic epilepsy, and bipolar disorder (clonazepam). Their mechanism of action is explained by their binding to receptors which are connected to GABA receptors and chloride channels (p. 58).

Beyond routine lab assessments (1), no specific tests are required for BZP treatment. The BZPs are contraindicated in cases of sensitivity to the individual drug and in acute narrow-angle glaucoma. They should not be used for substance abusers (except for alcohol withdrawal), and they should be avoided in pregnancy because of increased risk of congenital malformations.

The choice of an individual drug depends in large part on its half-life (56). Some authors claim that BZPs with shorter half-life are more useful in elderly patients, because drug half-life increases with age, and accumulation is possible (57) The BZPs that have longer half-life have less rebound anxiety, interdose anxiety, and withdrawal symptoms (58, 59). All BZPs can transiently impair memory. Usual daily doses are listed in Table 24.5. Initial dosage should be the lowest possible divided daily dose (e.g., 2 mg diazepam TID, 0.25–0.5 mg alprazolam TID). The dose should be gradually increased to the effective dose or maximum recommended dose. The usual length of treatment is 1–2 months, following which the BZP should be slowly tapered. Some authors advocate long-term BZP use in chronically anxious patients (60); this is widely debated (60). Some BZPs are available parenterally (IM or IV) (chlordiazepoxide, diazepam, lorazepam). IM absorption is poor compared to oral or IV doses. Several BZPs (e.g., alprazolam, clonazepam, lorazepan) (61) are effective for panic disorder, but because of abuse potential should be used only if conventional treatments are ineffective.

> Mr. F, a 38-year-old Euro-American maintenance man, has suffered from panic attacks for 3 years. He was tried on imipramine, buspirone and phenelzine, but could not tolerate these because of side effects. Trial with clonazepam 0.5 mg BID brought significant relief. He became

panic-free, and did not have any side effects for 2 years on the same dose of clonazepam.

Flurazepam hydrochloride, quazepam, temazepam, estazolam and triazolam are used for insomnia, with temazepam offering the fewest complications, and triazolam the least daytime sedation. IM lorazepam may be used for psychotic agitation in undiagnosed patients (2).

The most frequent side effects are drowsiness and mild cognitive impairment, particularly amnesia. The BZPs should not be combined with alcohol. The possibility of BZP abuse is high. They may be safely combined with other psychotropic drugs, but cautiously when combined with other sedating medication.

SEROTONERGIC ANXIOLYTICS

The only available drug from this group is the azaspirodecanedione hydrochloride buspirone. Gepirone is being tested. Buspirone is effective in generalized anxiety disorder (GAD) (62), but not panic disorder. The mechanism of action may be through the serotonergic system, but it also affects the noradrenergic system.

Beyond routine lab assessments (1), no other tests are required. Buspirone is contraindicated only in cases of sensitivity to it, or when the patient is taking MAOIs. The usual initial daily dose is 15 mg, the average daily dose 30 mg. The daily dose should not exceed 60 mg. It works well for at least several months in the treatment of GAD, perhaps longer. The usual side effects are headache, nausea, dizziness, and nervousness. It is not effective in BZP withdrawal (63). It should not be combined with MAOIs or neuroleptics, but can be combined with CAs.

BETA-BLOCKING AGENTS

The beta-blocking agents propranolol hydrochloride and atenolol are sometimes used in psychiatry. Propranolol's hypothesized mode of action is on peripheral autonomic symptoms of anxiety (e.g., palpitation, tremor, sweating) (64). It is helpful in generalized anxiety and performance anxiety, but not in panic disorder (61).

Cardiopulmonary status should be assessed, because propranolol is contraindicated in bronchial asthma, congestive heart failure, cardiogenic shock, sinus bradycardia (slowing of heart rate paced by the sinoatrial node) and second- or third-degree heart block. Propranolol should not be used in diabetes mellitus, Raynaud's disease (painful, discoloring blood vessel spasm in the fingers precipitated by cold), and depression; it may worsen depression. The usual starting dose is 10 mg BID. It may be gradually increased to 80–160 mg/day, using modest slowing of heart rate as a goal.

Common side effects are hypotension, bradycardia, bronchospasm, nausea, vomiting, dizziness, depression, and lethargy. As already noted, it is useful in lithium-induced tremor and neuroleptic-induced akathisia, but there is no indication for its therapeutic combination with other psychotropic drugs.

CLONIDINE

The antihypertensive clonidine, an alpha 2 adrenergic agonist (p. 56), has been used in panic disorder (0.4–0.6 mg/day), Tourette's syndrome, and opioid withdrawal. Its use in psychiatry dates back to the early 1980s (65). Unfortunately, tolerance (p. 305) develops frequently. The only contraindication to clonidine is allergy to it. Orthostatic hypotension is the most bothersome side effect.

SEDATIVE HYPNOTICS

Numerous drugs have been used for insomnia, most often benzodiazepines and barbiturates. Barbiturates are potent CNS depressants, anticonvulsants, anesthetics, and hypnotics, but their use has diminished because their potential for abuse is high and their therapeutic index (dose ratio between toxic and therapeutic effects) is low. No specific pretreatment tests are required.

The best known sedative hypnotics are pentobarbital (dose range 100–200 mg), phenobarbital (dose range 15–100 mg), secobarbital (range 100–200 mg), and butabarbital (range 50–100 mg). Some of the barbiturates are available in parenteral form. Amobarbital (200–500 mg slowly IV) is used in the Amytal interview to help mute catatonic patients talk, or for emergency sedation in newly admitted undiagnosed patients (3). Barbiturates should be used only for short-term management of insomnia. The most frequent side effects are sedation, slurred speech, ataxia, cognitive impairment, and dysphoria. Barbiturates should not be mixed with other CNS depressants, and they are contraindicated in porphyria. Other hypnotics (e.g., ethchlorvynol [dose range 500–750 mg], chloral hydrate [500–1000 mg]) have been used in the short-term management of insomnia (66).

ELECTROCONVULSIVE THERAPY

Various methods of inducing seizures have been used in psychiatry since the 1930s. In 1937, Cerletti and Bini used electrical current to induce seizures in psychotic patients. Originally, its use was hampered by fractures and other complications. Since the introduction of the muscle relaxant succinylcholine chloride and other precautions, electroconvulsive therapy (ECT) has become safe.

Electroconvulsive therapy is effective in major depression with melancholia, mania, schizophrenia with positive symptoms (p. 242) and schizoaffective disorder. It is particularly useful in debilitated patients with psychosis, in pregnant patients (49, 50), and in patients who have treatment-resistant depression. Numerous (67-70) studies have demonstrated the superiority of ECT to other treatments of severe depression.

The exact mechanism of action is not known, but the seizure is necessary for its antidepressant effect. ECT's only contraindication is increased intracranial pressure. The CAs, neuroleptics, MAOIs, lithium, and BZPs are usually discontinued before ECT.

The patient should not eat past midnight when ECT is administered in the morning, and can have only clear liquids for breakfast when it is administered in the afternoon. Usually 30 minutes before the procedure, atropine sulfate or glycopyrrolate is administered IM to minimize secretions and decrease the risk of arrhythmias. The mouth should be checked for dentures.

A psychiatrist performs the ECT, with anesthesia administered by an anesthesiologist or nurse-anesthetist using the short-acting barbiturate methohexital sodium, and succinylcholine-induced muscle relaxation. The seizure is induced by electrodes placed either bilaterally (bifrontotemporally) or unilaterally (usually over the nondominant hemisphere). Brief pulse currents are used. The seizure should last 30–60 seconds. Occurrence of seizure pattern on EEG or tonic-clonic muscular contraction (seen distal to a blood pressure cuff) confirms the adequacy of the seizure. Usually 5–10 procedures (3/week) are required.

The most frequent side effect of ECT is a transient retrograde amnesia. Headaches, posttreatment delirium (preventable with proper dosing of succinylcholine chloride, treatable with IV diazepam) may occur. Tachycardia and increased blood pressure accompany the seizure, and EEG slowing follows it. Memory impairment is less after unilateral ECT. Biweekly or monthly outpatient ECT may be used for maintenance therapy to prevent relapse (67).

The authors thank Cheryl Cussigh for her secretarial and editorial assistance.

SECTION V. DESTRUCTIVE AND INJURIOUS BEHAVIORS

25/Accidents

Gregory Franchini, M.D.

OBJECTIVES

GENERAL OBJECTIVE: Given a patient who has just experienced an accident, suggest strategies for preventing future accidents.

SPECIFIC OBJECTIVES:

1. State the trends in accidental death rates in the United States.
2. Discuss the demographic and clinical correlates of accidents.
3. Discuss the epidemiologic model of accident cause and prevention, including the phase-factor matrix.
4. Summarize prevention strategies for the following: injuries to children, adolescents, and the elderly; motor vehicle, home, occupational, and recreational safety; and firearms regulation.

In the time it takes to read this chapter, accidents, the fourth leading cause of death in the United States, will have killed six Americans, disabled over 500, and cost over $9 million (1). Unlike the three leading killers, cardiovascular disease, cancer, and stroke, accidents disproportionately affect the young. Accidents also are the leading cause of premature death in the United States, accounting for more years of life lost prior to age 65 than cardiovascular disease, cancer, and strokes combined.

ACCIDENT RATES, CAUSES, AND TRENDS

Accidents cause nearly 100,000 deaths and over nine million disabling injuries annually in the United States. Yearly, about 62 million persons seek medical care because of accidental injuries.

The overall accidental death rate has steadily declined during this century from about 100 deaths per 100,000 population in 1900 to about 38 per 100,000 by the 1990s. In that time, however, accidents have increased in relative importance. In the early 1900s (before the Model T), accidents were the seventh leading cause of death. By the mid-1960s, they had risen to their current position as the fourth leading cause, surpassing death from infections (3). Accidents have become one of the leading causes of death in the United States because of declines in mortality from the major communicable diseases rather than from any increase in accident mortality itself.

Motor vehicle accidents, falls, poisoning, drowning, and fires were among the leading causes of accidental death in 1990 (Table 25.1). The overall accidental death rate fell approximately 20% between 1980 and 1990 (from 47/100,000 population to 38/100,000),

Table 25.1.   Accidental Deaths, 1990[a]

Type of Accident	Total Deaths	Percent	Per 100,000
Motor vehicle	46,300	50.0	18.6
Falls	12,400	13.0	5.0
Poisoning by solids and liquids	5,700	6	2.3
Drowning	5,200	5.5	2.1
Fires, burns and death associated with fires	4,300	4.6	1.7
Suffocation by ingested object	3,200	3.4	1.3
Firearms	1,400	1.5	0.6
Poisoning by gases and vapors	800	1.0	0.3
All other types	14,200	15.0	5.7
TOTAL ACCIDENTS	93,500	100.0	37.5

[a]Adapted from National Safety Council estimates.

(Table 25.1) a drop that affected all age groups. Of the four major classes of accidents—motor vehicle, work, home, and "public"—all but home accidental deaths declined during the 1980s. Deaths increased significantly in two categories: suffocation by ingestion, which rose 20%, and poisoning by liquids and solids, which increased 77%. Both were attributable to increased accidental drug overdoses (1).

ARE ACCIDENTS ACCIDENTAL?

An accident is an "unforeseen occurrence, especially one of an injurious nature" (4). This implies that unintentional injuries occur randomly and are unpredictable and unpreventable. Yet research shows that causes can be determined, corrections undertaken, and accidents prevented (5, 6).

The epidemiologic model helps explain this reasoning: an accident is viewed not as occurring by chance (i.e., not accidental), but as the product of an interacting system of influences involving the injured person (the host), the source of injury (agent), and the environment in which the injury occurs (7).

Accidents may be studied using three elements: environmental hazard, exposure, and vulnerability (8). An environmental hazard is any situation that can harm someone. Exposure is a person's degree of interaction with that situation. Vulnerability is the person's capacity (e.g., coordination, judgment, knowledge) to deal with a situation. For an accident to occur, there must be disequilibrium between the three elements.

CORRELATES OF ACCIDENTS

Age

Accidents among Americans are the leading cause of death from the ages of 1–37 years. Deaths from accidents increase markedly during the teen years, and have a first peak at about 21 years of age. Accident fatalities gradually decrease between the ages of 21 and the late forties, then stabilize from age 40–60, and increase to the highest rates after age 74 (1).

For infants under 1 year of age, accidents are the fifth leading cause of death, but the number of accidental deaths for infants under the age of 1 year exceeds that for any age group prior to the teens. For Americans between the ages of 1–24 years, accidents account for nearly half the deaths, 66% of which are from motor vehicle accidents. Accidental death rates among the elderly aged 75 years or older are nearly three times those of any other age group, with falls causing the most morbidity and mortality (1).

Sex

The overall accidental death rate among men is over twice that of women. Males have more accidents than do females at all ages, except for nonmotor vehicle accidents among the elderly aged 75 years or older. This male preponderance is most marked from between the ages of 15 and 24 years. Yet males exhibit only slightly higher overall nonfatal injury rates than do females; thus, injuries to males *tend* to be more severe (9).

Ethnicity and Socioeconomic Status

Native Americans have the highest accidental death rates in all age groups; Asian-

Americans show the lowest rates in corresponding age groups. Euro-Americans experience the second highest rates among those aged 25 years or younger and among those aged 70 years or older. African-Americans show the second highest rates for the population 25–70 years of age (9).

Individual socioeconomic status (SES) is omitted in national mortality data. Instead, accident rates are related to per capita income of the area of residence of each fatality. Accidental motor and nonmotor vehicle death rates show a dramatic negative correlation with per capita income, decreasing from 71 per 100,000 population in the lowest income areas to 34 per 100,000 population in the highest income areas. In contrast, deaths from airplane crashes increase with income (for obvious reasons). Deaths from falls are unrelated to socioeconomic status (9).

Socioeconomic status influences ethnic differences in accidental death rates. When ethnicity and residence are taken together, accidental death rates for African-Americans and Euro-Americans are the same. (9)

Geographic Variations

For most accidental injuries (exceptions: falls and poisonings), death rates are higher in rural areas. The overall rural accidental death rate is twice the urban rate. Western mountain and east south central states show the highest overall rates. Reasons for rural-urban disparities are uncertain but may reflect differences in socioeconomic conditions, occupational exposures, and availability of emergency care (9). Individual states markedly differ, ranging from 23 per 100,000 population in New Hampshire to 79 per 100,000 population in Alaska (1).

Temporal Variations

Deaths from accidents are most frequent on weekends (especially Saturday) and in summer (especially July). Deaths from motor vehicle accidents, drownings, and motorcycle and bicycle accidents are most prominent in summer. Deaths from house fires, falls, and unintentional poisoning by motor vehicle exhaust peak in winter (9).

Occupation

In 1990 nearly 2 million work-related injuries caused over 10,000 fatalities and 75 million work days lost, and cost almost $64 billion (1). Mining and agriculture (Table 25.2) are the most hazardous industries, with accidental fatality rates of 43 and 42 per 100,000 population, respectively. The overall work force rate is 9 per 100,000 population (1).

The most common cause of accidental occupational deaths is motor vehicle accidents (over 35%), followed by falls (nearly 13%). About 60,000 workers experience permanently disabling injuries each year (1).

Younger and less experienced workers disproportionately incur work injuries and deaths. They are more likely to be assigned risky tasks and are less experienced at avoiding

Table 25.2.   Occupational Accidents, 1990[a]

Type of Industry	Number of Workers	Injuries	Deaths	Deaths/ 100,000
Mining	700,000	30,000	300	43
Agriculture	3,100,000	120,000	1,300	42
Construction	6,400,000	210,000	2,100	33
Transportation and Public Utilities	6,000,000	120,000	1,300	22
Government	17,600,000	290,000	1,600	9
Manufacturing	18,800,000	360,000	1,100	6
Trade	27,500,000	330,000	1,200	4
Services	37,300,000	340,000	1,600	4
ALL INDUSTRIES	117,400,000	1,800,000	10,500	9

[a]Adapted from National Safety Council estimates.

injury (10). Minorities are overrepresented in hazardous occupations (11).

Recreation

Although recreation fosters good health, it often leads to serious injury. Recreational activities are diverse and wide-ranging with no specific or widely accepted definition. Our knowledge and understanding of these activities are further hampered by limited information and inadequate collection of data. Data on incidence of injuries and death from hazardous sports (e.g., rock climbing, skydiving) and unorganized, informal recreation are sparse. There are more data on water sports, competitive sports, and playground activities (12).

Drownings are the fourth leading cause of accidental death in the United States. Death by drowning steadily decreased during the 1980s, with the greatest reductions among young adults aged 15–22 years. Men, more prone to risk-taking, drown four times as often as women. Most drownings occur in swimming or boating accidents and in natural bodies of water, although many young children drown in residential swimming pools. The highest rate of drowning occurs in children aged 5 years or younger, typically during lapses in adult supervision (13).

Many nondrowning recreational injuries are associated with water activities. Most are lacerations and abrasions, usually of the face and head, related to slippery surfaces, roughhousing, climbing ladders, or diving. Spinal cord injuries from diving, approximately 1,000 of which occur annually, are devastating: they account for 10% of all spinal cord injuries. Most result in permanent paralysis, and most victims are adolescent and young adult males. Alcohol plays a significant role in 41%–80% of aquatic spinal cord injuries (12).

Competitive sports are associated with over 1.5 million injuries a year, most of which (1.2 million) are in baseball, basketball, and football (1). Contact sports have higher rates than noncontact sports. Males are injured at approximately twice the rate of females, but rates are similar if contact sports are not included. The most prevalent injuries are strains (stretching or tearing of a tendon), sprains (stretching or tearing of a ligament), contusions, abrasions, and concussions (transient losses of consciousness because of a head injury). Only 2% of sports injuries require hospitalization (12).

Playground or playground equipment injuries number 200,000 yearly. Half occur at home, 25% at schools, and the remaining 25% at other public playgrounds. Although most injuries are minor, 25% are serious: concussions, fractures, crush wounds, or multiple injuries. The number of deaths from playground injuries is small, usually from head injuries. The vast majority of playground injuries are from falls to the playground surface (12).

Alcohol and Other Drugs

Alcohol plays a major role in accidents of all types. In 1990, alcohol was a factor in at least 22,000 fatal motor vehicle accidents, over 500,000 injuries, and nearly 1.4 million property damage accidents, costing over $20 billion (1). Almost half of fatally injured drivers, and substantial proportions of adult passengers and pedestrians killed in motor vehicle crashes, as well as in falls, drownings, and fires, have blood alcohol concentrations of 0.10% or higher (i.e., legally intoxicated) (14).

As property damage and the severity of injuries in crashes increases, so does the probability that alcohol is involved. The idea that alcohol protects a person against injury is a myth: alcohol increases susceptibility to injury in any type of collision (15).

The data on alcohol and nonvehicular accidents are less complete. An emergency room breathalyzer study detected alcohol in 22% of patients injured at home, 16% on the job, and 30% on the road (16).

The role of drugs other than alcohol in accidents is unclear. Benzodiazepines and barbiturates increase the effect of alcohol when used in combination and impair performance in experiments, but little is known about their role in accidents.

Psychiatric Illness, Personality Traits, and Life Stress

Patients who have been hospitalized for mental illness have motor vehicle accident rates similar to those of patients who have chronic systemic illnesses, which is more than the general population. Among the mentally ill group, the increased risk is accounted for primarily by alcoholics and persons who have antisocial and borderline personality disorders (pp. 272, 273). Some personality traits—low frustration tolerance, emotional instability, aggressiveness, and immaturity—are associated with higher frequencies of accidents (17). Although some studies (18–20) suggest a link between accidents and life stress (e.g., arguments, divorce), other studies (17, 21) find no such link.

ACCIDENT PREVENTION

In recent decades, an increasingly effective approach to accident prevention and control has developed using epidemiology. Early 20th century efforts focused on the individual, emphasizing educational measures such as pamphlets and posters, with limited effectiveness (12). DeHaven's 1940s work on aircraft and automobile structure (22) pointed to the critical role of vehicle design in passenger safety in crashes and established the central importance of biomechanics in injury prevention. In the late 1940s, Gordon (23) suggested that accidents shared many characteristics of classic infectious diseases and could be studied by using the same epidemiologic techniques. Gordon reasoned that each accident, like each disease outbreak, was the product not of one cause but of interrelationships between the host, the agent, and the environment (23).

Haddon (24) in the 1960s conceptualized the phase-factor matrix in which host, agent, and environment interact over time to cause injury. In this model the preevent phase involves all factors that determine whether an accident will occur. The event phase includes all factors that determine whether, and to what extent, an injury will occur. Finally, the postevent phase considers all factors that determine how well an injury is treated (24). Haddon determined that accident and subsequent injury prevention required the modification of only one of the factors involved, thus moving the focus of accident prevention from the host to include the agent and the environment. Using the phase-factor matrix, 10 strategies have been developed (Table 25.3) for preventing or minimizing injury (12).

Intervention involves three general approaches or combinations: (1) persons at risk may be persuaded to alter their behavior through educational measures; (2) individual behavior change may be required by new laws or better enforcement of existing laws; and (3) automatic protection may be provided through changes in product and environmental design.

Research on accidents has shown that requiring a change in behavior is more effective than persuading persons to change behavior through education (25). Providing automatic protection through engineering and technology is the most effective technique.

Physicians should try to influence their patients' behavior on an individual basis. Public educational programs in accident prevention have had limited success (24), but education may be more effective within the physician–patient relationship (25).

Preventing Injuries to Children and Adolescents

Accidents are the major health problem in children and adolescents in the United States, accounting for more deaths than all disease combined. Motor vehicle accidents are the leading cause of death for children and adolescents, followed by drowning, fires and burns, firearms, poisoning, falls, and mechanical suffocation (1).

Historically, active educational approaches were, by themselves, ineffective (26). Passive, automatic measures became the major focus. The most successful example is the Poison Prevention Package Act of 1970, which required child-resistant containers for specified medications and household substances (12). Since then, ingestions of substances covered by the Act decreased 50%. Corresponding reductions in poisoning deaths have been even more dramatic. Other successful interventions of this type included legislation requiring approved restraints for children in motor vehicles, smoke detectors in the home, flame-resistant sleep wear, and withdrawal of dangerous toys from the market. Withdrawal from the market of polystyrene-filled cushions that tended to cause rebreathing of expired air has reduced infant deaths from asphyxia (27).

Because a risk-free environment is impossible, combining active and passive prevention is necessary. Active or educational interventions by physicians have been found to be more effective when they are focused on a single safety concern geared toward the child's

developmental level rather than on a comprehensive safety overview (28).

The American Academy of Pediatrics has developed an Injury Prevention Program (29) in which children's physicians discuss with parents specific safety topics at each well-child visit (Table 25.4). Unfortunately, pediatricians spend an average of less than 1 minute per well-child visit to discuss safety with parents (30).

Preventing Injuries to the Elderly

Americans aged 65 years or older (12% of the population) account for over 25,000 (25%) accidental deaths annually. For the 75 and older age group, the rate, as stated earlier, is three times that of any other age group, and is mainly the result of falls, motor vehicle accidents, and suffocation by aspiration (inhaling a liquid or solid). Nearly five million elderly

Table 25.3. Ten Strategies to Prevent or Minimize Injury[a]

1. Control the amount of hazard created. Reduce production of poisons, gunpowder, radioactive materials, motorcycles, and automobiles. Drain and cover swimming pools off season.
2. Reduce the amount of hazard created. Package potentially toxic drugs in smaller, safe amounts. Limit the speed of vehicles and the height of diving boards, high chairs, and ladders. Restrict the availability of ammunition.
3. Prevent or reduce the risk of an accident. Make bathtubs less slippery. Require child-proof containers. Design hunting weapons that will not discharge inadvertently. Restrict contact sports.
4. Minimize the severity of injury should an accident occur. Require automobile air bags and seat belts, parachutes for airplane passengers, fire nets, safety valves on boilers. Maintain a flammability standard for children's sleep wear that limits the burning rate.
5. Take safety precautions when using hazardous materials. Spray poisons sparingly and only when people are absent. Transport hazardous materials when traffic is minimal and dispose of them responsibly. Ventilate noxious fumes by ventilation. Store target-shooting pistols at the shooting range, not at home.
6. Design safety precautions into products and activities. Insulate electrical cords. Distance gas tanks away from the body periphery of vehicles. Use helmets, shin guards, boxing gloves, padded clothing, and bullet-proof vests in the appropriate sports, occupations, and pasttimes. Require eye protection devices in racquet sports, and face masks and mouth guards for contact sports. Pad gymnasium walls.
7. Manufacture safer products. Make openings between crib slats too narrow to lodge a head and strangle a child and too wide to lodge an arm or hand. Remove projections, rounding and softening corners and edges of likely impact sites such as dashboards, playpens, bus window frames, and seat backs. Design light posts, sign posts, and goal posts to yield when struck.
8. Practice proper health promotion and responsible physical fitness. Improve health through balanced nutrition and exercise programs. Limit the number of innings each game that a Little Leaguer can pitch. Group school athletics and other sports by athletic skill level, physical fitness, and physical maturity as well as by age.
9. Counter damage already done by the hazard. Provide emergency medical care. Improve communication systems within emergency medical care components. Increase availability of ambulances equipped to support life. Ensure that emergency and paramedical personnel are highly trained and emergency care units are well staffed.
10. Stabilize, repair, and rehabilitate the injured person. Provide acute care and rehabilitation facilities. Develop specialized treatment facilities such as burn units, detoxification centers, and regional trauma centers. Modify the environment to accommodate the handicapped.

[a]Modified from the National Committee for Injury Prevention and Control. Injury prevention: meeting the challenge. New York: Oxford University Press, 1989.

Table 25.4. Topics to Address During Well-Child Visits[a]

Patient Age at Visit	Topic
Newborn	Car restraints
2–4 weeks	Crib environment
2 months	Infant furniture
4 months	Toy safety
6 months	Electrical burns and scalds
9 months	Ingestions
12 months	Falls
15 months	Cuts
18 months	Repetition of poisoning warnings
24 months	Yard safety
36 months	Repetition of toy safety (e.g., tricycle)
5 years	Fire prevention

[a]Adapted from the Committee on Psychosocial Aspects of Child and Family Health. Guidelines for health supervision II. Elk Grove Village, IL: American Academy of Pediatrics, 1985.

Americans sustain nonfatal injuries annually, 75% at home (31).

The elderly are more susceptible to injuries because of their general physiologic status (p. 165), and because of the effects of illness and medication. Falls are particularly noteworthy because they may be an early indication of a serious underlying medical condition (32).

Physicians can help prevent accidents in their elderly patients by fully evaluating and modifying, as appropriate, personal and environmental factors (31). Cognitive impairment, inattention and dizziness caused by overmedication or oversedation are often misdiagnosed as senility. Seizures should be properly diagnosed and treated. A patient's full drug regimen and compliance should be monitored. The best predictor of falls is past falls, about which the physician should inquire. Because most accidents in the elderly occur at home, a home hazards checklist (Table 25.5) should be given to the patient, family, visiting nurse, or other caretaker.

Between the ages of 65 and 74 years, motor vehicle accidents are the major cause of accidental death. Physicians should screen for cognitive, motor, or sensory impairment, any of which could make a patient a dangerous driver. Alternative transportation must then be arranged if driving is prohibited or restricted.

Table 25.5 Home Hazard Checklist[a]

STAIRS
Adequate illumination
Top and bottom steps painted
Nonskid treads
Handrail: detached, graspable, end of rail shaped to signify bottom of stairway
Risers painted in easily visible color

LIVING AREAS
Carpets
Edges tacked down completely
Wall-to-wall with thick, shock-absorbent pads
No throw rugs
Floors
No highly polished floor surfaces
Nonskid wax
Thresholds removed
No extension cords
Access pathways free of low-lying furniture or other objects
Baseboard lighting in halls
Other
Emphasis on control of pets and small children to avoid causing trips
No low couches, sharp-cornered furniture, or chairs on casters
Light switches easily accessible at door or room
Lighted switches

BATHROOM
Nonskid rubber mats in shower or bath
Handrails in bath and by toilet
Adequate lighting in bath and night light on access path
Water temperature regulated at 43°C (110°F) or lower
Clearly marked hot and cold faucets, preferably with separate controls
Seat in tub

KITCHEN
Adequate illumination
Stove controls large and clearly marked
Large, easily grasped, protected handles on pots and pans
Stored items easily accessible

MISCELLANEOUS
Smoke detectors with regularly checked, working batteries
Adequate access and escape doors and windows
Consider personal alarm system keyed to emergency system to be worn by high-risk patient

[a]Adapted from Snipes GE. Accidents in the elderly. Am Fam Phys 1982;26:117-122.

Motor Vehicle Safety

Motor vehicle accidents caused 46,000 deaths and nearly two million disabling injuries in the United States in 1990 (1). Costs from motor vehicle accidents exceed $89 billion annually (1). Teenage and young adult males show disproportionately high rates of death and disability from motor vehicle accidents.

All states passed legislation in the 1980s that resulted in stricter penalties for alcohol-impaired driving convictions. This includes mandatory participation in rehabilitation, provisions about blood alcohol concentration that presumes drunk driving, and an increase in the minimum legal drinking age to 21 years in all states (12). Attitudes toward alcohol use are changing. Groups such as Mothers Against Drunk Driving and Students Against Drunk Driving have led to stronger social sanctions against and responsibility for uncontrolled drinking (33).

The most effective approach to motor vehicle accident prevention involves a combination of legislation and enforcement, education and behavioral change, and engineering and technology. Strict enforcement of safety belt use and child restraint laws have reduced motor vehicle injury and death in both adults and children (12). Congress enacted the 55-mph speed limit in 1974 for fuel conservation. Repeated evaluations of this Act have shown that it has led to reductions in accidental injury and death. Recent increases in speed limits to 65 mph on rural interstate highways, on the other hand, have been accompanied by increases in fatalities, averaging 22% in states that raised speed limits (2).

Physicians should discuss with their patients the importance of using seat belts, air bags, defensive driving, restraints for children, and helmets and protective outer wear for motorcyclists. These efforts are essential for high-risk patients, including substance abusers. Physicians should be adept at identifying and referring these persons (p. 297) as well as those whose personality traits (p. 343), medical conditions, or life circumstances make them particularly vulnerable to motor vehicle accidents.

Technology has given us laminated windshields, collapsible steering columns, padded dashboards, antilock braking systems, automatic seat belts, and air bags. These effective measures were implemented only after a collaborative effort (which included organized medicine) to induce government to set auto safety standards.

Home Safety

Home accidents resulted in 21,500 deaths (23% of all accidental deaths) and 3.2 million disabling injuries in 1990, costing over $23 billion. The major causes of accidental home death are falls, poisonings, fires and burns, suffocation or asphyxiation, and firearms (1). Preschool children and the elderly are most at risk (12). Successful interventions (described in the preceding sections) include poison prevention packaging, flammable fabric laws, home hazard assessments, and smoke detectors.

Occupational Safety

Formal efforts to reduce occupational injuries in the United States date back to the late 1800s. By 1930 most industrial states had passed occupational safety laws, few of which were adequately enforced. It was not until the late 1960s that public attention again became focused on occupational safety.

In 1970, Congress passed the Occupational Safety and Health Act, which included creation of the Occupational Safety and Health Administration (OSHA) with authority to "set standards, inspect workplaces, cite violations, impose penalties, and seek injunctions to shut down operations in cases of imminent danger (12, 34)." OSHA was also given the task of training employers and employees in "recognition, avoidance, and prevention of unsafe or unhealthful working conditions." The Act also mandated the establishment of the National Institute for Occupational Safety and Health to conduct research, recommend standards, and undertake hazard evaluations.

Although it has helped, OSHA is limited. Fewer than 2% of U.S. workplaces are inspected annually. Many standards must still be established or updated. OSHA does not cover all federal workers and exempts small businesses. Penalties for violations of its regulations are not severe enough to induce employers to improve conditions (12, 24, 34).

The model commonly used in occupational safety efforts is the hierarchy of controls (12). In this model, engineering controls that operate at the source of the hazard (e.g., modifying a machine to enhance safety) are considered the most effective interventions and are preferable to other measures. The second level of intervention uses environmental or administrative controls such as ventilation systems or physically separating workers from machines to prevent transmission of the hazard to the workers. The third and least effective level involves personal protective measures (e.g., safety goggles, masks). Worker training and educational programs to prevent injuries provide a necessary adjunct to these controls.

Recreational Safety

Water-related activities have multiple safety interventions. Educational approaches include swimming instruction (much effort required) for children, cardiopulmonary resuscitation (CPR) training, and swimming area warning signs (12).

Effective accident-reducing legislation includes ordinances requiring adequate fencing around swimming pools and restriction of alcoholic beverages in water recreation areas. Successful technologic interventions include improved boat design and flotation devices.

Some sports programs teach coaches CPR and first aid. Rule enforcement by officials and prohibition of dangerous techniques exemplify prevention that requires behavioral change. Technologic interventions such as face masks in football and eye guards in some racquet sports can also reduce injuries (12).

Most serious playground injuries involve falls to the playground surface. One factor is the surface material. Asphalt and concrete surfaces produce more serious injuries than others (e.g., wood chips, sand) and should be banned from playgrounds.

Firearms Regulation

Firearms resulted in the accidental deaths of 1400 Americans in 1990. Of these, the highest fatality rates (36%) occurred in the 15–24-year-old age group, males predominating (1). Over half of accidental firearm deaths occur at home, many involving children and adolescents using their parents' guns (12). One household in five has a handgun. Although these account for only 20% of the firearms in use today, they are involved in most criminal and accidental firearm injuries (33).

Interventions for preventing accidental firearm injuries include (a) reducing the availability of guns, especially easily concealed ones, through federal gun control laws; and (b) in cases in which handguns are legal, (1) locking up guns and keeping them unloaded and out of reach of children; (2) using locked trigger guards; (3) fostering the use of single-shot guns, which must be reloaded between firings, to reduce the likelihood of accidental firings; (4) minimizing inadvertent discharge by better gun design; and (5) storing ammunition in a separate, locked location (33). Little is known about the effects of firearm safety courses, which should be evaluated.

Interventions in Daily Medical Practice

An office-based approach to accident prevention has four components: awareness, identification, intervention, and follow-up. Awareness involves acknowledgement that accidents are a major health problem and, as such, come under the responsibility of physicians. This requires that physicians view accidents as they would other disease processes and take a prevention-minded approach. Another component is identification of patients most at risk for accidents. Health hazard or health risk appraisal instruments (35, 36) contain questions about a person's health-related behavior. Physicians can compare answers to mortality data to estimate the patient's risk of dying at a specific future time, and determine the risk that could be eliminated by specific behavioral changes. The physician presents the risks and benefits of the behavioral changes to the patient and initiates a discussion. Thus, risks are identified, approaches are determined, and opportunity for discussion is provided. Multiple health hazard or health risk appraisal instruments are available from the National Health Information Clearinghouse (36).

Each patient presents the physician with the opportunity to explore accident behavior from a past, present, and future perspective. The patient seen following an accident brings helpful clues to a physician's examination. Input from the patient, family members, friends, coworkers, and law enforcement agents may help ascertain if the accident is part of a pattern (8).

Past history may reveal previous accidents, near misses, or minor mishaps. Preexisting illnesses may influence accident behavior. History of injury, hospitalizations, and operations may contribute. Social history may reveal family, occupational, or financial difficulties. A review of medication, drug, and alcohol use provides critical information.

The physical examination addresses the presenting disorder but may also reveal scars, gait disturbances, and other findings indicating prior accidents. It may also reveal stigmata of substance abuse (e.g., needle marks, alcohol on breath). Motor or sensory deficits that could increase the patient's accident risk may be elicited. Examination of mental status may detect problems with alertness, orientation, memory, complex motor functions, reading ability, pattern recognition and other cognitive functions, irritability, agitation, depressed or labile moods, and delusions or hallucinations, all of which may increase vulnerability to accidents.

COUNSELING, FOLLOW-UP, AND MAINTENANCE

Once a patient is identified as being at risk, the person should be counseled about risk factors, risk-reducing behavioral change; and efforts to achieve that change. The approach chosen depends on the skill level and training of the physician (37). One approach is to encourage the patient to adopt self-care measures for which prepared materials are available. A second is referral of the patient to a more experienced clinician. The third requires physician training in behavioral therapies. Whichever level is chosen, continued interest and encouragement on the part of the physician will further foster behavioral change.

As the patient modifies behavior, continued interaction with the physician is important. At follow-up, progress should be monitored and feedback and encouragement given. Reiterating goals and helping the patient cope with relapses are part of this process. The ultimate goal is for the patient to learn to regulate his or her own accident-related behavior (38).

26/Suicide

Martin D. Plutzer, M.D., and Howard S. Sudak, M.D.

OBJECTIVES

GENERAL OBJECTIVE: Given a patient interview, discuss the patient's suicide risk and the initial care you will provide.

SPECIFIC OBJECTIVES:
1. Discuss the extent to which suicide is preventable.
2. State risk factors for suicide based on epidemiologic and clinical data.
3. Summarize psychodynamic theories and biologic correlates of suicide.
4. Discuss history-taking in suicidal patients.
5. Discuss the care of suicidal patients.

Former Pennsylvania State Treasurer Bud Dwyer was convicted of conspiracy, mail fraud, perjury, and racketeering. One day before his 1987 sentencing, he held a press conference. With cameras rolling he removed a .357 magnum handgun from his briefcase and placed the barrel in his mouth. Before a stunned and terrified audience who shouted, "no, no, Bud, don't do it," he quickly pulled the trigger. The top of his skull splattered against the wall while blood poured from his mouth and nose as he slumped to the floor.

Suicide is the eighth leading cause of death in the U.S. (1) Although the fatal act itself is not usually as dramatic as what the nation witnessed with Bud Dwyer, the impact on those left behind may be as profound. Bud Dwyer was an angry man who claimed he was unjustly accused. He used the forum of a televised press conference to force us to watch in horror his final act. Typical of the irrationality of suicide, he believed this was his only solution. He had suffered multiple losses, including his job and reputation. His attempt to control his destiny to avoid being sentenced suggested an attempt to cope with feelings of hopelessness and helplessness. Likely, he was depressed. He gave a clue about his intention. The evening before his death he told his wife "I think we should have a *last* family dinner together before I'm sentenced."

Despite the dramatic gravity of cases like Dwyer's, and the high frequency of suicide, there is good news: The majority of suicidal patients have psychiatric disorders that can be treated effectively (2, 3). Thousands of lives are saved annually by proper psychiatric intervention. According to Murphy (4), next to lung cancer, suicide is the second most preventable cause of death in the U.S.

Patients who contemplate suicide often visit their physicians. In one study (3), 67% of persons who kill themselves had visited their primary physician in the month before the suicide, and 40% had visited in the prior week. In another study (2), 54% had been treated for psychiatric illness in the year before the suicide, and 31% had been treated in the final month. Alert, well-trained physicians can identify the risk and intervene preventively. An education program on suicide for general practitioners on the Swedish island of Gotland led to a drop in Gotland's suicide rate (compared to the suicide rates both in Gotland and the Swedish mainland) (5).

Suicide is an intentional act. Although this seems obvious, less obvious is the relation between suicide and other self-destructive behaviors. Consider the following: (1) while high on alcohol, a teenager loses control of her car and drives into a tree; (2) a chainsaw "accidentally" recoils, nicking the operator's jugular vein; (3) a woman smokes, overeats and otherwise neglects her general health despite warnings from her physician; (4) while high on drugs, a man provokes a fight and is stabbed; (5) a man elopes (escapes) from the hospital, goes to a notoriously violent neighborhood, yells ethnic insults at people in the street, and is shot to death.

These behaviors represent conscious or unconscious wishes for punishment, excitement or death. How do we know whether the person is unintentionally self-destructive or intentionally suicidal? Are these points on a continuum? In ambiguous cases, a psychological autopsy (a mortality review conducted by clinicians or researchers) may help determine motivation and other factors. Robins's book *The Final Months* (2) consists of 134 psychological autopsies.

EPIDEMIOLOGY OF SUICIDE

Suicide rates are reported as the rate per 100,000 population at risk. Suicide is the eighth leading cause of death overall, but the second leading cause of death in 15–24 year olds (in some reports, it is the third [after homicide] leading cause) (6–10). This is a tragic, often-preventable loss of decades of productive life for these young people. But this does not mean that 15–24 year olds have a higher rate than older adults. Epidemiologi-

cally, this reflects that young adults tend to be relatively healthy, with few deaths from stroke, cancer, and heart disease (6–8).

Statistically, suicide tends to increase with increased age. Males commit (complete) suicide 2–3 times as often as females. Native American rates are highest of any U.S. ethnic group. Euro-American rates (both sexes) are 2–3 times as high as African-American. Asian-American and Hispanic rates are closer to the white than the black rate. Married persons have lower rates than either widowed, separated, or divorced persons. Rates are about 10/100,000/year overall, a rate that has changed little over the past 50 years (6–8).

The increase in suicide rates with age is largely the result of the striking rise with age seen in Euro-American men. Even for them, however, there is diphasic curve with a moderate peak in 15–29 year olds, then a slight decrease, then a marked increase. For nonwhite males, the rate in 20–24 year olds is as high as the rate for comparably aged white males, but then decreases with increased age. After age 20–24, the rates for women increase and then peak and plateau in middle age, but the rise in rates by age is not nearly as dramatic as for men (11).

For suicide attempts rather than completions, the rate among women is 3–4 times that of men. Attempts peak in the 15–30 age group and decline thereafter. Suicide attempters are more likely to have personality disorders (p. 269) than those who complete suicide. No one knows the precise ratio of attempts to completions (many attempts never receive medical attention), but most experts estimate there are at least 10 times as many attempts as completions. With 25,000–29,000 deaths by suicide yearly in the United States, this would conservatively put the number of attempted suicides annually at 250,000–290,000.

Equally as important as the differences between attempters and those who kill themselves are their similarities. Approximately 10% of persons who attempt suicide eventually kill themselves (i.e., the populations of attempters and completers overlap). *One of the best predictors of future suicide, therefore, is prior attempt.* Suicide attempters often receive poor care in emergency rooms (ERs). They are dismissed as manipulative, culpable, and attention-seeking (which is disparaging), and (perhaps most critical) they make ER personnel uneasy about themselves. Furthermore, all attempters need to be taken seriously. Even if they appear to have minimal intent to die or choose a method of low lethality, they use ineffectual and dangerous methods of dealing with their upsets, and warrant assistance (8).

Although the net or overall rate of suicide has changed relatively little since 1900, certain patterns within that net rate have changed markedly. Between 1950 and 1975, adolescent rates increased 200–300-fold; rates for persons aged 50 years or older declined by almost as much (11). Overall rates rose during the Great Depression and declined during World War I and II. These are period effects (rate changes during one time period). Thus, the net, overall rate for all ages stayed almost the same (11). Despite numerous theories (6, 8, 11–13), no one has proved why rates for age groups change over time.

Epidemiologists are also concerned with epidemics (increases in incidence beyond what is expected) of suicide, and with contagion effects (harmful influences that induce people to commit suicide), especially in adolescents. Television or newspaper publicity about suicides (real or fictional) appear to generate an increased number of adolescent suicidal deaths. It is important not to portray suicide as a heroic or romantic death, lest we inadvertently encourage others (14, 15).

Suicide rates vary according to geography, religion, occupation, and economic climate, as well as sex, ethnicity, age, and socioeconomic status. Rates are high in Japan, Eastern Europe (particularly Hungary [although reliable data are difficult to obtain]), Scandinavian countries (primarily Protestant), and Austria (primarily Catholic). Strikingly low rates are reported for Ireland (16, 17). In the United States, rates are lower for Catholics than for Protestants or Jews. Within the United States, rates are highest in the western mountain states. In states with large cities, rates are highest in neighborhoods of apartment houses in which high proportions of single, separated, divorced, and widowed persons tend to live.

Women who are physicians, attorneys, chemists, and other professionals have suicide rates higher than nonprofessional women (18–21). Whether this is because of role strain (being both a professional and [usually] the primary caretaker of children), selection of women with particularly high standards, or the higher prevalence of affective disorder among women (22) is not known. These are not mutually exclusive hypotheses. Review of nine studies (23–31) of physician suicide reveals no consistent, replicable tendency to suicide in any medical specialty. Among professionals, suicide rates are highest among those persons publicly shamed (e.g., Bud Dwyer), disbarred, defrocked, unlicensed, or otherwise censured, particularly if they also lose their livelihood (once Bud Dwyer had been sentenced, he would have lost his pension). They often have good reputations before the publicity, and 20% kill themselves in the year following disgrace (32).

Suicide rates are high in jails, especially for young, first-time offenders, so-called "good kids" without prior criminal records. One factor in jail suicides may be hostility of jailers towards prisoners, leading to careless surveillance.

Many investigations have shown increased rates as the economy declines and unemployment increases (33). Facile explanations are unsatisfactory, however, because poor persons do not have higher rates of suicide or depression than those who are economically privileged (34, 35).

PSYCHODYNAMIC THEORIES

Considering the lengths to which most people go to live, why would others want to kill themselves? It is especially difficult for the physician, firmly grounded in the ethic of sustaining life, to understand the will to die. Consider also the strength of the will to live. Holocaust victims survived unbelievable horrors, disaster victims survive days without food or water, and patients who have terminal or life-threatening diseases cling to life, refusing to die (p. 401).

Why, then, do people want to die? Most actually are ambivalent: a wish to live opposes a wish to die. They seek relief from pain, suffering, and desperation. According to psychoanalytic theory, suicide results from illogical unconscious ideas, such as the magical perception that when you kill yourself you do not really die (36–38). Few persons who kill themselves are aware that they have a treatable condition that is causing their wish to die. There are several psychoanalytic explanations for such paradoxic behavior.

Suicide is the mirror opposite of homicide. Most persons who kill themselves are angry, but cannot or do not know how to cope with that anger. (Fortunately, you do not have to recognize this anger to identify a person as suicidal.) Unacceptable murderous rage with fantasies of revenge toward someone is unconsciously turned against oneself. Suicide simultaneously mobilizes both the destruction of the other person and punishment for such wishes (36–38). Hostility may be expressed in the wish to make the survivors suffer with guilt (i.e., "It's our fault. If we'd been nicer, he wouldn't be dead").

> A man killed himself by driving into an embankment, after mailing a suicide note to his internist reading "Damn you and your God-damned Aldomet" (alphamethyldopa, an effective antihypertensive that can produce depression as a side effect).
>
> When she feels angry at her doctor, a patient threatens to kill herself and leave a note to the newspaper blaming her doctor. She is amused at what this would do to her doctor's reputation.
>
> Another patient threatens to kill himself and leave his psychiatrist all his money. The patient enjoys the thought of the psychiatrist being sued by the patient's enraged family.

Another motive for suicide may be to discharge guilt. Depressed persons usually have low self-esteem and guilt, which may reach delusional proportions. Suicide may serve as a punishment and an escape from guilt feelings.

> A suicidal, psychotically depressed physician believed he had AIDS and was spreading it to his patients. He did not have AIDS, but was unconsciously using this delusional idea to punish himself for a prior sexual relationship with a former patient.

Another paradoxic motive is represented by a suicide attempt by someone who has an overpowering fear of death, who tries to control fate counterphobically rather than passively submitting to it. As with other unconsciously motivated ideas, death's finality is denied. Other unconscious motives include the fantasy of death as a rebirth, a chance to live again. There may be an associated idea of joining someone who has died (often, a dead parent) and living together forever.

BIOLOGIC CORRELATES

Suicidal behavior, like other behaviors (normal and abnormal), is a final common pathway that reflects biologic and environmental vulnerabilities. What is the evidence for a biologic predisposition?

Nonhuman animals exhibit self-destructive behavior (39). Cross-cultural studies reveal similar suicide rates in nonindustrial as well as industrial cultures (40).

Twin and adoption studies (pp. 64, 65) strongly suggest a biologic vulnerability. In one study of 149 twin pairs, nine of 60 identical twins were concordant for suicide, compared to none of 98 fraternal pairs (41). An adoption study demonstrated that suicide in a biologic parent tended to predict suicide among adoptees, whereas suicide in the adoptive parent did not (42). In this case, whether it is psychiatric illness (especially depression) or suicidal behavior that is heritable is unknown. The clinical implication is that a family history of suicide statistically increases a patient's risk.

Efforts have been made to find biologic markers to identify those at risk. For example, serotonin (p. 56) is thought to regulate aggression and impulse control. In a study of hospitalized patients who made suicide attempts, those with decreased 5 hydroxyindoleacetic acid (5-HIAA), a metabolite of serotonin, in the cerebrospinal fluid (CSF) were 10 times as apt to kill themselves during the next year than those with normal or elevated 5-HIAA values (43). Another study showed that decreased CSF 5-HIAA was associated with violent suicide methods (guns, jumping, hanging) (44). Autopsy studies of the frontal cortex of suicide victims show increased serotonin (5-HT-2) receptor sites and decreased presynaptic imipramine (p. 327) binding (45).

Such results should be interpreted cautiously. Biochemical research in suicide presents promising findings, but the small number of studies conducted to date suffer from methodologic constraints (46). On the other hand, "If genetic predisposition plays a role in determining suicidal behavior, independent of psychiatric illness . . . a biological factor independent of psychiatric diagnosis may be identified in individuals at risk for suicide (40)."

CLINICAL APPROACH

Interviewing

Suicide is a crisis of intense emotions, suffering, and need for escape. As discussed earlier, most persons who commit suicide spontaneously communicate their self-destructive wishes to somebody (usually a relative, friend, or doctor) before they die. Most are ambivalent about dying and are usually willing (in fact, relieved) to talk about it if asked. Physicians should not hesitate to ask; asking will not cause patients to commit suicide. Indeed, suicidal patients have trouble communicating with doctors who are unreceptive to discussing suicide. Having an index of suspicion (based upon the information presented below) for patients who are depressed, agitated, psychotic, or hopeless may be life-saving.

When asking about depression, agitation, or other moods associated with suffering, a logical progression is to ask next about suicide. For example, if a person acknowledges feeling depressed, consider this sequence: "When you feel this way (i.e., depressed), do you also feel life is not worth continuing? Are things so bad that you would like to go to sleep and not awaken? Have you thought about killing yourself? How would you do it? Do you have a plan? Do you have the means to carry it out? What would happen if you killed yourself? How would (others) react? Might you act on these feelings?"

Diagnoses Associated with Suicide

Depression and alcoholism are the two most important diagnostic risk factors, accounting for 70% of completed suicides (47). Schizophrenics are also at high risk (48). Chronic general medical illness (e.g., AIDS, Huntington's chorea, lupus erythematosus, chronic renal failure, epilepsy) and terminal illness are also associated with increased risk of suicide (49–53). There is an increased frequency of suicidal ideation and attempts in patients with panic disorder (54).

A history of depression and alcoholism also may be denied or disguised. For example, a depressed person may not be sad, but instead have an anxious or restless mood. An alcoholic may deny or lie about his or her problem. Some alcoholics become depressed only in withdrawal or only when intoxicated.

> An alcoholic man was admitted to a psychiatric ward while depressed, suicidal, and intoxicated. When he sobered up, he looked normal. Because of his improved condition, he was given a pass 3 days later. While on pass, he drank and immediately became sad and combative. He returned to the ward in that condition, and late that night hanged himself in his hospital room.

Elderly melancholic patients often have severe cognitive impairment (pseudodementia) and are diagnosed as demented, but their depressive illness goes unrecognized (55).

The History

As said earlier, most persons who commit suicide communicate their intent beforehand, usually giving conspicuous clues (2). Clues include talking of suicidal wishes or of someone else's suicide, making a will, putting affairs in order, and giving away valued possessions.

Most persons who kill themselves have made prior attempts, Most who attempt suicide do not die (56), however. The ratio of attempts to suicides is between 10–20:1, except for persons aged 65 years or older, when the ratio ratio changes to 4:1 (43, 57).

Losing an important relationship could precipitate a suicide. This is especially true in alcoholics (58). Other evidence of self-destructive behavior can be important, e.g., driving while intoxicated. The loss of a parent early in life from death, divorce, or separation is also associated with increased suicide risk (58).

ADOLESCENT RISK FACTORS

The rate of suicide has been increasing among teens aged 15–19 years (12). Between 1950 and 1980, the rates for white males aged 15-24 years increased 300%, for white females 200%, for African-American males and females 300%. In one survey, 25% of college students had periodic suicidal thoughts (59). As in adults, depression was strongly correlated with suicide attempts. However, half the students who made attempts were not depressed. Both substance abuse and hopelessness increased the risk of an attempt, as did a prolonged desire to be dead.

GERIATRIC RISK FACTORS

Although between 1950–1980 the suicide rates for the elderly aged 65 or older dropped as much as rates rose for adolescents (60), the elderly rate is still the highest of any age group, and suicide rates among this group have recently risen (57). When the elderly attempt suicide, they frequently "succeed", because they almost fully expect to die (61). Loneliness, general medical illness, or disability are frequent antecedents in the elderly.

Mental Status Examination

Almost any finding on the mental status exam that indicates psychiatric illness, especially depression, increases the risk of suicide. Sadness or anxiety sustained (i.e., the mood does not lighten) throughout a sensitively conducted interview should concern the practitioner. Auditory hallucinations commanding someone to kill him- or herself (command hallucinations) are especially dangerous if the patient takes them seriously. Fortunately, many patients identify command hallucinations as symptoms of their illness, or as coming from malicious people who need not be obeyed. Agitation (p. 188) usually reflects suffering, often with an associated desire to alleviate the suffering promptly. Again, feelings of hopelessness (62–65) or helplessness represent a serious risk, as (of course) does suicidal ideation itself.

WHY DOCTORS MISS THE DIAGNOSIS

Well-trained, concerned physicians are skilled at suicide prevention, saving many lives (5). Doctors in a position to prevent suicide sometimes do not address the risk, however, with fatal outcome (2, 3).

Suicidal people, especially middle-aged women of lower socioeconomic status, typically seek help from their primary care doctors (66). Unfortunately, their doctors sometimes do not ask about suicide potential, or do not acknowledge it when the patient spontaneously presents it (2, 3, 67–69). Some doctors act pejoratively towards a suicide attempter, or fail to recognize that a physiologically trivial attempt may precede a completed suicide. Why is this?

For many physicians, their training does not help them. In most nonpsychiatric residencies, psychiatric illness is deemphasized, isolated, and compartmentalized. General medical illness and systemic symptoms are stressed instead. Specialization further narrows the physician's focus. Accidents and risk-taking are often not recognized as suicidal equivalents. Many studies have demonstrated that more than 50% of depressed patients are misdiagnosed (67).

Doctors feel frustrated by patients who resist referral to a psychiatrist. Some do not refer effectively (e.g., patients' fears about psychiatric treatment are not addressed). Some physicians do not interview well (66, 69, 70). Despite teaching of psychiatric data and skills in medical school, there is little reinforcement of this teaching in nonpsychiatric clerkships and residencies. Indirect or nonverbal communication is often ignored. Some interviews are too directive and controlling, with inadequate listening and silence. Some doctors fear the patient will misinterpret inquiries about suicide to mean the doctor thinks they are crazy. Some physicians are embarrassed to ask about sex, substance abuse, depression, and suicide, maintaining that these subjects are too personal or "too psychiatric" (71).

Countertransference feelings (p. 311) can impede effective care. Recognizing self-destructive patient behavior would compel doctors to acknowledge similar feelings in themselves. A doctor could believe the world would be better off if the person were dead, or agree with the patient that the situation is hopeless. A doctor angry at a patient, or mistakenly believing that suggesting suicide paradoxically prevents it, could even suggest that a patient kill himself.

> An intern suggested (thinking this would have the opposite effect) that a patient kill himself. Later that day, the patient did so.

Professionals often become angry at patients who attempt to destroy their lives. Most of their training has been in saving lives. Practitioners often fear their patients' destructiveness, preferring not to ask rather than open Pandora's box. Some physicians engage in power struggles with patients in which they refuse to be "manipulated." For example, the doctor may take the inflexible position that the patient cannot manipulate the physician into hospitalizing him or her because of a suicide threat. Of course, a small number of parasu-icidal (pseudosuicidal) (72) patients will falsely claim suicidal intent in order to be admitted, and some should not be admitted. The decision not to admit a patient threatening suicide requires considerable experience, however, and is best made by a psychiatrist (who should explain his or her reasoning in the chart).

INDICATIONS FOR PSYCHIATRIC CONSULTATION

Sometimes we hear from patients who make serious suicide attempts that a prior suicide attempt was mislabeled as a suicide gesture (i.e., an attention-seeking move with no suicidal intent), that they had been "treated" in an ER and sent home without psychiatric consultation. Such patients may feel no one cares, and the consequent increased hopelessness may prove fatal. A common problem is how (beyond gastric lavage or suturing) to help a patient who takes a small overdose of relatively innocuous pills just to obtain attention, or superficially cuts his wrists to express anger at his spouse during an argument. Although the vast majority of such attempts do not lead to completed suicide (56), such behavior is a strikingly maladaptive way of coping, can result in death, and requires prompt, sincere psychiatric intervention on an outpatient or inpatient service.

Psychiatric consultation is indicated for the following: (1) A suicide attempt regardless of severity. Many hospitals require (appropriately) psychiatric consultation in this circumstance. (2) Someone states the desire to die. (3) A family member believes the patient may kill him- or herself. (4) The physician feels an accident is a suicide equivalent, particularly when the patient has multiple suicide risk factors (e.g., is a depressed substance abuser with past suicide attempts, a recent loss, and hopeless feelings). (5) A patient complies poorly with medical advice, continuing to jeopardize his or her health despite admonitions. A rule of thumb is that whenever the word suicide is thought or spoken, psychiatric consultation should be obtained. It is better to err on the side of caution. When a psychiatrist is in doubt, a colleague's second opinion should be sought. According to Murphy (4:573), "most suicidal crises do not end in death. At the same time, a miscalculation is irretrievable. Overtreatment is not the mistake it might be with other conditions."

INITIAL MANAGEMENT ONCE THE PATIENT IS IDENTIFIED AS SUICIDAL

Prevention of suicide is the primary goal. To save a person's life, emergency involuntary psychiatric hospitalization, and follow-up commitment, including (in some circumstances) breach of confidentiality (when the assistance of family, friends, or police is needed), may be necessary. Such a breach is ethical (p. 434). A passive, laissez-faire stance with a suicidal patient is irresponsible. A good doctor-patient relationship helps. Once you believe a person to be imminently suicidal, you are obliged to arrange protection for that person. This may require family, friends, police, or paramedics to serve as escorts to a secure facility. Patients will tell their doctors of their intent if they thinks the doctor cares. Remember, the suicidal person is ambivalent. The suicidal crisis is usually brief. At some point, whether minutes or months after the physician's initial intervention, most patients are grateful to be alive.

> A middle-aged woman heard voices telling her to jump off a bridge. Although initially resistant to hospitalization, she agreed to it and was treated with medication and psychotherapy. On feeling better, she thanked her doctor for saving her life.

Once a physician diagnoses the patient as suicidal, adequate precautions should be taken. These could include hospitalization in a locked ward of a psychiatric hospital, or continuous one-to-one guarding in any ward. Patients can kill themselves in hospitals by jumping from windows, hanging themselves, running head first into a wall, or escaping and committing suicide by any means.

DEFINITIVE TREATMENT AND FOLLOW-UP

The suicidal crisis is usually brief (i.e., hours to weeks), so the need for intense observation is usually limited. After instituting safeguarding of the patient, treatment should be directed at the underlying condition (Chapters 20–24). After psychiatric evaluation, some patients may be treated as outpatients. The keys are a good diagnosis and a strong doctor-patient relationship. Psychotherapeutic goals include allowing the patient to spontaneously express angry feelings without criticism, reducing guilt, improving self-esteem, and challenging self-deprecatory cognitions (pp. 78, 312). The patient should not be badgered into expressing anger, however. Nor should too much medication be prescribed. One guideline in determining dosage is that if a patient took all at once all the medicine that was prescribed, it would not be fatal.

> A married mother of two daughters sought treatment following her husband's learning of her affair with her best friend's husband. A teacher, she began having difficulty concentrating at work and suffered other symptoms of depression including intense guilt. She thought of overdosing to atone for her actions. She was treated as an outpatient with antidepressants (not much was prescribed at one time) and psychotherapy designed to reduce guilt and understand her behavior. The psychiatrist told her that her condition had a good prognosis. She agreed not to act on her suicidal thoughts, and to call her psychiatrist if she felt the need to act on her self-destructive impulses (she didn't need to call). The suicidal crisis passed and her depression lifted.

Treating suicidal patients is a difficult, life-and-death (but usually rewarding) process. Monitor your own responses. It is easy to become anxious, angry, despairing, or callous. Resist giving simplistic, clichéd advice (e.g., "pull yourself together," or "think of what this is doing to your family"). This may intensify the patient's guilt, and is insensitive. Maintain a regular, cordial relationship with key family members, who can provide valuable history, persuade an ambivalent patient to consent to care, and bring the patient to the hospital in an emergency. Most family members are helpful and caring. Occasionally, a family member is willfully destructive or troublingly ambivalent. An example of the latter is a mother whose son made a suicide attempt by cutting his wrist. The next day she brought him a razor to shave with in the hospital, unaware of the message she was communicating.

The months following hospital discharge are a time of increased risk for suicide because of incomplete recovery or early relapse (73). Consequently, prompt follow-up outpatient visits are mandatory. If the patient misses an appointment, a follow-up phone call is in order.

27/Violence

Abraham Heller, M.D., and Frederick S. Sierles, M.D.

OBJECTIVES

GENERAL OBJECTIVE: Given a patient examination, discuss the patient's violence risk and the initial care you would provide.

SPECIFIC OBJECTIVES:

1. State several similarities and differences between aggression exhibited by humans and that exhibited by other animals.
2. Summarize the epidemiology of violence in the United States.
3. Discuss the ability of physicians to predict violence.
4. Summarize the clinical assessment of a patient's violence risk.
5. Discuss strategies for violence prevention in the clinical setting.
6. State several limitations of and strategies for violence prevention in the community.

All mammals exhibit some form of aggressive behavior. For predators, killing prey provides food. For all animals, aggression protects self, family, and territory. Within a species, aggression establishes an animal's place in the dominance hierarchy. Ethologists maintain that dominance hierarchies foster the survival of groups of animals to maximize group efficiency in defense against attack (1). For many species (e.g., humans, lions, cichlid fish, praying mantids, bees, termites, and ants), aggression may include within-species (intraspecific) homicide, even massacre (2). Aggression is greatest among species whose bonding between members is closest (2). Humans fit into this overall scheme, manifesting predatory behavior, rageful and defensive aggression, and dominance hierarchies to which aggressive behavior often contributes. Technology enormously extends the capacity of man to be dangerously aggressive. Humans have annihilated millions of people by holocaust, caused extinction of many other species, and poisoned the environment by pollution. This, despite the fact that humanity is the only species with written codes of ethics and law.

VIOLENCE IN AMERICA

The United States is currently the most violent industrialized country, and our violent crime rates are increasing. In 1991, there were an estimated 24,020 homicides, the highest number in our history (3, 4). Homicide is the tenth leading cause of death in the U.S. Each year, 102,000 rapes are reported (5), and it is estimated (3) that 650,000 rapes actually occur. Yearly, over 1.5 million assaults are reported (3). (An assault is an *attempt*, successful or not, to injure someone.) Homicide is the second leading cause of death in Americans aged 15–25 years (5).

One reason is the widespread ownership of guns that is minimally regulated by legislation (6, 7). The Second Amendment guarantees a right to keep and bear arms: "A well-trained militia being necessary to the security of a free State, the right of the people to keep and bear arms shall not be infringed (8)." Thus phrased, this Amendment is unclear, leading to passionate debate over whether this right exists *only* to maintain a militia. Regardless, this right may be, but rarely is, limited by federal or state legislation (8).

Violence also is glorified in the media. There is an expanding body of evidence that this media depiction (not unique to the U.S.) increases peoples' tendencies to act violently, especially people who are violence-prone (9, 10).

EPIDEMIOLOGY

Males, teenagers, young adults, and the poor are most prone to violence, as all community studies record. The same triad—male, young, and poor—is overrepresented among *victims* of homicide (5, 11–14). Women who are poor are more likely than other women to be raped or otherwise attacked. Most homicides are committed by acquaintances, friends, and family members (5). Each year, however, homicides of strangers or near-strangers (e.g., murders during robberies, gang homicides [15], drive-by killings, and shooting of nontargeted bystanders) becomes more frequent. By far, the most common homicide committed in the United States is by an acquaintance, over a love triangle or in an argument (often about money or property) (5). The vast majority of homicides are intraracial (i.e., Euro-Americans tend to kill Euro-Americans, Asian-Americans each other) (5, 16). Women murdered in the U.S. are often killed by husbands or boyfriends (5).

Males are nine times as likely to commit violent crimes as are females, although rates of violence for females are increasing (11). Unlike suicide, homicide is more frequently committed by teenagers or young adults than by the middle-aged and elderly. The combined effect of sex and age is considerable; for example, males aged 15–20 years represent 8.5% of the population but 35% of arrests for violent crimes (17).

Poverty and its components—minimal education, poor health, family instability, and overcrowded and inadequate housing (p. 96)—are highly associated with violence. Poverty probably accounts for the considerable ethnic differences in the frequency of violence (14). For example, homicide is the leading cause of death of African-Americans aged 15–34 years (18). The age-adjusted homicide death rate for African-Americans of all ages is six times that for Euro-Americans. African-Americans represent 12% of the U.S. population, but 49% of its murder victims (5).

For decades, homicide rates have been greater in the Southern than in the Northern states (5, 13). However, as is the case for ethnic groups, once socioeconomic status is accounted for, the geographic difference disappears (13). There is some debate about whether the crucial factor in the relation between violence and poverty is the absolute degree of poverty in a locality or is inequities in income distribution (13, 19).

Noted above, availability of handguns is another contributing factor: 65% of homicides are committed with firearms, primarily handguns (5). A gun kept at home for self defense is 167 time more likely to be used in a suicide than to kill a home intruder, 21 times more likely to kill a family member during a disagreement, and 6 times more likely to cause an accidental death (20). A loaded gun in the home is 100 times more likely to kill a family member or friend than a burglar (20, 21). The most common fates of readily available loaded handguns in the home are, in decreasing order of frequency, to be stolen, to be used in a suicide or homicide, and to be used by a burglar to shoot the homeowner (21, 22). About 2.9% of high school students nationwide (23), and 6.6% of urban high school students (24), carried a handgun to school during the past year. The effects of handgun control are discussed below.

In 1965, the U.S. homicide rate began to increase progressively and dramatically, and reached an all time high in 1991. During the Great Depression of the 1930s, there was another peak, modest in comparison to the present one (25).

Other Demographic Correlates

Violence is more frequently committed by persons whose parents were separated or divorced (26), whose parents were criminals (26), and who were abused as children (27, 28). It is committed more frequently by persons who are separated, divorced, or unemployed (26). Within families, violence is more likely to occur between family members not genetically related than between blood kin (29). For example, people are more likely to kill stepparents than biological parents, adopted than biological children. Among women, violence is more likely to be committed during the paramenstruum (the time immediately before, during, and after menstruation) (30). Violence is more often committed by people living in overcrowded conditions, but less likely to occur if bystanders are present (13, 14, 19, 31, 32). Violent crime is more frequent during summer months than during the rest of the year (5). A country's domestic violence rates tend to decrease while it is engaged in a war on foreign soil, and tend to increase after it has concluded the war (4).

Health professionals frequently have clinical responsibility for assessing and treating violent persons, and are therefore at risk for being assaulted. Of 115 psychiatrists on one university's faculty, 42% reported having been assaulted by a patient (33). In another survey of 101 mental health professionals, 24% reported being assaulted by at least one patient during the prior year (34). Interestingly, the youngest and least experienced physicians have the greatest exposure to violent patients (35).

CLINICAL PREDICTION

Physicians in any speciality may have to assess whether a patient poses a threat of violence.

Can clinicians predict violence? If so, what factors must they consider in the assessment? Until the 1980s, it was often maintained that clinicians could not predict whether a patient would be violent. This was based largely on follow-up studies in patients previously hospitalized as criminally insane. In these studies, "only" 14%–35% of patients were arrested during the years after they were discharged to the community (11, 36). This meant that a given prediction that a person would be violent was more likely to be wrong than to be right. There were several weaknesses in this reasoning. First, there is no evidence that data from institutions for the criminally insane can be extrapolated to the general population. Second, the patients in question were treated prior to discharge, presumably reducing their risk of violence (37). Third, and most important, it is unreasonable to expect clinicians to predict an uncommon event with *certainty* (11).

Recent research has shown that clinicians can, by assessing the risk factors discussed below, identify patients with an increased *likelihood* of acting violently during the days following their evaluation (37–41). Violence assessment is accomplished from the patient's history (including data obtained from other sources such as family and prior medical records) and physical examination (including the mental status and behavioral neurologic exams). Assessment continues during the course of the patient's care. Laboratory data may facilitate diagnosis at any point.

Thus, psychiatrists or other physicians testifying at commitment hearings should not state with certainty that a person will injure someone else. Rather, they should state that, compared to the general population, the patient is statistically more likely (or not likely) to be violent, and give the evidence for this conclusion (11).

Clinical Assessment of Risk

As in assessing suicide risk, assessing violence risk hinges much more on individual clinical factors (e.g., the patient is irritable and agitated) than on demographics (e.g., the patient is young, male, or poor). For example, in studies by McNiel and Binder (37–39) of hospitalized psychiatric patients, the best predictors of violent behavior during the week after admission were both the clinician's general conclusion about whether the patient would be violent, and whether the patient had been violent during the days before admission.

Factors in the patient's history that increase the statistical likelihood of future violence include incidence of past violence, certain psychiatric illnesses, owning weapons, alcohol or street drug intoxication, certain mental status findings, and (to a lesser extent) certain laboratory findings.

PAST VIOLENCE

As a rule, past behavior tends to predict future behavior. This is certainly the case for violent behavior (11, 26, 37, 42–47). Past chronic offenders are more likely than controls to act violently (42). Persons paroled after imprisonment for violent offenses are more likely to be violent than parolees who had been imprisoned for nonviolent offenses (43). Viet Nam veterans who engaged in fragging (placing a live grenade in the quarters of a hated fellow soldier, typically an officer) during wartime were more likely than controls to have engaged in antisocial acts prior to the fragging (44). Viet Nam combatants who showed militarily excessive violence (e.g., atrocities) during combat were more likely than controls to have been violent previously (45). Among murdered children, in 90% of cases the victims or their siblings had been abused or neglected prior to the killings (46). In 85% of domestic (family) homicides, the police had been called to the residence at least once prior to the murder, and at least five times in over half the cases (47). And as noted above, violence just prior to psychiatric admission is highly associated with in-hospital violence during the week following admission.

Circumstances of past violence are also important. For example, a patient may be self-controlled while in the hospital and abstinent from alcohol, but combative while intoxicated (48).

PSYCHIATRIC ILLNESS

The vast majority of psychiatric patients are never violent, and only a small proportion of violent crimes in the community are committed by persons previously treated for mental illness (49, 50). Nevertheless, compared to the general population, psychiatric patients are more likely to be arrested for violent crimes (51). The latter statistic includes patients who have antisocial personality disorder, a disorder in which many patients are prone to violence but often unresponsive to treatment. In one report (51), violent behavior was the reason for 10% of psychiatric admissions. In some hospitals, violence or threatened violence is the main reason for admission in far more than 10% of cases.

In the community, crime in general and violent crime in particular are most frequently associated with diagnoses of antisocial personality disorder, alcoholism (p. 292), drug dependence (p. 292), and somatization disorder (p. 266) (26, 52, 53). Intoxication with alcohol or other drugs is very common during commission of violent crimes. In one comparison of murderers and nonviolent criminals, the murderers were much more likely to have been intoxicated with alcohol or other drugs during the crime than were the nonviolent criminals (54% vs. 5%, respectively) (54). In many other studies, large percentages of murderers (range 19%–88%, median 54%) were intoxicated at the time of the crime (54, 55).

Drugs other than alcohol that are associated with violence include barbiturates and other sedative-hypnotics, cocaine and amphetamines, hallucinogens (including phencyclidine), and anabolic steroids (13, 48, 54, 56). With the exception of steroids, these drugs are disinhibiting (i.e., they reduce self-control). The exact contribution of drugs to violent acts is less clear, however. For instance, among a group of habitually violent teenagers, it was known that "reds [secobarbital] make you rowdy," and that these adolescents often took alcohol or secobarbital *in anticipation* of acting violently (55, 57).

Among psychiatric outpatients (58), assaultive behavior occurs most often in patients who have personality disorders (p. 269). Within the hospital, diagnoses most often made for assaultive patients are mania, schizophrenia, delirium, dementia and focal (e.g., psychomotor epilepsy) brain disease, personality disorder, and alcoholism (48, 59). Because of past clinician tendencies to overdiagnose schizophrenia (p. 243), the association of violence with accurately diagnosed schizophrenia is not known.

Some psychiatric disorders of childhood are associated with violence in childhood or adulthood. These include conduct disorder (p. 145), attention deficit hyperactivity disorder (p. 144), and mental retardation (p. 143) (48). An increased likelihood of violence in adults also occurs with a childhood history of the triad of enuresis, firesetting, and cruelty to animals (60, 61), or a history or severe head trauma or coma during childhood (62–64).

Epileptics (30, 62–67), persons who suffer from posttraumatic stress disorder (PTSD [68]), and XYY males (males born with one X and two Y sex chromosomes) (30, 69, 70) *may* be violent, but it is unclear whether violence is more frequent in these persons than in matched controls in the general population. When epileptics act aggressively, it is most likely during periods of postictal (postseizure) confusion or during periods between seizures. Violence rarely occurs during the seizure itself. The association of PTSD with violence is discussed on p. 265.

The association between depression and violence towards others is also unclear. Violence is often listed as an infrequent feature of depressive illness (48). On the other hand, in England, 25% of homicides are followed by suicide of the perpetrator (71), suggesting an association between depression and homicide in some cases (72).

ADDITIONAL ALERTING DATA FROM PATIENT HISTORY

Patients who report (or whose relatives or friends report) violent and vengeful thoughts and intentions have an increased risk of violence. Ownership and willingness to use weapons increase the risk, as does the likelihood of the patient becoming intoxicated after returning home. Violent threats and gun acquisition were prominent in the case of Joseph Wesbecker (73), who on September 14, 1989 killed eight coworkers and injured 12 others with a semiautomatic assault rifle before killing himself with a pistol.

> Mr. Wesbecker was a 47-year-old, twice-divorced Euro-American man, a father of two adult sons. He lived with his second ex-wife. During the year prior to his death, he received disability payments while on leave for psychiatric illness from the printing firm in which he had previously been employed for 17 years. He had been treated for various psychiatric diagnoses for 5 years, and had been hospitalized voluntarily three times with complaints of confusion, depression, headaches, anger, sleeplessness, isolation, and anxiety. He was not known to be a substance abuser. During this 5-year period, he had attempted suicide several times and had expressed wishes to harm others, including his foreman at the printing company.
>
> During his final months on the job, he felt that the company had "done me dirty" by exposing him to toluene (an ink thinner) and making him work at a machine the operation of which he found too stressful. He told his company and a labor attorney about this and was subsequently placed on disability leave. In the time that followed, his concerns and symptoms, including delusions of persecution by the company, only intensified. He obtained numerous firearms (including automatic weapons) legally by filling out forms, honestly replying "no" to the inquiry "Have you ever been adjudicated mentally defective or have you ever been *committed* to a mental institution?"
>
> He told a close friend of his intentions to kill people at the printing company. The friend reported these threats to coworkers, who dismissed the warnings. Then, one morning, armed with several of his weapons, he entered the plant through a side door and killed the coworkers.

MENTAL STATUS FINDINGS

The mental status examination provides important clues to both short-term and long-term violence risk. The following findings (55,

74–76) are associated with increased short-term risk: (1) an agitated, irritable, angry or labile mood; (2) threatening gestures, a menacing gait, muscle clenching, and shouting; (3) expression of violent or vengeful thoughts or intentions, either spontaneously or in response to questions; (4) delusions of persecution, especially delusions of being poisoned; (5) command hallucinations upon which the patient feels impelled to act (many patients who experience command hallucinations resist and reject what they are told); (6) signs of drug intoxication, including ataxic gait, dysarthric speech, dilated pupils, flushed skin, elevated pulse and blood pressure, or the odor of digesting alcohol on the breath; (7) and signs of diffuse or focal brain disease (e.g., cognitive dysfunction with diminished alertness in delirium, choreoathetoid movements in Huntington's disease), antisocial personality disorder, alcoholism, mania, and schizophrenia.

Symptoms and signs of these disorders are discussed in Chapters 20 and 22. If patients with the above findings are not properly treated, the violence risks persist in both the short term and the long term.

LABORATORY STUDIES

Just as there are no pathognomonic lab tests for psychiatric syndromes, there are no laboratory tests with sensitivity and specificity (p. 29) sufficient to substitute for clinical judgment in the prediction of violence. There are some statistical associations of certain lab findings with violent behavior, however, and laboratory testing is sometimes a valuable adjunct to diagnosis.

Lab testing may be valuable in diagnosis of drug intoxication (e.g., urine drug screening, breathalyzer or blood alcohol testing) or of general medical conditions associated with violence (e.g., computerized tomographic scanning in Huntington's chorea) (48).

There is also an association between electroencephalographic (EEG) abnormality and sociopathy, criminality and violence (62, 63, 76–78). Among habitually aggressive criminals, the majority have abnormal EEGs, most often slowing in the anterior temporal and lateral frontal regions of the brain (76, 77). Several retrospective studies (30) have shown reduced levels of 5 hydroxyindoleacetic acid (5-HIAA) in the cerebrospinal fluid (CSF) of violent offenders, but this does not justify routine use in daily practice of lumbar puncture for measurement of CSF 5-HIAA levels.

VIOLENCE PREVENTION

The management of violent behavior is its prevention (75). Prevention of violence can be divided into (1) prevention in the clinical setting and (2) prevention in the community.

Violence Prevention in the Clinical Setting

In medical centers, violence prevention encompasses the center's resources and logistics, clinical assessment and interviewing skill, and treatment.

CRISIS TEAM, RESTRAINT, AND SECLUSION

All hospitals that provide frequent emergency room (ER) psychiatric assessments or that have psychiatric inpatient units should have during each shift a crisis team consisting (ideally) of nursing personnel, a physician, other staff, and a security officer (55). This team is prepared to arrive within minutes to manage a violent person whose irritable or threatening behavior cannot be managed by conventional interpersonal and pharmacotherapeutic techniques. Crisis team members are formally trained in conversing with irritable or psychotic patients, and in physical control and restraint procedures. The crisis team is summoned by a phone call, a paging system, or an emergency remote buzzer system triggered by a panic button located in offices in which new patients are evaluated. The experienced crisis team may provide, if needed, an often-reassuring show of force to an often frightened, albeit menacing, patient. If the patient cannot be persuaded by discussion to accept restraints and medication, the team will impose medication or restraints, using the techniques for which it has been trained, for the protection of the patient and others. Detailed elsewhere (49, 75, 79), the physical control, restraint, and seclusion procedure includes one team member directing the procedure, one controlling each of the patient's limbs, one controlling the head to prevent biting, and one to administer medication previously drawn in a syringe. Choice of medication depends on the situation (see below).

For patients who present an obvious, immediate risk of violence (e.g., yelling, threatening, pacing), the crisis team should be called. Before the crisis team arrives, it is often best for staff to maintain a conversation with the patient while keeping a distance of 10–15 feet. This distance (as near the door as possible without causing the patient alarm) allows conversation to occur while permitting the staff member to exit safely if necessary. If the patient then begins to approach the staff member, the latter could raise a hand and firmly state "stop," but if this fails, the staff member should promptly leave the room (76).

Many inpatient psychiatric units maintain locked rooms (seclusion rooms) in which combative or severely agitated patients are managed according to guidelines detailed elsewhere (49, 75, 79). For restrained patients, these include (1) a nurse who assesses the patient every 15 minutes (or more if necessary), during which time the restraint on one extremity is loosened; (2) a staff member who sits with the patient, whose upper limb is freed for eating, during mealtimes; (3) toileting every 4 hours under careful supervision; and (4) a physician's assessment every 8–12 hours, or more often if needed. Properly diagnosed and treated, patients rarely need restraints or seclusion for more than 24 hours.

EMERGENCY ROOM

One site of high risk for assaults is the ER of hospitals (usually public hospitals) to which relatives or police routinely bring patients with behavioral problems for assessment or admission. In this setting, patients and staff often are unfamiliar with each other, the diagnosis is not known, the patient and family are experiencing a crisis, and the patient may be intoxicated. Emergency room procedures vary depending on whether the ER is in a general or a psychiatric hospital.

Initial Assessment in the General Hospital Emergency Room

In the general hospital, ER physicians and staff (not consultants) see the patient first, make preliminary general medical and psychiatric assessments, request psychiatric or other consultation if indicated, and restrain patients if necessary. Initial ER assessments include obtaining a chief complaint, a history of the present illness, other pertinent history, vital signs (blood pressure, pulse, respiration, temperature), a focused physical exam (not a complete exam) responsive to the presenting problems and, if needed, crucial lab tests (e.g., testing for glucose and ketones in symptomatic diabetics).

Important corroborative data can be obtained from hospital charts or from relatives, friends, or police who accompany the patient. The relative or friend should be asked to wait, and occasionally it is best if the friend or relative participates in the interview (e.g., when requested by the patient, or when the patient cannot present a clear history). Because they have observed the patient prior to arriving in the ER, police should not be allowed to "drop off" the patient and leave without first providing the physician with information about the patient's recent appearance and behavior (48). In some ERs, when patients exhibit symptoms and signs suggesting violence risk, the patient's clothing is discreetly checked for weapons after he or she has changed into a hospital gown. In some especially high-risk ER settings, hospital security personnel check patients and visitors with metal detectors prior to patient or visitor entry into the ER.

Based on data about the patient that is already available (e.g., a phone call from a referring physician) and on the patient's greeting behavior, ER personnel determine whether the patient can be seen by the ER physician alone (which is usually the case), will require nursing staff or security personnel to attend or to wait nearby, or will require restraint.

Patients who exhibit obvious behavioral problems should be interviewed and physically examined in a relatively large room in which both patient and physician can escape easily. Regardless of clinician interviewing skill, small "cubicle" offices intensify patient and physician anxiety and are unsafe for patients presenting psychiatric emergencies. Unless the patient is too agitated to sit (in which case a detailed interview is unlikely), both patient and physician should sit. Seating should be at an angle so that patient and physician are not squarely facing each other (49, 79).

Following the initial assessment, ER psychiatric consultation should usually be obtained if the patient reports homicidal or suicidal thoughts or intent, is psychotic, exhibits other behavior that suggests a need for psychiatric admission, or whose serious illness is complicated by abnormal behavior that is not readily explained (e.g., a patient with a neck injury who is also catatonic [p. 188]). The ER physician should call the consulting psychiatrist who may provide preliminary recommendations in advance of his or her arrival and will estimate the time of arrival. In some circumstances (typically when both doctors perceive that the patient's ER visit is not for a genuine emergency), a phone conversation alone may suffice. In the latter circumstance, the psychiatrist could advise about any aspect of the patient's care, including drug side effects, refilling of prescriptions for psychotropic drugs (why the patient "ran out" of medications must be explained), and referrals for outpatient psychiatric care.

Emergency Room Psychiatric Evaluation

Regardless of whether the ER psychiatric assessment is conducted in a general hospital (where the psychiatrist is consultant to the ER physician) or a psychiatric hospital (where the psychiatrist is responsible for the entire assessment), it is preferable that the decision to admit the patient to the psychiatric unit is made by a psychiatrist following an examination. This examination is diagnostically and therapeutically crucial, constituting a specialist's evaluation of an unmedicated patient in a time of crisis. For this reason, and because the psychiatrist usually has more time than the ER physician to evaluate the patient, this exam should be more thorough and should usually take at least 30 minutes.

The examination is best conducted in an office designed for such evaluations. It should be well lighted and large, allow easy access for the patient or doctor to walk out, have an emergency button (that sets off a buzzer in a designated area but not in the examination room), and be clear of objects such as ashtrays that could be used as weapons (49). If there is no emergency buzzer system, other strategies are used. Based on the circumstances and the patient's general behavior, these may include having security or other staff either attend the interview, listen through the door (which could be left ajar), or be available to respond to the doctor's seemingly neutral inquiry or phone call in which a prearranged code word summons help (80).

There should be good access to a clinical laboratory and medical/surgical consultants (48). When the interview is conducted in a regular ER exam room or a nursing office temporarily vacated for the interview, interruptions (including requests to vacate the room) are inevitable and interview efficiency reduced. Whether a family member or friend should be present during the interview is decided the same as for the ER physician's examination.

Once the stage is set and the interview begins, it is conducted like other initial interviews (p. 179). The history must cover the patient's present illness and address violent or suicidal ideation or behavior (as discussed above), current living circumstances, past psychiatric history, drug use history, and family history of psychiatric illness (p. 180).

Like the interview's content, the style of an initial interview in which violence risk is assessed is essentially the same as that of any other initial interview. As discussed in Chapter 16, style is responsive to the degree to which the patient is open, spontaneous, articulate, and insightful. Patients being assessed for violence risk, no less than other patients, appreciate an interview conducted with respect, empathy, responsiveness to their concerns, and reasonable thoroughness. Patients appreciate amenities, such as a comfortable chair, and other expressions of concern for the patient's comfort (48). Interview thoroughness adds credibility to the physician's conclusions and recommendations.

From the time the doctor and patient meet, the patient's mental status is assessed. Assessment of alertness and a brief screening test of cognitive functioning (e.g., a "mini-mental state" examination) are necessary.

To conclude the interview, the physician should summarize the assessment and treatment recommendations and explain these to the patient and (with the patient's consent) any relative or friend who may have accompanied the patient. If admission is indicated, its rationale should be explained in terms that dovetail with the patient's concerns. (E.g., "You said you couldn't control your temper. We can assist you with that problem in the hospital.") All patients with treatable illnesses who pose a short-term violence risk should be admitted, voluntarily (preferably) or involuntarily.

Sometimes the potentially violent patient will already have requested hospital admission. Many violent patients requiring admission make no such request. If admission is required because of short-term violence risk, the patient does not accept the recommendation for admission, and the relative or friend (if present) is willing to fill out a brief petition for involuntary admission, the admission should be effected promptly. The psychiatrist should avoid confrontation at this point, however, at most stating "I'd like to arrange for you to be admitted."

If the patient refuses, the doctor should not state definitively that the patient will be admitted involuntarily until the crisis team or security personnel have arrived on the scene.

This summoning begins with the physician telling the patient matter-of-factly or with staged absentmindedness, "Wait here, I'll be back in a few minutes," or by pressing the emergency buzzer and changing the topic or leaving the room.

Once the decision to admit to the psychiatric inpatient service has been made, the admissions process includes a search for weapons. It is accomplished most easily and discreetly at the time of the physical exam in the ER (see above); otherwise it is done immediately on admission to psychiatric units in which newly admitted patients are required to change into hospital gowns.

Discharging Patients from the Emergency Room

When patients are discharged home following an ER assessment, the physician should include in the chart a statement about the patient's short- and long-term homicide and suicide risk, the differential and working diagnosis, and a follow-up plan. If suicide or homicide was a consideration, the rationale for the discharge decision should be explained.

As discussed on page 272, most patients diagnosed with antisocial personality disorder have an increased long-term risk for violent behavior, and often request psychiatric admission for various appropriate (e.g., admission to a chemical dependency or detoxification unit) or medically inappropriate (e.g., no place to stay) reasons. Also as discussed previously, sociopaths should not be admitted to general psychiatric wards unless they have a treatable complication (e.g., a drug-induced psychosis). Sociopathic patients often disrupt general psychiatric wards (81). Consequently, physicians often must discharge from the ER sociopaths who have requested admission and made threats about what they will do if they are not admitted (e.g., "I can't promise what I will or won't do if you discharge me"). Such patients should be told that they are responsible for their actions, are capable of self-control, and will be arrested if they act violently. If they continue to demand admission, they should be escorted from the premises by security staff. They are, of course, entitled to referral for social services (e.g., for temporary placement), or outpatient medical care or substance dependency programs if indicated. The rationale for discharging the patient, despite increased *long-term* risk of violence, should be explained in the patient's chart.

EXTREME CIRCUMSTANCES

On rare occasions, a patient will brandish a weapon in an ER, ward, or clinic. If feasible, patients and staff should be evacuated, the area locked, and security called. Also on (fortunately) rare occasions, a patient will threaten a clinician with a weapon in the office. This merits immediate use of the emergency buzzer. The physician may agree to an initial reasonable request, but soon thereafter, the physician should tell the patient, repeatedly if necessary, that it is in everyone's best interest that the patient place the weapon out of reach on the desk or table, and that nothing helpful can be accomplished until this occurs. Other types of rare, extreme circumstances are discussed in detail elsewhere (82).

INPATIENT TREATMENT

Once the patient has been admitted to the inpatient psychiatric unit, treatment is based on diagnosis and individual patient characteristics. If the patient is undiagnosed, an observation period of one to several days may be helpful to clarify the diagnosis. During this time, if sedation is required, intramuscular (IM) or intravenous (IV) lorazepam 1–2 mg. or IV or IM amobarbital 300–500 mg are rapid-acting substances that induce sleep but do not mask symptoms once they wear off (76). Once the diagnosis is made, emergency medication, if needed, is chosen based on diagnosis (49, 76). For example, IM neuroleptics (e.g., haloperidol 10–30 mg) are highly effective in manic patients. Violence is less frequent in inpatient units that have a high staff to patient ratio, where staff are well trained and feel supported, and where clear ward

rules allow for granting of privileges based on improvements in the patient's behavior (76).

Discharge from Inpatient Unit

The patient should be discharged once he or she has received maximal treatment benefit, is no longer dangerous, and a feasible follow-up plan has been made. The latter includes having a relative or friend sell weapons if the patient kept weapons at home, making an appointment for a follow-up visit at a site where continued outpatient care is possible, prescribing medications to last until that appointment, making a strategy for prompt reassessment if an emergency arises, and verifying that the patient has kept the follow-up appointment. This should be discussed with the patient's family and detailed in the patient's chart. Predischarge passes are given under the same circumstances and using the same strategies (55).

When a competent patient wishes to sign out of the hospital against medical advice, cannot be persuaded to remain in the hospital for care, and poses no *short-term* threat of violence, the physician is obligated to discharge the person. The family should be informed about recommended treatments and about the long-term risk, and told of the impossibility of holding a patient involuntarily based on a long-term prediction.

OUTPATIENT TREATMENT

Like inpatient treatment, psychotherapy and pharmacotherapy for outpatient treatment are determined by the patient's diagnosis and individual characteristics. In addition, certain drugs may be modestly effective that are not specific to the patient's psychiatric illness but that may reduce aggressive behavior in patients who are impulsively aggressive. These include lithium carbonate (p. 330) in patients who have no apparent mood disorder (83, 84), carbamazepine (p. 332) in patients who have no mood disorder or epilepsy (84, 85), and propranolol (p. 334) for patients who have diffuse (e.g., dementia) or focal brain disease not treatable with other drugs (84, 86).

There is another important intervention, a simple one that is often overlooked. When patients discuss their ideas about killing someone else, it is usually helpful for the patient to realize the consequences of the act for himself or herself. Most patients can be told that the likely consequences of a violent crime is arrest and imprisonment, and the fact of being in psychiatric treatment regardless of diagnosis is not likely to hold sway with a judge or jury. Patients willing and able to contemplate and comprehend this advice are probably less likely to act violently (84). However, this advice alone does not relieve the physician of his or her legal duty, if the need arises, to protect or warn potential victims of violence according to the Tarasoff precedent discussed in Chapter 34.

Violence Prevention in the Community

Reducing violence in the community is an obligation of society in general, not just of the medical profession. For example, although epidemiologic evidence (see below) strongly suggests that legislation to reduce people's access to handguns and automatic weapons would reduce the nation's death toll, the public must reconsider the *unlimited* Second Amendment right to bear arms.

Good medical care itself contributes to violence reduction. The involvement of medicine is underscored by the American Medical Association and the Surgeon General's Office which have identified violence prevention as a major public health priority (3). Because violence has so many determinants, however, not all of which are medical, its prevention is not as straightforward as the development of a new vaccine or antibiotic.

MEDICAL CARE

To the extent that neuropsychiatric illness contributes to violent behavior (p. 361), factors increasing the risk of neuropsychiatric illness need to be addressed by good prenatal care (Chapter 10), child health care (Chapter 11) including standard childhood immunizations, accident prevention (Chapter 25), and early neuropsychiatric diagnosis and treatment (Chapters 20–24). These should be available to all Americans. Unfortunately, access to health care and the quality of care for the poor and minorities is inadequate (Chapter 35). A scandalous example is our record of immunizing minority children, a record that is the poorest among the world's industrialized countries.

Community mental health agencies can provide classes in parenting for young mothers, as well as family counseling for marital difficulties (87). An effective, caring parent is less likely to be abusive and more likely to serve as a positive role model for his or her children.

Persons at high statistical risk for committing or being victimized by violence could be screened for real-life risk and treated accordingly (87, 88). This screening requires asking patients whether they have been violent or victimized by violence. Most victims do not report this spontaneously or even easily if asked. Given that 20% of visits by women to some ERs result from abuse by a mate (88), and because 30% of murders of women are committed by mates (89), ERs and gynecologists' offices are good sites to question women about family violence (87). If it has occurred, then a continuum of multiple resources (e.g., social support services, family counseling, psychiatric and general medical care) must be provided.

Prevention also includes the legal duty to protect or warn potential victims according to the Tarasoff precedent, discussed in Chapter 34. Following the Wesbecker case (p. 362), Monahan (90) recommended that workplaces develop systems for reporting and addressing employee threats, which should include making treatment available when indicated.

HANDGUN CONTROL

There is evidence that handgun control reduces the frequency of homicide. Washington, D.C., passed a gun-licensing law in 1976, following which the city's frequency of homicide decreased considerably during the period

1977–1988. The overall decline was associated with a reduction in handgun homicide without it being "replaced" by homicides by other means. Nearby communities, which passed no such legislation, maintained the same homicide rates (6). Similarly, an epidemiologic study (7) that compared Vancouver and Seattle (cities that are the same in climate, geography, demographic characteristics, and overall crime rates) found that Vancouver, which had legislation to control handgun use, had a significantly lower homicide rate than Seattle.

IMPROVED CONDITIONS FOR HIGH-RISK POPULATIONS

Hardest to accomplish, but essential to reducing the problem, is improving the conditions of living and providing alternatives to violence for poor urban children, teenagers, and young adults—the people most at risk for being violent or victimized by violence. Prevention must begin at conception with good prenatal and child health care, and continue throughout childhood, teenage, and young adulthood with good, well-monitored day care centers for child supervision while parents work, preschool (e.g., Head Start) programs followed up by education in safe primary and secondary schools, community and summer camp activity programs (91), and good jobs available in the community. Because violence is less frequent when bystanders are present, neighborhood Community Watch programs are helpful (49). How the nonmedical components of the above are best accomplished is beyond the scope of this book.

COMBATING THE DRUG EPIDEMIC

There are several associations of drug and violent crime, including the high frequency of intoxication by people before and during the commission of crimes, and the violence (e.g., armed robbery) associated with obtaining money to support a drug habit and with the large sums of money involved in the business of drug dealing. Consequently, any *effective* efforts to reduce access to drugs, attractiveness of drug use (by education and advertising campaigns), and abuse of drugs and its consequences (through substance dependence programs) will be helpful. Drug abuse and its treatment are discussed in Chapter 22. A radical alternative (not endorsed here) to reducing access to drugs is reducing the strong link between drugs and money by legalizing drugs. The nonmedical components of the "war on drugs" are also beyond the scope of this book.

IMPRISONMENT OF VIOLENT CRIMINALS

Most violent crimes are committed by callous, habitual criminals, the majority of whom are sociopaths (26). Society holds these persons responsible for their criminal behaviors, and assigns their apprehension, trial, and separation from society to the criminal justice system. The mission of the criminal justice system for violent habitual offenders is primarily the protection of society and secondarily the rehabilitation of the offender. Psychiatric assessment is not usually required to identify callous, habitual offenders. The criminal justice system readily identifies them.

SECTION VI.
GENERAL HEALTH

28/Sleep and Sleep Disorders

Charles R. Hillenbrand, M.D.

OBJECTIVES

GENERAL OBJECTIVE: Given an examination of a patient, identify and explain normal and abnormal sleep phenomena.

SPECIFIC OBJECTIVES:
1. Summarize the anatomy, biochemistry, physiology, and chronobiology of normal sleep.
2. Discuss the phenomenology of normal sleep.
3. Describe the disorders of excessive daytime sleepiness, including sleep apnea, narcolepsy, and obesity-hypoventilation disorder.
4. Summarize the insomnia disorders, including transient insomnias, persistent sleep-onset insomnia (p. 77), abnormal periodic leg movements of sleep, iatrogenic insomnia, and insomnia associated with psychiatric disorders.
6. Discuss parasomnias, including somnambulism and night terrors.

For centuries, sleep was regarded as the mere absence of wakefulness; it is now known to be an active process that competes with waking. Two types of mental activity occur during sleep: quiet sleep and dreaming sleep. These two states differ from each other and from waking in many respects (Table 28.1); in sleep disorders there is mixing of states (1).

NORMAL SLEEP

Anatomy and Physiology

Sleep is a recurring activity that operates within a 24-hour cycle; hence, it is a circadian (Latin *circa*, about, and *diem*, day) rhythm. The rhythm is tied to the changes in environmental lighting. Information about changes in light passes through the retina to the suprachiasmatic nucleus of the hypothalamus in the retinohypothalamic tract (Fig. 28.1 [2]). An interplay between this structure and the pineal gland results in nocturnal elevation of melatonin, a compound that synchronizes internal rhythms.

The brainstem is common to all vertebrates and makes up most of the reptilian brain. It processes sensory inputs through sensory perception (consciousness) and evaluation (memory), and it directs the appropriate motor output. It consists of 98 nuclear groups. Nuclei contain serotonergic, dopaminergic, noradrenergic, and cholinergic cells (pp. 53–60), ideally located to perform regulatory tasks by influencing other neurons. The brainstem is involved in spontaneous rhythmic behaviors (e.g., blood pressure, respiratory control), periodic rhythmic behaviors (quiet and dreaming sleep), learning (through modulation of the

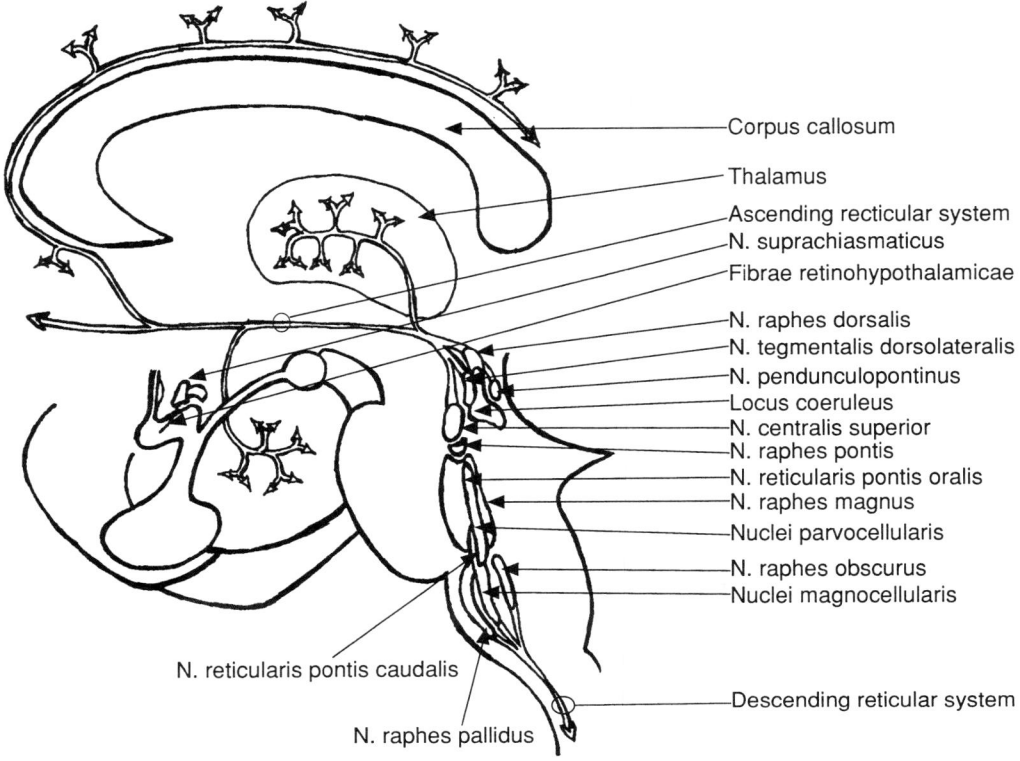

Figure 28.1. The anatomy of sleep. (Modified from Nieuwenhuys R, Woogd J, van Huijzen C. The human central nervous system. 3rd ed. New York: Springer-Verlag, 1988.)

forebrain and local circuits), and consciousness (3–5).

During awakening, serotonergic input from the raphe nuclei in the brainstem (p. 57) may cause accumulation of a tiredness factor which triggers secretion of hypnogenic (sleep-inducing) factors theorized to be polypeptides from the area postrema of the hypothalamus. This organ lies outside the blood-brain barrier and is responsive to brain and systemic influences. Along with multiple other factors (e.g., amount of stress, activity level, boredom), the hypnogenic factors cause a threshold to be exceeded, initiating a series of activities (6, 7).

Neurons ordinarily fire in patterns revealed only by computer analysis. They show characteristic rhythms in algebraic summation on the electroencephalogram (EEG) (Fig. 28.2 [8]). The wake brain has beta (13–40 Hz) and alpha (8–13 Hz) waves (pp. 198, 199), suggesting in-

formation processing; such waves are low voltage and fast, reflecting the enormous variety of active neurons. With the influence of the hypnogenic factors, the neurons start firing synchronously. As sleep nears, and a person rests comfortably with eyes closed, the alpha tracing dominates.

As sleep begins, light drowsiness appears, reflected by loss of alpha in favor of mixed slower frequencies. Expectably, the voltage diminishes, then the rate slows. The eyes then move slowly back and forth horizontally (slow eye movements [SEM]), repeating every 4 seconds. By a naming convention adopted in 1968, this is Stage 1 sleep. Active symmetric muscle movements (sleep startles) may occur, as pontine motor control is temporarily interrupted by sleep mechanisms. A very brief dream may occur, and a person wakened may insist he or she was not asleep.

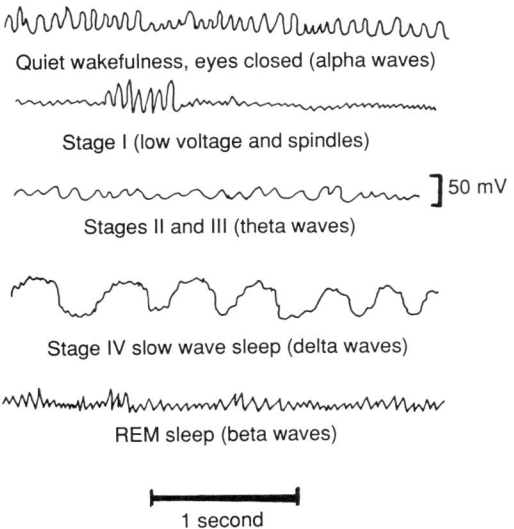

Quiet wakefulness, eyes closed (alpha waves)

Stage I (low voltage and spindles)

] 50 mV

Stages II and III (theta waves)

Stage IV slow wave sleep (delta waves)

REM sleep (beta waves)

1 second

Figure 28.2. EEG during wakefulness and sleep. (Modified from Guyton A.C. Textbook of medical physiology. 8th ed. Philadelphia: Saunders, 1991:663.)

The EEG continues to slow and sleep spindles appear. These waveforms may combine with a multiphasic sharp wave (vertex wave) to form the K-complex waveform; this activity could represent either lingering environmental stimulus processing, or processing of internal perceptions. These two features characterize Stage II sleep, and are superimposed upon a background of 1–5 Hz activity spreading anteriorly from the occiput.

Stage III consists of the slow wave background of Stage II, the delta wave (0.5–3 Hz) comprising 20%–50% of the tracing and coming to occupy progressively more of it.

Stage IV is indicated by delta waves in all head regions, occupying 50% of the tracing. This tendency for synchronized neuronal firing characterizes the first 3 hours of sleep, then gradually lessens (5, 9).

Superimposed on this initial tonic slowing is a phasic activation occurring about every 90 minutes. This activity is apparently mediated by pontine structures including the nucleus reticularis pontis caudalis (NRPC) and the nucleus reticularis pontis oralis (NRPO), as well as medullary structures including the gigantocellular nuclei, ventral reticular nuclei,

and parvocellular nuclei. The NRPC, NRPO, and other nuclei are noradrenergic (NA) (pp. 55, 56) and influence eye movements through the cranial nerve nuclei. The medullary nuclei project to the thalamic and hypothalamic NA neurons. Medullary nuclei including the locus ceruleus (LC) ascend via the medial forebrain bundle to these same areas and to all areas of the cortex. Cholinergic pontine nuclei include the pedunculopontine tegmental (PPT) nuclei and dorsolateral tegmental nuclei (LDT). The PPT goes to the thalamus and frontal cortex, whereas the LDT goes to the raphe nuclei, thalamus, septum, and cortex. These cholinergic nuclei likely regulate the occurrence or density of the PGO spike (spikes occurring in *p*ons, lateral *g*eniculate bodies of the thalamus, and *o*ccipital cortex) discharges characterizing this phase of sleep, as well as muscular atony (absent muscle tone), and the cardiovascular and respiratory changes of this phase.

With activation of these structures, the EEG changes to mixed low voltage frequencies (mainly theta, some alpha), resembling the awake tracing. PGO spike activity seems to alert the cortex by mimicking the sensory input of wakefulness to elicit dream imagery, and stimulating forebrain processes to enhance learning and memory. Sections of the LC cluster with the LDT neurons to influence spinal inhibitory interneurons through the ventrolateral reticulospinal pathway to cause generalized inhibition of spinal motoneurons, producing the inhibition of motor tone (exception: eye and respiratory movements) during this stage. The eyes, which had been moving slowly, move rapidly in visible lateral bursts, giving this stage the name rapid eye movement (REM) sleep. This phasic activity repeats every 90 minutes or so, initially brief but later lasting 20 minutes. Depending on the length of the night's sleep, there can be 4–6 REM epochs, occupying a total of 20%-25% of the night's sleep (4–6, 10, 11).

For infants, 50% of sleep time is REM; this diminishes to 25% in young adults and may decrease further with aging. The amount of slow wave sleep (SWS, Stages 3 and 4) also decreases with aging and can disappear in the

Table 28.1.   Sleep Characteristics

	Awake	NREM	REM
MOVEMENT	Frequent, voluntary	Infrequent, involuntary episodic gross movements	Inhibited, frequent small brief twitches
MENTATION	Logical, progressive recalled	Logical, progressive recalled	Illogical, bizarre not recalled unless wakened
SENSATION/ PERCEPTION	Vivid, externally generated	Dull or absent	Vivid, internally generated
POSTURE	Variable, erect	Recumbent	Recumbent
CONSCIOUSNESS	Awake	Asleep	Asleep
EYES	Open, moving	Closed, slowly or not moving	Closed, moving
EEG	Desynchronized, fast low voltage	Synchronized, slower higher voltage	Desynchronized, fast low voltage
MUSCLE TONE	Strong	Diminished	Diminished to absent

Modified from Mahowald MW, Schenck CH. Status dissociatus—a perspective on states of being. Sleep 1991;14:69–79.

sixth decade. The reasons for these decreases are not known.

Although the purposes of sleep are not known with certainty, sleep appears to serve multiple functions. It is restorative, perhaps allowing the regeneration of physiologic properties of the CNS needed for proper functioning. It may be protective; suppressing cortical activity may prevent exhaustion of cortical neurons. It is instinctive (a behavior with an innate organized pattern). It is energy-conserving: warm-blooded animals can gain energy by turning down their bodily thermostats and being inactive. It is immobilizing, enhancing survival by rendering animals immobile and nonresponsive, increasing safety during ecologically adverse parts of the day (12). It may enhance learning by allowing time for neuronal repair and processing of newly learned data.

Normal Sleep Phenomenology (Table 28.1)

As sleep starts, unilateral contractions of an entire upper or lower limb may occur, termed a sleep startle (hypnic jerk). These occur more often while antidepressant medication (p. 327) is taken. During the night, the sleeper may initiate (usually brief) conversation (somniloquy [sleeptalking]). Somniloquy does not reflect dreaming, because it occurs in non-REM (NREM) sleep (but not during intense delta activity), often in Stage II. The speech is inco-

herent, though it may seem responsive to comments from an awake partner. Amnesia for it in the AM is the rule, unless it is so loud that the sleeper wakens.

Dreams, emotionally charged vivid multisensory hallucinations starring the dreamer, occur almost exclusively in REM sleep. This type of dream may be reported outside of REM sleep, but likely reflects the same mechanisms of dreaming (but not driving REM EEG stages). Typically, if wakened from NREM sleep, the sleeper reports ordinary waking mentation. It is debated whether dreams have "meaning," as hypothesized by Freud (13); some theories reject notions of psychologically important meaning, noting instead that dreaming accompanies physiologic memory and information-processing occurring in many areas of the brain in parallel (14). The oddity of dream thought could derive from the absence of external stability orientation (10). The nightmare (anxiety dream) is a somewhat longer REM phenomenon, followed by waking with anxiety while recalling the dream. One major difference between a dream and a nightmare is the intensity of the PGO activity immediately preceding it; the greater the PGO activity (owing to stress, medications [e.g., antidepressants], or withdrawal from medications with anticholinergic or REM-suppressant activity) the more likely the dream will have nightmarish qualities. The reaction to the dream, not its content, makes a nightmare; some bizarre dreams are fun, and some ordinary dream scenes from waking life may feel threatening.

Penile and clitoral engorgement occur during REM sleep; they are part of the autonomic arousal characterizing REM sleep, not sexual arousal of the sleeper. On occasion, the pleasant feelings may be included in dream content (as may environmental events [e.g., a ringing telephone]), but one may waken from a dream of studying math with engorged erectile tissues as often as from a sexually alluring dream. Full bladders have nothing to do with this. Sexual climax (called nocturnal emission in men) during sleep is also a REM phenomenon reflecting autonomic arousal.

Recent evidence (15) suggests that sleep is a variant of the circadian rhythm termed a circasemidian rhythm, with occurrences at the body temperature minima (nocturnal sleep) and maxima (afternoon nap). The latter is the siesta culture nap, the last nap given up by children as they mature, and a frequent nap time for narcolepsy patients. Naps occur from 12–2 PM for 76% of the world's nappers, most of whom live within 45 degrees of latitude north or south of the equator (15).

During sleep, there is increased production by the hypothalamus of the vasoconstricting (blood vessel narrowing via smooth muscle constriction) peptide vasopressor (VP). This facilitates urinary continence during sleep by halving urine output. This usual nighttime rise in VP does not occur in enuretic people (16). The experimental drug desmopressin, a nonvasopressor analog of VP, reduces urine volume during sleep and could be a helpful adjunct in the treatment of enuresis (17–19).

ABNORMAL SLEEP

Excessive Daytime Sleepiness (EDS)

This group of disorders (including narcolepsy and sleep apnea) is characterized by intense sleepiness (i.e., readiness to fall asleep in permissive [e.g., in a dull classroom or while reading] or nonpermissive [e.g., driving a car] settings). Fatigue and boredom are not sleepiness. Ordinary sleepiness between 12–2

PM is not a disorder. The sleepiness following an inadequate night's sleep is discussed with the insomnia disorders (p. 377). Sleepiness occurs commonly in older persons: in sleep labs they fall asleep within 15 minutes; 35% fall asleep while reading, 45% while watching television, 3% talking with friends, and 5% while driving. These phenomena are often related to sleep apnea (20–23).

NARCOLEPSY

Narcolepsy was named by Gelineau in 1880, and its symptom tetrad (unwanted sleep episodes, cataplexy, sleep paralysis, and hypnogogic or hypnopompic hallucinations) was identified in 1934. It occurs in 0.05% of the population, most often males aged 10–20, although it can occur from childhood to the fifth decade (24). Many patients have a link between this disorder and the major histocompatibility complex class II antigen called DR2 (25); there are recent reports of links with the HLA-DQ1 (HLA-DWw1) antigen (26). Between 30%–50% of offspring will show either narcolepsy (6%–18%) or EDS alone (24%–34%) (24).

The key feature is unwanted episodes of sleep, in both permissive and nonpermissive settings, several times daily. Onset is irresistible, typically within 5 minutes (24), and the duration of sleep ranges from 15–60 minutes with the person waking refreshed. In addition to napping, the person may have excessive daytime drowsiness, impaired work performance, poor memory, or automatisms (involuntary repetitive actions such as scratching or chewing) while half asleep. This can result in the patient being called lazy and unfairly censured, lead to divorce, or cause auto accidents (20).

The second feature is cataplexy, an abrupt decrease of muscular tone ranging from brief weakness or sagging of the knees to paralysis (except for respiratory and ocular muscles). This can occur unpredictably, or follow laughter, anger, or other strong emotion. It causes the victim to lose tone in posture-maintaining muscles with head bobbing on the neck, elbows slipping off a desk as the arms lose tone, and buckling of the knees. Milder attacks are the most common. It can be terminated by someone's touch.

Closely allied is muscle weakness or paralysis as sleep nears or ends (sleep paralysis). Typically this frightens the sleeper, and an anxiety dream may intrude into wakefulness. The episode lasts a few seconds or minutes and, although distressing, is benign. It ends after the sleeper makes a strong effort to waken, or falls asleep again. Like cataplexy, it can be terminated by someone's touch.

The fourth manifestation is the intrusion of dreams into waking consciousness at sleep onset (hypnogogic hallucinations) or sleep end (hypnopompic hallucinations). They often consist of poorly formed, darkly colored objects seeming to approach the sleeper, but also can consist of more typical colorful dream imagery. Auditory intrusions may occur as random sounds, mumbled snatches of conversation, or machinery or household noises. The cataplexy, sleep paralysis, and hallucinations are called narcolepsy's ancillary (auxiliary) symptoms; they may occur on rare occasions in nonnarcoleptic sleepers—their regular recurrence, not their occurrence, characterizes narcolepsy.

In the sleep lab, narcoleptics typically fall asleep within 5 minutes. Uniquely, their sleep routinely starts with the REM stage. A small number of patients develop REM-related daytime hallucinations that respond to treatment for narcolepsy, but not to treatments for psychotic disorders (27). Two other sleep disturbances occur more often in narcoleptics than in other persons: periodic movements of sleep (which disturb nocturnal sleep), and obstructive sleep apnea.

Narcolepsy can be viewed as an attack of dreaming sleep, but little is understood of its etiology (28, 29). For years, treatment has been stimulants for sleep attacks and antidepressants for the ancillary symptoms. Studies have confirmed the usefulness of methylphenidate, dextroamphetamine, protriptyline, and pemoline (p. 332) (30, 31).

SLEEP APNEAS

The sleep apneas account for more than 75% of patients (84% of men, 60% of women) who have excessive daytime sleepiness (22). Among the general population of elderly, it is even more frequent (27%–75% of men, up to 32% of women aged 65 years or older) (21).

Obstructive sleep apnea consists of episodes of upper airway collapse and obstruction during sleep with cessation of airflow causing hypoxemia. Interruption of sleep restores airway motor tone and patency. More often, snoring partially overcomes the obstruction. The snoring, a successful attempt to force air past the obstructed oro- and hypopharynx, is very loud and becomes louder (can be over 80 dB). It is interrupted by periods of total airway obstruction with absence of airflow despite strenuous respiratory efforts; these obstructive periods in turn end with a snorting-gasping loud inspiration.

Central sleep apnea consists of cessation of all respiratory efforts during sleep lasting more than 10 seconds. It occurs most often in those unaccustomed to high altitudes where the lower ambient oxygen increases ventilatory drive, which can then destabilize breathing (32). It also occurs in patients who have heart failure, frontal lobe damage, and chronic hyperventilation (e.g., people in pain or highly anxious), all of whom have respiratory instability interacting with decreased responsiveness (uncovered by sleep) to accumulation of CO_2. Obesity and use of alcohol can aggravate this. In infants, cyanosis (p. 189) on awakening, resolving later in the morning, can be an early sign. Central sleep apnea accounts for some cases of sudden infant death syndrome (SIDS).

Not surprisingly, sleeping with brain hypoxia owing to either type of sleep apnea has behavioral consequences. Morning dullness of intellect, inattention, poor concentration, memory loss, irritability, moodiness, loss of sexual appetite and arousal, and nocturnal enuresis, can all occur. This condition can simulate major depression with suicidal ideas and psychotic experiences. Sleepiness when attention is not demanded (e.g., watching TV) is most typical, but may intrude progressively into situations of greater attentional demand (e.g., auto accidents occur twice as often in these patients as in the general population) (20). This can occur in children, manifest as school disturbances or snoring *between* bouts of upper respiratory infection.

Furthermore, cardiovascular impairments are common. The frequent arousals provoke elevation of catecholamine levels, with increased systemic and pulmonic artery pressures (32–34). In over half of obstructive sleep apnea patients, sustained hypertension occurs; these patients make up about 25% of hypertensives. Cardiac irregularities occur in nearly 40%, primarily during the apneic pauses.

Treatment includes minimizing risk factors (e.g., avoiding alcohol or other sedatives, repairing anatomic abnormalities such as hypertrophied tonsils). Bypassing the airway obstruction by surgical incision through the midline of the neck into the trachea (tracheostomy) or airway sustenance (e.g., nasal continuous positive airway pressure [CPAP]) eliminates apnea, relieving symptoms promptly and dramatically in nearly all patients (35).

A rare related disorder is Ondine's curse (daytime hypoventilation and nocturnal sleep apnea). Similarly rare is the Pickwick syndrome, named for the immensely obese snoringly hypersomnolent Joe, a servant at Charles Dickens's Pickwick Club.

Insomnia Disorders

Insomnia disorders are, naturally, characterized by insomnia (a complaint of an inadequate or abnormal night's sleep [either difficulty falling asleep, wakings during the night, or a shorter than usual sleep time]). Thirty-five percent of the general population have trouble sleeping, with 17% considering it serious (36). Daytime consequences include fatigue, sleepiness, impairment of usual functioning, and anxiety.

TRANSIENT INSOMNIAS

Transient insomnias last less than 3 weeks, often 1–2 days. The most common accompanies an unfamiliar sleeping environment, persisting a few days and requiring no treatment other than reassurance. Noisy and uncomfortably warm or cool circumstances also provoke insomnia, with noisiness causing repeated wakings, movements, and shifts between sleep stages, and uncomfortable temperatures causing increases in wakefulness and loss of REM. These stimuli show variable impacts on each person. Emotional stressors generally have a longer lasting impact, often 2–3 weeks. Treatment consists in adherence to one's usual sleep time without napping, regardless of sleepiness, to avoid shifting circadian rhythms. Brief use of a short-acting benzodiazepine (BDZ) hypnotic (p. 333), perhaps every second or third night, may help the person maintain normal patterns during the stress.

Jet lag symptoms include malaise, tiredness, and difficulty falling asleep (if flying east, because of trying to fall asleep during the usual wake time) or waking during later sleep hours (if flying west, because of trying to stay asleep during usual wake hours). Diets and behavioral changes are ineffective. Short-acting BDZs can allow regular sleep with daytime alertness.

The sleep disturbances of shift work change persist, with interrupted and shortened sleep and daytime sleepiness. Often efforts to adapt to a new sleep-wake schedule are frustrated by resumption of the usual sleep schedule on weekends and holidays. The impact of these abnormalities is notable, and includes gastric ulceration and attentional and mood disturbances. The best treatment is avoiding shift work; failing that, strictly adhering to the new sleep schedule for the rest of the shift assignment, including nonworking days, is next best. When possible, changed shifts should advance (e.g., from 8 AM to 4 PM) as forward shifts are less disruptive physiologically. Using a short-acting BDZ for the first day or two of a new shift to facilitate adjustment to the new sleep time may help, but chronic BDZ use is contraindicated in this case.

PERSISTENT SLEEP ONSET INSOMNIA

(See Chapter 6, page 77.)

PERIODIC LEG MOVEMENTS IN SLEEP

A common cause of insomnia, periodic leg movements in sleep consists of bilateral, asymmetric sustained contractions of leg muscles lasting 0.5–5.0 seconds and recurring every 20–40 seconds (37, 38). The movements occur in lighter stages of sleep later in the night. The prevalence increases after age 30, rising to 50% in the elderly (21). The regularity of the leg contractions may derive from a reticular pacemaker (39, 40). The movements are accompanied by K complexes or by alpha EEG waves (signs of arousal), but the patient is unaware of the movements. A bed partner notices very restless sleep with a tendency to disrupt the bedclothes. The sleeper may even fall out of bed. Such movements are found in a variety of neurologic and metabolic illnesses, and in sleep apnea and narcolepsy. Of many suggested treatments, the most consistent improvement occurs either with levodopa (an anti-Parkinson agent that is metabolized to dopamine) supplemented with benserazide (which reduces the conversion of levodopa to dopamine everywhere in the body except the brain), with bromocriptine 2.5–5.0 mg HS, or with clonazepam 0.5–1.5 mg HS (37, 39).

Some of these cases are accompanied by the restless legs syndrome, characterized by a creeping unpleasant dysesthesia occurring deep in the legs or hands coupled with an irresistible urge to move the extremities (which relieves the feelings) before falling asleep. The sufferer may pedal the legs, or rub or hit the limbs against the bed, or may have to leave the bed to move around. Unfortunately, when rest is again attempted, the feelings return. The intensity of the feelings diminishes as the night passes so the person can eventually sleep. Once the person is asleep, periodic leg movements of sleep occur in virtually all cases.

IATROGENIC INSOMNIA

Patients given sleeping medications in the hospital are often abruptly withdrawn from them on discharge from inpatient care. With most sedatives, a rebound insomnia follows, lasting several days. If called and informed of this complaint, the physician (unaware of the cause of the problem) may renew the hypnotic agent. If a nonbenzodiazepine agent is used, tolerance (p. 305) rapidly occurs. Eventually, the patient could take more than 7 doses of hypnotic medication spread through the day (from fear of taking such a large quantity at one time). If reluctant to describe this development to the primary physician, the patient may seek agents from additional doctors, often using several pharmacies. If the patient's sources dry up, or if the patient needs hospitalization, he or she may inadvertently experience a withdrawal seizure or delirium on sudden cessation of the medication.

Treatment involves several steps. The patient should be educated about the cause of the problem and reassured about eventual recovery. Medication availability must be controlled. All prescribing physicians and utilized pharmacies used must be contacted and advised that the sole source of hypnotics will be the primary physician. The entire dose is then given *hora somni* (HS, at bedtime). The amount is lowered by one daily dose after each week, so a person taking seven daily doses would require 6 weeks to stop the medication. Although such a slow decrease is not needed to prevent acute withdrawal, it is necessary to allow the patient to sleep enough to prevent the person from seeking another physician for more sleeping pills. It requires 4–6 weeks without the hypnotic to recover the pretreatment sleep quality.

PSYCHIATRIC DISORDERS

Insomnia accompanies most exacerbations (worsenings) of severe psychiatric disorders, including bipolar disorder, manic phase, major depression, the schizophrenias, delusional disorder, the anxiety disorders, and coarse brain diseases. Major affective disorder is the second most common cause (6%) of excessive daytime sleepiness. Treat the underlying disorder. Lorazepam may be successfully used for sedation in such patients.

Parasomnias

The parasomnias are characterized by behaviors during sleep that are usually associated with wakefulness. Although the nocturnal behaviors resemble waking behavior, they are different physiologically (41). These behaviors commonly start in childhood or adolescence, distressing the patient and family (42); occasionally, injurious behavior occurs (43)

SOMNAMBULISM (SLEEPWALKING)

Somnambulism is seen in children during the first 3 hours of sleep, when delta wave EEG activity is most intense; in adults, it may occur outside of SWS (44) but most often comes from deep sleep. The sleeper suddenly sits up in bed with eyes open and a dulled facial expression. The person may pick at the bedclothes before arising, and then clumsily walk in or out of the room. Some visual agnosia (p. 44) is present: the sleepwalker can avoid some but not all obstacles in his or her path; dangerous falls and collisions have been reported. The episode is measured in minutes, usually less than 10, and the somnambulist returns to sleep, in bed or wherever the person is when the walk ends. Sleepwalking occurs in 15%–30% of normal children, but persists in only 3% to puberty. Perhaps 1% of adults continue to sleepwalk. Family history is positive in 80%, and prevalence is higher in monozygotic (p. 64) than dizygotic twins. There is no characteristic psychopathology in children who sleepwalk. The episode is heralded by bursts of high-voltage delta activity on EEG followed by lighter NREM stages, most often in the first SWS epoch of the night.

PAVOR NOCTURNUS (NIGHT TERRORS)

Night terrors are closely related to sleepwalking. Patients with one often have the other, sometimes simultaneously. Both are familial (p. 64). Sleep EEG pathology is also similar. From intense delta sleep, there is a burst of high-voltage slow waves, an increase in motor tone, tachycardia, and a gasping inspiration followed by hyperventilation. The child sits up, a terrified look on the face, and then screams and mutters. He or she may then run out of the room. The child then rapidly falls into deep sleep as the episode terminates. Pavor nocturnus persists in 6% of schoolchildren, tends to disappear at puberty, but persists in about 1% of adults. Night terrors in adults are termed incubus, which awakens the adult patient.

Treatment of somnambulism and pavor nocturnus is similar. Education of the patient and family is essential; demonstration of the positive family history often fosters acceptance and may reveal adult untreated patients. Protection of the sleeper is necessary to avoid accidental injury; harmful objects should be removed from the room, and locks may have to be applied to windows and doors. BDZ medication, particularly clonazepam, often blocks these behaviors. Curiously, clonazepam's ability to block SWS is not related to its effectiveness in this condition (44, 45).

29/Sex and Sexual Dysfunctions

Joel M. Silberberg, M.D., and Richard L. Grant, M.D.

OBJECTIVES

GENERAL OBJECTIVE: Given a patient examination, discuss the patient's sexual functioning and describe sexual problems or dysfunctions if present.

SPECIFIC OBJECTIVES:

1. Compare current societal attitudes in the United States about sex with attitudes that prevailed in the 1960s and 1970s.
2. Summarize the anatomy and physiology of the sexual response cycle for both sexes.
3. Discuss normal variability in sexual behavior and list factors that influence this variability.
4. State the population prevalences of sexual problems and dysfunctions.
5. List the levels of inquiry about sexual dysfunctions.
6. Discuss the sources of sexual dysfunctions.
7. Summarize the major sexual dysfunctions.
8. Define and summarize the paraphilias.

The science of sexual medicine is the anatomy, physiology, psychology, and disorders of the sexual response cycle. The art of sexual medicine is developing trust, rapport, and nonjudgmental sensitive awareness with patients who seek the physician's help in this most private and personal area. Both are the subject of this chapter. Students begin medical school with prejudices and anxieties (1). Unless you become aware of your own attitudes and can put them in proper perspective, a patient's sexual problem may either repulse or overexcite you and thereby diminish your therapeutic effectiveness. Understanding and effectively treating a person with a sexual complaint also means understanding the crucial role the social system plays in symptom formation and relief.

CHANGING ATTITUDES ABOUT SEXUALITY

You may not be aware that you may subscribe to misconceptions or value judgments about sexuality. Physicians must transcend personal opinion to be aware of the range of normal sexual behaviors and be effective practitioners (2). Much occurred in the 1980s to change American attitudes about sexuality formed during the sexual revolution of the 1960s, which was then influenced by the researchers Alfred Charles Kinsey (3, 4) and William Masters and Virginia Johnson (5). Acquired immunodeficiency syndrome (AIDS) provided an opening for people to discriminate against homosexuals and to make premarital or extramarital sex "dirty" again, as in the era before Masters and Johnson. For some people, AIDS has become a phobia that can interfere with their sexual, social, and professional lives.

> Mr. A. was a successful businessman and a fine husband and parent. But he took a dare from friends while on a business trip and received fellatio from a prostitute while he was wearing a condom. Since then, despite testing negative for HIV antibodies every 6 months for 2 years, he refuses to touch his children or kiss his wife for fear of transmitting AIDS to them.

The 1980s saw the arrival of many triple-s (single, successful, satisfied) women, whose education and income made marriage less an expected event than a viable option (6). What happens when such a woman, once married, wants to become pregnant at 35 years of age and complains of infertility? What if her husband develops sexual problems during this stressful time? Infertility testing often entails sex on demand, which may lead to sexual dysfunction in both partners. Brief sex therapy can reduce sex-related stress (7).

> Ms. and Mr. B. were an emotionally and sexually happy couple until Ms. B. wanted to become pregnant, and had difficulty conceiving. Mr. B. resented having to be ready to impregnate her at the most fertile point in her menstrual cycle, and under these (to him) unromantic conditions he developed secondary erectile dysfunction. The couple responded well to brief sex therapy which focused on decreasing Mr. B.'s performance anxiety about "sex on demand." The sensate focus exercises that the physician prescribed for the couple—that deemphasize performance, emphasize pleasure, and initially forbid intercourse (8)—were integral to the success of the therapy.

HISTORY

For centuries literature and art gave us the only insights on sexuality. Conception yielded to scientific study in the early 19th century, before which abstinence was the only contraception. In the late 1800s, Henry Havelock

Ellis (9) and Sigmund Freud (10) reported on sexual feelings and behavior in Victorian Europe. The world, however, changed greatly in the next half century with rapid industrialization, mass communications, two world wars, a cure for some venereal diseases, and invention of the condom. Kinsey's research in the 1940s and 1950s (3, 4) enlightened us about normal sexual behavior. For instance, he reported that nearly all men and three fourths of women recall masturbating at some time.

Oral contraceptives became available. In the 1960s, Masters and Johnson began reporting about studies of human sexuality in a laboratory setting. Special cameras and equipment were devised and normal and sexually dysfunctional volunteers studied. Their treatises *Human Sexual Response* (5) and *Human Sexual Inadequacy* (8) were turning points. The work elucidated, among many other things, that the clitoris is the only human organ with no other function but pleasurable arousal, and that there is greater frequency of masturbatory than coital orgasms. They demonstrated the role of sexual misinformation, performance anxiety, and emotions in sexual dysfunction, and that a brief, intensive, dual-therapist intervention is effective in more than 80% of sexual dysfunctions.

ANATOMY AND PHYSIOLOGY OF THE SEXUAL RESPONSE CYCLE

For centuries, the sex organs have been a subject of interest or shame, praised and vilified, concealed and exhibited in art and literature. Concealment promotes desire and is socially prudent, but when excessive it perpetrates ignorance.

> Mr. & Mrs. C. presented to a sexual dysfunction clinic because of her "primary anorgasmia." Married for 10 years, they were a loving, well-educated couple. But neither knew where her clitoris was, or what it did. They responded well to brief sex therapy that centered around education, a sexological examination (p. 389), and exercises to allow them to feel less ashamed about their sexual anatomy.

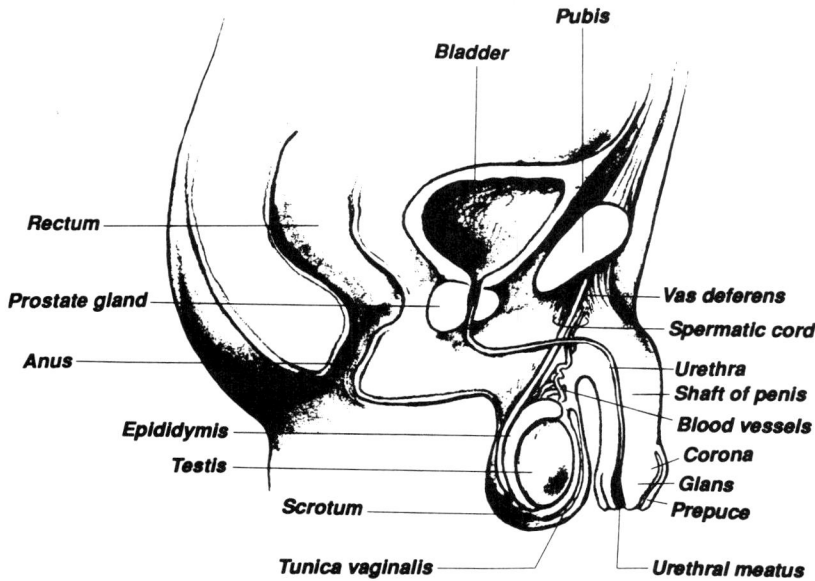

Figure 29.1. Male genitalia. (Reprinted with permission from Bates B. A guide to physical examination and history-taking. Philadelphia: Lippincott, 1988.)

The penis has three functions: urination, procreation, and pleasure. The only function of the clitoris is pleasurable sexual arousal.

In both sexes, the reproductive system is located partly inside the body cavity and partly outside. The male external sex organs (Fig. 29.1 [11]) are the penis and scrotum. Although the testes are outside the pelvic cavity, they are not considered external genitalia. The penis contains three cylinders of spongy tissue (two corpora cavernosa, one corpus spongiosum). The urethra, which conveys both urine and ejaculate, runs through the corpus spongiosum. Spongy tissue is rich in blood vessels and nerves and contains many cavities. In the flaccid state these cavities contain little blood, but during sexual arousal they fill with blood within their tough fibrous coats, and the penis "hardens." An erection is *not* caused by muscular contraction. The corpus spongiosum terminates in the glans of the penis which is richly supplied with nerves and extremely sensitive. At the tip of the glans is a longitudinal slit for the urethal opening. The foreskin (prepuce) is a sleeve of skin that folds over the corona of the glans at the neck of the penis. Small glands under the prepuce and in the corona secrete smegma, a cheesy substance (function unknown). Accumulation of smegma produces a characteristic odor and increases susceptibility to venereal infections. Circumcision is excision of the foreskin, done for religious reasons. In some countries, physicians advocate it to prevent accumulation of smegma under the prepuce.

Circumcision is obligatory only when the foreskin is so tight that it cannot be retracted over the glans (phimosis) and may cause irritation, infection, problems with urination, and sexual dysfunction. In the absence of phimosis, excitability of the circumcised and uncircumcised penis are the same. The size of the flaccid penis is not related to build, race, potency, or personality. The smaller flaccid penis grows proportionately larger when erect. Most erect penises are about the same size; hence, the size of the flaccid penis is of no consequence in relation to potency or subjective sexual satisfaction.

The scrotal sac is richly innervated and divided by a septum into two compartments,

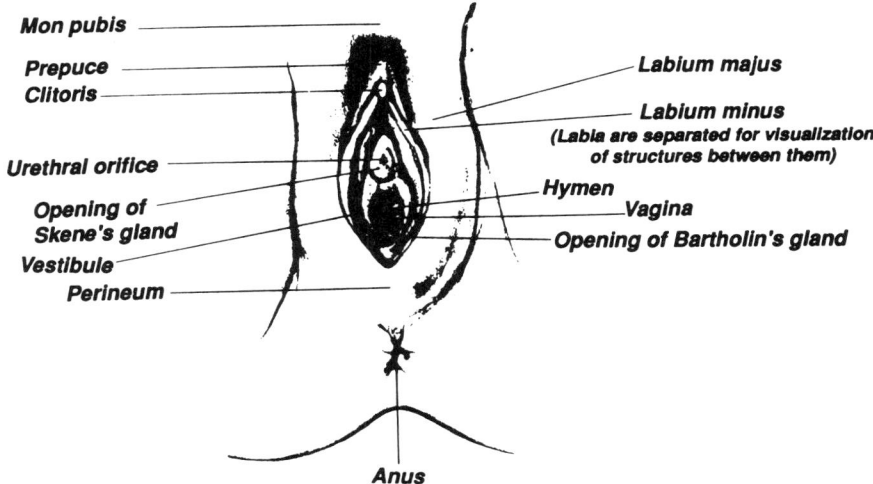

Mon pubis
Prepuce
Clitoris
Urethral orifice
Opening of
Skene's gland
Vestibule
Perineum

Labium majus
Labium minus
(Labia are separated for visualization
of structures between them)
Hymen
Vagina
Opening of Bartholin's gland

Anus

Figure 29.2. Female external genitalia. (Reprinted with permission from Bates B. A guide to physical examination and history-taking. Philadelphia: Lippincott, 1988.)

each containing a testicle (right higher than left) and a spermatic cord which enters the abdominal cavity through the inguinal canal.

> Mr. C. reported an unconsummated marriage of 5 years. He did not want his wife to see that he was "abnormal." He was embarrassed that his left testicle hung lower than his right one. The physician informed him that this was normal, allowing him to cross his legs without injuring himself. This allowed the couple to enter sex therapy and successfully address other issues that were interfering with their sexual intimacy.

The male internal sex organs consist of the testes (which produce sperm and testosterone), and a system of ducts (epididymis, vas deferens, ejaculatory duct, urethra) for sperm storage and transport. The seminiferous tubules in the testes produce sperm, and Leydig cells in the interstitial tissue of the testes produce testosterone directly into the bloodstream, making the testis an endocrine (ductless) gland. Sperm are stored in the tortuous, c-shaped epididymis which adheres to the posterior surface of the testis and journeys out of the scrotal sac through the inguinal canal as the vas deferens. The vas terminates at the antero-superior aspect of the prostate gland in

an ampulla and joins the duct of the seminal vesicle to form the ejaculatory duct.

The seminal vesicle contributes fluids that nourish and promote motility of sperm. The ejaculatory duct then joins the urethra of the bladder to form the prostatic urethra, which continues first as the membranous urethra and then as the penile urethra. The bulbourethral (Cowper's) glands, which flank the penile urethra, secrete an alkaline solution that protects sperm in the male urethra and the vagina (both acidic). The fluid from Cowper's gland and the seminal vesicle often contain sperm for several weeks after a vasectomy (tying off the vas deferens). Couples should be advised about this to avoid unplanned pregnancies.

The external genitals of the female are collectively called the vulva ("covering") of the pudendum (interestingly, "a thing of shame" in Latin). The vulva includes the mons pubis, labia majora and minora, clitoris, and vaginal opening (Fig. 29.2). The mons pubis is the soft, rounded elevation of fatty tissue over the pubic symphysis. The labia majora meet anteriorly at the anterior commissure and merge posteriorly with surrounding tissues. The anus is separate from the external genitals and lies further posteriorly. The labia minora are two pink hairless folds of skin located between the

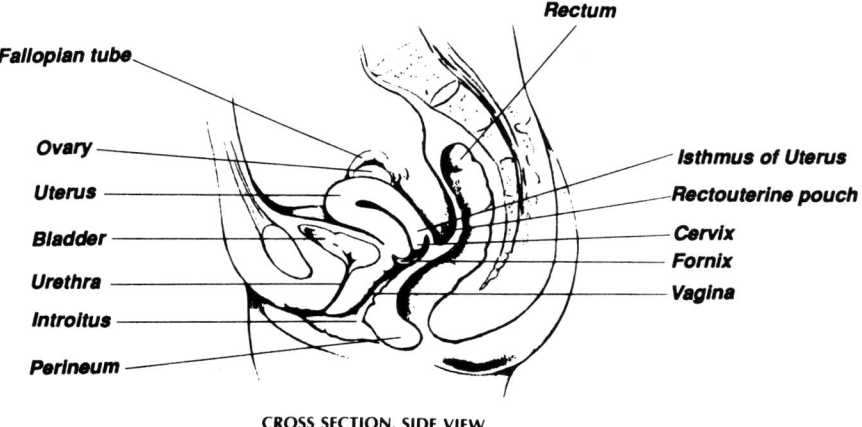

CROSS SECTION, SIDE VIEW

Figure 29.3. Female internal genitalia. (Reprinted with permission from Bates B. A guide to physical examination and history-taking. Philadelphia: Lippincott, 1988.)

major labia. They enclose a space called the vaginal vestibule which contains, from posterior to anterior, the ducts of the greater vestibular (Bartholin's) gland, the vaginal orifice, the urethral orifice, and the clitoris with its prepuce and two corpora cavernosa, the tips (crura) of which are attached to the pubic bone. The clitoris and labia majora and minora are richly supplied with blood vessels and nerves and are highly sensitive. The clitoris becomes engorged with blood during excitement.

> Mr. D. complained that Ms. D. did not have an orgasm with intercourse, but had orgasm with oral or manual stimulation. The therapist explained that only 20–30% of couples have simultaneous orgasms, and that a woman's orgasm during intercourse is caused by direct or indirect pressure of the man's pubis and penis on the clitoris. (Vaginal orgasm may be a myth; there is no compelling evidence for the existence of the G-spot [Graphenberg spot]. The excitement of vaginal containment of the penis, lubrication from the vaginal wall, and other stimuli facilitate orgasm.) Informing the couple that different sexual positions would increase clitoral stimulation (e.g., a pillow under her buttocks) during intercourse helped solve their problem.

The hymen (a membrane partially blocking the vaginal orifice) varies in shape and size. It may be torn accidentally or *withstand* intercourse, making its intactness unrelated to virginity.

The internal female sex organs are the paired ovaries and uterine (fallopian) tubes, the uterus, and vagina (Fig. 29.3). The ovary contains numerous follicles (each containing one ovum) in various stages of development. These follicles start maturing at puberty, and each month one follicle ruptures (ovulation). The fallopian tubes catch the ovum and fertilization occurs in the infundibular (funnel-shaped) third of the uterine tube.

The vagina has anterior and posterior walls and (like the pleural cavity) is a potential space rather than a permanent space. It communicates at its upper end with the cervical canal and is poorly supplied by nerves. It contains the penis, provides pleasure, receives sperm, and forms part of the birth canal during delivery. With the exception of severe cephalopelvic disproportion (p. 129), the vagina allows an infant's head to pass through during delivery. Hence, properly stimulated, it can accommodate the largest penis. The introitus (vaginal entrance) is different. It is richly innervated, and the ring of the bulbocavernosus muscle around it permits some control over the size of the opening. If a woman is tense, her introitus will be tense. Occasionally muscular spasm of the introitus (vaginismus) occurs because of pain or anxiety.

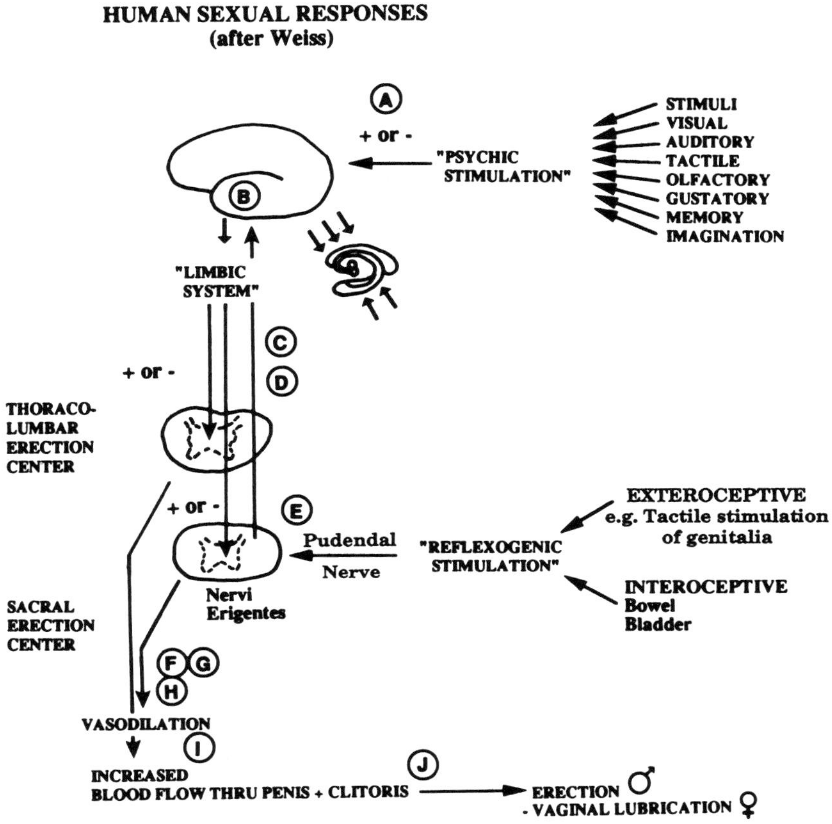

HUMAN SEXUAL RESPONSES
(after Weiss)

Figure 29.4. Physiology of human sexual response. (Reprinted with permission from Weiss HD. The physiology of human penile erection. Ann Intern Med 1972;76:793–799.)

In men and women, the nipples are richly innervated, sensitive, and important in arousal. This sensitivity is unrelated to nipple size and shape.

Masters and Johnson (5, 8) described a sexual response cycle (excitement, plateau, orgasm, resolution, and [in men] a refractory phase). The excitement phase is brought on by sensory stimulation involving visual, olfactory, tactile, auditory or gustatory perception, or fantasy. There is penile erection in the man and vaginal lubrication (by transudation [passage of liquid through a membrane with salt contents intact and no cells present] from the vaginal wall) in the woman. The nipples become erect. The clitoris becomes hard and the labia minora engorged. Reflexogenic stimulation also occurs by means of exteroceptive (e.g., tactile) stimulation and interoceptive (e.g., full bladder or bowel) mechanisms (Fig. 29.4 [12]). The length of a couple's excitement phase depends on their lifestyle, culture, and communication. To reach this stage, older men and women tend to require more tactile stimulation than in their earlier years. The plateau phase is an intensification of the excitement phase and is accompanied by up to 50% increase in testicular size with full testicular elevation, increased diameter and coloring of the glans, and Cowper's gland secretion. In the woman, the breasts may enlarge up to 25%, the clitoris elevates and retracts, and the labia minora become brighter red. Heart rate, blood pressure, and respiratory rate increase. There is reddening (sex flush) over the neck, chest, and forehead. Contraction of large muscle groups occurs.

A sense of ejaculatory (male) or orgasmic (female) inevitability is reached and orgasm occurs. In the man, 4–5 rhythmic contractions force the seminal fluid through the urethra. In the woman, 4–16 involuntary contractions of the lower third of the vagina, followed by sustained contractions of the uterus, occur. Extragenital responses include carpopedal spasm (hyperextension of the foot and claw-like contractions of the toes), hyperventilation (respiratory rate may peak at >40/min), myotonia (general muscle tension), and involuntary contraction of facial muscles, causing frowns or grimaces. Orgasm lasts 3–15 seconds, with a peak of pleasure.

> Ms. E felt that her husband did not like sex with her. She was relieved when the physician informed her that Mr. E's scowls were part of his orgasm and not disapproval of her.

Resolution entails relaxation, disgorgement of the genitalia, and emotional well-being. The duration of this stage varies proportionately with the length of prior stages.

After orgasm men have a refractory period lasting minutes to hours (depending on age, amount of alcohol, frequency of sex/masturbation, etc.), whereas women are potentially multiorgasmic. The female response resembles that of a man's in the biphasic nature of arousal and plateau to orgasmic inevitability, followed by orgasm and resolution. The essential difference is timing. Unmodified by the encounter with the partner, the man's total timing averages less than 3 minutes, the woman's usually 12–15 minutes. If a couple understands this, they will accommodate the woman's slower response without recriminations of frigidity, or the man's faster response without accusations of lack of consideration or unmanliness.

The *Diagnostic & Statistical Manual, 3rd Edition (Revised version)* (p. 240) (13) consolidates the excitement and plateau phases into one phase (excitement), and precedes it with an appetitive phase (phase of initial desire). The orgasm and resolution phases remain as described by Masters and Johnson.

Age-related changes in anatomy and physiology of sexuality cause anxiety and dysfunction if not understood. For both sexes the capacity for sexual arousal and enjoyment is lifelong. The need to be held and touched remains strong. The skin is the body's largest organ, is highly innervated, and responds pleasurably to touch throughout life. Expected changes for men over 50 years of age include delayed and partial erections (become fuller and sustained with prolonged foreplay), a less acute angle of the erect penis to the abdominal wall (because of decreased elastic tissue), prolonged plateau and ejaculatory inevitability period (increased ejaculatory latency), rapid detumescence, and an increased refractory period. Expected changes for women in this same age group include reduced vaginal lubrication (estrogen- or lubricant jelly-responsive) and reduced orgasm intensity. Education about changes expected with aging, and on valuing one's partner, leads to acceptance of and adaptation to the physiologic impact of aging.

INDIVIDUAL DIFFERENCES IN SEXUAL BEHAVIOR

The song "What Were Once Vices Are Now Habits" sums up individual differences in sexual behavior. The culture, religion, and individual psychology all determine what is considered normal. For some couples, intercourse several times yearly may be normal.

> Mr. F thought his wife was abnormal. He wanted sex twice a day and she was in the mood "only" 4 times a week.
>
> Mr. G became exceptionally aroused when he wore a woman's garment during foreplay with his wife. She accepted this behavior, which took place in the privacy of their home.
>
> On the other hand, Mr. H can *only* be aroused sexually when he cross-dresses. He has become obsessed with this behavior to the point that it is a financial and emotional drain on his wife and family; in fact, he no longer desires sex with his wife.

Individual differences are seen in masturbation and menstruation as well as sex. Masturbation is stimulation of one's genitals by hand movements, or by friction of the genitals against clothing or objects (e.g., a pillow, vibrator). One person can masturbate another (mutual masturbation). For both sexes, masturbation produces a more intense body response than intercourse; partners must adjust to each other's reactions. With masturbation the heart rate, blood pressure, breathing, and muscle tone are all more elevated than with intercourse.

In normal maturing, the discovery of sustained touch soon leads to masturbation. Children should be told that masturbation is OK, but that it should be done in private. There are many myths about it. It does not cause infertility, insanity, impotence, poor athletic performance, or perversions. In fact, it is a normal development to be mastered to promote normal adulthood sexual intimacy. Sex therapy exercises include masturbation as a step in alleviating sexual dysfunctions. The taboo may be too strong, however, for its use with some patients.

Historically, negative terms (e.g., the curse) were applied to menstruation. In some cultures, menstruation is still considered dirty. In many communities in India, women are not allowed to enter a temple when menstruating. Orthodox Jewish women take a ceremonial bath (Mikvah) before resuming sexual intercourse with their husband when the menstrual period is over. Cultural taboos aside, the time of the menstrual flow may be a good time for sex. Menstruation provides relief from the premenstrual engorgement of the vagina and uterus, impregnation rarely occurs, and lubrication is more than usual. The menstrual cycle may be used as an alibi (by husband or wife) to avoid sexual intimacy, until eventually sex is avoided before, during, and after menstruation (13). One patient wore sanitary pads for 20 days because her aunt told her "that will keep him away from you."

SEXUAL HISTORY AND SEXOLOGIC EXAMINATION

Taking a sexual history is the same as taking the rest of a medical history, and there is much common content. For example, certain illnesses (i.e., diabetes) and drugs (e.g., antihypertensives, alcohol) can lead to impotence. It is often necessary, however, to ask questions (which may be anxiety-provoking for both physician and patient) not usually asked in a routine interview, about masturbation, homoerotic sex play, first sexual experience, sexual orientation, rape, incest, extramarital affairs, sexual fantasies, favorite and painful sexual positions, orgasm, anal sex, oral sex, and fetishes (p. 398). This is facilitated by your being nonjudgmental and comfortable with your sexuality.

Sometimes, the sexologic exam, performed by physicians with specialized training, may be crucial to the success of brief therapy (23). In this, the physician educates each partner, in the presence of the other, about the genital anatomy and physiology. This technique counters myths and misinformation.

SEXUAL DYSFUNCTIONS

A sexual dysfunction is present when there is persistent disruption of any stage of the sexual response cycle (6). Sexual dysfunctions may occur when there is disturbance of any of the following: (1) the general health, including the integrity of the central and peripheral nervous systems and homeostasis of the endocrine system; or (2) structural and functional integrity of the genitalia, including adequacy of the blood supply.

The sexual dysfunctions (Table 29.1) may occur singly or in combination, may be lifelong to the time of evaluation (primary) or occur after normal initial function (secondary), and may be present in all settings where sexuality might occur (global) or limited to some settings and no others (situational). For example, a 42-year-old man who had rapidly ejaculated throughout his life began to experience

Table 29.1. Lifetime Prevalence Rates for Sexual Dysfunctions[a]

Inhibited female orgasm	5%–30%
Inhibited male orgasm	5%
Premature ejaculation	35%
Male erectile disorder	10%–20%
Hypoactive sexual desire disorder	
Men	1%–15%
Women	1%–35%

[a]Reprinted with permission from Nathan SG. The epidemiology of the DMS-III psychosexual dysfunctions. J Sex Marital Ther 1986; 12: 267–281.

erectile dysfunction with his wife after 20 years without erectile difficulty. However, he had normal erections for masturbation (primary premature ejaculation and secondary erectile dysfunction).

Prevalence

The divergence of statistics about the epidemiology of sexual dysfunctions results from variations in age, health, sexual knowledge, and sexual experience of the population sampled, whether the population is a random or convenience sample, and whether specific sexual dysfunctions are separated from nondysfunctional sexual problems created by lack of knowledge about function, disagreements about timing or frequency of sex, type of sexual practices, insufficient foreplay, the location and conditions under which sex occurs, or dissatisfaction with the nonsexual aspects of the relationship. An analysis of 22 general population surveys alone yielded the lifetime prevalence rates in Table 29.1 (15).

In a nonrandom survey (16) of 100 ostensibly happily married couples, 40% of the men reported erectile or ejaculatory difficulties and 63% of the women had arousal or orgasmic dysfunctions at some time during their current marriage. The occurrence of sexual difficulties rose to 50% in men and 77% in women when nondysfunctional sexual problems were added to the list. Despite the above, only 21% of the women and 33% of the men were dissatisfied with the sexual aspect of their relationship. If persons have sexual dysfunctions or problems yet are satisfied overall, then sex-

uality is more complex than just the quality and quantity of sex alone.

Levels of Inquiry in Evaluating for Sexual Dysfunctions

Twice as many sexual difficulties are identified if physicians ask directly than if they wait for the patient to initiate the subject (17). Physician attentiveness to patient sexuality varies. For example, at one medical school, only 1% of the local physicians refer almost 33% of the patients of the sexuality clinic.

When you can name the sexual dysfunctions, you have a ready list of sexual difficulties to screen for in a comprehensive medical evaluation. Screening level questions are few, and preferably open-ended (e.g., What difficulties do you have with erections? rapid ejaculations? having climaxes? your sexual interest?) rather than closed-ended (e.g., Do you have difficulty with erections?), do not search for causes, and are aimed at determining the presence or absence of a *current* problem. If no current problem is present, further questions waste time. Readily available, self-administered, paper-and-pencil questionnaires (18–20) help to gather information at the problem exploration level when the physician suspects the presence of a sexual difficulty. Such instruments save you time, and initially, patients may be more self-disclosing on questionnaires than with face-to-face questions (21, 22).

An affirmative response to a screening or problem exploration level question requires a second level of inquiry (the present illness development level) by history, physical, and lab evaluation. The goal of this is to understand the problem identified sufficient to initiate the third level—the treatment (management) level, either by referral or by yourself. Most physicians do not possess expertise sufficient to apply a full range of treatment level interventions, discussed at length elsewhere (8, 23–29). Do not mistake screening level problem identification with present illness development level understanding, and then intervene with a simplistic management plan. Sexual difficulties (like other medical difficulties) are inextricably biological, social, and psychological in etiology and treatment (23).

Sources of Sexual Dysfunctions

Dichotomizing causes for sexual (or other behavioral) dysfunctions under such rubrics as somatic/organic/physical versus psychological/functional has been a misleading convenience in the past and is a destructive atavism in the present. Only for convenience have the primary impetuses for sexual dysfunctioning been considered to arise solely from the person's environment (e.g., lack of privacy) or interpersonal interaction (e.g., resentment), mood states (e.g., anxiety), endocrine imbalances (e.g., hypothyroidism), local or systemic effect of diseases, or drug effects. Only infrequently do we identify an exclusive single source of a sexual dysfunction. For example, some patients develop erectile dysfunction after starting antihypertensive medication. Yet when switched to antihypertensives with much lower frequencies of sexual side effects, the erectile dysfunctions often remain because other elements have come into play.

Once you identify a sexual dysfunction using screening level inquiry, therefore, your search for contributing factors susceptible to remediation ranges across the patient's psychology, interpersonal environment, general health, and substance intake.

MISINFORMATION

A lack of sexual information, or misinformation, can disrupt normal sexual function.

> Ms I's dyspareunia (painful intercourse [p. 397]) resolved when she and Mr. I were instructed to wait until she achieved vaginal lubrication during her arousal before he inserted his penis.
> Ms. J became orgasmic and Mr. J lost his rapid ejaculation after they were informed that their private masturbation was normal, that it was permissible to enjoy sex, and that each person was responsible for his or her own pleasure by

telling the other what types of stimulation each desired in addition to intercourse itself.

PSYCHOLOGICAL FACTORS

Psychological factors contributing to sexual dysfunctions are low self-esteem; dissatisfaction with one's body; preoccupation with external events; distraction by past traumatic events; thinking that sexuality is messy, embarrassing, awkward, dirty, or wrong; fearing discovery, pregnancy, sexually transmitted disease, pain, or harm; anxiety about sexual performance; and exacerbation (reoccurrence, worsening) of almost any Axis I (p. 240) psychiatric disorder. The presence of any psychiatric disorder should occasion an inquiry about accompanying sexual difficulty. Chief among the disorders associated with sexual dysfunctions and problems are the affective disorders, the schizophrenic "spectrum," and somatization disorder (pp. 241, 246, 266, 270, 271). A psychiatric disorder does not automatically account for a sexual dysfunction, however, until other problems have been considered and rules out (excluded).

Another important influence on sexuality has to do with thoughts, feelings, and behaviors derived from complex programs in the brain. Not only is the brain programmed toward gay, straight, or bisexual sex object choice (30), but it also is programmed for an individualized pattern of erotic arousal which Money calls a lovemap (31). The lovemap depicts the idealized partner with regard to appearance, ethnicity, intelligence, grooming, sexual behavior style, aroma, affectional expressions, and other diverse attributes that can be sexually arousing. A lovemap also encompasses our own preferred erotic behaviors within the relationship. For optimal sexual enjoyment, incorporating both partners' lovemaps is necessary. Given the uniqueness of lovemaps, optimal sexuality requires the partners to communicate, verbally or nonverbally, specifically what would be most gratifying. Deficient acceptance of a partner's lovemap is another source of sexual dysfunction.

INTERPERSONAL INFLUENCES

Most sexuality is part of interpersonal interaction. The relationship is essential in the management of sexual dysfunction. Couples rely on each other for rewards and gratifications (32). With dyadic dysfunction, the components essential to intimacy—trust, considerateness, respect, mutuality—are reduced and replaced by conflict, resentment, anger, insecurity, or withdrawal. Some partners bring out the worst in each other, initiating or contributing to any sexual dysfunction.

> Ms. K discovered that Mr. K was having an affair with her best friend. Previously orgasmic, she became anorgasmic with intercourse with Mr. K. The anorgasmia persisted long after the affair ended.
>
> Mr. L had experienced occasional nondistressing erectile dysfunction throughout his harmonious marriage to Ms. L. He had no problems with erections for masturbation while away on business trips. Some 15 years into their 23-year marriage, she had an "awakening" that included becoming orgasmic and beginning a career as a minister. Mr. L's erectile problems intensified, but reversed with treatment when Mr. and Ms. L permitted each other to express dissatisfaction with the other.

Other interactions that impair function include placing demands on the partner, timing sexual approaches poorly, requesting sexual behaviors that the partner dislikes, becoming repulsive (e.g., gaining weight, not shaving, neglecting hygiene), and frustrating the partner's sexual desires (23).

Examples of difficulties in implementing mutually satisfying lovemaps are (1) he does not say "I love you" during foreplay, which she would find especially stimulating; (2) she lies motionless during intercourse, whereas he prefers her active participation; (3) her climaxes with cunnilingus are her most satisfying; he finds this disgusting; (4) she finds his 63-pound weight gain repulsive; and (5) rapid intromission (penile penetration) and ejaculation is his most exciting pattern, but she likes leisurely foreplay and languorous intercourse.

In one sexuality clinic, for one third of couples, both partners had a sexual dysfunction. Also, most men and women with a sexual dysfunction have more than one. Treatment, therefore, best addresses both partners' psychological and interpersonal difficulties and general health. Particular attention is given to deficits in either partner's ability to express preferences and dislikes.

OTHER CAUSES

There is another caveat concerning compartmentalized thinking about sexual dysfunction: the presence of a disease (e.g., diabetes) known to be associated with erectile dysfunction has in the past halted a search for other causes for the dysfunction.

> Mr. M, 44 years of age, with a 3-year history of diabetes, was told by his physician that his year-long erectile difficulties were caused by the diabetes and that nothing could be done. But his history revealed a growing preoccupation with impotence in the context of a recent marriage. Brief sex therapy resulted in a full resolution of the problem.

Thus, discovering a disease that could account for a sexual dysfunction does not necessarily explain it.

Common systemic causes of sexual dysfunctions and the mechanisms mediating them (23, 27, 28, 33) are listed in Table 29.2. Some diseases overlap several categories. Consequently, when evaluating a sexual dysfunction, a thorough history, and a physical and lab assessment should accompany your present illness level development. Conversely, having diagnosed a disease, your questions about its impact on sexuality often reveal an important problem meriting attention.

Malignancies, systemic infections, metabolic diseases, and other diseases of the cardiovascular, pulmonary, genitourinary, gastrointestinal, hepatic, musculoskeletal, and endocrine systems all can affect sexual desire and arousal. Mediating variables include the distracting effect of pain and other suffering, debilitation, or endocrine imbalances.

Table 29.2. Disease Sources of Sexual Dysfunction, Mechanisms of Dysfunctions and Principal Type of Dysfunction[a]

| Disorders* | Mechanisms of Dysfunctions | Type of Dysfunction | | |
		Inhibited desire	Decreased arousal	Orgasmic difficulties
Biochemical/physiologic disorders	Systemic effects: general debility, pain, depression, or changes in hormones	+	+	
Tumor, infection, or invasive process	Systemic or direct	+	+	
Anatomic or mechanical interference	Local genital	+	+	+
Postsurgery with neurologic or vascular damage	Local genital	2°	+	+
Neurologic disorders	Damage to higher centers	+		
	Spinal and peripheral nerve damage		+	+
Vascular disorders	Local reduction of blood flow		+	+
Endocrine disorders	Systemic and hormonal	+	+	
Genetic or congenital disorders	Diverse	.............Variable.............		

*See text for selected specific examples. (Modified from Nadelson CC, Marcotte DB, eds. Treatment interventions in human sexuality. New York: Plenum Press, 1983: 12–13.)

Destruction of testicular or ovarian function from carcinoma or infection leads to sexual dysfunction through hormonal dysregulation or direct invasive effects. Mechanical disruption of genital function (often with pain) can be caused by genital cancers or infections (e.g., vaginitis, salpingitis [fallopian tube infection], urethritis, prostatitis) or trauma which compromises the nerve or vascular supply. Cancer surgery likewise may inadvertently or of necessity damage genital structures or vascular supply.

Many neurologic disorders affect sexual function. Brain disease (e.g., temporal lobe epilepsy [p. 47]) usually decreases sexual desire but occasionally increases it. Spinal cord disorders and disorders of peripheral nerves that serve the genitalia (e.g., amyotrophic lateral sclerosis, spina bifida, multiple sclerosis [p. 199]) disrupt genital function directly, causing arousal as well as erectile and orgasmic dysfunction. However, some patients with spinal cord transection can experience arousal and erection on a reflex basis based on touching.

Compromise of the arteries and veins to the penis owing to any mechanism (e.g., penile vein thrombosis, sickle cell anemia, leukemia) causes arousal and erectile difficulties and secondary orgasmic dysfunction. This includes obstruction at the aortic bifurcation (Leriche syndrome) or in the internal iliac artery or its branches.

Diseases that reduce or disrupt endocrine homeostasis (e.g., primary testicular failure, functioning pituitary or adrenal adenomas, adrenal or pituitary failure, hypo- and hyperthyroidism) can lead to disorders of sexual desire and directly affect genital functioning. In men, screening for abnormalities of serum testosterone and prolactin are routine for the evaluation of erectile difficulties and sexual desire disorders. Low testosterone levels, however, may be a consequence as well as a cause of sexual dysfunction.

In the presence of primary, global sexual dysfunctions, consider genetic disorders. There is usually prior evidence for Kleinfelter's syndrome, androgen insensitivity (p. 157), Turner's syndrome, or adrenogenital syndrome. The mechanisms for sexual dysfunction may be hormonal, or the result of end-organ deficits or learning. These syndromes are complex, and not all patients who have them have sexual dysfunctions. Following extensive (including neurohormal and chromosomal) evaluation, hormonal treatment is usually needed for full sexual functioning (23, 34).

PHARMACOLOGIC CAUSES

Several classes of medications commonly have side effects on sexual function: the antihypertensives, other cardiovascularly active compounds, and psychotropic medications.

Table 29.3.   Medications and Drugs and Their Effect on Sexual Function

Drug	Inhibited desire	Type of Dysfunction Decreased arousal	Orgasmic difficulties
Antidepressants			
Tricyclics	+	+	+
Monoamine oxidase inhibitors	+		+
Lithium	+	+	
Trazadone (priapism)			+
Neuroleptics (antipsychotics)			
Phenothiazines	+	+	+
Thioxanthines	+	+	+
Butyrophenones	+	+	
Anxiolytics and sedatives			
Benzodiazepines	+		+
Phenobarbital	+	+	
Soporifics	+		+
Antihypertensive and cardiovascular			
Diuretics: thiazides, spironolactone	+	+	
Alpha-methyldopa	+	+	+
Clonidine	+	+	+
Beta-blockers: propranolol, atenolol	+	?	+
Reserpine	+		+
Guanethidine	+	+	+
Digoxin (gynecomastia)	+	+	
Anticonvulsants			
Phenytoin	+		
Primidone	+		
Miscellaneous Medications			
Fenfluramine—an anorectic	+	+	
Cimetidine	+	+	
Carbonic anhydrase inhibitors-glaucoma	+	+	
Clofibrate—for antihyperlipoproteinemia	+	+	
Drugs of abuse			
Alcohol (chronic use/high dose)	+	+	+
Cannabis (chronic use/high dose)		+	
Cocaine (chronic use/high dose)	+	+	
Opiates (chronic use/high dose)	+	+	+
Amphetamines			+
Cigarettes/nicotine		?	

Composite of data from Bancroft J. Human sexuality and its problems. 2nd ed. Edinburgh: Churchill Livingstone, 1989; Leiblum SR, Segraves RT. Sex therapy with aging adults. In: Leiblum SR, Rosen RC, eds. Principles and practice of sex therapy. 2nd ed. New York: Guilford Press, 1989; and Lieberman ML. The sexual pharmacy. New York: New American Library, 1988.

These and other drugs commonly associated with the major sexual dysfunctions are listed in Table 29.3 (23, 27, 33). Drugs may contribute to sexual dysfunctions through anticholinergic parasympathetic and sympathetic ganglionic-blocking, antiadrenergic, antiandrogenic, beta-adrenergic, progestational, antihistaminic, and dopamine antagonist actions. Beyond the sexual effects of a particular drug, the effects of drug combinations create a bewildering labyrinth for the physician. Patients should be routinely asked about sexual functioning, and resources regularly consulted such as *The Sexual Pharmacy* (information on the sexual side effects of over 200 drugs [33]), and the *Physician's Desk Reference* (listing side effects of each drug [35]).

Major Sexual Dysfunctions

SEXUAL DESIRE DISORDERS

When Helen Singer Kaplan (36) expanded Masters and Johnson's (8) conceptualization of the human sexual response cycle to include the appetitive phase, the taxonomy of sexual dysfunctions became more comprehensive and a common difficulty received appropriate recognition.

This remarkably heterogeneous category recognizes two types of sexual desire disorders: hypoactive sexual desire disorder and sexual aversion disorder. Both represent the lower end of a spectrum of interest that logically must also have an opposite, hyperactive sexual desire (not yet formally recognized).

Hypoactive desire disorder and aversion disorder both have a persistent deficiency of desire for sexual activity or the absence of sexual fantasies. Sexual aversion disorder involves disgust or revulsion to sexual activity, almost always accompanied by disinterest in sexual activity. Causes, durations, and prognoses vary.

> Sexuality was satisfactory for Mr. & Mrs. N until 15 years into their marriage when he suddenly developed erectile dysfunction. Within 2 years of onset of this difficulty, he reported no interest in sexuality of any kind with anyone. The hypoactive sexual desire disorder was resolved when his erectile dysfunction was reversed by brief sex therapy that retrained a sexuality focused on penetrative intercourse to one of erotic sensuality, only part of which included erectile competence.
>
> Mr. O is a 42-year-old, single, socially adept, successful businessman whose few attempts at intercourse early in adult life were with prostitutes with whom he felt disgust and had no erections. Reared by a drug-abusing, prostitute mother who died when he was 18 years old, and sexually abused by an adult man when he was 9 years old, he has erections for masturbation using fantasies of idealized women, but thoughts of actually engaging in intercourse cause nausea and revulsion.

> Ms. P's loss of interest in sex disappeared when she received a new antihypertensive medication.

THE AROUSAL DISORDERS

Greatly delayed, insufficient, or absent arousal in women and men results in female sexual arousal disorders and male erectile disorders. Like desire disorders, the causes are legion and cross the spectrum of biopsychosocial etiologies.

Compared to male erectile disorders, reduced or absent female sexual arousal is infrequently seen. Rarely an isolated complaint, it is usually associated with psychological or interpersonal difficulties, or problems with general health (e.g., side effects of anticholinergic drugs [antihistamines, over-the-counter cold medications, neuroleptics, antidepressants, or cannabis]). Most women overcome this difficulty with artificial lubrication. The problem often surfaces when another dysfunction (e.g., acquired hypoactive sexual desire disorder, inhibited female orgasm) appears. A woman's difficulty in arousal usually leads to dyspareunia owing to insufficient lubrication.

By contrast, a burgeoning industry of technical, surgical, and pharmacologic aids, a network of self-help groups (e.g., Impotence Anonymous), the promulgation of purported aphrodisiacs (e.g., innocuous herbal compounds, ground rhinoceros horn) and inaccurate, simplistic public utterances about the frequency and causes of male erectile disorders bespeak ages-old fears of loss of erectile function in men (e.g., cited in Egyptian papyri and the works of Hippocrates and Galen). Stereotypically, most men and many women believe that sexuality equals penetrative intercourse. Granted the rise of pharmacologically induced erectile dysfunction, the contemporary overemphasis on "organic" causes and solutions obscures the need for detailed assessment of erectile dysfunction before embarking on treatment. A modicum of thoughtfulness often supplants needless pharmacologic interventions.

Mr. Q complained of "loss of my manhood." Only after considerable history-taking was it learned that his wife detected no change in his erectile capacity. Instead, at 41 years of age, he noticed for the first time that he no longer became spontaneously aroused just by visual or fantasy stimuli. Spontaneous nocturnal and masturbatory erections were undisturbed. Generalized and genital erotic touching then became the ingredients for his full erections. Reassurance that his change was a part of the normal aging process was helpful.

Mr. R, 57 years of age, had been married to his wife, 37 years old, for 12 congenial years while they reared her two children from a previous marriage and a 10-year-old son from the current marriage. Ms. R returned to her nursing career full time. He developed increasing erectile dysfunction. He did not masturbate, and when asked to try, found minimal erectile function. He had no AM erections. He could ejaculate with a flaccid penis. His general health was good, he took no medications, and rarely drank alcohol. The gradual onset of erectile failure in the three areas of function—with a partner, upon awakening, and with masturbation—had the conventional hallmarks of "organically based" (again, a misnomer) impotence. The therapist began contemplating the use of surgery (e.g., penile implant) or medication (e.g., yohimbine). However, nocturnal penile tumescence monitoring (measurement of penile expansion) in the sleep lab revealed adequate REM sleep-related erections. In brief sex therapy, the reduction of Mr. R's fear of losing his younger wife to a younger man restored his erections.

ORGASMIC DISORDERS

Dysfunctions in the orgasmic phase of the sexual response cycle run the gamut from "too quick"—premature ejaculation—to greatly delayed or absent—inhibited female orgasm or inhibited male orgasm. Except in cases in which the male partner has notably delayed orgasm, we have not heard the complaint from a woman or her partner that she climaxed too quickly. Orgasmic disorders have many caveats and stipulations based on the clinician's judgment. First, normal arousal must have been present. If arousal is adequate, the type, duration, and adequacy of stimulation

requires explication. Women who climax with manual or oral stimulation but not intercourse are identified as having inhibited female orgasm. This often responds, however, to education about direct or indirect friction of the penis against the clitoris.

A man may have premature ejaculation with vaginal intercourse but not with oral or manual stimulation by the partner or with masturbation. Beyond the men who climax before intromission or immediately on penetration with minimal movement, what constitutes prematurity is subjective. Some men prefer rapid climaxes, befitting their lovemap, but the partner is dissatisfied. Physicians should consider age (because of increased ejaculatory latency with aging), novelty of the sexual situation (decreased latency), and the patient's history of sexual frequency (higher frequency correlates with longer latency).

There are several common presentations of premature ejaculation: one is straightforward complaints by a younger man and his partner of lifelong, rapid ejaculation with no other dysfunctions. A more complex type of acquired premature ejaculation occurs in older men and is associated with difficulties achieving or maintaining erections, usually in the context of interpersonal problems.

Mr. S, age 49, began experiencing erectile failure intermittently with his wife, age 48. Within 10 months, even with a normal erection, his ejaculatory latency with intercourse had decreased from 10 minutes to less than 1 minute. Throughout this brief intercourse, he worried that he would lose his erection.

Another is a lifelong premature ejaculation that has troubled the partner, but elicits contentiousness only in middle age as the woman partner learns that sex need not be as it was. Of all the treatments of sexual dysfunctions, therapy of uncomplicated premature ejaculation (using a stop-start technique) has the best outcome (24).

Thirty percent of women do not climax with intercourse (8). Some do not want to climax with each sexual exchange. The latter is not a dysfunction; it becomes a source of conflict between partners if the man's lovemap defines his partner's climax as important. Another contribution to inhibited female orgasm lies in the marital relationship.

> Ms. T was orgasmic during courtship, but after marriage her husband became inattentive. She lost interest in sex and could not climax with him when she complied with his requests for sex.

Inhibited male orgasm is infrequent. Medications and street drugs account for most cases. Antiandrogenic antihypertensives (e.g., guanethidine) and neuroleptics (e.g., thioridazine) frequently cause ejaculatory delay or failure. Sometimes related to drug effects, there is a rare dissociation of orgasms from emissions. Sometimes this is caused by retrograde (backwards into the bladder) ejaculation, but often it is not (23). The reverse situation, mediated by anxiety, can occur. Rapid emission with minimal or no orgasmic sensation can occur with a flaccid penis.

> Mr. U, 57 years old, had a sexually functional affair with a colleague at work but had no erections with his wife. Attempts at intercourse with her were accompanied with profuse seminal emissions and minimal tumescence. The underlying problem was Mr. W's anger because of his perception of his wife's alliance with their 27-year-old daughter against him over money and the daughter's overdependency.

SEXUAL PAIN DISORDER

There are many sources of recurrent or persistent genital pain, most often in women. Painful intercourse in men is not common; when it occurs, it is usually caused by local inflammatory conditions (e.g., herpes, urethritis, prostatitis) or anatomical abnormalities (chordee [downward penile concavity from infection or congenital defect], Peyronie's disease [lateral penile concavity from fibrous tissue, cause unknown]), and rarely to interpersonal causes. For women, the end points of many biopsychosocial etiologies are vaginismus or dysparunia. Vaginismus is involuntary spasms of pelvic diaphragm musculature, with pain in the outer third of the vagina. Dyspareunia occurs in any location—from the vulva to deep in the pelvis, with numerous causes.

Vaginismus may be severe enough to prevent the penetration of the introitus with any object, or specifically where a partner's fingers may penetrate easily but penile intromission elicits painful spasm. The physician's ability to perform a speculum (a rounded metallic vaginal examination instrument) and bimanual pelvic examination does not always preclude vaginismus.

In addition to many pelvic diseases, injuries to the birth canal during delivery can lead to dyspareunia. A frequent mistake concerning nonvaginismic coital pain is physician referral for "psychogenic" pain, where examination reveals a structural cause.

> After the birth of her second child, Ms. V complained of low sexual desire, and withheld from Mr. V that she was having painful intercourse, fearing he would not believe her. She could be orgasmic with oral and manual stimulation, but likewise would not reveal that to Mr. V. The pain was always in the same place, under the same conditions, a history suggestive of an anatomically based dyspareunia (compared to a history of diffuse or variable pain). Surgical correction cured the dyspareunia.
>
> Ms. M, age 47, began experiencing menometrorrhagia (mid-cycle uterine bleeding plus excessive menstrual flow). Her refusal of a pelvic exam led her gynecologist to a previously unrevealed history that she *never* had allowed a pelvic exam. She also never had vaginal intercourse despite one pregnancy. Her husband confirmed this, stating that sexuality was conducted with either anal intercourse or intercrural intercourse with his penis displaced posteriorly and inferiorly across her introitus. Both were orgasmic. She had vaginismus with all attempts at penetration, including her own digital insertion. Gradual dilatation with progressively wider vaginal dilators, paired with relaxation training, cured the vaginismus.

Table 29.4.   A Selected List of Paraphilias[a]

Acrotomophilia (amputee partner)	Mysophilia (filth)
Apotemnophilia (self-amputee)	Narratophilia (erotic talk)
Asphyxiophilia (self-strangulation)	Necrophilia (corpse)
Autagonistophilia (on stage)	Pedophilia (child)
Autassassinophilia (own murder staged)	Pictophilia (pictures)
Autonepiophilia (diaperism)	Peodeiktophilia (penile exhibitionism)
Biastophilia (violent assault)	Sadism (humiliation or suffering of other person)
Coprophilia (feces)	Scoptophilia (watching coitus)
Ephebophilia (youth)	Somnophilia (sleeper)
Erotophonophilia (lust murder)	Stigmatophilia (piercing; tattoo)
Fetishism (inanimate object)	Symphorophilia (disaster)
Frotteurism (rub against stranger)	Telephone scatophilia (lewdness)
Gerontophilia (elder)	Troilism (couple + one)
Hyphephilia (fabrics)	Urophilia or Undinism (urine)
Kleptophilia (stealing)	Voyeurism or Peeping-Tomism
Klismaphilia (enema)	Zoophilia (animal)
Masochism (own humiliation or suffering)	

[a]Reprinted with permission from Money J. Venuses penuses. Buffalo: Prometheus Books, 1986:441.

PARAPHILIAS

The paraphilias are deviations from the usual lovemap development. They are strong, persistent sexual urges and fantasies that involve nonhuman objects, suffering or humiliation of a partner or oneself, children, or nonconsenting partners. To be identified as paraphilic, a person must have acted on the urges or be distressed by them.

Differences between men and women in sexual arousal and expression are those of threshold, not type (37). Visual cues have a lowered threshold for men (i.e., they are more responsive to visual cues); the threshold for tactile arousal is lower in women (31). The overwhelmingly greater frequency of paraphilias in men may result from this sex-dimorphic threshold difference to visual arousal.

Because the hallmark of a paraphilia is its lovemap imagery, paraphilias are appetitive phase disorders. Also, paraphilias are usually accompanied by reduced capacity to form strong, lasting closeness with another person (31).

Money (34) described over 40 paraphilias, the most common of which are listed in Table 29.4. Four paraphilias (exhibitionism, fetishism, transvestic fetishism, voyeurism) enact no direct contact with another person for their enactment. The hands-on paraphilias are frotteurism, sexual masochism, sexual sadism, and pedophilia, all of which can have long-lasting negative effects (30, 38, 39) on unwilling (which is most) objects (i.e., victims) of the paraphilic's attention.

The recent increased emphasis on treatment of the paraphilias and the negative consequences for many victims (30, 38, 39) increases the possibility that the physician will be asked to play some role (e.g., referral for specialized treatment, which may include psychotherapy, behavior modification, or the antiandrogen drug medroxyprogesterone). Paraphilias most often come to the physician's attention through the complaints of a partner, victim, or law enforcement agency.

A common concern of patients is whether their own sexual practices are deviant. Essential to a paraphilia is the persistence and intensity of the paraphilic behavior. Many persons have unusual or creative fantasies and may enact them with a consenting partner. Examples are role-playing a "pick-up" in a bar by a married couple, pretending that one partner is captured for sex by the other, taking risks of making love where others might see, using objects to enhance arousal, or viewing one another in sexual posturing. Reassure patients that such practices are not disorders when they are part of a larger repertoire and involve the partner's consent.

30/Psychophysiology and Psychoneuroimmunology

Irwin N. Hassenfeld, M.D.

OBJECTIVES

GENERAL OBJECTIVE: Given the history and examination of an ill patient, state how the person's attitude and personality traits might affect the outcome of his or her illness.

SPECIFIC OBJECTIVES:

1. Discuss the following psychophysiologic concepts: conditioned visceral responses, fight-or-flight reaction, homeostasis, general adaptation syndrome, specificity hypothesis, and the giving up, given-up complex.
2. Summarize the relations to illness of stress, cognitive appraisal, hardiness, and type A personality. Illustrate the statement "Stress is in the eye of the beholder."
3. Define and give examples of problem-focused coping and emotion-focused coping.
4. List components of the immune response to illness.
5. Summarize experimental data on how mental and immune function, conditioning of the immune system, and the placebo effect interact.
6. Discuss the relation of sense of control, social support, and hope on the course of illness.
7. Discuss Spiegel's study of the effect of psychotherapy on women who have breast cancer.

Psychophysiology is the study of how mental processes affect health. Some persons can warm their hands just by thinking about it (1). Some asthmatic patients wheeze at the sight of an artificial flower (2). Warts can be made to appear and disappear by hypnosis (3, 4). Among Californian Chinese women aged 75 or older over a 15–year period, there was a 35% annual drop (below the expected rate) in mortality before the Harvest Moon Festival, and a 35% rise above expected the week after the Festival (5). This also occurred among elderly Jewish men around Passover (6). People under heavy stress have increased risk for colds (7).

HISTORY

William Beaumont (1785–1853), an American military surgeon, treated a French-Canadian trapper, Alexis St. Martin, for a gastric fistula from a gunshot wound. Beaumont described changes in St. Martin's exposed gastric mucosa during various emotional states (8).

Ivan Pavlov (1849–1919), the Nobel Prize-winning Russian physiologist, demonstrated that visceral responses can be conditioned (p. 75) (9). In Pavlov's classic experiment, a symbolic conditioned stimulus (the sound of a bell) triggered autonomic nervous system responses (salivation) in dogs.

Walter Cannon (1871–1945), an American physiologist and neurologist, described a fight or flight response needed for survival and mediated by the sympathetic nervous system: emotions stimulated by threats caused increased pulse, blood pressure, and respiration, with increased blood supply, oxygen, and glucose available to the striated muscles, heart and brain, and increased blood coagulability with decreased blood loss. Blood supply to other viscera decreased. Following the challenge there is reconstitution whereby the parasympathetic (acetylcholine-mediated [p. 58]) nervous system predominates (10, 11).

Influenced by Claude Bernard, Cannon conceptualized homeostasis (10, 11): the organism strives to maintain an internal equilibrium in the face of challenges. The finely tuned balance between sympathetic and parasympathetic nervous systems promotes homeostasis. Cannon also suggested the role of adrenal malfunction in anecdotes of voodoo death (12), in which a healthy believer in voodoo dies after receiving a curse. (Richter suggested parasympathetic overactivity with cardiac slowing as the cause of voodoo death [13].).

Hans Selye (1907–1982), a Canadian neuroendocrinologist, discovered that when injected with crude ovarian extract, rats developed gastric ulcers, adrenal enlargement, and involution of the thymus and lymph nodes (14). Further, other organ extracts, infectious agents, heat, cold, and pain also caused these changes. These responses to a variety of stresses were termed the general adaptation syndrome (GAS) (15). The GAS has three stages: an alarm reaction resembling Cannon's fight-or-flight; resistance to the continued presence of the stressor manifested by chronically heightened physiologic states, posited by Selye to lead to diseases of adaptation (e.g., ulcers, essential hypertension); and exhaustion, manifested by depletion of the pituitary and adrenal cortex and decreased resistance to disease. Whereas Cannon emphasized adrenal medullary hormones and autonomic nervous discharge, Selye emphasized hypothalamic-pituitary-adrenocortical activity (16).

I. Arthur Mirsky, an American psychiatrist, predicted which Army recruits would develop peptic ulcers during basic training (17). He demonstrated that physiologic (high serum pepsinogen levels), psychologic (anxious anticipation of loss of emotional support), and social (separation from family) events must all operate for development of ulcer disease. An example of Franz Alexander's controversial specificity hypothesis is that specific psychological conflicts or personality traits lead to specific diseases (18).

George Engel, an American internist and psychoanalyst, studied an infant who had a gastric fistula (19). Her gastric mucosa responded to the approach of her trusted doctor, and to food, with increased secretion. When she was depressed, or when strangers approached, her gastric mucosa was hypoactive. Engel also described the detrimental effects on patients of hopelessness and helplessness (the giving-up, given-up complex), which impedes host defenses and may lead to disease (e.g., stroke) (20). He also urged (and coined the phrase) a biopsychosocial approach (pp. 3–15) to patient care, wherein biological, psychological, and social factors must all be simultaneously addressed to maximize health (21).

STRESS CONCEPT

Thomas Holmes, a public health physician, and Richard Rahe, a psychiatrist, developed a Schedule of Recent Events Questionnaire to quantify stressors (life events that can produce the complex response called stress). For example, they weighted death of a spouse 100 and change in residence 20. The questionnaire does not consider the *meaning* of the events to the person. They consistently found a modest but statistically significant association between life change and numerous illnesses (22). Negative events (e.g., losses) are more detrimental to health than positive ones (e.g., birth of a child) (23).

Despite the above data, stress is sometimes overrated as a cause of illness. Some emotional arousal is necessary for motivation: students often observe that if they do not experience some anxiety before an exam, they will not prepare maximally. Patient compliance tends to be better when patients have some anxiety about their illness (24, 25).

Further, the effects of events on us reside not exclusively in the events themselves, but in our perception of them. Stress, like beauty, is in the eye of the beholder. An injury can mean personal disaster or a ticket home from the front lines. As a formerly depressed patient told me, "What I used to think of as an obstacle, I now see as a challenge." How we evaluate the significance of events is called cognitive appraisal (26).

The will to live and a fighting spirit are expressions of a commitment to life often critical for surviving life-threatening disease (27). For someone who believes the world is a dangerous place filled with unscrupulous people, stressors are everywhere. The optimist who believes he or she can make things happen has built-in protection (mediated by the immune system [pp. 403–406]) against everyday stress. Faith in a higher power, your physician, or the support of someone about whom you care can also modify appraisal of stressors.

As a personality construct, hardiness also is pertinent. Hardy persons have a firm sense of self and belonging, feel their efforts can make a difference; and believe their fate is largely in their own hands (internal locus of control [p. 103]). Persons high on a scale of hardiness, especially those who have opportunities to be challenged and to exert control, have reported fewer stressful events and illnesses as compared with nonhardy persons (28–31).

Another personality cluster is Type A. The Type A personality "is aggressively involved in a chronic incessant struggle to achieve more and more in less and less time, and if required to do so, against the opposing efforts of the other things or other persons" (32:6).

Initial research (32, 33) on this issue suggested that the type A personality was prone to coronary artery disease. Although five studies failed to demonstrate a relation between global Type A measures and the extent of coronary artery disease (CAD)(34), they did reveal a consistent link between the hostility (expressed and suppressed) component of the Type A profile and CAD outcome.

Coping With Stress

Cognitive appraisal involves evaluation of potential stressors; coping is the response to this evaluation. Of the two basic ways of coping with stressors, problem-focused and emotion-focused (26, 35), either may be adaptive or maladaptive, and both can occur in combination.

Problem-focused coping is directed at managing or altering the problem causing the distress (26).

> Because of budget cuts at his school, a professor, nearing retirement, lost his secretary. Because he was active in several professional societies and had a research proposal and journal articles in the works, he was distressed and demoralized. So he took a typing course, and taught himself to use a computer.

Emotion-focused coping is directed at regulating emotional response to the problem (26), especially when the threat cannot be averted. Denial, avoidance, and minimization are examples of emotion-focused coping with life-threatening illness. These are protective in the short run but hurtful in the long run. For example, during and soon after a myocardial infarction (p. 4), denial facilitates recovery and reduces the risk of complications. But before and after hospitalization, denial and avoidance are maladaptive (36).

Other factors that contribute to coping include social skills, problem-solving abilities, and finances. Perceived social support during illness is important. Receiving moral and practical support from family and friends may enhance recovery (37).

Physiologic Responses

Recent work paints a more detailed picture of physiologic responses to stress than did

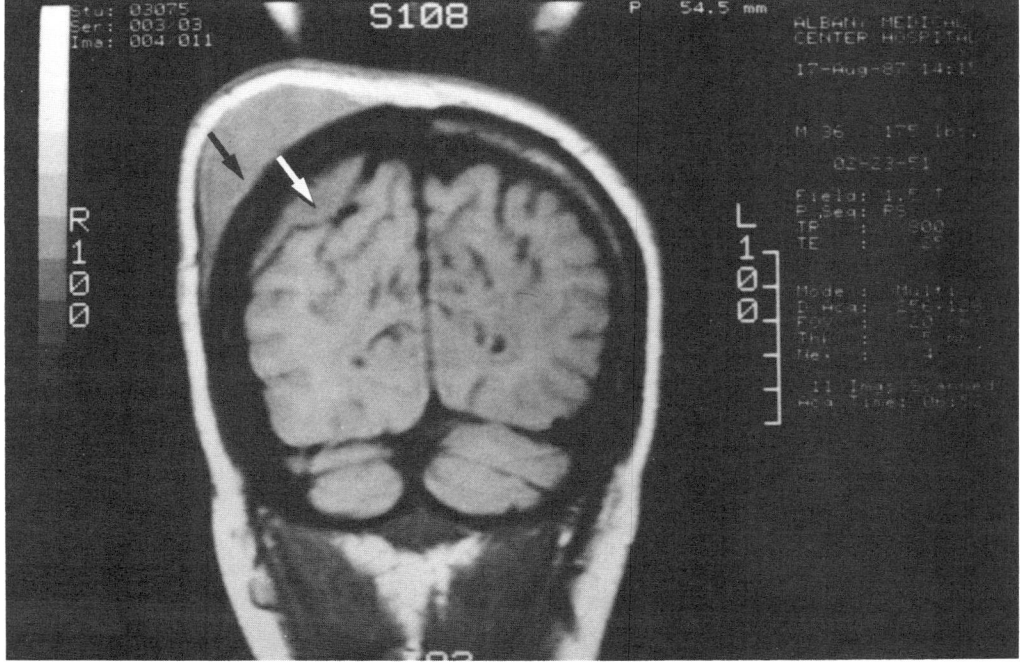

Figure 30.1. Magnetic resonance image showing Mr. Curran's tumor

Selye's GAS (15). Different kinds of stressors elicit different autonomic responses.

The defense reaction occurs during active coping (fight or flight). Heart rate and cardiac output increase. Striate muscle activity increases, accompanied by vasodilation in these muscles. There is an increase in catecholamine and cortisol secretion. Effort without distress is accompanied by an increase in catecholamines (especially norepinephrine [p. 55]) and suppression of cortisol. Effort associated with negative emotions such as embarrassment or feeling harassed leads to preferential secretion of epinephrine (38).

Facing stressors for which no coping strategies are apparent, the organism manifests vigilant inaction during which there is decreased skeletal movement, increased blood pressure and resistance to the passage of blood through the arterioles, vagus nerve-mediated bradycardia (slow pulse) and decreased cardiac output, increases in corticotropin (ACTH) and cortisol secretion, and decreased levels of brain norepinephrine. When active coping be-

comes possible, adrenal medullary secretion of epinephrine and hypothalamic-pituitary-adrenocortical activity diminish.

Physiologic response to threat is a complex interaction of the sympathoadrenomedullary (SAM) and hypothalamic-pituitary-adrenocortical (HPAC) systems. The SAM system is preferentially active during problem-focused coping; the HPAC system is preferentially active during emotion-focused coping.

PSYCHONEUROIMMUNOLOGY

Over the past decade, psychoneuroimmunologists have studied the interactions of mental processes and immunity. Preliminary findings sparked the imagination of Cousins (39) and Siegel (40), who helped popularize the young field with best-selling books. An unfortunate consequence of popularization is cynicism in the scientific community. Despite this, psychoneuroimmunologic findings shed light on puzzling clinical phenomena such as spontaneous remission (clearing up with no appar-

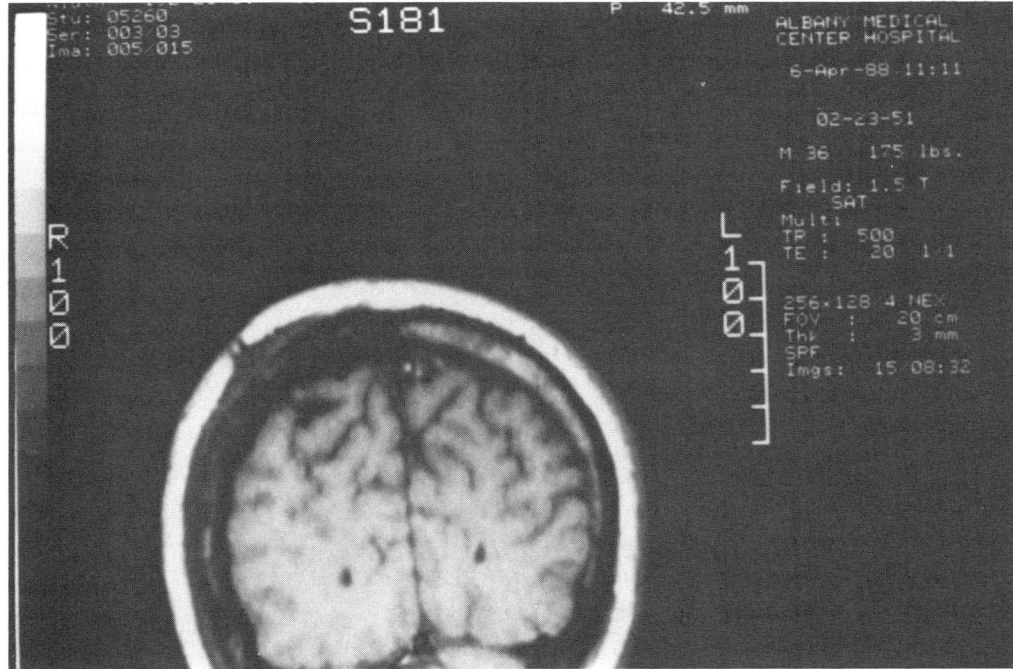

Figure 30.2. Magnetic resonance image showing disappearance of Mr. Curran's tumor

ent reason) of serious diseases such as multiple sclerosis, lupus erythematosus, and (rarely) cancer.

Mr. Curran, a painter, had recently returned from a stay in Florence where he had finished work on a piece based on Michaelangelo's David. In Florence, Mr. Curran had noticed a small bump on his head which slowly grew. He forgot about it in the excitement of returning home; by now, it appeared the size of a golf ball on magnetic resonance imaging (MRI) (p. 214). He was told it was a lymphoma (cancerous overproduction of lymphocytic white cells) eroding his skull and pressing on his brain (Fig. 30.1).

He was scheduled for a craniotomy, but his neurosurgeon cancelled it to obtain a second opinion at another center. The diagnosis was confirmed by a second MRI, but a recommendation was made for chemotherapy and radiation instead of surgery. Before the treatment began, another MRI revealed that the tumor had disappeared (Fig. 30.2).

There are other dramatic cases like this in the literature (41–45), raising the question of what causes a malignant tumor to melt away within 2 months? Calling it a spontaneous remission, and saying that these things sometimes happen, is unsatisfactory. We will return to Mr. Curran's case after we examine data on the relationships between mind, the immune system, disease, and healing.

Overview of Immune System

We are surrounded by pathogenic microorganisms and foreign substances that threaten our health. Mutations during cell division may be triggered by viruses, chemicals, or radiation. Mutant cells may proliferate uncontrollably and form tumors. Our immune systems protect us from these invaders by recognizing self and not self, and incapacitating the foreign substances or antigens. Damaged and mutant cells are recognized as not self.

The immune system can be likened to a department of defense. It has its separate military branches (T-cell killer lymphocytes for local skirmishes and police actions, B-cell lymphocytes for wars, and commando units made up of natural killer [NK] cells) which sometimes cooperate in assaulting the enemy (bacteria, parasites, viruses, and tumor cells). It has intelligence and counter-intelligence agents (antibodies, helper T cells) who tirelessly patrol the bodily fluids looking for foreign agents and marking them for destruction, a data storage facility (long-lived lymphocyte memory cells), a command control structure (helper [which are multifunctional] and suppressor T cells), and ambassadors (macrophages) which present the foreign antigen to the helper cells. Like all defense departments, it sometimes makes mistakes and attacks its own troops (autoimmune disease); overreacts to the enemy (hypersensitivity reactions); and does not recognize its allies (transplant rejection). Like any effective military, it is not autonomous—it is influenced by and influences other agencies of the body politic (CNS, endocrine system).

Communication Between Brain, Immune, and Glandular Cells

Animal research has revealed communication links between brain, endocrine, and immune systems which allow them to influence one another: stimulation of the anterior hypothalamus enhances immune responsivity, whereas stimulation of the posterior portion inhibits immune activity (46). Certain hypothalamic neuron populations fire at increasing rates and peak in step with increases and peaks in immune response. Removal of the thymus gland results in atrophy of these hypothalamic neurons (47). Receptors for neuropeptides are found in high concentrations in the limbic system, intestinal lining, and lymphocytes. Immune cells produce the same neuropeptides as those produced in the brain (48). Some peptide hormones produced in the brain stimulate T cells to produce lymphokines (substances released by lymphocytes that have come in contact with antigens, activating macrophages, and cell-mediated immunity) such as interleukin-2 and interferon (49).

Other peptide hormones inhibit lymphokine production.

Brain cells possess receptors for interleukins and can produce interferon directly. Corticotropin-releasing factor (CRF) stimulates production of adrenocorticotropic hormone (ACTH), which in turn stimulates production of cortisol (which inhibits immune response), and also stimulates leukocytes to produce ACTH and beta-endorphins, which also lowers natural killer (NK) cell activity (50). Epinephrine stimulates release of suppressor T cells, reducing cellular immune activity (51). Norepinephrine (NE) enhances NK cell activity. Lymphocytes produce and have receptors for NE (52, 53). Acetylcholine (p. 58) is produced by lymphocytes, which also have receptors for this neurotransmitter (52). The thymus contains a substantial number of vagus nerve fibers (the vagus [wandering] nerve is the 10th cranial nerve, with major acetylcholinergic functions) (54). Networks of adrenergic and cholinergic nerve fibers also have been found in the spleen, lymph nodes, and marrow (55, 56).

Can the Mind Influence Immune Function?

The evidence of regular communication between the brain and the immune system suggests ways by which mental functions can influence immunity.

About 15 years ago, the psychologist Robert Ader made a startling discovery (57). He was experimenting with rats classically conditioned (p. 75) to avoid saccharine-flavored water using the drug cyclophosphamide (an immunosuppressant that causes nausea) as the unconditioned stimulus. Ader noted that the experimental rats contined to die from infection even after he stopped the cyclophosphamide. He concluded that the rats had inadvertently *learned* to suppress their immune system. Ader's experiments were independently replicated many times (58–63).

Ader also subjected a strain of rats, susceptible to an autoimmune disease similar to lupus erythematosus (LE), to the above protocol

(64). Those LE rats who learned to suppress their immune system, curtailing the autoimmune process, lived longer than control LE rats. Another investigator conditioned mice to delay growth of implanted tumors (65). Mice were also given a drug that elevates NK cell activity, and simultaneously exposed to camphor smell. Later the camphor smell alone elevated NK cell activity and increased survival.

Case reports suggest that conditioned learning of the immune system also occurs in humans. A man allergic to horses had an asthma attack whenever he saw horses in a movie. A woman began sneezing in response to an artificial rose (2).

Another line of evidence evolved from placebo studies. A placebo is an inactive substance or procedure given by a physician to a patient to induce a therapeutic change. The placebo effect is the altered experience of the patient to the substance or procedure. The anesthesiologist Henry K. Beecher systematically demonstrated the power of situation and expectation on pain due to injury (66). He observed, contrary to common belief, that the *greater* the pain and anxiety, the more effective the placebo. The placebo effect is mediated by endogenous opiates which also modulate immune response. Warts, caused by a viral infection, can be made to appear and disappear by hypnosis (3, 4). This may be mediated by the immune system.

Can the Mind Influence Course of Disease and Healing?

Investigations in humans and other animals have shown that certain stresses can reduce the vigor of the immune response to antigens. More accurately, how life events are perceived (rather than the events themselves) determines the effect on the immune system. Three clusters of attitudes, emotional responses, and social factors are important modulators of immune function: perception of control and helplessness, perception of social support and loneliness, and hope, optimism, faith, pessimism, and hopelessness.

CONTROL AND HELPLESSNESS

Particularly inhibiting of immune responsivity are pervasive feelings of loss of control and helplessness. Such feelings occur in our lives at one time or another, but might not affect health if short-lived. Feelings of helplessness and loss of control of one's life for protracted periods is, however, noxious for one's health.

In one study (67), rats were divided into three groups. One group received electric shocks from which they could escape. A second received inescapable shocks. Controls received no shocks. The next day, all the rats were exposed to shocks, after which their in vitro (in a test tube) cellular immunity was measured. Lymphocyte proliferation in response to mitogens (standard measures of cellular immunity) were suppressed only in the inescapable shock group.

Kiecolt-Glaser's studies of medical students (68) bear out the inhibiting effect on the immune system of not feeling in control. Whatever aspect of immune response is measured (NK cell activity, percent of helper T cells, interferon production by stimulated lymphocytes, geometric mean titer of Epstein-Barr virus [EBV, the one that causes "mono"]) long before, immediately before, and during final exams in the first 2 years of medical school, the immune response is weaker during the exam period. In contrast, when immune system activity is measured during the first week of the first third-year clerkship, robust immune responses (raised proportion of helper T lymphocytes) are found as compared with the level 1 month earlier.

The beginning of the third year is a stressful period for students, who worry that they do not know enough to participate in patient care. The important difference between these two situations, which produce such differing immune reactions, lies in contrasting perceptions. During the first 2 years, students' grades depend on exam performance. Because there are more facts than they can learn, they often feel at the mercy of the professor who can give an easy or hard exam. By contrast, the third year is seen by most students as a challenge they will master despite initial anxiety. When you feel equal to a challenge your immune system is enhanced, but when you feel at the mercy of others (e.g., professors), immune function weakens.

CONTROL, HELPLESSNESS, AND DISEASE

It is easier to study the effect of attitudes on acute illnesses (e.g., flu) than on chronic ones (e.g., cancer), because the course of the latter is usually extended and its time of onset often unclear. We all carry viruses that can cause disease. One factor that determines whether the virus will make us sick is how we feel. West Point cadets were studied throughout their 4 years (69). Among those cadets who were exposed to and seropositive for EBV, only some developed mononucleosis during their 4 years at West Point. Those who contracted the disease were those whose motivation for a military career was high (they also had overachieving fathers), but could not achieve grades that would make a career as an Army officer possible. They felt their fate was no longer in their hands.

Being a very sick hospitalized patient means yielding control of basic decisions (when to eat, sleep, go to the bathroom) and subordinating your routines to the hospital's routine. Your response to this may affect the outcome. Of 75 poor-prognosis patients diagnosed with recurrent breast cancer who were followed for 1 year (70), those whose disease was best controlled were those who complained the most. They also had the highest levels of blood NK cell activity.

> Mr. Curran never felt helpless. On the contrary, the diagnosis mobilized a burst of activity, aimed at prevailing. Here is how he described this period: "Friends who were into holistic medicine sent us vitamins. We took everything and turned down nothing . . . I was doing intense visualization and everything I could think of to beat this." You do not have to believe that vitamins and visualization help cancer to consider the *possibility* that these activities increased Mr.

> Curran's sense of control, bolstering his immune system and dissolving his tumor.

SOCIAL SUPPORT, LONELINESS, AND MOURNING

During certain stages of bereavement (p. 173), the immune system is less responsive (71–74). Bartrop (71) demonstrated suppression of lymphocyte mitogens PHA and ConA at 2 months of bereavement, but not earlier in spouses of patients who had died in accidents or from prolonged illnesses. A second study (72) measured lymphocyte responsiveness in men before and after the death of their spouse from metastatic breast cancer. Significant lymphocyte suppression occurred in these men only after their spouses' death. When NK activity of women about to be widowed by their husbands' lung cancer was compared with controls who had well husbands, NK activity was lower in the former group (73). Persons anticipating or suffering a loss experience activation of adrenal cortical and medullary secretion and activation of the sympathetic nervous system.

Are adrenocortical functions responsible for reduced NK activity during bereavement? A study (73) compared three groups of women: a bereaved group whose husbands had recently died of lung cancer; a group whose husbands were ill with metastatic lung cancer; and a control group who had well husbands. The bereaved women had reduced NK activity and elevated cortisol levels. The women who were anticipating their husbands' death also had depressed NK activity, but their cortisol levels were not elevated. This suggests that reduction of NK in anticipatory mourning is not mediated by adrenocortical activity. Changed immunity during bereavement may be related to the increase in mortality among widowers over that of married men of the same age (75, 76).

Kiecolt-Glaser found that medical students with the most depression of immune function scored highest on a measure of loneliness (68). Unmedicated psychiatric inpatients who scored high on the loneliness scale had poorer mitogenic response compared to patients low on this scale (77). Can we die of loneliness? Not directly, but consider this: in one study (78) 2700 persons were rated for psychosocial variables including number of friends, closeness to relatives, group participation. After 10 years, those rated lonely had 1.5–3 times the mortality of those rated social.

Caring for a relative who has Alzheimer's disease (AD) is often lonely and hopeless because, unlike most other chronic diseases, AD impairs the victim's personality and makes meaningful relationships harder. The AD caregivers have poorer cellular immune function (percentage of total T lymphocytes and helper T cells, helper-suppressor ratio, and antibody to EBV) than controls (79).

A study (80) of women with advanced metastatic breast cancer revealed that premorbid mental health, coping, and social support had little effect on survival, but that social support during the illness was crucial. Support from family and friends when you are healthy are no assurance that this support will be there for the long haul when you fall victim to a disease like cancer (p. 409). When a person develops cancer, traffic is usually in the opposite direction.

HOPE, OPTIMISM, FAITH, PESSIMISM, AND HOPELESSNESS

Only the human species can contemplate the future. Expectations have a powerful impact on health. Women scheduled for breast biopsy were assessed psychologically before the biopsy results were known (27). Three months later those who had a biopsy diagnosis of cancer were interviewed. Four of five of these women who expressed hopelessness in that interview were dead within 5 years, compared with 2 of 20 who were hopeful. Negative expectations can also trigger immune overreaction in susceptible persons. Children who have serious asthma and feel hopeless are at greater risk for fatal asthma attacks than those who do not feel this way (81).

Solomon (82) found that long-time AIDS survivors engage in active coping activity and participate actively in their medical care and exercise programs. Most highly correlated with survival and relatively positive immune function is the ability to say no, comfortably, to unwelcome requests. Hope and optimism may be derived from faith (e.g., faith in oneself, the doctor, or a higher power).

PSYCHOTHERAPY IN BREAST CANCER PATIENTS

Spiegel (82) followed 86 patients who had metastatic breast cancer, having hypothesized that psychological intervention would reduce anxiety, depression, and pain without affecting disease outcome. During the initial year, the randomly selected experimental group (EG, N = 50) had weekly group psychotherapy plus self-hypnosis for pain control. Both the experimental and control groups (CG, N = 36) received standard oncological care. During the first year, survival was the same in the EG and CG. After the first year (group therapy had stopped), the EG developed a remarkable advantage, living on average 18 months longer than the CG. This study looked at other variables (staging, type of surgery, chemotherapy, radiation, metastatic spread) that might account for the difference in survival, but only the psychosocial intervention accounted for the variance. Interestingly, prepsychotherapeutic psychological assessments failed to predict survival. It is uncertain whether *men* who have advanced metastatic disease would benefit similarly from group psychotherapy; this needs to be studied.

ACKNOWLEDGMENT

Supported by a grant from the Schaffer Foundation, Albany Medical College.

31/Chronic Disease and Disability

Irwin N. Hassenfeld, M.D.

OBJECTIVES

GENERAL OBJECTIVE: Given the history and examination of a patient with a chronic illness or disability, discuss the psychological aspects of the patient's care.

SPECIFIC OBJECTIVES:
1. Compare acute and chronic illness as they relate to the sick role and the doctor-patient relationship.
2. Discuss common helpful and hurtful attitudes and behaviors of family, friends, and doctors of chronically ill or disabled persons.
3. Summarize the advantages of, and issues involved in, being treated by a chronically ill or disabled physician.
4. Discuss strategies for coping effectively with chronic disease or disability, and state how the physician can facilitate use of these strategies.

Having a chronic illness changes a person—physically, emotionally, socially, professionally, and often financially.

Julie was worn out. This time around, she had been battling a flare-up of her lupus for over a year. Systemic lupus erythematosus is an autoimmune disease of connective tissue that affects many organ systems. Its course is characterized by remissions and exacerbations (spontaneous improvements and worsenings).

Julie's right side hurt. The pain medication only worked for a little while. She did not want anything stronger. It really "zonked" her out, and she had to work with complex computer programs and be emotionally available to her teenage son, Derek. She was grateful that when things were really bad, meditating could get her through it.

Because of the disease and the steroid treatment, she was much weaker than usual, and

Derek had to help her carry up the groceries. Derek, who was getting ready to strike out on his own, was not particularly attentive or reliable. Julie was an independent person who hated depending on Derek, or anyone else for that matter. Worst of all was the uncertainty: She did not know, and her doctor could not tell her, when the disease would remit. She had had a 20-year remission during which she reared a family and built a career, most of the time without the help of her ex-husband. During this period, Julie did not think of her disease. She was an upbeat person who, characteristically, looked to the future and did not dwell on things about which she could do nothing. Now, however, her natural optimism was beginning to wear thin.

A chronic illness is always there, even when it remits—having the illness without the symptoms is just waiting for the other shoe to drop. An acute illness such as the flu or infec-

408

tious mononucleosis can make you weak and miserable; the pain and discomfort can leave you unable to function. There is comfort in knowing, however, that the illness will soon pass and things will return to normal. People who have chronic diseases have no such comfort. They must adjust to a new way of being.

THE SICK ROLE AND DOCTOR-PATIENT RELATIONSHIP

Sociologists write about the sick role (p. 100). To play this role well, patients try to get well as soon as possible by complying with the doctor's recommendations. This role was defined with acute illness in mind. The kind of doctor-patient relationship implied in the definition, with the doctor active and the patient compliant, is inappropriate for the patient who has a chronic illness.

With acute illness, the emphasis in the doctor-patient relationship is on the technical knowledge of a doctor practiced on a consenting patient. Of course, the personality of both the patient (e.g., locus of control [p. 103]) and the doctor must be taken into account. But if the patient has an infection and needs a shot of penicillin, the doctor and patient do not have to "hit it off" for the antibiotic to work. Under general surgical anesthesia, there is no patient participation. On the night before my surgery I was amazed at my reaction when the surgeon told me that the next day, while on the operating table, I would cease to be a person to him and would become instead a technical problem to be solved. My reaction was to feel *relieved*. During surgery, we want technical competence, not bedside manner.

With chronic illness, as essential as the doctor's expertise is, the patient becomes a much more active participant in the process of care. Chronically ill persons must monitor their blood sugar or pressure or examine their breasts for lumps. They must note the therapeutic and side effects of medication and accurately report them to the doctor. This model of the doctor-patient relationship is one of mutual participation, a working partnership (1). Both parties make their unique contributions to the treatment process: the doctor, medical knowledge and skills; the patient, exclusive knowledge of feelings and sensations and the responsibility for carrying out much of the therapeutic plan.

Julie had great respect for her doctor, but she knew better than anyone else whether she or her disease had the upper hand. She was fortunate to have a doctor who listened to her and was guided by her feelings. They were partners who worked together to find ways for her to live as fully as possible. For example, she knew that her kidneys "spilled" protein, so her urine needed to be checked every few months. She would therefore collect a weekend's worth of urine at intervals and deliver it to the lab, which reported the results to her and to the doctor. She would then call the doctor, and together they would decide whether to adjust her medication.

REACTIONS OF OTHERS

Another way that chronic illness differs is in how other people react to the patient. Having an acute illness such as mono elicits sympathy and support from healthy persons. Some send cards. Others offer to buy groceries and cook meals, even as they worry about catching the disease. Falling ill with a chronic disease such as lupus may elicit the same responses, but over time the sympathy and support tend to gradually diminish until, like Julie, the person is fending alone. Even family can eventually run out of concern. Then the person feels forgotten.

On a recent weekend, Julie felt desperately alone. Her muscles were so weak that she could hardly walk on a level surface. Climbing the stairs to her second floor apartment was out of the question. Derek was staying with his girlfriend. Her married daughter, Paula, had not called. Julie did not know how she would manage if she ran out of food. The thought of suicide crossed her mind, but she quickly rejected it—she would get through the weekend somehow.

People readily identify with the patient who has mono. When lupus strikes, empathy is harder to sustain. It is scary for healthy people to contemplate having a chronic disease that never goes away, changes your life, and may shorten it. Chronically ill persons have a higher suicide rate than the general population (2). Empathy for patients who have chronic, life-shortening illness is in particularly short supply. That is why support groups of patients with similar problems can be so helpful.

Stigma and Isolation

When the poet John Donne wrote, "No man is an island" (3), he was observing that, although humans may think of themselves as autonomous beings, we are all of us social beings who need to belong. Usually we take for granted our need to belong. When we become disabled, disfigured, or chronically ill, this reality stands out in bold relief. Even temporary disability can make us aware of this, as happened to a woman who, because of a minor accident, was temporarily on crutches and fell while entertaining guests. She wrote "What I remember most keenly about my moment on the carpet is how much I wanted to be part of the group—to help, and to keep up with the conversation to the very last second. I didn't want to be omitted, deleted, or put in parentheses, even out of kindness (4:43)".

This sense of isolation is multiplied many times when the illness or disability is permanent. The writer Flannery O'Connor shared her experience of lupus: "In a sense sickness is a place, more instructive than a long trip to Europe, and it's always a place where there's no company, where nobody can follow" (5: 163). A most dramatic example of the stigma and isolation incurable illness confers is described by Dr. David Rabin, a physician who, at age 45, developed ALS (amyotrophic lateral sclerosis [Lou Gehrig's disease]), a progressive, incurable disease of unknown cause which results in a selective degeneration of motor neurons in the brain and spinal cord, leading to disability and death.

Dr. Rabin was invited to participate in a medical conference, and although he limped severely and needed a cane, he and his wife (also a physician) accepted the invitation, looking forward to seeing old friends and colleagues. This is how they described the meeting.

> "San Marino is not much bigger than its famous postage stamps. The speakers were all housed in the same hotel, had their meals in the same dining room, traveled on the same bus to the conference hall, and spent their leisure time in the same small lounge. . . . Yet, despite the physical proximity, my wife and I might have been on a desert island. People walked by us with eyes averted or were suddenly mesmerized by the floor. The dining room had a long, narrow, rectangular shape, and for reasons of convenience we were seated early and of course chose the table nearest the door. As the other guests came in to dinner, they literally made a beeline to the corner of the room most distant from ours. If eye contact was unavoidable, there would be a hurried "Hello, David" and off the person would go, almost jet-propelled. . . . What frightened people away was, I suppose, the knowledge that I had an incurable illness. To be candid, it was nothing short of brutal treatment" (6: 39).

The hurt and anger the Rabins felt is what many chronically ill persons feel when they are avoided by former friends. The Rabins dealt with these feelings, in part, by writing an article (7) to communicate to doctors what it is like for disabled patients. Of course, countering isolation by writing is not always an option. It is regrettable that when people have a chronic illness or disability and deserve to be treated with understanding and compassion, they instead are often shunted aside and treated as nonentities.

How, then, can physicians, who could treat a fellow physician this way, care for patients who have chronic illnesses? For the most part, doctors are able to work with patients by not identifying (p. 87) with them, a feat much harder to accomplish when a colleague is stricken with an incurable illness. It is a precarious balancing act for many physicians. If they are too successful at being objective by putting too much distance between themselves and their patients, they will not empathize and will be perceived as cold and uncaring. Too little distance and they are in danger of losing their objectivity by becoming too personally involved.

In caring for chronically ill patients, two rules of thumb are suggested. If you notice it is difficult to find time to see the patient, you are probably putting too much distance between the two of you. If, on the other hand, you find yourself thinking about the person when you are with other patients or your family, you may need to pull back a little.

Physician Avoidance and Insensitivity

A dramatic example of a physician who avoided a family was reported to me by Calvin, whose wife had undergone heart surgery. She had suffered with heart problems all her life. Ten years before, two of her heart valves had been replaced by a famous heart surgeon. Because her heart was failing, she again turned to this surgeon for help and was admitted to the intensive care unit. Calvin and their daughter Ann traveled to the hospital to be with her. She underwent surgery to replace her valves. Postoperatively, her condition worsened for 10 days. Calvin and Ann tried, in vain, to speak to the surgeon to ask what was happening. The internist told them that an x-ray film showed that several sutures holding the valves in place had unraveled and that the surgeon had scheduled another operation.

After the operation, the patient suffered a stroke. When the family finally saw the famous surgeon and his entourage in the waiting room, they asked about the stitches. He angrily shouted, "What stitches?" and added, "If you would stop pressuring me and let me do my job, your wife and mother would be better off."

Calvin and Ann were humiliated and outraged at the surgeon's outburst. But they did not tell him how they felt for fear that it would affect her care. We can only guess what prompted the surgeon's behavior. A good bet is that he was frustrated by the patient's failure to respond to his ministrations, compounded by the fatigue and irritability of a 16-hour day. But blaming the family when the patient does not get well is cruel and unfair. The surgeon's apology the next day did little to undo the hurt he had caused.

Being Treated by Chronically Ill or Disabled Doctors

One way to find an empathic doctor is to select one who is also chronically ill or disabled. Physicians and nurses who have chronic illnesses or disabilities are often particularly skilled at relating helpfully to their incurable patients. Patients are sometimes skittish about receiving care from such a doctor because of concern that the physician may be unavailable when needed most or may die prematurely and leave the patient in the lurch. For example,

> After my surgery I was unable to work. Another physician agreed to see my patients during this period. When I returned a month later, one of my patients told me that she had decided to seek care from another physician. She said she could not take the risk that I would get sick again and be unavailable to her. When I agreed that I could not guarantee that I'd stay well, but that I understood her concerns, she asked whether I could be her back-up doctor if her new psychiatrist became ill.

Patient concerns about going to chronically ill physicians are unfortunate but understandable. When we go to a doctor we want that person not only to be competent, but also to be wiser, stronger, and healthier than other mortals.

Most chronic illnesses are not life-threatening, and few disabilities are completely disabling. Just as Robert Dole and Franklin Roosevelt had illustrious careers, physicians can practice excellently despite chronic illness and disability. The real problem is the perception that a disabled doctor (e.g., one in a wheelchair) is defective and therefore cannot be a good doctor (8). This belief is patently false and prejudiced.

Combatting Stereotypes

When a disabled person visits a doctor, it is usually for something other than disability. It is vital that the doctor see past the disability and listen to the patient. Unfortunately, many physicians see only the disability, so the patient may have to remind the doctor of the human presence behind the handicap. Robin Stephens, a woman who has cerebral palsy, calls this attitude conditioned impersonal regard (9), and describes it thus:

> "Many doctors discount the reason the person with a disability is seeing them because they assume the physical disabilities are overwhelming. The reality is that the reason the person is in to see that particular doctor may or may not have anything to do with his or her disability. For example, I know my body, the way it usually is, the way it usually reacts; I know my normal patterns. When I go to see a doctor, there's something wrong with my usual pattern; I come for advice about what I can do to resolve the problem. Sometimes there's nothing that can be done; sometimes there are several options. An honest appraisal of the situation is what is wanted and needed from a medical consultation.
>
> Because of their uncertainty, many doctors are unable to look at the whole person. I am a whole person. Doctors may use one sense at a time to make their initial examination. When they use only their eyes, they may see only my wheelchair, or only a helpless woman, or only a flailing uncontrolled body. When doctors use only their ears, they may hear only a mumbled voice, only think how difficult I am to understand. Or only hear a quarter of what's going on. If they use only their sense of touch, they may feel only a tight, spastic hand, only a body that jumps when they touch it, or only a head that moves when I speak. None of these assessments describe who I am. Yet, many doctors have never gone further than these images of me. My reaction as a patient to being seen only in parts is to feel closed off, uncertain, and frustrated (9)."

Physicians can start to combat the stereotypes that Stephens describes by addressing their own fears. When we are with a disabled person, it reminds us of our own vulnerability to disease. We use various defense mechanisms (p. 87) to quiet our fears. They include depersonalizing the encounter emotionally to distance ourselves from the disabled person and avoiding looking at the person. Recognizing and taking responsibility for our own fears make it less likely that we will use these mechanisms. Facing personal fears enables the future physician to confront and even enlighten peers when they express prejudice toward the chronically ill and disabled.

Two other common, but unhelpful, attitudes toward disabled persons are pity and overregard. Pity, unlike sympathy, is condescending. The disabled rarely feel sorry for themselves and want to be considered for what they can do rather than what they cannot. The second attitude—the perception of the disabled as a superperson—is equally untenable in the other extreme. Accomplishing the ordinary tasks of living is considered amazing and heroic. Stephens (9) calls this attitude conditioned ridiculous regard, describing physicians who display this attitude as so busy being congratulatory of the patient's accomplishments that they miss important facts and cannot imagine their full potential. Some disabled persons live the role of the hero by giving no quarter to their disability.

> A professor, who had polio as a child, needed crutches to walk. Assigned a fourth floor office in a building without an elevator, he said nothing. For 2 years he left for work an hour early so that he would have time to climb the stairs to his office. When he realized how costly in time and effort this was, he requested and obtained a first floor office.

Stephens expressed a more constructive attitude toward disability, calling her motorized wheelchair a "freedom tool" that allows her to conserve the energy she expends walking and to use it for other activities.

There are about 43 million disabled Americans. The disabled are a minority that anyone can join. Persons between the ages of 35–60 years are four times as likely to become disabled as to die (10). The ubiquitousness of disability led Stephens to refer to the unaffected as the "temporarily able-bodied." Recent landmark legislation, the 1990 Americans with Disabilities Act (Public Law 101-336), now guarantees disabled persons equal access to jobs and services in the private sector. Governmental agencies and public-supported institutions are already prohibited by the Rehabilitation Act of 1973 from rejecting a qualified person because of a handicap, and, with passage of Public Law 101–336 must now provide disabled persons access to buildings. The government pays approximatly $60 billion a year to disabled persons who are not working (12). One million disabled persons receive Social Security Disability Insurance (SSDI) and an additional three million receive Supplemental Security Income (SSI) who have less than $2,000 in liquid assets (10). Both are Federal programs. By decreasing discrimination and mandating universal accessibility, many more disabled persons will be able to contribute to the economy by working, paying taxes, and spending their earnings.

Legislation can only address the most blatant discrimination in housing and the workplace. The prejudice in people's hearts cannot, of course, be legislated away.

> Some years ago a young married woman was referred to me because she was depressed. She had Friedrich's ataxia (a progressively disabling neurologic disease that begins in childhood, causes corticospinal and posterior spinocerebellar tract degeneration, and results in early death). I dreaded the appointment, assuming she was depressed about her disease, and wondered what I could possibly do to help.
>
> She arrived in a wheelchair, accompanied by her husband. It turned out that her distress had nothing to do with her disease. She was managing well with the children and with the house. She was unhappy because she and her husband were not communicating. A few sessions with both of them were all that was needed. I learned from this woman the importance of not jumping to conclusions about disabled people.

COPING WITH CHRONIC ILLNESS AND DISABILITY

Persons who have a chronic illness or disability must overcome two obstacles to maintaining self-esteem and finding a meaningful way of living. First, they must accept the reality of their condition and make peace with the limitations it imposes. It is natural, in the early stages, to deny these limitations and expect to do all things as before. In time, with griefwork (the process of emotionally working through a loss), most disabled persons can alter their lives and expectations, accounting for limitations. Not doing so leads to frustration and bitterness. Physicians are in a unique position to help their patients accept the limitations that illness imposes. During regularly scheduled appointments, physicians can promote their patients' grieving, and when the patient is ready, facilitate reappraisal.

A second task that patients face is that of putting their illness or disability into perspective, *not* letting it replace their former identity. A perception of Ted Smith as cardiac cripple must not replace that of Ted Smith the father, husband, carpenter, and beekeeper.

> Ralph was stricken with multiple sclerosis (MS) (p. 199) when he was 30 years old. He had always prided himself on his physical prowess. He was bigger and stronger than most. He grew up poor and motherless. His size and strength were his security. When MS struck, the rug was pulled out from all 6'7" of him. He felt extremely vulnerable. He could no longer rely on his body to perform as he willed it. If he could not be the powerful, agile person he used to be, who was he? For many years after he was diagnosed with MS, he saw his full-time job as basic survival and his identity as that of an MS patient. Then, he began to develop and value a latent artistic talent, an important new part of his identity.

Unless the chronically ill or disabled person can transcend the ill or handicapped identity, that label will restrict the person in his or her own eyes and those of others. For the person to have a satisfying life, it is rarely sufficient to possess a handicap. More is required.

Grieving Losses

"When I found out that I had MS, it felt like I had lost my best friend." That is how Ralph described his reaction to learning the diagnosis. When the disease struck, draining his strength and coordination, he felt that he had lost his faithful bodyguard. Most persons who become chronically ill or disabled feel a palpable sense of loss, similar to that felt when a loved one dies (p. 173). It is normal for chronic illness and disability to trigger grief. The time it takes to grieve varies from person to person; it can last several months or several years.

> A retired schoolteacher sought treatment for recurrent depression. With medication and psychotherapy she regained her usual optimism and humor. She remained on medication and psychotherapy to prevent recurrences. When her husband died, she underwent a normal course of grief. Four and one-half years after her husband's death, she finally felt like her old self again. She knew this had occurred when her ability to enjoy a beautiful sunset had returned.

Grief may be protracted beyond the time that general health improves. A longitudinal study (13) showed that a year after the diagnosis of cancer was made, the psychologic health of one third of the patients studied had declined, even though most showed no comparable decline in their general health. Two or more years after diagnosis, two thirds were doing poorly psychologically, with no concurrent deterioration in their general health.

Grief is a family affair. In the above study, although the general health of the patients had improved, the psychologic health of one third of family members and friends deteriorated. Their distress persisted even longer than that of the patients. These families could benefit from family therapy aimed at facilitating grief-work.

ACKNOWLEDGMENT

Supported by a grant from the Schaffer Foundation, Albany Medical College.

32/Limb Amputation

John C. Racy, M.D.

OBJECTIVES

GENERAL OBJECTIVE: Given a patient who requires limb amputation, discuss the patient's care from a psychosocial perspective.

SPECIFIC OBJECTIVES:
1. List the conditions frequently associated with limb amputation.
2. Discuss the following factors that affect a person's adaptation to amputation: age, personality traits, occupation, social support, mental health, medical indications for the amputation, preoperative preparation, surgical technique, introduction of the prosthesis, and teamwork in rehabilitation.
3. Summarize the preoperative and postoperative stages of adaptation to amputation.
4. Discuss the following considerations relating to amputation: phantom phenomena, body image, and sexuality.

Because of their exposed structure and demanding functions, limbs are particularly vulnerable to injury and poor healing and sometimes require amputation. Techniques of limb amputation, which is one of the oldest surgical procedures (1), can be found in the writings of Hippocrates and in other ancient documents.

Throughout recorded history, the exchange of limb for life has necessitated amputation by whatever means under the most adverse conditions. Before anesthesia was introduced, amputation required rapid surgical execution and was often fatal. Anesthesia and asepsis made it possible to operate more slowly and under better conditions.

INDICATIONS

Until recently, the most common reason for amputation was severe trauma, often in combat. In peacetime, and with greater longevity of the population, the reasons for amputation have shifted to chronic conditions, particularly vascular disease and the complications of diabetes (p. 196). Less common indications today are trauma, tumor, and revision of congenital deformity (2).

EPIDEMIOLOGY

There are approximately 500,000 amputees in the United States, 75% of whom are men, the majority aged 50–75 years (3). Eighty-five percent of amputations involve a lower limb. Thirty thousand to 50,000 lower extremity amputations are performed annually (2). Limb amputation is a triple challenge: it produces changes in body image, and it entails losses of function and sensation (3). Although limb amputation is the subject of this chapter, many principles of management of limb amputation apply to amputation of other structures.

FACTORS AFFECTING ADAPTATION TO AMPUTATION

Many variables affect a person's adaptation to amputation. These include age, mental health, occupation, economic factors, social support, general health, reasons for the procedure, surgical technique, surgical complications, efficacy of a prosthetic (artificial substitute) device, and teamwork of caregivers.

Age

Adaptation to amputation varies with age (4). Newborns who have a missing limb and babies who sustain amputation show remarkable resilience and modest residual effects. School-age children and adolescents are particularly sensitive to peer response. Young adults tend to adapt best because of good general health and a better developed identity. In old age, the success of adaptation depends on many factors. Common problems in the elderly—social isolation, poverty, reduced organ function (e.g., lower immunity) and disease (e.g., vascular disease)—tend to diminish adaptive capacity.

People's concerns also tend to vary with age. For adolescents, major concerns include identity, social status, and sexuality. For adults of all ages, major concerns include livelihood, functional capacity, sexuality, and social connections.

Mental Health

The relation between personality traits and reaction to amputation is complex (5). Optimism and pride foster adaptation. Those who are excessively invested in their appearance and in power tend to react negatively to the loss of a limb. Similarly, persons who are self-conscious, mistrustful, or pessimistic tend to show more distress than others. Resentment and denial are also associated with poor adaptation. Some dependent individuals derive

gain from the disability (secondary gain) because it legitimizes their dependency.

Depressed mood, which may occur before or after the amputation, can be part of a vicious cycle. It delays acceptance of the loss and receptiveness to a prosthesis. This, in turn, delays recovery and intensifies depression. Depression is the most important psychological correlate of poor adaptation (6). Treatment of the depression depends on the form the depression takes (p. 253).

Occupation

Obviously, those whose occupation entails frequent, adroit use of a limb (e.g., machine operators, artisans, and musicians) are likely to suffer more from the loss. Those whose occupation is based more on language suffer less from the loss.

An association between economic resources and adaptation is also predictable. Persons who are able to maintain their livelihood or, failing that, can draw on substantial reserves or liberal disability policies, tend to do better than those for whom the amputation entails serious economic loss. Unemployment is associated with greater psychological distress, and may be a predictor of phantom pain (see below) (7).

Social Support

Amputees routinely speak of the crucial importance of social support and acceptance. Most notable is the attitude of the spouse, followed by that of parents and children (8).

A mother in her 30s who had lost her hand in a paper shredder tried to conceal both the amputated stump and her prosthesis. One day she overheard her children boast to their schoolmates that their mother had an artificial limb. Further, they reported to her that their schoolmates responded admiringly, "Wow, a bionic Mom!" Not only did this amuse her, but it gave her a lift and contributed to her adjustment.

Another form of support is the self-help group, formal or informal (9).

Reasons for the Surgery

When the amputation results from trauma sustained in a socially sanctioned activity, such as combat or the discharge of one's duties, there are some compensations. Similarly, when the loss of a limb means the cure of a malignant tumor, the person has the advantage of preparation and of choice.

For the elderly, amputation usually follows prolonged suffering from diabetes or vascular disease. Relief from pain can help in adjustment, but poor general health does not. When amputation is necessitated by the negligence or malice of others, it is more likely to produce resentment and conflict. Litigation may complicate and prolong rehabilitation (6, 10).

Preoperative Preparation

When the situation allows for preparation, postoperative adjustment tends to be better (11, 12). Most amputees appreciate when the surgeon takes the time to discuss the need for surgery, the procedure itself, the disposition of the amputated limb, and common postoperative symptoms, including phantom phenomena. Preoperatively and postoperatively, they usually welcome the opportunity to meet with an amputee who successfully underwent the experience and mastered the prosthesis.

Surgical Technique

Amputation is a technically difficult procedure, and surgical success rests on the judgment and the skill of the surgical team. A balance must be struck between preserving as much tissue as possible and creating a functioning stump that is less vulnerable to complications (e.g., infection, pain) and that will accept a prosthesis in the future (13). Surgical complications can delay adaptation. These include persistent infection, pain, awkward configuration of the stump, and continued need for medication and surgical intervention (9).

Prosthesis

The early introduction of a prosthesis seems to foster successful adaptation. When it is absent or delayed, there is more anxiety, sadness, and self-consciousness. Psychologically, it is crucial to integrate the prosthesis into the body image (14) and to direct attention toward future function rather than past loss. Amputees are often pleasantly surprised on awakening from the amputation to find a prosthesis next to their intact leg. One indicator of successful adaptation is the appearance of the prosthesis in dreams (7, 15).

Teamwork in Rehabilitation

The procedures of amputation and rehabilitation, like most complex processes, require a sustained team effort. In addition to the surgeon, there are important roles for family members, nurses, rehabilitation therapists, social workers, counsellors, and vocational experts (16).

STAGES OF ADAPTATION

There are two phases of adaptation to amputation: preoperative and postoperative.

Preoperative Phase

Noted above, much is gained when there is adequate opportunity for discussion and preparation. Preoperative concerns revolve around (1) practical issues, such as pain, loss of function, loss of income, prosthesis, and the need for ongoing treatment, and (2) symbolic issues, such as changed appearance, limb disposal, acceptance by others, and sex. Many persons experience anticipatory grief similar to the experience of those approaching mortality (5). Experts counsel that amputation should be presented as positively as possible, labeling it reconstructive surgery, not merely the removal of a limb. Expectations of relief from pain and improved lifestyle should be emphasized (17). Family members should be included in the educational process and follow-up phases.

Postoperative Phase

The postoperative phase can be conveniently divided into three stages: the period immediately following surgery, rehabilitation in the hospital, and the home experience.

IMMEDIATE POSTOPERATIVE STAGE

During the hours or days immediately following surgery, the person's greatest concerns are recovery from surgery, the relief of pain, and (sometimes) disposition of the limb. Most go through a psychologically numb phase in which they have little emotional reaction. Some experience relief, if surgery reduces or removes pain and suffering (11).

HOSPITAL REHABILITATION STAGE

The hospital rehabilitation stage is the most critical period, involving challenges for the patient, the family, and the team. It calls for flexibility and optimism. From early concerns with pain and disfigurement, the focus shifts to restoration of function, social reintegration, and vocational adjustment. Some amputees show denial (pp. 44, 87, 169) through bravado or humor (18). Others go through stages of grief, including numbness, pining for the lost limb, feelings of disorganization, and reorganization (19). During this stage, phantom experiences (described below) occur. Adjustment during this phase can be helped by early prosthetic fitting, acceptance by friends and family, and contacts with successfully rehabilitated amputees (20).

HOME REHABILITATION STAGE

Home rehabilitation may be particularly difficult for some amputees who have done well in the structured hospital environment with the team's support. Difficulties may arise when these supports are withdrawn. Further, attending to one's needs and navigating around the house may be extremely stressful, in contrast to the ordered life of the hospital.

Only now may the impact of the loss become evident. Many amputees describe a "second realization" and a return of sadness. Some regress and resume the sick role (pp. 100, 409). Others manifest denial by pretending that little has changed.

Retrospectively, most successful amputees caution against excessive sympathy and indulgence by the family.

> Shortly after her return home, an amputee was guided by her husband to a sink full of dishes. She washed them while in tears, resenting her husband. Later she was amused to learn that the scenario was contrived by her husband (who usually did the dishes) and her doctor to counteract her feelings of uselessness. She said it was the best thing that they could have done for her.

Although fostering self-sufficiency and pride is best achieved without duplicity, this vignette depicts a creative exception.

Many amputees reject the handicapped label and prefer to view themselves as normal (1). This is easiest for those whose lower leg prosthesis can be concealed appropriately by clothing. Nevertheless, some self-consciousness lingers. At a pool party that an amputee group had organized for themselves and their guests (mostly family members), the only people who went into the pool were the guests (1).

SPECIAL CONSIDERATIONS

Special considerations with amputation include phantom phenomena, body image changes, and effects on sexuality.

Phantom Phenomena

Phantom phenomena are perceptions that seem to emanate from the absent limb or other amputated structure. They can occur even in persons who have congenitally absent limbs.

Phantom limb phenomena are more frequent in upper extremities than in lower ones, and are more frequent in the preferred hand

and limb than in the nonpreferred hand and limb. Almost universal are phantom sensations other than pain that include perception of the limb as if it were whole, limb motion, constriction, heat, cold, and itching (13, 21). Curiously, some amputees experience relief of itching by scratching the prosthesis.

For each person, the quality of the sensation changes over time. In telescoping, a common pattern, the phantom limb initially feels normal in size and shape and then appears to contract over time, until only the hand or foot seems to protrude from the stump (21, 22). Unless patients scheduled for amputation are told about phantom phenomena, some will not spontaneously report these phenomena to the physician, thinking they will be viewed as crazy (23, 24).

Phantom pain is more serious but not universal. It can prevent effective use of a prosthesis (25). Its reported prevalence varies from 1%–97% of patients (26), a striking variability largely explainable by different sampling techniques that range from prospective studies of randomly selected patients to retrospective studies of patients referred for treatment of pain (26).

Phantom pain shows no statistical association with age, sex, medical indication (e.g., blood vessel insufficiency, traumatic injury) for the procedure, or (once response to pain is taken into account) personality traits or psychiatric illness. Most authors believe that phantom pain is more likely if there was pain in the affected structure prior to the amputation and pain in the stump postoperatively (22, 26). It may be triggered or intensified by cool, damp weather (27). There is no clear treatment of choice (22, 28). Treatments reported to be helpful include transcutaneous electrical nerve stimulation, vibratory stimulation, and biofeedback-assisted relaxation (29–31).

HYPOTHESIZED MECHANISMS FOR PHANTOM PHENOMENA

It is hypothesized (32) that during gestation, neural matrices are automatically formed in the developing cerebral cortex for recognition, motor control, and memory of each body part. Subsequent perception and use of the body part enhances functioning of these matrices. Sensory nerves from the structure are received in the cerebral cortex. Following amputation, these matrices continue to function and continue to receive sensory input from the same sensory nerves originally attached to the original structure, although these sensory nerves are now shortened and emanate from the stump. Phantom pain could result from sensitization of these remaining neurons, diminished inhibition of the sensation, and reduced blood flow in the stump (25, 32). It has also been speculated (19) that incomplete grieving for the lost limb contributes to phantom pain.

Body Image

Successful adaptation is reflected when, in the Draw-a-Person Test (p. 211), the lost limb is omitted (7, 18). Those who adapt poorly trend to draw a larger-than-usual limb with increased markings. Dreams of the prosthesis denote better integration than dreams that deny the loss. The amputee contends with three body images: intact, amputated, and with prosthesis (33). Even among the more successful, some self-consciousness and discomfort may occur in social situations.

Sexual Behavior

Amputation affects sexual behavior in three ways: (1) fear of rejection by the partner; (2) loss of a functioning body part, such as the hand, and (3) loss of sensation. Although the prosthesis may restore body image and much function, it is usually of little help in sexual activity. Crucial elements are acceptance by the partner and the assurance that one is not a "freak." Fortunately, the passage of time often aids this process. Some members of an amputee group spoke of having better sex as a function of having better communication with their partners (1).

CONCLUSION

The surgical loss of a limb presents a triple challenge: loss of function, loss of sensation, and loss of physical integrity. At best, these losses are balanced by relief of pain, improvement in function, and restoration of social and vocational activity. When successfully approached as a team effort, the adjustment to amputation bears testimony to people's resilience, social support, and modern medicine.

SECTION VII.
BEHAVIOR AND SOCIETY

33/Medical Ethics

Roger C. Sider, M.D.

OBJECTIVES

GENERAL OBJECTIVE: Given the evaluation and treatment of a patient, summarize the ethical issues related to the patient's care.

SPECIFIC OBJECTIVES:
1. State why there has been more interest in medical ethics in the past 2 decades than at any other time in history.
2. Summarize the following four general philosophic approaches to ethics: utilitarianism, deontology, teleology, and virtue-based.
3. Summarize the characteristics of clinical ethics in contrast to philosophic ethics.
4. Discuss the following: beneficence, autonomy, informed consent, common good, public interest, and competence.
5. Discuss the following medical ethics issues: resource allocation, involuntary treatment, choice of therapeutic modality, duty to warn, suicide, AIDS reporting, and abusive behaviors by physicians.

HISTORY

From the time of Hippocrates to the mid-20th century, medical ethics maintained a consistent tradition. Modeled after the Hippocratic Oath (1), medical ethics provided a noncontroversial framework for practice. The essentials of the vow—confidentiality, proscription of sexual intimacy with patients, the commitment to act in a patient's best interest, and the obligation of loyalty to one's colleagues—were universally accepted. This compact between physicians and society began to fragment in the U.S. in the 1960s. Several factors accounted for this. Scientific and technical progress in medicine after World War II changed the nature of medical care. Powerful, life-sustaining treatments became routinely available, creating novel life-and-death decision-making dilemmas (2). The dying could now be kept alive much longer and were sometimes maintained in persistent vegetative states (i.e., irreversible comas that require ongoing external life supports).

There was an erosion of trust in physicians. Patients (whose parents accepted their doctor's recommendations unquestioningly) began asking if the doctor really knew best. Pluralism was growing, with a lost consensus on many social values. Prescribed answers, whether from physician or priest, were no longer based on widely shared mores. Medical specialization and the increased mobility of physicians and patients lessened the degree to which doctors and patients knew one another. The image of the beloved, pre-World War II, small town general practitioner caring for three generations in the same community was replaced by one of specialists whose patients were virtual strangers.

MEDICAL ETHICISTS

Medical ethicists comprise two professions. Most are philosophers and theologians who work in universities, medical schools, and bioethics institutes. Some are physicians, most of whom have no graduate training in philosophy. In rare instances, they are physicians who also have Ph.D.s in philosophy, like Tris Engelhardt (3) and Howard Brody (4).

LAW, ETHICS, AND MEDICINE

Medical ethics and the law are not identical. Morality precedes any legal corpus. Professional ethics, grounded in our obligation to patients, sometimes runs counter to law (e.g., Nazi eugenics statutes). We must evaluate the morality of legal doctrine before using the law to justify behavior. *What is legal is not always ethical, and vice versa.*

PHILOSOPHIC APPROACHES TO ETHICS

Philosophers approach medical ethics as a domain of applied morality, using moral theories as guidelines for action. There is no universally accepted moral theory, because there is no source of moral knowledge on which everyone agrees: some contend the source of ethical value is reason, some intuition, others divine revelation. We will presume, however, that moral knowledge is possible, even if certainty is not. Otherwise, we would be radical skeptics, and this chapter would be pointless.

There are four approaches to ethics: utilitarian, deontologic, teleologic, and virtue-based.

Utilitarianism

Utilitarian (consequentialist) theories teach that there is one fundamental moral duty—to produce the greatest good for the greatest number. Elaborated in the 19th century by Bentham (5) and Mill (6), it attempted to provide a mathematic method for decision making: calculate the good and bad consequences of an action or policy, then do what produces the greatest good. Utilitarianism values the general good more than that of an individual.

There are several permutations and combinations within utilitarianism. Some hold a monistic, hedonistic view, that there is one moral good: happiness or pleasure. Others believe pluralistically that several goods (e.g., health, knowledge) are primary. At a different level, because it is impossible to agree on what is intrinsically valuable, utilitarians ask whether the goods to be maximized are universal for everyone (agent-neutral), or based on individualized choices. Currently the individualistic alternative has more support.

Another dichotomy is between rule and act utilitarianism. Although for all utilitarians, the rule of utility is the ultimate source of moral appeal, there is a disagreement over whether this applies to individual acts (e.g., an act utilitarian might say there are circumstances in which it would be ethical for a poor person to steal food) or general rules. For the rule utilitarian (7), moral action is action according to rules (e.g., do not steal) that maximize the good. Rule utilitarians and deontologists may agree on basic ethical principles, but they justify them differently.

Deontology

Deontologists believe that certain acts are right, others wrong, not because of their consequences but because of intrinsic rightness or wrongness. Deontologists typically hold that to lie to a patient is wrong, even if good consequences follow. Moreover, deontologic or principle-based theories are more concerned with preserving existing good than with creating more good. The deontologist believes that persons have inviolable rights and duties. Specifying and justifying these rights and duties lend variety to deontologic theories. Some philosophers, following Kant (8), hold that morality may be derived from a single principle, the categorical imperative ("act only on that maxim whereby you can at the same time will that it should become a universal law"). Others (9) contend there are several irreducible principles (e.g., fidelity, beneficence [p. 426], justice). Conflict between irreducible principles (e.g., between beneficence and autonomy regarding involuntary hospitalization) sometimes occurs. If so, deontologists prioritize the principles, or little guidance results.

Teleology

A third approach is teleologic, in which there is an effort to understand the goals of human existence, which become the good toward which morality directs us. First elaborated by Aristotle (10), teleologic ethics is influential in Catholicism, initially through Aquinas (11). The search for the natural good of persons has proved difficult. In particular, it is argued that one cannot derive the moral "ought" from what "is" in nature. Yet an ethic based on natural goods is attractive. Health (biopsychosocial well-being) is a specifiable good toward which we aim.

Virtue

Virtue theorists contend that the fundamental question in ethics is personal, "What kind of person should I be?" Instead of focusing on rules, rights, or natural goods, one should attend to character. Virtue theories hold that the right motivation is the best predictor of moral conduct. MacIntyre (12) contends that virtue develops in practices serving human needs (e.g., a life of practicing medicine instills virtues fundamental to medical practice). This is disparaged by some ethicists who say that bioethics is not concerned with physicians becoming better persons. Such a pity!

Summary

Although ethical theories differ, in practice there is often congruence in application. The appropriateness of informed consent, for ex-

ample, usually justified deontologically, can be supported by rule utilitarians as well as teleologic and virtue ethicists. Here, what differs is the way in which actions are morally justified. Sometimes, appeal to different theories leads to different moral actions. For example, Oregon withholds Medicaid coverage for some extremely expensive but life-saving procedures and devotes more resources to inexpensive primary prevention efforts that affect large numbers of Oregonians. Other states adopt different strategies.

SPECIAL FEATURES OF CLINICAL ETHICS

Philosophers tend to see all areas of applied ethics as similar. Whether one is a physician, priest, or politician, the moral principles and reasoning processes are the same. This presumes generalizability and universality in ethics. Clouser (13) contends that medical ethics is simply "the 'old ethics' trying to find its way around in new, very puzzling circumstances" (13:386).

Yet many clinicians believe medicine warrants a modified approach to ethical problem solving. Medicine is practical, not theoretical. Kierkegaard distinguished between theoretician and participant in answering the question "Is knowledge changed when it is applied?"

"Imagine a pilot, and assume that he had passed every examination with distinction, but that he had not as yet been at sea. Imagine him in a storm; he knows everything he ought to do, but he has not known before how terror grips the seafarer when the stars are lost in the blackness of night; he has not known the sense of impotence that comes when the pilot sees the wheel in his hand become a plaything for the waves; he has not known how the blood rushes into the head when one tries to make calculations at such a moment; in short, he has had no conception of the change that takes place in the knower when he has to apply his knowledge" (14).

Several aspects of medical practice help shape clinical ethics: grounding of the therapeutic professions in health values, the relational context of health care, its case-centered focus, the pervasiveness of uncertainty, and the use of professional codes.

Health Values

The ethical responsibilities of physicians are not limited to those of fellow citizens. Physicians are ethically bound to care for the sick and restore health, and they have a mandate to act only in this context. Health values establish the boundaries for medical interventions; physicians are not free to negotiate services beyond those of health care.

Relational Context

Effective medical care involves physician-patient bonding. The physician is not a dispassionate observer. The influence of the therapeutic bond on clinical reasoning is double-edged. At its best it ensures that the physician will be empathically disposed toward the patient, facilitating care. The doctor-patient bond may disrupt the physician's rationality, however. Some philosophers (rationalists) view moral reflection as an objective process from which emotions should be removed. Clinicians, in contrast, find their reflection informed by their emotional commitment to the patient. For this reason, among others, clinicians sometimes feel that advice regarding a moral dilemma is better assisted by consultation with a clinical colleague than with a philosopher-ethicist.

Case-Centered Focus

Most physicians treat patients one-to-one or, at most, in small groups, and must focus more on the good of their patients than on social policy. This is one basis for the patient's trust. Because of this focus, clinical ethics is concerned with the rich detail of each patient's history and clinical status. Philosopher-ethicists sometimes reduce the case history to "ethical essentials." Clinicians have difficulty viewing clinical data as irrelevant.

Clinical Complexity and Uncertainty

There is ambiguity in practice that often renders ethical decision making imprecise. This contrasts with the logical clarity of deriving deductive arguments from ethical principles. The sources of this ambiguity include the complexity of data, uncertainty of diagnosis and prognosis, and ambivalent patient wishes. Moreover, sometimes only somber or tragic choices are available. Physicians often must be content with what is relatively better, not what is absolutely good.

Professional Codes

Clinical ethics is further distinguished by commitment to professional codes. Membership in the American Psychiatric Association (APA), for example, requires adherence to its *Principles of Medical Ethics: With Annotations Especially Applicable to Psychiatry* (15). Members charged with ethical violations have allegations reviewed by a district ethics committee of peers, which then may recommend disciplinary action to the APA. Professional ethics codes have been criticized for resembling "codes of etiquette" that simply serve the physician's guild. Their importance has increased recently, however. Sexual misconduct is the most common ground for disciplinary action.

OTHER IMPORTANT CONCEPTS

Patient Good (Beneficence)

Beneficence connotes acts of kindness or mercy. In ethics, it asserts an obligation to do good for others. In medical ethics, beneficence is the demand on the physician to provide care for the patient's good (in the patient's best interest). This legitimizes medical advice and treatment. Pellegrino and Thomasma (16) place beneficence at the core of medicine. Controversy has arisen about whether patient best interest is a subjective (patient choice) or objective (natural good) value. Is the definition and value of my health my determination, or ought my physician to apply a definition of health in deciding what to recommend? Much rests on this question, especially when patients appear to disregard their health.

Patient Autonomy and Informed Consent

Autonomy is Greek for self-governance. In ethics, it is the prerogative of persons to choose for themselves. But what makes a choice autonomous is unclear. In the strictest accounts, it requires that the choice be independent, consistent, rational, and authentic. It is arguable whether choices are ever fully autonomous; Beauchamp and Childress (17) view autonomy as present in degrees.

Physicians should enhance and respect the patient's ability to choose whether and how to be treated. This requires that others not impose constraints, and that sufficient information is given to allow patients to make informed decisions. Respect for autonomy undergirds informed consent (see also p. 435), which consists of four elements: disclosure, understanding, voluntariness, and consent. Disclosure is the provision of information to the patient about the decision at hand. How much and what type of information is disputed. The professional practice standard regards the traditional practices of a local physician as the norm. This is criticized on the grounds that it may result in inadequate disclosure, whereby the patient cannot make a truly informed choice. Another standard is the reasonable person standard. Here, the information provided should be what a reasonable person in the patient's situation would find relevant and understandable. This, too, has been criticized as unclear.

These difficulties suggest the subjective standard, in which the idiosyncrasies of the individual patient are the criterion on which the nature of disclosure is based. This encourages physicians to be attuned to their patients' individual wishes.

The second element is understanding. A patient is said to understand a treatment if he or she has reasonable beliefs about its nature and consequences. Information is useful only when understood in the context of the decision to be made.

Voluntariness, the third element, entails freedom from coercion. Obviously, there are influences on the decision-making process, but the patient must experience the decision as his or her own. Next of kin and caregivers must respect this. Disclosure, understanding, and voluntariness culminate in the consent itself.

Studies (18) reveal that informed consent works less neatly in practice than in theory. Patients sometimes express little interest in information, or do not use it in decision making. They frequently defer to their physician (even waiving the right to be informed [p. 435]), and the degree to which they understand what they are told is often frustratingly low. On the other hand, many patients know more than physicians about how their illness, or its treatment, affects them.

Common Good and Public Interest

Physicians legitimately focus their ethical concern at the individual level, the best interest of their patients. But physicians also belong to communities that have medically pertinent concerns. These concerns might be framed in terms of the common good or in terms of public interest.

The common good, rooted in Greek political thought, is a communal vision of individuals banded together by a shared pursuit of common goals, with individual good bound to the common good; individuals flourish only as they and the community flourish together. The public interest is a more recent (17th century) concept. Society is viewed as a rational alliance of self-interested persons whose individual good is defined by their private interests. The public interest is the organization that best promotes the flourishing of its citizens' private interests. These two visions compete in American life, neither dominant.

Confidentiality

The 1989 edition of the *Principles of Medical Ethics of the American Medical Association* (19) states, "A physician shall . . . safeguard patient confidences within the constraints of the law." Confidentiality rules have been based on deontologic, utilitarian, and virtue grounds. The first holds that both respect for personal autonomy and the implicit promises in the fiduciary (held in confidence and trust) doctor-patient relationship obligate the physician to protect confidentiality. Utilitarians argue that confidentiality fosters the candor and trust necessary for effective care. Although confidentiality is a special obligation, it is not absolute. Situations in which it may have to be breached are discussed on p. 434.

Competence

Competence, a legal term, may also be viewed in ethics when its importance hinges on respect for autonomy. Persons can only function autonomously if they are competent. Therefore, our obligation to obtain informed consent and respect patients' autonomy is meaningful only when the patient is competent to make the decision at hand. The *law presumes competence* in all patients, as for all citizens. Also, the law regards competence not as one entity, but rather a specific capacity in regard to a given task (p. 435).

Drane (20) suggested a sliding scale of rigor in the assessment of competence, with the scale anchored by two endpoints in a risk-benefit spectrum. At one end are patients for whom the recommended treatment is effective and relatively safe. Because the risk is low and the benefit high, only a modest standard of competence (awareness and assent) is required. Patients at the other end have chronic illness for which only partially effective treatment exists, or the treatment poses major risks. In the latter, the risk-benefit calculus is less one-sided. Accordingly, a more stringent standard (the capacity for an understanding choice) is applied. Although ambiguous, this establishes a helpful principle, that the more risky or uncertain the effectiveness of the treatment, the more care should be taken in establishing competency for informed consent.

Incompetence is common in patients who have brain dysfunction. Yet competence must be presumed, and incompetent status assigned only after careful assessment. When patients are clearly incompetent to give consent for treatment, two questions arise: Who should make the decision for the patient? By what criteria should it be made?

There has been disagreement about who can best serve as proxy decision makers, family, health professionals, or the courts. Although the courts have been called the best arbiter of treatment decisions, many clinicians and ethicists do not agree (21). The courts are often too slow to resolve urgent clinical situations, and there is no evidence that the courts render judgments superior to others (22). Family members and health care professionals may not be ideal candidates as proxy decision makers either because they may have conflicts of interest.

A helpful recent federal law, the Patient Self-Determination Act (1991) requires that hospitals reimbursed by Medicare ask newly admitted adult patients if they have executed advance directives, and if the patient has not done so, to assist the patient in writing advance directives if he or she wishes (23, 24). These directives include a living will and durable power of attorney for health care. In a living will, the patient may give general treatment guidelines (e.g., do whatever is necessary for my comfort, but nothing further) or specific directions (e.g., provide food and water by tube if necessary, but do not attempt cardiopulmonary resuscitation). Also, the patient designates a durable power of attorney for health care, or patient advocate. Any person 18 years of age or older is eligible if that person is selected by the patient and agrees to serve. The advocate is authorized (preferably, guided by the living will) to make treatment decisions whenever the patient is unable to do so (e.g., reversible delirium, irreversible coma).

Another question concerns the criteria by which proxy decisions should be made. Two standards exist: patient best interest and substituted judgment. Patient best interest, beneficence, asks proxies to weigh the risks and benefits of treatment options and then judge what is best for the patient. This does not always yield a decisive answer. But for most patients whose behavioral abnormalities are accessible to treatment (e.g., depression, reversible delirium), the best-interest standard favors treatment, following which the patient's competence is then restored.

Substituted judgment posits that the incompetent patient's autonomy must be preserved regardless of competence. The proxy should decide as he or she believes the patient *would have decided* if competent. In its *Cruzan* decision (25), the U.S. Supreme Court held that substituted judgment is a valid basis for decisions in cases concerning cessation of life supports for patients in a persistent vegetative state, as long as the patient's prior wishes were clearly expressed (as in a living will).

PROBLEM AREAS

Allocation of Resources

The United States is currently struggling to define a just system of distributing costs and benefits of health care. This is a problem of distributive justice, with two contrasting approaches: libertarian and egalitarian. The libertarian approach (4, 26) holds that individual liberty is the central value of a health care system. A free market is advocated unless participants freely choose an alternative. In the free market, people are paid proportional to the economic contribution of their work, then buy goods and services on the open market. Self-pay or payment through voluntary private health insurance is the preferred method of payment for health care. Strict libertarians reject egalitarian arguments that this system is unfair to the poor. They agree that it may be unfortunate that some citizens cannot pay for care, but view this as just, because underwriting the cost of care for the poor involves involuntary removal of resources from wealthier citizens to pay for others' health. For the libertarian, the state's role is limited to insuring just procedures for operation of the market (e.g., acquisition and transfer of property).

Many ethicists reject libertarian approaches not because they are uncaring or unwise, but because they are unethical. Egalitarians maintain that some goods and services should be distributed equally. Rawls (27) argues that legitimate communal arrangements are those that advance the good of the least advantaged. Because inequalities of birth (the natural lottery) and circumstance (the social lottery) are undeserved, a just society strives for equality for the disadvantaged; this is the system people would choose if required in advance to choose the system while ignorant (the veil of ignorance) of their own lottery standing. Rawls holds that because sickness and disability are often undeserved, a just system benefits everyone based on need. This requires universal access to good care. Additional services might be available to those able to pay more.

Involuntary Treatment

Legally, voluntary consent for admission to a psychiatric hospital takes priority over coercive restraint (least restrictive alternative). Yet legal jurisdictions in Western democracies allow for involuntary treatment. Two criteria are used: (1) mentally ill, and (2) dangerous to self or dangerous to others. Even if dangerous, psychiatric commitment is not appropriate for someone not mentally ill. Conversely, mental illness is a necessary but not sufficient criterion for involuntary admission. Dangerousness to self (by virtue of suicidal risk or inability to care for oneself, or to solicit others to care for oneself) or others must also exist.

The ethical justification for involuntary treatment of a mentally ill person at risk of harm to self derives most directly from the principle of beneficence. Where the threat of harm is to another person, the physician is only indirectly acting in the patient's best interest (pp. 368, 426). In these cases the physician is also an agent of the state operating under legal mandate.

Choice of Therapeutic Modality

The choice of therapeutic modality is an ethical issue in psychiatry (28). Consider the choice between individual and marital therapy in this case:

> A 40-year-old homemaker calls a psychiatrist to make an appointment. She describes the situation as follows: "Our marriage has been slowly deteriorating over several years, but recently I have begun to consider a divorce. I'm anxious, depressed, and unable to cope. My husband seems unaware and unconcerned."

Should the psychiatrist be primarily concerned with the health of the marital unit or that of the patient? Should the doctor see the patient alone or with her husband? Marital therapy focuses on the health of the marriage as well as that of each partner, whereas individual therapy focuses on the health of the patient. Usually, both individual and marital health are enhanced through either treatment. Sometimes, however, one partner in a divorce benefits at the expense of other family members (29), regardless of who obtains what treatment. Where goods conflict, therefore, choice of therapeutic modality often equals selection of the primary goal of the therapy. Accordingly, the choice of modality should be discussed with the patient prior to treatment.

Duty to Protect or to Warn

In the 1976 *Tarasoff* (30) decision, a U.S. jurisdiction for the first time determined that therapists have a duty to warn potential victims of their patient's violent intentions if treatment of the patient cannot assure the potential victim's safety. The Tarasoff decision stated that, "When a therapist determines, or pursuant to the standards of his profession should determine, that his patient presents a serious danger of violence to another, he in-

curs an obligation to use reasonable care to protect the intended victim against such danger . . . it may call for him to warn the intended victim or others likely to apprise the victim of the danger, to notify the police, or to take whatever other steps are reasonably necessary under the circumstances." Many states have enacted legislation based on the *Tarasoff* decision.

A duty to warn requires for its ethical justification a demonstration either that it serves the patient's best interest, or that the clinician has obligations to potential victims of his or her patient's intended violent acts. A case can be made for both. Because acting violently often results in grave personal and legal consequences, reasonable steps you take to protect your patient from committing violence serves important patient interests. Warning third parties should usually occur after the patient has been advised of your intention, and only if the patient declines to communicate the warning him- or herself. The second justification for the duty to warn is your obligation to foster the health and safety of the community, here the safety of those at risk from the patient's possible violent actions.

Suicide

In the philosophic literature, suicide has been examined in terms of the concepts of "rational suicide" and the right to die (31). "Rational" suicide is hypothesized as one in which the agent is competent, understands suicide's irreversibility, weighs other consequences, and then kills himself. Some philosophers, who place autonomy atop their value list, advocate noninterference with "autonomous" suicide, or even assisted suicide (31). In two well-publicized recent cases (32, 33), physicians assisted patient suicides, and grand juries would not indict the doctors for homicide.

Physicians are, however, expected to intervene preventively where suicidal risk is present. For one, retrospective studies (34) of completed suicides show that over 95% were suffering from a treatable mental disorder at the time of their death, most commonly affective disorder, schizophrenia, and substance abuse. Psychiatrists question, therefore, how frequently autonomous suicide actually occurs. Beyond this, however, lies your fundamental ethical responsibility to preserve life and health, to care for your patient, and to pursue his or her best interest (at least by the natural good concept of beneficence).

AIDS Reporting

The AIDS epidemic poses dilemmas for physicians, arising out of the conflict between the duty to protect patient confidentiality and the duty to protect (or warn) potential victims of high-risk behaviors. In 1988, the APA published its *AIDS Policy: Confidentiality and Disclosure* (35), which condones breach of confidentiality only after all other alternatives have been considered. But if HIV-positive patients continue to place others at risk, and will not acknowledge their HIV-positive status to those persons, disclosure by the physician is ethically permissible. In such cases, it is permissible to report HIV-positive cases to the appropriate public health agency.

The justification for the breach of confidentiality is both legal, as in the Tarasoff case, and moral. Ethically, it rests on the life-threatening risk to potential victims and physicians' historic obligation to reduce the spread of communicable disease. The APA policy, although it has general professional support, is opposed by some. Perry (36) contends that breaches of confidentiality in the name of a duty to warn will drive patients away from treatment, fueling the AIDS epidemic.

UNETHICAL BEHAVIORS BY PHYSICIANS

Sexual Abuse of Patients

The health professions are plagued by reports of sexual contact with patients. A 1973 study, based on an anonymous self-report survey (with a 46% return rate), found that of male physicians in California, 10% reported sexual contact with patients (37). Male physician-female patient is by far the most frequent type.

Codes of ethics since Hippocrates have proscribed such behavior. Many state legislatures have legislated mandatory reporting, civil penalties and, in a few states, criminal penalties. Concerning sexual involvement with former patients, the APA's position is that "sexual activity with one's former patients generally exploits emotions deriving from treatment and therefore almost always is unethical" (15).

Sexual Involvement with Trainees

Recently sexual involvement of physicians with trainees has come under scrutiny. The APA's position that "sexual involvement between a faculty member or supervisor and (a resident) or student, in those situations in which an abuse of power can occur, often takes advantage of inequalities in the working relationship and may be unethical because: (*a*) any treatment of a patient being supervised may be deleteriously affected; (*b*) it may damage the trust between teacher and student; and (*c*) teachers are important role models for their trainees and affect the trainees' future professional behavior" (38:1402).

Research Abuse of Patients

In 1966, Beecher reported that of 50 published studies only two mentioned consent. In some of these, patients were unknowingly subjected to risk (39). Since then, stringent regulatory guidelines have been established. The ethical foundation of research with human subjects is informed consent. Subjects must know in advance the nature, purpose, risks, and benefits of the study, that they are free to decline to participate, and if they decline, their usual care will not be jeopardized. In addition, federally funded research grant applications, and many universities, require that research involving human subjects receive prior approval from institutional review boards.

Exposure of a patient to risk does not itself render a study unethical. People have a remarkable capacity for altruistic behavior. The opportunity to assist medical science, oneself, and future patients often motivates assumption of risk.

34/Forensic Medicine

Sanford Jacobson, M.D.

OBJECTIVES

GENERAL OBJECTIVE: Given a patient's history and examination, summarize the legal aspects of that patient's care.

SPECIFIC OBJECTIVES:

1. Summarize the legal considerations in establishing and maintaining the doctor-patient relationship.
2. Discuss confidentiality and testimonial privilege in medical care.
3. Summarize informed consent.
4. List the conditions necessary for a successful medical malpractice suit and state the relation between actual physician malpractice and the litigation that follows.
5. Discuss the legal aspects of charting, supervision of employees, and medical education and research.
6. State the legal standards used for the various types of competence.

The role of the law in medical practice is increasing, both in the legal regulation of medical practice and in the involvement of physicians in litigation. Almost all medical periodicals have articles on legal issues. Indeed, one practitioner (1) described his specialty as "belegaled." The philosophies of the law and of medicine differ. Today, medicine is based on scientific knowledge and its application. The law is less concerned with scientific truth than with fairness and justice according to rules and precedents.

In general, when you practice medicine well, the law supports your efforts. Physicians and attorneys often work together to help a patient. Patients who are injured, need guardians, must make wills, or are involved in litigation may require a physician-attorney relationship. Physicians will require an attorney to represent them if they are sued. When serving as an expert witness, you work closely with an attorney. The services of attorneys can be invaluable, as illustrated by the following case:

While on pass from the psychiatric unit of a hospital, an alcoholic patient shot his girlfriend to death. The girlfriend's family sued the hospital and each of the patient's doctors for $1 million apiece. The hospital's case was strong: the patient's treatment was competent, the pass was therapeutically warranted, the patient's prepass mental status was normal, and the patient had expressed no anger at his girlfriend. However, the plaintiff's case evoked sympathy: a woman was dead, her three children motherless, and the hospital and doctors well insured.

The hospital's legal defense team, consisting of two young African-American women and their consultant, an elderly Euro-American man, was

432

superb. Their courtroom defense included the patient's testimony that his care had been good, that prior to the pass he had never contemplated killing his girlfriend (on the first day of his pass, his girlfriend spontaneously confessed to an affair with another man), the testimony of the girlfriend's lover that the affair had indeed occurred, and the statement by the plaintiff's expert witness psychiatrist (on cross-examination) that the diagnosis and treatment of the patient were competent.

The defense won the case. For 12 years subsequently, the patient's doctors sent a Christmas card with a note of gratitude to the defense team.

DOCTOR-PATIENT RELATIONS

Except for initial evaluations (e.g., in the emergency room) where you have contracted to assess patients and are the only physician available, you have no obligation to accept a given patient (2). When you accept a patient, a relationship exists, establishing a contract (which does not depend on payment of a fee). Although you are expected to exercise reasonable skill and care, you must not guarantee results. In some situations in which you evaluate a patient at the request of a third party (e.g., an insurance company), no doctor-patient relationship exists. In this situation, you should clarify your role explicitly for the patient, and you should not inadvertently establish a doctor-patient relationship.

A cardiologist was asked to perform an independent medical examination for an insurance company on a beneficiary who was receiving disability payments because of a cardiac disorder. During his examination and review of the records, the physician told the patient that he might achieve better results in the management of his hypertension if he took an additional medication. He gave the patient a prescription (a mistake), with instructions to take it along with his current medication. Two days later, the patient developed light-headedness and felt weak. When he called the cardiologist, the cardiologist advised him to call his treating physician, because the cardiologist was only a consultant. Indeed, the prescription had established a doctor-patient relationship.

Do not inadvertently establish doctor-patient relations by giving advice, prescribing medication, taking call for a colleague, or simply making an appointment. For example, when taking call for a colleague it is often advisable to defer the prescription, by telephone, of new medication without seeing the patient and reviewing the records. Each situation is unique.

All states, through Good Samaritan statutes, allow your rendering of care in an emergency outside your usual practice setting, with limitation of liability you might incur in a more usual doctor-patient relationship. The standard of care in a Good Samaritan situation might fall below the usual standard of practice that would apply to a malpractice action (2). No continuing obligation to treat the patient develops. A *premature* departure after initiating treatment (abandonment) is unacceptable. A Good Samaritan situation does not arise in an emergency involving a patient previously under your care.

Be cautious in terminating a doctor-patient relationship. Treatment can be terminated by mutual agreement between you and the patient, or when either the patient or you chooses to dissolve the relationship. You must give the patient suitable notice that the arrangement is to be terminated. The patient should have time and assistance in securing another physician (if further care is needed), and information should be available to the new physician. Failure to pay a bill or cooperate in treatment, or missing an appointment, does not itself justify ending your responsibility to the patient.

In general, you need not provide treatment you believe fruitless or inappropriate (e.g., laetrile for cancer) (3, 4). There are rare exceptions: In the Helga Wanglie case, the court upheld a family's demand that an irreversibly comatose patient be maintained on life supports (hoping for a miracle), despite multiple medical and lay opinions that this was pointless (3, 4).

Confidentiality and Privilege

Confidentiality is the right of a patient to maintain privacy and prevent disclosure to other parties (2, 5). Testimonial privilege is the right of a patient to prevent the disclosure of confidential information in a court proceeding (2, 5). Confidentiality statutes vary by state. In some, they apply to psychiatrists, other mental health professionals, and other physicians. In others, these statutes apply only to mental health professionals. Even in the absence of a statute, there are common law and case law protections of a patient's communications with a physician, so it is still unwise under most circumstances for you to disclose information without legal authority (such as signed consent for release of information). For physicians, confidentiality is an ethical obligation that is usually protected by law. Sometimes, however, disclosure of information is mandatory, such as when authorized in writing by the patient, when the law obligates reporting of certain communicable diseases (e.g., syphilis, typhoid, measles, tuberculosis), or when you receive a subpoena. Do not respond automatically to subpoenas, particularly when the patient is not aware of the request. Some subpoenas result from thoughtless "fishing expeditions" by attorneys who usually withdraw the subpoena if persuaded that your testimony would not enhance their case.

There are further exceptions to confidentiality: child abuse (p. 142), life-and-death emergencies (e.g., calling a relative or police when a suicidal patient has eloped from the hospital), danger to a third party, peer review, insurance companies (usually entitled to a limited amount of information with signed consent from the patient), other professionals (e.g., physicians, nurses) treating the patient, and clerical personnel who record information for the medical record (2). Confidentiality continues after a patient's death, and disclosure can be made only by court order or when permission is granted by the legal representative of the deceased.

You may be required to testify in court. This often is desired by the patient, who may in other situations oppose it. In the latter case, you must confirm that the communications of the patient are not protected by testimonial privilege. Usually the patient's attorney will invoke this privilege, but the right belongs to the patient. No testimonial privilege exists with child abuse, civil commitment (involuntary hospitalization), some aspects of child custody disputes, court-ordered evaluations, or when the patient's medical record is an issue in litigation (2). Also, either side may successfully argue that aspects of the testimony requested are irrelevant to the case.

I had been treating a 37-year-old woman, a mother of three children, with psychotherapy and antidepressants for 2 years. Her symptoms were those of depression, emotional instability, and periodic extreme anger. She had never physically abused her children, but sometimes directed angry outbursts at them. During treatment, she decided to divorce her husband and seek custody of the children; her husband also sought custody. Although her communications to me were confidential and would normally be subject to testimonial privilege, the issue of child custody jeopardized those confidences. The court allowed a limited amount of testimony with respect to her fitness as a mother, but disallowed inquiry into issues deemed irrelevant to custody. Thus, her rights to privacy were substantially protected, but some of her testimonial privilege was lost. This was decided exclusively by the court; none of this could be presumed by me.

Although physicians often communicate information to spouses (an educative process often in the patient's best interest, usually suggested or agreed to by the patient), there is no absolute obligation to do so. The patient is entitled to privacy with respect to disclosure to a spouse, with a few exceptions such as life-threatening emergencies (e.g., a patient's serious suicide risk) in which a relative's assistance may be critical.

You may wonder whether you have a duty to disclose knowledge of a crime. Technically, the failure to report a crime is a misprision (serious misdemeanor). But rarely is anyone prosecuted for this. It is a federal crime to threaten the life of the President, successors to the presidency, and visiting heads of state (6). Conceivably, failure to report such a threat might result in prosecution. The reporting of a threat on the life of the President is protected (in Veterans Affairs medical centers, it is required).

Sometimes, a patient's friend or relative confides "secret" information (sometimes in the patient's best interest, sometimes not) to a physician, and requests confidentiality of that communication. You have no obligation to honor that request. Depending on your best judgment, you may report the secret to the patient (this is usually best), or temporarily withhold the information while insisting that the messenger confront the patient directly (7). Burnum (7) has proposed several situations in which ongoing withholding of the secret may be in the patient's best interest.

Informed Consent

In 1914, Justice Cardozo (8) stated that "every human being ... has a right to determine what shall be done with his own body." When a physician treats a patient without his or her consent, that physician may be committing a battery. Simply obtaining the patient's consent is not enough. Consent must be informed (p. 427). The content of information provided should include (1) the diagnosis; (2) the treatment; (3) alternative treatments; (4) the likelihood of success of the proposed and alternative treatments; (5) the risks of the proposed and alternative treatments; and (6) the course of the illness if untreated. In life-threatening emergencies, informed consent is not always required (e.g., most physicians do not give detailed information before sedating combative psychotic patients). Likewise, an incompetent person and, in many instances, children cannot give consent, but there must be a substituted consent (p. 429). Rarely, because of the patient's mental condition, you might claim a right (therapeutic privilege) not to obtain informed consent, documenting in the chart that had you tried to obtain in-

formed consent, the patient would have refused, reacted dangerously, or suffered harm. This is a medicolegally risky strategy, to be weighed against the extent to which the situation is life-threatening.

Another exception to obtaining informed consent is when the patient waives the right to be informed. This must be documented.

> A 32-year-old woman had panic disorder. The treating psychiatrist suggested imipramine (p. 327) to prevent future panic attacks. When he began to discuss side effects, the patient stated "I don't want to know," because of her tendency to be fearful. She said she would trust the physician's judgment and take the medication. The psychiatrist tried persuading her to just listen to a list of possible side effects—she reiterated her position. The psychiatrist prescribed the medication and 8 days later the patient developed a generalized pruritic (itchy) rash which disappeared on withdrawal of the imipramine. Did the patient's actions constitute a waiver? Fortunately, no legal complications resulted because of a satisfactory physician-patient relationship. But the risk of so-called waivers is obvious. The physician should have asked the patient to waive the information in writing, or promptly documented the refusal in the chart.

A short-lived exception to our obligation to inform came in the Supreme Court's 1991 *Rust v. Sullivan* decision, bitterly challenged by organized medicine and then disregarded by federal regulation in 1992. The Court supported a federal agency's decision that physicians in federally funded family planning clinics could not discuss abortion as an option for pregnant women not wishing to continue a pregnancy. This contradicted, for several months, our obligation (and right) to discuss alternative treatments (9).

In general, a parent has authority to consent to treatment for his or her child but there are ambiguities, such as when the parents are divorced, the minor is living independently or is pregnant, or in cases of sexually transmitted diseases or substance abuse. Some states allow for the treatment of minors with these needs without parental consent, and some even provide for confidentiality from the parents. Minors living alone usually can be treated like adults (emancipated minors), particularly when self-supporting, but this is rarely defined clearly. A minor needing immediate emergency treatment would not usually require parental consent. In ambiguous areas involving minors, seek legal guidance, because the law is constantly evolving, and novel situations occur daily.

MALPRACTICE

Most physicians will be involved in a malpractice action during their careers (2). In a malpractice action, the plaintiff (the party bringing suit) alleges a wrongful action on the part of the defendant, the physician (and frequently, the hospital, other professional staff, or the physician's employer). This alleged civil wrong is a tort, a noncriminal act committed by one person harming another. Most malpractice suits claim negligence (doing something incorrectly or failing to do what is necessary), alleging failure to meet a standard of care. To establish a malpractice action, the plaintiff must demonstrate that (*1*) the physician had a duty to provide care; (*2*) there was dereliction of that duty; (*3*) damages resulted; and (*4*) the damages were directly related to the breach of the duty owed the patient.

Physicians may be sued for things other than malpractice such as violating a patient's civil rights (e.g., refusing to give an appointment to a patient because of race) or contractual disputes (conflicts over fees). Simply breaching your duty to a patient would probably not be sufficient for you to lose a malpractice action. There must be damages from the malpractice.

A physician inadvertently wrote an incorrect prescription for one patient, prescribing Premarin (conjugated estrogen) instead of Provera (progesterone). The patient filled the prescription and took the medication for 2 days before the error was detected. The physician corrected the error and began the proper treatment. Although the physician had been derelict, no damages resulted, so a successful action would have been unlikely.

In most civil suits, the plaintiff must prove his or her case by preponderance of the evidence (more likely than not = 51%). This differs from criminal cases, whose standard is beyond a reasonable doubt (estimated by some to be 90%–95% probability) (5).

When awarded, damages are of two types: compensatory and punitive. The usual basis is compensatory, for medical costs, lost income, pain, suffering, or lost capacity for enjoyment. Rarely, punitive damages are awarded when the behavior is egregious, or when the outcome (e.g., quadriplegia, vegetative state, death) is devastating.

In an excellent malpractice litigation system (one that deters malpractice and is perceived as fair), most cases of negligence leading to damage should result in malpractice claims, and most malpractice claims should be based on actual negligence leading to damage. Only 1.53% of cases of damage owing to negligence lead to claims, however, and only 48% of malpractice claims follow actual adverse events owing to negligence (10).

PATIENT'S RECORD

You must maintain an ongoing current record of your care of a patient. Not doing so may result in a presumption of negligence. Although you may be tempted to alter a patient's record to hide a mistake, any attempt to do so is foolhardy. Sophisticated evidence-dating techniques (or testimony of witnesses) may allow detection of changes in the record made well after the initial entry (11), overshadowing any defense you have. Also, post-catastrophe or postmortem explanatory chart entries, even properly written, carry far less weight than do ongoing preinjury ones.

Patients have a right to a copy of their medical record. Unfortunately this reduces the frankness and vividness of present-day charting. Where you feel that harm will likely come to patients if they view their record, you may withhold the record.

VICARIOUS LIABILITY

You and your hospital may be liable for the actions of your employees or agents. This is called respondeat superior (12). For you and the hospital to be liable, though, the act must have been performed by your employee within the scope of employment.

TEACHING AND RESEARCH

Well-trained, well-supervised students tend to write good, detailed histories, tend not to manifest the arrogance to which many of us attendings are prone, and push us to serve as good role models. Patients in a teaching facility incur no special obligation, and have the right to refuse some or all participation by medical students in their care. Students must inform patients that they are supervised trainees, although some appreciative patients refer to students as "my doctor." Rarely do legal problems, or even unpleasantries, arise because students participate in care.

There is no justification for jeopardizing the patient's health for teaching purposes. Research subjects are due a special level of informed consent, particularly with respect to risks and alternative treatments. You must avoid even the appearance of duress with respect to any teaching or research subject.

Legal Rights of Medical Students

At the bedside, the actions of medical students are judged under the doctrine of respondeat superior. Academically, students may seek legal relief when subject to a dismissal. Dismissal usually occurs for academic reasons but occasionally is for disciplinary reasons. Courts generally defer to a school's academic judgments. Disciplinary dismissals are more apt to be scrutinized. Well-documented, habitually poor performance in areas other than examinations (e.g., lateness, poor hygiene, poor interpersonal relationships) is a legitimate consideration in decisions about promotion and graduation (13–15).

The student is entitled to fair treatment based on reasonable (not capricious) academic decisions. Due process (of law) does not mean a formal hearing but usually requires that the student receive timely notice of his or her deficiencies and an opportunity to correct them. The toughest situations usually arise late in the medical school careers of students whose past performance was inadequate but not promptly called to the student's attention (along with written notification of risks for dismissal and conditions for maintaining academic standing) with good follow up (15).

The most common reasons for lawsuits by students are their efforts to (1) discharge or rearrange debts incurred for medical education, (2) dispute National Health Service Corps (p. 447) clinical assignments, or (3) challenge admission (to medical school), dismissal, and readmission decisions (16, 17).

PHYSICIAN AS EXPERT WITNESS

There are many situations in which you may be an expert witness: when you testify for a patient you have treated, consult to a party in a suit, or are a court-appointed expert. As an expert, you may give your opinion. Technically other witnesses may testify only about facts, not opinions. However, nonexpert witnesses are often asked for their rationales for actions. Expert status is based on education, knowledge, and experience (18). Criminal defendants may also be entitled to expert witnesses, as they are to an attorney, even if they cannot afford them (19). Prepare for testifying by familiarizing yourself with the record, the issues, and often the pertinent literature. Physician testimony in depositions and in court is detailed elsewhere (18).

COMPETENCE

Competence of all citizens is presumed, and declaration of incompetence can only be made by a court. But you may be consulted by a court in a competency issue, and clinically you must assess (not declare) whether patients

Table 34.1. Behavioral Capacity and The Law

Behavioral Capacity	Legal Issue	Legal Standard	Comments
Testamentary capacity	Making a will	Person knows he or she is making a will; knows nature and extent of property; knows heirs (natural objects of bounty)	Must be free of duress
Incompetence/incapacity	Managing personal affairs and property	Capable of performing functions in question	Trend towards limited (vs. total) guardianship
Testimonial capacity	Being a witness	Knows meaning of oath (to tell truth); remembers the events in question; able to communicate	Special considerations for children
Involuntary hospitalization	Remaining at liberty	Because of mental illness, dangerous to self or others, *or* unable to care or solicit care for self	Different standards in different localities
Right to treatment	Treatment vs. detention	Evidence of adequate professional care	Also applies to criminal cases
Right to refuse treatment	Involuntary treatment	Dangerousness vs. personal autonomy; able to make a reasonable choice vs. impaired by mental illness	Applies to involuntary hospitalization also
To stand trial	To be tried	Knows nature and consequences of charges; able to participate cooperatively in his defense	Not identical with insanity defense
Defense of insanity	Lack of guilt owing to insanity	*McNaghten*: at time of offense, did not know nature, consequences, and wrongness of act; Irresistable impulse: at time of offense, could not conform conduct to requirements of law; American Law Institute (A.L.I.) Code: not a habitual offender *and* meets McNaghten *or* irresistable impulse standard; *Durham*: offense was the product of a mental illness	Different standards in different states; most use A.L.I. or McNaghten

meet competency standards. *Legal standards of competent mental functioning vary according to the legal issue.* Incompetence for trial differs from incompetence for managing one's affairs or consenting to a treatment. When the term incompetence is used, ask "incompetent for what?" Legal standards for competence are covered in Table 34.1. The following case demonstrates the confusion regarding incompetence.

A senior psychiatric resident was consulted by the surgical service. A 78-year-old diabetic woman who had impaired arterial circulation to her lower extremities refused surgery. She indicated that she was willing to bear the consequences, ultimately loss of the limb and even death. The surgical resident wanted the psychiatric resident to "declare" the woman incompetent. Although alert and not demonstrating obvious impairment of cognition, she

was clinically depressed. The psychiatric resident correctly indicated that he had no legal authority to declare the woman incompetent, and though he might initiate procedures for involuntary psychiatric hospitalization, this would not authorize surgery.

Ultimately that authority had to come from the court after a petition and hearing for incompetency and (if the patient is declared incompetent in court) appointment of a guardian. Because no relatives were available, the hospital administrator was contacted and an emergency petition was initiated. During that process, the patient, after further consultation with the psychiatric resident, agreed to surgery. But was she competent to give informed consent for the surgery? In this or similar situations the record should describe why the patient can give informed consent. If the patient is unable to consent but there is no emergency, guardianship will probably be required.

35/Health Care Financing and Delivery

Freda C. Lewis-Hall, M.D., Frederick S. Sierles, M.D., and Jennifer J. Conway

---

OBJECTIVES

GENERAL OBJECTIVE: Given proposed reforms of America's health care system, explain the need for and intended consequences of those reforms.

SPECIFIC OBJECTIVES:

1. Explain why the achievements of American medicine and its current health care delivery system are paradoxical.
2. Describe the trends in national health care expenditures since 1965.
3. State some of the major causes of those trends.
4. Explain the significant consequences of rising health care costs.
5. Discuss the major cost-containment strategies that have been implemented within the last 20 years and why they have not been particularly successful in controlling the rate of growth in health care spending.
6. Summarize why Canadian and several European systems of health care are being considered as models for reforming America's health care system.
7. Summarize the structure of America's health care delivery system.

THE PARADOX OF AMERICAN MEDICINE

Modern medicine, to which the United States has made many important contributions, is one of the 20th century's greatest achievements. General health and life expectancy in most industrialized nations are greatly improved as a result of such medical miracles as antibiotics, vaccines, organ transplantation, and life-saving drugs. In America, these great innovations have produced a health care system whose technological innovations and high quality are matched by few other countries. Americans have become accustomed to an exceptional standard of care, access without delays, and the freedom to choose their doctor and place of care.

Intruding ominously on this proud heritage is a U.S. health care system whose spending is spinning out of control. As much as we have defeated plagues and diseases and learned how to make spare parts for everything except the brain, Americans have created a system of health care whose costs within the last two decades have grown alarmingly out of proportion to the care its citizens receive and to what the nation spends on other goods and services. For millions of Americans—the poor, minorities, and, increasingly, the working and middle classes—health care is no longer the basic right we have come to expect, but instead has become a two-tiered system that discriminates on the basis of ability to pay.

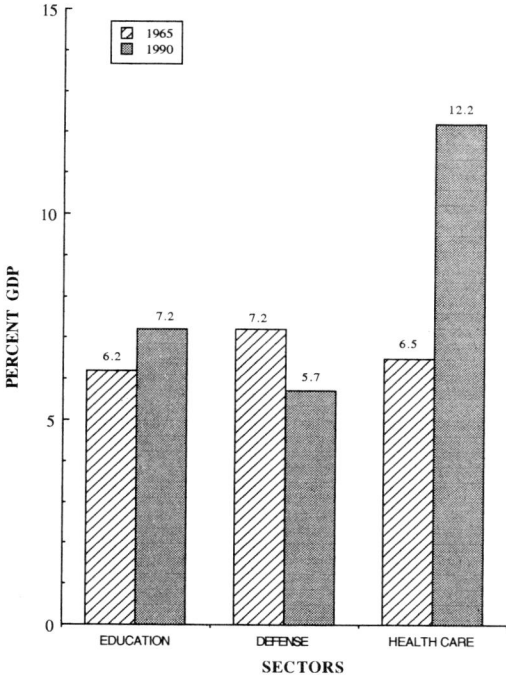

Figure 35.1. Education, defense, and health care as a share of the gross domestic product (1965 and 1990).

AMERICA'S HIGH COST OF HEALTH CARE

The United States spends more per capita for health care ($2,566 in 1990) than any other industrialized nation at the same time that nearly 26 million adults and 10 million children are uninsured and lack access to basic medical and dental care (1–3). The United States and South Africa are the only two industrialized nations in the world without universal health coverage for their citizens.

In 1990, America's total spending for medical care topped $666 billion, or $1.8 billion a day. These expenditures, the second largest annual increase in three decades, were 10.5% higher than in 1989 and consumed 12.2% of the country's gross domestic product (GDP) (1). In 1965, the nation spent $41.6 billion on health care (6.5% of the GDP). Predictions are that if current laws and practices remain unchanged, the United States will spend $1.6 trillion for health care by the year 2000, consuming 16.4% of the GDP (4). Indications of how disproportionate health care has become as a share of the U.S. economy can be seen in Figure 35.1. Whereas in 1965, health care was roughly comparable to education and defense as a share of the GDP, in 1990 a very different picture prevailed (5, 6), with education rising slightly, defense declining, and health care skyrocketing.

The United States faces a crisis in health care financing. Government health programs are in serious financial difficulty. The trust fund for Medicare, Part A, the federal hospital insurance program, is projected to be exhausted by 2005 (3). Federal spending for health care as a percent of the government's total expenditures rose from less than 5% in 1965 to 15.1% in 1990, and is projected to rise to 24.1% by the year 2000 (4). State-run Medicaid programs (which are funded jointly by the federal and state governments) also are in jeopardy, barely able to help the 40% of the poor currently financed under the program; in 1980, Medicaid financed 65% of the poor (3). The U.S. Congressional Budget Office predicts that real Medicaid expenditures will increase by almost 120% between 1990 and 1996, consuming 7% of all federal spending on health care by 1996 compared to 3% in 1990 (7).

Employers, who finance most of the nation's private health insurance, have been on a collision course with health care providers for at least the last decade as employers' payments for health care, 14% of aggregate after-tax profits in 1965, *exceed* after-tax profits today (8). The prospect of persistent, double-digit increases in medical costs has forced many companies to reduce health benefits to their employees and in some cases trim their workforce. At the same time, insurance companies continue to raise premiums—which are out of reach to most small employers and therefore their employees—and growing numbers of Americans worry about affording their coverage, losing it, or not being able to pay for truly catastrophic medical expenses.

CAUSES OF HEALTH CARE INFLATION

It is said that there are two kinds of prices in America today: regular prices, which seem to follow some reasonable process of supply and demand, and health care prices, which follow their own perverse course. Since Medicare was enacted in 1965, and the federal government began reimbursing providers on a fee-for-service basis (i.e., a method of paying providers in which each service carries a fee), health care expenditures have grown more rapidly than the rest of the economy. There are many reasons why health care costs keep rising, some considerably more confounding than others.

Natural economic factors such as general inflation, rising income levels, the introduction of new services and new technologies, and sociodemographic changes in the population explain a reasonable amount of this increase. For example, projections are that as the fastest growing segment of society, America's elderly will account for 21.8% of the population by the year 2050 (in 1990, they represented 12.7%) (9). Because the likelihood of illness increases with age and the elderly are the heaviest users of health services, their increasing numbers will consume a greater percentage of public and private sector health care costs.

Other, more difficult explanations are embedded in the failure of the health care market to perform the way markets for other goods and services do. In short, rather than being competitive and allowing the market to work naturally, the health care market shields consumers from the impact of their purchasing decisions. Additional factors that contribute to rising health care costs include physician-induced demand for medical services, the medical malpractice environment, and administrative costs.

Consumer Incentives and Employee Health Benefits

Historically the consumer, or patient, has not been an active participant in the health care decision-making process, leaving decisions over seemingly complex medical treatment to providers (10). Moreover, insurance, typically offered through the employer (by Blue Cross and Blue Shield plans, health maintenance organizations, and other forms of managed care) or the government (by Medicare and Medicaid) (p. 452), traditionally has carried little or no out-of-pocket costs for consumers. Unlike some government entitlement programs (e.g., Medicaid and Aid to Families with Dependent Children), Medicare is not needs based, or "means tested"; Medicare premiums and deductibles are the same regardless of a person's income. As a result, all taxpayers end up supporting the affluent who receive the same coverage under Medicare as the poor and middle class. Of all the federal entitlement programs today, only $1 of every $5 goes to the poor; the rest goes to the middle class and wealthy (11).

Some health economists (3, 12–15) believe that tax subsidies to insurance, which exempt employers' premium payments from taxation, and generous medical insurance in which employees have minimal or no copayments or cost-sharing, are an important cause of persistently high rates of increase in health care spending. Tax subsidies historically have tended to warp the insurance choice process, resulting for consumers in the purchase of coverage that is excessive and distorted. That is, cost sharing affects the demand for medical services. When people choose generous coverage knowing that premiums are tax free or that cost sharing is low, there is a tendency to overuse services. In a major health insurance study conducted over a number of years in the 1970s (14, 15), researchers found that patients used more medical services and that costs for care were 50% higher when their insurance paid the entire bill.

Physician-Induced Demand

If we recall that patients historically have been relatively passive participants in their medical care decisions, leaving those decisions to their doctors, we realize how significant a role doctors play in influencing the demand for medical services (10). In a conventional economic market, consumers actively participate in their purchasing decisions and influence market patterns. In health care, providers traditionally have influenced those patterns; patients simply do not know what laboratory tests or procedures are important or even necessary (although current trends suggest this is beginning to change).

Recent studies have shown that when efforts are made to control physicians' fees as a cost-containment strategy, physicians compensate by providing additional services (16–18). For example, in studying patterns of physician spending over a three-year period (1984–1986) in which Congress imposed a fee freeze on Medicare services to doctors, it was found that significant increases in surgical procedures and diagnostic tests resulted in Medicare spending 30% more for physician services by the end of the freeze than when the freeze began (17).

The 1989 landmark reform of Medicare, Part B, the federal Supplementary Medical Insurance program that pays for physicians' services (p. 445), has fundamentally changed the "customary, prevailing, and reasonable" (CPR) approach that has been the health insurance industry's payment standard for physicians for the past 30 years. Rather than basing payment on a combination of individual physician charges and prevailing geographic rates, physicians will now be paid a fixed amount on the basis of a predetermined schedule of fees. This "resource-based relative value scale" will be based on the relative resource consumption of various services adjusted according to the physician's geographic location. This reform is expected to provide Congress with an opportunity to observe whether and how much physicians actually increase their volume of services (19). Numerous other studies have shown that physicians also order unnecessary tests (20–26), charge excessively for those tests (prices may vary up to 17-fold for the same lab test) (27, 28), overuse expensive technology (29), and perform unnecessary procedures (widespread geographic variations

have been found in hysterectomy rates, prostatectomies, tonsillectomies, and other procedures as a result of physician practice patterns, not patient characteristics) (30).

Medical Malpractice

Although malpractice insurance premiums represent a small share of costs for physicians in many specialties, practitioners in some specialties pay over $100,000 annually for those premiums. Medical malpractice premiums cost physicians $4.7 billion in 1987, typically account for 15% of physicians' fees for services (31, 32), and contribute markedly to inflation.

Malpractice litigation has made notorious the concept of "defensive medicine," which technically refers to decision making by doctors to reduce legal liability. Some doctors interpret the concept to mean ordering needless tests or charting unnecessarily, missing the point that the best protection against a damaging lawsuit is good diagnosis and treatment, not excessive testing and charting. Some analysts argue for the social benefits of malpractice as a form of deterrence and quality control (33), and that defensive medicine deters malpractice and leads physicians to spend more time with patients and maintain more extensive medical records (34). Perhaps so, but this underplays the fact that for physicians, the satisfactions of skillful patient care (e.g., patient health and appreciation, intellectual challenge, professional reputation, and referrals from colleagues) have always been powerful reinforcers.

In some ways, the malpractice crisis has reduced the quality of care. It has caused many physicians to perform fewer or no high-risk procedures by refusing to treat certain patients for whom a poor outcome is more likely, and it has caused others to retire. In other important ways, the health care system appears capricious: less than 2% of medical negligence leads to a malpractice claim, and health care providers are rarely identified and held accountable for substandard care (35). In a better malpractice system, many more cases of negligence that lead to injury would result in successful malpractice claims, and most claims would be based on injury from actual malpractice. An even better way to prevent negligence would be improved peer or supervisory review of physician practice.

Administrative Costs

Health care is not only expensive but also inefficient and increasingly bureaucratic. Health care administrative costs in the United States are estimated to consume 20%–25% of total spending on health care, or between $400–$500 per capita (36). In Canada (whose health care system is being considered as a possible model of reform [p. 446] because it shares common features with ours), administrative costs absorb 8.4%–11% of the country's health care bill, or approximately $120–$160 per capita (36). American physicians spend 4.4% of their time in billing compared to Canadian physicians' 1% (36). In the United States, considerable overhead costs are spent on paperwork to comply with regulations for insurance reimbursement (37, 38). An average patient visit to a physician's office, for example, generates 10 pieces of paper related to billing requirements (39). Instructions for a one-page billing form consume 35 pages in one state's Medicaid manual, a process so convoluted that most payment denials are caused by problems with paperwork, not patient eligibility or health (39, 40).

In addition to being inflationary, bureaucracy is dysfunctional. It steals time from direct patient care, lacks intellectual challenge, and threatens physicians' autonomy in medical decision making. This condition, particularly perverse in some managed care systems, infuriates doctors. "In managed care's arsenal of cost-control weaponry, probably none is more potent—except for restricting hospital admission—than superseding the physician's autonomy by a managerial-review process in which armies of clerks, administrators, auditors, form processors, peer reviewers, functionaries, and technocrats of every description insinuate themselves into a complex system that

authorizes, delivers, and pays for medical service" (37:608).

CONSEQUENCES OF HEALTH CARE INFLATION

The greatest consequence of America's rising health care costs is a two-tiered system of health care that closes out persons who are unable to pay (41). Because health care costs have skyrocketed within the last decade, that inability to pay is no longer a problem only for America's poor. It is now increasingly a problem as well for its working and middle classes who, if unemployed, self-employed, or working for a small employer, cannot afford basic coverage (42). Many employees who are insured cannot afford rising copayments, lose their coverage if they become unemployed, or are denied insurance because of a preexisting medical condition (insurers refer to this group as high risk). This latter insurance industry trend has created a phenomenon known as "job lock" in which employees are locked into one job (a basic violation of a person's economic liberty) because a preexisting condition prevents them from receiving insurance coverage under a new employer (43).

Another indictment of America's wasteful, expensive health care system is the discrepancy between the health statistics for minorities, many of whom are poor, and those of the general population (44, 45). Life expectancy for black men is 65.2 years (6.1 years less than white men) and for black women is 73.5 years (4.8 years less than white women). The infant mortality rate for blacks is more than twice that for whites (17.9 per 1,000 live births vs. 8.6/1,000) (46). In Harlem, the rate of survival for men beyond age 40 years is lower than in Bangladesh (47). The health indices for immigrants and migrant workers also are disproportionately high (45). (In countries that have universal access to health care, everyone receives care, citizen, immigrant, and visitor alike.) The health care system, although an important factor, is not solely responsible for these disparities; health indices are influenced by socioeconomic status and education as well as access (46, 48).

Because America's poor are more apt to be uninsured (49–51), they are likelier to be ill than the general population. They tend to seek care later in their illness, to need hospital care when ill, and to be sicker and require longer stays when hospitalized (52). The poor and uninsured are less apt to seek care and more apt to seek it in the public sector and in costly settings (53). For example, most of the nation's medically indigent are treated in hospital emergency rooms (ERs) rather than in outpatient settings, a pattern largely responsible for much of the nation's current severe problem with ER overcrowding (54). Many analysts cite this overcrowing as an important example of the need for health care reform.

For patients who receive charity care in public hospitals, as well as in for-profit non-teaching hospitals, mortality rates are higher, even when the patient diagnosis and demographic characteristics are accounted for (55). Moreover, as stated earlier, Medicaid's increasingly limited coverage of the poor and its meager reimbursement to physicians and hospitals for indigent care tend to discourage providers from treating the poor and the poor from seeking care (44, 56–59).

COST-CONTAINMENT STRATEGIES

Within the last 20 years a number of public and private sector strategies to control U.S. health care costs have been implemented. Their lack of success in controlling the rate of growth in the nation's overall health care costs testifies to how complex the problem is. The numerous strategies have succeeded in doing primarily three things: (1) increasing the role and responsibility of consumers in the health care process by raising their out-of-pocket costs (now a standard feature of most employee health care plans and Medicare); (2) establishing managed care and utilization review plans as an integral part of the health care system (health maintenance organizations, the most well-known managed care

strategy, have disproportionately high administrative costs as explained earlier [36] and are not particularly effective in holding down the rate of increase in costs [60]); and (3) regulating the health care industry through provider price controls, which have succeeded in controlling some prices only to force others to increase through the practice of increasing volume and shifting costs from services priced lower or set at a fixed rate to services or procedures priced higher (17, 61). This is sometimes referred to as the "balloon" effect: in squeezing costs at one end, costs balloon at the other end, so that overall costs are not reduced, simply shifted.

Several federal reforms enacted over the last 20 years are particularly notable for fundamentally affecting how the nation's health care delivery system is managed and, in most instances, financed.

In an effort to control mounting health care utilization by providers following enactment of Medicare, Congress passed the Professional Standards and Review Organization Act (PSRO) in 1972. Although the Act sought to establish a national utilization review program and set of uniform standards for necessary and appropriate care, extreme variability across states in their standards of practice and performance rendered the system largely ineffective.

In 1973 Congress passed the Health Maintenance Organization Development Act, which encouraged the creation of more HMOs to foster increased competition and greater efficiency in the health care system and to promote the notion that prepaid practice plans supported preventive care. (The first HMO dates to 1910; by the time President Richard Nixon signed the 1973 Act, only about 30 HMOs were operating in the U.S. By 1975 there were 166 HMOs serving 5.8 million enrollees; in 1991, 34.1 million members were enrolled in 556 HMOs [62]).

The HMO Act of 1973 stimulated competition as a mechanism for controlling health care costs, and several studies have shown that HMOs are effective in controlling costs by reducing hospitalization and unnecessary laboratory tests (61, 63, 64). What HMOs have not done, as stated earlier, is to control the rate of increase or growth in health care costs; HMO costs are increasing at the same rate as or faster than traditional indemnity plans (65).

Through the 1982 Tax Equity and Fiscal Responsibility Act and Title VI of the Social Security Amendments of 1983 which authorized prospective payment for inpatient hospital services, Congress enacted stricter controls over Medicare reimbursement for inpatient costs. Passage of prospective payment in 1983, in which hospitals were reimbursed a fixed price (rather than the customary cost-based price) per diagnosis-related disease group (DRG), represents the most significant change to the Medicare program since its enactment in 1965.

Medicare's prospective payment system (PPS) enabled the federal government to predict and control Medicare expenditures more readily and provided hospitals with financial incentives to operate more efficiently. Although the DRG system saves costs in the short run, some studies report poorer outcomes for patients, especially the elderly, under the system (66–68). To monitor quality and protect against potential abuses, Congress created the Peer Review Organization (PRO) program in 1984. The PRO program arose from the failure of the old PSRO program to address Medicare's vulnerability to paying for inappropriate patient care and patients' vulnerability to lower quality care. (Under PPS, hospitals could have an incentive to increase admissions as a way of increasing their payments, to increase readmissions by not performing all procedures in a single admission, and to classify inappropriately a diagnosis to boost their payments and reduce inpatient services that might affect the patient's quality of care—all a form of "gaming" the system.) Many PROs today are transformed PSROs with much greater responsibility for comprehensive medical review that focuses on delivering high-quality care (69).

In 1989 Congress passed the second most significant reform since Medicare's enactment. Within the Omnibus Budget Reconcili-

ation Act of 1989 was a provision that created a resource-based physician fee schedule and set limits on the amount physicians may charge patients above that fee schedule. Implementation of the Medicare Fee Schedule for physicians under Medicare, Part B, began in January 1992 and is scheduled to be fully implemented by 1996 (70).

PROPOSALS FOR REFORM

As rapidly rising costs buy less care for fewer Americans, a growing number of health care legislators and policy makers, industry leaders, employers, and consumer groups have called for national health reform (44, 71–77). Despite numerous calls for change and for national political leadership on the issue since at least the last half of the 1980s, national health reform did not move to the top of the nation's political agenda (78, 79) until the November 1991 state elections (although the issue had been extensively debated in Congress and a number of legislative proposals drafted in the several years before). In Pennsylvania's U.S. Senate race, Democratic Senator Harris Wofford soundly defeated then U.S. Attorney General Richard Thornburgh. Senator Wofford's historic win, attributed to his campaign message that the richest nation in the world should not ignore the health needs of its uninsured and underinsured, abruptly reversed President George Bush's plans to avoid addressing national health reform until at least after the 1992 presidential election, if at all. Within 3 months of Senator Wofford's election, President Bush released his long-awaited health reform plan—in time to make it a 1992 campaign issue. His plan joined what would become more than 70 reform proposals introduced by members of the 102nd Congress. (The sheer volume of legislative proposals introduced that term itself epitomizes the social, political, and economic morass that the American health care system has become.)

Although the 70-odd proposals differ in how the health care system would be administratively structured, in the degree of government versus private sector control, and in the degree of public responsibility, most fall into one of three basic reform strategies: *(1)* incremental changes (President Bush's strategy), which favor a series of market-based reforms (e.g., tax credits, insurance market reform, tort reform, and public health care program changes) enacted over time that preserve and improve on the existing health care and health insurance systems; *(2)* employer-based programs, which require that all employers buy insurance for their employees or pay to enroll them in a public insurance program (known legislatively as "play or pay"); and *(3)* a single-payer system (as in Canada), the most sweeping of reforms, in which all current insurance programs would be channeled through one payer—a kind of federal reserve system that would oversee and monitor health care costs—and insurance would not depend on employment status (80).

In considering various reforms, U.S. policy makers have studied the Canadian national health insurance system and several European systems of health care (e.g., Germany, France, Switzerland), all of which have been relatively successful in controlling the growth in their health expenditures (81, 82). They have accomplished this while providing universal access and achieving life expectancy and infant mortality rates that are at least as good as those in America, and in some cases better. Although each universal health insurance system has its imperfections and is struggling with the same cost pressures as the United States, all are being looked to as models for reforming America's system of care (83–86).

For example, the United States has placed great emphasis on utilization control to reduce health care costs (e.g., PSROs and PROs), but other nations have maintained much lower spending levels without reducing utilization. In Canada and most European nations, inpatient admissions rates, average lengths of hospital stay, and physician visit rates are generally higher than those in the United States. As a result, U.S. policy makers have focused their attention on the way these nations pay for health care services. Indeed, much of the dif-

ference in health care spending levels between the United States and its European counterparts has been attributed to the presence of a single payer or united group of payers for health services. These highly influential payers have been able to control overall spending by forcing health care providers to accept global budgets and fee schedules. It is for this reason that a single-payer system is so appealing as a possible reform strategy. (It is not clear, however, whether a single-payer system would minimize high overhead costs; over half of existing paperwork in the United States is provider accountability to various government and private agencies for services performed.)

The crucial difference between the health care systems in the United States and other countries is that our values of pluralism, individualism, freedom of choice, a private, free-market economy, and collective bargaining do not favor a single, strong, centralized system of control (87–90). Canadians and Europeans place such great value on public health and equal access to care that they are willing to accept a centralized, often government-controlled system, to pay considerable shares of their annual wages for that coverage, to tolerate queues and waiting lists, and to travel sometimes great distances for medical treatment. It is not at all clear whether Americans are yet willing to make such sacrifices and accept the inevitable compromises necessary to benefit the greater good. It also is not clear whether there is sufficient political courage to balance or, if necessary, override the concerns of the many powerful vested interests that seek to maintain their hegemony.

Whatever is decided, health care is clearly one of America's most important domestic issues for the remainder of the 20th century and beyond. Not to confront it, or to do so with only piecemeal, partisan solutions that lack political courage and social vision, is to leave a terrible legacy that jeopardizes America's future and shames the great achievements of American medicine. For medicine and its practitioners, perhaps the greatest challenge lies in deciding what their

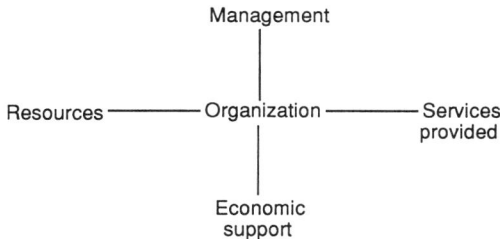

Figure 35.2. Components of the health care system.

roles and responsibilities are in reshaping America's health care system. No matter what the mandated reforms, values and priorities can never be legislated.

U.S. HEALTH CARE SYSTEM STRUCTURE

Health care systems have five components: resources, organization, management, financing, and provision of services (Fig. 35.2) (91).

Resources

Health care resources consist of manpower, facilities, commodities, knowledge, and information. Health manpower produces, deploys, and uses the other resources and functions of the system. The U.S. health care industry employs over 8 million persons (excluding housekeepers and kitchen and maintenance workers), approximately 54% of whom work in hospitals, 16% in nursing and personal care facilities, 11% in physicians' offices, 6% in dentists' offices, 0.8% in chiropractors' offices, and 12% in "other" sites (92, 93). The characteristics of the various health occupations are described in Table 35.1.

PHYSICIANS

In 1950, the United States had about 220,000 physicians (medical and osteopathic), which at the time was perceived as an undersupply. To achieve a better balance between supply and need, in 1959 the federal Bane Commission recommended that medical schools increase their number of yearly graduates until they reached a threshold of 11,000 by 1975 (92, 94). In the early 1970s, most ob-

servers still perceived an undersupply (95), although others thought the problem was less one of numbers than of physician overspecialization and geographic maldistribution (96–99). Medical school expansion (from 85 schools in 1960 to 127 in 1980 [now numbering 126]), together with increased class sizes in many schools (100), overshot the mark suggested by the Bane Commission, producing 15,000 graduates in 1975 and peaking at 16,327 in 1984 (92). Lefkowitz (101) observes that to have anticipated and dealt with the perceived oversupply would have required careful national planning—hard to do in this country. Moreover, large numbers of foreign/international medical graduates (IMGs) came to the United States to practice. In 1992, about 643,000 physicians were practicing in the United States; 615,000 MDs, 27,600 DOs, and about 139,000 IMGs, including 8,300 graduates of Canadian medical schools (102, 103).

Some attempt to resolve the maldistribution was made through the National Health Service Corps (NHSC), which provides scholarships to health professions students in return for service proportional to the years of medical school scholarship aid. The NHSC physician serves in federally designed health manpower shortage and medically underserved areas—usually rural and inner city hospitals. The scholarship money is jointly provided by the federal government and the community in which the graduate is placed (92, 104–106). Although the NHSC has influenced many of its physicians to settle and practice in rural areas (106), the problem of maldistribution remains, not only in rural areas but also in underserved urban areas, because of federal cutbacks to the program since the mid-1980s (107) and lack of interest among physicians in serving in NHSC-designated areas.

Most observers today still believe the nation lacks enough physicians (108–113), although the view is controversial (114, 115). The 1980 Graduate Medical Education National Advisory Council (GMENAC) Report predicted that the United States would reach an oversupply of physicians by 1990 in all but

Table 35.1. Characteristics of Various Health Care Occupations

Discipline	Number (in thousands)	Nature of Work	Conditions/Hours	Training	1986 Median Net Income
Licensed Practical Nurses	631	Care for the ill under the direction of physicians and registered nurses	40 hrs/wk; day evening and night shifts in hosps.	Licensure state-approved programs	$15,600
Registered Nurses	1,406	Care for the ill and maintain health in a variety of settings	40-60 hrs/wk; 66% in hospitals, less than 10% in others	License, Asso, Degree, Bachelor's	$23,900
Health Services Managers	274	Plan, organize and coordinate the delivery of health care	Long hours; 55% in hospitals, 17% in nursing homes	Ph.D, Master's, Bachelor's or Associates	$81,000
Psychologists	110	Study emotional, cognitive or social aspects of human behavior	Dependent on specialty, in education, hosps. and government	Ph.D., Psy.D., private practice licensure	$39,500
Social Workers	365	Direct counselling or referrals for people requiring help with life circumstances.	40 hrs/wk; 40% in state or county government	Ph.D., Master's or Bachelor's. 41 States require licensure	$23,500
Speech and Language Therapists	45	Diagnose and treat impairments of speech and language	60% school systems, elementary through university	Master's in Speech Language	$25,000
Occupational Therapists	29	Teach people to develop and maintain skills in daily living	40 hrs/wk; Private practice and rehabilitation	Bachelor's	$26,000
Physical Therapists	61	Aid in restoring functional mobility, relieving pain and limiting disability	35% hospitals, 20% private practice, 14% nursing homes	License and Bachelor's	$22,000
Recreational Therapists	29	Leisure activities in persons who are disabled	60% nursing homes, psychiatric and rehab hospitals	Certification Nat'l Council Therapeutic Recreation	$19,000
Dentists	151	Diagnose and treat problems of the teeth and tissues of the mouth	42 hrs/wk and some evenings and weekends	Licensure DDS, DDM	$59,000
Dental Hygienists	87	Provide preventive dental care/perform X-Rays	35 hrs/wk including evening and weekends	Licensure-written board exam	$17,500
Podiatrists	13	Treat diseases of the foot	37 hrs/wk; private practice	Licensure 4-year podiatric residency	$63,000
Dieticians/Nutritionists	40	Food selection and preparation; weight loss strategies	40 hrs/wk; hospitals and nursing homes	Bachelor's Registration in American Dietetic Association	$20,400
Pharmacists	151	Provide information and dispense medications	Community pharmacies	License Bachelor's Pharm B Pharm D	$31,000
Physician Assistants	26	Perform tasks related to diagnosis and treatment under a physician's supervision	38% physicians offices, 38% hospitals, 20% clinics	Complete accredited program	$23,400
Laboratory Technicians	239	Perform clinical laboratory tests	365 days/year; day, evening and night shifts	Bachelor's, special training	$20,000

five specialties: child psychiatry, emergency medicine, preventive medicine, general psychiatry, and hematology/oncology (114). No 1990 GMENAC follow-up occurred.

Each specialty has a typical frequency and intensity of visits and annual income. Radiologists see the most patients per week (about 225), in low-intensity visits. Family physicians and pediatricians also see many patients (169 and 145 a week, respectively), at varying intensity. The fewest patients are seen by surgeons (107/wk) and psychiatrists (54/wk), but at the highest intensity per visit (procedural for surgeons, interpersonal for psychiatrists) (116). The highest incomes are in procedure-oriented specialties that have relatively little interpersonal contact and high malpractice premiums (93).

Because of a perceived physician oversupply, high tuition costs and malpractice premiums, and the encroachment of managed care, the number of medical school applicants fell from 32,893 in 1985 to 26,915 in 1989 (117). In 1991, the applicant pool increased again; whether this is a trend or an anomaly is uncertain.

High medical school tuition costs are a serious problem; 90% of medical students have loans, and the average student graduating in 1990 owed $46,224. During the 1980s for the first time ever, willingness to incur *huge* debts influenced students' choice of medical career. Loan repayment influences specialty choice and the quality of residency education. (Most resident physicians moonlight; before the 1980s only a minority did so.) The greatest debts are incurred by minority students, those most apt to practice in underserved minority communities (106).

HEALTH CARE FACILITIES

Hospitals

In 1989, there were 6,720 hospitals in the United States: 5,455 community (2,958 urban, 2,497 rural) and 1,265 noncommunity hospitals. Of the community hospitals, 3,220 are nongovernment, not-for-profit voluntary, 1,466 are public, and 769 are for-profit, investor-owned.

Noncommunity hospitals consist of 340 federal hospitals (veterans and military), 741 nonfederal psychiatric hospitals, and 184 specialty hospitals for TB and other respiratory diseases, long-term care, and short-term care (118).

Community hospitals are defined as nonfederal, short-term urban and rural hospitals (excluding psychiatric hospitals, those that treat alcoholism and chemical dependency, and hospital units of institutions such as prisons and college infirmaries) that provide acute care to the public. In 1989 they accounted for 82% of all hospitals and 92% of all hospital admissions in the United States. The average community hospital then had 171 beds, an average length of stay (ALOS) of 7.2 days, and an occupancy rate of 66%. The average ratio of full-time employees to patients is 3.8 to 1 (118, 119).

In 1989, hospitals reported 286 million outpatient visits. This 6% increase over the previous year (whose 10% increase over 1987 rates was the highest rate of growth in outpatient use in more than a decade) reflects the trend toward greater use of outpatient care since enactment of prospective payment in 1983. Outpatient services currently are not subject to federal PPS reimbursement policies. More than eight of every ten community hospitals have organized outpatient service departments. Since 1980, 440 community hospitals have ceased to provide inpatient care services (118).

The 2,497 rural community hospitals in 1989 accounted for one fifth of all hospital inpatient days and outpatient visits and nearly one half of all community hospitals (118). Most (71%) have fewer than 100 beds. The rural hospital is a vital link in a community's health care system and economy. As a major, if not sole, source of health services, its presence is critical in being able to attract and retain physicians and other health care professionals to the area. Rural hospitals since 1984 have, however, suffered serious financial difficulties because of changes in rural economies and distortions in the standardized amounts paid to all urban and rural community hospitals under the federal government's original PPS policy. Because more urban than rural hospitals can better afford the latest developments in medical technology, rural hospitals have also experienced rapid declines in admissions. In 1989, 35% of rural hospitals reported overall financial losses. Their closure rate has increased from an average of 14 (0.5% of rural hospitals) per year between 1980 and 1985 to an average of more than 40 (1.6%) per year between 1986 and 1989 (120). Between 1980 and 1989, patient days fell 32% (vs. 13% for urban hospitals), the number of beds declined by 17%, and occupancy rates fell from 69% in 1980 to 57% in 1989 (118). Although steps are being taken to correct PPS payment inequities between urban and rural hospitals, financial difficulties are expected to continue to plague rural hospitals somewhat more disproportionately than urban hospitals for at least as long as the U.S. economic outlook remains unstable (120).

Federal hospitals serve veterans through Veterans Affairs medical centers, military personnel, native Americans, including native Alaskans, and merchant seamen. In 1989, the ALOS in federal hospitals was 14 days (118, 119). The VA hospitals have a total annual budget of $11 billion, which changes minimally each year (121). About 15% of the 30 million U.S. veterans use the VA system; the typical user has a disability acquired on active military duty and is poor and male (95%). Those who use the VA prefer it to care in community hospitals under Medicare and Medicaid coverage out of loyalty and because it is cheaper (Medicare requires a 20% copayment). Most VA hospitals are affiliated with medical schools (102 of the 126 schools), a strong association that began after World War II when the VA faced an extreme shortage of doctors to care for the nation's 100,000 veterans then hospitalized. Extensive teaching and VA-funded research occur in VA hospitals. The system is viewed by many as a national asset and cost-effective model for national health insurance; others perceive it as a "sacred cow" with redundancies and inefficiencies (121, 122).

Teaching hospitals are nonfederal members of the Council of Teaching Hospitals (COTH) of the Association of American Medical Colleges (AAMC). These hospitals provide more care to the poor, free care, and specialized services than community hospitals; they also have more outpatient visits and surgical procedures and are more apt to be located in cities (119).

When municipal hospitals are strongly affiliated with medical schools (e.g., New York's Bellevue, Chicago's Cook County, Los Angeles County General), technical medical quality tends to be superior to that of the average community hospital (119). Urban public hospitals provide much of the care of the poor, the uninsured, and persons who have special social problems, including 5 million undocumented aliens (119, 123). Many local government hospitals suffer, however, from poor surroundings, amenities, overall staffing, buildings, equipment, budgeting, and management, compounded by patronage and a cumbersome civil service system (123).

Long-Term Care

Long-term care (LTC) services are "rehabilitative, medical, and supportive social services of various kinds for people who have functional limitations or chronic health conditions and who need ongoing health care or assistance with normal activities of daily living" (124:ix). Services include nursing home care and a range of home health and community-based services.

About 75% of LTC is unpaid or informal care given by family members (especially spouses, daughters, and daughters-in-law) and friends (124–126). Formal, paid care for services received through the health care market amounted to $57.8 billion in 1988, 77% or $44.2 billion of which was for nursing home care, and $13.6 billion for home and community-based care (124). Payments from private sources were 47%, all but 4% of which was out-of-pocket; the balance (53%) was from government (federal, state, and local) through Medicare, Medicaid, and Veterans Affairs programs (124). Between 38% and 40% of persons admitted to nursing homes in 1985 met costs primarily from their own income or assets; public programs contributed the balance (127). Only 1.9 million people carry private LTC insurance (128), which became available in the mid-1980s (largely because of Congressional and public pressure) and, with rare exception, remains a risky investment because generally too few services are covered at too high a price. Spending on LTC could triple over the next 30 years (129).

In 1986, the United States had 16,388 nursing homes, with an average of 92 beds and average occupancy rate of 92%. The 1.5 million residents of nursing or personal care homes are disproportionately female, 75% require another person's help with at least two activities of daily living, and about 40% suffer from dementia (124). The demand for LTC is expected to increase dramatically as the "baby boom" generation begins to reach age 65 after 2010. As death rates continue to decline, the elderly population is expected to become more concentrated in those aged 85 or older. As a percentage of the total population, this group is expected to increase from 1.3% in 1990 to 2.7% in 2030, reaching 5.1% in 2050 (124). Changing demographic trends will translate into a trebling of nursing home use between 1990 and 2050 (from 1.7 million persons in 1990 to 2.5 in 2010, 3.7 million in 2030, and 5.2 million in 2050) (124).

Other formal LTC services are home health care and community-based services, about which comprehensive data are limited. Estimates are that between 6,000 and 8,000 home health agencies provide skilled medical care for persons who have acute conditions rather than personal care for persons who have chronic conditions (124). Nearly 1,000 adult day care centers assist mainly elderly, functionally dependent, white, unmarried women while their caregivers are at work. Most centers serve an average of 20 clients a day for about $30 per person per day (124). About 1,500 hospice programs provide care for the terminally ill at a cost that is typically lower than traditional care (130).

Organization and Financing

Decision making in the health care system is pluralistically influenced by many interest groups (131, 132). This adds to the system's complexity and inability to move cohesively, as explained earlier in this chapter. Within the government, there are federal, state, and local agencies that finance and administer services. Numerous private sector professional associations and organizations also influence the system.

FEDERAL GOVERNMENT

The most influential federal health care agency is the Department of Health and Human Services (DHHS). A major division of DHHS is the Health Care Financing Administration (HCFA), which administers Medicare and Medicaid.

Medicare, which was enacted in 1965 and became effective July 1, 1966, is a federally administered program that provides hospital and medical insurance to persons aged 65 years and older, disabled persons under age 65 who receive cash benefits under Social Security or Railroad Retirement programs (the latter because the government took over the running of AMTRAK), and persons of all ages who require dialysis for chronic kidney disease (130).

Medicare, Part A, covers most hospital and some long-term care services, but *not* nursing home care; Part B covers most physician services (including second opinion consultations about the advisability of surgery), as well as some medications and durable equipment purchases or rentals. Medicare also pays for care of Medicare-eligible persons enrolled in HMOs or PPOs that have Medicare contracts, and for some ambulance services.

More than 6,300 hospitals participate under the Medicare Prospective Payment System (PPS). In 1989, 33.6 million persons were enrolled in Medicare (14.6 million men, 19 million women). The Health Care Financing Administration projects that by 2050, 69 million persons aged 65 years and over will be eligible for coverage, 15 million of whom will be over age 85 (133).

Medicaid, also enacted in 1965, covers 50 different state programs that fund health care for the poor. According to a variety of formulas, costs are borne jointly by states and the federal government. Medicaid recipients include low-income families with dependent children where one parent is absent or incapacitated, and the low-income aged and disabled. States vary widely in their granting of Medicaid eligibility, leaving millions of medically indigent residents who fall outside the safety net (50, 134).

The DHHS also administers the Public Health Service (PHS). The PHS, in turn, oversees a number of agencies, including the Centers for Disease Control, which oversees the control of communicable diseases; the Food and Drug Administration (FDA), which regulates the safety and efficacy of foods and drugs; the National Institutes of Health, a major source of research funding; the Indian Health Service, which serves more than 1 million Native Americans, including Alaskan natives, through 50 hospitals and 340 clinics (135); and the Alcohol, Drug Abuse, and Mental Health Administration.

Non-DHHS Cabinet-level agencies with health care functions include the Departments of Labor (workplace safety), Interior (mineworkers' health), Agriculture (farm workers' health and control of animal disease), Defense (health of active duty military and their families), Veterans Affairs (health of disabled veterans), Justice (federal prison system health), and Treasury (narcotics-related health issues).

STATE AND LOCAL GOVERNMENT

The public health programs of state health agencies and local public health departments can be divided into four primary program areas: personal health, environmental health, health resources, and laboratory services. In addition, the agencies perform general administrative and service functions. Not all states perform the same services. In some states, designated expenditures for mental health care may be controlled by a separate mental health agency. In 1989, 55 state health agencies (includes the District of Columbia, American Samoa, Guam, Puerto Rico, and the Virgin Islands) spent a total of $11.8 billion for their public health programs for maternal and child health, communicable diseases, handicapped children, dental health, chronic disease, mental health, state health agency-operated institutions, home health care, and services to special population groups (128). At the state level, 275 public psychiatric hospitals, with about 130,000 beds and a budget of $8 billion, employ 220,000 people (118). Because of the availability of neuroleptic drugs (p. 324) in the 1960s, the federal Community Mental Health Centers Act of 1963 supported massive deinstitutionalization of state mental hospitals in which residents were discharged into the community for care. States do not adequately fund community-based care, so that many mentally ill persons, including those discharged from state mental hospitals, receive inadequate or no care. Many of the deinstitutionalized mentally ill have become homeless.

States sponsor 73 of the 126 U.S. medical schools (136), many of which have affiliated state-operated community hospitals. State departments of registration and education (sometimes called departments of professional regulation) set standards for obtaining and maintaining state licenses.

There were nearly 3,000 local public health departments in 1989 (128). Many of these agencies, particularly in urban areas, face the same or worse budgetary woes as state governments in stretching increasingly scarce resources across a broader spectrum of increasingly costly needs. Urban public health departments are especially hard hit in their efforts to combat the plight of the urban poor, who are at high risk for such ills as infant mortality, child abuse, teen pregnancy, childrens' health care, substance abuse, AIDS, and mental health care (137).

PRIVATE SECTOR ORGANIZATIONS

Many private and professional associations and organizations influence the nation's health care system (in the Greater Washington, DC Metropolitan Area alone there are over 700 organizations involved in health affairs [138]). Several of the more prominent (but only the tip of the iceberg) medical associations are listed below.

The American Medical Association (AMA). Founded in 1847, the AMA is the most influential professional organization for physicians. It lobbies for the medical profession, sponsors conferences, and publishes several journals and other periodicals, including *JAMA (the Journal of the American Medical Association), Archives of Internal Medicine, Archives of General Psychiatry,* and *American Medical News.* It also oversees local medical societies, runs the Joint Commission on the Accreditation of Healthcare Organizations (JCAHO) which inspects hospitals every 2 years, and advises physicians on various issues.

The National Medical Association (NMA). The NMA provides for African-American physicians many of the services that the AMA provides its members; NMA members may also belong to the AMA or AMWA (below). Services include lobbying, publication of the *Journal of the National Medical Association,* support of the Student NMA, national conferences, and a variety of tutorial, legal, and counseling services for African-American medical students.

The American Medical Women's Association (AMWA). Women physicians who are members of AMWA (and may also be members of the above-named associations) receive many of the services that the AMA and NMA offer.

The Association of American Medical Colleges (AAMC). The AAMC publishes *Academic Medicine,* holds national conferences, provides workshops for medical school faculties, publishes a weekly news report, and performs medical school accreditation inspections for the Liaison Committee on Medical Education (LCME). Three departments work under AAMC's board of directors: the Council on Teaching Hospitals, the Council of Academic Societies, and the Council of Deans.

The National Board of Medical Examiners (NBME). A private corporation, NBME produces national accrediting examinations for medical students who have completed basic sciences (Step I), clerkships (Step II), and the first year of postgraduate medical training (Step III). NBME certification, based on passing Steps I–III of the United States Medical Licensure Examination (USMLE), is accepted for accreditation by all states as long as it is completed within a requisite number of years prior to application for a state license. The NBME also assists some specialty boards with certifying examinations.

The Educational Council for Foreign Medical Graduates (ECFMG). This Council represents the AAMC, the American Hospital Association (AHA), the AMA, and the Federation of State Medical Boards. It devised "an effective mechanism for measuring educational attainment in the absence of intimate knowledge of the educational background of foreign physicians." To this end, ECFMG verifies the following: that a foreign medical school is of acceptable quality; that an IMG attended that school; and (through USMLE) that an IMG has sufficient knowledge to practice medicine.

The American Hospital Association (AHA). The AHA represents the nation's community hospitals. It produced the *Patient Bill of Rights* and lobbies on behalf of hospitals. The Coordinating Committee on Medical Education (CCME) consists of representatives of the AAMC, AMA, AHA, the American Board of Medical Specialties, and the Council of Medical Specialty Societies. The CCME has four branches: its Liaison Committee on Medical Education (LCME), which accredits medical schools, with AAMC personnel doing much of the on-site inspection; the Accreditation Committee on Graduate Medical Education (ACGME), whose Residency Review Councils (RRCs) accredit residency training programs; the Liaison Committee on Continuing Medical Education, which oversees continuing medical education; and the Liaison Committee on Allied Health Education, which reviews education in the allied health services.

HEALTH CARE FINANCING

The government has since 1979 funded nearly two fifths of all health spending; private sources fund the remainder through private health insurance (33.1% in 1989), out-of-pocket payments (23.5%), and other sources (4.4%, e.g., philanthropy, interest and dividend income) (140). The government funds public programs (through Medicare [17%], Medicaid [10%], and programs for the military, veterans, federal civilian employees, and native Americans [15%]), which represented more than 42% of total national health expenditures in 1989 (140). It also reimburses a portion of personal health care costs (i.e., nonhospital, out-of-pocket) as a third-party insurer. The role of Medicare and Medicaid in the nation's health care financing and delivery system were discussed at length earlier.

In 1989, personal health care spending (consumer out-of-pocket payments, and third-party payments made on behalf of patients by private health insurers and government) totalled $530.7 billion. Although only 23.5% ($124.8 billion) of this was out-of-pocket compared to 53% in 1965, the dollar amount per person was nearly five times that in 1965—$486 vs. $100, respectively (140, 141).

On average, each person visits a physician 5.5 times a year. Nearly 8% of the population was hospitalized at least once a year in 1990 (about 23% lower than the 10.3% rate in 1982) (139).

Private Health Insurance

Approximately 87% of the civilian noninstitutionalized population (214 million Americans) received some form of health insurance coverage in 1989 (128). Private health insurance covered 189 million persons through some form of commercial insurance, Blue Cross-Blue Shield plan, self-funded employer plan, or managed care plan (health mainte-

nance organization [HMO] or preferred provider organization [PPO]). About 96 million persons are insured under group policies, and nearly 10 million carry individual or family policies (128).

Blue Cross and Blue Shield insurers are nonprofit membership plans that work in concert to offer both individual and group health insurance. They cover hospital care (Blue Cross) and physician fees (Blue Shield), using annual deductibles and copayments for most services. The "Blues" administer some HMOs and PPOs, and account for 50% of private coverage.

"Managed care" is a fairly new concept that has emerged within the last 5 years to characterize the competitive, integrated, cost-conscious approach to health services financing and delivery that the 1973 HMO Act set in motion (p. 444). Its common characteristics are (1) arrangement with selected providers to furnish a comprehensive set of health care services to members; (2) explicit standards for the selection of health care providers; (3) formal programs for ongoing quality assurance and utilization review; and (4) significant financial incentives for members to use providers and procedures covered by the plans and for physicians to practice cost-conscious medicine.

The most common managed care plans are HMOs and PPOs, both of which have existed longer than the managed care concept they embody. They developed as competitive alternatives to traditional indemnity plans that reimburse on a fee-for-service basis, which is now the antithesis of most cost-conscious reimbursement systems (e.g., Medicare, Part A and B, in addition to HMOs and PPOs). HMOs and PPOs differ fundamentally in several ways, although there have been attempts to combine features of both. Within the last several years, the distinctions between the two types of managed care plans have become increasingly blurred as they compete to increase their market share and, in so doing, begin to offer many of the same features.

At heart, an HMO is simply a prepaid health plan that combines insurance coverage with actual health care delivery, in which payment is based on a set monthly fee, or "capitation" per enrollee. The fixed contract fee provides a strong incentive for providers to promote wellness among their enrollees (which translates into fewer visits and therefore lower costs and higher profits for the HMO) and to control costs and excessive services among their physicians. Enrollees are required to use only those providers associated with the HMO, and there is no fee for individual services. The cost controls and designation of specific physician providers in HMO systems can create some problems for patients and physicians in the HMO, but these issues are beyond the scope of this book. Most HMOs employ full-time, salaried physicians to provide care, although some contract their services to outside physicians.

In contrast to an HMO, a PPO is simply an arrangement negotiated between one or more providers (physicians and hospitals) and a group of health care purchasers (generally employers or insurance carrier), in which purchasers are given lower prices for services and providers are assured a larger supply of patients. Some PPOs are owned by physicians in competition with HMOs for patients (142). The PPO does not replace conventional insurance, and providers continue to be paid on a fee-for-service basis according to a negotiated discount or fee schedule (128). Patients are not locked into a specific provider. Instead, they have much greater choice of practitioners under a PPO than under an HMO, although there are generally financial incentives in their coverage to encourage them to use PPO physicians (usually in the form of substantially lower deductibles and copayments). Largely a phenomenon that emerged in the 1980s, PPOs are growing rapidly, rising from 241 in 1984 (143) to 824 in 1990 (58).

References

1/ Acquired Immunodeficiency Syndrome: A Biopsychosocial Paradigm

1. Engel GL. The need for a new medical model: a challenge for biomedicine. Science 1977;196:129–136.
2. Scully RE, Mark EJ, McNeely WF, McNeely BU, eds. Case records of the Massachusetts General Hospital. N Engl J Med 1990;322:43–51.
3. Engel GL. The clinical application of the biopsychosocial model. Am J Psychiatry 1980;137:535–544.
4. Polan HJ, Auerbach MI, Viederman M. AIDS as a paradigm of human behavior in disease: impact and implications of a course. Acad Psychiatry 1990;14:197–203.
5. Levy RM, Bredesen DE. Central nervous system dysfunction in AIDS. J AIDS 1988;1:41–64.
6. Bacchetti P, Moss AR. Incubation period of AIDS in San Francisco. Nature 1989;338:251–253.
7. Blanche S, Rouzioux C, Moscato MG, et al. A prospective study of infants born to women seropositive for human immunodeficiency virus type 1. N Engl J Med 1989;320:1643–1648.
8. Dean L, Hall WE, Martin J. Chronic and intermittent AIDS-related bereavement in a panel of homosexual men in New York City. J Palliative Care 1990;4:54–57.
9. Henderson DK, Fahey BH, Willy M, et al. Risk for occupational transmission of human immunodeficiency virus type 1 (HIV-1) associated with clinical exposures: a prospective evaluation. Ann Intern Med 1990;113:740–746.
10. Gerbert B, Maguire BT, Bleecker T, et al. Primary care physicians and AIDS: attitudinal and structural barriers to care. JAMA 1991;266:2837–2842.
11. Centers for Disease Control. Update: transmission of HIV infection during invasive dental procedures—Florida. MMWR 1991;40:37–38.
12. Centers for Disease Control. Recommendations for preventing transmission of human immunodeficiency virus and hepatitis B virus to patients during exposure-prone invasive procedures. MMWR 1991;40(No. RR-8):1–9.
13. Altman LK. U.S. backs off on plan to restrict health workers with AIDS virus. New York Times 1991;Dec. 3.
14. World Health Organization. Weekly Epidemiologic Record 1992;67:9–10.
15. USDHHS, Centers for Disease Control. HIV/AIDS Prevention Newsletter. Dec. 1991;2:3.
16. Preble EA. Impact of HIV/AIDS on African children. Soc Sci Med 1990;31:671–680.
17. USDHHS, Centers for Disease Control. HIV/AIDS Surveillance, Jan. 1992.
18. USDHHS, National Center for Health Statistics. Advance report of final mortality statistics, 1989. Monthly Vital Statistics Report 1992;40(Suppl 2):1–45.
19. USDHHS, National Center for Health Statistics. Monthly Vital Statistics Report 1992;40:16–17.
20. USDHHS, Centers for Disease Control. AIDS in women—United States. MMWR 1990;39:845–846.
21. Chu SY, Buehler JW, Berkelman RL. Impact of the human immunodeficiency virus epidemic on mortality in women of reproductive age, United States. JAMA 1990;264:225–229.
22. Landesman S, Minkoff H, Holman S, et al. Serosurvey of human immunodeficiency virus infection in parturients. JAMA 1987;58:2701–2703.
23. Kilbourne BW, Buehler JW, Rogers MF. AIDS as a cause of death in children, adolescents, and young adults (ltr). Am J Public Health 1990;80:499–500.
24. USDHHS, Centers for Disease Control. Estimates of HIV prevalence and projected AIDS cases: summary of a workshop, October 31–November 1, 1989. MMWR 1990;39:110–112,117–119.
25. Hernandez SR. Laboratory testing and management of HIV infected patients. In: Cohen PT, Sande MA, Volberding PA. The AIDS knowledge base. Waltham, MA: Massachusetts Medical Society, 1990;4.2.2:4,5.
26. McGrath MS. Immunology of AIDS: overview. In: Cohen PT, Sande MA, Volberding PA. The AIDS knowledge base. Waltham, MA: Massachusetts Medical Society, 1990;3.3.1:1,2.
27. Price RW, Brew B, Sidtis J, et al. The brain in AIDS: central nervous system HIV-1 infection and AIDS dementia complex. Science 1988;239:586–592.
28. Cummings JL, Benson DF. Dementia: a clinical approach. 2d ed. Boston: Butterworth-Heinemann, 1992:179.
29. Navia BA. AIDS dementia complex. In: Cummings JL, ed. Subcortical dementia New York: Oxford University Press, 1990.
30. Gabuzda DH, Levy SR, Chiappa RH. Electroencephalography in AIDS and AIDS-related complex. Clin Electroenceph 1988;19:1–6.
31. Rabins PV, Folstein MF. Delirium and dementia: diagnostic criteria and fatality rates. Br J Psychiatry 1982;1140:149–153.
32. Perry SW. Organic mental disorders caused by HIV: update on early diagnosis and treatment. Am J Psychiatry 1990;147:696–710.
33. Perry SW, Jacobsberg LB, Fishman B, et al. Psychiatric diagnosis before serologic testing for the human immunodeficiency virus. Am J Psychiatry 1990;147:89–93.

34. Kubler-Ross E. On death and dying. London: Macmillan, 1969.

35. Lipowski Z. Physical illness, the individual and the coping process. Psychiatry in Med 1970;1:91–102.

36. Luber MP. Part I: Psychiatric skills review. In: Polan HJ, ed. Neuropsychiatry of HIV for primary care providers. New York: New York-Caribe AIDS Education Center, New York University, 1991.

37. Marzuk PM. Suicidal behavior and HIV illness. Intl Rev Psychiatry 1991;3:367–374.

38. Becker M, ed. The health belief model. Thorofare, NJ: Slack, 1974.

39. Johnson RW, Ostrow DG, Joseph J. Educational strategies for prevention of sexual transmission of HIV. In Ostrow DG, ed. Behavioral aspects of AIDS. New York: Plenum, 1990:73.

40. Kelly JA, St. Lawrence JS, Diaz Y, et al. HIV risk behavior reduction following intervention with key opinion leaders of population: an experimental analysis. Am J Public Health 1991;81:168–171.

41. Peterson JL, Marin G. Issues in the prevention of AIDS among black and hispanic men. Am Psychologist 1988;43:871–877.

42. Penkower L, Dew MA, Kingsley L, et al. Behavioral, health and psychosocial factors and risk for HIV infection among sexually active homosexual men: the multicenter AIDS cohort study. Am J Public Health 1991;81:194–196.

43. Maduro R. Curanderismo and Latino views of disease and healing. West J Med 1983;139:868–874.

44. Rabkin JG, Williams JBW, Neugebauer R, et al. Maintenance of hope in HIV-spectrum homosexual men. Am J Psychiatry 1990;147:1322–1326.

45. Morris PLP, Raphael B. Depressive disorder associated with physical illness: the impact of stroke. Gen Hosp Psychiatry 1987;9:324–330.

46. Patrick DL, Morgan M, Charlton JRH. Psychosocial support and change in the health status of physically disabled people. Soc Sci Med 1986;22:1347–1354.

47. Wolf TM, Balson PM, Morse EV, et al. Relationship of coping style to affective state and perceived social support in asymptomatic and symptomatic HIV-infected persons: implications for clinical management. J Clin Psychiatry 1991;52:171–173.

48. Perez-Stable EJ. Cuba's response to the HIV epidemic. Am J Pub Health 1991;81:563–567.

49. van Haastrecht HJA, van den Hoek JAR, Bardoux C, et al. The course of the HIV epidemic among intravenous drug users in Amsterdam, the Netherlands. Am J Public Health 1991;81:59–62.

50. Hintz S, Kuck J, Peterkin JJ, et al. Depression in the context of human immunodeficiency virus infection: implications for treatment. J Clin Psychiatry 1990;51:497–501.

51. Rabkin JG, Harrison WM. Effect of imipramine on depression and immune status in a sample of men with HIV infection. Am J Psychiatry 1990;147:495–497.

52. Schmidt FA, Bigley JW, McKinnis R, et al. Neuropsychological outcome of zidovudine (AZT) treatment of patients with AIDS and AIDS-related complex. N Engl J Med 1988;319:1573–1578.

53. Holmes VF, Fernandez F, Levy JK. Psychostimulant response in AIDS-related complex. J Clin Psychiatry 1989;50:5–8.

54. Perry SW, Markowitz JC. Counseling for HIV testing. Hosp Comm Psychiatry 1988;39:731–739.

55. Perry SW, Fishman B, Jacobsberg L, et al. Effectiveness of stress prevention training after HIV Testing. Arch Gen Psychiatry 1991;48:143–147.

56. Reiser D, Rosen D. Medicine as a human experience. Baltimore: University Park Press, 1984:1984.

57. Viederman M. Psychotherapeutic approaches to the medically ill. In Michels R, ed. Psychiatry. Philadelphia: Lippincott, 1985.

58. Pizzo PA, Wilfert CM, eds. Pediatric AIDS: the challenge of HIV infection in infants, children and adolescents. Baltimore: Williams and Wilkins, 1991.

59. Pizzo PA, Eddy J, Falloon J, et al. Effect of continuous intravenous infusion of zidovudine (AZT) in children with symptomatic HIV infection. N Engl J Med 1988;319:889–896.

60. Brouwers P, Belman AL, Epstein LG. Central nervous system involvement: manifestations and evaluation. In: Pizzo PA, Wilfert CM, eds. Pediatric AIDS: the challenge of HIV infection in infants, children and adolescents. Baltimore: Williams and Wilkins, 1991.

61. Stiehm RE, Wara DW. Immunology of HIV. In: Pizzo PA, Wilfert CM, eds. Pediatric AIDS: the challenge of HIV infection in infants, children and adolescents. Baltimore: Williams and Wilkins, 1991.

62. Joshi VV. Pathologic findings associated with HIV infection in children. In: Pizzo PA, Wilfert CM, eds. The challenge of HIC infection in infants, children and adolescents. Baltimore: Williams and Wilkins, 1991.

63. Septimus A. Psycho-social aspects of caring for families of infants infected with human immunodeficiency virus. Seminars in Perinatol 1989;13:49–54.

2/ Basic Research and Statistical Methods

1. Swain JF, Rouse IL, Curley CB, Sacks FM. Comparison of the effects of oat bran and low-fiber wheat on serum lipoprotein levels and blood pressure. New Engl J of Med 1990;322:147–152.

2. Nuland SB. Doctors: the biography of medicine. New York: Vintage Books, 1988.

3. McCain G, Segal EM. The game of science. 5th ed. Pacific Grove, CA: Brooks/Cole, 1988.

4. Garrison FH. An introduction to the history of medicine. 4th ed. Philadelphia: Saunders, 1966.

5. Koch R. Untersuchungen über die Aetiologie der Wundinfektionskrankheiten. Berlin, 1878.

6. Lister J. On the antiseptic principle in the practice of surgery. Lancet 1867;2:95,353,668.

7. Cohen J, Cohen P. Applied multivariate regression/correlation analysis for the behavioral sciences. 2nd ed. Hillsdale, NJ: Lawrence Erlbaum, 1983.

8. Tabachnick BG, Fidell FS. Using multivariate statistics. New York: Harper & Row, 1983.

9. Guilford JP, Fruchter B. Fundamental statistics in psychology and education. 6th ed. New York: McGraw-Hill, 1978.

10. Winer BJ. Statistical principles in experimental design. 2nd ed. New York: McGraw-Hill, 1971.

11. Anastasi A. Psychological testing. 6th ed. New York: Macmillan, 1988.

12. Helzer J, Robins L, Taibleson M, Woodruff R, Reich T. Reliability of psychiatric diagnosis 1. Arch Gen Psychiatry 1977;34:129–133.

13. Hubbard JP. Measuring medical education: the tests and the experiences of the National Board of Medical Examiners. Philadelphia: Lea and Febiger, 1978:65,66.

14. Gunzberger LK, Frazier RG, Yang LM, Rainey ML, Wronki T. Premedical and medical performance in predicting first-year residency performance. J Med Educ 1988;62;379–384.

15. Cook TD, Campbell DT. Quasi-experimentation: design and analysis issues for field settings. Chicago: Rand McNally, 1979.

16. Sierles FS. Behavioral science for the boreds. 2nd ed. North Miami Beach: Medmaster, 1989.

17. Franks P, Harp J, Bell B. Randomized, controlled trial of clonidine for smoking cessation in a primary care setting. JAMA 1989;262:3011–3013.

18. Jenkins DJA, Wolever TMS, Vuksan V, et al. Nibbling versus gorging: metabolic advantages of increased meal frequency. New Engl J Med 1989;321:929–934.

19. Gehlbach SH. Interpreting the medical literature. 2nd ed. New York: Macmillan, 1988.

20. London SJ, Colditz GA, Stampfer MJ, Willett WC, Rosner B, Speizer FE. Prospective study of relative weight, height, and risk of breast cancer. JAMA, 1989;262:2853–2858.

21. Werler MM, Allen AM, Shapiro S. The relation of aspirin use during the first trimester of pregnancy to congenital cardiac defects. New Engl J Med 1989;321:1639–1642.

3/ Neurology of Behavior

1. Mayeux R, Kandel ER. Natural language, disorders of language, and other localizable disorders of cognitive functioning. In: Kandel ER, Schwartz JH. Principles of neural science. 2nd ed. New York: Elsevier, 1985:688–703.

2. Mesulam M-M. Patterns in behavioral neuroanatomy: association areas, the limbic system, and hemispheric specialization. In: Mesulam M-M, ed. Principles of behavioral neurology. Philadelphia: FA Davis, 1985:1–70.

3. Barbas H, Mesulam M-M. Organization of afferent input to subdivisions of area 8 in rhesus monkey. J Comp Neurol 1981;200:407–431.

4. Mesulam M-M. A cortical network for directed attention and unilateral neglect. Ann Neurol 1981;10:309–325.

5. Mesulam M-M, Van Hoesen GW, Pandya DN, Geschwind N. Limbic and sensory connections of the inferior parietal lobule (area PG) in rhesus monkey: a study with a new method for horseradish peroxidase histochemistry. Brain Res 1977;136:393–414.

6. Brinkman C, Porter R. Supplementary motor area and premotor area of monkey cerebral cortex: functional organization and activities of single neurons during performance of a learned movement. In: Desmedt JE, ed. Motor control mechanisms in health and disease. New York: Raven Press, 1983.

7. Geschwind N. The anatomical basis of hemisphere differentiation. In: Diamond S, Beaumont J, eds. Hemisphere function in the human brain. New York: Halstead Press, 1977:7–24.

8. Levy J. The origin of lateral asymmetry. In: Harnad S, Doty R, Goldstein L. Lateralization in the nervous system. New York: Academic Press, 1977:195–209.

9. Nottebohm F. Origins and mechanisms in the establishment of cerebral dominance. In: Gazzaniga MS, ed. Handbook of behavioral neurobiology, Neuropsychology. Vol. 2. New York: Plenum, 1979:295–344.

10. Broca P. Perte de la parole. Ramollissement chronique et destruction partielle du lobe anterieur gauche du cerveau. Bull Soc d'anthropologie 1861;II:235–238.

11. Goodglass H. Studies on the grammar of aphasics. In: Goodglass H, Blumstein S, eds. Psycholinguistics and aphasia. Baltimore: Johns Hopkins University Press, 1973:183–215.

12. Robinson RG, Benson DF. Depression in aphasic patients: frequency, severity, and clinical-pathological correlations. Brain Lang 1981;14:282–291.

13. Lipsey JR, Robinson RG, Pearlson GD, Rao K, Price TR. Nortriptyline treatment of post-stroke depression: a double-blind study. Lancet 1984;1:297–300.

14. Robinson RG, Kubos KL, Starr LB, Rao K, Price TR. Mood disorders in stroke patients. Brain 1984;107:81–93.

15. Albert ML, Goodglass H, Helm NA, Rubens AB, Alexander MP. Clinical aspects of dysphasia. New York: Springer-Verlag, 1981.

16. Benson DF. Aphasia, alexia, and agraphia. New York: Churchill-Livingstone, 1979.

17. Faber R, Abrams R, Taylor MA, Kasprisin A, Morris C, Weisz R. Comparison of schizophrenic patients with formal thought disorder and neurologically impaired patients with aphasia. Am J Psychiatry 1983;140:1348–1351.

18. Wernicke K. Der aphasische Symptomencomplex. Breslau, West Germany: Cohn and Weigert, 1874. (Engl trans.: Cohen RS, Wartofsky MW, eds. The symptom-complex of aphasia. Boston studies in the philosophy of science, Reidel Dordrecht-Hollands, 1969;IV:34–97).

19. Benson DF, Geschwind N. Aphasia and related disorders: a clinical approach. In: Mesulam M-M, ed. Principles of behavioral neurology. Philadelphia: FA Davis, 1985:193–238.

20. Dejerine J. Sur un cas de cecite verbale avec agraphie, suivi d'autopsie. Mem Soc Biol 1891;3:197–201.

21. Dejerine J. Contibution a l'étude anatomoclinique et clinique des differentes varietes de cecite verbale. Mem Soc Biol 1892;46:61–90.

22. Ross ED, Mesulam M-M. Dominant language functions of the right hemisphere? Arch Neurol 1979;36:144–148.

23. Ross ED. The aprosodias. Arch Neurol 1981;38:561–569.

24. TenHouten WD, Hoppe KD, Bogen JE, et al. Alexithymia: an experimental study of cerebral commissurotomy patients and normal control subjects. Am J Psychiatry 1986;143:312–316.

25. Sifneos PE. The prevalence of "alexithymic" characteristics in psychosomatic patients. Psychother Psychosom 1973;22:255–262.

26. Shipko S, Alvarez WA, Noviello N. Towards a teleologic model of alexithymia: alexithymia and post-traumatic stress disorder. Psychother Psychosom 1983;39:122–126.

27. Hoppe KD. Split brains and psychoanalysis. Psychoanal Q 1977;46:220–244.

28. Zeitlin SB, Lane RD, O'Leary DS, Schrift MJ. Interhemispheric transfer deficit and alexithymia. Am J Psychiatry 1989;146:1434–1439.

29. Gazzaniga MS. The social brain: discovering the networks of the mind. New York: Basic Books, 1985.

30. Hemphill RE, Klein R. Contribution to the dressing disability as a focal sign and to the imperception phenomena. J Mental Sci 1948;94:611–622.

31. Kleist K. Kriegsverietzungen des Gehirns in ihrer Bedeutung für die Hirnlokalisation und Hirnpathologie. In: Von Schjerning O, ed. Handbuch der ärztlichen Erfahrung im Weltkriege, Vol. 4 Leipzig: Barth, 1923.

32. Damasio AR. Disorders of complex visual processing: agnosias, achromotopsia, Balint's syndrome, and related difficulties of orientation and construction. In: Mesulam M-M, ed. Principles of behavioral neurology. Philadelphia: FA Davis, 1985:259–288.

33. Geschwind N. The apraxias: neural mechanisms of disorders of learned movement. Am Sci 1975;63:188–195.

34. Cummings JL. Disorders of verbal output: mutism, aphasia, and psychotic speech. In: Cummings JL. Clinical neuropsychiatry. New York: Grune & Stratton, 1985.

35. Cummings JL. Visuospatial and visual-perceptual disturbances. In: Cummings JL. Clinical neuropsychiatry. New York: Grune & Stratton, 1985:48–56.

36. Christodoulou GN. The syndrome of Capgras. Br J Psychiatry, 1977;130:556–564.

37. Christodoulou GN. Delusional hyper-identification of the Fregoli type. Acta Psychiatr Scand, 1976;54:305–314.

38. Christodoulou GN. The delusional misidentification syndromes. Basel, Switzerland: Karger, 1986.

39. Benton AL, Van Allen MW. Impairment in facial recognition in patients with cerebral disease. Cortex 1968;4:344–358.

40. Luria AR. Disorders of "simultaneous perception" in a case of bilateral occipito-parietal brain injury. Brain 1959;82:437–449.

41. Hecaen H, Albert ML. Human neuropsychology. New York: John Wiley & Sons, 1978.

42. Kinsbourne M, Warrington EK. A disorder of simultaneous form perception. Brain 1962;85:461–486.

43. Weinstein EA, Kahn RL. The syndrome of anosognosia. Arch Neurol Psychiatry 1950;64:772–791.

44. Weinstein EA, Kahn RL, Malitz S, Rozanski J. Delusional reduplication of parts of the body. Brain 1954;77:45–60.

45. Christodoulou GN. Syndrome of subjective doubles. Am J Psychiatry 1978;135:249–251.

46. Benson DF, Gardner H, Meadows JC. Reduplicative paramnesia. Neurology 1976;26:147–151.

47. Schilder P, Stengel E. Asymbolia for pain. Arch Neurol Psychiatry 1931;25:598–600.

48. Adams RD, Victor M. Principles of neurology. New York: McGraw-Hill, 1981:111.

49. Benson DF, Denkla MB. Verbal paraphasia as a source of calculation disturbance. Arch Neurol 1969;21:96–102.

50. Levin HS. The acalculias. In: Heilman KM, Valenstein E, eds. Clinical neuropsychology. New York: Oxford University Press 1979:128–140.

51. Grewel F. The acalculias. In: Vinken PJ, Bruyn GW, eds. Disorders of speech, perception, and symbolic behavior, Handbook of clinical neurology. Vol. 4. New York: Elsevier, 1969:181–194.

52. Grewel F. Acalculia. Brain 1952;75:397–407.

53. Benson DF, Weir WF. Acalculia: acquired anarithmetria. Cortex 1972;8:465–472.

54. Fuster JM. The prefrontal cortex. New York: Raven Press, 1980.

55. Stuss DT, Benson DF. The frontal lobes. New York, Raven Press, 1986.

56. Nauta WJH. The problem of the frontal lobe: a reinterpretation. J Psychiatry Res 1971;8:167–187.

57. Damasio A. The frontal lobes. In: Heilman KM, Valenstein E, eds. Clinical neuropsychology. New York: Oxford University Press 1979:360–412.

58. Nauta WJH. Fibre degeneration following lesions of the amygdaloid complex in the monkey. J Anat 1961;95:515–531.

59. Blumer D, Benson DF. Personality changes with frontal and temporal lobe lesions. In: Benson DF and Blumer D, eds. Psychiatric aspects of neurologic disease. New York: Grune & Stratton, 1975:151–169.

60. Damasio AR, Van Hoesen GW. Emotional disturbances associated with focal lesions of the limbic frontal lobe. In: Heilman KM, Satz P, eds. Neuropsychology of human emotion. New York: Guilford Press, 1983:85–110.

61. Ross ED, Stewart RM. Akinetic mutism from hypothalamic damage: successful treatment with dopamine agonists. Neurology 1981;31:1435–1439.

62. Papez JW. A proposed mechanism of emotion. Arch Neurol Psychiatry 1937;73:161–171.

63. MacLean PD. The triune brain, emotion and scientific bias. In: Schmit FO, Worden FG, eds. The neurosciences, second study program. New York: Rockefeller University Press, 1970:336–349.

64. von Economo C. Encephalitis lethargica (Trans: Newman KO). London: Oxford University Press, 1931.

65. Gibbs FA. Ictal and non-ictal psychiatric disorders in T.L.E. J Nerv Ment Dis, 1951;113:522–528.

66. Victor M, Adams RD, Collins GH. The Wernicke-Korsakoff syndrome. Philadelphia: FA Davis, 1971.

67. Adams RD, Victor M. Principles of neurology. 2nd ed. New York: McGraw-Hill, 1977.

4/ Neurochemistry of Behavior

1. Kandel ER, Siegelbaum S. Principles underlying electrical and chemical synaptic transmission. In: Kandel ER, Schwartz JH, eds. Principles of neural science. 2nd ed. New York: Elsevier, 1985:87–107.

2. Koester J. Resting membrane potential and action potential. In: Kandel ER, Schwartz JH, eds. Principles of neural science. 2nd ed. New York: Elsevier, 1985:49–57.

3. Koester J. Voltage-gated channels and the generation of the action potential. In: Kandel ER, Schwartz JH, eds. Principles of neural science. 2nd ed. New York: Elsevier, 1985:75–86.

4. Grebb JA, Reus VI, Freimer NB. Neurobehavioral chemistry and physiology. In: Goldman HH, ed. Review of general psychiatry. San Mateo: Lange, 1988:121–135.

5. Kandel ER. Factors controlling transmitter release. In: Kandel ER, Schwartz JH, eds. Principles of neural science. 2nd ed. New York: Elsevier, 1985: 120–131.

6. Schwartz JH. Molecular steps in synaptic transmission. In: Kandel ER, Schwartz JH, eds. Principles of neural science. 2nd ed. New York: Elsevier, 1985:169–175.

7. Coyle JT. Neuroscience and psychiatry. In: Talbott JA, Hales RE, Yudofsky SC, eds. Textbook of psychiatry. Washington, DC: American Psychiatric Press, 1988:3–32.

8. Baraban JM, Worley PF, Snyder SH. Second messenger systems and psychoactive drug action: focus on the phosphoinositide system and lithium. Am J Psychiatry 1989;146:1251–1260.

9. Worley PF, Baraban JM, Snyder SH. Beyond receptors: multiple second messenger systems in brain. Ann Neurol 1987;21:217–229.

10. Schramm M, and Selinger Z. Message transmission: receptor-controlled adenylate cyclase system. Science 1984;225:1350–1356.

11. Avissar S, Schreiber G, Danon A, Belmaker RH. Lithium inhibits adrenergic and cholinergic increases in GTP binding in rat cortex. Nature 1988;331:440–442.

12. Creese I, Burt DR, Snyder SH. Dopamine receptor binding predicts clinical and pharmacologic potencies of antischizophrenic drugs. Science 1976;192:481–483.

13. Wong DF, Wagner HN, Tune LE, et al. Positron emission tomography reveals elevated D_2 dopamine receptors in drug-naive schizophrenics. Science 1986;1558–1563.

14. Cowan WM, Cuenod M, eds. The use of axoplasmic transport for studies of neuronal connectivity. Amsterdam: Elsevier, 1975.

15. Creese I. Dopamine and antipsychotic medications. In: Hales RE, Frances AJ, eds. Psychiatry update. Vol 5. Washington: American Psychiatric Press, 1985:17–36.

16. Seeman P, Lee T, Chau-Wong M, Wong K. Antipsychotic drug doses and neuroleptic/dopamine receptors. Nature 1976;717–719.

17. Ereshefsky L, Watanabe MD, Tran-Johnson TK. Clozapine: an atypical antipsychotic agent. Clin Pharmacy 1989;8:691–709.

18. Kane J, Honigfeld G, Singer J, Meltzer H. Clozapine for the treatment-resistant schizophrenic. Arch Gen Psychiatry 1988;45:789–796.

19. Kane J. The current status of neuroleptic therapy. J Clin Psychiatry 1989;40:322–328.

20. Schwartz JH, Chemical messengers: small molecules and peptides. In: Kandel ER, Schwartz JH, eds. Principles of neural science. 2nd ed. New York: Elsevier, 1985:148–158.

21. Mesulam M-M. Patterns in behavioral neuroanatomy: association areas, the limbic system and hemispheric specialization. In: Mesulam M-M ed. Principles of behavioral neurology. Philadelphia: FA Davis, 1985.

22. Weiner RI, Ganong WF. Role of brain monoamines and histamine in regulation of anterior pituitary secretion. Physio Rev 1978;905–976.

23. Snyder SH. Drugs and neurotransmitter receptors in the brain. Science 1984;224:22–31.

24. Paul SM, Janowsky A, Skolnick P. Monoaminergic neurotransmitters and antidepressant drugs. In: Hales RE, Frances AJ, eds. Psychiatry update. Vol 5. Washington: American Psychiatric Press, 1985:37–48.

25. Torgersen S. Genetic factors in anxiety disorders. Arch Gen Psychiatry 1983;40:1085–1089.

26. Friedman S, Sunderland G, Rosenblum LA. A non-human model of panic disorder. Psychiatry Res 1988;23:65–75.

27. Sunderland G, Friedman S, Rosenblum LA. Imipramine and alprazolam treatment of lactate-induced acute endogenous distress in non-human primates. Am J Psychiatry 1989;146:1044–1047.

28. Thoren P, Asberg M, Cronhelm B, Jornestedt L, Traskman L. Clomipramine treatment of obsessive-compulsive disorder. Arch Gen Psychiatry 1980;37:1281–1285.

29. Flament MF, Rapaport JL, Berg CJ, et al. Clomipramine treatment of childhood obsessive-compulsive disorder: a double-blind controlled study. Arch Gen Psychiatry 1985; 42:977–986.

30. Zohar J, Mueller EA, Zohar RK, et al. Behavioral and neuroendocrine effects of μ-chlorophenylpiperazine, a serotonin agonist, in obsessive-compulsive patients and normal controls (abstract). Presented at the annual meeting of the Society for Biological Psychiatry, Washington, DC. 1986.

31. Jenike MA, Baer L, Summergrod P, et al. Sertraline in obsessive-compulsive disorder: a double-blind comparison with placebo. Am J Psychiatry 1990;147:923–928.

32. Karacan I, Moore C. Physiology and neurochemistry of sleep. In: Hales RE, Frances AJ, eds. Psychiatry update. Vol. 5. Washington: American Psychiatric Press, 1985:266–293.

33. Schneider-Helmut D, Spinweber CL. Evaluation of L-tryptophan for treatment of insomnia: a review. Psychopharmacol 1986;89:1–7.

34. Adam K, Oswald I. One gram of L-tryptophan fails to alter the time taken to fall asleep. Neuropharmacology 1979;18: 1025–1027.

35. Belongia EA, Hedberg CW, Gleich GJ, et al. An investigation of the cause of the eosinophilia-myalgia syndrome associated with tryptophan use. N Engl J Med 1990;323:357–365.

36. Peroutka SJ, Sleight AJ, McCarthy BG, et al. The clinical utility of pharmacological agents that act at serotonin receptors. J Neuropsychiatry 1989;1:253–262.

37. Singer DJ, GABA and the behavioral effects of anxiolytic drugs. Life Sci 1985;36:1503–1513.

38. Enna SJ. Gamma-aminobutyric acid (GABA), pharmacology and neuropsychiatric illness. In: Hales RE, Frances AJ, eds. Psychiatry update. Vol. 5. Washington, DC: American Psychiatric Press, 1985:67–82.

39. Tallman JF, Gallager DW. The GABA-ergic system: a locus of benzodiazepine action. Ann Rev Neurosci 1985;8:21–44.

40. Coyle JT. The cholinergic systems in psychiatry. In: Hales RE, Frances AJ, eds. Psychiatry update. Vol. 5. Washington: American Psychiatric Press, 1985:49–66.

41. Coyle JT, Price DL, DeLong MR. Alzheimer's disease: a disorder of cortical cholinergic innervation. Science 1983; 1184–1190.

42. Cote L, Crutcher MD. Motor functions of the basal ganglia and diseases of transmitter metabolism. In: Kandel ER, Schwartz JH, eds. Principles of neural science. 2nd ed. New York: Elsevier, 1985:523–535.

43. Jeste DV, Grebb JA, Wyatt RJ. Psychiatric aspects of movement disorders and demyelinating diseases. In: Hales RE, Frances AJ, eds. Psychiatry update. Vol 5. Washington: American Psychiatric Press, 1985:159–189.

44. Schwarcz R, Meldrum B. Excitatory amino acid antagonists provide a therapeutic approach to neurological disorders. Lancet 1985;2:140–143.

45. Kreiger DT. Brain peptides: what, where, and why? Science 1983;222:975–985.

46. Watson SJ, Kelsey JE, Lopez JF, Akil H. Neuropeptide biology: basic and clinical lessons from the opioids. In: Hales RE, Frances AJ, eds. Psychiatry update. Vol. 5. Washington: American Psychiatric Press, 1985:83–97.

47. Kelly DD. Central representations of pain and analgesia. In: Kandel ER, Schwartz JH, ed. Principles of neural science. 2nd ed. New York: Elsevier, 1985:331–343.

48. Kandel ER. Genes, nerve cells, and the remembrance of things past. J Neuropsychiatry 1989;1:103–125.

49. Kandel ER. From metapsychology to molecular biology: explorations into the nature of anxiety. Am J Psychiatry 1983; 140:1277–1293.

50. Kandel ER. Psychotherapy and the single synapse. New Engl J Med 1979;301:1028–1037.

5/ Genetics of Personality and Psychiatric Illness

1. Murray RK, Granner OK, Mayes PA, Rodwell VW, eds. Harper's biochemistry, 22nd ed. Norwalk, CT: Appleton & Lange, 1990:324–316.

2. Hershkowitz NN. Genetic disorders of brain development: animal models. In: Gaull GE, ed. Biology of brain dysfunction. Vol 2. New York: Plenum, 1973.

3. Buchsbaum MS, Coursey RD, Murphy DL. The biochemical high risk paradigm: behavioral and familial correlates of low platelet monoamine oxidase activity. Science 1976;194: 339–341.

4. Nies A, Robinson DS, Lamborn KR, Lampert RP. Genetic control of platelet and plasma monoamine oxidase activity. Arch Gen Psychiatry 1973;28:834–838.

5. Rice J, McGruffin P, Goldin LR, Shaskan EG, Gershon ES. Platelet monoamine oxidase (MAO) activity: evidence for a single major locus. Am J Hum Genet 1984;36:36–43.

6. Wyatt RJ, Murphy DL, Belmaker K, Cohen S, Donnelly CH, Pollin W. Reduced monoamine activity in platelets: a possible genetic marker for vulnerability to schizophrenia. Science 1973;179:916–918.

7. Nies A, Robinson DS, Harris LS, Lamborn KR. Comparison of monoamine oxidase substrate activities in twins, schizophrenics, depressives and controls. Adv Biochem Psychopharmacol 1974;12:59–70.

8. Maier SF, Seligman MEP. Learned helplessness: theory and evidence. J Exp Psychol 1976;105:3–46.

9. Sherman AD, Sacquitne JL, Petty F. Specificity of the learned helplessness model of depression. Pharmacol Biochem Behav 1989;16:449–454.

10. Shanks N, Hymie A. Provoked behavioral changes in six strains of mice. Behav Neurosci 1988;102:6:894–905.

11. Rieder RU, Kaufman CA. Genetics. In: Talbott JA, Hales RE, Yudofsky SC, eds. The American Psychiatric Press textbook of psychiatry. Washington, D.C.: American Psychiatric Press, 1988.

12. Porter IH. Heredity and disease. New York: McGraw-Hill, 1986:298–299.

13. Loughlin JC, Willerman L, Horn JM. Human behavior genetics. Ann Rev Psychol 1988;39:101–133.

14. Hopper JL, Culross PR. Covariation between family members as a function of cohabitation history. Behav Genet 1983;13:459–471.

15. Campion E, Tucker G. A note on twin studies, schizophrenia and neurological impairment. Arch Gen Psychiatry 1973;29:460–464.

16. Fogel BJ, Nitowsky HM, Gruenwald P. Discordant abnormalities in monozygotic twins. J Pediatr 1965;66:64–72.

17. Kaelber CT, Pugh TF. Influence of uterine relations on the intelligence of twins. N Engl J Med 1966;280:1030–34

18. Gottesman II, Shields J. Schizophrenia: the epigenetic puzzle. London: Cambridge University Press, 1982:100–128.

19. Plomin R, Daniels D. Why are children in the same family so different from one another? Behav Brain Sci 1987;10:1–60.

20. Loehlin JC, Horn JM, Willerman L. Personality resemblance in adoptive families. Behav Genet 1981;11:309–330.

21. Loehlin JC, Nichols RC. Heredity, environment and personality: a study of 8850 sets of twins. Austin: University of Texas Press, 1976.

22. Rainer JD. Genetics and psychiatry. In: Kaplan HI, Sadock BJ, eds. Comprehensive textbook of psychiatry IV. Vol. 1, 4th ed. Baltimore: Williams & Wilkins, 1985.

23. Cloninger CR, Bohman M, Sigvardsson S. Importance of alcohol abuse: cross-fostering analysis of adopted men. Arch Gen Psychiatry 1981;38:861–868.

24. Cadoret RJ, Gath A. Inheritance of alcoholism in adoptees. Br J Psychiatry 1978;132:252–258.

25. Bohman M, Sigvardsson S, Cloninger R. Maternal inheritance of alcohol abuse: cross-fostering analysis of adopted women. Arch Gen Psychiatry 1981;38:965–969.

26. Plomin R, Defries JC, McClean GE. Behavioral genetics: a primer. 2nd ed. New York: WH Freeman, 1990.

27. Kendler KS, Robinette CD. Schizophrenia in the National Academy of Sciences—National Research Council Twin Registry: a 16-year-update. Am J Psychiatry 1983;140:1551–1563.

28. Gershon ES, Goldin LR, Weissman MM, Nurnberger JL, Jr. Family and genetic studies of affective disorders in the eastern United States: a provisional summary. In: Perris C, Struwe G, Janssen B, eds. Biological psychiatry. Amsterdam: Elsevier, 1981:157–162.

29. Gershon ES, Hamovit TJ, Guroff JJ, et al. A family study of schizoaffective, bipolar I, bipolar II, unipolar and normal control probands. Arch Gen Psychiatry 1982;39:1157–1167.

30. Nurnbarger JI, Gershon ES. Genetics of affective disorder. In: Friedman E, ed. Depression and antidepressants: implications for courses and treatments. New York: Raven Press 1981:23–39.

31. Bartelson A, Harvald B, Hague M. Controversies and consistencies in psychiatric genetics. Acta Psychiatr Scand 1985;71:61–75.

32. Mendelwitz J, Rainer JP. Adoption study supporting genetic transmission in manic depressive illness. Nature 1977;3268:327–329.

33. Gershon ES. Genetics. In: Goodwin FK, Jamison KR, eds. Manic depressive illness. New York: Oxford University Press, 1990:379.

34. Andreasen N, Black D. Introductory textbook of psychiatry. Washington, D.C.: American Psychiatric Press, 1990.

35. Taylor MA, Abrams R. Reassessing the bipolar-unipolar dichotomy. J Affective Disord 1980;2:195–217.

36. Winokur G. Unipolar depression. In: Winokur G, Clayton P, eds. The medical basis of psychiatry. Philadelphia: Saunders, 1986.

37. Winokur A, March V, Mendels V. Primary affective disorder in relatives of patients with anorexia nervosa. Am J Psychiatry 1980;130:695.

38. Bohman M, Cloninger R, Sigvardsson S, von Knorring AL. The genetics of alcoholism and other disorders. J Psychiatric Res 1987;21:447–452.

39. Murry RM, Clifford C, Gurling HMD, Topham A, et al. Current genetic and biological approaches to alcoholism. Psychiatric Dev 1982;1:179–192.

40. Mednick SA, Moffick TE, Stack S. The cause of crime: new biological approaches. New York: Cambridge University Press, 1987.

41. Guze SB, Wolfgram ED, McKinney JK, et al. Psychiatric illness in the families of convicted criminals: a study of 519 first-degree relatives. Dis Nerv Syst 1967;28:651–659.

42. Torgersen S. Genetic factors in anxiety disorders. Arch Gen Psychiatry 1983;40:1085–1089.

43. Noyes RJ, Crowe RR, Harris EL, Hamra BJ, McChesny CM, Chaudhry DR. Relationship between panic disorder and agoraphobia: a family study. Arch Gen Psychiatry 1986;43:227–232.

44. Hudson JT, Laffer PS, Pope HG. Bulimia related to affective disorder by family history and response to dexamethasone suppression test. Am J Psychiatry 1982;139:685.

45. Defries JC, Dector SN. Genetic aspects of reading disability: a family study. In: Aaron PG, ed. Reading disorders: varieties and treatments. New York: Academic Press, 1982:255–279.

46. St. George-Hyslop PH, Tanzi RE, Polinsky RJ, et al. The genetic defect causing familial Alzheimer's disease maps on chromosome 21. Science 1987;235:883–889.

47. Nussbaum R, Brennard J, Chinault C. et al. Molecular analysis of the hypoxanthine phosphoribosyl transferase locus. In: Casky CT, White RL, eds. Recombinant DNA ap-

plication to human disease. New York: Harbor Laboratory, 1983:81–90.

48. Comings DE, Comings BG, Devor EJ, Cloninger CR. Detection of major gene for Gilles de la Tourette syndrome. Am J Hum Genetics 1984;36:586–600.

49. Gusella JF, Wexter NS, Coneally PM, et al. A polymorphic DNA marker genetically linked to Huntington's disease. Nature 1983;306:234–238.

50. Cloninger CR, Reich T, Guze SB. The multifunctional model of disease transmission. III. Familial relationship between sociopathy and hysteria. Br J Psychiatry 1975;127: 11–12.

51. Cloninger CR, Sigvardsson S, von Knorring AL, Bohman M. An adoption study of somatoform disorders. II. Identification of two discrete somatoform disorders. Arch Gen Psychiatry 1984;41:863–871.

52. Insel TR, Hoover C, Murphy DC. Parents of patients with obsessive compulsive disorder. Psychological Medicine 1983;13:807–811.

53. McGriffin P, Mawson D. Obsessive-compulsive neurosis: two identical twin pairs. Br J Psychiatry 1980;137:285–287.

54. Gershon ES. Inheritance of major psychiatric disorder. Trends Neurosci 1982;5:241–242.

55. Lotter V. Epidemiology of autistic conditions in young children. I. Prevalence. Soc Psychiatry 1966;1:124–137.

56. Folstein S, Rutter M. Infantile autism—a genetic study of 21 twin pairs. J Child Psychol Psychiatry 1977;18:297–331.

57. Ritvo ER. The syndrome of autism: a medical model. Integr Psychiatry 1983;1:101–109.

58. Crowe, RR, Noyes R, Pauls DL, Slyman D. A family study of panic disorder. Arch Gen Psychiatry 1983;40:1065–1069.

59. Plomin R. Environment and genes. Amer Psychol 1989;44: 2:105–111.

60. Stevenson J, Graham P, Friedman G. McLoughlin V. A twin study of genetic influences on reading and spelling. J Child Psychol Psychiatry, 1987;28:229–247.

61. Plomin R. The nature and nurture of cognitive abilities. In: Sternberg RJ, ed. Advances in the psychology of human intelligence, vol. 4. Hillsdale, NJ: Erlbaum, 1988:1–33.

62. Egger M. Mental retardation. In: Sierles FS, ed. Clinical behavioral science. New York: Spectrum, 1982:279.

63. Talbott JA, Hales, RE, Yudofsky SC, eds. Textbook of psychiatry. Washington, D.C.: American Psychiatric Press, 1988:1261.

64. Plomin R, Defries JC. Origins of individual differences in infancy. The Colorado Adoption Project, 1985.

65. Wilson RS, Matheny AP Jr. Behavior-genetics research in infant development: the Louisville twin study. In: Plomin R, Dunn J, eds. The study of temperament. Hillsdale, NJ: Erlbaum, 1986.

66. Henderson ND. Human behavior genetics. Am Rev Psychol 1982;33:403–440.

67. Pogue-Geile MF, Rose RJ. Development genetic studies of adult personality. Dev Psychol 1985;21:547–557.

68. Rushton JP, Fulker DW, Neale MC, Nias DK, Eysenck HJ. Altruism and aggression—the heritability of individual differences. J Pers Soc Psychol 1986;50:1192–1198.

69. Tellegen A, Lykken DT, Bouchard TJ Jr., et al. Personality similarity in twins reared apart and together. J Pers Soc Psychol, 1988;54:6:1031–1039.

70. Martin NG, Eaves LJ, Heath AC, et al. Transmission of social attitudes. Proc Natl Acad Sci USA 1986;83:4364–4368.

71. Begley S, Murr A, Spring K, et al. All about twins. Newsweek; November 23, 1987.

72. Cloninger, CR. A unified biosocial theory of personality and its role in the development of anxiety states. Psychiatr Dev 1986;3:167–226.

73. Cloninger CR. A systematic method for clinical description and classification of personality variants: a proposal. Arch Gen Psychiatry 1987;44:573–588.

74. Wilson GD. Personality. In: Eysenck HJ, Wilson GD, eds. Textbook of human psychology. Baltimore: University Park Press, 1976.

75. Siever LJ, Klar H, Coccaro E. Psychological substrates of personality. In: Klar H, Siever L, eds. Biological response styles: clinical implications. Washington, DC: American Psychiatric Press, 1985.

76. Plomin R. Development genetics and psychology. Hillsdale NJ: Eribaum, 1986.

77. von Knorring L, Monakhov K, Perris C. Augmenting/reducing: an adaptive switch mechanism to cope with incoming signals in healthy subjects and psychiatric patients. Neuropsychobiology 1978;4:150–159.

78. Sepinwall J, Cook L. Mechanism of action of the benzodiazepines: behavioral aspects. Fed Proc 1980;39:3021–3031.

79. Brown GL, Goodwin FK, Ballenger JC, Gover PF, Major LF. Aggression in humans correlates with cerebrospinal fluid amine metabolites. Psychiatry Res 1983;10:253–261.

80. Frith CD, Dowdy J, Ferrier IN, Crow TJ. Selective impairment of paired associate learning after administration of a centrally-acting adrenergic agonist (clonidine). Psychopharmacology 1985;87:490–493.

81. Kovacs GL, Bohus B, Versteeg DHG. Facilitation of memory consolidation by vasopressin: mediation by terminals of the dorsal noradrenergic bundle? Brain Res 1979;172:73–85.

82. Bohman M, Cloninger CR, Sigvardsson S, von Knorring AL. Predisposition to petty criminality in Swedish adoptees. I. Genetic and environmental heterogeneity. Arch Gen Psychiatry 1982;39:1233–1241.

83. Cloninger CR, Sigvardsson S, Bohman M, von Knorring AL. Predisposition to petty criminality in Swedish adoptees. II. Cross-fostering analysis of gene-environment interaction. Arch Gen Psychiatry 1982;39:1242–1247.

84. Sigvardsson S, Bohman M, von Knorring AL. Predisposition to petty criminality in Swedish adoptees. III. Sex differences and validation of male typology. Arch Gen Psychiatry 1982;39:1248–1253.

85. Bohman M, Cloninger R, Von Knorring AL, Sigvardsson S. An adoption study of somatoform disorder. III. Cross-fostering analysis and genetic relationship to alcoholism and criminality. Arch Gen Psychiatry 1984;41:872–878.

86. Watson JD. The human genome projects: past, present and future. Science 1990;248:44–49.

87. Beckford JAR, Ellison RM. The high incidence of Huntington's chorea in the Duchy of Cornwall. J Ment Sci 1953;99: 623.

88. Kurlan K, Kidd KK, Pauls D. Linkage analysis approach to hereditary movement disorders. J Neurogenet 1989;5:3: 161–171.

89. Braunwald E, Isselbacher KJ, Petersdorf RG, Wilson JD, Martin JB, Fauci AS. Harrison's principles of internal medicine, 11th ed. New York: McGraw-Hill, 1987:308–309.

90. Akiskal HS, Dekerminjian H, Rosenthal RH et al. Cyclothymic disorder: validating criteria for inclusion in the bipolar affective group. Am J Psychiatry 1977;134:1227–1233.

91. Nurnberger JI, Jr., Goldin LR, Gershon ES. Genetics of psychiatric disorders. In: Winokur G, Clayton P, eds. The medical basis of psychiatry. Philadelphia: Saunders, 1986.

92. Tsuang MT. Genetic counseling for psychiatric patients and their families. Am J Psychiatry 1978;135:1465–1475.

6/ Learning and Behavior Modification

1. Marks IM. Fears, phobias and rituals: panic, anxiety and their disorders. New York: Oxford, 1987.
2. Emmelkamp PMG. Behavior therapy with adults. In: Garfield SL, Bergen AE, eds. Handbook of psychotherapy and behavior change. 3rd ed. New York: Wiley, 1986.
3. Barlow DH. Anxiety and its disorders: the nature and treatment of anxiety and panic. New York: Guilford Press, 1988.
4. Foa EB, Steketee G, Milby JB. Differential effects of exposure and response prevention in obsessive-compulsive washers. J Consult Clin Psycholo 1980;48:71–79.
5. Marks I. Blood-injury phobia: a review. Am J Psychiatry 1988;145:1207–1213.
6. Melamed BG, Siegel LJ. Reduction of anxiety in children facing hospitalization and surgery by use of filmed modeling. J Consult Clin Psychol 1975;43:511–521.
7. Bandura A, Grusec JE, Menlove FL. Vicarious extinction of avoidance behavior. J Pers Soc Psychol 1967;5:16–23.
8. Bandura A. Psychotherapy based on modeling principles. In: Bergin AE, Garfield SL, eds. Handbook of psychotherapy and behavior change: an empirical analysis. New York: Wiley, 1971.
9. White WC, Davis MT. Vicarious extinction of phobic behavior in early childhood. J Abnorm Child Psychol 1979;2:25–32.
10. Bandura A, Ross D, Ross S. Imitation of film-mediated aggressive models. J Abnorm Soc Psychol 1963;66:3–11.
11. Bandura A. Principles of behavior modification. New York: Holt, Rinehart, Winston, 1969.
12. Pfeffer C, Plutchick R, Mizruchi M. Predictors of assaultiveness in latency-age children. Am J Psychiatry 1983;140:31–35.
13. Bandura A. Social learning theory. Englewood Cliffs, NJ: Prentice-Hall, 1977.
14. Pavlov IP. Conditioned reflexes. New York: Dover, 1927.
15. Beaton JM. Learning theory and human behavior. In: Wedding D. Behavior and medicine. St. Louis: Mosby Year Book, 1990:267–268.
16. Skinner BF. About behaviorism. New York: Vintage, 1974.
17. Skinner BF. Beyond freedom and dignity. New York: Knopf, 1971.
18. Dorsett PG. Behavioral and social learning psychology. In: Stoudemire A. Human behavior: an introduction for medical students. Philadelphia: Lippincott, 1990:92.
19. Taylor MA. The practice of neuropsychiatry. New York: Free Press, 1992.
20. Ayllon T, Azrin NH. The token economy: a motivational system for therapy and rehabilitation. New York: Appleton-Century-Crofts, 1968.
21. Parsons T. Definitions of health and illness, in the light of American values and social structure. In: Jaco E, ed. Patients, physicians, and illness. New York: Free Press, 1972.
22. Lichtenstein E, Penner MD. Long-term effects of rapid smoking treatment for dependent cigarette smokers. Addict Behav 1977;2:109–112.
23. American Lung Association. Freedom from smoking in 20 days: a self-help quit smoking program. 1986.
24. Cantela JR. The treatment of alcoholism by covert sensitization. Psychother: Theory, Res, Pract. 1970;2:83–90.
25. Gatchel RJ, Baum A, Krantz DS. An introduction to health psychology, 2nd ed. New York: Random House, 1989:227,228,303–305.

26. Veitia MC, McGahee CL. Ordinary addictions: tobacco and alcohol. In: Wedding D. Behavior in medicine. St. Louis: Mosby Year Book, 1990:300.
27. Stuart RB. Behavioral control of overeating. Behav Res and Ther 1967;5:357–365.
28. Stunkard AJ. Behavioral medicine and beyond: the example of obesity. In: Pomerleau OF, Brady JP, eds. Behavioral medicine in theory and practice. Baltimore: Williams & Wilkins, 1979.
29. Lacks P, Bertelson AD, Gans L, et al. The effectiveness of three behavioral treatments for different degrees of sleep onset insomnia. Behav Ther 1983;14:593–605.
30. Bootzin RR, Nicassio PM. Behavioral treatments of insomnia. In: Hersen M, Eisler RE, Miller PM. Progress in behavior modification, vol 6. New York: Academic Press, 1978.
31. McClusky MA, Milby JB, Switzer PK, Williams V, Wooten V. Efficacy of behavioral versus triazolam treatment in persistent sleep-onset insomnia. Am J Psychiatry 1991;148:121–126.
32. Reynolds G. A primer of operant conditioning. Glenview, IL: Scott, Foresman, 1975.
33. Beck AT, Rush AJ, Shaw BF, et al. Cognitive therapy of depression. New York: Guilford, 1979.
34. Beck AT, Emery G, Greenberg BL. Anxiety disorders and phobias. a cognitive perspective. New York: Basic Books, 1985.
35. Miller NE. Learning of visceral and glandular responses. Science 1969;163:434–445.
36. Cox DJ, Hobbs W. Biofeedback as a treatment for tension headaches. In: White L. Tursky B. Clinical biofeedback; efficacy and mechanisms. New York: Guilford, 1982.
37. Hollroyd KA, Penzien DB, Hursey KG, Tobin DL, et al. Change mechanisms in EMG biofeedback training: cognitive changes underlying improvements in tension headache. J Consult Clin Psychol 1984;52:2039–2053.
38. Gatchel RJ. Biofeedback in the treatment of fear and anxiety. In: Gatchel RJ, Price KP, eds. Clinical application of biofeedback: appraisal and status. Elmsford NY: Pergamon, 1979.
39. Hatch JP, Gatchel RJ, Harrington R. Biofeedback: clinical applications in medicine. In: Garchel RJ, Baum A, Singer JE, eds. Behavioral medicine and clinical psychology: overlapping areas. Hillsdale NJ: Erlbaum, 1982.
40. Luborsky L, Crits-Christoph P, Brady JP, Kron RE, Weiss T, Engelman K. Antihypertensive effects of behavioral treatments and medications compared. N Engl J Med 1980; 302:586.
41. Beatty J. Biofeedback in the treatment of migraine: simple relaxation or specific effects. In: White L, Tursky B, eds. Clinical biofeedback: efficacy and mechanisms. New York: Guilford Press, 1982.
42. Shapiro D, Surwit R. Learned control of physiological functioning in disease. In: Leitenberg H, ed. Handbook of behavior modification and behavior therapy. Englewood Cliffs NJ: Prentice-Hall, 1976:92–94.
43. McFall RM, Marston A. An experimental investigation of behavior rehearsal in assertive training. J Abnorm Psychol 1970;76:295–303.
44. McFall RM, Lillesand DV. Behavioral rehearsal with modeling and coaching in assertive training. J Abnorm Psychol 1971;77:313–323.
45. McFall RM, Twentyman CT. Four experiments on the relative contribution of rehearsal, modeling and coaching to assertive training. J Abnorm Psychol 1973;81:199–218.

46. Wolpe J. Psychotherapy by reciprocal inhibition. Stanford CA: Stanford University Press, 1958.

47. Jacobson E. Progressive relaxation. Chicago: University of Chicago Press, 1938.

48. Gatchel RJ. Effectiveness of two procedures for reducing dental fear: group-administered desensitization and group education and discussion. J Am Dent Assoc 1980;101:634–637.

49. Rimm DC, Masters JC. Behavior therapy: techniques and empirical findings. New York: Academic Press, 1974.

50. Coates T, Thoreson C. Treating sleep disorders: few answers, some suggestions and many questions. In: Turner S, Calhoun K, Adams K, eds. Handbook of clinical behavior therapy. New York: Wiley, 1981:240–283.

51. Physician's desk reference. Oradell, NJ: Medical Economics, 1989:2296.

52. Brewer C. Combining pharmacological antagonists and behavioral psychotherapy in treating addictions: why it is effective but unpopular. Br J Psychiatry 1990;157:34–40.

53. Miller W, Hester R. The effectiveness of alcoholism treatment: what research reveals. In: Miller WR, Heather N, eds. The addictive behaviors: processes of change. New York: Plenum, 1986.

54. Miller W. The effectiveness of alcoholism treatment modalities. In: Causes and consequences of alcohol abuse. Washington, DC: U.S. Govt. Printing Office, 1988.

55. Miller W. The effectiveness of treatment for alcohol problems: reasons for optimism. In: Drug abuse and alcoholism: New prospects for recovery. London: Routledge, 1990.

56. Burns DM. Tobacco and health. In: Wyngaarden JB, Smith LH Jr., eds. Cecil textbook of medicine. 17th ed. Philadelphia: Saunders, 1985:46–50.

57. Evans RI, Rozelle RM, Maxwell SE, et al. Social modeling films to deter smoking in adolescents: results of a three year field investigation. J Appl Psychol 1981;66:319–414.

58. Ockene JK. Physician-delivered interventions for smoking cessation: strategies for increasing effectiveness. Prev Med 1987;16:723–737.

59. Pederson LL. Compliance with physician advice to quit smoking: a review of the literature. Prev Med 1982;22:71–84.

60. Leventhal H, Prohaska TR, Hirschman RS. Preventive health behavior across the life span. In: Rosen JC, Solomon LJ, eds. Prevention in health psychology. Hanover NH: University Press of New England, 1985.

61. Grunberg NE. The effects of nicotine and cigarette smoking on food consumption and taste preferences. Addict Behav 1982;7:317–331.

62. Solberg LI, Maxwell PL. A practice office-based smoking cessation program. Patient Health Educ Proc 1987;9:35–38.

63. Nelson RO, Hayes SC, Spong RT, Jarrett RB, McKnight DL. Self-reinforcement: appealing misnomer or effective mechanism? Behav Res Ther 1983;21:577–566.

64. Goldiamond I. Self-reinforcement. J App Behav Anal 1976;9:509–514.

65. Ossip-Klein DJ, Bigelow G, Parker SR, Curry S, Hall S, Kirkland S. Task force 1. Classification and assessment of smoking behavior. Health Psychol 1986;5:3–11.

66. Fagestrom KO, Melin B. Nicotine chewing gum in smoking cessation: efficiency, nicotine dependency, therapy duration and clinical recommendations. Nat Inst Drug Abuse Res Mono 1985;52:102–110.

67. Hall SM, Kellen JD. Psychological and pharmacological approaches to smoking relapse prevention. Nat Inst Drug Abuse Res Mono 1985;52:131–143.

68. Pi-Sunyer FX. Obesity. In: Wyngaarden JB, Smith LH, Bennett JC. Cecil textbook of medicine, 19th ed. Philadelphia: Saunders, 1992:1162–1170.

69. Stunkard AJ, Sorensen TIA, Hanis C, et al. An adoption study of human obesity. N Engl J Med 1986;314:193–198.

70. Brook CGD, Huntley RMC, Slack J. Influence of heredity and environment in determination of skinfold thickness in children. Br Med J 1975;2:719–721.

71. Medlund P, Cederlof R, Floderus-Myrhed B, et al. A new Swedish twin registry. Acta Med Scand (Suppl) 1976;600:1–111.

72. Borjeson M. The aetiology of obesity in children: a study of 101 twin pairs. Acta Paediatr Scand 1976;65:279–287.

73. Feinleib M, Garrison RJ, Fabsitz R, et al. The NHLBI twin study of cardiovascular disease risk factors: methodology and summary of results. Am J Epidemiol 1977;106:284–295.

74. Fabsitz R, Feinleib M, Hrubec Z. Weight changes in adult twins. Acta Genet Med Gemellol 1980;29:273–279.

75. Morris L, King NJ. Obesity. In: King NJ, Remenyi A, eds. Obesity: a behavioral approach. Orlando FL: Grune & Stratton, 1986.

76. Stunkard AJ. Behavioral medicine and beyond: the example of obesity. In: Pomerleau OF, Brady JP, eds. Behavioral medicine: theory and practice. Baltimore: Williams and Wilkins, 1979.

77. Stuart RB. Behavioral control of overeating. Beh Res Ther 1967;5:357–365.

78. Lissner L, Odell PM, D'Agostino RB, et al. Variability of body weight and health outcomes in the Framingham population. N Engl J Med 1991;324:1839–1844.

7/ Psychoanalytic and Psychodynamic Theories

1. Horowitz MJ. Introduction to psychodynamics: a new synthesis. New York: Basic Books, 1988.

2. Fine R. The history of psychoanalysis. Northvale, NJ: Jason Aronson, 1990.

3. Jones E. The life and work of Sigmund Freud. New York: Basic Books, 1953.

4. Gay P. Freud: a life for our time. New York: WW Norton, 1988.

5. Freud S. (1925) An autobiographical study. Standard edition of the complete psychological works of Sigmund Freud. London: Hogarth, 1958.

6. Swales PJ. Freud, his teacher, and the birth of psychoanalysis. In: Stepansky P, ed. Freud: appraisals and reappraisals. Hillsdale, NJ: Analytic Press, 1986.

7. Freud S. (1895) Studies on hysteria. Standard ed. London: Hogarth, 1955.

8. Freud S. (1900) The interpretation of dreams. Standard ed. London: Hogarth, 1953.

9. Freud S. (1920) Beyond the pleasure principle. Standard ed. London: Hogarth, 1955.

10. Freud S. (1923) The ego and the id. Standard ed. London: Hogarth, 1961.

11. Laplanche J, Pontalis JB. The language of psychoanalysis. New York: WW Norton, 1973.

12. Hartmann H. Ego psychology and the problem of adaptation. New York: International Universities Press, 1958.

13. Freud S. (1933) New introductory lectures on psychoanalysis. Standard ed. London: Hogarth, 1962.

14. Freud S. (1926) Inhibitions, symptoms, and anxiety. Standard ed. London: Hogarth, 1959.
15. Vaillant GE. The natural history of alcoholism: causes, patterns and paths to recovery. Cambridge, MA: Harvard University Press, 1983.
16. Freud S. (1911) Psychoanalytic notes on an autobiographical account of a case of paranoia (dementia paranoides). Standard ed. London: Hogarth, 1958.
17. Freud S. (1914) On narcissism. Standard ed. London: Hogarth, 1957.
18. Boyer LB. Analytic experiences in work with regressed patients. In: Giovacchini PL, Boyer LB, eds. New York: Jason Aronson, 1982.
19. Freud S (1905) Three essays on the theory of sexuality. Technical factors in the treatment of the severely disturbed patient. Standard ed. London: Hogarth, 1953.
20. Freud S. (1915) Instincts and their vicissitudes. Standard ed. London: Hogarth, 1957.
21. Freud S. (1914) Papers on technique. Standard ed. London: Hogarth, 1958.
22. Jung CG. Memories, dreams, reflections. New York: Random, 1961.
23. Satinover J. Jung's lost contribution to the dilemma of narcissism. J Am Psychoanal Assoc 1986;34:401–438.
24. Ansbacher HL, Ansbacher RR, eds. The individual psychology of Alfred Adler. New York: Basic Books, 1956.
25. Wyss D. Psychoanalytic schools: from the beginning to the present. New York: Jason Aronson, 1973.
26. Fine R. The development of Freud's thought. Northvale, NJ: Jason Aronson, 1987.
27. Reich W. Character analysis. New York: Orgone Institute Press, 1945.
28. Abraham K. Selected papers on psychoanalysis. New York: Basic Books, 1953.
29. Alexander F. Psychoanalysis and psychotherapy. New York: Norton, 1956.
30. Alexander R. Psychosomatic medicine. New York: Norton, 1950.
31. Horney K. Neurosis and human growth. New York: Norton, 1950.
32. Sullivan HS. Schizophrenia as a human process. New York: Norton, 1962.
33. Sullivan HS. The interpersonal theory of psychiatry. New York: Norton, 1953.
34. Freud A. The ego and the mechanisms of defense. New York: International Universities Press, 1966.
35. Hartmann H. Essays in ego psychology. New York: International Universities Press, 1964.
36. Erikson E. Childhood and society. New York: Norton, 1950.
37. Mahler MS, Pine P, Bergman A. The psychological birth of the human infant. New York: Basic Books, 1975.
38. Spitz R. The first year of life. New York: International Universities Press, 1965.
39. Horner AJ. Object relations theory and the developing ego in therapy. Northvale, NJ: Jason Aronson, 1979.
40. Blanck R. Blanck G. Beyond ego psychology. New York: Columbia University Press, 1986.
41. Klein M. The psychoanalysis of children. London: Hogarth, 1949.
42. Caper R. Immaterial facts: Freud's discovery of psychic reality and Klein's development of his work. Northvale, NJ: Jason Aronson, 1988.
43. Fairbairn WRD. A revised psychopathology of the psychoses and psychoneuroses. Int J Psychoanal 1941;22:250–279.
44. Fairbairn WRD. An object relations theory of the personality. New York: Basic Books, 1954.
45. Winnicott DW. Human nature. New York: Schocken, 1988.
46. Winnicott DW. Transitional objects and transitional phenomena. Psychoanal 1953;34:89–97.
47. Kernberg O. Borderline conditions and pathological narcissism. Northvale, NJ: Jason Aronson, 1975.
48. Goldstein WN. Kernberg on the borderline: a simplified version. In: Ross JM, Myers WA, eds. New concepts in psychoanalytic psychotherapy. Washington, DC: American Psychiatric Press, 1988.
49. Goldberg A. Psychoanalytic self psychology. In: Rothstein A, ed. Models of the mind: their relationships to clinical work. New York: International Universities Press, 1985.
50. Kohut H. The analysis of the self. New York: International Universities Press, 1971.
51. Kohut H. The restoration of the self. New York: International Universities Press, 1977.
52. Kohut H Wolf E. The disorders of the self and their treatment: an outline. Int J Psychoanal 1978;59:414–425.

8/ Medical Sociology

1. Zborowski M. Cultural components in response to pain. J Soc Issues 1952;8:16–30.
2. Zola I. Culture and symptoms: an analysis of patients presenting complaints, Am Sociol Rev 1966;31:615–630.
3. Milunsky A. Choices, not chances: an essential guide to your heredity and health. Boston: Little, Brown, 1989: 120,121.
4. Maduro R. Curanderismo and Latino views of disease and healing. West J Med 1983;139:868–874.
5. Kiev A. Curanderismo. New York: Free Press, 1968.
6. Lieban R. The field of medical anthropology. In: Landy D, ed. Culture, disease and healing. New York: Macmillan, 1977.
7. Himmelstein DU, Woolhandler S, and the Writing Committee of the Working Group on Program Design. A national health program for the United States: a physician's proposal. N. Engl J Med 1989;320:102–108.
8. Sin AL, Sonnenberg FA, Manning WG, et al. Inappropriate use of hospitals in a randomized trial of health insurance plans. N Engl J Med 1986;315:1259–1266.
9. Brian EW, Gibbens SF. California's Medi-Cal co-payment experiment. Med Care (Suppl) 1974;12:1–303.
10. Ginzberg E: Health care reform—why so slow? N Engl J Med 1990;322:1464–1466.
11. Kimbell M. Fee controls prompt doctors to reduce Medicare services. Health Week May 30, 1989.
12. Wilensky G. Underwriting the uninsured: targeting providers or individuals. In: Sloan FA, Blumstein JF, Perrin JM, eds. Uncompensated hospital care: rights and responsibilities. Baltimore: Johns Hopkins University Press 1986:148–166.
13. Davis K, Rowland D. Uninsured and underserved; inequities in health care in the United States. Milbank Mem Fund 1983;61:149–176.
14. Harwood A. The hot-cold theory of disease: implications for treatment of Puerto Rican patients. JAMA 1971;26:1153–1158.
15. Snow LF. Traditional health beliefs and practices among lower-class black Americans. West J Med 1983;139:820–828.
16. Stern RS, Weissman JS, Epstein AM. The emergency department as a pathway to admission for poor and high-cost patients. JAMA 1991;266:2238–2243.

17. Friedman E, Haglund MM, McNamara P. The sagging safety net: emergency departments on the brink of crisis. Hospitals 1991(Feb. 20):26–40.

18. Stunkard A. From explanation to action in psychosomatic medicine: the case of obesity. Psychosom Med 1975;37: 195–236.

19. Antonovsky A. Social class, life expectancy and overall mortality. Milbank Mem Fund Q 1967;45:31–73.

20. Richardson WC. Poverty, illness and the use of health services in the United States. Hospitals 1969;43:34–40.

21. Kegeles SS, Kirscht JP, Haefner DP, Rosenstock IM. Survey of beliefs about cancer detection and taking Papanicolao tests. Public Health Rep 1965;80:815–824.

22. Kasl SV, Cobb S. Health behavior, illness behavior and sick role behavior. I. Arch Environ Health 1966;12:246–266.

23. Kasl SV, Cobb S. Health behavior, illness behavior and sick role behavior. II. Arch Environ Health 1966;12:531–541.

24. Moody PM, Gray RM. Social class, social integration, and the use of preventive health services. In: Patients, physicians and illness: a source book in behavioral science and health. New York: Free Press, 1972:240–370.

25. Susser M, Hopper K, Richman J. Society, culture and health. In: Mechanic D, ed. Handbook of health, health care, and the professions. New York: Free Press 1983;23–49.

26. Jenkins CR. Social environment and cancer mortality in men. N Engl J Med 1983;308:395–398.

27. Kosa J. The nature of poverty. In: Kosa J, Zola IK. Poverty and health. Cambridge MA: Harvard University Press, 1976:1–39.

28. Hollingshead AB, Redlich FC. Social class and mental illness. New York: Wiley, 1958.

29. Srole L, Langer TS, Michael SI. Mental health in the metropolis: the midtown Manhattan study. New York: McGraw, 1962.

30. Leighton DC, Harding JS, Macklin DB, et al. The character of danger. New York: Basic Books, 1963.

31. Baker SP, O'Neill B, Karpf RS. The injury fact book. Lexington KY: D.C. Heath, 1984.

32. Duff S, Hollingshead AB. Sickness and society. New York: Harper and Row, 1968.

33. Rainwater L. The lower class, health, illness and medical contributions. In: Millon T, ed. Medical behavioral science. Philadelphia: Saunders, 1975.

34. Goodwin DW, Guze SB. Psychiatric diagnosis. New York: Oxford, 1989:243.

35. Guze SB, Woodruff RA Jr, Clayton PJ. A study of conversion symptoms in psychiatric outpatients. Am J Psychiatry 1971;128:643–646.

36. Dunham HW. Community and schizophrenia. Detroit: Wayne State University Press, 1965.

37. Sierles FS. Behavioral science for the boreds. Miami: Medmaster, 1989;17–19.

38. Verbrugge L. Longer life but worsening health? trends in health and mortality of middle-aged and older persons. Milbank Mem Fund Q 1984;62d:475.

39. Cullen MR, Cherniack MG, Rosenstock L. Occupational medicine I. N Engl J Med 1990;322:594–599.

40. Cullen MR, Cherniack MG, Rosenstock L. Occupational medicine II. N Engl J Med 1990;322:675–683.

41. Cullen MR, Cherniack MG. The spectrum of occupational disease. Arch Intern Med 1989;149:1621–1626.

42. Anonymous. Occupational medicine: health hazards of the work place. Patient Care 1979;13:183–192.

43. Leigh JP. Estimates of the probability of job-related death in 347 occupations. J Occup Med 1987;29:510–519.

44. Leigh JP. Specific illnesses, injuries and job hazards associated with absenteeism. J Occup Med 1989;31:792–797.

45. Ressignol AM, Locke JA, Burke JF. Employment status and the frequency and causes of burn injuries in New England. J Occup Med 1989;31:751–757.

46. Andreasen NC. Creativity and mental illness: prevalence rates in writers and their first degree relatives. Am J Psychiatry 1987;144:1288–1292.

47. Veitia MC, McGahee L. Ordinary addictions: tobacco and alcohol. In: Wedding D, ed. Behavior in medicine. St. Louis: Mosby Year Book, 1990.

48. Mechanic D. Social psychologic factors affecting the presentation of bodily complaints. N Engl J Med 1972;286: 1132–1139.

49. Tessler R, Mechanic D. Psychological distress and perceived health status. J Health Soc Behav 1978;19:254–262.

50. Dubos R. Mirage of health. New York: Doubleday, 1959.

51. USDHHS, Centers for Disease Control. HIV prevalence estimates. MMWR 1990(Nov. 30).

52. USDHHS, Centers for Disease Control. Mortality patterns—United States, 1987. MMWR 1990;39(12):193–201.

53. Virchow RK. Cellular pathology as based upon physiological and pathological histology. London: Churchill, 1860.

54. Pennebaker JW, Skelton JA. Psychological parameters of physical symptoms. Pers Soc Psychol Bull 4:524–530.

55. Parsons T. Definitions of health and illness, in the light of American values and social structure. In: Jaco E, ed. Patients, physicians and illness. New York: Free Press, 1972.

56. Salloway JC. Health care delivery systems. Boulder, CO: Westview Press, 1982.

57. Rosenstock I. Historical origins of the health belief model. Health Educ Mono 1974;2:334.

58. Becker M, Maiman L, Kirscht J, Haefner D. The health belief model and prediction of dietary compliance: a field experiment. J Health Soc Behav 1977;18:159.

59. Becker M. The health belief model and personal health behavior. San Francisco: Society for Public Health Education, 1974.

60. Coe M. Sociology of medicine. New York: McGraw-Hill, 1978.

61. Salloway JC, Pletcher WR, Collins JJ. Sociological and social psychological models of compliance with prescribed regimen: in search of synthesis. Sociological Symposium 1978;23:100–121.

62. Suchman E. Stages of illness and medical career. J Health Hum Behav 1965; 6:2–16.

63. Andersen R, Newman J. Societal and individual determinants of medical care utilization in the United States. Milbank Mem Fund Q 1973;51:95–124.

64. Wallston BS, Wallston KA, Kaplan GD, Maides S. Development and validation of the health locus of control scale. J Consult Clin Psychol 1976;44:580–585.

65. Wallston KA, Maides S, Wallston BS. Health-related information-seeking as a function of health-related locus of control and health values. J Res Pers 1976;10:215–222.

9/ Evolutionary Biology and Human Behavior

1. Linnaeus CV. Systema naturae. New York: Weldon and Wesley, 1964.

2. Johanson DC, Taieb M. Plio-pleistocene hominid discoveries in Hadar, Ethopia. Nature 1976;260:293–297.

3. Simons EL. Human origins. Science 1989;245:1343–1350.

4. Leakey LSB, Tobias PV, Napier JR. A new species of the genus Homo from the Olduvai Gorge. Nature 1964;202:7–9.

5. British Museum of Natural History. Man's place in evolution. London: Cambridge University Press, 1980.

6. Stringer CB, Andrews P. Genetic and fossil evidence for the origin of modern humans. Science 1988;239:1263–1268.

7. Lewin R. Africa: cradle of modern humans. Science 1987; 237:1292–1295.

8. Lovejoy CO. The origin of man. Science 1981;211:341–350.

9. Lewin R. Four legs bad, two legs good. Science 1987;235: 969–971.

10. Calvin WH. The throwing madonna. New York: McGraw-Hill, 1983:28

11. Daly M, Wilson M. Evolutionary social psychology and family homicide. Science 1988;242:519–523.

12. Hamilton WD. The genetical evolution of social behavior. J Theoretical Biol 1964;7:1–52.

13. Crawford CB, Anderson JL. Sociobiology: an environmentalist discipline. Am Psychol 1989;44:1449–1459.

14. Ehlers CL, Frank E, Kupfer DJ. Social zeitgebers and biological rhythms. Arch Gen Psychiatry 1988;45:948–952.

15. Wilson EO. Sociobiology: the new synthesis. Cambridge: Belknap, 1975.

16. Lewin R. The origin of the modern human mind. Science 1987;236:668–670.

17. Lewin R. Practice catches theory in kin recognition. Science 1984;223:1049–1051.

18. Trivers RL. The evolution of reciprocal altruism. Q Rev Biol 1971;46:35–57.

19. Maynard Smith J, Price GR. The logic of animal conflict. Nature 1973;246:15–18.

20. Charlesworth W. Resources and resource acquisition during ontogeny. In: MacDonald KB, ed. Sociobiological perspectives on human development. New York: Springer-Verlag, 1987:25–76.

21. Gould SJ. Hen's teeth and horse's toes. New York: Norton, 1984:329.

10/ Pregnancy

1. Brenner PF, Mishell DR. Control of human reproduction: contraception, sterilization, and pregnancy termination. In: Scott JR, DiSaia PJ, Hammond CB, Spellacy WN, eds. Danforth's obstetrics and gynecology. 6th ed. Philadelphia: Lippincott, 1990:709–728.

2. Shoupe D, Mishell DR. Norplant: subdermal implant system for long-term contraception. Am J Obstet Gynecol 1989;160:1286–1292.

3. Kochenour NK: Normal pregnancy and prenatal care. In: Scott JR, DiSaia PJ, Hammond CB, Spellacy WN, eds. Danforth's obstetrics and gynecology. 6th ed. Philadelphia: Lippincott, 1990:123–159.

4. Cruikshank DP. Cardiovascular pulmonary renal and hematologic diseases in pregnancy. In: Scott JR, DiSaia PJ, Hammond CB, Spellacy WN, eds. Danforth's obstetrics and gynecology. 6th ed. Philadelphia: Lippincott, 1990:433–459.

5. Rakic P. Specification of cerebral cortical areas. Science 1988;241;170–176.

6. Benedek T. The psychobiology of pregnancy. In: Anthony EJ, Benedek T, eds. Parenthood, its psychology and psychopathology. Boston: Little, Brown, 1970:137–151.

7. Bibring GL, Dwyer TF, Huntington DS, Valenstein AF. A study of the psychological processes in pregnancy and of the earliest mother-child relationship. I. Some propositions and comments. In: Eissler RS, Freud A, Hartmann H, Kris M, eds. The psychoanalytic study of the child. New York: International Universities Press, 1961:9–24.

8. Lips HM. A longitudinal study of the reporting of emotional and somatic symptoms during and after pregnancy. Soc Sci Med 1985;21:631–640.

9. Bailey LA, Hailey, BJ. The psychological experience of pregnancy. Int J Psychiatry Med 1986–1987;16:263–274.

10. Mamelle N, Gerin P, Measson A, Munoz F, Collet P. Assessment of psychological modifications during pregnancy: contribution of Derogatis symptom check-list (SCL 90-R). J Psychosom Obstet Gynecol 1987;7:39–50.

11. Brown MA. A comparison of health responses in expectant mothers and fathers. West J Nurs Res 1988;10:527–549.

12. Brown S. Drawing women into prenatal care. Fam Plann Perspect 1989;21:73–80.

13. Brown WA. Psychological care during pregnancy: an opportunity in preventive medicine. In: Psychological care during pregnancy and the postpartum period. New York: Raven, 1979:1–10.

14. Physician's Desk Reference. Oradell, NJ: Medical Economics Company, 1991.

15. Reading AE, Campbell S, Cox DN, Sledmere CM. Health beliefs and health care behaviour in pregnancy. Psychol Med 1982;12:379–383.

16. Anderson HF, Merkatz IR. Preterm labor. In: Scott JR, DiSaia PJ, Hammond CB, Spellacy WN, eds. Danforth's obstetrics and gynecology. 6th ed. Philadelphia: Lippincott, 1990.

17. Reed KL. Ultrasound in obstetrics. In: Scott JR, DiSaia PJ, Hammond CB, Spellacy WN, eds. Danforth's obstetrics and gynecology. 6th ed. Philadelphia: Lippincott, 1990: 293–314.

18. Phipps S, Zinn AB. Psychological response to amniocentesis: I. Mood state and adaptation to pregnancy. Am J Med Genet 1986;25:131–142.

19. Marteau TM, Johnston M, Shaw RW, Michie S, Kidd J, New M. The impact of prenatal screening and diagnostic testing upon the cognitions, emotions and behaviour of pregnant women. J Psychosom Res 1989;33:7–16.

20. Simpson JL. Genetic factors in obstetrics and gynecology. In: Scott JR, DiSaia PJ, Hammond CB, Spellacy WN, eds. Danforth's obstetrics and gynecology. 6th ed. Philadelphia: Lippincott, 1990:237–272.

21. Stotland NL. Psychological implications of recent developments in peripartum care. Adv Psychosom Med 1985;12: 91–104.

22. Istavan JA. Stress, anxiety, and birth outcomes: a critical review of the evidence. Psychol Bull 1986;3:331–348.

23. Molfese VJ, Bricker MC, Manion LG, Beadnell B, Yaple K, Moires KA. Anxiety, depression and stress in pregnancy: a multivariate model of intra-partum risks and pregnancy outcomes. J Psychosom Obstet Gynecol 1987;7:77–92.

24. Omer H, Everly GS. Psychological factors in preterm labor: critical review and theoretical synthesis. Am J Psychiatry 1988;145:1507–1513.

25. Brown WA. The pregnany adolescent. In: Psychological care during pregnancy and the postpartum period. New York: Raven, 1979:49–62.

26. Muran D. Pediatric and adolescent gynecology. In: Pernoll ML, Benson RC, eds. Current obstetric and gynecologic diagnosis and treatment 6th ed. Norwalk, CT: Appleton & Lange, 1987:563–585.

27. Welles-Nystrom BL, de Chateau P. Maternal age and transition to motherhood: prenatal and perinatal assessments. Acta Psychiatr Scand 1987;76:719–725.

28. Lee RE. When midcareer mothers first return to work: counseling concerns. J Couns Dev 1984;63:35–39.

29. Grunebaum A, Minkoff H, Blake D. Pregnancy among obstetricians; a comparison of births before, during, and after residency. Am J Obstet Gynecol 1987;157:79–83.

30. Schwartz RW. Pregnancy in physicians: characteristics and complications. Obstet Gynecol 1985;66:672–676.

31. Phelan ST. Pregnancy during residency: II. Obstetric complications. Obstet Gynecol 1988; 72:431–436.

32. Klebanoff MA, Shiono PH, Rhoads GG. Outcomes of pregnancy in a national sample of resident physicians. N Engl J Med 1990;15:1040–1045.

33. Tatum HJ. Contraception and family planning. In Pernoll ML, Bensen RC, eds. Current obstetric and gynecologic diagnosis and treatment. Norwalk, CT: Appleton & Lange, 1987:586–611.

34. Kochanek KD. Induced terminations of pregnancy: reporting states, 1987. Monthly vital statistics report final data from the National Center for Health Statistics 1990;38(9) (suppl January 5).

35. Dagg PKB. The psychological sequelae of therapeutic abortion—denied and completed. Am J Psychiatry 1991;148: 578–585.

36. David HP. Post-abortion and post-partum psychiatric hospitalization. Ciba Found Symp 1985;115:150–164.

37. Pare CMB, Raven H. Psychiatric sequelae to therapeutic abortion: followup of patients referred for termination of pregnancy. Lancet 1970;1:635–638.

38. Resnick PJ. Murder of the newborn: a psychiatric review of neonaticide. Am J Psychiatry 1970;126:1414–1420.

39. Matejcak Z, Dytrych Z, Schuller V. Children born from unwanted pregnancies. Acta Psychiatr Scand 1978;57:67–90.

40. Zlatnik FJ. The puerperium: normal and abnormal. In: Scott JR, DiSaia PJ, Hammond CB, Spellacy WN, eds. Danforth's obstetrics and gynecology. 6th ed. Philadelphia: Lippincott, 1990:189–194.

41. Paffenberger RS. Epidemiologic aspects of postpartum mental illness. Br J Prev Soc Med 1964;18:189–195.

42. Hapgood CC, Elkind GS, Wright JJ. Maternity blues; phenomena and relationship to later post partum depression. Aust NZ J Psychiatry 1988;22:299–306.

43. Kennerley H, Gath D. Maternity blues reassessed. Psychiatr Dev 1986;1:1–17.

44. Casiano ME, Hawkins DR. Major mental illness and childbearing, a role for the consultation-liaison psychiatrist in obstetrics. Psychiatr Clin North Am 1987;10:35–51.

45. Brockington IF, Cernik KF, Schofield EM, Downing AR, Francis AF, Keelan C. Puerperal psychosis, phenomena and diagnosis. Arch Gen Psychiatry 1981;38:829–833.

46. Munoz RA. Postpartum psychosis as a discrete entity. J Clin Psychiatry 1985;46:182–184.

47. Katona CLE. Puerperal mental illness: comparisons with non-puerperal controls. Br J Psychiatry 1982;141:447–452.

48. Kadrmas A, Winokur G, Crowe R. Postpartum mania. Br J Psychiatry 1979;135:551–554.

49. Brockington IF, Kelly A, Hall P, Deakin W. Premenstrual relapse of puerperal psychosis. J Affective Disord 1988;14: 287–292.

50. McNeil TF, Kaij L, Malmquist-Larsson A. Women with nonorganic psychosis: mental disturbance during pregnancy. Acta Psychiatr Scand 1984;70:127–138.

51. McNeil TF, Kaij L, Malmquist-Larsson A. Women with nonorganic psychosis: pregnancy's effect on mental health during pregnancy. Acta Psychiatr Scand 1984;70:140–148.

52. Paffenbarger, Jr. RS. Epidemiological aspects of mental illness associated with childbearing. In: Brockington IF, Kumar R, eds. Motherhood and mental illness. New York: Grune & Stratton, 1982:19–36.

53. Davidson J, Robertson E. A follow-up study of postpartum illness, 1946–1978. Acta Psychiatr Scand 1985;71:451–457.

54. Mortola JF. The use of psychotropic agents in pregnancy and lactation. Psychiatr Clin North Am 1989;12:69–87.

55. Repke JT, Berger NG. Electroconvulsive therapy in pregnancy. Obstet Gynecol 1984;63:395–415.

56. Abrams R. Electroconvulsive therapy. New York: Oxford, 1989:77, 78.

57. Molitch ME, Reichlin S. The amenorrhea, galactorrhea and hyperprolactinemia syndromes. Adv Intern Med 1980;26: 37–65.

58. Milner GL, Hayes GD. Pseudocyesis associated with folie a deux. Br J Psychiatry 1990;156:438–440.

59. Seibel MM, Ranoux C, Kearnan M. In vitro fertilization: how much is enough? N Engl J Med 1989;321:1052–1053.

60. Herz EK. Infertility and bioethical issues of the new reproductive technologies. Psychiatr Clin North Am 1989;12: 117–131.

61. Hughes CL, Hammond CB. Infertility. In: Scott JR, DiSaia PJ, Hammond CB, Spellacy WN, eds. Danforth's obstetrics and gynecology. 6th ed. Philadelphia: Lippincott, 1990: 807–820.

62. Wright J, Allard M, Lecours A, Sabourin S. Psychosocial distress and infertility: a review of controlled research. Int J Fertil 1989;34:126–142.

63. Rosenwaks Z, Davis OK. In vitro fertilization and related techniques. In: Scott JR, DiSaia PJ, Hammond CB, Spellacy WN, eds. Danforth's obstetrics and gynecology. 6th ed. Philadelphia: Lippincott, 1990:821–843.

64. Blaser A, Maloigne-Katz B, Gigon U. Effect of artificial insemination with donor semen on the psyche of the husband. Psychother Psychosom 1988;49:17–21.

65. Alexander NJ, Ackermann S. Therapeutic insemination: the infertile woman. Obstet Gynecol Clin North Am 1987;14: 905–929.

66. Berger DM, Eisen A, Shuber J, Doody KF. Psychological patterns in donor insemination couples. Can J Psychiatry 1986;31:818–823.

67. Callan VJ, Hennessey JF. Emotional aspects and support in in vitro fertilization and embryo transfer programs. J In Vitro Fertil Embryo Transfer 1988;5:290–295.

68. de Zoeten MJ, Tymstra T, Alberda AT. The waiting list for IVF: the motivations and expectations of women waiting for IVF treatment. Hum Reprod 1987;2:623–626.

69. Harrison KL, Callan VJ, Hennessey JF. Stress and semen quality in an in vitro fertilization program. Fertil Steril 1987;48:633–636.

70. Hall RCW, Beresford TP, Quinones JE. Grief following spontaneous abortion. Psychiatr Clin North Am 1987;10: 405–420.

71. Leppert PC, Pahlka BS. Grieving characteristics after spontaneous abortion: a management approach. Obstet Gynecol 1984;64:119–122.

72. LaRoche C, Lalinec-Michaud M, Engelsmann F, Fuller N, Copp M, McQuade-Soldatos, Azima R. Grief reactions to perinatal death—a follow-up study. Can J Psychiatry 1984; 29:14–19.

73. Berezin N. After a loss in pregnancy, help for families affected by a miscarriage, a stillbirth or the loss of a newborn. New York: Simon & Schuster, 1982.

11/ Child and Adolescent Development and Psychopathology

1. Hinde RA. Family influences. In: Rutter M, ed. Developmental psychiatry. Washington, DC: American Psychiatric Press, 1980:48.
2. Dunn J. Individual differences in temperament. In: Rutter M, ed. Developmental psychiatry. Washington, DC: American Psychiatric Press, 1980:101.
3. Dixon SD. The newborn examination: innate readiness for interaction with the environment. In: Dixon SD, Stein MT, eds. Encounters with children: pediatric behavior and development. Chicago: Mosby Year Book, 1987:63.
4. Frith U. Reading and spelling skills. In: Rutter M, ed. Developmental psychiatry. Washington, DC: American Psychiatric Press, 1980:223.
5. Dixon SD, Stein MT. Basic perspectives: biases and format. In: Dixon SD, Stein MT, eds. Encounters with children: pediatric behavior and development. Chicago: Mosby Year Book, 1987:3.
6. Felice ME. 11 to 13 years: early adolescent—the age of rapid changes. In: Dixon SD, Stein MT, eds. Encounters with children: pediatric behavior and development. Chicago: Mosby Year Book 1987:319.
7. Antinucci F, Miller R. How children talk about what happened. J Child Lang 1975;3:167–189.
8. Adelson E, Fraiberg S. Gross motor development of infants blind from birth. Child Dev. 1974; 45:114–126.
9. Branch C, Millner B, Rasmussen T. Intracarotid sodium amytal for the lateralization of cerebral speech dominance. J. Neurosurg 1964;21:399–405.
10. Madge N, Tizard J. Intelligence. In: Rutter M, ed. Developmental psychiatry. Washington, DC: American Psychiatric Press, 1980:245–265.
11. Rutter M, Birch H, Thomas A, Chess S. Temperamental characteristics in infancy and later development of behaviour disorders. Br J Psychiatry 1964;110:651–661.
12. Graham P, Rutter M. Psychiatric disorders in the young adolescent: a follow-up study. Proc R Soc Med 1973;66:1226–1229.
13. Cowen EL, Pederson A, Babijian H, Izzo LD, Trost MA. Long-term follow-up of early detected vulnerable children. J Consult Clin Psychol 1973;41:438–446.
14. Roff M, Sells SB, Golden MM. Social adjustment and personality development in children. Minneapolis: University of Minnesota Press, 1972.
15. Green R. Gender identity in childhood and later sexual orientation: follow-up of 78 males. Am J Psychiatry 1985;142:339–342.
16. Walker E, Lewine RJ. Prediction of adult-onset schizophrenia from childhood home movies of the patients. Am J Psychiatry 1990;147:1052–1056.
17. Crisp AH, Douglas JW, Ross JM, Stonehill E. Some developmental aspects of disorders of weight. J Psychosom Res 1970;14:327–345.
18. Brown JV, Bateman R. Relationships of human mothers with their infants during the first year of life: effects of prematurity. In: Bell RW, Smotherman WP, eds. Maternal influences and early behavior. Holliswood, NY: Spectrum, 1978.
19. Rutter M. Individual differences. In: Rutter M, Hersov LA, eds. Child psychiatry: modern approaches. Oxford, UK: Blackwell, 1977:3–21.
20. Stein MT. Interviewing in a pediatric setting. In: Dixon SD, Stein MT, eds. Encounters with children: pediatric behavior and development. Chicago: Mosby Year Book, 1987:31, 33.
21. Sarma PSB. Child development. In: Sierles FS, ed. Clinical behavioral science. Jamaica NY: SP Medical & Scientific Books, 1982:245–271.
22. Freedman DG, Keller B. Inheritance of behavior in infants. Science 1963;40:196.
23. Wilson RS. Mental development in twins. In: Oliverio A, ed. Genetics, environment and intelligence. North Holland: Elsevier, 1977:305–334.
24. Corballis MC. Is left-handedness genetically determined? In: Herron J, ed. Neuropsychology of left-handedness. New York: Academic Press, 1980:159–176.
25. Fischbein S. Onset of puberty in MZ and DZ twins. Acta Genet Med Gemellol 1977;26:151–157.
26. Holmes LB. Genetic counseling. In: Behrman RE, Vaughan VC, Nelson WE, eds. Nelson textbook of pediatrics. Philadelphia: Saunders, 1987:272.
27. Farran D, Ramey C. Social class differences in dyadic interaction during infancy. Child Dev 1977;48:97–103.
28. Clarke-Stewart KA. Interactions between mothers and their young children: characteristics and consequences. Monogr Soc Res Child Dev 1973;38:1–109.
29. Newson J, Newson E. Four years old in an urban community. London: Allen and Unwin, 1968.
30. Mitchell RE. Some social implications of high density housing. Am Soc Rev 1971;36:18–29.
31. Hess RD, Shipman VC. Early experience and the socialization of cognitive modes in children. Child Devel 1968;36:869–888.
32. Nelson K. Structure and strategy in learning to talk. Monogr Soc Res Child Dev 1973;38(1):2.
33. Powers MJ, Benn RT, Morris JN. Neighbourhood, school and juveniles before the courts. Br J Criminol 1972;111–132.
34. Edwards A. Sex and area variations in delinquency rates in an English city. Br J Criminol 1973;13:121–137.
35. West DJ, Farrington DP. Who becomes delinquent? second report of the Cambridge study in delinquent development. London: Heinemann, 1977.
36. Quinton D. Cultural and community influences. In: Rutter M, ed. Developmental psychiatry. Washington, DC: American Psychiatric Press, 1980:77–91.
37. Ugurel-Semin R. Moral behavior and moral judgment of children. J Abnorm Soc Psychol 1952;47:463–474.
38. Berkowitz L, Friedman P. Some social class differences in helping behavior. J. Pers Soc Psychol 1967;5:217–225.
39. Lev-Ran A. Gender role differentiation in hermaphrodites. Arch Sex Behav 1974;3:391–424.
40. Hampson JL, Hampson JG. The ontogenesis of sexual behavior in men. In: Young WC, Corner GW, eds. Sex and internal secretions. Vol. II, 3rd ed. Baltimore: Williams & Wilkins, 1961.
41. Rutter M. Psychosexual development. In: Rutter M, ed. Developmental psychiatry. Washington, DC: American Psychiatric Press, 1980:322–339.
42. Green R. Sexual identity of 37 children raised by homosexual or transsexual parents. Am J Psychiatry 1978;135:692–697.

43. Popper CW. Disorders usually first indent in infancy, childhood or adolescence. In: Talbott JA, Hales RE, Yudofsky SC, eds. Textbook of psychiatry. Washington, DC: American Psychiatric Press, 1988:649–736.

44. Willemsen E. Understanding infancy. San Francisco: WH Freeman, 1979.

45. Oppell WC, Harper PA, Rider RV. The age of attaining bladder control. Pediatrics 1968;42:614–626.

46. Caudell W, Platt DW. Who sleeps by whom? parent-child involvement in urban Japanese families. Psychiatry 1966; 29:344–366.

47. Klackenburg A. Primary enuresis: when is a child dry at night? Acta Paediatr Scand 1955;44:513–518.

48. Lovibund SH. Conditioning and enuresis. Oxford, UK: Pergamon, 1964.

49. Lozoff B, Paludetto R, Lotz S. Transitional object use in the United States, Japan and Italy. Paper presented to the Ambulatory Pediatric Association, Carmel, CA, 1985.

50. Altus WD. Birth order and its sequelae. Science 1966;151: 44–48.

51. Rutter M, Mittler P. Environmental influences on language development. In: Rutter M, Marlin JAM, eds. The child with delayed speech. Clinics Devel Med. No. 43. London: Heinemann, 1972.

52. Clarke AM, Clarke ADB, eds. Early experience: myth and evidence. London: Open Books, 1976.

53. Scarr S, Weinberg RA. IQ test performance of black children adopted by white families. Am Psychologist 1976;31: 726–739.

54. Coleman JS. Equality of educational opportunity. Washington, DC: U.S. Government Printing Office, 1966.

55. Reynolds D, Jones D, St. Leger S. Schools do make a difference. New Society 1976;37:321–323.

56. Rutter M, Maughan B, Mortimore P, Ouston P. Fifteen thousand hours. London: Open Books, 1979.

57. Salvia J, Sheare J, Algozzine B. Facial attractiveness and personal-social development. J Abnorm Child Psychol 1975;3:1171–178.

58. Lerner RM, Lerner JV. Effects of age, sex, and physical attractiveness on child-peer relations, academic performance, and elementary school adjustment. Dev Psychol 1977;13: 585–589.

59. Hartup WW. Children and their friends. In: McGurk H, ed. Issues in childhood social development. London: Methuen, 1978.

60. Thomas A, Chess S. Genesis and evolution of behavioral disorders: from infancy to adult life. Am J Psychiatry 1984; 141:1–9.

61. Torgerson AM, Kringlen E. Genetic aspects of temperamental differences in infants. J Am Acad Child Psychiatry 1978;17:433–444.

62. Brazelton TB, Koslowski B, Main M. The origins of reciprocity: the early mother-infant interaction. In: Lewis, M, Rosenblum LA, eds. The effect of the infant on its caregiver. New York: Wiley, 1974:49–76.

63. Thomas A. Current trends in developmental theory. Am J Orthopsychiatry 1981;51:580–609.

64. Lorenz K. Studies in animal and human behavior. Vol. 1. Cambridge, MA: Harvard University Press, 1970.

65. Condon WS, Sandler LW. Synchrony demonstrated between movement of the neonate and adult speech. Child Dev 1974;43:456–462.

66. MacFarlane A. Olfaction. In: The development of social preference in the human neonate. Ciba Found Symp No. 33, 1975.

67. Rutter M. Attachment and the development of social relationships. In: Rutter M, ed. Developmental psychiatry. Washington, DC: American Psychiatric Press, 1987:267–279.

68. Dixon SD, Yogman M, Tronick E, et al. Early infant interaction with parents and strangers. J Am Acad Child Psychiatry 1981;20:32–52.

69. Dixon SD. Three to four months: having fun with the picture-book baby. In: Dixon SD, Stein MT, eds. Encounters with children: pediatric behavior and development. Chicago: Mosby Year Book, 1987:131–141.

70. Bendell-Estrofff D, Snyder DM. Birth and infancy. In: Wedding D, ed. Behavior in medicine. Chicago: Mosby Year Book, 1991:3–17.

71. Rajecki DW, Lamb ME, Obmascher P. Toward a general theory of infantile attachment: a comparative review of aspects of the social bond. Behav Brain Sci 1978;1:417–464.

72. Ainsworth MDS. The development of infant-mother attachment. In: Caldwell BM, Riocciuti HN, eds. Review of child development research. Vol. 3. Chicago: University of Chicago Press, 1973.

73. Rheingold HL, Eckerman CO. The infant separates himself from his mother. Science 1970;168:78–83.

74. Cox FN, Campbell D. Young children in a new situation with and without their mothers. Child Dev 1968;39:123–131.

75. Bower TGR. A primer of infant development. San Francisco: WH Freeman, 1977:61.

76. Maccoby EE. Social development: psychological growth and the parent-child relationship. New York: Harcourt, Brace, Jovanovich, 1980.

77. Bowlby J. Attachment and loss. vol 2. Separation: anxiety and anger. London: Hogarth Press, 1973.

78. Maccoby EE, Feldman SS. Mother-attachment and stranger-reactions in the third year of life. Monogr Soc Res Child Devel 1972;37, serial no. 146.

79. Stayton DJ, Ainsworth MDS. Individual differences in infant responses to brief, everyday separations as related to other infant and maternal behaviors. Develop Psychol 1973;9:226–235.

80. Ainsworth MDS. Infancy in Uganda: infant care and the growth of attachment. Baltimore: Johns Hopkins Press, 1967.

81. Stevens A. Attachment and polymatric rearing: a study of attachment formation, separation anxiety and fear of strangers in infants reared by multiple mothering in an institutional setting. Unpublished DM thesis, University of Oxford, 1975.

82. Schaffer HR, Emerson PE. The development of social attachments in infancy. Monogr Soc Res Child Devel 1964; 29, serial no. 94.

83. Blehar MC, Lieberman AF, Ainsworth MDS. Early face-to-face interaction and its relation to later infant-mother attachment. Child Dev 1977;48:182–194.

84. Tizard B, Hodges J. The effect of early institutional rearing on the development of eight-year-old children. J Child Psychol Psychiatry 1978;19:99–118.

85. Tizard J, Tizard B. The social development of 2-year-old children in residential nurseries. In: Schaffer HE, ed. The origins of human social relations. London: Academic Press, 1971.

86. Goldfarb W. The effects of early institutional care on adolescent personality. J Exp Educ 1943;12:106–129.

87. Spitz RA. Anaclitic depression. Psychoanal Study Child 1946;2:313–342.

88. Volpe JJ. Neurology of the newborn. Philadelphia: Saunders, 1971.

89. Dixon SD. The prenatal visit: making an alliance with a family. In: Dixon SD, Stein MT. Encounters with children: pediatric behavior and development. Chicago: Mosby Year Book 1987:39–55.

90. Berger LR. Modern motor milestones. Pediatrics 1978;62: 1037.

91. Chistopherson CR. Children's behavior during automobile rides: do car seats make a difference? Pediatrics 1977;60: 69–74.

92. Wiswell T, Roscelli J. Corroborative evidence for the deceased incidence of urinary tract infections in early infancy. Pediatrics 1986;78:1031–1045.

93. Williamson P, Williamson M. Physiologic stress reduction by a local anesthetic during newborn circumcision. Pediatrics 1983;71:36–42.

94. Legg C, Sherick I, Wadland W. Reaction of preschool children to the birth of a sibling. Child Psychiatry Hum Dev 1974;5:3–39.

95. Parke RD, Power TG, Tensley BR, et al. The father's role in the family system. Semin Perinatol 1979;3:25–34.

96. Kaiser P. Five days to four weeks. In: Dixon SD, Stein MT, eds. Encounters with children: pediatric behavior and development. Chicago: Mosby Year Book, 1987:99–109.

97. Klaus MH, Fanaroff AA. Care of the high-risk neonate. Philadelphia: Saunders, 1973.

98. Brazelton TB, Robey J. Observations of neonatal behavior: the effect of perinatal variables, in particular that of neonatal medication. J Child Psychiatry 1965;14:613.

99. MacKeith R, Wood C. Infant feeding and feeding difficulty. Edinburgh: Churchill-Livingstone, 1977.

100. Crooks CK, Lipsitt L. Neonatal nutritive sucking: effects of taste stimulation upon sucking rhythm and heart rate. Child Dev 1976;47:518–522.

101. Condon WS, Sandler LW. Synchrony demonstrated between movement of the neonate and adult speech. Child Dev 1974;43:456–462.

102. Sagi A, Hoffman ML. Empathic distress in newborns. Dev Psychol 1976;12:175–176.

103. Melzoff AN, Moore MK. Imitation of facial and manual gestures by the human neonate. Science 1977;198:75–78.

104. Erikson EH. Childhood and society, 2nd ed. New York: WW Norton, 1963.

105. Freud S. Three essays on sexuality (1905). In: Standard edition of the complete psychological works of Sigmund Freud, vol. 7. London: Hogarth, 1953.

106. Rutter M. Emotional development. In: Rutter M, ed. Developmental psychiatry. Washington, DC: American Psychiatric Press, 1980:306–321.

107. Lester BM, Boukydis CFK. Infant crying: theoretical and research perspectives. New York: Plenum, 1985.

108. Brazelton TB. Crying in infancy. Pediatrics 1962;29:579–588.

109. Wessel MA, Cobb JC, Jackson ED, et al. Paroxysmal fussing in infancy, sometimes called colic. Pediatrics 1954;14: 421.

110. Stein MT. Five weeks to two months. In: Dixon SD, Stein, MT, eds. Encounters with children: pediatric behavior and development. Chicago: Mosby Year Book, 1987.

111. Hunziker VA, Barr RG. Increased carrying reduces infant crying: a randomized control trial. Pediatrics 1986;77:641.

112. Kaiser P, Dixon S. Seven to eight months: separation and strangers. In: Dixon SD, Stein MT, eds. Encounters with children: pediatric behavior and development. Chicago: Mosby Year Book, 1987:169–179.

113. Greenberg DJ, Hillman D, Grice D. Infant and stranger variables related to stranger anxiety in the first year of life. Dev Psychol 1973;9:207–212.

114. Howlin P. Language. In: Rutter M, ed. Developmental psychiatry. Washington, DC: American Psychiatric Press, 1980:198–220.

115. Stewart DM, Hamilton ML. Imitation as a learning strategy in the acquisition of vocabulary. J Exp Child Psychol 1976; 21:380–392.

116. Piaget J. The origins of intelligence in children. New York: International Universities Press, 1953.

117. Chandler L. Gross and fine motor development. In: Cohen M, Gross P, eds. The developmental resource: behavioral sequences for assessment and program planning. vol. 1. New York: Grune & Stratton, 1979.

118. Dixon SD, Hennessy MJ. One year old. In: Dixon SD, Stein MT, eds. Encounters with children: pediatric behavior and development. Chicago: Mosby Year Book, 1987: 199–219.

119. Newson J, Newson E. Patterns of infant care in an urban community. London: Allen and Unwin, 1963.

120. Foye H, Sulkes S. Developmental and behavioral pediatrics. In: Behrman RE, Klugman R, eds. Nelson essentials of pediatrics. Philadelphia: Saunders, 1990:1–56.

121. Gundy JH. The pediatric physical examination. In: Hoekelman RA, Blatman S, Brunell PA, Friedman SB, Seidel HM, eds. Principles of pediatrics: health care of the young. New York: McGraw-Hill, 1978:33–76.

122. Conaway LP, Walker CE. Childhood. In: Wedding D. Behavior in medicine. Chicago: Mosby Year Book, 1991:19–39.

123. Stein MT. 18 months: asserting oneself, a push-pull process. In: Dixon SD, Stein MT, eds. Encounters with children: pediatric behavior and development. Chicago: Mosby Year Book, 1987:221–234.

124. Dixon SD. Two years old: learning the rules—language and cognition. In: Dixon SD, Stein MT, eds. Encounters with children: pediatric behavior and development. Chicago: Mosby Year Book, 1987:237–254.

125. Lewis C, Lewis M. The impact of television commercials on health-related beliefs and behaviors of children. Pediatrics 1974;53:431–435.

126. Shaffer D. The development of bladder control. In: Rutter M, ed. Developmental pediatrics. Washington DC: American Psychiatric Press, 1980:129–137.

127. Brazelton TB. Working and caring. Reading, MA: Addison-Wellesley, 1985.

128. Rutter M. Separation experiences: a new look at an old topic. J Pediatr 1979;95:147–154.

129. Drabman RS, Jarvie B. Counseling parents of children with behavior problems: the use of extinction and time-out techniques. Pediatrics 1977;59:78–85.

130. Levine MD, Carey WB, Crocker AC, et al. Developmental and behavioral pediatrics. Philadelphia: Saunders, 1983.

131. Broun R, Cazden C, Bellugi U. The child's grammar from I to III. In: Hill JP, ed. Minnesota symposia on child psychology. vol. 2. Minneapolis: University of Minnesota Press, 1969.

132. Davidson HP. A study of the confusing letters, B.D.P.Q. J Genet Psychol 1935;47:458–468.

133. Helms DB, Turner JS. Exploring child behavior: basic principles. Philadelphia: Saunders, 1978.

134. Toumen BCL. Laterality. In: Rutter M, ed. Developmental pediatrics. Washington, DC: American Psychiatric Press, 1980:154–164.

135. Whiting BB, Whiting JWM. Children of six cultures. Cambridge, MA: Harvard University Press, 1975.

136. Dixon SD. 2 1/2 years: the emergence of magic. In: Dixon SD, Stein MT, eds. Encounters with children: pediatric behavior and development. Chicago: Mosby Year Book, 1987: 257–267.

137. Conn JH, Kanner L. Children's awareness of sex differences. J Child Psychiatry 1947;1:3–57.

138. Jacklin C, Maccoby E. Issues of gender differentiation. In: Levine MD, et al, eds. Developmental-behavioral pediatrics. Philadelphia: Saunders, 1983.

139. Rutter M. Normal psychosexual development. J Child Psychol Psychiatry 1971;11:259–283.

140. Gundy JH. The pediatric physical examination. In: Hoekelman RA, Blatman S, Brunell PA, Friedman SB, Seidel HM, eds. Principles of pediatrics: health care of the young. New York: McGraw-Hill, 1978:33–76.

141. Putnam N. Seven to ten years: growth and competency. In: Dixon SD, Stein MT, eds. Encounters with children: pediatric behavior and development. Chicago: Mosby Year Book, 1987:305–317.

142. Walk RD. Perception. In: Rutter M, ed. Developmental psychiatry. Washington, DC: American Psychiatric Press, 1980:177–184.

143. Dunn J. Feeding and sleeping. In: Rutter M, ed. Developmental psychiatry. Washington DC: American Psychiatric Press, 1980:119–128.

144. Barker RG, Wright HF. Midwest and its children. New York: Harper & Row, 1955.

145. Sullivan HS. The interpersonal theory of psychiatry. New York: Norton, 1953.

146. Malinowski B. The sexual life of savages in North Western Melanesia. New York: Harcourt, Brace & World, 1929.

147. Ford CS, Beach FA. Patterns of sexual behavior. New York: Harper, 1951.

148. Ramsey CV. The sexual development of boys. Am J Psychol 1943;56:217–233.

149. Kales J, Jacobson A, Kales A. Sleep disorders in children. Prog Clin Pathol 1968;8:63.

150. Gastant H, Broughton RJ. A clinical and polygraphic study of episodic phenomena during sleep. In: Wortis J, ed. Recent advances in biological psychiatry. New York: Plenum, 1965.

151. Schofield M. The sexual behavior of young people. London: Longmans, 1965.

152. Bee H. The developing child, 3rd ed. New York: Harper & Row, 1981.

153. Tizard J. Progress and degeneration in the IQ debate: comments on Urbach. Bri J Phil Soc 1976;27 :251–274.

154. Rohlberg L. Development of moral character and moral ideology. In: Hoffman ML, Hoffman LW, eds. Review of child development research, vol. 1. New York: Russell Sage, 1974.

155. Aten MJ, McAnarney ER. A behavioral approach to the care of adolescents. St. Louis: Mosby, 1981.

156. Alan Guttmacher Institute. 11 million teenagers: what can be done about the epidemic of adolescent pregnancies in the United States. New York: Planned Parenthood Federation of America, 1976.

157. Hancock JR, Walker CE. Adolescence. In: Wedding D, ed. Behavior in medicine. Chicago: Mosby Year Book, 1991: 41–55.

158. Emans SJH, Goldstein D. Pediatric and adolescent gynecology. 2nd ed. Boston: Little, Brown, 1982.

159. Masters W, Johnson V. Homosexuality in perspective. Boston: Little, Brown, 1979.

160. Kinsey A, Pomeroy W, Martin C. Sexual behavior in the human male. Philadelphia: Saunders, 1948.

161. Goodwin DW, Guze SB. Psychiatric diagnosis. 4th ed. New York: Oxford University Press 1989:243,244,248.

162. Johnston LD, O'Malley PM, Bachman JG. Drug abuse among American high school students. Washington DC: US Dept. of Health and Human Services, 1986.

163. Felice ME, Friedman SB. Behavioral considerations in the health care of adolescents. Pediatr Clin North Am 1982;29: 399–412.

164. Felice ME. Mid-adolescence—the dating game. In: Dixon SD, Stein MT, eds. Encounters with children: pediatric behavior and development. Chicago: Mosby Year Book, 1987: 331–342.

165. Zelnick M, Kim YJ, Kantner JF. Probabilities of intercourse and conception among US teenage women. Fam Plann Perspect 1979;11:177–183.

166. Sibler TJ, Woodward K. Sexually transmitted diseases in adolescence. In: Pan American Health Organization. The health of adolescents and youths in the Americas. Scientific Publication No. 489. Washington, DC: Regional Office of the World Health Organization, 1985.

167. Bates B. A guide to physical examination and history-taking. 5th ed. Philadelphia: Lippincott, 1991.

168. Long JT, Fitzpatrick SB, Reese JM, et al. Basic issues in adolescent medicine. Curr Probl Pediatr 1984;14:1–50.

169. Mech EV. Adoption: a policy perspective. In: Caldwell BM, Ricciuti H, eds. Review of child development research. Chicago: University of Chicago Press, 1973.

170. Stein MT. Children's encounters with illness. In: Dixon SD, Stein MT, eds. Pediatric behavior and development. Chicago: Mosby Year Book 1987:367–374.

171. Hetherington EM. Divorce: a child's perspective. Am Psychol 1979;34:851–858.

172. Wallerstein JS, Blakeslee S. Second chances: men, women and children a decade after divorce. New York: Ticknor and Fields, 1989:7,141,157,233.

173. Hetherington EM, Cox M, Cox R, The aftermath of divorce. In: Stevens JH Jr, Matthews M, eds. Mother-child, father-child relations. Washington, DC: National Association for the Education of Young Children, 1978.

174. Wallerstein JS. Separation, divorce and remarriage. In: Levin MD, Carey WB, Crocker AC, Gross RT, eds. Developmental-behavioral pediatrics. Philadelphia: Saunders, 1983:241–255.

175. Cherlin AJ, Furstenburg FF, Chase-Lansdale PL, Kiernan KE, Robins PK, Morrison DR, Teitler JO. Longitudinal studies of effects of divorce on children in Great Britain and the United States. Science 1991;252:1386–1389.

176. Kessler DB, Hyden P, Craig JA. Physical, sexual and emotional abuse of children. Ciba Clin Symposia, 1991;43:2–32.

177. Russell DEH. The incidence and prevalence of intrafamilial and extrafamilial abuse of female children. Child Abuse and Neglect, 1983;7:133–146.

178. Forman MA, Kerschbaum WE, Hetznecker WH. Dunn JM. Assessment and interviewing. In: Behrman RE, Vaughan VC, Nelson WE, eds. Nelson textbook of pediatrics. 13th ed. Philadelphia: Saunders, 1987:50–54.

179. Boyle WE. The pediatric history. In: Hoekelman RA, Blatman S, Brunell PA, Friedman SB, Seidel HM, eds.

Principles of pediatrics: health care of the young. New York: McGraw-Hill, 1978:25–32.

180. Lambert L, Hart S. Who needs a father? New Society 1976;37:80.

181. Chess S, Hassibi M. Behavior deviations in mentally retarded children. J Am Acad Child Psychiatry 1970;9:282–297.

182. Phillips I, Williams N. Psychopathology of mental retardation: a study of 100 mentally retarded children. Am J Psychiatry 1975;132:1265–1271.

183. Volkmar FR, Cohen DJ. Neurobiological aspects of autism. N Engl J Med 1988;318:1390–1392.

184. Bregman JD, Dykens E, Watson M, et al. Fragile X syndrom—variability of phenotypic expression. J Am Acad Child Psychiatry 1987;26:463–471.

185. Davies K. Breaking the fragile X. Nature 1991;351:439–440.

186. Rumsey JM, Rapoport JL, Sceery WR. Autistic children as adults—psychiatric, social and behavioral outcomes. J Am Acad Child Psychiatry 1985;24:465–473.

187. Rapoport JL, Buchsbaum MS, Weingartner H, et al. Dextroamphetamine—its cognitive and behavioral effects in normal and hyperactive boys and normal men. Arch Gen Psychiatry 1980;37:933–943.

188. Weiss G, Hechtman LT. Hyperactive children grow up. New York: Guilford Press, 1986.

189. Petti TA. Depression in children: a significant disorder. Pscyhosomatics 1981;22:44–447.

190. Philips I. Childhood depression: interpersonal interactions and depressive phenomena. Am J Psychiatry 1979;136:511–515.

191. Pfeffer CR. Suicidal behavior of children: a review with implications for research and practice. Am J Psychiatry 1981;138:154–159.

192. Anthony EJ. An experimental approach to the psychopathology of childhood. Br J Med Psychol 1957;30:146–175.

193. Levine MD. Encopresis—its potentiation, evaluation and alleviation. Pediatr Clin N Am 1982;29:315–330.

194. Koffman M, Elizur E. Infants who become enuretics: a longitudinal study of 161 kibbutz children. Monogs Soc Res Child Dev. vol. 42 Serial no. 170.

195. Garfinkel PE, Garner DM. Anorexia nervosa: a multidimensional perspective. New York: Brunner/Mazel, 1982.

12/ Adult Development

1. Neugarten BL, Neugarten G. The changing meaning of age. Psychol Today 1987;21:29–33.

2. Kenney RA. Physiology of aging. 2d ed. Chicago: Yearbook Medical Publishers, 1982.

3. Finch, C.E. and Schneider, EL. The biology of aging. 2nd ed. New York: Van Nostrand Reinhold, 1985.

4. Kimmel DC. Adulthood and aging. 2d ed. New York: Young, Wiley and Sons, 1980.

5. Schaie KW, Geiwitz J. Adult development. In: Aging. Boston: Little, Brown, 1982.

6. Roose S, Pardes H. Biological considerations. In: Oldham J, Liebert R, eds. The middle years. New Haven: Yale University Press, 1989.

7. American Heart Association. Fact sheet, January, 1990.

8. Hillerman T. The dark wind. New York: Harper & Row, 1982.

9. Erikson E. Childhood and society. New York: Norton, 1950.

10. Clayton V. Erikson's theory of human development as it applies to the aged: wisdom as contradictive cognition. Hum Dev 1975;18:119–128.

11. Erikson EH, Erikson JM, Kivnick H. Vital involvement in old age. New York: Norton, 1986.

12. Benedek T. Climacterium, a developmental phase. Psychoanal Q 1950;19:1–14.

13. Jacques E. Death and the mid-life crisis. Int J Psa 1965;46:502–514.

14. Vaillant G. Adaptation to life. Boston: Little, Brown, 1977.

15. Vaillant GE, Vaillant CO. Natural history of male psychological health, XII. Am J Psychiatry 1989;147:32–37.

16. Levinson DJ. The seasons of a man's life. New York: Knopf, 1979.

17. Levinson DJ. Toward a conception of the adult life course. In: Smelser NJ, Erikson EH, eds. Themes of work and love in adulthood. Cambridge MA: Harvard University Press, 1980.

18. Levinson DJ. A conception of adult development. Am Psychol 1986;41:3–13.

19. Gould R. Transformations. New York: Simon & Schuster, 1978.

20. Gould R. Transformation during early and middle adult years. In: Themes of work and love in adulthood. Cambridge MA: Harvard University Press, 1980.

21. Rosenfeld A, Stark E. The prime of our lives. Psychol Today 1987;21:62–722.

22. Wallerstein J, Blakeslee S. Second chances. New York: Ticknor & Fields, 1989.

23. Neugarten BL. Time, age and the life cycle. Am J Psychiatry 1979;136:887–894.

24. Rossi AS. Life span theories and women's lives. Signs: J Women in Cult Soc 1984;6:4–32.

25. Baruch GK et al. Lifeprints: new patterns of love and work for today's woman. New York: McGraw-Hill, 1983.

13/ Gender-Related Psychology

1. Bickel J. Women in medical education: a status report. N Engl J Med 1988;319:1579–1584.

2. Cooperstock R. Sex differences in the use of mood-modifying drugs: an explanatory model. J Health Soc Behav 1971;12:238–244.

3. Seiden AM. Overview: research on the psychology of women. II. Women in families, work and psychotherapy. Am J Psychiatry 1976;133:1111–1123.

4. Sutherland E. Veroff J. Achievement motivation and sex roles. In: O'Leary VE, Unger RK, Wallson BS. eds. Women, gender, and social psychology. Hillsdale, NJ: Lawrence Erlbaum Assoc. 1985.

5. Williams JH. Psychology of women: behavior in a biosocial context. 3d ed. New York: Norton, 1987:129;461–463.

6. Mechanic D. Social psychologic factors affecting the presentation of bodily complaints. N Engl J Med 1972;286:1132–1139.

7. Robins LN, Helzer JE, Weissman MM, Orvaschel H, Gruenberg E, Burke JD, Jr, Regier DA. Lifetime prevalence of specific psychiatric disorders in three sites. Arch Gen Psychiatry 1984;41:949–958.

8. Fidell L 1980. Sex role stereotypes and the American physician. Psychol Women Q;4:313–327.

9. Prange AJ, Loosen PT, Wilson IC, Lipton MA. The therapeutic use of hormones of the thyroid axis in depression. In: Post RM, Ballenger JC, eds. Neurobiology of mood disorders. Baltimore: Williams & Wilkins, 1988:318,319.

10. Waldron I. Why do women live longer than men? Soc Sci Med 1976;10:349–362.

11. Howell MC. What medical schools teach about women. N Engl J Med 1974;291:304–307.

12. Prather JE, Fidell LS. Sex differences in the content and style of medical advertisements. Soc Sci Med 1975;9:23–26.

13. Hawkins JW, Aber CS. The content of advertisements in medical journals: distorting the image of women. Women Health 1988;14:43–59.

14. Sells J. Pediatrician and parent: a challenge for female physicians. Pediatrics 989;84:55–361.

15. Muller, Ralph. Personal communication.

16. Stotland, N.L. Social change and women's reproductive health care. New York: Praeger, 1988.

17. Eichler M, Reisman AL, Borins E. Presentation on gender bias in research published in medical journals. Can Psych Assn meeting 1989. Reported in Psychiatr News January 5, 1990.

18. Khatamee MA, Leinberger-Sica A, Matos P, et al. Sex preselection in New York City: who chooses which sex and why. Int J Fertil 1989;34:353–354.

19. Lewis M. Parents and children: sex-role development. School Rev 1972;80:229–240.

20. Elia I. The female animal. New York: Henry Holt, 1988.

21. Waldron I, Jacobs JA. Effects of multiple roles on women's health—evidence from a national longitudinal study. Women Health 1989;15:3–19.

22. Berta P, Hawkins JR, Sinclair AH, Taylor A, Griffiths BL, Goodfellow PN, Fellous M. Genetic evidence equating SRY and the testis-determining factor. Nature 1990;348:448–450.

23. Jager RJ, Anvret M, Hall K, Scherer G. A human XY female with a frame shift mutation in the candidate testis-determining gene SRY. Nature 1990;348:452–454.

24. Arey LB. Developmental anatomy. 7th ed. Philadelphia: Saunders, 1974.

25. Masica DN, Money J, Erhardt AA. Fetal feminization and female gender identity in the testicular feminization syndrome of androgen insensitivity. Arch Sex Behav 1971;1:131–142.

26. Popper CW. Disorders usually first evident in infancy, chilhood or adolescence. In: Talbott JA, Hales RE, Yudofsky SC, eds. Textbook of psychiatry. Washington, DC: American Psychiatric Press, 1988.

27. Tanner JM. Fetus into man. Cambridge, MA: Harvard University Press, 1978.

28. Miller JB. Women's psychological development: theory and application. Women's mental health occasional paper series. National Institute of Mental Health, 1986.

29. Maccoby EE, Jacklin CN. The psychology of sex differences. Vol. I. Stanford, CA: Stanford University Press, 1974:352.

30. Williamson NE. Sex preferences, sex control and the status of women. Signs 1976;1:847–862.

31. Lamb ME and Lamb J. The nature and importance of father-infant relationships. Family Coord 1976;25:379–385.

32. Konopka G. Young girls: a portrait of adolescence. Englewood Cliffs NJ: Prentice-Hall, 1976.

33. Wakefield WM. Awareness, affection and perceived similarity in the parent-child relationship. J Gen Psychol 1970;111:91–97.

34. Huston AC. Sex typing. In: Mursen PH, series ed., Hetherington EM, volume ed. Handbook of child psychology, vol 4: Socialization, personality and social development, 4th ed. New York: Wiley 1983, 387–467.

35. Well J, Self P, Daton D. Maternal behavior and perceived sex of infant. Am J Orthopsychiatry 1976;46:135–139.

36. Klaus MH. Human maternal and paternal behavior. In: Klaus MH, Kennell JH, eds. Parent-infant bonding. St. Louis: Mosby, 1982:38–98.

37. Weintraub M. Clemens LP, Spockloff A, Ethridge T, Gracely E, Myers B. The development of sex role stereotypes in the third year: relationships to gender labeling, gender identity, sex-typed toy preferences, and family characteristics. Child Dev 1984;55:1493–1503.

38. Erhardt AA, Meyer-Bahlburg HFL. Effects of prenatal sex hormones on gender-related behavior. Science 1981;211:1312–1318.

39. Parke RD, Suomi SJ. Adult male-infant relationships: human and nonprimate evidence. In: Immelman K, Barlow G, Main M, Petrinovich L, eds. Behavioral development: the Bielefeld interdisciplinary project. New York: Cambridge University Press, 1980.

40. Power TG, Parke RD. Play as a context for early learning: lab and home analyses. In: Segel IE, Laosa LM, eds. The family as a learning environment. New York: Plenum, 1984.

41. Green R. The sissy boy syndrome and the development of homosexuality. New Haven: Yale University Press, 1987.

42. Hyde JS, Rosenberg BFG, Behrman J. Tomboyism. Psychol Women Quart 1977;2:73–75.

43. Brown DG, Lynn DR: Human sexual development. An outline of components and concepts. J Marriage Fam 1966;28:155–162.

44. Sherman J. On the psychology of women. Springfield, IL: C.C. Thomas, 1971.

45. Hines M. Prenatal gonadal hormones and sex differences in human behavior. Psychol Bull 1982;92:56–80.

46. Berenbaum SA. Congenital adrenal hyperplasia: intellectual and psychosocial functioning. In: Holmes CS, ed. Psychoneuroendocrinology: brain, behavior and hormone interactions. New York: Springer-Verlag, 1990.

47. Maccoby EE. Gender as a social category. Dev Psychol 1988;24:755–765.

48. Linn MC, Petersen A. A meta analysis of gender differences in spatial ability: implications for mathematics and science achievement. In: Hyde JS, Linn MC, eds: The psychology of gender: advances through meta-analysis. Baltimore: Johns Hopkins, 1986.

49. Scharfman M. Puberty and the adolescent. In: Simons R, ed. Understanding human behavior in health and illness, 2nd ed. Baltimore: Williams & Wilkins 1985.

50. Kumura D. Sex differences in cerebral organization for speech and praxic functions. Can J Psychol 1983;37:19–35.

51. Gur RC, Gur RE, Obrist WD, Hungerbuhlker JP, Younken D, Rosen AD, Skolnick BE, Reivich M. Sex and handedness differences in cerebral blood flow during rest and cognitive activity. Science 1982;217:659–661.

52. Swabb DF, Fliers E. A sexually dimorphic nucleus in the human brain. Science 1985;228:1112–1115.

53. Gilligan C. In a different voice: psychological theory and women's development. Cambridge: Harvard, 1982.

54. Scully D, Bart P. A funny thing happened on the way to the orifice: women in gynecology textbooks. In: Huber J, ed. Changing women in a changing society. Chicago: University of Chicago Press, 1973:283–288.

55. Schechter MD, Graham LC. The normal development of the seven to ten year old child. In: Greenspan SI, Pollock GH, eds. The course of life, vol. II. Latency, adolescence and youth. Adelphi, MD: Mental Health Study Center. 1980.

56. Fagot BI. Sex differences in toddlers' behavior and parental reaction. Dev Psychol 1974;10:554–558.

57. Block JH. Another look at sex differentiation in the socialization behaviors of mothers and fathers. In: Sherman J, Denmark FL, eds. The psychology of women: future directions of research. New York: Psychological Directions, 1978.

58. Eisenberg C. Medicine is no longer a man's profession. N Engl J Med 1989;321:1542–1544.

59. Delaney J, Lupton MJ, Toth E. The curse: a cultural history of menstruation. New York: Dutton 1976.

60. Gitlin MJ, Pasnau RO. Psychiatric syndromes linked to reproductive functions in women: a review of current knowledge. Am J Psychiatry 1989;146:1413–1422.

61. Stotland NL. Psychiatric issues in abortion. Washington, DC: American Psychiatric Press, in press.

62. Weissman MM. The myth of involutional melancholia. JAMA 1979;242:742–744.

63. Winokur G. Depression in the menopause. Am J Psychiatry 1973;130:92–93.

64. Kempe CH. Silverman FN, Steele BF et al. The battered child syndrome. JAMA 1962;181:17.

65. Silver L, Dublin, Lourie R. Does violence breed violence? Contributions from a study of the child abuse syndrome. Am J Psychiatry 1969;126:152–155.

66. Hilberman E. The rape victim. Washington, DC: American Psychiatric Association, 1976.

67. National Institute of Mental Health. Victims of rape. Washington, DC: U.S. Govt. Prntg Office, 1977; pub. no. 241–186/1133.

68. Kaplan HI, Sadock BJ. Synopsis of psychiatry, 5th ed. Baltimore: Williams & Wilkins, 1988.

14/ Geriatric Development

1. Levinson DJ. The seasons of a man's life. New York: Knopf, 1978.

2. Zisook S, ed. Grief and bereavement. Psychiatr Clin North Am 1987;10(3).

3. Erikson EH. The life cycle completed. New York: Norton, 1982.

4. Vaillant GE. Adaptation to life. Boston: Little, Brown, 1977.

5. Viorst J. Necessary losses. New York: Simon & Schuster, 1986:265–304.

6. Abrams WB, Fletcher AJ. The Merck manual of geriatrics. Rahway, NJ: Merck, Sharp & Dohme Research, 1990.

7. Gurland BJ, Cross PS. Epidemiology of psychopathology in old age. Psychiatr Clin North Am 1982;5:11–26.

8. Bumagin VE, Hirn KF. Helping the aging family. Glenview, IL: Scott, Foresman, 1990.

9. Pollock GH. Aging or aged: development or pathology in the course of life: psychoanalytic contributions toward understanding personality development. Rockville, MD: National Institute of Mental Health 1980;3:549–585.

10. Pies R. Elder abuse: clinical detection and intervention. Geriatr Med Today 1987;6:24–31.

11. Ford CV, Shordone RJ. Attitudes of psychiatrists towards elderly patients. Am J Psychiatry 1980;137:571–575.

12. Hickey T. Changing health perceptions of older patients and the implication for assessment. Geriatr Med Today 188;7:59–66.

13. Kohn RR. Causes of death in very old people. JAMA 1982; 247:2793–2797.

14. Weale R. The eyes of the elderly. Geriatr Med Today 1985; 4:29–37.

15. Morello R, Fox D. The aging eye. Geriatr Med Today 1989; 8:83–87.

16. Weinstock FJ. Cataracts and the primary care physician. Geriatr Med Today 1989;8:101–120.

17. Podoshin L, Fradis M, Ben-David J, Levy S. Hearing and old age. Geriatr Med Today 1984;3:22–32.

18. Kohrs MB. Age related changes in taste acuity. Geriatr Med Today 1985;5:88–101.

19. Colarusso CA, Nemiloff RA. Adult development: a new dimension in psychodynamic theory and practice. New York: Plenum, 1981.

20. Miche DD. Causes of impotence in elderly men and considerations for treatment. Geriatr Med Today 1988;7:38–44.

21. Heslop HE, Beard MEJ, Sainsbury R. Heart related illness in the elderly. Geriatr Med Today 1985;4:21–26.

22. Lye M. Clinical recognition of hypothermia in the elderly. Geriatr Med Today 1985;4:3:63–66.

23. Cornell R. Aging and the skin. Geriatr Med Today 1986;5: 26–37.

24. Lakatta E. Age related changes in the heart. Geriatr Med Today 1985;4:86–97.

25. Reichel W, ed. The geriatric patient. New York: Hospital Practice Publishing Co., 1978.

26. Nochomovitz ML, Cherniack NS. Age-related changes in respiratory function. Geriatr Med Today 1984;3:49–60.

27. Rothschild B. Age-related changes in skeletal muscle. Geriatr Med Today 1986;5:87–95.

28. Tamarin F. Falls in the elderly: Risks and prevention. Geriatr Med Today 1988;7:83–86.

29. Fam A. Osteoarthritis in the geriatric patient. Geriatr Med Today 1987;4:18–49.

30. Lawton MP. Annual review of gerontology and geriatrics. Vol. 9. New York: Springer, 1989.

31. Lindeman RD. Changes in kidney function with age. Geriatr Med Today 1984;3:41–47.

32. Shock NW, et al. Normal human aging: the Baltimore longitudinal study of aging. Washington, DC: U.S. Department of Health and Human Services, 1984.

33. Sibley GNA, Smith JC. Differential diagnosis of urinary incontinence in geriatric women. Geriatr Med Today 1983;2: 67–79.

34. Kay M. Immunological changes associated with normal aging. Geriatr Med Today 1985;4:30–39.

35. Gardner I. Aging and susceptibility to infection. Geriatr Med Today 1986;5:29–41.

36. Link S. Pneumonia in the elderly. Geriatr Med Today 1987; 6:85–88.

37. Derose J. Avoiding drug related problems in the elderly. Geriatr Med Today 1989;8:64–66.

38. Lehmann HE. Affective disorders in the aged. Psychiatric Clin North Am 1982:27–34.

39. Goldman R. Aging and geriatric medicine. In: Wyngaarden JB, Smith LH, eds. Cecil textbook of medicine. Philadelphia: Saunders, 1985:23.

40. Baker H. Hypovitaminosis in the elderly. Geriatr Med Today 1983;2:161–66.

41. Roehrs T, Zorick R, Roth T. Sleep disorders in the elderly. Geriatr Med Today 1984;3:76–86.

42. Sinaki M. Beneficial musculoskeletal effects of physician activity in the older woman. Geriatr Med Today 1989;8:53–72.

43. Grisso JA, Kelsey JL, Strom BL, et al. Risk factors for falls as a cause of hip fractures in women. N Engl J Med 1991; 324:1326–1331.

44. Maddocks PD. A five-year follow-up of untreated psychopaths. Br J Psychol 1970;116:511–515.
45. Robins LN. Deviant children grown up. Baltimore: Williams & Wilkins, 1966.
46. Pies R. Psychiatric presentations of medical illness. Geriatr Med Today 1987;6:39–53.
47. Jeste DV, Zisook S., eds. Psychosis and depression in the elderly. Psychiatr Clin North Am 1988;11(1).
48. Jarvik LF. Dementia in old age: reflections on nomenclature. Psychiatr Clin North AM 1982;5:105–106.
49. Cohen GD. Prevalence of psychiatric problems in older adults. Psychiatr Annals 1990;20:433–438.
50. Popkin MK. The organic brain syndromes presenting with little or no cognitive impairment. In: Winokur G, Clayton P, eds. The medical basis of psychiatry. Philadelphia: Saunders, 1986.
51. Andreasen NC, Black DW. Introductory textbook of psychiatry. Washington, DC: American Psychiatric Press, 1990: 168.
52. Tarsy D. Movement disorders with neuroleptic drug treatment. Psychiatr Clin North Am 1984;7:453–471.
53. Kay DWK, Roth M. Environmental and hereditary factors in the schizophrenias of old age ("late paraphrenia") and their bearing on the general problem of causation in schizophrenia. J Ment Sci 1961;107:649–686.
54. Butler R. Overview of aging. In: Usdin G. Aging: the process and the people. New York: Brunner/Mazel, 1978:1–19.
55. Folstein MF, Folstein SW, McHugh PR. "Minimental State": a practical method of grading the cognitive state of patients for the clinician. J Psychiatr Res 1975;12:189–198.
56. McCue J. Routine medical screening of the relatively symptomatic elderly patient. Geriatr Med Today 1987;6:233–45.

15/ Dying, Death, and Bereavement

1. Kubler-Ross E. On death and dying. London: Macmillan, 1969.
2. Weisman AD. Coping with cancer. New York: McGraw-Hill, 1979.
3. Marks R, Sachar E. Undertreatment of medical inpatients with narcotic analgesics. Ann Intern Med 1973;68:173–181.
4. Seravalli E. The dying patient, the physician, and the fear of death. N Engl J Med 1988;319:1728–1730.
5. Levy MH. Symptom control manual. In: Cassileth BR, Cassileth PA, eds. Clinical care of the terminal cancer patient. Philadelphia: Lea & Febiger, 1982.
6. Sierles FS. Correlates of malingering. Behav Sci Law 1984; 2:113–118.
7. Cassileth PA. Common medical complications. In: Cassileth BR, Cassileth PA, eds. Clinical care of the terminal cancer patient. Philadelphia: Lea & Febiger, 1982.
8. Danis M, Southerland LI, Garrett JM. A prospective study of advance directives for life-sustaining care. N Engl J Med 1991;324:882–888.
9. Emanuel LL, Barry MJ, Stoeckle JD, et al. Advance directives for medical care—a case for greater use. N Engl J Med 1991;324:889–895.
10. Youngner SJ, Landefeld CS, Coulton CJ, Juknialis BW, Leary M. Brain death and organ retrieval, a cross-sectional survey of knowledge and concepts among health professionals. JAMA 1989;261:2205–2210.
11. Plum F. Prognosis in severe brain damage and diagnosis of brain death. In: Wyngaarden J, Smith L, eds. Cecil textbook of medicine. 17th ed. Philadelphia: Saunders, 1985.
12. Vales-Dapena M: The postautopsy conference with families. Arch Pathol Lab Med 1984;108:497–499.
13. Nemetz PN, Ludwig J, Kurland LT. Assessing the autopsy. Am J Pathol 1987;128:362–374.
14. Anderson RE, Fox RC, Hill RB. Medical uncertainty and the autopsy: occult benefits for students. Hum Pathol 1990; 21:128–135.
15. Centers for Disease Control. Autopsy frequency—United States: 1980–1985. MMWR 1988;37:191–194.
16. Parkes CM. Bereavement. Br J Psychiatry 1985;146:11–17.
17. Lewis CS. A grief observed. New York: Phoenix Press, 1984.
18. Clayton P, Desmarais L, Winokur G. A study of normal bereavement. Am J Psychiatry 1968;125:64–74.
19. Hirsch J, Hofer M, Holland J, Solomon F. Toward a biology of grieving. In: Osterweis M, Solomon F, Green M, eds. Bereavement reactions, consequences, and care. Washington, DC: National Academy Press, 1984.
20. Engel GL. Psychologic stress, vasodepressor (vasovagal) syncope, and sudden death. Ann Intern Med 1978;89:403–412.
21. Worden JW. Grief counseling and grief therapy: a handbook for the mental health practitioner. New York: Springer Publishing Co., 1982.
22. Storr A. Solitude: a return to the self. New York: Macmillan, 1988.
23. Pruyser P. Existential impact of professional exposure to life-threatening or terminal illness. Bull Menninger Clin 1984;48:357–367.

16/ Interviewing

1. American Psychiatric Association. Diagnostic and statistical manual of mental disorders. 3rd ed. Washington DC: American Psychiatric Association, 1980.
2. Goodwin DW, Guze SB. Psychiatric diagnosis. 4th ed. New York: Oxford University Press, 1989.
3. Engel G. Morgan W. Interviewing the patient. Philadelphia: Saunders, 1973.
4. Bernstein L, Bernstein RS. Interviewing: a guide for health professionals. 4th ed. Norwalk, CT: Appleton-Century-Crofts, 1985.
5. Billings JA, Stoeckle JD. The clinical encounter: a guide to the medical interview and case presentation. Chicago: Mosby Year Book, 1989.
6. Coulehan JL, Block MR. The medical interview: a primer for students of the art. Philadelphia: FA Davis, 1987.
7. Enelow AJ, Swisher SN. Interviewing and patient care. 3rd ed. New York: Oxford University Press, 1986.
8. Leon RL. Psychiatric interviewing: a primer. New York: Elsevier, 1989.
9. Guckian JC, ed. The clinical interview and physical examination. Philadelphia: Lippincott, 1987.
10. Othmer E, Othmer SC. The clinical interview: using the DSM-III-R. Washington DC: American Psychiatric Press, 1989.
11. Stevenson I. The diagnostic interview. 2nd ed. New York: Harper & Row, 1971.
12. Swartz MH. Textbook of physical diagnosis, history and examination. Philadelphia: Saunders, 1989.
13. Bates B. The guide to physical examination and history-taking. 5th ed. Philadelphia: Lippincott, 1991.
14. DeGowin EL. Bedside diagnostic examination. 5th ed., rev. by DeGowin RL. New York: Macmillan, 1987.
15. Hall ET. The hidden dimension. Garden City, NY: Doubleday, 1966.

16. Cox A, Hopkinson K, Rutter M. Psychiatric interviewing techniques. II. Naturalistic study: eliciting factual information. Br J Psychiatry 1981;138:283–291.
17. Haas AP, Hendin H, Singer P. Psychodynamic and structured interviewing: issues of validity. Compr Psychiatr 1987;28:47–53.

17/ The Psychiatric Evaluation

1. Andreasen N. Brain imaging: applications in psychiatry. Science 1988;239:1381–1388.
2. Nasrallah HA, Coffman JA. Computerized tomography in psychiatry. Psychiatric Ann 1985:15:2339–249.
3. Cox SM, Ludwig AM. Neurologic soft signs and psychopathology 1. Findings in schizophrenia. J Nerv Ment Dis 1979;168:161–165.
4. Quitkin F, Rifkin A, Klein DF. Neurologic soft signs in schizophrenia and character disorders. Arch Gen Psychiatry 1979;33:845–853.
5. Erlenmeyer-Kimling L, Cornblatt B, Friedman D, et al. Neurological, electrophysiological, and attentional deviations in children at risk for schizophrenia. In: Henn FA, Nasrallah HA, eds. Schizophrenia as a brain disease. New York: Oxford University Press, 1982.
6. Taylor MA, Abrams R. Cognitive impairment in schizophrenia. Am J Psychiatry 1984;141:196–201.
7. Taylor MA, Abrams R. Cognitive impairment in mania. Compr Psychiatry 1986;27:186–191.
8. Abrams R, Taylor MA. Cognitive dysfunction in melancholia. Psychol Med 1987;17:359–362.
9. Stevens JR. Neurology and neuropathology of schizophrenia. In: Henn FA, Nasrallah HA, eds. Schizophrenia as a brain disease. New York: Oxford University Press, 1982.
10. Abrams R, Taylor MA. Differential EEG patterns in affective disorder and schizophrenia. Arch Gen Psychiatry 1979; 36:1355–1358.
11. Vianna U. The electrocephalogram in schizophrenia. In: Lader MH, ed. Studies of schizophrenia. Br J Psychiatry special publ ser no. 10. Kent, England: Headley Bros., 1975:54–58.
12. Tucker GJ, Detre T, Harrow M, et al. Behavior and symptoms of psychiatric patients and the electroencephalogram. Arch Gen Psychiatry 1965;12:278–286.
13. Mathysse S, Williams R. Neurohistologic studies in schizophrenia. In: Henn RA, Nasrallah HA, eds. Schizophrenia as a brain disease. New York: Oxford University Press, 1982.
14. Allen CB, David MB, David KL. Psychoendocrinology in clinical psychology. In: Hales RE, Frances AJ, eds. American Psychiatric Association Annual Review, vol. 6. Washington DC: American Psychiatric Press, 1987.
15. Pitts FN, McClure JN, Jr. Lactate metabolism in anxiety neurosis. N Engl J Med 1967;277:1329–1336.
16. Taylor MA. The practice of neuropsychiatry. New York: Free Press, 1992 (in press).
17. Koran LM, Sox HC, Marton Kl, et al. Medical evaluation of psychiatric patients—results in a state mental health system. Arch Gen Psychiatry 1989;46:733–740.
18. Koranyi EK. Morbidity and rate of undiagnosed physical illnesses in a psychiatric clinic population. Arch Gen Psychiatry 1979;36:414–419.
19. Hall RCW, Popkin MK. Psychological symptoms of physical origin. Female Patient 1977;2:43–47.
20. Barnes RF, Mason JC, Greer C, et al. Medical illness in chronic psychiatric outpatients. Gen Hosp Psychiatry 1983; 5:191–195.
21. Hall RCW, ed. Psychiatric presentations of medical illness—somatopsychic disorders. Jamaica, NY: SP Medical and Scientific Books, 1980.
22. Martin MJ. A brief review of organic diseases masquerading as functional illness. Hosp Commun Psychiatry 1983; 34:328–332.
23. Oppenheim G. Physical illness diagnosed as psychiatric: patients at special risk. Gen Hosp Psychiatry 1982;4:241–243.
24. Hall RCW, Gruzenski W, Popkin MK. Differential diagnosis of somatopsychic disorders. Psychosomatics 1979;20: 381–389.
25. Cummings JL. Clinical neuropsychiatry. Orlando, FL: Grune & Stratton, 1985.
26. Spitzer RL, First MB, Williams JBW, Kendler K, Pincus HA, Tucker G. Now is the time to retire the term "organic mental disorders." Am J Psychiatry 1992;149:240–244.
27. Anonymous. Some drugs that cause psychiatric symptoms. Med Letter Drugs Therapeutics 1989;31:113–116.
28. Weissberg MP. Emergency room medical clearance: an educational problem Am J Psychiatry 1979;136:787–790.
29. Teitelbaum ML. Toward better integration of medical and psychiatric care. JAMA 1982;248:977.
30. Shulman R. Psychogenic illness with physical manifestations and the other side of the coin—a practical approach. Lancet 1977;2:524–526.
31. Krummel S, Kathol RG. What you should know about physical examinations in psychiatric patients—results of a survey. Gen Hosp Psychiatry 1987;9:275–279.
32. Anderson WH. The physical examination in office practice. Am J Psychiatry 1980;137:1188–1191.
33. Summer WK, Munoz RA, Read MR. The psychiatric physical examination—Part I: methodology. J Clin Psychiatry 1981;42:95–98.
34. McIntyre JS, Romano J. Is there a stethoscope in the house (and is it used)? Arch Gen Psychiatry 1977;34:1147–1151.
35. Sierles FS, Weil MH. Should psychiatrists teach the physical examination to medical students? A case report and national survey. J Psychiatric Educ 1984;8:121–126.
36. Yater WM, Oliver WF. Symptom diagnosis. New York: Appleton-Century Crofts, 1961.
37. Wyngaarden JB, Smith LH Jr., eds. Cecil textbook of medicine, 17th ed. Philadelphia: Saunders, 1985.
38. Schwartz SO, Hartz WH, Robbins JH. Hematology in practice. New York: McGraw-Hill, 1961.
39. Hampton JR, Harrison MJG, Mitchell JRA, et al. Relative contributions of history taking, physical examination and laboratory investigation to diagnosis and management of medical outpatients. Br Med J 1975;2:486–489.
40. Summer WK, Munoz RA, Read MR, Harch CD. The psychiatric physical examination—Part II: findings in 75 unselected psychiatric patients. J Clin Psychiatry 1981;42:99–101.
41. Luria RE, McHugh P. Reliability and clinical utility of the "Wing" Present State Examination. Arch Gen Psychiatry 1974;30:866–871.
42. Abrams R, Taylor MA. A rating scale for emotional blunting. Am J Psychiatry 1978;135:226–229.
43. Andreasen NC. Affective flattening and the criteria for schizophrenia. Am J Psychiatry 12979;136:944–947.
44. Andreasen NC. Thought, language and communication disorders. II. Diagnostic significance. Arch Gen Psychiatry 1979;36:1325–1330.
45. Folstein MF, Folstein SE, McHugh PR: Mini-mental state: a practical method for grading the cognitive state of patients for the clinician. J Psychiatr Res 1975;12:189–198.

46. Taylor MA. The neuropsychiatric mental status examination. Costa Mesa, CA: PMA Publishing, 1981.

47. Melges FT. Mental status examination. In: Rosenbaum CP, Beebe JE, eds. Psychiatric treatment—crisis, clinic, consultation. New York: McGraw-Hill, 1975:529–538.

48. MacKinnon RA, Yudofsky SC. Principles of the psychiatric evaluation. Philadelphia: Lippincott, 1991.

49. Feinglass EJ, Arnett FC, Îorsch CA et al. Neuropsychiatric manifestations of systemic lupus erythematosus: diagnosis, clinical spectrum, and relationship to other features of the disease. Medicine 1976;55:323.

50. Kronfol Z, Schlesser M, Tsuang MT. Catatonia and systemic lupus erythematosus. Dis Nerv Sys 197;38:729.

51. Morrison JR. Catatonia: retarded and excited types. Arch Gen Psychiatry 1973;28:39–41.

52. Abrams RA, Taylor MA. Catatonia: a prospective clinical study. Arch Gen Psychiatry 1976;33:579–581.

53. Andreasen NC. Thought, language and communication disorders. I. Clinical assessment, definition of terms, and evaluation of their reliability. Arch Gen Psychiatry 1979;36:1315–1321.

54. Kleist K. Schizophrenic symptoms and cerebral pathology. J Ment Sci 1960;106:246–255.

55. Fromkin V. A linguist looks at schizophrenic language. Brain Lang 1975;2:498–503.

56. Gerson SN, Benson DF, Frazier SH. Diagnosis: schizophrenia versus posterior aphasia. Am J Psychiatry 1977;134:1966–1969.

57. Faber R, Abrams R, Taylor MA, Kasprisin A, Morris C, Weisz R. Comparison of schizophrenic patients with formal thought disorder and neurologically impaired patients with aphasia. Am J Psychiatry 1983;140:1348–1351.

58. Taylor MA, Sierles FS, Abrams R. General hospital psychiatry. New York: Free Press, 1985.

59. Schneider K. Clinical psychopathology. Hamilton MW, trans. New York: Grune & Stratton, 1959.

60. Taylor MA. Schneiderian first-rank symptoms and clinical prognostic features in schizophrenia. Arch Gen Psychiatry 1972;26:64–67.

61. Carlson GA, Goodwin FK. The stages of mania. Arch Gen Psychiatry 1973;128:221–228.

62. Carpenter WT, Strauss JS, Muleh S. Are there pathognomic signs of schizophrenia? Arch Gen Psychiatry 1973;28:847–852.

63. Berenbaum SA, Abrams R, Rosenberg S, Taylor MA. The nature of emotional blunting: a factor-analytic study. Psychiatr Res 1986;20:57–67.

64. Andreasen NC. Reliability and validity of proverb interpretation to assess mental status. Compr Psychiatry 1977;18:465–472.

65. Jacobs JW, Bernhard MR, Delgado A, et al. Screening for organic mental symptoms in the medically ill. Ann Intern Med 1977;86:40–46.

66. Pfeiffer E. A short portable mental status questionnaire for the assessment of organic brain deficit in elderly patients. J Am Geriatr Soc 1975;23:433–441.

67. Heimburger RF, Reitan RM. Easily administered written test for lateralizing brain lesions. J Neurosurg 1961;18:301–312.

68. Dubin WR, Weiss KJ, Zeccardi JA. Organic brain syndrome—the psychiatric impostor. JAMA 1983;249:60–62.

69. Taylor MA, Sierles FS, Abrams R. The neuropsychiatric evaluation. In: Hales RE, Yudofsky SC, eds. Textbook of neuropsychiatry. Washington, DC: American Psychiatric Press, 1987:3–15.

70. Harry SW, Markowitz J. Organic mental disorders. In: Talbott JA, Hales RE, Yudofsky SC, eds. Textbook of psychiatry. Washington DC: American Psychiatric Press, 1988:302,303.

71. Dubin WR, Hanke N, Nickens HW, eds. Psychiatric emergencies. New York: Churchill-Livingstone, 1984:26–29.

72. Hall RCW, Gardner ER, Stickney SK, LeCann AF, Popkin MK. Physical illness manifesting as psychiatric disease—analysis of a state hospital inpatient population. Arch Gen Psychiatry 1980;37:989–995.

73. Barnes RF, Mason JC, Greer C, et al. Medical illness in chronic psychiatric outpatients. Gen Hosp Psychiatry 1983;5:191–195.

74. Smail P, Stockwell T, Canter S, Hodgson R. Alcohol dependence and phobic anxiety states. I. A prevalence study. Br J Psychiatry 1984;144:53–57.

75. Kaplan HI, Sadock BJ. Pocket handbook of clinical psychiatry. Baltimore: Williams & Wilkins, 1990:296.

76. Carroll BJ, Feinberg M, Greden JF, et al. A specific laboratory test for the diagnosis of melancholia: standardization, validation and clinical utility. Arch Gen Psychiatry 1981;38:15–22.

77. Rosse RB, Giese AA, Deutsch SI, Morihisa JM. Concise guide to laboratory diagnostic testing in psychiatry. Washington DC: American Psychiatric Press, 1989:68–76.

78. Veragoni VK. The incidence of abnormal dexamethasone in schizophrenia: a review and meta-analytic comparison with the incidence in normal controls. Can J Psychiatry 1990;35:128–132.

79. Allen CB, Davis BM, Davis KL. Psychoendocrinology in clinical psychiatry. In: Hales RE, Frances AJ, eds. American Psychiatric Assoc Ann Rev, vol 6. Washington DC: American Psychiatric Press, 1987.

80. Tyner FS, Knott JR, Mayer WB, Jr. Fundamentals of EEG technology, vol. 2: clinical correlates. New York: Raven, 1989.

81. Tucker GJ, Detre T, Harrow M, et al. Behavior and symptoms of psychiatric patients and the electroencephalogram. Arch Gen Psychiatry 1965;12:278–286.

82. Abrams R, Taylor MA. Differential EEG patterns in affective disorder and schizophrenia. Arch Gen Psychiatry 1979;36:1355–1358.

83. Vianna U. The electroencephalogram in schizophrenia. In: Lader MH, ed. Studies of schizophrenia. Br J Psychiatry special pub ser. no. 10. Kent, England: Headley Bros, 1975:54–58.

84. McCall WV, Shelp FE, McDonald WM. Controlled investigation of the amobarbital interview for catatonic mutism. Am J Psychiatry 1992;149:202–206.

85. Tomb DA. Psychiatry for the house officer, 3rd ed. Baltimore: Williams & Wilkins, 1988:14–15.

86. Liebowitz MR, Fyer AJ, Gorman JM, et al. Lactate provocation of panic attacks. Arch Gen Psychiatry 1984;41:764–770.

87. Rainey JM, Aleen A, Oritz A, Yeragani V, Pohl R, Berchou R. A laboratory procedure for the induction of flashbacks. Am J Psychiatry 1987;144:1317–1319.

88. Dubin WR, Weiss KJ, Dorn JM. Pharmocotherapy of psychiatric emergencies. J Clin Psychopharmacol 1986;6:210–222.

89. Kaplan HI, Sadock BJ, eds. Synopsis of psychiatry, 5th ed. Baltimore: Williams & Wilkins, 1988:190–191.

90. Murray GB. Confusion, delirium and dementia. In: Hackett TP, Cassem NH, eds. Handbook of general hospital psychiatry. 2nd ed. Littleton, MA: PSG Publishing, 1987:111.

91. Menninger KA. A manual for psychiatric case study. New York: Grune & Stratton, 1962.

18/ Psychological Testing

1. 1988–1989 Survey of graduate departments of psychology. Office of Demographic, Employment, and Educational Research: American Psychological Association and Council of Graduate Department of Psychology. Unpublished report, 1991.
2. Matarazzo JD. Wechsler's measurement and appraisal of adult intelligence. 5th ed. New York: Oxford University Press, 1972.
3. Terman LM, Merrill MA. Stanford-Binet Intelligence Scale. Manual for the third revision, Form L–M. Boston. Houghton Mifflin, 1973.
4. Wechsler D. Wechsler Adult Intelligence Scale–Revised manual. San Antonio: The Psychological Corporation, 1981.
5. Bornstein RA, Matarazzo JD. Wechsler VIQ versus PIQ differences in cerebral dysfunction: a literature review with emphasis on sex differences. J Clin Neuropsychol 1983;4: 319.
6. Wechsler D. Manual for the Wechsler Intelligence Scale for Children–Revised. New York: Psychological Corporation, 1974.
7. Wechsler D. Manual for the Wechsler Preschool and Primary Scale of Intelligence. New York: Psychological Corporation, 1967.
8. Halstead WC. Brain and intelligence. Chicago: University of Chicago Press, 1947.
9. Lezak MD. Neurophysical assessment. 2nd ed. New York: Oxford University Press, 1983.
10. Golden CJ. A standardized version of Luria's neuropsychological tests. In Filskov S and Ball TJ, eds. Handbook of clinical neuropsychology. New York: Wiley-Interscience, 1981.
11. Goodglass H, Kaplan E. Assessment of aphasia and related disorders. Philadelphia: Lea and Febiger, 1972.
12. Wechsler D. Wechsler Memory Scale–Revised manual. San Antonio: The Psychological Corporation/Harcourt Brace Jovanovich, 1987.
13. Raven JC. Guide to the Standard Progressive Matrices. London: HK Lewis, 1960, New York: Psychological Corporation, no date.
14. Osterrieth PA. Le test de copie d'une figure complexe. Arch Psychologie, 1944;30:206–356.
15. Hutt ML. The Hutt adaptation of the Bender-Gestalt test. 3rd ed. New York: Grune & Stratton, 1977.
16. Berg EA. A simple objective test for measuring flexibility in thinking. J Gen Psychol 1948;39:15–22.
17. Johnstone EC, Crow TJ, Frith CD, et al. Cerebral ventricular size and cognitive impairment in schizophrenia. Lancet 1976;2:924–926.
18. Donnelly EF, Weinberger DR, Waldman IN, et al. Cognitive impairment associated with morphological brain abnormalities on computed tomography in chronic schizophrenic patients. J Nerv Ment Dis 1980;168:305–308.
19. Golden CJ, Moses JA, Zelazowski R, et al. Cross-validation of the Luria Neuropsychological Battery to differentiate chronic schizophrenics with and without ventricular enlargement. J Consult Clin Psychol 1982;50:87–95.
20. Lubin B, Larsen RM, Matarazzo JD. Patterns of psychological test usage in the United States: 1935–1982. Am Psychol 1984;39:451–454.,
21. Graham JR, Lilly RS. Psychological testing. Englewood Cliffs, NJ: Prentice Hall, 1984.

22. Graham JR. The MMPI: a practical guide. 2nd ed. Oxford. Oxford University Press, 1987.
23. Hathaway SR. Minnesota Multiphasic Personality Inventory–2. Minneapolis: University of Minnesota Press, 1989.
24. Millon T. Millon Clinical Multiaxial Inventory manual. 3rd ed. Minneapolis: Minnesota Interpretive Scoring Systems, 1983.
25. Derogatis LR. SCL-90-R: Administration, scoring, and procedures manual–II. 2nd ed. Baltimore: Clinical Psychometric Research, 1983.
26. Gough HG. California Psychological Inventory manual. Palo Alto, CA: Consulting Psychologist Press, 1957.
27. Cattell RB. Manual for forms A and B sixteen personality questionnaire. Champaign, IL: Institute for Personality Testing, 1949.
28. Beck AT, Ward CH, Mendelson M, Mock J, Erbaugh JK. An inventory for measuring depression. Arch Gen Psychiatry, 1961;4:561–571.
29. Jenkins CD, Zyzanski SJ, Rosenman RH. The Jenkins activity survey manual. New York: Psychological Corporation, 1979.
30. Exner JE, Jr. The Rorschach: a comprehensive system. Vol 1. New York: John Wiley & Sons, 1974.
31. Exner JE. The Rorschach: a comprehensive system. Vol. 2: current research and advanced interpretations. New York: Wiley-Interscience, 1978.
32. Exner JE, Armbruster GL, Viglione D. The temporal stability of some Rorschach features. J Pers Assess 1978;42: 474–482.
33. Exner JE, Wylie JR. Some Rorschach data concerning suicide. J Pers Assess 1977;41:339–348.
34. Murray HA. Explorations in personality. New York: Oxford University Press, 1938.
35. Goodenough F. Measurement of intelligence by drawings. New York: World Book, 1926.
36. Harris DB. Children's drawings as measures of intellectual maturity. New York: Harcourt, Brace and World, 1963.
37. Buck JN. The House-Tree-Person technique: Revised manual. Beverly Hills, CA: Western Psychological Services, 1966.

19/ Brain Imaging in Psychiatry

1. Reiman EM, Mintun MA. Positron emission tomography. Arch Intern Med 1990;150:729–731.
2. Benes FM, Davidson J, Bird ED. Quantitative cytoarchitectural studies of the cerebral cortex of schizophrenics. Arch Gen Psychiatry 1986;43:31–35.
3. Bogerts B, Meertz E, Schonfeldt-Bausch R. Basal ganglia and limbic system pathology in schizophrenia. Arch Gen Psychiatry 1985;42:784–791.
4. Jakob H, Beckmann H. Prenatal developmental disturbances in the limbic allocortex in schizophrenics. J Neural Trans 1986;65:303–326.
5. Andreasen NC. Nuclear magnetic resonance imaging. In: Andreasen NC, ed. Brain imaging: applications in psychiatry. Washington DC: American Psychiatric Press, 1989:67–121.
6. Ogawa S, Lee TM, Tank DW, Kay AR. Magnetic resonance micro-imaging of blood oxygenation in brain. (Abstr). Society for Neuroscience Annual Meeting, Phoenix, AZ. 1989; 15:pt 1:856.
7. Deicken RF, Van Dyke C, Fein G, Sappey-Marinier D, Hubesch B, Weiner M. Phosphorous magnetic resonance spectroscopy of deep white matter lesions in human brain.

(Abstr). Am Col Neuropsychopharmacology Annual Meeting 1989;149.

8. Penn RD, Belanger MG, Yasnoff WA. Ventricular volume in man computed from CAT scans. Ann Neurol 1978;3: 216–223.

9. Synek V, Reuben J. The ventricular-brain ratio using planimetric measurement of EMI scans. Br J Radiol 1976;49: 233–237.

10. Coffman JA. Computed tomography. In: Andreasen NC, ed. Brain imaging: applications in psychiatry. Washington DC: American Psychiatric Press, 1989:1–65.

11. Brown R, Colter N, Corsellis JAN, et al. Postmortem evidence of structural brain changes in schizophrenia. Arch Gen Psychiatry 1986;43:36–42.

12. Nyback H, Wiegel FA, Berggren BM, et al. Computed tomography of the brain in patients with acute psychosis and in healthy controls. Acta Psychiatr Scand 1982;65:403–413.

13. Andreasen NC, Dennert JW, Olson SA, et al. Hemispheric asymmetries and schizophrenia. Am J Psychiatry 1982;139: 427–430.

14. Nasrallah HA, Olson SC, McCalley-Whitters M, et al. Cerebral ventricular enlargment in schizophrenia: a preliminary follow-up study. Arch Gen Psychiatry 1986;43:157–159.

15. Obiols-Llandrich JE, Ruscallada J, Masferrer M. Ventricular enlargement in young chronic schizophrenics. Acta Psychiatr Scand 1986;73:42–44.

16. Turner SW, Toone BK, Breet-Jones JR. Computerized tomographic scan changes in early chronic schizophrenia—their relationship to perinatal trauma, family history and alcohol intake: preliminary findings. Psychol Med 1986;14: 219–225.

17. Roberts GW, Colter N, Lofthouse R, Bogerts B, Zech M, Crow TJ. Gliosis in schizophrenia: a survey. Biol Psychiatry 1986;21:1043–50.

18. Johnstone ED, Crow TJ, Frith CD, et al. Cerebral ventricular size and cognitive impairment in schizophrenia. Lancet 1976;2:924–926.

19. Nasrallah HA, Jacoby CG, McCalley-Whitters M. Cerebellar ventricular enlargement in subtypes of chronic schizophrenia. Arch Gen Psychiatry 1982;39:774–777.

20. Weinberger DR, Torrey EF, Neophytides AN, et al. Lateral ventricular enlargement in chronic schizophrenia. Arch Gen Psychiatry 1979;36:735–739.

21. Weinberger DR, Luchins DJ, Morihisa JM, et al. Asymmetrical volumes of the right and left frontal and occipital regions of the human brain. Ann Neurol 1982;11:97–100.

22. Johnstone EC, Crow TJ, Frith CD, et al. The dementia of dementia praecox. Acta Psychiatr Scand 1978;57:305–324.

23. Donnelly EF, Weinberger DR, Waldman IN, et al. Cognitive impairment associated with morphological brain abnormalities on computed tomography in chronic schizophrenic patients. J Nerv Ment Dis 1980;168:305–308.

24. Golden CJ, Moses JA, Zelazowski R, et al. Cerebral ventricular size and neuropsychological impairment in young chronic schizophrenics, measurement by the standardized Luria-Nebraska neurophysiological battery. Arch Gen Psychiatry 1980;37:619–623.

25. Golden CJ, MacInnes WD, Ariel RN, et al. Cross-validation of the ability of the Luria-Nebraska Neuropsychological Battery to differentiate chronic schizophrenics with and without ventricular enlargement. J Consult Clin Psychol 1982;50:87–95.

26. Williams AO, Reveley MA, Kolakowska T, et al. Schizophrenia with good and poor outcome. II. Cerebral ventricular size and its clinical significance. Br J Psychiatry 1985; 146:239–246.

27. Weinberger DR, Cannon-Spoor E, Potkin SC, et al. Poor premorbid adjustment and CT abnormalities in chronic schizophrenia. Am J Psychiatry 1980;137:1410–1413.

28. DeLisi LE, Schwartz CC, Targum SD, et al. Ventricular brain enlargement and outcome of acute schizophreniform disorder. Psychiatry Res 1983;9:9–16.

29. Pearlson GD, Garbacz DJ, Breakey WR, et al. Lateral ventricular enlargement associated with persistent unemployment and negative symptoms in both schizophrenia and bipolar disorder. Psychiatry Res 1984;12:1–9.

30. Pearlson GD, Garbacz DJ, Moberg PJ, et al. Symptomatic, familial, perinatal and social correlates of computerized axial tomography (CAT) changes in schizophrenic and bipolars. J Nerv Ment Dis 1985;173:42–50.

31. Andreasen NC, Smith MR, Jacoby CG, et al. Ventricular enlargement in schizophrenia: definition and prevalence. Am J Psychiatry 1982;139:292–296.

32. Luchins DJ, Lewine RJ, Meltzer HY. Lateral ventricular size, psychopathology and medication response in the psychoses. Biol Psychiatry 1984;19:29–34.

33. Luchins DJ, Jackman J, Meltzer HY. Lateral ventricular size and drug-induced parkinsonism. Psychiatry Res 1983; 9:9–16.

34. Luchins DJ, Lewine RJ, Meltzer HY. Lateral ventricular size in the psychoses: relation to psychopathology and therapeutic and adverse response to medication. Schizophr Bull 1983;19:518–523.

35. Reveley AM, Reveley MA, Clifford CA, Murray RM, Cerebral ventricular size in twins discordant for schizophrenia. Lancet 1982;540–541.

36. Largen JW, Smith RC, Calderon M, et al. Abnormalities of brain structure and density of schizophrenia. Biol Psychiatry 1984;19:991–1013.

37. Takahashi R, Inaba Y, Inanaga K, et al. CT scanning and the investigation of schizophrenia. In: Perris C, Struwe G, Jansson B, ed. Biological psychiatry. Amsterdam: Elsevier, 1981.

38. Tanaka Y, Hazama H, Kawahara R, et al. Computerized tomography of the brain in schizophrenic patients. Acta Psychiatr Scand 1981;63:191–197.

39. Shelton RC, Weinberger DR, Doran A, et al. Cerebral structural pathology in schizophrenia. Presented at the Fourth World Congress of Biological Psychiatry, Philadelphia, 1984.

40. Pandarangi AK, Dewan MJ, Lee SH, et al. The ventricular system in chronic schizophrenic patients, a controlled tomography study. Br J Psychiatry 1984;144:172–176.

41. Nasrallah HA, Kuperman S, Jacoby CG, et al. Clinical correlates of sulcal widening in schizophrenia. Psychiatry Res 1983;19:237–242.

42. Reveley MA, Reveley AM, Baldy R. Left cerebral hemisphere hypodensity in discordant schizophrenic twins. Arch Gen Psychiatry 1987;44:625–632.

43. Suddath RL, Christison GW, Torrey EF, Casanova MF, Weinberger DR. Anatomical abnormalities in the brains of monzygotic twins discordant for schizophrenia. N Engl J Med 1990;322:789–794.

44. Nurnberger JI, Goldin LR, Gershon ES. Genetics of psychiatric disorders. In: Winokur G, Clayton P, ed. The medical basis of psychiatry. Philadelphia: Saunders, 1986:486–521.

45. Kelsoe JR, Cadet JL, Pickar D, Weinberger DR. Quantitative neuroanatomy in schizophrenia. Arch Gen Psychiatry 1988;45:533–541.

46. Suddath RL, Casanova MF, Goldberg TE, Daniel DG, Kelsoe JR, Weinberger DR. Temporal lobe pathology in schizophrenia: a quantitative magnetic resonance imaging study. Am J Psychiatry 1989;146:464–472.

47. Andreason NC, Nasrallah HA, Dunn V et al. Structural abnormalities in the frontal system in schizophrenia: a magnetic resonance imaging study. Arch Gen Psychiatry 1986; 43:136–144.

48. Mathew RJ, Partain CL, Prakash R et al. A study of the septum pellucidum and corpus callosum in schizophrenia with MR imaging. Acta Psychiatr Scand 1985;72:414–421.

49. Coffman JA, Andreasen NC, Nasrallah HA, Left hemisphere density deficits in chronic schizophrenia. Biol Psychiatry 1984;19:1237–1247.

50. Matthew RJ, Partain CL. Midsagittal sections of the cerebellar vermis and fourth ventricle obtained with magnetic resonance imaging of schizophrenic patients. Am J Psychiatry 1985;142:970–971.

51. Nasrallah HA, Andreasen NC, Coffman JA. A controlled magnetic resonance imaging study of corpus callosum thickness in schizophrenia. Biol Psychiatry 1986;21:274–282.

52. Besson JAO, Corrigan FM, Cherryman GR et al. Nuclear magnetic resonance brain imaging in chronic schizophrenia. Br J Psychiatry 1987;150:161–163.

53. Fujimoto T, Yokoyama Y, Fujimoto A et al. Spin-lattice relaxation time measurement in schizophrenic disorders. Abstracts, Society for Magnetic Resonance Imaging 1984.

54. Pearlson GD, Verhoff AF. Computerized tomographic scan changes in manic depressive illness. Lancet 1981;2:170.

55. Johnstone EC, Owens DCG, Crow TJ, et al. A CT study of 188 patients with schizophrenia, affective psychosis and neurotic illness. In: Perris C, Struwe G, Jansson B, eds. Biological psychiatry. Amsterdam: Elsevier, 1981:237–240.

56. Nasrallah HA, McCalley-Whitters M, Jacoby CG. Cerebral ventricular enlargement in young manic males: a controlled CT study. J Affect Dis 1982;4:15–19.

57. Weinberger DR, DeLisi LE, Perman GP, et al. CT scans in schizophreniform disorder and other acute psychiatric patients. Arch Gen Psychiatry 1982;39:778–783.

58. Rieder RO, Mann LS, Weinberger DR, et al. Computed tomographic scans in patients with schizophrenia, schizoaffective, and bipolar affective disorder. Arch Gen Psychiatry 1983;40:735.

59. Luchins DR, Lewine RRJ, Melzer HY. Lateral ventricular size, psychopathology, and medication response in the psychoses. Biol Psychiatry 1984;19:29.

60. Tanaka Y, Hazama H, Fukuhara T, et al. Computerized tomography of the brain in manic-depressive patients: a controlled study. Folia Psychiatr Neurol 1982;36:137–144.

61. Dewan MJ, Haldipur V, Lane EE, et al. Bipolar affective disorder. I. Comprehensive quantitative computed tomography. Acta Psychiatr Scand 1988;77:670–676.

62. Besson JAO, Henderson JA, Foreman I, et al. An NMR study of lithium-responding manic depressive patients. Magn Reson Imaging 1987;5:273–277.

63. Nasrallah HA, Olson SC, Coffman JA, et al. Cranial, cerebral and frontal size in affective disorders and schizophrenia: an MRI study. Paper presented at the Am Coll Neuropsychopharmacology Annual Meeting, Dec. 1988. San Juan, PR.

64. Jacoby RJ, Levy R, Bird JM: Computer tomography and the outcome of affective disorder: a follow-up of elderly patients. Br J Psychiatry 1981;139:288.

65. Targum SC, Rosen LN, Citren CM. Delusional symptoms associated with enlarged ventricles in depressed patients. South Med J 1983;76:985–987.

66. Scott ML, Golden CJ, Ruedrich SL, et al. Ventricular enlargement in major depression. Psychiatry Res 1983;8:91–93.

67. Dolan RJ, Calloway SP, Mann AH. Cerebral ventricular size in depressed subjects. Psychol Med 1985;15:873–878.

68. Schlegel S, Kretzschmar K. Computed tomography in affective disorders. I. Venticular and sulcal measurements. Biol Psychiatry 1987;22:4–14.

69. Nasrallah HA, Jacoby CB, McCalley-Whitters M. Cerebellar atrophy in schizophrenia and mania: a comparative CT study. J Clin Psychiatry 1982;43:439–441.

70. Lippman S, Manshadi M, Baldwin H, et al. Cerebellar vermis dimensions on computerized tomographic scans of schizophrenia and bipolar patients. Am J Psychiatry 1982; 139:667.

71. Weinberger DR, Luchins DJ, Morihisa JM, et al. Asymmetrical volumes of the right and left frontal and occipital regions of the human brain. Ann Neurol 1982;11:97–100.

72. Nasrallah HA, Coffman JA, Olson SC. Structural brain-imaging findings in affective disorders: an overview. J Neuropsychiatry 1989;1:21–26.

73. Shima S, Shikano T, Kitamura T, et al. Depression and ventricular enlargement. Acta Psychiatr Scan 1984;70:275–277.

74. Cazzullo CL, Sacchetti E, Vita A, et al. Cerebral ventricular size and age of onset in major depression. IRCS Med Sci 1984;12:917–918.

75. Kellner H, Rubinow DR, Gold PW, et al. Relationship of cortisol hypersecretion to brain CT scan alters in depressed patients. Psychiatry Res 1983;8:191–197.

76. Johnstone EC, Ownes DGC, Crow TJ, et al. Hypothyroidism as a correlate of lateral ventricular enlargement in manic-depressive and neurotic illness. Br J Psychiatry 1986; 148:317–321.

77. Standish-Barry HMAS, Bouras N, Hale AS, et al. Ventricular size and CSF transmitter metabolite concentrations in severe endogenous depression. Br J Psychiatry 1986;148:286–392.

78. Bentson JR, Reza M, Winter J, et al. Steroids and apparent cerebral atrophy on computed tomography scans. J Comput Assist Tomogr 1978;2:16–19.

79. Okuno T, Ito M, Konishi Y, et al. Cerebral atrophy following ACTH therapy. J Comput Assist Tomogr 1980;2:16–19.

80. Nasrallah HA, Coffman JA, Burnstein BA, et al. Cognitive deficits and MRI findings in bipolar disorder compared to controls. Paper presented at Am Coll Neuropsychopharmacology Annual Meeting, Dec. 1988. San Juan, PR.

81. Coffey CE, Holt P, Weiner RD, Webb M, Djang WT, Wilkinson WE. Quantitative brain magnetic resonance imaging in the depressed elderly. [Abstract]. Am Coll Neuropsychopharmacology, Annual Meeting Dec. 1989:203.

82. Hauser P, Altshuler LL, Berrettini W, Dauphinais ID, Gelernter J, Post RM. Temporal lobe measurement in primary affective disorder by magnetic resonance imaging. J Neuropsychiatry 1989;1:128–134.

83. McDonald W, Husain MH, Doraiswamy PM, et al. Diminished caudate volumes in major depression. Presentation at Am Psychiatric Assoc Meeting, New York, NY, May 1990.

84. Krishnan KRA, Doraiswamy PM, Lurie SN, et al. Pituitary enlargement in depression. (Unpublished manuscript)

85. Preskorn S, Hartman B, Irwin C, et al. Roles of the central adrenergic system in mediating amytriptyline-induced alteration in the mammalian blood-brain barrier *in vivo*. J Pharmacol Exp Ther 1982;233:388–395.

86. Fiegel GS, Krishnan KRR, Doraiswamy PM, Rao VP, Nemeroff CB, Boyko OB. Subcortical hyperintensities on brain magnetic resonance imaging: a comparison between late age onset and early onset elderly depressed subjects. (Unpublished manuscript.)

87. Coffey CE, Figiel GS, Djang WT, Saunders WB, Weiner RD. White matter hyperintensity on magnetic resonance imaging: clinical and neuroanatomic correlates in the depressed elderly. J Neuropsychiatry 1989;1:135–144.

88. Tomlinson BE, Blessed G, Roth M. Observations on the brain of nondemented old people. J Neurological Sci 1968; 7:331–356.

89. Robinson RG, Starkstein SE. Current research in affective disorders following stroke. J Neuropsychiatry 1990;2:1–14.

90. Luxenberg JS, Swedo SE, Flament MF, Friedland RP, Rapoport J, Rapoport SI. Neuroanatomical abnormalities in obsessive-compulsive disorder detected with quantitative X-ray computed tomography. Am J Psychiatry 1988;145: 1089–1093.

91. Modell JG, Mountz JM, Curtis GC, Greden JF. Neurophysiologic dysfunction in basal ganglia/limbic striatal and thalamocortical circuits as a pathogenic mechanism of obsessive-compulsive disorder. J Neuropsychiatry 1989;1:27–36.

92. LaPlane D, Levasseur M, Pillon B, et al. Obsessive-compulsive and other behavioral changes with bilateral basal ganglia lesions. Brain 1989;112:699–725.

93. Ontiveros A, Fontaine R, Breton G, Elie R, Fontaine S, Dery R. Correlation of severity of panic disorder and neuroanatomical changes on magnetic resonance imaging. J Neuropsychiatry 1989;1:404–408.

94. Courchesne E, Corchesne RY, Press GA, et al. Hypoplasia of cerebellar vermal lobules VI and VII in autism. N Engl J Med 1988;813:1349–1354.

95. Bauman M, Kemper T. Histoanatomic observations of the brain in early infantile autism. Neurology 1985;35:866–874.

96. Ritvo ER, Freeman BJ, Scheibel AB, et al. Lower Purkinje cell counts in the cerebella of four autistic subjects: initial findings of the UCLA-NSAC autopsy research report. Am J Psychiatry 1986;143:862–866.

97. Heh CWC, Smith R, Wu J, et al. Positron emission tomography of the cerebellum in autism. Am J Psychiatry 1989; 146:242–245.

98. Cala LA, Mastaglia FL. Computerized tomography in chronic alcoholics. Alcoholism 1981;5:283–294.

99. Ennzmann DR, Lane B. Cranial computed tomography findings in anorexia nervosa. J Comput Assist Tomogr 1977; 1:410–414.

100. Nussbaum M, Shenker IR, Mar J, et al. Cerebral atrophy in anorexia nervosa. J Pediatr 1980;96:867–869.

101. Heinz ER, Martinex J, Haenggell A. Reversibility of cerebral atrophy in anorexia nervosa and Cushing's syndrome. J. Comput Assist Tomogr 1977;1:415–417.

102. Kohlmeyer K, Lehmkuhl G, Poutska F. Computed tomography of anorexia nervosa. Am J Neuroradiol 1983;4:437–438.

103. Rapoport JL, Ismond DR. Biological research in child psychiatry. J Am Acad Child Psychiatry 1982;21:543–548.

104. Nasrallah HA, Loney J, Jacoby CG, et al. Cerebral atrophy in young adults with history of hyperactivity in childhood. Psychiatry Res 1986;17:241–246.

105. Raichle ME. Circulatory and metabolic correlates of brain function in normal humans. In: Brookhart JM, Mountcastle VB, ed. Handbook of physiology—the nervous system V. Baltimore MD: Am Physiol Soc 1977: V, chap 16, 643–674.

106. Lassen NA, Perl W. Tracer kinetic methods in medical physiology. New York: Raven, 1979.

107. Shipley RA, Clark RE. Tracer methods for in vivo kinetics. New York: Academic, 1972.

108. Godfrey K. Compartmental models and their application. New York: Academic, 1983.

109. Cohen LB, DeWeer P. Structural and metabolic processes directly related to action potential propagation. In: Brookhart JM, Mountcastle VB, eds. Handbook of physiology. The nervous system. Bethesda: Am. Physiol. Soc, 1977: 1(vol 1):137–159.

110. Creutzfeldt OD. Neurophysical correlates of different functional states of the brain. In: Ingvar DH, Lassen NA, ed. Brain work: the coupling of function, metabolism and blood flow in the brain. Copenhagen: Munksgard, 1975:22–47. (Alfred Benzon Symp. 8).

111. Lightman SL, Hunt SP, Iversen LL. Effects of opiates and osmotic stimuli on rat neurohypophyseal metabolic activity monitored with [^{3}H] 2-deoxyglucose. Neuroendocrinology 1982;35:104–110.

112. Schwartz WJ, Smith CB, Davidsen L, et al. Metabolic mapping of functional activity in the hypothalamo-neurohypophysial system of the rat. Science 1979;205:723–725.

113. Siejo BJ. Brain energy metabolism. New York: Wiley, 1978.

114. Leniger-Follert E. Mechanisms of regulation of cerebral microflow during bicuculline-induced seizures in anaesthetized cats. J Cereb Blood Flow Metab 1984;4:150–165.

115. Leniger-Follert E, Hossmann KA. Simultaneous measurements of microflow and evoked potentials in the somatomotor cortex of the cat brain during specific sensory activation. Pfluegers Arch 1979;380:85–89.

116. Leniger-Follert E, Lubbers DW. Behavior of microflow and local PO2 of the brain cortex during and after direct electrical stimulation. Pfluegers Arch 1976;366:39–44.

117. Lubbers DW, Leniger-Follert E. Capillary flow in brain cortex during changes in oxygen supply and state of activation. In: Cerebral vascular smooth muscle and its control. Amsterdam: Elsevier/North-Holland 1978:21–42. (Ciba Found Symp 56).

118. Sandman CA, O'Halloran JP, Isenhart R. Is there an evoked vascular response? Science 1984;224:1355–1357.

119. Ter-Pogossian MM, Ficke DC, Mintun MA, Herscovitch P, Fox PT, Raichle ME. Dynamic cerebral positron emission tomographic studies. Ann Neurol 1984;15:46–47.

120. Yarowsky PM, Kadekard PM, Sokoloff L. Frequency-dependent activation of glucose utilization in the superior dependent activation of glucose utilization in the superior cervical ganglion by electrical stimulation of cervical sympathetic trunk. Proc Natl Acad Sci 1983;80:4179–4183.

121. Fox PT, Raichle ME, Mintun MA, Dence G. Nonoxidative glucose consumption during focal physiologic neural activity. Science 1988;241:462–464.

122. Fox PT, Raichle ME. Focal physiological uncoupling of cerebral blood flow and oxidative metabolism during somatosensory stimulation in human subjects. Proc Natl Acad Sci USA 1986;83:1140–1144.

123. Fox PT, Raichle ME. Cerebral blood flow and oxidative metabolism are focally uncoupled in physiological activation: a positron-emission tomographic study. In: Raichle ME, Powers WJ, ed. Cerebrovascular diseases. New York: Raven Press, 1987:129–140.

124. Ingvar DH. Pattern of brain activity revealed by measurement of regional cerebral blood flow. In: Ingvar DH, Lassen NA, ed. Brain work. Copenhagen: Munksgaard, 1975: 397–413.

125. Ingvar DH. Serial aspects of language and speech related to prefrontal cortical activity: a selective review. Hum Neurobiol 1983;2:177–189.

126. Roland PE. Organization of motor control by normal human brain. Hum Neurobiol 1984;2:205–216.

127. Reiman EM, Fusselman MJ, Fox PT, Raichle ME. Neuroanatomical correlates of anticipatory anxiety. Science 1989;243:1071–1074.

128. Lassen NA, Ingvar DH. Radioisotope assessment of regional cerebral blood flow. Prog Nucl Med 1972;1:376–409.

129. Landau WM, Freygang WH, Roland LP, Sokoloff L, Kety SS. The local circulation of the living brain: values in the unanesthetized cat. Trans Am Neurol Assoc 1955;80:125–129.

130. Sokoloff LM, Reivich C, Kennedy MH, Patlak CS, Pettigrew KD, Sakurada O, Shinohara M. The [14C] deoxyglucose method for the measurement of local cerebral glucose utilization: theory, procedure and normal values in the conscious and anesthetized albino rat. J Neurochem 1977; 28:897–916.

131. Phelps ME, Huang SC, Hoffman EJ, Selin C, Sokoloff L, Kuhl DE. Tomographic measurement of local cerebral glucose metabolic rate in humans with [^{18}F]2-fluro-2-deoxy-D-glucose: validation of method. Ann Neurol 1979;6:371–388.

132. Sokoloff L. The radioactive deoxyglucose method: theory, procedure and applications for the measurement of local glucose utilization in the central nervous system. Adv Neurochem 1982;4:1–82.

133. Mazziotta JV, Phelps ME, Meadors AK, Ricci A, Winter K, Bentson JR. Anatomical localization schemes for use in positron computed tomography using a specially designed headholder. J Comput Assist Tomogr 1982;6:848–853.

134. Fox PT, Perlmutter JS, Riachle ME. A sterotactic method of anatomical localization for positron emission tomography. J Comput Assist Tomogr 1985;9:141–153.

135. Talairach J, Szikla G, Tournous P, et al. Atlas d'anatomie stereotaxique du telecephale. Paris: Masson, 1967.

136. Passingham R, Friston KJ, Nutt J, Heather JD, Frackowiak RSJ. Neuroanatomical localisation in PET images. J Cereb Blood Flow and Metabolism 1919;9(Suppl1):S196.

137. Drevets WC, Raichle ME, Fox PT, Preskorn SH, Videen TO. Trait and state cerebral blood flow abnormalities in depression. [Abstract]. Soc Neurosci Ann Meeting, Phoenix, AZ;15(l)30.

138. Raichle ME. Positron emission tomography. Ann Rev Neurosci 1983;6:249–267.

139. Fox PT, Mintun MA, Raichle ME, Meizen FM, Allman JM, Van Essen DC. Mapping human visual cortex with positron emission tomography. Nature Lond. 1986;323:806–809.

140. Devous MD. Imaging brain function by single-photon emission computer tomography. In: Andreasen NC, ed. Brain imaging: applications in psychiatry. Washington DC: American Psychiatric Press 1989;147–234.

141. Ingvar D, Franzen G. Abnormalities of cerebral blood flow distribution in patients with chronic schizophrenia. Acta Psychiatr Scand 1974;50:425–462.

142. Franzen G, Ingvar D. Absence of activation in frontal structures during psychological testing of chronic schizophrenics. J Neurol Neurosurg Psychiatry 1975;38:1027–1032.

143. Ingvar D, Franzen G. Distribution of cerebral activity in chronic schizophrenia. Lancet 1974;ii:1484–1486.

144. Ariel R, Golden C, Berg R, et al. Regional cerebral blood flow in schizophrenics. Arch Gen Psychiatry 1983;40:258–263.

145. Weinberger DR, Berman KF, Zec RF. Physiologic dysfunction of dorsolateral prefrontal cortex in schizophrenia. I. Regional cerebral blood flow evidence. Arch Gen Psychiatry 1986;43:114–124.

146. Berman KF, Zec RF, Weinberger DR. Physiologic dysfunction of dorsolateral prefrontal cortex in schizophrenia. II. Role of neuroleptic treatment, attention, and mental effort. Arch Gen Psychiatry 1986;43:126–135.

147. Farkas T. Wolf AP, Jaeger J, Brodie JD, Christman DR, Fowler JS. Regional brain glucose metabolism in chronic schizophrenia. Arch Gen Psychiatry 1984;41:293–300.

148. Buchsbaum MS, Ingvar DH, Kessler R, et al. Cerebral glucography with positron tomography. Arch Gen Psychiatry 1982;39:251–259.

149. Buchsbaum M, DeLisi L, Holcomb H, et al. Anteroposterior gradients in cerebral glucose use in schizophrenia and affective disorders. Arch Gen Psychiatry 1984;41:1159–1166.

150. DeLisi L, Holcomb H, Cohen R, et al. Positron emission tomography in schizophrenic patients without neuroleptic medication. J Cereb Blood Flow Metab 1985;5:201–206.

151. Wolkin A, Jaeger J, Brodie J, et al. Persistance of cerebral metabolic abnormalities in chronic schizophrenia as determined by positron emission tomography. Am J Psychiatry 1985;142:564–571.

152. Gur RE, Resnick SM, Alavi A, et al. Regional brain function in schizophrenia. Arch Gen Psychiatry 1987;44:119–125.

153. Mathew R, Duncan G, Weinman M, Barr D. Regional cerebral blood flow in schizophrenia. Arch Gen Psychiatry 1982;39:1121–1124.

154. Gur RE, Skolnick BE, Gur R, et al. Brain function in psychiatric disorders. I. Regional cerebral blood flow in medicated schizophrenics. Arch Gen Psychiatry 1983;40:1250–1254.

155. Gur RE, Gur RC, Skolnick BE, et al. Brain function in psychiatric disorders. III. Regional cerebral blood flow in unmedicated schizophrenics. Arch Gen Psychiatry 1985;42:329–334.

156. Sheppard G, Gruzelier J, Manchanda R, et al. 150-Positron emission tomographic scanning predominantly never-treated acute schizophrenic patients. Lancet 1983;ii:1448–1452.

157. Garnett ES, Nahmias C, Firnau G, Cleghorn J. Patterns of local cerebral glucose metabolism in untreated schizophrenics. J Cereb Blood Flow Metab 1985;Suppl. 1:5,S220.

158. Volkow ND, Brodie JD, Wolf AP, Angrist B, Russell J, Cancro R. Brain metabolism in patients with schizophrenia before and after acute neuroleptic administration. J Neurol Neurosurg Psychiatry 1986;49:1199–1202.

159. Early TS, Reiman EM, Raichle ME, Spitznagel EL. Left globus pallidus abnormality in never-medicated patients with schizophrenia. Proc Natl Acad Sci 1987;84:561–563.

160. Widen L, Blomquist T, Greitz T, Litton JE, Bergstrom M, Ehrin E, Ericson K. PET studies of glucose metabolism in patients with schizophrenia. Am J Nucl Med Radiol 1983;4:550–552.

161. Weinberger DR, Berman KF. Speculation on the meaning of cerebral metabolic hypofrontality in schizophrenia. Schizophrenia Bull 1988;14:157–168.

162. Goldberg TE, Berman F, Mohr E, Weinberger DR. Regional cerebral blood flow and cognitive function in Huntington's disease and schizophrenia. Arch Neurol 1990;47:418–422.

163. Daniel DG, Weinberger DR, Jones DW, et al. The effect of amphetamine on CBF (XE-133 dynamic SPECT) in schizophrenia. (Abstr.) American College of Neuropsychopharmacology Annual Meeting Dec. 1989:122.

164. Cohen RM, Semple WE, Gross M et al. Dysfunction in a prefrontal substrate of sustained attention in schizophrenia. Life Sciences 1987;40:2031–2039.

165. Kling AS, Metter EJ, Riefe WH, et al. Comparison of PET measurement of local brain glucose metabolism and CAT measurement of brain atrophy in chronic schizophrenia and depression. Am J Psychiatry 1986;143:175–180.

166. Baxter LR, Phelps ME, Mazziotta JC, et al. Cerebral metabolic rates for glucose in mood disorders. Arch Gen Psych 1985;42:441–447.

167. Schwartz JM, Baxter LR, Mazziotta JC, Gerner RH, Phelps ME. The differential diagnosis of depression: Revelvance of positron emission tomography studies of cerebral glucose metabolism to the bipolar-unipolar dichotomy. J Am Med Assn 1987;258:1368–1373.

168. Buchsbaum MS, Wu J, DeLisi LE, et al. Frontal cortex and basal ganglia metabolic rates assessed by positron emission tomography with [^{18}F]2-deoxyglucose in affective illness. J Aff Dis 1986;10:137–152.

169. Kishimoto H, Takazu O, Ohno S, et al. ^{11}C-Glucose metabolism in manic and depressed patients. Psychiatry Res 1987;22:81–88.

170. O'Connell RA, Van Heertum RL, Billick SB, et al. Single photon emission computed tomography (SPECT) with [^{123}I]IMP in the differential diagnosis of psychiatric disorders. J Neuropsych 1989;1:145–153.

171. Devous MD, Rush AJ, Schlesser Ma, et al. Single-photon tomographic determination of regional cerebral blood flow in psychiatric disorders. J Nucl Med 1984;25:57.

172. Cohen RM, Semple WE, Gross M, et al. Evidence for common alterations in cerebral glucose metabolism in major affective disorders and schizophrenia. Psychopharmacology 1989;2:241–254.

173. Baxter LR, Schwartz JM, Phelps ME, et al. Reduction of prefrontal cortex glucose metabolism common to three types of depression. Arch Gen Psychiatry 1989;46:243–250.

174. Guenther W, Moser E, Mueller-Spahn F, von Oefele K, Buell U, Hippius H. Pathological cerebral blood flow during motor function in schizophrenic and endogenous depressed patients. Biol Psychiatry 1986;21:889–899.

175. Risberg J. Regional cerebral blood flow measurement by ^{133}Xenon inhalation: methodology and applications in neuropsychology and psychiatry. Brain and Lang 1980;9:9–34.

176. Landau P, Gordon E, Kraiuhin C, et al. Cerebral blood-flow (RCBF) and the P300 event related potential (ERP) in the diagnosis of dementia and depression. Austral New Zeal J Med 1988;18:421.

177. Berman KF, Doran AR, Pickar D, Weinberger DR. Regional cerebral blood flow during cognitive activation in depression: a comparison with normal subjects and patients with schizophrenia. (Abstr) Am Coll Neuropsychopharmacology Ann Meeting, Maui, Hawaii, Dec. 1989;199.

178. Gustafson L, Johanson M, Risberg J, Silfverskiold P. Regional cerebral blood flow in organic dementias, affective disorders and confusional states. Third World Congress of Biological Psychiatry, Stockholm, 1981.

179. Ingvar DH, Franzen G. Normal and abnormal mentation related to cerebral circulation and metabolism. Third World Congress of Biological Psychiatry, Stockholm, 1981.

180. Silfverskiold P, Risberg J. Regional cerebral blood flow in depression and mania. Arch Gen Psychiatry 1988;46:253–259.

181. Sackeim HA, Prohovnik I, Moeller JR, et al. Regional cerebral blood flow in mood disorders. I. Comparison of major depressives and normal controls at rest. Arch Gen Psychiatry 1990;47:60–70.

182. Gur RE, Skolnick BE, Gur RC, et al. Brain function in psychiatric disorders. II. Regional cerebral blood flow in medicated unipolar depressives. Arch Gen Psychiatry 1984;41:695–699.

183. Uytdenhoef P, Portelange P, Jacquy J, Charles G, Linkowski P, Mendlewicz J. Regional cerebral flow and lateralized hemispheric dysfunction in depression. Brit J Psychiatry 1983;143:128–132.

184. Schwartz JM, Baxter LR, Phelps ME, Mazziotta JC, Guze BH. Caudate nucleus metabolism with respect to specific cortical regions discriminates bipolar depressed, unipolar depressed, and normal control populations. (Abstr.) Ann Meeting Am Coll Neuropsychopharmacology, Dec. 1989, Nashville: 197.

185. Rush AJ, Schlesser MA, Stokely EM et al. Cerebral blood flow in depression and mania. Psychopharmacol Bull 1982;18:6–8.

186. Reivich M, Gur R, Alavi A. Positron emission tomographic studies of sensory stimuli, cognitive processes and anxiety. Hum Neurobiol 1983;2:25–33.

187. Reiman EM, Raichle ME, Butler FK, Herscovitch P, Robins E. A focal brain abnormality in panic disorder, a severe form of anxiety. Nature 1984;310:683–685.

188. Reiman EM, Raichle ME, Robins E, et al. Neuroanatomical correlates of a lactate-induced anxiety attack. Arch Gen Psychiatry 1989;46:493–500.

189. Reiman EM, Raichle ME, Robins E, et al. The application of positron emission tomography to the study of panic disorder. Am J Psychiatry 1986;143:469–477.

190. Baxter LR, Phelps ME, Mazziotta JC, Guze BH, Schwartz JM, Selin CE. Local cerebral glucose metabolic rates in obsessive-compulsive disorder. Arch Gen Psychiatry 1987;44:211–218.

191. Baxter LR, Schwartz JM, Mazziotta JC, et al. Cerebral glucose metabolic rates in nondepressed patients with obsessive-compulsive disorder. Am J Psychiatry 1988;145:1560–1563.

192. Nordahl TE, Benkelfat C, Semple WE, Gross M, King AC, Cohen RM. Cerebral glucose metabolic rates in obsessive compulsive disorder. Neuropsychopharmacology 1989;2:23–28.

193. Swedo SE, Schapiro MB, Grady CL, et al. Cerebral glucose metabolism in childhood-onset obsessive-compulsive disorder. Arch Gen Psychiatry 1989;46:518–523.

194. Farde L, Hall H, Ehrin E. Quantitative analysis of D_2 dopamine receptor binding in the living human brain by PET. Science 1986;231:258–61.

195. Persson A, Ehrin E, Erkisson L, Farde L, Hedstrom CG et al. Imaging of [C]-labelled RO 15-1788 binding to benzodiazepine receptors in the human brain by positron emission tomography. J Psychiatr Res 1985;19:609–622.

196. Sedvall G, Farde L, Persson A, Wiesel FA. Imaging of neurotransmitter receptors in the living human brain. Arch Gen Psychiatry 1986;43:995–1005.

197. Wong DF, Wagner HN, Tune LE et al. Positron emission tomography reveals elevated D_2 dopamine receptors in drug-naive schizoprenics. Science 1986;234:1558–63.

198. Welch MJ, Katzenellenbogen JA, Mathias CJ et al. N-(3[^{18}F]Fluoropropyl)-spiperone: the preferred ^{18}F labeled spiperone analog for positron emission tomographic studies of the dopamine receptor. Nucl Med Biol 1988;15:83–97.

199. Farde L, Wiesel F, Stone-Elander S, et al. D_2 dopamine receptors in neuroleptic-naive schizophrenic patients. Arch Gen Psychiatry 1990;47:213–219.

200. Martinot J, Peron-Magnan P, Huret J et al. Striatal D_2 dopaminergic receptors assessed with positron emission tomography and [^{76}Br] bromospiperone in untreated schizophrenic patients. Am J Psychiatry 1990;147:44–50.

201. Innis RB, Woods SW, Zoghbi S et al. SPECT imaging of the dopamine D_2 and benzodiazepine receptors in non-human primate brain (Abstr.) Am Coll Neuropsychopharmacology Ann Meeting, Dec. 1989, Maui, Hawaii; 138.

202. Crawley JCW, Crow TJ, Johnstone EC et al. Uptake of 77Br-spiperone in the striata of schizophrenic patients and controls. Nucl Med Commun 1986;7:599–607.

203. Farde L, Wiesel F, Halldin C, Sedvall G. Central D_2-dopamine receptor occupancy in schizophrenic patients treated with antipsychotic drugs. Arch Gen Psychiatry 1988;45:71–76.

204. Karson CN, Coppola R, Morihisa JM, Weinberger DR. Computed electroencephalographic activity mapping in schizophrenia. Arch Gen Psychiatry 1987;44:514–517.

205. Pfurtscheller G, Ladurner G, Maresch H, Vollmer R. Brain electrical activity mapping in normal and ischemic brain. In: Pfurtscheller G et al. Brain ischemia: quantitative EEG and imaging techniques. Prog Brain Res 1984;62:287–302.

206. Buchsbaum MS, Cappelletti J, Coppola R, Regal F, King AC, van Kammen DP. New methods to determine the CNS effects of antigeriatric compounds: EEG topography and glucose use. Drug Dev Res 1982;2:489–496.

207. Morihisa JM, Duffy FH, Wyatt RJ. Brain electrical activity mapping (BEAM) in schizophrenic patients. Arch Gen Psychiatry 1983;40:719–728.

208. Morstyn R, Duffy FH, McCarley RW. Altered topography of EEG spectral content in schizophrenia. Electroenceph Clin Neurophysiol 1983;56:263–271.

209. Guenther W, Breitling D, Banquet JP, Marcie P, Rondot P. EEG mapping of left hemisphere dysfunction during motor performance in schizophrenia. Biol Psychiatry 1986;21:249–262.

210. Small JG, Milstein V, Small IF, Miller MJ, Kellams JJ, Corsaro CJ. Computerized EEG profiles of haloperidol, chlorpromazine, clozapine and placebo in treatment resistant schizophrenia. Clin Electroencephalogr 1987;18:124–135.

211. Small JG, Milstein V, Kellams JJ, Miller MJ, Boyko OB, Small IF. EEG topography in psychiatric diagnosis and drug treatment. Ann Clin Psychiatry 1989;1:7–17.

212. Morihisa JM, Duffy FH. Focal cortical arousal in the schizophrenias. In: Duffy FH, ed. Topographic mapping of brain electrical activity. Boston: Butterworth 1986:371–379.

213. Karson CN, Coppola R, Daniel DG, Weinberger DR. Computerized EEG in schizophrenia. Schizophrenia Bull 1988;14(2):193–197.

214. Itil TM, Saletu B, Davis S. EEG findings in chronic schizophrenics based on digital computer period analysis and analog power spectra. Biol Psychiatry 1972;5:1–13.

215. Flor-Henry P. Lateralized temporal-limbic dysfunction and psychopathology. Ann NY Acad Sci 1976;280:777–797.

216. Torello MW, McCarley RW. The use of topographic mapping techniques in clinical studies in psychiatry. In: Duffy FH, ed. Topographic mapping of brain electrical activity. Boston: Butterworth, 1986:383–387.

217. Duncan CC. Event-related brain potentials: A window on information processing schizophrenia. Schizophrenia Bull 1988;14:199–203.

218. Buchsbaum MS, Awsare SV, Holcomb HH et al. Topographic differences between normals and schizophrenics: the N120 evoked potential component. Neuropsychology 1986;15:1–6.

219. Schatzberg AF, Elliott GR, Lerbinger JE, Marcel B, Duffy FH. Topographic mapping in depressed patients. In: Duffy FH, ed. Topographic mapping of brain electrical activity. Boston: Butterworth, 1986:389–391.

20/ Psychopathology

1. Robins E, Guze SB. Establishment of diagnostic validity in psychiatric illness: its application in schizophrenia. Am J Psychiatry 1970;126:107–111.

2. Klein DF. The pharmacological validation of psychiatric diagnosis. In: Robins LN, Barrett JE, eds. The validity of psychiatric diagnosis. New York: Raven, 1989.

3. American Psychiatric Association. Diagnostic and statistical manual of mental disorders, 3rd ed. Washington, DC: American Psychiatric Association, 1980.

4. Cohen J. A coefficient of agreement for nominal scales. Educ Psychol Meas 1960;20:37–46.

5. Spitznagel EL, Helzer JE. A proposed solution to the base rate problem in the kappa statistic. Arch Gen Psychiatry 1985;42:725–728.

6. Feighner JP, Robins E, Guze SB, Woodruff RA, Winokur G, Munoz RA. Diagnostic criteria for use in psychiatric research. Arch Gen Psychiatry 1972;26:56–63.

7. Spitzer RL, Endicott J, Robins E. Research diagnostic criteria: rationale and reliability. Arch Gen Psychiatry 1978;35:773–782.

8. American Psychiatric Association. Diagnostic and statistical manual of mental disorders, 3rd ed, rev. Washington DC: American Psychiatric Association, 1987.

9. Morel BA. Traite des maladies mentales. 1860:491,560,566,712.

10. Kraepelin E. Psychiatrie. Leipzig:Weiner, 1893.

11. Kraepelin E. Manic depressive insanity and paranoia. New York: Arno Press, 1921/1976.

12. Kraepelin E. Dementia praecox and paraphrenia. (Trans. Barclay RM, ed. Robertson GM). Huntington, NY: RE Krieger, 1971/1919.

13. Bleuler E. Dementia praecox or the group of schizophrenias (trans. Tinkin J). New York: International Universities Press 1911/1950.

14. Crow TJ. Positive and negative schizophrenic symptoms and the role of dopamine. Br J Psychiatry 1980;137:383–386.

15. Andreasen NC, Olsen S. Negative v. positive schizophrenia: definition and validation. Arch Gen Psychiatry 1982;39:789–794.

16. Andreasen NC, Olsen SA, Dennert JW, et al. Ventricular enlargement in schizophrenia: relationship to positive and negative symptoms. Am J Psychiatry 1982;139:297–302.

17. Abrams R, Taylor MA. A rating scale for emotional blunting. Am J Psychiatry 1978;135:225–229.

18. Andreasen NC, Black DW. Introductory textbook of psychiatry. Washington, DC: American Psychiatric Press, 1991.

19. Andreasen NC. Thought, language and communication disorders. 2. Diagnostic significance. Arch Gen Psychiatry 1979;36:1325–1330.

20. Carlson GA, Goodwin FK. The stages of mania. Arch Gen Psychiatry 1973;28:221–228.

21. Abrams R, Taylor MA. The importance of schizophrenic symptoms in the diagnosis of mania. Am J Psychiatry 1983;138:658–661.

22. Goodwin DW, Alderson P, Rosenthal R. Clinical significance of hallucinations in psychiatric disorders: a study of 116 hallucinatory patients. Arch Gen Psychiatry 1971;24:76–80.

23. DeVaul RA, Hall RCW. Hallucinations. In: Hall RCW, ed. Clinical presentations of medical illness: somatopsychic disorders. Jamaica NY: Spectrum 1980;;91–103.

24. Schneider K. Clinical psychopathology. New York: Grune and Stratton, 1959:133.

25. Carpenter WT Jr, Strauss JS, Mulch S. Are there pathognomonic symptoms in schizophrenia? Arch Gen Psychiatry 1973;28:847–852.

26. Andreassen NC, Akiskal HS. The specificity of Bleulerian and Schneiderian symptoms: a critical reevaluation. Psychiatr Clin North Am 1983;6:41–54.

27. Hamilton M, ed. Fish's outline of psychiatry. 3rd ed. Bristol: John Wright & Sons, 1978.

28. Taylor MA. Schneiderian first-rank symptoms and clinical prognostic features in schizophrenia. Arch Gen Psychiatry 1972;26:64–67.

29. Quitkin F, Rifkin A, Klein DF. Neurologic soft signs in schizophrenia and character disorders. Arch Gen Psychiatry 1976;33:845–853.

30. Cox SM, Ludwig AM. Neurological soft signs and psychopathology. 1. Findings in schizophrenia. J Nerv Ment Dis 1979;168:161–165.

31. Taylor MA. The behavioral neurologic examination. In: Sierles FS, ed. Clinical behavioral science. New York: SP Medical and Scientific Books, 1982:14.

32. Taylor MA. The practice of neuropsychiatry. New York: Free Press, 1992.

33. Pope HG, Lipinski JF. Diagnosis in schizophrenia and manic depressive illness: a reassessment of the specificity of "schizophrenic" symptoms in the light of current research. Arch Gen Psychiatry 1978;35:811–828.

34. Kramer M. Some problems for international research suggested by observations in differences in first admission rates to the mental hospitals of England and Wales and of the United States. Proc Third World Congress of Psychiatry 1961;3:153–160.

35. Cooper JE, Kendell RE, Gurland BJ et al. Psychiatric diagnosis in New York and London: a comparative study of mental hospital admissions. London: Oxford University Press, 1972. Maudsley Monographs no. 20.

36. Taylor MA, Abrams R. Manic depressive illness and good prognosis schizophrenia. Am J Psychiatry 1975;132:741–742.

37. Sharpe S, Gurland BJ, Fleiss JL et al. Comparisons of American, Canadian and British psychiatrists in their diagnostic concepts. Can Psychiatric Assoc J 1974;19:235–245.

38. Strauss JS, Gift TE. Choosing an approach for diagnosing schizophrenia. Arch Gen Psychiatry 1977;34:1248–1253.

39. Baldessarini R. Frequency of diagnosis of schizophrenia vs. affective disorder from 1944 to 1968. Am J Psychiatry 1970;127:759–763.

40. Kendell RE, Cooper JE, Gowiley AJ, et al. Diagnostic criteria of American and British psychiatrists. Arch Gen Psychiatry 1971;25:123–130.

41. Tsuang MT, Loyd DW. Schizophrenia. In: Winokur G, Clayton P, eds. The medical basis of psychiatry. Philadelphia: Saunders, 1986:80–101.

42. Helzer JE, Brockington IF, Kendell RE. Predictive validity of DSM-III and Feighner definitions of schizophrenia: a comparison with Research Diagnostic Criteria and CATEGO. Arch Gen Psychiatry 1981;38:791–797.

43. Stephens JH, Astrup C, Carpenter WT et al. A comparison of nine systems to diagnose schizophrenia. Psychiatry Res 1982;6:127–143.

44. Cutting J. Outcome in schizophrenia: overview. In: Kerr TA, Snirh RP, eds. Contemporary issues in schizophrenia. Washington DC: American Psychiatric Press, 1986;433–440.

45. Tsuang MT, Woolson RF, Fleming JA. Long term outcome of major psychoses. I. Schizophrenia and affective disorder compared with psychiatrically symptom free surgical conditions. Arch Gen Psychiatry 1979;36:1295–1306.

46. Black DW, Yates WR, Andreasen NC. Schizophrenia, schizophreniform disorder, and delusional (paranoid) disorders. In: Talbott JA, Hales RE, Yudofsky SC, eds. Textbook of psychiatry. Washington DC: American Psychiatric Press 1988:357–401.

47. Vaillant GE. Prospective prediction of schizophrenic remission. Arch Gen Psychiatry 1964;11:509–518.

48. McCabe MS, Fowler RC, Cadoret RJ et al. Symptom differences in schizophrenics with good and poor prognosis. Am J Psychiatry 1972;128:1239–1243.

49. McGlashan TH. The prediction of outcome in chronic schizophrenia. IV. The Chestnut Lodge follow-up study. Arch Gen Psychiatry 1986;4:167–176.

50. Tsuang MT, Winokur G. Criteria for subtyping schizophrenia: clinical differentiation of hebephrenic and paranoid schizophrenia. Arch Gen Psychiatry 1974;31:43–47.

51. Kendler KS, Gruenberg AM, Tsuang MT. Outcome of schizophrenic subtypes defined by four diagnostic systems. Arch Gen Psychiatry 1984;41:149–154.

52. Taylor MA. Catatonia: A review of a behavioral neurologic syndrome. Neuropsychiatry Neuropsychol Behav Neurol 1990;3:48–72.

53. Goodwin DW, Guze SB. Psychiatric diagnosis. 4th ed. New York: Oxford, 1989.

54. Kendler KS, Gruenberg AM, Tsuang MT. Subtype stability in schizophrenia. Am J Psychiatry 1985;142:827–832.

55. Nielson J, Nielson JA. A census study of mental illness in Samso. Psychol Med 1977;7:491–503.

56. Tsuang MT, Winokur G, Crowe RR. Morbidity risks of schizophrenia and affective disorders among first degree relatives of patients with schizophrenia, mania, depression and surgical conditions. Am J Psychiatry 1980;137:497–504.

57. Robins LN, Helzer JE, Weissman MM et al. Lifetime prevalence of specific disorders in three sites. Arch Gen Psychiatry 1984;41:949–958.

58. Anthony JC, Folstein M, Romanoski AJ, et al. Comparison of the lay Diagnostic Interview Schedule and a standardized psychiatric diagnosis. 1985;42:667–675.

59. Goldberg EM, Morrison SL. Schizophrenia and social class. Br J Psychiatry 1963;109:785–802.

60. Wender PH, Rosenthal D, Kety SS, Schulsinger F, Welner J. Social class and psychopathology in adoptees. Arch Gen Psychiatry 1973;28:318–325.

61. Salokangas RRK. Social class of the parents of schizophrenic patients. Proceedings of the 18th Nordic Psychiatric Congress. Acta Psychiatr Scand 1976, 54 suppl 265:30.

62. Dunham HW. Community and schizophrenia. Detroit: Wayne State University Press, 1965.

63. Hare EH. Season of birth of schizophrenia and neurosis. Am J Psychiatry 1975;132:1168–1171.

64. Hare EH, Moran P. A relation between seasonal temperature and the birth rate of schizophrenic patients. Acta Psychiatr Scand 1981;63:396–405.

65. Torrey EF, Torrey BB, Peterson MR. Seasonality of schizophrenic births in the United States. Arch Gen Psychiatry 1977;34:1065–1070.

66. Tsuang MT, Woolson RF. Mortality in patients with schizophrenia, mania, depression and surgical conditions. Br J Psychiatry 1977;130:162–166.

67. Tsuang MT. Suicide in schizophrenics, manics, depressives and surgical controls: a comparison with general population suicide mortality. Arch Gen Psychiatry 1978;35:153–155.

68. Frangos E, Athanassenas G, Tsitourides S, et al. Prevalence of DSM-III schizophrenics among the first degree relatives of schizophrenic probands. Acta Psychiatr Scand 1985;72:382–386.

69. Gottesman II, Shields J. Schizophrenia: the epigenetic puzzle. Cambridge UK: Cambridge University Press, 1982.

70. Kendler KS, Masterson CL, Davis KC. Psychiatric illness in first-degree relatives of patients with paranoid psychosis, schizophrenia and medical illness. Br J Psychiatry 1985;147:524–531.

71. Fischer M, Harvald B, Hauge M. A Danish twin study of schizophrenia. Br J Psychiatry 1969;115:981–990.

72. Allen MG, Cohen S, Pollin W. Schizophrenia in veteran twins: a diagnostic review. Am J Psychiatry 1972;128:939–945.

73. Suddath RL, Christison GW, Torrey EF, Casanova MF, Weinberger DR. Anatomical abnormalities in the brains of monozygotic twins discordant for schizophrenia. N Engl J Med 1990;322:789–794.

74. Heston LL. Psychiatric disorders in foster home-reared children of schizophrenic mothers. Br J Psychiatry 1966;112:819–825.

75. Kendler KS, Gruenberg AM. An independent analysis of the Danish Adoption Study of Schizophrenia. Arch Gen Psychiatry 1984;41:555–564.

76. Kety SS. Mental illness in the biological relatives of schizophrenic adoptees: findings relevant to genetic and environmental factors in etiology. Am J Psychiatry 1983;140:720–727.

77. Fischer M. Psychoses in the offspring of schizophrenic twins and their normal co-twins. Br J Psychiatry 1971;118:43–52.

78. Mednick SA, Machar RA, Huttunen MD, et al. Adult schizophrenia following prenatal exposure to an influenza epidemic. Arch Gen Psychiatry 1988;45:189–192.

79. Andreasen NC, Wosek P. Adjustment disorders in adolescents and adults. Arch Gen Psychiatry 1980;37:1166–1170.

80. Wilcox JA, Nasrallah HA. Childhood head trauma and psychosis. Psychiatry Res 1982;21:303–306.

81. Lynn M. Barr CE, Cannon TD, et al. Fetal neural development and schizophrenia. Schizophr Bull 1989;15:149–160.

82. Rakich P. Specification of cerebral cortical areas. Science 1988;241:170–176.

83. Snyder SH. The dopamine hypothesis in schizophrenia: focus on the dopamine receptor. Am J Psychiatry 1976;133:197–202.

84. Rosen JN. Direct analysis: Selected papers. New York: Grune and Stratton, 1953:9.

85. Searles HF. The effort to drive the other person crazy: an element in the etiology and psychotherapy of schizophrenia. Br J Med Psychol 1959;32:1–18.

86. Wynne LC, Rychoff I, Day J, et al. Pseudomutuality in the family relations of schizophrenics. Psychiatry 1958;21:205–220.

87. Bateson G, Jackson DD, Haley J et al. Toward a theory of schizophrenia. Behav Sci 1956;1:251–264.

88. Falloon IRH, Boyd JL, McGill CW, et al. Family management in the prevention of exacerbations of schizophrenia: a controlled study. N Engl J Med 1982;306:1437–1440.

89. Falloon IRH, Boyd JL, McGill CW, et al. Family care for schizophrenia: a problem-solving approach to mental illness. New York: Guilford, 1984.

90. Leff J. Schizophrenia and sensitivity to the family environment. Schizophr Bull 1976;2:566–574.

91. Baldessarini RJ. Chemotherapy in psychiatry. Cambridge, MA: Harvard University Press, 1985.

92. Baldessarini RJ. Drugs and the treatment of psychiatric disorders. In: Gilman AG, Rall TW, Nies AS, Taylor P, eds. Goodman and Gilman's the pharmacologic basis of therapeutics. New York: Pergamon, 1990:383–435.

93. Davis JM. Overview: Maintenance therapy in psychiatry. I. Schizophrenia. Am J Psychiatry 1975;132:1237–1245.

94. Crow TJ, MacMillan JF, Johnson AL, et al. The Northwick Park Study of first episodes of schizophrenia: II. A randomized controlled study of prophylactic neuroleptic treatment. Br J Psychiatry 1986;148:120–127.

95. Johnson DAW. Antipsychotic medication: clinical guidelines for maintenance therapy. J Clin Psychiatry 1985;46:6–15.

96. Christison GW, Kirch GD, Wyatt RJ. When symptoms persist: choosing among alternative somatic treatments for schizophrenia. Schizophr Bull 1991;17:217–245.

97. Safferman A, Lieberman JA, Kane JM, et al. Update on the clinical efficacy and side effects of clozapine. Schizoph Bull 1991;17:247–261.

98. Ellsworth RB. Characteristics of effective treatment milieu. In: Gunderson JG, Will DA, Mosher LF, eds. Principles and practice of milieu therapy. New York: Jason Aronson, 1983.

99. Leff J, Krupers L, Berkowitz R et al. A controlled trial of intervention in the families of schizophrenic patients. Br J Psychiatry 1982;141:121–134.

100. McGlashan TH. The Chestnut Lodge follow-up study: II. Long-term outcome in schizophrenia and the affective disorders. Arch Gen Psychiatry 1984;41:586–601.

101. Hogarty GE, Goldberg SC, Schooler NR. The Collaborative Study Group. Drug and sociotherapy in the aftercare of schizophrenic patients. III. Adjustment of nonrelapsed patients. Arch Gen Psychiatry 1974;31:609–618.

102. Lewis AJ. Melancholia: a historical review. In: Lewis AJ, ed. The state of psychiatry: essays and addresses. New York: Science House, 1967.

104. Leonhard K. The classification of endogenous psychoses. 5th ed. Robins E, ed. Berman R, trans. New York: Irvington Publishers, 1957/1979.

105. Cerletti U, Bini L. Un nuovo metodo di shockterapie "L'elettro-shock." Bull Acad Med Roma 1938;64:136–138.

106. Cade JFJ. Lithium salts in the treatment of psychotic excitement. Med J Aust 1949;2:349–352.

107. Freud S. Mourning and melancholia. In: Freud S. The complete psychological works of Sigmund Freud, vol. 14. Strachey J, trans. London: Hogarth, 1955:237–259.

108. Abraham K. Selected papers on psychoanalysis. Bryan D, Strachey A, trans. New York: Basic Books, 1911/1968.

109. Mendlewicz J, Rainer JD. Adoption study supporting genetic transmission in manic-depressive illness. Nature 1977; 268:327–329.

110. Klerman GL, DiMascio A, Weissman MM, et al. Treatment of depression by drugs and psychotherapy. Am J Psychiatry 1974;131:186–191.

111. Rush AJ, Beck AT, Kovacs M, et al. Comparative efficacy of cognitive therapy and pharmacotherapy in the treatment of depressed outpatients. Cognitive Ther Res 1977;1:17–37.

112. Weissman MM. The psychological treatment of depression: evidence for the efficacy of psychotherapy alone, in comparison with, and in combination with pharmacotherapy. Arch Gen Psychiatry 1979;36:1261–1269.

113. Carroll BI, Feinberg M, Greden JF, et al. A specific laboratory test for the diagnosis of melancholia: standardization, validation and clinical utility. Arch Gen Psychiatry 1982;38: 15–22.

114. Clayton P. Bipolar illness. In: Winokur G, Clayton P, eds. The medical basis of psychiatry. Philadelphia: Saunders, 1986.

115. Winokur G. Unipolar depression. In: Winokur G, Clayton P. eds. The medical basis of psychiatry. Philadelphia: Saunders, 1986:60–79.

116. Carroll BJ. Diagnostic validity and laboratory studies: the rules of the game. In: Robins LN, Barrett JE, eds. The validity of psychiatric diagnosis. New York: Raven Press, 1989;229–246.

117. Hirschfeld RMA, Goodwin FK. Mood disorders. In: Talbott JA, Hales RE, Yudofsky SC. Textbook of psychiatry. Washington DC: American Psychiatric Press, 1988:403–441.

118. Carney MWP, Roth M, Garside RF. The diagnosis of depressive syndromes and the prediction of ECT response. Br J Psychiatry 1965;111:659–674.

119. Kiloh LG, Garside RF. The independence of neurotic depression and endogenous depression. Br J Psychiatry 1963; 109:451–463.

120. Rush AJ. A phase II study of cognitive therapy of depression. In: Williams JBW, Spitzer RL, eds. Psychotherapy research: where are we and where should we go? New York: Guilford, 1984:216–233.

121. Robinson DS, Fries A. Ravaris CL, et al. The monoamine oxidase inhibitor, phenelzine, in the treatment of depressive anxiety states: a controlled clinical trial. Arch Gen Psychiatry 1973;29:407–413.

122. DiMascio A, Weissman MM, Prusoff BA, et al. Differential symptom reduction by drugs and psychotherapy in acute depression. Arch Gen Psychiatry 1979;36:1450–1456.

123. Goodwin FK, Jameson KR. Manic-depressive illness. New York: Oxford University Press, 1990.

124. Baker M, Dorzab J, Winokur G, et al. Depressive disease: classification and clinical characteristics. Compr Psychiatry 1971;12:354–365.

125. Maes M, Cosyns P, Maes L, et al. Clinical subtypes of unipolar depression: I. A validation of the vital and nonvital clusters. Psychiatry Res 1990;34:29–41.

126. Maes M. Schotte C, Maes L, et al. Clinical subtypes of unipolar depression. II. Quantitative and qualitative clinical differences between the vital and nonvital depressive groups. Psychiatry Res. 1990;34:43–57.

127. Maes M, Maes L, Schotte C, et al. Clinical subtypes of unipolar depression. III. Quantitative differences in various biological markers between the cluster analytically generated nonvital and vital depression classes. Psychiatry Res 1990; 34:59–75.

128. Widlocher DJ. Psychomotor retardation: clinical, theoretical and psychometric aspects. Psychiatr Clin N Am 1983;6: 27–40.

129. Folstein MF, Folstein SW, McHugh PR. "Minimental State": a practical method of grading the cognitive state of patients for the clinician. J Psychiatr Res 1975;12:189–198.

130. Styron W. Darkness visible: a memoir of madness. New York: Random House, 1990.

131. James W. The varieties of religious experience. In: Silverman C, ed. The epidemiology of depression. Baltimore: Johns Hopkins University Press, 1968.

132. Guze SB, Robins E. Suicide and primary affective disorders. Brit J Psychiatry 1970;117:437–438.

133. Abrams R, Taylor MA. The importance of mood-incongruent symptoms in melancholia. J Affective Disord 1983;5: 179–181.

134. Kendler KS. Mood-incongruent psychotic and affective illness: a historical and empirical review. Arch Gen Psychiatry 1991;48:362–369.

135. APA Task Force on Laboratory Tests in Psychiatry. The dexamethasone suppression test: an overview of its current status in psychiatry. Am J Psychiatry 1987;144:10.

136. Alamura C, Guercetti G, Percudoni M. Dexamethasone suppression test in positive and negative schizophrenia. Psychiatry Res 1989;30:69–75.

137. Targum SD. Neuroendocrine challenge studies in clinical psychiatry. Psychiatric Ann 1983;13:383–395.

138. Gold MS, Pottash ALC, Extein I, Sweeney DR. Diagnosis of depression in the 1980's. JAMA 1981;245:1562–1564.

139. Gold PW, Loriaux DL, Roy A, et al. Response to corticotropin-releasing hormone in the hypercortisolism of depression and Cushing's disease: physiologic and diagnostic implications. N Engl J Med 1986;314:1329–1335.

140. Gillin JC, Sitaram N, Wehr TA, et al. Sleep and affective illness. In: Post RM, Ballenger JC, eds. Neurobiology of mood disorders. Baltimore: Williams & Wilkins, 1984.

141. Kellner CH, Rubinow DR, Gold PW, et al. Relationship of cortisol hypersecretion to brain CT scan alterations in depressed patients. Psychiatry Res 1983;16:775–799.

142. Dolan RJ, Calloway SP, Thacker PF, et al. The cerebral cortical appearance in depressed subjects. Psychol Med 1986;16:775–799.

143. McDonald W, Husain MH. Doraiswamy PM, et al. Diminished caudate volumes in major depression. Abstract presented at 143rd annual meeting, American Psychiatric Association. New York: May 1990:20.

144. Tucker GJ, Detre T, Harrow M, et al. Behavior and symptoms of psychiatric patients and the electroencephalogram. Arch Gen Psychiatry 1965;12:278–286.

145. Abrams R, Taylor MA. Cognitive dysfunction in melancholia. Psychol Med 1987;17:359–362.

146. Liebowitz MR, Klein DF. Hysteroid dysphoria. Psychiatr Clin North Am 1979;2:555–575.

147. Hall RCW. Depression. In: Hall RCW, ed. Psychiatric presentations of medical illness: somatopsychic disorders. Jamaica NY: SP Medical and Scientific Books, 1980:37–63.

148. Robinson RG, Kubos KL, Starr LB, Rao K, Price TR. Nortryptiline treatment of post-stroke depression: a double-blind study. Lancet 1984;1:297–300.

149. Fras I, Litin EM, Pearson JS. Comparison of psychiatric symptoms of carcinoma of the pancreas with those in some other intra-abdominal neoplasms. Am J Psychiatry 1967; 123:1553–1562.

150. Hong B, Smith MD, Robson AM, Wetzel RD. Depressive symptomatology and treatment in patient with end-stage renal disease. Psychological Med 1987;17:185–190.

151. Schwab JJ. Psychiatric illness produced by infections. Hosp Med 1969;5:98–108.

152. McAlpine D. The benign form of multiple sclerosis: results of a long-term study. Brit Med J 1964;2:1029–2032.

153. Hall RCW, Reading A. Steroid psychosis. Neu Phys 1971; 20:20–23.

154. Goodwin FK. Ebert MB, Bunney WE, Jr. Mental effects of reserpine in man: a review. In: Shader RI, ed. Psychiatric complications of medical drugs. New York: Raven, 1972: 73–101.

155. Popkin M, Callies A, Mackenzie T. The outcome of antidepressants in the medically ill. Arch Gen Psychiatry 1985;42:1160–1163.

156. Cloninger CR, Martin RL, Guze SB, Clayton PJ. The empirical structure of psychiatric comorbidity and its theoretical significance. In: Maser JD, Cloninger CR, eds. Comorbidity of mood and anxiety disorders. Washington DC: American Psychiatric Press, 1990;439–462.

157. Guze S, Woodruff R, Clayton P. Secondary affective disorder: a study of 95 cases. Psychol Med 1972;1:426–428.

158. Clayton P, Desmarais L, Winokur G. A study of normal bereavement. Am J Psychiatry 1968;125:168–178.

159. Taylor MA, Abrams R. Cognitive impairment patterns in schizophrenia and affective disorder. J Neurol Neurosurg Psychiatry 1987;50:895–899.

160. Nasrallah HA, Coffman JA, Olson SC. Structural brain imaging findings in affective disorders: an overview. J Neuropsychiatry 1989;1:21–26.

161. Dewan MJ, Haldipur V, Lane EE, et al. Bipolar affective disorder. I. Comprehensive quantitative computed tomography. Acta Psychiatr Scand 1988;77:670–676.

162. Lippman S, Manshadi M, Baldwin H, et al. Cerebellar vermis dimensions in computerized tomographic scans of schizophrenia and bipolar patients. Am J Psychiatry 1982; 139:667–670.

163. Rosenthal J, Strauss A, Minkoff L, et al. Identifying lithium responsive bipolar depressed patients using nuclear magnetic resonance. Am J Psychiatry 1986;143:779–780.

164. Akiskal HS, Dekerminjian AH, Rosenthal RH, et al. Cyclothymic disorder: validating criteria for inclusion in the bipolar affective group. Am J Psychiatry 1977;134:1227–1233.

165. Akiskal JS, Mallya G. Criteria for the "soft" bipolar spectrum: treatment implications. Psychopharmacol Bull 1987; 23:68–73.

166. Dunner DL, Fieve RR. The effect of lithium on depressive subtypes. In: Deniker A, Radouco-Thomas B, Villeneuve C, eds. Neuropsychopharmacology. New York: Pergamon Press, 1978.

167. Schwartz JM, Baxter LR, Mazziotta JC, Gerner RH, Phelps ME. The differential diagnosis of depression: relevance of positron emission tomography studies of cerebral glucose metabolism to the bipolar-unipolar dichotomy. JAMA 1987; 258:1368–1374.

168. Taylor MA, Abrams R, Hayman MA. The classification of affective disorders: a reassessment of the bipolar-unipolar dichotomy—a clinical, laboratory and family study. J Affect Dis 1980;2:95–109.

169. Clayton P. Bipolar illness. In: Winokur G, Clayton P, eds. The medical basis of psychiatry. Philadelphia: Saunders, 1986.

170. Winokur G, Pitts FN. Affective disorder. VI. A family history study of prevalences, sex differences and possible genetic factors. J Psychiatr Res 1965;3:113–123.

171. Nicholi AM. Harvard dropouts: some psychiatric findings. Am J Psychiatry 1967;124:651–658.

172. Zis AP, Goodwin FK. Major affective disorder as a recurrent illness: a critical review. Arch Gen Psychiatry 1979;36: 835–839.

173. Keller MB, Shapiro RW, Lavori PW, Wolfe N. Relapse in major depressive disorder. Arch Gen Psychiatry 1982;39: 911–915.

174. Anonymous. Mood disorders: pharmacologic prevention of recurrences. Public Health Service Monog. vol 5, no 4, 1986.

175. Bratfos O, Haug JL. The course of manic-depressive psychoses: a follow-up investigation of 215 patients. Acta Psychiatr Scand 1968;44:89–112.

176. Kerr TA, Schapira K, Roth M. The relationship between premature death and affective disorders. Brit J Psychiatry 1969;115:1277–1282.

177. Clayton PJ. The epidemiology of bipolar affective disorder. Compr Psychiatry 1981;22:32–43.

178. Myers JK, Weissman MM, Tischler GL, et al. Six-month prevalence of psychiatric disorders in three communities. Arch Gen Psychiatry 1984;41:959–967.

179. Weissman MM, Boyd JH. The epidemiology of affective disorders, rates and risk factors. In: Grinspoon L, ed. American Psychiatric Association annual review, vol 2, Washington DC: American Psychiatric Press, 1982:406–428.

180. Weissman MM, Leaf PJ, Bruce ML, et al. The epidemiology of dysthymia in five communities: rates, risks, comorbidity and treatment. Am J Psychiatry 1988;145:815–819.

181. Hohman LB. A review of one hundred and forty-four cases of affective disorders: after seven years. Am J Psychiatry 1937;94:303–308.

182. Keller MB, Klerman GL, Lavori PW, et al. Treatment received by depressed patients. JAMA 1982;248:1848–1855.

183. Andreasen NC. Creativity and mental illness: prevalence rates in writers and their first-degree relatives. Am J Psychiatry 1987;144:1288–1292.

184. Coryell W, Endicott J, Keller M, et al. Bipolar affective disorder and high achievement: a familial association. Am J Psychiatry 1989;146:983–988.

185. Johnson GFS, Leeman MM. Onset of illness in bipolar manic-depressives and their affectively ill first degree relatives. Biol Psychiatry 1977;12:733–741.

186. Cadoret R. Evidence for genetic inheritance of primary affective disorder in adoptees. Am J Psychiatry 1978;135: 463–466.

187. Paykel ES. Contribution of life events to causation of psychiatric illness. Psychol Med 1978;8:245–253.

188. Seligman MEP. Helplessness: on depression, development, and death. San Francisco: Freeman, 1975.

189. Bibring E. The mechanism of depression. In: Greenacre P, ed. Affective disorders. New York: International Universities Press, 1965:13–48.

190. Kohut H. The analysis of the self. New York: International Universities Press, 1971.

191. Alexander F. Psychoanalysis and psychotherapy. New York: W.W. Norton, 1956.

192. Post RM, Rubinow DR, Ballenger JC. Conditioning, sensitization and kindling: implications for the course of affective illness. In: Post RM, Ballenger JC, eds. The neurobi-

ology of mood disorders. Baltimore: Williams & Wilkins, 1984:432–466.

193. Beck AT, Rush AJ, Shaw BF, et al. Cognitive therapy of depression. New York: Guilford Press, 1979.

194. Klerman GL, Weissman MM, Rounsaville BJ, et al. Interpersonal psychotherapy in depression. New York: Basic Books, 1984.

195. Janicak PG, Davis JM, Gibbons RD, et al. Efficacy of ECT: a meta-analysis. Am J Psychiatry 1985;142:297–302.

196. Hunan S, Lachenbruch PA, Winokur G, Clayton P. An efficacy study of electroconvulsive therapy and antidepressants in the treatment of primary depression. Psychol Med 1982; 12:615–624.

197. Nelson JC, Bowers MB Jr. Delusional unipolar depression: description and drug response. Arch Gen Psychiatry 1978; 35:1321–1328.

198. Carlson GA, Goodwin FK. The stages of mania: a longitudinal analysis of the manic episode. Arch Gen Psychiatry 1973;28:221–228.

199. McCabe MS. ECT in the treatment of mania: a controlled study. Am J Psychiatry 1976;133:688.

200. Prien RF, Kupfer DJ, Marisky PA, et al. Drug therapy in the prevention of recurrences in unipolar and bipolar affective disorders. Arch Gen Psychiatry 1984;41:1096–1104.

201. Schou M. Lithium as a prophylactic agent in unipolar affective illness. Arch Gen Psychiatry 1979;36:849–851.

202. Coxhead N, Silverstone T, Cookson J. Carbamazepine versus lithium in the prophylaxis of bipolar affective disorder. Acta Psychiatr Scand 1992;85:114–118.

203. Noyes RN. Anxiety and phobic disorders. In: Winokur G, Clayton P, eds. The medical basis of psychiatry. Philadelphia: Saunders, 1986:152–170.

204. Regier DA, Burke JD, Burke KS. Comorbidity of affective and anxiety disorders in the NIMH Epidemiologic Catchment Area Program. In: Maser JD, Cloninger CR, eds. Comorbidity of mood and anxiety disorders. Washington DC: American Psychiatric Press, 1990:113–122.

205. Helzer JE, Robins LE, McEvoy L. Posttraumatic stress disorder in the general population: findings of the Epidemiologic Catchment Area Survey. N Engl J Med 1987;317: 1630–1634.

206. Robins LN, Helzer JE, Weissman MM, et al. Lifetime prevalence of specific psychiatric disorders at three sites. Arch Gen Psychiatry 1984;41:958–967.

207. Hollander E, Liebowitz MR, Gorman JM. Anxiety disorders. In: Talbott JA, Hales RE, Yudofsky SC, eds. Textbook of psychiatry. Washington DC: American Psychiatric Press, 1988;443–491.

208. Clancy J, Noyes R Jr, Hoenk PR, Slymen D. Secondary depression in anxiety neurosis. J Nerv Ment Dis 1978;160: 846–850.

209. Mackenzie TB. Obsessive-compulsive neurosis. In: Winokur G, Clayton P, eds. The medical basis of psychiatry. Philadelphia: Saunders, 1986:115–122.

210. Alloy LB, Kelly KA, Mineka S, Clements CM. Comorbidity of anxiety and depressive disorders: a helplessness-hopelessness perspective. In: Maser JD, Cloninger CR, eds. Comorbidity of mood and anxiety disorders. Washington DC: American Psychiatric Press, 1990:499–543.

211. Klass ET, DiNardo PA, Barlow DH. DSM-III-R personality diagnoses in anxiety disorder patients. Compr Psychiatry 1989;30:251–258.

212. Alnaes R, Torgerson S. DSM-III personality disorders among patients with major depression, anxiety disorders, and mixed conditions. J Nerv Ment Dis 1990;178:693–698.

213. Rasmussen SA, Tsuang MT. Clinical characteristics and family history in obsessive-compulsive disorder. Am J Psychiatry 1986;143:317–322.

214. Joffe RT, Swenson RP, Regan JJ. Personality features of obsessive-compulsive disorder. Am J Psychiatry 1988;145: 1127–1129.

215. Mavissakalian M, Hamann MS, Jones B. Correlates of DSM-III personality disorder in obsessive-compulsive disorder. Compr Psychiatry 1990;31:481–489.

216. Spielberger CD. Anxiety and behavior. New York: Academic Press, 1966;3–20.

217. Freud S. New introductory lectures on psychoanalysis. Standard ed. London: Hogarth Press, 1933;1962.

218. Cullen W. First lines of the practice of physic. Edinburgh: Bell and Bradfute, 1812;327,330.

219. Cohen M, White P. Life situations, emotions, and neurocirculatory asthenia (anxiety neurosis, neurasthenia, effort syndrome). Assoc Res Nerv Dis Proc 1950;29:832–869.

220. Marks IM, Lader M. Anxiety states (anxiety neurosis): a review. J Nerv Ment Dis 1973;156:3–18.

221. Crowe RR, Noyes R, Paul DL, Slymen D. A family study of panic disorder. Arch Gen Psychiatry 1983;40:1065–1069.

222. Noyes R Jr, Clancy J, Hoenk PR, Slymen DJ. The prognosis of anxiety neuroses. Arch Gen Psychiatry 1980;37:173–178.

223. Weissman MM, Klerman GJ, Markowitz JS. Suicidal ideation and suicide attempts in panic disorder and attacks. N Engl J Med 1989;321:1209–1213.

224. Coryell W, Noyes R Jr, Clancy J. Panic disorder and primary unipolar depression. Arch Gen Psychiatry 1982;39: 701–703.

225. Quitkin F, Robkin J. Hidden psychiatric diagnoses in the alcoholic. In: Soloman J, ed. Alcoholism and clinical psychiatry. New York: Plenum, 1982.

226. Katon W. Panic disorder in the medical setting. National Institute of Mental Health DHHS pub. (ADM) 89-1629. Washington, DC, Supt of Documents, US Govt Printing Office, 1989.

227. Liberthson R, Sheehan DV, King ME, Weyman AE. The prevalence of mitral valve prolapse in patients with panic disorders. Am J Psychiatry 1986;143:511–515.

228. Markiewicz W, Stoner J, London E, Hunt SA, Popp RL. Mitral valve prolapse in one-hundred presumably healthy females. Circulation 1976;53:464.

229. Rackley CE. Vavular heart disease. In: Wyngaarden JB, Smith LH Sr, Bennett JC, eds. Cecil textbook of medicine. Philadelphia: Saunders, 1992:321–331.

230. Klein DF, Gorman JM. Panic disorders and mitral prolapse. J Clin Psychiatry Monog 1984;2:14–17.

231. Klein DF. Interview. Currents 1985;4:5–10.

232. Tyrer P. Classification of anxiety disorders: a critique of DSM-III. J Affective Dis 1986;11:99–104.

233. Pitts FN, McClure JN. Lactate metabolism in anxiety neuroses. N Engl J Med 1967;277:1329–1336.

234. Liebowitz MR, Fryer AJ, Gorman JM, et al. Specificity of lactate infusion in social phobia versus panic disorders. Am J Psychiatry 1985;142L947–950.

235. Liebowitz MR, Fryer AJ, Gorman JM, et al. Lactate provocation of panic attacks. Arch Gen Psychiatry 1984;41:764–770.

236. Reiman EM, Raichle ME, Robins E, et al. The application of positron emission tomography to the study of panic disorder. Am J Psychiatry 1986;143:469–477.

237. Van den Hout M, Griez E. Panic symptoms after inhalation of carbon dioxide. Brit J Psychiatry 1984;144:503–507.

238. Gorman JM, Askanazi J, Liebowitz MR, et al. Response to hyperventilation in a group of patients with panic disorder. Am J Psychiatry 1984;141:857–861.

239. Rainey JM, Pohl RB, Williams M, et al. A comparison of lactate and isoproterenol anxiety states. Psychopathology 1984;17(suppl 1):74–82.

240. Fontaine R, Breton G, Dery R, et al. Temporal lobe abnormalities in panic disorder: an MRI study. Biol Psychiatry 1990;27:304–310.

241. Uhde TW, Kellner CH. Cerebral ventricular size and panic disorder. J Affect Dis 1987;12:175–178.

242. Edlund JM, Swann AL, Clothier J. Patients with panic attacks and abnormal EEG results. Am J Psychiatry 1987; 144:508–509.

243. Torgerson S. Genetic factors in anxiety disorders. Arch Gen Psychiatry 1983;40:1085–1089.

244. Torgerson S. Genetics of neurosis: the effects of sampling variation upon the twin concordance ratio. Brit J Psychiatry 1983;142:126–132.

245. Reich J, Noyes JR, Troughton E. Dependent personality disorder associated with phobic avoidance in patients with panic disorder. Am J Psychiatry 1987;144:323–326.

246. Green MA, Curtis GC. Personality disorders in panic patients: response to termination of anti-panic medication. J Pers Disord 1988;2:303–314.

247. Cloninger CR. A unified biosocial theory of personality and its role in the development of anxiety states. Psychiatric Dev 1986;3:167–226.

248. Cloninger CR. A systematic method for clinical description and classification of personality variants: a proposal. Arch Gen Psychiatry 1987;44:578–588.

249. Sarason IG. Theories of anxiety and its treatment. J Drug Res 1982;7:7–15.

250. Redmond DE. New and old evidence for the involvement of a brain norepinephrine system in anxiety. In: Fann I, Pokorny AD, et al, eds. Phenomenology and treatment of anxiety. New York: SP Medical & Scientific Books, 1979.

251. Guttmacher LB, Murphy DL, Insel TR. Pharmacologic models of anxiety. Compr Psychiatry 1983;24:312–326.

252. Gray JA. The neuropsychology of anxiety. Oxford: Clarendon Press, 1982.

253. Breuer T, Freud S. Studies on hysteria. In: Strachey J, ed. Standard edition of the complete psychological works of Sigmund Freud. London: Hogarth Press, 1961.

254. Zitrin CM, Klein DF, Woerner MG, Ross DC. Treatment of phobias. I. Comparison of imipramine hydrochloride and placebo. Arch Gen Psychiatry 1983;40:125–138.

255. Sheehan DV, Ballenger J, Jacobson G. Treatment of endogenous anxiety with phobic, hysterical and hypocondriacal symptoms. Arch Gen Psychiatry 1980;37:51–59.

256. Klein DF. Importance of psychiatric diagnosis in prediction of clinical drug effects. Arch Gen Psychiatry 1980;37:63–72.

257. Mavissakalian M, Perel J, Bowler K, Dealy R. Trazodone in the treatment of panic disorder and agoraphobia with panic attacks. Am J Psychiatry 1987;144:785–787.

258. Bezchlibnyk-Butler KZ, Jeffries JJ. Clinical handbook of the psychotropic drugs. 3rd ed. Toronto: Hogrefe & Huber, 1991.

259. Aronson TA. A naturalistic study in imipramine in panic disorder and agoraphobia. Am J Psychiatry 1987;144:114–119.

260. Ballenger JC, Burrows GD, DuPont RO, et al. Alprazolam in panic disorder and agoraphobia: results from a multicenter trial: efficacy in short-term treatment. Arch Gen Psychiatry 1988;45:413–422.

261. Gorman JM, Fyer AF, Gliklich J, et al. Effect of imipramine on prolapsed mitral valves of patients with panic disorder. Am J Psychiatry 1981;138:977–978.

262. Shear MK, Ball G, Fitzpatrick M, et al. Cognitive-behavioral therapy for panic: an open study. J Nerv Ment Dis 1991;179:468–472.

263. Welkowitz LA, Papp LA, Cloitre M, et al. Cognitive-behavior therapy for panic disorder delivered by psychopharmacologically oriented clinicians. J Nerv Ment Dis 1991;179: 473–477.

264. Marks IM, Tobena A. What do the neurosciences tell us about anxiety disorders? Psychol Med 1986;16:9–12.

265. Charney DS, Heninger GR, Sternberg DE, et al. Plasma MHPG in depression: effects of acute and chronic administration of desipramine treatments. Psychiatry Res 1981;5: 217–229.

266. Stone EA. Problems with the current catecholamine hypotheses of antidepressant agents: speculations leading to a new hypothesis. Behav Brain Sci 1983;6:535–577.

267. Price RW. Rabies. In: Wyngaarden JB, Smith LH, Bennett JC, eds. Cecil textbook of medicine. Philadelphia: Saunders, 1992:2186–2187.

268. Westphal C. Die Agoraphobie: Cine neuropathische Erscheinsuing. Arch Psychiat Nervenk 1871–1872;3:138–171,219–221.

269. Kantor JS, Zitrin CM, Zeldes SM. Mitral valve prolapse syndrome in agoraphobics. Am J Psychiatry 1980;137:467–469.

270. Smail P, Stockwell T, Canter S, Hodgson R. Alcohol dependence and phobic anxiety states. I. A prevalence study. Br J Psychiatry 1984;144:53–57.

271. Harris EL, Noyes R, Crowe RR, Chaudhry DR. A family study of agoraphobia: report of a pilot study. Arch Gen Psychiatry 1983;1061–1064.

272. Moran C, Andrews G. The familial occurrence of agoraphobia. Brit J Psychiatry 1985;146:262–267.

273. Mathews AM, Gelder MG, Johnston DW. Agoraphobia: nature and treatment. New York: Guilford, 1981.

274. Gittleman R, Klein DF. Relationship between separation anxiety and panic and agoraphobic disorders. Psychopathology 1984 (suppl 1);17:56–65.

275. Gelder MG, Marks IM, Wolff H. Desensitization and psychotherapy in the treatment of phobic states: a controlled clinical inquiry. Br J Psychiatry 1967;113:53–73.

276. O'Sullivan G, Marks I. Followup studies of behavioral treatment of phobic and obsessive compulsive neuroses. In: Roth M, ed. Treatment outcome of phobic and related disorders. Psychiatr Ann 1991;21:368–373.

277. Liebowitz MR, Gorman TM, Fyer AT, Klein DF. Social phobia: a review of neglected anxiety disorder. Arch Gen Psychiatry 1985;42:729–736.

278. Solyom L, Ledwidge B, Solyom C. Delineating social phobia. Brit J Psychiatry 1986;149:464–470.

279. Marks IM. The classification of phobic disorders. Brit J Psychiatry 1970;116:377–386.

280. Goodwin DW. Phobia: the facts. New York: Oxford University Press, 1983.

281. Mullaney JA, Trippett CJ. Alcohol dependence and phobias: clinical description and relevance. Brit J Psychiatry 1979;135:563–573.

282. Liebowitz MR, Fyer AJ, Gorman JM, et al. Specificity of lactate infusions in social phobia v. panic disorders. Am J Psychiatry 1985;142:947–950.

283. Weissman MM. Epidemiology of panic disorder and agoraphobia. In: Ballenger JC, ed. Clinical aspects of panic disor-

der, frontiers of clinical neuroscience. vol 6. New York: Wiley-Liss, 1990:57–65.

284. Marks I. Fears and phobias. London: Academic Press, 1969.

285. Goldstein AJ, Chambless DLA. A reanalysis of agoraphobia. Behav Ther 1978;9:47–59.

286. Freud S. The analyses of a phobia in a five-year-old boy. In: Strachey J, ed. Standard edition of the complete works of Sigmund Freud. vol 10. London: Hogarth Press, 1961.

287. Paul GL. Outcome of systematic desensitization. II. Controlled investigation of individual treatment, technique variations, and current status. In: Franks CM, ed. Behavior therapy: appraisal and status. New York: McGraw-Hill, 1969.

288. Esquirol JED. Mental maladies: a treatise on insanity (Hunt ED, trans). Philadelphia: Lee and Blanchard, 1845.

289. Dowson J. The phenomenology of severe obsessive-compulsive neurosis. Brit J Psychiatry 1977;131:75–78.

290. Stern R, Cobb J. Phenomenology of obsessive-compulsive neurosis. Brit J Psychiatry 1978;132:233–239.

291. Akhtar S, Wig N, Varma V, et al. A phenomenological analysis of symptoms of obsessive-compulsive neuroses. Brit J Psychiatry 1975;127:342–348.

292. Rachman SJ, Hodgson RJ. Obsessions and compulsions. Englewood Cliffs, NJ: Prentice-Hall, 1980.

293. Kringlen E. Obsessional neurotics: a long-term follow-up. Brit J Psychiatry 1965;111:709–722.

294. Ingram IM. Obsessional neurosis in mental hospital patients. J Ment Sci 1961;107:382–402.

295. Coryell W. Obsessive-compulsive disorder and primary unipolar depression: comparisons of background, family history, course and mortality. J Nerv Ment Dis 1981;169:220–224.

296. Pollitt J. Obsessional states. Brit J Psychiatry 1975;9:133–140.

297. Rasmussen SA, Tsuang MT. The epidemiology of obsessive compulsive disorder. J Clin Psychiatry 1984;45:450–457.

298. Lo WH. A followup study of obsessional neurotics in Hong Kong. Brit J Psychiatry 1967;113:823–832.

299. Black A. The natural history of obsessional neurosis. In: Beech HR, ed. Obsessional states. London: Methuen, 1974.

300. Hollingsworth C, Tanguay P, Grossman L, et al. Long-term outcome of obsessive-compulsive disorder in childhood. J Am Acad Child Psychiatry 1980;19:134–144.

301. Welner A, Reich T, Robins E, et al. Obsessive-compulsive neuroses: record, family and followup studies. Compr Psychiatry 1976;17:527–539.

302. Nickoloff SE, Radant AD, Reichler R, et al. Smooth pursuit and saccadic eye movements and neurological soft signs in obsessive-compulsive disorder. Psychiatry Res 1991;38:173–185.

303. Marks IM, Stern RS, Mawson D, Cobb J, McDonald R. Clomipramine and exposure for obsessive-compulsive neurosis. Brit J Psychiatry 1980;136:1–25.

304. Zielinski CM, Taylor MA, Juzwin KR. Neuropsychological deficits in obsessive-compulsive disorder. Neuropsychiatry, Neuropsychol Behav Neurol 1991;4:110–126.

305. Nordahl TE, Benkelfat C, Semple WE, et al. Cerebral glucose metabolic rates in obsessive compulsive disorder. Neuropsychopharm 1989;2:23–28.

306. Baxter LR, Phelps ME, Mazziotta JC, et al. Local cerebral glucose metabolic rates in obsessive-compulsive disorder. Arch Gen Psychiatry 1987;44:211–218.

307. Luxenberg JS, Swedo SE, Flament MF, et al. Neuroanatomic abnormalities in obsessive-compulsive disorder detected with quantitative x-ray computed tomography. Am J Psychiatry 1988;145:1085–1093.

308. Capstick N, Seldrup J. Obsessional states: a study of the relationship between abnormalities occurring at the time of birth and the subsequent development of obsessional symptoms. Acta Psychiatr Scand 1977;56:427–431.

309. Hoover CF, Insel TR. Families of origin in obsessive-compulsive disorder. J Nerv Ment Dis 1984;172:207–215.

310. Turner SM, Beidel DC, Nathan RS. Biological factors in obsessive-compulsive disorders. Psychol Bull 1985;97:430–450.

311. Rosenberg CM. Familial aspects of obsessive neurosis. Brit J Psychiatry 1978;132:233–239.

312. Cornings DE, Cornings BG. Hereditary agoraphobia and obsessive compulsive behavior in relatives in patients with Giles de la Tourette's syndrome. Br J Psychiatry 1987;151:195–199.

313. Inouye E. Similar and dissimilar manifestations of obsessive-compulsive neurosis in monozygotic twins. Am J Psychiatry 1965;121:1171–1175.

314. Schilder P. The organic background of obsessions and compulsions. Am J Psychiatry 1938;94:1397.

315. Grimshaw L. Obsessional disorder and neurological illness. J Neurol Neurosurg Psychiatry 1964;27:229–231.

316. Rapoport JL. The neurobiology of obsessive-compulsive disorder. JAMA 1988;197:102–150.

317. Freud S. Notes on a case of obsessional neurosis. In: Strachey J, ed. Standard edition of the complete works of Sigmund Freud. vol 10. London: Hogarth, 1909/1961.

318. Freud S. Inhibition, symptoms and anxiety. In: Strachey J, ed. Standard edition of the complete works of Sigmund Freud. vol 20. London: Hogarth, 1925/1961.

319. Thoren P, Asberg M, Cronholm B, et al. Clomipramine treatment of obsessive compulsive disorder: a controlled clinical trial. Arch Gen Psychiatry 1980;37:1281–1289.

320. Clomipramine Collaborative Study Group. Clomipramine in the treatment of patients with obsessive-compulsive disorder. Arch Gen Psychiatry 1991;48:730–738.

321. Pato MT, Pigott T, Hill JL, et al. Controlled comparison of buspirone and clomipramine in obsessive compulsive disorder. Am J Psychiatry 1991;148:127–129.

322. Perse TL, Greist JH, Jefferson JW, et al. Fluvoxamine treatment of obsessive-compulsive disorder. Am J Psychiatry 1988;145:1521–1525.

323. Jenike MA, Buttolph L, Baer L, et al. Open trial of fluoxetine in obsessive-compulsive disorder. Am J Psychiatry 1989;146:909–911.

324. Salzman L, Thaler FH. Obsessive-compulsive disorders: a review of the literature. Am J Psychiatry 1981;138:286–296.

325. Marks I, Hodgson R, Rachman S. Treatment of chronic obsessive-compulsive neurosis by in-vivo exposure. Brit J Psychiatry 1975;127:349–364.

326. Marks IM. Review of behavioral psychotherapy. I.Obsessive-compulsive disorders. Am J Psychiatry 1981;138:584–592.

327. Rudin G. Ein Beitrag zur Frage der Zwangskrankheit, instesonhere iherer heridetaren Beziehungen. Arch Psychiatr Nerveakr 1953;191:14–54.

328. Jenike MA, Baer L, Ballentine T, et al. Cingulotomy for refractory obsessive-compulsive disorder. Arch Gen Psychiatry 1991;48:548–555.

329. Barlow DH, Blanchard EB, Vermilyea JA, et al. Generalized anxiety and generalized anxiety disorder: description and reconceptualization. Am J Psychiatry 1986;143:40–44.

330. Katon W, Vitaliano PP, Anderson K, et al. Panic disorder: residual symptoms after attacks abate. Compr Psychiatry 1987;28:151–158.

331. Noyes R, Clancy J, Garvey MJ, et al. A family study of generalized anxiety disorder. Am J Psychiatry 1987;144:1019–1024.

332. Anderson DJ, Noyes RJ Jr, Crowe RR. A comparison of panic disorder and generalized anxiety disorder. Am J Psychiatry 1984;141:572–579.

333. Brier A, Charney DS, Heninger GR. The diagnostic validity of anxiety disorders and their relationship to depressive illness. Am J Psychiatry 1985;142:787–797.

334. Cloninger CR, Martin RL, Clayton P, et al. A blind follow-up and family study of anxiety neuroses: preliminary analysis of the St. Louis 500. In: Klein DF, Rabkin J, eds. Anxiety: new research and changing concepts. New York: Raven, 1981.

335. Hoehn-Saric R. Comparison of generalized anxiety disorder with panic disorder patients. Psychopharmacol Bull 1982; 18:69–77.

336. Breslau N, Davis GC. DSM-III generalized anxiety disorder: an empirical investigation of more stringent criteria. Psychiatry Res 1985;14:231–238.

337. Grinker RR, Spiegel JP. War neuroses in North Africa: the Tunisian campaign. New York: Josiah Macy Foundation, 1943.

338. McNally R. Psychopathology of post-traumatic stress disorder (PTSD): boundaries of the syndrome. In: Basoglu M, ed. Torture and its consequences. Cambridge, UK: Cambridge University Press, 1991.

339. Rothbaum BO, Foa EB. Subtypes of PTSD and duration of symptoms. Paper prepared for the DSM-IV work group on post-traumatic stress disorder, 1989.

340. McFarlane A. Vulnerability to posttraumatic stress disorder. In: Wolf ME, Mosnaim AD, eds. Posttraumatic stress disorder: etiology, phenomenology and treatment. Washington DC: American Psychiatric Press, 1990;2–20.

341. McFarlane AC. The aetiology of post-traumatic morbidity: predisposing, precipitating and perpetuating factors. Br J Psychiatry 1989;154:221–228.

342. Andreasen NC. Neuropsychiatric complications in burn patients. Int J Psychiatry Med 1974;5:161–171.

343. Solomon Z, Kotler M, Shalev A, Lin R. Delayed onset PTSD among Israeli veterans of the 1982 Lebanon war. Psychiatry 1989;52:428–436.

344. Sierles FS, Chen JJ, McFarland RE, Taylor MA. Posttraumatic stress disorder and concurrent psychiatric illness: a preliminary report. Am J Psychiatry 1983;140:1177–1179.

345. Escobar JI, Randolph E, Puente G, et al. Posttraumatic stress disorder in Hispanic Vietnam veterans. Clinical phenomenology and sociocultural characteristics. J Nerv Ment Dis 1983;171:585–596.

346. Davidson J, Swartz M, Storck M, et al. A diagnostic and family study of posttraumatic stress disorder. Am J Psychiatry 1985;142:90–93.

347. Boman B. Are all Vietnam veterans like John Rambo? In: Wolf ME, Mosnaim AD, eds. Posttraumatic stress disorder: etiology, phenomenology and treatment. Washington DC: American Psychiatric Press, 1990;80–93.

348. Mazer M. Two ways of expressing psychological disorder: the experience of a demarcated population. Am J Psychiatry 1972;128:933–937.

349. Boman B. Post-traumatic stress disorder (traumatic war neuroses) and concurrent psychiatric illness among Australian Vietnam veterans: a controlled study. JR Army Medical Corps 1985;131:128–131.

350. Shaw DM, Churchill CM, Noyes R, et al. Criminal behavior and posttraumatic stress disorder in Vietnam veterans. Compr Psychiatry 1987;28:403–411.

351. Yager J. Post-combat violent behavior in psychiatrically maladjusting soldiers. Arch Gen Psychiatry 1976;174:137–144.

352. Hearst N, Newman TB, Hulley SB. Delayed effects of the military draft on mortality: a randomized natural experiment. N Engl J Med 1986;314:620–624.

353. Lerer B, Bleich A, Kotler M, et al. Posttraumatic stress disorder in Israeli combat veterans: effects of phenelzine treatment. Arch Gen Psychiatry 1987;44:976–981.

354. Kudler H, Davidson J, Meador K, et al. The DST and posttraumatic stress disorder. Am J Psychiatry 1987;144:1068–1071.

355. Halbreich U, Olympia J, Glogowski J, et al. The importance of past psychological trauma and pathophysiological process as determinants of current biologic abnormalities. Arch Gen Psychiatry 1988;45:293–294.

356. Rainey JM Jr., Aleem A, Ortiz A, et al. A laboratory procedure for the induction of flashbacks. Am J Psychiatry 1987; 144:1317–1319.

357. Kulka RA, Schlenger WE, Fairbank JA, et al. National Vietnam Veterans Readjustment Study (NVVRS): description, current status, and initial PTSD prevalence estimates. Research Triangle Park, NC: Research Triangle Institute, 1988.

358. Foy DW, Sipprelle RC, Rueger DB, et al. Etiology of posttraumatic stress disorder in Vietnam veterans: analysis of nonmilitary, military and combat exposure influences. J Consult Clin Psychol 1984;52:79–87.

359. Steketee G, Foa EB. Rape victims: post-traumatic stress responses and their treatment: a review of the literature. J Anx Disord 1987;1:69–86.

360. Breslau N, Davis GC. Posttraumatic stress disorder: the etiological specificity of wartime stressors. Am J Psychiatry 1987;144:578–583.

361. Shore JH, Tatum EL, Vollmer WM. Evaluation of mental effects of disaster, Mount St. Helen's eruption. Am J Public Health 1986;76 (Suppl):76–83.

362. Solomon Z, Kotler M, Mikalincer M. Combat-related posttraumatic stress disorder among second-generation Holocaust survivors: preliminary findings. Am J Psychiatry 1988; 145:865–868.

363. Wolf ME, Mosnaim AD, eds. Posttraumatic stress disorder: etiology, phenomenology and treatment. Washington DC: American Psychiatric Press, 1990.

364. Briquet P. Traite di l'Hysterie. Paris: JB Bailliere et Fils, 1859.

365. Purtell JJ, Robins E, Cohen ME. Observations on clinical aspects of hysteria: a quantitative study of 50 hysteria patients and 156 control subjects. JAMA 1951;146:902–909.

366. Perley MJ, Guze SB. Hysteria: the stability and usefulness of clinical criteria. N Engl J Med 1961;266:421–426.

367. Guze SB, Perley MJ. Observations on the natural history of hysteria. Am J Psychiatry 1963;119:950–965.

368. Robins E, O'Neal P. Clinical features of hysteria in children. Nerv Child 1953;10:246–271.

369. Smith GR Jr. Somatization disorder in the medical setting. Rockville MD: National Institute of Mental Health DHHS

Pub No (ADM) 90-1631. Washington DC: Supt of Docs US Govt Print Off, 1990.

370. Smith GR, Monson RA, Ray DC. Patients with multiple unexplained symptoms. Arch Intern Med 1986;146:69–72.

371. Swartz M, Landerman R, George L, et al. Somatization disorder. In: Robins LN, Regier D, eds. Psychiatric disorders in America. New York: Free Press, 1990.

372. Zoccolillo MS, Cloninger CR. Excess medical care of women with somatization disorder. So Med J 1986;79:532–535.

373. Martin RL, Roberts WV, Clayton PJ. Psychiatric status after hysterectomy. JAMA 1980;244:350–353.

374. Young SJ, Alpers DH, Norland CC, Woodruff RA Jr. Psychiatric illness and the irritable bowel syndrome. Gastroenter 1976;70:162–166.

375. Reich J, Tupin JP, Abramowitz SI. Psychiatric diagnosis of chronic pain patients. Am J Psychiatry 1983;140:1495–1498.

376. Lillienfeld SO, van Valkenburg C, Larntz K, Akiskal HS. The relationship of histrionic personality disorder to antisocial personality and somatization disorders. Am J Psychiatr 1986;13:718–722.

377. Kaminsky MJ, Slavney PR. Hysterical and obsessional features in patients with Briquet's syndrome (somatization disorder). Psychol Med 1983;13:111–120.

378. Guze SB, Woodruff RA Jr, Clayton PJ. Hysteria and antisocial behavior: further evidence of an association. Am J Psychiatry 1971;127:957–960.

379. Folks DG, Ford CV, Regan WM. Conversion symptoms in a general hospital. Psychosomatics 1984;25:285–291.

380. Morrison JR. Suicide in a case of Briquet's syndrome. J Clin Psychiatry 1981;42:123.

381. Ries RK. Single case study. DSM-III differential diagnosis of Munchausen's syndrome. J Nerv Ment Dis 1980;168:629–632.

382. Sierles FS. Correlates of malingering. Beh Sci and the Law 1984;2:113–118.

383. Coryell W. Diagnosis-specific mortality: primary unipolar depression and Briquet's syndrome (somatization disorder). Arch Gen Psychiatry 1981;38:939–942.

384. Cloninger CR. Somatoform and dissociative disorders. In: Winokur G, Clayton P, eds. The medical basis of psychiatry. Philadelphia: Saunders, 1986;123–151.

385. Bianchi GN. Patterns of hypochondriasis: a principal components analysis. Br J Psychiatry 1973;122:541–548.

386. Flor-Henry P, Fromm-Auch D, Tupper M, Schopflocher D. A neuropsychological study of the stable syndrome of hysteria. Biol Psychiatry 1981;16:601–626.

387. Ludwig AM. Hysteria: a neurobiological theory. Arch Gen Psychiatry 1972;27:771–786.

388. Bendefeldt F, Miller LL, Ludwig AM. Cognitive hysteria. Arch Gen Psychiatry 1976;33:1250–1254.

389. Almgren PE, Nordgren L, Skantze H. A retrospective study of operationally-defined hysterics. Br J Psychiatry 1978;132:670–673.

390. Mears R, Horvath TB. "Acute" and "chronic" hysteria. Brit J Psychiatry 1972;121:653–657.

391. Cloninger CR, Martin RL, Guze SB, Clayton PJ. Somatization disorder in men and women: a prospective follow-up and family study. Am J Psychiatry 1986;143:873–878.

392. Woodruff RA Jr. Hysteria: an evaluation of objective diagnostic criteria by the study of women with chronic medical illnesses. Br J Psychiatry 1967;114:1115–1120.

393. Weissman MM, Myers JK, Harding PS. Psychiatric disorders in a U.S. urban community: 1975-76. Am J Psychiatry 1978;135:459–462.

394. Martin RL, Cloninger CR, Guze SB. The evaluation of diagnostic concordance in follow-up studies. II.A blind follow-up of female criminals. J Psychiatric Res 1979;15:107–125.

395. Rinieris PM, Stefanis CN, Lycouras EP, Varsou EK. Hysteria and ABO blood types. Am J Psychiatry 1978;135:1106–1107.

396. Rounsaville BJ, Harding PS, Weissman MM. Single case study: Briquet's syndrome in a man. J Nerv Ment Dis 1979;167:364–367.

397. Coryell W. A blind family history study of Briquet's syndrome: further validation of the diagnosis. Arch Gen Psychiatry 1980;37:1266–1269.

398. Arkonac O, Guze SB. A family study of hysteria. N Engl J Med 1963;268:239–242.

399. Cloninger CR, Reich T, Guze SB. The multifactorial model of disease transmission. III. Familial relationships between sociopathy and hysteria. (Briquet's syndrome). Br J Psychiatry 1975;127:11–22.

400. Guze SB, Cloninger CR, Martin RL, Clayton PJ. A follow-up and family study of Briquet's syndrome. Br J Psychiatry 1986;149:17–23.

401. Guze SB, Wolfgram ED, McKinney JK, Cantwell DP. Psychiatric illness in the families of convicted criminals: a study of 519 first-degree relatives. Dis Nerv Syst 1967;28:651–659.

402. Cadoret RJ. Psychopathology in adopted-away offspring of biologic parents with antisocial behavior. Arch Gen Psychiatry 1978;35:176–184.

403. von Knorring A-L. Adoption studies on psychiatric illness. Umea University Medical Dissertations, Series No 101. Umea, Sweden: Umea University, 1983.

404. Schalling D. Psychopathy-related personality variables and the psychophysiology of socialization. In: Hare RD, Schalling D, eds. Psychopathic behavior: approaches to research. New York: Wiley, 1978;85–106.

405. Lane RD, Schwartz GE. Levels of emotional awareness: a cognitive-developmental theory and its application to psychopathology. Am J Psychiatry 1987;144:133–143.

406. Bohman M, Cloninger R, von Knorring AL, Sigvardsson S. An adoption study of somatization disorder. III. Cross-fostering analyses and genetic relationship to alcoholism and criminality. Arch Gen Psychiatry 1984;41:872–878.

407. Morrison J. Childhood sexual histories of women with somatization disorder. Am J Psychiatry 1989; 146:239–241.

408. Shapiro D. Neurotic styles. New York: Basic Books, 1965.

409. Schafer R. Clinical application of psychological tests. New York: International Universities Press, 1948.

410. Smith GR Jr, Monson RA, Ray DC. Psychiatric consultation in somatization disorder. N Engl J Med 1986;314:1407–1413.

411. Gunderson JG. Personality disorders. In: Nicholi AM, ed. New Harvard guide to psychiatry. Cambridge, MA: Harvard University Press, 1988.

412. Pfohl B, Stangl D, Zimmerman M. DSM-III personality disorders: diagnostic overlap and internal consistency of individual DSM III criteria. Compr Psychiatry 1986;27:21–34.

413. Pope HG, Jonas JM, Hudson JI, et al. The validity of DSM-III borderline personality disorder: a phenomenologic family history, treatment response and long-term follow-up study. Arch Gen Psychiatry 1983;40:23–30.

414. Oldham JM, Skodol AE, Kellman HD, et al. Diagnosis of DSM-III-R personality disorders by two structured interviews: patterns of comorbidity. Am J Psychiatry 1992;149: 213–220.

415. Mellsop G, Varghese F, Joshua S, Hicks A. The reliability of Axis II of DSM-III. Am J Psychiatry 1982;139:1360–1361.

416. Spitzer RL, Forman JBW, Nee J. DSM-III field trials. I. Initial interrater diagnostic reliability. Am J Psychiatry 1979;136:815–817.

417. Tyrer P, Alexander J. Classification of personality disorder. Br J Psychiatry 1979;135:163–167.

418. McGlashan TH. Schizotypal personality disorder: Chestnut Lodge follow-up study. VI. Long-term follow-up perspectives. Arch Gen Psychiatry 1986;43:329–334.

419. Akiskal HS, Chen SE, Davis GC, et al. Borderline: an adjective in search of a noun. J Clin Psychiatry 1985;46:41–48.

420. Pfohl B. Personality disorders. In: Winokur G, Clayton P. The medical basis of psychiatry. Philadelphia: Saunders, 1986;442–457.

421. Reich J, Yates W, Nguaguba M. Prevalence of DSM-III personality disorders in the community. Soc Psychiatry Psychiatr Epidemiol 1989;24:12–16.

422. Kendler K. Gruenberg A. Genetic relationship between paranoid personality disorder and the "schizophrenic spectrum" disorders. Am J Psychiatry 1982;139:1185–1186.

423. Siever L, Klar H. A review of DSM-III criteria for the personality disorders. In: Frances A, Hales R, eds. Psychiatry update: The American Psychiatric Association annual review, vol 5. Washington, DC: American Psychiatric Press, 1986;279–314.

424. Freeman PS, Gunderson JG. Treatment of personality disorders. Psychiatr Ann 1989;19:147–153.

425. Kendler KS, Gruenberg A, Strauss JS. An independent analysis of the Copenhagen sample of the Danish adoption study of schizophrenia. II. Relationship between schizotypal personality disorder and schizophrenia. Arch Gen Psychiatry 1981;38:982–984.

426. Torgerson S. Relationship of schizotypal personality disorder to schizophrenia: genetics. Schizophr Bull 1985;11: 554–563.

427. Torgerson S, Psychol C. Genetic and nosological aspects of schizotypal and borderline personality disorders: a twin study. Arch Gen Psychiatry 1984;41:546–554.

428. Siever L. Biological markers in schizotypal personality disorder. Schizophr Bull 1985;11:564–574.

429. Widiger TA, Frances AJ. Personality disorders. In: Talbott JA, Hales, RE, Yudofsky SC, eds. Washington, DC: American Psychiatric Press, 1988;621–648.

430. Stone M. Schizotypal personality: psychotherapeutic aspects. Schizophr Bull 1985;11:576–584.

431. Goldberg S, Schultz P, Schultz R, et al. Borderline and schizotypal personality disorders treated with low-dose thiothixene plus placebo. Arch Gen Psychiatry 1986;43:680–686.

432. Liebowitz M, Stone MH, Turkat I. Treatment of personality disorders. In: Frances AJ, Hales RE, eds. Psychiatry update: The American Psychiatric Association annual review, vol 5. Washington, DC: American Psychiatric Press, 1986; 356–393.

433. Prichard JC. A treatise on insanity and other disorders affecting the mind. London: Sherwood, Gilbert & Piper, 1835.

434. Rush B. Medical inquiries and observations upon the diseases of the mind. New York: Hafner, 1962.

435. Cleckley H. The mask of sanity. St. Louis: Mosby, 1941.

436. Robins LN. Deviant children grown up. Baltimore: Williams & Wilkins, 1966.

437. Robins LN, O'Neal P. Morbidity, mortality and crime: Problem children thirty years later. Am Sociol Rev 1958;23: 162–171.

438. Guze SB, Goodwin DW, Crane JB. Criminality and psychiatric disorders. Arch Gen Psychiatry 1969;20:583–591.

439. Guze SB. Criminality and psychiatric disorders. London: Oxford University Press, 1976.

440. Frances AJ. The DSM-III personality disorders section: a commentary. Am J Psychiatry 1980;137:1050–1054.

441. Cloninger CR. The antisocial personality. Hosp Pract 1978; 13:97–106.

442. Taylor MA, Sierles FS, Abrams R. General hospital psychiatry. New York: Free Press, 1985.

443. Loeb J, Mednick S. Prospective study of predictors of criminality: electrodermal response patterns. In: Mednick S, Christiansen K, eds. Biosocial bases of criminal behavior. New York: Gardner, 1977.

444. Woodruff RA Jr, Guze SB, Clayton PC. The medical and psychiatric implications of antisocial personality (sociopathy). Dis Nerv Syst 1971;32:712–714.

445. Cloninger CR, Guze SB. Psychiatric illness and female criminality: the role of sociopathy and hysteria in antisocial women. Am J Psychiatry 1970;127:303–311.

446. Crowe RR. An adoption study of antisocial personality. Arch Gen Psychiatry 1974;31:785–791.

447. Guze SB, Goodwin DW, Crane JB. A psychiatric study of the wives of convicted felons: an example of assortative mating. Am J Psychiatry 1970;126:1773–1776.

448. Koller KM, Kastanos JN. Family background in prison groups: a comparative study of parental deprivation. Brit J Psychiatry 1970;117:371–380.

449. Jonsson G. Delinquent boys, their parents and grandparents. Acta Psychiat Scand 1967;195(suppl):43.

450. Johnson A, Szurek S. The genesis of antisocial acting out in children and adults. Psychoan Q 1952;21:323.

451. Liss R, Frances AJ. Court-mandated treatment: dilemmas for hospital psychiatry. Am J Psychiatry 1975;132:924–927.

452. Vaillant GE. Sociopathy as a human process: a viewpoint. Arch Gen Psychiatry 1975;32:178–183.

453. Kernberg O. Borderline conditions and pathological narcissism. New York: Jason Aronson, 1975.

454. Grinker RR Sr, Werble D, Drye R. The borderline syndrome. New York: Basic Books, 1968.

455. Schmideberg M. The borderline patient. In: Arieti S, ed. American handbook of psychiatry 1959;1:398–418.

456. Snyder S, Pitts WM. Electroencephalography of borderline personality disorder. Acta Psychiatr Scand 1984;69:129–134.

457. Carroll BJ, Greden JF, Feinberg M, et al. Neuroendocrine evaluation of depression in borderline patients. Psychiatr Clin N Am 1982;4:89–99.

458. Pfohl B, Stangl D, Zimmerman M. The implication of DSM-III personality disorders for patients with major depression. J Affect Dis 1984;7:309–319.

459. Siever LJ, Coccaro ER, Zemishlany Z, et al. Psychobiology of personality disorders: pharmacological implications. Psychopharmacol Bull 1987;23:333–336.

460. Herman JL, van der Kolk BA. Traumatic antecedents of borderline personality disorder. In: van der Kolk BA, ed. Psychological trauma. Washington, DC: American Psychiatric Press, 1987.

461. Waldinger R. Intensive psychodynamic psychotherapy with borderline patients: an overview. Am J Psychiatry 1986;144: 267–274.

462. Cowdry RW, Garner DL. Pharmacotherapy of borderline personality disorder: alprazolam, carbamazepine, trifluoperazine and tranylcypromine. Arch Gen Psychiatry 1988;45:111–119.

463. Kernberg O. Severe personality disorders. New Haven: Yale University Press, 1984.

464. Kohut H. The restoration of the self. New York: International Universities Press, 1977.

465. Lilienfeld S, Van Valkenburg C, Larntz K, et al. The relationship of histrionic personality disorder to antisocial personality and somatization disorders. Am J Psychiatry 1986; 143:728–732.

466. Rosenberg CM. Personality and obsessional neurosis. Br J Psychiatry 1967;113:471–477.

467. Tyrer P, Casey P, Gall J. Relationship between neurosis and personality disorder. Br J Psychiatry 1983;142:404–408.

468. Freud S. Character and anal erotism. In: Strachey J, ed. The standard edition of the complete psychological works of Sigmund Freud. London: Hogarth Press, 1908/1953-1974. IX: 169–175.

469. Winokur G. Delusional disorder (paranoia). Compr Psychiatry 1977;18:453–479.

470. Kendler KS. Demography of paranoid psychosis (delusional disorder): a review and comparison with schizophrenia and affective illness. Arch Gen Psychiatry 1982;39:890–902.

471. Kasanin J. The acute schizoaffective psychoses. Am J Psychiatry 1933;13:97–123.

472. Taylor MA. Are schizophrenia and affective disorder related? A selective literature review. Am J Psychiatry 1992; 149:22–32.

473. Slater ETO. The diagnosis of "hysteria." Br Med J 1965;1: 1395–1399.

474. Slater ETO, Glithero E. A follow-up of patients diagnosed as suffering from "hysteria." J Psychosom Res 1965;9:9–13.

475. Alexander F. Psychosomatic medicine. New York: Norton, 1950.

21/ Dementia and Delirium

1. Folstein M, Folstein S, McHugh P. "Mini-mental state": a practical method for grading the cognitive state of patients for the clinician. J Psychiatric Res 1975;12:189–198.

2. Cummings J. Clinical neuropsychiatry. Orlando, FL: Grune and Stratton, 1985.

3. DeVaul RA, Hall RCW. Hallucinations. In: Hall RCW, ed. Psychiatric presentations of medical illness: somatopsychic disorders. Jamaica NY: Spectrum, 1980;91–103.

4. Lipowski ZJ. Delirium: Acute brain failure in man. Springfield IL: C.C. Thomas, 1980.

5. Perry SW, Markowitz J. Organic mental disorders. In: Talbott JA, Hales RE, Yudofsky SC, eds. Textbook of psychiatry. Washington DC: American Psychiatric Press, 1988: 279–311.

6. Popkin MK. Organic brain syndromes presenting with global cognitive impairment: delirium and dementia. In: Winokur G, Clayton P, eds. The medical basis of psychiatry. Philadelphia: Saunders, 1987:3–19.

7. Lipowski ZJ. Organic mental disorders: An American perspective. Br J Psychiatry 1984;144:542–546.

8. Rabins PV, Folstein MF. Delirium and dementia: diagnostic criteria and fatality rates. Br J Psychiatry 1982;140:149–153.

9. Kay DWK, Beamish P, Roth M. Old age mental disorders in Newcastle upon Tyne. Br J Psychiatry 1964;110:146–148.

10. Popkin MK, Mackenzie TB. The provisional diagnosis of dementia: three phases of evaluation. In: Hall RCW, Beresford TP, eds. The handbook of psychiatric diagnostic procedures. Jamaica NY: Spectrum, 1984.

11. Cummings J, Benson DF, LoVerme S. Reversible dementia: illustrative cases, definition and review. JAMA 1980; 243:2439.

12. Rabins PV. The prevalence of reversible dementia in a psychiatric hospital. Hosp Comm Psychiatry 1981;32:490–492.

13. Wise MG. Delirium. In: Hales RE, Yudofsky SC, eds. Textbook of neuropsychiatry. Washington DC: American Psychiatric Press, 1987.

14. Pro JD, Wells CE. The use of the electroencephalogram in the diagnosis of delirium. Dis Nerv Sys 1977;38:804–808.

15. Kennard MA, Bueding E, Wortis WB. Some biochemical and electroencephalographic changes in delirium tremens. Quart J Stud Alc 1945;6:4–14.

16. Millar HR. Psychiatric morbidity in elderly surgical patients. Br J Psychiatry 1981;138:17–20.

17. Black DW, Warrack G, Winokur G. The Iowa record-linkage study: II. Excess mortality among patients with organic mental disorders. Arch Gen Psychiatry 1985;42:78–81.

18. Weddington WW. The mortality of delirium. Psychosomatics 1982;23:122–1235.

19. Epstein LJ, Simon A. Organic brain syndrome in the elderly. Geriatrics 1967;22:145–150.

20. Hodgkinson HM. Mental impairment in the elderly. J R Coll Phys Lond 1973;7:305–317.

21. Robins LN, Helzer JE, Weissman MM, et al. Lifetime prevalence of specific psychiatric disorders in three sites. Arch Gen Psychiatry 1984;41:949–958.

22. Small GW, Liston EH, Jarvik LF. Diagnosis and treatment of dementia in the aged. West J Med 1981;135:469–481.

23. Berdine RW. Dementia. In: Rowe JW, Berdine RW, eds. Health and disease in old age. Boston: Little, Brown, 1982.

24. Jacobs JW, Bernhard MR, Delgado A, et al. Screening for organic mental syndromes in the medically ill. Ann Int Med 1977;86:40–46.

25. Fields SD, MacKenzie CR, Charlson MD, et al. Reversibility of cognitive impairment in medical inpatients. Ann Int Med 1986;146:1593–1596.

26. Lipowski ZJ. Transient cognitive disorders (delirium, acute confusional states) in the elderly. Am J Psychiatry 1983;140: 1426–1436.

27. Knights EB, Folstein MF. Unsuspected emotional and cognitive disturbances in medical patients. Ann Int Med 1977; 87:723–724.

28. Levine PM, Silberfarb PM, Lipowski ZJ. Mental disorders in cancer patients: a study of 100 psychiatric referrals. Cancer 1978;42:1385–1391.

29. Gehi M, Strain JJ, Weltz N, Jacobs J. Is there a need for admission and discharge screening for the medically ill? Gen Hosp Psychiatry 1980;3:186–191.

30. Folstein MF. Psychiatric disturbances in neurological patients: detection, recognition and course. Ann Neurol 1978; 4:225–228.

31. Mace NL, Rabins PV. The 36-hour day. 2nd ed. Baltimore: Johns Hopkins University Press, 1991.

32. Cummings JL, Benson DF. Dementia: a clinical approach. 2nd ed. Boston: Butterworth, 1991.

33. Mayeux R, Rosen WG, eds. The dementias. New York: Raven Press, 1983.

34. Wilkins RH, Brody IA. Alzheimer's disease. Arch Neurol 1969;21:109–110.

35. Jellinger J. Neuropathological agents and dementia. Acta Neurol Belg 1976;76:83–102.

36. Sourander P, Sjogren H. The concept of Alzheimer's disease and its clinical implications. In: Wolstenholme GEW, O'Connor M, eds. Alzheimer's disease and related conditions: A CIBA Foundation Symposium. London: Churchill: 11–36.

37. Tomlinson BE, Blessed G, Roth M. Observations on the brains of demented old people. J Neurol Sci 1970;11:205–242.

38. Terry RD, Katzman R. Senile dementia of the Alzheimer type. Ann Neurol 1983;14:497–506.

39. Katzman R. The prevalence and malignancy of Alzheimer's disease: a major killer. Arch Neurol 1976;33:217–218.

40. Taylor MA. The practice of neuropsychiatry. New York: Free Press, 1992.

41. Heston LL, Mastri AR, Anderson VE, White J. Dementia of the Alzheimer type: Clinical genetics, natural history and associated conditions. Arch Gen Psychiatry 1981;38:1085–1090.

42. Heston LL, Mastri AR. The genetics of Alzheimer's disease: associations with hematologic malignancy and Down syndrome. Arch Gen Psychiatry 1977;34:976–981.

43. St. George-Hyslop PH, Tanzi RE, Polinsky RJ, et al. The genetic defect causing familial Alzheimer's disease maps on chromosome 21. Science 1987;235:885–889.

44. Wells CE, Duncan GW. Neurology for psychiatrists. Philadelphia: FA Davis, 1980.

45. Blessed G, Tomlinson BE, Roth M. The association between quantitative measures of dementia and of senile change in the cerebral gray matter of elderly subjects. Br J Psychiatry 1968;114:797–811.

46. Ball MJ. Neuronal loss, neurofibullary tangles, and granulovascular degeneration in the hippocampus with aging and dementia: a quantitative study. Acta Neuropathol 1977;37:111–118.

47. Whitehouse PJ, Clark AW, Price DI, et al. Alzheimer's disease (AD): loss of cholinergic neurons in the nucleus basalis. J Neuropathol Exp Neurol 1981;40:323.

48. Coyle JT, Price DL, DeLong MR. Alzheimer's disease: a disorder of central cholinergic innervation. Science 1983; 219:1184–1190.

49. Ashford JW, Soldinger S, Schaeffer J, et al. Physostigmine effects on 6 patients with dementia. Am J Psychiatry 1981; 38:829–830.

50. Davis KL, Mohs RC, Tinklenberg JR. Enhancement of memory by physostigmine. N Engl J Med 1979;301:946.

51. Peters BH, Levin HS. Effects of physostigmine and lecithin on memory in Alzheimer's disease. Ann Neurol 1979;6: 219–221.

52. Fisman M, Merskey H, Helmes E, et al. Double blind study of lecithin in patients with Alzheimer's disease. Can J Psychiatry 1981;26:426–428.

53. Mohs RC, Davis KL. Choline chloride effect on memory in the elderly. Neurobiol Aging 1980;1:21–25.

54. Thal LJ, Rosen W, Sharpless NS, Crystal H. Choline chloride fails to improve cognition in Alzheimer's disease. Neurobiol Aging 1981;2:205–208.

55. Perry EK, Tomlinson BE, Blessed G, et al. Neuropathological and biochemical observations on the noradrenergic system in Alzheimer's disease. J Neurol Sci 1981;51:279–287.

56. Johannesson G, Hagberg B, Gustafson L, Ingvar DH. EEG and cognitive impairment in senile dementia. Acta Neurol Scand 1979;59:2225–2240.

57. Goad DL, Davis CM, Liem P, Fuselier CC, McCormack JR, Olsen KM. The use of selegiline in Alzheimer patients with behavioral problems. J Clin Psychiatry 1991;52:342–345.

58. Hachinski VC, Lassen NA, Marshall J. Multiinfarct dementia: a cause of mental deterioration in the elderly. Lancet 1974;2:207–209.

59. Cummings JL. Multi-infarct dementia: diagnosis and management. Psychosomatics 1987;28:117–126.

60. Corsellis JAN. Aging and the dementias. In: Blackwood W, Corsellis JAN, eds. Greenfield's neuropathology. London: Edward Arnold, 1976;796–848.

61. Lishman WA. Organic psychiatry. London: Blackwell Scientific Publishers, 1978.

62. Wechsler AF, Verity M, Rosenscheen S, Fried I, Scheibel AB. Pick's disease. Arch Neurol 1982;39:87–90.

63. White P, Goodhardt MJ, Keet JP, Hiley CR, Carrasco LH, Williams IEI, Bowen DM. Neocortical cholinergic changes in elderly people. Lancet 1977;1:668–670.

64. Cummings JL, Duchen LW. The Kluver-Bucy syndrome in Pick's disease. Neurology 1981;31:1415–1422.

65. Lilly R, Cummings JL, Benson DF, Frankel M. The human Kluver-Bucy syndrome. Neurology 1983;33:1141–1145.

66. McGeachie RE, Fleming JO, Sharer LR, Hyman RA. Diagnosis of Pick's disease by computed tomography. J Comput Assist Tomogr 1979;3:113–115.

67. McHugh PR, Folstein MF. Subcortical dementia. Address to the American Academy of neurology. Boston, April 1973 (unpublished).

68. Albert ML. Subcortical dementia. In: Katzman R, Terry RD, Bick KL, eds. Alzheimer's disease: senile dementia and related disorders. New York: Raven, 1978.

69. Cummings JL, Benson DF. Subcortical dementia: review of an emerging concept. Arch Neurol 1984;41:874–879.

70. Benson DF. Subcortical dementia: a clinical approach. In: Mayeux R, Rosen W, eds. The dementias. New York: Raven Press, 1983.

71. Martin JB, Gusella JF. Huntington's disease: pathogenesis and management. N Engl J Med 1986;315:1267–1276.

72. Gusella JF, Wechsler NS, Conneally PM, et al. A polymorphic DNA marker genetically linked to Huntington's disease. Nature 1983;306:234–238.

73. Folstein SE, Phillips JA III, Meyers DA, et al. Huntington's disease: two families with different clinical factors show linkage to the G8 probe. Science 1985;229:776–779.

74. Gusella JF, Tanzi RE, Anderson MA, et al. DNA markers for nervous system diseases. Science 1984;225:1320–1326.

75. Bruyn GW, Bots GTAM, Dom R. Huntington's chorea: current neuropathological status. Adv Neurol 1979;23:83–93.

76. Bird ED. Chemical pathology of Huntington's disease. Annu Rev Pharmacol Toxicol 1980;20:533–551.

77. Graybiel AM. Neuropeptides in the basal ganglia. In: Martin JB, Barchas J, eds. Neuropeptides in neurologic and psychiatric disease. New York: Raven Press, 1986:135–161.

78. Perry TL, Hansen S, Kloster M. Huntington's chorea, deficiency of gamma-aminobutyric acid in brain. New Engl J Med 1973;288:337–342.

79. Terrence CF, Delaney JF, Alberts MC. Computed tomography for Huntington's disease. Neuroradiology 1977;1: 173–175.

80. Barr AN, Heinze WT, Dubben GD, Valvassou GE, Seegar O. Bicaudate index in computerized tomography in Huntington's disease and cerebral atrophy. Neurology 1978;28: 1196–1200.

81. Folstein SE, Franz ML, Jensen BA, Chase GA, Folstein MF. Conduct disorder and affective disorder among the offspring of patients with Huntington's disease. Psychol Med 1983;13:45–52.

82. Folstein SE, Abbott MH, Chase GA, Jensen BA, Folstein MF. The association of affective disorder with Huntington's disease in a case series and in families. Psychol Med 1983; 13:531–542.

83. Beckford JAR, Elleson RM. The high incidence of Huntington's chorea in the Duchy of Cornwall. J Ment Sci 1953; 99:623.

84. Hayden MR. Huntington's chorea. New York: Springer-Verlag, 1981.

85. Bruyn GW. Huntington's chorea: historical, clinical and laboratory synopsis. In: Vinken PJ, Bruyn GW, eds. Handbook of clinical neurology. Vol. 6. Diseases of the basal ganglia. Amsterdam: Elsevier, 1968;6:298–378.

86. Lyle DE, Gottesman II. Premorbid psychometric indicators of the gene for Huntington's disease. J Consult Clin Psychol 1977;45:1011–1022.

87. Adams RD, Victor M. Principles of neurology. 4th ed. New York: McGraw-Hill, 1989:938–943.

88. Jankovic J. The extrapyramidal disorders. In: Wyngaarden JB, Smith LH, Bennett JC, eds. Cecil textbook of medicine. 19th ed. Philadelphia: Saunders, 1992:2135–2136.

89. Javoy-Agid F, Agid Y. Is the mesocortical dopaminergic system involved in Parkinson's disease? Neurology 1980;30: 1326–1330.

90. Greenfield JG, Bosanquet FD. The brain-stem lesions of parkinsonism. J Neurol Neurosurg Psychiatry 1953;16:213–226.

91. Gilroy J, Meyer JS. Medical neurology. London: Macmillan, 1969.

92. Mayeux R, Stern Y, Rosen J, Leventhal J. Depression, intellectual impairment, and Parkinson's disease. Neurology 1981;31:645–650.

93. Pirozzolo FÔ, Hansch EC, Mortimer JA, Webster DA, Kuskowski MA. Dementia in Parkinson's disease: a neuropsychological analysis. Brain Cogn 1982;1:71–83.

94. Taylor MA, Sierles FS, Abrams R. General hospital psychiatry. New York: Free Press, 1985.

95. Franz DN. Drugs for Parkinson's disease: centrally acting muscle relaxants. In: Goodman LS, Gilman A, eds. The pharmacologic basis of therapeutics. 5th ed. New York: Macmillan, 1975.

96. Abrams R, Douyon R, Serby M, Klutchko B, Rotrosen J. ECT and Parkinson's disease revised. A "naturalistic" study. Am J Psychiatry 1989;146:1451–1455.

97. Goetz CG, Olanow MD, Koller WC, et al. Multicenter study of autologous adrenal medullary transplantation to the corpus striatum in patients with advanced Parkinson's disease. N Engl J Med 1989;320:337–341.

98. Deiss A. Wilson's disease. In: Wyngaarden JB, Smith LH, Bennett JC, eds. Cecil textbook of medicine. 19th ed. Philadelphia: Saunders, 1992;1132–1133.

99. Scheinberg IH, Sternlieb I. Wilson's disease. Philadelphia: WB Saunders, 1984.

100. Benson DF. The hydrocephalic dementias. In: Benson DF, Blumer D, eds. Psychiatric aspects of neurologic disease. New York: Grune and Stratton, 1975:83–89.

101. Wells CE. Diagnosis of dementia: a reassessment. Psychosomatics 1984;25:183–190.

102. Wells CE. Pseudodementia. Am J Psychiatry 1979;136: 895–900.

103. McHugh PR. Occult hydrocephalus. Quart J Med 1964;33: 297–308.

104. Udvarhelyi GB, Wood JH, James AE Jr, Bartelt D. Results and complications in 55 shunted patients with normal-pressure hydrocephalus. Surg Neurol 1975;3:271–275.

105. Hughes CP, Siegel BA, Coxe WS, Gado MH, Grub RL, Coleman RE, Berg L. Adult idiopathic communicating hydrocephalus with and without shunting. J Neurol Neurosurg Psychiatry 1978;41:961–971.

106. Navia BA, Jordan BD, Price RW. The AIDS dementia complex. I. Clinical features. Ann Neurol 1986;19:517–524.

107. Sparling PF. Sexually transmitted diseases. In: Wyngaarden JB, Smith LH, Bennett JC, eds. Cecil textbook of medicine. 19th ed. Philadelphia: Saunders, 1992:1751–1770.

108. Kirschbaum WR. Jakob-Creutzfeld disease. New York: Elsevier, 1968.

109. Gajdusek DC. Unconventional viruses and the origin and the origins and disappearance of kuru. Science 1977;197: 943–960.

110. Duff P, Wolf J, Collins G, DeVoe AG, Streeten B, Cowen D. Possible person-to-person transmission of Creutzfeld-Jacob disease. N Engl J Med 1974;290:692.

111. Bernoulli C, Siegfried J, Baumgartner G, Regli F, Rabinowitz T, Gajdusek DG, Gibbs CJ Jr. Danger of accidental person-to-person transmission of Creutzfeld-Jakob disease by surgery. Lancet 1977;1:478–479.

112. Chiofalo N, Fuentes A, Galvez S. Serial EEG findings in 27 cases of Creutzfeld-Jakob disease. Arch Neurol 1980;37: 143–145.

113. Burger LJ, Rowan J, Goldensohn ES. Creutzfeldt-Jakob disease: an electroencephalographic study. Arch Neurol 1972;26:428–433.

114. Douglas RG. Introduction to viral diseases. In: Wyngaarden JB, Smith LH, Bennett JC, eds. Cecil textbook of medicine. 19th ed. Philadelphia: Saunders, 1992:1798–1800.

115. Berger JR, Koszovitz B, Post MJD, et al. Progressive multifocal leukoencephalopathy associated with human immunodeficiency virus infection. A review of the literature with a report of sixteen cases. Ann Intern Med 1987;107:78.

116. Price RW. Progressive multifocal leukoencephalopathy. In: Wyngaarden JB, Smith LH, Bennett JC, eds. Cecil textbook of medicine. 19th ed. Philadelphia: WB Saunders, 1992:2191.

117. Houff SA, Major EO, Katz DA, et al. Involvement of JC virus-infected mononuclear cells from the bone marrow and spleen in the pathogenesis of progressive multifocal leukoencephalopathy. N Engl J Med 1988;318:301.

118. Narayan O, Penney JB Jr, Johnson RT, Herndon RM, Weiner LP. Etiology of progressive multifocal leukoencephalopathy. N Engl J Med 1973;289:1278–1282.

119. Richardson EP Jr. Progressive multifocal leukoencephalopathy. In: Vinken PJ, Bruyn FW, eds. Multiple sclerosis and other demyelinating diseases. vol. 9. Handbook of clinical neurology. New York: Elsevier, 1970:485–499.

120. Holmes KK, Mardh P-A, Sparling PF. Sexually transmitted diseases. New York: McGraw-Hill, 1990.

121. Gjestland T. The Oslo study of untreated syphilis: an epidemiologic investigation of the natural course of the syphilitic

infection based upon a re-study of the Boeck-Bruusgaard material. Acta Derm Venereol 1955;35(suppl 34).

122. Bruetsch WL. Neurosyphilitic conditions. In: Arieti S, ed. American handbook of psychiatry. New York: Basic Books, 1959:1003–1020.

123. Hahn RD, Webster B, Werckhardt G, et al. Penicillin treatment of general paresis (dementia paralytica). Arch Neurol Psychiatry 1959;81:557–590.

124. Alexander MP. Traumatic brain injury. In: Benson DF, Blumer D, eds. Psychiatric aspects of neurologic disease. vol. 2. New York: Grune and Stratton, 1982.

125. Black DW. Subdural hematoma—a retrospective study of the "great neurologic imitator." Postgrad Med 1985;78: 107–114.

126. Ross RJ, Cole M, Thompson JS, Kim KH. Boxers-computed tomography, EEG and neurological evaluation. JAMA 1983;249:211–213.

127. Corsellis JAN, Bruton CJ, Freeman-Broune D. The aftermath of boxing. Psychol Med 1973;3:270–303.

128. Mawdsley C, Ferguson FR. Neurological disease in boxers. Lancet 1963;2:795–801.

129. Jordan BD, Zimmerman RD. Computed tomography and magnetic resonance imaging in boxers. JAMA 1990;263: 1670–1674.

130. Folstein MF, McHugh PR. Dementia syndrome of depression. In: Katzman R, Terry RD, Bick KL, eds. Alzheimer's disease: senile dementia and related disorders. New York: Raven Press, 1978;87–93.

131. Taylor MA, Abrams R. Cognitive impairment in schizophrenia. Am J Psychiatry 1984;141:196–201.

132. Golden CJ, Moses JA Jr, Zelazowski R, et al. Cerebral ventricular size and neuropsychological impairment in young chronic schizophrenics. Arch Gen Psychiatry 1980;37:619–623.

133. Andreasen NC, Olsen SA, Dennert JW, Smith MR. Ventricular enlargement in schizophrenia: Relationship to positive and negative symptoms. Am J Psychiatry 1982;139: 297–302.

134. Bleuler E. Dementia praecox; or, the group of schizophrenias. Zenkin J, trans., New York: International Universities Press, 1950.

135. Engel GL, Romano J. Delirium, a syndrome of cerebral insufficiency. J Chron Dis 1959;9:260–277.

136. Strub RL, Black FW. Organic brain syndromes: an introduction to neurobehavioral disorders. Philadelphia: FA Davis, 1982.

137. Goldstein K. After effects of brain injuries in war. New York: Grune and Stratton, 1942.

138. Wyngaarden JB, Smith LH, Bennett JC, eds. Cecil textbook of medicine. 19th ed. Philadelphia: Saunders, 1992.

139. Wilson JD et al, eds. Harrison's principles of internal medicine. 12th ed. New York: McGraw-Hill, 1991.

140. Wilson LM. Intensive care delirium. Arch Intern Med 1972;130:225–226.

22/ Substance Abuse

1. Gorman JM, Rooney JF. Delay in seeking help and onset of crises among Al-Anon wives. J Drug Alc Abuse 1979;6:223–233.

2. Moore RD, Bone LR, Geller G, Mamon JA, Stokes E, Levine DM. Prevalence, detection, and treatment of alcoholism in hospitalized patients. JAMA 1989;261:403–407.

3. Clark AW, Kay J, Clark DC. Patterns of psychoactive drug prescriptions by house officers for nonpatients. J Med Educ 1988;63:44–50.

4. Galanter M, Kaufman E, Taintor Z, Robinowitz CB, Meyer RE, Halikas J. The current status of psychiatric education in alcoholism and drug abuse. Am J Psychiatry 1989;146: 35–39.

5. Maynard L, Goldberg R, Ockene J. Behaviors and attitudes among medical students concerning cigarette smoking and alcohol consumption. J Med Educ 1986;61:921–922.

6. Conard S, Hughes P, Baldwin DC Jr, Achenback KE, Sheehan DV. Cocaine use by senior medical students. Am J Psychiatry 1989;146:382–383.

7. Gallant DM, Alcoholism: the physician's imperative for follow-up care. Alc: Clin Exp Res 1987;11:411–412.

8. Schuckit MA, Zisook S, Mortala J. Clinical implications of DSM-III diagnoses of alcohol abuse and alcohol dependence. Am J Psychiatry 1985;142:1403–1408.

9. Robins LW, Helzer JE, Weissman MM, Orvaschel H, Gruenberg E, Reiger DA. Lifetime prevalence of specific psychiatric disorders. Arch Gen Psychiatry 1984;41:949–958.

10. Adams WL, Garry PG, Rhyne R, Hunt WC, Goodwin JS. Alcohol intake in the healthy elderly: changes with age in a cross-sectional and longitudinal study. J Am Geriatr Soc 1990;38:211–216.

11. Petersson B, Kristenson H, Krant P, Trell E, Sternby WH. Alcohol related deaths: a major contributor to mortality in urban middle-aged men. Lancet 1982;2:1088–1090.

12. Berglund M. Suicide in alcoholism. Arch Gen Psychiatry 1984;41:888–891.

13. Gallant DM. Recent advances in research and treatment of alcoholism and drug abuse. CME textbook of the American Society of Addition Medicine, 1991.

14. Oster GO, Russell MW, Huse DM, Adams SF, Imbimbo J. Accident- and injury-related health care utilization among benzodiazepine users and nonusers. J Clin Psychiatry 1987; 48:17–21.

15. Gallant DM. Alcoholism: a guide to diagnosis, intervention and treatment. New York: Norton, 1987.

16. Snail P, Stockwell T, Canter S, Hodgson R. Alcohol dependence and phobic anxiety states. I. a prevalence study. Brit J Psychiatry 1983;40:125–138.

17. Westmeyer J. Predisposing factors. In: Westermeyer J. Primer on chemical dependency. Baltimore: Williams & Wilkins, 1976:23–29.

17a. Kinzie JD, Leung PK, Boehnlein J, et al. Psychiatric epidemiology of an Indian village: a 19–year replication study. J Nerv Ment Dis 1992;180:33–39.

18. Bohman M, Sigvardsson S, Cloninger CR. Maternal inheritance of substance abuse: cross-fostering analysis of adopted women. Arch Gen Psychiatry 1981;38:965–969.

19. Cloninger CR, Bohman M, Sigvardsson S. Inheritance of alcohol abuse: cross-fostering analysis of adopted men. Arch Gen Psychiatry 1981;38:861–868.

20. Cloninger CR. Neurogenetic adoptive mechanisms in alcoholism. Science 1987;236:410–416.

21. Woodruff RA, Clayton PJ, Cloninger CR, Guze SB. A brief method of screening for alcoholism. J Clin Psychiatry 1976; 37:434–435.

22. Schwartz B, Lauderdale RM, Montgomery L, Burch EA, Gallant DM. Immediate versus delayed feedback on urine reports of methadone maintenance patients. Addict Behav 1987;12:29–31.

23. Peek GJP, Keating JW, Ward RJ, Peters TJ. Alcohol swabs and venipuncture. Lancet 1989;1:1388.

24. Goodwin FK. Neurotoxic effect of phencyclidine. JAMA 1989;262:1439.

25. Shaw JM, Kolesar GS, Sellers EM, Kaplan HL, Sandor PS. Development of optimal treatment tactics for alcohol withdrawal. I. Assessment and effectiveness of supportive care. J Clin Psychopharmacol 1981;1:382–389.

26. Gallant DM: Improvements in treatment of alcohol withdrawal syndromes. Alc: Clin Exp Res 1989;13:721–722.

27. Murphy SM, Owen RT, Tyrer PJ. Withdrawal symptoms after only six weeks' treatment with diazepam. Lancet 1984; 2:1389.

28. Ries RK, Roy-Byrne PP, Ward NG, Neppe V, Cullison S. Carbamazepine treatment for benzodiazepine withdrawal. Am J Psychiatry 1989;146:536–537.

29. O'Brien CP, Childress AR, Arndt IO, McLellan AT, Woody GE, Meany I. Pharmacological and behavioral treatment of cocaine dependence: conflicted studies. J Clin Psychiatry 1988;49:17–22.

30. Wei H, Young D. Effect of clonidine on cigarette cessation and in the alleviation of withdrawal symptoms. Br J Addict 1988;83:1221–1226.

31. Schuckit MA. Caffeine: the most widely used drug. Drug Abuse Alc News 1989;18:1–3.

32. Harper C. Wernicke's encephalopathy: a more common disease than realized: a neuropathological study of 51 cases. J Neurol Neurosurg Psychiatry 1979;42:226–231.

33. Waugh M, Jackson M, Fox GA, Hawke SH, Tuck RR. Effect of social drinking on neuropsychological performance. Br J Addict 1989;84:659–667.

34. Goodwin FK. HIV-related disease in IV drug use. JAMA 1989;261:970.

35. Ricaurte G, Bryan G, Strauss L, Seiden L, Schuster C. Hallucinogenic amphetamine selectively destroys brain serotonin nerve terminals. Science 1985;229:986–989.

36. Negrete JC. Cannabis and schizophrenia. Br J Addict 1989; 84:349–356.

37. Fielding JE, Phenow KJ. Health effects of involuntary smoking. N Engl J Med 1988;319:1452–1460.

38. Little RE, Anderson KW, Erviln CH, Worthington-Roberts B, Clarren SK. Maternal alcohol use during breast feeding and infant mental development at one year. N Engl J Med 1989;321:425–430.

39. Institute of Medicine Report. Prevention and treatment of alcohol problems: research opportunities. Washington DC: National Academy Press, 1989–1990.

40. Rawon RA, Marinelli PJ, Obert JL, Smith DP. Chemical dependency treatment outcome: alcoholism and cocaine addicts (Abstr.). Annual Meeting of the ACNP, San Juan, 1989.

41. Gallant DM, Faulkner MA, Stoy B, Bishop MP, Langdon D. Enforced clinic treatment of paroled criminal alcoholics. Q J Stud Alcohol 1968;29:77–83.

42. Gallant DM, Bishop MP, Mouledoux A, Faulkner MA, Brisolara A, Swanson MA. The revolving door alcoholic: an impasse in treatment. Arch Gen Psychiatry 1973;28:633–635.

43. Gallant DM, Bishop MP, Stoy B, Faulkner MA, Paternostro L. The value of a "first contact" group intake session in an alcoholism outpatient clinic: statistical confirmation. Psychosomatics 1966;7:349–352.

44. Marlatt GA, Gordon JR. Relapse prevention maintenance strategies in the treatment of addictive behaviors. New York: Guilford Press, 1985.

45. Miller WR, Taylor CA. Relative effectiveness of bibliotherapy, individual and group self-control training in the treatment of problem drinkers. Addict Behav 1980;5:13–20.

46. McCrady BS, Noel NE, Abrams DB, Stout RL, Nelson HF, Hay WM. Comparative effectiveness of three types of spouse involvement in outpatient behavioral alcoholism treatment. J Stud Alcohol 1986;47:459–467.

47. Chick J, Ritson B, Connaughton J, Stewart A, Chick JO. Advice versus extended treatment for alcoholism: a controlled study. Br J Addic 1988;83:159–170.

48. Helzer JE, Robins LN, Taylor JR, Carey BA, Miller RH, Combs-Orme T, Farmer A. The extent of long-term drinking among alcoholics discharged from medical and psychiatric facilities. N Engl J Med 1985;312:1678–1682.

49. Glaser FB, Ogborne AC. Does A.A. really work? Brit J Addict 1982;77:123–129.

50. Fuller RK, Roth HP. Disulfiram for the treatment of alcoholism: an evaluation in 128 men. Ann Intern Med 1979; 90:901–904.

51. Azrin NH, Sisson RW, Meyers R, Godley M. Alcoholism treatment by disulfiram and community reinforcement therapy. J Behav Ther Exp Psychiatry 1982;13:105–112.

52. Kristenson H, Ohlin H, Haltin-Nosslin M-J, Trell E, Hood B. Identification and intervention of heavy drinking in middle-aged men: results and follow-up of 24–60 months of long-term study with randomized controls. Alcohol: Clin Exp Res 1983;7:203–209.

53. Vaillant GE. What can long-term follow-up teach us about relapse and prevention of relapse in addiction? Br J Addict 1988;83:1147–1157.

54. de la Fuente J-R, Morse RM, Niven RG, Ilstrup DM. A controlled study of lithium carbonate in the treatment of alcoholism. Mayo Clinic Proc 1989;64:177–180.

55. Bullock ML, Culliton PD, Olander RT. Controlled trial of acupuncture for severe recidivist alcoholism. Lancet 1989; 1:1435–1438.

56. Anglin MD, Speckart GR, Booth MW, Ryan TM. Consequence and costs of shutting off methadone. Addict Behav 1989;14:307–326.

57. Brewster JM. Prevalence of alcohol and other drug problems among physicians. JAMA 1986;255:1913–1920.

58. Crenshaw R, Bruce DA, Eraker PL. An epidemic of suicide among physicians on probation. JAMA 1980;243:1915–1917.

59. Healy K. Bolivia and cocaine: a developing country's problem. Br J Addict 1988;83:19–23.

60. Brooke J. Peruvian farmers razing rain forest to sow drug crops. New York Times, August 13, 1989.

61. Nadelman EA. Drug prohibition in the United States. Science 1989;245:939–946.

62. Hartnoll R, Lewis R, Mitcheson M, Bryer S. Estimating the prevalence of opioid dependence. Lancet 1985;1:203–205.

63. Becker DM, Conner HF, Waranch HR, Stillman F, Pennington L, Lees PSJ, Oski F. The impact of a total ban on smoking in the Johns Hopkins Children's Center. JAMA 1989;262:799–802.

64. Teplen LA, Abram KM, Michael SK. Blood alcohol level among emergency room patients: a multivariate analysis. J Stud Alc 1989;50:441–447.

23/ Psychotherapy

1. American Psychiatric Association. A psychiatric glossary, 2nd ed. Washington, DC: American Psychiatric Press, 1964.

2. Frank JD. General psychotherapy: the restoration of morale. In: Arieti S., ed. American handbook of psychiatry, vol. 5. New York: Basic Books, 1975:117–132.

3. Waldinger R. Psychiatry for medical students. Washington, DC: American Psychiatric Press, 1984.

4. Gabbard GO. Dynamic psychiatry. Washington DC: American Psychiatric Press, 1990.

5. Nemiah JC. Psychoanalysis and individual psychotherapy. In: Karasu TB, ed. The psychiatric therapies. Washington, DC: American Psychiatric Press, 1984;319–337.

6. Hamilton NG. Self and others: object relations theory in practice. Northvale, NJ: Jason Aronson, 1988.

7. Kohut H. The analysis of the self. New York: International Universities Press, 1971.

8. Bion WR. Learning from experience. London: Heinemann, 1962.

9. Kernberg OF. Object relations theory and clinical psychoanalysis. New York: Jason Aronson, 1988.

10. Brenner C. An elementary textbook of psychoanalysis, revised ed. New York: International Universities Press, 1973.

11. Freud A. The ego and its mechanisms of defense. New York: International Universities Press, 1946.

12. Freud S. The dynamics of transference. Standard ed. of the complete work of Sigmund Freud 1912;12:97–108.

13. Hamilton NG. The containing function and the analyst's projective identification. Int J Psychoanal 1990;71:445–453.

14. Rush AH. Cognitive therapy. In Karasu, T.G., ed. The psychiatric therapies. Washington, DC: American Psychiatric Press, 1984;397–414.

15. Beck AT. Cognitive therapy and the emotional disorders. New York: International Universities Press, 1976.

16. Weman DS. The practice of supportive psychotherapy. New York: Brunner/Mazel, 1984.

17. Hales RE, Ursano RJ. The brief psychotherapies. In: Cavenar JO, ed. Psychiatry, Vol. 1, Revised ed. Philadelphia: Lippincott, 1988.

18. Balint M, Ornstein P, Balint E. Focal psychotherapy. New York: Plenum, 1975.

19. Sifneos P. Short-term psychotherapy and emotional crisis. Cambridge, MA: Harvard University Press, 1972.

20. Mann J. Time-limited psychotherapy of depression. New York: Basic Books, 1984.

21. Kerman GL, Weissman MM, Rounsaville BJ, et al. Interpersonal psychotherapy of depression. New York: Basic Books, 1984.

22. Myers JK, Weissman MM, Tischler GL, et al. Six-month prevalence of psychiatric disorders in three communities. Arch Gen Psychiatry 1984;41:959–967.

23. Luborsky L, Singer B, Luborsky L. Comparative studies of psychotherapies. Arch Gen Psychiatry 1975;32:995–1008.

24. Smith ML, Glass GV, Miller TI. The benefits of psychotherapy. Baltimore: Johns Hopkins University Press, 1980.

25. DiMascio A, Weismann MM, Prusoff BA, et al. Differential symptom reduction by drugs and psychotherapy in acute depression. Arch Gen Psychiatry 1979;36:1450–1456.

26. Weissman MM. The psychological treatment of depression. Arch Gen Psychiatry 1979;36:1261–1269.

27. Blackburn IM, Bishop S, Glen AIM, et al. The efficacy of cognitive therapy in depression: a treatment trial using cognitive therapy and pharmacotherapy, each alone and in combination. Br J Psychiatry 1981;139:181–189.

28. Kovacs M, Rush JA, Beck AT, et al. Depressed outpatients treated with cognitive therapy or pharmacotherapy. Arch Gen Psychiatry 1981;

29. Weissman MM, Klerman GL, Prusoff BA, et al. Depressed outpatients: results one year after treatment with drugs and/or interpersonal psychotherapy. Arch Gen Psychiatry 1981;38:51–55.

30. Spiegel D, Kraemer HC, Bloom JR, Gottheil E. Effect of psychosocial treatment on survival of patients with metastatic lung cancer. Lancet 1989;2:888–891.

31. Bergin AE, Garfield SL, eds. Handbook of psychotherapy and behavior change. New York: Wiley, 1974.

32. Beels CC. Family Therapy. In: Talbott JA, Hales RE, Yudofsky SC, eds. Textbook of psychiatry. Washington DC: American Psychiatric Press 1988;929–949.

33. Kaplan HS. The new sex therapy. New York: Brunner Mazel, 1974.

34. Heiman JR, LoPiccolo L, LoPiccolo J. The treatment of sexual dysfunction. In: Gurman AS, Kniskern DP, eds. Handbook of family therapy. New York: Brunner Mazel, 1981:592–627.

35. Gurman AS, Kniskern DP, Pinsof. Research on the process and outcome of marital and family therapy. In: Garfield SL, Bergin AE, eds. Handbook of psychotherapy and behavior change. New York: Wiley, 1986;565–624.

36. Vaughn C, Leff J. The measurement of expressed emotion in the families of psychiatric patients. British J Psychol 1976;15:157–165.

37. Pratt JH. The principles of class treatment and their application to various chronic diseases. Hospital Social Service 1922;6:404.

38. Grunebaum H. A soft-hearted review of hard-nosed research on groups. Int J Gr Psychiatry 1975;25:185–197.

39. Grunebaum H, Kayes W. When to refer for group psychotherapy. Am J Psychiatry 1977;132:130–133.

40. Rutan JS, Stone WN. Psychodynamic group psychotherapy. New York: Macmillan, 1984.

41. Weiner ME. Homogeneous groups. In: Frances AJ, Hales RE, eds. Psychiatry update: American Psychiatric Association annual review. Washington, DC: American Psychiatric Press, 1986.

42. Yalom ID. The theory and practice of group psychotherapy, 3rd ed. New York: Basic Books, 1985.

43. Yalom ID, Houts PS, Zimberg SM. Prediction of improvement in group psychotherapy. Arch Gen Psychiatry 1967;17:159–168.

24/ Psychopharmacology and Electroconvulsive Therapy

1. Rosse RB, Morihisa JM. Laboratory and other diagnostic tests in psychiatry. In: Talbott JA, Hales RE, Yudofsky SC, eds. Textbook of psychiatry. Washington, DC: American Psychiatric Press, 1988:247–277.

2. Bick PA, Hannah AL. Intramuscular lorazepam to restrain violent patients. Lancet 1986;i:206.

3. Taylor MA, Sierles FS, Abrams R. General hospital psychiatry. New York: Free Press, 1985.

4. Spiker DG, Weiss JC, Dealy RS, et al. The pharmacological treatment of delusional depression. Am J Psychiatry 1985;142:430–436.

5. Glassman AH, Kantor SJ, Shostak M. Depression, delusions and drug response. Am J Psychiatry 1975;132:716–719.

6. Wiener JM, ed. Diagnosis and psychopharmacology in childhood and adolescent disorders. New York: Wiley & Sons, 1985.

7. Delay J, Deniker P, Harl JM. Utilisation en therapetique psychiatrique d'une phenothiazine d'action centrale elective (4560 R.P.). Ann Med-Psychol 1952;110:112–117.

8. Guy W. ECDEU assessment manual for psychopharmacology, revised. Washington, DC: U.S. Department of

Health, Education and Welfare, Public Health Service 1976:534–537.

9. Kane JM. The current status of neuroleptic therapy. J Clin Psychiatry 1989;50:322–328.

10. Lipinski JF Jr., Zubenko GS, Cohen BM, Barreira PJ. Propranolol in the treatment of neuroleptic-induced akathisia. Am J Psychiatry 1984;141:412–415.

11. Adler L, Angrist B, Peselow E, Corwin J, Rotrosen J: Efficacy of propanolol in neuroleptic-induced akathisia. J Clin Psychopharm 1985;5:164–166.

12. Levenson JL. Neuroleptic malignant syndrome. Am J Psychiatry 1985;142:1137–1145.

13. Kuhn R. Über die Behandlung depressiver Zustande mit einem Iminodibenzylderivat (G22355). Schweiz Med Wochenschr 1957;87:1135–1140.

14. Hollander E, Liebowitz MR, Gorman JM. Anxiety disorders. In: Talbott JA, Yudofsky SC, eds. Textbook of psychiatry. Washington DC: American Psychiatric Press, 1988: 443–491.

15. Pope HG, Hudson JI, Jonas JM, Yurgelum-Todd D. Bulimia treated with imipramine: a placebo-controlled, double-blind study. Am J Psychiatry 1983;140:554–558.

16. Hughes PL, Wells LA, Cunningham CJ, Illstrup DM. Treating bulimia with desipramine: a double-blind, placebo-controlled study. Arch Gen Psychiatry 1986;43:182–186.

17. Feinmann C, Harris M, Cawley R. Psychogenic facial pain: presentation and treatment. Br Med J 1984;288:436–438.

18. Shaffer D. Enuresis. In: Rutter M, Hersov L, eds. Child psychiatry: modern approaches. Oxford: Blackwell, 1977: 581–612.

19. Campbell M, Green WH, Anderson LT, Deutsch SI. Child and adolescent psychopharmacology. Beverly Hills: Sage Publications, 1985.

20. Sulser F. Mode of action of antidepressant drugs. J Clin Psychiatry 1983;44:5(Sec 2),14–20.

21. Anton RF, Burch EA. Amoxapine versus amitriptyline combined with perphenazine in the treatment of psychotic depression. Am J Psychiatry 1990;147:1203–1208.

22. Balon R. Biological predictors of antidepressant treatment outcome. Clinical Neuropharm 1989;12(3):195–214.

23. Baldessarini RJ. Current status of antidepressants: clinical pharmacology and therapy. J Clin Psychiatry 1989;50:117–126.

24. Kupfer DJ, Perel JM, Frank E. Adequate treatment with imipramine in continuation treatment. J Clin Psychiatry 1989;50:250–255.

25. Pollack MH, Rosenbaum JF. Management of antidepressant-induced side effects: a practical guide for the clinician. J Clin Psychiatry 1987;48:3–8.

26. West ED, Dally PJ. Effects of iproniazid in depressive syndromes. Br Med J 1959;1:1491–1494.

27. Nutt D, Glue P. Monoamine oxidase inhibitors: rehabilitation from recent research? Br J Psychiatry 1989;154:287–291.

28. Liebowitz MR, Fyer AJ, Gorman JM, Campeas R, Levin A. Phenelzine in social phobia. J Clin Psychopharmacol 1986; 6:93–98.

29. Frank JB, Kosten TR, Giller EL, Jr., Dan E. A randomized clinical trial of phenelzine and imipramine for posttraumatic stress disorder. Am J Psychiatry 1988;145:1289–1291.

30. Walsh BT, Stewart JW, Wright L, Harrison W, Roose SP, Glassman AH. Treatment of bulimia with monoamine oxidase inhibitors. Am J Psychiatry 1982;139:1629–1630.

31. Zametkin A, Rapoport JL, Murphy DL, Linnoila M, Ismond D: Treatment of hyperactive children with monoamine oxidase inhibitors. I. Clinical efficacy. Arch Gen Psychiatry 1985;42:962–966.

32. Wender PH, Wood DR, Reimherr FW, Ward M. An open trial of pargyline in the treatment of attention deficit disorder, residual type. Psychiatry Res 1983;329–336.

33. Wyatt RJ, Fram DH, Buchbinder R, Snyder F. Treatment of intractable narcolepsy with a monoamine oxidase inhibitor. N Engl J Med 1971;285:87–91.

34. Lascelles RG. Atypical facial pain and depression. Br J Psychiatry 1966;112:651–659.

35. Cade JFJ. Lithium salts in the treatment of psychotic excitement. Med J Aust 1949;36:349–352.

36. Akiskal HS, Djenderedjian AH, Rosenthal RH, Khani, MK. Cyclothymic disorder: validating criteria for inclusion in the bipolar affective disorder group. Am J Psychiatry 1977;134: 1227–1233.

37. Winokur G. The schizoaffective continuum: Euclid's second axiom. Ann Clin Psychiatry 1989;1:19–24.

38. Pope HG, Jr., Lipinski JF, Cohen BM, Axelrod DT. "Schizoaffective disorder": an invalid diagnosis? A comparison of schizoaffective disorder, schizophrenia, and affective disorder. Am J Psychiatry 1980;137:921-927.

39. Garfinkel PE, Garner DM. Anorexia nervosa: a multidimensional perspective. New York: Brunner/Mazel, 1982.

40. Atre-Vaidya N, Taylor MA. Effectiveness of lithium in schizophrenia: Do we really have an answer? J Clin Psychiatry 1989;50:170–173.

41. Sheard MH. Effects of lithium in human aggression. Nature 1971;230:113–114.

42. Sheard MH, Marini JL, Bridges CI, Wagner E. The effect of lithium on impulsive aggressive behavior in man. Am J Psychiatry 1976;133:12:1409–1413.

43. Tupin JP, Smith DB, Clanon TL, Kim LL, Nugent A, Groupe A. The long-term use of lithium in aggressive prisoners. Comp Psychiatry 1973;14:311–317.

44. Swartz CM. Correciton of lithium levels for dose and blood sampling time. J Clin Psychiatry 1987;48:60–64.

45. Gelenberg AJ, Kane JM, Keller MB, et al. Comparison of standard and low serum levels of lithium for maintenance treatment of bipolar disorder. N Engl J Med 1989;321: 1489–1493.

46. NIMH/NIH Consensus Development Conference statement. Mood disorders: pharmacologic prevention of recurrences. Am J Psychiatry 1985;142:4:469–476.

47. Swartz CM. Serum lithium during treatment of bipolar disorder. N Engl J Med 1990;322:1159–1160.

48. Schou M. Lithium prophylaxis: myths and realities. Am J Psychiatry 1989;146:573–576.

49. Repke JT, Berger NG. Electroconvulsive therapy in pregnancy. Obst Gynecol 1984;63:395–415.

50. Abrams R. Electroconvulsive therapy. 2nd ed. New York: Oxford, 1992.

51. Prien PF, Gelenberg AJ. Alternatives to lithium for preventive treatment of bipolar disorder. Am J Psychiatry 1989; 146:840–848.

52. Fawcett J. Valproate use in acute mania and bipolar disorder: an international perspective. J Clin Psychiatry 1989;50: 3:(Suppl):10–12.

53. Okuma T, Kishimoto A, Inouye K, et al. Anti-manic and prophylactic effects on manic-depressive psychosis. Folia Psychiatr Neuro Jpn 1973:283–297.

54. Post RM, Rubinow DR, Ballenger JC. Conditioning, sensitization, and kindling: implications for the course of affective illness. In: Post RM, Ballenger JC, eds. Neurobiology of mood disorders. Balitimore: Williams & Wilkins, 1984.

55. Satel SL, Nelson JC: Stimulants in the treatment of depression: a critical overview. J Clin Psychiatry 1989;50:241–249.

56. Norman TR, Judd FK, Marriott PF, Burrows GD. Physical treatment of anxiety: the benzodiazepines. In: Roth M, Noyes R, Burrows GD, eds. Handbook of anxiety. Amsterdam: Elsevier, 1988:355–384.

57. Jenike MA. Handbook of geriatric psychopharmacology. Littleton MA, PSG Publishing Co., 1985.

58. Adam K, Oswald I. Can a rapidly eliminated hypnotic cause daytime anxiety? Pharmacopsychiat 1989;22:115–119.

59. Gillin JC, Spinweber CL, Johnson LC. Rebound insomnia: a critical review. J Clin Psychopharmacol 1989;9:161–172.

60. Rickels K. Antianxiety therapy: potential value of long-term treatment. J Clin Psychiatry 1987;48:12:(Suppl):7–11.

61. Balon R, Pohl R, Yeragani VK. Biological treatment of anxiety disorders. In: Pohl R, Gershon S, eds. The biological basis of psychiatric treatment. Prog Basic Clin Pharmacol, vol. 3. Basel: Karger, 1990:284–310.

62. Ortiz A, Pohl R, Gershon S. Azaspirodecanediones in generalized anxiety disorder: buspirone. J Aff Dis 1987;13:131–143.

63. Lader M, Olajide D. A comparison of buspirone and placebo in relieving benzodiazepine withdrawal symptoms. J Clin Psychopharm 1987;7:11–15.

64. Granville-Grossman KL, Turner P. The effect of propranolol on anxiety. Lancet 1966;1:788–790.

65. Hoehn-Saric R, Merchant AF, Keyser ML, Smith VK. Effects of clonidine on anxiety disorders. Arch Gen Psychiatry 1981;38:1278–1282.

66. Gillin JC, Byerley WF. The diagnosis and management of insomnia. N Engl J Med 1990;322:239–248.

67. Weiner RD. The psychiatric use of electrically-induced seizures. Am J Psychiatry 1979;136:1507–1517.

68. Janicak PG, Davis JM, Gibbons RD, Ericksen S, Chang S, Gallagher P. Efficacy of ECT: a meta-analysis. Am J Psychiatry 1985;142(3):297–302.

69. Homan S, Lachenbruch PA, Winokur G, Clayton P. An efficacy study of electroconvulsive therapy and antidepressants in the treatment of primary depression. Psychol Med 1982;12:615–624.

70. Avery D, Winokur G. Suicide, attempted suicide and relapse rates in depression. Arch Gen Psychiatry 1978;35:749–753.

71. Fink M. Convulsive therapy: a manual of practice. In: Frances AJ, Hales RE, eds. Review of psychiatry. Vol 7. Washington DC: American Psychiatric Press, 1988:482–494.

25/   Accidents

1. Accident facts. Chicago: National Safety Council, 1991.

2. Accident facts. Chicago: National Safety Council, 1990.

3. Spiegelman M, Erhardt CL. Mortality in the United States by cause. In: Erhardt CL, Berlin JE, eds. Mortality and morbidity in the United States. Cambridge, MA: Harvard University Press, 1974:22,25.

4. Dorland's illustrated medical dictionary, 27th ed. Philadelphia: W.B. Saunders.

5. Haddon W, Suchman, EA, Klein D. Accident research; methods and approaches. New York: Harper & Row, 1964.

6. MacMahon B, Pugh TF. Epidemiology: principles and methods. Boston: Little, Brown, 1970.

7. Margolis LH, Runyan CW. Accidental policy: an analysis of the problems of unintended injuries of childhood. Am J Orthopsychiatry 1983;53:629.

8. Henker FO. Accident-proneness and how to prevent it. Clin Orthop Related Res 1987;222:30–34.

9. Baker SP, O'Neill B, Karpf RS. The injury fact book. Lexington: D.C. Heath & Company, 1984.

10. Hagglund G. What causes accidents and injuries? Madison, WI: University of Wisconsin School of Social Work, 1980.

11. Robinson JC. Racial inequality and the probability of occupation-related injury or illness. Milbank Q 1984;62(4):568.

12. National Committee for Injury Prevention and Control. Injury prevention: meeting the challenge. New York: Oxford University Press, 1989.

13. Gulaid J, Sattin R. Drownings in the United States, 1978–1984. MMMR 1988;37:27–33.

14. Waller J. Alcohol and unintentional injury. In: Kissin B, Begleiter H, eds. The biology of alcoholism. New York: Plenum, 4:307–349.

15. Waller PF, Stewart RJ, Hansen AR, et al. The potentiating effects of alcohol on driver injury. JAMA 1986;256:1461.

16. Thum D, Wechsler H, Demone HW. Alcohol levels of emergency service patients injured in fights and assaults. Criminology 1973;10:487–497.

17. Tsuang MT, Boor M, Fleming JA. Psychiatric aspects of traffic accidents. Am J Psychiatry 1985;142:538–546.

18. Selzer ML, Rogers JE, Kern S. Fatal accidents: the role of psychopathology, social stress, and acute disturbance. Am J Psychiatry 1968;124:1028–1036.

19. McMurray L. Emotional stress and driving performance: the effect of divorce. Behav Res Highway Safety 1970;1:100–114.

20. Selzer ML, Vinokur A. Life events, subjective stress, and traffic accidents. Am J Psychiatry 1974;131:903–906.

21. Isherwood J, Adam KS, Hornblow AR. Life event stress, psychosocial factors, suicide attempt and auto-accident proclivity. J Psychosocial Res 1982;26:371–383.

22. DeHaven H. Mechanical analysis of survival in falls from heights of fifty to one hundred and fifty feet. War Med 1942:586–596.

23. Gordon JE. The epidemiology of accidents. Am J Public Health 1949;39:504–515.

24. Haddon W, Baker SP. Injury control. In: Clark D, MacMahon B, eds. Preventive and community medicine. Boston: Little, Brown, 1981:10.

25. Robertson LS. Behavior and injury prevention: whose behavior? In: Matarazzo JD, et al., eds. Behavioral health. New York: John Wiley & Sons, 1984:980–989.

26. Sobel R. Accident proneness. In: Noshpitz JD, ed. Basic handbook of child psychiatry, Vol.2. New York: Basic Books, 1979:637.

27. Kemp JS, Thach BT. Sudden death in infants sleeping on polystyrene-filled cushions. N Engl J Med 1991;324:1858–1864.

28. Dershewitz RA, Christophersen ER. Childhood household safety. AJDC 1984;138:85–88.

29. Committee on Psychosocial Aspects of Child and Family Health. Guidelines for health supervision II. Elk Grove Village IL: American Academy of Pediatrics, 1985.

30. Reisinger KS, Bires JA. Anticipatory guidance in pediatric practice. Pediatrics 1980;66:889–892.

31. Snipes GE. Accidents in the elderly. Am Fam Physician 1982;26:117–122.

32. Tinetti ME, Ginter S. Identifying mobility dysfunction in elderly patients: standard neuromuscular examination or direct assessment? JAMA 1988;259:1190–1193.

33. Smith GS, Falk H. Unintentional injuries. In: Amler RW, Dull HB, eds. Closing the gap: the burden of unnecessary illness. New York: Oxford University Press, 1987:143–163.

34. Assessment of OSHA and NIOSH activities. Preventing injury and illness in the workplace. (Report no. OTA-H-256) Washington, DC: Office of Technology Assessment 1985; (Apr):257–272.

35. Weiss SM. Health hazard/health risk appraisals. In: Matarazzo JD, et al., eds. Behavioral health. New York: Wiley, 1984:275–294.

36. National Health Information Clearinghouse. P.O. Box 1133, Washington, DC 10013.

37. Segall A. Physician education in clinical prevention. In: Matarazzo JD, et al., eds. Behavioral health. New York: Wiley, 1984:1204–1213.

38. Gutmann MC, Jackson TC. Facilitating behavior change. In: Sheridan DP, Winograd IR, eds. The preventive approach to patient care. New York: Elsevier, 1987:49–68.

26/ Suicide

1. U.S. Department of Health and Human Services. Health: United States, 1990 Washington DC: U.S. Government Printing Office, PHS 91–1239.

2. Robins E. The final months. New York: Oxford University Press, 1981.

3. Barraclough B, Bunch J, Nelson B, et al. A hundred cases of suicide: clinical aspects. Br J Psychiatry 1974;125:355–373.

4. Murphy GE. Suicide and attempted suicide. In: Winokur G, Clayton P, eds. The medical basis of psychiatry. Philadelphia: Saunders, 1986:572–579.

5. Rutz W, von Knorring L, Walinder J. Frequency of suicide on Gotland after systematic postgraduate education of general practitioners. Acta Psychiatrica Scand 1989;80:151–154.

6. Holinger PC. Violent deaths in the United States. In: Holinger PC, ed. Suicide. New York: Guilford Press, 1987:41–55.

7. Buda M, Tsuang MT. The epidemiology of suicide: implications for clinical practice. In: Blumenthal SJ, Kupfer DJ, eds. Suicide over the life cycle. Washington DC: American Psychiatric Press, 1990:17–37.

8. Sudak HS, Ford AB, Rushforth NB. Suicide in the young. Boston: Wright PSG, 1984.

9. Blumenthal SJ. Youth suicide: risk factors, assessment and treatment of adolescent and young adult suicidal patients., Psychiatr Clin N Am 1990;13:511–555.

10. Pfeffer C.R. Suicidal behavior among children and adolescents. In: Frances AJ, Hales RE, eds. Review of psychiatry, vol 7. Washington, DC, American Psychiatric Press, 1988: 386–402.

11. Holinger PC. Violent deaths in the United States. In: Violent death rates, United States, 1914–1984 by type of mortality, age, sex and race. Vital Statistics of the United States 1987:219–259.

12. Solomon MI, Murphy GE. Cohort studies of suicide: In: Sudak HS, ed. Suicide in the young. Boston: Wright PSG, 1984:1–14.

13. Murphy GE, Wetzel RD. Suicide risk by birth cohort in the United States. Arch Gen Psychiatry 1980;37:519–523.

14. Phillips DP, Carstensen LL. Clustering of teen aged suicides after television news stories about suicide. N Engl J Med 1986;315:685–689.

15. Gould MS, Shaffer D. The impact of suicide in television movies. N Engl J Med 1986;315:690–694.

16. Hendin HH. Suicide in Scandinavia. New York: Grune & Stratton, 1964.

17. Moller HJ, Schmidtke A, Welz R, eds. Current issues of suicidology. Berlin: Springer-Verlag, 1988.

18. Carlson GA, Miller DC. Suicide, affective disorders and women physicians. Am J Psychiatry 1981;138:1330–1335.

19. Pitts FN, Schuller AB, Rich CL, et al. Suicide among U.S. women physicians, 1967–1972. Am J Psychiatry 1979;136: 695–696.

20. Mausner JS, Steppacher RC. Suicide in professionals: a study of male and female psychologists. Am J Epidemiology 1973;98:436–445.

21. Li FP. Suicide among chemists. Arch Env Health 1962;19: 518–520.

22. Weissman MM, Klerman GL. Sex differences and the epidemiology of depression. Arch Gen Psychiatry 1977;34:98–111.

23. Rich CL, Pitts FN, Jr. Suicide by psychiatrists: a study of medical specialists among 18,730 consecutive physician deaths during a five-year period. J Clin Psychiatry 1980;41: 261–263.

24. Blachly PH, Disher W, Roduner G. Suicide by physicians. Bulletin of Suicidology. Rockville, MD: National Institute of Mental Health pub. 312–0260–69–3, 1969.

25. Arnetz BB, Horte LG, Hedberg A, Theorell T, Allander E, Malker H. Suicide patterns among physicians related to other academics as well as to the general population: results from a national long-term prospective study and a retrospective study. Acta Psychiatr Scand 1987;75:139–143.

26. Brauchitsch VH. The physician's suicide revisited. J Nerv Ment Dis 1976;162:40–45.

27. Richings JC, Khara GS, McDowell M. Suicide in young doctors. Br J Psychiatry 1986;149:475–478.

28. Helliwell PJ. Suicide amongst anaesthetists in training. Anaesthesia 1983;38:1097.

29. Waterson DJ. Psychiatric illness in the medical profession—incidence in relation to sex and field of practice. Can Med Assn J 1976;115:311–317.

30. Harrington JM, Shannon HS. Mortality study of pathologists and medical laboratory technicians. Br Med J 1975;4: 329–332.

31. Rose KD, Rosow I. Physicians who kill themselves. Arch Gen Psychiatry 1973;29:800–805.

32. Crashaw KR, Bruce JA, Eraker PL, et al. An epidemic of suicide among physicians on probation. JAMA 1980;243: 1915–1917.

33. Brenner MH. Mortality and the national economy: a review, and the experience of England and Wales, 1936–1976. Lancet 1979;2:568–573.

34. Hendin H. Black suicide. Arch Gen Psychiatry 1969;21: 407–411.

35. Williams J. Why are blacks less prone to suicide than whites? New York Times, vol. 131, February 9, 1982:19.

36. Kubie L. Multiple determinants of suicidal efforts. J Nerv Ment Dis 1964;138:3–8.

37. Freud S. Mourning and melancholia. In: Jones E, ed. The collected papers of Sigmund Freud. New York: Basic Books, 1959.

38. Rado S. The problem of melancholia. Int J Psychoan 1928; 9:420–438.

39. Stevenson J. Suicide. In: Talbott JA, Hales RE, Yudofsky SC, eds. Textbook of psychiatry. Washington DC: American Psychiatric Press, 1988:1027.

40. Arana G, Hyman S. Biological contributions to suicide. In: Jacobs D. Brown H, eds. Suicide understanding and responding. Madison, WI: International Universities Press, 1989:74.

41. Haberlandt WF. Aportacion a la genetica del suicidio. Folio Clin Int 1967;17:319–322.

42. Schulsinger F, Kety SS, Rosenthal D, Wender PH. A family study of suicide. In: Schou M, Stromgren E, eds. Origins, prevention and treatment of affective disorders. New York: Academic Press, 1979:277–278.

43. Asberg M, Trackman L, Thoren P. 5–HIAA in the cerebrospinal fluid: a biochemical suicide predictor. Arch Gen Psychiatry 1976;33:1193–1197.

44. Van Praag HM. Depression, suicide and the metabolism of serotonin in the brain. J Affect Dis 1982;4:275–290.

45. Stanley M, Mann JJ. Increased serotonin-2 binding sites in frontal cortex of suicide victims. Lancet 1983;1:214–216.

46. Stanley M, Stanley B, Traskman-Bendz L, et al: Neurochemical findings in suicide completers and suicide attempters. In: Maris R, ed. Biology of suicide. New York: Guilford, 1986:215.

47. Robins E. Suicide. In: Kaplan H, Sadock B, eds. Comprehensive textbook of psychiatry. IV. Baltimore: Williams & Wilkins, 1985:1311–1315.

48. Bleuler M. The schizophrenic disorders. New Haven: Yale University Press, 1978.

49. Beckford JAR, Ellison RM. The high incidence of Huntington's chorea in the Duchy of Cornwall. J Ment Sci 1953;99:623.

50. Dorpat TL, Ripley HS. A study of suicide in the Seattle area. Comp Psychiatry 1960;11:349–359.

51. Dorpat TL, Anderson WF, Ripley HS. The relationship of physical illness to suicide. In: Resnik HLP. Suicidal behavior: diagnosis and management. Boston: Little, Brown, 1963.

52. Fawcett J. Suicidal depression and physical illness. JAMA 1972;219:1303–1306.

53. Abram HS, Moore GL, Westervelt FB Jr. Suicidal behavior in chronic dialysis patients. Am J Psychiatry 1971;127:1199–1204.

54. Weissman M, Klerman GJ, Markowitz JS. Suicidal ideation and suicide attempts in panic disorder and attacks. N Engl J Med 1989;321:1209–1213.

55. Folstein MF, Folstein SW, McHugh PR. "Minimental State," a practical method of grading the cognitive state of patients for the clinician. J Psychiatric Res 1975;12:189–198.

56. Ettlinger RW. Suicide in a group of patients who had previously attempted suicide. Acta Psychiatrica Scand 1964;40:363–378.

57. Tolchin M. When life is too much: suicide rises among elderly. New York Times, July 19, 1989:1,10.

58. Adam KS, Bouckoms A, Stremer D. Parental loss and family stability in attempted suicide. Arch Gen Psychiatry 1982;39:1081–1085.

59. Levy J, Deykin E. Suicidality, depression and substance abuse in adolescence. Am J Psychiatry 1989;146:1462–1467.

60. Robins L, Kulbok P. Epidemiologic studies of suicide. In: Review of psychiatry. Washington DC: American Psychiatric Press, 1988;7:289–304.

61. Pfeiffer E, Busse EW. Affective disorders. In: Busse EW, Pfeiffer E, eds. Mental illness in later life. New York: American Psychiatric Association Press, 1973:125.

62. Pokorny AD, Kaplan HB, Tsai SY. Hopelessness and attempted suicide: a reconsideration. Am J Psychiatry 1975;132:954–956.

63. Wetzel RD. Hopelessness, depression and suicidal intent. Arch Gen Psychiatry 1976;33:1069–1073.

64. Wetzel RD, Margulies T, Davis R, et al. Hopelessness, depression and suicide intent. J Clin Psychiatry 1980;41:159–160.

65. Beck AT, Kovacs M, Weissman A. Hopelessness and suicidal behavior: an overview. JAMA 1975;234:1146–1149.

66. Coombs D, Miller H, Alarcon R. Psychosocial factors influencing the recognition of suicidal behavior by primary care physicians. Am J Prev Psychiatry Neurol 1989;2:21–25.

67. Reich P, Kelly MJ. Suicide attempts by hospitalized medical and surgical patients. N Engl J Med 1976;294:298–301.

68. Farberow NL, Schneidman ES, Leonard CK. Suicide attempts among general medical and surgical hospital patients with malignant neoplasms. Med Bull Vet Adm 1963;9:1–11.

69. Platt FW, McMath JC. Clinical hypocompetence: the interview. Ann Intern Med 1979;91:898–902.

70. Moore RD, Bone CR, Geller GG, Mamon JA, Stokes EJ, Levine DM. Prevalence, detection and treatment of alcoholism in hospitalized patients. JAMA 1989;261:403–408.

71. Reiser D, Rosen D. Medicine as a human experience. Rockville, MD: Aspen, 1984:106–107.

72. Beck AT, Beck R, Kovacs M. Classification of suicidal behaviors. I. Quantifying intent and medical lethality. Am J Psychiatry 1975;132:285–287.

73. Pokorny AD, Kaplan HB. Suicide following psychiatric hospitalization. J Nerv Ment Dis 1976;162:119–125.

27/ Violence

1. Charlesworth W. Resources and resource acquisition during ontogeny. In: McDonald KB, ed. Sociobiological perspectives on human development. New York: Springer-Verlag 1987:25–76.

2. Lorenz K. On aggression. New York: Harcourt Brace Jovanovich, 1970.

3. Novello AC. From the Surgeon General, US Public Health Service. JAMA 1992;267:3003.

4. Gurr TR, ed. Violence in America: the history of crime. Newbury Park CA: Sage Publications, 1989.

5. Federal Bureau of Investigation. Uniform Crime reports for the United States 1990. Washington DC: US Government Printing Office, 1990.

6. Loftin C, McDowall D, Wiersma B, Cottey TJ. Effect of restrictive licensing of handguns on homicide and suicide in the District of Columbia. N Engl J Med 1991;325:1615–1620.

7. Sloan JH, Kellerman AL, Reay DT. Handgun regulations, crime, assaults and homicide. A tale of two cities. N Engl J Med 1988;319:1256–1262.

8. Cullop FC. The Constitution of the United States: an introduction. New York: New American Library, 1969.

9. National Institute of Mental Health. Television and behavior: 10 years of scientific progress and implications for the eighties. Washington DC: U.S. Government Printing Office, 1982.

10. Centerwell BS. Television and violence: the scale of the problem and where do we go from here. JAMA 1992;267:3059–3063.

11. Monahan J. Predicting violent behavior: an assessment of clinical techniques. Beverly Hills: Sage, 1981.

12. Lion JR, Tardiff K. The long-term treatment of the violent patient. In: Hales RE, Frances AJ, eds. American Psychiatric Association Annual Review, Vol. 6. Washington DC: American Psychiatric Press, 1987:537–545.

13. Messner SF. Research on social and cultural factors in criminal violence. In: Tardiff K, ed. The violent patient. Psychiatr Clin N Am 1988;11:511–535.

14. Centerwall BS. Race, socioeconomic status and domestic homicide: Atlanta 1971–81. Am J Public Health 1984;74:813–815.

15. Hayner D. Gang killings soar. Chicago Sun-Times, June 9, 1992:1,16.

16. Griffith EEH, Bell CC. Recent trends in suicide and homicide among blacks. JAMA 1989;262:2265–2269.

17. Zimring FE. Background in confronting youth crime: report of the Twentieth Century Fund Task Force in Sentencing Policy Toward Young Offenders. New York: Holmes & Meier, 1978.

18. Secretary's Task Force on Black and Minority Health. Report of the Secretary's Task Force on Black and Minority Health. Vol 1. Washington DC: U.S. Department of Health and Human Services, 1985.

19. Messner S, Tardiff K. The social ecology of urban homicide: an application of the routine activities approach. Criminology 1985;23:241–267.

20. Kellerman AL, Reay DT. Protection or peril: an analysis of firearm-related deaths in the home. N Engl J Med 1986;314:1557–1560.

21. Bell CC. Neuropsychiatry and gun safety. J Neuropsychiatry 1990;2:145–148.

22. Bell CC. Preventive strategies for dealing with violence among blacks. Community Ment Health J 1987;23:217–228.

23. Callahan CM, Rivara FP. Urban high school youth and handguns: a school-based survey. JAMA 1992;267:3038–3042.

24. American School Health Association, et al. The National Adolescent School Health Survey. Oakland, CA: Third Party Publishing Co., 1989.

25. Zahn M. Homicide in the twentieth century. In: Gurr TR, ed. Violence in America. Newbury Park, CA: Sage 198;219.

26. Guze SB. Criminality and psychiatric disorders. New York: Oxford University Press, 1976.

27. Kempe CH, Silverman FN, Steele BF, et al. The battered child syndrome. JAMA 1962;181:17.

28. Silver L, Dublin D, Lawrie R. Does violence breed violence? Contributions from a study of the child abuse syndrome. Am J Psychiatry 1969;126:152–155.

29. Daly M, Wilson M. Evolutionary social psychology and family homicide. Science 1988;242:519–523.

30. Burrowes KL, Hales RE, Arrington E. Research on the biologic aspects of violence. In: Tardiff K, ed. The violent patient. Psychiatr Clin North Am 1988;11:499–509.

31. Anderson AC. Environmental factors and aggressive behavior. J Clin Psychiatry 1982;43:280–283.

32. Sampson RJ. Structural density and criminal victimization. Criminology 1983;21:276–293.

33. Madden DJ, Lion JR, Penna MW. Assaults on psychiatrists by patients. Am J Psychiatry 1976;133:422–425.

34. Whitman RM, Armao BB, Dent OB. Assault on the therapist. Am J Psychiatry 1976;133:426–429.

35. Tardiff KJ. A survey of psychiatrists in Boston and their work with violent patients. Am J Psychiatry 1974;131:1008–1014.

36. Cocozza J, Steadman H. The failure of psychiatric predictions of dangerousness: clear and convincing evidence. Rutgers Law Rev 1976;29:1084–1101.

37. McNiel DE, Binder RL, Greenfield TK. Predictors of violence in civilly committed acute psychiatry patients. Am J Psychiatry 1988;145:965–970.

38. McNiel DE, Binder RI. Predictive validity of judgments of dangerousness in emergency civil commitment. Am J Psychiatry 1987;144:197–200.

39. McNiel DE, Binder RL. Clinical assessment of risk of violence among psychiatric inpatients. Am J Psychiatry 1991;148:1317–1321.

40. Rofman ES, Askinazi C, Fant E. The prediction of dangerous behavior in emergency civil commitment. Am J Psychiatry 1980;137:1061–1064.

41. Yesavage JA, Werner PD, Becker JMT, et al. Short-term civil commitment and the violent patient. Am J Psychiatry 1982:139;1145–1149.

42. Wolfgang ME. A sociocultural overview of criminal violence. In: Hays JR, Roberts TK, Solway KS, eds. Violence and the violent individual. New York: SP Medical and Scientific Books, 1981.

43. Wenk EA, Robinson JO, Smith GW. Can violence be predicted? Crime and delinquency 1972;18:393–402.

44. Bond TC. The why of fragging. Am J Psychiatry 1976;133:1328–1333.

45. Yager J. Post combat violent behavior in psychiatrically maladjusting soldiers. Arch Gen Psychiatry 1976;33:1332–1335.

46. Kaplun D, Reich R. The murdered child and his killers. Am J Psychiatry 1976;133:809–812.

47. Police Foundation. Domestic violence and the police: studies in Detroit and Kansas City. Washington DC: Police Foundation, 1977.

48. Reid WH, Balis GU. Evaluation of the violent patient. In: Hales RE, Frances AJ. American Psychiatric Association annual review. Vol. 6. Washington DC: American Psychiatric Press, 1987.

49. Tardiff KJ. Violence. In: Talbott JA, Hales RE, Yudofsky SC, eds. Textbook of psychiatry. Washington DC: American Psychiatric Press, 1988:1037–1057.

50. Tardiff K. A survey of assault by chronic patients. In: Lion JR, Reid WH, eds. Assaults within psychiatric facilities. New York: Grune and Stratton, 1983.

51. Rabkin JG. Criminal behavior of discharged mental patients: a critical review of the research. Psychol Bull 1979;86:1–27.

52. Hare RD. Psychopathy and violence. In: Hays JR, Roberts TK, Solway KS, eds. Violence and the violent individual. New York: SP Medical and Scientific Books, 1981.

53. Virkkunen MN. Reactive hypoglycemic episodes among habitually violent offenders. Neuropsychobiol 1982;8:35–40.

54. Langevin R, Paitich D, Orchard B, et al. The role of alcohol, drugs, suicide attempts and situational strains in homicide committed by offenders seen for psychiatric assessment: a controlled study. Acta Psychiatr Scand 1982;66:229–242.

55. Taylor MA, Sierles FS, Abrams R. General hospital psychiatry. New York: Free Press, 1985.

56. Nurco D, Ball J, Shaffer J, et al. The criminality of narcotic addicts. J Nerv Ment Dis 1985;173:94–102.

57. Tinklenberg JR, Murphy PL, Murphy P, et al. Drug involvement in criminal assaults by adolescents. Arch Gen Psychiatry 1974;30:685–689.

58. Tardiff K, Koenigsberg HW. Assaultive behavior among psychiatric outpatients. Am J Psychiatry 1985;142:960–963.

59. Reid WH, Bollinger M, Edwards G. Assaults in hospitals. Bull Am Acad Psychiatry Law 1985;13:1–4.

60. Hellman DS, Blackman N. Enuresis, firesetting and cruelty to animals: a triad predictive of adult crime. Am J Psychiatry 1966;123:1431–1435.

61. Macdonald JM. The murderer and his victim. Springfield, IL: CC Thomas, 1961.

62. Bell CC. Coma and the etiology of violence, part 2. J Natl Med Assn 1987;79:79–85.

63. Lewis DO, Moy E, Jackson LD, et al. Biosocial characteristics of children who later murder: a prospective study. Am J Psychiatry 1985;142:1161–1167.

64. Lewis DO. Delinquency, psychomotor epileptic symptoms and paranoid ideation: a triad. Am J Psychiatry 1976;133:1395–1398.

65. Elliot F. Neurological findings in adult minimal brain dysfunction and the dyscontrol syndrome. J Nerv Ment Dis 1982;170:680–687.

66. Gunn J, Bonn J. Criminality and violence in epileptic prisoners. Br J Psychiatry 1971;118:337–343.

67. Whitman S, Coleman T, Patmon C, et al. Epilepsy in prison: elevated prevalence and no relationship to violence. Neurology 1984;34:775–782.

68. Boman B. Are all Vietnam veterans like John Rambo? In: Wolf ME, Mosnaim AD, eds. Posttraumatic stress disorder: etiology, phenomenology and treatment. Washington DC: American Psychiatric Press, 1990:80–94.

69. Neilson J, Christensen A, Schultz-Larson J, et al. A psychiatric-psychological study of patients with the XYY syndrome found outside of institutions. Acta Psychiatrica Scand 1973;49:159–168.

70. Schiavi R, Theilgaard A, Owen D, et al. Sex chromosome abnormalities, hormones and aggressivity. Arch Gen Psychiatry 1984;41:93–99.

71. West DJ. Murder followed by suicide. London: Heinemann, 1965.

72. Atkinson JH. Managing the violent patient in the general hospital. Postgrad Med 1982;71:193–201.

73. Kuzmits FE. When employees kill other employees: the case of Joseph T. Wesbecker. J Occup Med 1990;32:1014–1020.

74. Dubin WR. Evaluating and managing the violent patient. Ann Emerg Med 1981;10:481–484.

75. Soloff PH. Emergency management of violent patients. In: Hales RE, Frances AJ, eds. American Psychiatric Association annual review. Vol 6. Washington DC: American Psychiatric Press, 1987:510–536.

76. Taylor MA. The practice of neuropsychiatry. New York: Free Press, 1992.

77. Stafford-Clark D. The foundations of research in psychiatry. Brit Med j 1959;2:1199.

78. Williams D. The significance of an abnormal electroencephalogram. J Neurol Psychiatry 1957;4:257–268.

79. Tardiff K. The psychiatric uses of seclusion and restraint. Washington DC: American Psychiatric Press, 1984.

80. Reid WH. Clinical evaluation of the violent patient. In: Tardiff K, ed. The violent patient. Psychiatr Clin N Am 1988;11:527–537.

81. Liss R, Frances AJ. Court-mandated treatment: dilemmas for hospital psychiatry. Am J Psychiatry 1975;132:924–927.

82. Thackrey M. Therapeutics for aggression: psychological/physical crisis intervention. New York: Human Sciences Press, 1987.

83. Sheard MH. Review: Clinical pharmacology of aggressive behavior. Clin Neuropharmacol 1985;7:173–178.

84. Lion JR, Tardiff K. The long-term treatment of the violent patient. In: Hales RE, Frances AJ, eds. American Psychiatric Association annual review. Vol 6. Washington DC: American Psychiatric Press, 1987:537–547.

85. Luchins DJ. Carbamazepine in psychiatric syndromes: clinical and neuropharmacologic properties. Psychopharmacol Bull 1984;20:569–571.

86. Silver JM, Yudofsky S. Propranolol for aggression: literature review and clinical guidelines. Intl Drug Ther Newsletter 1985;20:9–12.

87. Bell CC, Jenkins EJ. Preventing black homicide. In: The state of black America 1990. National Urban League, 1990:143–155,319–323.

88. Stark E, Flitcraft A. Medical therapy as repression: the case of the battered woman. Health and Medicine 1982:29–32.

89. Federal Bureau of Investigation. Crime in the United States: 1986. Washington DC: U.S. Department of Justice, 1987.

90. Monahan J. Violence in the workplace. J Occup Med 1990;32:1021.

91. Mason J. From the Assistant Secretary for Health, U.S. Public Health Service. JAMA 1992;267:3003.

28/ Sleep and Sleep Disorders

1. Mahowald MW, Schenck CH. Status dissociatus—a perspective on states of being. Sleep 1991;14:69–79.

2. Nieuwenhuys R, Voogd J, van Huijzen C. The human central nervous system. 3d ed. New York: Springer-Verlag, 1988.

3. Klemm WR. Historical and introductory perspectives on brainstem-mediated behaviors. In: Nemeroff CB, ed. Neuropeptides and psychiatric disorders. Washington DC: American Psychiatric Press, 1991:3–32.

4. Vertes RP. Fundamentals of brainstem anatomy: A behavioral perspective. In: Nemeroff CB, ed. Neuropeptides and psychiatric disorders. Washington DC: American Psychiatric Press, 1991:33–104.

5. Widerlov E, Hellig M, Bjartell A, Ekman R. Involvement of neuropeptide γ and delta sleep-inducing peptide in neuropsychiatric illness. In: Nemeroff CB. Neuropeptides and psychiatric disorders. Washington DC: American Psychiatric Press, 1991:225–260.

6. Drucker-Colin R, Arankowsky-Sandoval G, Prospero-Garcia O, Jiminez-Anguino A, Merchant H. The regulation of REM sleep: some considerations on the role of vasoactive intestinal peptide, cetylcholine, and sensory modalities. In: Mancia M, Marini G, eds. The diencephalon and sleep. New York: Raven Press, 1990:313–341.

7. Krueger JM, Obal F Jr, Opp M, Toth L, Johannsen L, Cady AB. Somnogenic cytokines and models concerning their effects on sleep. Yale J Biol Med 1990;63:157–172.

8. Guyton AC. Textbook of medical physiology. 8th ed. Philadelphia: Saunders, 1991:663.

9. Monti JM. Slow wave sleep in health and disease (circa 1987). In: Wauquier A, Dugovic C, Radulovacki M. Slow wave sleep. New York: Raven Press, 1989:311–322.

10. Hobson JA. The dreaming brain. New York: Basic Books, 1988.

11. Hobson JA, Lydic R, Baghdoyan HA. Evolving concepts of sleep cycle generation: from brain centers to neuronal populations. Behav Brain Sci 1986;9:371–448.

12. Daan S, Beersma D. Circadian gating of human sleep-wake cycles. In: Moore-Ede MC, Czeisler CA. Mathematical models of the circadian sleep-wake cycle. New York: Raven Press, 1984:129–158.

13. Freud S. The interpretation of dreams. Standard edition. London: Hogarth Press, 1955.

14. Cartwright RD. Dreams and their meaning. In: Kryger MH, Roth T, Dement WC. Principles and practice of sleep medicine. Philadelphia: Saunders, 1989:184–190.

15. Broughton R, deKonick J, Gagnon P, Dunham W, Stampi C. Sleep-wake biorhythms and extended sleep in man. In: Montplaisir J, Godbout R, eds. Sleep and biological rhythms. New York: Oxford University Press, 1990:25–41.

16. Rittig S, Knudsen UB, Jonler M, Norgaard JP, Pedersen EB, Djurhuus JC. Adult enuresis. The role of vasopressin and atrial natriuretic peptide. Scand J Urol Nephrol 1989; 125 (suppl):79–86.

17. Janknegt RA, Smans AJ. Treatment with desmopressin in severe nocturnal enuresis in childhood. Br J Urol 1990;66: 535–537.

18. Sukhai RN, Mol J, Harris AS. Combined therapy of enuresis alarm and desmopressin in the treatment of nocturnal enuresis. Eur J Pediatr 1989;148:465–467.

19. Terho P. Desmopressin in nocturnal enuresis. J Urol 1991; 145:818–820.

20. Aldrich MS. Automobile accidents in patients with sleep disorders. Sleep 1989;12:487–494.

21. Ancoli-Israel S. Epidemiology of sleep disorders. Clin Geriatr Med 1989;5:347–362.

22. App WE, Boatwright GW, Ostrander SE, Unruh MM, Winslow DH. Disorder of excessive somnolence: a case series of 1,000 patients. J Ky Med Assoc 1990;88:393–396.

23. Gottlieb GL. Sleep disorders and their management: special considerations in the elderly. Am J Med 1990;88(3A): 29S–33S.

24. Richardson JW, Frederickson PA, Lin SC. Narcolepsy update. Mayo Clin Proc 1990;65:992–998.

25. Parkes JD, Lock CB. Genetic factors in sleep disorders. J Neurol Neurosurg Psychiatry 1989;(suppl):101–108.

26. Douglass AB, Harris L, Pazderka F. Monozygotic twins concordant for the narcoleptic syndrome. Neurology 1989; 39:140–11.

27. Douglass AB, Hays P, Pazderka F, Russell JM. Florid refractory schizophrenias that turn out to be treatable variants of HLA-associated narcolepsy. J Nerv Ment Dis 1991;179: 12–18.

28. Mamelak M. A model for narcolepsy. Can J Psychol 1991; 45:194–220.

29. Marczynski TJ. Adenosine presynaptic inhibition and transmitter "spillover": hypothesis of etiopathogenesis of narcolepsy. Med Hypotheses 1989;29:265–273.

30. Mitler MM, Hajdukovic R. Relative efficacy of drugs for the treatment of sleepiness in narcolepsy. Sleep 1991;14: 218–220.

31. Mitler MM, Hajdukovic R, Erman M, Koziol JA. Narcolepsy. J Clin Neurophysiol 1990;7:93–118.

32. Westbrook PR. Sleep disorders and upper airway obstruction in adults. Otolaryngol Clin North Am 1990;23:727–743.

33. Kimoff RJ, Cosio MG, McGregor M. Clinical features and treatment of obstructive sleep apnea. Can Med Assoc J 1991;144:689–695.

34. Parish JM, Shepart JW Jr. Cardiovascular effects of sleep disorders. Chest 1990;97:1220–1226.

35. Sanders MH, Kern N. Obstructive sleep apnea treated by independently adjusted inspiratory and expiratory positive airway pressures via nasal mask: physiologic and clinical implications. Chest 1990;98:317–324.

36. Manfredi RL, Vgontas A, Kales A. An update on sleep disorders. Bull Menninger Clin 1989;53:250–273.

37. Coccagna G. Restless legs syndrome/periodic leg movements in sleep. In: Thorpy MJ. Handbook of sleep disorders. New York: Marcel Dekker, 1990:457–478.

38. Coleman RM. Periodic movements in sleep (nocturnal myoclonus) and restless legs syndrome. In: Guilleminault C, ed. Sleeping and waking disorders (indications and techniques). Menlo Park, CA: Addison-Wesley, 1982:265–295.

39. Snodgrass SR. Myoclonus: analysis of monoamine, GABA, and other systems. Faseb J 1990;4:2775–2788.

40. Lugaresi E, Cirignotta F, Coggagna G, Montagna P. Nocturnal myoclonus and restless legs syndrome. In: Fahn S, Marsden CD, Van Woert M, eds. Advances in neurology, vol. 43. Myoclonus. New York: Raven, 1986:295–307.

41. Fisher BE, McGuire K. Do diagnostic patterns exist in the sleep behaviors of normal children? J Abnorm Child Psychol 1990:18:179–186.

42. Kahn A, Van de Merckt C, Rebuffat E, Mozin MJ, Sottlaux M, Blum D, Hennart P. Sleep problems in healthy preadolescents. Pediatrics 1989;84:542–546.

43. Mahowald MW, Rosen GM. Parasomnias in children. Pediatrics 1990;17:21–31.

44. Kavey NB, Whyte J, Resor SR Jr, Gidro-Frank S. Somnanbulism in adults. Neurology 1990;40:749–752.

45. Fisher C, Kahn E, Edwards A, et al. A psychophysiologic study of nightmares and night terrors. I. Physiological aspects of the stage 4 terror. J Nerv Ment Dis 1973;157:75–98.

29/ Sex and Sexual Dysfunctions

1. Leif HI Fink PJ, Hammett VO, eds. Sex education of the physician: sexual function and dysfunction. Philadelphia: FA Davis, 1969.

2. Woods SM. A course for medical students in the psychology of sex: training in socio-cultural sensitivity. Am J Psychiatry 1969;125:1508–1519.

3. Kinsey AC, Pomeroy WB, Martin CE. Sexual behavior in the human male. Philadelphia: Saunders, 1948.

4. Kinsey, AC, Pomeroy WB, Martin CE, Gebhard PH. Sexual behavior in the human female. Philadelphia: Saunders, 1953.

5. Masters WH, Johnson VE. Human sexual response. Boston: Little, Brown, 1966.

6. Renshaw DC. Single, successful—and pregnant: the new phenomenon: how it involves you. Female Patient 1986;2: 54.

7. Ansbacher R, Adler, JP. Infertility workup and sexual stress. Med Aspects Hum Sexuality 1988;55:8, 15, 23.

8. Masters WH, Johnson VE. Human sexual inadequacy. Boston: Little, Brown, 1970.

9. Ellis H. Studies in the psychology of sex. New York: Random House, 1942.

10. Freud S. The standard edition of the complete psychological works of Sigmund Freud. Strachey J, ed. London: Hogarth Press and Institute of Psychoanalysis, 1957–1965.

11. Bates B. A guide to physical examination and history-taking. 4th ed. Philadelphia: Lippincott, 1988.

12. Weiss HD. The physiology of human penile erection. Ann Intern Med 1972;76:793–799.

13. American Psychiatric Association. Diagnostic and statistical manual. 3rd ed, rev. Washington DC: American Psychiatric Press, 1986.

14. Renshaw DC. Sex and the female psyche. Compr Ther 1978;20:415.

15. Nathan SG. The epidemiology of the DSM–III psychosexual dysfunctions. J Sex Marital Ther 1986;12:267–281.

16. Frank E, Anderson C, Rubinstein D. Frequency of sexual dysfunction in normal couples. N Engl J Med 1978;299:111–115.

17. Burnap DW, Golden JS. Sexual problems in medical practice. J Med Educ 1967;42:673–680.

18. Derogatis LR, Lopez MC, Zinzeletta EM. Clinical applications of the DSFI in the assessment of sexual dysfunction. In: Brown RA, Field JR, eds. Treatment of sexual problems in individual and couples therapy. Costa Mesa, CA: PMA Publishing, 1988:167–186.

19. Lopiccolo J, Steger JC. The sexual interaction inventory: a new instrument for assessing sexual dysfunction. In: Lopiccolo J, Lipiccolo K, eds. Handbook of sex therapy. New York: Plenum, 1978:113–122.

20. Rust J, Golombok S. The Golombok-Rust inventory of sexual satisfaction. Windsor: NFER-Nelson, 1986.

21. Sorensen R. Adolescent sexuality in contemporary America. New York: World, 1972.

22. Knudsen DD, Pope H, Irish DP. Response differences to questions on sexual standards: an interview-questionnaire comparison. Public Opinion Q 1967;31:290–297.

23. Bancroft J. Human sexuality and its problems. 2nd ed. Edinburgh: Churchill Livingstone, 1989.

24. Arentewicz G, Schmidt G, eds. The treatment of sexual disorders. New York: Basic books, 1983.

25. Brown, RA, Field, JR, eds. Treatment of sexual problems in individual and couples therapy. Costa Mesa, CA: PMA Publishing, 1988.

26. Kaplan HS. The new sex therapy. New York: Brunner/Mazel, 1974.

27. Leiblum SR, Rosen RC, eds. Principles and practice of sex therapy. 2nd ed. New York: Guilford Press, 1989.

28. Lopiccolo J, Lopiccolo L. Handbook of sex therapy. New York: Plenum, 1978.

29. Nadelson CC, Marcotte DB, eds. Treatment interventions in human sexuality. New York: Plenum, 1983.

30. Money J. Gay, straight, and in-between. New York: Oxford, 1988.

31. Money J. Lovemaps. New York: Irvington, 1986.

32. Scanzoni J. Social exchange and behavioral interdependence. In: Burgess RL, Huston TL, eds. Social exchange in developing relationships. New York: Academic Press, 1979:61–98.

33. Lieberman ML. The sexual pharmacy. New York: New American Library, 1988.

34. Money J. Venuses penuses. Buffalo: Prometheus Books, 1986.

35. Anonymous. Physician's desk reference. Oradell, NJ: Medical Economics Company, 1991.

36. Kaplan HS. Disorder of sexual desire. New York: Brunner/Mazel, 1979.

37. Money J. Love and love sickness: the science of sex, gender difference and pair bonding. Baltimore: Johns Hopkins University Press, 1980.

38. Brown GR, Anderson B. Psychiatric morbidity in adult inpatients with childhood histories of sexual and physical abuse. Am J Psychiatry 1991;148:55–61.

39. Finkelhor D. Child sexual abuse. New York: Free Press, 1984.

30/ Psychophysiology and Psychoneuroimmunology

1. Green E, Green A. Beyond biofeedback. New York: Delacorte Press, 1977.

2. Mackenzie JN. The production of so-called "rose cold" by means of an artificial rose. Am J Med Sci 1886;9:45–57.

3. Ullman M. On the psyche and warts. Psychosom Med 1959;21:473.

4. Surman OS. Hyposis in the treatment of warts. Arch Gen Psychiatry 1973;23:439–441.

5. Philips DP, Smith DG. Postponement of death until symbolically meaningful occasions. JAMA 1990;263:1947–1951.

6. Philips DP, King EW. Death takes a holiday: mortality surrounding major social occasions. Lancet 1988;2:728–752.

7. Cohen S, Tyrrell DAJ, Smith AP. Psychological stress and susceptibility to the common cold. N Engl J Med 1991;325:606–612.

8. Beaumont W. Experiments and observations on the gastric juice and the physiology of digestion. Plattsburgh: FP Allen, 1833.

9. Pavlov IP. Lecture on conditioned reflexes. WH Gantt, ed./trans. New York: International Publishing, 1941, 2 vols.

10. Cannon WB. Bodily changes in pain, hunger, fear and rage. New York: Appleton, 1929.

11. Cannon WB. The wisdom of the body. New York: Norton, 1932.

12. Cannon WB. Voodoo death. Am Anthropologist 1942;44:169.

13. Richter C. On the phenomenon of sudden death in animals and man. Psychosom Med 1957;19:191.

14. Selye H. A syndrome produced by diverse noxious agents. Nature 1936;138:32.

15. Selye H. The stress of life. New York: McGraw-Hill, 1956.

16. Selye H. Forty years of stress research: principal remaining problems and misconceptions. Can Med Assoc J 1976;115:53–56.

17. Mirsky IA. Physiologic, psychologic and social determinants in the etiology of duodenal ulcer. Am J Digest Dis 1958;3:285–314.

18. Alexander F. Psychosomatic medicine: its principles and applications. New York: W W Norton, 1950:68–70.

19. Engel GL, Reichsman, Segal HL. A study of an infant with a gastric fistula. Psychosom Med 1956;18:374.

20. Schmale AH, Engel GL. Psychoanalytic theory of somatic disorder: conversion, specificity and the disease onset situation. J Amer Psychoan Assoc 1967;15:344–365.

21. Engel GL. The clinical application of the biopsychosocial model. Am J Psychiatry 1980;137:535–544.

22. Holmes TH, Rahe RH. The social readjustment rating scale. J Psychosom Res 1967;11:213–218.

23. Johnson, JH, Sarason IG. Recent developments in reasearch on life stress. In: Hamilton V, Warburton DM, ed. Human stress and cognition. Chichester, England: Wiley, 1979:205–233.

24. Ley P, Spelman MS. Communicating with the patient. London: Staples Press, 1967.

25. Leventhal H. Fear communications in the acceptance of preventive health practices. Bull NY Acad Med 1965;41:1144-1168.

26. Lazarus RE, Folkman S. Stress appraisal and coping. New York: Springer, 1984.

27. Greer S, Morris T, Pettingale KW. Psychological response to breast cancer: effect on outcome. Lancet 1979;11:785–787.

28. Kobasa SC, Stressful life events, personality and health: an inquiry into hardiness. J Pers Soc Psychol 1979;37:1–11.

29. Schmied LA, Lawler KA. Hardiness, type A behavior, and the stress-illness relation in working women. J Per Soc Psychol 1986;51:1218–1223.

30. Wiebe DJ, McCallum DM. Health practices and hardiness as mediators in the stress-illness relationship. Health Psychol 1986:425–438.

31. Estes RA. Personality and immune function. North Chicago, IL, 1990 (unpublished doctoral dissertation:30,31).

32. Friedman M, Rosenman RH. Type A behavior and your heart. New York: McGraw-Hill, 1974.

33. Brand R. Coronary-prone behavior as an independent risk factor for coronary heart disease. In: Dembroski TM, Weiss SM, Shields JL, Haynes LG, Feinleib M, eds. Coronary prone behavior. New York: Springer-Verlag, 1978.

34. Dembroski TM, MacDougall JM. Beyond global type A: relationships of paralinguistic attributes, hostility and anger-in to coronary heart disease. In: Field TM, McCabe PM, Schneiderman N, eds. Stress and coping. Hillsdale, NJ: Lawrence Erlbaum Associates, 1985.

35. Weisman A. Coping with cancer. New York: McGraw-Hill, 1979.

36. Hackett T, Cassem N. Development of a quantitative rating scale to assess denial. J Psychosom Res 1974;18:93–100.

37. Dean A, Lin N. The stress buffering role of social support. J Nerv Ment Dis 1977;169:403–417.

38. Field TM, McCabe PM, Schneiderman N, eds. Stress and coping. Hillsdale, NJ: Lawrence Erlbaum Associates, 1985.

39. Cousins N. Head first: the biology of hope. New York: E. P. Dutton, 1989.

40. Siegel BS. Love, medicine and miracles: lessons learned about self-healing from a surgeon's experience with exceptional patients. New York: Harper & Row, 1986.

41. Klopfer B. Psychological variables in human cancer. J Proj Tech 1957;21:331–340.

42. Fegan C, Morgan G, Whittaker JA. Spontaneous remission in a patient with chronic myeloid leukemia. Br J Hematol 1989;72:594–595.

43. Wolf JW. Prolonged spontaneous remission of case of malignant lymphoma. Mod Med 1989;86:275–277.

44. Barletta C, Buzzetti R, Vagri D, Savo D. Cushing's disease and prolonged spontaneous remission, clinical case. Minerva Endocrinol 1989;14:137–141.

45. Terai A, Terachi T, Yoshida S, Kadota K. Pheochromocytoma presenting as shock and followed by spontaneous remission. Urol Int 1989;44:58–60.

46. Stein M, Schleifer SJ, Keller SE. Hypothalamic influences on immune responses. In: Ader R, ed. Psychoneuroimmunology. New York: Academic Press, 1981:429–448.

47. Aarlie JA. The immune system and the nervous system. J Neurology 1983;229:137–154. Functional communication between the immune and neuroendocrine systems, Physiol Rev 1989;69:1–32.

48. Blalock JE, Harbour-McMenamin D, Smith EM. Peptide hormones shared by the neuroendocrine and immunologic systems. J Immunol 1985;135:858s–861s.

49. Blalock JE, Harbour-McMenamin D, Smith EM. Peptide hormones shared by the neuroendocrine and immunologic systems. J Immunol 1985;135:858s–861s.

50. Fauci AS. Corticosteroids and circulating lymphocytes. Transplant Proc 1975;7:37–48.

51. Alqvist J. Hormonal influences on immunologic and related phenomena. In: Ader R, ed. Psychoneuroimmunology. New York: Academic Press, 1981:355–403.

52. Pert CB, Ruff MR, Weber RJ, Herkenham M. Neuropeptides and their receptors: a psychosomatic network. J Immunol 1985;135:820s–826s.

53. Livnat S, Felton SY, Carlson SL, Bellinger DL, Felton DL. Involvement of peripheral and central catecholamine systems in neuro-immune interactions. J Neuroimmunol 1985;10:5–30.

54. Bullock K. Neuroanatomy of lymphoid tissue. In: Guillemin R, Cohn M, Menechuk T, eds. Neural modulation of immunity. New York: Raven Press, 1985.

55. Guillemin R, Cohn M, Menechuk T, eds. Neural modulation of immunity. New York: Raven Press, 1985.

56. Felten DL, Felten SY, et al. Noradrenergic sympathetic neural interactions with the immune system: structure and function. Immunol Rev 1987;100:225–260.

57. Ader R, Cohen N. Behaviorally-conditioned immunosuppression. Psychosom Med 1975;37:333–340.

58. Gorczynski RM, Kennedy M, Ciampi A. Cimetidine reverses tumor growth enhancement of plasmacytoma tumors in mice demonstrating conditioned immunosuppression. J Immunol 1985;134:4261–4266.

59. Klosterhalfen W, Klosterhalfen S. Pavlovian conditioning of immunosuppression modifies adjuvant arthritis in rats. Behav Neurosci 1983;97:663–666.

60. O'Reilly CA, Exon JH. Cyclophosphamide-conditioned suppression of the natural killer cell response in rats. Physiol Behav 1986;17:759–764.

61. Russell M, Dark KA, Cummins RW, et al. Learned histamine release. Science 1984;225:733–734.

62. Rogers MP, Reich P, Carpenter CB. Behaviorally conditioned immunosuppression: replication of a recent study. Psychosom Med 1976;38:447–451.

63. Kusnecov AW, Swyer M, King MG, et all. Behaviorally-conditioned suppression of the immune response by anti-lymphocyte serum. J Immunol 1983;130:2117–2120.

64. Ader R, Cohen N. Behaviorally conditioned immunosuppression and murine systemic lupus erythematosus. Science 1982;215:1534–1536.

65. Ghanta VK, Hiramoto RN, Solvason HB, Spector H. Neural and environmental influences on neoplasia and conditioning of NK activity. J Immunol 1985;135:848s–852s.

66. Beecher HK. The powerful placebo. JAMA 1955;159:1602–1606.

67. Laudenslager ML, Ryan SM, Drugan RC, Hyson RL, Maier SF. Coping and immunosuppression: inescapable, but not escapable, shock suppresses lymphocyte proliferation. Science 1983;221:568–570.

68. Kiecolt-Glaser JK, Garner W, Speicher CE, Penn GM, Holiday J, Glaser R. Psychosocial modifiers of immunocompetence in medical students. Psychosom Med 1984;46:7–14.

69. Kasl SV, Evans AS, Niederman JC. Psychosocial risk factors in the development of infectious mononucleosis. Psychosom Med 1979;44:445–466.

70. Levy SM, Herberman RB, Maluish AM, Schlein B, Lippman M. Prognostic risk assessment in primary breast cancer by behavioral and immunological parameters. Health Psychol 1985;4:99–113.

71. Bartrop RW, Lazarus L, Luckherst E et al. Depressed lymphocyte function after bereavement. Lancet 1977;1:834–836.

72. Schleifer SJ, Keller SE, Camarino M, et al. Suppression of lymphocyte stimulation following bereavement. JAMA 1983;250:374–377.

73. Irwin M, Daniels M, Weiner H. Immune and neuroendocrine changes during bereavement. In: Zisook S, ed. Grief and bereavement. Psychiatr Clin North Am 1987;10:449–465.

74. Linn MW, Linn BS, Jensen J. Stressful events, dysphoric mood, and immune responsiveness. Psychol Rep 1984;54:219–222.

75. Young M, Benjamin B, Wallis C. Mortality of widowers. Lancet 1963;2:454.

76. Helsing KG, Szklo M, Comstock EW. Factors associated with mortality after widowhood. Am J Pub Health 1981;71:802–809.

77. Kiecolt-Glaser JK, Ricker D, George J, et al. Urinary cortisol levels, cellular immunocompetency and loneliness in psychiatric patients. Psychosom Med 1984;15:23.

78. House JS, Landis KR, Umberson D. Social relationships and health. Science 1988;241:540–545.

79. Kiecolt-Glaser JK, Glaser R. Major life changes, chronic stress and immunity. In: Bridge TP, et al., eds. Neuropsychological, neuropsychiatric and substance abuse aspects of AIDS. New York: Raven Press, 1988.

80. Cassileth BR, Luak EJ, Miller DS, Brown LL, Miller C. Psychosocial correlates of survival in advanced malignant disease. N Engl J Med 1985;312:368–373.

81. Miller BD, Strunk RC. Circumstances surrounding the deaths of children due to asthma: a case control study. Am J Dis Child 1989;143:1294–1299.

82. Solomon GF. Coping styles, personality thought to play role in battle against HIV infection. Psychiatr News, July 21, 1989.

83. Spiegel D, Kraemer HC, Bloom JR, Gottheil E. Effect of psychosocial treatment on survival of patients with metastatic lung cancer. Lancet 1989;2:888–891.

31/ Chronic Disease and Disability

1. Szasz TS, Hollender MH. A contribution to the philosophy of medicine: the basic models of the doctor-patient relationship. Arch Intern Med 1955;97:585–592.

2. Robins E. The final months: a study of 134 successful suicides. New York: Oxford University Press, 1981.

3. Donne J. Devotions upon emergent occasions, no. 6 (1624). Raspa A, ed. New York: Oxford University Press, 1987.

4. Anonymous. The talk of the town. New Yorker, vol 65, Nov. 20, 1989:43–44.

5. O'Connor F. The habit of being. Fitzgerald S, ed Letters. New York: Farrar Straus Giroux, 1979:163.

6. Rabin D, Rabin PL. The pariah syndrome: the social disease of chronic illness. In: Rabin D, Rabin PL, eds. To provide safe passage: the humanistic aspects of medicine. New York: Philosophical Library, 1985:38–47.

7. Rabin D, Rabin PL, Rabin RC. Compounding the ordeal of ALS: isolation from my fellow physicians. N Engl J Med 1982;307:506–509.

8. Wainapel SF. The physically disabled physician. JAMA 1987;257:2935–2938.

9. Stephens R Ahhhhhhhhhh! (or what, me open up about doctors?). In: Gerhardt J, King P, Guyer W, eds. So the team may know: interdisciplinary rehabilitation in orthopedic medicine. Vol. 1: Evaluation and therapy. New York: Hogrefe-Huber, 1992.

10. Roth WC. Let us work. Parade Magazine, September 17, 1989:16.

11. Americans with Disabilities Act (PL 101–336). U.S. Code, Vol. 42, secs. 12101–12112 (1990).

12. De Parle J. Realizing the rights of the disabled. NY Times December 17, 1989:sec. 4:1.

13. Ell K, et al. Studies of the psychological effects of cancer. Psychiatr News, September 15, 1989;24.

32/ Limb Amputation

1. Bradway JK, Malone JM, Racy J. Psychological adaptation to amputation: an overview. Orthot Prosth 1984;38:46.

2. Racy J. Psychological aspects of amputation. In: Moore WS, Malone JM, eds. Lower extremity amputation. Philadelphia: Saunders, 1989:330–340.

3. Von Bertalanffy L. General systems theory. New York: Braziller, 1968.

4. Miller JG, Miller JL. General living systems theory. In: Kaplan HI, Sadock BJ, eds. Comprehensive textbook of psychiatry IV. Baltimore: Williams & Wilkins, 1985:13–24.

5. Marmor J. Systems thinking in psychiatry: some theoretical and clinical implications. Am J Psychiatry 1983;140:833–838.

6. Engel GL. The clinical application of the biopsychosocial model. Am J Psychiatry 1980;137:533–544.

7. Sabelli HC, Carlson-Sabelli L. Biological priority and psychological supremacy: a new integrative paradigm from process theory. Am J Psychiatry 1989;146:1541–1551.

8. Barash DP, Lipton JE. Sociobiology. In: Kaplan HI, Sadock BJ, eds. Comprehensive textbook of psychiatry IV. Baltimore: Williams & Wilkins, 1985:70–77.

9. Freud S. Civilization and its discontents. Trans. by Strachey J. New York: Norton, 1961.

33/ Medical Ethics

1. Jones WHS, trans. Hippocrates, vol. 1. Cambridge, MA: Harvard University Press, 1923.

2. Curran WJ. Beyond the best interests of the child—bone marrow transplantation among half-siblings. N Engl J Med 1991;25:1818–1819.

3. Engelhardt HT Jr. The foundations of bioethics. New York: Oxford University Press, 1986:336–374.

4. Brody H. Ethical aspects of the doctor-patient relationship. In: Wedding D, ed. Behavior and medicine. St. Louis: Mosby Year Book, 1990:199–207.

5. Bentham J. An introduction to the principles of morals and legislation. New York: New American Library, 1974.

6. Mill JS. On liberty. Indianapolis: Bobbs-Merrill, 1956.

7. Hooker W. Physician and patient; or a practical view of the mutual duties, relations and interests of the medical profession and the community. New York: Baker and Scribner, 1849:357ff,378–381.

8. Kant I. Fundamental principles of the metaphysic of morals. New York: Liberal Arts Press, 1949.

9. Ross WD. The right and the good. Oxford: Clarendon Press, 1930.

10. Thomson JAK. The ethics of Aristotle. 2nd ed. New York: Penguin Books 1976.

11. McInery R. Ethica thomistica: the moral philosophy of Thomas Aquinas. Washington, DC: Catholic University Press, 1982.

12. MacIntyre A. After virtue. Notre Dame: University of Notre Dame Press, 1981.
13. Clouser KD. Medical ethics: some uses, abuses, and limitations. N Engl J Med. August 21, 1975;13:384–387.
14. Kierkegaard S. Thoughts on crucial situations in human life. In: Oden TC, ed.: Parables of Kierkegaard. Princeton, NJ: Princeton University Press, 1978:38.
15. The principles of medical ethics with annotations especially applicable to psychiatry. Washington, DC: American Psychiatric Press, 1989.
16. Pellegrino ED, Thomasma DC. For the patient's good. New York: Oxford University Press, 1988.
17. Beauchamp TL, Childress, JF. Principles of biomedical ethics. 3rd ed. New York: Oxford University Press, 1989:69.
18. Lidz CW, Meisel A, Zerubavel E, Carter M, Sestak RM, Roth LH. Informed consent. New York: The Guilford Press, 1984.
19. The Council on Ethical and Judicial Affairs of the American Medical Association. Current opinions. Chicago: AMA, 1989.
20. Drane JF. The many faces of competency. The Hastings Center Report, 1985;15,2:17–21.
21. Gutheil TG. Rogers v commissioner: Denouement of an important right-to-refuse-treatment case. Am J Psychiatry 1985;142:2:213–214.
22. Schouten R, Gutheil TG. Aftermath of the Rogers decision: assessing the costs. Am J Psychiatry 1990;147:1348–1352.
23. Emanuel LL, Barry MJ, Stoeckle JD, Ettelson LM, Emanuel EJ. Advance directives for medical care—a case for greater use. N Engl J Med 1991;324:889–895.
24. LaPuma J, Orentlicher D, Moss RJ. Advance directives on admission: clinical implications and analysis of the Patient Self-Determination Act of 1990. JAMA 1991;266:402–405.
25. Cruzan vs. Director, Missouri Dept of Health. Docket no. 88-1503, 1989.
26. Nozick R. Anarchy, state, and utopia. New York: Basic Books, 1974.
27. Rawls J. A theory of justice. Cambridge, MA: Harvard University Press, 1971.
28. Sider RC, Clements C. Family or individual therapy: the ethics of modality choice. Am J Psychiatry 1982;139:1455–1459.
29. Wallerstein JS, Blakeslee S. Second chances. New York: Ticknor & Fields; 1990.
30. Stone AA. Law, psychiatry, and morality. Washington, DC: American Psychiatric Press; 1984;161–190.
31. Battin MP, Mayo D, eds. Suicide: the philosophical issues. New York: St. Martins Press, 1980.
32. Wilkerson I. Doctor is charged with murder in suicide by device he invented. NY Times, Dec. 4, 1990:1,15.
33. Quill TE. Death and dignity—a case of individualized decision-making. N Engl J Med 1991;324:691–693.
34. Robins E. The final months: a study of 134 successful suicides. New York: Oxford University Press, 1981.
35. AIDS policy: confidentiality and disclosure. Am J Psychiatry 1988;145:4:541–542.
36. Perry S. Warning third parties at risk of AIDS: APA's policy is a barrier to treatment. Hosp Commun Psychiatry 1989; 40:158–161.
37. Kardener SH, Fuller M, Mensh IN. A survey of physicians' attitudes and practices regarding erotic and nonerotic contact with patients. Am J Psychiatry 1973;142:1077–1081.
38. Margolis PM. Annual reports to the membership. Am J Psychiatry 1990;147:1402.

39. Beecher HK. Ethics and clinical research. N Engl J Med 1966;274:1354–1360.

34/ Forensic Medicine

1. Rappaport JR. Editorial. Bull Amer Acad Psychiatry Law 1977;5:iv–vii.
2. Taraska, JM. Legal guide for physicians. New York: Matthew Bender, 1988.
3. Angell M. The case of Helga Wanglie: a new kind of right to die case. N Engl J Med 1991;325:511–512.
4. Miles SH. Informed demand for "non-beneficial" medical treatment. N Engl J Med 1991;325:512–515.
5. Simon RI. Concise guide to clinical psychiatry and the law. Washington, DC: American Psychiatric Press, 1988:57–72.
6. 8 USC Sec 871, 3056.
7. Burnum JF. Secrets about patients. N Eng J Med 1991;324: 1130–1133.
8. Schloendorff v. Society of New York Hospital, 211 N.Y. 125, 105 N.E. 92, 93 (1914).
9. Annas GI. Restricting doctor-patient communications in federally funded clinics. N Engl J Med 1991;325:362–364.
10. Localio AR, Lawthers AG, Brennan TA, Laird NM, Hebert LE, Peterson LM, Newhouse JP, Weiler PC, Hiatt HH. Relationship between malpractice claims and adverse events due to negligence by physicians—results of the Harvard Medical Practice Study III. N Engl J Med 1991;325: 245–251.
11. Brunelle RL, Cantu A. A critical evaluation of current ink dating techniques. J Forensic Sci 1987;32:1511–1521.
12. Ginzburg, HM. The evolution of psychiatric-legal diagnostic dilemmas. In: Simon RI, ed. Review of clinical psychiatry and the law. Washington, DC: American Psychiatric Press, 1988:241–294.
13. Board of Curators of Univ. Missouri v. Horowitz. 98 S. Ct 948 (1978).
14. Ewing v. Univ. of Michigan. 106 S. Ct. 507 (1985).
15. Irby, DM, Milam, S. The legal context for evaluating and dismissing medical students and residents. Acad Med 1989; 64:639–643.
16. Helms LB, Helms CM. Forty years of litigation involving medical students and their education. I. General educational issues. Acad Med 1991;66:1–7.
17. Helms LB, Helms CM. Forty years of litigation involving medical students and their education. II. Issues of finance. Acad Med 1991;66:71–76.
18. Tanay E, Robertson JD. The psychiatrist in the courtroom. In: Simon RI, ed. Review of clinical psychiatry and the law. Washington, DC: American Psychiatric Press, 1988:341–363.
19. Ake v. Oklahoma, 105 S. Ct. 1087 (1985).

35/ Health Care Financing and Delivery

1. Levit KR, Lazenby HC, Cowan CA, Letsch SW. National health expenditures, 1990. Health Care Finan Rev 1991; 13(1):29–54.
2. Employee Benefit Research Institute. Sources of health insurance and characteristics of the uninsured, analysis of the March 1991 current population survey. EBRI Special Report SR-14, Issue Brief 123. Washington, DC: EBRI, February 1992.
3. Congress of the United States, Congressional Budget Office. Rising health care costs: causes, implications, and strategies. Washington, DC: US Government Printing Office, April 1991.

4. Sonnenfeld ST, Waldo DR, Lemieux JA, McKusick DR. Projections of national health expenditures through the year 2000. Health Care Finan Rev 1991;13(1):1–27.

5. U.S. Department of Education. Digest of Education Statistics, 1991. Washington, DC: Department of Education, 1991.

6. Office of the President of the United States. Economic report of the President 1991. Washington, DC: Office of the President, 1991.

7. U.S. Congressional Budget Office. CBO staff memorandum: factors contributing to the growth in the Medicaid program. Washington, DC: CBO, May 1992.

8. Levit KR, HC, Letsch SW, Cowan CA. National health care spending, 1989. Health Affairs 1991;10(1):117–130.

9. U.S. Senate Special Committee on Aging, American Association of Retired Persons, Federal Council on Aging, U.S. Administration on Aging. Aging America: trends and projections, 1987–88 edition. Washington, DC: U.S. Senate Special Committee on Aging, 1988.

10. Starr P. The social transformation of American medicine. New York: Basic Books, 1982.

11. Rist RC. Declining options/increasing needs. Transaction: Social Sci Mod Society 1989;26(6):39–45.

12. Pauly MV. Health care issues and American economic growth: innovation in financing health care. In: Advances in the study of entrepreneurship, innovation, and economic growth. Greenwich, CT: JAI Press, 1990;4:97–125.

13. Pauly MV. Taxation, health insurance, and market failure in the medical economy. J Econ Lit 1986;24:629–675.

14. Newhouse JP, Manning WG, Morris CN, et al. Some interim results from a controlled trial of cost sharing in health insurance. N Engl J Med 1981;305:1501–1507.

15. Manning WG, Newhouse JP, Duan N, et al. Health insurance and the demand for medical care: evidence from a randomized experiment. Amer Econ Rev 1987;77:251–277.

16. Gabel JR, Rice TH. Reducing public expenditures for physician services: the price of paying less. J Health Politics Policy Law 1985;9:595–609.

17. Mitchell JB, Wedig G, Cromwell J. The Medicare physician fee freeze: what really happened? Health Affairs 1989; 8(1):21–33.

18. Holahan J, Dor A, Zuckerman S. Understanding the recent growth in Medicare physician expenditures. JAMA 1990; 263:1658–1661.

19. Pauly MV, Eisenberg JM, Radany MH, et al. Paying physicians: options for controlling cost, volume, and intensity of services. Ann Arbor, MI: Health Administration Press, 1992.

20. Tierney WM, Miller ME, McDonald CS. The effect of test ordering on informing physicians of the charges for outpatient diagnostic tests. N Engl J Med 1990;322:1499–1504.

21. Maloney TW, Rogers DE. Medical technology—a different view of the contentious debate over costs. N Engl J Med 1979;301:1413–1419.

22. Williamson JW, Alexander M, Miller GE. Continuing education and patient care research: physician response to screening test results. JAMA 1967;201:938–942.

23. Dixon RH, Laszlo J. Utilization of clinical chemistry services by medical house staff: an analysis. Arch Intern Med 1974;134:1064–1067.

24. Olsen DM, Kane RL, Proctor PH. A controlled trial of multiphasic screening. N Engl J Med 1976;294:925–930.

25. Shapiro MF, Hatch RL, Greenfield S. Cost containment and labor-intensive tests: the case of the leukocyte differential count. JAMA 1984;252:231–234.

26. Hubbell FA, Greenfield S, Tyler JL, Chetty K. Wyle FA. The impact of routine admission chest x-ray films on patient care. N Engl J Med 1985;312:209–212.

27. Shroeder S, Kenders K, Cooper J, Pumme T. Use of laboratory tests and pharmaceuticals: variations among physicians and effect of cost audit on subsequent use. JAMA 1973; 225:969–973.

28. Pauly MV, Eisenberg JM, Highland J. Methods for pricing the technical component of diagnostic tests. Final report to the Health Care Financing Administration, Grant No. 99-C-99169/5. Springfield, VA: National Technical Information Service, June 1989 (Vol 1, PB89 9232789, Vol 2, PB89 232797).

29. Aaron H, Schwartz W. The painful prescription: rationing hospital care. Washington, DC: Brookings Institution, 1984.

30. Wennberg JE. Dealing with medical practice variations: a proposal for action. Health Affairs 1984;3(2):6–32.

31. Maneul BM. Professional liability—a no-fault solution. N Engl J Med 1990;322:628–630.

32. Reynolds RA, Rizzo JA, Gonzalez ML. The cost of medical professional liability. JAMA 1987;257:2776–2881.

33. Danzon PM. Medical malpractice: theory, evidence, and publice policy. Boston, MA: Harvard University Press, 1985.

34. Schwartz W, Kamesar M. Doctors, damages and deterrents. N Engl J Med 1979;298:1282–1290.

35. Localio AR, Lawthers AG, Brennan TA, et al. Relations between malpractice claims and adverse events due to negligence—results of the Harvard Medical Practice Study III. N Engl J Med 1991;325:245–251.

36. Woolhandler S, Himmelstein DU. The deteriorating administrative efficiency of the U.S. health care system. N Engl J Med 1991;324:1253–1258.

37. Grumet GG. Health care rationing through inconvenience: the third party's secret weapon. N Engl J Med 1989;320: 571–577.

38. Evans RG, Lomas J, Barer ML, et al. Controlling health expenditures—the Canadian reality. N Engl J Med 1989; 320:571–577.

39. Wohl S. The medical industrial complex. New York: Harmony Books, 1984.

40. Computer Science Corporation. Medical management information system provider manual—physicians. Albany, NY: Computer Science Corporation, 1988.

41. Freeland M. Schendler CE. National health expenditure growth in the 1980s: an aging population, new technologies, and increasing competition. Health Care Finan Rev 1983; 4(3):1–58.

42. Trost C. At risk—middle-class families often lack insurance for children's health. The Wall Street J 1992;June 5:1,A5.

43. Lewin T. The price of health. New York Times 1991;Apr 28:1.

44. Himmelstein DU, Woolhandler S, and the Writing Committee of the Working Group on Program Design. A national health program for the United States: a physicians' proposal. N Engl J Med 1989;320:102–108.

45. U.S. Department of Health and Human Services, National Center for Health Statistics. Monthly vital statistics report. Hyattsville, MD: DHHS, NCHS, 1988:7.

46. Manton KG, Patrick CH, Johnson KW. Health differentials between blacks and whites: recent trends in mortaliy and morbidity. Mibank Q 1987;65(Suppl 1, Pt 1):125–199.

47. McCord C. Freeman HP. Excess mortality in Harlem. N Engl J Med 1990;322:173–177.

48. Davis K, Lillie-Blanton M, Lyons B, Mullan F, Powe N, Rowland D. Health care for black Americans: the public sector role. Milbank Q 1987;65(Suppl 1, Pt 1):213–247.

49. Wilensky G. Underwriting the uninsured: targeting providers or individuals. In: Sloan FA, Blumstein JF, Perrin JM, eds. Uncompensated hospital care: rights and responsibilities. Baltimore: Johns Hopkins University Press, 1986:148–166.

50. Davis K, Rowland D. Uninsured and underserved: inequities in health care in the United States. Milbank Mem Fund Q 1983;61:149–176.

51. Sulvetta M. Swartz K. The uninsured and uncompensated care: a chartbook. Washington, DC: National Health Policy Forum, George Washington University, 1986.

52. Epstein AM, Stern RS, Weissman JS. Do the poor cost more? A multihospital study of patients' socioeconomic status and use of hospital resources. N Engl J Med 1990;322:1122–1128.

53. Ries P. Health care coverage by age, sex, race and family income: United States, 1986. In: Advance data from Vital and Health Statistics of the National Center for Health Statistics. No. 139. Hyattsville, MD: Department of Health and Human Services, NCHS, 1987 (DHHS pub. no. [PHS]87–1250).

54. Friedman E. The sagging safety net: emergency departments on the brink of crisis. Hospitals 1992;Feb 20:26–30.

55. Hartz AJ, Krakauer H, Kuhn EM, et al. Hospital characteristics and mortality rates. N Engl J Med 1989;321:1720–1725.

56. Sin AL, Sonnenberg FA, Manning WG, et al. Inappropriate use of hospitals in a randomized trial of health insurance plans. N Engl J Med 1986;315:1259–1266.

57. Brian EW, Gibbens SF. California's Medi-Cal co-payment experiment. Med Care 1974;12(Suppl):1–30.

58. Ginzberg E. Health care reform—why so slow? N Engl J Med 1990;322:1464–1466.

59. Kimbell M. Fee controls prompt doctors to reduce Medicare services. Health Week, May 30, 1989.

60. Feldstein PJ, Wickizer TM, Wheeler JRC. Private cost containment: the effects of utilization review programs on health care use and expenditures. N Engl J Med 1988;318:1310–1314.

61. Luft HS. Assessing the evidence on HMO performance. Milbank Mem Fund Q 1980;58:501–536.

62. Interstudy. The Interstudy competitive edge: biannual report of the managed care industry. Excelsior, MN: Interstudy 1(1), 1991.

63. Manning WG, Leibowitz A, Goldberg GA, Rogers WH, Newhouse JP. A controlled trial of the effect of a prepaid group practice on use of services. N Engl J Med 1984;310:1505–1510.

64. Epstein AM, Begg C, McNeil BJ. The use of ambulatory testing in prepaid and fee-for-service group practices. N Engl J Med 1986;314:1089–1094.

65. Newhouse JP, Schwartz WB, Williams AP, Witsberger C. Are fee-for-service costs increasing faster than HMO costs? Med Care 1985;23:960–966.

66. Knickman JR, Thorpe KE. Financing for health care. In: Kovner AR, ed. Health care delivery in the United States, 4th ed. New York: Springer, 1990:263.

67. Guterman S, Eggers PW, Riley G, Greene TF, Terrell SA. The first 3 years of Medicare prospective payment: an overview. Health Care Finan Rev 1988;9(3):67–77.

68. Fitzgerald JF, Moore PS, Dittus RS. The care of elderly patients with hip fracture: changes since implementation of the prospective payment system. N Engl J Med 1988;319:1392–1397.

69. Ernst & Whinney. The impact of PROs on hospitals. Washington, DC: Ernst & Whinney, 1987 (E&W Pub. No. J58693).

70. U.S. Congress, Physician Payment Review Commission. Annual report to Congress, 1989. Washington, DC: PPRC, 1989.

71. Relman AS. Reforming the health care system. N Engl J Med 1990;323;991–992.

72. Pauly MV, Danzon P, Feldstein P, Hoff J. A plan for "responsible national health insurance." Health Affairs 1991;10(1):5–25.

73. Cantor JC, Barrand NL, Desonia RA, Cohen AB, Merrill JC. Business leaders' views on American health care. Health Affairs 1991;10(1):98–105.

74. Butler S. Haislmaier E, eds. A national health system for America. Washington, DC: The Heritage Foundation, 1989.

75. Rockefeller JD. A call for action: the Pepper Commission's blueprint for health care reform. JAMA 1991;265:2507–2510.

76. Enthoven A, Kronick R. Universal health insurance through incentives reform. JAMA 1991;265:2532–2536.

77. Todd JS, Seekins SV, Krichbaum JA, Harvey LK. Health access America—strengthening the US health care system. JAMA 1991;265:2503–2506.

78. Blumenthal DB, Berenson RA. Health care issues in presidential campaigns. N Engl J Med 1989;321:908–912.

79. Blumenthal D. The timing and course of health care reform. N Engl J Med 1991;325:198–200.

80. Noble LE. Healthcare reform stews in Congressional pressure cooker. Health Care Finan Mgt 1992;Jan:21–39.

81. Schieber GJ, Poullier JP. International health spending: issues and trends. Health Affairs 1991;10(1):106–116.

82. U.S. General Accounting Office. Health care spending control: the experience of France, Germany, and Japan. Washington, DC: USGAO, November 1991.

83. Blendon RJ, Leitman R, Morrison I, Donelan K. Satisfaction with health systems in ten nations. Health Affairs 1990;9(2):185–192.

84. Hurst JW. Reforming health care in seven European nations. Health Affairs 1991;10(3):7–21.

85. U.S. General Accounting Office. Canadian health insurance: lessons for the United States. Washington, DC: USGAO, June 1991.

86. Iglehart JK. Canada's health care system faces its problems. N Engl J Med 1990;322:562–568.

87. Etheredge L, Jones S. Managing a pluralist health system. Health Affairs 1991;10(4):93–105.

88. Blendon RJ, Edwards JN, Szalay U. The health insurance industry in the year 2001: one scenario. Health Affairs 1991;10(4):170–177.

89. Cohodes DR. Insurance reform: industry, heal thyself! Health Affairs 1991;10(4):178–180.

90. Kirkland L. A labor leader's view of insurance reform. Health Affairs 1991;10(4):181–184.

91. Roemer MI. Comparative health systems. In: Last JM, ed. Maxcy-Rosenau public health and preventive medicine, 12th ed. Norwalk, CT: Appleton-Century Crofts, 1986.

92. Jonas S. Population data for health and health care. In: Kovner AR, ed. Health care delivery in the United States, 4th ed. New York: Springer, 1990:39.

93. U.S. Department of Labor. Occupational outlook handbook. Washington, DC: Bureau of Labor Statistics, April 1988:140.

94. Fordham CC. The Bane Report revisited. JAMA 1980;244:354.

95. Carnegie Commission on Higher Education. Higher education and the nation's health. New York: McGraw-Hill, 1970.

96. Fein R. The doctor shortage. Washington DC: Brookings, 1967.

97. Castleton KB. Are we building too many medical schools? JAMA 1971:216.

98. Navarro V. A critique of the present and proposed strategies for redistributing resources in the health sector and a discussion of alternatives. Med Care 1974;12:721.

99. Sednior B, Smith BA. The number of physicians as a constraint on delivery of health care. JAMA 1972;222:178.

100. Schofield JR. New and expanded medical schools. San Francisco: Jossey-Bass, 1984.

101. Lefkowitz B. Health planning: lessons for the future. Rockville, MD: Aspen, 1983.

102. American Medical Association. Physician characteristics and distribution in the United States, 1992. Chicago, AMA, 1992.

103. American Osteopathic Association. Active doctors of osteopathy, 1989. Chicago: AOA, 1990.

104. Smith BWH, Gerard RJ. Federal Health Service Corps. N Engl J Med 1982;306:1045.

105. Mullan FSM. The National Health Service Corps. Public Health Reports 1979(July-Aug. Suppl).

106. Stamps PL, Kuriger FH. Location decision on National Health Service Corps physicians. Am J Public Health 1983;73:906.

107. Hughes RG, Barker DC, Reynolds RC. Are we mortgaging the medical profession? N Engl J Med 1991;325:404–407.

108. Health Resources and Services Administration, Bureau of Health Professions (based on data from the AMA). Physician distribution and licensure in the U.S., 1975, and physician characteristics and distribution in the U.S., 1986.

109. Bailey BJ. Manpower issues for a surgical specialty: the impact of oversupply. JAMA 1985;253:1025.

110. Graduate Medical Education National Advisory Committee (GMENAC). Interim report (DHEW pub. no. HRA 79-633). Washington, DC: US Government Printing Office, 1979.

111. Harris JE. How many doctors are enough? Health Affairs 1986;5(4):73–83.

112. Iglehart JK. The future supply of physicians. N Engl J Med 1986;314:860–864.

113. Luft HS, Arno P. Impact of increasing physician supply: a scenario for the future. Health Affairs 1986;5(4):31–46.

114. Schloss FP. Beyond GMENAC: another physician shortage from 2010 to 2030? N Engl J Med 1988;318:920–922.

115. Schwartz WB, Sloan FA, Mendelson DW. Why there will be little or no physician surplus between now and the year 2000. N Engl J Med 1988;318:892–897.

116. Medical care chartbook, 7th ed. Ann Arbor: Health Administration Press, 1980.

117. Association of American Medical Colleges College Application Service. Washington, DC: AAMC Annual Survey Research, 1989.

118. American Hospital Association. Hospital statistics, 1990–91 ed. Chicago: AHA, 1990.

119. Kovner AR. Hospitals. In: Kovner AR, ed. Health care delivery in the United States, 4th ed. New York: Springer, 1990:141–174.

120. American Hospital Association. Environmental assessment for rural hospitals 1992. Chicago: AHA, 1991.

121. Hollingsworth JW, Bondy PK. The role of the Veterans Administration hospitals in the health care system. N Engl J Med 1990;322:1851–1857.

122. Relman AS. The future of the Veterans Administration hospital system: two points of view. N Engl J Med 1978;298:623.

123. Friedman E. Public hospitals: is "relevance" in the eye of the beholder? Hospitals 1980;May1:83.

124. U.S. Congressional Budget Office. Policy choices for long-term care. Washington, DC: CBO, June 1991.

125. Stone RI. Exploding the myths: caregiving in America. US House of Representatives, Select Committee on Aging, Pub. No. 99-611, January 1987.

126. Liu K, Manton KG, Liu BM. Home care expenses for the disabled elderly. Health Care Finan Rev 1985;7(2):51–58.

127. Sekscenski ES. Discharges from nursing homes: 1985 National Nursing Home Survey. Series 13: Data from the National Health Survey, No. 103. Hyattsville, MD: US DHHS, National Center for Health Statistics, March 1990.

128. Health Insurance Association of America. Source book of health insurance data, 1991. Washington, DC: HIAA, 1991.

129. Rivlin AM, Wiener JM. Caring for the disabled elderly. Washington, DC: Brookings Institution, 1988.

130. Tames S. The booming hospice industry. Med Health Persp 1987;41:6.

131. Marmor TR. Political analyses and American medical care. New York: Cambridge University Press, 1983.

132. Brecher C. The government's role in health care. In: Kovner AR, ed. Health care delivery in the United States, 4th ed. New York: Springer, 1990.

133. US DHHS, Health Care Financing Administration. The Medicare handbook. Pub. No. 10050. Baltimore: HCFA 1990.

134. US DHHS, Health Care Financing Administration. Program Statistics: Medicare and Medicaid data book. 1990. Baltimore: HCFA, 1990.

135. Wagner L. Blending old traditions with modern medicine. Modern Healthcare 1988;August 26:22.

136. Jolly P, Taksel L, Beran R. U.S. medical school finances. JAMA 1988;260:1077.

137. Hoerlin BY. Connecting: Challenges in health and human services in the Philadelphia region. Philadelphia: The Pew Charitable Trusts, 1989.

138. National Health Council, Inc. Health groups in Washington: a directory, 11th ed. Washington, DC: The Council, 1991.

139. US DHHS, National Center for Health Statistics. Current estimates from the National Health Interview Survey, 1990. Series 10, No. 181, DHHS Pub. No. (PHS) 92-1509. Hyattsville, MD: National Center for Health Statistics, December 1991.

140. Lazenby HC, Letsch SW. National health expenditures, 1989. Health Care Finan Rev 1990;12(2):1–26.

141. Gibson RM. National health expenditures, 1978. Health Care Finan Rev 1979;1(1):1–36.

142. de Lissovoy G, Rice T, Ermann D, Gabel J. Preferred provider organizations: today's models and tomorrow's prospects. Inquiry 1986;23:7–15.

143. American Medical Care and Review Association and Institute for International Health Initiatives. Directory of preferred provider organizations and the industry report on PPO development. Bethesda, MD: AMCRA, 1985.

Index

Page numbers in italics denote figures; those followed by "t" denote tables.